nations in transit 1998

Freedom House

This publication was made possible through support provided by the U.S. Agency for International Development, under the terms of Grant No. DHR-0001-G-00-6030-00. The opinions expressed herein are those of the author(s) and do not necessarily reflect the views of the U.S. Agency for International Development or Freedom House.

nations in transit 1998

civil society, democracy and markets
in east central europe and
the newly independent states

edited by Adrian Karatnycky, Alexander Motyl,
and Charles Graybow

Transaction Publishers
New Brunswick (U.S.A.) and London (U.K.)

This publication was made possible through support provided by the U.S. Agency for International Development, under the terms of Grant No. DHR-0001-G-00-6030-00. The opinions expressed herein are those of Freedom House and do not necessarily reflect the views of the U.S. Agency for International Development.

This book is printed on acid-free paper that meets the American National Standard for Permanence of Paper for Printed Library Materials.

Library of Congress Catalog Number: 98-50279
ISBN: 0-7658-0623-1
Printed in the United States of America

Library of Congress Cataloging-in-Publication Data

Nations in transit 1998 : civil society, democracy and markets in East Central Europe and the newly independent states / edited by Adrian Karatnycky, Alexander Motyl, and Charles Graybow.
p. cm.
ISBN 0-7658-0623-1 (pbk. : alk. paper)
1. Europe, Eastern—Politics and government—1989- 2. Former Soviet republics—Politics and government. 3. Civil society—Europe, Eastern. 4. Civil society—Former Soviet republics. 5. Europe, Eastern—Economic conditions—1989- 6. Former Soviet republics—Economic conditions. I. Karatnycky, Adrian. II. Motyl, Alexander J. III. Graybow, Charles.
JN96.A58N384 1999
320.94'09171'7—dc21 98-50279
CIP

contents

ACKNOWLEDGMENTS

Nations in Transit 1998 could not have been completed without the dedicated and expert advice of the project's academic consultants. Freedom House is grateful to Professor Alexander Motyl, who serves as Associate Director of the Harriman Institute at Columbia University and who coordinated the advisers' group and provided editorial expertise for the country reports; Boris Shor, who coordinated the *Nations in Transit 1997* survey and who wrote several country essays and provided editorial guidance on all sections of the survey dealing with economics and privatization; Stephen Handelman, who is a fellow at the Harriman Institute and who edited the sections dealing with corruption; and Dr. Martha Brill Olcott, who serves as a fellow at the Carnegie Endowment for International Peace and a professor at Colgate University and who provided invaluable advice on the country reports for the Caucasus and Central Asia.

Freedom House also thanks the members of the project's Academic Oversight Board, which was primarily responsible for determining the ratings for each country. In addition to Mr. Handelman, Dr. Motyl, and Dr. Olcott, the board includes Dr. Jozef von Brabant, Senior Economist at the United Nations; Dr. Richard Ericson, Professor of Economics at Columbia University; and Dr. Charles Gati of the School of Advanced International Studies at Johns Hopkins University. Most of these board members also reviewed and provided commentary on the country reports.

Freedom House also thanks Professor Allen Lynch of the University of Virginia and Mr. Handelman for their analytic essays. It also thanks those consultants who researched and wrote the individual country reports: Gordon Bardos, Columbia University (Yugoslavia); Lowell Bezanis (Kyrgyz Republic and Turkmenistan); Robinder Bhatty, Columbia University (Armenia, Azerbaijan, and Georgia); Dr. Roger Kangas, Johns Hopkins University (Uzbekistan); Pauline Jones Luong, Davis Center for Russian Studies, Harvard University (Kazakhstan); Tibor Papp, Columbia University (Hungary); Aili Piano, (Estonia and Latvia); Inna Pidluska, Ukrainian Center for Independent Political Research (Ukraine); and Boris Shor, Columbia University (Czech Republic, Moldova, Romania, Russia, and Poland).

Freedom House is grateful to Daniel Fata for proofreading the text, to the Lithuanian Free Market

Institute for the country report on Lithuania, and to the Institute for Public Affairs and MESA-10 for their collaboration on the Slovakia report. Freedom House also greatly appreciates the work of those organizations that provided information and assistance to this project. These included the Associated Press, Banka International, the Center for Economic Policy Research (Brussels), the Center for International Private Enterprise, the Center for the Study of Constitutionalism in Eastern Europe, the U.S. Department of Commerce, *East European Constitutional Review*, the European Bank for Reconstruction and Development, the European Union Market Access Database, the Economist Intelligence Unit, the *Financial Times,* Human Rights Watch, the International Monetary Fund, the *New York Times*, the Organization for European Cooperation and Development, Radio Free Europe-Radio Liberty, Reuters, U.S. Embassies, the U.S. Department of State, the Winston Foundation for World Peace, the World Bank, and World News Connection.

At Freedom House, Charles Graybow shouldered the major burden of coordinating this survey's data gathering and wrote the country reports for Bulgaria, Bosnia, Mongolia, and Tajikistan. George Zarycky, a principal writer of the survey, provided expert oversight for the entire survey and wrote the country reports for Albania, Azerbaijan, Belarus, Macedonia, Poland, Romania, and Russia. Kristen Guida coordinated the survey materials on press freedom and wrote the country reports for Croatia and Slovenia. Freedom House President Adrian Karatnycky developed the project, edited the study, and, along with Dr. Motyl, provided overall guidance for the data-gathering and analysis. Arch Puddington, Vice President for Research, coordinated the work of the research staff. Freedom House Senior Fellow Marshall Freeman Harris, a Balkan affairs expert and former State Department official, served as text editor. Jason Muse assisted in preparing charts, tables, and follow-up research. Tara Kelly assisted with the layout and design.

A more detailed explanation of the process and personnel involved in the survey may be found in the Methodology section.

INTRODUCTION

Nations in Transit: From Change to Permanence

Adrian Karatnycky

It has been nine years since the fall of the Berlin Wall. Seven years have passed since the failed August 1991 coup began the sequence of history-making events that resulted in the dissolution of the Soviet Union in December 1991. This is a significant span of time in the life of states. Certainly, it is ample time to take a hard look at the gains and reversals that have occurred in a great expanse that includes the countries of Central Europe; Eastern Europe; the Black, Baltic and Caspian Sea littorals; and Central Asia.

The people of this vast territory lived under Soviet rule, Soviet dominion, or other Marxist-Leninist regimes. This territory includes an extraordinary range of cultures, religions, and traditions: traditionally Catholic, Protestant, and Orthodox Christian societies, Islamic societies, and even Buddhist societies. It includes a wide range of ethno-linguistic communities, including countries in which the majority cultures are Turkic, Slavic, and Baltic. Included, as well, is a wide range of European, Asian, and Indo-European civilizations. The expanse of countries under review in this study, *Nations in Transit 1998*, traverses an extraordinary range of history and experience. Once politically and economically homogeneous as a consequence of the compulsory assimilation imposed by totalitarian communism, these societies have resumed divergent paths of political and economic development, in which indigenous culture and belief once again are playing a central role.

Nations in Transit 1998 tracks the political and economic evolution of an extensive territory inhabited by more than 415 million people. It charts the divergent paths of political and economic transformation that have been taken by the 28 countries formerly under the rule of Communist dictatorship. *Nations in Transit 1998* is the third such comprehensive study of the ebb and flow of democratic and market reform in the territory inhabited by the Soviet Union, its satellites, and other Marxist-Leninist regimes in Eastern Europe. It systematically monitors, examines, and evaluates on a comparative basis the changes that have occurred in these strategically and economically vital states. This report covers the events and policies of the period from January 1997, to the end of March 1998. Commissioned by the U.S. Agency for International Development, the first such Freedom House survey focused on developments from January 1994 until June 1995. The second survey, *Nations in Transit 1997*, covered events through December 1996.

The initial survey completed in 1995 contained a checklist of 36 questions examining political, civic, and economic changes. In 1997, Freedom House added additional data to the survey results to trace more precisely the dynamics of economic change. In addition, the 1997 survey introduced a rating system that assesses the degree of progress made in each of the discrete political and economic categories. The 1998 survey is even more comprehensive. It contains a new section dealing with corruption and a more detailed set of questions concerning economic reforms. The survey addresses 52 questions organized in the following categories: political process, civil society, independent media, rule of law, governance and public administration, corruption, macro-economic policy, micro-economic policy, and privatization. Moreover, this year's survey has been expanded to include Bosnia and Herzegovina, Yugoslavia (Serbia-Montenegro), and Mongolia.

Nations in Transit 1998 rates the countries under review on the basis of a scoring system that allows the countries to be compared to one another in eight categories. (See section on Methodology on page 39). In addition to the numerical system of scoring employed (with one representing the highest level of economic and political reform and seven the lowest score), the Academic Oversight Board recommended that a broader alphabetical grade be applied in evaluating corruption Taken together, the survey's rating system allows for rigorous examination of the relationship between economic and political reforms, for the examination of these reforms in their relationship to the problem of corruption, and for the comparative assessment of 28 countries undergoing significant political and economic change.

The ratings reflect the consensus of a panel of leading U.S. Academic experts and senior Freedom House staff. The systematic tracking of political, governmental, civic, economic, and legal transformations in the former Communist states of Central and Eastern Europe, the Caucasus, and Central Asia can be a critical tool for policymakers and analysts. The United States and other Western governments have invested billions of dollars in foreign aid and assistance programs aimed at promoting reforms. Additional tens of billions in loans have been invested to strengthen the economies and societies of the region. This survey helps assess the efficacy of that investment and can serve as a tool to guide policymakers in determining where best to direct limited resources. The survey is also valuable because it is the only such annual comprehensive study of change in a strategically vital part of the world.

The Findings

What do the 1998 survey findings show? The survey divides the states under review into three broad categories: consolidated democracies and market economies; transitional polities and transitional economies, some of which have made considerable progress in reforming their political and economic systems; and consolidated autocracies and statist economies (See Table A on page 7).

In 1998, seven countries qualify as consolidated democracies and consolidated market economies: the Czech Republic, Estonia, Hungary, Latvia, Lithuania, Poland, and Slovenia. Seventeen countries are designated as transitional polities and transitional economies: Albania, Armenia, Azerbaijan, Bosnia and Herzegovina, Bulgaria, Croatia, Georgia, Kazakhstan, Kyrgyzstan, Macedonia, Moldova, Mongolia, Romania, Russia, Slovakia, Ukraine, and Yugoslavia (Serbia-Montenegro). These transitional societies range from countries with relatively open political and economic systems (Bulgaria, Romania, and Georgia) to relatively autocratic states that tolerate only limited political opposition (Kazakhstan and Azerbaijan). The survey designates four countries as consolidated autocracies and statist economies: Belarus, Tajikistan, Turkmenistan, and Uzbekistan.

Significantly, the survey finds a strong correlation between the degree of political change that has occurred within each country and its economic

Democratic vs. Economic Reforms

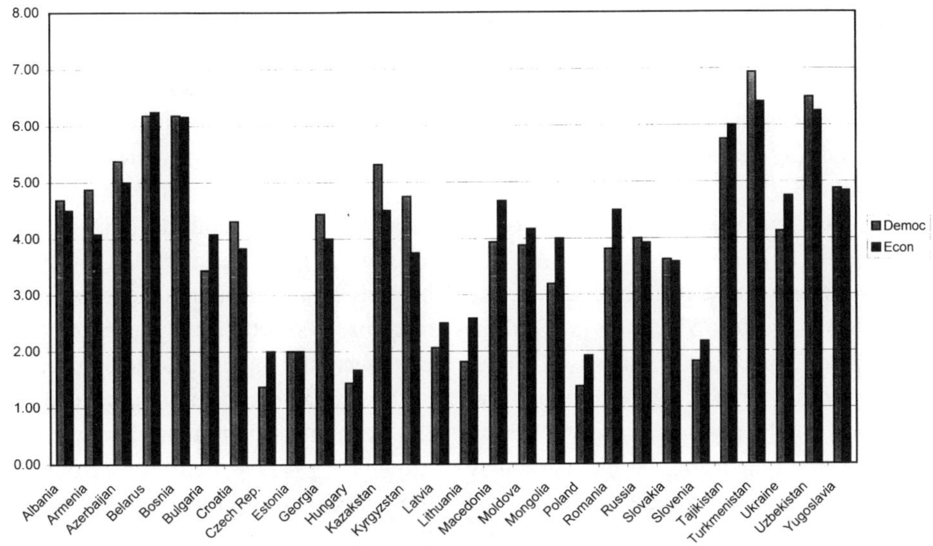

reforms. With the exception of the Baltic states, the former Soviet republics have not established consolidated democracies or market economies. Eight of these post-Soviet states are transitional polities and economies, and four are consolidated autocracies and statist economies. The situation differs significantly from that in Central and Eastern Europe. There, the survey found seven states that had consolidated democratic and market reform. The survey also found forward momentum or the potential for further economic and political progress in the majority of Central and East Europe's transitional countries.

Reform and Economic Growth

The survey's most important finding is the strong correlation between economic growth and political and economic reform. To examine the correlations between reform and economic performance, a combined average score is provided for political and economic reform. (See Table B on page 12). Countries with a combined average rating of one to three are designated as consolidated market democracies. Countries with a combined average score of between three and 5.5 are designated as transitional countries. The third category, consolidated autocracies and statist economies, includes countries that have combined average economic and political ratings in a range from 5.5 to seven points.

According to this rating system, the consolidated market democracies achieved an average growth rate of 4.7 percent in 1997. The transitional countries showed wide variations, ranging between 11.3 percent growth (for Georgia) and minus 7.5 percent (for Bulgaria). As a group, they achieved an average growth rate in 1997 of only 1.39 percent. Among the four consolidated statist autocracies, the gross domestic product declined on an average of 2.85 percent — even with a 7.0 percent growth rate recorded in 1997 by Belarus.

An equally important relationship established by the survey is the relationship between economic growth and the degree of corruption. (See Table C page 13). *Nations in Transit 1998* finds that countries rated "A" or " B" and judged to be the region's least corrupt averaged 4.7 percent growth in 1997. Countries with a grade of "C" for corruption averaged 1.97 percent growth. Those countries at the bottom of the scale, with a grade of "D," registered an average growth rate of 1.63 in 1997.

Two countries were excluded from these growth related statistics: Yugoslavia (Serbia-Montenegro) and Bosnia and Herzegovina. There are several reasons why they were excluded from the calculations. In the first quarter of 1998, both countries were emerging from a period marked by sharp economic decline resulting from protracted civil and interstate wars. In the case of Yugoslavia (Serbia-Montenegro), a U.N.-sanctioned boycott of goods and services affected economic performance in 1996 and would have distorted economic growth figures for 1997 and 1998, when the embargo was lifted. Similarly, war and ethnic cleansing had so disrupted economic life as to make the year-to-year statistical measurement of economic growth unreliable in Bosnia and Herzegovina. Moreover, while the survey did rate the political and civic institutions of Bosnia and Herzegovina, in the period under review (January 1997, to March 1998), Bosnia was just emerging from protracted ethnic war fueled by outside support from Yugoslavia and Croatia. Moreover, the Dayton Accords and the significant military and political presence of the West in Bosnia meant that the country was effectively a foreign protectorate, making it difficult to assess the character of sovereign political and economic development.

In light of the significant correlations between economic performance and reform, it should be noted that GDP trends were not taken into account by the Oversight Board and senior Freedom House staff as assessments were made. The Freedom House *Nations in Transit* ratings were determined solely on the basis of the legal framework, policies, and practices of the countries surveyed. In this context, the lessons of the survey are dramatic. States that undertake fundamental reforms and that guard against corrupt practices are far more likely to have productive economies than corrupt states and unreformed dictatorships. States that take half-measures or pursue episodic or inconsistent reforms also fail to generate sustained growth and lag far behind countries that implement sweeping and deep reforms. In short, there appears to be no evidence of a successful middle ground of piecemeal reform.

Regrettably, even as the evidence demonstrates the correlation between change and economic growth, in 1997-98 there were no new entrants into the ranks of consolidated market democracies At the same time, the survey found that in the short- and mid-term there is potential for further significant reform momentum in Georgia, Bulgaria, Bosnia and Herzegovina, Romania, and Slovakia. There was little evidence of progress toward further economic and political reform in the remaining transitional countries and little evidence of chances for political and economic openings in the consolidated statist autocracies. Indeed, the survey finds that, in the majority of the transitional states, not to speak of the consolidated autocratic states, the pace of change has slowed significantly.

The middle range of "transitional" countries includes a very divergent group of states, including those making progress, those experiencing significant setbacks in reform, and a large number of countries in which the reform process has stalled. The lack of reform momentum is particularly evident in the non-Baltic states that emerged from the collapse of the Soviet Union. Among these countries only one— Georgia— made significant gains. The majority of the countries registered no significant positive or negative change. In the cases of Russia and Ukraine, there were setbacks in

Table A

Rankings and Classifications East Central Europe and NIS*

DEMOCRACY RANKINGS

CONSOLIDATED DEMOCRACIES

	DEMOC	ECON
Poland	1.45	1.92
Czech Republic	1.50	2.00
Hungary	1.50	1.67
Lithuania	1.95	2.58
Slovenia	1.95	2.17
Estonia	2.05	2.00
Latvia	2.15	2.50

TRANSITIONAL GOVERNMENTS

	DEMOC	ECON
Mongolia	3.25	4.00
Bulgaria	3.55	4.08
Slovakia	3.65	3.58
Romania	3.85	4.50
Macedonia	3.95	4.67
Moldova	4.00	4.17
Russia	4.10	3.92
Croatia	4.25	3.83
Ukraine	4.25	4.75
Georgia	4.55	4.00
Kyrgyz Rep.	4.70	3.75
Albania	4.75	4.50
Armenia	4.80	4.08
Yugoslavia	4.90	4.83
Bosnia	5.35	5.67
Kazakhstan	5.35	4.50
Azerbaijan	5.55	5.00

CONSOLIDATED AUTOCRACIES

	DEMOC	ECON
Tajikistan	5.95	6.00
Belarus	6.20	6.25
Uzbekistan	6.40	6.25
Turkmenistan	6.90	6.42

ECONOMY RANKINGS

CONSOLIDATED MARKET

	ECON	DEMOC
Hungary	1.67	1.50
Poland	1.92	1.45
Czech Rep.	2.00	1.50
Estonia	2.00	2.05
Slovenia	2.17	1.95
Latvia	2.50	2.15
Lithuania	2.58	1.95

TRANSITIONAL ECONOMIES

	ECON	DEMOC
Slovakia	3.58	3.65
Kyrgyz Rep.	3.75	4.70
Croatia	3.83	4.25
Russia	3.92	4.10
Georgia	4.00	4.55
Mongolia	4.00	3.25
Armenia	4.08	4.80
Bulgaria	4.08	3.55
Moldova	4.17	4.00
Albania	4.50	4.75
Kazakhstan	4.50	5.35
Romania	4.50	3.85
Macedonia	4.67	3.95
Ukraine	4.75	4.25
Yugoslavia	4.83	4.90
Azerbaijan	5.00	5.55
Bosnia	6.17	6.25

CONSOLIDATED STATIST

	ECON	DEMOC
Tajikistan	6.00	5.95
Belarus	6.25	6.20
Uzbekistan	6.25	6.40
Turkmenistan	6.42	6.90

* This year's scores reflect the period through April 1998.

political progress and economic reform efforts. (See Table D page 14). Among the consolidated autocracies, Belarus slipped further toward repression and statism in the period under review.

The stagnation experienced by the "transitional countries" has great importance for the West and for the United States. This is so because reform has stalled in Russia, a nuclear power, and in Ukraine, a country whose independence is central to the new geopolitical balance in Eastern Europe.

The findings suggest that the very notion that most governments and societies in the region are in transition requires reappraisal. Much of our thinking about democratic and free market transitions in the region was shaped by the dramatic openings that resulted in the collapse of communism and of the Soviet Union and its imperial system. In the first years after the collapse of the old order, opposition forces, mainly associated with dissident political groups, won political power as a result of elections in many Central and East European countries. In Albania, Poland, Hungary, Czechoslovakia, and Bulgaria, anti-Communist reformers generally pursued a program of fundamental economic and political reform. In its initial phases, economic reform and the collapse of the Soviet bloc trading system precipitated a steep decline in the living standards of the majority of the population in Central and Eastern Europe. In all but one case, the Czech Republic, ex-Communist parties eventually recaptured power in the mid-1990s as public discontent over the costs of economic reform led to the defeat of anti-Communist parties. In Poland and Hungary, the ex-Communist parties held to the sound pro-market economic policies of their anti-Communist predecessors, albeit with less vigor. After a few years, the pendulum shifted due to public discontent with ex-Communist rule. Late 1997 marked the political comeback of anti-Communist and non-Communist reform parties. Essentially, the same pattern occurred in the Baltic states of Latvia, Lithuania, and Estonia.

In the non-Baltic former Soviet states, political change proceeded along a different trajectory. Initially anti-Communist reformers swept into power only in Armenia, Azerbaijan, Georgia, and Kyrgyzstan. In Tajikistan, opposition forces briefly shared power in coalition with the local nomenklatura. Only Kyrgyzstan's President Askar Akayev has survived from this initial generation of non-Communist and anti-Communist leaders. The rest fell in coups (Azerbaijan and Georgia), through resignations forced by military and political pressure (Armenia), and through civil war (Tajikistan). With the exception of Georgia, the successor governments have proved to be less reform-minded than their predecessors.

This is not to say that the changes that occurred in the former Soviet Union were not dramatic. Nevertheless, their nature is better explained by the collapse of empire and nationalist passions than by the rise of indigenous reform forces pressing for change.

The Historical Context

All states in the region, including those in which reforms never took root, have moved very far from the Marxist-Leninist model. This is because most of the states underwent both national revolutions and political and economic transformations. Thus, states where authoritarian rule and statist economies prevailed were changed by virtue of the fact that most were new entities, usually with dramatically different populations and boundaries— the result of the voluntary separation or secession of states or significant population migrations. Even the dictatorships that resisted free market reform were changed by a new balance of forces in the aftermath of the Soviet Union's collapse.

Of the 28 countries under examination, only six exist today within the boundaries of 1989: Albania, Bulgaria, Hungary, Mongolia, Poland,

and Romania. Three states—Russia, the Czech Republic and the rump Yugoslavia (Serbia-Montenegro)— inherited the infrastructure of their more multi-national precursors: the Soviet Union, Czechoslovakia, and the Socialist Federal Republic of Yugoslavia.

This set of circumstances opened the possibility for far-reaching reform. Change was accompanied in most countries by the challenge of establishing the rudimentary institutions of statehood. Even in places where authoritarian rule remained and democratic political reform was stymied, new interest groups began to influence political, state, and economic development. Nation-building represented a rare opportunity for fundamental reform. At the same time, it was occurring in places with little or no experience of sovereign rule. As Alexander Motyl suggested in *Nations in Transit 1997*, the task of nation-building — of creating sovereign state, civic, and economic institutions — is extremely complex. It should therefore not be surprising that only a minority of the new states succeeded in establishing durable democracies and free market economies.

Of the new states that emerged from the collapse of the former Soviet Union, only the former Baltic republics could draw upon a tradition of state independence from the inter-war years. Moreover, these states had benefited from the fact that in the years leading up to independence, there had been a high degree of civic and political activism and efforts by indigenous leaders to shape the contours of sovereign government. When compared to the hyper-centralism of the Soviet Union, there likewise had been a degree of decentralization in the Socialist Federal Republic of Yugoslavia before disintegration and the secession of Slovenia, Croatia, Macedonia, and Bosnia and Herzegovina.

Clearly, the non-Baltic Soviet republics were ill-equipped for political and economic transition. In most cases, leaders of these proto-states had not used the period before the collapse of Soviet rule to strengthen economic and political structures in their republics. Although most of the Soviet-era republic leaders came to abandon the Communist party after the failure of the August 1991 coup, all had emerged from the nomenklatura system, and few had been proponents of genuine statehood for their republics. Under Leonid Brezhnev as little as 6 percent of the Soviet economy was under the control of the putatively sovereign republics. Indeed, almost until the very last days of his rule, President Mikhail Gorbachev, too, had not been a proponent of decentralization. Faced with mounting pressures from secessionist movements in the outlying republics in the mid- and late-1980s, Gorbachev and the central Soviet leadership had devolved little authority to the leaders of the 15 Soviet republics. In the Russian Federation, for example, Gorbachev had been reluctant to cede power that would have strengthened his political opponent Boris Yeltsin. Moreover, even in the earliest days of his reform efforts, Gorbachev relied on centralized power in an effort to implement controlled reform from above. In truth, Gorbachev's reign strengthened central authority to propel what he styled "glasnost and perestroika." On this foundation, the challenge of building effective and stable state systems was to prove a complex, onerous, and, for many, an unattainable task.

The challenge facing the new states was to create new governmental and civic institutions *de novo*. This meant the establishment of tax systems, armed forces, finance ministries, and judicial systems. Such realities must be kept in mind when we examine the degree of progress in the new post-Communist states.

Another critical factor affecting institutional and economic development was political strife and war. The countries that emerged from the disintegration of Yugoslavia were ravaged by cross-border conflict, separatism, and bloody ethnic cleansing. While most analysts agree that the collapse of the Soviet Union was not accompanied by widespread warfare and that peace was preserved between the region's largest new states (Ukraine, Russia, Belarus, Kazakhstan, and Uzbekistan), civil wars and secessionist struggles did rage in the smaller republics (Armenia, Azerbaijan, Georgia, Moldova, and Tajikistan), and Russia confronted a separatist war in Chechnya.

The majority of post-Soviet states faced challenges to territorial integrity from internal secessionist movements and secessionist sentiments. Each of the Caucasus states (Georgia, Azerbaijan, and Armenia) was engulfed in conflicts that arose as a result of separatist movements seeking to carve out new boundaries. Russia (with Chechnya) and Moldova (with the self-styled Transdniester Republic) confronted armed force in breakaway regions. Tajikistan saw a protracted civil war fueled by regional clan interests as much as political rivalry. Ukraine faced a peaceful, but potentially destabilizing problem in the predominantly ethnic Russian Crimean peninsula. In most cases, these conflicts undermined the prospects for democratic transition. In Georgia, they encouraged autocratic rule by the country's first democratically elected President. In Azerbaijan, the struggle over the breakaway Armenian enclave of Nagorno-Karabakh precipitated events that toppled reformist President Abulfaz Elchibey. In Armenia, nationalist radicalism and growing militarism that resulted from the struggle over Nagorno-Karabakh contributed to tainted elections and a military-inspired "soft coup" that resulted in the resignation of President Levon Ter-Petrossian in early 1998.

While Russia had initially accepted the orderly secession of the former Soviet Republics, in the years that followed, Russian officials appeared at times to encourage separatist movements in a bid to become hegemonic guarantors of peace and stability among the non-Russian states. When the breakaway region of Chechnya proclaimed statehood, Russia initiated a bloody civil war that resulted in tens of thousands of deaths and the destruction of numerous Chechen cities and villages. The struggle over Chechnya, too, undermined Russia's democratic development by strengthening authoritarian forces linked to the military-industrial complex and the military and security services, by helping to increase the popularity of the Communist party, and by eroding support for the country's broader reform agenda.

In the former Soviet Union, decades of totalitarian rule meant that civil society did not emerge as a powerful force. While the years leading up to the Soviet Union's disintegration had seen a high level of political protest and mobilization in the non-Russian republics, and although the months leading up to this collapse had witnessed similar trends in Russia, such demonstrations and other spontaneous forms of civic activism did not lead to the establishment of permanent and effective civic organizations and political parties. As importantly, most trade unions in the former Soviet Union changed little from their Soviet-era predecessors and did not emerge as effective or responsible advocates of worker interests. Civic groups were weak and political parties even weaker — with the exception of indigenous Communist parties. While some reformers were co-opted into service in the governments of such states as Russia, Ukraine, Moldova, and even Belarus in the early years of statehood, in no case did the reins of power ever pass fully and for a sustained period to a group of committed non-Communist and anti-Communist reformers, as had been the case in Central and Eastern Europe. In other words, the Central European model of rapid and fundamental change was not followed.

In 1998, the evidence indicates that the period of dynamic transformation in many of these states is over. While evidence of year-to-year incremental improvements is still to be found in some Central and East European countries covered by this report, such changes continue to bypass the non-Baltic post-Soviet states. This, in turn, suggests that we need to rethink the reform process in the former Soviet Union. Progress there is clearly not inevitable. For, while the countries that *Nations In Transit* describes as consolidated democracies have made dramatic and even revolutionary strides in opening their economies, their societies, and their governments, the vast majority of gains occurred over a brief period and were focused on Central and Eastern Europe. This year's report suggests that many countries perceived to be in transition are, in fact, not undergoing slow but incremental transitions toward greater freedom, but rather are stagnating or suffering reversals in their path to reform.

Transition and Stagnation

Societies may be regarded as transitional when they are in the process of incremental, progressive change. Still other societies may be labeled as transitional because — despite having experienced significant reform — there are still important social, economic, and political threats to their political and economic arrangements.

Other societies that are considered transitional show little motion toward reform or even experience setbacks. They are considered to be transitional largely because they occupy what analysts believe is a midpoint in their political development. Yet if the political and economic arrangements in such societies persist over time and interest groups within these societies resist incremental political and market change, it is well worth asking whether such countries are indeed at a transitional mid-point or whether they represent relatively stable new political and economic arrangements that are neither free market nor socialist.

Two post-Soviet countries that are regarded to be in transition — Russia and Ukraine — merit particular attention. Together, Russia and Ukraine represent nearly two-thirds of the Soviet Union's population. Both countries have made strides in privatizing state industries, in bringing their budgets into greater balance, in restraining inflation, and in adopting a number of characteristics of the market system. Nevertheless, they have failed to create the basis for an entrepreneurial economy in which small business is the driving engine for economic growth.

Politically, Russia and Ukraine have made significant strides. Their citizens need not fear the expression of political beliefs. Political parties and civic groups can freely organize and engage in the public square. Both countries have conducted relatively open and competitive elections with parties advocating a broad range of policy options. In both countries there is no state censorship and the news and information media give voice to a broad range of opinion. While politics and culture are far more open than in the period of Gorbachev's glasnost, there are important constraints on democratic practice and the rule of law. In Russia and Ukraine, large economic interest groups have taken over most non-state mass media, usually with the support of allies within government. With the exception of the Communists, political parties are weak and underfinanced, and some are susceptible to the control of industrial and financial oligarchs. The judicial systems are not fully independent, the rule of law is weak, and corruption is rampant.

It may be tempting to view this set of events as symptomatic of a transitional mid-point in the evolution toward full-fledged democracy and an entrepreneurial free market. The dynamics of change in these countries suggest, however, that neither deep democratic reform nor a free market system is in the offing. Trends, likewise, do not augur a radical reversal toward state socialism, such as is sought by the Communists.

Instead, we are dealing with new political and economic conditions that have the characteristics of an established system. This is not to say that this system will not be subject to the ebb and flow of market forces and to the pressure of emerging

Table B
Correlation Between GDP Growth and Reform*

CONSOLIDATED DEMOCRACIES AND ECONOMIES

	% CHANGE IN GDP 1997	RATING**
Czech Rep.	1.00	1.75
Estonia	9.00	2.03
Hungary	4.40	1.58
Latvia	4.00	2.33
Lithuania	3.80	2.27
Poland	6.90	1.69
Slovenia	3.80	2.06
AVERAGE	4.70	1.96

TRANSITIONAL POLITIES AND ECONOMIES

	% CHANGE IN GDP 1997	RATING
Albania	-7.00	4.63
Armenia	3.10	4.44
Azerbaijan	5.80	5.28
Bulgaria	-7.50	3.82
Croatia	5.30	4.04
Georgia	11.30	4.28
Kazakhstan	2.00	4.93
Kyrgyz Rep.	9.00	4.23
Macedonia	1.40	4.31
Moldova	-3.00	4.08
Mongolia	3.30	3.63
Romania	-6.60	4.18
Russia	.40	4.01
Slovakia	6.50	3.62
Ukraine	-3.20	4.50
AVERAGE	1.39	4.27

AUTHORITARIAN POLITIES AND STATIST ECONOMIES

	% CHANGE IN GDP 1997	RATING
Belarus	7.00	6.23
Tajikistan	2.20	5.98
Turkmenistan	-23.00	6.66
Uzbekistan	2.40	6.33
AVERAGE	-2.85	6.30

*Bosnia and Yugoslavia were excluded from the calculations in view of the effect of internal conflict and sanctions in those countries in 1997.

**The combined average rating is the average of the cumulative scores on political and economic reform.

political forces. At the same time, this system is not protected from economic distress, market turmoil, and currency instability. It is likely, however, that in the foreseeable future, the political and economic arrangements that exist today are likely to persist in both Russia and Ukraine, and the project of true reform may take many years to achieve.

How, then, can we describe the new system that has emerged in Russia and — to a lesser degree— in Ukraine? Some reformers, including Russian economist Andrei Ilarionov, have suggested that Russia is a country in which the state has been privatized while the private sector has been made a part of the state. This process has been accompanied by the emergence of a powerful new financial-industrial oligarchy that has been given special favors by the state. Indeed, the emergence of this new Russia and Ukrainian oligarchy has been accompanied by something that very much resembles what Max Weber called the "patrimonial state". Patrimonial systems are characterized by a state that dispenses licenses to insiders, offers privileged and selectively applied subsidies, provides special favors and services, targets tax amnesties, and exerts pressures against new competitors. The losers in this insular system are new economic players, who are excluded from the privileged circle or denied access to economic life, and consumers, who are forced to pay for the goods and services of monopolies and oligopolies that may not be the most efficient producers.

In Russia, the new economic oligarchs have achieved economic power and political influence in symbiotic relationship with the post-Communist state. Their rise to wealth and power has been aided by the support of patrons in the state and inside relevant ministries. As Harvard economist Jeffrey Sachs has stated, the "Moscow authorities committed

Table C
Levels of Corruption and Changes in GDP*

	% CHANGE IN GDP 1997	RATINGS
LOWER LEVELS		
Czech Rep	1.00	B
Hungary	4.40	A
Estonia	9.00	B
Latvia	4.00	B
Lithuania	3.80	B
Poland	6.90	A
Slovenia	3.80	A
AVERAGE	4.70	
MID-LEVELS		
Belarus	7.00	C
Bulgaria	-7.50	C
Croatia	5.30	C
Georgia	11.30	C
Macedonia	1.40	C
Moldova	-3.00	C
Mongolia	3.30	C
Romania	-6.60	C
Slovakia	6.50	C
AVERAGE	1.97	
HIGHEST LEVELS		
Albania	-7.00	D
Armenia	3.10	D
Azerbaijan	5.80	D
Kazakhstan	2.00	D
Kyrgyz Rep.	9.00	D
Russia	.40	D
Tajikistan	2.20	D
Turkmenistan	-23.00	D
Ukraine	-3.20	D
Uzbekistan	2.40	D
AVERAGE	-.83	

*Bosnia and Yugoslavia were excluded from the calculations in view of the effect of internal conflict and sanctions in those countries in 1997.

a fundamental tactical error in giving up control over raw materials industries in a series of illicit transactions to a group that emerged from the inner circles of power." At various times, representatives of these oligarchs — some of them economic forces that emerged in the late 1980s and early 1990s and others former Soviet industrial managers labeled "red directors" — are offered posts within the government. In some cases, as with the financial-industrial oligarch Boris Berezovsky, they hold government posts while simultaneously controlling and managing vast private economic interests.

Such a system necessarily allows for the rapid concentration of inordinate power by this new economic oligarchy. If representatives of this privileged private sector, who already command considerable power by virtue of their wealth, their media holdings, and their influence in elections also hold key government posts, they have unchecked power. If, through such state posts, they can shape policies that affect their own economic fortunes, the systemic seeds of corruption are sown. Clearly, the exercise of state power in conjunction with vast financial resources and control over important segments of the media gives these oligarchs immense power leverage over politicians who do not command vast private economic resources. At the same time, the fragile Russian government and its leaders, including reformers, can ill afford to make enemies of these powerful interests. As a result, representatives of the economic elite are regularly offered places in the state power structures.

Participation by the oligarchs in power-sharing becomes a necessity because neither Russia's President Yeltsin nor Ukraine's President Leonid Kuchma have the backing of their parliaments. Indeed, at times the oligarchs side with anti-reform forces in the parliament to block tax reform or to protect privileged in-

Table D
Trends in Reform 1998*

CONSOLIDATED DEMOCRACIES

	POLITICAL			ECONOMIC		
	1997	1998	TREND**	1997	1998	TREND
Czech Rep.	1.38	1.50		1.88	2.00	
Estonia	2.00	2.05		2.13	2.00	
Hungary	1.44	1.50		1.63	1.67	
Latvia	2.06	2.15		2.50	2.50	
Lithuania	2.06	1.95		2.50	2.58	
Poland	1.44	1.45		2.00	1.92	
Slovenia	1.88	1.95		2.38	2.17	❸
AVERAGE	1.76	1.79		2.15	2.12	

TRANSITIONAL GOVERNMENTS

	POLITICAL			ECONOMIC		
	1997	1998	TREND	1997	1998	TREND
Albania	4.50	4.75	❺	4.00	4.50	❺
Armenia	4.75	4.80		4.00	4.08	
Azerbaijan	5.44	5.55		5.13	5.00	
Bulgaria	3.81	3.55	❸	5.38	4.08	❸
Croatia	4.25	4.25		3.88	3.83	
Georgia	4.75	4.55	❸	4.13	4.00	
Kazakhstan	5.25	5.35		4.38	4.50	
Kyrgyz Rep.	4.75	4.70		3.75	3.75	
Macedonia	3.88	3.95		4.50	4.67	
Moldova	3.81	4.00		4.00	4.17	
Romania	3.88	3.85		4.63	4.50	
Russia	3.75	4.10	❺	3.50	3.92	❺
Slovakia	3.81	3.65		3.38	3.58	❺
Ukraine	3.88	4.25	❺	4.25	4.75	❺
AVERAGE	4.32	4.38		4.21	4.24	

CONSOLIDATED AUTOCRACIES

	POLITICAL			ECONOMIC		
	1997	1998	TREND	1997	1998	TREND
Belarus	5.88	6.20	❺	6.00	6.25	❺
Tajikistan	6.00	5.95		6.13	6.00	
Turkmenistan	6.94	6.90		6.38	6.42	
Uzbekistan	6.44	6.40		6.25	6.25	
AVERAGE	6.32	6.36		6.19	6.23	

*Bosnia, Mongolia, and Yugoslavia were not ranked in 1997.

**Trend arrows represent changes in ratings of .2 or higher.

Table E
Major Transition Indicators

Country	Free and Fair Parliamentary Elections?	Free and Fair Presidential Elections?	Private Share of GDP*	Post-Communist Constitution?	1997 Freedom House Rating
Albania	Yes (1997)**	Not Direct	75	No	Partly Free
Armenia	No (1995)	No (1996)	64	Yes (1995)	Partly Free
Azerbaijan	No (1995)	No (1993)	30	Yes (1995)	Partly Free
Belarus	No (1995)	No (1994)	15	Yes (1994, '96)	Not Free
Bosnia	Yes (1996)*****	Yes (1996)**	N/A	Yes (1995)******	Partly Free
Bulgaria	Yes (1997)	Yes (1996)	45	Yes (1991)	Free
Croatia	Yes (1995)***	No (1997)	55	Yes (1990)	Partly Free
Czech Rep.	Yes (1996)	Not Direct	75	Yes (1992)	Free
Estonia	Yes (1995)	Not Direct	67	Yes (1992)	Free
Georgia	Yes (1995)	Yes (1995)	55	Yes (1995)	Partly Free
Hungary	Yes (1998)	Not Direct	86	No	Free
Kazakhstan	No (1995)	No (1991)	72	Yes (1995)	Not Free
Kyrgyz Rep.	Yes (1995)	Yes (1995)	50	Yes (1993)	Partly Free
Latvia	Yes (1995)	Not Direct	60	No****	Free
Lithuania	Yes (1996)	Yes (1992)	70	Yes (1992)	Free
Macedonia	Yes (1994)***	Yes (1994)	70	Yes (1991)	Partly Free
Moldova	Yes (1998)	Yes (1996)	45	Yes (1994)	Partly Free
Mongolia	Yes (1996)	Yes (1997)	90	Yes (1992)	Free
Poland	Yes (1997)	Yes (1995)	65	Yes (1997)	Free
Romania	Yes (1996)	Yes (1996)	55	Yes (1991)	Free
Russia	Yes (1995)	Yes (1996)***	70	Yes (1993)	Partly Free
Slovakia	Yes (1994)	Not Direct	83	Yes (1992)	Partly Free
Slovenia	Yes (1996)	Yes (1997)	50	Yes (1991)	Free
Tajikistan	No (1995)	No (1994)	20	Yes (1994)	Not Free
Turkmenistan	No (1994)	No (1992)	N/A	Yes (1992)	Not Free
Ukraine	Yes (1998)	Yes (1994)	45	Yes (1996)	Partly Free
Uzbekistan	No (1994)	No (1991)	45	Yes (1992)	Not Free
Yugoslavia	No (1996)	No (1997)	40	Yes (1992)	Not Free

* = Source: European Bank for Reconstruction and Development, mid-1997 ** = Significant Irregularities *** = Some Irregularities

**** = The 1992 Constitution is in force ***** = Significant Irregularities in Muslim-Croat Federation; Free but Not Fair elections in Serbian Republic ****** = Annex 4 of the Dayton Agreement is the Constitution of Bosnia and Herzegovina

Table F
Nations in Transit 1998 Ratings Summary

	PP	CS	IM	GPA	ROL	CO	P	MA	Mi	Democ	Econ
Albania	4.50	4.25	4.75	5.00	5.25	D	4.00	5.00	4.50	4.69	4.50
Armenia	5.75	3.50	5.25	4.50	5.00	D	3.75	4.25	4.25	4.88	4.08
Azerbaijan	5.50	5.00	5.50	6.25	5.50	D	5.00	5.00	5.00	5.38	5.00
Belarus	6.25	5.75	6.50	6.25	6.25	C	6.00	6.25	6.50	6.19	6.25
Bosnia	5.00	5.00	4.75	6.00	6.00	C	5.50	6.00	6.00	5.35	5.67
Bulgaria	2.75	3.75	3.50	4.00	3.75	C	4.00	4.00	4.25	3.44	4.08
Croatia	4.25	3.50	4.75	4.00	4.75	C	4.00	3.75	3.75	4.31	3.83
Czech Rep.	1.25	1.50	1.25	2.00	1.50	B	2.00	2.00	2.00	1.38	2.00
Estonia	1.75	2.25	1.75	2.25	2.25	B	2.00	2.00	2.00	2.00	2.00
Georgia	4.50	4.25	4.25	5.00	4.75	C	4.00	4.00	4.00	4.44	4.00
Hungary	1.25	1.25	1.50	1.75	1.75	A	1.50	1.75	1.75	1.44	1.67
Kazakhstan	5.50	5.00	5.50	5.50	5.25	D	4.25	4.50	4.75	5.31	4.50
Kyrgyz Rep.	5.00	4.50	5.00	4.50	4.50	D	4.25	3.50	3.50	4.75	3.75
Latvia	2.00	2.25	1.75	2.50	2.25	B	2.50	2.50	2.50	2.06	2.50
Lithuania	1.75	2.00	1.50	2.50	2.00	B	2.25	2.75	2.75	1.81	2.58
Macedonia	3.50	3.75	4.00	4.00	4.50	C	4.00	5.00	5.00	3.94	4.67
Moldova	3.50	3.75	4.25	4.50	4.00	C	4.00	4.25	4.25	3.88	4.17
Mongolia	2.75	3.25	3.25	3.50	3.50	C	4.25	4.00	3.75	3.19	4.00
Poland	1.25	1.25	1.50	1.75	1.50	A	2.25	1.75	1.75	1.38	1.92
Romania	3.25	3.75	4.00	4.00	4.25	C	4.50	4.50	4.50	3.81	4.50
Russia	3.50	4.00	4.25	4.50	4.25	D	3.25	4.25	4.25	4.00	3.92
Slovakia	3.50	3.00	4.00	3.75	4.00	C	3.25	3.75	3.75	3.63	3.58
Slovenia	2.00	2.00	1.75	2.50	1.50	A	2.50	2.00	2.00	1.81	2.17
Tajikistan	5.75	5.25	6.00	6.75	6.00	D	6.25	6.00	5.75	5.75	6.13
Turkmenistan	7.00	7.00	7.00	6.75	6.75	D	6.75	6.25	6.25	6.94	6.42
Ukraine	3.50	4.25	4.75	4.75	4.00	D	4.50	4.50	5.25	4.13	4.75
Uzbekistan	6.50	6.50	6.50	6.25	6.50	D	6.25	6.25	6.25	6.50	6.25
Yugoslavia	5.00	5.00	4.50	5.00	5.00	D	4.50	5.00	5.00	4.88	4.83

Category Note:

PP-Political Process CS-Civil Society IM-Independent Media GPA-Government and Public Administration ROL-Rule of Law
CO-Corruption P-Privatization MA-Macroeconomic Policy MI-Microeconomic Policy

Continued from page 11

dustries. Co-opting the economic oligarchs into state structures is necessary to maintain a coalition of forces that can stave off assaults on the executive from anti-reform parliaments. In the absence of strong political parties and truly independent media, it also secures the needed financial support of these economic circles for expensive presidential and legislative campaigns. At the same time the integration of these oligarchic interests into the state requires compromises that weaken governmental reform agendas.

From this perspective, what some would regard as Yeltsin's capricious rule or Kuchma's lack of resolve can also be understood as maneuvering to allow powerful economic interest groups to participate in the governing elite in a fashion that denies them sufficient time to consolidate power within the state and thus to challenge the state's democratically elected leaders. Thus, the seemingly endless personnel shifts in the upper reaches of government in Russia and Ukraine are a response to the systemic problem of the concentration of power by the financial-industrial elites.

It is significant that, while free market reformers have frequently participated in the shaping of the state's reform agenda and while the radical anti-market Communists dominate in the Ukrainian and Russian legislatures, the policies of neither political force has prevailed. Political life, instead, is developing along a third path: a patrimonial system in which the state is symbiotically linked to the new oligarchic economic interests.

What accounts for this state of affairs? This essay has already indicated some of the historical and developmental reasons that account for the different problems that confronted the new post-Soviet states and that contributed to their specific path of patrimonial development. Another related factor is the sustained political role of strong Communist and leftist anti-reform forces in Russia and Ukraine. In Ukraine, the Communist-led left has successfully and repeatedly delayed the implementation of reforms required by the international financial community as a precondition for credits. The left has stifled tax reforms and blocked or slowed privatization through legislative action and inaction. In Russia, where the President has more autonomy and power than his Ukrainian counterpart, the Communist left has regularly delayed personnel changes in key ministries and impeded the formation of new government teams. Frequently, in an effort to govern on the basis of some consensus and to stave off mass protest, the Russian and Ukrainian executive branches have co-opted representatives of these parties and movements by offering them key state posts.

In Russia and Ukraine, political and economic development is complicated not only because it occurs in the context of Communist opposition to reform, but also because it develops in the context of a leftist opposition that is opposed to the very existence of the Russian and Ukrainian states. In both countries, the Communist Party seeks the restoration of the Soviet Union and consequently an end to the state sovereignty of Russia and Ukraine.

Can This State of Affairs Persist?

The evidence of history suggests that patrimonial, corporatist regimes can survive for long periods. Consider the cases of such Latin American states as Brazil and Argentina from the 1950s to the mid-1980s and, more recently, of Indonesia and Malaysia. The leaders of such states can at times pursue policies that maintain currency stability, restrain the growth of the state sector, maintain budgets that are in reasonable balance, and establish policies that allow for export-driven economic growth. Indeed, such systems can be stable and even productive for sustained periods.

In the end, however, crony capitalism, monopolism, and corruption within such systems prove inefficient impediments to sustained economic growth. Such systems provoke crises, and, with the gradual emergence of middle class entrepreneurial interests and discontent among workers, such crises in patrimonial systems can lead to democratic change and fundamental free market reform. Such auspicious outcomes, however, are far from guaranteed. Economic crises can also engender instability that leads to the direct engagement of the military and security structures in political life and deals severe setbacks to human liberty. Democratic and free-market outcomes are therefore not the inevitable consequence of political and economic crises in patrimonial systems; rather, they are a likely outcome provided there are significant and organized democratic and reform forces. The nurturing of such ideas, values, and forces should therefore be a locus of U.S. engagement in the region.

Russia, Ukraine, and many of the other states of the former Soviet Union are in the midst of a prolonged crisis that started with the economic decline of the mid-1980s. Nevertheless, with the exception of a brief period of mass activism, strikes, and political ferment in the late 1980s — much of it provoked by the forces of nationalism — there has been little sustained social mobilization or civic activism in these countries. Indeed, the absence of a strong independent civil society suggests that the current systems in Russia and elsewhere will persevere for some time. They are not likely to be supplanted by a new reform-based free market democracy nor by an old-style statist system led by the Communists and the far left.

Implications for Policy

It is not the intention of this survey to make specific policy recommendations, but there are some lines of approach that appear to issue naturally from the findings. First, the record of change in many of the countries in the region has been impressive. Despite difficulties, the vast majority are far freer and more open than under the state socialism of the Communist era. There are now seven consolidated market democracies among the 28 states under review. Several more appear poised to make—or have the potential to make— the transition to stable democratic market systems in the near future.

Second, while the study finds that several states have seen the consolidation of authoritarian rule and state-dominated economies and while there is evidence that the momentum for reform has slowed in the former republics of the Soviet Union, it would be a mistake to conclude that U.S. assistance has been squandered. The assumption that the post-Communist world was on a trajectory of inevitable democratic and free-market reform was flawed from the outset. In truth, reform in the post-Communist world has been an extremely complex and difficult task conducted against the will of powerful entrenched interests and with resistance by broad segments of the population accustomed over generations to dependence on a custodial state. Aid and assistance, even when it has not produced fundamental reform, has in many cases had the effect of preventing reversals of limited progress.

Third, even in countries in which considerable progress has been made, there may still be a requirement for the intelligent investment of resources to help strengthen democratic practices, improve economic policies, promote respect for the rights of minorities, and perfect the rule of law.

It is equally important, however, that limited government resources be intelligently focused on clear goals. This requires making difficult distinctions about where particular countries are headed and what mix and degree of aid and assistance can be applied effectively. If societies resist change, this need not mean an end to assistance efforts – only their deployment in behalf of initiatives that over time can create the framework for democratic and economic change.

Apart from the countries that are consolidating their democracies, there are three types of societies in which U.S. AID is likely to be engaged. The first category is authoritarian societies such as Belarus or Uzbekistan, in which democracy and the free market have been completely stifled. In such closed societies, collaboration with indigenous governments and anti-democratic ruling elites is not likely to produce serious reforms. Here, approaches should emphasize the successor generation in education efforts aimed at strengthening democratic and free market values. Programs can focus on support for authentic independent civic groups that are pressing for change and may require assistance in the form of support for printing of uncensored newspapers and books. Some assistance can be targeted for human rights monitoring and the building of coordianted international pressure. Efforts to strengthen foreign broadcasting into such closed societies are a component of a long-term strategy aimed at promoting democracy and reform.

The second category is represented by transitional countries, such as Romania or Bulgaria—in which reformers are in power and are moving toward fundamental change. In such countries programs of technical assistance and the investment of significant resources can make a difference in securing democracy and a free market economy and are likely to involve close collaboration with the state, civic, and private economic sectors. There are also transitional countries such as Slovakia, where reformers are not yet in power, but where civil society and independent media are strong, and in which democratic political processes hold open the prospect of a change in government. These, too, merit the investment of considerable resources to complete political and economic transitions.

The third, and perhaps the most difficult, category for policymakers is represented by such countries as Ukraine and Russia, in which powerful indigenous economic interests stifle reform, corruption is rampant, and anti-reform Communist political parties block or retard progress; and in which reformist civic groups and the independent media are relatively weak. In these countries, aid and assistance can best be focused on strengthening change agents such as public policy research institutes, independent civic groups, independent media, educational organizations and institutions, and groups seeking to build respect for human rights and the rule of law. Here, investments of resources can productively be made to strengthen democratic and free-market values and respect for the rule of law within the successor generation, which ultimately will be in a position to secure a successful transition.

As this report is being completed, the currency and equity markets of the region are beset by turmoil and significant political and social tension. In Russia, this turmoil has seen a shift to the left in the government, as part of an effort to placate a hostile Communist-led parliament. The full consequences of the region's turmoil will not be known for months, if not years. Regardless of the effects of the current economic difficulties in many of the former Communist countries, this report--which provides a clear and unbiased assessment of the status of the key components of healthy democratic, civic, and economic life--can serve as an important resource in sorting out what has and has not been achieved and in determining the best approaches for promoting constructive change in a critical and potentially volatile part of the world.

Adrian Karatnycky is President of Freedom House, co-author of three books on Soviet and post-Soviet politics, and editor of Nations in Transit.

Notes

1. The Board believed that incomplete data on issues related to corruption as well as the fact that the judgments are influenced by perceptions of corruption in addition to actual instances of corrupt practices, make it impossible to provide a more nuanced grading system than the "A to D" scale used herein.

2. It should be kept in mind that economic statistics for Belarus are regarded by most economists as unreliable, as output remains heavily subsidized by the state, some commodity prices are fixed by the state, and currency exchange rates are state-controlled.

NATIONS IN TRANSIT

Stealing the Dream: "Bandit Capitalism" in the Post-Communist States

Stephen Handelman

You could call it shock therapy. In the nearly ten years since the collapse of the Soviet empire, corruption has replaced the command economy as the region's most conspicuous, and oppressive, feature. Even as the governments of central Europe and the former Soviet Union have settled into different levels of economic and political development, not one has been able to avoid the classic temptations of power.

The extent to which political corruption is "normal" behavior for nations in transit or a sign of system failure has, justifiably, become a subject of earnest debate among Western policymakers and investors. They have few precedents to work with. There has never been a similar case this century in which so many separate countries have simultaneously faced the challenge of constructing a new economic system and a new political framework in which it can operate.

The reports on corruption in this year's Freedom House survey illustrate how formidable that challenge has been. They are, in their own way, an ironic response to the radical "shock" reforms prescribed by the West in the 1990s. As a reminder that human behavior rarely moves in step with political ideals, the shock this time is on us. The reports tell, in many respects, the story of a return to business as usual.

The transformation of the former Communist economies released a dazzling burst of entrepreneurial energy. But in far too many countries that energy was pressed into the service of older, familiar and darker forces.

Scandals involving fraud, conflict-of-interest, embezzlement, graft, money-laundering and murder have appeared from Poland to Kazakhstan, and from the Balkans to Belarus. A class of newly rich elites shuttles between ministry offices and company boardrooms in a pattern that derives as much from the amoral universe of the old Communist *nomenklatura* as from the opportunities offered by the capitalist marketplace.

Communist authorities relied on their monopoly of political power to control th e disbursement of patronage. Now, their successors collude with so-called "bandit capitalists" whose achievement of monopoly control over strategic sectors of the economy guarantees a steady source of income to the public treasury and, not coincidentally, the governments' continuation in power. The persistence of old habits of state-sponsored larceny calls into question many of the assumptions held at the beginning of the post-Cold War era.

Needless to say, political corruption in central Europe and Eurasia has been "modernized" by the accelerating globalization of business in the 1990s, and by the creation of a cyber-economy where millions of dollars can be transferred across borders at the click of a mouse button. Those factors have made the goal of transparent markets and honest government equally elusive to developing nations elsewhere in the world — and to some "advanced" states as well. Nevertheless, the experience of the countries reviewed here raises uniquely difficult questions.

Are free-market systems as easy to transplant as we thought? Did the pressure for speedy and radical economic reforms somehow distort a process that should have been left to evolve naturally? Were there stabilizing elements in the old systems that could have been preserved?

The answers to these questions will shape not only the disposition of billions of dollars in aid and investment to the region, but future political strategies. And they challenge us in turn to re-examine our own theories of the link between free markets and democracy.

Even if corruption is, as some maintain, a natural stage along the path to prosperity, it threatens to devalue the entire exercise of democratization and, potentially, paves the way for authoritarian or corporatist regimes to come to power on anti-corruption platforms. While such a development arguably might improve prospects for stability, it would also negate the dreams which spurred many of the revolutions in the first place. Whether they view these developments with concern or not, most analysts would now agree that corruption and crime are key factors in evaluating the post-Communist experiments with free-market democracy. It seems obvious now, but in the days of triumphant "end-of-history" analyses, few people gave them weight. An unwillingness to accept the evidence on the ground may even have helped to exacerbate the problem, as foreign investment and aid poured in with little regard to how it was going to be used and who were the ultimate beneficiaries.

Some early studies were already noting the damage to the social fabric of post-Communist societies by indiscriminate policies that targeted the welfare-state paternalism of the old system without providing legal protection from the strains of the new markeplace. One early symptom of trouble was the soaring crime rate in countries where personal safety had been one of the few unambiguous advantages of Party rule. Another was the rush to pyramid and other dubious investment schemes which exploited the popular belief that the free market meant easy and instant personal wealth. Of course, Communist societies were neither crime-free nor devoid of scheming for private gain, but the sense of collective endeavor kept many of the worst materialistic tendencies under restraint. Even corrupt Party mandarins took care to keep their luxuries away from public view.

The impact of post-Communist profiteering has been just as jarring for countries outside the region. Those who expected the new markets of Russia and Central Europe to settle down following a brief period of lawlessness were brought up short by evidence that criminal behavior was being exported beyond the borders of the old empire.

Over the past decade, Russian and East European mafiya groups have set up subsidiary operations everywhere their transnational business interests have taken them, leaving in the process a bloody trail of victims in New York, Los Angeles, Miami Beach, London, Frankfurt and dozens of other cities. In the same period, resources from the former Soviet Union have been dumped in the bazaars of international commerce by traders exploiting the breakdown of export and customs controls (usually with the active or passive connivance of their governments). Gold, oil, diamonds, aluminum, nickel, submarines, weapons, drugs and even nuclear materials are just some of the plundered goods.

The absence of strict banking regulations turned many central European countries and Russia itself into centers for international money-laundering. And, perhaps even more ominously, the massive amounts of cash flowing out of the East (an estimated $120 billion in five years from Russia alone) provided opportunities for bribery and corruption on a world scale. Corruption in the East has been the equivalent of a global infectious disease.

Yet finding a way to stop the contagion has been complicated by the fact that those most directly affected do not always see the problem in the stark, moral terms that outsiders do.

Outrage at the scandals rippling across the region has usually been limited to a few politicians, academics and members of the intelligentsia. The kind of popular outcry that could be translated into a political movement has so far been missing. In the streets and shops, it is more likely to be seen as proof that the old rules of the game have not changed.

The example of Albania, where the collapse of pyramid schemes triggered a prolonged episode of violence that eventually took down a government, has not been repeated elsewhere. While it would be foolhardy to rule out a wider backlash in the future, corruption at the top, more often than not, has served as a license for petty graft and chicanery at the bottom.

The ability to circumvent legal structures was essential to survival in the old regimes, and the evidence of daily reality shows such skills remain highly valued. A recent survey taken by Russia's Public Opinion Foundation asked Russians to select the qualities they believed necessary for success. Overwhelming majorities picked "good connections" and dishonesty. Only 39 percent chose "hard work." Another poll found that 77 percent believed "corruption will continue far into the future."

All the same, few governments can afford to appear sanguine about corruption, even if they have been notoriously unable to deal with it. President Boris Yeltsin has called it "Russia's most serious problem," and he announced in 1997 his fifth "war on crime" in as many years. Yeltsin's diagnosis has been repeated in state after state.

In June 1997, justice ministers from across Europe gathered in Prague to underline their concerns that the impact of modern crime stretches beyond international borders. The most passionate warnings came from the former Communist states.

"(We) believed corruption would no longer pose a big problem in an emerging market economy since the reasons for it would have ceased to exist," Justice Minister Pal Vastagh of Hungary admitted ruefully. His Ukrainian counterpart, Serhii Holovaty, spoke of the "institutionalisation" of corrupt practices in the East. "Because of the absence of accountability within hierarchical power structures, the scope for fraud, corruption, and self-aggrandizement is broad, to put it mildly," he said. "The distinction between organized crime and certain aspects of government activity is often indistinguishable."

But distinctions do exist. A review of the various corruption scandals that absorbed the governments of central Europe and the newly independent states last year turns up marked differences in both scale and gravity.

Many of the scandals are tied to the process of privatization, and in most cases they did not directly affect workers and their families. Although the voucher programs in Russia, for example, were designed to make everyone feel part of the exercise of disposing state property, in reality the sell-offs occupied the undivided attention only of small groups of financiers, managers and public officials. Once the enterprises came into private hands, they became pieces of someone's expanding empire rather than targets for modernization and investment. The real cost of such asset-stripping must be counted in lost opportunities rather than dollars.

Ironically, some of the most corruption-riddled privatization deals were the result of policies aimed at co-opting the former Communist establishment. In the early 1990s, Moscow's "Young Turks," led by Yegor Gaidar and Anatoly Chubais, believed the best way to avoid having their reform plans sabotaged by the old-line managers of state enterprises was to buy them out. In what was described as an exchange of power for property, managers were offered the first opportunity to purchase majority shares at rigged prices. Just how much of a bargain they were given is indicated by an estimate from The Financial Times of London, which assessed the collective value of some 15,000 companies sold off by the state at $14 billion — a sum equal to the market capitalization of one U.S. cereal company (Kellogg).

Adding insult to injury, much of the money used to purchase state enterprises came from funds secretly diverted from the Party treasury during the final years of perestroika. Thus, the state's own money was used to defraud itself.

With similar lack of foresight, the reformers tried to kickstart other sectors of the embryonic private economy by giving favored bankers the right to collect customs duties and handle other government budget funds. Within a few years, the accumulating interest on those funds helped bankers who had started out with limited capital and even less financial experience acquire vast power, previously unimaginable riches, and large, secret armies to protect themselves. But any hope that the beneficiaries of the government's largesse would repay their good fortune in the form of investments in productive sectors of the economy dissipated when the banks turned into political players in their own right.

In 1996, the seven most prominent bankers funneled cash to a desperate Boris Yeltsin facing reelection against what then seemed a resurgent Communist Party. "Capitalism's bared fangs," in the words of Boris Berezovsky, one of the banker-saviors, successfully eliminated the threat — only to turn its avaricious instincts on the remaining pieces of the state economy.

Over a four-month period last summer, the largest Russian banking and industrial monopolies waged a war among themselves that was as merciless and consuming as any mafiya turf struggle, over the privatization of Syazinvest, the state telecommunications giant. The fallout from that battle was so intense that Yeltsin called the bankers, many of whom had worked as officials in his government, into his office for peace talks. The banking oligarchs, who by their own admission control fifty per cent of the Russian GDP (some even made Forbes Magazine's list of world billionaires) have erased the remaining lines between the public and the private interest. Corporate battles are now a form of political struggle — and vice versa.

Although Russia offers the most egregious examples of how the fortunes of politicians are tied to jockeying for advantage in the new economy, the Freedom House reports illustrate how the syndrome has repeated itself in each of the transitional states.

The huge flows of foreign investment pouring into the Caucasus and Central Asia, where newly confirmed oil and gas reserves have sparked a pipeline-building boom, intensified the already flourishing institutional criminality of the region. In Kazakhstan, top ministers dismissed for financial improprieties mysteriously turn up as local managers of international resource exploration firms and then, just as mysteriously, return to their old government posts. A former Kazakh premier candidly described the process as a division of natural resources "among the oligarchy."

Not surprisingly, the first line of defense in many of the emerging economies has been the easiest to sabotage. Police and judicial structures are fragile everywhere. More than 100 prosecutors and judges were under investigation for bribery in Bulgaria last year, and scandals have touched the most senior police authorities in nearly every country. It is not simply that they are too poorly paid, too poorly trained and too poorly equipped to fight white- collar criminals whose sophistication would challenge Western law enforcement authorities. There is little motivation to enforce laws which would put them into conflict with the ministers who control their salaries, a problem demonstrated by the long, sad list of prosecutors, police chiefs and judicial investigators who have been dismissed from their jobs or even jailed for probing too intimately.

Like the police, civil servants have been bellweathers of the ex-socialist states' inability to cope with the contradictions of the new economy. Paid starvation wages, and forced to watch in frustration as their political masters rake in millions, many have found profiteering hard to resist. Some 2,500 Russian officials were under investigation for bribery in 1997, a figure that probably bears no relationship to the extent of the problem. Yet civil servants make easy scapegoats. If the auditors in the Russian Duma are to be believed, investigations into the disappearance of billions of dollars from state coffers, involving some of the state's most senior ministers, have been quietly shelved.

The standard cures prescribed for corruption in developing nations include the development of a coherent body of commercial and civil law, the training of an independent judiciary, and the molding of a professional, non-partisan civil service. These would be helpful — if belated — but they do not address the real problem. Post-Communist societies are already awash in laws, but they lack the framework of mutual consent and collective will to make them meaningful.

In May 1997, Yeltsin issued a decree ordering every top official in the Russian government to disclose all sources of income. The responses were eye-opening. Then-Prime Minister Viktor Chernomyrdin, for instance, claimed an income of $8,000 and property worth $46,000. But he also admitted he owned a sport utility vehicle worth over $19,000 — an apparent extravagance for someone with such modest holdings. He did not say whether it was a gift, and he was apparently not asked. Chernomyrdin has stoutly denied allegations that he is one of Russia's wealthiest men, thanks to his stock holdings in Gazprom, the state gas company he once ran and whose fortunes he was presumably able to affect as prime minister. Other officials provided equally dubious reports, but even those who were disarmingly frank, such as the leader of the Kalmyk government who reported his income as $1 million, aroused no further questions.

It is reasonable to ask why any government would go through such a potentially embarrassing exercise and then compound the problem by doing nothing with the answers it received. The only reasonable answer is that such a government considers itself strong enough to do exactly what it chooses.

One of the curious facts about corruption in the post-communist world is that governments have been empowered, rather than weakened by it. Selling access and influence may fatten individual pockets but it also underlines a government's control over the keys to wealth. The distribution of property rights is one of those keys, and it explains why the ownership of land and property remains a bitterly disputed issue in many ex-socialist countries. Governments' retention of the power to determine who can own what and for how long may be the most significant factor in the systemic corruption of most of the former Soviet republics.

From the beginning of the post-Communist era in Russia, small business owners and budding entrepreneurs shared one fear — that everything they owned or operated might be expropriated at the stroke of a bureaucrat's pen. The fears of re-nationalization and, lately, the fear of prosecution (if a business rival with compromising information should happen to win the favor of power brokers) continue to motivate the chaotic accumulation of capital. It also underlies the contemptuous attitude towards legal niceties. If everything can end tomorrow, why bother about details?

Some of those fears may seem exaggerated, but they have been sharpened by an exploitive tax regime and the arbitrary enforcement of administrative decrees. Large numbers of people have thus been driven out of the legitimate economy and, in a Catch-22, have made themselves even more vulnerable to criminal and government predators. A "gray" or "black" economy has reappeared in almost all states. In both Russia and Ukraine, for instance, the shadow economy is estimated to account for nearly 50 per cent of GDP.

Other "traditional" forms of economic relationships have revived. In St. Petersburg, a spokeswoman for the municipal health department blithely explained to a reporter that employees were expected to rely on "non-budget funds" (bribes) to compensate for their low salaries — a practice that dates from Czarist times.

Such developments give inordinate power and authority to the species that was supposed to have expired with the end of the Communist era, namely, the *nomenklatura* mandarin. In Ukraine, where a sophisticated government infrastructure, huge resources, and an entrepeneurial culture should have created a European success story, the web of Soviet-era connections threatens to suffocate key sectors of the economy. Agriculture, for instance, has been weakened by the open connivance of government ministers and former state enterprise managers to inflate prices and dampen production. Similarly, in the Baltics, a wave of bank scandals was traced to old-boy networks of former apparatchiks and security officials.

Using experienced bureaucrats to manage the economic transition may have been unavoidable in the early years, but their working patterns of secrecy, corruption and influence-peddling now act as an intolerable drag on the development of open market economies.

An even darker tendency becomes apparent when the links between corruption and violence are examined.

A few days after then-Russian Central Bank chairman Sergei Dubinin exposed the diversion of over half-a-billion dollars in government funds by a former minister, shots were fired at the windshield of his car. In Belarus, a leading government official named Yevhenii Mikolataly was killed by a car bomb before he could go ahead with his plan to expose the corrupt practices of two government ministers. More than 80 Russian bankers have been murdered in mob-style assassinations.

In the Balkans, the association between corruption and politically-motivated violence is made graphically clear in the Freedom House report from that region. Last year, three close allies of Yugoslav President Slobodan Milosevic were gunned down in mafiya-style hits. One of the victims, Zoran Todorovic, had become a millionaire several times over on the strength of his ability to exploit international sanctions that pushed up the price of goods he smuggled in from the West. However, as his interests gradually expanded into oil and other resource sectors the protection provided by his government friends could not save him from the retribution of equally well-placed competitors.

Corruption has deepened governments' dependence on organized crime. The traditional mafiya clans in Russia, the Caucasus and Eastern Europe were often used by governments in the fading years of communism to keep order in the black economy. They have been largely overtaken by more professional and better-armed criminal organizations, often led by ex-military or intelligence officials, who carry out the blackmail, extortion and assassinations required to keep order in the jungle of post-Communist capitalism.

Russia's troubled parliament provides a sobering case study of the criminalization of politics. Like its counterparts elsewhere, the Duma has pushed for greater accountability from government ministers. But it developed a credibility problem of its own. Thanks to constitutional guarantees of immunity from prosecution, the parliament has been sprinkled with con artists and gangsters of all types. When one deputy accused his colleagues of accepting bribes from large corporations and state enterprises, there were immediate calls for his expulsion.

Public knowledge of the excesses of corrupt officials and gangster-businessmen is due in large part to the work of an active, probing media — one of the most encouraging developments in the post-Communist world. Yet the press role as watchdog has also been seriously compromised as leading oligarchs buy up newspapers and TV stations to promote their own ends. The most revealing glimpses of high-level Russian corruption were published in newspapers controlled by those who lost out in the Syazinvest auction. As in the shrill political denunciations of the Communist era, it has become important to recognize the motives behind the charges — which often tends to blunt the outrage, regardless of their accuracy. Since so few corruption cases ever come to trial, most citizens feel justified in a refusal to regard the nefarious schemes of their political leaders as having anything to do with their own lives.

This may be the most destructive wound that corruption has inflicted on the body politic of the new states. Citizens, when they are not themselves investing in some get-rich-quick scheme, have come to regard entrepreneurial capitalists and government ministers with equal distaste. A cynical populace is hardly fertile ground for the cultivation of a free-market democracy.

In every country, there is no shortage of political voices eager to exploit the steadily increasing gap between the lifestyles of the region's new rich and the majority of their compatriots. Nationalist, authoritarian, and anti-capitalist appeals continue to resonate among large sectors of the population.

The foregoing summary and the special corruption reports from Freedom House contributors this year suggest the beginning of some answers to the questions posed at the start of this essay. Western advisors and analysts were clearly over-optimistic in their conviction that post-communist economies could be transformed by the implantation of result-oriented economic instruments, values and techniques that have worked well elsewhere. Especially when the bureaucracy overseeing such changes is forced to make dangerous compromises to achieve them.

We underestimated the residual power of the older systems (and their managers), while badly overestimating the ability of reformers to shape the political directions of the new economies. And we failed to account for the pervasive contempt and suspicion for legal authority that remains the most abiding legacy of the Communist era. Western policymakers and international financial institutions have made the establishment of a civil society and transparent markets a factor in assistance and exchange programs, but very often the flood of investment and aid, and the growing concern for the economic stability of the larger economies, tends to push such considerations from the top of the agenda. Until attitudes of openness, honesty and trust in government take root in the popular culture, there is little hope of short-term change — even less hope that outsiders can affect the outcome significantly.

Nevertheless, that doesn't release outsiders from the responsiblity of paying close and persistent attention to the political motives and the connections of "partners" seeking deals or help, the kind of ongoing scrutiny which might have helped avoid last year's embarrassing quarrel in

Russia involving Harvard-sponsored economists and the U.S. Agency for International Development. The operative approach must be, as in dealing with any outbreak of malignancy, to do no harm.

As crony capitalism is replaced by overt corporatist control over governments in many areas of the former Soviet bloc, there's every likelihood that the distance between reformers' hopes and reality will get even larger. The situation was summed up in a few pithy words by Irina Yasina, director of a financial information company in St. Petersburg. "The nation and the government," she said, "are living their own separate lives."

The old Party bosses, now departed from the scene, would have wondered what all the fuss was about.

Stephen Handelman is the author of Comrade Criminal: Russia's New Mafiya.

NATIONS IN TRANSIT

The Year In Context

Allen Lynch

In his remarkable 1993 study entitled *Making Democracy Work*[1], Harvard political scientist Robert Putnam examined the consequences and sought to account for the differences in implementation of wide-reaching administrative reforms in each of Italy's 20 provinces since 1970. One of Putnam's unexpected conclusions reflected the continuing influence of distant history: one of the most reliable indicators of how effectively a particular region or city had exploited the opportunities of the greater freedom allowed by administrative decentralization turned out to be that region's level of civic development in the late Middle Ages! While nearly all of Italy's regions benefited significantly from the devolution of power from Rome, the gap in political, civic, and relatedly economic development between Italy's "North" and "South" remained as large, if not larger, after the experience of reform as before.

Likewise, the emerging patterns of political and economic development in post-communist Europe during the first post-Soviet decade suggest strongly that history and politics are strongly intertwined in these states' transit from their recent and common communist experience. Each state's experience under communism, which itself was conditioned by particularities of history and circumstance, continues to project a major if inevitably declining influence upon the prospects for freedom, prosperity, stability, and security in the years ahead.[2] To be sure, specific policy choices and ongoing political and economic configurations are serving to differentiate the post-communist states: *ex uno plura* is a plausible summary of this emerging reality. But the differentiation across the post-Communist region is not random in nature. The emergence of four relatively distinct groups of states that are defined in terms of geographical regions (corresponding to the nature and degree of post-Communist development toward political and economic freedom) implies that there are deeply rooted forces at work that impel or constrain a given state's political and economic prospects. The four regions may be broadly defined as: East-Central Europe (extending to the Baltic states and including Slovenia and Croatia), South-Eastern Europe (with Bosnia and Albania being understood as wards of the great powers), the Slavic core of the Commonwealth of Independent States, as well as the Caucasus, and Central Asia. As a general rule, it appears that the closer that a given state is to "the West" (conceived as the broader Group of Seven advanced industrial democracies)—geographically, historically, economically, culturally, and diplomatically—the greater are its chances for managing the intrinsic challenges of establishing simultaneously political democracy and market capitalism in a mutually reinforcing and self-sustaining fashion. Interestingly, the consolidated capitalist democracies are all located in East-Central Europe while the consolidated repressive regimes, with the exception of Belarus, are all located in Central Asia; the "in-between" states, i.e., those whose fundamental political and economic conditions and direction remain fluid, indeterminate and potentially unstable in the short- to medium-term future, are for the most part located literally "in-between" East-Central Europe and Central Asia.

How are we to explain this close correspondence between political-economic direction and geographical location? Five factors appear to account for a given state's capacity to manage the dilemmas of the post-Communist transition. Two factors are historical in nature, and concern the impact of the communist political legacy and the legacy of imperialism in a given state; two additional factors concern political choices made in the last decade but which are conditioned by the exit from both communism and imperialism, i.e., the degree of political democratization and the degree of economic marketization undertaken in the given state; the fifth and final factor is the impact of the international environment—economically, diplomatically, militarily—on a given transitional state. As we shall see, beyond a certain threshold of economic and political development, it is arguably external factors that have had the greatest single impact upon a given state's ability to negotiate the path of economic, political, and social revolution (for that is what it is) in the wake of the communist collapse.

It may be helpful at this point to clarify several points that are often obscured in discussions about democracy and democratic transitions. The first and most important is that an important distinction exists between democracy as a set of values and democracy as a set of institutions.[3] It is far from clear that the kinds of values that today many commonly consider democratic (e.g., equality, liberty, tolerance) are as a matter of principle best and always advanced by democratic politics. Indeed, Aristotle held that the ideal form of government, one that would advance the common weal and respect that which was due the individual, was an enlightened despot of Solomonic judgment and capabilities. Conceding for the moment the difficulties of finding such an individual, not to mention ensuring that his or her successors would maintain the tradition, the fact remains that it has very frequently been the case that indisputably democratic institutions have thwarted as well as advanced democratic values. Conversely, indisputably authoritarian institutions have often promoted liberal values, both politically and economically.

Consider, for instance, that slavery was abolished in the United States through the vehicle of the bloodiest war that had been experienced in either Europe or North America in the century between 1815-1914, whereas Tsarist Russia abolished its comparable institution of serfdom in 1861 by decree, and quite peaceably at that. Moreover, U.S. Democratic institutions proved insufficient to guarantee the civil rights of emancipated slaves for fully a century thereafter. In Latin America, the modeling of post-colonial constitutions after 1825 on the U.S. Constitution, with its emphasis on checking and blocking the accumulation of central state power, served under the very different economic and social conditions of the region to perpetuate feudalistic elites' grip on power: such imported democratic structures hindered rather than advanced the democratization of society. In recent times, the sudden convening of (genuinely) free elections in multinational Bosnia-Herzegovina in the early 1990s had the (predictable) effect of providing democratic legitimacy to three purely and exclusively nationalist political parties (i.e., Croat/Catholic, Serb/Orthodox, and Bosniak/Muslim), thereby fueling the genocidal war that soon ensued. Civil wars in the multi-ethnic societies of Georgia and Moldova were also triggered by the institution of free elections in societies which lacked a sufficient pre-existing social and political consensus to make elections a factor for stability and unity rather than discord and strife.

The Napoleonic civil code, which remains central to the legal structures of contemporary democratic Western Europe, was of course imposed by Napoleonic means. Likewise, some of the most outstanding successes in democratic development have been imposed by foreign conquest and rule: the Allied conquest and domination of Germany and Japan between 1945-1949/50, in which both states were compelled to adopt democratic institutions, is only the most recent and dramatic case of this kind. Previously it was the British Empire, through foreign conquest and imperial administration, which laid the groundwork for democracy in North America, Australia, New Zealand, India, South Africa, the Caribbean, and elsewhere (even Ireland), in the process becoming the greatest propagator of democracy in history. The relatively liberal yet imperial administration of the late Habsburg era—by contrast to the harsher rule of the Ottomans and the Russian Tsars— is itself one of the historical factors that work in favor of Czech, Slovene, and even Croat efforts to establish liberal economic, social, and political institutions in the post-Communist period.

Finally, there are some pressing issues of democratic participation that most democracies, as currently structured, seem ill prepared to address. In most industrial democracies, the majority of the population is middle class, and thus relatively prosperous. It is increasingly clear that prosperous democratic majorities are not necessarily sensitive to claims for economic and social inclusion from poor and marginal minorities, especially when such majority-minority cleavages are associated with ethnic and/or racial divides as well. Democratic theory assumes that majorities and minorities are complex and will alternate over time. A social, economic, and political condition in which entrenched minorities do not effectively participate in the common life of the polity, in part because they do not see how such participation can address their social and economic circumstances, is not easily compatible with democratic values; yet it is far from clear that current liberal democratic institutions and practices are capable of mobilizing majority coalitions on behalf of such marginalized economic and social minorities. If this is true of such established democracies as France (see the rise of the anti-Arab *Front National*), Germany (see German resistance to citizenship for its long-resident Turkish inhabitants), and the United States (i.e., the intersection of race and poverty), one should not be surprised that the incomparably more fragile institutions of the many multinational societies of post-Communist Europe have encountered substantial difficulties in reconciling ethnic/national heterogeneity with liberal politics. (Perhaps indicatively, five of the seven consolidated democracies in the region—Poland, the Czech Republic, Hungary, Slovenia, and Lithuania—are ethnically homogeneous, or nearly so.)

What has just been said is not offered in order to make the case for an authoritarian transition to democracy but rather to suggest the complexity of the relationship between democratic values and democratic institutions. Clearly, each is dependent upon the other in an organic fashion and precisely because of this; it is difficult to see how one model of democratic governance can be transplanted from the North Atlantic experience to the post-communist experience without substantial adaptations and unexpected consequences. Discussion about the transition to "democracy" often overlooks just how varied democratic experience is within the North

Atlantic (or G-7) world itself. Consider just a few of the variations that are typically found among democratic polities:

- presidential versus parliamentary systems;
- direct versus proportional representation (or a mix of both);
- unitary versus federal (or federal versus confederal);
- written versus unwritten constitutions;
- common-law versus civil code legal foundations;
- bipolar versus multipolar party systems (and sometimes unipolar);
- active judicial review versus judicial restraint;
- thresholds for representation in parliament or not; and
- absolute versus qualified majorities.

Under these circumstances, the effectiveness of particular democratic institutions needs to be viewed in light of local circumstances as well as democratic principles, as has in fact always been the case in the Western world. It should also be noted that, since the states under review are undergoing economic and social as well as political transformations, there is historically an even wider variation in political systems associated with the functioning of market economies. Whereas all liberal democracies have a capitalist economic foundation, many capitalist economies do not operate with liberal democratic political systems. Market economics are a historically demonstrated and necessary prerequisite to liberal political development, but they are very far indeed from being a sufficient enabling condition for democracy. This is of particular importance since the attempt throughout post-communist Europe to construct democracy and capitalism at the same time is historically unprecedented and arguably one that is fraught with tensions and dilemmas not captured by the notion of a linear "democratic-capitalist transition".

We have argued that five factors define the prospects for political and economic transformation in the post-Communist countries under review: the impact of communist and imperial legacies, respectively; the scope and pace of democratization and marketization, respectively; and the influence of the international environment. In last year's report, Alexander J. Motyl advanced a persuasive explanation of the trajectory of post-Communist outcomes, arguing that the capacity of governments to undertake effective political and economic reforms is strongly influenced by historical legacies and in particular by two factors stemming from the legacy of the communist period: (a) the degree of totalitarianism experienced by the given country, and (b) the degree of imperial rule experienced.[4] These legacies are important because it appears that the stronger the impact of totalitarianism and imperialism, the smaller the scope for the development of civil society and for the growth of competent local elites, respectively. As Motyl framed the issue, countries with a lesser degree of imperial rule have a greater capacity to embark on reform (in the form of qualified indigenous elites), while countries which avoided the harshest extremes of the totalitarian system over longer periods of time possess a greater capacity to respond to the reform process (in the form of a relatively active civil society). Polities with both features are thus those most able to embark successfully upon the path of reform. The East-Central European states, which alone have consolidated liberal political and economic systems, tended to exercise the most autonomy under the Communist system. Motyl noted that the actual degree of reform since 1989-91 correlates closely with the extent of totalitarianism and imperial rule, with the exceptions being those states that have been involved in desperate military conflicts (i.e., ex-Yugoslavia, Armenia and Azerbaijan, Georgia and Tajikistan).

In short, the nature of the imperial legacy influences the nature and capacity of the state, while the nature of the totalitarian legacy influences the capacity of civil society. Both an effective state and a vital civil society are essential to a stable consolidation of democratic authority. To ask which comes first is to engage in "chicken-and-egg" argumentation: the relationship is an organic one that evolves over longer rather than shorter periods of time. Still, the skill of the gardener and gardening strategy can make a decisive difference to the nature and prospects of the garden, so long as an organic rather than a mechanistic perspective is maintained.

In this respect, it seems warranted to take up a point mentioned but not developed by Motyl, i.e., the relative impact of the international environment upon the political and economic transformations of the post-Communist states. Many of the dilemmas and difficulties of post-Communist reform have been analyzed by a broad range of scholars: the difficulty of building so many new social, economic, political, and other institutions practically from the ground up in the wake of the Communist collapse; the problem of simultaneity, i.e., constructing these new institutions at the same time when some—as the long and often painful democratic evolution of the West suggests—are demonstrated prerequisites for the success of others; as well as the apparent tension between democratization and marketization, i.e, in the short-term disenfranchising large sectors of the country economically and socially while at the same time giving them the ballot to express their resentment at the putative cause of their immiseration.[5] All post-Communist countries have been confronting these challenges and dilemmas. Certainly, some have been more successful than others in negotiating their way around the numerous pitfalls to earnest reformers. Yet are the differences in initial conditions among the post-Communist countries sufficient to account for the greater success of the East-Central European states in consolidating political and economic transformations? (Czechoslovakia, for example, along with the German Democratic Republic and Romania, was arguably the most strictly controlled Communist state between 1969-1989, with almost no scope for civil society or economic experimentation before the collapse.) Consider that the most successful case of democratization and marketization, as between 1945-1949, has been imposed in Germany, i.e., the incorporation of the German Democratic Republic—perhaps the most totalitarian of all of the ex-communist countries—into the Federal Republic of Germany. *Pace* Ronald Reagan, you *can* solve problems by throwing money at them, but you need a great deal of money indeed to do so. By transferring about $100 billion per year every year since 1990 into the former GDR, the German state has fulfilled the function of a super Marshall Plan in the region.

Clearly, no other ex-Communist state has remotely comparable prospects for economic integration into the G-7 world as has the ex-GDR. Yet just as clearly, some are much better positioned than others to obtain resources that can help them absorb some of the inevitable costs and instabilities of the post-Communist region. It is now evident that Germany (and hence NATO and the European Union)—out of an understandable desire to stabilize her new eastern frontiers—will simply not allow Poland, the Czech Republic and Hungary to remain outside of the sphere of North Atlantic economic, political, and even security integration. Geography and size, as well as legacy and policy, matter. Comparison of trade, investment, and aid flows eastward underscore that a few countries, which happen to be those who are also able to make best use of the resources, are exceptionally well positioned to become absorbed into the North Atlantic political-economic-security community.[6] Thus, direct foreign investment in Hungary between 1989-1996, which amounted to just under $15 billion, accounts for about 10% of Hungary's GDP, while the figure for Russia, which attracted approx. $6 billion for the same period, is less than one-half of one percent of the country's GDP.

Purely diplomatic attention matters as well. Across the southern periphery of the former Soviet Union, from Moldova through Georgia, Armenia, Chechnya, and Tajikistan, the Russian state has employed military force unilaterally without concern that by so doing it might call its broader relationship with the G-7 world into question. By contrast, the persistent and demonstrable message from Western Europe and the United States in 1993 and 1994 that Russian resistance to withdrawal from the Baltic states would jeopardize Russian-Western relations, reinforced rather than undermined a developing consensus in the Russian government that the Baltic states were "different", in significant measure because the most powerful Western states plausibly declared that they were different. The prospects for democracy in both the Baltic states as well as in Russia itself were thereby improved. Likewise, the prospect of early admission into NATO and the European Union for Hungary and comparable hopes in Romania, have impelled those states to insulate the delicate issue of the substantial Hungarian minority in Romania from their bilateral relationship.

This should not be surprising. The period since 1989-91 is not the first, or even the second liberal moment of the twentieth century. In the years before 1914 as well as in the mid-1920s, the fact that the most powerful states and empires in the world were democracies in their core polities meant that liberal democracy was the apparent wave of the future throughout much of the world. This emulation effect is quite common in world politics. Success is imitated, failure spurned. It was the inability of the Western world to manage its international relations more than the specific failings of democracy that saw the rise of new authoritarian and even fascist emulators throughout East-Central Europe in the mid-1930s, as the international successes of Nazi Germany and Fascist Italy appeared to presage an anti-democratic wave throughout the world. Today, in the post-Communist and post-cold war world order, the leading democratic state, i.e., the United States of America, is arguably more powerful relative to the next most powerful states than has been true of any Occidental polity since Imperial Rome during the Hadrian-Trajan apogee. (The U.S. Military budget, e.g., is larger than that of the next 10 most powerful states combined.) Among the next dozen or so most prosperous and powerful states, only China is not a democracy or aspiring to become one. It flatters most Americans to imagine that the United States is strong because it is special; most of the world has concluded that the United States is special because it is strong. Democrats should actually take heart from such a reality, because it means that the power of the democratic world can serve to counteract and absorb some of the inevitable tensions and costs of the post-communist transitions. The exercise of power, however, is never cost-free and seldom cheap. Absent the kinds of resources that the German state has been pumping into eastern Germany since 1990 (upwards of $700 billion), the choice of interventionist strategy becomes all important.

Where to focus attention? In its own *Transition Report 1997; Enterprise Performance and Growth*, the European Bank for Reconstruction and Development (EBRD), after noting the impressive sheer scope of privatizing former state enterprises throughout much of the post-Communist region, concluded that one of the main reasons for pessimism about economic prospects throughout the region is the weakness of "institutions, policies and practices which underpin a well-functioning market economy and the investment that supports growth. In responding to these challenges, good governance will be crucial."[7] In other words, the establishment of a competent state, one that is able to exercise the regulatory functions and legal consistency requisite to a modern market economy, is essential to translate the privatization of the former Communist economy into productive and self-sustaining economic growth. In the critical area of financial institutions (i.e., banking reform, interest rate liberalization, securities markets, and non-bank financial institutions), the EBRD adjudges that not a single country among the 25 that it examined possesses "standards and performance norms of advanced industrial countries."[8] The focus here is clearly on strengthening the state.

On the other hand, a careful reading of the U.S. State Department's *Country Reports on Human Rights Practices for 1997* shows that, outside of the East-Central European region, human rights are frequently abused by states that are too strong (because irresponsible) in the wrong areas, i.e., in the ways that they treat their own individual citizens. Political and civil society are too weak to compel responsible human rights behavior on the part of the state. Consider the gravamen of abuses contained in the U.S. State Department's report on a state that has often been considered one of the more hopeful democratic aspirants, the Russian Federation:

- "Many members of the security forces, particularly within the internal affairs apparatus, continued to commit human rights abuses....law enforcement and correctional officials tortured and severely beat detainees and inmates....virtually without restraint."
- "between 10,000 and 20,000 detainees and prison inmates may die in penitentiary facilities annually...."
- "Police and other security forces...continued their practice of targeting citizens from the Caucasus and darker-skinned persons in general for arbitrary searches and detentions...."
- "Lengthy pre-trial detention remained a serious problem. The Government made little progress in the implementation of constitutional provisions for due process, fair and timely trial, and humane punishment. In addition, the judiciary was often the subject of manipulation by political authorities....Authorities infringed on citizens' privacy rights."
- "While the President and the Government have supported human rights and democratic practices in their statements and policy initiatives, they have not institutionalized the rule of law required to protect them. While most abuses occur at lower levels and not by central direction, Government officials do not investigate the majority of cases of abuse and do not dismiss or discipline the perpetrators."
- "The judiciary does not yet act as an effective counterweight to other branches of government."
- "Domestic violence [against women] remains a major problem, as victims rarely have recourse to protection from the authorities."
- "The law establishes minimum conditions of workplace safety and worker health, but these standards are not effectively enforced."[9]

Clearly, under such conditions, an improvement in human rights practices involves the exertion of effective pressure upon existing governments, from within in the form of a stronger civil and political society and from without in the form of sustained international attention and appropriate incentives, positive and negative. In broad terms, an apparently contradictory picture emerges: the improvement of long-term economic prospects involves a strengthening of the state (within appropriate regulatory spheres), while the improvement of respect for human rights involves a weakening of the capacity of the state to act in arbitrary and capricious ways against its citizens. Such a tension is real, and cannot be wished away. Nevertheless, a careful comparative analysis of the states in transit suggests certain avenues of approach that may increase the scope of both economic progress and individual freedom. Consider the following rankings of the states in transit that I have constructed independently of Freedom House, based upon data and evaluations from the European Bank for Reconstruction and Development[10] and the U.S. Department of State[11], as well as my own research. The rankings include an economic rating, based on a combination of GDP per capita (measured in terms of Purchasing Power Parity), the coherence of the financial as well as legal institutions necessary for the functioning of a modern market economy, as well as the state's prospects for accession to the European Union; the political ranking is based upon degree of respect for human rights, civil liberties and due process of law by the government. The rankings are in descending order, according to the degree to which governmental practice promotes modern market practice and respect for human rights and due process of law.

Thus, I: The states *performing at or very close to Western standards* economically are: the Czech Republic, Estonia, Hungary, and Poland; such states politically are: the Czech Republic, Lithuania, and Slovenia.

II. Those states *approaching Western standards* economically are: Slovakia[12] and Slovenia; politically, they are: Estonia, Hungary, Latvia, and Poland.

III. States that have made *substantial progress in establishing and implementing Western standards* of performance economically are: Croatia, Latvia, and Lithuania; politically, they are: Bulgaria, Kyrgyzstan, Macedonia, Moldova, Romania, and Ukraine.

IV. The state where *contradictory progress* has been made in establishing and implementing Western standards economically is: Russia; politically, the states are: Croatia and Russia.

V. *Substantial difficulties* in establishing and implementing Western standards economically have been witnessed in: Bulgaria, Georgia, Kazakhstan, Kyrgyzstan, Macedonia, Moldova, and Romania; politically, such states are: Azerbaijan, Georgia, and Tajikistan.

VI. States where *little or no progress* is evident in establishing and implementing Western norms are, economically: Albania, Armenia, Azerbaijan, Belarus, Bosnia-Herzegovina, Serbia-Montenegro, Tajikistan, Turkmenistan, and Ukraine; politically: Albania, Armenia, Belarus, Bosnia-Herzegovina, Kazakhstan, Serbia-Montenegro, Turkmenistan, and Uzbekistan.

What conclusions may be drawn from these comparisons, which are broadly comparable to those produced by Freedom House and other reputable organizations and scholars? First, there is a broad (though far from perfect) correspondence between the coherence of governmental institutions in the economic area and respect for human rights and due process of law. In the long term, strengthening the state need not mean weakening society or the rights of its constituent individuals. Second, a number of states with poorer economic records and less coherent state institutions in the financial and legal sectors generally respect the human rights of their citizens and observe due process of law. These include Bulgaria, Lithuania, Macedonia, Moldova, Romania, and Ukraine. Third, certain states, especially Croatia, perform much less well in the sphere of respect for human rights and due process than their levels of economic development and coherence of governmental institutions would otherwise suggest. Fourth, a number of states are either at, approaching, or making quite substantial progress in approaching Western standards of both economic and human rights performance. These include the Czech Republic, Slovenia, Hungary, Estonia, Poland, Latvia, Lithuania, as well as Slovakia. With the possible exception of Slovakia, progress toward consolidating market democracy seems assured (barring external Russian pressure upon the Baltic states) and there is little that the West can do beyond what it is already doing to promote progress in respecting liberal norms and practices. Current Western policies of progressively integrating these states into Western political, economic, and security institutions will only accelerate their consolidation of Western political and economic norms and practices. Slovakia, whose capricious and authoritarian leader Vladimir Meciar has drawn attention away from a fairly impressive economic and even legal record, should warrant special attention to ensure progress in consolidating democratic norms. Separately, since external factors are the only real threat to the prospects for Baltic democracy, the United States and its European allies should continue to make clear to the Russian government that intervention in the Baltic states will have grave consequences for Russian-Western relations. This stands to become more complicated as one of the instruments that is accelerating the consolidation of market democracy in East-Central Europe, i.e., the expansion of NATO to include Poland, Hungary and the Czech Republic, also challenges Russian definitions of Russian security along the ex-Soviet periphery, which most definitely includes the Baltic states.

Fifth, a number of states have few prospects (or apparent desire) to establish Western-oriented norms in politics and economics. States whose leaders appear ill-disposed in these directions include Turkmenistan, Tajikistan, Belarus, Serbia, and Uzbekistan; Albania may have better intentions, but its state capacity is so weak that (like Bosnia), barring its conversion into an international trusteeship, its has few medium-term liberal prospects.

Finally, there are a number of states which are experiencing contradictory or slow progress in establishing Western-oriented economic and political norms and where external engagement could make the most difference in eventual outcomes. These include, in descending order of their progress to date: Croatia, Russia, Kyrgyzstan, Bulgaria, Romania, Kazakhstan, Georgia, Macedonia, Moldova, Armenia, and Azerbaijan.

Where might concerted external attention and intervention make the most difference? Since states rarely act except in relation to their self-interest, however defined, candidates for special international attention will need to meet two kinds of tests: their domestic economic and political systems must be susceptible to external sanctions, positive and negative; and the states themselves must be of sufficient significance to the states with the power to act effectively that resources can be mobilized both domestically and internationally to make a difference in the states concerned. In this light, the most promising and least promising states may be safely ignored: there is little chance that additional external attention or intervention is either likely or can make a significant difference to the respective states' prospects. Among the rest of the intermediate states, two candidates stand out for special attention from the West: Croatia and Ukraine, each of which occupies a critical role in relation to its own regional security as well as Western interests, each of which has shown itself to be especially sensitive to criticism from Western governments, and each of which has made notable progress in one but not the other dimension of liberal reform (i.e., Croatia has made considerable progress in market reform and general capacity to govern, while politically and in respect of human rights its record is far from enviable; contrarywise, Ukraine, which continues to resist comprehensive structural reform of its economy, has nevertheless, in the words of the U.S. State Department's 1997 human rights report, "continued the process of building a law-based civil society. Reports of human rights violations remained at the same low level as in 1996."[13]) Given the centrality of Ukrainian stability for the critical Russian-Ukrainian bilateral relationship, the more manageable scope of problems in Ukraine as compared to Russia, and the predominance of strategic over domestic issues in Russian-Western relations, Ukraine as well as Croatia would appear to be the leading candidates for sustained Western attention and policy intervention in order to encourage a more healthy balance between economic and political progress in each country. As for the rest: history can be cruel, as the twentieth century, that most cruel of all centuries, convincingly demonstrates.

[1]Robert Putnam, *Making Democracy Work* (Cambridge, MA: Harvard University Press, 1993).

[2]Minton F. Goldman, *Revolution and Change in Central and Eastern Europe* (Armonk, NY: M.E. Sharpe, 1997), pp.3-52.

[3]See the discussion by Hans Kohn in the 14th edition (1947) of the *Encyclopedia Brittanica* under the entry, "Democracy".

[4]See Alexander J. Motyl's introduction to *Nations in Transit* (New York: Freedom House, 1997).

[5]See Adam Przeworski *et al.*, *Sustainable Democracy* (UK: Cambridge University press, 1995).

[6]For an analysis of East-Central Europe's greater chances of economic integration into the capitalist world economy, see Roderick Martin, "Central and Eastern Europe and the International Economy: The Limits to Globalization," *Europe-Asia Studies*, Vol. 50, no.1 (1998), pp.7-26.

[7]European Bank for Reconstruction and Development, *Tranisition Report 1997. Enterprise Performance and Growth Economic Transition in Eastern Europe and the former Soviet Union* (London: EBRD, 1997), p. vi.

[8]*Ibid.*, p.14.

[9]U.S. Department of State, *Country Reports on Human Rights Practices for 1997* (Washington, D.C.: U.S. Government Printing Office, 1998), pp.1244-1245, 1248, 1253, 1264, 1268.

[10]Derived and adapted from Table 2.1 of, European Bank for Reconstruction and Development, *Transition Report 1997. Enterprise Performance and Growth. Economic Transition in eastern Europe and the former Soviet Union* (London: EBRD, 1997), p.14.

[11]Derived and adapted from U.S. Department of State, *Country Reports on Human Rights Practices for 1997* (Washington, D.C.: U.S. Government Printing Office, 1998), *passim*.

[12]The EBRD report (*op. cit.*, p.14) ranked Slovakia and Slovenia equally in terms of degree of small-scale privatization, enterprise governance and restructuring, and price liberalization; Slovakia was rated superior to Slovenia in terms of its securities markets and non-bank financial institutions, while private sector GDP was estimated at 75% for Slovakia and 50% for Slovenia; Slovenia was adjudged superior in terms of its large-scale privatization and competition policy, and marginally superior in its trade and foreign exchange system, banking reform and interest rate liberalization.

[13]*Country Reports on Human Rights*, *op. cit.*, p.1361.

EXPLANATORY NOTES

Charles Graybow

Nations in Transit 1998 measures the progress and setbacks in democratic and economic reform in 28 post-Communist countries. It is an updated and expanded edition of versions published in 1995 and 1997.

The 1998 edition features an expanded list of questions in each country report; divides the economics section into separate macroeconomic and microeconomic sections; and adds a new section on corruption. The 1998 edition also includes three new countries: Bosnia-Herzegovina, Mongolia, and Yugoslavia.

Each country report is divided into nine major sections. The Political Process section examines the context of elections and whether they were free and fair; the development of multiparty systems; and popular participation in the political process. The Civil Society section assesses the growth of nongovernmental organizations, their organizational capacity and financial sustainability, and the legal and political environment in which they function; the development of free trade unions; and interest group participation in the policy process.

The Independent Media section looks at the legal framework for and actual status of press freedom, including harassment of journalists and editorial independence; the emergence of a financially viable private press; and Internet access for private citizens. The Governance and Public Administration section considers the actual power of legislative bodies; decentralization; the responsibilities, election and management of local government; and legislative and executive transparency.

The Rule of Law section highlights constitutional reform and human rights protection; criminal code reform; the judiciary and judicial independence; and the status of ethnic minority rights. The Corruption section considers the perception of corruption in the civil service; business interests of top policy makers; laws on financial disclosure and conflict of interest; and anticorruption initiatives.

The legal framework for privatization and the actual state of the privatization process are covered in the Privatization section. The Macroeconomic Policy section covers tax reform; fiscal and monetary policy; and banking reform. Finally, the Microeconomic section covers property rights; price liberalization; the ability to operate a business; international trade and foreign investment; and the energy sector.

Freedom House developed the initial survey, and expanded the subsequent editions, after consultations with the United States Agency for International Development. Freedom House staff researched and wrote many of the country reports, and selected consultants for the remainder. Consultants were generally specialists at the Ph.D. level, recommended by recognized authorities on their respective regions. In addition, in-country think tanks wrote initial drafts of several of the country reports.

All reports were edited for content by Alexander

Motyl, Associate Director of the Harriman Institute at Columbia University; Martha Brill Olcott, a fellow at the Carnegie Endowment for International Peace and a professor at Colgate University; Stephen Handelman, an authority on corruption, and Boris Shor, a former *Nations in Transit* coordinator.

The research team used a wide variety of sources in compiling the data. These included research reports from non-governmental organizations; dozens of local newspapers and magazines; analytic reports by multilateral lending institutions; and data released by the governments themselves.

Country reports are current through March 31, 1998. An exception is the report for Hungary, which includes data from a second round of elections that occurred in April. Where the data indicate a significant positive or negative trend in a given category, compared to the previous report, up or down arrows are assigned to that category.

The 1998 report includes many new questions. For example, in the Independent Media section, there is a new question on Internet access. Moreover, subquestions have been added to many questions. To use another example, in the Rule of Law section, the question on reform of the criminal code adds subquestions on searches and warrants, treatment of suspects and prisoners, and the efficiency of the judicial system.

There is an important caveat regarding the new Corruption section. It is difficult to assess corruption using directly verifiable data or statistics. Instead, observers can only gauge the *perception* of corruption in a country based on anecdotal reports from ordinary citizens, businessmen, and others. Freedom House has, however, included some questions in this section that require more tangible answers, such as whether laws requiring financial disclosure have been passed and what major anti-corruption initiatives have been implemented. This allows us to consider how serious governments are in tackling corruption.

In most instances, the facts in *Nations in Transit 1998* are self-explanatory. Interpretation, however, is necessary in some areas. For example, membership figures for trade unions and civic associations are notoriously unreliable. Similarly, while simple conversion of enterprises or state farms into joint-stock enterprises may technically be described as privatization, in several countries the state remains a significant shareholder through the agency of a privatization fund or directly as a minority shareholder. These instances are pointed out in the text.

Economic statistics should be treated with caution. In many of the countries surveyed, the administrative capacity for accurate measurement of economy dynamics is lacking. Worse, governments in the least developed countries (Belarus, for example) often put out statistics that put a positive spin on conditions for political purposes. Finally, in any country, statistics gathered by the government and financial institutions often fail to capture the size and importance of the rather large "shadow" economy.

Using the data in the country reports it is possible to assess how developments in one section relate to and influence those in another, as well as how countries measure up against one another across a wide range of areas. Taken together, the three editions of *Nations in Transit* allow policymakers and others to identify longitudinal trends in the countries surveyed, providing a basis to judge progress and identify areas of need.

Ratings Methodology

For all 28 countries surveyed, Freedom House rated each of the nine sections (Political Process, Civil Society, etc.), thus allowing for comparative analysis within and among countries. This was done on a one-to-seven scale, with a one representing the highest and a seven the lowest level of progress. As with *Freedom in the World*, Freedom House's annual comparative survey of political rights and civil liberties, *Nations in Transit* does not rate governments *per se*; rather, it rates the rights and freedoms an individual enjoys as affected by governments, business oligarchies, powerful social movements, and insurgencies and other groups that function outside of the normal political and civic process. Furthermore, ratings are based on the degree of freedom, and on constitutional and legal guarantees.

These ratings, however, should be taken as comparative or ordinal, not absolute. Their major significance is in allowing for comparison of institutional reform in a particular area between various countries. These ratings would, therefore, answer the following questions: 1) Is the Romanian political process more or less open than the Ukrainian political process? 2) Has the Czech Republic carried out deeper macroeconomic reforms than Russia? The *Nations in Transit* ratings not only allow us to characterize countries as, for example, democracies or authoritarian states, but enable us to makeassessments of how democratic or authoritarian a country is.

The ratings process involved three main steps. First, the authors of the individual reports created preliminary ratings for each section of their countries. Next, the *Nations in Transit* Academic Oversight Board met in New York in May 1997. This Board was chaired by Alexander Motyl and included the following experts: Jozef van Brabant, Principal Economics Affairs Officer, United Nations; Richard Ericson, Professor of Economics, Columbia University; Charles Gati, School of Advanced International Studies, Johns Hopkins University; and, journalist and scholar Stephen Handelman. Using the preliminary ratings as source material, the Board established ratings by consensus following extensive discussion and debate. Finally, a Ratings Committee of Freedom House staff reviewed the ratings for consistency. It also assigned trend arrows to category ratings to reflect a significant increase or decrease in liberalization as compared to the previous report.

Freedom House also created two additional ratings: "democratic reform" and "economic reform." The former is an unweighted average of the first five categories which deal with political liberalization, and the latter is an unweighted average of the three categories relating to economic liberalization. These give a quick summary of the political and economic reforms in a given country.

Freedom House Surveys

The results of Freedom House's annual *Freedom in the World* comparative survey of political rights and civil liberties and *Survey of Press Freedom* are included in order to facilitate comparisons among countries. *Freedom in the World* uses a unique methodology to rate countries on a one-to-seven scale for both political rights and civil liberties, with a one indicating the greatest degree of enjoyment of political rights or civil liberties, and a seven representing the least. *Freedom in the World* also places countries in the categories of "Free," "Partly Free," and "Not Free," which are useful for making broad comparisons among countries. The *Freedom in the World* ratings and category designations are included in the header for each country report.

Freedom House's *Survey of Press Freedom* also rates countries as "Free," "Partly Free" and "Not Free." These results are included in the Independent Media section, question 8.

It is important to note that *Freedom in the World* and the *Survey of Press Freedom* judge individual categories of political rights, civil liberties, and press freedom differently than does *Nations in Transit*. As a result, ratings are not identical or directly comparable. There is, however, a high degree of correlation between the *Freedom in the World* ratings and the *Nations in Transit* ratings.

ALBANIA

Freedom in the World Ratings, 1989-1998

	1989-90	1990-91	1991-92	1992-93	1993-94	1994-95	1995-96	1996-97	1997-98
Political Rights	-	-	5	4	3	3	3	4	4
Civil Liberties	-	-	5	3	4	4	4	4	4
Status	-	-	PF	PF	PF	PF	PF	PF	PF

Polity: Transitional
Economy: Transitional
Population: 3,282,000
PPP: $2,853
Ethnic Groups: Albanians (96 percent; two main ethnic/ linguistic groups: Ghegs, Tosks), Greeks (2.5 percent)
Capital: Tirana

Political Process 4.5/7

1. When did national legislative elections occur? Were they free and fair? How were they judged by domestic and international election monitoring organizations? Who composes the government? Legislative elections were held in June and July 1997, amid a political crisis precipitated by the collapse of pyramid investment schemes earlier in the year and subsequent social unrest which resulted in the control of the southern part of the country by armed gangs opposed to the government of President Sali Berisha and the ruling Democratic Party (PD). In May, the PD-dominated parliament, which had earlier re-elected Berisha president, adopted a new election law that increased the number of seats from the legislature 140 to 155, with 115 decided by majority voting and 40 by proportional representation. After domestic and international pressure, President Berisha modified the law to include greater proportional representation. After two-rounds of voting, the opposition ex-Communist Socialist Party (PS) won 99 seats; the PD won 29; the Social Democratic Party of Albania, 8; The Human Rights Unity Party (Greek), four; the nationalist Balli Kometar, three; the Democratic Alliance of Albania, two; and the Republican Party of Albania, one. International observers called the vote "adequate and acceptable" but cited instances of pre-election violence, cases of fraud, and irregularities. President Berisha resigned on July 24. The new parliament elected PS leader Fatos Nano as prime minister and Rexhep Mejdani as president. The government and ministries are dominated by the PS and the Social Democrats. The PD boycotted the new parliament on several occasions. A five-month boycott ended in March 1998.

2. When did presidential elections occur? Were they free and fair? Under the Albanian system, the president is elected by parliament. In March 1997, the then PD-dominated parliament (the

PD controlled 97 of 140 seats) re-elected President Berisha. After the Socialists won the June-July parliamentary election, Berisha resigned. The new parliament elected Rexhep Mejdani, an independent, to a five-year term.

3. Is the electoral system multi party-based? Are there at least two viable parties functioning at all levels of government? Independent parties have been allowed to exist since December 1990. The major parties, which span the political spectrum, include the Socialist Party, the Democratic Party, the Social Democratic Union of Albania, the Albanian Republican Party, and the Social Democratic Party of Albania. Since the 1997 parliamentary elections, the Socialists have controlled the legislature. They have controlled a majority of seats in local councils since municipal elections in 1996. The two major parties function at all levels.

4. How many parties have been legalized? Are any particular parties illegal? Approximately 40 parties are registered. In 1992, the People's Assembly banned all parties identifiable as "fascist, anti-national, chauvinistic, racist, totalitarian, Communist, Marxist-Leninist, Stalinist, or Enverist," the last reference to former long-time Communist leader Enver Hoxha. After the political events in 1997 that led to the fall of the PD regime, the Albanian Communist Party sought legalization. On March 25, 1998, a government bill upheld the ban on political parties "whose program envisions the seizure of power and reliance on Stalin- and Enver-type traditions." The Islamic Democratic Union was denied registration in 1993 and 1996 due to its religious basis.

5. What proportion of the population belongs to political parties? Precise membership figures are unreliable. In 1997, polls continued to show low party identification among voters, particularly after the political turmoil early in the year. The Socialists continue to claim more than 100,000 members, however, the figure cannot be verified independently .

6. What has been the trend of voter turnout at the municipal, provincial, and national level in recent years? In national elections, voter turnout in 1991 was 59 percent; in March 1992, 95 percent; in May and June 1996, 89 percent (first round), and 59 percent (second round, however, this figure was disputed by the opposition, which put it at 30 percent); and in June 1997, 66 percent. In local elections, voter turnout in July 1992, was 70.5 percent; and in October 1996, 75 percent. Approximately 75 percent voted in a November 1994 constitutional referendum.

Civil Society 4.25/7

1. How many nongovernmental organizations (NGOs) have come into existence since 1988? What is the number of charitable/non-profit organizations? Are there locally led efforts to increase philanthropy and volunteerism? What proportion of the population is active in private voluntary activity? According to the Albanian Civil Society Foundation, Albania has approximately 350 NGOs. While a number of environmental, human rights, women's, and youth organizations have obtained foreign support, most Albanian NGOs lack essential resources, adequate coordination among themselves, and links to the international NGO community. There are more than a dozen NGOs dealing with health issues and social services. Like other post-Communist societies, Albania does not have developed philanthropic traditions or institutions. While most NGOs rely on volunteers, information on public participation is not available.

2. What is the legal and regulatory environment for NGOs (i.e., ease of registration, legal rights, government regulation, taxation, procurement, and access-to-information issues)? To what extent is NGO activism focused on improving the regulatory environment? NGOs in Albania must be registered as such with the government. With over 350 organizations registered, there are no serious bureaucratic obstacles to registration. In collaboration with the Washington-based International Center for Non-Profit Law, the Albanian Civil Society Foundation recently commissioned a study of the legal framework of Albanian NGOs.

3. What is the organizational capacity of NGOs? Do management structures clearly delineate authority and responsibility? Is information on NGO management available in the native language? Is there a core of experienced practitioners/trainers to serve as consultants or mentors to less-developed organizations? Most NGOs have weak organizational structures, lack fund-raising and media outreach capabilities, and face shortages of essential equipment, due mostly to lack of funds. Major NGOs such as public policy institutions, environmental and business groups, and women's organizations have management structures that delineate authority and responsibility. For example, The Independent Sociological Center has a board of directors, a nine-member staff, and 20 part-time workers. In Albania, NGOs receive training primarily from foreign governments and institutions, among them the United Nations Development Program (UNDP), U.S. Agency for International Development (USAID) (through its Democracy Network program), the Danish Ministry of Foreign Affairs, and the Soros Foundation. These extensive programs provide training in management, sustainability, fund-raising, media and government outreach, and other key areas.

4. Are NGOs financially viable? What is their tax status? Are they obliged to and do they typically disclose revenue sources? Do government procurement opportunities exist for private, not-for-profit providers of services? Most NGOs are not financially viable without the assistance of Western governments, institutions, and organizations. Major and well-organized NGOs that receive international assistance typically disclose revenue sources as part of the condition of the grants. The Women's Center in Tirana is exclusively funded by international governmental organizations and private foundations in the West. The Albanian Center for Economic Research receives all of its $60,000 annual budget from international sources. NGOs are not tax-exempt, but charitable and humanitarian groups have received tax and customs concessions.

5. Are there free trade unions? How many workers belong to these unions? Is the number of workers belonging to trade unions growing or decreasing? What is the numerical/proportional membership of farmers' groups, small business associations, etc.? Workers obtained the right to form independent unions in 1991 under Article 1 of Law 7516. The Independent Confederation of Trade Unions of Albania, with an estimated 280,000 members, was created as an umbrella organization from a number of smaller unions. A separate Confederation of Trade Unions represents some school, petroleum, postal, and telecommunications workers and estimates its membership at between 130,000-150,000. There are also independent unions not affiliated with either federation. According to the Law on Major Constitutional Provisions and other legislation, all workers (excluding employees of military enterprises) have the right to strike. Union membership has declined over the last several years from 1.2 million to approximately 550,000 due to the expansion of the private sector and high unemployment in the state sector. The private sector includes between 900,000-1 million workers, mostly in agriculture, small shops, and enterprises; very few of them have formed unions to represent themselves. Some unions have organized to represent workers in foreign-owned shoe and textile factories. Industrial policy is putatively decided by representatives of the state, employees, and employers. In 1997, unions opposed a value-added tax (VAT), and miners at the Port of Durres went on strike for a few days in October 1997. There are several nongovernmental organizations that represent the interests of the more than 500,000 private farmers. More than 65 percent of Albanians still live off of the land or in rural communities. The Agrarian Party won one seat in the 1997 elections. Other farm workers' groups include the Agricultural and Farmers' Associations and the Albanian Agricultural Union. An Agrarian Trade Bank offers credits and loans to farmers. Business associations and professional and scientific groups exist in Tirana and the larger cities, but exact membership figures are unavailable.

6. What forms of interest group participation in politics are legal? What types of interest groups are active in the political and policy process? The 1991 Law on Majority Constitutional Provisions (the extant constitution) guarantees the right of both individuals and groups to petition the government. Article 23 establishes the right to initiatives at the national level. Any group of 20,000 voters has the right to initiate legislation in parliament, although in 1997 there were no instances of public exercise of this right. The legal framework does not establish formal opportunities for public participation in governmental or parliamentary decision-making. Petitions and public demonstrations are still the main mechanism for public pressure on the government. Massive protests and social unrest were seen in the first half of 1997. NGOs have become increasingly active in the political process. Public policy institutes such as the Albanian Center for Economic Research, the Center for Economic and Social Studies, the Institute of International and Strategic Studies, the Research Center for Rural Development, the Professional and Business Women's Association, the Institute of Management and Public Administration, as well as several well-organized environmental groups, disseminate their findings and recommendations to parliament and the government.

7. How is the not-for-profit/NGO sector perceived by the public and government officials? What is the nature of media coverage of NGOs? To what extent do government officials engage with NGOs? According to the Albanian Civil Society Foundation, the image of NGOs among the public is weak and not always positive. In general, NGOs and the government do not have a broad working relationship as the concept of NGO input into government is resisted by officials. Government-controlled media and a highly partisan private press do not regularly cover NGO activities. Western assistance programs have focused on improving these relationships with training and assistance focused on outreach and the development of contacts with government, media, and the public.

Independent Media 4.75/7

1. Are there legal protections for press freedoms? On September 1, 1997, parliament—arguing that there was no need for a new press law because Article 1 of the Law on the Press states that "the press is free"—repealed 22 articles of the 1993 law that were commonly viewed as overly restrictive. The 1993 law allowed the government frequently to withhold information from the public by designating it as a state secret. It also included provisions on confiscation and the removal of publications from circulation for security reasons. These provisions were susceptible to abuses. Parliament also amended the statutes governing state radio and television by allocating broadcast time between the president, government, and opposition and guaranteeing political parties the right to define the content of their air time. The legislature also amended the broadcast law to provide more air time for presenting "alternative" views. The moves were triggered by a hunger strike by opposition deputy Pjeter Arbnori to protest the failure of television to air opposition views during a parliamentary plenary session. On September 8, the opposition accepted the government's proposal that airtime would be allocated in proportion to the party's share of seats in parliament as determined by the June 1997 elections. During the state of emergency in March (lifted in mid-April), blanket censorship and an information blackout were imposed by the government. The editorial offices of several opposition or independent newspapers were burned down or destroyed. The offices of *Koha Jone*, the most prominent opposition newspaper, were incinerated on March 3. The newly elected Socialist government maintained that, by repealing the more egregious sections of the 1993 statute, it was showing tolerance to the new Democratic Party opposition. Nevertheless, the possibility of state interference with the press remains; the second part of Article 1 declares that "freedom of the press shall be protected by law" and such "protection" can take many forms. In January 1998, the first officially registered Albanian private television station, SHIJAK-TV, was vandalized by government supporters.

2. Are there legal penalties for libeling officials? Are there legal penalties for "irresponsible" journalism? Have the laws been enforced to harass journalists? While parliament removed restrictive aspects of the press law, the Penal Code criminalizes various forms of defamation. Insulting representatives of foreign countries and public officials on duty, including judges and other members of a trial panel, carry penalties of fines or imprisonment for up to three years. Under law, persons can face fines and imprisonment for three months to five years for denigrating the President of the republic or the Albanian nation and its symbols or for printing "false information." Several journalists were heavily fined for libel in 1996, but there were few such cases in 1997. During the political instability in the first half of 1997, scores of journalists were detained, beaten, harassed, and arrested.

3. What proportion of the media is privatized? What are the major private newspapers, television stations, and radio stations? Most of the print media are in private hands, as political parties, unions, and various societies publish their own newspapers. In May 1997, Albania passed the Law on Public and Private Radio-Television, the first statute that contained specific provisions relating to private broadcast media. Areas of potential concern in the law were a capital requirement of $40,000 for each station applying for a license; the pervasiveness of content regulation in the licensing process; the possibility of political domination of the licensing council; and legal liability under civil and criminal laws for journalists and broadcasting executives for untrue broadcasts that cause damage to private persons. The first private station to get a license was SHIJAK-TV. Its offices were vandalized in January 1998, allegedly by pro-government supporters. Alba-TV, another private station, began operations as an Italian-Albanian joint venture in January 1997. State-controlled television and radio dominate the airwaves, but Albanians have access to a wide range of electronic media. Satellite dishes are prevalent. Approximately 250 newspapers, magazines, and journals are registered, but many are published sporadically or not at all due to financial and economic circumstances. The larger ones include *Zeri i Popullit* ("Voice of the People," with a circulation of 50,000), a daily tied to the Socialist Party; *Rilindja Demokratike* ("Democratic Awakening," 30,000), which is published by the Democratic Party; *Baskimi* ("Unity," 30,000), the journalists' union daily; *Respublika* ("Republic"), a daily published by the Republican Party; and *Progresui Agrar*, which is published by the Agrarian Party. The largest independent papers include *Koha Jone*, with a circulation of almost 30,000; *Dita Infomacion*; *Albania; Popullit Po*; and *Gazeta Shqiptare*. Erotic publications have a significant circulation, reportedly averaging 30,000 copies per day. It is estimated that only 500,000 people, or one-sixth of the population, read a daily newspaper. Approximately 65 percent do not read one at all, as they live in rural areas beyond the reach of the inadequate newspaper distribution networks. Leading private radio stations are Radio Koha, Radio Ime, Radio Klan, and Radio Stinet.

4. Are the private media financially viable? Newspaper publishers in Albania face high levels of taxation, in addition to such problems as the availability of newsprint, limited printing facilities, and a poor distribution infrastructure. Potential commercial advertising income is limited. Newspapers affiliated with the major political parties have the advantage of party support, and pro-government publications enjoy reduced rates at the *Demokracia* printing plant. The government raised its VAT from 12.5 percent to 20 percent as recommended by the International Monetary Fund. Shpetim Nazarko, publisher of *Dita Informacion* and head of the Association of Publishers, said in 1997 that the print media in Albania is nearly bankrupt. In August 1997, the publishers of nine of the largest news papers called for the abolition of the VAT and the advertising tax, reduction of customs taxes for paper, and reduction of phone rates. A four-day strike by nine of the largest papers in November 1997, highlighted the serious financial dilemmas faced by the print media. After the strike, the government removed the VAT on advertising, discontinued the tax on profits, eliminated the customs tax on newsprint and computers, and provided each publication with two telephones that are charged at domestic rates. In August, Alba-TV broadcasts were interrupted allegedly because the station owed money to the facility that houses its studio. Most private radio stations in Tirana were founded in the latter half of 1997. Several, such as Radio Koha and Radio Klan, benefit from being owned by organizations that also own other for-profit ventures that can provide them with capital. Radio Ime and other stations operate on capital and equipment that their owners have accumulated.

5. Are the media editorially independent? Are the media's news-gathering functions affected by interference from government or private owners? Government, party, and union newspapers generally expound the views of their sponsors. The print media remain polarized between pro-government newspapers, which espouse the official line, and opposition newspapers, which are stridently anti-government. In electronic media, the government elected in June 1997, has created a more tolerant climate by allowing greater access to opposition views. It has also been more tolerant of press criticism. During the social and political unrest in the first half of 1997, journalists were often prevented from doing their jobs by police and other authorities. In February, for example, police assaulted several journalists, including foreign reporters, covering street demonstrations in and around Tirana. A month earlier, Muharrem Meko, a correspondent for *Zeri i Popullit*, was arrested in southern Albania after witnessing and covering violent anti-government demonstrations. In February 1998, the Albanian Journalists' League protested the kidnapping by police of a journalist from *Albania* as well as attacks on journalists from *55*, *Tribuna Demokratike*, and the Enter independent news agency.

6. Is the distribution system for newspapers privately or governmentally controlled? There are two distribution companies in Albania responsible for delivering all daily newspapers. One company is jointly owned by *Albania* and *Zeri i Popullit*. The other is owned by *Koha Jone*. Both companies have been accused of "overcharging, under-delivering, and in some cases, stealing from the newspapers they are charged with distributing," according to an assessment report of the Albanian media by ProMedia. Newspapers also complain that neither of the distribution companies provides them with accurate numbers regarding sales and circulation. Politics also played a role in distribution. During the anti-government upheaval in the south, pro-government and PD papers were barred from distribution. In August 1997, a spokesman for the Albanian Journalists' League reported that a group of masked gunmen stopped an Albanian Press distribution vehicle, burned the newspapers, and insisted that newspapers that criticize Prime Minister Fatos Nano would not be transported on that road.

7. What proportion of the population is connected to the Internet? Are there any restrictions on Internet access to private citizens? Government offices, universities, political parties, and NGO's are connected to the Internet. Figures for the population at large are not available. There are no legal restrictions to internet access, but most citizens cannot afford computer or internet service in this largely rural, impoverished country.

8. What has been the trend in press Freedom as measured by Freedom House's *Survey of Press Freedom*? Freedom House's annual *Survey of Press Freedom* rated Albania Not Free from 1988 to 1990 and Partly Free from 1991 to 1994. Based on the period from 1994 to March 1996, Albania was downgraded to Not Free due to continued government control and dominance of the electronic media and persecution of journalists. In 1997, the rating was upgraded to Partly Free after parliament eliminated the restrictive aspects of the press law, provided the opposition greater access to government television, and removed several crippling taxes.

Governance and Public Administration 5/7

1. Is the legislature the effective rule-making institution? Parliament is the effective rule-making institution, although, before his resignation following parliamentary elections in June 1997, President Berisha exercised significant powers to rule by decree. Parliament elects the president. By naming an independent as president, the new parliament aimed to buttress its authority. A constitutional draft delineating governmental authority is expected by the end of 1998.

2. Is substantial power decentralized to subnational levels of government? What specific authority do subnational levels have? Local elections in 1992 marked the introduction of a new, more decentralized system. Relations between the federal government and subnational levels, however, were badly disrupted throughout most of 1997 due to the violent social unrest, particularly in the south. Albania is divide into 26 districts (*rrethet*), more than 310 communes, and 61 municipalities. A Local Council, elected directly by universal suffrage, is the governing body of each subdivision. Under the democratized process, the local administrative authorities enjoy more autonomy from the central administration. Municipalities and communes enjoy greater material, financial, and executive rights at the expense of the center. The position of mayor (formerly executive chairman) is much more important. Mayors are empowered to make decisions in the critical housing sector, and the local authorities are responsible for distributing state payments to poor families. The commune, the smallest local authority, has its own administrative apparatus, including specialists such as doctors and policemen, and may also provide public services. Nevertheless, decentralization remains an important problem. All plans depend on finding adequate funding and developing a local tax base, a daunting challenge in such a poor country.

In October 1996, following a new round of local elections, the government stated that it would reform the laws on the Organization and Operation of Local Government and the Law on Prefectures so that "a legal basis will be created for local finances." The amended law, which met with European Council approval, was intended to improve significantly the procedures for cooperation with the central government and the demarcation of responsibilities for local government. The law, however, was never implemented due to the deteriorating political situation. The Socialist victory in the national elections put the government at odds with local governments controlled by the Democratic Party, which had won the October 1996 local elections. Moreover, the violence in the south destroyed administrative buildings in many municipalities, communes, and districts. In February 1998, Lush Perpali, Albanian Secretary for local authorities, stated that "decentralization of local authorities is a priority and urgent problem" and that Albania was working closely with the European Council's Congress of local and regional authorities of europe and the World Bank to improve local government. Three associations including the chairmen of communes, mayors, and district chairmen were established. The opposition claims that thousands of local government officials were dismissed due to their party affiliation. In October 1997, leaders of the National Association of Albanian Mayors held a news conference to ask that local government be more independent and have more powers in managing tax revenues and budgets. Elections in 15 municipalities and communes were scheduled for late 1998.

3. Are subnational officials chosen in free and fair elections? The Organization for Security and Cooperation in Europe refused to monitor the October 1996 local elections because the government tried to limit the number of monitors. The Council of Europe found no serious violations in the voting, but the opposition Socialists claimed intimidation of voters and tampering with the count. Official results showed that the Democratic Party won 61 percent of city councils, including Tirana, and 58 percent of commune seats. Reuters reported that Socialists won only 6 percent of city hall and commune seats, down from 50 percent in 1992. The new Socialist government has called new elections for 15 municipalities and communes to be held in late 1998. The opposition has charged that there is no legitimate legal reason for early local elections.

4. Do the executive and legislative bodies operate openly and with transparency? Is draft legislation easily accessible to the media and the public? National and executive bodies operate with limited transparency. Parliamentary sessions are open to the public and televised, but government-controlled media can be selective in their coverage of events. In August 1997, PD deputy Pjeter Arbnori went on a hunger strike to protest selective television coverage of a plenary session, which he charged had censored the opposition debate. Opposition and independent journalists are still frequently denied access to government officials. Government-owned and private media do publish important draft legislation, but statutes are not readily available to the public.

5. Do municipal governments have sufficient revenues to carry out their duties? Do municipal governments have control of their own local budgets? Do they raise revenues autonomously from the central state budget? Most municipal revenues continue to come from the state government, and the distribution of funds remains a nettlesome political issue. According to Albanian law that was passed after consultations with Western officials during the previous government, local tax revenues collected by local authorities should go to those local authorities. The new central government, however, has not been releasing the required level of local revenue to local authorities, most of whom represent the opposition Democratic Party. The government has estimated that the damage incurred by local authorities in the 1997 unrest exceeded 500 million *leks*. In 1998, 265 million leks were allocated for local authorities, with part of the money coming from an anticipated $1 million credit from the World Bank. Most towns and cities have insufficient revenues to carry out badly needed infrastructure repair.

6. Do the elected local leaders and local civil servants know how to manage municipal governments effectively? Municipal governments generally lack trained and qualified personnel. Because many civil servants are appointed on the basis of political patronage rather than ability, electoral transitions have led to a dearth of professional personnel. The United Nations Development Program, the Council of Europe, and other Western institutions continue to run programs to improve the quality and accountability of local leadership.

7. When did the constitutional/legislative changes on local power come into effect? Has there been a reform of the civil service code/system? Are local civil servants employees of the local or central government? The 1992 local elections marked the introduction of the current structure. Municipalities and communes assumed greater responsibility in land distribution, privatization, social housing assistance, and maintenance. The 1996 Law on the Organization and Operation of Local Governments and the Law on Prefectures, which would have better defined financial responsibilities and authority, were never passed. The Law on Civil Service in Albania (No. 8095) was adopted in March 1996, although the government did not issue the necessary by-laws to make it complete. It made most civil servants employees of local government. In practice, however, the law is flouted. Article 15 of an amended law debated in early 1998 would limit the number of political appointees. Since taking power, the Socialists have dismissed 15,000 public administration employees and thousands of other workers and have replaced most of them with partisan appointees. Changing the Law on Civil Service was a contentious and unresolved issue in early 1998.

Rule of Law 5.25/7

1. Is there a post-Communist constitution? How does the judicial system interpret and enforce the constitution? Are there specific examples of judicial enforcement of the constitution in the last year? The Law on Majority Constitutional Provisions (No. 7491) of April 29, 1991, serves as a "temporary" constitution. A referendum on a new constitution supported by the Democratic Party government was held in November 1994, but was rejected by 60 percent of the voters. Subsequent attempts to discuss a mechanism for drawing up a constitution failed. After the Socialist victory in the June 1997 elections, the government pledged to make drafting a constitution a top priority. A 21-member parliamentary commission was created in the fall of 1997, but the opposition refused to participate. In March 1998, the commission adopted a preamble. The commission approved the form of the regime as a parliamentary republic with a unitary state. A nine-member Constitutional Court was created in 1992, with five members appointed by parliament and four by the president. Under Chapter IIIA, Section II, Article 17 of the constitution, the court is "the highest authority that protects and guarantees respect for the constitution and the legislation, as well as making definitive interpretations of the constitution." In a November 1997 ruling, the court angered the government by ruling that Article 7 of the Transparency Law was unconstitutional. Under the law, the government had sent administrators to investigate VEFA, an investment company allegedly involved in pyramid schemes. That ruling sparked a constitutional crisis between the courts and parliament (see Question 5).

2. Does the constitutional framework provide for human rights? Do human rights include business and property rights? Chapter I, Article 4 of the constitution states that "the Republic of Albania recognizes the human rights and fundamental freedoms of the individual and national minorities, accepted by international documents." Chapter V (Fundamental Freedoms and Human Rights) includes articles guaranteeing the right to life, freedom of expression, the abolition of torture, the prohibition of forced labor, individual freedom and personal security, no punishment without a legal basis, presumption of innocence, standard criminal procedure, freedom of conscience and religion, the right to organize, freedom of movement, the right to private property and inheritance, trade union freedom, and the right to petition. Business rights are guaranteed by law.

3. Has there been basic reform of the criminal code/criminal law? Who authorizes searches and issues warrants? Are suspects and prisoners beaten or abused? Are there excessive delays in the criminal justice system? The bulk of the criminal code was implemented in 1995 under a new Penal Code that the government said was "free of ideology that characterized the code of former totalitarian society" and that "conforms to international standards" as recommended by the Council of Europe and international covenants. While the code, which took effect on June 1, 1995, enhanced defendants' rights and reduced sentences, several articles and subsequent laws dealing with libel, defamation, and past political activity were restrictive. In February 1998, parliament passed an anti-crime bill that included laws on "Special Forces and Rapid Intervention Forces," "The Criminal Police," "The Use of Weapons," and "The Ethics Code for the Albanian Police." The laws were aimed at curbing police abuses and addressing armed violence. In November 1997, parliament proposed amendments to the 1995 Law on the Verification of Officials (No.8043) that would establish a screening commission to bar high-level security officials or Communist operatives from serving in top political, judicial, and cultural posts. The law would also allow citizens to obtain access to their security files. Nafiz Bezhani, chairman of the State Commission on the Verification of Officials' Personal Records, said the new statute was an improvement over the 1995 law because, among other things, it included past criminal activities and was therefore not strictly political. By law, a police officer or prosecutor may order a suspect into custody, and criminal courts issue warrants for searches, although police often conduct searches without them. Albanian law enforcement institutions are corrupt and often resort to various forms of abuses, including ill-treatment of prisoners. Most police lack professional training. During the social unrest in early 1997, police attacked independent journalists and members of the political opposition, often with excessive force. In August 1997, interior ministry officials met with representatives of the Albanian Center for the Documentation of Human Rights to coordinate on a curriculum for seminars to train police officers in fundamental human rights principles and correct public behavior. The Penal Procedures Code requires that pretrial investigations be completed within three months. The prosecutor may extend this period by three-month intervals in especially difficult cases. The accused has the right to appeal these extensions to the district court. Pretrial detention conditions remained deficient throughout 1997.

4. Do most judges rule fairly and impartially? Do many remain from the Communist era? While judges rule fairly in criminal and civil cases, most lack adequate training. Most were appointed by the anti-Communist PD government. Many of the judges received their legal education only through accelerated and dubious six-month courses in 1993 at the Faculty of Law at Tirana. In addition to being short, many of the courses were taken by "correspondence." Graduates received their diplomas in the spring of 1994 and were instantly appointed as prosecutors and judges. After the change of government in June 1997, the Socialist government dismissed several prosecutors and court administrators, but there were no mass firings. With the Council of Europe's assistance in October 1997, a magistrates school was opened in Tirana to train future judges and prosecutors. In 1997, there were several publicized cases of judges and prosecutors freeing prisoners after receiving bribes or threats.

5. Are the courts free of political control and influence? Are the courts linked directly to the Ministry of Justice or any other executive body? Albania's judiciary has been hampered by political pressures, insufficient resources, and corruption. The judicial system comprises district courts, six courts of appeal, and the Court of Cassation. Each of these is divided into criminal, civil, and military jurisdictions. The Court of Cassation hears appeals from the court of appeals, while the separate, nine-member Constitutional Court reviews cases requiring interpretation of constitutional legislation or acts. The High Council of Justice, headed by the president, appoints and dismisses all other judges, and prosecutors serve at the pleasure of the Council, thereby, giving the executive broad authority and control over the judiciary. The Council has broad powers to fire, demote, transfer, and otherwise discipline district and appeals court judges for incompetence, commission of a serious crime, or questionable morality. In August 1997, parliament passed an amendment to the Law for the High Council of Justice. Under the previous government, nine members of the 13-member council (approximately 69 percent) were elected by fellow judges and prosecutors via secret ballot. Under the new law, the proportion of seats elected by judicial peers was reduced to just 38 percent, with the other 62 percent selected by parliament, which has a two-thirds Socialist majority. The opposition accused the government of undermining judicial independence. In September 1997, the Council dismissed three judges and relocated a number of others as disciplinary measures. In December, parliament passed a law on the "Organization of Justice," which gives judges the right to appeal their dismissals to the cessation court. In January 1998, eight judges went on a hunger strike to protest their actual or impending dismissals.

Parliament has the authority to approve and dismiss the nine judges of the Constitutional Court and the 100 members of the Court of Cessation. The judges may be dismissed only for mental incompetence or conviction of a serious crime. Constitutional Court justices serve maximum nine-year terms, rotating in three justices every three years. A constitutional crisis erupted in 1997 over the rotation issue. The court rejected a parliamentary amendment to constitutional provisions obliging the court to replace three of its members. Court Chairman Rustem Gjata maintained that the rotation had already occurred and that the new law was a political attempt to tamper with the judiciary. Parliament then accused Gjata of past service in the Communist-era intelligence services (*Sigurimi*), and he was ousted. The Democratic Party abstained from the vote. On March 19, 1998, rotation was carried out after a draw; of six members who took part in the draw, three — one appointed by the president and two by parliament — agreed to quit. Three of the nine Court members did not participate in the draw, as they had replaced other members in 1994.

6. What proportion of lawyers is in private practice? How does this compare with the previous year? Defense lawyers are in private practice, and attorneys in the major cities and commercial centers have business clients. Prosecutors are state employees. Lawyers have formed bar associations. The precise number of attorneys in private practice and comparative figures are unavailable.

7. Does the state provide public defenders? Defendants have the right to legal counsel, which is provided free of charge to those unable to afford a private lawyer. This right is generally respected in criminal and civil cases.

8. Are there effective anti-bias/discrimination laws, including protection of ethnic minority rights? The Law on Major Constitutional Provisions prohibits discrimination based on ethnicity, language, race, sex, or religion, but minority groups have been the subject of discrimination. Roma

(Gypsies) and Greeks, numbering about 70,000-80,000, make up the largest minority groups, and there are smaller groups of Romanian-speaking Vlachs and Roma. Improved relations with Greece in 1996 paved the way for Greek-language schools in the south. The Greek minority is represented in parliament by the Human Rights Unity Party; the Greek organization Omonia is well-organized and active. Tradition and custom have limited women's rights, but there are several organizations devoted to women's issues. Men receive preference in hiring, and, in 1997-98, unemployment among women increased.

Corruption	D

1. What is the magnitude of official corruption in the civil service? Must an average citizen pay a bribe to a bureaucrat in order to receive a service? What services are subject to bribe requests—for example, university entrance, hospital admission, telephone installation, obtaining a license to operate a business, applying for a passport or other official documents? What is the average salary of civil servants at various levels? Corruption has been endemic at all levels of government, private business, state enterprises, and the civil service since the end of the totalitarian regime in 1991. In 1997, the more egregious examples include cases of prosecutors and judges in Lac, Tepelene, Elbasan, and Tirana accepting bribes to release prisoners or detainees; the illegal issuance of diplomatic passports to persons connected to the outgoing PD government; wide-scale bribes of customs officials by smuggling operations (drugs, arms, fuel to Serbia, cigarettes, and women) with high-level government connections; attempts to bribe newspapers by money-lending and pyramid operators; charges against former Prime Minister Aleksander Meksi for bribery and manipulation of bids in the sale of the Selenica coal mines that involved money-lending with dubious financial institutions such as VEFA; the re-opening by the Italian court of a 1991 case in which current and then-Prime Minister Fatos Nano was implicated for corruption in the distribution of humanitarian aid; rampant corruption in the privatization and operating of state enterprises; and the illegal involvement of high-level federal officials in banking and other businesses. Corruption and bribery in the issuance of business licenses and permits have discouraged broad foreign investment. Anecdotal evidence by Albanians suggests widespread corruption in the issuance of passports and travel documents and widespread bribery to gain admittance to certain university faculties. Since the Socialists took power from the Democratic Party in mid-1997, both parties have leveled serious corruption charges against the other. The highly politicized party press has printed wild accusations. Most independent newspapers have been reluctant to expose or write about specific corruption cases for fear of retaliation by officials or organized crime, which has become pervasive. Police frequently accept bribes from criminals and shakedown motorists and small businesses. Average public-sector wages are less than $100 a month.

2. Do top policy-makers (the president, ministers, vice ministers, top court justices, and heads of agencies and commissions) have direct ties to business? How strong are such connections, and what kind of businesses are these? In 1997, there were widespread reports of collusion between high-level government officials and the various pyramid scheme failures, which triggered months of civil unrest and the ouster of the PD government and President Berisha. Several party officials, such as former finance minister Genc Ruli, allegedly had ties with pyramid groups. Several former PD ministers maintained posts in private firms in contravention of conflict-of-interest standards. Suzana Panariti, former Minister of Industry, Transportation, and Trade, remained president of the Tirana-based Arab-Islamic bank. Former finance minister Dylber Vrioni was allegedly paid for one year as president of the Italian-Albanian Bank. Former Prime Minister Alexander Meksi and former State Audit Chairman Blemri Celo maintained ties to several business interests. The Socialist government installed in mid-1997 has also faced charges that several of its leading ministers are connected to smuggling and shady private enterprises, particularly in the south, according to the head of a December 1997 European Union mission that investigated smuggling activities. Bashkim Fino, a Socialist economist who served as interim prime minister between March and July 1997, and was later named a deputy prime minister, allegedly maintained his financial interests in several companies during his official tenure.

3. Do laws requiring financial disclosure and disallowing conflict of interest exist? Have publicized anti-corruption cases been pursued? To what conclusion? Chapter III, Article 35 of the Law on the Major Constitutional Provisions states that a cabinet minister "should not have, except for the mandate of the deputy, any other state or professional function and should not take part in leading bodies of economic and trade organizations." Conflict-of-interest laws also bar elected officials from being involved in businesses or organizations over which they have domain. High-level government ministers and parliamentarians are required to report their assets under a 1995 law. There has been little institutional follow-up, however, in investigating the veracity of declarations because the law does not specifically outline verification procedures. In September 1997, Farudin Arapi, the transparency controller, asked the Bank of Albania's assist in drafting a law that would make it easier to trace accounts in foreign banks and give his office easier access to government officials' finances. The Albanian justice minister announced in August 1997 that he would draft a law compelling judges to declare their assets. One of the most publicized corruption cases involved the VEFA investment company. Under provisions of the Law on Transparency, the government sent administrators to investigate and assumed control over the company's financial dealings. In a controversial November 1997 ruling, the Constitutional Court ruled that the government's action was unconstitutional and voided Article 7 of the Transparency Law. In October 1997, Maksude Kadena, the head of the Sude pyramid scheme, was sentenced to five years imprisonment on fraud charges for embezzling $60 million.

4. What anti-corruption initiatives have been implemented? How often are anti-corruption laws and decrees adopted? In early 1997, a law on "Some Amendments in the Penal Code" (No. 8175) was enacted in order to combat organized crime and corruption. The statutes raised the punishment for "fiscal evasion" and "tax fraud." In addition to the Transparency Law, penal and civil codes include anti-corruption provisions that explicitly outlaw bribery, money-laundering, and graft. A tough anti-crime law was passed in 1997 to give police broader powers to confiscate weapons and use force. The lack of enforcement mechanisms and wide-spread corruption in the judiciary, however, have made enforcement sporadic or non-existent.

5. How do major corruption-ranking organizations like Transparency International rate this country? Transparency International has not rated Albania.

Privatization 4/7

1. What percentage of the GDP comes from private ownership? What percentage of the labor force is employed in the private sector? How large is the informal sector of the economy? According to the European Bank for Reconstruction and Development, in 1997, the private sector accounted for more than 75 percent of GDP. Approximately 75 percent of jobs come from the private sector. The country has a very high level of black market activity. Taxi and bus transportation is provided by black marketeers, and shortages and high tariffs have spawned extensive smuggling operations that bring in consumer goods, cigarettes, and cars. The informal credit market has strengthened the lek while undermining banks, and the black market has increased the supply of hard currency in the market.

2. What major privatization legislation has been passed? What were its substantial features? The Privatization Law (1991) and subsequent amendments regulate the privatization of small-scale entities (defined as those with less than 15 employees). Privatization of these units progressed rapidly in 1991-92, and privatization of retail shops is virtually complete. Approximately 108,000 assets and 6,000 small workshops and medium-sized enterprises were privatized under Law No. 7512. In 1995, the government announced a program of mass privatization to transform large- and medium-sized enterprises into shareholding companies. The plan outlined three privatization options: The state retains more than 50 percent of shares, thereby controlling administration and management; the state owns less than 50 percent and does not administer the enterprises; or the state sells 100 percent of enterprise shares. The fourth phase of privatization began in early 1996. Most of agriculture, construction, road transport, retail trade, and the food industry is now in private hands. The 1995-96 program was undermined by problems of restitution and ownership issues. In all, parliament has endorsed approximately 23 laws dealing with privatization of industry, housing, and land since 1992. The civil unrest in early 1997 derailed planned privatization of banks, infrastructure, and strategic enterprises. In early 1998, the Socialist parliament passed a law on the "Privatization Strategy in the Sectors of Special Importance," which covered the oil and gas sector (the Albpetrol Company); mines, telecommunications, ports, and airports, water pipelines and other infrastructure. The electric power and water pipeline sectors are to be privatized through management contracts with foreign investors. Privatization would be through auctions and tender, with an emphasis on strategic private investors, state share, and employee privatization vouchers. The voucher system has been a failure; only 16 percent of voucher issues have been used. There are 135 joint ventures, including 102 with foreign capital and 33 with private Albanian capital.

3. What proportion of agriculture, housing and land, industry, and small business and services is in private hands? *Agriculture:* Under Law No. 7501, more than 95 percent of all farmland has been privatized. Land was distributed in 3.5 acre plots to more than 500,000 private farmers. Agriculture accounts for more than 50 percent of GDP. Stock-raising and agricultural machinery are fully privatized, according to the government.

Housing and land: Housing was privatized under Law No. 7652 dated December 1992. Albanians were given the opportunity to buy houses and apartments, many at low rates. As a result, more than 95 percent of homes are in private hands. A controversial land restitution law that allows former landowners dispossessed by the Communists, or their heirs, to reclaim property, was never implemented. In February 1998, modifications to Law No. 7501 made it easier to transfer land, eliminated the restitution provision to avoid uprooting those who obtained land under 7501, and provided for the sale of land to foreigners.

Industry: Privatization has lagged in the state-owned industrial sector, which includes some 300 large-scale aging Soviet-era enterprises. Before social unrest rocked the country in early 1997, several large enterprises were put up for sale. A 70 percent stake in the Elbasan cement works was sold at auction, as was a 70 percent stake in a limestone quarry. A total of 15 companies in sectors from cement to wineries, oil product trading, printing, and textiles were sold in the first quarter of 1997, and 20 were slated for sale in the second quarter. Despite the collapse of pyramid schemes and unrest, several large-scale foreign investments occurred, with interest shown in Albanian companies by investors from Switzerland, Greece, Germany, Turkey, and Belgium. In early 1998, parliament adopted a bill on the "Privatization Strategy in the Sector of Special Importance," but there was no firm timetable offered for the privatization in such key sectors as telecommunications and power generation.

Small businesses and services: Small businesses and the service sector experienced a rapid growth and a surge in job creation over the last seven years. Nearly one million people were employed in the private sector, mostly in small- or medium-sized businesses such as restaurants, kiosks, auto servicing, trade and investment groups, and the financial sector.

4. What has been the extent of insider (management, labor, and nomenklatura) participation in the privatization process? What explicit and implicit preferences have been awarded to insiders? The privatization processes launched in 1991 and 1995 were characterized by "insider" privatization, with favorable treatment of high-level government officials and PD activists. Several government ministers and parliamentary deputies have held lucrative positions in newly privatized companies, though hard evidence of wrong-doing has been difficult to verify with certainty. Management and employees of privatized firms also had an advantage over the general population in securing stakes in companies.

5. How much public awareness of and support for privatization have there been? What is the nature of support and opposition to privatization by major interest groups? The privatization programs of the 1990s were launched with substantial fanfare and received broad coverage in the print and electronic media. More than one million Albanians were awarded privatization vouchers. Only 16 percent, however, invested in newly privatized companies. Most citizens preferred to sell the vouchers to vendors for quick cash, much of which was then invested in high-interest yielding pyramid schemes. Entrepreneurship has led to a mushrooming of small- and medium-sized businesses, mainly in the service sector. Resistance to mass privatization of large enterprises has come from trade unions, which fear mass lay-offs, and from certain elements in the Socialist government. The government intends to keep a so-called "golden share" in various strategic enterprises. Ylli Bufi, minister of public economy and Privatization, said in March 1998 that the state may hold a given share of assets in different sectors "in order to retain its decision-making right in case of major problems."

Macroeconomics 5/7

1. How has the taxation system been reformed? (What areas have and have not been overhauled? To what degree are taxpayers complying? Is tax compliance difficult to achieve? Has the level of revenues increased? Is the revenue-collection body overburdened? What is the overall tax burden?) Until 1990, the state budget relied essentially on three revenue sources: the turnover tax, enterprise profit transfers, and social security contributions. All three were paid by enterprises. Reforms since 1991 introduced new revenue sources: a personal income tax, a property tax, and customs duties. They have also replaced profit transfers with profit taxation. Albania has a top income tax rate of 24 percent, although data to determine the tax on the average income level are not available. The top corporate tax rate is 30 percent. A value-added tax (VAT) was introduced in July 1996. In October 1997, the VAT rate was raised from 12.5 percent to 20 percent. The social unrest earlier in the year disrupted tax collection. In January 1998, the government announced that in 1997, 10.8 billion leks were collected from the VAT and 8.4 billion leks from customs revenues. Both figures represented an increase from 1996. The 1998 budget anticipates a doubling of tax revenues. Smuggling and widespread tax evasion remain a serious problem and contributed to a budget deficit for 1997 of 50 billion leks, or 16 percent of GDP. The Socialist government promised revisions of laws dealing with income taxes, business taxes, farm taxes, and customs tariffs.

2. Does fiscal policy encourage private savings, investment, and earnings? (Has there been any reform/alteration of revenue and budget policies? How large are budget deficits and overall debt? Is the financing of the social insurance/pension system sustainable? What proportion of the budget is taken up by subsidies to firms and individuals?) Despite the dearth of private banks, lack of legislation to protect deposits, and the collapse of pyramid schemes, high interest rates on deposits have increased the number of bank deposits. The budget deficit for 1997 was 50 million leks, or 16 percent of GDP. The public debt at the end of 1997 was estimated to be 37.5 million leks, or about 63 percent of GDP, according to the chairman of the Parliamentary Commission on the Economy, Finance, and Privatization. To cope with the budget deficit, the government has issued T-Bills, which have been purchased mainly by commercial banks. This move, however, has increased the government's debt to the banks, which could result in higher taxes and lower public investment by the government. A large part of the 1998 budget is devoted to social welfare items, pensions, and subsidies for unemployment and housing. Without adjustments, these programs will continue to exacerbate budget deficits, although changes in the pension system would be particularly unpopular and politically risky. There has been very little reform of the non-contributory social insurance program, including retirement pensions and compensation for disability.

3. Has there been banking reform? (Is the central bank independent? What are its responsibilities? Is it effective in setting and/or implementing monetary policy? What is the actual state of the private banking sector? Does it conform to international standards? Are depositors protected?) The absence of a properly-functioning banking system has been one of the key institutional deficiencies hampering economic transition. Lack of trust in the state-owned banks and their inability to develop modern banking services contributed to the escalation of informal financial markets and pyramid schemes, as Albanians had savings and combined remittances from Albanians totaling more than $700 million at the end of 1996. The three state-owned banks — Savings Bank, National Commercial Bank, and Rural Commercial Bank — are burdened by a heavy weight of non-performing loans, which reached 60 percent of the loan portfolio at the Rural Bank. The weak legal environment for pursuing debt collection has exacerbated problems. A 1997 study by the U.S.-based economic analysts PlanEcon found that "Albania's two-tiered banking system is the least developed in the region. A majority of financial transfers take place outside the formal banking sector.... Reports have also surfaced of government officials abusing their positions to receive credits that are not guaranteed by collateral." Several foreign banks have entered the market. These are led by three major Greek banks; Piraeus Bank, the National Bank of Greece, and the Alpha Credit Bank. There are two joint-venture banks, The Italian-Albanian Bank and the Arab-Albanian Islamic Bank and one that is fully private. The joint-venture banks have focused on mobilizing short-term deposits and lending to selected customers mostly for trade financing. They have been reluctant to provide long-term investment financing. Though depositors in state banks are nominally protected, vague laws and a lack of transparency in bank procedures and transactions undermine the banking system. The World Bank and the European Bank for Reconstruction and Development have been working with the government to strengthen banks and the financial sector. The Central Bank is independent and charged with managing inflation and setting and implementing monetary policy. It has the right to issue licenses for commercial banks to operate, approve mergers and division of banks, and approve the issue of securities.

4. How sound is the national currency? (Is the value of the currency fixed or does it float? How convertible is the currency? How large are hard currency reserves? Has exchange rate policy been stable and predictable?) Until the political and financial crisis spurred by the collapse of pyramid schemes, the lek was one of the most stable currencies in the emerging markets of Eastern Europe. The exchange rate is freely determined in the interbank market, which competes with private dealers and foreign exchange bureaus. The exchange system is largely free of restrictions on current account transfers for profit repatriation. In late January and early February 1997, the lek fell 12 percent against the U.S. dollar. On February 3, the Central Bank intervened heavily in the foreign exchange market. It sold large amounts of dollars in order to stop the collapse of the currency after the lek lost more than 20 percent of its value. In the absence of a developed banking system, currency trading in Albania is still largely carried out in an informal street market. Albania's foreign currency reserves totaled around $280 million at the beginning of 1997. Inflation was 42 percent at the end of 1997. In introducing the 1998 budget, the finance minister said the government hopes to reduce inflation to 10 percent by the end of 1998.

5. Is there a functioning capital market infrastructure? (Are there existing or planned commodities, bond, and stock markets? What are the mechanisms for investing and lending? What government bodies have authority to regulate capital markets?) The Tirana stock exchange was established in May 1996 for trading government bonds, treasury bills, and privatization vouchers.

The market was organized within the Central Bank of Albania and regulated by a presidentially-appointed National Stock Exchange Commission. In 1995, Law No. 7979 established Investment Funds, joint-stock companies involved in investing, reinvesting privatization vouchers. The minimum capital requirement was established at about $20,000. Foreign entities and companies whose capital is partly owned by foreigners may subscribe to no more than 50 percent of the basic capital of the fund. The fund is managed by an administrator not employed by the concern. A lack of clear laws and enforcement led to a proliferation of pyramid schemes which promised investors exorbitant interest rates. The total value of deposits that the 16 pyramid funds received before the crisis exploded in early 1997—excluding the accrued interest at the time of the estimate—reached an astonishing $1.2 billion, or 50 percent of the country's GDP. Legal activities undertaken through the schemes could hardly have paid the unrealistic interest rates promised clients. The new Socialist government passed a law putting the few remaining such funds under external administration.

Microeconomics 4.5/7

1. Are property rights guaranteed? (Are there both formal and *de facto* protections of private real estate and intellectual property? Is there a land registry with the authority and capability to ensure accurate recording of who owns what? What are the procedures for expropriation, including measures for compensation and challenge? Have any seizures taken place?) Article 11 of the constitution asserts that the state and judicial and physical persons have the right to ownership, that all kinds of ownership are equally defended by law, and that assets that are objects of state property are set by law. A Law on the Registration of Real Estate mandates the maintenance of accurate records and transactions. Local land boards maintain land registry records, but corruption on the boards led to cases of officials purchasing land and property at reduced rates while ignoring claims of former owners. Former President Berisha admitted in March 1998, that "in the course of the implementation of this (land privatization) law, the recognized right of ownership was not respected to the extent that international standards and norms require." The issue of restitution to owners whose property was seized under the Communists has yet to be resolved. The constitution and real estate law guarantee compensation for expropriation. The Laws on Industrial Property Rights (No. 7819), which protects patents, designs, and trademarks, and the Law on Copyrights (No. 7654), which protects intellectual property, conform with European standards. Courts are ill-prepared to handle the increasing load of property disputes.

2. To what extent have prices been liberalized? What subsidies remain? Since 1992, price liberalization has been comprehensive. In 1996, the government lifted price controls on bread, flour, paraffin, and liquid fuel gas. Some 25 items remain subject to administrative price setting, among them milk, some dairy products, and utility rates.

3. Is it possible to own and operate a business? (Has there been legislation regarding the formation, dissolution and transfer of businesses, and is the law respected? Do there exist overly cumbersome bureaucratic hurdles that effectively hinder the ability to own and dispose of a business? Are citizens given access to information on commercial law? Is the law fairly applied? Does regulation (or licensing requirements) impose significant costs on busi-

ness and consumers? Do they create significant barriers to entry and seriously hamper competition? Since 1992, there have been several laws and codes passed dealing with the establishment of businesses, including Law No. 7764 on "Foreign Investments," Law No. 7638 on "Commercial Companies," and Law No. 7667 on "Commercial Registration and the Formalities that Must be Respected by Commercial Companies." There are four legal forms of commercial companies: partnerships, limited partnerships, limited liability companies, and joint-stock companies. Companies must be registered in the Commercial Register of the District Court of Tirana. Licenses are required in some cases. Companies must also register with the district tax office. Citizens do not have easy access to information about commercial law and other economic information. For example, when the government began issuing T-bills the public was not adequately informed, and most of the issues were bought by commercial banks.

4. Are courts effective, transparent, efficient, and quick in reaching decisions on property and contract disputes? What alternative mechanisms for adjudicating disputes exist? The court system is beset by corruption, overburdened with cases, and lacks qualified judges to adjudicate commercial, contract, and property disputes. There are no legal alternatives to adjudicating these types of disputes.

5. Is business competition encouraged? (Are monopolistic practices limited in law and in practice? If so, how? To what degree is "insider" dealing a hindrance to open competition? Are government procurement policies open and unbiased?) Privatization legislation and the constitution enshrine the principle of a free-market economy based on competition. While there is competition in small and medium-sized businesses, "insider" information and bureaucratic connections give some entrepreneurs an advantage. While monopolies are limited by law, which is overseen by a government agency, telecommunications, energy, and other sectors remain primarily in government hands, although plans were announced in 1998 to privatize these operations. Procurement policies are generally open, with information readily available to bidders and companies on the Internet.

6. To what extent has international trade been liberalized? To what degree has there been simplification/overhaul of customs and tariff procedures, and are these applied fairly? What informal trade barriers exist? Foreign trade has been liberalized. In 1996, there were improvements in customs procedures and reductions of some tariffs aimed at improving competition. In January 1998, the government announced plans to reduce tariffs for consumer goods and agricultural products. Changes will allow foreign and domestic investors to bring in upgraded technology and paying proportional customs duties. In 1997, customs duties of 10 percent were imposed on imported grain, flour, and corn, and tariffs were increased from seven to 20 percent on vegetables, fruits, and meats. Average tariffs are between 15 and 20 percent. Trade liberalization in Albania was implemented in two stages. Between 1993 and 1996, the government removed restrictions on exports and imports, as long as international standards were respected. Export taxes were removed and import differentiated tariffs established. In April 1998, the government reported a trade deficit of 22 billion leks, with imports at 38.5 billion leks and exports at 6.1 billion in the first quarter of the year. While the government is seeking to further liberalize trade policy, the main barriers include corruption in the customs service and poor infrastructure.

7. To what extent has foreign investment and capital flow been encouraged or constrained? The Law of Foreign Investment (Law 7764) was passed in 1993, and privatization and related legislation have expedited foreign investment. Political instability, civil unrest, poor infrastructure, corruption, a small local market, an underdeveloped legal system, and a weak banking and financial sector led to a dramatic decrease in direct foreign investment in 1997. According to the Albanian Center for the Promotion of Foreign Investment, direct foreign investment totaled $26 million in 1997 (compared to $70 million in 1996), the lowest level in five years. Tax Free Zones, which were approved in 1996 to encourage investment, have not been established. The government has sought to promote investment in the privatization of the telecommunications and energy sectors. Countries with significant investment in Albania include Italy, Germany, and the United Kingdom, which is developing oil exploration. The World Bank, IMF, and the European Bank for Reconstruction and Development (EBRD) have development programs in Albania aimed at helping improve the environment for foreign investment.

8. Has there been reform in the energy sector? (To what degree has the energy sector been reconstructed? Is the energy sector more varied, and is it open to private competition? Is the country overly dependent on one or two countries for energy [including whether exported fuels must pass through one or more countries to reach markets]?) In 1996, the government announced a four-year program to improve the energy infrastructure and to privatize the energy sector. An energy policy introduced that year called for the use of all sources of energy, such as wood, coal, petroleum, electricity, and gas - in accordance with the specific conditions of each Albanian district - with gas and oil considered priority sources. Approximately 86 percent of the country's electricity is produced by hydro-electric facilities. Increased demand has severely overloaded the electricity transmission system and caused frequent power outages and serious damage to transformers. Construction began on a new electrical substation in Durres, with a $9 million donation from the Swiss government. The second stage of the reconstruction of the country's electrical grid also began in 1996 with credits from the Italian government. The EBRD has focused attention on the energy infrastructure, in particular by upgrading two main hydro-electric facilities, and three smaller installations. The World Bank has earmarked $123 million to modernize power transmission and distribution systems. The country is not overly dependent on one country for energy. Premier Oil, a British firm, has made a 25-year investment to drill for oil.

ARMENIA

Freedom in the World Ratings, 1989-1998

	1989-90	1990-91	1991-92	1992-93	1993-94	1994-95	1995-96	1996-97	1997-98
Political Rights	-	-	5	4	3	3	4	5	5
Civil Liberties	-	-	5	3	4	4	4	4	4
Status	-	-	PF	PF	PF	PF	PF	PF	PF

Polity: Transitional
Economy: Transitional
Population: 3,749,000
PPP: $2,208
Ethnic Groups: Armenian (93 percent), Azeri (3 percent)
Capital: Yerevan

Political Process **5.75/7**

1. When did national legislative elections occur? Were they free and fair? How were they judged by domestic and international election monitoring organizations? Who composes the government? The parliamentary bloc of the Armenian National Movement (ANM) collapsed in early February 1998, when President Levon Ter-Petrossian was forced to resign under pressure from the Ministries of Defense, Internal Affairs, and National Security, and prime minister Robert Kocharian, the former President of the Nagorno-Karabakh republic. On January 28, the "Intellectual Armenia" party had quit the ruling *Hanrapetutyun* bloc. By February 3, at least 25 other members of parliament had quit Hanrapetutyun. The group's disintegration accelerated in the following days.

Many of the defectors joined *Yerkrepah*, a party representing veterans of the Karabakh War. Yerkrepah was organized as a veterans union in late 1994 under the auspices of the Ministry of Defense, with approximately 3,500 members in chapters across Armenia. In 1995, members of Yerkrepah were accused of attacking the offices of several foreign religious organizations. In the fall of 1996, Yerkrepah units attacked protestors demonstrating against fraud in the presidential elections. The group registered as a political party in October 1997, and entered parliament with a strength of 17 seats, which it gained by recruiting sitting, independent members.

Following Ter-Petrossian's resignation, Acting President Kocharian re-legalized the *Dashnaktsutyun* party, a hardline nationalist group that enjoyed strong links to the Armenian diaspora in North America and Europe and that had been banned by the Ter-Petrossian regime in 1995 following allegations of involvement in terrorism, murder, and drug trafficking. While the party currently holds no seats in parliament, it is expected to do well in future parliamentary elections and, together with Yerkrepah, will form the core of the post-Hanrapetutyun government bloc.

Parliamentary elections for the National Assembly last occurred on July 5, 1995. International observers characterized the election as "free, but unfair." Nine opposition parties were refused certification by the Central Election Commission, and the single largest opposition party, the Armenian Revolutionary Federation (ARF), was banned in January 1995, after members were charged with involvement in drug trafficking and murder. A total of 190 deputies — a figure that is to drop to 131 deputies in the 1999 elections — were elected in two rounds of voting to represent 150 single-member districts and 40 proportional representation seats reserved for parties and blocs that polled more than five percent of ballots cast. Fifty-four percent of eligible voters participated.

In the proportional voting, the ANM-led Republican bloc won 20 seats. The *Shamiram* party, which is led by wives of government officials, won eight seats. The Communist Party won six seats. The National Democratic Union, which was among the President's severest critics, and the National Self-Determination Association, which is led by former Soviet-era political prisoner Paruir Hairikian, won three seats each. In the majoritarian races, run-off and repeat elections were held on July 29. All but ten of the legislature's 190 seats were filled, with the president's Republican bloc controlling two-thirds of the seats.

2. When did Presidential elections occur? Were they free and fair? Presidential elections last took place in Armenia on March 16, 1998, following the forced resignation of Ter-Petrossian under pressure from his prime minister Robert Kocharian (former President of the Nagorno-Karabakh Republic) and the ministers of Defense, National Security, and Internal Affairs. Under the Armenian Constitution, the Speaker of Parliament succeeded the president. A long-time Ter-Petrossian ally, the speaker resigned immediately. The succession then passed to Prime Minister Kocharian.

The March 16 elections included 12 candidates. The front-runners were Acting President Kocharian, running as the incumbent with the support of the security ministries; Karen Demirchyan, the Soviet-era Communist chief who had been running a factory since his retirement in 1990; and Vazgen Manukyan, the head of the National Democratic Union. Acting President Kocharian won 38.76 percent of the vote. Demirchian received 30.67 percent.

As neither contender received a majority, a run-off election took place on March 30. Acting President Kocharian won this round with 59.48 percent of the vote. Demirchian received 40.52 percent.

The March 16 election was declared "not free or fair" by the monitoring mission of the Organization for Security and Cooperation in Europe (OSCE). In light of the serious fraud in the country's presidential elections in September 1996, an especially large group of monitors had been dispatched. The head of the mission cited numerous irregularities and violations of the electoral laws. Initially, the OSCE reacted more positively to the March 30 vote. It noted that while the election fell short of OSCE standards in some areas, this had not affected the outcome of the vote. On April 3, the OSCE's Office for Democratic Institutions and Human Rights (ODIHR) stated that new evidence of serious irregularities had come to light. The OSCE then extended the term of its observer mission in order to investigate further.

Previous presidential elections took place on September 22, 1996, and were won by Ter-Petrossyan. Official figures credit him with 51.75 percent of the vote — just enough to avoid a run-off election with the main opposition candidate, Vazgen Manukian. Manukian, a former prime minister and defense minister, was leader of the National Democratic Union and the National Accord bloc (the coalition of opposition parties that contested the election) and officially polled 41.3 percent.

International observers (OSCE/ODIHR and the International Foundation for Electoral Systems) strongly criticized the elections. They cited discrepancies between the number of votes cast and the number of registered voters, as well as numerous other irregularities. Opposition supporters accused the government of stealing the election and took to the streets in large-scale protests that turned violent. In response, the government ordered troops and armored vehicles into the streets of the capital, and arrested between 50 and 250 opposition supporters, including six parliamentary deputies.

On November 22, 1996 the Constitutional Court rejected an opposition petition to annul the election. The decision was widely expected, given that members of the court were appointed by the Ter-Petrossian administration. No further avenues of appeal exist. President Ter-Petrossian was formally re-inaugurated on November 11, before the Court had made its ruling.

3. Is the electoral system multi-party based? Are there at least two viable political parties functioning at all levels of government? The electoral system is multi-party based. The opposition is highly fragmented but was able to unite under a single candidate to contest the 1996 presidential elections. The 1995 constitution reorganized the 39 Soviet-era administrative districts into ten large districts, plus the city of Yerevan. District governors are appointed by the central government and have the power to remove locally elected officials. The only elected local governments are village councils representing no more than several hundred people each. Elections to these councils were held on November 11, 1996. The unified opposition boycotted these elections to protest government fraud and vote-tampering in the presidential election.

4. How many parties have been legalized? Forty-nine political parties have been registered in Armenia since 1990. Between 21 and 25 of these appear to remain active in some capacity. The uncertainty derives from the coalitions and unions which were created between parties in the run-ups to the parliamentary and presidential elections in 1995 and 1996, respectively.

Dashnaktsutyun, the Armenian Revolutionary Federation (ARF), was banned in 1995 but re-legalized on February 9, 1998, by then-Acting President Kocharian. Eight party members accused of murder, drug-trafficking, and plotting to overthrow the government were sentenced to prison terms of between three and 13 years. Three others were sentenced to death. Thirty-one other members of the party, including ARF leader Vahan Hovannesyan, are being tried in a separate case in which they are charged with attempting a *coup d'etat* during the November 1995, parliamentary elections.

Major parties include the National Democratic Union, the Union for National Self-Determination, the Armenian National Movement, Yerkrepah, and the ARF.

5. What proportion of the population belongs to political parties? Less than ten percent of the population belongs to political parties. This figure reflects no significant change from 1996-97.

6. What has been the trend of voter turnout at the municipal, provincial and national levels

in recent years? In general, voter turnout has been steadily declining since the achievement of independence. The figures are as follows: In the May 1990 elections to the Supreme Soviet, approximately 50 percent of the population participated; in the Independence Referendum of September 21, 1991, 90 percent; in the presidential election of October 16, 1991, 70 percent; in the Constitutional Referendum of July 5, 1995, 55.6 percent; in the parliamentary elections of July 5, 1996, 50 percent; in the presidential elections of September 22, 1996, 58.25 percent; and, in the presidential election of March 16, 1998, 64.8 percent.

Civil Society 3.50/7

1. How many nongovernmental organizations have come into existence since 1988? What is the number of charitable/nonprofit organizations? Are there locally-led efforts to increase philanthropy and volunteerism? What proportion of the population is active in private voluntary activity? Over one thousand NGOs are currently registered in Armenia. Approximately 60 of these claim to engage in charitable work. The largest such organizations are affiliated with the International Red Cross, the Armenian Church, and the Adventist Church. There is little locally-led effort to increase philanthropy and volunteerism. Most Armenians are far too poor to engage in such activities. Extended family networks and patronage links, however, are extensive and often serve a similar function.

2. What is the legal and regulatory environment for NGOs (i.e., ease of registration, legal rights, government taxation, procurement, and access-to-information issues)? To what extent is NGO activism focused on improving the legal and regulatory environment? NGOs must register with the Ministry of Justice in order to operate. Registration delays have been used in the past to harass some NGOs. The revised Armenian tax code of June 1997, although not yet finalized, appears to increase the tax burden on NGOs, although not to a great extent.

NGOs have not been particularly active in lobbying the government for changes, but have on occasion acted in the face of unacceptable government conduct. Following attacks on minority religious groups operating charities in the summer of 1995, diaspora-based NGOs threatened the government with a shutdown of their operations if the attacks did not cease. The threat appeared to be effective.

3. What is the organizational capacity of NGOs? Do management structures clearly delineate authority and responsibility? Is information available on NGO management issues in the native language? Is there a core of experienced practicioners/trainers to serve as consultants or mentors to less-developed organizations? Over a thousand NGOs exist in Armenia, and organizational and managerial capacity varies dramatically among them. The Armenian Assembly of America maintains a well-equipped office in Yerevan and operates a NGO training center that provides assistance and information in Armenian, Russian, and English on management and funding issues.

4. Are NGOs financially viable? What is their tax status? Are they obliged and do they typically disclose revenue sources? Do government procurement opportunities exist for private,

not-for-profit providers of services? NGOs are heavily dependent on state assistance and grants from a few large Western donors. They are obliged to disclose revenue sources in order to establish tax liability. Procurement opportunities exist, but government procurement is an extremely murky business, and it is difficult to determine what factors influence the awarding of government contracts.

The tax status of NGOs is somewhat uncertain due to recent revisions in the Armenian tax code. Not-for-profit organizations are not liable for profit taxes but are subject to taxation on property, vehicles, and employee incomes.

5. Are there free trade unions? How many workers belong to these unions? Is the number of workers belonging to trade unions growing or decreasing? What is the numerical/proportional membership of farmer's groups, small business associations, etc.? Article 25 of the 1995 constitution promises freedom of association, including the "right to form or join trade unions."

Most trade unions are holdovers from the Soviet period, and operate under the umbrella of the Soviet-era Confederation of Labor Unions. These include the Journalists, Writers, Artists, and Cinematographers unions, all of which are politically active.

Some new unions have been created since a January 1993 presidential decree that prohibited government retaliation in the event of a strike. Directors of newly-privatized companies, however, can dissolve employee unions at will. Demonstrations and strikes by state and private-sector workers over unpaid wages and management closing of unions occurred during the summer of 1996. The proportion of workers who belong to trade unions is decreasing slowly as privatization of government-owned companies proceeds.

The Federation of Independent Labor Unions was founded on December 12, 1997 to compete with the Confederation. Two farmers' groups are registered: the Assistance to Farms Union and the Association of Farmers of Armenia. Membership figures are unavailable.

A small number of business associations exist in Armenia, the most active of which are craftsmen's associations. The largest businessmen's association, made up largely of the owners of larger state-owned enterprises privatized in 1995, was headed by Telman Ter-Petrossian, President Ter-Petrossian's elder brother, until his death in 1997. Membership figures are unavailable, and the future of this organization and other business associations with connections to the Armenia National Movement are uncertain in the wake of the collapse of the Ter-Petrossian government.

6. What forms of interest group participation in politics are legal? What types of interest groups are active in the political and policy process? Armenian law requires that all NGOs register as political, public, or religious in nature. Political organizations generally refer to political parties. Public organizations form the bulk of registered NGOs, which range from the Red Cross to the UFO Society of Armenia. Religious organizations are the smallest group. Public and religious organizations are not permitted to engage in political activity, including lobbying. Interest groups are allegedly sometimes consulted informally about policy ideas affecting them, but this is frequently the result of personal or kinship relations between government policy-makers and interest group members.

Interest groups active in the policy process are frequently associated with political parties and movements either in the government or allied with particular ministries. For example, prior to its incarnation as a political party, the veteran's union Yerkrapah agitated for increased social and tax benefits for veterans of the Karabakh War. Yerkrapah's close ties to the Ministry of Defense, however, make it difficult to label these activities as "lobbying", as opposed to a public statement of Ministry preferences.

7. How is the not-for-profit/NGO sector perceived by the public and government officials? What is the nature of media coverage of NGOs? To what extent do government officials engage with NGOs? Public attitudes towards the NGO sector are generally positive, but often tinged with a strain of xenophobia expressed as suspicion of the motives of foreigners. Media coverage of NGOs is again usually positive, depending on the types of activities in which the NGO is engaged and the nature of its political connections. Most NGOs have described the attitude of government officials as helpful, if sometimes distant.

Independent Media 5.25/7

1. Are there legal protections for press freedom? Press freedom, which is nominally protected by the Law on Press and Mass Media, has been substantially curtailed by the government. All print, audio, and video media with distributions of 100 copies or more must register with the Ministry of Justice. Many newspapers routinely permit government censors to review material prior to publication in order to avoid suspension.

Several independent or opposition newspapers have been forcibly closed by the Ministry of Justice. Eight newspapers affiliated with the banned ARF were closed in January 1995. In April 1996, *Lragir*, an independent newspaper, was forced to close, although it subsequently resumed publication under a different name. In the same month, the Ministry of Justice assigned control of a newspaper affiliated with an opposition party to a breakaway, pro-government faction of that party.

2. Are there legal penalties for libeling officials? Are there legal penalties for "irresponsible" journalism? Have these laws been enforced to harass journalists? The Law of Press and Mass Media permits libel suits against journalists and media organizations. Advocating "war, violence, ethnic and religious hostility, prostitution, drug abuse, or other criminal acts" and publishing "state secrets," "false and unverified reports," and the details of citizens' private lives without permission is illegal. A first offense carries a three-month suspension of license to publish. A second offense warrants a six-month suspension.

In July 1996, the editor of the Armenian government newspaper, *Respublika Armeniya*, was fired after one of his reporters informed the international news agency INTERFAX that then-prime minister Hrant Bagratyan and defense minister Vazgen Sarkisyan had been shot and wounded by a Turkish soldier while meeting with the governor of the Turkish border province of Kars. The story was quickly exposed as a prank, but not before INTERFAX ran the news.

In early September 1996, the head of Armenian State Radio, along with several editors, was fired after being successfully sued for slander by the head of a Yerevan bread factory.

In March 1996, *Lragir* was prevented from publishing for three months after it printed an article advocating the annexation of Armenian-populated regions of southern Georgia.

3. What proportion of media is privatized? What are the major private newspapers, television stations, and radio stations? There are a number of private cable television broadcasters operating around Armenia. The largest are Mayr Hayrenik in Yerevan, and Shant, in Gyumri. Their programming is largely restricted to pirated western movies and Mexican soap operas. There are also two independent radio stations based in Yerevan; High-FM and Lasto Radio, and one independent radio station in Gyumri. There are a large number of private newspapers claiming to be independent or openly affiliated with opposition political parties. Five independent news agencies exist.

Almost all media organizations use state-owned offices and facilities whether they are independent or not. Media operations, however, are exempt from paying rent on state-owned premises that they occupy, but it is not clear whether this exemption is actually honored. Some media outlets insist that they are still required to pay.

4. Are the private media financially viable? Only the four largest newspapers publish regularly. Smaller newspapers appear irregularly as finances permit. Fiscal support from diaspora groups and western organizations is avidly sought. The private radio and cable stations are reportedly profitable.

5. Are the media editorially independent? Are the media's news gathering functions affected by interference from government or private owners? A wide variety of opinions is represented in the media. Nevertheless, the dependence of most media organizations on powerful patrons — such as political parties, diaspora groups, or wealthy and well-connected individuals — encourages a tendency towards partisanship. In fact, the idea that the media should be independent of influence by their financial supporters has little currency in Armenia and seems restricted to a small group of journalists who have been exposed to Western journalistic training.

6. Is the distribution system for newspapers privately or governmentally controlled? A government agency, *Haymamul*, controls newspaper distribution. Almost all of the country's major newspapers, nine news agencies, and one radio station staged a one-day strike on December 3, 1997 to protest inefficient newspaper distribution. The chief of the government's Department of Information and Book Publishing, which controls Haymamul, was subsequently fired on December 9.

In the larger cities, newspapers are distributed largely through kiosks and some state-owned bookstores. Although most kiosks are now privately owned, their operation requires a government-issued license. As a result, the majority of kiosk owners are government supporters or tend to be risk-averse about which newspapers to carry. Newspaper readership in any case has declined precipitously. According to a recent poll, only three percent of the population reads a newspaper on a regular basis.

7. What proportion of the population is connected to the Internet? Are there any restrictions on Internet access to private citizens? There are no formal restrictions on Internet access for private citizens. Poverty and poor telephone communications combine to place the Internet beyond the reach of most Armenians. Only a tiny fraction of the population has Internet access, generally through employment at an NGO with an office account or at the universities. The country's one private Internet service provider, Arminco, is based in Yerevan.

Although there are no digital lines at present, Armentel, a newly formed telecommunications joint venture between the Ministry of Communications and the U.S. company Transworld, is beginning to install fiber optic cables and modern phone switches. Armentel has been granted a legal monopoly on long-distance service in Armenia.

Under a funding program sponsored by NATO and intended to facilitate Internet access in the CIS, a conference was held in Yerevan in May 1997, to discuss Internet development in Armenia. The Eurasia Foundation has given almost $70,000 in grants since 1995 to fund Internet-related activities. In addition, the Armenian Internet User's Group, a small, but active Yerevan-based NGO, is promoting Internet use and access.

7. What has been the trend in press freedom as measured by Freedom House's *Survey of Press Freedom*? The trend in press freedom has been strongly negative from the beginning of 1995, when ARF news agencies and newspapers were forcibly closed, through the summer of 1996, when the independent newspaper *Lragir* was closed.

The Committee to Protect Journalists (CPJ) criticized press freedom in Armenia in January 1998, and observed that, while formal censorship had been abolished after independence, official pressure on journalists took the form of threats, intimidation, and occasional violent actions, although such incidents had declined in 1997. CPJ characterized government controls over television as amounting to formal censorship

The fall of the Ter-Petrossian government and the establishment of its successor may lead to an increase in press freedom as previously banned opposition papers are permitted to resume publication.

Governance and Public Administration 4.50/7

1. Is the legislature the effective rule-making institution? Only parliament has the power to pass laws. Presidential decrees, regional governor decrees, and some decisions by local executive committees, however, have the power of law. The 1995 constitution strongly shifts power to the president at the expense of the parliament.

2. Is substantial power decentralized to subnational levels of government? What specific authority do subnational levels have? Power in Armenia is highly centralized in the office of the president. Provincial governors and the mayor of Yerevan, whose rank is equivalent to a provincial governor, are accountable to the president rather than the local population or the parliament.

Each of the ten provinces is divided into urban and rural districts governed by locally-elected Councils of Elders and a locally-elected District Administrator, who may organize his or her own staff. The president can remove District Administrators upon the recommendation of the provincial governor.

3. Are subnational officials chosen in free and fair elections? In each of the ten provinces, district governments are elected by secret ballot. Voters elect a five-to-fifteen-member Council of Elders, and a District Administrator (if rural) or City/Village Mayor (if urban), for a term of three years. The Council of Elders approves the district budget, supervises its implementation, and assesses local taxes and fees.

Elections on November 11, 1996 to the District Councils were boycotted by the opposition in protest against fraud and vote-tampering by government supporters in the September 1996 presidential election.

4. Do the executive and legislative bodies operate openly and with transparency? Is draft legislation easily accessible to the media and the public? Parliamentary debates in Yerevan are widely publicized in the national press. Local government traditionally functions in near-total secrecy, but it is too soon to determine whether the new structure has led to any improvements. Draft legislation is generally available to the media and public, but there have been instances of some bills being introduced with little prior public notice.

5. Do municipal governments have sufficient revenues to carry out their duties? Do municipal governments have control of their own local budgets? Do they raise revenues autonomously or from the central state budget? Municipal governments have not been immune to the fiscal crisis that has gripped Armenia since independence. All taxation is controlled by the central government. Municipal governments make budget requests to the Ministry of Finance, which forwards them to the president after review. Allocations to specific municipalities are given in the yearly budgets presented by the president to parliament. It is unclear how much latitude local governments enjoy to spend funds once they are received.

6. Do the elected local leaders and local civil servants know how to manage municipal governments effectively? An August 30, 1994 U.S. AID report on local government cited severe accountability problems in local government, with a "large percentage" of deputies elected to local governments refusing to be held accountable by the electorate or to hold accountable the executives that they themselves elected. It is not clear to what extent the new arrangements mandated in the 1995 constitution may affect this state of affairs. The emerging pattern of Armenian politics — rampant clientism and increasing authoritarianism at the national level — is not encouraging.

Local civil servants with technical specializations are frequently very competent, although emigration has reduced their ranks considerably and led to calls in parliament to restrict the right to emigrate for some classes of citizens.

7. When did the constitutional/legislative changes on local power come into effect? Has there been a reform of the civil service code/system? Are local civil servants employees of the local or central government? The constitution was officially adopted on July 7, 1995. Actual changes to the organization and election of local powers were delayed pending the passage of the appropriate legislation by parliament. This was accomplished before the November 11 local elections. Local civil servants, the majority of whom are holdovers from the Soviet era, are employed by the national government.

Rule of Law 4.75/7

1. Is there a post-communist constitution? How does the judicial system interpret and enforce the constitution? Are there specific examples of judicial enforcement of the constitution in the last year? On July 5, 1995, Armenia adopted a new constitution that was ratified by referendum and strongly criticized by opposition groups for its shift of power to the presidency at the expense of the parliament. The president is directly elected and may not serve more than two consecutive terms (Article 50). He may dissolve parliament (Article 54), appoint and remove the prime minister, appoint four of the nine members and the president of the Constitutional Court and the Court of Appeals, appoint or remove any judge serving in any court other than the Constitutional Court, and appoint and remove the Prosecutor-General and any other prosecutor. He may also declare martial law (Article 55).

While there are no specific instances of judicial enforcement of the constitution in the last year, constitutional procedures for effecting the transfer of power after the removal or incapacitation of the president were followed after President Ter-Petrossian's resignation on February 3, 1998.

2. Does the constitutional framework provide for human rights? Do the human rights include business and property rights? Chapter Two of the 1995 constitution guarantees a full range of civil and political rights, including the rights to life, confidentiality, privacy, freedom of movement and residence, freedom of emigration, freedom of speech and thought, freedom of association, choice of employment, and the right to vote. In addition, citizens are guaranteed health care, education, and an adequate standard of living.

The right to own and inherit property is guaranteed in Article 28. The state may seize private property "only under exceptional circumstances, with due process of law, and with prior equivalent compensation." Non-citizens may not own land except under special circumstances. Intellectual property rights are guaranteed in Article 36.

3. Has there been basic reform of the criminal code/criminal law? Who authorizes searches and issues warrants? Are suspects and prisoners beaten or abused? Are there excessive delays in the criminal justice system? The 1995 constitution guarantees the presumption of innocence and a person's right not to incriminate himself, as well as a "public hearing by a fair and impartial court."

Much of the Soviet-era criminal code remains in effect. Suspects and prisoners are frequently abused by the police, and there have been instances of prisoners dying due to mistreatment while in custody. According to the office of the Armenian Prosecutor-General, 56 inmates died in 1995; 60 in 1996; and 14 in 1997, out of a total prison population of between 5,000 and 6,000. The deaths were attributed to harsh prison conditions and disease. Six of the 14 deaths in 1997 were attributed to pneumonia, and another 400 convicts were said to be suffering from the disease.

4. Do most judges rule fairly and impartially? How many remain from the Communist era? Impartiality and fairness of judges varies dramatically depending on the nature of the case being tried. Sensitive political cases are almost never resolved against the state.

The 1995 constitution grants a three-year grace period to create the new judicial institutions it describes. Replacement of Soviet-era judges has been a very high priority for the Ter-Petrossian government since the ratification of the constitution. As of autumn 1996, the government was reportedly pursuing the replacement of judges energetically.

5. Are the courts free of political control and influence? Are the courts linked directly to the Ministry of Justice or any other executive body? The Armenian judicial system was thoroughly controlled by the Ter-Petrossian government, and judges rarely acted against its wishes. It is unclear whether the new Kocharian Administration will attempt to exercise the same level of control.

The 1995 constitution mandates that all judges be appointed by the president and may be removed by him at his discretion; in the case of members of the Constitutional Court, he may remove the offending judge after a determination is made by the court.

Article 95 of the constitution creates a body called the Judicial Council, which is chaired by the president and includes two legal scholars, nine judges, and three prosecutors, all of whom are appointed by the president. The Council acts as a supervisory and disciplinary body for the judiciary. It prepares lists of judges and prosecutors to be considered for appointments, promotions, or dismissals.

6. What proportion of lawyers are in private practice? How does this compare with the previous year? As in 1996-97, the majority of lawyers remain in state employ.

7. Does the state provide public defenders? The 1995 constitution guarantees defendants legal representation by court-appointed attorneys. This guarantee is usually honored.

8. Has there been comprehensive reform of anti-bias/discrimination laws, including protection of ethnic minority rights? Article 37 of the 1995 constitution states, "Citizens belonging to national minorities are entitled to the preservation of their traditions and development of their language and culture." Few ethnic minorities remain in Armenia. An area on the Turkish frontier populated largely by ethnic Kurds has been the site of numerous operations by Armenian security forces seeking to prevent Kurdish guerrillas fighting in Turkey from establishing a foothold.

In September 1997, parliament amended the Law on Religious Organizations to raise the requirement for registration as a minority from 50 members to 200. Religious organizations must now submit a list of all their members before being allowed to operate legally.

Corruption D

1. What is the magnitude of official corruption in the civil service? Must an average citizen pay a bribe to a bureaucrat in order to receive a service? What services are subject to bribe requests — for example, university entrance, hospital admission, telephone installation, ob-

taining a license to operate a business, applying for a passport or other official documents? What is the average salary of civil servants at various levels? Civil service corruption is widespread. Citizens must pay bribes frequently for all manner of services. An unpublished U.S. government report compiled in the summer of 1996 detailed instances of corrupt practices by almost every Armenian government agency. Most of these practices relate to the requirement of bribes for the performance of official duties. Other corrupt practices concern illegal importation of gasoline, diesel fuel, cigarettes, and various luxury goods and foodstuffs from Georgia and Iran. (*Illegal* refers to importers being permitted to evade payment of customs and excise duties in exchange for payoffs in cash or kind to government officials.) Some institutions, such as the American University of Armenia, have managed to remain relatively free of such practices as bribes for admission or graduation. The average salary is approximately $10 per month.

2. Do top policy-makers (the president, ministers, vice-ministers, top court justices, and heads of agencies and commissions) have direct ties to businesses? How strong are such connections and what kinds of businesses are these? The Ter-Petrossian Administration was frequently criticized for extensive corruption. Much of this concerned activities by officials of the ANM rather than top officials in the executive. It is too soon to determine whether the Kocharian Administration will perform any better.

3. Do laws requiring financial disclosure and disallowing conflict of interest exist? Have publicized anti-corruption cases been pursued? To what conclusion? Armenian law does not currently require financial disclosure by holders of public office, and there are no specific prohibitions against conflict of interest. No high-ranking official has ever been prosecuted for corruption.

4. What major anti-corruption initiatives have been implemented? How often are anti-corruption laws and decrees adopted? As prime minister, Kocharian made anti-corruption initiatives a central theme of his policies. He has indicated that he intends to pursue similar policies as president. A wave of corruption prosecutions of ANM officials from the Ter-Petrossian regime is expected.

5. How do major corruption-ranking organizations like Transparency International rate this country? Transparency International has not rated Armenia.

Privatization 3.75/7

1. What percentage of the GDP comes from private ownership? What percentage of the labor force is employed in the private sector? How large is the informal sector of the economy? According to the European Bank for Reconstruction and Development (EBRD), approximately 64 percent of Armenia's GDP was produced by the private sector in 1997. The informal economy, driven by private entrepreneurs and businessmen, may be almost equal in size to the formal economy. The private sector employs one-half of the labor force.

2. What major privatization legislation has been passed? What were its substantive features? In 1991, Armenia introduced a comprehensive land privatization program, as established in the

Privatization Law adopted on February 17, 1991, and the Privatization and Denationalization Law of July 1992. A Housing Privatization law took effect on September 1, 1993. The term of this law has been extended to December 31, 1996, due to slow progress. In May 1995, legislation clarifying collateral requirements and bankruptcy was passed by parliament.

In January 1995, the government agreed to privatize 900 medium and large enterprises by the end of the year. This target was lowered to 700 enterprises in mid-September and 350 shortly thereafter.

In November 1996, the government created a new Ministry of Privatization and Foreign Investment, which was given exclusive authority over the privatization of medium and large industries. In addition, the government postponed — and subsequently ended — the distribution of vouchers for the 1996-97 privatization program. The value of the vouchers, which had a face value of $46, had fallen to $6 to $7 in open trading.

In early March 1998, the government finalized the sale of 90 percent of the equity in Armentel, the Armenian telecommunications firm that holds a legal monopoly on Armenian long-distance service, the state owned Greek Telecommunications Organization (OTE) in partnership with France Telecom, Greece's Hellenic Bottling Company, and the EBRD. OTE paid $142.5 million, assumed Armentel's $46.7 million debt, and promised to invest $300 million in modernizing Armenian telecommunications over the next decade. OTE also received exclusive rights to the market for fixed and mobile telecommunications services in Armenia for at least 15 years. Transworld Telecommunications, a U.S. firm that owned 49 percent of Armentel, received $62 million from the sale and surrendered all of its shares.

The Armentel deal, with its switch to international tenders and cash auctions, may establish a precedent for the future of privatization under the Kocharian Administration.

3. What proportion of agriculture, housing and land, industry, and business and services is in private hands? *Agriculture*: Almost all of the 800 former state and collective farms have been divided, with 300,000 new private farms created. Approximately 95 percent of total agricultural output is produced by private farms. *Land*: Eighty-seven percent of agricultural land has been privatized with freely transferable land titles. *Housing*: Approximately 80 percent of the housing stock is in private hands. *Business and Services*: Approximately 88.4 percent (1,700) of medium- and large-sized enterprises were privatized through September 1997. Privatization of small firms was largely completed by March 1998.

Government sources cited the reluctance of ministries to surrender control over enterprises and the low values for which enterprises were being sold. In part, this reflected corruption and favoritism in the privatization process. It also reflected the poor condition of the enterprises being privatized.

Revenues derived from privatization have been disappointing, with earnings of 342 million *dram* ($700,000) against projections of 3.5 billion dram ($700,000,000).

4. What has been the extent of insider (management, labor, and nomenklatura) participation in the privatization process? What explicit and implicit preferences have been awarded to insiders? While most medium- and large-sized firms were sold by public subscription, many were privatized through insider buyouts. Moreover, under the voucher privatization program, management and employees could purchase shares in privatized companies at a preferential rate. Varying numbers of shares were reserved for purchase by voucher. The process was heavily criticized for corruption and the generation of low revenues for the state and was subsequently cancelled.

5. How much public awareness of and support for privatization has there been? What is the nature of support and opposition to privatization by major interest groups? Public support for privatization has declined as wrenching economic changes have not produced discernible improvement in the average standard of living. An indirect indication of the decline in public support for the adoption of western economic practices is shown in the strong support for Demirchyan's campaign for the presidency in the March 16 and March 30, 1998 elections. Even with substantial vote fraud, Demirchyan polled 40 percent in the March 30 run-off after running on a campaign platform based on promises to restore Soviet-era institutions and living standards.

Resistance to privatization has been voiced by unions and left-wing parties on behalf of the work forces of medium and large state enterprises. Some of this opposition had more to do with opposition to the Ter-Petrossian government than genuine representation of worker opinions, which appear to be more concerned with wage arrears. Privatization has not yet resulted in massive layoffs at many industries, since capital has not been available to undertake renovation and reconstruction of outdated equipment.

Resistance has also been offered by the Union of Industrialists and Entrepreneurs, an association of factory managers and owners headed by Telman Ter-Petrossian. The Union favors protecting Armenian heavy industry from international pressure.

Criticism of the privatization of some high-profile industries — most prominently the famous Yerevan Cognac Factory — has also been voiced on nationalist grounds as a plunder of national resources by foreigners.

Macroeconomics 4.25/7

1. Has the taxation system been reformed? (What areas have and have not been reformed? To what degree are taxpayers complying? Has the level of revenues increased? Is the revenue collection body overburdened? What is the overall tax burden?) The taxation system has been extensively reformed with an eye towards encouraging foreign investment and privatization. The new Law on Taxes (May 12, 1997) complements the Law on Duties (July 19, 1996). The tax law establishes six different types of taxes: profit/corporate, income, value-added, excise, property, and land. Employers are also required to pay a social security tax for employees. The law has undergone a series of amendments by parliament and is not expected to be finalized until well into 1998. The political instability of early 1998 is expected to delay finalization.

Newly privatized industries and new companies formed with foreign investment are granted a two-year exemption from profit taxes. If the company is liquidated before the fifth year of operation, however, it must pay the total amount of taxes which otherwise would have been due since the third year of registration. Under an agreement reached with the IMF in May 1997, the government promised to begin ordering firms to sell off assets to meet tax arrears.

Armenia imposes a 20 percent Value Added Tax (16 2/3 percent on consumer goods) and a variety of excise taxes at varying rates on luxury goods. Employers pay a social security payroll tax of 37 percent. Profits are taxed at 12 to 30 percent for most firms. Private farmers are taxed at a flat 15-percent rate.

In total, Armenian enterprises have to pay an effective tax rate of some 70 percent. Tax evasion is therefore a major problem and the shadow economy is enormous. Total tax revenue reached 12.3 percent of GDP in May 1997.

2. Does fiscal policy encourage private savings, investment and earnings? (Has there been any reform/alteration of revenue and budget policies? How large are budget deficits and overall debt? Is the financing of the social insurance/pension system sustainable? What proportion of the budget is taken up by subsidies to firms and individuals? The national budget for 1997 was 151.9 billion dram ($325 million). At 30.5 billion dram ($65 million), military spending remained a heavy drain on the budget. Social spending was set at 16.8 billion dram ($30 million), which represented a concession to parliamentary pressure for increased support for social programs. The deficit of 33.9 billion dram ($71 million) was covered almost entirely by loans from international institutions and foreign assistance. Thirty billion dram ($62 million) was earmarked for debt servicing (excluding the debt to Russia, which has been restructured), but only one-third of that amount had been spent by October 1997. Consumer price inflation was 21.1 percent — substantially above the government's prediction of 10 percent and the 1996 rate of 5.7 percent.

The 1998 budget set government expenditures at 174 billion dram ($350 million), with the deficit projected to be 5.5 percent of GDP. Tax revenues were projected to increase by 28 percent due to improved value-added and excise tax collection; government projections of increased revenue collection have been greatly overstated in the past. GDP growth is projected to reach 5.2 percent, while inflation is expected to rise to 13 percent.

Armenia's major creditors are Russia, the International Monetary Fund (IMF), and the World Bank. The national debt is substantial. According to the Association of Armenian Banks, the official debt was $660 million at the end of 1997. The trade deficit stood at $480 million.

The Russian debt of $73.7 million was restructured in September 1997 to be repayable over 11 years, beginning in 2000, at five percent annual interest. In 1994, Armenia pledged a 15 percent stake in its Medzamor nuclear power station, the Nairit chemical plant, the Yerevan cognac distillery, and the Armelektromash electrical engineering factory as collateral for a 110 billion dram (approximately $22 million) credit.

Subsidies to the state sector — estimated at the equivalent of $30 million in 1996, with total government spending at $318 million — remain high and are a source of concern to international lending agencies.

In 1996, Armenia's foreign debt was 34.9 percent. In 1997, it reached 46.3 percent. At current rates of borrowing, the foreign debt will reach 50 percent of GDP by the end of 1998, the upper limit allowed by Armenian agreements with international lending agencies.

The pension system was moderately reformed at the end of 1995. It gradually increased the retirement age, flattened the pension structure, and reduced payments to working pensioners. The government has announced its desire to introduce private pension accounts in the future.

3. Has there been banking reform? Is the Central Bank independent? What are its responsibilities? Is it effective in setting and/or implementing monetary policy? What is the actual state of the private banking sector? Does it conform to international standards? Are depositors protected? The Central Bank of Armenia (CBA) acts independently. This is evidenced by the 30+ bank closures in 1995 and 1996. It has also been very effective in setting monetary policy and has self-consciously patterned its behavior on that of the U.S. Federal Reserve. The IMF, however, has expressed strong dissatisfaction with the pace of reform of the banking sector, and has pressed for mergers among Armenian banks to increase their capitalization and ability to extend credits to private enterprises.

The Central Bank was criticized by the IMF in January 1997 for exceeding agreed-upon limits to borrowing to cover shortfalls in the state budget.

The introduction of banking reforms in 1995 seems to have had a positive effect on the sector. The 35 percent limit on foreign interest in financial institutions was lifted. Minimum capital requirements were raised. By 1997, they were $350,000. They are scheduled to rise to $600,000 in 1998. Banks are required to report daily or weekly to the CBA. The performance of audits by recognized independent auditing firms is mandated yearly. While international accounting standards were introduced in January 1996, banks have been slow to use them. In 1997, the CBA promised to review the role of government ministers in banks, and the government discontinued budget transfers to the savings bank.

By mid-1997, there were 32 commercial banks operating in Armenia; 30 of these were solvent by international standards. Their combined capital was the equivalent of only $20 million. There were also five foreign banks.

The banking system does not enjoy public confidence. Individuals are almost entirely excluded from the banking system. Private banks are principally owned and funded by wealthy, well-connected individuals, who in many cases either head state-owned industries or are related to the heads of such industries, which in turn are heavily dependent on the credit extended by the banks. Well-connected individuals can secure interest-free loans without regard to credit histories, assets, or collateral; in such cases, arrangements for repayment are only rarely made.

There is no protection for depositors and little incentive to use the system e.g., no interest is offered on deposits and high fees are applied for both deposits and withdrawals. Controls on interest rates were eliminated in 1994, and directed credits were ended in early 1995.

Private banks tend to restrict their lending to short-term loans with very high rates of interest (6 to 9 percent per month, or 50 to 70 percent per year) and collateral equaling or exceeding the value of the loan. Such financing as is available is provided through subsidized loan programs funded by multilateral institutions.

4. How sound is the national currency? (To what extent has inflation eroded its value? Is the value of the currency fixed, or does it float? Is the currency convertible? How large are the hard currency reserves? Has exchange rate policy been stable and predictable?) Between 1994 and 1996, the central bank took largely successful steps to stabilize the currency, bring down high interest rates, and curb inflation. Maintaining low inflation, however, has been a difficult, expensive, and ongoing battle. The central bank was forced to draw Armenian hard currency reserves down from the equivalent of $13 million to $4.5 million by December 1996. Inflation rose in 1997 to 10.9 percent.

The dram is fully convertible for current account transactions.

5. Is there a functioning capital market infrastructure? Are there existing or planned commodities, bond, and stock markets? What are the mechanisms for investment and lending? What government bodies have authority to regulate capital markets? There is a minimally functioning capital market at present, although three "stock exchanges" do exist. These serve as conduits for the purchase of international stocks and currency and also deal in the Privatization Certificates issued to citizens during the earlier economic reforms. There is no effective regulation, and deals are made on the basis on personal connections.

A share registry system has been implemented, and a unit in the Ministry of Finance has been assigned authority to regulate capital markets. A treasury bill market has been operating since October 1995.

Microeconomics 4.25/7

1. Are property rights guaranteed? Are there both formal and de facto protections of private real estate and intellectual property? Is there a land registry with the authority and capability to ensure accurate recording of who owns what? What are the procedures for expropriation, including measures for compensation and challenge? Property rights, including intellectual property rights, are guaranteed in Articles 28 and 36 of the 1995 constitution. Private real estate is protected in fact as well as in law. No cases of state seizure of land seem to have occurred since 1993. Expropriation may be challenged in court, and the 1995 constitution requires that fair value compensation be paid. Intellectual property rights are far less secure, particularly foreign entertainment products such as movies, music, and computer software.

A land registry exists with the authority to record ownership.

2. To what extent have prices been liberalized? What subsidies remain? The majority of prices have been freed. Price controls remain on the following goods: urban transport, energy, utilities, sewerage, state-owned housing, telecommunications, and irrigation.

3. Is it possible to own and operate a business? Has there been legislation regarding the formation, dissolution and transfer of businesses, and is the law respected? Do there exist overly cumbersome bureaucratic hurdles that effectively hinder the ability to own and dispose of a business? Are citizens given access to information on commercial law? Is the law applied fairly? Does regulation (or licensing requirements) impose significant costs on business and consumers? Do they create significant barriers to entry and seriously hamper competition?) It is possible to own and operate a business. Legislation governing the creation and conduct of private enterprises includes the Law on Enterprises and Entrepeneurial Activities (June 13, 1994), the law on Private Business (December 24, 1993) and foreign investments law (July 31, 1994). The recently-amended tax code attempts to lighten the tax burden on small entrepeneurs.

Nonetheless, business operations can be very difficult in those cases where government licenses must be obtained. The legal system is generally ineffective in contract enforcement. While reform has made a difference, many informal barriers to entry and free competition continue to make business difficult. A new Bankruptcy Code was enacted in January 1997. So far, only 35 firms have been declared bankrupt. The Ministry of Finance now requires all firms to use international accounting standards.

4. Are courts effective, transparent, efficient, and quick in reaching decisions on property and contract disputes? What alternative mechanisms for adjudicating disputes exist? Armenia's courts continue to struggle with the burdens of Soviet-trained personnel and vulnerability to political pressure. In civil and commercial cases, judges have reportedly asked for bribes in exchange for favorable rulings.

There is little faith in the courts, and most entrepeneurs are reluctant to resort to legal measures. Difficulties with competitors or state agencies are generally resolved by means of appeal to politically connected patrons.

Trials begin less than six months after papers are filed. It takes between seven months and one year for final judgment to be executed. The Soviet-era State Arbitrage Board was reformed by the 1995 constitution to function as a commercial court.

5. Is business competition encouraged? (Are monopolistic practices limited in law and in practice? If so, how? To what degree is "insider" dealing a hindrance to open competition?) Business competition is officially encouraged, but legislation has not yet been passed to provide for enforcement. Monopolistic practices are widespread, if rather more subtle than in 1992 and 1993, when gang warfare between competing factions seeking to dominate trading in gasoline, luxury goods, and other imports made shootouts in Yerevan a common occurrence. Insider dealing is a severe hindrance to competition.

The Law on Protection of Economic Competition was submitted to parliament in late 1996, and the Law on Natural Monopolies was submitted by early 1997.

6. To what extent has international trade been liberalized? To what degree has there been simplification/overhaul of customs and tariff procedures, and are these applied fairly? What informal trade barriers exist? Armenia has one of the most liberal trade regimes in the CIS. In December 1995, a complicated five-band tariff structure was transformed into a two-band structure with rates of 0 and 10 percent.

Informal barriers to trade are substantial and arise from crippling shortages of credit and poor infrastructure.

The conflict with Azerbaijan has meant the closing of the most heavily used roads and railways and greatly complicates Armenian access to international markets. A single rail line runs from the Georgian port of Batumi into Armenia. There are two roads, but only one of these is capable of supporting heavy trucks is in poor repair on the Georgian side. There are few road connections to Iran, one of Armenia's major trading partners, and these are also in poor condition.

Armenia has negotiated bilateral free trade agreements with 35 countries, although only the one with Russia has been put into effect. Armenia applied for accession to the WTO in January

1995, and is expected to become a member in 1998.

7. To what extent has foreign investment and capital flow been encouraged or constrained? Armenia strongly encourages foreign investment and international trade. Customs and tariff procedures have been overhauled, and real efforts have been made to control abuses by officials, particularly at Zvartnots International Airport. There are no restrictions on the repatriation of profits by foreigners. Foreign investors also receive a variety of tax privileges.

Direct foreign investment totalled $70 to $80 million at the end of 1997. The lion's share of investment was divided between proceeds from the Armentel privatization, the U.S.-Armenian gold mining joint venture Global Gold, and investments by Midland Bank Armenia and Coca Cola Bottlers Armenia.

Of 766 joint ventures partly or wholly funded by foreign capital at the end of 1997, 404 were engaged in trade. Russia was the most important investor with 193 enterprises, followed by Iran, the United States, France, Georgia, Germany, and Syria.

In June 1997, the government announced its intention to sell Armental and 13 other major firms to foreign investors.

8. Has there been reform of the energy sector? To what degree has the energy sector been restructured? Is the energy sector more varied, and is it open to private competition? Is the country overly dependent on one or two other countries for energy (including whether exported fuels must pass through one or more countries to reach markets)? Armenia produces no gas or oil and, during the Soviet era, relied principally on Azerbaijani energy. An Armenian-American joint venture has begun drilling for oil at a site near Yerevan, but no results have been achieved thus far. Exploratory coal mining is being conducted in the Ijevan region.

The collapse of Armenian manufacturing between 1989 and the present has to some extent relieved pressure on the meager domestic power supplies available and enabled Armenia to eliminate shortages to residential customers; in fact, negotiations are underway to supply excess generating capacity to Georgia.

Armenia undertook substantial reform of the electrical power sector in 1996 and early 1997. The state electricity firm has been separated into generation, transmission and distribution subunits, and the government has increased enforcement of bill collection on consumers. Power rates are set by an interministerial committee and remain well under market value, but are scheduled to increase steadily through 1997. Under an agreement with the World Bank, electricity prices will rise to six cents per kilowatt-hour by January 1999 in order to make the energy sector profitable.

The Armenian section of a heavy-duty power line was completed in February 1997 to link Armenia with the Iranian power grid. The line is carry 65 MW per day.

Oil is imported from Russia (via Georgia) and Iran by rail. Natural gas is imported from Turkmenistan via Russia and Georgia. Additionally, private entrepreneurs selling improved distribution are active in the three major cities. The government is encouraging these entrepreneurs through preferential tax exemptions.

At present Armenia relies heavily on domestically generated hydropower, mostly from generating stations at Lake Sevan. In 1995, this accounted for 70 percent of Armenian electricity generation. The Soviet-built Metsamor nuclear power station resumed power generation in October, 1995 after being closed for safety reasons in the wake of the December 1988 earthquake. It is expected to provide 27 percent of Armenia's energy consumption. Russian loans permitted Metsamor to re-open. The plant is dependent on continued Russian financing for nuclear fuel and regular maintenance. A second reactor, to be built with French assistance, is to be completed by 2005.

AZERBAIJAN

Freedom in the World Ratings, 1989-1998	1989-90	1990-91	1991-92	1992-93	1993-94	1994-95	1995-96	1996-97	1997-98
Political Rights	-	-	5	5	6	6	6	6	6
Civil Liberties	-	-	5	5	6	6	6	5	4
Status	-	-	PF	PF	NF	NF	NF	NF	PF

Polity: Transitional
Economy: Transitional
Population: 7,409,000
PPP: $1,463
Ethnic Groups: Azeri (82 percent), Russian (7 percent), Armenian (5 percent)
Capital: Baku

Political Process 5.5/7

1. When did national elections occur? Were they free and fair? How were they judged by domestic and international election monitoring organizations? Who composes the government? Elections to the unicameral, 125-member National Assembly (*Milli Majlis*), created under the 1995 constitution, were held in November 1995. Runoffs and re-runs took place on February 4, 1996. One hundred members were returned from single-member constituencies and 25 from party lists by proportional representation. Legislators are elected to five-year terms. President Haidar Aliyev's *Yeni Azerbaijan* (New Azerbaijan) party and its allies won 115 seats. The Azerbaijan Popular Front (AzPF) won four. The Azerbaijan National Independence Party won three, while the New Muslim Democratic Party (*Musavat*) won one. Five leading opposition parties and approximately 600 independent candidates were barred from participating. The Organization for Security and Cooperation in Europe (OSCE) found the balloting to be "not free and fair," while the Council of Europe characterized it as marred by "irregularities and clear cases of fraud." The constitution, which had been adopted earlier by referendum, strengthened the already wide-reaching powers of the president over the government, legislature, and judiciary. Prime Minister Artur Rasizade heads a government dominated by Yeni Azerbaijan and its allies. No opposition parties are represented in the cabinet.

2. When did presidential elections occur? Were they free and fair? President Aliyev, a former member of the Soviet Politburo, was directly elected to a five-year term on October 3, 1993 (in an election for which the 65-year age-limit was rescinded), reportedly with 98 percent of the vote. He had become acting head of state in June 1993 after the overthrow of President Elchibey, who had been elected in free and fair elections in June 1992. The October 3 vote was declared "undemocratic" by international observers. Presidential and parliamentary elections were scheduled for the second half of 1998.

3. Is the electoral system multiparty-based? Are the at least two viable political parties functioning at all levels of government? The electoral system is nominally multi-party-based. With the exception of the AzPF, however, most opposition and pro-government independent parties have no effective organizations outside the capital city of Baku. Yeni Azerbaijan has become the dominant party, both at the national and local levels.

4. How many parties have been legalized? Are any particular parties illegal? More than 45 parties applied for official registration prior to the November 1995 parliamentary vote, but only 32 were recognized by the Ministry of Justice. The government-appointed Central Election Commission barred most of these from taking part in the vote. Several parties merged or ran in coalitions. In January 1996, the Ministry of Justice asked the Supreme Court to bar three opposition organizations, the Democratic Youth Organization, the Labor Party, and the Gardashlyg Society, on the grounds that they sought to "undermine Azerbaijani statehood." In September 1995, the Supreme Court banned the Azerbaijan United Communist Party (AVKP) for alleged anti-state activities but reversed its decision later in the month. Several leaders of the Islamic Party were arrested for allegedly spying for Iran in 1997. On March 26, 1998, the Ministry of Justice issued a statement in which it threatened to take legal action against political parties and public movements engaged in "illegal activities" or not officially registered with the ministry. The statement specifically accused the opposition Brotherhood, Evolution, and Moderan Turan party of engaging in "illegal acts and activities." The ministry also announced that it considered the Democratic Congress, Round Table, Azerbaijan National Committee of the Helsinki Civil Assembly, the Youth Organization Turan, and the Society for the Protection of Oilmen's Rights illegal parties and movements.

5. What proportion of the population belongs to political parties? Few political parties in Azerbaijan can claim large public support, with most — such as Etibar Mamedov's Azerbaijan National Independence Party (ANIP) — centered on a high-visibility, Baku-based leader. The ruling Yeni Azerbaijan claims over 100,000 members, and membership figures for the AzPF have ranged from 10,000 to 50,000. Membership figures are unreliable, however, and polls have shown low voter-party identification and participation figures in the single digits. In a 1996 article on the possibility of municipal elections, *Zerkalo*, a Russian-language publication, "calculated" that "no more than ten percent of the population...belongs to political parties or actively supports them." It also noted that more than likely "these figures are exaggerated."

6. What has been the trend in voter turnout at the municipal, provincial, and national levels in recent years? In the 1992 presidential elections, 74 percent voted. In the presidential elections of October 1993, there was a 98 percent turnout; in the November 1995 legislative elections, 79.8 percent cast ballots; in the run-offs of February 1996, 79.4 percent voted.

Civil Society 5.00/7

1. How many nongovernmental organizations (NGOs) have come into existence since 1988?

What is the number of charitable/nonprofit organizations? Are there locally led efforts to increase philanthropy and volunteerism? What proportion of the population is active in private voluntary activities (from polling data)? There are approximately 950 NGOs officially registered in Azerbaijan. Of these, however, only approximately 90 to 110 are active, according to a January 1998 report by the U.S. NGO, ISAR-Azerbaijan. NGOs include women's groups, charitable organizations, environmental associations, and public policy institutes. The strongest NGOs are those that work on refugee issues and that have contacts with international organizations such as the United Nations High Commission for Refugees. There are also well-established groups working on health and children's issues. Several NGOs deal with charitable work, although the exact number is unavailable. Among these are the Humanitarian Informational Analytical Agency *Saniya*, the Jewish Women's Society of Azerbaijan, and the Charity Center *Havva*. While the country lacks established philanthropic institutions, some oil companies have funded NGOs, but these are non-controversial and deal with such issues as endangered species and the promotion of Azerbaijan's new Latin alphabet. There are no available polling data on private voluntary activity, but most NGOs rely heavily, if not exclusively, on volunteers.

2. What is the legal and regulatory environment for NGOs (i.e., ease of registration, legal rights, government regulation, taxation, procurement and access-to-information issues)? To what extent is NGO activism focused on improving the legal and regulatory environment? NGOs in Azerbaijan operate in a generally hostile environment. The 1992 Law on Social Organizations allowed for the formation of NGOs, but stipulated that they must register with the Ministry of Justice and barred the establishment of any organization hostile to the state. Azerbaijan has only very vague laws regulating NGOs and defining what NGOs do. NGO registration is very difficult, and even the least controversial groups, such as the Azerbaijan English Teacher's Association, find that the process can take up to nine months. Some human rights groups find it virtually impossible to register. Some of the more active NGOs have been subject to harassment in the form of repeated government audits. The Center for Not-For-Profit Law began to collaborate with local groups in late 1997 to develop favorable NGO legislation.

3. What is the organizational capacity of NGOs? Do management structures clearly delineate authority and responsibility? Is information available on NGO management issues in the native language? Is there a core of experienced practitioners/trainers to serve as consultants or mentors to less developed organizations? The larger, more developed NGOs such as the Human Rights Center of Azerbaijan, the Center for Strategic and International Studies, and the FAR Center for Political and Economic Studies, have full-time staff and leadership structures and delineate authority and responsibility. ISAR and other Western and international institutions regularly present training seminars and workshops aimed at increasing the capacity of NGOs to become effective and self-sustaining organizations. ISAR's NGO Resource Center provides information and reference materials on topics important to developing NGOs. The Center holds over 600 volumes in Russian, Azeri, and English, and has Internet access. The Center facilitates communications between local NGOs and international partners by providing NGOs with technical assistance and e-mail accounts. International groups are working to train a core of practitioners, but, for the most part, NGOs must work with local people, many of whom have little understanding of NGO work.

4. Are NGOs financially viable? What is their tax status? Are they obliged and do they typically disclose revenue sources? Do government procurement opportunities exist for private, not-for-profit providers of services? Most successful NGOs rely almost exclusively on assistance from Western or international organizations and operate on a grant-to-grant basis. Since there are no laws on grants, a grant to an NGO is technically taxable at a 40- to 60-percent tax-rate. NGOs working on refugee issues have become implementing partners in large projects run by international agencies. NGOs that receive foreign assistance are obliged to disclose revenue sources and keep accurate records as conditions for receiving operating grants and for government audits. A few charitable organizations and public policy institutes have done work for the Azeri government, but, in general, procurement opportunities are limited.

5. Are there free trade unions? How many workers belong to these unions? Is the number of workers belonging to trade unions growing or decreasing? What is the numerical/proportional membership of farmers' groups, small business associations, etc.? The largest labor organization is the Azerbaijan Confederation of Trade Unions or, as it is sometimes known, the Azerbaijan Labor Federation, which depends on government support. It is a hold-over from the Communist era and claims 2.5 million members out of a work force of 2.8 million — in the industrial, public service, and government sectors. In June 1997, the government and the union signed a collective agreement on wages and social security. The only truly independent union, the Free Trade Union Of Azerbaijan Oil and Gas Industry Employees, which claims more than 85,000 members, suffered a setback in May 1997, when the Azerbaijan State Oil Company (SOCAR) formed a new, pro-government union. The Committee to Defend the Rights of Azerbaijani Oil Workers operates outside established trade union structures and the Turan Independent Association of Trade Unions is a small organization. Accurate union membership figures are unavailable. The emerging private service sector is non-union, and the emasculation of the Free Trade Union of Azerbaijan Oil and Gas Industry Employees suggests reduced independent union influence in the expanding energy sector. Small business proprietors are represented politically by the small Party of Entrepreneurs. In addition, small business associations function in Baku, but their number and membership is not known. The Baku-based Independent Consumers Union represents consumer interests. Although much of agriculture has been privatized, there is no major party representing agrarian interests. Farmers have, however, formed informal cooperatives.

6. What forms of interest participation in politics are legal? What types of interest groups are active in the political and policy process? There are no legal barriers against interest group participation in politics. Nevertheless, opposition parties have been harassed and their leaders have been detained. Some public demonstrations have been forcibly stopped by the police. NGOs are not an integral part of the political and policy process, although several public policy institutes and refugee relief organizations do exercise influence through the independent media and contacts within the government. The right to petition is nominally guaranteed by the Section III, Article 57, of the constitution.

7. How is the not-for-profit/NGO sector perceived by the public and government officials? What is the nature of media coverage of NGOs? To what extent do government officials engage with NGOs? Both public and government perception of indigenous and foreign NGOs engaged in refugee relief, and assistance is generally positive. The public is largely unaware of the activities of other NGOs, such as public policy research groups. The opposition press reports on the activities of NGOs that are opposed to government policies, but the state-run media do not report on NGO activities. With the exception of relief and assistance NGOs, there is little engagement between government officials and NGOs.

Independent Media 5.50/7

1. Are there legal protections for press freedom? The 1995 constitution and a 1992 press law ostensibly guarantee free media. In reality, however, the print media in Azerbaijan are subject to censorship and other forms of harassment, and the state-run electronic media are firmly in the hands of the government and President Aliyev. In November 1996, parliament amended the law on mass media to require licensing in addition to registration with the Ministry of Justice before newspapers could begin or continue to operate. When editors demanded clarification, they were not told the criteria for licensing. While Article 3 of the 1992 press laws explicitly prohibits censorship, a 1993 amendment in light of the conflict with Armenia over Nagorno-Karabakh allowed military censorship. Newspapers, particularly opposition ones, often publish with white space where a censored story would have run. Article 4 continues to bar unspecified "abuse of media freedom." No law currently regulates television and radio.

2. Are there legal penalties for libeling officials? Are there legal penalties for "irresponsible" journalism? Have these laws been enforced to harass journalists? Among the materials banned under Article 4 of the press law, a remnant of the Soviet-era code, are "assaults on the honor and dignity of citizens." The criminal code limits the criticism of government officials through several articles. Article 121, on libel, punishes "false and dishonoring" comments; Article 122 punishes insults; and Article 188.6 specifically prohibits "critical comments on the activity" of the President of the republic. Under Article 188.6, four young journalists from the newspaper *Chesme* were arrested and tried in 1995. They were pardoned by President Aliyev and released on the eve of the 1995 parliamentary elections. In December 1997, Salavan Mamedov, editor of the weekly *Istintaq*, was arrested and charged under Article 121 for making "false and dishonoring comments" against a former prosecutor in the Lenkoran district in Baku.

3. What proportion of the media is privatized? What are the major newspapers, television stations, and radio stations? Approximately 375 newspapers are registered throughout the country, but less than 50 appear on a regular basis. Most popular newspapers are published in Baku. Most newspapers, magazines, and journals are privately owned. Private newspapers include *Ayna/Zerkalo* a weekly, with a circulation of 20,036; *Avrasiya* a weekly with a circulation of 20,000; *Gunay* produced three times a week with a distribution of 41,000 in Azeri and 24,000 in Russian; and *Press-Fakt*. Party financed papers include the opposition *Azadliq* (published by the Azerbaijan Popular Front, three times a week, 26,012), *Yeni Musavat* (Musavat, irregular, 7,000), *Istigal* (Social Democratic Party, weekly, 5,000), and *Millat* (Azerbaijan National Independence Party, semiweekly, 17,302). Government-supported newspapers include *Azerbaijan* (parliament, three times a week, 4,749), *Bakinskiy Rabochiy* (president's office, three times a week, 3,204), and *Yeni Azerbaijan* (ruling New Azerbaijan Party, weekly, 10,280). Forty-seven radio and television companies are registered with the government, but only eight are currently operating. Among the independent television companies in operation, ANS (Azerbaijan News Service) has the most powerful transmitter and provides 16 hours of news and entertainment a week to 1.2 million viewers, or 13 percent of the population, in Baku, Sumgait, and the Absheron Peninsula. Sara-TV in Baku only provides entertainment programs. There are local independent stations in Guba and Tauz. Two stations operate in Ganja. The State Television and Radio Company reaches the entire country, with AzTV-1 and AzTV-2 providing news, entertainment, and public affairs programming. Foreign television includes ORT and RTR (Russian) and two Turkish channels (TRT-1 and a private station). Other foreign broadcasts can be received with a satellite dish. State radio broadcasts nationwide and abroad in Azeri, Russian, English, Turkish, Farsi, Arabic, French, and German. The main independent radio stations are ANS-Radio and Sara-BTR.

4. Are the private media financially viable? Most private newspapers operate with precarious finances, depend on government-controlled printing facilities, and face a tax rate of 20 percent. *Ayna* and *Zerkalo* are financed by advertising sales. *Avrasiya* is financed by two Turkish brothers with support from a Turkish bank. *Panorama* has close connections to the government, while *Gunay* and *Press-Fakt* have wealthy patrons. Most of the major parties finance newspaper organs. ASN television, founded in 1992 by two Azeri brothers and permitted to register by hard-line President Ayaz Mutalibov, had been periodically closed by President Aliyev and his predecessor. It is the Caucasus partner of Internews, a California-based foundation funded in part by U.S. Agency for International Development.

5. Are the media editorially independent? Are the media's news gathering functions affected by interference from government and private owners? Government-controlled newspapers and state-run television and radio adhere strictly to the government line. Party newspapers reflect the views of their sponsors, and opposition papers are often openly critical of government policies. ANS Television is editorially independent. Government interference with media includes outright censorship, harassment and violence against journalists, and denial of access to state television to political opponents. These infringements on press freedom have a deleterious impact on news-gathering.

6. Is the distribution system for newspapers privately or governmentally controlled? The government has a virtual monopoly on distribution outside Baku because most newspapers rely on the post office. In Baku, the larger private and party newspapers have their own distribution networks and are sold in private kiosks and retail stores.

7. What proportion of the population is connected to the Internet? Are there any restrictions on Internet access to private citizens? The authorities have yet to address the issue of freedom of information on the Internet. Free access to the Internet is limited and available only at the Academy of Sciences and a few other academic institutions. Private subscribers can gain access by subscribing for a fee through two companies, Intrans and Compuserve. The number of private users is not known.

8. What has been the trend in press freedom as measured by Freedom House's *Survey of Press Freedom*? Since 1992, Freedom House's *Survey of Press Freedom* has rated Azerbaijan as Not Free due to censorship, violence against journalists, and a dominant government role in printing and distribution.

Governance and Public Administration 6.25/7

1. Is the legislature the effective rule-making institution? Under the constitution, parliament is the primary rule-making body (Section V, Article 81), but presidential decrees also have the force of law (Section VI, Article 113). The 125-member legislature is dominated by President Aliyev's Yeni Azerbaijan Party and its allies, who control all but ten seats.

2. Is substantial power decentralized to subnational levels of government? What specific duties do subnational levels have? Power is not decentralized. Azerbaijan is divided into 59 *rayons*, 11 cities and municipalities, and the Nakichevan Autonomous Republic. (Nagorno-Karabakh, the Armenian enclave, had its autonomy stripped by the Azerbaijan Supreme Soviet on November 26, 1991.) Under the constitution (Section VI, Article 124), local executive power lies in the hands of governors appointed by President Aliyev. While Nakichevan has its own parliament, executive power rests with a governor appointed by President Aliyev in consultation with the chairman of the Nakichevan parliament and the republic's prime minister. The constitution (Section IX, Articles 142-146) defines the role of municipalities, which impose taxes, approve the local budget, implement local programs of social security and social development, and implement ecological policies.

3. Are subnational officials chosen in free and fair elections? Governors are appointed by the president. There have been no municipal elections in Azerbaijan since the adoption of the 1995 constitution. In 1996, a parliamentary Commission of Local Self-Government began deliberations about a draft law on municipal elections. In May 1997, the opposition newspaper *Azadliq* blamed the government for not adopting a municipal elections law and laws dealing with the powers and financing of local governments. It charged that federal ministries were not anxious to give up their control of finances, police, and other functions to decentralization. There was speculation that local elections would be held by November 1997, but they were not.

4. Do the executive and legislative bodies operate openly and with transparency? Is draft legislation easily accessible to the media and the public? Executive and legislative bodies operate with limited transparency. The opposition media have access to draft legislation through a handful of opposition deputies, but, with Yeni Azerbaijan dominating parliamentary commissions and the government, some draft legislation and decrees are not readily available unless the government chooses to release them through the government-controlled media. Parliament is not obliged by the constitution to hold sessions open to the public.

5. Do municipal governments have sufficient revenues to carry out their duties? Do municipal governments have control over their own local budgets? Do they raise revenues autonomously or from the central state budget? Although municipalities can raise some local taxes, most funding comes from the state budget. Local officials submit budgets to the Ministry of Finance, which then submits those to the office of the President. Several draft laws on local financing were submitted and discussed in 1996 and 1997, but the current, centralized system of allocation remains in place.

6. Do the elected local leaders and local civil servants know how to manage municipal governments effectively? Shortages of financial resources have hampered attempts by the mayors of Baku, Sumgait, and other cities to make badly needed infrastructure repairs and provide adequate services from trash pick-up to health care. International organizations such as the U.N. Development Program and the European Bank for Reconstruction and Development (EBRD) have launched projects to improve local water supply and delivery systems, waste disposal, and other infrastructure projects in Baku and other cities. Other hindrances include the lack of skilled municipal administration specialists and a patronage system that allows ill-trained and often corrupt personnel to hold municipal posts.

7. When did the constitutional/legislative changes on local power come into effect? Has there been reform of the civil service code/system? Are local civil servants employees of the local or central government? The 1995 constitution (Chapter Four: Local Self-Government, Section IX, Articles 142-146) broadly outlines the general structure and duties of organs of local power. Parliament, however, has yet to pass a local election law or legislation delineating local authority in terms of financing, police, taxation, and related issues. The civil service code has not been amended since the Soviet era, and local civil servants are effectively employees of the central government.

Rule of Law 5.50/7

1. Is there a post-Communist constitution? How does the judicial system interpret and enforce the constitution? Are there specific examples of judicial enforcement of the constitution in the last year? A new constitution was passed by public referendum in November 1995. Article 30 in Section VII establishes a Constitutional Court, which consists of nine members appointed by the parliament at the recommendation of the president, and which is charged with interpreting the constitutionality of laws, among other duties. An October 1997 draft law on the Constitutional Court stated that the chairman and his deputy would be elected by the judges. The judges would be nominated by the president for ten-year terms subject to the approval of parliament. The president, parliament, the cabinet of ministers, the procurator general's office, and the parliament of Nakichevan will have the right to appeal directly to the Constitutional Court, but ordinary citizens will not enjoy this right. Citizens can appeal to the court through a parliamentary deputy, who then must collect an as yet unspecified number of signatures from other deputies.

2. Does the constitutional framework provide for human rights? Do human rights include business and property rights? The constitution (Chapter Two: Major Rights, Freedoms and Responsibilities, Section III, Principal Human Rights and Civil Rights and Freedoms) outlines such basic rights as the right to property, the right to intellectual property, the inviolability of the home, the right to strike, national and ethnic rights (Article 44), freedom of speech, freedom of conscience, freedom of assembly and association, freedom of information, the right to participate in the political life of society and the state, the presumption of innocence, and freedom of enterprise and business (Article 59).

3. Has there been basic reform of the criminal code/criminal law? Who authorizes searches and issues warrants? Are suspects and prisoners beaten and abused? Are there excessive delays in the criminal justice system? The basic criminal code of Azerbaijan is the Soviet-era legislation adopted in December 1960, although certain amendments have been made. In 1992, the government of President Elchibey liberalized the laws by eliminating some overtly political crimes and expanding defendants' rights to appeal. Under President Aliyev, the death penalty was made applicable to crimes involving national security. In March 1998, parliament adopted a measure that would impose the death penalty in time of war or threat of war for "serious crimes in exceptional circumstances." Procurators and police must ask courts for warrants, but police often conduct searches without warrants. Arbitrary arrests without legal warrant occur. In 1997 and 1998, dozens of opposition journalists and members of the Azerbaijan Popular Front, Musavat, and other opposition parties were detained by police for short periods. There have been persistent reports of political prisoners and other detainees being beaten and abused. In August 1997, for example, 30 defendants in a trial of former OPON (special police) members complained of beatings and torture by electric shocks. Defendants in coup-attempt proceedings have also complained of medical neglect and abuse. Prison conditions are poor, and the government has repeatedly denied requests by the Red Cross and various embassies for permission to visit all prisons. The slowness of judicial reform has led to delays in court proceedings. Corruption is rampant among policemen, who arbitrarily demand payments from enterprises, motorists, and citizens.

4. Do most judges rule fairly and impartially? Do many remain from the Communist era? Judges tend to rule fairly in most criminal and civil cases, although corruption and bribery are a problem. In 1992, many Communist-era judges were replaced during the democratic regime of President Elchibey. With the return of President Aliyev, the former Communist leader, hard-line judges with little tolerance for the political opposition have been named to the bench. According to a report by the non-partisan Human Rights Center of Azerbaijan, there were 900 political prisoners at the end of December 1997. In June 1997, a new judicial law on courts and judges went into effect and created a three-tier judicial system and the institution of jurors. The appropriate agencies of the executive authority, most likely the Ministry of Justice, will select jurors, but no timetable for the introduction of jurors has been announced. Under the law, the state guarantees the inviolability of judges, grants them the right to bear arms, and provides them with an apartment within six months after appointment to the job. The law does not have a mechanism for monitoring the execution of judicial decisions, and no mention is made of methods for combating the acceptance of bribes by court officials. Higher salaries were mandated to discourage corruption.

5. Are the courts free of political control and influence? Are the courts directly linked to the

Ministry of Justice or any other executive body? The constitution provides for a judicial system of limited independence. A 1997 judicial reform law created county appellate courts and an appellate Supreme Court. The court structure includes: county and city courts; county and city courts to consider heinous crimes; martial courts to consider heinous crimes and replace existing military tribunals; local economic courts; economic courts to consider disputes involving international contracts; the Supreme Court of Nakichevan; courts of appeal; and the republic-level Economic Court and Supreme Court of Azerbaijan. Flora Akhmedova, Chairman of the Economic Court of Azerbaijan, maintained that the draft law was unconstitutional because, under the constitution, the highest court for deciding economic disputes is the Economic Court, whose decisions are not subject to appeal in the Supreme Court. Her objections were ignored. The President appoints Supreme Court and Constitutional Court judges (subject to parliamentary approval) and directly appoints lower level judges with no confirmation provisos. The judicial system is inefficient, corrupt, and subject to the influence of executive authorities. The government organizes prosecutors at the district, municipal, and republic levels. The prosecutors are appointed by the President and answerable to the Minister of Justice.

6. What proportion of lawyers are in private practice? How does this compare to the previous year? Information on lawyers in private practice is unavailable.

7. Does the state provide public defenders? By law, the state is required to provide public defenders. According to human rights organizations, this right is ignored in practice.

8. Are there effective anti-bias/discrimination laws, including protection of ethnic minority rights? While the constitution guarantees ethnic and minority rights, the few Armenians which remained after the anti-Armenian riots in the late 1980s and early 1990s have complained of discrimination. According to the Human Rights Center of Azerbaijan, ethnic Lezgins, Meskhetian Turks, and Kurds have also been the targets of harassment and discrimination. The constitution provides for equal rights for women before the law, and there are provisions in the criminal code concerning violence against women. These provisions address rape, forced abortion, forced marriage or divorce, and abduction. Women constitute half of the population of this traditionally male-dominated society. There are more than 16 women's organizations, and women have equal educational opportunities. Women are prominent in political parties, and female participation in the traditionally male-dominated spheres of law and business management is increasing, according to the U. N. Development Program.

Corruption D

1. What is the magnitude of official corruption in the civil service? Must an average citizen pay a bribe to a bureaucrat in order to receive a service? What services are subject to bribe requests — for example, university entrance, hospital admission, telephone installation, obtaining a license to operate a business, applying for a passport or other official documents? What is the average salary of civil servants at various levels? Bribery is ubiquitous in the Azerbaijani government. Ordinary citizens are subject to demands for bribes from petty bureaucrats at almost all levels. Almost any area in which officials are permitted to exercise discretionary judgment is subject to demands for bribes. These include operating a business, applying for a passport, and applying to and graduating from universities.

The average wage in the civil service is $30 per month. The official poverty line is set at $89 per month.

2. Do top policy-makers (the President, ministers, vice-ministers, top court justices, and heads of agencies and commissions) have direct ties to businesses? How strong are such connections, and what kinds of businesses are these? Top policy-makers frequently disguise business interests with family connections. For example, while a given official may not ostensibly own any businesses, members of his family frequently own enterprises that depend on the protection and access that the official can grant. Some of the most popular businesses are those involving duty-free imports under false pretenses. An example of this is the duty-free importation of medical supplies by an NGO controlled by a family member. The goods are then sold for profit domestically or within other parts of the FSU. Other examples include the diversion of state subsidies for industry and "black" production i.e., off-the-books production of state-enterprise goods that are then sold privately by factory managers and their patrons.

3. Do laws requiring financial disclosure and disallowing conflict of interest exist? Have publicized anti-corruption cases been pursued? To what conclusion? Azeri laws concerning financial disclosure and conflict of interest date to the Soviet period and are generally inadequate. There have been several highly publicized trials of major government officials for corruption. Almost without exception, however, these have been Mutalibov or Elchibey administration members who are considered political enemies of the Aliyev government.

In October 1997, anti-corruption investigations led to the firing of several officials in the Azeri NGO sector and local government bodies for misappropriation of funds and goods intended for refugees from the Karabakh conflict. In addition, several high-ranking officials from Azerigaz, the state natural gas firm, were fired by the cabinet of ministers for embezzlement.

In January 1998, the Turkish government released its "Sussurluk Report" on corruption within the Turkish security services. The report provided details of the misappropriation of Turkish development aid to Azerbaijan. The assistance funds were used to build the luxury Avrupa Hotel, which was then deeded to a Turkish organized crime group in order to pay off gambling debts incurred by a family member. President Aliyev angrily denied that any member of his family was involved and later fired Foreign Minister Hasan Hasanov, who was charged with corruption regarding the misappropriation of the Turkish funds. The case has not yet come to trial. The President also closed all casinos in Azerbaijan by decree and declared that such activities undermined Azeri cultural values and promoted money-laundering.

4. What major anti-corruption initiatives have been implemented? How often are anti-corruption laws and decrees adopted? There have been periodic anti-corruption campaigns in Azerbaijan since President Aliyev came to power. The bulk of these have been directed at members of previous governments. The most recent action by the government was the closure of the country's casinos in response to the Turkish government's revelations of the involvement of Turkish mafia organizations in the establishments.

5. How do major corruption-ranking organizations like Transparency International rate this country? A business survey by Control Risk, a British risk management firm, rated Azerbaijan the third-most corrupt country in the world.

Privatization 5/7

1. What percentage of the GDP comes from private ownership? What percentage of the labor force is employed in the private sector? How large is the informal sector of the economy? The EBRD estimates that approximately 30 percent of GDP is from the private sector. Less than 25 percent of the labor force works in the private sector. These figures are relatively in comparison with those from neighboring Armenia and Georgia. They also reflect the slow start of Azeribaijan's privatization programs and the importance of government-controlled oil revenues to the country's GDP.

The size of the informal economy is conservatively estimated at 40 percent of GDP.

2. What major privatization legislation has been passed? What were its substantive features? The government passed a privatization law in January 1993 to establish ground rules for the establishment of joint-stock enterprises and the auction of small- and medium-sized enterprises.

In 1995, the Azerbaijani government pledged to make significant efforts to privatize in the industrial and agricultural sectors. The Law on Privatization, which was approved by parliament on July 21, 1995, called for privatization to begin on September 1, 1995. Eight thousand small enterprises were to be privatized by the end of 1995. Fifty large- and medium-sized enterprises were to be privatized by the end of March 1996. The distribution of vouchers for mass privatization of other enterprises was also to begin by the end of 1996. The privatization program never really began, however, and none of these goals were met.

Genuine privatization actually began in Azerbaijan in February 1997 with the launch of a three-year program through which 70 percent of enterprises would be privatized by the end of 1998. The program divided enterprises into small (less than 50 workers for industry and less than 10 for service), medium (50 to 300 workers for industry and 11 to 50 for service), and large (more than 300 workers for industry and more than 50 for service).

The country's privatization legislation divides enterprises into four categories: non-privatizable (the national bank, railroads, water utilities, historical monuments, and pension funds), privatizable by presidential decree (fuel, energy, petrochemical production, telecommunications, and bread- and wine-making), privatizable by decree of the Council of Ministers (oil and oil products, construction, road maintenance, and medical services), and fully privatizable. Companies privatizable by presidential decree are privatized by the same method as fully privatizable companies, except that a non-voting share is reserved for the state.

In 1997, each Azeri citizen received a book containing four privatization vouchers. Veterans of the Karabakh War and families of the victims of the January 1990 Soviet army attack on Baku received two books. A total of 32 million vouchers were distributed. The vouchers can be traded on the open market. Foreign investors can take part in both cash and voucher auctions, but, for voucher auctions, they must buy an "option" from the State Property Committee at a cost of 100,000 *manat* ($25) per voucher.

Almost immediately after the initial distribution of the vouchers in late February 1997, panic-selling ensued as Azeris rushed to cash their vouchers. While the government had estimated that each voucher was worth the equivalent of $200, the street price fell in two days to approximately $22.50. Following pleas by the State Property Commission to halt sales, the price rose to $120. As of March 1998, the vouchers were trading at a price of 195,000 manat (approximately $47). The market price of the vouchers has tended to increase sharply shortly before privatization auctions and to decline afterwards.

Voucher auctions, which began in June 1997, take place at regular intervals. In any given auction, approximately 50 enterprises are offered for sale. Bidding takes place in six major cities. Share prices are determined by the number of vouchers offered for each share in the auctions.

Privatization procedures involve a combination of cash and voucher auctions. Fifty large- and medium-sized industrial plants — including a large air-conditioner factory and precision-machinery, petrochemical, and metal-refining enterprises — are scheduled to be privatized in the first half of 1998. Eighty-five hotels and 11 guest-houses are also to be offered. There has been little interest in the large industrial concerns. In 1997, the government privatized 1,100 medium- and large-sized enterprises in 16 voucher and 15 cash auctions. A total of 13,000 small enterprises have already been privatized, in most cases through purchases by their workers. As of November 1997, 340 large industries out of a total of 2,000 had been privatized. The government expected the total to reach 400 by the end of 1997.

On December 3, 1997, President Aliyev issued decrees to mandate the privatization of six state-owned construction firms.

3. What proportion of agriculture, housing and land, industry, and small business and services is in private hands? The cotton industry was privatized in the summer of 1997 amid significant participation by foreign investors. A presidential decree ordering the privatization of the tea, tobacco, and wine industries is expected by the summer of 1998.

Privatization of agricultural land is handled separately from privatization of industry. Legislation was passed in 1994, and privatization began in 1995. It has proceeded slowly and unevenly, however, due to resistance on the part of regional authorities. Foreigners are not permitted to purchase leases. The Azeri government claimed that approximately 2,000 private farms had been created by July 1995. In some sparsely populated regions, leases were granted to refugees and internally-displaced persons.

The Law on Land Reform was passed in August 1996. It envisions that 22 percent of land will be privately owned. Forty-five percent will be state-owned, and 33 percent will be municipally-owned.

There has been little actual privatization of housing or industry. Citizens living in Baku can buy, sell, and trade apartments but not entire buildings. Nevertheless, there is a booming private sector in retail commerce and services.

4. What has been the extent of insider (management, labor, and nomenklatura) participation in the privatization process? What explicit and implicit preferences have been awarded to insiders? The government has restricted the number of voucher options that foreigners can purchase. Fifteen percent of the shares must be sold to enterprise employees. Another 55 percent must be sold at open voucher auctions. The remaining 30 percent must be sold in cash auctions, in which foreigners can participate. Foreigners can buy up to ten percent of the shares in state-owned enterprises.

The privatization of small firms has been dominated by insiders, who generally bought the firms that they had already been leasing from the state in order to obtain *de jure* recognition of their *de facto* ownership rights.

5. How much public awareness of and support for privatization has there been? What is the nature of support and opposition to privatization by major interest groups? The government has moved more slowly on privatization in part because they claim to fear the effects of the large layoffs that could result from the process. In addition, there has been substantial resistance to privatization among the managers and politicians who benefit financially from diversion of subsidies to state-controlled industries. These groups have managed to shelve efforts led by U.N. Special Representative Paolo Lembo to create a free trade zone in the industrial city of Sumgait.

The attitude of the presidentially-appointed regional government appears to be the single greatest factor influencing the progress of privatization in rural areas.

Workers and managers in small industries and the agricultural sector have been the strongest supporters of privatization, particularly of their own firms.

The IMF has been the most influential group supporting privatization. Its pressure and threats – including a possible cutoff of loans and credits — were instrumental in prodding the government to beginning a privatization program in 1997.

Macroeconomy 5.00/7

1. Has the taxation system been reformed? (What areas have and have not been overhauled? To what degree are taxpayers complying? Is tax compliance difficult to achieve? Has the level of revenues increased? Is the revenue-collection body overburdened? What is the overall tax burden?) Tax system reforms began in the spring of 1995 in response to rampant tax evasion, declining revenues, and pressure from international financial institutions. The size of the tax administration was increased, and tax inspectors were ordered to collect tax arrears aggressively from state- and privately-owned enterprises and NGOs. Import tariffs and major taxes have increased, while the number of exemptions from profit- and value-added taxes has declined. The finance ministry reported a collection rate of nearly 100 percent for 1996. Nevertheless, taxation remains unpredictable.

Tax revenue as a proportion of government revenue remains low. The state is heavily dependent on foreign credits and signing bonuses on oil-exploration leases. Tax compliance varies among taxpayers. Foreign companies are generally compliant. Azeri citizens often evade taxes. In any case, their incomes are so low — studies show that between 40 and 90 percent of the population is below the poverty line — as to make collection pointless.

Foreign and local businesses are frequently subject to tax claims by various authorities.

2. Does fiscal policy encourage private savings, investment and earnings? (Has there been any reform/alteration of revenue and budget policies? How large are budget deficits and overall debt? Is the financing of the social insurance/pension system sustainable? What proportion of the budget is taken up by subsidies to firms and individuals?) A policy of fiscal austerity by Azerbaijan was begun in 1995 and ratified in a three-year IMF agreement signed in December 1996. It has continued to the present day.

Azerbaijan's GDP dropped by 61 percent between 1991 and 1995. The new austerity program, combined with a cease-fire with Armenia and the beginning of the long-awaited boom in foreign investment, resulted in a growth rate of 1 percent in 1996 and 5.8 percent in 1997. Growth for 1998 is projected to be 7 percent.

The budget is unusually dependent on oil revenues for financial stability. In the first quarter of 1998, oil revenues accounted for 43 percent of the total intake. This represented a drop from 52 percent in 1997 due to lower oil prices on the world market.

Azerbaijan's 1997 budget was $758 million. The deficit was $163 million, which represented a signficant increase over the 1996 figure of $117 million. The deficit was to be covered mainly by treasury bills and signing bonuses paid by international oil companies for on-shore fields and contracts and production-sharing agreements (PSAs) in the Caspian Sea. These payments are quite substantial. For example, a single PSA signed by Azerbaijan with a consortium of Amoco, Unocal, Itochu, and Delta Nimir included a $75 million signing bonus for the Azerbaijani government.

Servicing the national debt was projected to cost $100 million. Budgetary subsidies were eliminated entirely under the auspices of the IMF-sponsored fiscal reform plan. Indirect subsidies through state-owned banks were also decreased.

In 1992, the Social Protection Fund was created as Azerbaijan's social insurance program. Almost one-third of government expenditures are transfers through the fund. Pension arrears are a constant problem.

3. Has there been banking reform? (Is the central bank independent? What are its responsibilities? Is it effective in setting and/or implementing monetary policy? What is the actual state of the private banking sector? Does it conform to international standards? Are depositors protected?) The banking system is small and not very significant in an economy that is still dominated by cash transactions.

Azerbaijan had more than 150 state-owned and private banks in 1996. A number of these were closed by the National Bank in September 1996, in the face of an incipient debt crisis. In addition, the National Bank assumed control of foreign exchange holdings and lending by state-owned banks, and a Treasury office was established within the finance ministry to monitor and control expenditures. While no formal decree was issued, in practice the government decided to cease the issuance of licenses to foreign banks until such time as the domestic banking sector was functioning effectively. Seven foreign banks were licensed to operate in Azerbaijan in July 1997.

The National Bank and Ministry of Finance have successfully implemented a stabilization package approved by the IMF. This has led to a dramatic drop in inflation (see Question 2 above) and made Azerbaijan the leading CIS state in macroeconomic statistics.

As of July 1997, there were four state-owned banks, 93 private banks, and six foreign-owned banks. Only one of the state-owned banks is viable, while the other three are engaged in bankruptcy procedures. The private banks are weak.

Azeri bankers estimated that the reforms would cause the number of banks to drop by 50 percent or more. On July 1, 1997, the capital requirement for Azeri banks was increased from $100,000 to $600,000. The requirement is set to double to $1,200,000 by July 1998.

Banking reform has been identified by the IMF as a priority for Azerbaijan in the period from 1998 to 2000. In particular, the IMF has indicated that several state-owned banks should be privatized.

4. How sound is the national currency? (Is the value of the currency fixed, or does it float? How convertible is the currency? How large are the hard currency reserves? Has exchange rate policy been stable and predictable?) Under an IMF-sanctioned stabilization plan, Azerbaijan has succeeded in restoring stability to the national currency, the manat, which floats freely. Inflation declined from 1600 percent in 1994 to 0.4 percent in 1997. The manat even appreciated somewhat in even nominal terms against the U.S. dollar. Hard currency reserves were approximately $500 million in November 1997.

The manat is not widely convertible to hard currencies outside of Azerbaijan, although it is convertible within the country. In mid-July 1997, Azerbaijan inaugurated an inter-bank currency market in order to pave the way for the manat to achieve full convertibility after Azerbaijan begins to receive large-scale revenues from oil exports in 2001. The new market permits banks to trade currency privately among themselves after the daily auction held at the Baku Interbank Currency Exchange (BICEX). At the beginning of 1998, the average daily turnover of foreign exchange at the BICEX daily auction was approximately $3 million.

5. Is there a functioning capital market infrastructure? (Are there existing or planned commodities, bond, and stock markets? What are the mechanisms for investment and lending? What government bodies have authority to regulate capital markets?) There is an active market in government-issued privatization vouchers, which are traded both at government-run voucher shops and on the black market. There is no formal stock exchange at which shares in enterprises can be traded, but government records of share ownership can be updated to reflect changes.

Legislation governing the operations of investment funds has been passed but at present no such funds exist in Azerbaijan.

Microeconomics 5.00/7

1. Are property rights guaranteed? (Are there both formal and de facto protections of private real estate and intellectual property? Is there a land registry with the authority and capability to ensure accurate recording of who owns what? What are the procedures for expropriation, including measures for compensation and challenge? Have any seizures taken place? Property rights are guaranteed in the 1995 constitution, but specific legislation to codify these rights has not yet been adopted. There is little real protection for property rights, and predatory practices by government agencies and powerful criminal organizations are common.

The beginning of the privatization process has led to great improvements in the land and asset registry system, which is generally accurate.

Azerbaijan has adopted a copyright law and is a signatory of several international intellectual property rights conventions.

There are no formal mechanisms for securing compensation or challenging an expropriation. The issue is expected to grow in prominence as private property is expropriated for pipeline routes. When asked about procedures for compensation in such cases, central government officials have admitted that the issue has not been considered.

2. To what extent have prices been liberalized? What subsidies remain? The rapid expansion of the private retail sector has, to a considerable extent, overtaken price liberalization. While state-owned stores that sell subsidized bread and other staples remain in operation, large and vigorous markets that sell a wide variety of goods exist in almost every city and town of any size. Gasoline prices were liberalized in 1995. Power and telecommunications prices remain artificially low.

3. Is it possible to own and operate a business? (Has there been legislation regarding the formation, dissolution and transfer of businesses, and is the law respected? Do there exist overly cumbersome bureaucratic hurdles that effectively hinder the ability to own and dispose of a business? Are citizens given access to information on commercial law? Is the law applied fairly? Does regulation (or do licensing requirements) impose significant costs on business and consumers? Do they create significant barriers to entry and seriously hamper competition?) It is possible to own and operate a business, and private retail trade is growing very rapidly. Nevertheless, there has been almost no significant legislation to clarify rules for the formation, dissolution, and transfer of businesses. Such matters are handled on an *ad hoc*, cash basis by the principals involved.

To the extent that they exist, bureaucratic procedures pertaining to property ownership and sale are extremely complex and frequently corrupt. It is not uncommon for tax assessments to be levied by any of a variety of government agencies in an unpredictable manner. There is little public knowledge of laws that affect commercial activities, and such laws are rarely applied.

Laws are often vague, and only implementing decrees are more specific. There is no official outlet for publicizing changes in laws. While decrees are usually published by newspapers, new regulations are rarely published. A new bankruptcy law was adopted in 1997.

4. Are courts effective, transparent, efficient, and quick in teaching decisions on property and contract disputes? What alternative mechanisms for adjudicating disputes exist? Azeri courts are slow, inefficient, and frequently corrupt. They are not independent of the government. The judicial system is not an effective enforcer of contracts or property rights. The Economic Court, which has jurisdiction over commercial disputes, is particularly corrupt. Foreign court and arbitration decisions are not enforceable in Azerbaijan.

It can take between one and a half to two and a half years for a court case to be heard and for judgment to be executed. Disputes are therefore frequently mediated by political or economic patrons.

5. Is business competition encouraged? (Are monopolistic practices limited in law and practice? If so, how? To what degree is "insider" dealing a hindrance to open competition? Are

government procurement policies open and unbiased?) The rapid and sweeping privatization effort that began in 1997 was in part a reaction to strong IMF criticism of the state sector of the economy, which the IMF had likened to a system of government-sanctioned monopolies.

There are no laws prohibiting insider- or self-dealing. Insider privileges in procurement remain commonplace.

6. To what extent has international trade been liberalized? To what degree has there been simplification/overhaul of customs and tariff procedures, and are these applied fairly? What informal trade barriers exist? In accordance with an agreement with the IMF, Azerbaijan has taken several steps to simplify customs and tariff procedures. Decree Number 62 of the Cabinet of Ministers mandates that as of July 1, 1997, all imported goods are subject to a 15-percent import tariff. Certain specifically identified products, however, are exempt or subject to tariffs of five percent. Imported goods are also subject to a value-added tax of 20 percent. Most previously allowed exemptions have been eliminated.

In January 1997, the State Ministry of Natural Resources was converted into a state company called "Azercontract." On June 25, 1997, the Ministry of External Economic Relations and the Ministry of Trade were combined in a new Ministry of Trade.

The July 1, 1997 decree represents an advance on the existing law, which did not clearly define which imported goods were duty-free. Determination of this status was left to individual customs inspectors and was to be based on the intended use of the goods. In practice, this led to widespread abuses, as importers presented false accounts of the intended use of the goods in question and customs inspectors demanded bribes in exchange for favorable determination of duty-free status.

The Ministry of Foreign Economic Relations is the primary government agency for the regulation of international trade. It establishes maximum and minimum prices for a wide range of imported goods and must give its consent to contracts at prices outside of these limits. Imports of certain goods — such as arms, military equipment, nuclear materials, narcotics, toxic chemicals, and certain categories of scientific and technical information related to military production — must be cleared through the Cabinet of Ministers.

Azeri export regulations indicate a concern with non-payment for exported products. This has been a perennial post-Soviet-era problem in much of the region, where large amounts of finished goods and raw materials were exported from state firms for minimal amounts and then resold by private individuals on international markets for much higher prices. In Azerbaijan, this practice was particularly common with cotton, petroleum products, and such abundant commodities of non-ferrous minerals, such as copper.

Failure to register income from exports is a favored tax evasion technique; by banking proceeds from foreign sales abroad, businessmen seek to cloak the size of their incomes from government scrutiny.

7. To what extent has foreign investment and capital flow been encouraged or constrained? Foreign investment in Azerbaijan rose five-fold to $342 million in 1996. It rose still further still to $1 billion in 1997.

A 1992 law guarantees equal treatment of foreign and local investors. In January 1997, foreign investment regulations were overhauled by a Presidential decree that greatly simplified procedures for investment.

Firms that are more than 30 percent state-owned must submit export contracts to the government for registration. Non-state-owned firms can do so with local customs authorities.

8. Has there been reform of the energy sector? (To what degree has the energy sector been restructured? Is the energy sector more varied, and is it open to private competition? Is the country overly dependent on one or two other countries for energy (including whether exported fuels must pass through one or more countries to reach markets)? The Azerbaijan oil and gas sector has the potential to become one of the most important in the world. According to one estimate, Caspian Sea reserves are at the level of those of the North Sea. Almost every oil company in the world is establishing a presence in the country.

Azeri oil exports rose in 1997 to 292,000 metric tons of crude oil, which was worth $23.4 million, and 2.9 million metric tons of petroleum products – such as gasoline, diesel fuel, and kerosene – that were worth $262.2 million. Overall production declined slightly from 1996 levels to 9.02 million metric tons. A total of 14,200 metric tons of liquefied natural gas with a value of $2.4 million were also exported. Azerbaijan imported 260,900 metric tons of crude oil with a value of $20.4 million and 77,600 metric tons of oil products with a value of $13.05 million.

Production targets for natural gas were not met by a substantial margin. Azerbaijan imported 27,570 metric tons of liquefied natural gas, primarily from Turkmenistan, for domestic consumption.

In September 1992, the two state oil companies, Azerineft and Azneftkimiya, were merged to form SOCAR. Large-scale manufacturing related to the energy sector remains in state hands and continues to receive subsidies. Much of the energy sector is slated to remain in state hands and will not be privatized, although the government reportedly considered offering 30 percent of SOCAR to strategic investors. The EBRD has made several large loans to Azerbaijan for upgrading power generation and distribution systems.

Under the terms of a Cabinet of Ministers decree on the reform of export laws, SOCAR has, since the summer of 1997, been able to demand pre-payment for deliveries to domestic and foreign customers, thereby substantially lowering the rate of domestic consumption. Only the state Ministries of Agriculture and Defense are exempt from this practice. In the first quarter of 1998, Azerbaijan's two largest oil refineries reported losses of $8.8 million due to falling world oil prices.

Azerbaijani oil exports to international markets must cross through Russia, Georgia, or Iran. Oil produced by the Azerbaijan International Operating Company (AIOC), a consortium of western oil companies and SOCAR, began shipping oil through Russia to the port of Novorosiisk in November 1997. An 11-day stoppage in February 1998, for unspecified "technical reasons" by the Russian pipeline operator Transneft underlined Azerbaijan's continuing dependency on Russian goodwill for energy exports to succeed. The AIOC is moving rapidly to complete a pipeline to a new export terminal in Supsa, Georgia. This is expected to be ready by October 1998. The new line will not cross Russian territory. American pressure has thus far succeeded in blocking shipments of oil through Iran to terminals in the Persian Gulf.

Electricity prices were increased recently, but are still very low. The last increase in December 1996 set rates at 50 manat ($.0125) per kilowat hour.

BELARUS

Freedom in the World Ratings, 1989-1998

	1989-90	1990-91	1991-92	1992-93	1993-94	1994-95	1995-96	1996-97	1997-98
Political Rights	-	-	4	4	5	4	5	6	6
Civil Liberties	-	-	4	3	4	4	5	6	6
Status	-	-	PF	PF	PF	PF	PF	NF	NF

Polity: Consolidated Autocracy
Economy: Consolidated Statist
Population: 10,330,000
PPP: $4,398
Ethnic Groups: Belarusan (79.4 percent), Russians (11.9 percent), Poles (4.2 percent), Ukrainians (2.4 percent), Jews (1.4 percent)
Capital: Minsk

Political Process 6.25/7

1. When did national legislative elections occur? Were they free and fair? How were they judged by domestic and international election monitoring organizations? Who composes the government? In November 1996, President Lukashenka conducted a controversial referendum that changed the 1994 constitution, extended the presidential term, broadened already substantial powers, and created a new bicameral parliament. A 110-member lower house, the Chamber of Representatives, which was formed by pro-Lukashenka members of the existing parliament (elected in 1995) was dissolved. A 64-member upper house, called the Council of the Republic, was created by a combination of presidential appointments and the results of January 1997 elections by the six oblast councils and the Minsk City Council. The transition left 86 electoral districts unrepresented because the new constitution reduced the number of representatives (from 260), and a full parliament had never been seated due to the executive interference in the 1995 vote. Western governments do not recognize the legitimacy of the new parliament, which functions as little more than a rubber-stamp. The last popular, contested elections — for the unicameral 260-seat parliament, which was created under the March 1994 constitution — were held on May 14, 1995, with a run-off on May 28. A complex voting system produced only 108 deputies after the second round, which left the body well short of the two-thirds quorum of 174 seats as required by the constitution. The Soviet-era parliament that was elected in 1990 was supposed to fill the vacuum until the autumn elections, but it did not meet until September. Ignoring the constitution, President Lukashenka did not recognize its legitimacy and ruled by decree. He stripped deputies from the holdover parliament of their immunity and threatened to impose presidential rule. Turnout for the November 29, 1996 parliamentary elections was higher. It brought the total to 139 deputies, but this figure was still short of a quorum. In the December 10 runoff, the election of 59 additional deputies brought the total to 198.

Of these, the Communist Party of Belarus won 42 seats; the Agrarian Party, 33; the United Civic Party, nine; the Party of Popular Accord, eight; the Social Democratic Hramada, two; and the Party for All Belarusan Unity and Accord, two. Six other parties won one seat each, including Lukashenka's Belarusian Patriotic Movement (BPR). Ninety-five deputies were "unaffiliated." Many of these subsequently formed the pro-Lukashenka Accord (*Zgody*) faction in parliament. No candidates from the democratic Popular Front, which helped to lead the country to independence, were elected. International observers, who deemed no round of the 1995 vote as free and fair, cited such irregularities as family voting, infringements on the mass media, and a lack of information about parties and candidates. After the November 1996, referendum, seats for the 110-member body were filled as follows: the Communist Party of Belarus, 24; the Agrarian Party, 14; and the Party of Popular Accord, five. Seven parties won one seat each. Sixty "independents" were also chosen. President Lukashenka has instituted de facto presidential rule in Belarus. The prime minister is Syarghei Linh, a leader of the BPR, and the cabinet consists exclusively of Lukashenka loyalists.

2. When did presidential elections occur? Were they free and fair? The post of president was created by the Communist-dominated, 360-member Soviet-era parliament in March 1994, after it ousted Stanislaw Shushkevich, a reformer and parliamentary chairman, as head of state, and overwhelmingly adopted the country's post-Soviet constitution. The constitution called for a strong presidency. The first round of presidential elections occurred on June 23, 1994. A second round took place on July 10. In the first round, Lukashenka, then a 39-year-old non-party populist who had campaigned on an anti-corruption platform, won with 45 percent of the vote. Prime Minister Vyacheslav Kebich, a pro-Russian Communist, finished second with 17 percent. In the run-off, Lukashenka won an overwhelming 80 percent of the vote. The elections were judged free and fair by international monitors.

3. Is the electoral system multiparty-based? Are there at least two viable political parties functioning at all levels of government? Section I, Article 5 of the constitution states that "political parties and other public associations acting within the framework of the constitution and laws of the Republic of Belarus shall contribute toward ascertaining and expressing the political will of the citizens and participate in elections." Section II, Article 36 enshrines "freedom of association." While a number of parties contested the 1990 and 1995 parliamentary elections, President Lukashenka has consolidated his rule by dissolving the elected parliament, governing by decree, and undermining opposition parties. Parties face harassment and restrictions such as a lack of access to state-run media and bans on literature and publications. In 1996, Lukashenka forçed key leaders of the Belarus Popular Front, a democratic nationalist party, to seek asylum in the West. In 1997, scores of opposition party leaders and members were arrested and detained, and the headquarters of the Popular Front were raided on several occasions.

4. How many parties have been legalized? Are any particular parties illegal? As of March 1998, 35 political parties were registered in Belarus, but no more than a dozen function in several oblasts. In addition to the Communists and the Popular Front, other major groupings include the Belarus Peasant Party (Agrarians), the United Civic Party (including the United Democratic Party of Belarus), the Social Democratic Hramada (Assembly), the Belarus Christian-Democratic Union, and the Union of Collective Farmers. In October 1994, parliament passed controversial legislation requiring that parties convene a founding meeting of at least 500 signed members in order to be registered. No specific parties have been officially outlawed, but Article 5 of the constitution bans the creation of parties that "aim to change the constitutional system by force, or propagate war, or ethnic, religious, and racial hatred."

5. What proportion of the population belongs to political parties? The proportion of the population belonging to political parties is minuscule; membership figures are unreliable. In 1997, the government sent registered parties questionnaires about membership figures; 23 parties failed to submit answers. The Belarusan Popular Front, founded in 1989, reported that it had 2,228 members and that "approximately 10,000 people work for the BPF as volunteers." Approximately one million people voted for BPF candidates in the 1990 parliamentary elections and the 1994 presidential vote. The Communist Party of Belarus, a successor to the Soviet-era party, maintains a strong organizational structure and won 42 seats — more than any other party — in the 1995 parliamentary elections. According to the party leader, official membership is 7,011. The Party of Communists of Belarus lists 10,429 members; the United Civic Party, 2,500; the Social Democratic Hramada, 1,729; and the Belarusan Peasant Party, 1,647.

6. What has been the trend of voter turnout at the municipal, provincial, and national levels in recent years? Since 1990, voter turnout at the municipal, provincial, and national levels has been decreasing. The participation figures for the country's seven million eligible voters in important elections is as follows: in the March 17, 1991 referendum on preserving the Soviet Union, 83 percent turnout; in the 1994 presidential elections, 70 percent; in the May 1995 referendum on such issues as parliamentary elections, economic integration, and the designation of Russian as a state language, 64.7 percent in the first round and 56.4 percent in the second; and, in the June 12, 1995 local elections, 47.6 percent. In the November 29 and December 10, 1995 parliamentary runoffs, elections were invalidated in several districts in which the turnout was less than 50 percent. Approximately 36,808 candidates competed for 28,000 local deputy seats in 6,698 electoral districts. In the November 29 and December 10 local by-elections, 51 percent and 53 percent voted, respectively. A total of 913 local deputies were elected, thereby fulfilling the two-thirds quorum for local sessions to be able to convene. In the November 24, 1996 referendum on changing the constitution to extending the presidential term and powers, 84.05 percent voted. International analysts and Belarus' political opposition, however, hold that the November 24 referendum and the November 29 and December 10 local by-election figures were inflated.

Civil Society 5.75/7

1. How many nongovernmental organizations (NGOs) have come into existence since 1988? What is the number of charitable/nonprofit organizations? Are there locally led efforts to increase philanthropy and volunteerism? What proportion of the population is active in private voluntary activity (from polling data)? There are 1,963 registered public associations in Belarus. These include educational, women's, cultural, environmental, youth, religious, media, and business groups.

Total membership in these organizations is estimated to be between 75,000 and 100,000. Most NGOs still lack experience, skills, funds, staff, and overall organization and are far less developed outside of major cities and towns. Western organizations and programs have a network of charitable and social welfare organizations that work with local groups, among them United Way of Belarus, the Prenatal Care Project, City of Hope, and For the Children of Chernobyl. Even charitable NGOs have faced government pressure, and arbitrary and contradictory tax policies have led several European and U.S.-based humanitarian groups to cease operations, thereby depriving Belarusans of millions of dollars worth of medical, food, and other aid. In April 1997, the government launched an investigation of Children of Chernobyl and other social support groups. In September 1997, the Soros Foundation closed its operations in Belarus after its director was barred from the country and its property was seized by authorities. The foundation had invested $6 million in Belarus, primarily for education, medical, and ecological programs. A predominantly state-run economy has worked against the development of private philanthropic institutions, and the repressive political climate has made citizens wary of involvement with public associations and NGOs. There is no polling data on private voluntary activity, although the 1986 Chernobyl nuclear disaster, which left 2.5 million Belarusans living in the contaminated areas, did spur an active ecological movement and groups to aid the victims.

2. What is the legal and regulatory environment for NGOs (i.e., ease of registration, legal rights, government regulation, taxation, procurement, and access-to-information issues)? To what extent is NGO activism focused on improving the legal and regulatory environment? A 1997 United Nations report on human rights in Belarus criticized the government's "lack of tolerance of NGOs." Local groups face serious political and bureaucratic obstacles to registration. In 1997, several Western-based aid groups, including the Irish-based Chernobyl Children Project and City of Hope, announced that they were planning to cease operations after the government reneged on previously agreed tax and customs exemptions. The main Belarusan distribution NGO, Nadzeya Ekspres, also faced "unjust taxation," according to its director. While NGOs such as the Independent Society for Law Research continue to work to improve the legal and regulatory environment, attempts to work with the government have been resisted. In May 1997, President Lukashenka closed the Law Institute, an independent organization working to improve legal rights in Belarus.

3. What is the organizational capacity of NGOs? Do management structures clearly delineate authority and responsibility? Is information available on NGO management issues in the native language? Is there a core of experienced practitioners/trainers to serve as consultants or mentors to less-developed organizations? The larger NGOs, particularly some environmental, human rights, and women's groups and health assistance organizations that work with Western institutions, have a leadership structure and full-time and volunteer staff, issue publications, and delineate authority and responsibility. Several Western organizations have NGO development programs to improve local management. Among these is the European Union's Tacis program, which works with 34 NGOs to strengthen their institutional capacity. Outside of the European Union, the United States is the principal supporter of the reform process in Belarus. One key goal of NGO development programs is to train a core of practitioners to assist less-developed NGOs outside of the major cities.

4. Are NGOs financially viable? What is their tax status? Are they obliged to and do they typically disclose revenue sources? Do government procurement opportunities exist for private, not-for-profit providers of services? Most NGOs in Belarus rely almost exclusively on technical and financial assistance from Western governments and organizations to sustain their activities. Those NGOs that receive assistance are required to keep accurate accounting records as a condition of their grants. The government has used frequent arbitrary audits to harass NGOs. Most NGOs are not tax-exempt. While Western charitable and humanitarian groups working in the country were promised tax-exemption under a February 1997 law signed by President Lukashenka, organizations such as City of Hope and Nadzeya Ekspres were subsequently informed by the State Tax Committee that they owed millions in taxes and fines. Government procurement opportunities for NGOs and not-for-profit organizations are non-existent.

5. Are there free trade unions? How many workers belong to these unions? Is the number of workers belonging to trade unions growing or decreasing? What is the numerical proportion of membership of farmers' groups, small business associations, etc.? In August 1995, the president banned the activities of the Independent Free Trade Union of Belarus, the Minsk Metro Trade Union, and the Railroad and Transport Facilities Workers' Union – a move that led to a transport workers strike. Several strike leaders were arrested and sentenced to brief terms of forced labor. In December 1997, largely in response to international pressure, the government ordered the Ministry of Justice to re-register the Free Trade Union of Belarus and register the Congress of Democratic Trade Unions, which had earlier been denied registration. Approximately 25,000 workers reportedly belong to independent trade unions. The Federation of Trade Unions of Belarus (FTUB), a successor to the Soviet-era union, claims five million members in a total workforce of 5.1 million; however, this figure cannot be verified independently. Employees at state-run enterprises are discouraged from joining independent trade unions. Workers are often automatically inducted into the FTUB and their union dues are deducted from their wages. With unofficial unemployment measured at approximately 30 percent, union membership is significantly lower than official figures suggest. In 1997, a presidential decree on "Immediate Measures to Strengthen Labor and Executive Discipline" gives employers greater leeway in terminating labor contracts, even for minor violations of the Labor Code. An estimated 19 percent of the workforce is involved in agriculture, which is still mostly collectivized. A small percentage of farmers belong to the Union of Cooperatives. Agrarian interests are represented by the Peasant Party and the Union of Collective Farmers. With much of the economy in state hands, the proportional membership of small business associations remains small (official figures are unavailable). Business, trade, and professional groups include the National Brokers Guild, the Union of Entrepreneurs and Lessees, the Science and Industry Association, and the Belarusan Association of Journalists

6. What forms of interest group participation in politics are legal? What types of interest groups are active in the political and policy process? There are no specific regulations governing interest group participation in politics. Article 40 of the 1994 and 1996 versions of the constitution enshrined the right to petition the government and state bodies as well as freedoms of association and assembly. Demonstrations are the main vehicle for public expression regarding government policies. Faced with mounting public protests, Lukashenka issued a decree in March 1997 to severely curtail the right of assembly. Rallies were banned in certain locations, and local authorities were given the power to impose strict limits on the number of participants. The decree also prohibited the display of unregistered flags and symbols, as well as placards deemed to threaten the state. This decree and subsequent laws impose severe penalties, including heavy fines and detention, on organizers and demonstrators who violate the law. Unsanctioned marches have been violently broken up by the police. Managers of state-run enterprises and collectives lobby the government, but President Lukashenka's totalitarian style precludes any meaningful interest group participation in policy decision-making.

Independent Media 6.5/7

1. Are there legal protections for press freedom? Both the 1994 and the amended 1996 constitutions enshrine freedom of expression, access to information, and a free press, but restrictions abound. In October 1997, the Chamber of Representatives passed several amendments to the press law to further curtail freedom of the media. While "defaming" the president is prohibited by the press law as well as the 1994 and 1996 versions of the constitution, the new amendments extended the stricture to include "higher officials," such as the prime minister and members of the government. The amendments also gave the State Committee for the Press the right to suspend the activity of a media organ for a period of three months to a year without going through the courts. Publications with a circulation of less than 500 copies had been exempt from registration, but now must register. Perhaps the most serious restriction barred the importation of newspapers that "include reports that may do harm to the political and economic interests of the Republic of Belarus." In 1995, non-state newspapers such as the independent *Svaboda, Belaruskaya hazeta, Belaruskaya delovaya gazeta,* and *Imya,* were banned from using the main state publishing house. This restriction forced them to move their printing operations to Lithuania. While confiscations were sporadic, the new amendment suggests that authorities are determined to stop the influx of independent papers from abroad. In July 1997, the Council of Ministers adopted a resolution that strictly regulates foreign media correspondents in Belarus. It mandates re-accreditation of all foreign journalists and obliged foreign correspondents to "check the reliability of news; to present objective information for publication; and not to allow the publication or broadcasting of deliberately false reports." It also held foreign correspondents responsible for "attacks on the morality, honor, and dignity of citizens and officials, in particular spreading reports discrediting the honor, dignity, and working reputation of the president of the Republic of Belarus."

In 1997, there were numerous examples of the government's campaign against the press. In November, the Supreme Economic Court banned the publication of *Svaboda*, the largest independent newspaper. (In January 1998, it reappeared under the new name of *Naviny*, and was resumed distribution on a limited basis). In April 1994, the editorial staff of *Pahonya*, the only independent newspaper in Grodno, was evicted from its offices. In July, the Ministry of Foreign Affairs revoked the accreditation of Pavel Shremet, a Belarusan citizen and bureau chief for the Russian TV station ORT, in response to his critical commentary on government expenditures for the celebration of Minsk's 930th anniversary. Three other ORT employees, all of whom were Russian citizens, were subsequently arrested, thereby setting off a major diplomatic confrontation with Moscow. The three were ultimately released, but, on January 28, 1998, Sheremet was found guilty of illegally trying to cross the Belarus-Lithuanian border and given a suspended sentence. In March 1998, the government announced that state officials were officially forbidden from making official documents and comments available for publication in the independent media. Although the Belarusan legislature passed a draft law in 1994 to prohibits the existence of a press monopoly, the government maintains a virtual economic monopoly over the press through its ownership of nearly all printing and broadcasting facilities and its management of the distribution of all print media through official outlets.

2. Are there legal penalties for libeling officials? Are there legal penalties for "irresponsible" journalism? Have these laws been enforced to harass journalists? Provisions in the 1997 amendments to the media law extended proscriptions barring defamation of the president to include other top level officials. The media law and a resolution on foreign correspondents prohibit "false reports" and unsubstantiated news. In November 1997, the editor of *Imya* received a warning that satirical collages in several issues defamed the president and that the newspaper could be stripped of its license. Although the newspaper appealed the charges, it stopped printing the collages.

3. What proportion of media is privatized? What are the major newspapers, television stations, and radio stations? Approximately one-half of the press, or approximately 500 mostly local newspapers and 39 magazines, have been privatized. Independent newspapers, however, have been severely harassed and restricted by censorship, intimidation of journalists, and arbitrary fines and taxation. The government remains the owner and chief financial backer of nine major publications. Of eight daily national papers, six are government-controlled or partially subsidized. They include: *Narodnaya Hazeta, Sovietskaya Belarus, Zvyazda, Respublika, Belarusa Niva, and Znamia Yunosti*. There is one state news agency, Belinfarm. The office lease of Belapan, an independent news agency, was broken with one day's notice in February 1996, but it continues to function. More than 40 radio and 165 television entities have been licensed by the Ministry of Information. Of the total number of registered TV and radio stations, 16 were founded by the government (two with foreign partners), 104 by non-state small enterprises and joint-stock companies, 27 by public organizations, 17 by private persons, and 19 by legislative bodies. Only one-quarter of these are on the air. The State Committee on Television and Radio controls broadcasting. State-owned television controls one national station and several local stations. A number of small privately-owned television stations are local operations that broadcast entertainment. BITA, a national network broadcasting on Channel 8, was closed by the government. In 1997, the Television Broadcasting Network (TBN) was attempting to unite 16 non-state private local television companies into a national network; the effort met with state resistance. Belarus television faces stiff competition for viewers from the Russian stations ORT, RTR, and NTV. Some Russian broadcasts have been suspended for broadcasting unflattering reports of the government. Several Russian personnel from ORT were detained near the Lithuanian-Belarusian border in July 1997. The state owns the only national radio station, which broadcasts on three channels. One of the most popular radio stations is Radio-Roks-Minsk, which is registered in Moscow and broadcasts programs from Russia's capital. The country's only independent radio station, Radio 101.2, was forced off the air by the government in August 1996.

4. Are the private media financially viable? The government-controlled and subsidized newspapers are financially viable, although, in a country of ten million people, the total circulation of all dailies and periodicals does not exceed 800,000. The slow pace of reform, which has led to high inflation rates and a sharp drop in output, poses financial problems for the independent press. Shortages of printing supplies, especially paper imported from Russia, can upset printing schedules because state publications receive priority. Official publications receive other privileges, including state subsidies, which give mainstream papers a financial edge over privately-owned competitors. Exorbitant taxation and heavy fines have been used to try to bankrupt independent newspapers that criticize the president and the government.

5. Are the media editorially independent? Are the media's news gathering functions affected by interference from government or private owners? Most of the major independent newspapers that are still functioning oppose the policies of the government. State-run newspapers and television and radio stations are unswervingly loyal to the regime. During mass demonstrations in March 1997, journalists, including those from the Russian and foreign media, were prevented from doing their jobs by police. Journalists were beaten and harassed and had equipment and film confiscated by authorities.

6. Is the distribution system for newspapers privately or governmentally controlled? The government controls most of the distribution of national newspapers. Privately-owned newspapers are distributed both by the government through official outlets and privately through the post office, hand delivery, street vendors, and kiosks. When independent newspapers were forced to publish in Lithuania after the government denied access to state printing facilities, the postal service was ordered to refuse delivery of newspapers not printed in Belarus, and Belarusan border guards were ordered to confiscate such publications. In March 1997, the Council of Ministers issued a decree (Number 218) that prohibited and restricted the movement of goods across the customs border. The decree specifically prohibits the import and export of printed, audio, and video materials or others news media containing information that could damage the economic and political interests of the country. On March 25, 1997 border guards detained the editor of *Narodna Volya* as he returned to Belarus from Lithuania with the day's edition of the newspaper. Kiosks have been barred from carrying opposition newspapers.

7. What proportion of the population is connected to the Internet? Are there any restrictions on Internet access to private citizens? Information on Internet access is not currently available.

8. What has been the trend in press freedom as measured by Freedom House's *Survey of Press Freedom*? Freedom House's annual *Survey of Press Freedom* rated Belarus "Partly Free" from 1992 through 1993, and "Not Free" from 1994-98. Since his election, Lukashenka has engaged in a concerted campaign to intimidate or eliminate the opposition press. The government maintains control of most electronic media, which only broadcast government-approved information and deny access for other views. The government maintains a virtual monopoly on printing and distribution facilities.

Governance and Public Administration 6.25/7

1. Is the legislature the effective rule-making institution? The bicameral parliament is wholly subservient to President Lukashenka, who essentially rules by decree. Lukashenka-appointed loyalists now predominate on the Constitutional Court, which, by the end of 1996, had ruled that 17 of 19 presidential decrees were unconstitutional.

2. Is substantial power decentralized to sub-national levels of government? What specific authority of sub-national levels have? Section V of the constitution covers "Local Government and Local Self Government." The country is divided into six oblasts and one municipality — Minsk, the capital. Major cities serve as administrative centers of the oblasts. Local administration is centered on local councils (Soviets of Deputies), which are elected for four-year terms, and local executive and administrative authorities, which are appointed and dismissed by Lukashenka. Under Article 121 of the 1996 constitution, the jurisdiction of the local councils includes the "ratification of programs of economic and social development; the adoption of local budgets and reports on their fulfillment; the establishment of local taxes and fees in accordance with the law; the determination, within the limits specified by law, of the procedure for administration and disposal of communal property; and the scheduling of local referenda." Local councils may be dissolved by the upper house of parliament for violations of law. A four-year-old law on local self-government is not observed in practice.

3. Are sub-national officials chosen in free and fair elections? Local, regional, and other sub-national officials are appointed either by the corresponding legislative bodies or by the head of the local or regional executive branch of power. The president has the right to appoint governors, who had previously been popularly elected, and who, in turn, appoint subordinate officials. Local elections are scheduled for 1999 for district, city, and regional councils (soviets). According to the president, they will be held under a majoritarian system with no party lists; a final law has yet to be approved.

4. Do executive and legislative bodies operate openly and with transparency? Is draft legislation easily accessible to the media and the public? The national parliament has become little more than a rubber stamp for presidential edicts and decrees. Presidential decrees, parliamentary resolutions, and legislation are publicized by the government-run broadcast and print media on the whims of the executive; government bodies operate without transparency.

5. Do municipal governments have sufficient revenues to carry out their duties? Do municipal governments have control of their own local budgets? Do they raise revenues autonomously or from the central state budget? Municipal governments generally have sufficient revenues to carry out their duties and, to a large extent, have control of their own local budgets. They raise revenues autonomously through local taxation or municipal ownership of industries or businesses.

In April 1997, the Brest regional Executive Council introduced a 5-percent local tax on the sale of alcohol. The revenue is to be used for the procurement of fertilizer for state, collective, and private farms. Most local funds, however, are based in the central state budget.

6. Do the elected local leaders and local civil servants know how to manage municipal governments effectively? Most elected and appointed local leaders and local civil servants do not know how to manage municipal governments effectively. Many continue to practice managerial methods commonly used during the Soviet period.

7. When did constitutional/legislative changes on local power come into effect? Has there been a reform of the civil service code/system? Are local civil servants employees of the local or central government? In terms of the constitution, changes in local power came into effect with the adoption a new constitution in 1994 and subsequent amendments in 1996. Legislation on local power was first adopted in 1991, although the law on local self-government has proven to be ineffective. Major legislative changes regarding local power occurred at the Supreme Soviet of September-November 1994. The president was given the right to appoint local governors and heads of executive committees in the provinces. The centralization of power led to resignations and protests by some local officials. A Civil Service Law was adopted by the Supreme Soviet on November 23, 1993. In September 1997, President Lukashenka issued a decree (Number 16) on "Some Measures to Introduce Proper Order into the System of Material and Social Support of Civil Service Employees and Persons of Equal Status." The decree states that the Council of Ministers will set new salary rates. The decree bans civil servants from "carrying out during working hours paid work (activity) which bears no relation to discharging duties ensuing from their position." Local civil servants are employees of the local government.

Rule of Law 6.00/7

1. Is there a post-Communist constitution? How does the judicial system interpret and enforce the constitution? Are there specific examples of judicial enforcement of the constitution in the last year? Belarus's first post-Communist constitution was adopted by the thirteenth session of the Supreme Soviet of the Republic of Belarus on March 15, 1994. A controversial November 1996 referendum adopted amendments that extended the presidential term from five to seven years, gave the president the right to annul decisions of the local councils, set elections dates, call parliamentary sessions, and dissolve parliament. The president appoints judges, including five of 11 Constitutional Court members, as well as one-third of the members of the Council of the Republic. In 1996, the Constitutional Court ruled that the referendum and new amendments to the constitution were unconstitutional. Lukashenka ignored the decision, and seven members were dismissed or resigned in January 1997. The court is little more than a rubber-stamp for executive decisions. In April 1997, the court abrogated its own resolution regarding the 1996 referendum. The chairman, a Lukashenka appointee, explained that the court will not examine any presidential decrees because, according to the constitution, the court has no right to begin proceedings on its own initiative. In return for their compliance, Article 18 of the "Law on the Constitutional Court" entitles justices to receive lifelong pensions upon retirement. It also gives the court the power to disband parliament.

2. Does the constitutional framework provide for human rights? Do human rights include business and property rights? The constitution approved by referendum in November 1996 contains language that protects human rights. Article 2 states that the "individual, his rights, freedoms and guarantees for their attainment manifest the supreme goal and value of the state and society." Article 21 safeguards "rights and liberties," but Article 23 allows for the "restriction of personal rights and liberties" in the interests of "national security" and "public order." Article 13 states that "property may be the ownership of the state or private" and that the state "shall regulate economic activities on behalf of the individual and society." These rights are abused in practice. Despite constitutional guarantees, abuses include violations of judicial procedure, press freedom, free assembly, and other basic political rights and civil liberties. In March 1997, following a series of demonstrations, Lukashenka issued a decree (Number 5) to restrict freedom of assembly.

3. Has there been basic reform of the criminal code/criminal law? Who authorizes searches and issues warrants? Are suspects and prisoners beaten or abused? Are there excessive delays in the criminal justice system? The Criminal Code of 1991 was amended in May 1994, and includes provisions, including "dangerous crimes against the state" (Articles 61-70) and defamation of the president, that are subject to political abuses. Article 61 bars plots to "seize state power by unconstitutional means," while Article 67 prohibits "calls for the overthrow or alternation of the constitutional state." Article 68 bans anti-state "propaganda." On October 24, 1997, Lukashenka issued a decree (Number 21) on "Immediate Measures to Fight Terrorism and Other Especially Dangerous Violent Crimes," which lengthened mandatory sentences for certain crimes and extended the maximum time that a suspect may be held in custody without charge from three to 30 days. It also allows police to search suspects without a warrant. On December 20, 1997, parliament approved new codes on criminal procedure and corrective labor. These included nearly 40 amendments to the previous codes, including measures drawn from Decree Number 21. The Corrective Labor Code introduced a new form of punishment called "arrest," which allows a suspect to be held for 30 days without charge. The new code also ordered the construction of special "arrest houses" throughout the country, as well as the development of special camps for convicts serving life sentences. The Belarusan Helsinki Committee and the Belarus League for Human Rights reported numerous instances of prisoner abuse by police, including beatings, psychological duress, and the denial of medical care. Lengthy investigations are a common form of punishment in Belarus. Under law, once a suspect is charged, a trial must be initiated within two months, although in some cases the procurator general can extend pretrial detention to 18 months to allow for further investigation. In August 1997, two young men, both members of the Belarus Popular Front youth organization, were arrested and charged with "malicious hooliganism" for writing anti-government graffiti. Both were held in a prison with ordinary criminals. In mid-February 1998, the court finally reached a verdict in their case and sentenced one man to 18 months in prison and the other to a suspended sentence. In another case, Tamara Vinnikova, a former head of the National Bank, was detained for more than a year in a KGB prison where she was denied medical care for tuberculosis and cancer. The investigation failed to accumulate sufficient evidence for an indictment, but as of March 1, 1998 she was under house arrest and forbidden from speaking to the press.

4. Do most judges rule fairly and impartially? How many remain from the Communist era? Under the Lukashenka regime, judges are under heavy pressure to conform to government influence, particularly in cases deemed remotely political. Judges owe their positions to the president. The 1997 U.S. State Department human rights report states, "Although the procurator's office categorically denies it, 'telephone justice' (the practice of executive and local authorities dictating to the courts the outcome of trials) is widely reported to continue." A majority of judges served under the Communist regime, but firm statistics are unavailable.

5. Are the courts free of political control and influence? Are the courts linked directly to the Ministry of Justice or any other executive body? The judicial system is essentially the same three-tiered structure that existed during the Soviet era: district, city or province, and republic. Judges continue to be influenced by the political leadership. Judges are dependent on the Ministry of Justice for sustaining the court infrastructure and on local executive branch officials for providing their personal housing. The president appoints six of the 12 members of the Constitutional Court, including the chairman. The remaining six are appointed by the Council of the Republic, which itself is composed partly of presidential appointees and partly of loyalists chosen by the pro-government oblast and Minsk city councils.

6. What proportion of lawyers is in private practice? Statistics on the number of lawyers in private practice may not be accurate because many lawyers employed by the state also have second or third jobs in the private sector. In May 1997, Lukashenka issued a decree (Number 12) that subordinated all lawyers to the Ministry of Justice, which now controls the licensing of lawyers. Several lawyers, including a number of the president's opponents, have been stripped of their licenses.

7. Does the state provide public defenders? Under law, the state is to provide public defenders to indigent defendants, but, according to human rights groups, this provision is often ignored in practice.

8. Are there effective anti-bias/discrimination laws, including protection of ethnic minority rights? In late 1992, parliament adopted a national minorities law that, in addition to forbidding discrimination, expressly prohibits official inquiries, in written or verbal form, regarding a person's nationality. Thirteen percent of the population is Russian. Poles constitute 4.1 percent, while 2.9 percent is Ukrainian. Non-Slavs constitute less then 2 percent. A 1992 law on freedom of religious beliefs and organizations provides broad guarantees for freedom of religion. There is still bureaucratic resistance, however, to religion in general and the major churches. Anti-Semitism persists. In a May 1995 referendum, 80 percent of voters supported a presidential proposal to make Russian an official language. Virtually no higher or technical education is available in the Belarusan language. Women are under-represented in upper levels of government and business management, even though the level of education of women is higher than that of men.

Corruption C

1. What is the magnitude of official corruption in the civil service? Must an average citizen

pay a bribe to a bureaucrat in order to receive a service? What services are subject to bribe requests — for example, university entrance, hospital admission, telephone installation, obtaining a license to operate a business, applying for a passport or other official documents? What is the average salary of civil servants at various levels? In some ways, Belarus' totalitarian regime makes corruption in the civil service more difficult, and the World Bank reports that corruption is less of a problem than in Russia. Nevertheless, corruption in the civil service is a problem, particularly in the customs and border patrol. In October 1997, criminal proceedings were launched against the chief of the local customs service in Pinsk in the Brest region for the acceptance of bribes. Civil servants often moonlight during working hours, and the government has taken steps to raise civil service salaries to discourage corruption. Virtually all services are susceptible to bribery; In June 1997, Lukashenka signed a parliamentary law on "Measures for Fighting Organized Crime and Corruption." Critics say that the president has used the corruption law as a pretense to crack down on businessmen and the private sector, political opponents, and officials opposed to his policies. Many well-publicized cases of high-level corruption may be political in nature (See Question 2 below). This makes information on individual cases less than reliable.

2. Do top policy makers (the president, ministers, vice-ministers, top justices, and heads of agencies and commissions) have direct link to businesses? How strong are such connections and what kinds of businesses are these? Allegations of high-level corruption persist, but many have a political dimension. In late 1996, participants at a meeting held within the framework of the national roundtable forum issued an Appeal to the Citizens and Supreme Soviet of the Republic of Belarus. The appeal, which was based on the independent news agency Belapan's allegations of corruption in central government bodies, accused Lukashenka and his immediate circle of "illegally setting up numerous funds" and a parallel state budget. It also accused them of having links with the Torgexpo company and the Makhmud Esambayev Fund. The also criticized what they called "donations" to the president and high-level officials by enterprises and private persons and "resources from the shadow economy." In March 1998, a Belarusian businessman who appeared on Interpol's wanted list stated after his arrest in Poland that he had an "impressive number of documents proving that Lukashenka and his entourage are corrupt." He also said that Lukashenka had private accounts in European banks. Opponents of Lukashenka have characterized his high-profile anti-corruption campaign, which was launched in the summer of 1997, as another lever of repression. In October 1997, Vasil Staravoytav, the head of Rassyet, the country's most successful agricultural joint-stock companies, was arrested and charged with embezzlement. He had been a long-time critic of Lukashenka's support of collectivized farming. Agricultural minister Vasil Lyavomov was also arrested and charged with embezzlement. On November 12, 1997, the United Civil Party issued a statement accusing Lukashenka of starting a "criminal prosecution campaign to make management at all levels absolutely obedient to him." The statement, made after the arrests of Staravoytav and Lyavomov, also noted that former National Bank chairman Tamara Vinnikova, Vladimir Taranov, general director of the Fandok company, and Alyaksandr Kudimov, a member of parliament, had been arrested previously on corruption-related charges. In February 1998, police detained Belarusan businessman Andrey Klimov, a member of the dissolved parliament and a known supporter of the opposition, on suspicion of major financial embezzlement. Klimov's successful construction enterprise had allowed him to launch a bank and a newspaper. Klimov was also one of the signatories of an appeal to the Constitutional Court to impeach Lukashenka.

3. Do laws requiring financial disclosures and disallowing conflict of interest exist? Have publicized anti-corruption cases been pursued? To what conclusion? There are laws requiring financial disclosures of parliamentarians and senior politicians and conflict-of-interest laws. Several anti-corruption cases have been pursued. In a highly-publicized case, National Bank chairwoman Tamara Vinnikova, was fired and detained in January 1997 for alleged corruption. She was held without charge for almost a year before being placed under house arrest. The investigation has yet to provide evidence to substantiate any wrongdoing. Proceedings against former Lyavomov and Staravoytav are ongoing.

4. What major anti-corruption initiatives have been implemented? How often are anti-corruption laws and decrees adopted? The Criminal Code, which was amended in 1994, contains several articles that outlaw bribery, embezzlement, abuse of power, and corruption. In June 1997, parliament passed and Lukashenka signed a law on "Measures to Fight Organized Crime and Corruption." In February 1998, Lukashenka ordered the establishment of a state committee for financial control over legislation on entrepreneurship and taxes. The body is part of the main investigation department at the State Tax Committee and will be responsible for protecting tax inspectors and preventing corruption in tax-collecting bodies. The president has vowed to continue issuing decrees to enhance the government's power to fight crime and corruption.

Privatization 6.00/7

1. What percentage of the GDP comes from private ownership? What percentage of the labor force is employed in the private sector? How large is the informal sector of the economy? Much of the Belarus economy remains in state hands. An April 1997 EBRD report estimates that by mid-1997 the private sector accounted for approximately 15 percent of GDP. (Some estimates suggest that, if the private informal economy were included, the non-state sector would account for 40 percent of GDP.) As of February 1998, approximately 25 percent of the workforce was employed in the private sector.

2. What major privatization legislation has been passed? What were its substantive features? Privatization in Belarus proceeded rapidly between 1991 and 1995. Since then, President Lukashenka's commitment to a state command-and-control economy has dramatically slowed the process. The key legislation was the January 1993 law on "Destatization and Privatization of Government Property," which attempted to create the conditions for a "socially-oriented" market economy. A voucher program was adopted in July 1993 to make each citizen eligible to receive a non-transferable voucher. The value of the voucher depended on the citizen's number of years in the workforce. The program foresaw three procedures for privatization: employee ownership, conversion to a joint-stock firm, and the auction of the enterprise. The Council of Ministers Committee on the Administration of Government Property was to manage the process, beginning with small retail enterprises. The committee aimed to privatize two-thirds of the state sector's approximately 2,500 firms, with 50 percent of the privatization to be accomplished through vouchers. These goals were not realized as delay after delay plagued the process. Finally, the voucher privatization process was effectively suspended by Lukashenka in March 1995, when all the investment funds responsible for managing the vouchers were frozen. Some of the funds restarted in August 1995. By January 1996, approximately 65 percent of Belarusan citizens received their vouchers, the distribution of which ended in June 1996. In 1996, the privatization process at the local level slowed, with 88 small enterprises being sold or transformed during the first seven months of the year. Approximately 415 small enterprises were privatized in 1995. In January 1997, the government reported that of the approximately 2,500 firms, 1,580 were sold at auctions, competitive sales, or bought by working collectives, while 908 were transformed into joint-stock companies. In all, only 18 percent of enterprises have been privatized, while 55 percent have been privatized in Russia. In October 1997, Lukashenka rejected the government's privatization schedule, which, he claimed, was "selling off the country." On March 20, 1998, he issued decree Number 3, which addressed the privatization of state property. The decree suspended clauses in the 1993 privatization law on approval of annual privatization programs. Local authorities will now retain the right to adopt their own program for privatization of municipal property. The decree stipulates that state and leased enterprises will be transformed into joint-stock companies, along with proposals from employees coordinated with government structures. Previously, such issues were handled by special privatization agencies. In buying property, leased enterprises can pay up to 50 percent of the price with privatization vouchers and receive a 20-percent discount for the rest of the property. In addition, payment can be deferred for up to three years, provided that at least 30 percent of the price is paid in advance.

3. What proportion of agriculture, housing and land, industry, and business and services is in private hands? *Agriculture*: Farmland has not been privatized to any significant degree. The World Bank reported in 1997 that only 52,000 hectares of land in was in private hands. It also found that 1,479 thousand hectares were in the hands of private subsidiary and private agricultural workers. Approximately 90 percent of agriculture, which accounts for 14 percent of GDP, remains in state hands. *Housing and Land*: Approximately 60 percent of the housing units in Belarus had been privatized by January 1997. Most of these units were transferred to current tenants. The government has balked at allowing for the private ownership and transfer of non-agricultural land. *Industry:* Privatization of large industrial enterprises is virtually non-existent. Approximately 85 percent of industry remains in state hands. In February 1998, the deputy minister for the management of state property explained, "Slower privatization rates in the leading economic branches — industry, construction, transport — can be explained by the fact that the privatization of a number of major enterprises in these sectors should be preceded by long preparatory work for restructuring and improving them." *Business and Services*: The service sector, particularly trade, public catering, retail shops, and other small-sized enterprises, has been significantly privatized, thereby accounting for more than 48 percent of privatization. According to a memorandum of understanding between the World Bank and Belarus, the privatization of the service sector will be completed in 1999.

4. What has been the extent of insider (management, labor, and nomenklatura) participation in the privatization process? What explicit and implicit preferences have been awarded

to major interest groups? Communist-era managers have retained control of the few former large- and medium-sized enterprises that have been privatized, and the state owns a considerable amount of shares in joint-stock companies. State representatives chosen from specialists of branch ministries have control over economic activity of such companies, including Slavneft, an energy company that was formed from the restructuring of three separate companies in which Belarus and Russia hold major shares.

5. How much public awareness of and support for privatization has there been? What is the nature of support and opposition to privatization by major interest groups? Public awareness of privatization is difficult to gauge, but before 1995, the government publicized privatization and encouraged Belarusan citizens to purchase vouchers. Since 1995, Lukashenka has increasingly criticized privatization and taken measures to slow down and hamper the process. State-enterprise managers, particularly in money-losing operations, support continued state subsidies and oppose privatization, as do state and collective farm directors and agro-business enterprises. A July 1997 poll released by U.S Information Agency found that 54 percent of respondents expressed a preference for an economy in which some enterprises, shops, and farms were owned by the state, and some were privately owned.

Macroeconomics 6.25/7

1. Has the taxation system been reformed? (What areas have and have not been overhauled? To what degree are taxpayers complying? Is tax compliance difficult to achieve? Has the level of revenues increased? Is the revenue-collection body overburdened? What is the overall tax burden?) Belarus' basic tax laws were adopted in 1991 and 1992, with some modifications in 1995. There is no unified tax code. Tax rates change frequently and without prior notice through presidential or parliamentary decree and often apply retroactively. In one week in May 1996, for example, five tax code changes were published. In January 1997, President Lukashenka issued a decree on the "Improvement of the Collection of Fixed Sums of Profit Tax and Firm Sums of Income Tax," which listed basic rates of profit tax collected from enterprises and retail outlets. In July, Lukashenka announced a five-year tax exemption for the Ford motor company, which had opened a new plant outside Minsk, but he unexpectedly lifted most of the exemptions in October. In August, the State Tax Committee announced some changes to the amount of local taxes to be paid by enterprises. The following basic taxes are levied in Belarus: an income tax with marginal rates of 12, 15, 20, and 30 percent; a value-added tax (VAT) of, in general, 20 percent, but only 10 percent on some agricultural and household goods; an excise tax of 10 to 75 percent of gross sales; a corporate profit tax of 30 percent of income before taxes; a land tax based on acreage; a fixed asset tax of 1 percent of assets; a payroll income tax (12-30 percent of employee salary); a profit repatriation tax of 0 to 15 percent; a road maintenance tax of 1 percent; a Chernobyl tax of 12 percent of total payroll; a "retail prices regulation fund" of 3 percent of gross sales; an employment fund of 1 percent; a pension fund of 1 percent; a social insurance fund of 40.8 percent of total payroll; and a hard currency tax of 10 percent. As elsewhere in the former Soviet Union, tax compliance has been a problem, according to the government. In August 1997, the State Committee for Taxation reported that in the first six months of the year, 29,639 enterprises that were registered for tax, or 29.2 percent of the total, were checked. Breaches of tax law were established at 21,103 enterprises, or 71 percent of those checked. Over the same period, the committee checked 20,002 non-state-owned enterprises and disclosing tax violations in 13,349. Among businessmen-proprietors, 24,426, or 54 percent of those checked, were found to have breached tax rules. In February 1998, Lukashenka ordered the establishment of a state committee for financial control over legislation on entrepreneurship and taxes. The body is part of the main investigation department at the State Tax Committee and will be responsible for protecting tax inspectors and preventing corruption in tax-collecting bodies.

2. Does fiscal policy encourage private savings, investment and earnings? (Has there been any reform/alteration of revenue and budget policies? How large are budget deficits and overall debt? Is the financing of social insurance/pension system sustainable? What proportion of the budget is taken up by subsidies to firms and individuals?) Macroeconomic policies led to positive economic growth in 1996 and 1997, but relied mainly on a Soviet-type model of rapid credit expansion and large amounts of directed low-cost credit that has created serious inflationary pressure. In 1994, inflation exceeded 2,300 percent, but it fell to 50 percent in 1996. In 1997, it jumped to 80 percent. Inflationary pressure has affected the exchange rate and the trade account of the balance of payments. As a result, at the start of 1998, Belarus faced a pronounced liquidity crisis. Living standards of the population continue to drop, and unofficial unemployment could be as high as 30 percent. According to the Ministry of Finance, state budget revenues in 1997 totaled 111,285.6 billion *rubles*. The share of the income and profit taxes in the total revenue was 14.9 percent. The income tax from individuals accounted for 10.2 percent; the VAT, 30.1 percent; excise duties, 13.1 percent; and customs duties, 8.4 percent. The deficit was 1,401 billion rubles, or 1.2 percent of GDP. The 1998 budget was for 115,151,521.7 million rubles, with a projected deficit of 1,657 billion rubles. Subsidies to industry and agriculture total approximately 5,374,655 million rubles, while expenditures for healthcare, pensions, and social welfare total 15,116,966.5 million rubles. The World Bank reported that the official external debt at $900 million, or 6.9 percent of GDP. The pension system is sustainable, if only because pensioners make up a sizable proportion of supporters of Lukashenka, who is highly unlikely to restructure the budget to reduce expenditures on social welfare outlays.

3. Has there been reform of the banking sector? (Is the central bank independent? What are its responsibilities? Is it effective in setting and/or implementing monetary policy? What is the actual state of the private banking sector? Does it conform to international standards? Are depositors protected?) The 1990 Law on the National Bank and the Law on Banks and Banking Activities established the National Bank of Belarus (NBB). The NBB is not significantly independent and is under severe political pressure from Lukashenka to loosen monetary policy. It is also being forced to shoulder the burden of eliminating wage and pension arrears – a task in which it can succeed only by printing more money. By mid-1997, the policy had weakened the official exchange rate of the Belarusan ruble by 70 percent from its late-1996 rate. In January 1997, Lukashenka dismissed NBB chairwoman Tamara Vinnikova, who was subsequently charged with causing "damage to the state of major proportions" and of corruption during her tenure at Belarus-Bank. The NBB tightly controls the approximately 20 banks in Belarus. Seven state-dominated banks control 90 percent of bank assets, which in August 1997 totaled 9.7 trillion rubles. The two largest were merged in August 1995 to form Belarus-Bank. These banks are mostly owned by groups of state enterprises that enjoy special privileges in their banks' lending activity. State banks are experiencing severe difficulties. BelarusBank and the Belarus Savings Bank have barely remained solvent. There are several small private banks. In April 1997, the Belarusan Bank for Development was registered. Interest rates were somewhat liberalized in October 1994. A significant amount of credit, however, is still funneled at preferential rates to politically-connected firms, especially in agriculture, through state-owned banks. In November 1997, the director of the World Bank's Belarus and Ukraine department stated that "progress had not been impressive" in reforming the banking sector.

4. How sound is the national currency? (Is the value of the currency fixed or does it float? How convertible is the currency? How large are the hard currency reserves? Has exchange rate policy been stable and predictable? Lukashenka's inflationary policies of printing more money to cover state credits and subsidies put severe pressure on the Belarusan ruble and finally led to its collapse in March 1998. On March 17, Lukashenka ordered firms and shops to return their prices to March 1 levels in order to reverse the price rises triggered by sharp falls in the ruble in the first half of the month. He also told foreign-exchange kiosks to post backdated rates. The currency regained 20 percent of its value, but no dealers were actually willing to buy it. The president blamed the continuing fall of the currency on Russian speculators in Moscow and, on March 23, told Belarusan banks to limit settlements with non-resident sellers. This drove the ruble's value still further down in Moscow. It proved difficult to sell the currency at much less than 70,000 rubles to the dollar, yet the Belarus National Bank stood by an official rate of 33,460. Currency kiosks were posting a rate of 42,000. Since March 1997, the value had plunged by 50 percent. In December, 1997 new regulations on purchasing foreign currency went into effect. The national bank announced that as of December 1, banks and companies licensed to buy and sell foreign currency would be free to set exchange rates according to supply and demand. In January 1998, the NBB issued a "currency control" policy aimed at meeting the demands of foreign currency, reducing the foreign trade deficit, building international liquidity reserves, and creating conditions for making the ruble convertible. The NBB said that it planned to liberalize currency exchange, cancel mandatory currency sales, sell all non-cash currency at a market exchange rate, develop the off-exchange currency market, and lift restrictions on the sale of hard currency to non-residents. The Belarusan ruble was introduced in May 1992. Its face value was cut to ten percent of its former value in August 1994, due to an inflation-induced currency shortage. The ruble was heavily overvalued through constant intervention by the NBB. The policy of maintaining an overvalued currency seems unsustainable as the NBB's foreign currency reserves fall further.

5. Is there a functioning capital market infrastructure? (Are there existing or planned commodities, bond, and stock markets? What are the mechanisms for investment and lending? What government bodies have authority to regulate capital markets?) A 1992 Law on Securities and Stock Exchanges led to the creation of a stock market. A security exchange exists with market-makers and brokers. There is a small amount of trading in government securities and bonds. A minimal regulatory framework exists for the issuance and trade of securities. As in other sectors, however, the legal rules are unclear. The State Inspector for Securities oversees and administers the activities of the stock market.

Microeconomics 6.50/7

1. Are property rights guaranteed? (Are there both formal and de facto protections of private real estate and intellectual property? Is there a land registry with the authority and capability to ensure accurate recording of who owns what? What are the procedures for expropriation, including measures for compensation and challenge? Have any seizures taken place?) Article 44 of the constitution guarantees the right of property. Article 86 of the Civil Code states that the "right to property represents the right of the person to possess, use, and dispose of his property, which is independent of other rights." Article 100 defines property as residences, dachas, gardening houses, plots of land, transport facilities, shares, stocks, securities, items of household and personal use, etc. The status of land as property is more problematic. Land, with some exceptions, cannot yet be privately owned by Belarusans. The exceptions are land used for gardening (no more than 0.37 acres), housing (0.62 acres), and farming (2.5 acres). Land can be leased to both citizens and foreigners for up to 99 years. Foreigners need state permission to own land. In the November 1996 referendum, only 15 percent voted in favor of free trade in land. Land must be used only for a strictly defined purpose, which can only be changed with the permission of municipal councils. The transfer and lease of land may be performed only when the purpose is unchanged. Identification and confirmation of land rights is an ongoing issue. Regarding expropriation, Article 44 of the constitution states, "The compulsory alienation of assets shall be permitted only by reason of public need, under the conditions and the procedures specified by law, with timely and full compensation for the value of the alienated assets." Civil law also calls for compensation for expropriation. The Interbank Currency Exchange was nationalized in May 1996, and the Komorovsky Market was nationalized as of January 1997. The government has given only token compensation for expropriated property. Shareholders of the Interbank Currency Exchange were paid only the nominal costs of their shares, not their real value. Belarus is a member of the World Organization of Intellectual Property, the Paris Convention on the Protection of Industrial Property, and the Treaty on Patent Cooperation. Belarus created a framework for the protection of intellectual property in February 1993.

2. To what extent have prices been liberalized? What subsidies remain? In 1995, Belarus adopted a stabilization program supported by the International Monetary Fund (IMF) and the World Bank in order to restore macro-economic balance and bring the country gradually toward a market economy. Initially, Belarus made progress in terms of price and trade liberalization, and financial sector management. By mid-1995, progress virtually stopped, as the Lukashenka government appeared to abandon plans to adopt a liberal economic model and reverted to many aspects of a command economy. Price controls were re-established and increased throughout 1997. In October 1996, Lukashenka decreed a partial freeze and complete regulation of prices. The edict froze prices for basic sorts of bread, milk, and dairy products and set maximum payments for rent. As for other goods and services, the edict prohibited any increases "without a corresponding increase in wages." In February 1997, the prime minister stated that while the government was committed to a free market, the prices of housing services, medicines, bread, milk, and baby food would be controlled. Price controls led to periodic shortages of certain goods due to the cost to producers to buy raw materials. In September 1997, Lukashenka reiterated his support for price controls, and warned that "failure to obey my instructions in this regard will meet with extremely severe treatment from me." Subsidies remain for meat, bread, milk, dairy products, other foodstuffs, medicines, and some goods and services.

3. Is it possible to own and operate a business? (Has there been legislation regarding the formation, dissolution, and transfer of businesses, and is the law respected? Do there exist overly cumbersome bureaucratic hurdles that effectively hinder the ability to own and dispose of a business? Are citizens given access to information on commercial law? Is the law applied fairly?) Does regulation (or do licensing requirements) impose significant costs on business and consumers? Do they create significant barriers to entry and seriously hamper competition?) In addition to the privatization law, there are numerous laws, parliamentary decrees, and presidential edicts governing business, among them the laws on "Enterprises" (1990), "Entrepreneurship" (1991), "Procedures for Opening and Functioning of the Representations of Foreign Firms and Organizations and their Branches/Subsidiaries" (1991 decree of the Cabinet of Ministers), "Particularities of Formation of Foreign Enterprises on the Territory of Belarus (1992 decree of the Cabinet of Ministers), the "List of Activities Requiring a Special Permit (License) and of the Bodies to Issue Such Permits (Licenses)" (decree of the Cabinet of Ministers 1995), and other laws on foreign investment. Arbitrary presidential decrees by Lukashenka, who is essentially hostile to a free market economy, and parliamentary decrees have created an uncertain environment for business. Examples include the April 1997 grant and subsequent rescinding of a five-year tax exemption to the Ford Motor Company. Commercial and tax laws are applied inconsistently and arbitrarily by local bureaucrats. A 1996 ban on new and amended business registrations by both foreigners and natives lasted four months and resulted in huge losses — including 40,000 lost jobs, according to one unofficial estimate — to firms and a tax revenue shortfall to the state. Presidential Decree Number 208 modified the ban and required the re-registration of all firms by January 1, 1997 under penalty of a shutdown. The move was enacted ostensibly to eliminate "illegal" firms and "specify, unify, and systematize" the data in the Belarusan business register. The decree authorized the shutdown of firms that, among other things, engaged in activities outside of the founding charter of the firm, failed to provide timely statistical information, and suffered losses in the previous fiscal year. The decree also directed the Council of Ministers to devise proposals to "adjust" the number of private sector firms in trade and "middleman" activities. Laws, regulations, decrees, bureaucratic hurdles, price controls, and a dominant state sector have discouraged business development and foreign investment, which has been decreasing since 1995.

4. Are courts effective, transparent, efficient, and quick in reaching decisions on property and contract disputes? What alternative mechanisms for adjudicating disputes exist? The courts, which are dominated by Lukashenka appointees and follow government policy, are unreliable in terms of adjudicating contract and other business disputes. An effective dispute resolution system does not exist. Moreover, government regulatory policies are not transparent, with policies changing overnight.

5. Is business competition encouraged? (Are monopolistic practices limited in law and in practice? If so, how? To what degree is "insider" dealing a hindrance to open competition? Are government procurement policies open and unbiased?) State interference in the economy, including price controls, have undermined business competition in Belarus. Between 1994 and mid-1995, the State Anti-Monopoly Ministry, which was established in 1991, moved to end major trading conglomerates. Since then, under Lukashenka's orders, the ministry has enforced state control of firms and control prices. It is charged with determining prices and profit margins for enterprises accounting for 30 percent of industrial output, far more than one would expect "natural" monopolies to be producing. In July 1996, it was converted into the Ministry of Entrepreneurship and Investment. "Insider" dealing has hindered competition, with state managers and other government officials benefiting from "nomenklatura" privatization, although even this is limited by the president's commitment to a statist economy. In practice, private businesses are often at a disadvantage relative to their state-owned counterparts because they are more often subject to audits and inspections and frequently have more difficulties securing bank credits. Under law, government procurement policies are open, but this is not the case in practice.

6. To what extent has international trade been liberalized? To what degree has there been simplification/overhaul of customs and tariff procedures, and are these applied fairly? What informal trade barriers exist? According to the Ministry of Foreign Economic Relations, Belarus' 1997 foreign trade amounted to $15.8 billion, which represented a 25 percent increase in real prices over those in 1996. Exports totaled $7.1 billion, while imports totaled $8.6 billion. Foreign and domestic companies face a number of obstacles to foreign trade. These include a February 1995, presidential decree requiring that goods being imported into Belarus be delivered within 60 days of the date of prepayment, and the NBB's prohibition on commercial banks' issuance of more than $10,000 in prepayment for goods to be imported, unless the foreign bank provides a guaranteed of full repayment if the goods are not delivered; and the requirement that all import or export transactions obtain clearance (a passport) from customs, an appropriate bank, and sometimes the Ministry of Foreign Economic Relations. Import duties are paid as a percentage of the contract price of the product being imported. Import duties range from 5 to 90 percent. Among the goods exempt from import duties are medical equipment and medicine, items imported for charter capital as part of a foreign investment in a joint venture, and goods imported to replace items in accordance with a contract. As a result of the customs union with Russia, tariffs have been introduced on some goods that were previously duty-free. In June 1997, the Council of Ministers issued a decree (Number 793) that introduced a pre-shipment check of certain products brought to Belarus outside of the countries of the former Soviet Union (except for the Baltics). Informal barriers to trade also include corruption in the customs service.

7. To what extent have foreign investment and capital flow been encouraged or constrained? The investment climate in Belarus is poor due to lack of checks and balances and the concentration of power in the presidency. Two basic regulations govern foreign investment: a November 1991 foreign investment law and an amendment passed in June 1993. These laws establish some incentives for foreign direct investment, particularly for firms with a foreign ownership share of more than 30 percent. The State Committee on Foreign Economic Relations regulates foreign investment. There is no comprehensive system of laws regulating everyday business matters, however, and business and economic figures are unreliable. In addition, no effective dispute resolution system exists. The laws that do exist, particularly those concerning taxes and customs, have been inconsistently and arbitrarily enforced. According to presidential decree Number 208, which applies to foreign and domestic business, a host of agencies, among them the tax inspectorate, the state statistical agency, the presidential supervisory department, and the KGB, can initiate the closure of a business for a wide variety of reasons, including a firm's failure to make a profit during any particular fiscal year. By law, foreign investment in banking, insurance, and stock exchanges may not exceed 50 percent of the outstanding shares.

8. Has there been reform of the energy sector? (To what degree has the energy sector been restructured? Is the energy sector more varied, and is it open to private competition? Is the country overly dependent on one or two other countries for energy [including whether exported fuels must pass through one or more countries to reach markets]?) Belarus imports 90 percent of its primary energy requirements, mainly from Russia. The World Bank reported that inadequate cost recovery from consumers, together with foreign exchange shortages, have contributed to arrears on payments for gas imports to Russia since mid-1995. These are being paid through barter and government-to-government agreements. Belarus has a sizable refining capacity for oil and gas. In July 1997, Lithuania suspended its electricity supply to Belarus for nonpayment. In March 1998, Gazprom, the Russian gas company, gradually began to decrease its deliveries to Belarus, also due to payment arrears. The government has considered resuming the construction of nuclear power stations to address the country's chronic energy crisis. There has been no major restructuring of the energy sector, nor are there immediate plans to privatize energy and electricity.

BOSNIA AND HERZEGOVINA

Freedom in the World Ratings, 1989-1998

	1989-90	1990-91	1991-92	1992-93	1993-94	1994-95	1995-96	1996-97	1997-98
Political Rights	-	-	-	6	6	6	6	5	5
Civil Liberties	-	-	-	6	6	6	6	5	5
Status	-	-	-	NF	NF	NF	NF	PF	PF

Polity: Transitional
Economy: Mixed -statist
Population: 3,588,000
PPP: na
Ethnic Groups: Pre-war – Slavic Muslim (44 percent), Serb (33 percent), Croat (17 percent)
Capital: Sarajevo

Political Process 5.00/7

1. When did national legislative elections occur? Were they free and fair? How were they judged by domestic and international election monitoring organizations? Who composes the government? Bosnia and Herzegovina held its first multiparty elections since World War II in November and December 1990, while still a republic of Yugoslavia. The three leading nationalist parties, formed along ethnic lines and appealing to their respective Muslim, Serb, and Croat constituencies, won a majority in the pre-independence, 240-member bicameral assembly. The League of Communists (SKJ), which since the end of World War II had been the only legal political party, won only 19 seats.

Bosnia's current constitution, which originated as Annex 4 of the November 1995 Dayton Accords that ended the 1992-95 war, established the country's legislative structure, as well as those of the country's two new entities: the Muslim-Croat Federation (the Federation) and the Serbian Republic. Bosnia's bicameral legislature consists of an upper House of Peoples, with 15 members (five Muslims and five Croats from the Federation and five from the Serbian Republic) chosen by the legislatures of the two entities, and a lower House of Representatives with 42 members (14 Croats and 14 Muslims from the Federation and 14 from the Serb Republic) directly elected by proportional representation from the two entities.

At the entity level, the Federation's bicameral legislature consists of an upper House of Peoples of the Federation, with 74 indirectly elected members, of whom at least 30 must be Muslims and 30 must be Croats, and a 140-member lower House of Representatives of the Federation, with members directly elected by proportional representation. The Federation president, with the concurrence of the vice president, nominates a government headed by a prime minister for legislative endorsement. Each minister must have a deputy who is not from his own constituent group.

The Serbian Republic has an 83-member unicameral National Assembly that is directly elected by proportional representation.

In December 1995, Rajko Kasagic was elected as prime minister of the Serbian Republic, although in May 1996, Bosnian Serb strongman Radovan Karadzic dismissed him in favor of hardliner Gojko Klickovic. This increased international pressure for the removal of Karadzic, an indicted war criminal, from public office (The Dayton Accords had prohibited persons indicted for war crimes by the International Tribunal for the Former Yugoslavia from holding office). Karadzic resigned as head of the Serbian Republic on July 19, 1996. Vice President Biljana Plavsic became president, pending elections.

Karadzic's departure cleared the way for presidential and legislative elections on September 14, 1996, under the auspices of the Organization for Security and Cooperation in Europe (OSCE). Voters chose deputies for the House of Representatives of Bosnia and Herzegovina, as well as for the House of Representatives of the Federation and the National Assembly of the Serbian Republic.

Final results for the House of Representatives of Bosnia and Herzegovina gave the Muslim-based Party of Democratic Action (SDA) 19 seats; the Serbian Democratic Party (SDS), nine; the Croatian Democratic Union (HDZ), eight; the multiethnic coalition Joint List, two; the multiethnic People's Union for Peace - Union for Peace and Progress (NSSM-SMP), two; and the multiethnic Party for Bosnia and Herzegovina (SBiH), two.

In balloting for the lower House of Representatives of the Federation, the SDA won 78 seats; the HDZ, 36; the Joint List, 11; SBiH, ten; the Muslim-based Democratic People's Union, three; and the Croatian Rights Party, two. In the elections for the National Assembly of the Serbian Republic, the SDS won 45 seats; the SDA, 14; the NSSM-SNP, ten; the Serbian Radical Party, six; the multiethnic Democratic Patriotic Bloc, two; SBiH, two; the Joint List, two; the Serbian Party of Krajina, one; and the Serbian Patriotic Party, one.

Despite substantial evidence of widespread electoral irregularities and intimidation — voter turnout was 108 percent, according to one estimate — and the broader problems of restrictions on freedom of movement, association, and expression, the OSCE certified the election results on September 29. On January 3, 1997, the parliament of Bosnia and Herzegovina approved the nomination of co-premiers Boro Bosic, a Serb, and Haris Silajdzic, a Muslim, and the country's joint government met for the first time.

On July 3, 1997, Bosnian Serb President Biljana Plavsic dissolved the hardliner-dominated Serbian Republic parliament, which she said was taking orders from "informal centers of power," a reference to Karadzic. New elections were held on November 22-23, 1997, with a 70- percent turnout. Thousands of Muslim and Croat refugees forcibly removed from Serb-held areas during the civil war voted by postal ballot. Pro-Karadzic Serbian hardliners lost their absolute majority, with the SDS winning 24 seats; the SDA-led Coalition for an Undivided Bosnia and Herzegovina, 16; Plavsic's new Serbian People's League (SPL), 15; the Serbian Radical Party, 15; the Socialist Party of Yugoslav President Slobodan Milosevic, nine; the Independent Social Democrats, two, and the Social Democratic Party, two. The vote was generally free but not fair due to restrictions on the media and the limited ability of alternative parties to campaign and organize.

Although the SDS remained the single largest party in the new Bosnian Serb parliament, on January 18, 1998, Serb moderates, supported by deputies representing Muslim and Croat refugees, backed a government headed by Milorad Dodik, a member of the Independent Social Democratic Party and the first Bosnian politician to hold high office without links to one of the main nationalist parties. The Dodik government allied itself with Bosnian Serb President Plavsic and supported the Dayton Accords, ending six years of rule by the Serbian ultranationalists who had launched the 1992-95 war. The SDS announced that it did not recognize the new government. In its first major decision, the Dodik government chose Banja Luka as the new seat of government of the Serbian Republic.

2. When did presidential elections occur? Were they free and fair? On November 18, 1990, Bosnia, as a constituent republic of Yugoslavia, held presidential elections in which the three leading ethnically-based nationalist parties appealed to their Muslim, Serbian, and Croatian communities and won all seven seats in the republican state presidency. In December, the three parties named Alija Izetbegovic, a Muslim, as president of the state presidency; Jure Pelivan, a Croat, as prime minister; and Momcilo Krajisnik, a Serb, as president (speaker) of the Assembly.

President Izetbegovic continued to head the state presidency through the 1992-1995 war. The 1995 constitution provided for a directly elected three-member presidency to serve a two-year term following the first election and four-year terms thereafter. In July 1996, Radovan Karadzic resigned as president of the Serbian Republic under mounting international pressure resulting from the Dayton Accords' stipulation that persons indicted as war criminals be banned from holding office. This permitted presidential and legislative elections to be held on September 14, 1996, under the auspices of the OSCE.

At the presidential level, balloting in the Muslim, Serbian, and Croatian communities for the three-member presidency of Bosnia and Herzegovina confirmed the dominance of the three main ethnically-based parties. President Izetbegovic of the SDA won 82.4 percent of the Muslim vote and defeated former Prime Minister Haris Silajdzic, who received 14 percent. Momcilo Krajisnik of the SDS won 67.3 percent of the Serbian vote and defeated Mladen Ivancic, who received 30 percent after running on a platform of ethnic reconciliation and the preservation of Bosnia as a unitary state. Kresimir Zubak of the HDZ won 88.7 percent of the Croatian vote and defeated Ivo Komsic, who received 11.1 percent. Izetbegovic won 40,000 more votes than Krajisnik, and, in accordance with the Dayton agreement, was elected chairman of the presidency of Bosnia-Herzegovina. In subsequent elections, the method of selecting the chairman will be determined by the Parliamentary Assembly. Voting was marred by widespread electoral irregularities and intimidation. The number of votes cast in the Muslim section of the presidential elections greatly exceeded the number of registered voters. Nevertheless, the OSCE certified the results.

At the entity level, the March 1994 Muslim-Croat Federation Agreement that established the Federation provided that indirectly elected representatives of the two communities would serve alternating one-year terms as president and vice president over a four-year period. On May 30, 1994, Kresimir Zubak, a Bosnian Croat, was elected to a six-month term as president. At the expiration of his term in November, however, he refused to relinquish the post. He argued that, if the vice president, a Muslim, became president, there would be no major office held by a Croat. On March 18, 1997, the Federation parliament elected Vladimir Soljic, a Croat and former Federation defense minister, as the new president.

In the September 14, 1996 Serbian Republic presidential elections, Biljana Plavsic, the former vice president who had replaced Karadzic as President of the Serbian Republic, won with 59.2 percent the vote. In 1997, a power struggle developed between Plavsic, who was based in Banja Luka, and Karadzic, who, from his stronghold in the town of Pale, continued to dominate Bosnian Serb affairs. In June, Plavsic began to criticize SDS leaders publicly for corruption and mafia-like practices. In July, the SDS, which was still controlled by Karadzic, expelled Plavsic from the party after accusing her of betraying Serbian interests by adhering to the Dayton Accords in spite of her own stridently nationalistic agenda. In June and July, police loyal to Karadzic staged what appeared to be two coup attempts against Plavsic. In early September, troops from the NATO-led Stabilization Force in Bosnia blocked buses carrying Karadzic supporters, many of whom were armed, to Banja Luka for an SDS rally that was reportedly being staged as cover for another coup attempt against Plavsic.

3. Is the electoral system multiparty-based? Are there at least two viable political parties functioning at all levels of government? Bosnia's first multiparty elections in 1990 brought to power three parties representing the Muslim, Serbian, and Croatian communities. After Croatia and Slovenia declared independence from the Republic of Yugoslavia on June 25, 1991, Belgrade sought to keep Bosnia in its federal system. In a February 29-March 1, 1992, referendum in Bosnia, 99.4 percent of participants approved secession from Yugoslavia. Most Serbs boycotted the vote.

On March 3, 1992, President Alija Izetbegovic formally declared Bosnia's independence. In mid-March, the leaders of the three main ethnic groups agreed to divide the country into three ethnically-derived autonomous units, although most Serbs still rejected the declaration of independence. On March 27, Bosnian Serbs nationalists proclaimed a self-styled Serbian Republic of Bosnia and Herzegovina under Radovan Karadzic. Together with the Serb-dominated Yugoslav army, they subsequently executed a brutal campaign to expand their territorial holdings, purge non-Serbs from captured areas, partition the republic along ethnic lines, and join Serb-held areas in a "Greater Serbia." As the attacks escalated in April, the United Nations authorized a U.N. Protection Force (UNPROFOR) to protect the civilian population and facilitate humanitarian aid distribution. Nevertheless, by mid-May, a Yugoslav army-led siege of Sarajevo, the capital, had created severe food and medicine shortages. By late 1992, Serbian nationalists controlled approximately 70 percent of Bosnia. Bosnian Croat forces, who had initiated their own separatist purges with backing from Croatia, held much of the remainder.

In April 1993, the self-styled Bosnian Serb parliament in Pale rejected a plan that had been advanced by U.N. mediator and former U.S. Secretary of State Cyrus Vance and European Community mediator and former British Foreign Secretary David Owen. The plan would have created a decentralized state divided into ten semi-autonomous provinces. In June, the Bosnian government agreed to a U.N. Security Council resolution that established "safe areas" in the besieged predominately Muslim enclaves of Bihac, Gorazde, Sarajevo, Srebrenica, Tuzla, and Zepa. Owen and Thorvald Stoltenberg, who replaced Vance as the U.N. mediator, then proposed a new peace plan that would divide the country even more formally into three ethnically-based states under a federal or confederal constitution. The leaders of the three ethnic communities endorsed the plan, which the Bosnia-Herzegovina Assembly accepted on condition that there would be no territorial transfers resulting from the "ethnic cleansing" that had become a hallmark of the war. Meanwhile, heavy fighting raged between the predominately Muslim Bosnian Army and Croatian forces for control of the southern city of Mostar. In late August, the Bosnian Croats formally proclaimed a Croatian Republic of Herzeg-Bosna under hardliner Mate Boban. By November, the Owen-Stoltenberg plan had effectively been negated by events on the ground. These events included renewed Serbian shelling of Sarajevo and intra-Muslim conflict in the northwest enclave of Bihac, where a dissident Muslim faction declared an Autonomous Province of Western Bosnia.

In February 1994, Boban resigned as head of the breakaway Croatian Republic, and the Muslim-led Bosnian government and Croatian forces agreed to a ceasefire. In March, Bosnian and Croatian leaders signed a Framework Agreement for a Federation of the Bosnian Muslim and Bosnian Croat populations. In May, they elected Kresimir Zubak as Federation president. In late August, Bosnian government troops captured Bihac, effectively abolishing the breakaway Bosnian Muslim province that had been established there.

In spite of a December 31, 1994, ceasefire, Bosnian Serb forces made new advances and renewed their shelling of Sarajevo, the last redoubt of the besieged Bosnian government, in May 1995. A U.N.-approved NATO-led air strike on an ammunition dump near Pale, the Bosnian Serb headquarters, triggered another crisis after Bosnian Serb troops took approximately 400 U.N. peacekeepers hostage.

In July 1995, Bosnian Serb forces captured Srebrenica and Zepa, two of the three "safe areas" in eastern Bosnia, in spite of United Nations Protection Force troops. In August, a shell apparently fired by Bosnian Serb forces killed 37 people in a Sarajevo market and provoked heavier NATO air strikes against Bosnian Serb military targets. In October, U.S. diplomatic intervention secured a 60-day ceasefire. At a Dayton, Ohio, air base in November, Bosnian President Izetbegovic, Croatian President Franjo Tudjman, and Serbian President Slobodan Milosevic reached a comprehensive peace agreement that nominally ended a conflict that had resulted in the deaths of more than 250,000 people, the rape and torture of tens of thousands of others, and the displacement — internally and abroad — of half of the country's surviving population of 4 million.

The General Framework Agreement for Peace in Bosnia-Herzegovina (the Dayton Accords) acknowledged Bosnia's status as a unitary state and maintained its internationally recognized borders. It also formally granted substantial autonomy to a Serbian entity and the Muslim-Croat Federation. The Federation received 51 percent of the country's territory, including all of Sarajevo, while the Serbian Republic received 49 percent. While Bosnian Muslims comprised an estimated 44 percent of Bosnia-Herzegovina's pre-war population, they now controlled only 27 percent of the territory. The parties pledged to cooperate with the International Tribunal for the Former Yugoslavia, which had been established in The Hague by the U.N. Security Council in 1993, and agreed that persons indicted by the tribunal would be ineligible to hold public office.

By late January 1996, the country's three forces had complied with the Dayton Accords by withdrawing to the designated ceasefire lines. During the year, a 60,000-strong, NATO-led Implementation Force (IFOR) served in Bosnia to implement and monitor the agreement. IFOR was succeeded by a smaller, NATO-led Stabilization Force (SFOR), with a similar mandate through June 1998.

The Dayton Accords mandated national, entity, and, for the Federation, cantonal elections within nine months. These elections were held on September 14, 1996. (See above.) The September 1997 municipal elections completed a cycle of multiparty elections at all levels.

4. How many parties have been legalized? Are any parties illegal? Soon after the end of World War II, Yugoslav strongman Josip Broz Tito made the Communist Party, which was redesignated in 1952 as the SKJ, the only legal political party. In 1989, non-Communist groups began to form in the republics, and, in early 1990, the government formally ended the SKJ's legal monopoly. In Bosnia, the SKJ was absorbed into the Democratic Party of Socialists, which was the local branch of the former "popular front" grouping, the Socialist League of the Working People of Yugoslavia.

Today, the three main political parties are nationalist parties formed around Bosnia's three ethnic groups. The Muslim based SDA was formed in May 1990, and is headed by Alija Izetbegovic, the chairman of the presidency of Bosnia and Herzegovina. The Crotian based HDZ was established in August 1990, and is headed by Kresimir Zubak, a member of the presidency of Bosnia. The SDS was formed in July 1990, and continues to be heavily influenced by Bosnian Serb strongman Radovan Karadzic. His rival, Serbian Republic President Biljana Plavsic, formed her own nationalist party, the SPL, after being expelled from the SDS.

The center-left Joint List is a multiethnic, four-party alliance that was formed prior to the September 1996 elections. It won representation in the House of Representatives of Bosnia-Herzegovina, the House of Representatives of the Federation, and the National Assembly of the Serbian Republic. Several other parties also gained representation in the September 1996 elections by running on anti-sectarian platforms. These include the Party for Bosnia and Herzegovina, which is led by former premier Haris Silajdzic.

The Provisional Election Commission (PEC), established under Annex 3 of the Dayton agreement, includes the chief of the OSCE mission, two international members appointed by the OSCE chief, a representative of the Western powers' High Representative, a representative appointed by Bosnia and Herzegovina, one representative for each of the two entities and their respective deputies, and three professional members and their deputies. The PEC is responsible for adopting electoral rules and regulations; registering parties and independent candidates; determining the eligibility of candidates and voters; ensuring a free and fair campaign; and certifying the results.

The registration process of political parties is relatively simple. Party organizers must obtain 200 signatures of eligible voters and sign a statement agreeing to abide by the Dayton Accords, a Code of Conduct, and the electoral rules. In the most recent nationwide elections, the September 1997 municipal polls, 82 parties were registered. The PEC has approved 67 parties to contest the September 1998 elections for the presidency of Bosnia, the President and Vice President of the Serbian Republic, the House of Representatives of Bosnia, House of Representatives of the Federation, the National Assembly of the Serbian Republic, the Cantonal Assemblies in the Federation, and all newly formed municipalities. While no parties are illegal, the PEC rejected four parties and three independent candidates on the basis of their not having fulfilled the criteria required by the PEC Rules and Regulations.

Despite this proliferation of parties, in practice security forces harass opposition parties in the

Serbian Republic, and the ruling parties intimidate opposition parties in the Federation. In the Bihac area of the Federation, supporters of Fikret Abdic, who led the breakaway Muslim mini-state during the war, continue to be harassed.

5. What proportion of the population belongs to political parties? There are no accurate figures on what proportion of the population belongs to political parties.

6. What has been the trend of voter turnout at the municipal, provincial and national levels in recent years? The OSCE determined that the turnout for the September 1997 municipal elections was between 80 and 85 percent of registered voters. Approximately 70 percent of registered voters participated in the November 1997 legislative elections in the Serb Republic.

Civil Society 5.00/7

1. How many nongovernmental organizations (NGOs) have come into existence since 1988? What is the number of charitable/nonprofit organizations? Are there locally led efforts to increase philanthropy and volunteerism? What proportion of the population is active in private voluntary activity (from polling data)? Information for the period covered by the report was unavailable.

2. What is the legal and regulatory environment for NGOs (i.e. ease of registration, legal rights, government regulation, taxation, procurement and access-to-information issues)? To what extent is NGO activism focused on improving the legal and regulatory environment? Information for the period covered by the report was unavailable.

3. What is the organizational capacity of NGOs? Do management structures clearly delineate authority and responsibility? Is information available on NGO management issues in the native language? Is there a core of experienced practitioners/trainers to serve as consultants or mentors to less developed organizations? Due to the destruction resulting from the 1992-95 war and the limited resources available for NGO development, civil society is weak. NGOs generally have limited organizational capacity. Numerous international organizations, however, are directly funding NGOs and facilitating the dissemination of information on NGO management issues in the Serbo-Croatian language. At present, there is no significant indigenous core of experienced practitioners who can serve as mentors to less developed organizations.

4. Are NGOs financially viable? What is their tax status? Are they obliged to and do they typically disclose revenue sources? Do government procurement opportunities exist for private, not-for-profit providers of services? Most NGOs are not financially viable and depend on grants from foreign governmental agencies and international and foreign NGOs.

5. Are there free trade unions? How many workers belong to these unions? Is the number of workers belonging to trade unions growing or decreasing? What is the numerical/propor-

tional membership of farmer's groups, small business associations, etc? The constitution guarantees the right of workers to join independent trade unions, and this right is respected in practice. The largest union is the Confederation of Independent Trade Unions, which evolved from the Communist-era Yugoslav Communist Trade Union Confederation. Strikes and collective bargaining are legal, although, due to the country's bleak economic situation, workers have limited leverage and such actions are rarely practiced.

6. What forms of interest group participation in politics are legal? What types of interest groups are active in the political and policy process? The constitution guarantees freedom of expression and association, and there are no explicit barriers to interest group participation in politics.

7. How is the non-for-profit/NGO sector perceived by the public and government officials? What is the nature of media coverage of NGOs? To what extent do government officials engage with NGOs? NGOs generally function without harassment. Coverage of NGOs by state-run broadcast media is limited, while private newspapers sometimes cover NGO activities and statements. Government officials generally offer little cooperation and do not engage with NGOs.

Independent Media 4.75/7

1. Are there legal protections for press freedom? The legal framework for the media consists of the Yugoslavia-era 1990 Law on Radio-Television Sarajevo, and the 1990 Law on Public Information Systems. Both are inadequate for the development and protection of an independent media in a post-Communist society. New laws on public and commercial broadcasting are being drafted. In 1997, the European Institute for the Media submitted two proposed draft broadcasting laws for the Federation. To have the force of law, these would have to be adopted as treaties by the Federation's cantons since the Federation's constitution vests authority for the regulation of the broadcast media at the cantonal level.

The constitution declares that the European Convention on Human Rights applies to the country and has precedence over other law. The Council of Europe has held that the principles invoked in the European Court's judgments concerning freedom of expression and broadcasting regulation, among other rights, are directly applicable.

Under Annex 1A of the Dayton Accords, international peacekeeping forces are granted ultimate authority to regulate the broadcast media. In May 1997, the countries that were participating in the implementation of the Dayton agreement granted their High Representative the right to censor or suspend any media outlet or program that persistently violates either the spirit or the letter of the accords.

The OSCE-led Provisional Election Commission established a Media Experts Commission (MEC) to assist authorities in the promotion of a free media environment during election campaigns, including freedom of movement of journalists and equal access to the media for parties. During the September 1997 municipal elections, the MEC enforced, *inter alia*, a prohibition against inflammatory speech and the right of journalists to travel within and between entities. In many cases, a media outlet chastised by the MEC for a violation did not commit further violations, although the MEC had limited power to impose penalties. Instead, it could submit matters to the PEC or to the

PEC's Election Appeals Sub-Commission (EASC). The MEC referred several cases to the EASC, only one of which was found to meet the EASC's rules of admissibility. The case, against HTV-Mostar, a Bosnian Croat-controlled station in western Mostar, arose after the station broadcast a combative speech by a former police commander. After the station refused to comply with the MEC's orders to adhere to professional media standards, the MEC referred the case to the EASC, which struck three HDZ candidates from the ballots for west Mostar municipalities. The MEC received no further complaints of violations by HTV-Mostar in the two weeks before the elections.

2. Are there legal penalties for libeling officials? Are there legal penalties for "irresponsible" journalism? Have these laws been enforced to harass journalists? Articles 80 and 81 of the Federal criminal code criminalize libel. On January 19, 1998, a municipal court convicted Senad Pecanin, the editor of the Sarajevo-based *Dani* magazine, of criminal libel against Fahrudin Radoncic, the editor of the daily newspaper *Dnevni Avaz*. Pecanin had published an investigative article on Radoncic's business practices. In the first criminal libel conviction in Bosnia and Herzegovina, the court gave Pecanin a two-month suspended prison sentence, which he will be required to serve if he is caught violating any law within the next year. There are no legal penalties for "irresponsible" journalism.

3. What proportion of media is privatized? What are the major private newspapers, television stations, and radio stations? Approximately 25 percent of the media outlets in Bosnia-Herzegovina are private. Of the state-run media, some were partially privatized in a process that was halted during the war and has not been restarted. The ownership and legal status of these semi-private papers remains uncertain.

Major private or semi-privatized newspapers in the Muslim-controlled areas of the Federation include *Oslobodjenje*, the oldest daily newspaper, which has a circulation of 10,000 and has been partially privatized; *Vecernje*, with a circulation of 8,000; *Dnevni Avaz*, an SDA-controlled private newspaper with a circulation of 20,000; *Ljiljan*, a private weekly with a circulation of 40,000; *Dani*, an independent monthly with a circulation of 33,000; and *Slobodna Bosna*, an independent bimonthly with a circulation of 30,000. In Bosnian Croat-controlled areas, there are small local newspapers, but no major print media. In the Serbian Republic, the private and semi-private press include the daily *Glas Srpski*, with a circulation of 25,000; the daily *Dnevne Nezavisne Novine*, with a circulation of 8,000; *Novi Prelom*, the Social Liberal Party's twice-weekly private paper, with a circulation of 5,000; and *Reporter*, an independent Banja Luka-based weekly, with a circulation of 5,000.

In broadcasting, private media in the Muslim-controlled area of the Federation include two television stations — Studio 99, which receives funding from the U.S.-based Open Society Institute, and TV Hayat — and several private and semi-private radio stations, including the Sarajevo-based Radio Stari Grad, half of which is owned by the municipality. In the Croat-controlled area of the Federation, the commercial HTV Mostar station strongly supports the HDZ, promotes hatred and intolerance, and, despite being nominally private, receives financial assistance from local authorities. In the Serb Republic, there are some private broadcasters, although most have links with political parties. These include three private television stations in Banja Luka — NTV Banja

Luka, Bel-TV, and ATV, which receives support from the Office of the High Representative — and numerous local radio stations.

There are also several foreign-funded media outlets. Several European countries sponsor the Alternative Information Network, which, since 1996, has provided articles free of charge to media. The Swiss government and the Soros Foundation fund Radio Fern, which can be heard by 80 percent of the population. The Open Broadcast Network (OBN) first broadcast in 1996 with the assistance of then-High Representative and former Swedish Prime Minister Carl Bildt. In 1997, it was re-launched under the administration of the Office of the High Representative and with new transmitters that cover approximately 60 percent of the country. The OBN, perhaps because it has played a role in breaking the monopoly of the state broadcasters, has been embroiled in confrontation with the government of Bosnia over allegations of misuse of funds and improper registration procedures.

4. Are the private media financially viable? Private media are generally not financially viable. With the economy ravaged in the aftermath of the war, most newspapers and magazines have difficulty in securing a circulation base. The population has limited purchasing power, with the cost of a daily newspaper being beyond the means of most people, and there are political barriers to distributing newspapers throughout the country. As a result, only an estimated five percent of the population reads newspapers. Most print media rely on international aid or the support of domestic political parties.

5. Are the media editorially independent? Are the media's news gathering functions affected by interference from government or private owners? The editorial orientation of the press in Bosnia is largely defined along communal lines, with the reach of most media outlets confined to the ethnically-controlled territory from which it originates. Most private media are nominally independent, although they can be broadly characterized as pro- or anti-government. Government-run broadcast media are generally an arm of the state and are used to rally support for nationalist leaders. The most egregious examples are in the Serbian Republic and in Bosnian Croat-controlled areas of the Federation. For example, Serbian Radio and Television (SRT), which has been particularly xenophobic, at one point portrayed NATO peacekeepers as Nazis.

In general, the print media present a broader range of opinion, from starkly nationalist to supportive of interethnic cooperation, than do the broadcast media. The print media face little overt censorship, although in June 1997, Sarajevo police confiscated issues of *Politika*, a satirical Lukavac-based monthly, from kiosks and street vendors and detained some people involved in publishing the magazine. *Politika*'s cover had compared Alija Izetbegovic, the president of the presidency of Bosnia, to former Yugoslav strongman Tito.

Due to financial constraints on the print media, television and radio are the main sources of news and information. The broadcast media are generally closely aligned with the ruling political parties. The broadcast media in the Muslim-controlled area of the Federation are the most diverse, although editorial lines still generally reflect the political position of local authorities. Radio-Television Bosnia-Herzegovina considers itself to be the official, national broadcaster, although it covers only 75 percent of the territory, its coverage favors the SDA, and opposition views receive limited coverage. The broadcast media in the Croat-controlled areas of the Federation are the least pluralistic and the most tightly controlled, with nearly all media adhering to the HDZ party line. In November 1997, HTV-Mostar's editor-in-chief resigned rather than follow an OSCE directive to apologize on air for his station's endorsement of ethnic enmity between the city's Croatian and Muslim communities.

In the Serbian Republic, the broadcast media are dominated by SRT. In 1997, the power struggle between President Biljana Plavsic and Radovan Karadzic played itself out in the broadcast media. SRT broadcasts controlled by Karadzic backers frequently challenged the Dayton Accords and made inflammatory statements against Plavsic and SFOR. In August, pro-Plavsic technicians and journalists in Banja Luka revolted against their pro-Karadzic management, stopped re-broadcasting news from Pale, and began their own broadcasts. On September 1, NATO troops seized a SRT television transmitter at Udrigovo, in northeast Bosnia, after SRT broadcasts incited Karadzic supporters to attack NATO troops in and around Brcko. NATO troops returned the tower to the control of the Pale-based hardliners on condition that they include one-hour, daily, prime time, unedited programs of opposing views supplied by Plavsic's supporters and NATO, and that they soften their anti-Plavsic, anti-NATO rhetoric. Meanwhile, High Representative Carlos Westendorp continued to insist that Momcilo Krajisnik, the Serbian member of Bosnia's presidency, and other politicians leave the SRT board of directors. On October 1, SFOR troops seized control of four television transmitters after SRT failed to implement the agreed conditions. The SRT Banja Luka outlet is now the only SRT station authorized by the High Representative to continue broadcasting, although the Banja Luka-based service has generally failed to voice pluralistic views. The numerous local private radio stations tend to be politically aligned with either the Pale- or Banja Luka-based Bosnian Serb political leaders.

Journalists face considerable difficulty in gathering news. Although journalists are increasingly traveling from one entity to another, especially from the Serb Republic to Muslim-controlled areas of the Federation, freedom of movement for journalists continues to be limited. Journalists from the Federation have been beaten and mistreated in the Serbian Republic, where they seldom receive protection from local police. On several occasions, Muslim journalists have been harassed in Bosnian Croat-controlled western Mostar. During the September 1997 municipal elections, Muslim journalists in Mostar had to obtain an OSCE escort to visit the western half of the city.

In the Serbian Republic, local authorities frequently demand that television crews and photographers obtain prior authorization to cover public events. They also arbitrarily bar reporters from conducting interviews. In September, an explosion destroyed the offices of *Alternativa*, the only opposition newspaper in the Serbian Republic town of Doboj.

Newspapers have also been publicly criticized by key political figures. While speaking at a November 1997 symposium, President Alija Izetbegovic called three private magazines "traitors" for publishing articles on new revelations about Muslim war crimes against Serbs in Sarajevo. A day later, the country's Muslim religious leader told the leading public television channel that people should mobilize against media outlets that attack "Muslim values."

Most experienced journalists left the country during the war and few have returned. Many of those who stayed have left journalism. As a result, most of Bosnia's journalists have little professional experience.

6. Is the distribution system for newspapers privately or governmentally controlled? The distribution system for newspapers is both privately and state controlled. Many newspapers rent space from the network of kiosks owned by the state. In the Serbian Republic and Bosnian Croat-controlled areas of the Federation, however, independent and opposition media have difficulty in gaining access to the state-run kiosks. In the Bosnian Croat-controlled areas, kiosks will not sell private newspapers that do not support the ruling HDZ, or that originate in the Federation's Muslim-controlled areas or the Serb Republic. After Izetbegovic denounced three publications as "traitors," at least one, the independent Sarajevo magazine *Dani*, experienced difficulties with state-owned printing facilities and the state distribution company.

The more financially secure papers take advantage of commercial distribution networks. *Oslobodjenje*, for example, has its own distribution network in addition to its contract with the privately-owned Opresa distribution network. *Dani*, a private monthly sold in the Federation, relies on individual newspaper sellers, the Opresa network, and, in Bosnian Croat-controlled areas, the Hrvatski Tisak distribution network. Even the commercial distribution network, however, has come under political influence. In 1997, as part of a plan to rehabilitate aging newspaper kiosks, the Sarajevo municipal government redistributed the contracts to operate kiosks. Preference has been given to kiosks owned by Avaz, the parent company to a pro-SDA newspaper, at the expense of Opresa, which distributes the editorially independent *Oslobodjenje*.

Few newspapers are distributed across entity lines. For example, the Serbian Republic daily *Dnevne Nezavisne Novine* has a distribution agreement with the Sarajevo daily *Vecernje Novine* to make both papers available in Sarajevo and Banja Luka.

7. What proportion of the population is connected to the Internet? Are there any restrictions on Internet access to private citizens? Information on the number of Bosnians who have Internet access is unavailable for the period under review. There are no restrictions on Internet access to private citizens.

8. What has been the trend in press freedom as measured by Freedom House's Survey of Press Freedom? Freedom House's Annual *Survey of Press Freedom* has consistently rated the media in Bosnia as "Not Free."

Governance and Public Administration 6.00/7

1. Is the legislature the effective rule-making institution? Under the constitution, the Parliamentary Assembly has responsibility for enacting legislation; deciding on the sources and amounts of revenues for the government; approving a budget; and ratifying treaties. While the legislatures are the effective rule-making institutions in Bosnia and in the two entities, the process is generally cumbersome and slow. Under the constitution, a proposed parliamentary decision can be declared to be "destructive of a vital interest" by any of the three communities by a majority of the delegates of that community. This option that has been repeatedly invoked. In order to pass, such a proposed decision then requires a majority vote in the House of Peoples by each of the three communities. In the Federation, laws must be approved by the Council of Ministers before being sent successively in draft and proposal form to each of the two houses of the Federation parliament, which then must approve them in identical form.

In the Serbian Republic, the parliament has been a pawn in the power struggle between President Biljana Plavsic and Radovan Karadzic. In August 1997, a month after Plavsic dissolved the hardliner-dominated parliament and called for fresh elections, the parliament passed a series of decrees aimed at undermining her authority, including measures to strip the president of her exclusive authority over the army; call for a postponement of the September 1997 municipal elections; and demand that her supporters surrender broadcast facilities that they had recently taken near Plavsic's base in Banja Luka.

2. Is substantial power decentralized to sub-national levels of government? What specific authority to sub-national levels have? Bosnia's municipal councils have limited powers. They are primarily responsible for providing health, education, and other social services; water, electricity, and sewer services; and issuing of marriage licenses.

3. Are sub-national levels chosen in free and fair elections? Bosnia-Herzegovina held its first local elections in seven years on September 13-14, 1997. Organized by the OSCE, 19,584 candidates vied for 4,789 seats on 136 municipal councils (75 in the Federation and 61 in the Serbian Republic), each of which have between 15 and 70 seats. With the exception of the 159 independent candidates, the seats were allotted by proportional representation.

The vote was a test of one of the key principles of the Dayton Accords: that people driven from their homes by "ethnic cleansing" should be able to return and participate in the local political process. The voting was initially scheduled to be held in conjunction with national and entity-level presidential and legislative elections in September 1996. It was postponed in August 1996, however, because massive fraud was uncovered in the registration process, particularly in the Serb Republic. The Dayton Agreement permitted displaced persons to register to vote in the municipality in which they were currently residing if they could prove they had lived there before August 1996, while refugees could register to vote in a municipality where they intended to reside. In order to obtain political legitimacy for the results of their "ethnic cleansing" campaigns during the war, Bosnian Serb leaders manipulated these rules by encouraging their supporters who were refugees or displaced persons to register in strategic locations such as the town of Brcko, even though they had not lived there before the war and did not intend to live there. Continuing problems with the registration process resulted in at least two more postponements.

In order to minimize the possibility of such fraud, the OSCE tightened the rules to require that refugees registering to vote in a municipality other than the one in which they resided in 1991 must demonstrate a connection to the municipality based on property, business, employment, or an invitation from a relative who had lived in that municipality before the war. Of 485,000 refugee voters, only a few thousand refugees ultimately attempted to register to vote in a municipality other than the one in which they lived in 1991, and only a few thousand received approval to do so. Many observers, however, argued that the fact that displaced persons were still able to vote in their new municipalities was a tacit acceptance of "ethnic cleansing." In addition, while the OSCE took effective action after discovering several major instances of fraud during the registration process, there were numerous reports of unchecked small-scale fraud.

In order to ensure maximum international supervision of the voting, the number of polling stations was reduced to 2,139 — almost half of the amount employed in the September 1996 elections, and a foreign supervisor was assigned to each station. An additional 300 international observers were deployed throughout Bosnia-Herzegovina on election day.

During their campaigns, both the SDS and the HDZ had pledged to boycott the elections, apparently over concerns that they would lose political control over strategic towns. Days before the vote, however, High Representative Carlos Westendorp convinced the parties to participate. Some observers criticized Westendorp for making major concessions in order to persuade the parties to participate. For example, the OSCE added 2,918 Serbian voters to the registration lists in the disputed town of Brcko after talks between Westendorp and then Serbian President Slobodan Milosevic, who wields considerable authority over the Bosnian Serbs. In addition, part of the divided city of Mostar was excluded from the polls.

In another controversial decision prior to the vote, the OSCE had ruled that the hardline Serb Radical Party would be decertified from the elections in Pale for deploying posters bearing Karadzic's picture, a violation of an electoral rule against displaying the likeness of indicted war criminals. On September 16 1996 Ambassador Robert Frowick, the chief of the OSCE mission, overturned the ruling after citing fears that it would endanger the lives of election observers and make it more difficult to implement the electoral results in the area.

While most observers credited the OSCE with organizing an administratively sound vote, there were some polling-day irregularities. Bosnian Croat officials in the formerly Serb-dominated town of Drvar in the Federation delayed Serbian voters, thereby forcing the OSCE to extend voting hours in the town. In addition, some Muslim refugees faced delays and intimidation while being taken by bus to vote in the Serbian Republic. In Zepce, Bosnian Croat officials failed to open three polling stations, which eventually opened without any Bosnian Croat officials manning them. The only violence was reported in the northwest Bihac region, where one man was wounded by gunfire and two hand grenades were thrown.

The overall environment in Bosnia was not conducive to a free and fair vote, particularly due to continuing restrictions on freedom of movement, association, and expression. The restrictions on freedom of movement were arguably of greater concern in the local elections than in the 1996 national and entity-wide balloting, since the elections were for municipal offices and a significant share of the population could not return to their municipalities of origin. In addition, approximately 67,000 people living on the Federation side of 18 municipalities divided by the Inter-Entity Boundary Line were not able to vote.

The ruling parties enjoyed far better access to the local media relative to opposition parties, particularly in the Croat-dominated areas of the Federation and in the Serbian Republic. Pale-based Bosnian Serb leaders refused to broadcast election-related Western-generated materials that offered pluralistic viewpoints. Television in areas under Muslim control generally only presented the views of the SDA. The activities of opposition parties received very limited coverage. In the Bosnian Croat-controlled part of the Federation, the media did not cover activities of non-Croatian parties or of Croatian parties that opposed that platform of the ruling HDZ. The OSCE disqualified several HDZ candidates in Mostar as punishment for broadcasting highly inflammatory statements on Mostar television.

After a turnout determined by the OSCE to have been between 80 and 85 percent of registered voters, the final results gave 45 parties or coalitions at least one seat on a municipal council. The three ruling parties won the most seats, although their power was diluted somewhat at the local level. Of the 4,789 municipal seats, an SDA-led coalition won 1,618; the SDS, 980; the HDZ, 640; the Serb Radical Party, 509; the Socialist Party of the Serbian Republic-Banja Luka, 329; the non-nationalist Social Democratic Party, 192; and the non-nationalist Joint List, 63. Refugee voters elected representatives to the majority of seats in six municipalities. Most notably, Muslim-based parties scored a majority in Srebrenica, the scene of brutal mass executions and purges by Serbian forces in June 1995. The Joint List captured a majority in Tuzla, the only municipality where a non-nationalist coalition won.

The only part of Bosnia in which the question of accession to either the Federation or the Serbian Republic was left unresolved by the Dayton Accords was the town of Brcko, which lies across a narrow corridor linking the northern and eastern parts of the Serbian Republic. Before the war, 20 percent of the town's population of 87,000 was Serbian. Serbian forces captured the town in 1992, killed approximately 3,000 Muslims and Croats, and forcibly expelled tens of thousands of others. The Dayton agreement required the parties to submit Brcko's political future to binding arbitration, with a Bosnian Serb administration governing the city until a final disposition.

The Bosnian government seeks the return of Brcko, arguing that failure to return the town would reward Serbian "ethnic cleansing." Bosnian Serb leaders argue that Brcko provides them with a secure link between the two parts of their entity. In February 1997, a U.S. arbitrator ruled that Brcko would remain under Serbian control, but be placed under international supervision until a final decision on its status was rendered in 1998. This gave the town's international supervisor, an American diplomat, the power to rule virtually by decree. He used this power to install a Muslim as the head of the city council, demand that several municipal departments be headed by non-Serbs, and integrate the police department.

4. Do the executive and legislative bodies operate openly and with transparency? Is draft legislation easily accessible to the media and public? The constitution requires each chamber of Bosnia's central parliament to deliberate publicly and to publish a complete record of its deliberations. In general, however, political and governmental institutions in Bosnia and its two entities operate with limited transparency. The governments of Bosnia and the entities generally try to prevent opposition media from gaining access to official news and information, with the result that the official media's interpretation of such news is generally the only view that the public receives.

Virtually all of the joint institutions of Bosnia barely function. Bosnian Serbs have been particularly obstinate in boycotting meetings of the joint presidency. In general, the country's national institutions have accomplished little. They have reached agreement on vital issues — such as a common passport, citizenship matters, and the composition of the diplomatic service — only under duress.

In the Serbian Republic in 1997, the power struggle between President Biljana Plavsic and Radovan Karadzic resulted in the division of many institutions into factions supporting Plavsic, who is based in Banja Luka, and Karadzic, who is based in Pale. While the situation has improved somewhat, much of Bosnian Serb territory remains under the control of war criminals and criminal underground leaders, and there is little semblance of a working government.

5. Do municipal governments have sufficient revenues to carry out their duties? Do municipal governments have control of their own local budgets? Do they raise revenue autonomously or from the central state budget? Municipal governments lack sufficient revenues to carry out their duties. In order to fulfill one of the chief goals of the Dayton Accords — to provide for the return of refugees and displaced persons to their pre-war homes — foreign donors have adopted a strategy of "conditionality," which links international reconstruction assistance to refugee returns. The United States and the European Union support the Open Cities program, which offers financial and rebuilding assistance directly to the cities and towns that allow refugees to return. The program has met with initial success in several Federation towns, including Konjic, Busovaca and Vogosca. A least three municipalities in the Serbian Republic are attempting to qualify for Open Cities money.

6. Do the elected local leaders and local civil servants know how to manage municipal governments effectively? Most municipal governments, particularly small ones, have very limited technical staff and lack sufficient management capability.

The ability of the winners of the September 1997 municipal elections to govern in the face of hardline local opposition is still limited. Some municipal councils were won by groups that had been "ethnically cleansed" from the area during the war. Others were won by multiethnic slates, and still others were won by opposition parties from within the area's dominant ethnic group.

In the Federation town of Drvar, Bosnian Croat authorities refused to allow the Zavicaj (homeland) coalition, which consists exclusively of Serbian refugees from the city, to take key positions in the government. The Muslim-based Democratic People's Union, a rival to the ruling SDA, won the municipal council in the northwestern Federation town of Velika Kladusa. When the municipal council tried to hold its first session in December 1997, approximately 100 people attacked Democratic People's Union deputies. In the northeastern town of Bijeljina, the local SDS branch illegally attempted to replace five elected municipal councilors who had switched their allegiance to President Biljana Plavsic.

On January 16, 1998, a mob stoned an armored car in which three Muslim politicians and an OSCE diplomat were traveling to Srebrenica. The officials were on their way to a meeting with Serbian lawmakers to negotiate a date for the first local assembly meeting at which members of both ethnic groups would be represented on the municipal council. By the spring, the OSCE had certified 135 councils as functioning, although it was not yet clear how many of these had truly operational councils.

7. When did the constitutional/legislative changes on local power come into effect? Has there been a reform of the civil service code/system? Are local civil servants employees of the local or central government? Information was not available for the period under review.

Rule of Law 6.00/7

1. Is there a post-Communist constitution? How does the judicial system interpret and en-

force the constitution? Are there specific examples of judicial enforcement of the constitution in the last year? Under the constitution, which was Annex 4 of the Dayton Accords, Bosnia is a unitary state with two "entities," the Muslim-Croat Federation (the Federation) and the Serbian Republic. The central republican government is in charge of foreign relations, trade and customs, monetary policy, finances of the institutions of the central government, international and interentity law enforcement, international and interentity communication, and inter-entity transportation. Bosnia is led by a presidency with three members — a Muslim, a Croat, and a Serb. The presidency is responsible for foreign policy; the execution of decisions of the Parliamentary Assembly; and the proposal of an annual budget. It also has civilian command authority over the armed forces. The constitution also provides for a Council of Ministers, a bicameral Assembly, a Constitutional Court, and a central bank.

The entities are specifically responsible for maintaining civilian law enforcement agencies. Defense, taxation, and other functions not specifically vested in the republic are reserved for the entities, although by agreement some of these may be assumed by the republic after five years. With a two-thirds majority vote, the legislatures of the Federation and of the Serbian Republic can veto a federal presidency decision that relates to the entity. Under the Dayton agreement, the High Representative of the foreign powers is to oversee implementation of the Accords' civilian provisions.

Both entities also have constitutions that must conform with the Dayton agreement and the constitution of Bosnia.

Judicial enforcement has been uneven, particularly at the entity level. The Constitutional Court of the Serbian Republic came under severe political pressure during the 1997 power struggle between Plavsic and Karadzic. On August 15, the court ruled against Plavsic's decision to disband the Serbian Republic's parliament and call early elections as unconstitutional, despite Plavsic's constitutional authority to dissolve the assembly. Judges, one of whom was badly beaten, came under severe pressure from Karadzic hardliners. Security forces also allegedly tapped the telephones of two constitutional court judges, including the one who was beaten.

2. Does the constitutional framework provide for human rights? Do the human rights include business and property rights? The constitution of Bosnia guarantees freedom from torture and inhuman or degrading treatment or punishment, the right to a fair trial, the right to privacy, freedom of religion, freedom of expression, freedom of assembly and association, the right to own property, and freedom of movement and residence. The constitution also states that such freedoms shall be enjoyed by all citizens without discrimination on the basis of sex, race, language, religion, or other grounds. In addition, it provides that all refugees and displaced persons have the right to return freely to their homes of origin. Refugees and displaced persons also have the right, in accordance with Annex 7 of the Dayton Accords, to have restored to them property that they lost due to civil war, or to be compensated for such property.

The constitution provides that the European Convention on Human Rights applies in Bosnia and has precedence over other law. The Council of Europe has held that all of the principles expressed in the European Court's judgments concerning freedom of expression, regulation of hate speech, and regulation of broadcasting are directly applicable.

Annex 6 of the Dayton Accords established a Human Rights Commission consisting of an Ombudsman and a Human Rights Chamber. The Ombudsman has the task of investigating first instance complaints regarding alleged human rights violations filed by citizens. Serious cases that the Ombudsman cannot settle are referred to the Human Rights Chamber, which is a judicial body that makes final and legally binding decisions.

The Bosnian conflict of 1992-95 produced the worst atrocities in Europe since World War II. Although all sides committed grave rights violations, the most egregious abuses were carried out by Serbian forces, who, *inter alia*, captured the Muslim "safe areas" of Srebrenica and Zepa in mid-1995 and executed thousands of the inhabitants. While the human rights situation has improved considerably since the end of the war, significant problems remain.

The right of refugees and displaced persons to return to their former homes — a key provision of the Dayton Accords — has been observed mainly in the breach. Particularly problematic has been the return of Muslims to Serb-controlled territory. According to a March 1998 report by the High Representative, a large number of displaced persons and refugees originate from areas where they would now be ethnic minorities. Approximately 93 percent of 1997 returns were to majority areas. There were only 10,000 "minority returns" during the year. Overall, approximately 75 percent of refugees (550,000 to 610,000) are still abroad. Only 190,000 refugees have returned. Similarly, more than three-fourths of the country's 950,000 internally displaced persons are still displaced. Returns of internally displaced persons dropped from 160,000 in 1996 to 50,000 in 1997, suggesting that most displaced persons able to go home have already done so and that further returns could remain limited as long as minority returnees are impeded. Refugee returns increased only slightly in 1997, from 85,000 to 100,000. Approximately 80 percent of the returns took place in the Federation. Only five percent of refugees originating from the Serbian Republic have returned. Half of the returnees have resettled in a place which is not their place of origin, with returns to the Serbian Republic being particularly difficult. Many returning refugees therefore remain internally displaced. Since 1996, only approximately 2,000 internally displaced persons have returned across the Inter-Entity Boundary Line.

In 1997, police in the Serbian Republic police and in Bosnian Croat-controlled areas of the Federation often forcibly prevented refugees from returning to or remaining in their homes. For example, Serbian Republic authorities prevented Muslims and Croats from returning to the strategic town of Brcko, even though in February 1997 a foreign supervisor was appointed, *inter alia*, to monitor the return of refugees.

In all three ethnically-controlled areas, members of ethnic minorities faced violence, intimidation, and other pressure by the authorities, state-organized civilian mobs, and thugs, who sought to make them move or prevent them from returning to their homes. In February 1997, Croats in the divided town of Mostar evicted some 100 Muslims from their homes. The evictions occurred only hours after a Croatian shooting attack on several members of a group of 500 Muslims visiting a cemetery left one dead and 34 wounded. U.N. police blamed Bosnian Croat policemen for the shooting. In early August 1997, drunken Bosnian Croat mobs, apparently organized by local authorities, forced hundreds of Muslims, who had only recently returned to their pre-war homes in the town of Jajce and three nearby Federation villages, to flee again. The mobs set several Muslim-owned houses on fire and at least one man was reportedly killed. In February 1998, Bosnian

Croat mobs beat Muslim refugees returning to the Croat-controlled Federation town of Stolac. Some refugees' houses were blown up or burned. The incidents appeared to have at least tacit approval from local authorities.

In the Serbian Republic, there were several attempts by state-organized thugs and civilians to intimidate and expel Muslim families in Teslic and other towns. The office of the international community's High Representative stated that there were indications that police may have been involved in the incidents. Authorities also reportedly pressured internally displaced Serbs not to return to their homes in the Federation.

A further barrier to the return of refugees and internally displaced persons is the failure of many towns to seat multiethnic, elected municipal councils due to strong-arm tactics by the ruling, nationalist parties. In towns such as Srebrenica, Muslims forced to leave as a result of "ethnic cleansing" are reluctant to return until elected members of their own ethnic group are seated on the municipal councils. In addition, many Croatian Serbs remain in the Serbian republic as refugees and often live in apartments vacated by Muslims and Croats during the war. A return of these refugees to Croatia would free apartments to their rightful owners.

In February 1998, Alija Izetbegovic, the president of the country's presidency, reluctantly agreed to stop preventing Serbs from returning to Sarajevo and accepted a goal of 20,000 returnees by the end of 1998. New Serbian Republic premier Milorad Dodik pledged to resettle 70,000 non-Serb refugees and displaced persons in the Serbian Republic in 1998.

Freedom of movement across the Inter-Entity Boundary Line improved in 1997. Freedom of movement in the Federation also improved, but continues to be restricted. In a positive development in January 1998, the country's leaders agreed on the design of a new motor vehicle license plate that makes it virtually impossible to tell whether the car is registered in the Federation or the Serb Republic. The previous license plates disclosed the car's city of registration and thereby increased the likelihood of harassment of occupants.

Another key issue is the status of indicted war criminals. In 1993, the U.N. Security Council established the International Tribunal for the Former Yugoslavia in The Hague. By the end of 1997, only 19 of the 78 persons indicted for war crimes by the Tribunal were in custody. Of the 78 accused, 57 are Serbian. In February and March 1998, four Bosnian Serbs indicted on war crimes charges surrendered to representatives of the Tribunal. It was the first surrender of Bosnian Serb suspects. In March 1998, a Bosnian Serb pleaded guilty to raping four Muslim women in 1991. The case marked the first time that an international court had won a conviction for rape as a war crime.

The Dayton Accords authorize the NATO-led SFOR troops to arrest indicted war criminals. In December 1997, Dutch commandos seized two Bosnian Croat war crimes suspects, and, in January 1998, U.S. forces captured another suspect. In general, however, SFOR personnel have avoided opportunities to arrest war criminals at checkpoints and other locations. At present, 46 Bosnian Serb war crimes suspects remain at large, including wartime leaders Radovan Karadzic and Ratko Mladic, who commanded the Bosnian Serb forces.

Police continue to violate human rights with impunity. Instances of punishment for violations are few. In the February 1997 shooting of Muslims by Bosnian Croat police officers in Mostar, the U.N. International Police Task Force (IPTF) identified five police officers who were involved in the incident. The higher court in Mostar issued suspended sentences for three officers and acquitted the two others. Also in 1997, however, the Sarajevo police force took disciplinary measures against several police officers after the IPTF substantiated seven cases of alleged abuse during the first six months of the year.

The power struggle in the Serb Republic between Karadzic and president Plavsic resulted in an open split in the police ranks. Ultimately, two interior ministers controlled two police forces. In August 1997, SFOR troops took control of all police buildings in Banja Luka, Plavsic's seat of power, and one police station in Doboj in north central Bosnia. The stations had been run by police loyal to Karadzic. In the ensuing months, the police increasingly shifted their loyalty to Plavsic.

In both entities, the IPTF is restructuring and training police forces on internationally-recognized standards of proper police procedure and human rights. By the end of 1997, six of the ten Federation cantons had formed multiethnic police forces. In all three ethnic areas, however, authorities maintain Communist-style secret police units that operate outside of the normal police chain of command and that have not been restructured.

In the Serbian Republic, there were restrictions on the right to privacy. In August 1997, after special police controlled by Plavsic seized control of the police station in Banja Luka, monitors from the IPTF found numerous tapes and transcripts that were part of an elaborate eavesdropping operation by hardliners loyal to Karadzic. The operation tapped the telephones, fax machines, and offices of Plavsic, two judges of the constitutional court, and other prominent figures in Banja Luka.

In addition to the approximately 7,000 persons missing — and presumed killed by the Bosnian Serb army — after the fall of Srebrenica in 1995, an additional 1,500 to 5,000 are missing and presumed killed in northern Bosnia. In July 1997, the International Committee of the Red Cross reported that it had received requests for information from family members of 19,380 persons missing from the war years. It also revealed that it had been able to account for 1,133 of these persons.

3. Has there been basic reform of the criminal code/criminal law? Who authorizes searches and issues warrants? Are suspects and prisoners beaten and abused? Are there excessive delays in the criminal justice system? The criminal procedure code is a holdover from the Yugoslav era and does not provide for adequate due process rights. Police have wide latitude to detain suspects for up to six months without filing formal charges. Relevant laws are being revised in the Federation with the aim of conforming them with international norms. Arbitrary arrests and detentions continue, although fewer cases were reported than in 1996. Some war-related prisoners are reportedly still being held. Police reportedly arbitrarily detained some members of ethnic minorities in the apparent hope of using them to bargain for the release of war prisoners of their own ethnic group.

Police and prison officials in all areas of the country are responsible for beating suspects and detainees. Prison conditions are poor and are below minimum international standards.

4. Do most judges rule fairly and impartially? Do many remain from the Communist era? The constitution provides for an independent judiciary, with the administration of justice reserved for the two entities. Judges often do not rule fairly and impartially. For example, the U.S. State

Department notes that in April 1997, a Serbian Republic municipal court in the town of Zvornik found seven Muslims guilty of murdering four Serbian civilians in May 1996, after a trial in which prosecutors reportedly failed to produce substantive evidence and in which the accused were denied their right to be represented effectively. In addition, the defendants were reportedly tortured.

While it is unclear how many judges remain from the Communist era, party affiliations, and political loyalty are still key criteria in judicial appointments.

5. Are the courts free of political control and influence? Are the courts linked directly to the Ministry of Justice or any other executive body? Courts in Bosnia are under the control or influence of the ruling parties. Judges are often pressured by government authorities. In July 1997, Bosnian Serb thugs loyal to Radovan Karadzic beat a judge on the Serbian Republic's Constitutional Court while the court was ruling on the legality of President Plavsic's dissolution of the legislature. Another problem is that local authorities often refuse to execute judicial rulings with which they disagree.

The courts are not linked directly to the Ministry of Justice or any other executive body. In addition to the civil and criminal courts, there is also a Constitutional Court, a Supreme Court, and a Human Rights Court. The Constitutional Court consists of nine members, four of whom are selected by the House of Representatives of the Federation. Two are selected by the Assembly of the Serbian Republic, and three are selected by the President of the European Court of Human Rights. The latter three judges cannot be citizens of Bosnia-Herzegovina or any neighboring state. After five years, the Parliamentary Assembly can provide a different method of selection of the three judges selected by the President of the European Court. The term for the Constitutional Court's initial judges is five years. Subsequent appointees will be able to serve until the age of 70. The Constitutional Court can rule on any constitutional dispute between the entities, or between Bosnia-Herzegovina and an entity or both entities, including whether any law is consistent with the constitution. In the Federation, there are municipal courts that have original jurisdiction in most civil and criminal cases, and cantonal courts, which have appellate jurisdiction over the ten cantons' municipalities.

6. What proportion of lawyers is in private practice? How does this compare with the previous year? Most lawyers are in private practice, although exact figures are not available.

7. Does the state provide public defenders? Exact information on this subject is not available for the period under review.

8. Are there effective anti-bias/discrimination laws, including protection of ethnic minority rights? The 1992-95 war was fought along ethnic lines, and ethnic and religious differences continue to be the major fault lines in society. The ethnic breakdown of Bosnia-Herzegovina is estimated at 40 percent Serb, 38 percent Muslim, and 22 percent Croat, although large numbers of Bosnians are of mixed ethnicity. The Dayton agreement ceded approximately 51 percent of the country's total territory to the Federation and 49 percent to the Serbian Republic.

The constitution prohibits discrimination on the basis of sex, race, language, religion, or other grounds. Nevertheless, the ruling parties continue to try to consolidate the power of their ethnic groups in areas under their control through discrimination and often violent harassment of minorities. This includes verbal aggression, vandalism, arson, assault, denial of access to housing for returning refugees, and other abuses. Discrimination against minority children and teachers in schools is also a problem.

Women face some discrimination in employment and generally do not hold positions of economic power. Although religious freedom is guaranteed by the constitution, Muslims outside of Muslim-controlled areas often feel pressured not to practice their religion in public. There have been several incidents of vandalism against Muslim religious objects, and there were two attacks on the Tomislavgrad mosque in 1997. Roman Catholic churches were also attacked.

Corruption C

1. What is the magnitude of official corruption in the civil service? Must an average citizen must pay a bribe to a bureaucrat in order to receive a service? What services are subject to bribe requests — for example, university entrance, hospital admission, telephone installation, obtaining a license to operate a business, applying for a passport or other official documents? What is the average salary of civil servants at various levels? Although difficult to quantify, there is reportedly considerable corruption in the civil service. In general, an average citizen reportedly must bribe a bureaucrat for basic services and to receive licenses.

2. Do top policy-makers (the President, ministers, vice-ministers, top court justices, the heads of agencies and commissions) have direct ties to businesses? How strong are such connections and what kind of businesses are these? Top officials have strong, direct, and often illicit ties to business. Former Bosnian Serb President Radovan Karadzic and his allies in the Serbian Republic town of Pale are reportedly heavily involved in smuggling timber into Yugoslavia and profit from illegal sales of fuel, tobacco, coffee, and alcohol. Karadzic reportedly paid Serbian Republic police loyal to him with profits from his cigarette and gasoline monopolies. In July 1997, Plavsic unsuccessfully attempted to remove the hardline interior minister, whom she accused of opposing efforts to create a viable customs administration that would curb the criminal activities of Karadzic and his allies.

Corruption often goes far beyond simple bribery or economic crime and reaches into politics and foreign relations. In July 1997, British Foreign Secretary Robin Cook charged that some senior Bosnia-Herzegovina officials were siphoning off huge amounts of international aid into personal accounts. In October 1997, High Representative Carlos Westendorp stated that corruption in the Federation was massive and systemic. He specifically accused the Agency for State Reserves of redirecting more than $13 million to institutions, including Iranian-trained spy agencies, outside of those established under the Dayton agreement.

3. Do laws requiring financial disclosure and disallowing conflict of interest exist? Have publicized anti-corruption cases been pursued? To what conclusion? Laws requiring financial disclosure and disallowing conflict of interest are inadequate. There have been few, if any, anti-corruption cases pursued through the courts.

4. What major anti-corruption initiatives have been implemented? How often are anti-corruption laws and decrees adopted? Few major anti-corruption initiatives have been implemented, and those that have been are often sidelined if they reach into the affairs of top officials. For example, in March 1998, the anti-fraud committee of the Federation accused the Federation government of blocking its inquiry into official misuse of international reconstruction aid.

5. How do major corruption-ranking organizations like Transparency International rate this country? Transparency International and other organizations that rate countries according to their levels of corruption have not yet rated Bosnia.

Privatization 5.50/7

1. What percentage of the GDP comes from private ownership? What percentage of the labor force is employed in the private sector? How large is the informal sector of the economy? In the absence of reliable statistics, it is difficult to determine what percentage of the GDP comes from private ownership and what percentage of the labor force is employed in the private sector. The public and "socially-owned" sectors of the economy account for 59 percent of jobs in the Federation and 67 percent in the Serbian Republic. According to the Office of the High Representative, the 1997 unemployment rate in the Federation was 32.5 percent and 40-50 percent in the Serbian Republic.

2. What major privatization legislation has been passed? What were its substantive features? In the Federation, several laws form the basis of privatization legislation. The 1996 Law on Privatization Agencies established the Federation Privatization Agency (FPA) and authorized the establishment of Cantonal Privatization Agencies (CPA), which will privatizate enterprises. In December 1997, the Federation parliament passed the Law on Settlement and Realization of Citizen Claims in the Process of Privatization, which regulates the handling of citizens' claims against property slated for privatization and authorizes the creation of vouchers to settle citizens' claims. The Federation parliament also passed the Law on Privatization of Enterprises, which defines procedures and methods for privatization of enterprises that have state or social capital. The FPA is preparing guidelines that define the methods for selling enterprises and providing details on enterprise privatization, the sale of apartments, citizens' participation in privatization, large enterprise privatization, privatization investment funds, and the role of the CPAs. Enterprises will be privatized through a combination of cash and vouchers.

The Federation Law on Privatization of Banks makes the Ministry of Finance responsible for the privatization of banks. These institutions will be privatized on a cash — rather than cash and voucher — basis for the purchase of bank shares or the assets and liabilities of insolvent banks that must be liquidated.

According to the Law on Opening Balance Sheets of Enterprises and Banks, which establishes the means of valuation for enterprises and banks slated for privatization, the external debt on the books of state-owned banks will be moved to an Asset Liquidation Account. Privatization certificates are to be issued to redeem depositors' claims on $2 billion of frozen currency accounts that were transferred to the National Bank of Yugoslavia before the war.

The privatization process may be slowed by an amendment to the Law on Opening Balance Sheet of Enterprises and Banks, which was adopted by the Federation House of Representatives and which proposes that, in situations in which the same assets are claimed by two different privatizing enterprises, privatization must be suspended until the relevant authority settles the dispute. The House of Peoples must either adopt the amendment or undertake a reconciliation of the two versions.

A Federation Law on Investment Funds and Management Companies is being prepared. The law will establish the basis for the creation of privatization investment funds, govern the participation of privatization investment funds in the privatization process, and establish procedures for the funds' investments in appropriate enterprises on behalf of citizens.

The Federation privatization process was to begin in June 1998 with small-scale privatization auctions of approximately 800 small firms and assets. Auctions for large-scale enterprises will begin in December. The entire process was scheduled to be completed by March 1999. Several CPAs, however, are finding it difficult to attract qualified staff, and cantons are experiencing difficulties in identifying assets and enterprises that fall under their jurisdiction.

In the Serbian Republic, the main privatization law is the Law on Privatization of Companies, which has serious deficiencies, including the exclusion of infrastructure and certain "strategic" enterprises. It provides for 55 percent of state ownership to be transferred to socially-oriented funds, a further 15 percent to be reserved for cash sales, and the remaining 30 percent to be sold through auctions against vouchers issued to citizens.

3. What proportion of agriculture, housing and land, industry, and small business and services is in private hands? Although no precise figures are available, nearly all agriculture is in private hands.

4. What has been the extent of insider (management, labor, and nomenklatura) participation in the privatization process? What explicit and implicit preferences have been awarded to insiders? Since the privatization process is in a rudimentary phase — it was suspended due to the war — it is difficult to determine the extent of insider participation in the privatization process and of explicit and implicit preferences that have been or will be awarded to insiders.

5. How much public awareness of and support for privatization has there been? What is the nature of support and opposition to privatization by major interest groups? In the Federation, several of the cantons have been slow in staffing the Cantonal Privatization Agencies, which will privatize enterprises. As a result, the distribution of public education materials has been limited. U.S.AID is working with both the Federation and Cantonal Privatization Agencies to educate the public on its rights and obligations under privatization laws and regulations. It is not clear what, if any, public education on privatization has been undertaken in the Serbian Republic. It is also difficult to gauge the nature of public support for privatization.

Macroeconomics 6.00/7

1. Has the taxation system been reformed? (What areas have and have not been overhauled? To what degree are taxpayers complying? Is tax compliance difficult to achieve? Has the

level of revenues increased? Is the revenue collection body overburdened? What is the overall tax burden?) The Dayton agreement makes the two entities responsible for taxation. The European Bank for Reconstruction and Development describes the tax system in both entities as "onerous and complex."

It is not clear to what extent taxpayers comply with the law or whether revenues are increasing. Payroll taxes average approximately 50 percent of gross salary. Legislation that remains valid calls for the payment of "war taxes" by returning displaced persons or refugees. Such taxes are often arbitrarily administered, with fluctuating rates, and are used to dissuade ethnic minorities from returning to their homes.

2. Does fiscal policy encourage private savings, investment and earnings? (Has there been any reform/alteration of revenue and budget policies? How large are budget deficits and overall debt? Is the financing of the social insurance/pension system sustainable? What proportion of the budget is taken up by subsidies to firms and individuals?) There has been little reform or alteration of revenue and budget policies. The fiscal policies of the central and entity-level governments have been largely irrelevant when compared with the effect of foreign aid on the economy. In certain areas, including Sarajevo, reconstruction aid and spending by SFOR soldiers and local employees of international organizations have greatly boosted the local economy. Other areas, however, have benefited little from the $1.6 billion in international reconstruction aid pledged in 1996. Initially, nearly all of the money went to the Federation. Through 1997, the Serbian Republic receiving only approximately five percent of the aid due to the leadership's failure to abide by the Dayton agreement. The January 1998 emergence of the new, more cooperative Serbian Republic government, however, may lead to increased reconstruction aid for the entity. In 1996, remittances by Bosnian citizens working abroad totaled $424 million.

International aid and foreign remittances are largely responsible for boosting the average wage to approximately $194 per month and cutting unemployment nearly in half from its 1996 level of 90 percent. In the Serbian Republic, however, the average wage is approximately $40 to 45 per month, and unemployment is still 80 percent.

There has been little progress in transferring social welfare responsibilities from state-owned enterprises directly to the government. The social safety net is not self-sustaining and depends on contributions from multinational institutions and other external funders.

3. Has there been banking reform? (Is the central bank independent? What are its responsibilities? Is it effective in setting and/or implementing monetary policy? What is the actual state of the private banking sector? Does it conform to international standards? Are depositors protected?) In June 1997, the Bosnian parliament passed a "Quick Start" package of laws that included a Central Bank Law. The bank, which formally began operations two months later, is independent and will operate for its first six years as a currency board. This means that it can only issue currency that is backed by an equivalent amount of foreign reserves. As such, monetary policy is largely out of the central bank's hands. The bank consists of one unit in the Serbian republic and another in the Federation. Each unit holds its own reserves.

As of June 1997, there were 27 licensed banks in the Federation and 11 in the Serbian Republic. These include 17 state-controlled banks, all of which are insolvent and base their lending on connections rather than on due diligence. Most private banks are small, undercapitalized, and incapable of meeting growing deposit and lending needs. Nevertheless, private banks now account for the majority of new loans extended. Accounting and regulatory standards are still not market-based and need to be updated. In October 1996, the Federation created a Federation Banking Agency responsible for licensing and supervision. By June 1997, it had refused to renew of licenses for 20 banks and indicated that some of the weaker banks were being sidelined.

There has been little progress on banking reform in the Serbian Republic.

4. How sound is the national currency? (Is the value of the currency fixed or does it float? How convertible is the currency? How large are the hard currency reserves? Has the exchange rate policy been stable and predictable?) After Bosnia's declaration of independence in 1992, the Yugoslav National Bank refused to provide Bosnia with Yugoslav *dinars*. The fledgling state planned to introduce a Bosnian dinar in July 1992, but this was delayed until October 1994, when the new currency entered circulation at a rate of one new dinar to 10,000 old Yugoslavian dinars.

Under the Dayton Accords, monetary policy is the responsibility of the central government. The Central Bank has begun to issue an interim currency, the *marka* (KM), which is fully convertible and, under the rules of the country's currency board, pegged at parity with the German *mark*. The KM is used throughout Bosnia for non-cash transactions. Cash payments are currently made in the temporary currencies established in the two entities, German marks, Croatian *kunas* (in Bosnian Croat-controlled areas), and Serbian dinars (in Bosnian Serb-controlled areas).

Political squabbles over the design of a permanent currency have delayed its implementation. In January 1998, High Representative Carlos Westendorp exercised his power to impose the designs of Bosnian currency. The Bosnian marka was to enter into circulation in April 1998.

5. Is there a functioning capital market infrastructure? (Are there existing or planned commodities, bond, and stock markets? What are the mechanisms for investing and lending? What government bodies have authority to regulate capital markets?) Bosnia currently lacks a functioning capital market infrastructure. In July 1997, the government and its London Club commercial bank creditors agreed that the country would accept responsibility for $404 million of debt, or 10.58 percent of the $4.2 billion owed by the former Yugoslavia. To cover this, Bosnia will issue $150 million of German mark-denominated bonds, with principal repaid over 20 years with a seven year grace period. Interest will be charged at a fixed rate of two percent for the first four years and rise to 3.5 percent by the end of the seventh year. For the last 13 years, interest will be payable at less than one percent over the benchmark London Interbank Offer Rate. Bosnia will pay the remaining $254 million of debt by issuing a second tranche of bonds that will be amortized over 12 years. These bonds will only be issued, however, after per capita income has risen above $2,800 or at least ten years after the issuance of the first tranche of bonds.

Microeconomics 6.00/7

1. Are property rights guaranteed? (Are there both formal and de facto protections of pri-

vate real estate and intellectual property? Is there a land registry with the authority and capability to ensure accurate recording of who owns what? What are the procedures for expropriation, including measures for compensation and challenge? Have any seizures taken place?) Property rights are tenuous throughout Bosnia, although they are somewhat better protected in the Federation than in the Serbian Republic. Property laws have generally been used as a tool to consolidate the results of "ethnic cleansing" by making the return of displaced persons and refugees impossible. In the Serbian Republic and, until recently, the Federation, residences can be occupied by others if the original occupants are absent even for short periods. Authorities have used this provision to block ethnic minority refugees from returning and to permit displaced persons to continue to occupy residences. Forcible evictions have been executed to a greater degree in the Serbian Republic than in the Federation.

In the Federation, the Law on Temporarily Abandoned Real Property Owned by Citizens, which was introduced during the war, provided that if the owners of private property left after April 30, 1991, the authorities could declare the property "abandoned" and grant temporary occupancy rights to a third party. While in theory the law did not permanently affect ownership rights, with the owners able to return at any time and reclaim their property, in practice the owner could not do so because there was no viable procedure for repossessing property and addressing the needs of current users. In March 1998, the Federation parliament passed the Law Regulating Application of the Law on Temporarily Abandoned Real Property Owned by Citizens. The new law allows owners of private property to file a claim to reclaim their property. The authorities must rule on claims within 30 days. If the property is vacant or occupied illegally, the owner may re-occupy the property immediately following the decision on the claim. If the property is occupied by an authorized temporary user, the current occupant has 90 days to vacate the property. In some circumstances, this period can be extended up to one year.

In March 1998, the Federation parliament also passed the Law on Cassation of the Application of the Law on Abandoned Apartments. This law applies to "socially-owned" apartments, meaning that persons were given occupancy rights by companies, government agencies, or social organizations. Previously, such socially-owned apartments had been regulated by the Law on Abandoned Apartments, which had permitted authorities to declare socially-owned apartments whose occupants had left as "abandoned" and grant temporary occupancy rights to other persons. In December 1995, the law was amended so that, if the original occupants did not claim and reoccupy their apartment by January 1996, their apartment would be declared permanently abandoned and could be permanently reallocated to a new occupant. This law blocked the return of tens of thousands of refugees and displaced persons to their homes. Under the new law, all decisions terminating the occupancy rights of refugees and displaced persons are null and void. Pre-war occupants or their authorized representatives must file claims for repossession of their apartment within six months after the law came into force or by October 1998. As with claims to private property, authorities must issue a decision within 30 days of the date a claim is filed. These decisions will confirm pre-war occupancy rights, terminate rights of temporary use of the apartment, and set a deadline by which the current user of the apartment must vacate the premises. If the apartment is vacant or occupied illegally, the pre-war occupant can repossess the apartment immediately. An authorized temporary user will be given 90 days to vacate the apartment, which can be extended if the pre-war occupant's designated return date is later. If the apartment is occupied by a person who has received a permanent occupancy right prior to February 7, 1998, the case may be referred for an additional decision concerning whether the pre-war occupant should be allocated a different apartment, thereby allowing the current occupant to remain in place.

The Federation parliament also transformed the pre-war Law on Housing Relations, which also applies to "socially-owned" apartments, into the Law on Taking Over the Law on Housing Relations. Under the old law, an occupancy right could be canceled, except in certain limited circumstances, when the occupant had not resided in the apartment for a continuous period of six months. The amended law provides that occupancy rights cannot be canceled automatically for failure to use an apartment after April 30, 1991, if the person with the occupancy right has the right to return under the Dayton Accords.

In December 1997, the Federation parliament passed the Law on the Sale of Apartments with Existing Tenancy Rights, which codifies the procedures for selling socially-owned apartments. The law provides three years of protection for soldiers and their families who live in apartments that were vacated and abandoned and who had been given tenancy by authorities. In March 1998, the Federation parliament amended the law so that persons who acquired occupancy rights to apartments that were declared "abandoned" since 1991 are not permitted to purchase the apartments in which they now reside. Meanwhile, under the Law on the Cassation of Application of the Law on Abandoned Apartments, pre-war occupants who left their apartments during the war will not be able to purchase their apartments until they have returned and resided in the apartment for six months. In addition, such pre-war occupants will not be permitted to sell the apartment for a period of five years from the date that the purchase of the apartment is registered.

In the Serbian Republic, property laws do not meet international standards and obstruct the return of refugees and displaced persons. In cases in which the owner or occupants fled their homes during the war, the Law on Abandoned Apartments declares the property to have been abandoned and to be "socially-owned." In practice, the law has been used as a tool for "ethnic cleansing," with non-Serbs in some cases being forcibly evicted from their apartments and houses, and their property declared abandoned. Many of the expelled persons never left the Serbian Republic and are now internally displaced. The new government has established a working group to develop property and housing law amendments. In addition, the High Representative is working with Serbian Republic authorities to ensure that the proposed laws comply with the Dayton Accords.

Annex 7 of the Dayton Accords established the Commission for Real Property Claims of Refugees and Displaced Persons (CRPC). Due to limited staffing, however, it has operated slowly. The CRPC is also maintaining and building an existing database of property registration records. This is complicated by the fact that each entity does not accept and recognize official property registration documents issued in the other entity.

2. To what extent have prices been liberalized? What subsidies remain? This information was not available for the period under review.

3. Is it possible to own and operate a business? (Has there been legislation regarding the formation, dissolution, and transfer of businesses, and is the law respected? Do there exist

overly cumbersome bureaucratic hurdles that effectively hinder the ability to own and dispose of a business? Are citizens given access to information on commercial law? Is the law applied fairly? Does the regulation (or do licensing requirements) impose significant costs on business and consumers? Do they create significant barriers to entry and seriously hamper competition?) According to the EBRD, business is "constrained by a legal and administrative framework that has yet to move much beyond that inherited from the old Yugoslav system." There is a need to develop an effective legal framework regarding contracts, bankruptcy, the establishment, dissolution, and transfer of businesses, and other areas of commercial law.

Businesses face numerous other constraints. The bureaucracy at all levels tends to be slow, cumbersome and inefficient. There is no regular postal service, telecommunications, or public transport between the Federation and the Serb Republic.

4. Are courts effective, transparent, efficient, and quick in reaching decisions on property and contract disputes? What alternative mechanisms for adjudicating disputes exist? The courts are not an effective means for reaching decisions in property and contract disputes. Bribery continues to be a problem. According to the Helsinki Committee for Human Rights, in the Serb Republic, people who do not have money to pay bribes can expect to wait at least one year before court proceedings begin. Even those that start earlier are often conducted at a very slow pace. On the other hand, according to the EBRD, there is generally a meaningful right of appeal from first-instance court decisions. There is also an independent right of judicial review of administrative action. On average, a party can expect to wait less than six months for a commercial case to be heard on the merits by a court in Sarajevo, and between two and three years for a final judgment calling for a payment to be executed. Court operations outside Sarajevo, however, are much slower. Municipal courts are particularly slow to reach decisions under the contentious Law on Abandoned Apartments.

The Dayton-mandated Commission for Real Property Claims by Displaced Persons and Refugees (CRPC) is also heavily backlogged. As of December 1997, it had received more than 70,000 claims, but had only managed to process 6,000 claims. The CRPC is also charged with issuing eviction orders and providing security for returning refugees and displaced persons, but the political will for enforcement is often lacking.

5. Is business competition encouraged? (Are monopolistic practices limited in law and practice? If so, how? To what degree is "insider" dealing a hindrance to open competition? Are government procurement policies open and unbiased?) Much of Bosnia's legal and administrative framework was inherited from the Yugoslav system. New regulations regarding business competition and monopolistic practices are therefore required. Many key industries function as monopolies. For example, Radovan Karadzic continues to operate cigarette and gasoline monopolies in the Serbian Republic.

Foreign investors have complained of a lack of transparency in the tender process for reconstruction projects financed by international aid. The World Bank is sponsoring a Public Works Employment Project that is subjecting proposals for local infrastructure projects to a strict and competitive appraisal process. The Federation government has established a Procurement Monitoring and Audit Unit to promote transparency in contracts that are let under World Bank financed projects. A similar organization is to be established in the Serbian Republic. Both entity governments have established several Project Implementation Units, with World Bank support, to ensure transparency in the implementation of World Bank-funded local infrastructure projects. Similarly, U.S.AID has established a Municipal Infrastructure and Services Program to supervise implementation of the reconstruction projects that the agency funds.

6. To what extent has international trade been liberalized? To what degree has there been simplification/overhaul of customs and tariff procedures, and are these applied fairly? What informal trade barriers exist? There has been some liberalization of the international trade regime. The Dayton agreement makes the central government responsible for trade matters. In February 1998, the Parliamentary Assembly passed the Permanent Customs Tariff Law, which repealed an interim June 1997 customs tariff law and replaced it with streamlined, uniform customs procedures for both the Federation and the Serbian Republic. The new law replaced 21 existing customs tariff rates with four rates of zero, five, ten, and 15 percent. The new law also abolished all existing *ad valorem* special assessment fees levied on imported goods, thereby leaving only a one percent customs entry fee in addition to the four new customs tariff rates. With the new law, the existing special trade relationships between the Federation and Croatia and between the Serbian Republic and Yugoslavia are being terminated.

7. To what extent has foreign investment and capital flow been encouraged or constrained? To date, most foreign direct investment in Bosnia has come from the neighboring countries of Italy, Germany, Austria, and Greece. Foreign investment has been concentrated in small and medium-sized companies in sectors such as food, clothing, and wood processing. The Free Zone Mostar is the first such free trade zone established under the Law on Free Zones. It offers investors exemptions from customs fees, duties, and taxes on exports from the zone, as well as other incentives.

In general, however, the government has done little to encourage foreign investment and capital flow. In addition, many potential investors remain wary of investing in the war-torn country.

8. Has there been reform of the energy sector? (To what degree has the energy sector been restructured? Is the energy sector more varied, and is it open to private competition? Is the country overly dependent on one or two other countries for energy [including whether exported fuels must pass through one or more countries to reach markets]?) There has been little reform of the energy sector, which remains largely under state control. Bosnia is relatively dependent on Russian gas imports. In February 1998, Russia cut natural gas supplies to Bosnia by 40 percent due to the country's failure to pay $12 million for gas supplied in 1996 and 1997. The government has stated that it is the responsibility of Energoinvest, the state-owned company that imports natural gas, to resolve what it considers to be a commercial problem. Inter-ethnic politics, however, are apparently a factor as well, with some Muslim leaders saying that a considerable portion of the gas has been used by the Serbian Republic, which should assume a share of the financial obligations.

BULGARIA

Freedom in the World Ratings, 1989-1998

	1989-90	1990-91	1991-92	1992-93	1993-94	1994-95	1995-96	1996-97	1997-98
Political Rights	7	3	2	2	2	2	2	2	2
Civil Liberties	7	4	3	3	2	2	2	3	3
Status	NF	PF	F	F	F	F	F	F	F

Polity: Transitional
Economy: Transitional
Population: 8,454,000
PPP: $4,604
Ethnic Groups: Bulgarian (86 percent), Turkish (9 percent), Roma (4 percent), Macedonian
Capital: Sofia

Political Process 2.75/7

1. When did national legislative elections occur? Were they free and fair? How were they judged by domestic and international election monitoring organizations? Who composes the government? Bulgaria held its first multiparty elections in June 1990, with the ex-Communist Bulgarian Socialist Party (BSP) winning 211 seats in the then-400 member National Assembly. The July 1991 constitution established a unicameral parliament with 240 members elected for a four-year term by proportional representation in multi-seat constituencies. Parties must pass a four percent barrier to gain seats. In October 1991, in the first elections held under the new constitution, the opposition Union of Democratic Forces (UDF) won a narrow plurality with 110 of the 240 seats. The BSP won 106 seats. After several months, political instability forced the UDF to yield to a non-party government. Further instability forced early elections in December 1994, in which the BSP won a clear majority with 125 seats. The fragmented UDF won 69, the Popular Union, 18; the Turkish-based Movement for Rights and Freedom (MRF), 15; and the pro-market Bulgarian Business Block (BBB), 13.

By the spring of 1996, the ex-Communists' reluctance to undertake far-reaching structural reforms had contributed to a banking crisis, and the currency, the *lev*, collapsed later in the year. In December 1996, as average wages plummeted, unemployment and inflation soared, and the country faced an impending default on its $9 billion foreign debt, BSP Prime Minister Zhan Videnov resigned. In January 1997, UDF President Zhelyu Zhelev rejected the BSP's choice of Interior Minister Nikolai Dobrev to replace Videnov, thereby leaving the country without a prime minister.

After a month of mass anti-government protests and paralyzing general strikes, the BSP agreed on February 5, 1997 to early elections. Fifty-nine percent of eligible voters participated in the April 19, 1997 poll. The UDF, which had evolved from a loose coalition of 15 anti-Communist groups into a unified party, dominated a four-party alliance that won 52 percent of the vote and 137 of 240 seats. The BSP won 22 percent and 58 seats. The Alliance for National Salvation, a coalition dominated by the ethnically Turkish-based MRF won 8 percent and 19 seats. Euroleft, an alliance of moderate BSP defectors, won 6 percent and 14 seats, while the pro-market (BBB) won 5 percent and 12 seats.

The UDF named Ivan Kostov, a former finance minister, as prime minister in the UDF-led government. On May 8, 1997, the new parliament adopted a Declaration of National Salvation that identified the UDF's key goals as the implementation of reforms agreed with the International Monetary Fund (IMF), the provision of a social safety net for workers whose jobs would be lost due to economic reforms, opposition to organized crime, the publication of secret police files on public figures, the return of land to its pre-Communist owners, and the pursuit of NATO and European Union (EU) membership. International observers characterized Bulgaria's four post-1989 elections as free and fair.

2. When did presidential elections occur? Were they free and fair? In November 1989, two weeks after the first pro-democracy rally in Bulgaria's post-war history, the National Assembly named Foreign Minister Petur Mladenov to replace strongman Todor Zhivkov, who had ruled since 1954. In July 1990, Mladenov was forced to resign after evidence emerged that he had endorsed the use of tanks to crush an anti-government demonstration in late 1989. The National Assembly elected UDF Chairman Zhelyu Zhelev as his successor.

Under the 1991 constitution, the president is directly elected for a five-year term. On January 19, 1992, in the second round of Bulgaria's first direct, multiparty presidential election, Zhelev won 53.5 percent of the vote and defeated BSP-backed Velko Valkanov, who received 46.5 percent of the vote. Thirteen candidates competed in the 1996 presidential vote. On October 27, in the first round, Petar Stoyanov of the UDF won 44.1 percent of the vote; Culture Minister Ivan Mazarov of the BSP, 26.9 percent; and Georgi Ganchev of the BBB, 21.9 percent. Other candidates received 4.6 percent of the vote. In the second round on November 3, Stoyanov defeated Mazarov with 59.7 percent of the vote. Voter turnout in the second round was 61.7 percent. Observers determined that the balloting was free and fair.

3. Is the electoral system multiparty-based? Are there at least two viable political parties functioning at all levels of government? Prior to 1989, the Bulgarian Communist Party (BCP) and a satellite party, the Bulgarian Agrarian Union, were the only legal political parties. Many of the post-1989 opposition parties united to form the UDF coalition, while the BCP transformed itself into the BSP. The current system includes parties ranging from ex-Communist to monarchist and nationalist. A total of 38 parties registered for the April 1997 parliamentary elections, and 31 parties and coalitions actually contested the vote under the terms of the Electoral Act by fielding candidates in at least one-third of the electoral districts. Since the country's democratic transition began, elections at all levels of government have been contested by more than two parties.

4. How many parties have been legalized? Are any parties illegal? At the time of the April 1997 parliamentary elections, the full spectrum of political ideologies was represented in Bulgaria's 205 registered political parties. The constitution prohibits the formation of political parties along religious, ethnic, or racial lines. Nevertheless, the predominantly ethnic-Turkish MRF operates freely and is represented in the National Assembly.

5. What proportion of the population belongs to political parties? Less than 10 percent of eligible voters are members of political parties.

6. What has been the trend of voter turnout at the municipal, provincial, and national levels in recent years? Approximately 87 percent of eligible voters participated in Bulgaria's October 1991, legislative elections. By contrast, only 59 percent voted in the 1997 legislative elections. In the 1996 presidential elections, voter turnout was 62.7 percent in the first round and only 53 percent in the second. Turnouts for municipal and provincial elections vary, but tend to be lower than in national elections.

Civil Society 3.75/7

1. How many non-governmental organizations (NGOs) have come into existence since 1988? What is the number of charitable/nonprofit organizations? Are there locally led efforts to increase philanthropy and volunteerism? What proportion of the population is active in private voluntary activity (from polling data)? While it is difficult to estimate the number of NGOs and charitable and nonprofit organizations in Bulgaria, there are more than 150 NGOs in Sofia alone. NGOs are active in fields such as human rights, women's affairs, culture, education, science, healthcare, social services, the environment, and business development. There are some locally-led efforts to increase philanthropy and volunteerism. For example, the Bourgas NGOs Development Center encourages charity and other citizen's initiatives to help needy persons. There are no accurate data on the proportion of the population that is active in private voluntary activity.

2. What is the legal and regulatory environment for NGOs (i.e., ease of registration, legal rights, government regulation, taxation, procurement and access-to-information issues)? To what extent is NGO activism focused on improving the legal and regulatory environment? Registration for NGOs is easy and straightforward. Of greater concern is the tax environment, which changed in 1996 with the introduction of a new Law on Profit Tax (LPT). Although generally an improvement over the previous tax law, analysts have found many of the LPT's provisions to be vague. For example, under the LPT, NGOs are liable for profit tax on vaguely defined "economic activities." It is not fully clear whether project grants are covered under the scope of economic activity. Profit tax consists of a 6.5 percent municipality tax and taxes to the central government that are levied at rates of 26 and 36 percent. The new law blurs the distinctions for tax purposes between associations and foundations. The one exception pertains to donations: Foundations do not pay taxes on donations, while associations — a term that covers most NGOs that depend on external funding do. NGOs are also liable for the normal 22-percent value-added tax (VAT), except in cases in which they sold services for a fee lower than or equal to the actual cost to the NGO. NGOs generally must also pay customs duties and other levies on imports. Donations to most types of NGOs are tax-deductible. According to the Sofia-based Center for the Study of Democracy's January 1997 survey of elite attitudes towards NGOs, there is considerable support for providing greater tax relief to charity organizations, foundations, citizens' associations, and other NGOs.

NGOs have been active in trying to improve the legal and regulatory environment as part of a broader effort to promote legal reform and educate citizens about their rights.

3. What is the organizational capacity of NGOs? Do management structures clearly delineate authority and responsibility? Is information available on NGO management issues in the native language? Is there a core of experienced practitioners/trainers to serve as consultants or mentors to less developed organizations? Bulgaria has a well-educated workforce, and NGOs benefit from organizational and technical expertise. There is a growing body of information on NGO management issues in the Bulgarian language. Several experienced NGOs are dedicated to supporting the institutional development of NGOs. For example, the Bourgas NGOs Development Center, founded in 1995, supports the development of NGOs in the Bourgas region by providing information, consultancy services, and other assistance.

4. Are NGOs financially viable? What is their tax status? Are they obliged to and do they typically disclose revenue sources? Do government procurement opportunities exist for private, not-for-profit providers of services? Bulgarian NGOs are hampered by a lack of funds, a dearth of trained activists, and limited international networking. Under the 1996 Law on Profit Tax, Bulgarian NGOs must pay taxes on "economic activity," a vaguely-defined term that involves the receipt of something of value in exchange for something else of value. Under this law, it is not clear whether NGO project grants are taxable. Profit tax consists of a 6.5- percent municipality tax and taxes to the central government at rates of 26 percent and 36 percent. Donations to associations (covering most NGOs that depend on funding for their operations) are taxable, while donations to foundations are tax-exempt. NGOs are also liable for the normal 22-percent VAT, except in cases in which they sold services for a fee lower than or equal to the actual cost to the NGO. NGOs are also generally charged with customs duties and other levies on imports. Donations to most types of NGOs are tax-deductible.

As Bulgaria continues its transition to a market economy, increasingly there are government procurement opportunities for NGOs.

5. Are there free trade unions? How many workers belong to these unions? Is the number of workers belonging to trade unions growing or decreasing? What is the numerical/proportional membership of farmers' groups, small business associations, etc.? Bulgarian workers are free to join independent trade unions. The two largest trade union confederations are the Confederation of Independent Trade Unions of Bulgaria (CITUB), the successor to the former Communist-controlled trade union, and *Podkrepa*, a confederation originally formed as a political opposition movement in 1989. Together they represent more than 2 million workers. Prior to Bulgaria's democratic transition, CITUB functioned as an arm of the state. More recently, it became critical of BSP governments and demanded the Videnov government's resignation over its mishandling of the economy. In October 1996, *Promyana* (Change), a UDF-supported coalition of trade unions and civic groups, was formed to advocate for early elections. By January 1997, it included 23 unions; it has not pursued official registration.

The share of the unionized work force is estimated variously at between 30 to 50 percent of the total workforce, but union ranks are decreasing as industrial restructuring shifts workers to smaller, non-unionized factories and businesses. Collective bargaining and the right to strike are legal, although labor advocates state that the government's enforcement of labor contracts is inadequate.

There are growing numbers of farmers' groups and small business associations. They include the Bulgarian Trade and Industrial Chamber, the Bulgarian Economic Chamber, and the Union for Private Economic Enterprise.

6. What forms of interest group participation in politics are legal? What types of interest groups are active in the political and policy process? There are few restrictions on interest group participation in politics. The constitution prohibits organizations that threaten the country's territorial unity or incite racial, ethnic, or religious hatred. Similarly, the Law on Political Parties prohibits the formation of ethnic-based political parties and organizations. Since 1990, the government has refused to register a self-styled Macedonian human rights group on the grounds that it is separatist in nature. The 1992 Labor Code recognizes the right to strike for all except key public sector workers but forbids "political strikes." Nevertheless, many workers did join the anti-government demonstrations and general strikes that forced the BSP government to resign in early 1997. Non-governmental organizations participate in politics through various means, including holding rallies and protest demonstrations, lobbying members of parliament, organizing petition campaigns, and working with the media.

7. How is the not-for-profit/NGO sector perceived by the public and government officials? What is the nature of media coverage of NGOs? To what extent do government officials engage with NGOs?

It its 1997 survey of elite attitudes towards NGOs, the Center for the Study of Democracy found that in general, all types of NGOs are viewed favorably rather than unfavorably by a two-to-one ratio. Charities and artists' unions are viewed particularly favorably. Many of those surveyed viewed NGOs as an institutional alternative to the government in some areas. According to the center, these results compared favorably with those of similar surveys conducted among the general public. Government attitudes towards NGOs range from positive to tolerant. Domestic human rights organizations operate freely. According to the U.S. Department of State, however, government officials, especially at the local level, are occasionally reluctant to provide information or cooperate actively with human rights investigations. In addition, human rights groups are denied access to National Investigative Service detention centers. The media frequently cover statements and reports by NGOs.

Independent Media 3.5/7

1. Are there legal protections for press freedom? The constitution provides for freedom of the press. In July 1996, parliament passed the Radio and Television Act, which placed state television and radio under the supervision of a National Council on Radio and Television (NCRT). The NCRT includes seven members whom parliament elects based on the distribution of party seats in the national assembly, two members who are appointed by the president, and two who are appointed by the government. The act authorized the NCRT to appoint and dismiss the directors of state-owned broadcast media. The act also banned libelous broadcasts and those that offend ethical norms or incite cruelty and violence. In addition, it banned propaganda and publicity for illegal religious denominations. Many journalists opposed the law on the grounds that it was too restrictive, particularly in its use of broad and vague concepts such as "morality." In November 1996, the Constitutional Court ruled 15 elements of the law to be unconstitutional, including provisions regulating the access of politicians and government officials to electronic media, banning the broadcast of subjective comments on facts, and governing the NCRT. The court argued that the procedures for selecting the NCRT tend to perpetuate partisan interference in the media. One provision that remained holds that state media are not obliged to grant free air time to the President, Speaker of the Parliament, Prime Minister, or their spokesmen.

In 1997, the incoming UDF-led government pledged to pass a new law that would minimize partisan interference in the state-owned broadcast media. In the interim, parliament appointed new radio and television directors, a move that the Constitutional Court declared unconstitutional in November 1997. Parliament then amended the act to establish a seven member NCRT, with four members elected by parliament and three appointed by the president. The BSP has appealed to the Constitutional Court on the grounds that the distribution of party quotas on the NCRT could still entrench partisan influence in the state broadcast media.

2. Are there legal penalties for libeling officials? Are there legal penalties for "irresponsible" journalism? Have these laws been enforced to harass journalists? During parliamentary debates prior to approval of the 1991 constitution, many members of parliament had argued that language in Article 41 stating that the right to express or publish an opinion should not be used to the detriment of the "rights and reputation" of others or to "the detriment of national security, public order, public health, and morality" was too vague. Nevertheless, the language remained in the final draft. There are no legal penalties for "irresponsible" journalism *per se*, but the penal code criminalizes libel, defamation, and slander. In 1997, a court convicted a journalist of libeling prominent political and business figures when she wrote that they had worked as government informants. Also in 1997, another journalist was released after serving a six-month term for libeling a prosecutor by accusing him of corruption.

3. What proportion of media is privatized? What are the major private newspapers, television stations, and radio stations? All print media are privately owned. Major private newspapers include *24 Chasa* (24 Hours), which has a circulation of 300,000; *Trud* (Labor), which has a circulation of 200,000; *Narodno Delo* (People's Cause), which has a circulation of 100,000; and *Zemya* (Earth), which has a circulation of 60,000. The UDF, BSP, and the trade union movement also publish major daily newspapers.

There are more than 60 private radio stations. The independent Darik Radio, established in 1993, increased its credibility and stature by broadcasting live from parliament on the night of January 10-11, 1997, when clashes between police and anti-government demonstrators injured 300 people. During the night it achieved an audience of 55 percent, compared with 25 percent for the state-run Bulgarian National Radio.

There are several privately-owned regional television stations. Foreign television broadcasts ended with the expiration of the stations' licenses in 1997.

4. Are the private media financially viable? Bulgaria's financial crisis caused severe hardship for the independent press. Two of the largest papers, *24 Chasa* and *Trud*, were bought by a German publishing group, *Westdeutsche Algemaine Zeitung* (WAZ), which now controls an estimated 70 to 80 percent of the daily newspaper market. WAZ slashed the papers' prices, which cut into the circulation and advertising revenues of other national and regional papers and forced many rival papers to dismiss journalists and reduce print-runs. As the economy began to recover from the crisis, the general financial situation for the private press improved somewhat, but high newsprint costs continue to be a constraint.

According to the 1996 Radio and Television Act, news and information shows can neither be sponsored nor interrupted by commercials. Advertisement time cannot exceed 15 percent of the total length of a program.

5. Are the media editorially independent? Are the media's news gathering functions affected by interference from government or private owners? The print media are editorially independent. The private press offer diverse views, although many newspapers are published by political parties or other politically-oriented organizations and tend to reflect the views of their owners. The quality of the private press varies. Some newspapers are mere "scandal sheets."

Some analysts have stated that political coverage in the state-run broadcast media favors the government. The Post and Telecommunications Committee issues and can withdraw licenses from broadcast media.

In general, there are few restrictions on the media's news-gathering functions. When the BSP was in power, the independent Darik Radio stated that its signal sometimes could not be received, for unknown reasons, in some of the seven towns from where it broadcasts. Some private stations complain that their licenses restrict them to weaker transmission strengths than those granted to state-owned stations.

In February 1997, the major political parties agreed to a plan for the allocation of media air time for the upcoming parliamentary elections. Based on the public opinion polls and the results of the last parliamentary and presidential elections, the Central Electoral Commission divided the 31 parties contesting the elections into two groups. The first group included five parties and coalitions that were each allowed to make addresses and nominate a representative to participate in all election debates. In the second group, the remaining 26 parties and coalitions were each allowed to nominate a representative to take part in two debates.

6. Is the distribution system for newspapers privately or governmentally controlled? Major media organizations have established their own distribution networks, but the government still largely controls the printing and distribution of newspapers.

7. What proportion of the population is connected to the Internet? Are there any restrictions on Internet access to private citizens? The most recent figures available — from 1994 – indicated that there are 0.9 Internet users per 100,000 Bulgarians. There are no restrictions on Internet access for private citizens.

8. What has been the trend in press freedom as measured by Freedom House's *Survey of Press Freedom*? Freedom House's annual *Survey of Press Freedom* rated Bulgaria as "Not Free" in 1988 and 1989, and "Partly Free" from 1990 through 1998.

Governance and Public Administration 4/7

1. Is the legislature the effective rule-making institution? The legislature, or National Assembly, is the effective rule-making institution, although, prior to the election of the UDF government in 1997, infighting, parliamentary boycotts, and a sharply polarized political climate often limited its effectiveness. In the early 1990s, then-President Zhelev had even argued in favor of a presidential republic during Bulgaria's transition period in order to adopt quickly new laws and stabilization measures. The depth of the 1996-97 economic crisis, the incoming UDF's parliamentary majority, and the Kostov government's commitment to radical economic reform led parliament to initiate and approve wide-ranging liberalizations, including the establishment of a currency board. Analysts reports that, since the UDF government took power, the parliament has adopted a more consensual legislative style, with informal agreements often reached prior to the introduction of draft laws.

The National Assembly passes most legislation and other acts by simple majority. In amending the constitution and in some other cases, however, a larger majority is necessary. Other important functions of the legislature are to approve the state budget, schedule elections, select and dismiss the prime minister and members of the Council of Ministers (cabinet), declare war or conclude peace, deploy troops, and ratify international treaties. The President can veto a law, in which case it is returned to the assembly for additional deliberation and a new vote. Parliament needs a two-thirds majority to override a presidential veto.

2. Is substantial power decentralized to sub-national levels of government? What specific authority sub-national levels have? Bulgaria has a three-tiered government structure, with the national government at the top, the nine *oblasti* (regions) on a second tier, and the 273 municipalities and 3,984 *naselini mesta* (settlements) on a third tier that constitutes the country's basic administrative territorial units.

Analysts have criticized Bulgaria's division of powers for failing to establish clear expenditure assignments among the different levels of government. It is often unclear which level of government — central, regional, or local — is responsible for which public sector services.

3. Are sub-national levels chosen in free and fair elections? The state Council of Ministers appoints regional governors. Mayors and municipal councils are directly elected for four-year terms in free and fair elections. In local elections, the UDF usually wins in the large cities, while the BSP still dominates in the smaller towns and villages.

4. Do the executive and legislative bodies operate openly and with transparency? Is draft legislation easily accessible to the media and public? Parliamentary sessions are broadcast, and members of parliament and the cabinet frequently hold regular press conferences. The gradual strengthening of the independent media, the public's growing political consciousness, and the expansion of civil society in Bulgaria have forced the executive and legislative bodies to become increasingly accountable, transparent and responsive to public demands. In general, draft legislation is readily accessible to the media and public.

5. Do municipal governments have sufficient revenues to carry out their duties? Do municipal governments have control of their own local budgets? Do they raise revenue autonomously or from the central state budget? Municipal governments generally have sufficient revenues to execute their duties. The budgets of municipalities have been autonomous since 1992. Revenues are raised through taxes and central government subsidies. Government ministers have been accused of preferential treatment in allocating subsidies to regions that voted for the ruling party.

6. Do the elected local leaders and local civil servants know how to manage municipal governments effectively? According to scholars, the weak administrative tradition in Bulgaria's Ottoman past made it easier for Communist authorities to impose stifling, control-bound administrative structures after World War II. In the post-Communist period, local officials and civil servants often lack sufficient managerial expertise.

7. When did the constitutional/legislative changes on local power come into effect? Has there been a reform of the civil service code/system? Are local civil servants employees of the local or central government? Changes in local administration took effect under the 1991 constitution, which establishes a decentralized power structure. Reforms of the civil service code are pending. Local civil servants are employees of the local, rather than central, government.

Rule of Law 3.75/7

1. Is there a post-Communist constitution? How does the judicial system interpret and enforce the constitution? Are there specific examples of judicial enforcement of the constitution in the last year? Parliament adopted Bulgaria's post-Communist constitution in July 1991. It establishes a parliamentary form of government in which power is shared between the legislature, the executive, and the judiciary.

The Constitutional Court, which is separate from the regular court system, has the power of judicial review. Of the court's 12 justices, four are elected by the National Assembly, four are appointed by the president, and four are elected by judicial authorities. The court has declared unconstitutional a number of articles and laws adopted by both BSP-led and UDF-led coalition governments. In November 1996, for example, the court declared unconstitutional 15 provisions of the Radio and Television Act that had been passed under a BSP-led government. In November 1997, the court struck down a decision by the UDF-led government to appoint the directors of the state-run broadcast media prior to the passage of a new media law.

2. Does the constitutional framework provide for human rights? Do the human rights include business and property rights? The 1991 constitution emphasizes the protection of fundamental human rights. The constitution prohibits torture and cruel, inhuman, or degrading punishment; protects against arbitrary arrest and detention; and guarantees detainees immediate access to counsel. The constitution also guarantees freedoms of speech, press, assembly, association, religion, internal movement, and emigration. In addition, it guarantees the right to privacy and bars racial, ethnic, gender, and other forms of discrimination. It specifically protects economic freedom (Article 19) and the right to own property (Article 17).

A key human rights concern continues to be the conduct of the police, which, along with the Central Service for Combating Organized Crime, the National Security Service (a civilian intelligence organization), internal security troops, border guards, and special forces, are nominally under the control of the Ministry of the Interior. Police treatment of criminal suspects continues to include excessive force, which caused several deaths in 1997. In January 1997, the Vienna-based International Helsinki Federation (IHF) accused Bulgarian authorities of "premeditated" brutality after police clashed with anti-government demonstrators outside of the parliament and injured nearly 300 people. The IHF described the police crackdown as a "well-orchestrated attack" that "had the elements of being well-planned, organized, and coordinated," and included deployments of police from outside the capital.

Police frequently harass members of minority groups, particularly the Roma. A 1996 Human Rights Watch report documented police abuse of Roma street children.

The Kostov government replaced the leadership and management of most of the internal security services, but the police are still not under full civilian control and operate in a climate of near impunity. Although some cases of police abuse have been investigated, there have been few convictions, and most allegations of police abuse go unpunished.

3. Has there been basic reform of the criminal code/criminal law? Who authorizes searches and issues warrants? Are suspects and prisoners beaten and abused? Are there excessive delays in the criminal justice system? In July 1997, the UDF-dominated parliament amended the Criminal Code to decriminalize numerous acts that had been illegal. Parliament also amended several provisions pertaining to criminal procedure to promote speedier trials and added articles aimed at fighting corruption and organized crime. Earlier amendments included a provision allowing death sentences to be reduced to life imprisonment.

Police are required to obtain a warrant from a prosecutor prior to arresting a suspect. If the arrest was necessary to stop a criminal act, a judge must rule on the legality of the detention within 24 hours. In March 1997, the Council of Europe's Committee for the Prevention of Torture stated that Bulgarian police were responsible for incidents of torture of criminal suspects during interrogation or detention and expressed serious concern over conditions in National Security Service detention facilities. The report also cited "atrocious conditions" in Bulgarian psychiatric hospitals. There are persistent reports of police abuses of prisoners.

4. Do most judges rule fairly and impartially? Do many remain from the Communist era? Judges generally rule fairly and impartially. Nevertheless, the judiciary is understaffed, wages for judges are inadequate, cases are backlogged, and corruption is widespread. A 1997 Gallup survey found that two-thirds of Bulgarians do not trust the judiciary.

Procedural safeguards for a fair trial are generally adequate and are observed in practice. All courts conduct hearings in public unless the proceedings involve state secrets or national security. Defendants have the right to examine evidence, receive access to legal counsel, and know the charges against them. They also receive adequate time to prepare a defense and have the right to confront witnesses. The laws guarantee a right of appeal, which is widely used. Human rights groups, however, have criticized the so-called Labor Education Schools, to which juvenile offenders can be sent after proceedings that do not provide the right to an attorney and that limit other due process safeguards. Some critics have also expressed concern that the system of handling asylum claims does not conform to international standards. As a result, some individuals with a legitimate claim to refugee status may have been forcibly returned to their country of origin in violation of the internationally-accepted principle of *non-refoulement.*

Since most lawyers and judges were educated under the Communist regime, they are still significantly influenced by Marxist notions that stress the overriding interests of the state.

5. Are the courts free of political control and influence? Are the courts linked directly to the Ministry of Justice or any other executive body? Under the 1991 constitution, the judiciary is independent. In practice, the courts are free of political control and influence. Judges are appointed by the 25-member Supreme Judicial Council, gain tenure after three years, and can be removed only under limited circumstances. The Supreme Court of Cessation and the Supreme Administrative Court serve as the courts of final appeal. The Supreme Court of Cessation exercises judicial oversight over the application of the law by all courts. The Supreme Administrative Court oversees the application of the law in administrative decisions and rules on challenges to the legality of the Council of Ministers' Acts.

6. What proportion of lawyers is in private practice? How does this compare with the previous year? While precise figures are not available, most attorneys in Bulgaria are in private practice.

7. Does the state provide public defenders? The state is only required to provide public defenders in serious criminal cases.

8. Are there effective anti-bias/discrimination laws, including protection of ethnic minority rights? Article 6 of the constitution bans racial, ethnic, religious, gender, and other forms of discrimination. The constitution makes the study of the Bulgarian language compulsory for every citizen, although "citizens whose mother tongue is not Bulgarian shall have the right to study and use their own language."

Freedom of worship is generally respected, although the government regulates churches and religious institutions through the Directorate or Religious Beliefs. Eastern Orthodox Christianity is constitutionally enshrined as the "traditional" religion, and the government has refused to register a number of religious groups, including Jehovah's Witnesses. Unregistered groups face some discrimination and harassment by officials and the general population. For example, police have on occasion disrupted religious gatherings and services. Muslims and some other registered religious minorities also report discrimination. A 1994 law that tightened registration requirements stripped 39 mostly Protestant associations of their formal status as "juridicial entities."

The two largest ethnic minorities are ethnic Turks, who constitute approximately 8.5 percent of the population, and Roma, who constitute approximately 2.6 percent of the population. There are smaller numbers of Bulgarian Muslims. The Roma face high levels of discrimination in obtaining benefits and employment, occasional violent attacks, and harassment and abuse by the police. Ethnic minority groups are often among the first to be dismissed from jobs. Women also face discrimination in employment opportunities and are often placed in low-wage jobs relative to their skills.

The constitution forbids the creation of political parties on ethnic, racial, and religious lines. Nevertheless, the Constitutional Court has rejected attempts to dissolve the ethnically Turkish-based MRF. In 1990, the government formally ended what had been an official campaign of legal persecution and forced assimilation against the ethnic Turkish minority. In January 1990, the government granted amnesty to 31 people who had been imprisoned since 1984 for opposing the assimilation campaign. In March 1990, parliament passed legislation that allowed ethnic Turks and Bulgarian Muslims to return to their original names, which had been forcibly changed. In November 1990, the government abolished Article 273 of the Criminal Code, which had criminalized "spreading untrue allegations" that lead to a "dissatisfaction with the government" or "confusion within society," and other similarly vaguely worded offenses. It also declared an amnesty for those imprisoned under the law. Parliament also amended Article 109, which addresses "anti-state agitation and propaganda," so that the provision now only prohibits the advocacy of violence, "fascism, or other undemocratic ideologies." In December 1990, the rights of ethnic Turks to choose their own names, speak Turkish, and practice Islam were restored. Approximately 60 ethnic Turks who had been imprisoned for "treason and espionage" were freed. The assimilation campaign was officially recognized as an illegal act and a violation of basic human rights.

Human rights organizations have complained that local prosecutors and magistrates sometimes fail to pursue vigorously crimes committed against minorities.

Corruption C

1. What is the magnitude of official corruption in the civil service? Must an average citizen must pay a bribe to a bureaucrat in order to receive a service? What services are subject to bribe requests — for example, university entrance, hospital admission, telephone installation, obtaining a license to operate a business, applying for a passport or other official documents? What is the average salary of civil servants at various levels? It is sometimes necessary to offer bribes in order to obtain licenses, and bureaucrats often apply regulations in an arbitrary manner. Vague provisions in a 1996 law on health care make it unclear in many cases whether a patient has to pay for services. As a result, patients routinely have to bribe doctors. Until a 1997 crackdown by the caretaker government and its UDF successors, the customs service had been particularly notorious for its corruption. During one weekend sweep in June 1997, police investigated 1,000 customs officials at 49 border points and found 883 luxury limousines owned by guards.

2. Do top policy-makers (the President, ministers, vice-ministers, top court justices, the heads of agencies and commissions) have direct ties to businesses? How strong are such connections

and what kind of businesses are these? Top policy makers generally do not have direct ties to businesses, although government officials wield ultimate control of state-owned enterprises.

3. Do laws requiring financial disclosure and disallowing conflict of interest exist? Have publicized anti-corruption cases been pursued? To what conclusion? Laws requiring financial disclosure and disallowing conflict of interest are generally inadequate. The government has admitted that organized crime and corruption are now the country's biggest problems. Due to widespread fear of retaliation, however, it has convinced few citizens to report bribery and fraud. Accordingly, relatively few publicized anti-corruption cases have been pursued. Nevertheless, approximately 100 officials, including prosecutors and judges, were under investigation for corruption in 1997.

4. What major anti-corruption initiatives have been implemented? How often are anti-corruption laws and decrees adopted? The caretaker government that organized the 1997 parliamentary elections initiated Bulgaria's first major anti-corruption campaigns. It streamlined and improved the supervision of the allocation of subsidies to tobacco and wheat farmers. The previous BSP governments had allowed favored companies to reap profits from massive illegal exports that exploited the differential between subsidized domestic prices and world prices. In 1995, firms owned by close friends of BSP premier Zhan Videnov had exported enough wheat to cause a severe grain shortage for several weeks. In the winter of 1996-97, a poor harvest and illegal exports had caused bread shortages and a twenty-fold increase in bread prices.

Another initiative, known as "Operation Mosquito," authorized police to ask drivers of luxury cars how they achieved their wealth, organized several high-profile crackdowns on racketeering groups, and ordered the army to assist in the collection of customs dues. In March 1997 alone, the customs service collected as much revenue as it had during all of 1996. "Operation Mosquito" also dissolved a lucrative insurance racket.

The Kostov government has continued the anti-corruption crackdowns against customs officers. It has also dismissed many officials and re-organized the 16 regional departments of the Main Customs Administration into four administrative centers.

In February 1998, banks complied with a new Law on Bad Credits by publishing information on credit granted during the preceeding seven years to private and state-run companies that had not paid their debts. The lists revealed the names of dozens of "credit millionaires" who had borrowed huge sums of money with no intention of repayment and led to the resignation of Deputy Transportation Minister Kalcho Hinov, whose private firm had accumulated more than $2 million in unpaid debts. The government has also taken action against several directors of state-run companies after the private Multigroup company made a series of revelations about corruption in state enterprises with which the company had conducted business. Multigroup made the allegations to embarrass the government, which attempted to exclude the company from Russian gas import deals.

In another development, the Bulgarian National Security Service has been investigating the Bulgarian State Bank for allegedly funneling illegal loans to other banks. In 1997, the government established a special financial police unit to tackle this type of corruption. It anticipated that the unit would become operational in 1998, but opposition members of parliament are attempting to abolish the unit by claiming that represents the return of the "police state." Similarly, an attempt to give permanent status to parliament's Anti-Crime Commission has encountered resistance.

Corruption in the armed forces has become endemic. For example, a special audit in November 1997, found widespread fraud in Bulgaria's U.N. peacekeeping operations, in which officers were running private businesses and illegally appropriating food and vehicles. On December 18, 1997, Defense Minister Georgi Ananiev, Prosecutor General Ivan Tatarchev, and Chief Military Prosecutor Emil Karamfilov signed an agreement to cooperate in eliminating military corruption. Meanwhile, the police have made credible claims of corruption in the ranks of the state prosecutors.

Prime Minister Kostov has stated he will delay further privatization until the country's anti-corruption drive proves successful.

5. How do major corruption-ranking organizations such as Transparency International rate this country? Transparency International and other major corruption-ranking organizations have not rated Bulgaria.

Privatization 4/7

1. What percentage of the GDP comes from private ownership? What percentage of the labor force is employed in the private sector? How large is the informal sector of the economy? Before beginning its economic reforms, Bulgaria had one of the largest state economic sectors in the former Soviet bloc, with a private sector share of GDP of only 6.4 percent. By 1997, the private sector accounted for approximately 45 percent of GDP. The informal sector is considerable and includes much of the activity in construction, transportation, and agriculture. The government estimates that as much as one-third of the labor force is engaged in black market activity.

2. What major privatization legislation has been passed? What were its substantive features? Bulgaria's privatization process began with the adoption in 1992 of the Transformation and Privatization of State-Owned and Municipal Enterprises Law. The act introduced various privatization methods, including open-tenders, auctions, management buyouts, and negotiations with potential buyers. It provides for privatization decisions at three levels that are determined by the size of the enterprise to be privatized. Enterprises with assets of less than 70 million leva are privatized by the respective branch ministries. Those with assets between 70 and 200 million leva are privatized by a new Privatization Authority (PA). Enterprises with assets of more than 200 million leva are privatized by the Privatization Agency upon approval of the Council of Ministers. Privatization can also be initiated by the management and/or the employees of an enterprise. Municipal property is privatized by municipal privatization agencies, which have statutes similar to those of the national PA.

The actual privatization process began slowly. To accelerate the process, the government introduced a debt conversion scheme that provided investors with a further incentive to participate in the privatization process. Additional provisions, such as the rescheduling of payments within five years with a one-year grace period, were introduced in order to facilitate employee participation in the process.

In July 1994, parliament adopted amendments that served as the legal basis for mass privatization. Under the amendments, every Bulgarian citizen of age 18 or older is entitled to receive 25,000 investment bonds in the form of vouchers in each wave of mass privatization. Mass privatization officially began in January 1996, with the goal of privatizing 1,063 joint stock companies in proportions of equity ranging from 25 percent to 90 percent.

The transformation of state-owned property was also effected through the restitution of small-scale urban property, including apartment buildings, warehouses, workshops, and industrial enterprises, to their former owners under a 1992 Law on Restitution.

In July 1996, Bulgaria signed an emergency $582 million loan agreement with the IMF. Under the agreement, the country had to close 64 loss-making state enterprises and thereby sacrifice at least 40,000 jobs. The agreement also barred 71 other ailing state enterprises from further lending. Due to the low credibility of the Bulgarian government, the IMF insisted on a "pay-as-you-go" approach: Money would be forthcoming as additional firms were closed or barred from lending. The agreement followed the rejection by international financial institutions of earlier and more modest Bulgarian proposals to restructure and close enterprises. The government failed to comply with the agreement, and, in September 1996, the IMF suspended the second tranche of loans.

By the end of 1996, less than 10 percent of state enterprise assets had been sold, and the state sector remained in deep crisis. Analysts blamed the failed policies on an overall lack of political will to restructure; an inefficient court system that turned bankruptcy proceedings into a quagmire; collusion of lower-level ministers and the boards of state-owned enterprises in blocking any significant restructuring or bankruptcy proceedings for obsolete Communist-era enterprises; and difficulties in establishing real estate property rights due to frequent administrative changes. Other problems included the large debts of some of the enterprises, as well as the existence of unfinished products or non-durable assets.

The caretaker administration that succeeded the BSP government closed nearly all of the 64 insolvent companies that had been targeted under the now-defunct IMF Fund deal. The incoming Kostov government made privatization plans that prioritized simplicity and speed under straightforward valuation and administrative procedures. It also attempted to minimize the involvement of the managers of state firms. The 30 largest enterprises, including the Kremikovsti steel complex, as well as the state telecommunications and airline companies, are slated to be sold or closed. Companies that fail to find buyers by the end of 1998 will be liquidated. In August and September 1997, the government made a tender to foreign consulting firms of contracts to privatize 27 of these large companies.

The government intends to privatize smaller mining, manufacturing, and food processing companies under a less rigorous timetable. In order to encourage foreign investment and better management, it has opted for a Hungarian-style cash privatization program that will be combined with a mass privatization voucher scheme. The program will affect approximately 1,050 smaller companies with a total value of $943 million. By October 1997, approximately 43 percent of the assets of these smaller companies had been exchanged in three auctions for coupons held by citizens or managed for them by investment funds. In all, approximately 32 to 35 percent of long-term assets of state-owned enterprises had been privatized by the end of 1997. Meanwhile, the state Banking Consolidation Company has pledged to sell majority stakes in five remaining state-owned banks by the end of 1998.

3. What proportion of agriculture, housing and land, industry, and small business and ser-

vices is in private hands? In December 1997, the Privatization Agency announced that the total "financial effect" of privatization, including payments contracted, liabilities undertaken, and promised future investments, in the first eleven months of 1997 was $1.4 billion, or 49 percent of the $2.9 billion privatization effected since 1993.

Approximately 24 percent of workers are employed in agriculture. Private farming accounts for 44 percent of Bulgaria's land and 90 percent of its livestock. In 1996, agriculture contributed only 12.5 percent of GDP, in part because inefficient and neglected state cooperatives still accounted for most farm land. In addition, the tiny plots of land that a non-Communist government began to surrender to private farmers in 1992 were generally not condusive to modern agriculture. In 1998, Bulgaria expects to export 150,000 tons of wheat. As the privatization process continues, a growing number of small business and services are in private hands.

4. What has been the extent of insider (management, labor, and nomenklatura) participation in the privatization process? What explicit and implicit preferences have been awarded to insiders? Under the BSP government, insider participation in the privatization process had been extensive. The combination of a non-transparent privatization process and a poorly supervised banking system encouraged widespread asset-stripping and the growth of shadowy financial "groups" with ties to the BSP. Many assets of state-owned farming cooperatives were privatized by well-connected ex-Communists who paid below-market prices with interest-free state loans from banks that later became insolvent. With the means of production in their hands, some local *nomenklatura* then used their connections with the Ministry of Agriculture to export much of the output. In addition, the sale of collective farms profited mainly government insiders. Under the UDF government, observers report that the privatization process is far more transparent and equitable.

5. How much public awareness of and support for privatization has there been? What is the nature of support and opposition to privatization by major interest groups? In 1997, during the the third round of privatization auctions, the privatization funds did not conduct a substantial advertising campaign. In the earlier rounds, they had openly declared where and how they would make their investments. In general, the BSP continues to resist privatization efforts. Ordinary citizens seem generally favorably disposed to the process, as evidenced by their participation in the mass privatization process and their 1997 electoral support for the UDF-led coalition, which ran on a platform that included calls for major economic restructuring.

Macroeconomics 4/7

1. Has the taxation system been reformed? (What areas have and have not been overhauled? To what degree are taxpayers complying? Is tax compliance difficult to achieve? Has the level of revenues increased? Is the revenue collection body overburdened? What is the overall tax burden?) Post-1989 governments have adopted a Tax Administration Code, an excise tax (1994), and a value added tax (1994). These reforms — particularly the introduction of the VAT — came later than in other formerly Communist countries. Tax compliance is not at satisfactory levels, and the Kostov government has taken enforcement measures — including increases in fines, penalty interest on overdue tax payments, and tightened control over border crossing-posts. Much tax avoidance involves manipulation of the VAT, particularly by exporters who invent fictitious goods and receive a tax credit.

The top income tax rate is 50 percent. The average income bracket is taxed at 20 percent – a decrease from 33 percent in 1996. The top corporate tax rate is 36 percent. The 1996 rate was 40 percent. The government plans to raise taxes for professionals and private sector workers and lower corporate taxation rates in 1998. It also intends to seek passage of an omnibus income tax law in 1999. It has also suggested that, after further financial stabilization, the VAT rate could be lowered.

2. Does fiscal policy encourage private savings, investment and earnings? (Has there been any reform/alteration of revenue and budget policies? How large are budget deficits and overall debt? Is the financing of the social insurance/pension system sustainable? What proportion of the budget is taken up by subsidies to firms and individuals?) The macro-economic policy of the BSP government led to the most severe financial crisis in Bulgaria in the post-Communist period. In 1996 and early 1997, the government's delays and mismanagement in implementing reforms in the banking and financial sector caused the lev to collapse and sent consumer prices soaring. In November 1996, the IMF proposed that a currency board be established to boost confidence in the economy and stabilize exchange rates. The BSP government rejected the proposal.

By this point, Bulgaria had failed to honor five previous IMF agreements. In April 1997, the interim government signed a one-year, $510 million stand-by accord with the IMF. When it assumed power, the UDF vowed to demand fiscal austerity and to establish credibility with international markets and lending institutions. In June 1997, parliament approved an austere budget. The move was part of a new IMF deal that was linked to the implementation of a currency board. With the introduction of the board and other stabilization measures, inflation fell from 484.2 percent for the first half of 1997 to 3.7 percent in July. In the last months of 1997, the rate stood at approximately about 1 percent per month on an annualized basis. In January 1998, it rose to 2.1 percent on an annualized basis. The fiscal deficit fell from 13.4 percent of GDP in 1996 to an estimated 2.6 percent in 1997.

The government is attempting to create a sustainable social welfare system. The current system relies on subsidies from the IMF, the World Bank, and the European Union. Of 8.4 million Bulgarians, approximately 2.5 million are pensioners. When the BSP government fell in February 1997, pensioners' benefits barely bought a loaf of bread a day. The average monthly pension reached $22.50 in April 1997. In December, with support from a $40 million World Bank loan, it reached $34 million. The government has also raised unemployment benefits to help the growing number of Bulgarians who have lost their jobs with the closure of bankrupt state enterprises. Public employees and workers in state-owned companies who are dismissed can choose between a lump-sum compensation and a monthly unemployment benefit. The 1997 budget allocated 27 percent of expenditures to social spending.

3. Has there been banking reform? (Is the central bank independent? What are its responsibilities? Is it effective in setting and/or implementing monetary policy? What is the actual

state of the private banking sector? Does it conform to international standards? Are depositors protected?) Under communism, all banking functions were performed by the Bulgarian National Bank (BNB), which was controlled by the Council of Ministers. The responsibilities of the BNB were limited to central banking and supervisory functions, including formulating and implementing monetary and credit policy, issuing bank notes, regulating bank activities, and ensuring the stability of the banking system. In practice, the BNB was only nominally independent, and the government's financial mismanagement led to a severe banking crisis.

Upon taking office in 1997, the Kostov government backed the IMF's November 1996, proposal for the establishment of a currency board to stabilize the lev, curb inflation, and boost currency reserves. In June 1997, parliament passed the Bulgarian National Bank Act, which included the legislation to initiate the currency board and mechanisms for banking supervision. Under the act, the restructured BNB cannot make loans to banks except in cases in which the stability of the banking system is threatened. Even then, the loans must be under very strict terms. In addition, the bank can no longer print money to finance government budget deficits or save loss-making state enterprises.

The currency board took effect on July 1, 1997, with the support of more than $1 billion from the IMF and the World Bank. By fixing the exchange rate at 1000 levs to the German *mark* and linking the volume of currency in circulation to the level of hard currency reserves, the currency board essentially removed monetary policy from the hands of the central bank.

In 1992, in the commercial banking sector, parliament passed the Law on Banks and Credit Activities which defined the range of financial transactions banks are licensed to operate, opened the banking sector to some foreign participation, and regulated the formation of shareholders' capital in a commercial bank. The government established a Bank Consolidation Company (BCC) to merge the large number (73 percent in 1991) of undercapitalized state-owned banks into a smaller number of stronger ones that would ultimately be privatized.

The BSP-led government's financial mismanagement was most obvious in the banking sector. Loose banking supervision allowed savings to be directed towards shadowy financial-industrial "groups," which had the effect of bankrupting several banks. In 1996, the country's foreign reserves declined dramatically due to poor export performance and the need to intervene on the domestic foreign exchange market to support the lev. As annual inflation reached 1,200 percent, many citizens simply took their money out of the banks. Under IMF pressure, the BNB closed 14 of the country's 35 banks, including five state-owned institutions, and began to consolidate and recapitalize the banking sector. By then, however, the banking system had virtually collapsed, as most of the banks still in operation were minor ones with severe liquidity problems.

The Kostov government is signing management contracts with foreign financial institutions to privatize the six state banks for privatization by the end of 1998. By early in the year, however, only the United Bulgarian Bank had been sold. Some analysts hold that the slow progress is due to disagreements between the IMF and the BCC over privatization methods. The IMF wants the BCC to focus more on attracting strategic investors than on raising funds for privatization through the stock exchange.

As part of its IMF deal, the government is also instituting international lending and supervisory standards in the banking industry. For example, it is forcing banks to adhere to the 8-percent capital adequacy ratio, a figure that will be increased to 12 percent by the end of 1998, as required under the Bank of International Settlement regulations. In October 1997, parliament passed the Law on Bad Credits, which mandated public disclosure of bank information regarding credit granted, but not re-paid during the past seven years to private and state-run companies. In February 1998, the banks complied by publishing the names of dozens of "credit millionaires" who had received huge loans with no intention of repaying them. In general, bank lending is down as banks try to avoid the profligate practices of the past. In addition, most banks have only been able to lend on a short-term basis since the bulk of their deposit base has been in short-term accounts. Banks are able to set their own deposit and loan rates.

The Kostov government has initiated deposit guarantees that allow small savers to retrieve the full amount of funds that were frozen when banks began to close in 1996.

4. How sound is the national currency? (Is the value of the currency fixed or does it float? How convertible is the currency? How large are the hard currency reserves? Has the exchange rate policy been stable and predictable?) Under the BSP government, financial mismanagement and crony capitalism drove the lev from a rate of 70 to the U.S. dollar at the beginning of 1996 to 645 by year's end. Inflation soared to 310 percent during the year and threatened to wipe out the average Bulgarian's meager savings. As the financial crisis worsened and political uncertainty mounted, the lev plunged to 3,000 to the U.S. dollar in February 1997. The BSP government's futile efforts to defend it depleted foreign reserves to approximately $400 million.

In mid-1997, the currency board pegged the currency at a rate of 1,000 lev to the German *mark*. The currency is now fully convertible, and the domestic currency supply is linked to the level of hard currency reserves. As of December 19, 1997, hard currency reserves stood at $1.3 billion, and the country was able to meet its foreign debt obligations. In general, the currency board has re-monetarized the economy and renewed economic growth. Due to the perceived stability of the currency, the benchmark interest rate fell from 42.4 percent in June to approximately 6 percent. Inflation has also been curbed, with prices rising only 2.2 percent in September 1997.

5. Is there a functioning capital market infrastructure? (Are there existing or planned commodities, bond, and stock markets? What are the mechanisms for investing and lending? What government bodies have authority to regulate capital markets?) In 1992, authorities created an interbank exchange market, which increased liquidity in the banking system. The primary securities market began to developed in 1990, when the first state securities were sold to the public. By the end of 1993, the government had issued three-, six-, and nine-month treasury bills, notes, and bonds. It had also issued long-term treasury bonds. The number of non-bank financial institutions, such as financial and brokerage houses and foreign exchange centers, grew quickly as a result of a liberal licensing policy.

Two local stock exchanges began to operate in 1992. By 1995, there were seven local bourses. Also in 1995, parliament adopted the Securities, Stock Exchanges, and Investment Companies Law, and a newly-created Securities and Exchange Commission began its regulatory activities. Bulgaria's first national stock exchange opened in Sofia on October 21, 1997. Financial authorities plan to tap into international capital markets with a $200 million inaugural Eurobond offering in 1998.

Microeconomics 4.25/7

1. Are property rights guaranteed? (Are there both formal and de facto protections of private real estate and intellectual property? Is there a land registry with the authority and capability to ensure accurate recording of who owns what? What are the procedures for expropriation, including measures for compensation and challenge? Have any seizures taken place? Private property is formally protected, and, in general, private property rights are respected in practice and enforced by the judiciary. Article 17 of the constitution states that "private property shall be inviolable." Other laws regulating property rights include the Ownership Law of 1990, which was last amended in 1996; the 1991 Law on Ownership and Use of Agricultural Land and subsequent amendments; the State Ownership Law of 1996; and the Municipal Ownership Law of 1996.

According to the laws on restitution and privatization, there are two ways of returning property to its original owners. First, if the estates have been preserved in their original form, the property right is restored entirely and immediately. Second, if the estates have been altered or incorporated into larger units, the former owners are entitled to compensation.

Foreign investors may own buildings and hold limited property rights over immovable property. Foreign persons acting in the capacity of local persons may acquire any land except arable land. Businesses with foreign participation may not own arable land, regardless of the share of foreign participation.

Under land reforms in the early 1990s, small parcels that averaged less than 2.5 hectares were returned to their pre-Communist owners and heirs. Nevertheless, only a small percentage of owners received official titles to their land. By October 1997, 70 percent of the 5.8 million hectares of land made available to private owners had been distributed, while only 18 percent of owners had received official titles. The remainder received temporary titles that could be contested in the courts. This has prevented the development of a land market and the offering of long-term leases to farming companies. Moreover, according to the U.S. Department of State, rural Roma are often discouraged from claiming land to which they are entitled under a law disbanding agricultural collectives. The Declaration of National Salvation approved by the new, UDF-dominated parliament in May 1997, made the return of all land to its rightful owners a high priority.

Laws nominally protect intellectual property, however, lax enforcement has spawned an industry for pirated computer software and music tapes. Western experts say that Bulgaria is second only to China in illegal production of music and video discs, compact discs, and computer software. Observers stated that only 10 percent of compact discs produced in Bulgaria are legal.

In March 1998, under a growing threat of American trade sanctions, the government closed all compact disk workshops, sealed production lines, established a special police unit to monitor the lines, and forced the workshops that sought to resume production to obtain licenses. On March 23, the Industry Ministry granted licenses to the first two companies under the new scheme. Although early indications were positive, the police presence will be too expensive to maintain permanently, and it is too early to determine whether the government's actions will be successful.

2. To what extent have prices been liberalized? What subsidies remain? In 1997, the interim government and the incoming UDF-led government broadly liberalized prices. In April, the interim government liberalized all prices except for select items such as wheat flour, bread, cooking oil, certain meats, cow's cheese, milk, road and rail transportation fares, and drinking water. On July 1, the Kostov government freed prices for wheat flour, bread, milk, meat, long-life salamis, cooking oil, butter, hard cheese, eggs, and sugar, but restricted traders from selling these products at prices higher than those marked on the packaging by the manufacturer. Prices for several commodities, including electricity, heating, domestic coal, postal services, and tobacco products, are still controlled.

3. Is it possible to own and operate a business? (Has there been legislation regarding the formation, dissolution, and transfer of businesses, and is the law respected? Do there exist overly cumbersome bureaucratic hurdles that effectively hinder the ability to own and dispose of a business? Are citizens given access to information on commercial law? Is the law applied fairly? Does the regulation (or do licensing requirements) impose significant costs on business and consumers? Do they create significant barriers to entry and seriously hamper competition?) Individuals may own and operate a business. Since 1991, several laws regulating the operations of business have been adopted. They include the Accountancy Law; the Protection of Competition Law; the Commercial Code; the Law on Business Activity of Foreign Persons; the Law on Banking and Credit Activities; the Transformation and Privatization of State-Owned and Municipal-Owned Enterprises Act; the Value-Added Tax Law; the Settlement Law; the Chamber of Accounts Law; and the Concessions Law. Citizens have full access to commercial law, and the courts respect and apply these laws fairly.

Although bureaucratic inefficiency imposes delays in the launch of a new business, difficulties in obtaining working capital constitute a greater problem. According to the Bulgarian Business Association, a prospective independent businessman needs basic start-up capital of approximately $5,000. With registration, legal fees, and other expenses, it costs approximately $8,500 to launch a small business such as a bakery. In addition, obtaining bank credit has become exceedingly difficult. By law, the minimum security for a bank loan is 80 percent. Burdened by bad debt, however, many banks demand up to 125 percent in security.

4. Are courts effective, transparent, efficient, and quick in reaching decisions on property and contract disputes? What alternative mechanisms for adjudicating disputes exist? Bulgarian courts are plagued by corruption and are characterized by poor administrative capacity, low salaries for judges and other officials, and significant backlogs. While their proceedings are generally transparent, they are also inefficient and often slow to reach decisions on property and contract disputes. There are few alternative mechanisms for adjudicating disputes.

5. Is business competition encouraged? (Are monopolistic practices limited in law and practice? If so, how? To what degree is "insider" dealing a hindrance to open competition? Are government procurement policies open and unbiased?) In 1991, parliament passed the Law on Protection of Competition to "guarantee the conditions necessary for free enterprise in manufacturing, trade and service, for a free determining of prices, and for the protection of consumers' interests." The law forbids "abuse with a monopoly position in the market, unfair competition, and other acts which could lead to restriction on competition in Bulgaria." The Law established an independent Commission for the Protection of Competition with regulatory and enforcement powers.

Nevertheless, insider dealing under BSP governments significantly hindered open competition. For example, managers of state food-processing plants often bought exclusively from private trading firms controlled by other nomenklatura. The trade firms were able to set prices so low that farmers were trapped in what one correspondent referred to as "nomenklatura feudalism." By contrast, the UDF government has strongly encouraged and enforced competition, and the business environment has improved markedly. Similarly, government procurement policies are increasingly open and unbiased.

6. To what extent has international trade been liberalized? To what degree has there been simplification/overhaul of customs and tariff procedures, and are these applied fairly? What informal trade barriers exist? In late 1989, the government abolished the Communist state's monopoly over foreign trade. All state-owned, municipal, cooperative, and private firms, including those with foreign participation, received direct access to international markets and the right to trade abroad independently or jointly with other firms. In December 1996, Bulgaria became a member of the World Trade Organization. In July 1997, the government eliminated a ban on agricultural produce exports.

In 1997, as part of its efforts to eliminate corruption and boost revenues, the government cracked down on rogue customs agents and incorporated the 16 regional departments of the Main Customs Administration into four regional centers. The average tariff rate is 17.97 percent. U.S. government agencies do not report any informal barriers.

7. To what extent has foreign investment and capital flow been encouraged or constrained? Under the BSP government, foreign investors had complained of inconsistencies in the application of legislation and of delays in privatization and other market reforms. The UDF-led government strongly encourages foreign investment and has taken numerous measures to improve the overall business climate, including the establishment of a currency board, fiscal austerity measures, and a renewed emphasis on privatization. There are no outright restrictions on foreign ownership, the foreign investment code generally is not restrictive, and the government has eliminated local content requirements for goods and services. Foreign investors are also eligible for some tax incentives. Nevertheless, investors still cite a lack of bureaucratic transparency as a considerable constraint on foreign investment. Some Western companies have also reported demands for bribes and kickbacks.

Foreign direct investment (FDI) during 1997 totaled $502 million, or nearly 39 percent of the 1.293 billion FDI since 1992. With $261.8 million invested since 1992, Germany is the largest single investor.

8. Has there been reform of the energy sector? (To what degree has the energy sector been restructured? Is the energy sector more varied, and is it open to private competition? Is the country overly dependent on one or two other country for energy [including whether exported

fuels must pass through one or more countries to reach markets|?) There has been only modest restructuring of the energy sector. After 1990, Bulgaria no longer had access to cheap energy from the Soviet Union. In 1996 and early 1997, the collapse of the lev caused huge losses for the state-owned Neftohim refinery, which lacked the cash to pay suppliers. Fuel shortages forced many petrol stations to close.

In 1997, as a first phase of restructuring, the interim government lifted energy prices to world levels, imposed a minimum commercial margin of 4 percent for distributors of natural gas, and transferred the National Electricity Company to the control of the state council of ministers. The UDF government, while constrained by Russia's considerable leverage as Bulgaria's sole supplier of natural gas, has sought to use the country's strategic location as a link between Russian and Caspian oil fields and foreign markets to secure more favorable terms for domestic gas deliveries. On several occasions since October 1997, authorities have stated that they had finalized a ten-year deal for the delivery of Russian gas on a commercial basis. The deal, between Gazexport, the export arm of Russian gas monopoly Gazprom, and Bulgargas, the Bulgarian state-owned gas company, would mark a departure from state-to-state deals, and exclude Multigroup and several other powerful private Bulgarian firms that have reaped huge windfalls from serving as intermediaries between Gazexport and the Bulgarian government. The deal has been repeatedly scuttled at the last minute. One reported reason is that Gazexport is under pressure from Russian officials to link the deal to changes in Bulgaria's pro-Western foreign policy. Another is that Multigroup is undermining the deal.

The Kostov government linked the gas agreement to talks on a proposed new pipeline that will pump 16 to 25 billion cubic meters of gas per year from Russia to western Turkey via Bulgaria and other countries. The Bulgarian leg of the pipeline will be wholly financed by transit fees for the gas. The government is also seeking alternative suppliers of oil and gas, including a proposed pipeline that would transport Turkmenistan gas to Turkey and Europe that would include branches to Bulgaria and other regional countries. Another option under consideration is the use of Bulgaria as a transit route for Azerbaijani oil.

The government plans to begin the privatization of the electricity industry in 1998. The first step in the restructuring of the state-owned National Electricity Company (NEC) will be to transfer low and medium voltage distribution networks to municipalities, which will be able to lease them to companies. The next stage will be to privatize small hydroelectric power plants and two thermoelectric plants. The remaining thermoelectric plants will then be privatized. The NEC will retain ownership of Bulgaria's sole nuclear power plant, one hydroelectric plant, and the high-voltage transmission networks.

CROATIA

Freedom in the World Ratings, 1989-1998

	1989-90	1990-91	1991-92	1992-93	1993-94	1994-95	1995-96	1996-97	1997-98
Political Rights	-	-	3	4	4	4	4	4	4
Civil Liberties	-	-	4	4	4	4	4	4	4
Status	-	-	PF	PF	PF	PF	PF	PF	PF

Polity: Transitional
Economy: Transitional
Population: 4,495,000
PPP: $3,972
Ethnic Groups: Pre-1995: Croat (77 percent), Serb (12 percent), Muslim (1 percent), Hungarian, Slovene, Czech, Albanian, Montenegrin, Ukrainian, others
Capital: Zagreb

Political Process 4.25/7

1. When did national legislative elections occur? Were they free and fair? How were they judged by domestic and international election monitoring organizations? Who composes the government? The Croatian parliament (*Sabor*) is divided into a lower house, the House of Representatives (*Zastupnicki dom*), and an upper house, the House of Districts (*Zupanijski dom*). The Croatian Democratic Union (HDZ) has dominated the Croatian political scene since the first free multiparty elections in April 1990. The HDZ became active several months before the 1990 elections but quickly acquired the character of a national movement for independence. In so doing, it mobilized the support of much of the Croatian diaspora, as well as a substantial portion of the domestic population.

The party incorporates a wide range of opinions from liberal to extreme nationalist, but the leadership has tended to be vehemently nationalist and anti-Communist. Franjo Tudjman, the party's president, and other HDZ leaders were themselves former Communists who fell out of favor with the Communist leadership. The party sealed control of parliament by winning a majority of seats in the House of Representatives in the August 1992 elections. It won control of the House of Regions in the February 1993 elections.

In 1995, the HDZ-led government capitalized on its success by re-taking military control of the Serb-occupied Krajina and Western Slavonia and announcing parliamentary elections for the lower house. In September 1995, parliament dissolved itself and paved the way for new elections. In the October 29 vote, the HDZ won 75 of 127 seats, and the center-right Croatian Social Liberal Party (HSLS), the nation's second largest party, won 12. Ten other parties won seats. In failing to win the two-thirds of lower-house seats required to amend the constitution, Tudjman was deprived of the opportunity to increase his presidential powers.

On November 7, 1995, Tudjman appointed a single-party HDZ government under Prime Minister Zlatko Matesa.

International observers, including the OSCE, cited such irregularities as legal and regulatory abuses related to electoral law and campaign access. An electoral law that was hastily presented to parliament and then passed with little debate in September 1995 was criticized by opposition leaders for favoring the HDZ. The law reduced the number of seats in the lower house from 138 to 127. Of these, 80 are to be elected by party lists, and 28 are to be elected by a direct district vote. The law also gave Croats living abroad a special franchise of nearly 10 percent of the seats in parliament. The franchise included ethnic Croats born and residing in Bosnia, but excluded ethnic Serbs who were born in Croatia and living as refugees in Serb-controlled areas. In addition, the new law increased the party threshold for gaining a seat in parliament from 3 percent to 5 percent of the total vote.

Reported irregularities in the election included arbitrary and non-transparent changes in constituency boundaries, restrictions on criticism of the government in the state-run media, and flawed election administration, including inaccurate and outdated voter lists.

In a recent memorandum on the Completion of the Peaceful Integration of Eastern Slavonia, the Croatian government announced that Croatian Serbs who were not living in Eastern Slavonia in 1991, but who had lived in another part of Croatia, i.e., refugees from Krajina and Western Slavonia would be entitled to vote.

On April 13, 1997, Croatia held elections for the Sabor and for municipal and county councils. The HDZ won 40 of 63 seats in the Sabor, while a coalition of the HSLS and the Croatian Peasants Party (HSS), which is the country's oldest political party and generally represents farmers, won 12. Seven other parties shared the remaining 11 seats. According to the OSCE, the clear bias of the state-run broadcast media toward the HDZ, and the party's regular attempts to control the print media limited the degree to which these elections could be considered free and fair.

2. When did presidential elections occur? Were they free and fair? In the presidential election on June 15, 1997, President Tudjman easily defeated Zdravko Tomac of the former Communist Social Democratic Party (SDP) by a margin of 61 percent to 21 percent. HSLS candidate Vlado Gotovac received 17.6 percent of the vote. Voter turnout was 57 percent.

International monitors denounced the election as severely biased. The OSCE characterized it "free, but not fair" and stated that it "did not meet minimum standards for democracies." Critics noted that national television and radio networks are tightly controlled by the HDZ and did not allow access to opposition candidates. They also reported that the HDZ-controlled electoral commission rejected all opposition complaints, including the HSLS's contention that its monitors were barred from several polling stations.

Previous elections in 1992 were determined by the Council of Europe to have been free and fair.

There is a constitutional limit of two terms for Croatia's president. Tudjman, however, may be eligible to run for a third term since his first, abbreviated two-year term began prior to the promulgation of the constitution on December 22, 1990.

3. Is the electoral system multiparty-based? Are there at least two viable political parties

functioning at all levels of government? The constitution guarantees a multiparty electoral system. Opposition parties compete with the HDZ; nine other parties are represented in parliament, although the HDZ dominates both houses.

The HDZ also dominates local government, with noticeable exceptions in Rijeka and Zagreb, where opposition parties have been in a bitter dispute for control of the city council since 1995. To date, Tudjman has rejected four of the opposition's nominees for mayor.

4. How many parties have been legalized? Are any particular parties illegal? More than 60 parties function legally in Croatia. The main political parties represented in parliament are the HDZ; the HSLS; the HSS; the SDP; the Croatian Independent Democrats, which was founded by HDZ dissidents in 1994; the Croatian Party of Rights (HSP), an extreme right-wing party; the Croatian People's Party, which was founded by former Communist dissidents active in the Croatian autonomy movement; the Serbian Democratic Party (SDS), which represents extreme Serbian nationalists; the Serbian People's Party (SNS), which represents Serbs who seek participation in the political life in Croatia), and the Istrian Democratic Assembly (IDA).

5. What proportion of the population belongs to political parties? Political parties must have at least 100 members and register with the Ministry of Administration. Parties are not required to report the number of members, so it is difficult to estimate the number of people actually belonging to a party. A 1994 survey of 24 parties conducted by the Croatian Central Bureau of Statistics showed a total membership of 726,531, with nine of the parties having a membership level of between 5000 and 10,000 people. Only one party has more than 100,000 members. The statistics do not specify by party.

6. What has been the trend of voter turnout at the municipal, provincial, and national levels in recent years? Turnout in the April 1997 elections for municipal councils and the House of Counties was slightly more than 71 percent statewide. In the June 1997 presidential election, turnout was 57 percent. In the October 1995 parliamentary elections, 68.8 percent voted. In the February 1993 elections for the House of Regions, voter turnout was 62.6 percent. Turnout in the 1992 presidential election was 75.6 percent.

Civil Society 3.50/7

1. How many non-governmental organizations (NGOs) have come into existence since 1988? What is the number of charitable/nonprofit organizations? Are there locally led efforts to increase philanthropy and volunteerism? What proportion of the population is active in private voluntary activity (from polling data)? There are approximately 4,000 non-governmental organizations, social organizations, and citizens associations in Croatia.

Since the war began in 1991, hundreds of NGOs have come into existence to meet the psychological and social needs of approximately 700,000 to 800,000 Croatian war victims. In addition, human rights, anti-war, and women's advocacy organizations document and publicize human rights abuses in Croatia as well as challenge government policies. Chief among these organizations are the Croatian Helsinki Committee for Human Rights; the Anti-war Campaign; the Group for Direct

Protection of Human Rights; the Dalmatian Solidarity Committee; and the Center for Peace, Nonviolence, and Human Rights. While many of these organizations were initially based in Zagreb, they have managed to build strong foundations and expand their own operations or offer technical and administrative support to local groups throughout Croatia, including Eastern Slavonia and formerly Serb-occupied Knin. Since NGOs did not exist in the Communist era the concept is still relatively new and misunderstood in Croatia. Some segments of society and the government equate "non-governmental" with "anti-government" or "anti-Croatian." The government has denounced human rights activities as "anti-national," and cases of physical attacks against activists have been reported.

2. What is the legal and regulatory environment for NGOs (i.e., ease of registration, legal rights, government regulation, taxation, procurement, and access-to-information issues)? To what extent is NGO activism focused on improving the legal and regulatory environment? A new Law of Associations was passed in June 1997 to replace its 1994 predecessor. The law regulates the founding, registration, duties, and administrative aspects of NGOs, social organizations, and citizens' associations. With this legislation, the government gave itself broad supervisory powers to monitor all aspects of existing associations and prevent others from being formed. For example, the activities of an association may be suspended if there is a "well founded" suspicion that its activities violate the constitution or any law. Until the association proves itself innocent in a court of law, the government can keep it closed indefinitely and appoint someone to manage and dispose of the association's property.

Financial contributions to NGOs are heavily taxed at a rate of 35 percent, although organizations financed through the state budget remain tax-exempt. The employees of NGOs are also heavily taxed.

Cooperation among NGOs is limited. This diminishes the organizations' ability to work collectively to improve their legal and regulatory environment. Nevertheless, more than 100 NGOs united in 1996 in a campaign to amend the draft Law on Associations. Although the effort was largely unsuccessful, it received media coverage, increased public awareness, and demonstrated the ability of NGOs to cooperate when they perceive a sufficient need.

3. What is the organizational capacity of NGOs? Do management structures clearly delineate authority and responsibility? Is information available on NGO management issues in the native language? Is there a core of experienced practitioners/trainers to serve as consultants or mentors to less developed organizations? According to a report by the Winston Foundation for World Peace, Croatian NGOs operate with less formal organizational development than those in the West. Most NGOs are headed by one or two motivated and well-connected people with a small support staff and/or several volunteers. The Center for the Development of Non-Profit Organizations, a resource center for NGO development issues, gathers information on legislation, funding, and other matters relevant to NGO work.

Leaders of NGOs often believe that they lack shared issues on which to cooperate. As a major human rights NGO, the Croatian Helsinki Committee for Human Rights (CHC) might be expected to offer training and support to smaller organizations with similar mandates. The CHC, however, is criticized for non-cooperation with such groups. Foreign efforts to provide training and guidance to less developed NGOs have been criticized for perpetuating the disempowerment of indigenous organizations and for failing to develop effective NGO leadership. These "quick fix" efforts often lack the commitment and sustained effort necessary to benefit the participants involved.

4. Are NGOs financially viable? What is their tax status? Are they obliged to and do they typically disclose revenue sources? Do government procurement opportunities exist for private, non-for-profit providers of services? NGOs have difficulty obtaining funding from local sources, mainly due to unfavorable social and economic conditions in Croatia. Leading sources of funding include the Open Society Institute, U.S. AID, and U.N. and other international governmental agencies. European governments and development agencies often sponsor one-time efforts such as public discussions and conferences. International private foundations provide support to a number of smaller NGOs.

If non-profit organizations lease offices or other premises, they are obliged to pay the value-added tax (VAT) on services at the rate of 10 percent. On January 1, 1998, a new VAT law entered into force with a universal rate of 22 percent for non-profit organizations. The rate on services is expected to increase from 10 to12 percent.

5. Are there free trade unions? How many workers belong to these unions? Is the number of workers belonging to trade unions growing or decreasing? What is the numerical/proportional membership of farmers' groups, small business associations, etc.? Article 43 of the constitution guarantees all workers the right to form or join trade unions. Article 60 guarantees the right to strike to all workers except those employed in the armed forces, the police, government administration, and public services. Croatia's labor movement includes five major labor confederations and several large unaffiliated unions. The five major confederations are the Union of Autonomous Trade Unions of Croatia (SSSH), the broadest entity, which claims 629,000 members in 26 branches and 81 territorial offices; the Association of Trade Unions of Croatia, which is the SSSH's main nationwide competitor and which claims 210,000 members in 210 enterprise unions and 10 branch unions in many commercial sectors; the Confederation of Independent Trade Unions of Croatia, which was organized in 1990 as a "more democratic" alternative to the SSSH and which claims 40,000 members; the Coordinating Council of Professional and Public Employees, which represents approximately 66,000 workers; and the Association of Trade Unions of Public Servants of Croatia, which has 26,000 members in higher education and science.

Despite Croatia's economic troubles and the recent increase in government repression against journalists, unions, and other civic groups, the trade union movement in Croatia constitutes a significant economic and political force. Trade unions have been very active in responding to high unemployment, rising inflation, and low average real wages.

In May 1997, union, government, and employer representatives signed an agreement to establish the Economic-Social Council (GSV), a tripartite body that addresses economic and social development policies. The GSV will be comprised of 18 members. Within one year, elections will be held to establish the representation of trade unions.

Trade unions are generally independent of the government and political parties. The HSS, however, is closely affiliated with farmers and fishermen and has actively participated in organizing farmers' demonstrations in protest against food imports, smuggling, and high commodity prices.

A new Labor Code was passed in 1995 and took effect on January 1, 1996. The code, which is supported by unions, revised the statutes governing collective bargaining contracts, protection for striking workers, and legal limitations on the ability of employers to bar employees during trade disputes. Under the code, unions may challenge firings in court, and illness may no longer be used to justify firings. Nevertheless, unions continue to complain of government threats to employees involved in labor disputes and of the replacement of strikers with new workers.

Farmers' interests are represented by the Croatian Peasants' Party. Craftsmen and workers in other small businesses of, in general, less than 200 employees are represented by the Croatian Chamber for Crafts and Small Businesses, a voluntary organization with a membership of approximately 85,000.

6. What forms of interest group participation in politics are legal? What types of interest groups are active in the political and policy process? Article 42 of the constitution guarantees the right to public protest. Article 42 protects "free association for the purposes of protection of interests or promotion of social, economic, political, national, cultural, and other convictions and objectives." Article 46 guarantees the right to "submit petitions and complaints, to make proposals to government and other public bodies." In practice, the government is responsive and accountable to citizens' protests only when they reach proportions that directly threaten government control.

In January 1997, several thousand railway workers launched the only significant strike of the year. In April, 2,000 textile workers organized a mass demonstration in Zagreb to demand collective negotiations with the government and the development of a long-term strategy for the industry. Labor unions held various assemblies and demonstrations, as did associations of war veterans, pensioners, and the families of persons missing from the war.

7. How is the not-for-profit/NGO sector perceived by the public and government officials? What is the nature of media coverage of NGOs? To what extent do government officials engage with NGOs? The government generally views NGOs with skepticism, and often with hostility, as governmental agencies perceive NGO work to be in competition with their own. Legislation such as the new Law of Associations is illustrative of the desire by government officials to exert control over the work of NGOs. According to the Winston Foundation for World Peace, the usual government response to NGOs is to ignore them. The result of this response is poor integration of public social services with NGO work.

NGOs rarely receive coverage in the media, which generally report on political and economic issues with a pro-HDZ bias and have little interest in providing information on human rights issues and the development of civil society. The limited coverage of NGOs and their work tends to be negative and critical.

Independent Media 4.75/7

1. Are there legal protections for press freedom? The constitution guarantees freedom of thought, expression, the press, and other media. In an October 1996, attempt to meet the Council of Europe's minimum standards for press freedom, Croatia's parliament passed a law to protect journalists from demands that they reveal their sources and from criminal charges in cases in which they publish false information unintentionally. Nevertheless, existing provisions prescribing fines and imprisonment for reporters who insult top state officials have been retained.

Electronic media are governed by the Law on Telecommunications. The Committee for Telecommunications, which grants broadcasting licenses, is appointed by parliament. Six of the committee's nine members are high-ranking members of the ruling party, two are cabinet members, and one is a special adviser to President Tudjman.

2. Are there legal penalties for libeling officials? Are there legal penalties for "irresponsible" journalism? Have these laws been enforced to harass journalists? In 1991, libel and the publication of state secrets were abolished as criminal offenses under the Penal Code, but parliament reinstated the provisions in two amendments in March 1996. One amendment provides for the punishment of persons who offend or slander the president, Speaker of Parliament, Prime Minister, or presidents of the supreme or constitutional courts. The other amendment criminalizes the publication of classified information "vital to state interests," a term which is not clearly defined. The penalties for such offenses include jail terms of six months to three years.

These laws are widely enforced in order to minimize critical coverage of the government. As of March 1998, approximately 500 libel suits were reportedly pending before the Croatian courts. Most were filed by HDZ members. In a particularly notable case, an editor and reporter from *Feral Tribune*, a satirical weekly newspaper, are being re-tried on appeal for "rudely and falsely slandering the president" before the same Zagreb municipal court judge who acquitted them of the same charge in September 1996. The charges stem from an article critical of President Tudjman's recommendation that Jasenovac, a concentration camp operated by Croatia's pro-Nazi regime during World War II and the gravesite of many thousands of victims of the regime, turned into a Croatian war memorial. In December 1997, 22 government ministers charged the independent weekly *Globus* with criminal libel after the publication featured an article on government corruption.

3. What proportion of media is privatized? What are the major private newspapers, television stations, and radio stations? The government retains a controlling interest in two of four daily newspapers, several weeklies, and HINA, the country's only news agency. It also has a monopoly on printing through the two major government-controlled newspaper publishing houses. The major private independent newspapers are *Novi List*, a daily with a circulation of 31,000; *Globus*, a weekly; and the weekly *Feral Tribune*. The private weekly *Slobodna Dalmacija* is now controlled by HDZ supporters.

Television is the major source of news for most Croats. In Zagreb, there are three national television channels and one local television station. Channel One, Channel Two, and Channel Three are part of the official state-owned Croatian Radio and Television Enterprise (HRT), which is managed by a director appointed by parliament. Under the 1994 Law on Telecommunications and Post, HRT has a virtual monopoly over nationwide broadcasting through its exclusive right to assign national broadcasting frequencies and the use of government transmitters. Five local television stations operate with varying degrees of independence in Zagreb, Split, Rijeka, Osijek, Cakovec, and Opuzen. One television programmer, Omladinska Televisija, has used privately-owned transmitters to broadcast several hours a day in northern Croatia without interference from the government. More than 50 local and independent radio stations operate throughout the country but with limited reception in any given area.

In November 1997, parliament rejected an opposition request to add debate on the television law to the legislative agenda. In October, Forum-21, a group of prominent opposition radio and television journalists called for the government to ease its control over the electronic media and grant control of one of the three HRT channels to the opposition. In April 1997, the independent Radio 101 was awarded two frequencies to improve reception. In 1996, its closure had prompted massive street demonstrations.

4. Are the private media financially viable? Private media are taxed at several points in the production process, and some papers have complained that more than 50 percent of their gross revenues are lost in taxes and distribution costs. Reportedly, the government-controlled printing houses do not charge pro-government media for their services. High-circulation independent newspapers such as *Globus* can thrive despite high taxes and distribution costs. The existence of independent newspapers is also threatened by the costly lawsuits brought against them by government officials.

5. Are the media editorially independent? Are the media's news gathering functions affected by interference from government or private owners? State-owned media generally favor the government and the ruling HDZ in their coverage. Broadcasters who exhibit too much independence — by criticizing officials, for example — are penalized or prevented from broadcasting. The independence of the print media is also compromised by self-censorship that results from official harassment and the threat of legal proceedings. In May 1997, an editor of *Feral Tribune* was visited at home and threatened by investigators from the Ministry of the Interior. The staff of the same paper received death threats in September after printing an interview with a Croatian police officer who confessed to murdering ethnic Serbs during Croatia's war for independence.

Media coverage of the 1997 presidential, parliamentary, municipal, and county elections was less than satisfactory. State-run television and radio generally honored their legal obligation to grant equal time to all political parties. According to a report by the OSCE, however, a coalition was treated as a single party, thus limiting the access of the constituent parties. The Croatian Helsinki Committee for Human Rights reported that, on evening television news broadcasts during the parliamentary and municipal election campaigns, the HDZ received between 60 and 75 percent of the coverage of candidates' activities. Opposition parties rarely received more than two percent. In radio, there are alternatives to government-run stations, such as Radio 101, but their range is generally limited.

According to the OSCE, the print media reflect a greater degree of diversity than the broadcast media, but some newspapers admit that their articles are government-biased. Most independent newspapers that have not fallen under HDZ control tend to be satirical publications. The result is a lack of objective newspaper coverage of opposition parties. The one exception is *Novi List*, which provided serious campaign coverage of the opposition.

6. Is the distribution system for newspapers privately or governmentally controlled? Tisak, the recently privatized national distribution network, is widely believed to remove independent newspapers very quickly from its shelves while charging them a high percentage of the cover price for its services. It has also reportedly refused to distribute controversial editions of newspapers and magazines. With its controll of almost two-thirds of the newspaper kiosks in Croatia, Tisak holds a virtual monopoly over distribution and is reportedly subject to considerable government influence.

7. What proportion of the population is connected to the Internet? Are there any restrictions on Internet access to private citizens? Of the two major Internet service providers in Croatia, CARNet is government-operated, and HPT-Internet is provided by the Croatian Post Office and Telecommunications. CARNet links all Croatian universities and their associates, as well as some primary and secondary schools. It has an estimated 65,000 users in Croatia. The number of HPT-Internet users is estimated at 30,000, according to a government source. It is considered the only significant commercial Internet service provider for the average citizen. HPT-Internet provides full Internet and Web access, e-mail, and reliable connections through MCI, according to a user newsgroup.

The only restriction on access for private citizens may be the price. The initial connection fee is 35 *kunas* (more than $5), while a monthly subscription fee is 70 kunas, which is taxed at a rate of 10 percent. The entire subscription fee must be paid in advance. America Online has three Internet service phone lines in Croatia via AOL Globalnet. There are also between 50 and 100 small Internet service-providers.

8. What has been the trend in press freedom as measured by Freedom House's *Survey of Press Freedom*? Freedom House's annual *Survey of Press Freedom* rated Croatia "Not Free" in 1992 and 1993, "Partly Free" from 1994 to 1996, and "Not Free" in 1997 and 1998.

Governance and Public Administration 4.00/7

1. Is the legislature the effective rule-making institution? Parliament is the supreme legislative body, but it may temporarily delegate power to the government to issue decrees subject to ratification by the Sabor. As the government has been dominated by a single party since Croatia's independence, it is difficult to determine whether rules originate with the parliament or President Tudjman.

Internal disagreements preclude effective, united opposition, although the IDA convened an August 1997 summit meeting of opposition parties in an attempt to unite them before the 1999 parliamentary elections. The group criticized the government's human rights record and tight control of the media and that constitution and the Law on Referenda be amended to allow citizens the right to initiate referenda. Currently, only the lower house of parliament or the president may do so. Infighting among opposition parties, however, makes the prospects of a united front seem bleak.

2. Is substantial power decentralized to sub-national levels of government? What specific authority do sub-national levels have? The constitution delegated substantial authority to local governments. Section VI, Article 128, guarantees the right to local self-government, which includes the right to "decide on needs and interests of local significance, particularly of localities and housing, public utilities, child care, social welfare, culture, physical culture, sport, and technical culture, and the protection and promotion of the environment." Article 130 states that local self-governing units shall, in conformity with law, be independent in the conduct of local affairs and "shall only be subjected to the supervision of legality by competent bodies of the Republic." Due to the war after the dissolution of Yugoslavia and the authoritarian tendencies of the president and the ruling HDZ, however, local governments have developed slowly and have relied heavily on the central government.

In February 1998, Council of Europe representatives who had been charged with drafting a report on the state of local and regional democracy in Croatia issued a statement that noted "encouraging progress" in a number of areas. It also noted, however, that one area in need of attention is the legal provision that makes the appointment of the local prefect, who represents state authorities and local government, subject to approval by the president and the state. The council also found the country's Local Administration and Autonomy Act, a 1992 law that defines the tasks for which municipalities, towns, and districts (*Zupanije*) are responsible, inadequate at defining the particular range of powers assigned to the different levels of government. In September 1997, parliament ratified the European Charter on Local Self-Government. The Council of Europe called the move a step forward, even though the government rejected a number of the charter's provisions.

Elections in Eastern Slavonia, where the largely ethnic Serb population was allowed to choose from ten political parties and 1,000 candidates in 25 municipalities and three towns, are expected to pave the way for the establishment of legitimate authority in the region and the return of refugees. In July 1997, the Serbian National Council, the advisory body that will represent Serbs in Croatia, convened and thereby gave Serbs a voice in Croatian politics for the first time in six years.

3. Are sub-national officials chosen in free and fair elections? Local elections are undertaken with a limited degree of freedom and fairness due to passive intimidation and active manipulation of election results by President Tudjman and the ruling HDZ. For example, opposition parties won 64 percent of Zagreb city council seats in the 1995 elections. The HDZ, which won only a third of the city council's 50 seats, boycotted the municipal assembly along with the HSP in an attempt to block the opposition from electing the mayor. The government ruled that no decisions taken by the opposition-dominated city council were valid since the HDZ's departure deprived it of a two-thirds quorum.

Nevertheless, the opposition elected Goran Granic as mayor of Zagreb and immediately requested a ruling from the Constitutional Court to determine if the government's action was legal. The court rejected the opposition's appeal and upheld the validity of the government's actions to annul the decisions of the city council. The court also called for a new constituent session of the city council to elect a new mayor on January 2, 1996, and if that failed, the appointment by the government of its own administrator until new elections could be called. Constitutionally, Zagreb is considered a separate territorial administrative unit, and the president must approve the mayor.

In the 1995 elections, observers also noted that non-Croats had been excluded from the lists of registered voters, and ethnic Serbs complained of intimidation at polling stations.

In local and regional elections held in April 1997, the HDZ retained control of most city councils, while the opposition retained its control of the councils in Split and Dubrovnik. In Zagreb, the HDZ won 24 of 54 seats in the city council. The HSLS and SDP won 23, while the HSS won three.

In May, two opposition defectors from the HSS gave the HDZ control of Zagreb, thereby ending the two-year stalemate. Acting mayor Marina Matulovic-Dropulic, who had been accused of corruption by opposition newspapers, was confirmed as mayor by the HDZ. In Eastern Slavonia, balloting was extended for an additional day due to irregularities such as incomplete voter lists, closed or delayed openings of polling stations, and confusion over registration. Pro-Croatian parties won in 15 municipalities in the region, while the SDS won absolute majorities in 10 municipalities. Until a week before election day, ethnic Serb political leaders had considered calling for a boycott of the vote. Approximately 56,240 Eastern Slavonia voters, most of whom were ethnic Croats in exile from the region, voted in other parts of Croatia.

OSCE observers reported "serious problems," including the late opening of polling stations, the absence of balloting papers, and misprinted ballots. The fairness of the elections was also adversely affected by media coverage that favored the HDZ. By law, all campaigning and campaign coverage was to have ended 24 hours before the elections, but Radio 101 sources claimed that there were three "election blackout" violations, two of which were television programs that provided coverage of HDZ candidates or rallies. The third was a newspaper article that attacked opposition party leaders. Western governments viewed elections in Eastern Slavonia as the beginning of the region's reintegration into Croatia. The fact that the elections were held at all was therefore considered more important than the degree of fairness of the voting. The highest voter turnout was in the two counties of Eastern Slavonia, where the average rate was 81.5 percent.

4. Do the executive and legislative bodies operate openly and with transparency? Is draft legislation easily accessible to the media and the public? Legislative bodies generally operate with transparency only when the issue concerned is uncontroversial or explicitly paints President Tudjman and the HDZ in a favorable light. Thus, laws on issues such as privatization and the denationalization of property are generally discussed publicly and receive prominent media attention, while debates on the return of refugees, the temporary seizure of ethnic Serbs' property, and citizenship tend to receive one-sided media coverage or none at all. Public finance statistics appear to be of reasonable quality, frequency, and reliability. Croatia has subscribed to the IMF's Special Data Dissemination Standard (SDDS), and its fiscal data, in general, meets the SDDS's specifications for coverage and timeliness.

Independent Croatian media report that HDZ members of parliament often stonewall the opposition by speaking beyond the set time-limit, thereby giving opposition members little or no opportunity to present their side of an argument. Opposition speakers are also assigned unfavorable time slots, including periods when there are too few members present to vote on an issue.

5. Do municipal governments have sufficient revenues to carry out their duties? Do municipal governments have control of their own local budgets? Do they raise revenues autonomously or from the central state budget? Municipal governments raise revenues autonomously, but they are often materially and financially incapable of undertaking post-war reconstruction, economic development, and the delivery of services to refugees and displaced persons who place a heavy burden on local social service agencies. Reportedly, substantial amounts of revenue collected locally are funneled directly to Zagreb. This is explained partly by the overwhelming financial needs of the central government during wartime. Nevertheless, Croatians living outside of Zagreb seem to be increasingly resentful of the use of exorbitant amounts of tax revenue collected during the war to pay for superficial improvements of the capital city at the expense of desperately-needed reconstruction and services in war-affected areas. For example, during the height of the war, the government authorized multimillion dollar "face lift" operations in Zagreb and completely overhauled the city's main tram line, renovated Ban Jelacic square, and built new highways through the city. Critics argue that these improvements were largely an effort by the HDZ to portray Croatia as "western," i.e., democratic, while others suggest that the improvements were an investment in Croatia's future and were meant to attract western investors in order to stimulate the economy.

A 1997-98 Council of Europe report found many aspects of the current system of financing local authorities unsatisfactory. According to the report, the tax system, while generous to local authorities in theory, actually produces very little revenue — and none at all in some regions —due to the country's poor economy. In addition, the report claimed that taxes provide insufficient funds to meet the needs of local authorities, regardless of whether a particular region was affected by the war. The council identified two problems with the distribution of funds to areas most seriously affected by the war. First, although the state distributes grants to the regions in which the economies have been most seriously affected by the armed conflict, local authorities are not involved in the redistribution of those grants. Second, there appear to be no precise rules governing the distribution of grants to local authorities. The council found that approximately 90 percent of local authorities' income is distributed by the government on a discretionary basis, thereby sharply limiting the actual scope of local self-government.

6. Do the elected local leaders and local civil servants know how to manage municipal governments effectively? The effectiveness of local leaders varies from region to region. In Dalmatia, a region vital to Croatia's tourism industry, local HDZ officials are considered to be capable and effective in managing the municipal government. Krajina, however, is said to be administered by radical HDZ loyalists imported from Bosnia's Herzegovina region primarily to frighten away any remaining ethnic Serbs and to deter those who fled in 1995 from returning.

7. When did the constitutional/legislative changes in local power come into effect? Has there been a reform of the civil service code/system? Are local civil servants employees of the local or central government? While the 1990 constitution guarantees the right of local self-government with responsibilities for provisions such as housing, social welfare, and public utilities, the constitution is vague on the jurisdiction of the central and local governments. In addition, the constitution provides for a strong central government and presidency. The primary local self-governing units are 21 *Zupanije*. With the notable exceptions of Eastern Slavonia and Krajina, elections for the more than 8,000 county and town councils took place in February 1993 and were easily dominated by the ruling HDZ. The next local elections were held in April 1997 and included Eastern Slavonia, which is currently under U.N. administration.

No significant reforms in the civil service system have taken place since 1990. The European Charter on Local Self-Government was ratified in 1997 and is scheduled to take effect on February 1, 1998. Nevertheless, Croatian authorities rejected a number of the Charter's provisions, including a requirement that local authorities be consulted on matters concerning them directly, a mechanism for financial equalization to protect the interests of financially weaker local authorities, a prohibition on grants earmarked for specific use by local authorities, and a recognition of the right of local authorities to belong to associations for the protection and promotion of their common interests. Most sub-national civil servants are technically employees of the local governments.

Rule of Law 4.75/7

1. Is there a post-Communist constitution? How does the judicial system interpret and enforce the constitution? Are there specific examples of judicial enforcement of the constitution in the last year? Croatia's post-Communist constitution, which was adopted on December 22, 1990, establishes a democratic, multiparty state and incorporates the principles of free trade. A Constitutional Court is charged with upholding and enforcing the constitution. Articles 122 through 127 of the constitution outline the composition and duties of the court, which includes 11 judges elected for a term of eight years by the House of Representatives at the proposal of the House of Districts. The chief judge is elected by the court to a five-year term. Duties include determining the conformity of laws with the constitution; protecting the constitutional freedoms and rights of citizens; resolving jurisdictional disputes between the legislative, judicial, and executive branches of government; and repealing or annulling laws or regulations that it deems unconstitutional.

Under Article 125.7 of the constitution, the Constitutional Court also oversees the constitutionality and legality of elections. Near the end of the April 1997, campaigns, the court issued five rulings against the HDZ, overturned four Electoral Commission decisions, and reversed three state television program rules. The decisions concerned the misuse of the Croatian Army for the promotion of the ruling party, a television report that suggested that Social Democrats are murderers, and a poster charging the Social Democrats with abuses of freedoms during the Communist regime.

In September 1997, the court annulled several provisions of the 1995 Law on the Temporary Takeover and Management of Specific Property, which had been passed soon after the liberation of large areas of Croatia under Serbian occupation. Deemed unconstitutional were Article 9, which provides that a person who is temporarily using property that is to be returned to its original owner cannot be dispossessed of it until he is provided with other accommodation by the Commission for the Temporary Takeover and Use of Property, and Article 11, which provides that the use of property will be regulated by an agreement on the normalization of relations between Croatia and rump Yugoslavia.

2. Does the constitutional framework provide for human rights? Do the human rights include business and property rights? The constitution's Section III, which is entitled "Fundamental Freedoms and Rights of Man and Citizen," guarantees full civil and political as well as economic, social, and cultural rights to all citizens of the Republic "regardless of race, color, sex, language, religion, political, or other opinion, national or social origin, property, birth, education, social status, or other properties," and provides that "all shall be equal before the law" (Article 14). The constitution also provides for the abrogation of several key rights when the state deems itself in danger or when it holds the freedoms and rights of people, public order, morality, or health to be in jeopardy (Articles 16 and 17). Vulnerable rights include the right to appeal (Article 18), the right to free movement (Article 32), the right to freedom and secrecy of correspondence (Article 36), and the right to free association (Article 43). Article 24 provides that "no one shall be arrested or detained without a written court order based on law," but adds that the "police may, without a court order, arrest a person reasonably suspected of having committed a serious criminal offense defined by law and shall immediately hand him over to the court."

Article 48 of the constitution guarantees the right to ownership and extends that right to foreigners under conditions "spelled out by law." Article 49 states, "Entrepreneurial and market freedom shall be the basis of the economic system." It also guarantees entrepreneurs equal legal status in the market. In addition, it states, "Foreign investors shall be guaranteed free transfer and repatriation of profit and the capital invested." Article 50, however, allows the government to restrict ownership, entrepreneurial freedom, and property rights in the interests of state security. The government has also passed several laws that restrict property rights. In October 1991, the government issued a decree of transfer ownership of property belonging to the former Yugoslav army or the former Yugoslav defense ministry to the Croatian government. In December 1991, parliament passed the Law Concerning the Temporary Use of Apartments. This measure granted the government administrative power over abandoned apartments, which were to be made available to displaced Croats, refugees, and members of the Croatian armed forces and their families. The decree and the law were used by the government to evict forcibly former members of the Yugoslav Army — mainly ethnic Serbs — from their homes. Evictions were often conducted by Croatian soldiers, military police, or unidentified persons in uniform. Those who were evicted had little recourse to due process or appeal. In September 1995, parliament passed a law on the Temporary Takeover and Administration of Specified Property, which effectively reverted ownership of property that ethnic Serbs, who had been forced to flee Krajina, had abandoned to the Croatian government. In 1997, several of the more discriminatory provisions of the law were annulled by the Constitutional Court, but there remains no effective mechanism by which ethnic Serbs can recover their property.

According to the U.S. Department of State's 1997 human rights report, the government implemented constitutional provisions for human rights in a discriminatory fashion. It limited press freedom by using the courts and administrative bodies selectively to close or restrict newspapers and radio stations that were critical of government officials. Provisions of the criminal code allow the government to prosecute individuals who insult high officials in the press or who make statements that might cause public instability — a provision that has at times been defined subjectively to allow judicial action to counter the expression of opinions contrary to those of the ruling party. In June 1997, the right of association was circumscribed by a new Law of Associations. In the 1997 presidential and local elections, the government seriously limited the right of citizens to change their government freely by its virtually complete control of the electronic media. It also used manipulation of laws, harassment, and economic pressure to control the political process.

Human rights advances in 1997 included the ratification in September of the European Convention on Human Rights, a notable acceleration in the return of internally displaced ethnic Serbs to their former homes in government-controlled territory, and the passage of a law to provide for primary education in minority languages.

3. Has there been basic reform of the criminal code/criminal law? Who authorizes searches

and issues warrants? Are suspects and prisoners beaten or abused? Are there excessive delays in the criminal justice system? Croatia adopted the criminal code of the former Socialist Federal Republic of Yugoslavia with only minor changes. The criminal procedure is divided into four stages: the pretrial phase, the preliminary inquiry or investigative phase, the trial process or main hearing, and the phase of review or legal remedies. Article 71 of the Croatian criminal code was amended in March 1997 to forbid the publication or broadcast of "untrue information" or material that may injure the honor and reputation of the President of the Republic and/or other high officials. The law provides for sentences of up to three years imprisonment.

Police may obtain arrest warrants by presenting evidence of probable cause to an investigative magistrate. Police may carry out arrests without a warrant if they believe that suspects may flee, destroy evidence, or commit other crimes. Such cases are not uncommon. The police then have 24 hours in which to justify their decision before the local investigative magistrate. There are credible reports that police beat suspects, particularly ethnic Serbs and mixed-marriage returnees detained after incidents of rioting in Hrvatska Kostajnica in May 1997.

According to the U.S. Department of State's 1997 human rights report, court cases often last for years due to overburdened and understaffed courts and the inexperience of many newly appointed personnel. The backlog of cases in many courts is huge. For example, in Osijek alone, a backlog of 6,000 commercial court cases has been reported.

4. Do most judges rule fairly and impartially? Do many remain from the Communist era? Lawyers, international monitors, and the Croatian Helsinki Commission for Human Rights claim that judges generally do not rule fairly and impartially when suspected Croatian war criminals are on trial. One notable example is the case of Mihajlo Hrastov, a member of Croatia's Special Police Force and a commander of the Special Police Forces of the Karlovac Police Department. Hrastov was accused of brutally killing a group of unarmed prisoners in front of witnesses in 1991. In 1992, the Karlovac county court acquitted Hrastov – a decision that produced a standing ovation from all present in the courtroom. Although the Supreme Court declared the decision void and initiated procedures for a new trial, the Karlovac county court has not yet set a date for the second trial. Meanwhile, on Karlovac County Day in 1996, Hrastov was recognized for outstanding public service.

By contrast, Milos Horvat, a Croatian Serb extradited from Germany to face charges of war crimes in Croatia, was found guilty of genocide in June 1997, and sentenced to 5 years in prison. The U.N. Center for Human Rights noted that "it was the widely held opinion of trial monitors that the evidence submitted by the prosecution was insufficient for a verdict of guilt, even less of genocide."

The U.N. Center, OSCE, and NGOs report that decisions issued in particular by the administrative courts, which rule on citizenship issues, are often improperly documented, arbitrary, and based on questionable standards of evidence. For example, one NGO documented more than 900 cases in Eastern Slavonia where ethnic Serbs, who had been forced to request citizenship through naturalization due to the loss or destruction of record books during the war, were denied citizenship with little or no explanation of the factual basis for the denial. Article 8 of the citizenship law provides two conditions for naturalization: that a "person has a place of residence for a period of not less than five years constantly on the territory of the Republic of Croatia" and that a "conclusion can be derived from his or her conduct that he or she is attached to the legal system and customs in the Republic of Croatia." The lack of a written explanation for denials under these provisions makes it virtually impossible to launch successful appeals.

In March 1997, the House of Representatives' Judicial Committee rejected a lustration bill that called for the eviction of Communist personnel from the state apparatus and judiciary. It is unclear how many judges remain from the Communist era. The HDZ-influenced High Judicial Council has removed many judges and appointed approximately 1,200 new ones.

5. Are the courts free of political control and influence? Are the courts linked directly to the Ministry of Justice or any other executive body? The Croatian judicial system includes municipal and district courts, a Constitutional Court, a Supreme Court, an Administrative Court, and a High Judicial Council that appoints judges and public prosecutors. The parliament's upper house nominates persons for membership on the High Judicial Council for election to eight-year terms by the lower house. The 11 judges of the Constitutional Court are elected to eight-year terms in the same manner. All judges, including those on the Supreme Court, are appointed for life by the High Judicial Council. Through parliamentary nomination and election, the HDZ wields influence over the High Judicial Council and thus over the selection of judges.

In recent years, the government has purged the judiciary of judges and attorneys who were not ethnic Croats or who were thought to hold political views different from the government's. Under legislation adopted in 1991, the High Judicial Council continued to review judicial appointments. In 1996, it removed six sitting judges because of their "independent views." Despite a shortage of experienced judicial officers — approximately 40 percent of judicial positions are vacant — six state attorneys in the Zagreb municipal attorney's office were dismissed in March 1997, allegedly because of their ethnic Serb or other non-Croatian origins. In Split in April 1997, nine dismissals were also allegedly based on ethnicity. Krunislav Olujic, the Chief Justice of the Supreme Court, was dismissed early in the year by the High Judicial Council for "behavior injurious to the reputation of the court." The council alleged that he had consorted with known criminals and had engaged in sex with underage persons. According to the U.S. Department of State's 1997 human rights report, the procedures of his trial were questionable, since three members of the council who were determining his fate were also witnesses who testified against him. The subsequent challenges to the grounds of the dismissal were accompanied by a public smear campaign carried out by state-owned television and pro-government newspapers. The OSCE and the U.N. Special Rapporteur for Human Rights denounced the proceedings against Olujic and expressed doubts as to the judiciary's independence from the HDZ.

The appointment of judges in Eastern Slavonia began in September 1997. An ethnically Serb Assistant Minister of Justice facilitated the process. Under an agreement between the government and the region's U.N. administration, ethnic Serb attorneys from the region may defer payment of the necessary fee to register with the bar association. This provided a measure of security for ethnic Serb defendants and proved to be a significant confidence-building measure.

6. What proportion of lawyers is in private practice? How does this compare with the previ-

ous year? Lawyers in private practice are required to register with the Croatian Bar Association (CBA), which was established in 1929. Trainees must complete one and a half years of training in a law office before taking the bar examination. They must then practice law for three years before becoming new members of the CBA. In 1996, there were reportedly 2,100 CBA members and 500 trainees.

7. Does the state provide public defenders? The right to counsel can be exercised at the beginning of criminal proceedings i.e., after an investigating judge decides to open an investigation or when a direct indictment is sought. A person who has not been formally charged is not guaranteed the right to counsel even though he or she may be in police custody. Access to counsel is further limited during the investigative phase and is only fully guaranteed during the trial phase.

Mandatory defense is provided under Article 70 of the Criminal Code. There are three types of circumstances in which the mandatory defense provision takes effect. First, a suspect's initial interrogation must be in the presence of defense counsel if the crime of which he is accused carries a penalty of 20 or more years of imprisonment. Second, if the penalty carries a penalty of ten or more years of imprisonment, the suspect must have access to counsel by the time the indictment is served. Third, defense becomes mandatory at the moment that the court decides to conduct a trial *in absentia*.

8. Are there effective anti-bias/discrimination laws, including protection of ethnic minority rights? The U.S. State Department noted a marked improvement in 1997 in the rights of ethnic Serbs in the area under U.N. administration. By September, approximately 145,000 ethnic Serbs had received identity documents at centers established by the Croatian Office of Displaced Persons and Refugees and the U.N. administration. Although estimates vary widely, at least 30,000 to 40,000 Serb applications to return from rump Yugoslavia remained pending with no action, while many refugees in Bosnia were unable to apply to return at all. As of December 1997, the U.N. High Commissioner for Refugees estimated that approximately 10,000 ethnic Serbs had returned to Croatia proper.

The government continues to tolerate serious abuses of ethnic Serbs. Adequate civil authority in the formerly occupied areas of Krajina and Western Slavonia has not yet been established, and the police have been unwilling or unable to take effective action against criminal activity against ethnic Serbs. Beatings and murders still occur, although less frequently than in the past.

In early 1997, according to a report by Human Rights Watch, the government circulated a list of thousands of ethnic Serbs suspected of committing war crimes. As a result of international pressure, the government reduced the list to 25 names. Nevertheless, police arrested hundreds of ethnic Serbs on war crimes and other criminal charges.

Despite opposition by minority leaders and opposition parliamentarians, the government adopted legislation regulating minority language education in September 1997. Although Ministry of Education officials claimed that the law incorporated every recommendation made by the Council of Europe — except in cases in which the guidelines would have "endangered the integrity of the Republic of Croatia and the right of Croatian children to be educated in their national language" — critics denounced the new law as overly restrictive.

Several laws enacted since the country re-took control of its Krajina region have been widely criticized by Croatian and international human rights organizations for promoting an "ethnically pure" Croatia by making it virtually impossible for ethnic Serbs to return to the region. In 1995, the Chamber of Representatives eliminated two pro-minority provisions of the Constitutional Law of Human Rights and Freedoms and the Rights of National Ethnic Communities or Minorities in the Republic of Croatia. One of the provisions had guaranteed self-governing, autonomous status to districts in which, under the 1981 census, minorities constituted more than 50 percent of the population. These districts included the districts of Knin and Glina. The other suspended provision had entitled minorities who constituted more than eight percent of the country's population to proportional representation in parliament and the supreme judicial bodies. The provisions were suspended indefinitely until the completion of a new, unscheduled census. As a result, ethnic Serb parliamentary representation, which is based on its "new" percentage of the population, dropped from 13 seats to three.

The Law on the Temporary Takeover and Administration of Specified Property allowed the Croatian government to sequester and administer movable and immovable property — everything from homes to cattle — that had been abandoned by persons who left the country after August 17, 1990. In practice, the law has been used to seize property abandoned by ethnic Serbs who fled Krajina and Western Slavonia and give it to displaced ethnic Croats from Eastern Slavonia and Bosnia.

Ethnic Serbs who seek to return to Croatia face enormous bureaucratic obstacles. The policy of the government has been to permit only the return of those who have relatives remaining in Croatia. The family member living in Croatia must apply on behalf of the returnee — a difficult task for some 10,000 elderly, mostly homebound Serbs who remain in the Krajina region. The application process for returning Serbs can take years to complete. Applicants are frequently rejected on the basis of Article 26 of the Law on Citizenship, which allows the government to deny citizenship to people who "pose a threat to national interests." The law distinguishes applicants with a claim to Croatian ethnicity. Accordingly, ethnic Croat are eligible even if they have never lived in the country, whereas ethnic Serbs and others who have lived in Croatia as citizens for years must apply for citizenship whether or not they fled the country. During the application process, the applicant is considered to be an alien and is denied rights such as medical care and other social service allowances, pensions, free education, and employment in the civil service.

In 1996, parliament passed the Law on the Limits of Special Government Protection. Commonly referred to as the "Law on Colonization," it designates certain formerly occupied areas for special government protection and development. Ethnic Croatian immigrants, displaced persons, refugees, soldiers, and disabled veterans are given property allotments and tax incentives to populate designated areas, thereby promoting long-term settlement of ethnic Croatians in areas in which ethnic Serbs had been in the majority.

Corruption C

1. What is the magnitude of official corruption in the civil service? Must an average citizen pay a bribe to a bureaucrat in order to receive a service? What services are subject to bribe requests — for example, university entrance, hospital admission, telephone installation, ob-

taining a license to operate a business, applying for a passport or other official documents? What is the average salary of civil servants at various levels? The domination of Croatian politics by a single party since independence has fostered the spread of corruption at all levels of government, according to opposition sources. In a notable March 1998 case, the Zagreb Municipal Court sentenced an assistant economic minister and his deputy to prison for 18 and 12 months, respectively, for taking bribes from the general manager of a chain of retail shops.

In April 1997, the independent newspaper *Globus* reported that, in a session of the Council for Defense and National Security, it was openly stated that Croatia had declined to do business with Boeing because Croatian negotiators had failed to extract adequate bribes from the company. *Globus* also reported that this was only one of many cases in which foreign investors or governments had complained of unfairness in open competition for major infrastructure projects.

According to *Banka International* magazine, Croatian state auditors reportedly have extensive case files on abuses of power and fraud in state institutions, although many of the cases never make it to court. In monetary terms, the magazine stated, such corruption accounts for the loss of approximately ten percent of the state budget.

The government document, "Principles of Fiscal Policy for 1998-2000: Strategy and Prospects," projects a reduction in the public spending share of GDP from 47 percent in 1997 to 44 percent in 1998. Government employees' real wages will be frozen, growing only at the rate of inflation. Half of all government salaries and benefits go to the army and police — five percent of GDP, or as much as the country's entire credit-investment program.

2. Do top policy makers (the President, ministers, vice-ministers, top court justices, and heads of agencies and commissions) have direct ties to businesses? How strong are such connections and what kinds of businesses are these? The Government's privatization program came under increasing criticism for allotting shares in prime enterprises to those loyal to the ruling party. Accusations of government cronyism are common.

3. Do laws requiring financial disclosure and disallowing conflict of interest exist? Have publicized anti-corruption cases been pursued? To what conclusion? A new Penal Code, a Code of Criminal Procedure, and a Money Laundering Law were passed by parliament in September 1997. The Money Laundering Law aims to prevent the laundering of money acquired through organized crime, corruption, or other financial wrongdoing. The Code of Criminal Procedure provides for the use of special measures by officials to infiltrate criminal groups and investigate suspected incidents of bribery and other offenses. The Penal Code provides for penalties, including prison sentences, for economic crimes such as embezzlement and bribery. In 1998, two top economic ministry officials charged with accepting bribes were sentenced to prison terms of 18 and 12 months. In November 1997, the parliamentary committee for domestic affairs and national security considered three former intelligence officials' allegations of corruption in the defense ministry.

According to *Banka International*, cases of fraud and other economic crimes are difficult to prosecute, often because leaks emerge from the State Auditors' Office to alert individuals who are being investigated. A Deputy State Attorney explained, "Usually, our main problem is compiling evidence. Facts are elusive, lawsuits are protracted, and there is an ever-decreasing number of guilty verdicts. Sentences have been watered down, as these sorts of crimes are regarded as less serious."

In September 1997, authorities linked seven military officers and four civilians to a major Balkan car-smuggling ring. Much of the activity appears to be linked to powerful and violent organized crime groups. Officials brought Mladen "Tuta" Maletilic, a gang leader, to trial. Maletilic allegedly has links to HDZ leaders in Mostar, Bosnia, where he supposedly terrorized Muslim residents on their behalf.

4. What major anti-corruption initiatives have been implemented? How often are anti-corruption laws and decrees adopted? Information on this subject is not available.

5. How do major corruption-ranking organizations like Transparency International rate this country? Transparency International has not rated Croatia.

Privatization 4.00/7

1. What percentage of the GDP comes from private ownership? What percentage of the labor force is employed in the private sector? How large is the informal sector of the economy? In November 1997, the EBRD reported that the private sector had produced 55 percent of GDP by mid-year – an increase from 50 percent in 1996. The gray economy accounts for an estimated 11 to 20 percent of GDP, although some analysts state that the figure is as high as 25 percent. According to the World Bank, the share of private sector employment in all registered enterprises was 45 percent in 1997.

2. What major privatization legislation has been passed? What were its substantive features? The Law on the Transformation of Socially Owned Enterprises was enacted in April 1991. It transformed approximately 2,600 enterprises into joint stock companies and was administered by the Croatian Privatization Fund (CPF). Companies were asked to submit their own privatization plans to the CPF by June 1992, for approval according to several options, including sale to external investors, debt/equity swaps, the introduction of fresh capital, and purchase by current and past employees. Businesses were valued at balance-sheet asset value. Croatian citizens were able to buy a certain number of shares at a discount. Two-thirds of shares not taken in the "self-privatization" program were transferred to a privatization fund. The other third was transferred to two State Pension Funds. By the end of September 1996, approximately 600,000 citizens — or 13 percent of the population — had become shareholders. CPF and the two State Pension Funds held a majority of stock in only 228 companies. In 1995, 42 percent of all employees — an increase from 1.7 percent in 1990 — worked in wholly-privatized companies. By mid-1995, approximately 3,000 applications for autonomous privatization had been received. Two-thirds of the applications were approved. More than 1,000 of these companies have been completely privatized. In another 900, the state has retained a minority stake.

The second phase of privatization began with the passage of the Privatization Law in 1996. This law provided for the creation of a new decision-making body, the CPF Board of Directors, which decides on sales of companies with a nominal value of more than 100 million *kuna*. It also gives the CPF Board of Directors the discretion to lower the asked price for shares of an enterprise and mandates the transfer of proceeds from the sale of shares in enterprises to the Croatian Bank for Reconstruction, which will disperse these funds mainly to reconstruction and infrastructure projects. The law also provides for the privatization of public enterprises or private companies in which the states holds 100 percent of the shares. After necessary laws are enacted, the CPF will conduct the privatization procedure. The 1996 Privatization Law also prolonged the period within which the installments for the purchase of shares by employees and former employees of transformed companies must be paid from five to 20 twenty years. It also required that the CPF transfer 1,821,232,000 kuna in shares to one of the country's three pension funds, the Croatian Self-Employed Businessmen's Pension and Disability Fund, which had not yet received an adequate amount of shares. The law also gave the Ministry of Privatization, which was established in 1994, the power to nominate people for appointment to supervisory boards of enterprises in which the CPF has shareholder status. It also mandated that every enterprise in which the CPF holds 25 percent or more of the equity file a quarterly report.

The law also creates a Mass Privatization Program, which entitles special classes of citizens — political prisoners before Croatian independence, ethnic Croatian war refugees, invalids, widows, and orphans — to receive vouchers that are denominated in investment points and that they can bid for shares in selected enterprises in a three-round procedure. An estimated 350,000 people qualify. Registration for voucher privatization began in June 1997, with entitled persons receiving a number of points based on degrees of disability or similar determining factors. When the distribution of vouchers began in January 1998, approximately 230,000 participants had registered. The initial round of auctions is scheduled for March 1998.

3. What proportion of agriculture, housing and land, industry, and small business and services is in private hands? According to the chief economist for Zagrebacka Banka, agriculture, housing, and land are approximately 80 percent privately owned; industry, 50 percent; and service industries, approximately 90 percent. Public utilities are still entirely state-owned, although the government planns to include some subsidiaries of INA, the state oil and gas conglomerate, in the voucher privatization program.

4. What has been the extent of insider (management, labor, and nomenklatura) participation in the privatization process? What explicit and implicit preferences have been awarded to insiders? External investors criticized the Law on Transformation for favoring insider buyouts by allowing managers to design their own privatization plans. Until the law was amended in March 1993, management and employees could take control of an entire company by purchasing 50 percent of the company's equity at a discount, thereby making it difficult for external investors to compete. As a result, 70 to 80 percent of all completely privatized enterprises are owned by the people who worked in them. The amended law allows managers and employees to own only 50 percent of the company's equity, with the remainder sold through public invitations or on the Zagreb Stock Exchange.

5. How much public awareness of and support for privatization have there been? What is the nature of support and opposition to privatization by major interest groups? As in many post-Communist regimes, Croatia's bureaucracy is firmly entrenched. Corruption exists, and privatization is often opposed by former Communist officials. The voucher privatization system, however, has been popular, with approximately 230,000 people participating in the program. During the 1992-96 phase of the country's privatization program, approximately 600,000 citizens became shareholders in companies.

Macroeconomics 3.75/7

1. Has the taxation system been reformed? (What areas have and have not been overhauled? To what degree are taxpayers complying? Is tax compliance difficult to achieve? Has the level of revenues increased? Is the revenue-collection body overburdened? What is the overall tax burden?) Croatia began to overhaul its tax system after independence. Reform is being implemented in phases. Institutional reform began with the 1990 Law on Indirect Taxation. New laws on income and profit taxes have been in effect since January 1, 1994. The VAT, which took effect on January 1, 1998, replaced the Turnover Tax on Goods and Services and is paid at final consumption. Excise duties for certain products —such as oil and oil products, tobacco products, coffee, beer, alcohol, soft drinks and the import of new cars — are paid when the goods are delivered from manufacturing plants or imported.

The new taxation system accords equal status to all taxpayers — i.e., domestic and foreign natural persons and legal entities. Croatia also honors all double taxation agreements made between the former Yugoslavia and other countries. In addition to the above-mentioned taxes, the current tax system includes taxes on real estate sales and games of chance, as well as taxes levied by local authorities.

The 22 percent VAT, which took effect on January 1, 1998, is applied to every stage in the cycle of goods or services from the producer to the end-user. At each stage, only the added value, that is, value created during that stage, is taxed. This is achieved by having each taxpayer deduct the amount of tax passed on to him by other taxpayers as part of their purchase price. Thus, the VAT is neutral for the taxpayer, who is an entrepreneur, and does not represent a business cost. Any enterprise that supplies goods or performs services that are defined as taxable is liable to pay the VAT. An enterprise is considered to include any natural person or legal entity that is independently and permanently engaged in an activity with the aim of gaining profit. As of March 1998, the Council of the Croatian National Bank stated that the introduction of the VAT caused a non-recurring increase in prices, which should be followed by a stabilization. Retail prices increased by .4 percent. Living costs increased by .7 percent, while manufacturers' prices fell by 0.1 percent.

The EBRD reported a 10 percent increase in profit tax from 1996 to 1997. The 8.7 percent economic growth in the first eleven months of 1997, as reported by *Banka International*, resulted from real growth as well as increased vigilance by the Tax Administration. In 1997, the basic rate of income tax was reduced from 25 percent to 20 percent. The standard rate of income tax remains at 35 percent. There is no capital gains tax.

The tax burden in Croatia is one of the heaviest among the countries in transition from communism. Tax revenue was 29.5 percent of GDP in 1995 and 29.3 percent of GDP in 1996.

2. Does fiscal policy encourage private savings, investment, and earnings? (Has there been

any reform/alteration of revenue and budget policies? How large are budget deficits and overall debt? Is the financing of the social insurance/pension system sustainable? What proportion of the budget is taken up by subsidies to firms and individuals?) In 1993, Croatia enacted a comprehensive stabilization program that continues to be the basis for current macro-economic policy. The program included three phases: arresting inflation, restructuring, and recovery. It stabilized the currency rate and reduced inflation from 37.3 percent in 1993 to 3.6 percent in 1997. As a result of this tight monetary policy, Croatia has experienced growing trade and current account deficits, low investment, and the failure of much of the business sector to extricate itself from debt, which spirals upward as a result of continued high real interest rates. The restructuring phase, which began in mid-1994, dealt with loss-making enterprises by privatizing debt-laden companies through debt-equity exchanges. It also increased competition in the banking sector by reducing lending rates.

According to the Croatian Investment Promotion Agency, the central government budget deficit in 1996 constituted 1 percent of GDP. In 1997, it rose to approximately 2.6 percent, which was financed entirely by foreign sources.

According to *Banka International*, approximately 800,000 Croatians are pensioners. There are approximately as many employees in business — not including workers in state administration, the armed forces, the police, and infrastructure enterprises — as there are pensioners. Due to severe falls in the spending power of their pension income, pensioners have become more outspoken, and opposition parties often use them as an example of how the government's economic policies have failed. Many basic food items and utilities that had been exempt or taxed at a lower rate under the former tax system have been brought into the scope of the new 22 percent VAT. To compensate partially, social security pensions were increased by 4.4 percent in December 1997. Increasing pensions was a top economic priority in 1997, an election year, amd precluded much-needed reform of the pension system. Croatia is faced with an increasingly aging population. According to a report by the IMF, Croatia's system-dependency ratio defined as the ratio of pensioners to working population was 54.3 percent in 1996, 43 percent in 1993, and 31 percent in 1990. In major advanced countries such as the United Kingdom and Japan, the average system dependency ratio is 39.2 percent.

Although a precise timetable has not been set, there are plans to replace the current pay-as-you-go pension system, which is funded by equal employer and employee contributions that total 25.5 percent of the payroll, with a three-pillar system based on a combination of compulsory and voluntary contributions paid into public pension funds and private investment funds.

In 1997, the state pension fund expenditure is forecast at 12.78 percent of GDP. There are no privately-owned pension funds so far. Health spending in 1997 was projected to be 8.78 percent of GDP. The Ministry of Employment and Social Welfare spends approximately 2.5 percent of GDP, principally on transfers to the unemployed and others on welfare benefits.

3. Has there been banking reform? (Is the central bank independent? What are its responsibilities? Is it effective in setting and/or implementing monetary policy? What is the actual state of the private banking sector? Does it conform to international standards? Are depositors protected?) The National Bank of Croatia (NBC) is responsible for the stabilization of the currency, the external liquidity of the country, and the supervision of the banking sector. It is formally independent, but accountable to parliament. NBC was strengthened in October 1994, when the government transferred deposits to it for safekeeping.

The banking system inherited faults in decision-making mechanisms and other problems from the former Socialist system. Decisions on large investments were made not on the basis of yields, but rather on development plans for socio-political communities. As a result, banks continue to have a high proportion of illiquid assets.

Since independence, the government has undertaken serious efforts to recapitalize and rehabilitate banks in Croatia. In November 1995, Slavonska Banka, the nation's sixth-largest bank, began its rehabilitation. In 1996, it was followed by Splitska Bank and Rijecka Banka, the third and fourth largest banks, respectively. In December 1996, the government decided to place Privredna Banka, the largest bank, into rehabilitation under the control of the Bank Rehabilitation Agency (BRA).

The 1994 Law on Bank Rehabilitation authorized the BRA to handle bank rehabilitation and insure savings deposits. The law established that the BRA would help banks already operating and established under the old banking law to bring their operations into line with the regulations of the new law. The law calls for the separation of bad loans from the balance sheet, the infusion of new capital in exchange for equity, the reorganization of management, and privatization. Earlier attempts to recapitalize failing banks had faltered, primarily because bonds were given to enterprises that were facing great financial difficulties. Under the new rehabilitation program, enterprises are obliged to cancel part of their capital against losses.

The rehabilitation of Slavonska Banka has been completed, and the bank is slated for privatization. Nevertheless, bank restructuring is a relatively new idea and systemic restructuring of other banks is progressing slowly. The process is likely to take several years. One result of the establishment of new banks and the restructuring of larger banks has been greater competition and the lowering of interest rates. The poor management of many banks in the process of restructuring, however, is reflected in significant numbers of bad loans on their balance sheets.

All 24 of the banks operating in 1989 were transformed into joint-stock companies. Since then, more than 30 new banks have been established and have been operating according to market criteria. The banking system is still controlled by a few large banks, but new ones have succeeded in gaining a significant share of the industry. The share of the eight largest banks' total assets had fallen from approximately 90 percent at the end of 1991 to approximately 73 percent by the end of 1995.

A deposit insurance plan implemented in mid-1997 fully insures kuna-denominated savings deposits up to 30,000 kuna and extends partial insurance up to 50,000 kuna. Strict rules for prudential regulations are in place, and the regulatory framework appears to be in accordance with EU directives. Nevertheless, rules concerning the allowed quantities and kinds of credit activities on lending to related parties appear to be insufficient. Banks submit quarterly reports on their capital-adequacy ratio, which is defined as the ratio between liable capital and total assets, plus off-balance asset items of the bank weighted in terms of the degree of risk. Capital adequacy fell in 1996 but has remained steady. Financial statements lack transparency in spite of legal obligations to use international accounting standards.

A foreign entity can establish a bank subject to reciprocal rights in its own country. Foreign banks may open branches and have representative offices, which are again subject to reciprocity. The law also regulates the supervision of banks, with the central bank enjoying powers that are customary in the West.

4. How sound is the national currency? (Is the value of the currency fixed, or does it float? How convertible is the currency? How large are the hard currency reserves? Has exchange rate policy been stable and predictable?) The Croatian kuna is a free-floating currency. It is freely convertible into foreign currency at exchange rates determined daily on the foreign exchange market. The NBC intervenes in the market occasionally to eliminate exchange rate fluctuations or maintain target exchange rates against the German *mark*. Exchange rates have remained stable since 1994.

According to the Croatian Institute for Culture and Information, prices in Croatia grew by 0.7 percent in December 1997, and 3.8 percent during December 1996. The average price level in 1997 was 3.6 percent higher than in 1996. After a 3 percent deflation that resulted from the adoption of a stabilization program that began in October 1993, inflation in Croatia has therefore been maintained at a rate comparable to stable market economies for three consecutive years. The annual inflation rate in 1995 was 3.7 percent and 3.4 percent in 1996. Of the countries in transition from communism, Croatia has retained the lowest inflation rate, even after an upturn of economic activity that was estimated at approximately 7 percent in real terms in 1997. According to the Croatian central bank, the maintenance of the inflation rate within the 3 to 4 percent range will remain an attainable objective in 1998.

The central bank's foreign currency reserves totaled $1.896 billion in 1995, or $491 million more than the 1994 reserves. Foreign currency reserves stood at $2.30 billion dollars in 1995 and $2.52 billion by the end of October 1997.

5. Is there a functioning capital market infrastructure? (Are there existing or planned commodities, bond, and stock markets? What are the mechanisms for investment and lending? What government bodies have the authority to regulate capital markets?) The Zagreb Stock Exchange was opened in 1991 by a group of 25 banks as a non-governmental, non-profit institution. It has developed slowly, and very few shares are listed and traded. The Securities and Exchange Commission was created in 1995 through a law that also provides for financial disclosure.

Croatia's financial system is generally characterized by the dominance of banking institutions, while capital markets are much less developed. Banks have a universal structure and, for now, are permitted to engage in the full range of capital market operations. Merchant and investment banks as such do not exist as separate legal entities. A bank is not permitted to participate in insurance deals, production, trade in goods, or future deals with commodities, with the exception of deals in gold, other precious metals, and coins.

In addition to the Zagreb Stock Exchange, an OTC market exists in Varazdin and Osijek. In the second half of 1996, encouraged by the successful flotation of shares in the pharmaceutical manufacturer Pliva and in Zagrebacka Banka, market capitalization and activity rose significantly. The OTC market has also become more active. Trading in shares and bonds — excluding auctions by the Privatization Fund — amounted to 4.5 million German marks in 1995, 370 million marks in 1996, and 230 million marks in the first five months of 1997. Of approximately 80 quoted companies, only three are fully listed.

Microeconomics 3.75/7

1. Are property rights guaranteed? (Are there both formal and de facto protections of private real estate and intellectual property? Is there a land registry with the authority and capability to ensure accurate recording of who owns what? What are the procedures for expropriation, including measures for compensation and challenge? Have any seizures taken place?) Property rights are guaranteed by the constitution, and intellectual property is protected under Article 68. A new criminal code that increased penalties for criminal copyright infringement took effect on January 1, 1998. Computer hacking, breaking into databases, and falsifying computer information are defined as crimes. Nevertheless, the Law on the Temporary Takeover and Administration of Specified Property effectively expropriated the property of many ethnic Serbs who fled Croatia in 1995. Although the courts revised some of the more discriminatory parts of the law in late 1997, ethnic Serbs still encounter difficulties in regaining property after it has begun to be administered by the Croatian authorities. In addition, there is still no effective mechanism by which ethnic Serb owners can recover their property. Ethnic Croatian displaced persons and refugees in possession of such property are, in general, still unwilling to return it to the original owners. Croatian authorities do little to assist the returning ethnic Serbs.

Forced evictions of ethnic Serbs, Croats, and others from former Yugoslav National Army (JNA) apartments occurred in 1997. According to the U.S. State Department, the Ministry of Defense arbitrarily revoked the tenancy rights of individuals who had lived in apartments for decades, and military police frequently took residences by force of arms, either by evicting current tenants or forcing them to share quarters. The authorities justified their actions on the basis of property laws that remove tenancy rights after a six-month absence or if the tenant was ruled to have "acted against the interests of the Republic of Croatia." The courts frequently used this legislation to deny tenancy rights to former JNA members and, in other cases, refused to recognize the rights of surviving family members to maintain the tenancy rights of their deceased or divorced spouses, even though these rights are specifically provided in the law. Membership in the JNA at any time by primary tenancy rights-holders was deemed sufficient to brand them as "enemies of the state." Ethnic Croats, however, were not immune from forced evictions, nor did all cases involve former JNA members. Many cases were reported in which desirable apartments were simply confiscated by individuals connected with either the military or the police. In one case in Zagreb, the owner of a home was allowed to stay, but was forced to share quarters with five others, all of whom were members of the police.

In October 1996, parliament passed the Law on Compensation for Property Taken During Yugoslav Communist Rule to regulate the denationalization of property confiscated or nationalized after 1945. The law gives preference, when it is possible, to restitution of property. In other cases, compensation is to be made. In the corporate sector, the rights of former owners or their heirs have been secured by freezing a percentage of equity in the CPF portfolio. Former owners of nationalized companies are to receive shares in the present company at an amount equivalent to the estimated value of their original property.

The land registry system is notably disorganized—a situation that was inherited from the socialist system and exacerbated by the fact that many official documents in occupied territories may have been destroyed during the war. Improvements are being made, however, and recent registrations are considered to be well-organized and are usually current within six months.

2. To what extent have prices been liberalized? What subsidies remain? All direct price controls have been removed, and prices in Croatia are generally set by the marketplace. Nevertheless, changes in the price of certain basic products, such as milk and bread, must be reported to the Ministry of Economy two weeks in advance, and changes in the prices of approximately one-third of products must be reported to the Ministry within three days after the change. The government has retained the right to disapprove these price changes, although this occurs rarely. The government may also influence pricing policy in companies under its direct or indirect control, particularly in the energy sector. Agricultural subsidies take the form of guaranteed prices. Utilities, which are state-owned, have not been scheduled for privatization, and the largest state-owned enterprises have not been privatized. Over 50 percent of economic activity in Croatia is therefore still controlled by the government.

3. Is it possible to own and operate a business? (Has there been legislation regarding the formation, dissolution, and transfer of businesses, and is the law respected? Do there exist overly cumbersome bureaucratic hurdles that effectively hinder the ability to own and dispose of a business? Are citizens given access to information on commercial law? Is the law applied fairly? Do regulation or licensing requirements impose significant costs on business and consumers? Do they create significant barriers to entry and seriously hamper competition?) The constitution guarantees the right to own and operate a business. In addition, it guarantees unrestricted transfer of profit and repatriation of capital, trade, and real estate investment; private ownership; and a profit-tax rate of 25 percent.

The full texts of laws affecting investment are published, usually within one month of passage. Draft laws are not often accessible to the public. Important court decisions are usually published or accessible by practitioners within 12 months of being issued. Sophisticated legal assistance on investment is available, particularly in Zagreb, and in general, is affordable to local investors.

A new bankruptcy law took effect on January 1, 1997. A debtor is considered insolvent when it is unable to meet its liabilities as they fall due or its liabilities exceed its assets. The law provides for reorganization. A panel of three judges supervises the settlement proceedings between the debtor and its creditors. A settlement may be approved by a simple majority of those creditors who participate in the proceedings. Bankruptcy proceedings are conducted by the Commercial Court within the jurisdiction of which the debtor has its registered office. A liquidator is required to verify claims, inquire into a debtor's financial position, sell assets, and satisfy claims. Transactions with third parties that are below fair value, concluded within a fixed time prior to liquidation, or not at arm's length may be reviewed and declared void.

4. Are courts effective, transparent, efficient, and quick in reaching decisions on property

and contract disputes? What alternative mechanisms for adjudicating disputes exist? As Croatian courts face a tremendous backlog due to shortages of judges and other problems, the settlement of commercial disputes often takes years. In late 1995, there were more than a million cases pending in Croatian courts.

When disputes arise, private parties may take their cases to court. Due to the general backlog of cases, however, parties may wait up to two years for a commercial case to be heard on its merits in Zagreb.

Croatia is a signatory of the following international conventions that regulate the mutual acceptance and enforcement of foreign arbitration: the 1923 Geneva Protocol on Arbitration Clauses, the 1927 Geneva Convention on the Execution of Foreign Arbitration Decisions, the 1958 New York Convention on the Acceptance and Execution of Foreign Arbitration Decisions, and the 1961 European Convention on International Business Arbitration.

5. Is business competition encouraged? (Are monopolistic practices limited in law and in practice? If so, how? To what degree is "insider" dealing a hindrance to open competition? Are government procurement policies open and unbiased?) Officially, competition is encouraged through a very liberal trade system and free entrance of foreigners to most industries. A Law on Competition and Monopoly was enacted in 1996 to address monopolistic practices, abuses from mergers, and other conditions that limit or prohibit trade. A competition protection agency is to be established to implement the policy.

Article 49 of the constitution forbids monopolies. In practice, however, some monopolies are still held by state-owned communications businesses such as the Croatian postal and telephone company; and the newspaper publishing houses Vjesnik and Slobodna Dalmacija. While guarding these public monopolies, Croatian authorities have been responsive to complaints about policies that hinder competition in other sectors. The Law on Transformation of Social Ownership initially favored insider-trading, but was amended in 1993 to make it easier for external investors to buy shares in a company on the Zagreb Stock Exchange. Through the Company Law, the Croatian government has leveled the playing field for foreign investors.

A Law on Trade, the first post-independence statute to regulate trade issues, took effect on February 1, 1996. It was prepared pursuant to EU legislation and World Trade Organization requirements. It defines unfair competition as acts that are contrary to good trade practices and that impede free competition or harm consumers. Under its terms, specific acts that may be considered unfair include methods of advertising or conducting sales that harm the goodwill or reputation of another merchant; the sale of goods that may cause confusion with respect to their origin, means of production, quantity or quality; the unjustified use of the name, trade name, trademark, or other designation of another entity or person, even with the owner's consent, that could cause confusion in the market; and the unlawful use of another's trade secrets. In addition to remedies of damages, the new law establishes fines for corporations and individuals, although there is no provision for injunctive relief.

6. To what extent has international trade been liberalized? To what degree has there been simplification/overhaul of customs and tariff procedures, and are these applied fairly? What

informal trade barriers exist? A customs system based on Western European models was implemented in 1992. It distinguishes between the protective role of the customs system as mandated by the GATT and the fiscal role of import duties. As of January 1, 1996, the main import levies in effect were tariffs ranging from 0 to 18 percent; a customs registration fee of one percent; a special import duty of 10 percent; and variable levies on agricultural imports. There are additional sales taxes or excise duties on cars, soft drinks, coffee, and other products that are entirely, or almost entirely, imported.

Traditionally, Croatia's leading export industries have been metal-manufacturing, textiles, chemicals, timber and wood processing, leather processing, food processing, and oil and gas. The total value of goods exported from the Republic of Croatia in 1996 was $4.5 billion, while imports into the Republic of Croatia amounted to $7.8 billion. Croatia's main trading partners are Germany and Italy, which accounted for 21 percent and 18.6 percent of exports, respectively, and 20.6 percent and 18.2 percent, respectively, of imports in 1996.

7. To what extent has foreign investment and capital flow been encouraged or constrained? The World Bank reports that Croatia is one of the most open economies in Central Europe. There are no limitations on foreign holdings. A foreigner may therefore purchase 100 percent of any Croatian company outside sensitive sectors, such as energy, utilities, and defense. In a 1996 move to encourage foreign investment, the Ministry of the Economy announced the establishment of a new agency that would serve as a "one-stop shop" to deal with all administrative problems faced by potential investors. This agency is still in development.

Free repatriation of profits and capital is guaranteed by the constitution, which also provides that rights acquired through foreign capital investments cannot be reduced by law or any other legal act. Foreign investors have the same rights, obligations, and legal status within an enterprise as domestic investors, provided that the condition of reciprocity is met. As an incentive, equipment imported as part of an investment by a foreign party is exempt from customs duties, provided that the investment is for a period of more than five years and that the foreign party's investment accounts for at least 20 percent of the total. Corporate tax is 25 percent. The current system of sales taxes was replaced by the VAT on January 1, 1998.

In order to stimulate and promote foreign direct investment, the government of Croatia, with assistance and support from the Foreign Investment Advisory Service of the World Bank, established the Croatian Investment Promotion Agency (CIPA), which began operations in September 1996.

Although CIPA was established and founded by the Government, it seeks to attract co-founders from the private domestic and foreign sector. All companies that operate in Croatia have been invited to join CIPA as co-founders. The companies that decide to join are expected to pay a nominal initial contribution and a yearly fee. In return, co-founders will have the opportunity to participate in the agency's principal decision making and advisory bodies.

The principal organ of CIPA is its Supervisory Council, which includes four members of the Croatian government, with the Prime Minister as its Chairman. Co-founders from the private sector will elect four other members of the Council. Two of these are to be Croatian co-founders. The other two are to be foreign co-founders. The governing organ of CIPA is expected to serve as a forum for a permanent dialogue between the government and the private sector.

CIPA's primary aim is to promote Croatia as a country with business opportunities and thereby attract direct foreign investments. The agency's activities will include identifying projects appropriate for foreign investments, informing foreign investors of these projects and opportunities, assisting foreign investors in their relations with government authorities, and stimulating a favorable environment for foreign investments in Croatia.

8. Has there been reform of the energy sector? (To what degree has the energy sector been restructured? Is the energy sector more varied, and is it open to private competition? Is the country overly dependent on one or two other countries for energy [including whether exported fuels must pass through one or more countries to reach markets]?) Privatization of the energy sector is scheduled to be completed by 1999. It is anticipated that the government will retain a substantial portion of the energy sector, 30 percent of shares will be transferred to the Pension Funds, and parliament will pass laws for each utility to regulate the distribution of the remaining shares. In 1994, the Croatian electricity enterprise HEP was converted into a state-owned joint stock company. The Ministry of Economy, which regulates the company, has decided to privatize only electricity generators. New power plants or the rehabilitation of existing power plants will be privately financed. INA, which accounts for the bulk of the oil and gas sector, will require comprehensive restructuring in order to be privatized. All direct price controls on energy have been removed, although some indirect controls remain due to continued government influence on major enterprises.

Croatia has been heavily dependent on imported energy. Mineral fuel imports cost approximately $860 million in 1990. Since then, they have stood at approximately $500 million.

CZECH REPUBLIC

Freedom in the World Ratings, 1989-1998

	1989-90	1990-91	1991-92	1992-93*	1993-94	1994-95	1995-96	1996-97	1997-98
Political Rights	6	2	2	2	1	1	1	1	1
Civil Liberties	6	2	2	2	2	2	2	2	2
Status	NF	F	F	F	F	F	F	F	F

Polity: Consolidated Democracy
Economy: Consolidated Market
Population: 10,357,000
PPP: $9,775
Ethnic Groups: Czechs (94 percent), Slovak (3 percent), Roma (2 percent)
Capital: Prague

* FH ratings through 1992-1993 are for the Czechoslovak Federal State

Political Process 1.25/7

1. When did national legislative elections occur? Were they free and fair? How were they judged by domestic and international election monitoring organizations? Who composes the government? The June 1996 parliamentary elections for the Czech Republic's Chamber of Deputies heralded the end of the transitional phase in the country's political scene, with the emergence of two strong parties on the left and right in the Western European mold. In a result nearly identical to that in 1992, the center-right Civic Democratic Party (ODS) won nearly 30 percent of the vote (68 seats). For the opposition, the center-left Czech Social Democrats (CSSD), led by Milos Zeman, was victorious. The party's 26-percent share (61 seats) quadrupled its returns from 1992. Unlike the typical Central and Eastern Europe social democratic party, which is a "reformed" Communist party, the CSSD comes from a long pre-Communist tradition of center-left politics. The other parties winning seats in the Chamber were the unreconstructed Communist Party of Bohemia and Moravia (KSCM), with 10.3 percent (22 seats); the Christian Democratic Union (KDU), with eight percent (18 seats); the extremist nationalist Republican Party, with 8 percent (18 seats); and the free-market Civic Democratic Alliance (ODA), with 6.3 percent (13 seats).

Of 200 parliamentary seats, the parties of the governing coalition managed only to win 99, a loss of six from their pre-election standings. As a result of its failure to win an outright majority, the ODS-led coalition was not assured of forming a government. The CSSD extracted concessions from the ODS-led coalition in return for its acquiescence in the formation of a minority government, which was named in July 1996, with Vaclav Klaus as Prime Minister.

In November 1997, allegations that the ODS had improperly accepted more than $200,000 in financial donations led the ODA and CDU to withdraw from the governing coalition and forced Klaus and his government to resign. Josef Tosovsky, who is not affiliated with any party, was named interim prime minister in January 1998, in a government that still included the three parties in the original coalition. While elections had been scheduled for 2000, the political deadlock in parliament and the interim government led to a change in the electoral law to allow for new elections in June 1998.

The 1992 constitution established a Senate along with the dominant Chamber. A lack of clarity in the constitutional text and political wrangling over electoral procedures, however, postponed Senate elections for four years. Two rounds of Senate elections were held in November 1996. Approximately 570 candidates registered to compete for Senate seats in 81 electoral districts. However, 100 of these registrations were rejected by the Central Electoral Commission due to technical errors, some of which were subsequently overturned by the constitutional court. Only three parties — ODS, KSCM, and CSSD — nominated a candidate in every district. ODS won the election, but with only a 39.6-percent share of the vote, which gave it 32 seats. The Social Democrats followed with 25 seats and 30.9 percent of the vote. The Christian Democrats won 13 seats; the ODA, seven; and the Communists, two. The second-round vote was viewed as a referendum on the ODS's performance. A total of 76 ODS candidates stood in the second round, but only 40 percent of them won. This poor showing was the result of a joint decision by all of the other parties, including ODS' coalition allies, to back whoever opposed the ODS candidate in a particular district. Over the objections of the ODS and with the support of the Social Democrats, the KDU successfully nominated its candidate, Petr Pithart, the Czechoslovak premier from 1990 to 1992, as Senate chairman.

In June 1990, the first post-1989 national legislative elections in Czechoslovakia were won by dissident Vaclav Havel's Civic Forum movement, which led peaceful demonstrations that brought down the hard-line Communist government. In the June 1992, national elections, two opposing parties each gained clear majorities in the different republics. Vaclav Klaus' center-right and pro-radical reform ODS, emerged victorious in the Czech lands. In the Slovak Republic, the Movement for a Democratic Slovakia (HZDS), which was headed by Vladimir Meciar, was the clear winner. Irreconcilable differences between the parties and their leadership led to the breakup of the Czechoslovak federation. With the countries' divorce on January 1, 1993, Klaus and Meciar became the leaders of their respective republics.

Foreign observers have determined that the 1990, 1992, and 1996 elections were free and fair.

2. When did presidential elections occur? Were they free and fair? Vaclav Havel was re-elected president of the Czech Republic by the parliament in January 1998. Under the constitution, presidents serve five-year terms. Since the dissolution of Civic Forum, Havel has had no political party affiliation.

Havel had been elected president of the Czechoslovak Federation in December 1989, by the Federal Assembly. He was then elected president of the Czech Republic by the Chamber of Deputies in January 1993.

3. Is the electoral system multiparty-based? Are there at least two viable political parties functioning at all levels of government? The electoral system is multiparty-based. Article 5 of the constitution states that the "political system is based on free and voluntary formation of and free competition between political parties."

In late 1989 and early 1990, parties began to form for the June 1990 legislative elections in

Czechoslovakia. At least two political parties function at different levels of government. Candidates often run independently in local elections, in which personal popularity can be more important than party membership. Independent candidates won approximately 40 percent of the vote in the November 1994 local elections. One newly elected senator is an independent, and another is a member of the extra-parliamentary Democratic Union Party.

4. How many parties have been legalized? Are any political parties illegal? More than 50 parties have emerged since the revolution of 1989. Fewer than 25 parties registered for the local elections in November 1994, and fewer than ten of these are of national importance. Twenty parties registered for the June 1996 parliamentary elections, but only six managed to clear the 5 percent threshold necessary for representation.

During their campaigns for the July 1996 elections, small parties complained of discrimination by the Central Electoral Commission, which is composed of individual party representatives who make decisions by majority vote. The commission ruled that the Free Democrats-Liberal National Social Party (FD-LNSP) was a coalition and not a single party, thereby raising its required share for Chamber representation from five to seven percent. The party complained that the Social Democrats and the other leftist parties were attempting to disqualify them through legalistic means. The Constitutional Court then ruled in favor of the FD-LNSP. Nevertheless, the FD-LNSP was unable to break even the 5-percent barrier.

In March 1996, internal affairs minister Jan Ruml announced that he would attempt to outlaw the new Party of Czechoslovak Communists, led by Miroslav Stepan, who is the only Communist imprisoned after 1989. Arguing that Stepan sought a "renewal of socialism," Ruml wanted to use the authority of the Crimes of Communism Act. Vaclav Klaus, however, later vetoed the move.

5. What proportion of the population belongs to political parties? The number of party members registered is between 8 and 12 percent of the adult population. In light of the relatively high level of voter turnout, however, this is not a very accurate measure of support.

6. What has been the trend of voter turnout at the municipal, provincial and national levels in recent years? Voter turnout in the Czech Republic has fallen since transition. In the first post-transition election in 1990, more than 90 percent of citizens voted. In the 1992 federal (Czechoslovak) elections, 85 percent of the population voted, although turnout was higher in the Czech republic than in the Slovak republic. Turnout in the November 1990 Czechoslovak local elections was 73 percent in the Czech lands and 63 percent in Slovakia, with an approximate national average of 70 percent. Excluding Prague, turnout in the November 1994 local elections averaged 54 percent in large cities and approximately 64 percent in towns and villages.

Voter turnout in 1996 was at two disparate levels. The Chamber election turnout was relatively high at 76 percent, while turnout for the Senate election was extraordinarily low with 35 percent in the first round, and 30 percent in the second round. The fact that the Senate is an unpopular institution — it is even less popular than the Chamber — together with the electoral fatigue resulting from two nationwide polls in quick succession — help to account for this result.

Civil Society 1.50/7

1. How many non-governmental organizations have come into existence since 1986? How many charitable/nonprofit organizations? Are there locally led efforts to increase philanthropy and volunteerism? What proportion of the population is active in private voluntary activity (from polling data)? As of early 1998, there were more than 30,000 NGOs operating in the Czech Republic. In 1988, there were approximately 2,000. As of mid-1995, there were approximately 2,500 foundations in the Czech Republic. Some international charitable organizations, such as the Salvation Army, have extensive operations in the Czech Republic.

2. What is the legal and regulatory environment for NGOs (i.e., ease of registration, legal rights, government regulation, taxation, procurement and access-to-information issues)? To what extent is NGO activism focused on improving the legal and regulatory environment? The growth of the NGO sector has been obstructed by economic constraints and delays in the passage of legislation on nonprofit organizations. In addition, a tax law passed in 1994 over the objections of President Havel ended the favorable treatment enjoyed by nonprofit organizations. In a compromise measure, the legislature empowered the Finance Ministry to enact appropriate regulations for nonprofit organizations. Draft laws have been long-delayed.

The right of public access to information is not enshrined in legislation, a deficiency that has drawn criticism from the European Union (EU).

3. What is the organizational capacity of NGOs? Do management structures clearly delineate authority and responsibility? Is information available on NGO management issues in the native language? Is there a core of experienced practitioners/trainers to serve as consultants or mentors to less developed organizations? The Prague Post Foundation hosts a monthly forum on Czech NGO management issues. The forum is known as the "International Roundtable for Not-For-Profit Organizations." Meetings are conducted in both English and Czech.

4. Are NGOs financially viable? What is their tax status? Are they obliged to and do they typically disclose revenue sources? Do government procurement opportunities exist for private, not-for-profit providers of services? Foreign sources of funding have supplied approximately half of the revenue used by Czech nonprofit organizations. NGOs have come to rely more and more on corporate and individual contributions as governmental, U.S., and EU (PHARE) assistance is slowly being phased out.

U.S. Agency for International Development is a major sponsor of Czech NGOs. The Democracy Network, a U.S. AID program designed to strengthen the nonprofit sector, has provided $1.5 million in assistance to NGOs.

5. Are there free trade unions? How many workers belong to these unions? Is the number of workers belonging to trade unions growing or decreasing? What is the numerical/proportional membership of farmers' groups, small business associations, etc.? The Communist Revolutionary Trade Union was abolished in March 1990. Most unionized workers belong to the Czech-Moravian Chamber of Trade Unions (CMKOS), which was established in April 1990 and currently includes 35 individual unions. Some unions are not a part of CMKOS, but these remain marginal.

Approximately two-thirds of all workers are members of a union. Despite this apparent strength, CMKOS generally remains politically independent. This is the result of many factors, the foremost being the severe mistrust that unions earned in the pre-1989 period as puppets of the Communist Party.

There are at least three farmers' groups. They are not very large, as farmers constitute only 5 percent of the workforce. Two small business associations merged in 1994 to consolidate their interests. Their membership and influence continue to grow.

6. What forms of interest group participation in politics are legal? The participation of interest groups in the political policy process is not yet legally regulated. Although some such activity exists, interest groups currently have relatively little power in the political process. Public petitions and demonstrations are legal and unrestricted.

7. How is the not-for-profit/NGO sector perceived by the public and government officials? What is the nature of media coverage of NGOs? To what extent do government officials engage with NGOs? While Havel has been supportive of NGOs, the limited powers of the presidency have also limited the impact of his support. The former Klaus government did not view NGOs as important political players. There is some indication, including a February 1998 resolution that recognized NGOs as important partners in social affairs, that the Tosovsky-led interim government views them more favorably,

In early 1998, an NGO publicity campaign entitled "30 Days" featured more than 290 events across the country and nearly 2,500 stories in the print and electronic media. TV-Nova was a major sponsor of the event.

The English-language *Prague Post* publishes a weekly column on a wide variety of issues that affect Czech NGOs. The column is translated and published in *Reflex*, a weekly newsmagazine.

Independent Media 1.50/7

1. Are there legal protections for press freedom? The Charter of Basic Rights and Freedoms protects the right to a free press. Current legislation protects both print and broadcast media, but is out of date. Much-debated revisions of the law had still not been adopted by the end of 1997. Czech journalists have criticized the draft laws for not requiring that state bodies give information to the press and for failing to protect journalists' rights to maintain the confidentiality of their sources.

2. Are there legal penalties for libeling officials? Are there legal penalties for "irresponsible" journalism? Have these laws been enforced to harass journalists? In April 1994, the Constitutional Court abolished a law that allowed for the prosecution of those accused of defaming government officials. A provision against defamation of the President and the Republic was retained, however, as was a provision allowing prosecution for the slander of government officials or departments.

In September 1997, Havel signed a law to repeal the provision against defamation of the president and the Republic. Until then, violators could be punished with prison terms of up to two years. The few people who were actually convicted under this law, however, only received suspended sentences. Even in these cases, Havel routinely pardoned the offenders.

There are no penalties for irresponsible journalism.

3. What proportion of media is privatized? What are the major private newspapers, television stations, and radio stations? The Czech Republic has scores of private newspapers and magazines. Of the Czech Republic's four television stations, two are private – TV-Nova, which enjoys a 71 percent market share, and TV Prima, which emerged from the struggling Premiera TV. There are 60 private radio stations, in addition to Czech Public Radio. Some major cities can connect to cable stations. Local stations are permitted but are not common, generally due to financial concerns). One private news agency, CTA, began operations in October 1994 and will compete with the state CTK agency.

4. Are the private media financially viable? From 1992 to 1995, print media costs increased 300 percent. This, together with the overcrowded nature of the market, has caused major turbulence, with the rapid disappearance of old publications and the quick appearance of new, merged, or re-formed publications. Many of these are more financially secure, primarily as a result of foreign investment. By March 1996, over half of the Czech press was foreign-owned. The largest holders are the Germans, followed by the Swiss and French. Media without foreign investment, government support or party support often have only limited solvency. Advertising rates and revenue have increased rapidly and are expected to reach 10.6 billion *koruna* ($393 million) in 1996.

5. Are the media editorially independent? Are the media's news-gathering functions affected by interference from government or private owners? The media are not always editorially independent. The case of Vladimir Stehlik, owner of the giant and bankrupt Poldi Steel Company, illustrates some of the problems with editorial independence in the Czech Republic. Both the government and TV-Nova have been very critical of Stehlik and his business practices, which are under investigation. Stehlik managed to purchase *Prace*, a trade-union daily, which now regularly attacks both the government and TV-Nova. Such editorial allegations are not uncommon: *Denni Telegraf*, for example, is widely viewed as a mouthpiece of the ODS.

A parliamentary commission has oversight powers for the Television and Radio Council. The Council regulates the telecommunications media by issuing and revoking licenses and monitoring programming. There is an independent journalists' association.

6. Is the distribution system for newspapers privately or governmentally controlled? There are three main printing companies in the Czech Republic. Typografia, a large printing company in Prague, is responsible for the printing of many national dailies. It is scheduled to be privatized.

7. What proportion of the population is connected to the Internet? Are there any restrictions on Internet access to private citizens? Paul Houcer, an editor of *Computerworld* magazine, estimates that there are as many as 250,000 regular Internet users in the Czech Republic. Approximately 15 percent are connected at home. Thirty percent are connected at school, while 55 percent are connected work.

8. What has been the trend in press freedom as measured by Freedom House's *Survey of Press Freedom*? Freedom House's annual *Survey of Press Freedom* rated Czechoslovakia "Partly Free" for 1989, and "Free" from 1990 through 1992. The Survey rated the Czech Republic "Free" from 1993 through the present. *The Economist* calculates that the Czech Republic has the world's fourth most free press, which ranks it ahead of both Germany (seventh) and Britain (ninth). Current press laws, however, do not provide for the right of media to have access to state information, and the legal protection of sources' confidentiality is not clearly provided.

Governance and Public Administration 2.00/7

1. Is the legislature the effective rule-making institution? The Czech parliament is an effective rule-making institution. In 1995, the Chamber of Deputies adopted approximately 300 statutes. Vaclav Klaus and the ODS effectively ran the legislature to advance their reform programs from 1992 to 1996. As a result of two inconclusive parliamentary elections in 1996, however, a tense political stalemate has slowed legislative action on a host of pressing issues.

2. Is substantial power decentralized to sub-national levels of government? What specific authority do sub-national levels have? In November 1990, under the Czechoslovak administration, several regional reforms took place. The ten-region system (seven Czech and three Slovak regions) of government under communism was eliminated, districts were placed under the administration of each republic, and municipal governments were converted into self-governing bodies. Thus, the Czech republic is subdivided, first, into 76 non-autonomous districts and, second, into thousands of autonomous local municipalities.

Article 8 of the constitution specifies that "self-government of territorial self-governing units is guaranteed," while Article 101 states that the state "may intervene in the activities of self-governing territorial divisions only if such intervention is required by protection of the law and only in a manner defined by law." Chapter 7 of the constitution deals specifically with local rule. It establishes the division of the Czech Republic into communities that "shall be the basic self-governing territorial divisions" and that shall be "administered by a community assembly." These include city councils that govern towns, villages and small cities, as well as district councils that govern sections of larger cities.

The constitution further states, however, that the "superior self-governing territorial divisions shall be lands or regions" that shall be "administered by an assembly of representatives." Thus, although the constitution establishes the order of authority, it does not specify in more detail the composition and features of this middle tier of government.

The continued process of regional reform has been a subject of intense debate in both successor republics to the Czechoslovak state. In the Czech Republic, the establishment of self-administrative regions has been complicated by fears of increased nationalist sentiment in the historical lands of Moravia and Silesia, as well as conflicts among parties. On the other hand, there is widespread feeling that failure to establish such regions could delay the country's entrance into the European Union.

An ODA-authored constitutional amendment on the establishment of a medium tier of elected government between the central government and the community councils was considered in March and April 1996. It was to establish nine regional bodies. The constitution actually calls for such bodies, but does not specify how they are to be composed or when they should be created. The bill was opposed principally by the ODS, which questioned whether creating these regional bodies was wise in a country as small as the Czech Republic. A January 1996 poll indicated that only 25 percent of Czechs considered the lack of such institutions to be a pressing problem. Nevertheless, 43 percent believed the creation of such bodies would improve state administration. Twenty-nine percent thought that these bodies would represent an improvement.

The coalition agreement signed after the June 1996, elections committed the government to establish these regions before the end of its term in 2000. ODA chairman and then-justice minister Jan Kalvoda proposed the establishment of 13 regions with considerable authority, including management of roads, schools, cultural institutions, health facilities, and forests.

3. Are sub-national officials chosen in free and fair elections? Article 102 of the constitution mandates that "Assembly members shall be elected by secret ballot on the basis of universal, equal and direct suffrage." According to the 1990 reforms, municipal or communal governments consist of assemblies chosen in local elections. These bodies then elect mayors and their deputies. District officials are appointed by the state, as districts are branches of the state. The first post-Communist local elections in 5,766 municipalities were held under these new rules in November 1990. Civic Forum won with 35.6 percent of the vote. This victory, which took place during a national debate over economic reform, gave a mandate to the government to continue on the path of radical reform.

The ODS won the largest percentage of support in the November 1994 local elections with 28 percent in the district councils and nearly 11 percent in the city councils. It was also victorious in Prague, with 41.2 percent of the vote. Josef Lux's KDU, however, received the greatest actual number of seats because its strength was in the more rural city councils where fewer voters were apportioned per seat. Despite expectations that they would do well, the Communists fared poorly. Independent candidates won slightly less than half of the city council seats and 13 percent of the district council seats.

The 1990 and 1994 local elections were generally deemed free and fair. The next local elections are scheduled for November 1998.

4. Do legislative bodies actually function? Is draft legislation easily accessible to the media and the public? In theory, the presence of the Senate should aid in stabilizing the political process in the Czech Republic. Article 33 of the constitution stipulates that, if the Chamber is dissolved, the Senate assumes legislative control until new elections are held. Due to the absence of a Senate, however, there was no practical constitutional way to dissolve the Chamber before November 1996. In the future, the low popularity of the Senate as an institution and the low turnout for its elections could undermine its legitimacy.

Local assemblies have the power to pass ordinances, call local referenda, and approve budgets. They have executive and legislative powers. Districts function as branches of the state and appear to operate smoothly.

5. Do the executive and legislative bodies operate openly and with transparency? Article 36 of the constitution guarantees that "meetings of both chambers [of parliament] shall be public" and that the "public may be excluded only under conditions defined by law." Legislative sessions are generally open to the public in practice and new laws are published. The transparency of local actions depends largely upon the quality of local media, which vary among regions.

6. Do municipal governments have sufficient revenues to carry out their duties? Do municipal governments have control of their own local budgets? Do they raise revenues autonomously or from the central state budget? Article 101 of the constitution stipulates that the self-governing regions have their own budgets and may have their own property. Former ODA Chairman Jan Kalvoda's proposed regions would have control of their own budgets. They would draw revenue from local taxes, property income, administrative fees, and state subsidies. Municipal governments have the power to approve budgets. It is estimated that municipalities received 43.5 percent of revenues from the state budget in 1995, versus 40.6 percent in 1994. With the exception of Prague, selling and renting real estate is an important source of revenue.

Municipalities are generally financially strapped, and mayors of small communities often do not receive financial compensation. Municipal governments in poor, industrialized areas such as northern Bohemia have reported difficulty in raising funds to attend to their communities' needs.

7. Do the elected local leaders and local civil servants know how to manage municipal governments effectively? There is substantial inefficiency at the local level due to the presence of incompetent, politically connected officials appointed by the Communists, as well as uncertainty about the procedural changes accompanying multiple reforms. These problems should diminish with time. Between 1989 and 1990, municipalities splintered and thereby increased in total number by 50 percent without regulatory consent. This situation has increased inefficiency. According to observers, petty corruption, such as small bribes to expedite matters, is common. For example, there have been allegations that civil servants request bribes in order to expedite the installation of telephone lines.

8. When did the constitutional/legislative changes on local power come into effect? Has there been a reform of the civil service code/system? Are local civil servants employees of the local or central government? A reformed civil service law has yet to be adopted in the Czech Republic. This has led to confusion about civil servants' status and responsibilities. Debate on drafts of such laws has been extensive.

Local reforms were enacted in November 1990. Further reforms were tabled until the division of the Czechoslovak state; specific legislation has not yet been passed. Reforms of the civil code have not yet been passed. Local civil servants are paid out of municipal budgets. District officials are appointed by the state.

Rule of Law 1.50/7

1. Is there a post-Communist constitution? How does the judicial system interpret and enforce the constitution? Are there specific examples of judicial enforcement of the constitution

in the last year? In December 1992, the Czech constitution was adopted by the Czech National Council. It took effect in January 1993 with the dissolution of the federal state.

2. Does the constitutional framework provide for human rights? Do the human rights include business and property rights? The Czechoslovak Federal Assembly adopted the Charter of Fundamental Rights and Freedoms in January 1991 to protect human rights. Although this charter is not in the constitution *per se*, according to Article 3 of the new Czech constitution, it is an "integral component of the constitutional system." Furthermore, Article 10 commits the Czech Republic to abide by ratified international treaties on human rights. Under Article 11 of the Charter, everyone has the right to own property.

3. Has there been basic reform of the criminal code/criminal law? Who authorizes searches and issues warrants? Are suspects and prisoners beaten or abused? Are there excessive delays in the criminal justice system? While the criminal code has undergone many revisions and amendments since 1989, including the adoption of a major law in 1993, an entirely reformed penal code still has not been adopted.

The civilian Internal Security Service (BIS) is independent of control by the Ministry of the Interior and reports to parliament and the Prime Minister's office. The police and BIS generally protect the individual rights that are guarenteed by law. Some members of the police, however, have been guilty of occasional abuses, which have been disproportionately directed at Roma and foreigners.

Police may hold suspects without charge for no longer than 24 hours, a right that was recently upheld in the Constitutional Court. Court cases themselves have been greatly delayed due to the lack of experienced judges and investigators and a still-evolving legal environment. The time it takes for a case to go to trial has increased from 89 days in 1989 to 212 days in 1997, during which time defendants are held in custody. Approximately 35 percent of prisoners are detainees awaiting trial.

4. Do most judges rule fairly and impartially? How many remain from the Communist era? Judges rule fairly and impartially. A large number of judges were dismissed between 1989 and 1992 for connections with the former Communist regime. Many resigned voluntarily and now have private legal practices. The 1991 law on the judiciary designated judges appointed after January 1990 to be life-appointees. Those appointed before 1990 were dismissed as of August 1992 unless they were re-appointed within twelve months. Once re-appointed, they can hold their positions for life. Many new judges have been hired since the transition from communism began.

On the Constitutional Court, which was established in 1993, there are now 15 presidentially-appointed judges with ten-year terms.

5. Are the courts free of political control and influence? Are the courts linked directly to the Ministry of Justice or any other executive body? The judiciary is independent in law and in practice. Article 82 of the constitution states that judges "shall be independent in the performance of their office" and that "no one may jeopardize their impartiality." In addition, a "judge may not be recalled or transferred to another court against his will; exceptions, ensuing in particular from disciplinary liability, shall be specified by law." Under Article 86, judges on the Constitutional Court are protected from interference. These protections are upheld in practice. New judges enjoy life tenure and are not demoted or transferred for political reasons.

Nevertheless, judges retain administrative connections with the Ministry of Justice, through which they are appointed and promoted. A 1995 Czech Helsinki Committee report took note of frequent interference in ongoing investigations and court trials by politicians making pronouncements through the media.

The earnings gap between judges and private sector attorneys is much larger than those in the West. In part as a result of Czech legal education, which trains lawyers and judges separately, and in part due to the public's mistrust of the profession under the Communists, magistrates do not yet enjoy Western-style non-pecuniary benefits of prestige and respect. They also do not always have adequate support in the form of law clerks, court reporters, bailiffs, and legal materials.

6. What proportion of lawyers is in private practice? How does this compare with the previous year? It is estimated that over half of all lawyers are employed by the private sector, including Czech and foreign groups, legal firms, and other corporations. This represents no significant change from 1996-97. Salaries for lawyers in the private sector are substantially larger than for those in the public sector. Lawyers must belong to the Czech Bar Association in order to practice law.

7. Does the state provide public defenders? The Charter of Fundamental Rights and Freedoms guarantees access to legal assistance by accused indigents. In practice, the state does provide public defenders in criminal and some civil cases. The International Helsinki Committee has found, however, that many who would otherwise be eligible for such aid do not receive it because the process involved is complicated.

8. Has there been a comprehensive reform of anti-bias/discrimination laws, including protection of ethnic minority rights? Hate crimes, particularly against Roma, are not unusual. There have been reports of neglect and even abuse by policemen, who are often slow to respond to calls for help by Roma who have been victimized in hate crimes. Observers have noted that local courts sometimes issue minor penalties for hate crimes, and deal more harshly with Roma than with Czechs. In June 1997, a judge in Hradec Kralove refused to penalize a Czech for hate crimes on the grounds that Czechs and Roma belonged to the same race. The justice ministry, however, appealed the decision, which was reversed by the Supreme Court in October 1997.

In January 1996, a special department was established to deal with extremist groups, and directives were issued to prosecutors to seek higher penalties in hate-crime cases. In December 1997, the parliament ratified the Council of Europe's Framework Convention for the Protection of National Minorities.

Approximately 3,500 people, most of whom are Roma, are de facto stateless. This is due to the cumbersome and overly bureaucratic naturalization procedures in Czech law.

Corruption **B**

1. What is the magnitude of official corruption in the civil service? Must an average citizen pay a bribe to a bureaucrat in order to receive a service? What services are subject to bribe requests — for example, university entrance, hospital admission, telephone installation, obtaining a license to operate a business, applying for a passport or other official documents? What is the average salary of civil servants at various levels? Observers report that the system of military contracting is the area most prone to corruption.

2. Do top policy-makers (the President, ministers, vice-ministers, top court justices, and heads of agencies and commissions) have direct ties to businesses? How strong are such connections, and what kinds of businesses are these? In May 1996, journalists uncovered evidence that contributions of $220,000 had been made to the ruling ODS in the names of a dead Hungarian and a Mauritian who had no known major sources of income. In November 1997, former foreign minister Josef Zieleniec stated that this money was likely to have come from a businessman involved in current privatization deliberations.

3. Do laws requiring financial disclosure and disallowing conflict of interest exist? Have publicized anti-corruption cases been pursued? To what conclusion? The privatization process has generally been free of major scandals. In October 1994, however, Jaroslav Lizner, the director of the Coupon Privatization Center, was arrested and charged with corruption in the privatization of the Klatovy Dairy. Lizner apparently accepted an 8 koruna ($300,000) bribe during a police sting operation.

The Czech Republic has been the scene of numerous shoot-outs involving mafia members from republics of the former Soviet Union. In August 1997, three people were wounded in a Prague gunfight between members of Tajik and Ukrainian mafias. Chechen gangsters were involved in an earlier shooting incident.

4. What major anti-corruption initiatives have been implemented? How often are anti-corruption laws and decrees adopted? The Czech Republic signed the Convention on Combatting Bribery of Foreign Public Officials in November 1997. This document makes the bribery of foreign officials as much a crime as bribery of domestic officials. It also requires stricter accounting and record-keeping to increase transparency and reduce the bureaucratic concealment of corruption.

5. How do major corruption-ranking organizations like Transparency International rate this country? In July 1997, Transparency International ranked the Czech Republic 27th in its list of 52 countries surveyed for its Corruption Perception Index (CPI). The country's CPI score was 5.20 in 1997 (on a one to ten scale on which low numbers indicate greater corruption, which represented a decline from 5.37 in 1996. Its corruption score is virtually the same as those of Hungary and Poland.

Privatization **2.00/7**

1. What percentage of the GDP comes from private ownership? What percentage of the labor force is employed in the private sector? How large is the informal sector of the economy? In 1990, Czechoslovakia had the largest state sector of all the emerging post-Communist CEE countries, with only a negligible portion of national output from the private sector. As of the end of 1996, almost 75 percent of GDP had been produced in the private sector.

2. What major privatization legislation has been passed? What were its substantive features? Restitution of Communist-confiscated property began in November 1990, and lasted until September 1991. Property with a value of 75 to 125 billion koruna was transferred into private hands through restitution. This included approximately 100,000 physical properties, such as houses, farms, and shops.

Privatization of small enterprises such as shops, service establishments, and restaurants followed the restitution process and created more controversy. Despite strong pressure for preferences in the form of closed rounds of auctions restricted solely to employees of the firms being privatized, the parliament rejected such preferences in the summer of 1990. After assets were selected to be privatized, the auctions were open to all Czech citizens, with no special preferences. The auctions began in January 1991, and were concluded at the end of 1993, although the majority of small enterprises were sold by April 1992. More than 22,000 small enterprises were sold, with shops constituting 58 percent of sales; service establishments, 18 percent; restaurants, 8 percent; and motor vehicles, 7 percent. The total value transferred through the program for the privatization of small enterprises amounted to more than 30 billion koruna, or more than $1 billion.

The foundation for large-scale privatization was created in April 1990, when laws established the legal foundation for converting state-owned enterprises (SOEs) into joint-stock companies. In the first half of 1990, the 100 large trusts that dominated the state sector were split into 330 independent enterprises, while the vast majority of Communist-appointed top-level directors were dismissed in favor of their deputies. With the need for speed and competition in mind, the large-scale privatization law was passed in April 1991. The initial large-scale privatization program was divided into two waves. The first began in February 1992, and the second was launched in April 1994. Privatization of each enterprise was based on the "privatization project." These were proposals for the future of each firm, including restructuring and some combination of five different privatization instruments: transformation into a joint-stock company (or "voucher privatization"), direct sale to predetermined buyers, public auction, free transfer to municipalities, and trust funds. Management was required to submit a basic privatization project, but anyone was allowed to submit competing projects. These projects were submitted to a "black box" decision-making process at the Ministry of Privatization. Mirroring the experience with restitution and small privatization, speed was emphasized as a primary goal.

The Ministry of Privatization's criteria for project selection gave priority to mass privatization components in competing proposals. As a result of this institutional bias, the voucher program became the core of the privatization program for large-scale enterprises. Three-fourths of medium and large enterprises in the beginning of the reform program had mass privatization components, however, the program had never been attempted on a large scale. Most Western academics and observers had predicted that it would fail.

Beginning in 1991, all Czechoslovak citizens aged 18 or more were made eligible to purchase a voucher booklet from one of 648 distribution centers. The nominal purchase price was 1,000 koruna (approximately $35, or one week's wages for the average worker). Trading was disallowed until the secondary market began after share allocation. Investment privatization funds (IPFs), which managed citizens' vouchers and promised large returns, piqued public interest in vouchers. Approximately 72 percent of voucher purchasers of vouchers invested their points in IPFs. Eventually, 264 IPFs formed in the Czech lands for the first wave and another 353 formed in the second wave. The largest IPFs were run by insurances companies and commercial and savings banks.

Privatization has slowed considerably since the process began. Shares worth 229 billion koruna ($8.3 billion) are still in state hands. In part, this is due to the fact that all of the easy sales have already been made. Currently, 77 percent of these unsold shares are in 56 "strategic" enterprises and will be exceedingly difficult to privatize for political reasons. The privatization of the remaining enterprises, which are owned directly by the state or indirectly through the National Property Fund (NPF), the state body that holds unprivatized equity, will be made on a case-by-case basis.

The other major portion of privatization is the gradual sale of residual state shares in enterprises privatized in the two waves of voucher privatization. By the end of 1995, these had been valued at 52 billion koruna ($2 billion). The government sold these shares at the pace of 2 billion koruna per month through 1996.

3. What proportion of agriculture, housing and land, industry, and small business and services is in private hands? *Agriculture*: Most agricultural land was privatized under restitution, a process that began in 1991. Other farms were put up for auction. As of mid-1995, it was estimated that approximately 90 percent of agriculture had been privatized, including all former cooperatives and most state farms.

Housing and Land: As part of property reform, the government passed a law soon after the 1989 revolution to give housing and land to the municipality in which they were located. Persons living in these units could then apply to buy them from the municipal government at a discounted price. This process may vary by municipality. In 1994, legislation was passed to provide for the discounted purchase of apartment houses by cooperative groups if members of the groups resided in the building. As of late 1994, it was estimated that approximately 40 to 60 percent of all housing units had been privatized.

Industry: It is estimated that the private share of industry exceeded 80 percent by early 1996. The remaining industries will be much more difficult to privatize. These industries are in the so-called strategic sector: communications, energy, mining and metallurgy, and transportation. In June 1995, a Dutch-Swiss consortium purchased a 27 percent stake in the SPT telecommunications monopoly. Twenty-six percent of the enterprise was sold for vouchers, while the remainder was held by the NPF.

Another important factor is the retention of ownership by the government through two major mechanisms. The first is the National Property Fund, which holds minority shares in firms sold through mass privatization. Studies have shown, however, that NPF board members have been extremely passive. Thus, state ownership of enterprise shares has not necessarily led to a politicization of business decisions. The second mechanism of government ownership is the complex web of cross-ownership in the financial sector. The largest banks are still state-owned.

They hold large equity stakes in investment funds, which in turn own newly-privatized companies. While there has not been significant evidence of government interference through these links in privatized firms, there is still some legitimate cause for caution. The ongoing privatization of state-owned banks is an important step toward finding a long-term solution to this problem.

Business and Services: Nearly all small businesses and services have been privatized. Out of a workforce of 5 million, the Czech Republic now has nearly 900,000 entrepreneurs, most of whom are involved with newly founded businesses rather than former state companies. Small businesses are the fastest growing portion of the private sector. They now provide 20 percent of industrial output.

4. What has been the extent of insider (management, labor, and nomenklatura) participation in the privatization process? What explicit and implicit preferences have been awarded to insiders? The "small privatization" process of retail, trade, and consumer service establishments was competitive. In auctions, winning bids were, on average, approximately 6.3 times the opening price. This indicates that insiders were not able to buy formerly state-owned businesses without substantial competition from outsiders. This contrasts with Poland, where winning bids were approximately the same as the opening price.

In the first two waves of sales of large enterprises in 1992 and 1994, outsiders were allowed to submit competing privatization projects. Competition was intense, with an average of 17 proposals received for each state firm. There was no institutional bias in favor of insiders. In fact, winning privatization projects had overwhelming voucher components. Observers have called the voucher process the least insider-dominated form of privatization.

5. How much public awareness of and support for privatization has there been? What major interest groups oppose and advocate privatization? The CSSD, led by a vocal Zeman, has been an opponent of the privatization process as conducted by the former governing coalition. It is particularly opposed to further privatization in the health care and energy sectors, as well as to the restitution of property to the church. The unreformed Communists are also major opponents of privatization, but they remain marginal as a political force.

Macroeconomics 2/7

1. Has the taxation system been reformed? (What areas have and have not been overhauled? To what degree are taxpayers complying? Is tax compliance difficult to achieve? Has the level of revenues increased? Is the revenue-collection body overburdened? What is the overall tax burden?) The old tax system was only slightly reformed between 1990 and 1992. This tax system relied mainly on implicit taxation in the form of turnover taxes and confiscation of SOE profits. In January 1993, the Czech Republic introduced a major tax reform through a value-added tax (VAT) and new corporate and individual income taxes. There have been three major goals of tax reform since the transition. The first of these was to subject the mushrooming private sector to normal taxation, especially as the government was essentially giving away its tax base through privatization and the restructure of SOEs. The second goal was to broaden the tax base. Accordingly, services were included for the first time. The final goal was to reduce the overall burden of taxation. This was accomplished by lowering tax rates, which had been as high as 85 percent with further levies on profits, and increasing depreciation allowances. The new taxes also achieved this goal by being much less distorting, which reduced taxation's excess burden on the economy.

Major taxes currently levied in the Czech Republic include a personal income tax of 15 to 40 percent; a corporate income tax of 35 percent; a social security fund tax of 12.5 percent for employees and 35 percent for employers; a VAT of 22 percent, but only 5 percent for some items; a social insurance tax of 35 percent. There is no capital gains tax.

The VAT was reduced by one percent in January 1995. Another tax reduction took effect in January 1996, when all corporate and personal income taxes were reduced by several percentage points. In January 1998, several tax rate reductions were introduced. The VAT rate on energy was reduced from 22 to 5 percent, and the corporate income tax rate was cut from 39 to 35 percent.

Enforcement of taxes is relatively lax, especially in small-scale enterprises. Underreporting profits and keeping two sets of accounting books (one accurate book and another for the tax collector) are widespread practices. Some shops reportedly ask customers if they want to buy a product "with Klaus or without Klaus", that is to say, with or without sales tax. Czech police and tax authorities complain that irregularities in the tax and commercial codes prevent proper investigation and prosecution of tax violations. According to one police estimate, only 10 percent of tax violators are caught. The problem is compounded by the frequent changes in the tax code in the early transition years and by the prevalence of easily hidden cash transactions.

The most spectacular decline in tax revenue in the region between 1989 and 1993 took place in the Czech Republic. While this record improved in the following years, a decline in tax revenue in the second half of 1996 has increased the government's willingness to increase tax compliance, especially in the area of the VAT.

2. Does fiscal policy encourage private savings, investment and earnings? (Has there been any reform/alteration of revenue and budget policies? How large are budget deficits and overall debt? Is the financing of the social insurance/pension system sustainable? What proportion of the budget is taken up by subsidies to firms and individuals?) The bulk of macro-economic reform began in September 1990. This included stabilization of the economy through a restrictive fiscal and monetary regime and the reduction in the size and interventionism of government. Czechoslovakia had inherited not only a swollen state enterprise sector, but also an expansive and intrusive government, even by the standards of Communist countries in the region. In 1989, government revenue and expenditure amounted to 62.1 percent and 64.5 percent, respectively, of GDP, compared with 41.4 percent and 48.8 percent for Poland. The governing coalition has reiterated its commitment to lowering government expenditures as a proportion of GDP by 1 percent annually.

The Czech Republic has come closest to the balanced budget ideal of all transition economies and actually achieved a surplus in 1993, 1994, and 1995. The budget deficit rose to 2.3 percent of GDP by the end of 1996. Local governments' budgets are generally balanced. Gross indebtedness is only 18 percent of GDP.

A balanced 1998 budget was passed in October 1997. This was a considerable achievement in the aftermath of the substantial budgetary cuts necessitated by the May 1997 currency crisis.

The solid general macroeconomic picture led Standard and Poor's to give the Czech Republic an "A" investment grade rating. The Organization for Economic Cooperation and Development (OECD) admitted the republic — the first post-Communist nation to gain admission — in December 1995.

Prior to 1989, Czechoslovakia had been spending an astonishing 25 percent of GDP on industrial subsidies. The massive decrease in this spending provided the bulk of the reduction in government expenditures between 1990 and 1992. Subsidies then fell to only 4.6 percent of GDP – an average rate for market economies. Curtailing the growth in the money supply and inexpensive credits to SOEs drastically reduced a large indirect subsidy. Together, these reductions in subsidies represented a genuine hardening of budget constraints of SOEs.

Subsidies for housing cost 13.7 billion koruna ($507 million) in the 1997 budget. Heating subsidies cost 4.5 billion koruna ($167 million), a decrease from the previous year's 6.9 billion koruna ($256 million). The new power of the CSSD-led opposition in parliament may lead to an increase in social expenditures, since its cooperation in other areas of economic policy is needed. Nevertheless, real reform is needed in health insurance and pension programs, where an awkward mix of state and market policies manages to be both unstable and inefficient.

The government's balanced 1998 budget was passed by parliament in October 1997.

3. Has there been banking reform? (Is the central bank independent? What are its responsibilities? Is it effective in setting and/or implementing monetary policy? What is the actual state of the private banking sector? Does it conform to international standards? Are depositors protected?) The State Bank of Czechoslovakia was established as the independent central bank in charge of monetary policy in 1990. Its Czech successor, the CNB, is independent by law. Article 98 of the Constitution notes that "the main purpose of [the CNB's] operations shall be to care for the stability of the currency" and that "intercessions in its operations may be effected only on the basis of law." It is also autonomous in practice. It is responsible for money market policy, the money supply, regulation of the banking sector, and the determination of interest rates. Most regulations accord with EU-standard banking regulations. The CNB's supervisory authority was augmented by two amendments to the banking code in 1994. These amendments also established deposit insurance, which guarantee deposits of up to 100,000 koruna (approximately $3600).

The Czech banking sector is one of the weakest and least reformed areas of the economy. It suffers from numerous problems, including a lack of experience in management and lending, cases of outright fraud, a lack of transparency, and inadequate supervision from above by the CNB. Bank-sector privatization also lags behind that of other sectors of the economy.

A more systemic problem in the banking sector is the complex web of interlocking ownership and credit arrangements between the banks, investment funds, the government, and the NPF. For example, the Investicnia Postovni Banka (IPB) directly or indirectly owns many Czech companies. At the same time, these companies are owners of the IPB bank. This sort of confused ownership undermines shareholder control of banks and leaves management free from the discipline imposed by profit-maximizing owners. In early 1997, however, the CNB proposed reforms to begin to address this problem. These include restrictions on ownership of non-bank firms, as well as a ban on shareholder ownership of more than a 10 percent stake in a bank.

In 1996, the Czech banking system underwent a severe crisis. Initially, the problems were confined to small banks that could not meet capital requirements. In August 1996, the Kreditni and Investicni Banka, the nation's sixth largest, collapsed. Its fall resulted in the loss of 12 billion koruna ($440 million). In September 1996, the CNB placed Agrobanka, the largest private bank and the fifth largest overall, under forced administration. An auditor estimated losses in that case to be 10 billion koruna ($330 million). In all, 12 of 60 banks failed in the crisis. Six of these are in bankruptcy, and the rest under forced administration. As of June 1996, 39 percent of bank loans were "classified," which means that "there exists uncertainty about their repayment."

In September 1996, Czech police charged five people with fraud in connection with the Kreditni collapse. The government soon established a special investigative team to examine issues of bank fraud. A special parliamentary commission was also formed. In April 1997, 11 people were charged in connection to the Agrobanka collapse. In May, two managers of Investicni bank were arrested on embezzlement charges.

A state company was established in October 1996 to buy bad loans from small banks in order to help stabilize them. Thus far, however, the collapses have only affected 4 percent of all banking assets. The costs of bank reconstruction in 1996 amounted to 37 billion koruna ($1.2 billion). Depositors were fully compensated by the Deposit Insurance Fund and credits provided by the CNB.

By early 1997, there were 54 licensed banks in the Czech Republic. Five banks dominate the sector, with 67 percent of its assets. Foreign banks hold 18 percent of its assets.

The pace of bank privatization has increased considerably, particularly of the four largest state-owned banks. In July 1997, the government announced the sale of its 36.3 percent stake in Investicnia Postovni Banka to Nomura International. In August, the state decided to sell the majority of the state's shares in the other three — Komercni Banka, Ceska Sporitelna, and Ceskoslovenska obchodnibanka — to strategic investors.

4. How sound is the national currency? (To what extent has inflation eroded its value? Is the value of the currency fixed or does it float? Is the currency convertible? How large are the hard currency reserves? Has exchange rate policy been stable and predictable?) Since May 1993, the value of the koruna has been fixed to a two-currency basket. Thirty-five percent is fixed to the dollar, and the remaining 65 percent is fixed to the German *mark*. In October 1995, the Foreign Exchange Law made the koruna fully convertible for current account transactions and partially convertible for capital account transactions. Firms are not restricted in borrowing funds from abroad.

From 1990 until 1995, the koruna's fixed exchange rate was quite stable due to a determined Central Bank and extensive foreign exchange reserves. Substantial capital flows made it necessary to widen the fluctuation band to plus or minus 7.5 percent in February 1996. International speculative attacks on the koruna increased in early 1997, when markets gambled that the CNB would not be able to sustain the fixed exchange rate. While initially attempting to resist international forces, the CNB was forced to float the koruna in May 1997. The initial level of devaluation was 15 percent, but the level fell to 10 percent by the end of the summer.

Fiscal and monetary discipline is responsible for the moderate inflation record of the Czech

Republic, which is the best in post-Communist Europe. Inflation dropped from 10 percent in 1994 to 8.8 percent in 1996.

5. Is there a functioning capital market infrastructure? (Are there existing or planned commodities, bond, and stock markets? What are the mechanisms for investment and lending? What government bodies have authority to regulate capital markets?) The Prague Stock Exchange (PSE) is the highest-capitalized equity market in the region. There are approximately 1,700 companies on the exchange, the majority of which were created by the two waves of voucher privatization. There are two alternatives to the PSE: the electronic RM-system for over-the-counter trades, and the Ministry of Finance-created Center for Securities. Both of these were originally created to trade privatization vouchers, but real shares are now traded on each.

Unfortunately, since its creation, the PSE has experienced numerous problems and has acquired the reputation of being an insiders' market. The biggest of these problems is the lack of transparency. Many of the traded companies fail to provide information on their operations to potential investors. They also do not inform current shareholders of arguably important events like earnings and mergers. Another problem is the high numer of bottlenecks in trading activity. These problems have led to chronically low liquidity.

In April 1998, a new Securities Commission began to address these problems. The commission's enforcement powers are limited, however, in that it can only make recommendations to the Ministry of Finance.

Liquidity is low because most of the companies on the exchange are not regularly traded on the PSE itself. Most transactions are made privately. The average daily trading volume in 1995 was only $30.9 million. In 1997, 1,000 blocks of shares were removed from the PSE for lack of trading activity. The PSE is currently more of an instrument of trading equity than of raising it.

Amendments to securities law took effect in July 1996. They increased protections for minority shareholders by requiring new majority owners to offer a buyout to all shareholders at a weighted six-month PSE share price. In addition, boards will be prevented from taking a company private without a 75 percent majority decision by all shareholders. They also increase transaction transparency by requiring the disclosure of major share acquisitions, mandating that listed firms publish their annual statements three months after the close of the fiscal year, and establishing stock-lending, which was previously unregulated, as a "legally binding contractual relationship."

The amendments also require licensing of investment funds, requiring the use of international accounting standards, mandating the segregation of investment fund assets from the assets they manage for their clients, and making them file quarterly reports on their portfolios. The enforcement of the last of these will be key, as investment funds in the past have ignored already-existing reporting rules.

The administrative capacity of the Ministry of Finance, however, may not be up to the task of Western-style regulation of the securities industry. Jan Ververka, the Ministry's chief of capital markets supervision, complained in November 1996 that his department is only able to regulate actively 20 percent of the 800 investment funds and brokerages. Several Western investors have noted that regulators sometimes ignore clear violations of existing rules.

Two commodity exchanges exist in the Czech Republic. The first is the Brno Farm Produce

Exchange, founded in July 1993. It deals mainly with agricultural commodities. The more general Czech-Moravian Commodity Exchange in Kladno was established in November 1995, and trades a wide variety of commodities.

As a result of a tight and well-managed fiscal policy, the Czech Republic's bond market is dominated by long-term private sector debt. The market is relatively small, however, and, as a result, a mature secondary market in bonds has yet to emerge. The total nominal value of publicly traded bonds was 10.7 percent of GDP in June 1996. Bonds accounted for 35.7 percent of PSE trading in 1995. Liquidity and transparency in the bond market, as in the equity market, leave much to be desired. The bond derivatives market is immature.

Microeconomics 2/7

1. Are property rights guaranteed? (Are there both formal and de facto protections of private real estate and intellectual property? Is there a land registry with the authority and capability to ensure accurate recording of who owns what? What are the procedures for expropriation, including measures for compensation and challenge? Have any seizures taken place? Property rights are guaranteed under Article 10 of the Charter of Fundamental Rights and Freedoms, which, under Article 3 of the new constitution, is "an integral component of the constitutional system."

The Czech Republic adopted a patent code in 1990 and a trademark law in 1988 and 1990. In June 1995, amendments to the trademark law harmonized the Czech intellectual property rights (IPR) "Law on Trademarks and Copyrights" with EU standards. These amendments make it easier to enforce, register, and sell trademarks, including those of foreign registry. The language on foreign registration was adopted after a small scandal in which the brother of a high-ranking government official registered names such as Jaguar, Toyota, Chevrolet, and Audi as his own. The Czech Republic is a signatory of numerous international IPR conventions. In April 1996, parliament adopted laws that strengthen the protection of computer software.

While Czech legal protections for intellectual property are adequate, enforcement is rather problematic, as in all other post-communist countries. For example, one major difficulty in implementation is the long delays in enforcing IPR laws against violators. The backlog of cases in the courts is approximately two years, enough time for substantial damage to have been incurred. As of the end of 1995, only 366 people had been convicted of IPR crimes. U.S. firms have estimated that more than $117 million was lost to copyright violations in 1997. This gap between law and practice has been recognized by the World Intellectual Property Organization, which has recently suggested that the Czech Republic be added to the list of countries impeding trade.

No expropriation has taken place since the end of Communist rule. Eminent domain is exercised under standards of international law, with due process and without discrimination.

Restitution of property nationalized by the Communists was completed by 1992. Nevertheless, due to the slow pace of courts, not all title has been transferred to new owners. This means that it is not always known who actually owns a particular property.

2. To what extent have prices been liberalized? What subsidies remain? Approximately 85 percent of government-controlled producer and consumer prices were liberalized in the beginning of 1991. After the first year of liberalization, 18 percent of GDP was valued in regulated prices. Between 1990 and the end of 1992, this figure fell from 85 percent to 5 to 6 percent. Among commodity groups, energy, housing rents, water, transportation (especially passenger), telecommunications, health care, and some agricultural products are still regulated.

Nevertheless, the government has made public its commitment to liberalize these prices within the next several years. Even when prices are controlled, adjustments have been made consistently in the upward direction. In July 1997, for example, public housing rents were raised between 22 and 100 percent, gas and electricity prices were raised 15 percent, and heating prices were increased by 39 percent.

The government has effectively suspended national wage bargaining between labor, employers, and the government under the Tripartite Council. In July 1995, wage regulation by the government was eliminated.

3. Is it possible to own and operate a business? (Has there been legislation regarding the formation, dissolution, and transfer of businesses, and is the law respected? Do there exist overly cumbersome bureaucratic hurdles that effectively hinder the ability to own and dispose of a business? Are citizens given access to information on commercial law? Is the law applied fairly? Does regulation (or do licensing requirements) impose significant costs on business and consumers? Do they create significant barriers to entry and seriously hamper competition?) Operating a business is relatively easy to do. Forming a business, however, necessitates nagivation through a lengthy and complex process of obtaining registrations and licenses.

The Czech Civil and Commercial Codes, which were adopted in 1992, are based heavily on the German and Austrian codes. The Commercial Code, which was adopted in January 1992, replaced 80 scattered regulations and codes and established the framework for inter-business transactions. Many of the provisions of the codes, however, remain vague.

The first Czech bankruptcy law was adopted in 1991. A second law was passed in 1993. The revised bankruptcy law of March 1996 streamlines and simplifies the bankruptcy process, thereby eliminating old bureaucratic obstacles. It now permits forced debt restructuring and prevents "looting" transactions. Nevertheless, the major Czech banks that are the largest creditors remain hesitant to force their debtors — inefficient and large ex-state-owned enterprises — into bankruptcy. The political repercussions of these state-owned banks imperiling the jobs of thousands of workers, for now, outweigh the financial costs incurred by not initiating bankruptcy proceedings. Moreover, bankruptcy remains an uncertain proposition for both debtor and creditor. This is due to the three-to-four-year backlog in bankruptcy courts and the lack of an established secondary market for seized assets. As with dispute resolution, courts do not have enough experience and resources. Bankruptcy statistics show, however, that, even before the recent amendments, firms and courts were gaining experience with the procedure and were disposing of cases more efficiently.

4. Are courts effective, transparent, efficient, and quick in reaching decisions on property and contract disputes? What alternative mechanisms for adjudicating disputes exist? The courts are frequently not effective in settling disputes. This is due to the burden of a very large number of new cases, inadequate number of judges, and the inexperience of these judges in dealing with complex commercial issues. This leads to significant time lags in rendering judgment. Commercial disputes are heard between seven months and two years from the date of filing. Decisions are reached between one and three years later. A large body of established precedent has also yet to be followed. Important trial judgments are published.

The Czech Republic is a member of the New York Convention on Arbitration and is therefore legally bound to recognize and enforce arbitration decisions.

5. Is business competition encouraged? (Are monopolistic practices limited in law and in practice? If so, how? To what degree is "insider" dealing a hindrance to open competition? Are government procurement policies open and unbiased?) The country's competition law was adopted in 1991. The Office for the Protection of Economic Competition is reponsible for policing anti-competitive behavior. The Czech Republic has been judged to have been one of the most successful competition policies in the region. Furthermore, an agreement was reached in January 1996 to coordinate and harmonize the competition policies of the Czech Republic and the European Commission.

As elsewhere in the region, however, the country's competition office is dominated by staff from the price-control ministries of the old regime. These people and, by extension, the ministry, often see their role as enforcing economic policy rather than establishing fair operating rules. For example, competition authorities have been involved in investigating the justification for insurance price-hikes. They have also meddled in industrial policy-making by allowing a firm to acquire 60 percent of the Czech coffee market in return for employment and investment guarantees. In addition, the problem of industry "capture" of regulatory agencies seems particularly acute across post-Communist Europe, with the Czech Republic as no exception. A snug relationship between managers and regulators has often led to competition policy regulators actually deterring new competition.

Insider trading of public companies is illegal. In practice, however, Czech equity markets have a reputation for being insider-dominated.

Czech procurement procedures are generally fair and open for large contracts at the central level. This is often not the case, however, at local levels, where political connections often count for much in awarding contracts. Another problem is that utility monopolies and other state-owned entities that are not receiving large budget transfers are not required to adhere to government procurement procedures. Finally, domestic firms receive a 10 percent price advantage over their foreign competitors. The impact of this is negligible, however, because most foreign investors establish legal entities in the Czech Republic. The competition ministry advocated procurement law amendments that took effect in July 1996. Improvements include the clarification and simplification of public tender procedures at both the local and federal levels. In addition, they institutionalize transparency-building devices, such as publishing winners and winning amounts, and they force government bodies to reveal selection criteria for tenders.

6. To what extent has international trade been liberalized? To what degree has there been simplification/overhaul of customs and tariff procedures, and are these applied fairly? What informal trade barriers exist? The Czech Republic's tariffs stand at an average rate of five percent. Nevertheless, some imported goods, such as certain foods, are charged as much as 68 percent. The government often applies lower tariffs to European exporters than it does to non-Europeans. Import protection levels, however, are substantially below OECD averages.

A deteriorating trade deficit in 1997 prompted two new measures. In April 1997, an import deposit scheme was adopted, only to be eliminated in August after much protest from the EU. In May, anti-dumping legislation was adopted.

With the exception of controlled goods, no export controls exist. Exports account for a large proportion of the Czech economy. In 1995, they accounted for 61 percent of GDP. In May 1994, the government established the Czech Export Bank to encourage exports by providing access to state-subsidized medium- and long-term financing.

Quantitative controls on imports were almost entirely abolished in 1990. To the extent that they exist, non-tariff restrictions are few, very liberal, and generally transparent. Certain imported goods require a license but these are not difficult to obtain. Product and labelling standards, while strict, are rapidly being harmonized with European and international standards. Product testing regulations were streamlined and liberalized in reforms that took effect in January 1997. In the early years, product testing was performed at state-run testing stations and often constituted a bureaucratic nightmare. Now, testing for most products is voluntary and performed at efficient private testing stations. Border customs stops are generally fairly simple for goods in transit to and from Western Europe but are much more onerous for those bound to and from Eastern Europe.

As a member of the General Agreement on Tariffs and Trade, the Czech Republic acceded to the World Trade Organization in January 1995. In addition, it is a founding member of the Central European Free Trade Agreement (CEFTA), which also includes Poland, Hungary, Romania, Slovakia, and Slovenia. All nonagricultural and food trade within CEFTA is scheduled to become duty-free in 1998. The Czech Republic is also a member of the European Free Trade Associate and has an association agreement with the EU. The EU Commission formally recommended that accession negotiations begin with the Czech Republic in July 1997. Membership, however, is not expected before 2002.

7. To what extent has foreign investment and capital flow been encouraged or constrained?
Generally, there is no legal discrimination against foreign firms. Foreigners can establish any form of business organization permitted to citizens. As part of its OECD accession agreement, the country promised not to give preferences to domestic firms in privatization sales. Profits earned on Czech investments can be repatriated, but with a 25 percent tax, which is standard for EU countries and which is lowered if double-taxation treaties are in effect. There are no land ownership restrictions on foreigners.

Nevertheless, in practice, there have been a few instances in which foreign firms have been treated differently. These have occurred in the petrochemical, telecommunications, media, and brewery sectors. These sectors are politically sensitive because they are highly visible and dominated by giant firms. Moreover, there are certain sectors that are explicitly reserved for domestic firms. These so-called strategic sectors include defense-related industries, pure-alcohol distilleries, national monuments, and, at least for now, telecommunications, and banking. Finally, although they were liberalized in 1996, government procurement procedures still give a 10 percent price advantage to domestic firms.

In the past, the government largely ignored calls to offer special tax incentives to foreign investors. With the political turmoil arising after the May 1997 currency crisis, this is in the process of changing.

On the strength of several major investment deals, foreign direct investment (FDI) reached a record $2.5 billion in 1995, but fell to a disappointing $900 million in 1996. Cumulative FDI over the 1990-1996 period was $6.4 billion. With its 30 percent share, Germany is the top investor. The United States, Switzerland and the Netherlands follow, each with approximately 14 percent.

There are few regulations that limit capital flow.

8. Has there been reform of the energy sector? (To what degree has the energy sector been restructured? Is the energy sector more varied, and is it open to private competition? Is the country overly dependent on one or two other countries for energy [including whether exported fuels must pass through one or more countries to reach markets]?)

Energy sector reforms in the Czech Republic date from 1992, when the distribution and production sub-sectors were separated. Shortly afterwards, Ceske Energeticke Zarody (CEZ), the state electricity monopoly, was "privatized." (The state has yet to sell the NPF's 67 percent share). Later, the country's ten large heat plants were sold to investment funds and individual shareholders. Furthermore, the privatization of state-owned enterprises in itself liberalized the energy sector because these cumbersome, over-sized entities operated their own power plants. In November 1994, the parliament passed legislation to establish the legal framework for energy production and trade.

Since then, liberalization of the energy sector has stalled. While private firms were producing 20 percent of the country's energy in 1994, by March 1996 the private sector share had only increased to 30 percent. The inadequate 1994 energy law has not been amended, the NPF stake in CEZ has not been sold, trade in electricity on the CEZ network has not been legalized, the nation's eight distribution companies have not been fully privatized, the creation of an independent regulatory commission has been delayed, and pricing is still not market-driven.

Due to state regulation and subsidy policies, the price of energy does not cover production costs. These controls ensure that households receive a far lower price for electricity by being subsidized through high prices charged to industry. This has led to the inefficient use of electricity in homes for such purposes as heating. Prices are currently increased twice a year in 15 percent increments. In September 1996, the government's economic ministers recommended a total liberalization of energy prices over a two-year period.

Domestic coal provides slightly more than half of the country's energy requirements. Eighty percent of the Czech Republic's natural gas needs are met through imports from Russia. Nuclear energy supplies 22 percent of the country's energy requirements. Until 1995, when an oil pipeline from Germany was completed, almost all oil supplies were imported from Russia. The pipeline will carry two million tons of crude oil, compared with the five million tons carried by the Russian pipeline.

Recent developments have demonstrated the state's willingness to allow foreign involvement in the energy sector. In October 1995, the Czech electricity transmission network was connected to UCPTE, the European transmission network. A consortium of Western oil companies, including Shell, Conoco, and Agip, finalized the purchase of a 49 percent ($138 million) stake in Ceske Refinerska in February 1996. The consortium has promised $480 million in investment. Unipetrol, the state-owned holding company, controls the other 51 percent.

ESTONIA

Freedom in the World Ratings, 1989-1998

	1989-90	1990-91	1991-92	1992-93	1993-94	1994-95	1995-96	1996-97	1997-98
Political Rights	-	-	2	3	3	3	2	1	1
Civil Liberties	-	-	3	3	2	2	2	2	2
Status	-	-	F	PF	F	F	F	F	F

Polity: Consolidated Democracy
Economy: Consolidated Market
Population: 1,477,000
PPP: $4,062
Ethnic Groups: Estonian (62 percent), Russian (30 percent), Ukrainian, German, others
Capital: Tallinn

Political Process 1.75/7

1. When did national legislative elections occur? Were they free and fair? How were they judged by domestic and international election monitoring organizations? Who composes the government? Estonia's first national legislative elections following the dissolution of the Soviet Union took place on September 20, 1992. Thirty-eight parties competed in the elections for the 101-seat parliament (*Riigikogu*). Eight political parties gained seats in parliament, with the right-of-center Pro Patria party securing 31 seats. The moderate Safe Home party won 17 seats. The leftist Center Party won 15 seats. In September 1994, Prime Minister Mart Laar of the Pro Patria party was ousted in a no-confidence vote. He was replaced in October by Environment Minister Andres Tarand. Although the Estonian constitution provides for parliamentary elections to be held every four years, the first parliament's term was shortened to three years to ensure that non-citizens could be naturalized and represented in the parliamentary process a year earlier. The second and most recent post-independence election was held on March 5, 1995. International observers deemed the vote to have been free and fair. Thirty political parties and electoral unions participated in the election, in which members of the legislature were elected by proportional representation. The vote marked a political shift in parliament, as the left-of-center Coalition Party/Rural Union alliance won a major victory over conservatives in the Pro Patria/Estonian National Independence Party (ENIP) coalition. The election results reflected popular dissatisfaction among the elderly and rural voters, who were hardest hit by the Pro Patria-led government's market reform policies. The Coalition Party/Rural Union won 32.2 percent of the vote and 41 seats in Parliament. The Reform Party/Liberals coalition, which led the right wing, won 16.2 percent of the votes and 19 seats. The Center Party won 14.2 percent and 16 seats. The Pro Patria/ENIP coalition won 7.8 percent and eight seats. The Moderates won 6 percent and 6 seats. The "Our Home is Estonia" movement receieved 5.9 percent and six seats. The Republican and Conservative People's Party received five percent and five seats. Our Home is Estonia, which represents several Russian-speaking parties, ran the first Russian candidate list in post-independence Estonia to be represented in parliament. Tiit Vahi, a moderate who was elected prime minister, formed a center-left coalition with the Center Party, while promising to continue the previous government's reforms. The government collapsed in October 1995, after the discovery that some Estonian politicians had been subjected to illegal surveillance, including wiretaps, and the implication of Interior Minister Edgar Savisaar in the scandal. Vahi dismissed Savisaar, whose Center Party, with its sixteen seats, left the ruling coalition. Vahi then submitted his cabinet's resignation. President Lennart Meri subsequently enlisted Vahi to form a new coalition in which the Reform Party joined the Coalition Party and the Rural Union. This fragile left-right coalition commanded 55 seats in Parliament and held until February 1997, when Vahi resigned following allegations that he had participated in the illegal procurement of luxury apartments for himself and others during the 1993-95 privatization process. In March, President Meri approved Mart Siiman, the leader of the parliamentary faction of the Coalition Party, as the new prime minister. Siiman pledged to maintain the previous government's policies and economic reforms, including its pursuit of European Union (EU) membership. In early 1998, the ruling minority coalition, which included the Coalition Party, Rural Union, Country People's Party, and Party of Pensioners and Families, was unable to increase its support in parliament after it failed to expand the membership of the coalition. Finding it increasingly difficult to carry out his political programs, including difficult legislative reforms necessary for EU membership, Siiman called for early legislative elections. The ruling coalition rejected the proposal, however, and asked him to remain as prime minister. The next parliamentary elections are scheduled for March 1999.

2. When did presidential elections occur? Were they free and fair? The first post-independence presidential elections were held on September 20, 1992, by direct election. Of the four candidates, Arnold Ruutel received 42 percent of the vote. Lennart Meri received 29.5 percent. Rein Taagepera received 23 percent, and Lagle Parek won 4 percent. Since no candidate received an absolute majority, parliament cast the deciding vote on October 5, when it elected Meri, whose Pro Patria party dominated the national legislature. After the deadline for an amendment to continue to elect the president directly had passed, the procedure reverted, as planned, to presidential elections by parliament. The most recent presidential elections took place on August 26-27 and September 20, 1996. Before the vote, candidate Ruutel's allies made unproved allegations about collaboration between the KGB and President Meri. In the 101-member parliament's first round of voting, Meri received 45 votes. Ruutel, a leader of the Country People's Party and Farmers' Assembly, received 35 votes. Since neither candidate received the necessary two-thirds vote of the legislature to win, a second round of voting was necessary. In that round, Meri won 49 votes, and Ruutel secured 34 votes. In the third round, Meri received 52 votes to Ruutel's 32.

The failure for a third time to reach a two-thirds majority for any candidate led to a vote by the electoral college, which included the full parliament and 273 local government representatives. Both candidates automatically entered into this round of voting. In addition, three new candidates were nominated by at least twenty-one members of the electoral college: Tunne Kelam of Pro Patria, Siiri Oviir of the Center Party, and independent candidate Enn Tougu. During the first round of voting on September 20, Meri received 139 votes. Ruutel won 85 votes, while Kelam won 76 votes.Tougu received 47 votes, while Oviir won 25. Since no candidate received a majority of the vote (50 percent plus one vote, or 187 votes), a second round was held on the same day with only the top two candidates. Meri was elected president with 196 votes to Ruutel's 126 votes. (There were also 44 blank ballots and six invalid ballots. Two members of the electoral college did not attend.) The constitution establishes a largely ceremonial presidency, Meri's active role remains the source of some controversy.

3. Is the electoral system multiparty-based? Are there at least two viable political parties functioning at all levels of government? The electoral system is multiparty-based at all levels of government. At the national level, 30 parties and coalitions competed in the legislative elections in March 1995. As of April 1998, there were thirteen political parties represented in parliament. At the local level, 18 political parties participated in the last local elections, which were held in October 1996. In the three major towns of Tallinn, Tartu, and Narva, the number of parties or coalitions elected to the town councils were six, seven, and five, respectively.

4. How many parties have been legalized? Are any particular parties illegal? In the 1992 Parliamentary elections, 38 parties participated. In the 1995 vote, the number decreased to 30. Until the last national election in 1995, parties could be legally registered with only 200 members. The 1994 Parties Registration Regulation, which took effect after the 1995 election, requires parties to have at least 1,000 members. Estonia's electoral law encourages the formation of larger, and therefore fewer, political parties by stipulating that parties running in national legislative elections receive at least 5 percent of the national vote in order to enter parliament. The exception to this is for individual candidates who receive a large proportion of the votes in an electoral district and are elected directly to the parliament. In addition, since the early 1990s, many smaller parties have merged with other like-minded parties to form coalitions in order to gain wider public support.

5. What proportion of the population belongs to political parties? According to information provided by political parties in late 1995, party membership was estimated at approximately 12,000. A survey conducted the same year, however, found that only approximately 7,000 people identified themselves as members of political parties. Under the constitution, only citizens of Estonia may be members of political parties.

6. What has been the trend of voter turnout at the municipal, provincial, and national levels in recent years? At the national level, 67 percent of eligible voters voted in the parliamentary elections of September 1992. Approximately 70 percent voted in the March 1995, elections. In the October 1993, local elections, 52 percent of eligible voters, who include non-citizen permanent residents, participated. Voter turnout varied considerably from town to town. Sixty percent voted in Tallinn, while 34 percent voted in Tartu. Forty-six percent cast their ballots in Parnu, while 66 percent voted in the predominantly ethnic Russian town of Narva. In the October 1996, local elections, the nation-wide turnout was again approximately 52 percent. In Tallinn, 52.3 percent voted, with a heavy non-citizen turnout of 87.5 percent. The total turnout in Tartu was 40.4 percent.

Civil Society 2.25/7

1. How many non-governmental organizations (NGOs) have come into existence since 1988? What is the number of charitable/nonprofit organizations? Are there locally led efforts to increase philanthropy and volunteerism? What proportion of the population is active in private voluntary activity (from polling data)? The year 1998 marked the beginning of significant changes in Estonia's nonprofit sector. The country began the large-scale process of reviving the voluntary associations that had been active before 1940. At the same time, large Soviet-style organizations, such as the sports associations Spartak and Dynamo, began to disappear in the face of dwindling government support. Between 1988 and 1991, many new, independent NGOs were established. Most of these were large, popular movements, such as the Green Movement, the Cultural Heritage Protection Society, and the Popular Front, which shared the goal of restoring Estonia's independence and which helped to set the tone for Estonia's newly emerging political parties. In the years immediately following the collapse of the Soviet Union in 1991, Estonia's nonprofit sector — including cultural associations, research and training centers, and foundations — grew at a rate of 400 new organizations annually.

In the 1990s, more than 5,700 civic groups and organizations have been documented by the Institute of International and Social Studies. Nevertheless, numerous community-level organizations have never been registered, and many organizations have ceased to exist. A 1996 report from the U.N. Development Program (UNDP) found that, in late 1995, there were 4,000 active associations, societies, and organizations, including approximately 440 professional and 500 religious associations, more than 800 sports associations, and 230 foundations. According to October 1996, data from the Statistical Office of Estonia, there were 3,145 registered non-profit organizations, including approximately 20 political parties and excluding all religious organizations. This number, however, is not exact because the Statistical Office lacks accurate data on the dissolution of NGOs. Nonprofit organizations represented in Estonia include those focusing on culture and recreation, education, research, health, social services, environment, religion, and business and professional interests. Of these, 64.2 percent are located in urban areas, with the 1,600 active organizations — the largest number — in Tallinn and 600 in Tartu. Approximately 75 percent of NGOs consider themselves to be proficient at dealing with local issues. Twenty percent consider themselves proficient with national issues.

It is virtually impossible to estimate the number of people active in the nonprofit sector. In 1993 and 1994, the last comprehensive surveys indicated that Estonians prefer large organizations with more than 100 members or small ones with less than 30 members. At least one in seven Estonians participates in nonprofit activities and, if church congregations and trade unions are included, the ratio increases to one in four. Two-thirds of NGO members are women, who have traditionally been more involved in the nonprofit sector. People aged 40 to 59 — a group that constitutes 39.3 percent of all participants — are most likely to join in the work of nonprofit organizations. According to the 1996 UNDP report, 14 percent of Estonians associated themselves with trade unions, 4.5 percent with religious organizations, 3.7 percent with professional associations, and 3.2 percent with sports clubs. There is a significant gap, however, between total membership numbers and actual active participants. For example, religious congregations claim that their members number 220,000, while, according to other sources, the number is no more than 45,000.

2. What is the legal and regulatory environment for NGOs (i.e., ease of registration, legal rights, government regulation, taxation, procurement, and access to information issues)? To what extent is NGO activism focused on improving the legal and regulatory environment? Between 1991 and 1994, the Citizens' Union Act regulated all NGOs established by private initiative, with no distinction between membership-based and non-membership organizations or political and non-political activities. The Nonprofit Associations and their Federations Act, which was adopted by parliament in March 1994, regulated membership organizations, but not other nonprofit organizations such as foundations. An least three private individuals were required in order to establish a nonprofit association, but legal bodies were not allowed to join. In October 1996, parliament passed the Nonprofit Associations Act and the Foundations Act. Both laws regulate the activities of governing bodies and address issues regarding the dissolution, merger, and separation of organizations more explicitly than previous acts. The Nonprofit Associations Act, which regulates the activities of all membership nonprofit organizations, states that profit cannot be the principle purpose of the not-for-profit association and that revenues may only be used to achieve statutory goals. It also specifies requirements for membership, orders of admission, secession, exclusion of members, and the rights and obligations arising from membership. The Foundations Act states that a foundation is a non-membership legal entity established to manage property and pursue stated objectives. It sets limits on the activities of foundations and states that, while a foundation is allowed to engage in economic activities, financial disbursements can only be made for charitable or social purposes.

3. What is the organizational capacity of NGOs? Do management structures clearly delineate authority and responsibility? Is information available on NGO management issues in the native language? Is there a core of experienced practitioners/trainers to serve as consultants or mentors to less developed organizations? Due to the relatively short period in which post-Communist NGOs have been operating in Estonia, many employees of nonprofit organizations have insufficient experience in proposal writing, accounting tasks, and budget elaboration. The board members of many NGOs are inactive or inexperienced. Many are well-known business professionals and politicians who serve on several boards and therefore often do not have the time to participate in board meetings. Although staff members may be qualified for their own positions, they generally lack the necessary knowledge and skills to guide their respective board members in their specific governance responsibilities. More positive developments in the nonprofit sector include an increasing willingness and ability among organizations to cooperate on joint projects and the development of an Estonian NGO Internet web site for NGOs to share information and inform the public of their activities. The Jaan Tonisson Institute and the Network of Estonian Non-Profit Organizations have consulted and conducted training programs with other not-for-profit associations, and the Soros Foundation's Open Estonia Foundation has sponsored various conferences on issues of importance to nonprofit groups. Recent training seminars for Estonian NGOs have focused on topics including fundraising, grant proposal-writing, and public relations and the media.

4. Are NGOs financially viable? What is their tax status? Are they obliged to and do they typically disclose revenue sources? Do government procurement opportunities

exist for private, not-for-profit providers of services? The Estonian not-for-profit associations and foundations do not have automatic tax exemption. The two main laws affecting NGO taxation are the Income Tax Act and the Value-Added Tax (VAT) Act, both of which have been amended frequently. The Income Tax Act states that non-refundable funds received from foreign donors, in addition to membership and entrance fees for nonprofit organizations, are tax-exempt. It also enables contributors to apply for tax exemption on donations and income from economic activities. The exact requirements for applying for tax-exempt status and deadlines are indicated in the Government Order of June 11, 1996. In order to qualify, an organization's activities must be connected with support to charity, science, culture, education, sports, health care, social welfare, environmental protection, or religious gatherings in the public interest. Local divisions of the Tax Department form the respective lists of organizations on a case-by-case basis each year, with the government making the final decision. According to the VAT Act, nonprofit organizations are not exempted from VAT, but the goods and services purchased or imported by the organization through non-refundable foreign aid are tax exempt.

According to the Nonprofit Associations Act, nonprofit organizations risk their status as organizations exempted from income taxes if they earn money selling publications or other products directly connected to their activities. This has complicated the work of small local organizations that do not receive state or international funding. In February 1997, a number of Estonian NGOs published a public appeal for the government to review the tax-exemption applications submitted to it by organizations in 1996 and 1997, to give written reasons for its rejections, to engage NGO representatives in the review process, and to issue an annual list of organizations that are exempt from income taxes. The organizations indicated that the current regulations may result in the closure of several small organizations that are already operating under difficult economic conditions.

No data are currently available on revenue sources for nonprofit associations and foundations, although it has been estimated that, in many cases, foreign assistance accounts for more than two thirds of all income. The level of private donations has been extremely low, and unfavorable tax rules have seriously limited the economic activities undertaken by NGOs. Approximately 50 NGOs have been supported by the state budget through the intervention of the Ministry of Social Affairs, Culture, and Education. The general tendency is for the government to support specific projects of organizations, rather than individual organizations as a whole. Since decisions regarding the funding of projects are made by the government's ruling coalition, NGOs that seek state funds may be faced with the choice of not criticizing the government in order to receive money, or leveling criticisms and then facing the possibility of not receiving state funds.

5. Are there free trade unions? How many workers belong to these unions? Is the number of workers belonging to trade unions growing or decreasing? What is the numerical/proportional membership of farmers' groups, small business associations, etc.? The constitution provides for the right to form and join a union or employee association. Unions may join federations freely and affiliate internationally. The right to strike is legal, and unions are independent of the government and political parties. The constitution and statutes prohibit retribution against strikers. In May 1997, approximately 2,000 teachers from 70 schools participated in a one-day teachers' strike to support demands for higher wages.

The Central Organization of Estonian Trade Unions (EAKL) was formed in 1990 as a wholly voluntary and exclusively Estonian organization that would replace the Estonian branch of the official Soviet labor confederation. The EAKL has 75,345 members. Another trade union, the Organization of Employee Unions, split from the EAKL in 1993 and has 55,000 members. A central union of food processing and rural workers was established in June 1997. There are approximately 30 unions in Estonia, and approximately one-third of the country's labor force belongs to one of the three main labor federations. Total union membership decreased from 800,000 in 1990 to 540,000 in 1992 and 330,00 in 1993. The reduced membership levels are due to the move from large-scale industrialized units into smaller production units and the services sector, which diminished the traditional union base. White-collar unions, however, have gained influence.

While Estonian workers now have the legally acquired right to bargain collectively, this right is still in its infancy. According to EAKL leaders, few collective bargaining agreements have been concluded between management and workers of a specific enterprise. The EAKL has, however, concluded framework agreements with producer associations. These provide the basis for specific labor agreements, including the establishment of the minimum wage. The EAKL also participated in the development of Labor Code provisions on employment contracts, vacation, and occupational safety. The code prohibits anti-union discrimination, and employees have the right to go to court to enforce their rights. Laws covering collective bargaining, collective dispute resolution, and shop stewards were enacted in 1993.

Entrepreneurs' organizations have been growing in Estonia since the mid-1990s. Two such alliances are the Estonian Small Business Association, which was established in 1988, and the Estonian Chamber of Commerce, which was reestablished as an independent organization in 1989. A number of territorial and branch alliances are also active. Several projects have been initiated and completed by the Estonian Small Business Association, which has cooperated with the United States, the Nordic countries, and several other European nations.

6. What form of interest group participation in politics is legal? What type of interest groups are active in the political and policy process? According to Article 48 of the Estonian constitution, only citizens of Estonia may be members of political parties, although non-citizens may form nonprofit and social groups. The constitution prohibits political parties or associations that direct activities toward the violent change of the country's constitutional system or that otherwise violate criminal law. Under Article 47, both citizens and non-citizens have the right, without prior permission, to assemble peacefully and conduct meetings. Permits for all public gatherings must be obtained three weeks prior to the date of the gathering. The authorities have wide discretion to prohibit such gatherings on the ground of public safety, but they seldom exercise this option. In 1997, there were no reports of government interference in mass gatherings or political rallies.

7. How is the not-for-profit/NGO sector perceived by the public and government officials? What is the nature of media coverage of NGOs? To what extent do government officials engage with NGOs? Although NGOs in Estonia have become increasingly active and professional throughout the 1990s, their influence on the public at large has been less pronounced. Most Estonians do not yet fully understand the significance of the role of the nonprofit sector in society, and many do not consider civic initiatives to be a solution to the country's various social, environmental, and other related problems. The media generally do not devote much attention to NGOs, in part because journalists would often rather cover more sensational topics, such as political and business scandals. In addition, many Estonian NGOs are not yet well-versed in public relations efforts regarding the media. Nevertheless, according to the Network of Estonian Nonprofit Organizations, an umbrella group, the role of NGOs in affecting developments in civil society is being increasingly, if slowly, acknowledged by the public.

Independent Media 1.75/7

1. Are there legal protections for press freedom? Article 45 of the Estonian Constitution states that "Everyone shall have the right to freely circulate ideas, opinions, persuasions, and other information by work, print, picture, and other means." The government respects these constitutional provisions. According to the Law on Radio and Television Broadcasting, which was adopted on May 19, 1994, television and radio stations have the right to make free decisions about the content of their transmissions and broadcasts. Any attempts to restrict these freedoms are punishable by law. As of May 1998, a new draft broadcasting law was being considered.

2. Are there legal penalties for libeling officials? Are there legal penalties for "irresponsible" journalism? Have these laws been enforced to harass journalists? Cases regarding libel are covered in civil and criminal codes, and the burden of proof in such cases rests with the media. There are no legal penalties for "irresponsible journalism". In August 1997, an Estonian court upheld the conviction of journalist Enno Tammer on charges of offensive remarks regarding Estonian politician Edgar Savisaar's second wife. Tammer was ordered to pay an $18 fine and $150 in court costs. The decision was criticized by some as a move against the right of free speech in Estonia.

3. What proportion of the media is privatized? What are the major private newspapers, television stations, and radio stations? There are three major private television stations: TV3, which is the second-largest channel in the country; TV1; and Kanal-2. ETV, the national state-owned public-service channel, enjoys the highest ratings in Estonia despite competition from the independent channels. Local television and radio stations are in private hands. Russian language programs, most of which are produced in Estonia, are broadcast over state and private television channels. Russian state television programs are widely available via cable, and there are many cable television channels. The Estonian Cable Association claims to link 33 cable operators that serve 75 percent of the 100,000 cable customers in the country. The Estonian Association of Cable Operators, a competing group, unites nine cable operators. There are several major independent radio stations. In the capital city of Tallinn alone, there are roughly 20 local commercial stations. The city's most popular commercial stations are Radio Kuku, which was founded in 1992 as the first commercial station, Uuno, and Raadio-100. A new Russian-language radio station, Radio Nostalgie, began its broadcasts in Tallinn in February 1998. Transmitted into Estonia via Moscow, it is the station with the widest audience in sixty Russian cities. All Estonian-language daily newspapers are privately owned and receive no subsidies from the state. There are several major national Estonian and Russian language dailies, in addition to various weekly publications. Foreign newspapers and magazines are also widely available. The three most popular daily newspapers are *Postimees* (The Postman), *Eesti Paevaleht* (The Estonian Daily) and *Sonumileht*. The two Russian-language dailies are *Vesti* and *Estoniya*. The weekly *Vesti Nedelja Plyus*, which is the largest-selling Russian language weekly, has a circulation of 17,000. The two main news agencies are the Estonian News Agency (ENA) and the Baltic News Service, a privately-owned regional agency that covers news in all three Baltic countris.

4. Are the private media financially viable? Many private media outlets continue to face economic difficulties and stiff competition. In late 1997, two daily newspapers launched free weekly papers in Tallinn. *Eesti Paevaleht* publishs *Linnaleht*, which it reportedly distributes throughout the city, and *Sonumileht* distributes its free paper *Pealinn* to its regular subscribers in the city. In September 1997, *Postimees*, *Eesti Paevaleht* and *Sonumileht* — the three major daily newspapers — simultaneously launched Sunday editions. *Eesti Paevaleht* announced the move first, but the other papers quickly followed out of fear of a loss of subscribers if they did not act immediately. Private newspapers are financed by a combination of advertisements, subscriptions, and sales, with the proportion of revenue from each source varying from paper to paper. State broadcast media continue to receive large subsidies, and the government has stated that these subsidies will continue. Until recently, ETV drew its revenues from both the state budget and advertising. Since the beginning of 1998, however, the country's three main private channels have paid a fixed sum to ETV to keep it free from advertising until the end of 1999. State budget financing constitutes 63.3 percent of the station's revenues. The compensatory payments from the private channels constitute 26.9 percent, and services rendered, sponsorship, and interest form the remaining 9.5 percent. The value of the Estonian advertising market in 1996 exceeded that of 1995 by 45 percent in terms of expenditure and by 20 percent in terms of actual volume. In recent years, Estonian media prices have increased an average of 25 to 35 percent a year, although they are still much less expensive than in most other European countries.

5. Are the media editorially independent? Are the media's news gathering functions affected by interference from government or private owners? The editorial independence of the media is generally respected by the government. The media routinely conduct probing and thorough investigative reporting. The Estonian Newspaper Association (EALL), an organization of publishers, unites 48 papers published in Estonia with a total daily circulation of 662,000 copies. It defends the common interests and rights of newspapers, seeks adherence to internationally recognized principles of democratic journalism, and fights against violations of the freedom of the press. In April 1997, seven organizations relaunched the Estonian Press Council, the self-regulatory watchdog for the media. The original Press Council was established in the early 1990s by the EALL, which was the sole financial backer of the Council for four years. In order to make the Council independent and increase its role, it was reconstituted as a separate NGO. The founding members of the new Press Council are the Newspaper Association, the Journalists Union, the Association of Media Trainers, the Broadcasting Association, Estonian Radio, Estonian Television, and the Consumer Protection Association. The aim of the Council is to maintain good journalistic practice by discussing complaints from the public and within the media. Council members hear cases involving journalistic improprieties and problems involving the authorities. Although its decisions are not legally enforceable, its findings can be publicized by the Estonian News Agency, thereby exerting pressure on the government to recognize the editorial independence of the country's media. In late 1997, however, critics questioned the editorial independence of ETV. In January 1998, an outcry in the national press resulted from reports that ETV had developed plans to launch new current affairs programs that would be funded by various government ministries. (ETV was already receiving an annual fixed sum from the state budget.) *Postimees*, the leading newspaper, warned in an editorial that, if ETV launched a defense program financed by the Defense Ministry, it would be close to becoming a propaganda tool. The negative publicity in the press led the authorities to reconsider, and the show was broadcast without funding from the Ministry. In one form of another, the Ministries of Agriculture, Environment, Justice, and Social Affairs have made extra financial contributions to programs broadcast on ETV since late 1997. Cases have been fewer, however, since the issue attracted the attention of the press and the Broadcasting Council, the supervisory body for public service stations.

6. Is the distribution system for newspapers privately or governmentally controlled? All newsprint, printing, and distribution facilities are now in the hands of privately owned companies.

7. What proportion of the population is connected to the Internet? Are there any restrictions on Internet access to private citizens? According to a study conducted in early 1997 by the market research company Baltic Media Facts, approximately 6 percent of Estonians used the Internet during the period between February and September 1997. There are 128 Internet-connected computers for every 10,000 people, or 19,200 Internet-connected computers for a total population of 1.5 million. Nevertheless, according to the RIPE Network Coordination Center, which acts as a regional Internet registry for Europe, Estonia is one of the most extensively connected countries in Eastern Europe, with more web sites *per capita* than any other country in the region, with the possible exception of Slovenia. Estonia also leads a number of EU countries in connections to the Internet. According to the most recent edition of Baltic Media Facts' annual survey of media in the Baltic states, there are 50 Internet service providers, and all major television and radio stations and newspapers have their own web sites. Approximately 89 per cent of Internet users are between the ages of 15 and 39, and the average age is 29. Approximately 62 per cent of Internet users in Estonia are men. Among reasons provided by respondents in a recent survey for not using computers or the Internet were fear of using computers, the cost of computers, and the belief that books and the press provide information comparable to that available on the Internet. The Soros Foundation's Open Estonia Foundation has conducted various projects to improve access to and the content of the Internet throughout the country, including increasing Internet-related services at educational, medical, and cultural institutions.

8. What has been the trend in press freedom as measured by Freedom House's Survey of Press Freedom? According to Freedom House's annual Survey of Press Freedom, Estonia was rated "Partly Free" in 1992 and "Free" from 1993 to 1998.

Governance and Public Administration 2.25/7

1. Is the legislature the effective rule-making institution? The national legislature is the effective rule-making institution. According to the Constitution, legislative power rests with parliament, which engages in various activities including the adoption of laws and resolutions, decisions on the conduct of referenda, and the passage of a national budget. Nevertheless, certain checks are imposed on legislative power through the work of the Legal Chancellor, an independent official who examines whether laws are in accordance with the constitution. If he finds a conflict and if appropriate changes are not made within twenty days, the Legal Chancellor appeals to the National Court — the court of constitutional review — to declare the law null and void.

2. Is substantial power decentralized to sub-national levels of government? What specific authority do sub-national levels have? According to Chapter Fourteen of the constitution, local governments are granted autonomy to direct and manage local issues. Until the October 1993, elections, there were two tiers of municipal government. The first included 250 primary units of local government — towns, townships, and boroughs. The second included fifteen counties and six large cities — Tallinn, Tartu, Parnu, Narva, Kohtla-Jarve, and Sillamae. The local administrative status of the boroughs as a smaller urban settlement was abolished in 1993, with some boroughs becoming towns and others designated as municipalities. In November 1994, the second tier was eliminated and absorbed into the national administration. By the October 1996 local elections, the borders of the remaining local governments had been altered, and there were 254 single-tier local government units, with 209 townships and 45 towns. All local issues are regulated and resolved by local governments.

3. Are sub-national officials chosen in free and fair elections? Estonia's first post-Soviet local elections were held on October 17, 1993. Approximately 3,400 candidates were elected by direct vote for city and district councils, with the centrist Coalition Party securing the largest number of seats nationwide. According to observers from the Council of Europe, the elections were conducted freely and fairly with no apparent irregularities. In May 1996, parliament amended the Local Elections Law. The amendments were drafted by President Meri, who had rejected the law because it required that potential political candidates who had graduated from non-Estonian-language schools pass oral and written Estonian language examinations. Meri stated that the law in its original form contradicted the constitution and a U.N. Convention on civil rights. The amended law still requires candidates to sign a statement asserting their proficiency in Estonian, but does not require proof in advance. Only citizens of Estonia are allowed to run in local elections, but non-citizens who have lived in their respective municipality for at least five years and have a permanent residence permit are allowed to vote in local elections.

The second and most recent local elections took place in October 1996, when 11,151 candidates competed for 3,453 seats in 273 election districts. The Reform Party/Liberals Coalition proved to be the most successful grouping in Tallinn and Tartu, where it won 15 seats on each city's council. Of the 882,726 registered voters — including 811,756 citizens and 70,970 non-citizen permanent residents — 52 cast their ballots. Approximately one-third of qualified non-citizens registered, and the vast majority of them also voted. According to a U.S. State Department human rights report, the elections were free and fair, although some qualified voters were excluded from the rolls due to technical errors.

4. Do the executive and legislative bodies operate openly and with transparency? Is draft legislation easily accessible to the media and the public? Sessions of parliament are public, unless the legislature, by a majority vote of two-thirds of its members, decides otherwise, and most voting in parliament is also public. All laws adopted by the parliament are published in an official document, the *Riigi Teataja* (State Gazette). In 1995, parliament adopted an anti-corruption law that made it possible to prosecute state officials for personal gains made from public service. The law also provides that the president, prime minister, and all 101 members of the legislature must declare all of their financial interests, holdings, and debts to the parliament's anti-corruption committee. Under the constitution, members of the executive branch may not hold any other public office or belong to the leadership or council of a commercial enterprise, although there have been reported cases of conflicts of interest involving government officials who own interests in business ventures.

5. Do municipal governments have sufficient revenues to carry out their duties? Do municipal governments have control of their own local budgets? Do they raise revenues autonomously or from the central state budget? Municipal governments receive funding from the state budget and also raise revenues autonomously. Laws governing local budget issues include the Local Taxation Law, the Law on the Region and Town Budget, and the Law on the Relationship between the Region and Town Budget and State Budget, all of which have been effective since 1994. Funds are allocated from the state budget to local budgets for compensating for tax exemptions, supplementing budget revenues, financing teacher salaries and capital expenditures, and financing expenditures associated with national responsibilities allocated to regions and towns by law. At the same time, local governments hold their own independent budgets and bank accounts and possess the right to levy and collect taxes and impose fees. The main source of income for local government is the individual income tax, which includes both income tax collected and paid by the state and local income taxes. In Tallinn, personal income tax constitutes 33.6 percent of the year's planned revenues. In December 1997, the Bank of Estonia issued a decree that makes local governmental borrowing more difficult. Estonian banks are now obliged to ensure that a local government is solvent and can provide sufficient guarantees before granting it a loan or buying its bonds. This move was a response to concerns that, while the state government had to operate with a balanced budget, local governments were free to operate with a deficit by borrowing from commercial banks.

6. Do the elected local leaders and local civil servants know how to manage municipal governments effectively? Local government leaders manage municipal governments effectively, although they would benefit from more training and experience. Legislation and a government decision provide that in districts in which more than one-half of the population speaks a language other than Estonian, the local government may conduct business in that language. In 1996, city governments in predominantly Russian-speaking communities conducted most internal business in Russian. In December 1996, however, the State Electoral Commission initiated hearings of a complaint filed by the Sillamae town council members against the council chairman who, according to the complaint, could not speak Estonian. In October 1997, the government brought formal court charges against the chairman for having filed a fraudulent Estonian language knowledge certificate.

7. When did the constitutional/legislative changes on local power come into effect? Has there been a reform of the civil service code/system? Are local civil servants employees of the local or central government? Self-governing status was conferred on local governments by the Presidium of the Supreme Council of Estonia, and, after the election of the new parliament in 1992, by the Estonian government. The constitution contains a chapter that guarantees local government autonomy. Other major laws pertaining to public administration and local government include the May 1993 Local Government Council Electoral Law, which is no longer valid; the June 1993 Law on the Organization of Local Government; the June 1993 Law on the Region and Town Budget; the August 1993 Law on the Relationship between the Region and Town Budget and the State Budget; and the September 1994 Local Taxation Law.

Administrative reforms were launched in Estonia in 1989, although it was not until 1995 that the slightly chaotic series of reforms became systematized. The Law on Public Service was adopted on January 25, 1995. The Government of the Republic Act was adopted in December 1995. Estonian language requirements for those employed in the civil service went into effect in 1993. The Law on Public Service as originally passed required state employees to be proficient in Estonian by the end of 1995. In December 1995, parliament amended the Law on Public Service to allow non-citizen local and national government employees without adequate Estonian language skills to continue working until February 1, 1997. No non-citizens were to be hired after January 1, 1996. This amendment reflected the government's awareness that, in some sectors, the number of employees with inadequate language skills remained high. In May 1997, three policemen were dismissed for insufficient skills in Estonian. Earlier in the year, 11 policemen were dismissed for not applying for Estonian citizenship by the established deadline. Five prosecutors and two judges were dismissed for presenting forged certificates regarding their knowledge of the language. Two have been restored to their positions, and criminal charges against one judge were dropped. Three of the prosecutors found employment as police inspectors.

According to the European Commission's opinion on Estonia's application for EU membership, the Estonian civil service is under-staffed, political pressures on civil servants are considerable, and public confidence in the civil service is low. As a result of Estonia's pursuit of EU membership, recent reforms in the country's civil service have been undertaken with the intent of ensuring that civil service legislation and practices meet EU standards. In June 1997, the Council of Senior Civil Servants adopted a strategy for training civil servants in issues related to European integration. The implementation of the strategy was scheduled to begin in late 1997 with the cooperation with foreign experts. Also in late 1997, the government formed a five-member commission, which was led by Prime Minister Mart Siiman, to consider a proposal for administrative reform, including the merger of several ministries and reducing the number of parliamentary deputies. The Law on Public Service provides for up to three months of paid educational leave during each five-year period of employment, as well as salary increments for advanced degrees and foreign language proficiency. Local civil servants are employees of the local government.

Rule of Law 2.25/7

1. Is there a post-Communist constitution? How does the judicial system interpret and enforce the constitution? Are there specific examples of judicial enforcement of the constitution in the last year? The current constitution was adopted with 93 percent support in a June 28, 1992 referendum. The constitution includes a chapter on the rights and obligations of citizens and non-citizens and establishes the separation and balance of authority of the executive, legislative, and judicial branches of government. It also contains sections on the national budget, foreign relations, national defense, and local government. The State Court, which is the highest court in Estonia, functions as a supreme court and is the court for constitutional review. It rules on the constitutionality of legislative acts and, if it finds legislation to be in violation of the constitution, it can declare it to be unconstitutional or render it null and void. The first constitutional review case was heard in June 1993. All residents, regardless of citizenship, can take complaints of alleged violations of human or constitutional rights directly to the State Court. Justices of the State Court review each case and have decided in favor of complainants. All decisions are in Estonian, but if a complaint is received in another language, such as Russian, the Court will provide a complimentary translation. In March 1998, the State Court ruled that a law on customs tariffs, which gives the government the right to impose such duties for up to six months, partly contradicts the constitution. The Court decided in favor of an appeal by the Legal Chancellor, who had argued that the parliament should have the right to establish customs tariffs. The Court's decision cannot be appealed.

2. Does the constitutional framework provide for human rights? Do the human rights include business and property rights? Human rights are protected in the constitution under Chapter Two, which is entitled "Fundamental Rights, Liberties and Duties." Under Article 12, no one can suffer from discrimination on the basis of nationality, race, color, sex, language, origin, creed, political or other persuasions, or financial or social status. The constitution guarantees freedom of conscience, religion and thought, and everyone has the right, without prior permission, to assemble and conduct meetings peacefully. According to Article 31, Estonian citizens have the right to engage in commercial activities and form profit- making associations and leagues. Unless otherwise determined by law, this right applies equally to citizens of foreign states and stateless persons living in Estonia. Article 32 guarantees that the property rights of everyone are inviolable and enjoy equal protections. The government generally respects the human rights of its citizens and the country's large non-citizen population, although problems exist in some areas, particularly in the mistreatment of prisoners and detainees and the use of excessive force by the police.

3. Has there been basic reform of the criminal code/criminal law? Who authorizes searches and issues warrants? Are suspects and prisoners beaten or abused? Are there excessive delays in the criminal justice system? Estonia has continued to overhaul its criminal procedure codes since regaining independence in 1991. An interim Criminal Code, which took effect on June 1, 1992, revised the Soviet-era Criminal Code and abolished political and economic crimes. A Code of Criminal Procedure was adopted in 1994. In May 1996, the Criminal Code was amended to give the police and prosecutors greater latitude in dealing with organized crime. New codes in a variety of fields were being drafted at the end of 1997. A multiyear plan is being compiled to replace the current criminal codes with new penal codes that fully meet European standards.

Under the law, a search warrant must be issued for the search and seizure of property. During the investigative stage, the prosecutor issues a warrant upon a showing of probable cause. After a case has gone to court, warrants are issued by the court.

There are no reports of political prisoners, political or other extrajudicial killings, or politically motivated disappearances. However, there continue to be credible reports that police use excessive force and verbal abuse during the arrest and questioning of suspects, and prison conditions remain poor. Punishment cells (*kartsers*) continue to be used in contravention of international standards. Most of the top leadership of one prefecture was dismissed for abuse of power. The government continues to adopt measures to address poor prison conditions and make prison staff more professional. Although the Tallinn Central Prison, which was built in 1765, remains overcrowded, the opening of a new wing that meets European standards has improved conditions. In December 1997, parliament passed a law to allow the number of prisoners to be reduced through a more extensive use of suspended sentences. Germany will launch a training program for Estonian prison officials in April 1998, and will introduce principles of European penal law and criminal care. Although the government has drafted a multi-year plan to refurbish and restructure all of the country's prisons and to close the Tallinn Central Prison, the plan had not been implemented by the end of 1997. According to the Ministry of Justice, there are nearly 4,700 detainees in Estonian prisons, although the optimal figure would be 2,500. Some suggestions made by Council of Europe representatives in 1993 have been implemented, but the fulfillment of others is still hampered by a lack of resources and high turnover among prison staff. A person may be held for 48 hours without being formally charged, and further detention requires a court order. A person may be held in pretrial detention for two months, but this period may be extended up to twelve months by court order. Police rarely violate these limits.

The rapid and extensive creation of new legislation following the restoration of Estonia's independence has brought with it a growing legal bureaucracy. Courts of law are understaffed and suffer from a lack of other resources—conditions that often result in long waits for court hearings.

4. Do most judges rule fairly and impartially? Do many remain from the Communist era? All judges were newly appointed or re-appointed upon reform of the court system, and the appointment of judges was completed in 1993. Although most judges are considered to rule fairly and impartially, there have been reports of corruption among some members of the judicial system.

5. Are the courts free of political control and influence? Are the courts linked directly to the Ministry of Justice or any other executive body? The constitution establishes an independent judicial branch. In practice, the judiciary is independent and experiences no interference from other government branches. Judges are appointed for life, but may be removed by court order. Under the constitution, judges cannot hold any other elective or appointive office. Criminal proceedings against a justice may be instituted only with the consent of the majority of members of parliament. The lower levels of the court system are linked financially to the Ministry of Justice, while, at the highest level, judges are paid from the state budget, independently of the Ministry. In May 1998, the government approved a judicial bill that had been in preparation for two years. According to Estonia's Justice Minister, the focus of the new legislation will be to improve the level of professionalism of judges and the courts' administration. Among the bill's provisions are the introduction of obligatory refresher training for current judges and an increase in the amount of time required to appoint new judges.

6. What proportion of lawyers is in private practice? How does this compare with the previous year? Most lawyers are in private practice. A number of foreign and domestic law firms employing foreign lawyers are operating in Estonia. Advokatuur, the bar association, maintains lists of practicing attorneys.

7. Does the state provide public defenders? Under the constitution, detainees must be informed promptly of the grounds for their arrest and given immediate access to legal counsel. If a person cannot afford legal assistance in a criminal case in which he has been detained, the state will provide counsel. A Law on Legal Aid, which would guarantee free legal assistance to those who cannot afford a lawyer in other cases, had not yet been adopted by the end of 1997.

8. Are there effective anti-bias/discrimination laws, including protection of ethnic minority rights? The Citizenship Law, which was enacted in February 1992, readopted the 1938 Citizenship Law, which stipulated that anyone born after 1940 to a citizen parent is a citizen by birth. The law included requirements for naturalization, including knowledge of the Estonian language, and a two-year residency period, which must be followed by a one- year waiting period. In January 1995, parliament adopted a new Citizenship Law that revised the 1992 law and combined provisions that had been scattered among several pieces of legislation. It extended the residency requirement for naturalization from two to five years and added a requirement for knowledge of the constitution and the Citizenship Law. Persons who had assumed legal residence in Estonia prior to July 1, 1990, are exempt from the five-year legal residence and one-year waiting period requirements. The law allows the government to waive the language, but not the civic knowledge, requirement for applicants who have had elementary or higher education in Estonian or who have performed valuable service to the country. In an effort to fulfill the remaining two of 30 recommendations made by the High Commissioner for National Minorities of the Organization for Security and Cooperation in Europe (OSCE), the government simplified the civic knowledge test. It also approved draft legislation on December 9, 1997, to amend the Citizenship Law to grant automatic citizenship to stateless children born after February 26, 1992, to legally resident stateless parents upon the parents' application. According to the Citizenship and Migration Department, the amendment could immediately affect 6,500 children and up to 1,500 children in each following year. As of February 1998, approximately 97,000 ethnic and non-ethnic Estonians have received Estonian citizenship by naturalization. An estimated 80,000 non-ethnic Estonians already hold Estonian citizenship by birth. More than 100,000 people have chosen to take the citizenship of Russia and other countries. While some officials of the Russian government and in the local Russian community continue to criticize the Citizenship Law as discriminatory, numerous international fact-finding organizations, including the Finnish Helsinki Committee and the OSCE, have determined that the law conforms to international standards. Nevertheless, bureaucratic delays and the language requirement have been cited as disincentives for securing citizenship. The government has established language training centers, but there is a lack of qualified teachers, financial resources, and training materials. There have been allegations that the examination process, which 75 to 90 percent of applicants pass, is arbitrary and that the language requirement is too difficult.

In July 1993, parliament enacted a Law on Aliens, which provided a one-year period during which non-citizens who came to Estonia prior to July 1, 1990, and were permanent residents of the former Estonian Soviet Socialist Republic could apply for temporary residence permits. Following delays and confusion in implementation, as well as criticism by international human rights observers, the application deadline was extended by another year to July 12, 1995. By that date, the vast majority of aliens — 327,737 of the estimated 370,000 — had filed applications. The government then extended the registration period until April 30, 1996. An indeterminate number of non-citizens — estimates ranged from 20,000 to 50,000 — still have not registered. In mid-1997, the government began a campaign to register this group of unregistered aliens and pledged not to take any measures against them. By October, approximately 1,500 had applied. In September, parliament approved an amendment to the Law on Aliens to allow those who had applied for residence by July 12, 1995, to change their temporary residence permits to permanent ones. The amendment took effect in 1998, two years earlier than the original act envisioned. The government encountered criticism for its slow pace in processing residence applications for approximately 19,000 Russian military pensioners. Approximately 35 percent of the first group of pensioners missed the deadline to present passports for residence permits. Although the Citizenship and Migration Board could deport the pensioners, the government is handling the issue on a case-by-case basis.

There are no restrictions on the right of non-citizens to foreign travel, emigration, or repatriation, although some individuals have complained of delays in obtaining travel documents. In late 1994, the government began to issue alien passports to resident aliens who had no other valid travel document. As of March 1998, approximately 168,000 individuals had applied for an alien passport, and approximately 166,00 had been issued.

The Law on Cultural Autonomy for citizens belonging to minority groups took effect in 1993. It applies to ethnic groups of citizens numbering at least 3,000 and entitles the group to apply for funds directly from the state budget to promote its activities. Some non-citizens have termed the law discriminatory since it limits cultural autonomy only to citizens. The government has stated that non-citizens can participate fully in ethnic organizations and that the law includes subsidies for cultural organizations. In April 1998, the Estonian Association of Ingermanland Finns announced its plans to apply for cultural autonomy status. It was the first ethnic minority group to do so since the adoption of the law five years earlier.

In response to continued allegations by the Russian government and members of the Russian community in Estonia of Estonia's poor treatment of its ethnic minorities, the Estonian president established a Human Rights Institute that first convened in 1992 to investigate reports of human rights violations against ethnic minorities. Due to tensions arising from the adoption of the Elections Law and Law on Aliens in 1993, the President established a roundtable of representatives of the parliament, the Union of Estonian Nationalities, and the Russian-speaking population's Representative Assembly. A non-governmental legal information center in Tallinn now provides free legal assistance to both citizens and non-citizens seeking advice on human rights-related issues. In September 1997, the Institute established an information center in the heavily ethni- Russian town of Kohtla-Jarve. In February 1998, the government approved a program to integrate non-citizens into Estonian society by increasing the role of Estonian as a language of interethnic communication. The government claims that the objective of the program, which has been praised by the Council of Baltic Sea States High Commissioner for Democratic Institutions and Human Rights, is not assimilation, but rather a reduction in the current barriers between the ethnic communities. In the context of repeated Russian allegations of human rights violations among the non-citizen population, both the OSCE mission in Estonia and the OSCE High Commissioner for National Minorities have declared that they could not find a pattern of human rights abuses.

Corruption B

1. What is the magnitude of official corruption in the civil service? Must an average citizen pay a bribe to a bureaucrat in order to receive a service? What services are subject to bribe requests, for example, university entrance, hospital admission, telephone installation, obtaining a license to operate a business, or applying for a passport or other official documents? What is the average salary of civil servants at various levels? Although corruption and prejudices exist within the civil service, estimates of the degree of official corruption vary. International and local nonprofit organizations have described the magnitude of corruption in Estonia as ranging from "not very high" to "relatively high." According to recent public opinion surveys, three of four Estonians consider corruption to be a serious threat to the country, and half regard corruption in the police force as an important or very important problem. Moreover, Estonia has the highest *per capita* crime rate in the Baltics — although crime rates have been dropping since 1994 – and, in most societies, there are clear links between criminality and corruption. The lack of well-trained and educated civil servants, as well as their low salaries relative to the private sector, contributes to corruption within government service. The average salary of civil servants ranges from $200 — primarily at the local government level —to $1,000 per month, and efforts are currently underway to increase salaries. Recently, President Meri requested that the income of high state officials be made public in order to increase the public's confidence in the civil service. In general, a citizen does not need to offer a bribe to obtain most personal services.

2. Do top policy-makers (the President, ministers, vice-ministers, top court justices, and heads of agencies and commissions) have direct ties to businesses? How strong are such connections and what kinds of businesses are these? The Public Service Act of January 25, 1995, defines the rules, regulations, and employee rights and obligations in the private sector. According to the Act, civil servants cannot belong to the board of directors or other controlling body of a commercial association. Although policy-makers may have close ties to businesses, they usually do not participate in the direct operations of enterprises. If a public servant is a director of a state enterprise, he or she cannot be paid. This rule, however, is frequently not followed in practice. Government employees are strictly prohibited from employment at an enterprise over which they exercise supervision. This prohibition extends to a period of three years after the official has left office. Current laws in Estonia do not prohibit higher-level civil servants from owning shares in companies. The Law on Corruption Prevention, which was passed on January 19, 1995, regulates the economic interests of public servants and defines employment restrictions. Civil servants must declare their sources of income — including property, shares or interests in business, and gifts that they have received — and they may not make or influence decisions in which there may be conflicts of interest. The declarations of the economic interests of higher civil servants are published.

3. Do laws requiring financial disclosure and disallowing conflict of interest exist? Have publicized anti-corruption cases been pursued? To what conclusion? Laws requiring financial disclosure and disallowing conflict of interest include the Criminal Code Anti-Corruption Law, the Law on Labor Contracts, and the Law on Bookkeeping. Investigative journalists in Estonia have covered various cases of corruption throughout the country over the last several years, and several publicized corruption cases have been pursued by the authorities. In one well-known case that began in late 1996, Estonian Supreme Court Chief Justice Rait Maruste took the unusual step of publicly denouncing a lower court's acquittal of an attorney who represented organized crime interests and who attempted to bribe a judge. Prosecutors claimed that the high-profile lawyer wanted the judge to release a defendant who had been remanded on charges of arms-dealing. A videotape recording made by the defense police on November 28, 1996, in the judge's chambers shows the lawyer asking the judge about the money and learning that the judge had already reported the incident to the police. The Harju County Court ruled on March 7, 1997 that the video was not sufficient proof that the lawyer had sought to bribe the judge because the lawyer and the judge had not agreed earlier for what the money would be used. In an Estonian newspaper interview soon after the ruling, Chief Justice Maruste denounced the decision as a setback for the integrity of the judicial system in Estonia. The ruling also shocked many political observers. Nevertheless, Maruste's remarks drew criticism from two opposition parliamentarians who claimed that he was exerting indirect pressure on the lower courts. On April 4, 1997, the Tallinn Circuit Court overturned the lawyer's acquittal. In an ironic twist, the Supreme Court justices had been nominated by a commission on which the lawyer had been a member. In another case in early 1997, Tallinn city officials were alleged to have inappropriately allowed the privatization of at least 181 apartments for privatization vouchers at a cost several times less than their real market value. The officials had declared that the vacant apartments were "residence areas" of enterprises and were occupied by persons affiliated with those enterprises. The occupants were then allowed to purchase the apartments with vouchers. The vouchers were intended to allow citizens to buy the flats in which they live at a nominal price. Then-Prime Minister and Coalition Party Chairman Tiit Vahi, whose daughter purchased one of the apartments, was implicated in the scandal and eventually resigned. The case is still pending. The police and courts often do not have enough experience or resources to fight corruption and pursue corruption cases.

4. What major anti-corruption initiatives have been implemented? How often are anti-corruption laws and decrees adopted? The Law on Corruption Prevention was adopted on January 19, 1995, and amendments are being considered in parliament. On November 11, 1996, parliament established the Committee on the Prevention of Corruption, which is chaired by a politician who had investigated public corruption cases in the Tallinn city government. Various seminars and conferences have been organized for civil servants and the public in order to raise awareness of corruption-related issues. The non-profit Jaan Tonisson Institute is analyzing Estonian laws pertaining to corruption by comparing them to similar laws in Western Europe. It plans to conclude its project by the end of 1998 by making proposals to the government for future anti-corruption legislation.

5. How do major anti-corruption-ranking organizations like Transparency International rate this country? Transparency International has not yet provided a ranking of the degree of corruption in Estonia. A 1997 OSCE report on the rule of law in Estonia stated that a "relatively high level of corruption among state and local authorities distances them from people and endangers individuals' right to due process."

Privatization 2.00/7

1. What percentage of the GDP comes from private ownership? What percentage of the labor force is employed in the private sector? How large is the informal sector of the economy? According to information provided by the Estonian Statistical Office and the European Bank for Reconstruction and Development (EBRD), the private sector constituted 67 percent of GDP in 1997. Data from the latest Estonian Labor Force survey indicated that the non-state sector of "pure" private sector and cooperatives accounted for 49 percent and 10 percent, respectively, of total employment in the first quarter of 1995. This represents an increase from 3 percent and 21 percent, respectively, in 1989. As for industrial sector employment, the Estonian Ministry of Economy reported a private sector share of 81 percent in mid 1996. The size of the informal sector of the economy remains a matter of dispute. According to a 1996 survey, the unofficial economy's share of GDP was 11.8 percent in 1995. In 1994, it stood at 25.1 percent. This decline may reflect improvements in the operating environment, as well as increases in the government's ability to enforce existing legislation and limit tax evasion. Other estimates, however, suggest that the informal sector is larger, particularly in the largely ethnic Russian north-east region of Estonia, where the unemployment rate is higher.

2. What major privatization legislation has been passed? What were its substantive features? Small-scale privatization began in Estonia began in June 1990, when the government adopted the Law on Ownership. In early 1992, the government launched an experimental pilot program to privatize seven companies. In August 1992, it began to privatize large-scale enterprises after establishing the Estonian Privatization Enterprise, which had a mandate to sell 38 selected concerns. The German *Treuhandanstalt* tender procedure was chosen, but, in mid-1994, a voucher-style privatization scheme was introduced to complement it.

The privatization of enterprises is regulated primarily by the June 17, 1993 Law on Privatization. Other relevant acts include the 1991 Law on the Fundamentals of Ownership Reform; the 1991 Land Reform Act; the 1991 Law on Foreign Investments; the

1992 Law on Bankruptcy; the 1993 Property Law; the 1993 Law on Securities Markets; and the 1994 government decrees on "Procedures for Public Offering of Shares of State-Owned Enterprises" and "Investment Funds." The process is administered by the Estonian Privatization Agency (EPA), which was founded in September 1993, and which assumed the functions of the Estonian Privatization Enterprise and the former State Property Department. The EPA is a government agency that reports to the Ministry of Finance and that is funded from the state budget. The basic methods of privatization have been sale by means of tender with preliminary negotiations, sale by public or restricted auction, and the public offer of shares. Privatization can also occur through the joint-venture method — the investment of state property as equity into a newly established company — the process of bankruptcy.

3. What proportion of agriculture, housing and land, industry, and small business and services is in private hands? *Agriculture:* Approximately 95 percent of farms had been privatized by 1996 – a slight increase from 93 percent in 1995. The number of total farms in Estonia increased from 13,513 in 1995 to 19,767 in 1996. The number of state-owned and cooperative farms decreased from 973 in 1995 to 873 in 1996.

Housing and land: The privatization of housing and land has been impeded by continuing uncertainty regarding the restitution of land and the slow process of land registration. Amendments to the Law on Land Reform were adopted in 1996 to accelerate land sales. They included provisions to give existing tenants and users priority in purchasing land, allow payments in installments, and abolish the previous requirement of conducting costly new surveys of each plot to be sold. The first auctions of undeveloped land were held, and the EPA concluded 169 land purchase agreements for a total of approximately $15 million. An estimated 14 percent of land under state ownership had been privatized by mid-1997. In 1996, approximately 70 percent of housing had been privatized.

Industry: With the exception of major utilities, the privatization of Estonian large-scale enterprises was virtually complete by the end of 1997. In 1998, the privatization program will continue to focus on sales of Estonia's strategic monopolies. Eesti Polevkivi, the oil shale mining company, and Eesti Telekom, the state telecommunications company, are likely to be sold during the year. Estonian Energy and Estonian Railways, which are considered to be among the most complicated transactions, are scheduled to be privatized in 1999.

Small business and services: Small-scale enterprise privatization was completed by the mid- 1990s. Approximately 80 percent of the 2,850 eligible small enterprises were privatized as early as 1993.

4. What has been the extent of insider (management, labor, and nomenklatura) participation in the privatization process? What explicit and implicit preferences have been awarded to insiders? In Estonia, there have been fewer allegations of corruption and insider-dealing than in many other formerly Communist countries. Workers and managers in firms that are being privatized receive no special concessions, but they can and often do submit bids and business plans. By 1996, they had won in approximately thirty cases. Estonia has made progress in identifying effective owners who are capable of running a durable, productive firm by promoting corporate governance rather than maximizing privatization revenues. When using the open tender process, the EPA decides among bids by taking into consideration, among other factors, the bid price, commitments to maintain or create jobs, pledges to invest, and the proposed business plan. As a result, most investors have met contractual obligations and have often surpassed them by wide margins.

5. How much public awareness of and support for privatization has there been? What is the nature of support and opposition to privatization by major interest groups? Among the methods used for privatization in Estonia is the voucher system, which is limited to Estonian citizens, who exchange vouchers for shares. Citizens may sell their vouchers to any bidder, exchange them for shares in companies or investment funds, use them to buy the housing in which they live, purchase land, or buy bonds from a Compensation Fund. This system has generated public support for the country's privatization program by countering the claim that divestiture benefits only the foreigner, the local elite, and the politically well-connected. Public perception has been particularly significant in Estonia, where claims that the privatization process was non-transparent won votes in the 1995 national legislative elections and contributed to the defeat of the incumbent coalition. It could be argued, however, that it was the few instances of insider-trading, rather than the scope and pace of the privatization program as a whole or the involvement of foreigners, that caused this dissatisfaction.

Macroeconomics 2.00/7

1. Has the taxation system been reformed? (What areas have and have not been overhauled? To what degree are taxpayers complying? Is tax compliance difficult to achieve? Has the level of revenues increased? Is the revenue-collection body overburdened? What is the overall tax burden?) Reform of Estonia's tax system began in 1991 and was based on the December 1989 Law of Taxation and other laws and government decrees on individual taxes. The Law on Taxation, which created the basis for introducing a tax system modeled on Western structures, gave the Estonian government the right to tax, established who could be taxed and on what basis, and issued a general order to permit tax allowances. The current tax structure, which has remained essentially unchanged since 1994, includes state and local taxes. State taxes include excises, income tax, VAT, social security tax, land tax, customs tax, gambling tax, and gift and inheritance tax. Local taxes may include sales and local income taxes. Estonia has a flat income tax rate of 26 percent and a top corporate tax rate of 26 percent. Widespread tax evasion was a serious problem in 1996, especially during the early part of the year. The government responding by establishing a special commission, strengthening customs posts, and raising fines for tax evasion. By the end of 1996, state budget revenues exceeded expenditures by $7.7 million, with approximately 92 percent of the revenue obtained through income tax, VAT, and excise duties. At the end of 1997, the year's budget revenue target had been exceeded by 6.3 percent – a figure that excludes the one-time income from the privatization of the Estonian Shipping Company. The "surplus" was channeled into an economic stabilization fund. This high level of revenue collection reflected better-than-expected VAT revenues and the growing effectiveness of the state revenue authorities in collecting taxes. Nevertheless, only 19.58 percent of the year's revenue target was collected in the first three months of 1998. Approximately 20.9 percent had been collected during the first quarter in 1997. Government officials predict that they will overcome the current shortfall in 1998, even though its revenue collection is not likely to improve until the second half of the year. The shortfall has been blamed in part on higher excise taxes which took effect on certain products at the beginning of 1998. Businesses reportedly acquired larger stocks of these items in late 1997 in anticipation of the tax increase.

2. Does fiscal policy encourage private savings, investment and earnings? (Has there been any reform/alteration of revenue and budget policies? How large are budget deficits and overall debt? Is the financing of the social insurance/pension system sustainable? What proportion of the budget is taken up by subsidies to firms and individuals?) The cornerstone of the success of Estonia's monetary reform was the introduction in June 1992 of the country's national currency, the *kroon* (crown). Pegged to the German *mark* at a rate of eight to one, the kroon's fixed exchange rate curbed inflation, promoted reorientation toward European markets, and supported long-term economic recovery and growth. With the kroon successfully launched, the Bank of Estonia decided at the beginning of 1993 to liberalize domestic holdings of foreign currency, thereby allowing individuals and Estonian firms to open unlimited foreign exchange accounts with local banks. The volume of deposits grew substantially in 1997 at nearly all commercial banks. Deposits totaled 21.3 billion kroons – an increase of 52.3 percent from the previous year. The total amount of individual deposits exceeds 7 billion kroons ($483 million), and the amount that Estonians will save annually is estimated at more than 30 million kroons ($2 million). The amount of individual deposits exceeded those of companies for the first time in March 1998, thereby demonstrating the public's growing confidence in the country's banking system. On the fiscal side, the government has maintained a balanced budget — as stipulated by law — since monetary reform, with revenues even slightly exceeding expenditures. The budget, therefore, creates no inflationary pressures in the economy. As a measure of inflation, the consumer price index (CPI) reached a relatively low rate during the mid 1990s. In 1993, annual CPI was 89.8 percent. It decreased to 41.7 percent in 1994, 28.9 percent in 1995, and 14.8 percent in 1996. By 1997, it had fallen to 11.2 percent. Analysts predict that it will stand between 9.6 and 10 percent in 1998. Unemployment has remained consistently low at rates between 4 and 6 percent in 1996 and 1997. After a decline during the early 1990s, GDP increased for the first time in 1993. It grew by approximately 4 percent in 1996 and 10 percent in 1997. The average gross monthly wage was approximately 4,000 kroons in the fourth quarter of 1997 – an increase of 21.7 percent from the same period in 1996. In early 1998, the government announced that it would increase pensions by an average of 102 kroons ($88) a month — twice the increase projected when the government's budget was adopted. This will cost approximately 370 million kroons ($257 million). The increase in pensions will necessitate a supplementary budget in 1998, in spite of earlier government pledges that it would avoid adopting one. At the same time, parliament approved an April 1998 pension reform bill that will move Estonia from a pay-as-you-earn system to a "three pillar system" that includes a minimum state-financed pension, a supplementary pension financed by compulsory contributions, and a voluntary private scheme. In addition to reducing strain on the budget, the reformed pension system is expected to boost savings, thereby contributing to sustainable rates of growth through increased investment.

3. Has there been banking reform? (Is the central bank independent? What are its responsibilities? Is it effective in setting and/or implementing monetary policy? What is the actual state of the private banking sector? Does it conform to international standards? Are depositors protected?) According to the Law on the Bank of Estonia of 1993, the country's central bank is administratively independent of the executive branch of the government. The Estonian Central Bank is one of the most autonomous central banks in the world and is well-protected from political manipulation. The Law on the Bank of Estonia provides that the Bank will implement monetary policies and set credit policies by buying and selling securities and foreign currencies, setting the Bank's interest rates, and issuing and withdrawing licenses and granting loans to credit institutions. It also provides that the Bank will determine the exchange rate of the Estonian kroon against foreign currencies, but this provision has been overtaken by the Law on the Security of the Estonian Kroon, according to which the official exchange rate is fixed against the German mark at a rate of eight to one. The Bank has received high marks for its regulation of commercial banks and has followed IMF recommendations to strengthen the capital adequacy of commercial banks and address short-term liquidity problems. The bank has also made clear that it will not save troubled commercial banks. In February 1998, it announced plans to sell its remaining five percent stake in Hoiupank, after which it will no longer hold any shares in commercial banks.

In 1992, insufficient banking legislation and a lack of professional skills and experience among many bank managers led to the insolvency of several of Estonia's banks and an ensuing banking crisis. In response, the Law on Credit Institutions and other stricter regulations were adopted. By 1994, most of the private banking sector had recovered. As of March 1998, 11 local commercial banks and one branch of a foreign bank were operating in Estonia — down from 40 authorized banks in 1992 and 20 in mid-1995. This decrease is the result of increasing competition, which is forcing smaller and less successful institutions to close or merge with other banks. After Estonia's stock market crash in October 1997, the Bank of Estonia announced several measures to tighten the supervision and regulation of commercial banks. As of January 1, 1998 the Bank had doubled the daily minimum balance requirement from 2 percent to 4 percent and had increased requirements for minimum capital plus reserves from 50 million 75 million kroons. All Estonian banks were able to meet the minimum of 75 million kroons by the January deadline. Despite the economic slump in late 1997, Estonia's commercial banks earned $62 million during 1997 — an increase of 84.6 percent from 1996. In April, 1998 parliament approved the formation of a deposit insurance scheme to encourage private savings and meet EUguidelines. According to the legislation, deposits up to 20,000 kroons ($1,385) will be covered through a special fund created by banking and credit institutions. After making an initial payment of 50,000 kroons, banks will pay 0.5 percent of the total sum of guaranteed deposits into the fund.

4. How sound is the national currency? (Is the value of the currency fixed or does it float? How convertible is the currency? How large are the hard currency reserves? Has exchange rate policy been stable and predictable? Estonia's reintroduction of its pre-Soviet currency on June 20, 1992 was instrumental in enabling the country to stabilize its economy well before other former Soviet republics. Under the country's currency board system, all kroons in circulation must by law be fully supported by foreign exchange reserves. Estonia has full current and capital account convertibility. In 1996, gross reserves, excluding gold, were approximately $630 million. Many foreign economic analysts have declared that the kroon is overvalued and called for the currency board to be abolished. By contrast, Estonian economists, government officials, and the International Monetary Fund (IMF) have insisted that the currency board serves Estonia well and that the kroon is reasonably valued. As evidence, they cite the country's growing exports — up 35 percent in one year — and the duration of loans being made by foreign banks to Estonian banks.

GEORGIA

Freedom in the World Ratings, 1989-1998

	1989-90	1990-91	1991-92	1992-93	1993-94	1994-95	1995-96	1996-97	1997-98
Political Rights	-	-	6	4	5	5	4	4	3
Civil Liberties	-	-	5	5	5	5	5	4	4
Status	-	-	NF	PF	PF	PF	PF	PF	PF

Polity: Transitional
Economy: Transitional
Population: 5,376,000
PPP: $1,389
Ethnic Groups: Georgians (70 percent), Armenian (8 percent), Russian (6 percent), Abkhazian, Azeri, Ossetian, others
Capital: Tbilisi

Political Process 4.50/7

1. When did national legislative elections occur? Were they free and fair? How were they judged by domestic and international election monitoring organizations? Who composes the government? The first multi-party parliamentary elections in Georgia were held in October 1990. Seats were allocated on the basis of party lists and single-candidate districts. The nationalist Round Table bloc led by Zviad Gamsakhurdia received 53 percent of the vote. The Communist Party won 29 percent. Gamsakhurdia's Round Table dominated the country's local elections in 1991. In May 1991, Gamsakhurdia won the presidential elections with 87 percent of the vote.

Gamsakhurdia was overthrown by a violent military coup in late 1991. Secessionist conflicts erupted in South Ossetia in late 1991, and in Abkhazia in August 1992. More than 200,000 people were displaced from their homes as a result of the fighting. Gamsakhurdia supporters staged an insurrection in western Georgia in the autumn of 1992.

Georgia's second parliamentary elections were held under these very difficult circumstances on October 11, 1992. South Ossetia, Abkhazia, and the areas held by pro-Gamsakhurdia insurrectionists did not participate in the vote. A new election law was implemented in order to permit the post-Gamsakhurdist authorities to gain democratic legitimacy. Twenty-six parties won seats in the new parliament. The biggest winner, the *Mshvidoba* ("Peace") bloc, won only 14 seats and 17 percent of the vote. Parliament's 235 seats, which were split between 85 single-member seats and 150 proportional representation seats, were divided between 24 parties. Most of the single member seats were won by independent candidates. Parliament proved fragmented and ineffective and rapidly lost the confidence of the people. By autumn 1993, most of the parties and blocs had collapsed. The largest informal grouping, which included approximately 125 members, united solely through its support for then-Chairman of Parliament Eduard Shevardnadze.

The most recent parliamentary elections were held on November 5, 1995, under a new constitution that restored a five percent threshold for representation. The constitution increased the powers to the president and reduced the number of parliamentary seats to 233. It also separated powers in an arrangement that was loosely based on the U.S. Constitution. Although 56 parties and blocs contested the elections, only three of these succeeded in gaining significant representation in parliament. Shevardnadze's Union of Georgian Citizens won 108 seats. The National Democratic Party won 35 seats with eight percent of the vote. The All-Georgian Revival Union, which is based in the autonomous region of Adjaria and is led by Adjarian Chairman Aslan Abashidze, won 27 seats with 7 percent of the vote. The remaining seats were won by minor opposition parties and independent candidates. Observers from the Organization for Security and Cooperation in Europe (OSCE) determined that the vote was generally free and fair, although it reported a number of violations in Adjaria and other regions. While the defeat of the pro-Gamsakhurdist insurrectionists led to western Georgia's participation in the elections, the breakaway regions of South Ossetia and Abkahzia were still excluded.

Parliament's term is four years. New elections are scheduled for the autumn of 1999.

2. When did Presidential elections occur? Were they free and fair? Presidential and parliamentary elections were held on November 5, 1995. Eduard Shevardnadze won with 75 percent of the vote. International observers characterized the vote as free and fair.

The first multiparty presidential elections were held on May 26, 1991. Zviad Gamsakhurdia, a nationalist dissident, won with 87 percent of the vote. After he was overthrown in December 1991, executive power was assumed by a provisional Military Council that abolished the Office of President. Shortly thereafter, the Military Council established the Political Council, an advisory body of individuals and parties that had opposed Gamsakhurdia.

The Military Council, which was dominated by warlords Jaba Ioseliani and Tengiz Kitovani, invited former Soviet Foreign Minister Eduard Shevardnadze to return to Georgia in March 1991 to lead the country out of crisis. It was then abolished, after which the Political Council was expanded and recast as the State Council. Executive functions were performed by the Presidium of the State Council, a collective presidency that included Kitovani, Ioseliani, Shevardnadze, and Provisional Prime Minister Tengiz Sigua. Shevardnadze served as Chairman of the Presidium, but Ioseliani and Kitovani had veto power. Government in Georgia effectively collapsed during this period as the members of the Presidium engaged in fierce political maneuvering.

The Presidium was abolished in October 1992 during the run-up to the parliamentary elections. Executive power was vested in the Chairman of the Parliament, a new, directly elected post. Shevardnadze won this position with 96 percent of the vote. In November 1992, the Law on State Power united the posts of parliamentary chairman and head of state. Again, Shevardnadze held the post.

In August 1995, parliament adopted a new constitution that restored the Office of President. Presidential elections followed on November 5, 1995. The December 8, 1995 Law on Executive Power, and the May 3, 1997 Law on State Institutions, redefined and greatly expanded the powers of the presidency.

3. Is the electoral system multiparty based? Are there at least two viable political parties functioning at all levels of government? The electoral system is multiparty based. Georgia is a unitary state; there are no elections other than those to the national parliament. Ten parties are represented in parliament, although, in practice, the body is dominated by three parties. The ruling Citizen's Union Party and its supporters control all parliamentary committees.

There is also a loose grouping of opposition parties, most of which are loyal to ousted President Gamsakhurdia. It lost its representation in parliament in the 1995 elections and is known colloquially as the "non-parliamentary opposition." Although it has been marginalized politically, this group publishes several newspapers and strongly opposes the Shevardnadze government. Gamsakhurdia supporters are accused of attempting to assassinate Shevardnadze in February 1998. Following this attempt and a subsequent police crackdown on Gamsakhurdia supporters, four members of the U.N. Military Observers Group, which monitors the Georgian-Abkhaz border, were taken hostage by Gamsakhurdia supporters. In order to end the crisis, the Shevardnadze government began talks with Moscow-based representatives of the pro-Gamsakhurdia faction.

The Autonomous Republic of Adjaria is governed by a Supreme Soviet and Chairman. In 1990, Gamsakhurdia named Aslan Abashidze as Chairman. Abashidze has increasingly centralized power in his own office and has unilaterally increased the powers of his security forces, thereby assuming powers that are formally assigned to central government agencies in Tbilisi. While relations with the Shevardnadze government have been strained at times, open clashes have been avoided. Nevertheless, Abashidze has charged that Georgian government officials are plotting to overthrow him and end Adjaria's autonomous status.

The secessionist regions of Abkhazia and South Ossetia, which remain unrecognized by any state, have each formed their own parliaments. Elections to the unrecognized 35-seat Abkhazian parliament in Sukhumi were held on November 23, 1995, amid protests from the Georgian government. A total of 87 candidates contested the elections.

The Georgian government maintains an Abkhaz government-in-exile that includes a Supreme Council and a Chairman. The Supreme Council was created on February 24, 1995, and includes Georgian members of parliament elected by refugees from Abkhazia during the November 1995 elections. These representatives are known as the "Abkhazeti."

Elections to the South Ossetian presidency in Tskhinvali were held on November 10, 1996, and were won by Ludvig Chibirov, the incumbent President of the Supreme Soviet. The Georgian government also protested against these elections but with less vehemence due to Chibirov's relatively moderate views on reintegration with Georgia.

4. How many parties have been legalized? Are any particular parties illegal? The Georgian Communist Party has claimed to be the target of an "anti-Communist vendetta," and several of its leaders have been jailed on charges of possession of illegal weapons and the creation of illegal armed groups. Government forces have disrupted rallies and demonstrations by representatives of ethnic Georgians forced to flee Abkhazia.

More than 100 parties and blocs have registered since the October 1992 elections. Many of these, however, have been moribund for some time.

5. What proportion of the population belongs to political parties? Party membership in Georgia is low; exact numbers, however, are unavailable. Membership figures provided by parties are wildly inflated. According to documents filed before the November 1995 elections, the 54 blocs and parties contesting the election claimed an aggregate membership of more than 500,000, or approximately 20 percent of the voting population. This figure, however, includes doubtful claims by the Stalin Communist Party that has 130,000 members as well as by the Agrarian Union claiming its membership to be 160,000 members. In general, the worst membership inflation is found among parties that were established between 1990 and 1992 and that adhere to a left-wing stance on economic and social issues. The ruling Citizens Union Party claimed a membership of 100,000 before the November 1995 elections.

6. What has been the trend of voter turnout at the municipal, provincial, and national levels in recent years? Voter turnout has declined since 1991, but stabilized in 1995. Turnout for the first multiparty elections in October 1990 was approximately 70 percent. Turnout for the May 1991 presidential elections was 83.4 percent. Approximately 86 percent cast ballots in the vote for Chairman of parliament on October 11, 1992. The turnout for the November 1995 presidential and parliamentary elections was approximately 68 percent.

Civil Society 4.25/7

1. How many NGOs have come into existence since 1988? What is the number of charitable/nonprofit organizations? Are there locally-led efforts to increase philanthropy and volunteerism? What proportion of the population is active in private voluntary activity (from polling data)? NGOs have proliferated dramatically in Georgia. A survey by the American organization National Democratic Institute revealed that, although there were no NGOs registered in 1992, by 1995, 60 were in operation and active in areas as diverse as environmental monitoring, human rights, electoral monitoring, conflict resolution, and social assistance.

2. What is the legal and regulatory environment for NGOs (i.e., ease of registration, legal rights, government regulation, taxation, procurement and access-to-information issues)? To what extent is NGO activism focused on improving the legal and regulatory environment? While confusion persists in the wake of tax code changes regarding the exact liability of NGOs, registration, procurement, and access are considerably simpler than in the two other Caucasian states. There is little activism directed at securing changes in the legal and regulatory environment.

3. What is the organizational capacity of NGOs? Do management structures clearly delineate authority and responsibility? Is information available on NGO management issues in the native language? Is there a core of experienced practitioners/trainers to serve as consultants or mentors to less developed organizations? Available NGO resources such as funding, management training, and mentoring have been unable to keep pace with the rapidly expanding NGO sector. The quality of NGO management varies widely among organizations. International NGOs such as the Open Society Institute, the NDI, and the Friederich Ebert Stiftung, among others, have undertaken efforts to supply advisory materials in Georgian and Russian languages and to advise Georgian

NGOs on organizational and management issues.

4. Are NGOs financially viable? What is their tax status? Are they obliged to and do they typically disclose revenue sources? Do government procurement opportunities exist for private, not-for-profit providers of services? The tax status of NGOs has deteriorated somewhat since 1992. In 1996, tax exemptions for some foreign and local NGOs were revoked. The new tax code restores some tax exemptions that are based on the type of activities in which the NGOs engage, such as the manufacture of prostheses and the import of children's literature or educational materials. Most NGOs remain heavily dependent on grants from a few large Western NGOs or state financial assistance.

5. Are there free trade unions? How many workers belong to these unions? Is the number of workers belonging to trade unions growing or decreasing? What is the numerical/proportional membership of farmers' groups, small business associations, etc.? There are trade unions in Georgia, although most of these are remnants of Soviet-era sectoral unions concentrated in state-owned industries. The 1995 constitution and labor code gave workers the right to organize. This right is respected, although members of the security forces are not permitted to unionize. There have been a number of demonstrations and even riots by workers in protest against non-payment of wages. The number of workers who belong to trade unions is slowly declining as businesses are privatized and more workers become active in the informal economy. No reliable information is available on membership in small business associations and farmers' groups.

6. What forms of interest group participation in politics are legal? What types of interest groups are active in the political and policy process? In general, most forms of interest group participation in politics are legal. It is illegal to advocate violence, the overthrow of the government, secession, or ethnic hatred. While the parliament is still learning to function in a transparent and open manner, interest groups are becoming more and more involved in government policy-making. NDI, for example, has functioned as a close adviser to several parliamentary committees and officials in the development of new legislation. Other groups have sought to provide independent sources of information on foreign and domestic affairs without necessarily lobbying the government actively.

7. How is the not-for-profit/NGO sector perceived by the public and government officials? What is the nature of media coverage of NGOs? To what extent do government officials engage with NGOs? The government's attitude towards NGOs is generally highly positive and reflects both a conscious desire to engage with Western organizations and an acknowledgment of Georgia's ongoing heavy dependence on foreign credits and assistance. For example, the World Food Program feeds 170,000 Georgians each year. Nevertheless, while the central government has made significant progress in achieving open and transparent governance, regions outside the capital have changed very little from the Communist era. Some organizations active in electoral monitoring in the regions have encountered hostility or suspicion from local authorities.

Independent Media 4.25/7

1. Are there legal protections for press freedom? The 1995 constitution provides for a free press. Article 24 states, "Every individual has the right to receive freely and to disseminate information and to express and disseminate his opinion orally, in written or any other form." Censorship is prohibited. The establishment of media monopolies is illegal.

2. Are there legal penalties for libeling officials? Are there legal penalties for "irresponsible" journalism? Have these laws been enforced to harass journalists? The 1991 press law requires that journalists "respect the dignity and honor" of the President and ordinary citizens and that they not undermine the state. The law provides for penalties against publications that "malevolently [use the] freedom of the press, [and] spread facts not corresponding to reality."

It is unclear how the 1991 law can be reconciled with the 1995 constitutional articles that guarantee freedom of expression. The parliament has indicated that the press law is one of a large group of laws that require revision to bring it into conformity with the constitution.

Partly as a result of the libel laws, the media practice self-censorship when discussing President Shevardnadze and his family and senior government officials. In 1997, there were no cases of journalists charged with libeling government officials.

3. What proportion of media is privatized? What are the major private newspapers, television stations, and radio stations? In Tbilisi, there are a number of privately owned local television stations that broadcast news and entertainment programs. Mexican and Brazilian soap operas are particularly popular. In addition, there are two state-operated stations, Channel 1 and Channel 2, and one state radio station, Station 1.

There are a large number of independent newspapers, most of which are very partisan and have small, regionally circumscribed circulations. The large government newspapers are *Sakartvelos Respublica*, which is published in Georgian, and *Svobodnaya Gruzia*, which is published in Russian.

4. Are the private media financially viable? Although the independent media are diverse and active, many journalists and publishers complain that economic difficulties cripple their efforts to publish or broadcast regularly. Shortages of electricity and vital raw materials, including newsprint and ink, have hampered media operations. Many newspapers are dependent on the patronage of powerful individuals or political parties, a condition that accounts in part for the frequently partisan tone of reporting.

5. Are the media editorially independent ? Are the media's news gathering functions affected by interference from government or private owners? In general, editorial independence has not been achieved in Georgia. While media are more independent from government control than in 1995, they are frequently not editorially independent from control by financial supporters. Private television, radio, and newspapers are frequently seen as the mouthpieces of particular individuals or groups that underwrite them.

The government has occasionally acted against media efforts to gather and broadcast news that it deems embarrassing. The most celebrated case occurred in July 1996, when the Ministry of Communications revoked the license of Rustavi-2, a popular, Tbilisi-based independent television station. The ministry claimed that the station did not hold the proper permits to broadcast on its frequency. The move was perceived as a reaction to Rustavi-2's coverage of a number of controversial stories on politics, government corruption, and ethnic relations. It was widely criticized within Georgia, and the Georgian Supreme Court filed a protest to request that the Tbilisi City Court force the ministry to restore the license. After nine months, Rustavi-2 was able to resume its broadcasts.

Citing the dangers of "opening old wounds," President Shevardnadze has opposed the opening of KGB archives from the Stalinist period.

6. Is the distribution system for newspapers privately or governmentally controlled? A state agency is charged with distributing newspapers and dominates distribution outside of Tbilisi. In the capital, some newspapers have attempted, with mixed results, to establish their own distribution networks.

7. What proportion of the population is connected to the Internet? Are there any restrictions on Internet access to private citizens? A small fraction of the population is connected to the Internet. Power shortages, general poverty, and poor telephone connections combine to make Internet access beyond the reach of most citizens. There is one private Internet service provider in Tbilisi. America On Line provides a local number to enable its members to obtain access to their accounts and the Internet.

8. What has been the trend in press freedom as measured by Freedom House's *Survey of Press Freedom*? According to Freedom House's annual *Survey of Press Freedom*, Georgia was rated "Partly Free" in 1992 and 1993, and "Not Free" in 1994 through 1996. The rating improved to "Partly Free" in 1997-98, in part due to the restoration of the broadcast permit of Rustavi-2 television, which continues to display independence in its news and programming.

Governance and Public Administration 4.50/7

1. Is the legislature the effective rule-making institution? The parliament is the effective rule-making institution in Georgia. It has become increasingly proficient in its law-making functions as its members have increased their level of experience. Seventy percent of members of the 1995 parliament had never held public office. Under the 1995 constitution, the president cannot dissolve parliament and must secure its agreement to the "main principles" of his budget before submission.

2. Is substantial power decentralized to sub-national levels of government? What specific authority do sub-national levels have? Georgia represents a paradox in decentralization. Legally, power remains highly centralized, particularly within the office of the president, who appoints most local officials without parliamentary review. In practice, however, poor communications and the financial and military weakness of the central government have endowed local governments with substantial autonomy. In particular, some regional governors, although ostensibly dependent on the president, operate their regions as virtually independent fiefdoms and ignore laws and directives from the central government when they disagree with them or find them inconvenient. The government rarely challenges these governors openly.

3. Are sub-national officials chosen in free and fair elections? Elections to local district self-government assemblies (*sakrebulo*) were held on March 31,1991, five days after Gamsakhurdia won his overwhelming presidential mandate. Although international observers did not monitor these elections, they were generally considered to be free and fair. Gamsakhurdia's Round Table party failed to achieve majorities in most sakrebulos. This led to fierce conflict between many sakrebulos and their presidentially-appointed prefects. The sakrebulos were based on the Soviet era People's Assemblies. Most of their limited power was concentrated in the hands of the prefects. Nevertheless, they served as the centers of opposition to the Gamsakhurdia regime and to the depredations of the prefects, who were often extremely corrupt.

After Gamsakhurdia's ouster, the Military Council tacitly acknowledged the sakrebulos' role by recognizing their powers and abolishing the offices of the prefects. The sakrebulos that were controlled by Gamsakhurdia's Round Table party, however, were disbanded.

The State Council replaced the prefects with *gamgeoba* (executives) and chairmen of gamgeoba or mayors. The power of these new executives, who were also appointed by the central government, grew steadily. By early 1994, the sakrebulos had been reduced to largely advisory bodies. In April 1994, their mandate expired, and they ceased to exist. In some districts, however, they have continued to function informally as advisors to the gamgeoba.

In 1995, regional administration in Georgia was reorganized by presidential decree, which called for the formation of nine *mkhare* (regions). These entities would be governed by presidentially-appointed *rtsmunebuli* (commissioners). Parliament subsequently accepted the decree, but significantly reduced the powers of the rtsmunebuli. It has also opposed subsequent efforts by the central government to increase their powers. At present, gamgeoba and chairmen of gamgeoba in towns, villages, communities, and settlements are appointed and dismissed by the district gamgeoba, provided that nominees are approved by the rtsmunebuli.

In September 1997, after prolonged debate and disagreement even within the ruling party, parliament adopted draft local government legislation that maintained the practice of presidential appointment of the chairmen of gamgeoba and rtsmunebuli.

4. Do the executive and legislative bodies operate openly and with transparency? Is draft legislation easily accessible to the media and the public? Parliament operates with increasing transparency and openness. The media and public are advised of upcoming debates and legislation, and parliamentary proceedings are televised. The executive continues to be relatively closed, although some ministries have become more accessible.

5. Do municipal governments have sufficient revenues to carry out their duties? Do municipal governments have control of their own budgets? Do they raise revenue autonomously or from the central state budget? Municipal governments are subject to the same economic privation as other levels of the Georgian government. They remain heavily dependent on transfers from the state budget and do not have sufficient revenues to operate effectively in many instances. Tbilisi and Kutaisi, the two major municipalities, are exempt from laws that require the mkhare to contribute fixed percentages of their revenues to the central budget. Municipalities raise some funds autonomously — they control the collection of property taxes, for example — but Georgia's economic situation does not permit the issuance of municipal bonds or other such measures. The new legislation on the powers of local self-government will institute some changes in municipal finance.

6. Do the elected local leaders and local civil servants know how to manage municipal governments effectively? There are no elected local leaders. Local civil servants are frequently corrupt, and political loyalty and family connections are often more important in securing civil service appointments than professional competence. Nevertheless, a solid core of competent technical professionals remain in the civil service.

7. When did the constitutional/legislative changes on local power come into effect? Has there been a reform of the civil service code/system? Are local civil servants employees of the local or central government? Local civil servants are employees of the central government. The civil service code is being restructured.

Rule of Law 5.00/7

1. Is there a post-Communist constitution? How does the judicial system interpret and enforce the constitution? Are there specific examples of judicial enforcement of the constitution in the last year? On August 24, 1995, parliament adopted a new constitution, which created a 235-seat bicameral national legislature. The parliament is divided into the Council of the Republic, which includes 150 seats allocated on the basis of proportional representation, and the Senate, which includes 80 seats in single-member constituencies. Five additional seats in the Senate are reserved for presidential appointees. Parliament sits for a four-year term and cannot be dissolved by the president.

A separate Constitutional Court was created in 1996. Its mandate includes arbitration in constitutional disputes between the branches of government and rulings on individual claims of human rights violations. As of mid-1997, the court had heard 37 cases, 36 of which were submitted by individual citizens who claimed that their rights had been violated. In five cases, the court ruled government actions unconstitutional. The case of *Zoidze v. the President of Georgia* resulted in the cancellation of an unconstitutional tax.

2. Does the constitutional framework provide for human rights? Do the human rights include business and property rights? The 1995 constitution guarantees freedom of speech, movement, and assembly, as well as freedom from torture, inhuman punishment, and discrimination on the basis of race, language, religion, or gender. Article 21 of the constitution guarantees the right to own and inherit property. Article 30 requires that the state foster conditions conducive to the development of free enterprise.

Article 43 creates the post of public defender, who is elected by parliament for a five-year term and is not accountable to the president or the parliament. The public defender is authorized to report on human rights violations to the appropriate authorities and to recommend criminal or other disciplinary procedures.

3. Has there been basic reform of the criminal code/criminal law? Who authorizes searches and issues warrants? Are suspects and prisoners beaten or abused? Are there excessive delays in the criminal justice system? The criminal code is predominantly a Soviet-era instrument with various new amendments. A new Criminal Procedures Code and a law of the procuracy (prosecutor's office) were passed in November 1997, but neither had taken effect by March 1998. These laws were designed to create a legal system with adversarial trials by reducing the pervasive powers of the procuracy, increasing the rights of defense attorneys, and enhancing the independence and authority of the judiciary. The police operate with relative impunity and frequently violate the constitution. While court-issued warrants are required by law, police frequently enter homes without them and stop vehicles without probable cause.

In June 1997, State Security Minister Shota Kviraya was forced to resign after opposition journalists and members of parliament charged him with ordering illegal wiretaps.

Georgia has observed an informal moratorium on executions since 1995. The death penalty was formally abolished in November 1997. In July 1997, Shevardnadze commuted the death sentences of 54 inmates. Prison conditions are grim and have been the subject of criticism by prisoners and international human rights groups. In 1997, Georgian death-row inmates staged hunger strikes in 1997 to protest "unbearable" conditions. Prisoners are frequently beaten and abused by the police. On June 9, 1997, Shevardnadze issued a decree requiring that law enforcement officers observe the legal and human rights of prison inmates and suspects. The decree mandated the prosecution of violators of these rights, ordered the institution of human rights courses at police and state security academies, and ordered the publication of a human rights handbook for distribution to police officers. Human rights activists report that the decree has not been enforced.

4. Do most judges rule fairly and impartially? Do many remain from the Communist era? The majority of Georgian judges were appointed during the Soviet era. The judiciary is held in low repute, and there are many anecdotal reports of judges taking bribes, making decisions based on political motives, and denying defendants access to counsel and necessary materials for their defense.

5. Are the courts free of political control and influence? Are the courts linked directly to the Ministry of Justice or any other executive body? The constitution prohibits judges from joining political parties or participating in political activities. The courts have been removed from the jurisdiction of the Ministry of Justice and are controlled by the Supreme Court. They remain vulnerable to pressure, however, particularly from the executive branch. The procuracy is widely seen, in the words of one observer, as the "spineless handmaiden of power" and has brought charges in some cases in clear contravention of the law.

In June 1996, a Tbilisi court sentenced Temur Zhorzholiani, a member of parliament and fierce critic of President Shevardnadze, to four years in prison on weapons charges. Observers suggested that he was arrested because of his ties to a state security officer who was suspected of complicity in the August 1995 attempt to assassinate Shevardnadze. The assassination plot was allegedly hatched by then-State Security Minister Igor Giorgadze.

6. What proportion of lawyers is in private practice? How does this compare with the previous year? The great majority of lawyers continue to work for the state. The proportion of lawyers in private practice is growing, however, along with the expansion of the NGO and private sectors. To date, these sectors have not greatly affected the dominant position of the state as employer. Precise figures are unavailable.

7. Does the state provide public defenders? The state is required to furnish legal counsel if the defendant cannot afford his or her own attorney. The criminal code has been amended to permit access to a lawyer from the moment of arrest. Bureaucratic procedures, however, frequently prevent this from taking place in practice.

8. Are there effective anti-bias/discrimination laws, including protection of ethnic minority rights? Article 38 of the 1995 constitution mandates equal treatment of all citizens regardless of ethnic, linguistic, or religious identity. Georgia has a tradition of tolerance for religious minorities. While the government has pledged to provide support for teaching minority languages, funds are seldom available due to the general scarcity of financial resources.

Corruption C

1. What is the magnitude of official corruption in the civil service? Must an average citizen pay a bribe to a bureaucrat in order to receive a service? What services are subject to bribe requests — for example, university entrance, hospital admission, telephone installation, obtaining a license to operate a business, applying for a passport or other official documents? What is the average salary of civil servants at various levels? Assessments of the business climate in Georgia consistently rate official corruption as one of the major impediments to doing business in the country. Citizens are subject to "fees" at all levels for even the most basic services, as well as arbitrary demands for payment by police and tax officials. Even the state itself is a frequent target for such practices. In autumn 1997, the state treasury was robbed of approximately 160 kilograms of gold ingots. Treasury officials are widely believed to be the culprits.

The average monthly wage for public sector employees is 35 *lari* ($28), although in some cases salaries exceed $100 per month. In 1997, the average monthly wage for the population as a whole was $50.

2. Do top policy-makers (the President, ministers, vice-ministers, top court justices, and heads of agencies and commissions) have direct ties to businesses? How strong are such connections, and what kinds of businesses are these? Some high-ranking officials have been accused of ties to various legal and illegal businesses. In June 1997, for example, the Minister of State Security was accused of controlling the illegal trade in cigarettes. There have been no corruption trials of high-ranking officials, however, and, in many cases, it is difficult to determine whether allegations are truthfully or politically motivated.

Most corrupt activities involving high-ranking government officials involve illegal trade in commodities — including electricity, oil, and manufactured goods – that are regulated by the ministry in which the official is employed. A second category of corruption involves the evasion of customs and excise duties on goods imported through Batumi and Poti and intended for use within Georgia or for re-export to Russia, Azerbaijan, Armenia, and Iran.

3. Do laws requiring financial disclosure and disallowing conflict of interest exist? Have publicized anti-corruption cases been pursued? To what conclusion? Laws on financial disclosure and conflict of interest date from the Soviet era and are inadequate, although some have been amended. Legal mechanisms for prosecuting corrupt officials appear to be ineffective, except in some cases in which the official in question belonged to the Gamsakhurdia regime or the Military Council. Former Prime Minister Tengiz Sigua, for example, was convicted of embezzling $15 million in state funds during his tenure in office. Although several high-level government officials, such as Georgia's ambassador to Italy, have been accused of corruption by members of parliament, there has been no prosecution of any high-ranking government official. Some high-ranking officials, however, have been fired for alleged corruption.

4. What major anti-corruption initiatives have been implemented? How often are anti-corruption laws and decrees adopted? No major anti-corruption initiatives have been undertaken. Several anti-corruption amendments to the Soviet-era code have been adopted, but with little effect.

5. How do major corruption-ranking organizations like Transparency International rate this country? Transparency International has not rated Georgia.

Privatization 4.00/7

1. What percentage of the GDP comes from private ownership? What percentage of the labor force is employed in the private sector? How large is the informal sector of the economy? The European Bank for Reconstruction and Development (EBRD) estimates that the private sector accounts for about 55 percent of Georgian GDP. The labor force in state enterprises has fallen by 35 percent since 1991. Unemployment is roughly 21 percent. The World Bank estimates the informal economy to be 40-45 percent of GDP.

2. What major privatization legislation has been passed? What were its substantive features? The main privatization law in Georgia is the Law on the Privatization of State-owned Enterprises, which was passed on August 9, 1991. This law is very general and a number of amendments and laws have been passed subsequently to regulate different aspects of privatization, including US Embassy Economic and Trade Overview 1997.

The agency responsible for privatization in Georgia is the Ministry of State Property Management. This ministry is based in Tbilisi and maintains 63 regional offices around Georgia. The Tbilisi office is mainly responsible for developing privatization strategy, while the regional offices are involved in the preparation and sale of state property and companies.

Georgia's privatization program, designed by World Bank consultants and the Georgian Ministry of State Property Management, began on April 27, 1994, with the introduction of privatization vouchers. The National Voucher Center prepared the documentation and schedules for special voucher auctions that lasted from June 1995 until July 1996. Of the 4 million vouchers distributed, private individuals acquired 66 percent, foreign investors received 20 percent, and legal entities, the remainder.

The first stage of privatization, which proved very successful, was the privatization of small-scale enterprises. As of September 9, 1996, 8,158 small enterprises out of 9,300 originally targeted for privatization were privatized. The second stage, referred to as "mass privatization," involves the transformation of medium and large enterprises into joint-stock companies for further sale to private investors. By early September 1996, 976 of 1,138 such enterprises to be privatized have been set up as joint-stock companies, and, of these, 550 have been privatized. In the next stage, referred to as cash privatization, and which will last until the end of 1997, the government plans to sell company shares separately and in blocks, and both citizens and foreigners have equal rights to access the cash auctions. Privatization has not begun in Abkhazia and South Ossetia.

Recent privatization legislation includes the Law on the Ownership of Agricultural Land, which was passed by parliament in March 1996 and which legalizes private ownership by Georgian citizens and allows land to be leased by foreigners and non-citizen residents. Popular participation in the mass privatization process has been low, with only one in every 17 or 18 families actually participating. The public has been unable to receive reliable information about enterprises that are to be auctioned due to an inadequate government publicity campaign. In addition, since large enterprises are generally perceived to be in poor financial condition, their auctions attract fewer investors, particularly domestically. Bidders tend to be enterprise insiders, such as workers and managers. Even though most employees of medium- and large-sized enterprises receive discounts on voucher prices, they generally face great difficulties in raising the money to complete their share subscriptions.

After the conclusion of mass privatization in 1996, cash auctions were employed as the primary means of privatization. In May 1997, a new law was passed to expedite the process. In July 1997, Georgia launched "no-minimum-price auctions" at which shares in 266 state-owned enterprises that had remained unsold at two previous auctions were offered to bidders without a reserve price. The shares were distributed in proportion to the amounts offered by bidders, as opposed to the customary practice of considering the number of bids that were made for shares at a fixed price. In addition, in August 1997, Shevardnadze rescinded a May 1996 decree that had suspended the privatization of 51 companies defined as "strategically important".

3. What proportion of agriculture, housing and land, industry, and small business and services is in private hands? *Agriculture*: According to statistics published by the Georgian Social-Economic Information Department, as of mid-1996, approximately 77 percent of agriculture had been privatized.

Housing and Land: A World Bank report estimates that virtually all housing has been privatized. By September 1996, 23 percent of agricultural land — including pastures, arable land, and land producing perennial crops — was under private ownership. The government planned to transfer an additional 920,000 hectares of land, i.e., 30 percent of all agricultural land, to private owners before April 1997.

Industry: According to the Georgian Social-Economic Information Department, 65 percent of industry is in private hands. Governmentally designated "strategic" industries, such as the energy sector and mining, will remain in state hands.

Small Business and Services: There are currently 65,000 registered small businesses.

4. What has been the extent of insider (management, labor, and nomenklatura) participation in the privatization process? What explicit and implicit preferences have been awarded to insiders? For small enterprises, employees are obliged to pay between 50 and 65 percent of the "striking price" in cash, with the remainder being paid in vouchers. These requirements are the same for non-employees.

Joint-stock companies, i.e., medium- and large-sized industries, have been divided into two privatization classes: JSC (I), in which 51 percent of shares will pass into private hands, and JSC (II), in which 51 percent or more of shares will be retained in state ownership due to the "strategic significance" of the firm.

Under the executive decree of May 29, 1994, management and employees of JSC (I) firms have the option of purchasing 51 percent of the shares in their companies. Up to 30 percent of the cost can be paid with vouchers. The balance must be paid in cash with a 30 percent discount. For JSC(II) firms, ten percent of shares is offered for sale to management and employees under the same terms as are offered to JSC(I) firms.

5. How much public awareness of and support for privatization has there been? What is the nature of support and opposition to privatization by major interest groups? The public is generally aware of privatization and accepts the need for the process. Proprietors of small enterprises and agricultural producers, who frequently cite the need for more discretion and freedom in choosing suppliers and marketing products, seem to be particularly enthusiastic supporters of privatization. Opposition to privatization is concentrated within the workforces of medium and large industries and in the left-wing political parties, including the three Communist parties. Opposition is generally cast in terms of job losses in the industrial workforce.

Macroeconomics 4.00/7

1. Has the taxation system been reformed? (What areas have and have not been overhauled? To what degree are taxpayers complying? Is tax compliance difficult to achieve? Has the level of revenues increased? Is the revenue-collection body overburdened? What is the overall tax burden?) Parliament passed a new tax code in June 1997 to supplant or incorporate all previous laws and amendments. The state tax service is the only body empowered to assess the tax liability of enterprises. Although there is no distinction in the tax code between foreign and domestically owned enterprises, tax inspectors have acted arbitrarily in some cases. Some investors have encountered difficulties in ascertaining which tax rates apply to particular activities.

As of January 1997, the corporate tax rate was set at 20 percent. Personal income tax ranges from 12 to 20 percent. In addition, there is a 20 percent value-added tax. Payroll taxes are set at rates of 15, 26, and 29 percent.

In March 1996, the government canceled tax privileges for most previously tax-exempt organizations and reinstated the income tax for private individuals on inheritance and gifts. Also in March, a new tax collecting body for large taxpayers was established. It limits the number of inspections by municipal, regional, and federal tax services, which previously had overlapping authority.

Measuring tax compliance is complicated by the population's decreasing reliance on cash transactions. Georgians rely heavily on in-kind trade and assistance from extended family members to maintain a subsistence-level existence. Additional reasons for tax evasion include the country's large shadow economy, insufficient punishment mechanisms for nonpayment, and the financial difficulties of many of the country's largest enterprises.

In spite of tax reforms, evasion remains endemic. The government finds it difficult to collect more than ten percent of the country's GDP in taxes, and low revenue collection remains a major problem.

2. Does fiscal policy encourage private savings, investment, and earnings? (Has there been any reform/alteration of revenue and budget policies? How large are budget deficits and overall debt? Is the financing of the social insurance/pension system sustainable? What proportion of the budget is taken up by subsidies to firms and individuals?) Fiscal policy encourages savings through an emphasis on fighting inflation. Earnings remain very low, and few mechanisms for investment exist.

The International Monteary Funds (IMF) has reported that the Georgian social support system is "unsustainable" in its current form. The social system currently costs approximately three percent of GDP, or one-third of the state budget. Substantial progress has been made in tightening the eligibility for benefits, which in turn has allowed increases in benefits to the poorest and most vulnerable sections of the population. The standard monthly benefit rate is only 9.8 lari ($7.70).

Georgia's national debt is very large. At the end of 1997, the country owed $1.485 billion, primarily to energy suppliers and international agencies such as the World Bank ($250 million), the IMF ($220 million), and the European Union ($125 million). Georgia's largest creditor is the Turkmenistan government, which supplies much of the country's natural gas supply. While Georgian budget deficits have actually fallen from 4.4 percent of GDP to an estimated 2 percent in 1998, the decline reflects a calculated policy of stringent spending controls and deliberate nonpayment of public sector expenses rather than an improvement in revenue collection.

Subsidies and directed credits to firms have been almost completely eliminated since the autumn of 1994. The remaining subsidies to firms are indirect, such as tolerance of payment arrears on energy bills. More energetic collection of energy tariffs, however, has partially solved this problem.

3. Has there been banking reform? (Is the central bank independent? What are its responsibilities? Is it effective in setting and/or implementing monetary policy? What is the actual state of the private banking sector? Does it conform to international standards? Are depositors protected?) The National Bank of Georgia (NBG) was created in August 1991, immediately after the collapse of the Soviet Union. Although supervised by parliament, the NBG is independent of other government controls and is responsible for government liabilities only when such responsibility is initiated by the NBG. Its primary functions are to provide national monetary policy and licensing; possess, save, and dispose of NBG official international reserves; and issue regulations and instructions for commercial banks, as well as to provide supervision over their legal activity. A new national bank law that was enacted in June 1995 strengthened the NBG's authority to implement anti-inflationary monetary policy and supervise the banking system. The NBG is credited with successfully organizing and implementing the monetary reform of 1995, including the introduction of the lari, and with maintaining a low rate of inflation during 1996.

In February 1996, parliament adopted an IMF-recommended commercial banking law, which strengthened the provisions for scrutinizing new private banks, developed capital provisions more fully, and increased the NBG's power to liquidate banks and regulate mergers and monopolies in the financial markets. In mid-1996, the national bank further tightened controls over bank solvency, liquidity, and stability, including the increase of charter capital. Currently, the minimum capital requirement for launching a bank is approximately $500,000.

The number of banks declined from 247 in 1995 to 70 in early 1998. In 1997, the government certified three former state banks — with combined assets of $133.7 million, or 54 percent of the total commercial bank assets in Georgia — in accordance with international standards.

The Central Bank (GNB) is independent and has strong regulatory powers. It certifies commercial banks and issues licenses for the conduct of specific activities. A license is required to conduct hard currency transactions.

Inadequate monitoring by the national bank and other controlling institutions produced a depositor crisis in April 1995, when 17 bankrupted banks and trust companies failed to pay between $11 million and $12 million to primarily private depositors. Since the beginning of 1996, commercial bank deposits have increased threefold, in part due to the public's growing trust in banking institutions and the national currency. Bank lending, however, remains problematic. Banks tend to hold their deposits rather than make new loans, and, when they do lend, they charge high interest rates. In June 1996, the average rate was 86 percent annually.

Although Georgian law does not limit the free flow of financial resources, the flow is restrained in practice due to poor and unreliable interbank communication — regular banking transactions within Georgia take three to seven days — a lack of financial resources in commercial banks, widespread cash settlements, and a lack of trust due to early-1990s scandals involving local financial companies. Most banks issue three- to six- month credit, which functions as money market instruments and is used for commercial operations. The interest rate is approximately five to eight percent per month. The EBRD, International Bank for Reconstruction and Development, and the European Partnership Fund plan to issue special purpose six-month credit at an 11 percent rate and one-year credit at a 14 percent rate. Existing legal, regulatory, and accounting systems that apply to the financial sector generally still derive from the Soviet era and are not consistent with international norms. The GNB is elaborating a new national accounting system to conform to international standards.

4. How sound is the national currency? (Is the value of the currency fixed or does it float?

How convertible is the currency? How large are the hard currency reserves? Has exchange rate policy been stable and predictable?) The lari has been stable against the dollar, — at a rate of 1.2 lari to US$1 — since its introduction in October 1995. The central bank maintains a "managed float" policy towards the currency, which is fully convertible on the current account. A license is required to conduct hard-currency transactions. Two foreign exchange markets operate in Georgia: the Tbilisi Interbank Currency Exchange and the Foreign Exchange Bureau Market.

Inflation fell from 19,000 percent in 1994 to 13.8 percent in 1996 and 7.9 percent in 1997.

5. Is there a functioning capital market infrastructure? (Are there existing or planned commodities, bond, and stock markets? What are the mechanisms for investment and lending? What government bodies have authority to regulate capital markets?) The capital market infrastructure in Georgia is in a very early state of development. The only available money market instruments are the GNB's credit facilities and interbank funds. The investment regulatory system is underdeveloped. Some regulations, however, have been adopted. These include a presidential decree on specialized investment funds, a licensing procedure for participants of securities markets, and GNB regulations on futures trading. Although special investment funds established in connection with the voucher privatization program were intended to promote the development of an equities market, they failed to perform adequately. Only four percent of vouchers were invested in the funds. Currently, ten specialized investment funds are operating. According to the Georgian Ministry of State Property Management, $19.5 million in shares are owned by more than 150,000 people. A total of $120 million are owned by 61,000 large shareholders.

In September 1997, the government issued short-term bonds worth 10 million lari. The Ministry of Finance regulates securities markets in the country. A stock exchange is expected to open soon.

Microeconomics 4.00/7

1. Are property rights guaranteed? (Are there both formal and de facto protections of private real estate and intellectual property? Is there a land registry with the authority and capability to ensure accurate recording of who owns what? What are the procedures for expropriation, including measures for compensation and challenge? Have any seizures taken place?) According to Article 21 of the constitution, the right to property and inheritance is guaranteed. Although Article 23 guarantees intellectual property rights, Georgian intellectual property laws are not well developed, and copyrights are left unregulated. The constitution permits the expropriation of property for "necessary social need" in cases determined by law or a decision of the court or through "urgent necessity." In all cases, however, full compensation mudst be made.

The Law on Ownership of Agricultural Land was passed in March 1996. Under the new law, land can now be bought, sold, leased, and inherited freely.

2. To what extent have prices been liberalized? What subsidies remain? The prices of more than 90 percent of consumer goods and services were liberalized in 1994. Many of the remaining prices were freed from control in 1995-6. As of early 1997, only prices for energy, housing, and transportation remained controlled. Electricity prices were increased 30 percent in January 1997.

3. Is it possible to own and operate a business? (Has there been legislation regarding the formation, dissolution, and transfer of businesses, and is the law respected? Do there exist overly cumbersome bureaucratic hurdles that effectively hinder the ability to own and dispose of a business? Are citizens given access to information on commercial law? Is the law applied fairly? Does regulation (or do licensing requirements) impose significant costs on business and consumers? Do they create significant barriers to entry and seriously hamper competition?) One of the first significant company laws in Georgia was the Law on Entrepreneurial Activity, which was adopted on October 28, 1994, and which became effective for most purposes on March 1, 1995. The law codified and fundamentally changed many corporate laws and regulations. It authorized six forms of business entities, including the joint-stock company and the sole proprietorship, and required that all companies introduce Western accounting methods by January 1, 1996. Other recent legislation includes a lease law, a bankruptcy law, and a law on ownership rights. Most recently, parliament adopted a Law on Investment Activity, which was passed in November 1996, and gives Georgian and foreign investors similar rights and guarantees.

Obstacles remain in the establishment and operation of businesses. Local courts must register new companies — including the company's charter and other required documents — assess the adequacy of the papers in meeting legal requirements, and record them. There have been cases of serious abuses and delays in the recording process, with some courts viewing their function as competitive with that of lawyers. In addition, a majority of Georgian entrepreneurs claims that existing tax rates are too onerous for local businesses and insist on reforms. The law requires that new businesses be registered with the local courts, a procedure that frequently proves time-consuming and onerous. A new bankruptcy code took effect in January 1997.

4. Are courts effective, transparent, efficient, and quick in teaching decisions on property and contract disputes? What alternative mechanisms for adjudicating disputes exist? The courts are rarely effective, transparent, or efficient in adjudicating property and contract disputes. Contract enforcement is still highly reliant upon informal negotiation and the support of powerful patrons and political contacts. Cases take six months to be heard, and judgments are executed within a year of the conclusion.

5. Is business competition encouraged? (Are monopolistic practices limited in law and practice? If so, how? To what degree is "insider" dealing a hindrance to open competition? Are government procurement policies open and unbiased?) Under Article 30 of the constitution, the state is required to foster conditions for the development of free enterprise and competition, and the monopolization of activity is prohibited except in cases envisaged by law. The Law on Monopoly Activity and Competition was adopted on September 26, 1996, after nearly two years of work by the Georgian Ministry of Economics, the IBRD, and the EBRD. Government officials involved in the law's preparation believe that it will protect the rights and interests of entrepreneurs, create favorable conditions for the development of business, and promote a competitive market. The agency charged with anti-monopoly enforcement has responsibility for all goods markets, while the GNB regulates the securities and financial markets. Business competition is hindered, however, by the continuation of Soviet-era patronage networks and by bureaucrats who create conflicts of interest by combining their official and private business activities. Government-granted monopolies exist in such sectors as rail, air, and sea transport; telecommunications; metal-mining; and energy.

Government procurement is not particularly open. The involvement of many officials in private business creates frequent conflicts of interest.

6. To what extent has international trade been liberalized? To what degree has there been simplification/overhaul of customs and tariff procedures, and are these applied fairly? What informal trade barriers exist? In mid-1995, the Georgian government significantly loosened foreign trade regulations. The export tax has been abolished, and most export restrictions were lifted by the end of 1996. A new unified import tariff structure has been introduced. Tariffs are at rates of 0.5 percent and 12 percent.

The government has announced its decision to adhere to World Trade Organization (WTO) standards for safety standards. It applied for WTO membership in June 1996.

The government has also pursued international funding to improve road, rail, and shipping infrastructure. Poor infrastructure constitutes a significant barrier to trade. Georgian shippers have attempted to decrease Russia's role as a middleman in trade between Europe, Ukraine, and Asia by investing in a new fleet of cargo ferries. In so doing, they have undercut Russian rates by more than 40 percent. Rail service has resumed between Tbilisi and Moscow, although the trains must be protected by armed guards.

Georgia anticipates that revenues from transit tariffs will exceed $300 million in 1997. Substantial "off-the-books" trade in commodities such as cigarettes and alcohol continue through the port of Poti to destinations in Azerbaijan and Caucasian Russia.

Trade between Russia and Georgia remains subject to unpredictable border-closings, which are usually initiated by the Russian side. Russian border guards have frequently adopted an aggressive posture towards Georgia through lengthy inspections of cross-border traffic and similar measures. On one occasion in 1997, they unilaterally moved their border posts into Georgian territory.

7. To what extent have foreign investment and capital flow been encouraged or constrained? In an effort to attract more foreign investment, parliament adopted a Law on Investment Activity in November 1996. The law abolishes a licensing procedure, which many foreign investors considered burdensome, and replaces it with more automatic registration. The law does not require foreign investors to reinvest profits locally. It also abolishes the previous tax withholding requirement of ten percent on repatriated profits or capital.

While some significant successes were achieved in 1997, Georgia attracted only $70 million in investment in 1996. Investors were discouraged by extensive corruption and fears of political instability arising from the repeated attempts by various groups to assassinate Shevardnadze.

8. Has there been reform of the energy sector? (To what degree has the energy sector been

restructured? Is the energy sector more varied, and is it open to private competition? Is the country overly dependent on one or two other countries for energy [including whether exported fuels must pass through one or more countries to reach markets]?) One of the most precarious areas of Georgia's economy has been the energy sector. The country has had to cope with difficulties in paying for imported energy, frequent electricity rationing due to armed conflict in various regions and the failure of customers to pay their bills, and the inefficiency of energy collection and distribution systems. Many customers have turned to bottled gas and kerosene to provide their energy needs.

Although Georgia's overall energy sector remains troubled, there have been recent improvements. In October 1995, a committee was established to satisfy preconditions for the restructuring of the energy sector. Eighteen small hydropower stations were privatized, three were leased to the private sector, and approximately 50 energy distribution companies were given to municipalities. Because of the importance of the energy sector for the overall development of Georgia's economy, foreign countries and organizations, including Germany, Turkey, and the EBRD, have been actively involved in its rehabilitation.

Although Georgia still depends heavily on Russia and Turkmenistan for energy supplies, this reliance is decreasing. After declining for several years, domestic oil extraction for the first eight months of 1996 was nearly 50 percent greater than during the entire year of of 1995. The growth of this sector has been attributed mainly to the activities of several joint ventures that were established in partnership with the Georgian Oil Depository. Recently, new prospective oil fields were discovered in Georgia, and plans are underway to construct a pipeline across Georgia for the transport of oil from Azerbaijan. In 1995, when Turkmenistan, Georgia's primary supplier of natural gas, cut shipments due to non-payment, Georgia began to import less expensive gas from Russia. Although Georgia currently produces no natural gas of its own, production from gas deposits near Tbilisi in expected soon.

Georgia was generating 18 to 25 percent more electricity per day in late 1996 than in 1995. Tbilisi's thermal power plant accounts for 30 to 50 percent of all electricity generated. The remainder is produced by hydroelectric plants. The nonpayment of electricity bills, however, remains an urgent problem. The government reports that consumers have been paying for only 11 percent of their electrical energy use and that Russian military bases owe $18 million for electricity and water supplies. As a result, the Ministry of Fuel and Energy increased the price of electricity supplied to households from 0.025 lari per kWh to 0.033 lari on January 1, 1997, and to 0.044 lari on March 1, 1997. The increase, however, was not sufficient to meet the conditions of the IMF, which had demanded that electricity prices be raised to 0.044 lari per kWh by January 1. As a result, the World Bank did not release a planned $10 million loan for the purchase of natural gas for electricity generation.

Electricity prices are still substantially below levels required for electricity generation to be profitable. At the end of 1997, Georgian industrial enterprises owed $28 million to Sakenergo, the Georgian state energy company. Domestic consumers owed $140 million.

Georgia also continues to be unable to pay fully for its imports of natural gas from Russia and Turkmenistan. Its failure to pay a $10 million bill from the Russian company Gazprom led the company to cut off supplies to Georgian power plants in November 1997. Georgia's debt to

Turkmenistan stood at $464.9 million at the end of 1997. The country has been able to offset the cost of Russian natural gas partially by charging transit fees of $80 per thousand cubic meters on Russian gas exports to Turkey. It has also encouraged Gazprom to increase these shipments.

Several Canadian and American companies have entered into production-sharing contracts with the Georgian government to develop oil fields in Georgia. In addition, Georgia has succeeded in attracting substantial foreign investment to develop and renovate its oil refining infrastructure. The Japanese firms Itochu and Marubeni have agreed to invest up to $550 million in building a new oil refinery at Supsa and modernizing an existing refinery at Batumi. Frontera Resources, a U.S. company, has also indicated it plans to to build a refinery in eastern Georgia.

Georgia is also serving as a transit country for the Western Route Export Pipeline, which is currently being built by the Azerbaijan International Oil Consortium and is scheduled to provide for the flow of Azerbaijani oil to European markets by the end of 1998.

HUNGARY

Freedom in the World Ratings, 1989-1998

	1989-90	1990-91	1991-92	1992-93	1993-94	1994-95	1995-96	1996-97	1997-98
Political Rights	4	2	2	2	1	1	1	1	1
Civil Liberties	3	2	2	2	2	2	2	2	2
Status	PF	F	F	F	F	F	F	F	F

Polity: Consolidated Democracy
Economy: Consolidated Market
Population: 10,197,000
PPP: $6,793
Ethnic Groups: Hungarian (96 percent), Romanian, Slovak, German, Roma, Croat and Bosnian Muslim refugees
Capital: Budapest

Political Process 1.25/7

1. When did national legislative elections occur? Where they free and fair? How were they judged by domestic and international election monitoring organizations? Who composes the government? The first multiparty national legislative elections since 1945 were held in March 1990. The Hungarian Democratic Forum (MDF) won the elections and Jozsef Antall, its leader, was elected prime minister in May 1990. The second national elections took place in May 1994 and were declared free and fair by international observers. They produced a governing coalition of the formerly Communist Hungarian Socialist Party (MSzP), which won 209 National Assembly (parliament) seats and 54.2 percent of the vote, and the liberal Alliance of Free Democrats (SzDSz), which won 70 seats and 18.1 percent of the vote. The MDF won 37 seats with 9.6 percent of the vote; the Independent Smallholders' Party 26 seats and 6.7 percent; the Christian Democratic People's Party 22 seats and 5.7 percent; the Federation of Young Democrats, 20 seats and 5.2 percent; the Agrarian Federation, one seat and 0.25 percent; and the Republican Party, one seat and .025 percent. The Agrarians and the Republicans joined the SzDSz parliamentary group.

A total of 1,602 candidates from 26 parties competed in the first round of the May 10, 1998, legislative elections. Of the 8.1 million-strong Hungarian electorate, 56.31 percent cast ballots with the following results: MSzP 32.25 percent; the Fidesz-Hungarian Civic Party (MPP) coalition 28.20 percent; the MSzP coalition partner, the SzDSz, 7.89 percent, and the two right wing nationalist parties, Istvan Csurka's Party of Hungarian Life and Justice (MIEP) and the FKGP gained 5.55 percent and 13.74 percent of votes respectively. In sum, five of the 26 parties who entered the first round of elections were able to beat the 5 percent threshold required in the parliamentary elections. After the second round, on May 24, the Fidesz-Hungarian Civic Party won 148 of 386 seats in parliament; the Socialists, 134; the Smallholders, 48; the Free Democrats, 24; the MDF, 17; and the extreme right-wing MIEP, 14. The prime minister designate was Civic Party leader Viktor Orban.

2. When did presidential elections occur? Were they free and fair? In May 1990, SzDSz member Arpad Goncz was elected president for a five-year term by the National Assembly. Goncz was re-elected to a second five-year term in June 1995. The second presidential election was controversial, as some political parties had preferred that the president be directly elected. The Independent Smallholders' Party presented a petition signed by more than 200,000 citizens in support of a referendum to determine the method of presidential elections, but the petition was ruled unconstitutional by the Constitutional Court. The Smallholders then boycotted the presidential vote in the National Assembly.

3. Is the electoral system multiparty-based? Are there at least two viable political parties functioning at the level of the government? Hungary's electoral system has been multiparty-based since 1989-1990. Six political parties are represented in the National Assembly. The government is a coalition of the MSzP and SzDSz parliamentary groups, and local elections are contested by a range of political parties and individuals. After the 1994 elections, the ruling coalition reduced state support for political parties. This decision may benefit the ruling MSzP in the next elections. On the local level, at least two viable parties competed in each electoral district.

4. How many parties have been legalized? Are any particular parties illegal? Since 1989, the Budapest City Court has registered nearly 200 political parties, as well as many movements and associations. Although no political parties have been declared illegal, the number of viable parties has declined in recent years. Some 20 parties competed in the May 1998 national elections. In addition, all political parties are barred from conducting activities in the workplace.

5. What proportion of the population belongs to political parties? No official figures of party membership are available, but none of the contemporary political parties is based on mass membership. No more than five percent of the electorate are members or active supporters of political parties.

6. What has been the voter turnout at the municipal, provincial, and national levels in recent years? In the first round of the 1990 legislative elections, 65.1 percent of eligible voters cast their ballots. In the first round of the May 8, 1994, legislative and local elections, the turnout was 68.92 percent, and in the second-round, 55.1 percent. The higher voter turnout for the first round in 1994 than in 1990 ran counter to pessimistic media critics who believed that the people had lost interest in politics. In the 1990 municipal elections, the turnout was at or below 20 percent in many areas. Turnout for the May 1998 parliamentary elections was over 57 percent.

Civil Society 1.25/7

1. How many nongovernmental organizations (NGOs) have come into existence since 1988? How many charitable/nonprofit organizations? Are there locally led efforts to increase phi-

lanthropy and volunteerism? What proportion of the population is active in private voluntary activity (from polling data)? Unlike in the other former Soviet satellite countries, NGOs began to function in Hungary in the mid-1980s. Their numbers increased dramatically in 1990. By 1995, approximately 40,000 were registered. In 1997, the total number was 55,774. An estimated 1.2 million citizens, or 12 percent of the country's population, are registered members of these organizations. According to public opinion polls, three to five percent of the population engaged in voluntary activity at least once monthly between 1992 and 1996, while nine percent were engaged in voluntary activity at least once yearly. Due to the absence of a comprehensive regulatory framework for NGO activities, business and political groups often register as foundations to establish a cover for the pursuit of private rather than public gain. It is therefore difficult to determine what proportion of registered NGOs is involved in charitable, not-for-profit activities.

2. What is the legal and regulatory environment for NGOs (i.e., ease of registration, legal rights, governmental regulations, procurement, and access-to-information issues)? To what extent is NGO activism focused on improving the legal and regulatory environment? Although a law on associations was enacted in January 1989, no comprehensive legislation to regulate NGO activities has been passed in Hungary. A new NGO law was the subject of debate in the National Assembly in March 1998. It would provide for a tax-deduction of up to five percent of taxable income that private individuals and companies contribute to the NGO of their choice rather than to a state agency. It would also establish transparent rules for registration and accounting. Proponents of the law argue that direct donations would reduce corruption and the role of the state in the NGO sector.

While the rights of NGOs in Hungary are guaranteed by the 1989 law, the relaxed regulatory environment creates incentives for the use of NGO status for personal enrichment and tax fraud. Several restaurants in Budapest, for instance, have paid wages in the form of non-taxable scholarships to their employees. Another fraud case involved the Hungarian Cable Television Company, which was initially funded by a government grant as the Open World Foundation. The board of directors later transferred the foundation's funds to a private firm. Similarly, the property of the Hungarian Socialist Worker's Party (MSzMP) was transferred to several civic associations before it was funneled into private and corporate hands. Between 1991 and 1994, more than 26 billion *forint* ($26 million) in state assets changed hands through false NGOs.

3. What is the organizational capacity of NGOs? Do management structures clearly delineate authority and responsibility? Is information available on NGO management issues in the native language? Is there a core of experienced practitioners/trainers to serve as consultants or mentors to less developed organizations? Hungary's highly diverse NGO sector includes organizations that are engaged in activities that range from charitable work to support for professional and educational associations and representation of groups such as women, retired persons, unionized workers, and entrepreneurs. In general, NGOs established and funded by Western partners, such as the Open Society Institute (OSI) and the PHARE networks, are well managed and organized. The quality of the organization and management of indigenous NGOs varies widely. In general, large NGOs such as the trade unions, the association of women, or the association of retired persons are better organized and managed than most small NGOs. Both OSI and PHARE, however, continue to train local practitioners and distribute information on the organization and management of NGOs. Since the early 1990s, local practitioners have gradually replaced their Western trainers at all levels in these organizations.

4. Are NGOs financially viable? What is their tax status? Are they obliged to and do they typically disclose revenue resources? Do government procurement opportunities exist for private, not-for-profit providers of services? Most charitable NGOs in Hungary are not financially viable and are dependent on grants from Western NGOs and the Hungarian government. Several Western NGOs, such as OSI and PHARE, offer fundraising training programs and provide incentives by offering matching grants to successful fundraisers. In 1997, OSI spent more than $1.6 million on training, consultation and advisory services, and the development of communication networks among NGOs. In addition, according to Sandor Striker, the deputy secretary of the Hungarian Ministry of Culture, the ministry has an annual budget of 120 million forint ($1.2 million) to support civic association projects that promote Hungarian culture.

Unlike in the for-profit sector, income gained from NGO activities is not subject to state and local taxes. This status, however, is often abused by private firms. According to Laszlo Kemeny, a political scientist, the state loses nearly 20 percent of its annual tax revenue due to such abuses.

5. Are there free trade unions? How many workers belong to these unions? Is the number of workers belonging to these unions growing or decreasing? What is the numerical/proportional membership of farmers' groups, small business associations, etc.? Approximately 1.2 million workers — nearly 30 percent of employees – are members of trade unions. This number has remained largely unchanged since the early 1990s. Approximately 400,000 workers are members of unions established since 1988. The two largest independent trade unions are the 100,000-member Democratic Confederation of Free Trade Unions (LIGA) and the 150,000-member Hungarian Workers Council. The National Federation of Hungarian Trade Unions (MSzOSz), the Communist-era federation, survived the political changes of 1990 and now enjoys considerable political and social influence. The MSzOSz, which represents the majority of organized workers in Hungary, is controlled by the MSzP and is therefore not free and independent. It claims to have 1.2 million members, although the actual figure is probably closer to 800,000.

In the Interest Reconciliation Council (IRC), a formal forum in which government officials discuss and mediate disputes between employers and employees, six trade unions are represented: the MSzOSz, the Association of Autonomous Trade Unions, the Trade Unions' Cooperative Forum, the Council of Interest-Representation Associations, LIGA, and the Workers' Councils (*Munkastanacsok*). In general, trade unions have opposed the austerity measures proposed by the government and employers.

Many smallholders' associations are active. There are also numerous independent entrepreneurial associations, the majority of which operate exclusively in Budapest. According to the National Statistical Bureau, farmers' associations have approximately 8,000 members, while small business associations, including regional chambers of commerce, have approximately 27,000 members.

6. What forms of interest group participation in politics are legal? What types of interest groups are active in the political and policy process? With the exception of Penal Code provisions and specific rules that disqualify judges, members of parliament, armed forces personnel, and civil servants, Hungarian law permits all forms of interest group participation in politics. The trade unions in the IRC are the most active NGOs in the country's political process. Professional associations, such as doctors' and teachers' groups, also actively lobby for improvements in such issues as medical insurance, school curricula, and teaching conditions.

7. How is the not-for-profit/NGO sector perceived by the public and government officials? What is the nature of media coverage? To what extent do government officials engage with NGOs? Public opinion polls suggest that NGO activities are generally perceived negatively in Hungary. According to polls conducted by the Central Statistical Bureau, 68 percent of respondents consider NGOs to be useless rather than useful for society. Less than 10 percent believe that they are useful. Seventy-two percent of the public believes that the most useful NGOs are those that are active in the provision of health care and education, but only 12 percent believe that NGOs play an important role in democratization. The government engages most actively with the representatives of the trade unions and entrepreneurs in the negotiations of the IRC.

Independent Media 1.25/7

1. Are there legal protections for press freedom? A law regulating television and radio broadcasting was passed in 1995, and legal protections for press freedom are explicitly guaranteed by the constitution. Although freedom of the press was nominally guaranteed even before 1989, it was only respected in practice after the country's sweeping political transformation in 1989-1990. In 1992, a 1977 decree that authorized governmental supervision of the news media was declared unconstitutional.

On December 21, 1995, the National Assembly passed a law to regulate television and radio broadcasting. The first section of the law mandates that, in broadcasts for the general audience, local broadcasts should constitute at least 20 percent of total broadcast time by 1999 and that commercial programs should not exceed 20 percent of the total. The law's second section mandates that, in public and commercial broadcasting, advertisements should not exceed an average of six minutes per hour. The law's third section mandates that 51 percent of programming should be produced in Hungary and that 70 percent of total programs should be produced in Europe. Many media experts agree that the new media law is one of the most comprehensive in the post-Communist states of East-Central Europe. They have also determined, however, that the law mandates an untenable change of pace for the state-owned Antena Hungaria national broadcast company.

2. Are there legal penalties for libeling officials? Are there legal penalties for "irresponsible" journalism? Have these laws been enforced to harass journalists? The law imposes penalties for libel and defamation of any individual, including officials. The Criminal Code specifies a number of press offenses, including defamation and incitement to hatred against the community. In these cases, the individual journalist is held primarily responsible for the criminal offense, but, under the general rules of criminal law, the editor may also be held responsible. The law also imposes civil liabilities. The defendant may be sued for damages in cases involving the violation of personal rights. Punishment for libel, however, is very light and has little if any deterrent impact, particularly on large publications. There are no known instances in which media laws have been used to harass journalists in Hungary.

On March 12, 1996, the parliament passed a Penal Code amendment that mandates a three-year prison sentence for "anyone who incites hatred or acts in any other way that is capable of inciting against the Hungarian nation or any other national, ethnic, or religious minority or race." The law was passed in the wake of several well-publicized cases in which defendants who had been charged with committing acts of racial hatred were acquitted after it was determined that they had been exercising their constitutional right to free speech. The country's debate over what constitutes an incitement to hatred and what constitutes protected free speech continues. The state prosecutor, for example, has banned not only the Magyar-language translation of *Mein Kampf,* but also the English version, although the work is being routinely read at Western universities.

3. What proportion of media are privatized? What are the major private newspapers, television stations, and radio stations? More than 80 percent of print media and approximately 70 percent of radio and television stations in Hungary are in private hands. There are three national public television channels, approximately 26 private commercial television stations, more than 200 regional cable outlets, and more than 30 radio stations. No national radio stations are privately owned, but several regional stations, including Radio Juventus and Radio Bridge, can be heard nationwide through transmitters. In 1996, the "media war" that began in 1994 when the government fired and replaced the directors of the state-owned radio and television finally ended. In 1997, the Radio and Television Regulatory Body offered concessions for television channels to foreign broadcasting companies. Among the most prominent bidders were Central European Media Enterprises; CLT-Bertelsmann, which owns RTL satellite television; MTM-SBS, a Hungarian-Swedish consortium; a consortium from French Channel TF1; and Westdeutsche Allgemeine Zeitung, a German firm. No single company is allowed to hold more than a 49 percent stake, and Hungarians must hold at least 26 percent. In the Hungarian Telegraph Agency, the country's major news agency, the U.S. firm Ameritech and Deutsche Telecom are 59.98-percent majority shareholders.

The country enjoys a wide variety of generally high-quality, uncensored national and local newspapers. *Nepszabdsag* (People's Freedom), which has the largest daily circulation (320,000), is a former Communist organ that is now privately owned by the Bertelsman Company, a German firm. The second largest is *Nepszava* (Voice of the People), which has a circulation of 140,000. *Mai Nap* (Today), the organ of the trade unions; the tabloid *Blikk;* the *Magyar Hirlap* (Hungarian Journal); and the *Kurir* (Courier) have a combined circulation of approximately 100,000 and are privately owned. One government agency is responsible for disseminating news received from official sources. Ferenczi, a private wire service owned by MTM Communications, also operates in Hungary.

4. Are the private media financially viable? In most cases, Hungary's media are financially viable. During the transition to a free market economy, however, many new publications appeared and proved not to be viable. Perhaps the greatest financial difficulties have been encountered by the country's national television and radio enterprise, which, in spite of $200 million in annual revenue, is still in debt due to its antiquated infrastructure. The company hopes to become solvent by selling concessions to private consortia. In general, private media; and especially organizations with a high percentage of foreign ownership, are profitable.

5. Are the media editorially independent? Are the media's news gathering functions affected by interference from government or private owners? Legally, the media are editorially independent. Some newspapers, however, are owned by banks and trusts that are in government hands, and some local newspapers are controlled by local self-governing administrators. For example, the majority state-owned Posta Bank owns at least four newspapers and Radio Bridge, a large private radio station. In addition, since many major publications were privatized during the Communist period, political opposition leaders argue that many editors reportedly remain loyal to the Communist successor MSzP. State-owned radio and television, according to the opposition leaders, are not editorially independent because, in 1994, the government fired and replaced the directors of the enterprise. In a move that, according to critics, may constitute a continuation of the country's "media law," the government has also announced plans to dismiss 1,000 radio and television employees due to financial constraints.

It cannot be proved that either of the government's highly criticized moves against radio and television employees was politically motivated. In addition, the reporting on major corruption scandals involving members of the government suggest that the media is independent and that no daily newspaper shows a clear pro-government bias.

6. Is the distribution system for newspapers privately or governmentally controlled? The major newspaper distributor in Hungary is the Hungarian Distributor's Office, a government entity. Government control in this sector, however, may reflect the prohibitively high costs of newspaper distribution more than a desire by the government to act as a censor or otherwise influence the process. In April 1998, the Hachette Distribution Service, a French firm, announced plans to cooperate with 18 Hungarian publishers and three local partners in the purchase of 82 percent of the national press distribution service. In 1995, foreign-owned publications formed a limited partnership to operate a new distribution service in response to the reported inefficiency and high cost of the state system.

7. What proportion of the population is connected to the Internet? Are there any restrictions on Internet access to private citizens? In 1997, approximately 0.7 percent of households were connected to the Internet compared to levels of 4 percent in Western Europe and 47 percent in the United States. In 1998, there were 34,000 registered Internet users and 74,000 host computers. Approximately 300,000 individuals, including 35,000 students, have access to the Internet. The major distributor of Internet services in Hungary is the Hungarian Telegraph Agency, which controls 30 percent of the market. There are no restrictions on private citizens' access to the Internet. "Internet Cafes" operate in most major cities. A total of 188 schools have Internet access. By 1999, the government hopes to connect every school to the Internet through its $2.5 million "Schoolnet" project.

8. What has been the trend in press freedom as measured by Freedom House's *Survey of Press Freedom*? Freedom House's Annual *Survey of Press Freedom* rated Hungary "Not Free" in 1988, "Partly Free" in 1989, "Free" from 1990 through 1992, "Partly Free" in 1993, "Free" in 1994, "Partly

Free" from 1995 to 1997, and "Free" in 1998.

Governance and Public Administration 1.75/7

1. Is the legislature the effective rule-making institution? The National Assembly is fulfilling its function as the country's supreme legislative body. Between its first session in May 1990 and March 1992, it passed more than 180 laws. In the Communist era, it adopted an average of four or five laws per year. Unlike in the Communist era, government degrees are now subordinate to legislative enactment.

During its 1993 session, the legislature voted on 117 acts and 103 resolutions and issued two statements. It passed 105 laws in 1994, 126 laws in 1995, and 70 in 1996.

In 1997, it failed to comply with a Constitutional Court decision requiring the adoption of a law on the proportional representation of minorities in the legislature. Political analysts attribute the failure to an unwillingness of members of parliament to address highly controversial issues in the months before new elections.

2. Is substantial power decentralized to sub-national levels of government? What specific authority do sub-national levels have? Chapter IX of the constitution vests substantial political power in the sub-national levels of government. Administratively, Hungary is divided into 19 counties, eight cities (including Budapest) with the status of counties, and approximately 150 towns and 3,000 villages with their own, sub-national governments. The council members at the local government level are directly elected to four-year terms. The county-level councils are elected by the lower level municipal governments.

Municipal governments have equal rights, but their duties differ. The rights of sub-national governments are protected by the judiciary, including the Constitutional Court. Local representatives may develop their own framework of laws and ordinances, provided that they are consistent with higher statutes, and may affiliate with other local bodies of representatives. Local authorities have the right to make policy autonomously, but they are often weak due to financial constraints.

3. Are sub-national offices chosen in free and fair elections? Local, regional, and other sub-national offices are chosen in free and fair elections. At the sub-regional level, however, Commissioners of the Republic are appointed by the government to supervise more than one county. The commissioners, who ensure that all local decrees correspond to national laws, can suspend any local directive that runs counter to national legislation. The most recent sub-national elections were held in December 1994. Law LXII of 1994 mandated the local election of mayors of all 3,147 communities in the country. Before the 1994 law was enacted, only communities with more than 10,000 inhabitants held such elections. The turnout in the 1994 local elections was 43.4 percent — 3.4 percent higher than in the 1990 elections. A total of 95,000 candidates competed for 21,495 offices.

4. Do the executive and legislative bodies operate openly and with transparency? Is draft legislation easily accessible to the media and the public? Hungary's executive and legislative bodies operate openly and with transparency under the scrutiny of the public, the media, the State Audit

Board, the Central Audit Office, and the Government Control Bureau.

The State Audit Board and the Central Audit Office were established in 1990 and 1993, respectively, to control the economy and manage the country's publicly financed central institutions. In late 1994, the Central Audit Office was replaced by the Government Control Bureau, an independent national organ of state administration. The Bureau has the right to control the central budget and the separate national funds — the two subsystems of public finances. It can also monitor the implementation of decisions by the cabinet.

The president holds veto power over the legislature. In December 1996, President Goncz vetoed two government-backed bills backed by the government.

5. Do municipal governments have sufficient revenue to carry out their duties? Do municipal governments have control of their own local budgets? Do they raise revenue autonomously or from the central state budget? In general, municipal governments have sufficient revenues to execute their duties, although the country's difficult economic situation places a significant burden on them. Municipalities receive revenues directly from the central state budget and from autonomously and locally raised real estate and business taxes. Funds received from the state are often earmarked for specific projects. Law XLVI of 1996 earmarked funds for Budapest for the construction of hospitals, the reconstruction and maintenance of national historical sites and monuments, and the modernization of infrastructure. In addition to municipal revenues tied to administrative districts, the central state budget earmarks funds for the self-government of minorities living in Hungary. These funds are proportional to the size of the respective minorities. In 1997, the National Roma Minority Self-Government received the most revenue — 90 million forint — from this source. The Bulgarian, Greek, Polish and Armenian minority self-governments received 7 million forint.

6. Do the elected local leaders and local civil servants know how to manage municipal governments effectively? Most local leaders elected during or after 1990 have proved to be competent and able to manage municipal governments. The government and local and international NGOs have launched projects on community development, democratic institution-building, and local self-government to increase the professional knowledge of local officials.

7. When did the constitutional/legislative changes on the local power come into effect? Has there been a reform regarding civil service code/system? Are civil servants employees of the local or central government? In 1991, parliament passed a reformist Law on Local Administration of Self-Governing Bodies. In 1994, the government of Socialist Prime Minister Gyula Horn modified and simplified it by providing for single-round local elections and direct elections of mayors in every community. The civil service code and system were reformed in 1991. A standard examination in public administration was mandated for national and local level civil service job applicants. Local civil servants are employees of the local governments, although their official status as civil servants is identical to those of central government employees.

Rule of Law **1.75/7**

1. Is there a post-Communist constitution? How does the judicial system interpret and enforce the constitution? Are there specific examples of judicial enforcement of the constitution in the last year? The constitution is a patchwork of amendments introduced in 1989 and 1990, when the parliament altered virtually all of the Communist-era constitution. While many legal experts agreed that the amended constitution met the requirements of a parliamentary democracy, they also found that its wording was often vague. This led to jurisdictional conflicts among government institutions and offices. After the 1994 legislative elections, the six parties represented in the National Assembly agreed to draft a new constitution.

In 1995, a newly-formed Constitutional Committee reached agreement on procedural rules for drafting and approving a new constitution. The coalition parties agreed that the opposition would contribute substantially to the process, including any modification of the National Assembly's Standing Order, which provides terms for constitutional changes. The coalition also agreed that the Constitutional Committee would have 24 members, or four members from each party represented in the parliament. The National Assembly then amended the constitution to state that the new rules in the Standing Order could only be enforced by a four-fifths majority. A new draft constitution has not yet been approved.

The constitution is interpreted by the Constitutional Court, and, in general, the legislature respects the court's rulings. On average, the court rules on approximately 150 cases annually. Of these, approximately 35 percent are found to be unconstitutional. Experts have determined that Hungary's Constitutional Court is one of the most active and independent constitutional courts in the post-Communist states. In 1997, the court upheld the right of ethnic minorities to be proportionally represented, with at least 13 seats, in the National Assembly. Today, one member of parliament represents the country's small German minority. The Roma, the country's largest minority group, are not represented at all. In March 1998, the National Assembly considered, but did not agree, on a bill to address this problem.

2. Does the constitutional framework provide for human rights? Do the human rights include business and property rights? The constitution declares that Hungary recognizes the inalienable and inviolable basic rights of man and that it is the foremost responsibility of the state to ensure the observance of those rights. Individual and human rights, freedom of speech and assembly, and social and property rights are extensively covered in the constitution. In 1996, the National Assembly passed a number of Penal Code amendments, including laws regulating press freedom, defamation, and the defense of minorities. Experts have determined that the country's laws governing business and property rights are fair and that they meet Western standards. There have been no post-Communist cases of government expropriation of private property or foreign-owned assets. Hungary's judiciary is, at times, corrupt and, in general, overburdened. Even rulings in relatively simple cases can take years. Nevertheless, the U.S. Department of Commerce has found that the system "protects and facilitates the acquisition and disposition of property rights."

3. Has there been basic reform of the criminal code/criminal law? Who authorizes searches and issues warrants? Are suspects and prisoners beaten and abused? Are there excessive de-

lays in the criminal justice system? The Hungarian Criminal Code has been substantially reformed since 1989. The death penalty for crimes against the state, aggravated detention as a punishment for crime, penal idleness as a crime, and the penalty of "reformative-educative labor" have all been abolished.

Between 1994 and 1996, the National Assembly passed four significant criminal laws. In 1994, Amendment IX in the Penal Code regulated the sale and use of firearms. In 1995, Amendment XLI changed the age limit for the prosecution of juvenile delinquents in cases of serious crimes. In 1996, Amendment XVII established harsh penalties for offenses against minorities. Also in 1996, Amendment LII imposed criminal penalties for crimes related to the smuggling of nuclear materials and acts that cause environmental destruction.

Only judges can authorize searches and issue arrest warrants. There are no known cases in which detainees or prisoners have been beaten or abused. Nevertheless, the massive increase in property and violent crime after 1990 has overburdened the criminal justice system.

4. Do most judges rule fairly and impartially? How many remain from the Communist era? A majority of judges is impartial and fair. Fifty-five percent of judges were appointed before 1989. New appointments have been slow, in part because it will take years to educate a new generation of lawyers, and in part because many graduates of Hungary's two law schools find more lucrative work in private firms.

5. Are courts free of political control and influence? Are the courts linked directly to the Ministry of Justice or any other executive body? Under the constitution, the judiciary is independent and is subordinate only to the law. To shield the judiciary from political influence, the constitution provides that judges cannot be members of any political party and cannot engage in any political activities.

The independence of judges in Hungary is guaranteed in several ways. First, the judiciary is financially independent from the executive branch of the government. Legislation provides that courts' budgets are not funded by the Ministry of Justice. Second, the promotion and remuneration of judges are determined exclusively by law. Third, with the exception of the Constitutional Court's chief justice, who is elected by the National Assembly, judges are appointed by the president of the republic after being proposed by the Minister of Justice with the consent of the Judicial Council. Fourth, a judge can cease to perform his duties either at his own request, after being declared incapable by his peers, or after being found guilty of professional misconduct by a disciplinary council. Finally, unless the president of the republic determines otherwise, judges enjoy immunity from prosecution and therefore cannot be arrested and detained or be subject to criminal proceedings.

6. What proportion of lawyers is in private practice? How does this compare with the previous year? Approximately 6,000 lawyers are employed by private law firms. In addition, companies, firms, trade unions, associations, and various other organizations employ nearly 25,000 counsels, solicitors, and advisers. In all, more than 80 percent of the country's lawyers are in private practice. The remainder is employed in the judiciary and governmental organizations.

7. Does the state provide public defenders? Under the constitution and the Penal Code, the state must provide public defenders if the accused has no means to obtain or pay for a private defense lawyer. International human rights organizations have found no deficiencies in the application of this law.

8. Has there been a comprehensive reform of anti-bias/discrimination laws, including the protection of ethnic minority rights? On July 7, 1993, the parliament passed the Bill on National and Ethnic Minority Rights after nearly two years of preparatory work and several draft texts. The law bans discrimination against minorities, whose rights to national and ethnic self-identity are considered to be part of universal human rights and basic freedoms. The law recognizes all ethnic peoples who have lived in Hungary for at least a century and who are Hungarian citizens with their own language, culture, and traditions. These groups include Armenians, Bulgarians, Croats, Germans, Greeks, Poles, Roma, Romanians, Ruthenians, Serbs, Slovaks, Slovenes, and Ukrainians. Nevertheless, Hungary's estimated 500,000 Roma continue to suffer de facto discrimination in employment and housing and have suffered severely from the effects of the economic restructuring of the country. They have also been the victims of attacks by skinheads and vigilantes. According to recent opinion polls, one out of every two Hungarians has a negative attitude towards the Roma.

In March 1996, after the acquittals of a number of perpetrators of hate crimes, parliament passed a penal code amendment that provides for up to three years of imprisonment for anyone who incites hatred or acts in any other way that is capable of inciting hatred against the Hungarian nation or any other national, ethnic, or religious minority or race.

In the 1994 elections, only one percent of mayoral posts were won by minorities. Approximately three percent of local government seats at all levels were won by minority candidates. This figure corresponds approximately to the percentage of minorities in the country's general population. Proportionally, the Germans are the best-represented minority, while the Roma, the largest minority group in Hungary, enjoy the least representation.

Corruption | A

1. What is the magnitude of official corruption in civil service? Must an average citizen pay a bribe to a bureaucrat in order to receive a service? What services are subjected to bribe requests — for example, university entrance, hospital admission, telephone installation, obtaining a license to operate a business, applying for a passport or other official documents? What is the average salary of civil servants at various levels? In 1996, popular confidence in the Horn government was shaken by corruption scandals in privatization deals. These scandals led to the dismissal or resignation of several high level government officials. Independent and parliamentary investigations revealed that billions of forint had reached private hands through insider-dealings in government circles. The greatest corruption, including insider-dealing and favoritism, appeared to be at the top levels of government and the civil service. In a scandal dubbed "oilgate," the country's industry and trade ministries favored companies with contracts related to the release of Russia's debt to Hungary. In another, the State Privatization and Holding Company made large payments to an external consultant who worked under an irregular contract. The board of the state company was later dismissed.

Data on lower-level corruption are not readily available. There are unconfirmed reports that law and medical school admission committees and doctors, who control access to scarce hospital beds, accept bribes. Bribes for licenses and other official documents are not unusual in cases in which applicants seek to obtain documents more rapidly.

In the first half of 1997, the monthly average net earnings of civil servants was as follows: Low-level bureaucrats, postal workers, and teachers earned 25,000 to 30,000 forint ($140 to $176). Doctors and university professors received 30,000 to 40,000 forint ($176 to $235). Cabinet ministers and members of parliament earned 150,000 forint ($882). For the same period, the monthly average net earnings for all Hungarians was 39,900 forint ($235). Blue-collar workers earned 31,400 forint ($185), while white-collar workers earned 58,000 forint ($341).

2. Do top policy-makers (the president, ministers, vice-ministers, top court justices, and heads of agencies and commissions) have direct ties to businesses? How strong are such connections and what kinds of businesses are these? Formally, the Conflict of Interest Law, which was enacted in January 1997, prevents top-policy makers and members of parliament from holding positions in companies in which the state-owned share is more than 10 percent. Members of parliament are not prevented from owning private companies or holding positions in them. Nevertheless, numerous corruption scandals — some of which have been related to the privatization of state-owned companies — suggest that informal ties exist between top government officials and businesses.

3. Do laws requiring financial disclosure and disallowing conflict of interest exist? Have publicized cases been pursued? To what conclusion? The law proscribes conflicts of interest, but does not require financial disclosures by elected and appointed civil servants. Civil servants are not allowed to hold shares in a company in which the state controls more than ten percent of the shares. Many governmental corruption cases were highly publicized in 1996 and 1997, and the persons involved, including the finance, welfare, and trade and industry ministers in the Horn government, were either forced to resign or dismissed. In addition, two vice presidents of the National Bank resigned in 1996. In November 1996, the interior minister fired top police officials in the wake of reports of internal corruption in the force.

4. What major anti-corruption initiatives have been implemented? How often are anti-corruption laws and decrees adopted? In January 1997, the Conflict of Interest Law was implemented after a veto by President Goncz, who objected that its provisions should also apply to state officials who assumed their positions before the 1994 elections. In July 1996, the legislature passed a revised law to require that public officials and civil servants who had worked in the Communist-era secret police be vetted. The law created tension and debate between the parties in the governing coalition. In the end, only 600 officials – out of 5,000 officials in the initial proposal — were screened.

5. How do major corruption-ranking organizations like Transparency International rate this country? In a 1995 survey by Transparency International, 60 industrialized countries were rated on a scale of 1 to 10, with 10 indicating the lowest degree of corruption. Hungary received a rating of 4.12. By comparison, New Zealand, which received a score of 9.55, was the least corrupt. Indonesia, with a score of 1.94, was the most corrupt.

Privatization 1.50/7

1. What percentage of the GDP comes from private ownership? What percentage of the labor force is employed in the private sector? How large is the informal sector of the economy? As of late 1994, the private ownership sector accounted for approximately 58 percent of GDP. By mid-1995, the figure had reached 60 percent. In 1996, after the partial privatization of the energy sector, it stood at nearly 70 percent. In 1997, 86 percent of the companies that had been owned by the state were in private hands, and the state retained ownership rights in only 296 companies of the 1,859 that were to be privatized. Privatization minister Judit Csiha claims that 90 percent of GDP, which stood at $4,094 per capita in 1997, is now from the private sector. According to the Central Statistical Bureau, nearly 70 percent of the work force is employed in the private sector, while the informal sector, the so called "black economy," is said to have accounted for an average of 30 percent of GDP since 1990.

2. What major privatization legislation has been passed? What were its substantive features? Privatization began in 1989 with the passage of Act Number 13, which provides for the transformation of state-owned companies into joint-stock and limited liability firms. The law calls for privatization in Hungary to take place through sale or open or closed tender. State property was privatized under the supervision of the Property-Managing Organization of the National Treasury, the State Property Agency, and the State Property Management Holding Company, which later became known as the State Privatization and Property Management Holding Company (APVRt) in 1995. In 1990, Act Number 74, also known as the "Pre-Privatization Act," established procedures for the privatization of small businesses through auctions. In 1992, Act Number 10 described the goals of privatization as the modernization of technology; increase of working capital; import of knowledge and marketing experience; support for domestic and foreign entrepreneurs; the development of the domestic capital market; and the creation of work opportunities.

The Horn government's "New Privatization Law" was drafted in November 1994 and passed by the parliament in January 1995 with 99 changes. The law, which launched a simplified privatization program under the sole control of the APVRt, targets state-owned, strategic industries, primarily related to mining, communications, transportation, banking, and energy. In the first of two rounds of privatization mandated by the law, the APVRt publicly announces the terms of the competition for a list of state-owned companies. Private domestic and foreign entities then submit bids. In the second round, the APVRt announces new terms for the sale of companies that did not sell in the first round. In the initial sale, which took place on September 29, 1995, 73 companies were listed. A total of 104 bids were made on 71 companies, 42 of which were sold. In the next sale, on January 10, 1996, only four of 37 offered companies were sold. The remaining 33 companies were liquidated in 1996 and 1997. Of the 1,859 state-owned companies in this program, only 296 remain under some degree of state ownership. Companies with an estimated total value of $1.87 billion remain to be sold.

3. What proportion of agriculture, housing and land, industry, and business and services is in private hands? *Agriculture:* The agriculture ministry estimates that approximately 90 percent of agricultural land is in private hands, but up to half of this property is owned by limited cooperatives. As of 1996, the state's share in forest lands remained at 85 percent. Some forests were restored to their former owners, but most remain under state ownership because of the domestic opposition to the government plan that proposes to sell land to foreigners.

Housing and Land: The Ministry of Agriculture estimates that approximately 97 percent of housing and land is privately owned or in the hands of municipalities. Foreigners could not purchase housing or land until the law was changed in 1994.

Industry: Approximately 65 percent of industry was privately-owned by the end of 1994. By 1996, this figure had increased to approximately 70 percent, mainly through the privatization of strategic and financial industries and the sale of state utilities to foreign and domestic investors. Today, according to the Central Statistical Bureau, 86 percent of formerly state-owned companies are in private hands. Manufacturing, mining, utilities, transport, communications, and financial services account for approximately 43.8 percent of Hungary's GDP. The ratio of domestically and foreign-owned private industries is approximately two to one.

Business and Services: The total number of small businesses that were privatized are 4,066 in 1991, 3,571 in 1992, 1,428 in 1993, and 416 in 1994. More than 70 percent of the business-and-services sector had been privatized by the end of 1994. Today, the private share is more than 80 percent, with the state continuing to own shares in so-called strategic services, such as banking, energy, telecommunications, and health care.

By the end of 1995, the state held only the legal minimum of 25 percent of the National Saving and Trade Bank remained under state control. In 1995, the stated owned 72 percent of the transportation, postal, and communications sector. By the end of 1997, this had declined to less than 30 percent. Approximately 45 percent of the health, education, and agricultural sector was held privately in early 1996. In 1997, the private share increased to 65 percent.

4. What has been the extent of insider (management, labor, and nomenklatura) participation in the privatization process? What explicit and implicit preferences have been awarded to insiders? Many members of the nomenklatura received preferential treatment in the privatization process between 1990 and 1993. During this period, the state-owned assets of the MSzMP were transferred into the hands of private firms through the use of foundations as intermediaries. The research of Gyorgy Lengyel, a Hungarian political scientist, reveals that nearly 75 percent of the industrial elite were former MSzMP members. The number of former MSzMP members who own formerly state-owned and privatized enterprises is especially high, while new enterprises have been established primarily by non-party members. The degree of insider participation declined as legislation requiring transparency — a strong demand of foreign investors — took effect.

5. How much public awareness of and public support for privatization has there been? What is the nature of support and opposition to privatization by major interest groups? As in most post-Communist societies, Hungarians have been dissatisfied with the increasing economic inequality and deprivation and the declining quality and scope of social entitlements in the country. Nevertheless, a majority of Hungarians, including trade unions and other interest groups, support the privatization process. In 1994, the Socialist Party repeatedly expressed its support for privatization, while at the same time pledging to champion equality and the rights of the poor to social entitlements.

According to surveys by Hungarian political scientists, 71 percent of the population believe in private ownership of property, 61 percent believe that land should not be sold to foreigners, and 44 percent believe that the economy should be free of state control. On the other hand, the proportion of those who believe that the free market is good for Hungary declined from 65 percent in 1991 to 38 percent in 1996.

Macroeconomics 1.75/7

1. Has the taxation system been reformed? (What areas have and have not been overhauled? To what degree are the taxpayers complying? Is tax compliance difficult to achieve? Has the level of revenues increased? Is the revenue collecting body overburdened? What is the overall tax burden?) The taxation system has undergone a number of reforms and changes. Between 1990 and 1996, the parliament passed 34 laws and amendments that regulate taxation. The most significant is Law XCI, which was passed in 1990 and regulates taxation and tariffs, nominates state agencies to monitor and enforce the law, and determines commercial and other activities and real estate and other objects that are subject to taxation and tariffs. The main sources of tax revenue are the sales, income, social security, and value-added taxes (VAT).

In 1996, in part due to the budget deficit, the Horn government proposed increasing the social insurance tax for small businesses from ten percent to up to 45 percent of net income.

Revenues from taxation posted their most significant increase in the 1994 fiscal year. They remained virtually at the 1994 level in 1995 in spite of the increases in social insurance tax. This could be attributed to taxpayer non-compliance with the new tax requirement and to the "black economy," which, according to current estimates, accounts for up to 30 percent of GDP.
In February 1996, as the National Customs and Revenue Office and the Tax and Finance Control Office grew even more overburdened, a separate Department for Major Taxpayers was formed.

Hungary's top income tax rate is 48 percent. The average rate of taxation of earned income is 44 percent. In 1995, a government decree reduced the corporate income tax by half to 18 percent. The capital gains tax is 18 percent, and the VAT is 12 percent.

2. Does fiscal policy encourage private savings, investment, and earnings? (Has there been any reform/alteration of revenue and budget policies? How large are budget deficits and overall debt? Is the financing of the social insurance/pension system sustainable? What proportion of the budget is taken up by subsidies to firms and individuals?) In 1995, legislators passed a budget to restrict the generous social entitlements, enact laws on supplementary budgets, abolish the tax on interest from savings, and establish the Committee for Coordination of Economic Protection, which polices "black economic" activities. The effect of the law, however, was limited by a 1996 ruling of the Constitutional Court, which found that the new austerity measures were not in accord with constitutional guarantees on social entitlements.

The 1997 budget deficit was 206.4 billion forint ($1.21 billion). The deficit of the social insurance and pension system accounted for approximately 32.7 billion forint of this amount. Hungary

has the highest per capita national debt of all of the post-Communist countries.
While no reliable figures are available on the country's total subsidies to firms and individuals, the $3 billion cost of the bailout of the banking sector over the past three years is illustrative.

3. Has there been banking reform? (Is the central bank independent? What are its responsibilities? Is it effective in setting and/or implementing monetary policy? What is the actual state of the private banking sector? Does it conform to international standards? Are depositors protected?) The banking sector has been reformed. According to a vice president of the National Bank of Hungary, the central bank operates independently from the government, but five-year, rather than three-year, appointments for vice presidents would guarantee more independence and stability. The central bank implements monetary policy by setting interests rates, maintaining the soundness of national currency, and regulating the banking sector.

By the end of 1995, the first year of privatization of the state banking sector, 58 percent of banks were privately owned. By the end of 1997, the private share had increased to 75 percent. According to the privatization law, the state may not own more than 25 percent of a bank. The banking industry is relatively competitive, and banks are free from burdensome government oversight. In addition, according to Kalman Mizsei, the country's leading expert, the openness of the banking sector is unprecedented, not only in the post-Communist countries, but also in Western Europe. The share of Hungarian banks owned by foreigners increased to 60 percent in the first quarter of 1997 and is expected to increase further.

Depositors are protected by deposit insurance. The Hungarian deposit insurance system and the National Deposit Insurance Fund (NDBA) were created under Act XXIV of 1993 and are currently regulated under Act CXII of 1996. The regulations are in accordance with international practices and standards. The NDBA, which is run by an independent board of directors, is supervised by the State Audit Office. If the interests of depositors necessitate credit, it may draw from the National Bank of Hungary or the state budget. Protection is limited to 1 million forint at each financial institution in which a depositor deposits money. The protection is extended to all depositors, including foreigners.

4. How sound is the national currency? (Is the value of the currency fixed, or does it float? How convertible is the currency? How large are the hard currency reserves? Has exchange rate policy been stable and predictable?) The Hungarian currency floats within a 4.5 percent intervention band, which is set by the National Bank of Hungary. It is floated against a basket that is based on the German *mark* (70 percent) and the U.S. dollar (30 percent). It is therefore freely convertible on hard currency markets. To maintain a stable exchange, the National Bank relies on a "crawling peg" devaluation system, which compensates for the difference between the domestic and foreign rates of inflation. The "crawling peg" rate, which currently stands at approximately 0.9 percent, is adjusted according to the inflation differential. Although exchange rate policy is stable and predictable, the forint has been jolted by two significant devaluations. In was devalued by eight percent in August 1994, and by nine percent in March 1995. The foreign exchange reserves were $6.8 billion in 1994, $12.0 billion in 1995, and $9.7 billion in 1996.

5. Is there a functioning capital market infrastructure? (Are there existing or planned commodities, bond, and stock markets? What are the mechanisms for investment and lending? What government bodies have the authority to regulate capital markets?) The Budapest Stock Exchange (BUX), which was established in 1990, was one of the first commodities, bond, and stock markets in the region. Its index contains 17 stocks. To qualify for the index, a stock must meet three of the following criteria: a minimum face value, a defined minimum price, a minimum number of transactions, and a cumulative minimum turnover of 10 percent of registered capital during the six months preceding the revision of the index. If more than 25 stocks meet at least three of these criteria, they are narrowed to 17 according to their weighed average calculated across the five criteria. The German Dax index was used as a blueprint for that of the BUX. The base value of the BUX was set at 1,000 points on January 2, 1991. Its historic low of 717.75 points was reached in 1992. In April 1998, it exceeded 9,000.

Individual and institutional investors can purchase and sell stocks, bonds, and commodities through more than 50 domestic and foreign brokerage firms. Prices are regulated by the market. Approximately 65 to 70 percent of investment capital in the BUX is from foreign investors. The lending rates for the domestic currency are set by the National Bank. They currently exceed 20 percent, thereby making domestic loans unattractive.

Microeconomics 1.75/7

1. Are property rights guaranteed? (Are there both formal and de facto protections of private, real estate, and intellectual property? Is there a land registry with the authority and capability to ensure accurate recording of who owns what? What are the procedures for expropriation, including measures for compensation and challenge?) Property rights are formally guaranteed by the constitution and are protected in practice by contract and property laws. The constitution mandates that public and private property shall be equally respected and granted equal protection, and that the Republic of Hungary shall acknowledge and promote the right to free enterprise and freedom of economic competition. The constitution also guarantees the right of inheritance. According to the head of a U.S. law firm in Budapest, the land registry, which records the ownership and transfer of real estate, has not been overburdened by the increased submission of claims that have resulted from privatization. Restitution is a less common direct form of property transfer. Former owners and their heirs are usually granted vouchers based on the size of their claims. The vouchers, which are tradable, can be applied toward the purchase of other state-owned property.

2. To what extent have prices been liberalized? What subsidies remain? According to the 1998 Index of Economic Freedom, Hungary has eliminated most price controls, yet the prices for public transport, vehicle fuel, and utilities, such as gas, electricity, and water continue to be subsidized by the state. There is also a minimum wage in Hungary.

3. Is it possible to own and operate a business? (Has there been legislation regarding the formation, dissolution, and transfer of businesses, and is the law respected? Do there exist overly cumbersome bureaucratic hurdles that effectively hinder the ability to own and dispose of a

business? Are citizens given access to information on commerce law? Is the law applied fairly? Does regulation or licensing requirements impose significant costs on businesses and consumers? Do they create significant barriers to entry and seriously hamper competition?) In addition to the constitutional protection of private enterprises, numerous laws regulate their formation and operation. The commercial code, which includes approximately 350 laws, is in conformity with Western standards, is sufficiently transparent, is applied fairly to all subjects, and is accessible. It also establishes clear rules for the ownership and disposal of businesses.

The acquisition of a business license is simple and relatively inexpensive in most cases. In order to protect consumers, however, some licensing procedures may require collateral or proof of a specific skill. The manager of a car repair facility, for instance, is required to have five years of experience in a related field of work, and the owner of a pawn shop is required to deposit a collateral of a specific value before he can receive an operating permit.

4. Are courts effective, transparent, efficient, and quick in reaching decisions on property and contract disputes? What alternative mechanisms for adjudicating disputes exist? Hungary's commercial court is cumbersome and complex. Actions brought before the court can take years. The U.S. Department of Commerce reports that, while at times corrupt, ineffective, and inefficient, Hungary's judicial system adequately facilitates the acquisition and disposition of property rights. No alternative legal mechanisms for the adjudication of contract and property rights exist.

5. Is business competition encouraged? (Are monopolistic practices limited in law and in practice? If so, how? To what degree is insider dealing a hindrance to open competition? Are government procurement policies open and unbiased?) Fair competition is guaranteed by the commercial code and by the effective elimination of state monopolies. The pace of privatization in Hungary suggests that the government has made substantial efforts to relinquish state monopolies in all spheres of production, and thus encourage competition in open and fair markets, including in the utilities, education, mining, and financial sectors. Nevertheless, confidence in the privatization process has been shaken by several corruption scandals that led to the dismissal of the entire state privatization board and the ministers in charge. Domestic investors also complain that they are disadvantaged against large Western corporations in the competition for privatized strategic industries. It appears that the government procurement policies are becoming less biased in the aftermath of corruption scandals in 1995 and 1996.

6. To what extent has international trade been liberalized? To what degree has there been simplification/overhaul of customs and tariff procedures, and are these applied fairly? What informal trade barriers exist? The level of trade protectionism is relatively high in Hungary. The average tariff rate is 12 percent, and the government maintains import quotas that affect mainly consumer products, such as automobiles, clothing, leather footwear, and some foodstuffs. Quotas on agricultural products have been replaced with tariffs. Such protectionist measures are aimed mainly at Hungary's trading partners from the Central European Free Trade Agreement, which focuses on import levies on agricultural products. The most recent dispute between Poland and Hungary emerged over the violation of these levies by Poland, which had imposed unacceptable import levies on Hungarian starch and fodder maize. At the same time, Hungary is among the six former communist countries that are expected to be admitted as the first new members of the European Union (EU). The country's trade policies are therefore expected to conform gradually to those of current EU-member states. The EU's February 1992 Maastricht treaty provides, *inter alia*, for the free movement of goods, services, capital, and citizens of member-states throughout the union.

7. To what extent has foreign investment and capital flow been encouraged or constrained? Hungary is very open to foreign investment and attracts more foreign investment than any other formerly Communist country. Foreign investment totaled nearly $16 billion at the end of 1997.

Laws on the privatization of strategic industries guarantee the solvency of companies and that investors can obtain their market share for a fair price and through an effective and transparent privatization process. In practice, these provisions have led to several lawsuits against the APVRt. In one case, a Belgian investor who had purchased a share of the state-owned utility company sued after, contrary to legislation, the government failed to deregulate energy prices.

Additional attractions for foreign investors are Hungary's relatively cheap and highly skilled labor force, its central location, and its relatively high degree of political stability. In addition, except for strategic industries, Hungary guarantees up to 100 percent ownership to foreign investors.

8. Has there been reform of the energy sector? (To what degree has the energy sector been restructured? Is the energy sector more varied, and is it open to private competition? Is the country overly dependent on one or two other countries for energy [including whether exported fuel must pass through one or more countries to reach markets]?) The privatization of the energy sector began in 1995. Currently, 75 percent of the sector is privately owned. The Hungarian Energy Office, an independent oversight body, was established in July 1994 to regulate energy sales and price-levels. On September 18, 1995, in the first round of energy sector sales, a 51 percent stake was sold for $460 million to 18 investors. Six electricity distributors and two electricity generating plants were sold in early December 1995 for a total of $1.3 billion. Electricite de France, Powerfin (a Belgian firm), and the German firms Bayernwerke and Isaar Amperwerke purchased between 47 and 49 percent of the distribution companies.

Domestic energy production is distributed among coal (23 percent), oil (30 percent), gas (29 percent), and nuclear and hydroelectric energies (17 percent). Approximately 50 percent of oil and gas is imported from Russia through Ukraine and Slovakia.

KAZAKHSTAN

Freedom in the World Ratings, 1989-1998

	1989-90	1990-91	1991-92	1992-93	1993-94	1994-95	1995-96	1996-97	1997-98
Political Rights	-	-	5	5	6	6	6	6	6
Civil Liberties	-	-	4	5	4	5	5	5	5
Status	-	-	PF	PF	PF	NF	NF	NF	NF

Polity: Transitional
Economy: Transitional
Population: 16,876,000
PPP: $3,037
Ethnic Groups: Kazakh (43 percent), Russian (35 percent), Ukrainian (6 percent), others
Capital: Astana

Political Process 5.50/7

1. When did national legislative elections occur? Were they free and fair? How were they judged by domestic and international election monitoring organizations? Who composes the government? Kazakhstan's most recent parliamentary elections were held in December 1995. The 1994 elections had been declared unconstitutional by the Constitutional Court of Kazakhstan in March 1995, because they did not conform with the constitutional principle of one person one vote. President Nazarbayev used this ruling to dissolve the increasingly unfriendly and independent parliament and rule by decree.

The December 1995 elections were the first since the adoption of a new parliamentary structure in an August referendum. The new two-chamber parliament includes a 67-member *Mazhlis* (Assembly), which is chosen in a general election, and a 40-member Senate, in which seven members are chosen by the president himself and the remainder by regional representatives. The new structure of the parliament directly reflects the preferences of President Nazarbayev, who had unsuccessfully lobbied the Supreme Soviet for a two-chamber parliament when the original constitution was adopted in 1993.

The regional representatives in the Senate, or upper house, were chosen on December 5, 1995 by the delegates from each of Kazakhstan's 19 oblasts (regional administrative-territorial divisions). Forty-nine candidates vied for 40 seats. Twenty-seven of the elected deputies are politically unaffiliated. The remainder includes six members of the pro-presidential Party of Popular Unity, five members of the pro-presidential Democratic party, and one each from the People's Congress and the Socialist (former Communist) parties. The Mazhlis, or lower house, was elected from single-member constituencies by popular vote on December 9, 1995. A total of 295 candidates — 128 self-nominated and 157 nominated by parties or public associations — competed for 67 seats. Only

41 candidates met the required 50 percent threshold for election, and, after considering all challenges, the Central Electoral Commission allowed only 32 of these to sit. On December 23, 1995, an additional 13 deputies were chosen. The remaining seats were not filled until February 4, 1996. Of the 67 deputies, 42 are independent. Twenty-five, including 11 from the Party of Popular Unity, are members of parties.

The opposition views the election and the new structure of the parliament mainly as vehicles for Nazarbayev to legitimize his authoritarian rule. The Organization for Security and Cooperation in Europe (OSCE), while calling the elections fair, has declined to give Kazakhstan's electoral system a "democratic" imprimatur. According to the International Foundation for Electoral Systems (IFES), Nazarbayev has pledged that the next parliamentary elections will be held no later than December 1999.

The president appoints the prime minister, with the Senate's consent, as well as all other ministers and deputy ministers. He also has the sole authority to dismiss members of the government and create new or disband existing ministries and state committees. Significant recent changes in the Kazakh government include the October 1997 resignation of Prime Minister Akezhan Kazhegeldin, who had served since 1995. Although Kazhegeldin allegedly resigned due to ill health, his resignation also followed his admission of service in the KGB during the Soviet era, accusations that he used his official position to acquire large shares in the Shymkent oil refinery, and harsh criticism of his aggressive privatization program. Nazarbayev immediately appointed Nurlan Balgimbaev, the head of the Kazakhstan National Petroleum Company (KazakhOil), to replace Kazhegeldin. Balgimbaev is a graduate of the Kazakh Polytechnical Institute and has spent most of his working life as an engineer in the oil sector. Between 1986 and 1992, he worked in the Soviet Union's oil and gas industry ministry in Moscow. He became Minister of the Oil and Gas Industry of Kazakhstan in October 1994, and chief of the state oil company that replaced the ministry in March 1997.

2. When did presidential elections occur? Were they free and fair? The last presidential elec tions occurred in December 1991. According to the first constitution, new presidential elections were to be held in December 1996. Under the new constitution, the next presidential elections are to be held in 2001. Vitalii Voronov, a former opposition parliamentary deputy, has claimed that since Nazarbayev was elected as "president of the Kazakh Republic of the U.S.S.R." in 1991, and since his term was extended in a 1995 referendum, he may be considered to be a first-time candidate for president of the Republic of Kazakhstan in the scheduled 2001 presidential elections. Opinion polls also show that Nazarbayev is the most viable candidate. According to a poll by Kazakhstan's Giller Institute of 1,400 people from six of the country's regions, Nazarbayev, who garnered the support of 41.6 percent of respondents, would win if the elections were held today. Meanwhile, a number of opposition parties are preparing their own presidential candidates. At a November 1997 meeting of opposition parties and movements, Murat Auezov, the leader of the *Azamat* (citizen) movement, announced his intention to run.

3. Is the electoral system multiparty-based? Are there at least two viable political parties functioning at all levels of government? Neither the newly-revised parliamentary electoral law nor the newly-revised constitution prevents parties from competing in elections. A total of six parties, as well as trade unions, farmers' organizations, and a socio-political movement representing the

Russian community (LAD), participated in the most recent parliamentary elections: the Party of Popular Unity, the Democratic Party, the Cooperative Party, the Communist Party, the People's Congress of Kazakhstan (NKK), the Socialist Party, and the Revival Party of Kazakhstan. Most of these parties were founded in 1995 and are considered "pro-presidential."

There are six political parties officially represented in the Kazakh parliament. Three of these — the Party of People's Unity, the Democratic Party, and the People's Cooperative Party — are pro-presidential. The other three — the Socialist, Communist, and NKK— are small opposition parties. Outside of parliament, small Kazakh ethnic and Slavic ethnic parties are active in some cities.

Many individuals in power at the national and local levels either claim no party affiliation or are members of the government party Union of People's Unity of Kazakhstan (SNEK), which was founded in March 1993, as a vehicle of support for President Nazarbayev. According to Article 5 of the constitution, state officials and employees are restricted from engaging in activity that will promote the ideology or organization of any party of which they are members. Membership in a party, however, is not prohibited.

4. How many parties have been legalized? Are any particular parties illegal? At the time of the 1994 parliamentary elections, there were four registered parties in Kazakhstan. By the end of 1996, the total had grown to 12. The Party of Democratic Order, which is led by Tolegen Zhukeyev, the secretary of Kazakhstan's Security Council, supports greater political and economic reform in the direction of building democracy and a market economy and claims no personal or political affiliation with President Nazarbayev. The Revival Party of Kazakhstan, which is led by writer, playwright, and former Supreme Soviet deputy Altynshash Dzhaganova, claims to protect the interests of women, children, the poor, the unemployed, and the disabled. The People's Cooperative Party of Kazakhstan (NKPK) was founded to represent rural workers and cooperative members. The Social Democrats, founded in 1990, remain unregistered by choice.

The most recent political organizations to emerge in Kazakhstan are the Democratic Party of Kazakhstan and the opposition movement Azamat. Azamat is the first large-scale opposition movement led by eminent public figures who are not part of the government. The Democratic Party of Kazakhstan held its founding conference in July 1995, and was registered just after the constitutional referendum in August 1995. Its basic goals are to support greater progress in economic and political reform and to foster respect and cooperation among all of Kazakhstan's ethnic groups. It considers itself one of three "centrist" parties in Kazakhstan. (The other two are SNEK and the NKK). The movement held its first congress in Almaty on April 20, 1996, and was registered by the justice ministry a few months later. Its 400 delegates elected a coordinating council of 49 members and three co-chairmen: Murat Auezov, Kazakhstan's former ambassador to China; Petr Svoik, the Socialist Party leader and the former chairman of the State Committee on Pricing and Anti-Monopoly Measures; and Turegeldy Sharmanov, a member of the Kazakh and Russian academies of medical sciences.

Interior minister Maksut Narikbayev threatened to ban the Communist Party in March 1996 for holding a series of unauthorized rallies in support of a Russian *Duma* resolution denouncing the Belavezha accords. The Communist Party arranged for rallies to be held in Almaty, Karaganda, Uralsk, and Semipalatinsk on March 17, the anniversary of the 1991 referendum on preserving the

Soviet Union. A number of party activists were fined. In April 1998, Narikbayev again attempted to ban the party by appealing directly to the justice ministry and claiming that the party's charter seeks to create "a unitary state with a socialist orientation and pro-Communist ideology" — goals that violate the principles of territorial integrity and sovereignty enshrined in Kazakhstan's constitution. Later in the year, the General Procuracy of Kazakhstan summarily prohibited the party from organizing any meetings or demonstrations to commemorate the anniversary of the Bolshevik Revolution.

On November 4, 1997, representatives of several opposition movements and parties attended the first session of a joint coordination committee on creating a union of opposition forces. They elected prominent opposition activist Galym Abelseyitov as chairman. The organization, which was called the People's Front of Kazakhstan, was officially established on February 27, 1998. The new organization includes representatives from the Communist Party, Socialist Party, the Workers Movement, Azamat, LAD, and Azat. Its expressed goal is to nominate a candidate for the presidency and "struggle against the regime of personalized power carried out by President Nazarbayev." Azamat chairman Petr Svoik was named First Deputy Leader, and Madel Ismailov was named Deputy Chairman. Following the conference, several delegates were detained by police.

In what many view as a response to the creation of a national front among the opposition parties, on January 8, 1998, 17 parties and movements signed a memorandum on cooperation with the government. They pledged support for both Nazarbayev and his reforms. Among the 17 groups are the Democratic and People's Cooperative parties, the Federation Union Council, and the Muslim Women's Union.

5. What proportion of the population belongs to political parties? In general, party identification among voters remains very low, as illustrated in the most recent parliamentary elections, in which the majority of deputies elected to the Senate and the Mazhlis are politically unaffiliated. A December 1996 IFES opinion revealed that 54 percent of the 1,500 individuals surveyed were more likely to vote for an unaffiliated candidate than one affiliated with any party.

SNEK and the Socialists, the two largest parties, claim 40,000 and 60,000 members, respectively. The People's Congress claims a membership of approximately 10,000. The NKPK claims 40,000 members. The Democratic Party of Kazakhstan claims 15,000 members. Popular identification with any of these parties stands at 5 percent or less, with the exception of the Communist Party, at 10 percent.

6. What has been the trend of voter turnout at the municipal, provincial, and national levels in recent years? Turnout in the December 1995 parliamentary elections was reported at more than 79 percent in the first round and approximately 65 percent in the second round. The turnout for the referenda of April and August 1995 was approximately 90 percent. More than 88 percent of eligible voters participated in the March 1991 referendum on the future of the Soviet Union. Approximately 74 percent participated in the March 1994 parliamentary elections and elections to local legislative assemblies (*maslikhats*).

Civil Society **5.00/7**

1. How many non-governmental organizations (NGOs) have come into existence since 1988? What is the number of charitable/non-profit organizations? Are there locally led efforts to increase philanthropy and volunteerism? What proportion of the population is active in private voluntary activity (from polling data)? The number of NGOs in Kazakhstan has grown from 500 in the early 1990s to more than 700 in 1996-97. These not-for-profit organizations provide a variety of free services, including environmental education, legal assistance, and cultural exchanges. None is organized for the sole purpose of promoting philanthropy and volunteerism.

The principal NGOs that exist and operate in Kazakhstan include the Almaty City Ecology Center, the Almaty City Uighur Cultural Center, the Almaty Helsinki Committee Artists' Union, the Businessman's Congress of Kazakhstan, the Chernobyl Union of the Republic of Kazakhstan Congress of Entrepreneurs, the Democratic Committee for Human Rights Ecofund of Kazakhstan, the Ecological Fund of Kazakhstan "Initiative" Green Salvation, the Intergovernmental Association of Uighurs, the Kazakhstan International Bureau for Human Rights and the Rule of Law, the Lop Noor Semipalatinsk Ecological Committee Neveda-Semipalatinsk, the Pokolenie Pensioners Movement, the Republican Society for the Legal Development of Kazakhstan, the Shalom Jewish Cultural Center, the Socio-Ecological Union, the Tatar-Baskin Social and Cultural Center, and the Ukrainian Cultural Center. All of these operate within Almaty, but others are based in Dzhambul, Dzezkazgan, Karaganda, Semipalatinisk, Uralks, and Ust-Kamenogorsk.

The main charitable NGO is the Almaty-based Charitable Fund for the Promotion of Business Undertakings by Orphans and the Protection of their Rights.

While there are no polling data on the proportion of the population that is engaged in private voluntary activity, the 1996 IFES-sponsored survey found that more than 40 percent of the population would consider joining an environmental, social welfare, or educational NGO. Only 19 percent of those surveyed said that they were aware of the existence of NGOs in their communities, while 74 percent did not know of any such groups.

2. What is the legal and regulatory environment for NGOs (i.e., ease of registration, legal rights, government regulation, taxation, procurement, and access-to-information issues)? To what extent is NGO activism focused on improving the legal and regulatory environment? On paper, the legal and regulatory environment for NGOs is favorable. Registration is rarely denied to organizations of a strictly apolitical nature, and NGOs enjoy the right of peaceful assembly and are not subject to taxation. In practice, however, local governments responsible for issuing permits for public meetings and demonstrations often refuse on spurious legal grounds.

As a result, groups are forced to hold "illegal" meetings and demonstrations, many of which are organized as protests against the government's repeated failure to pay back wages and pensions. On November 30, 1997, for example, several hundred members of opposition movements and trade unions staged a demonstration in front of the Kazakh parliament building in Almaty to protest restrictions on citizens' rights to meet in public. The gathering took place after Azamat was denied official permission to hold the protest from the Almaty Procurator General's office.

Leaders of these "unsanctioned' meetings and demonstrations have repeatedly been beaten, detained, fined, and imprisoned. Two miners accused of organizing an unsanctioned demonstration in Karaganda in June 1997 to protest pension reforms were put under "administrative arrest" and later sentenced to seven and 15 days in jail, respectively, without a court hearing. The men were originally fined one month's pay, but the Karaganda town council subsequently decided to put them in jail. Madel Ismailov, a leader of the Almaty's Workers Movement, was sentenced to one year of hard labor after being found guilty of organizing "events that could cause mass unrest in the capital." He was imprisoned while an investigation into the incidents took place. Yuri Venkov, the deputy leader of the movement, is scheduled to appear in court on April 13, 1998, on charges of organizing unsanctioned rallies.

Strikes by workers in 1997 and 1998 have met with a similar response. After a lengthy standoff between police and striking workers from the Janatas Phosphorus plant, for example, the prosecutor general opened a case against the Federation of Kazakh Trade Unions, which supported the strike, for using "financial support from abroad" and exploiting the protests to destabilize the country. A few weeks later, Kazakh authorities sent approximately 1,000 policemen and troops to disperse the striking workers, who were blocking the tracks at the Taraz railroad station. Some of the strikers were beaten and thrown into rail cars destined for Janatas, while 11 others were taken into custody. Thus far, charges have been brought against three of the detainees.

In the face of such oppression, NGOs are abandoning their largely futile efforts to improve the country's legal and regulatory environment. Their repeated attempts to lobby parliamentarians have failed, in large part because most legislation originates in the government's ministries or the presidential apparat rather than the parliament. In addition, the new constitution provides no stated right of legislative initiative on the part of citizens' groups. Meetings and demonstrations have therefore become the most effective means for NGOs to voice their grievances and gain the attention of governmental authorities.

3. What is the organizational capacity of NGOs? Do management structures clearly delineate authority and responsibility? Is information available on NGO management issues in the native language? Is there a core of experienced practitioners/trainers to serve as consultants or mentors to less developed organizations? The organizational capacity of NGOs is limited. Although most NGOs have executive boards or committees, they are limited in their ability to delegate tasks among members. Leaders and activists therefore tend to operate without clear delineations of authority and responsibility.

After several years of NGO activity in Kazakhstan, a core of experienced practitioners who can serve as consultants or mentors to less developed organizations is emerging. Counterpart Consortium has already begun to perform this service. In addition, "Interlegal" Kazakhstan, which was established in 1993, is providing legal and informational assistance to NGOs in Kazakhstan. Its activities include providing consultations on legal, financial, and management issues for NGOs; publishing a monthly bulletin on the same topics; and holdings seminars, training sessions, and conferences on NGO legislation and taxation, legal and court reform, charitable activity, and methods of interaction with the government.

4. Are NGOs financially viable? What is their tax status? Are they obliged to and do they typically disclose revenue sources? Do government procurement opportunities exist for pri-

vate, not-for-profit providers of services? NGOs depend entirely upon foreign sources of funding. There are no funding sources in Kazakhstan, and the dire socio-economic situation in the country prohibits private donations. The growing number of NGOs appears to be finding ways to circumvent the restrictions on foreign funding. These limitations have been in place since the adoption in early 1995 of an amendment to Article 106 of the Civil Code to prohibit foreign financing of public associations. According to this section of the Civil Code, NGOs are obliged to disclose revenue sources, although, in practice, they are rarely asked to do so. NGOs are also exempt from taxation.

5. Are there free trade unions? How many workers belong to these unions? Is the number of workers belonging to trade unions growing or decreasing? What is the numerical/proportional membership of farmers' groups, small business associations, etc.? The largest union remains a governmental organ that succeeded the Soviet-era General Council of Trade Unions. Most workers remain members of the state-sponsored trade unions established during the Soviet period. While the law gives workers the right to join or form unions of their own choosing and to stop automatic deductions of dues for the state unions, enterprises continue to ignore workers' requests and withhold dues for the state-sponsored trade unions. Moreover, workers who join independent unions are subject to threats and harassment by enterprise management without legal recourse.

At the same time, the Independent Trade Union Center, an active independent labor organization, has grown in popularity. In the early 1990s, the center claimed a membership of approximately 250,000. It now claims a membership of 500,000, out of a total workforce of about 5.6 million. These figures are unverifiable, however, and may be much lower. The Federation of Kazakh Trade Unions also became increasingly active in 1997-98 by sponsoring or supporting most of the strikes that took place during this period.

Membership in farmers' groups and small business associations remains very limited. Organizations of collective farmers and business people are neither popular nor influential. In February 1995, a few of Kazakhstan's business leaders organized the social movement New Generation, which lobbied Nazarbayev to support the privatization of land. This group appears to have had little influence and visibility in the last two years. There is also a small Kazakh Association of Businessmen in Almaty.

6. What forms of interest group participation in politics are legal? What types of interest groups are active in the political and policy process? The new constitution is more explicit about what forms of participation in politics by interest groups are legal. Section 3 of Article 5 prohibits public associations from activity that is "geared to a forcible change in the constitutional system" or "the incitement of social, racial, national, religious, or tribal discord." Public associations are also strictly prohibited from receiving any form of foreign aid.

No interest groups are actively involved in the political or policy process. According to the constitution, citizens' groups have no stated right to initiate legislation. In practice, they also have no access to those who initiate legislation. Both the Kazakhstan International Bureau for Human Rights and Rule of Law and the Kazakhstan Branch of "Interlegal" drafted legislation and lobbied parliamentary deputies since 1993, but they have had little success, particularly since 1995.

7. How is the not-for-profit/NGO sector perceived by the public and government officials? What is the nature of media coverage of NGOs? To what extent do government officials engage with NGOs? According to IFES, 45 percent of the Kazakh population believes that NGOs are "essential" or "necessary," while 41 percent believe that NGOs are "not very necessary" or "not necessary at all." Government officials, generally speaking, are much less receptive to NGOs. They tend to regard NGOs as annoyances rather than vehicles for constructive change and do not attempt to integrate them into the policy-making or legislative process. Instead, they have offered NGO leaders positions in the government and have established organizations to circumvent NGO activities. According to many NGO activists, this is what prompted the government to agree to set up a presidential commission on human rights in order to review complaints from citizens, mediate in disputes with authorities, and sponsor seminars to make citizens aware of their rights.

While the media do not cover NGO activities on a regular basis, they do cover major events. They provided continuous, but biased coverage of the 1997-98 strikes in southern Kazakhstan. In addition, media representatives occasionally attend NGO-initiated press conferences, even if the content is unfavorable to the government. The media participated in a press conference organized by the Society of Ethnic Russians in Kazakhstan in August 1997, for example, in which leaders of the country's Russian community harshly criticized Kazakhstan's new language policy.

Independent Media 5.50/7

1. Are there legal protections for press freedom? Articles 10 and 11 of Kazakhstan's previous constitution guaranteed freedom of speech and expression as well as "the right to receive and disseminate information by any legal means." Likewise, the new constitution also guarantees "freedom of speech and creativity" and the "right to obtain and disseminate information freely in any way not prohibited by law." It makes no explicit reference to press freedom. The 1991 Law on Media, which forbids censorship, is still in effect. In addition, in October 1995, President Nazarbayev amended the Law on Press and Mass Information by abolishing the Ministry of Press and Information and replacing it with the National Agency for Press and Mass Information of the Republic of Kazakhstan. The stated purpose of the new agency is to strengthen press freedom and provide state support for the publication of newspapers, magazines, and books. Instead, it is vested with very broad powers such as the right to prepare "proposals on improving legislation in the area of the press and mass media" that, according to many journalists, increase the government's control not only over state-owned, but also private media.

Several events in 1997 also illustrate that, in practice, press freedom is limited. In particular, the rule banning the "[incitement of] ethnic conflict" is interpreted quite broadly. The newspaper *Komsomolskaya Pravda* was banned in Kazakhstan after it printed an article in which Aleksandr Solzhenitsyn argued that parts of Kazakhstan are naturally and historically parts of Russia. Eleven members of the Kazakhstani Writers' Union filed a suit against the newspaper claiming that the article was an infringement on the "sovereignty and territorial integrity of our state." *Komsomolskaya Pravda*, which is the most popular newspaper in Kazakhstan, was banned for several months before the trial, but later allowed to operate. The state television news agency *Khabar* cancelled the Russian language news analysis program *Nedelya* after a broadcast featured an election appeal by Russian presidential candidate Aleksandr Lebed.

In May, the government initiated criminal proceedings against publications *Karavan*, *Kazakhskaya Pravda*, *Rabochaya Zhizn*, and *Biz-MY* and launched investigations of several others on charges of "igniting racial, ethnic, and religious hatred."

2. Are there legal penalties for libeling officials? Are there legal penalties for "irresponsible" journalism? Have these laws been enforced to harass journalists? Penalties for libel and irresponsible journalism are frequently invoked by Kazakhstan's authorities. The law against insulting the president and other officials remains active, and the constitution provides for the protection of the dignity of the president. Russian journalist Boris Suprynuk was convicted of insulting a public prosecutor and sentenced to two years' imprisonment in May 1995. In April 1998, Madel Ismailov, a leader of the Almaty's Workers Movement, was sentenced to one year in prison for "using the mass media for insulting the president" after he publicly criticized Nazarbayev during a rally. The Committee to Protect Journalists has determined that print journalists have resorted to self-censorship due to the increasing number of criminal libel suits and other official harassment.

3. What proportion of the media is privatized? What are the major private newspapers, television stations, and radio stations? According to Altynbek Sarsenbayev, the chairman of the National Agency for Press and Media, as of June 1996, there were more than 1,500 independent publications and 26 state-funded publications in Kazakhstan. The most popular independent newspaper continues to be *Karavan*, with the largest circulation in Central Asia. The Independent Trade Union and several political parties also publish their own newspapers. State-funded print media include Kazakh-language publications and those of the Uygur, Korean, and German ethnic minorities. The state continues to support the publication of Kazakh-language newspapers, magazines, and books that, Sarsenbayev argues, cannot be privatized due to severe limits on the generation of revenue through advertisements.

Beginning in November 1996, government officials used a variety of crude tactics — including claims of "interference with air traffic control" — to stop the broadcasts of independent radio and television stations in the capital. In December 1996, the government announced that it would hold a tender for broadcast frequencies. The tender, however, was not an auction to award the frequency to the highest bidder. Instead, the government Frequency Commission accepted applications and met with individual broadcasters to hear their arguments as to why they should be granted the frequencies. The cost of the license and annual fees were extremely high by local, regional, and international standards. Nevertheless, even independent broadcasters with the necessary funds were denied licenses. Several independent broadcasters were thus forced out of business, including the popular Radio Max and TV-M, which aired "Open Zone," a popular political program that provided a platform for the political opposition. As a result of the tender, there are now only four nominally non-state television channels and three independent radio stations in Almaty. The winners of the tender included Nazarbayev's daughter, who owns a partially state-run television company and a nominally private station.

Local officials employed the same tactics outside Almaty. In April, three popular channels in Akmola were suddenly told to close their transmitters. In May, the minister of transportation and communications held a tender for regional radio frequencies in seven provincial cities. Even in areas in which only one commercial station applied to participate in the tender, the licenses were not awarded to independent broadcasters.

In March 1998, the Kazakh International Bureau on Human Rights, an Almaty-based NGO, called on the country's Constitutional Council to review the 1997 auction due to its failure to "correspond to the spirit and letter of Kazakhstan's constitution." In addition, three television and radio stations appealed their failed bids.

4. Are the private media financially viable? The lack of adequate finances is the most severe difficulty faced by independent media in Kazakhstan. Although the plight of newspapers had been greater than that of radio and television stations, recent governmental actions have also imperiled these media. The 1997 auctions of broadcast frequencies, for example, has led to the closure of half of the country's independent radio and television stations.

Independent newspapers continue to be financed through advertising and direct sales.

5. Are the media editorially independent? Are the media's news-gathering functions affected by interference from the government or private owners? Since 1995, the media have become less editorially independent. For example, many newspapers published critical analyses of the draft constitution during the officially-designated "discussion period" in July 1995, and the press openly questioned the election of a new parliament with only limited powers before the December 1995 elections. Today, controversial issues such as the disappearance of the former prime minister and the appointment of his replacement, labor unrest and agitation for social rights, and the activities of Kazakh and foreign oil companies are either not addressed or subjectively covered by the media.

6. Is the distribution system for newspapers privately or governmentally controlled? The distribution system for newspapers remains under the control of the Soviet-era *Soyuzpechat* (Union Press). Nevertheless, many newspapers — including *Karavan* and *Delovaya Nedelya* — sell directly to kiosks. In addition, as in other Central Asian states, many private citizens continue to purchase newspapers at the point of production and sell them on the street at inflated prices.

7. What proportion of the population is connected to the Internet? Are there any restrictions on Internet access to private citizens? There are no formal restrictions on the access of private citizens to the Internet. Less than 5 percent of the population, however, has access to computers, high-quality telephone lines, English language skills, and other resources necessary for utilization of the Internet. The vast majority of Internet users are NGO leaders and activists who have received equipment through foreign funding.

8. What has been the trend in press freedom as measured by Freedom *House's Survey of Press Freedom*? Freedom House's annual *Survey of Press Freedom* rated Kazakhstan "Partly Free" from 1992 through 1993 and "Not Free" from 1994 - 1998.

Governance and Public Administration 5.50/7

1. Is the legislature the effective rule-making institution? The legislature is not the effective rule-making body in Kazakhstan. Powers have been increasingly concentrated in the executive branch since President Nazarbayev's role was strengthened in an April 1995 referendum. The presidential role was further increased in a 1996 decree that allows the president to determine the basic course of domestic and foreign policy and to serve as the symbol and guarantor of national unity, state power, the constitution, and citizens' rights. The decree also allows the president to order parliamentary elections, annul any existing law, and demand the government's resignation. It also states that the same person cannot be elected president to more than two consecutive terms. In the first half of 1997, the parliament adopted more than 150 draft laws, all of which were initiated and supported by the executive branch.

Moreover, the new constitution provides the president with greater influence over the inner-workings of the parliament. Many opposition leaders have claimed that the Senate, the parliament's new second chamber, is an extension of the presidency. The president appoints seven of the chamber's 40 deputies, and the remaining 33 members are elected by regional assemblies that are also, in effect, chosen by the president. In addition, the new constitution does not empower the legislature to control the budget, initiate changes in the constitution, or exercise oversight over the executive branch. For example, if the parliament fails within 30 days to pass an "urgent" bill brought by the president, the president may issue the bill by decree.

2. Is substantial power decentralized to sub-national levels of government? What specific authority do sub-national levels have? Constitutionally, Kazakhstan is a unitary state. Decisions are made at the national level and only implemented at the local levels by regional (*oblast*) administrative heads (*akims*). Under the new constitution, the akims are nominated by the prime minister and appointed and removed by the president without the scrutiny of either the legislative or judicial branches. Regional legislative bodies enjoy minimal authority.

Nazarbayev has repeatedly exercised his authority to appoint and replace akims. On April 10, 1996, he dismissed the head of East Kazakhstan Oblast for "serious mistakes and neglecting his duties." It was the fourth such firing in as many years in the oblast. Similarly, in 1997 Nazarbayev replaced two akims in Jambyl Oblast after they were unable to appease strikers who had not been paid for nearly three years.

At the same time, the akims in Western Kazakhstan are becoming increasingly independent due to the large degree of foreign investment in the country's oil and gas sector. They are now the main de facto enforcers of contracts negotiated with the central government.

3. Are sub-national officials chosen in free and fair elections? Akims for Kazakhstan's oblasts and two "special cities" — Almaty and Leninsk — are nominated by the prime minister and appointed and removed at the discretion of the president. Akims serving at other levels are appointed and removed at the discretion of their respective regional akims. The country's regional assemblies were dissolved at the end of 1992. In March 1994, new local legislative bodies (*maslikhats*) were elected to five-year terms. The voting was deemed free and fair. Local elections, however, are heavily controlled by the executive branch through the akims. Under the new constitution, future maslikhats will be elected to four-year terms. The next elections are scheduled to take place concurrently with those for the national legislature — no later than December 1999.

4. Do the legislative and executive bodies operate openly and with transparency? Is draft legislation easily accessible to the media and the public? At all levels of government in Kazakhstan, transparency is uncommon. This has been the case particularly since the dissolution of parliament in March 1994 — a parliament which had integrated several citizens' initiatives into its legislative reform program. After this dissolution and the adoption of the new constitution in August 1995, power was effectively concentrated in the hands of the executive branch.

As during the Soviet era, government-owned media publish draft legislation after the text is in a form that is acceptable to the central government.

5. Do municipal governments have sufficient revenues to carry out their duties? Do municipal governments have control of their own local budgets? Do they raise revenues autonomously or from the central state budget? Municipal governments do not have sufficient revenues to carry out their duties effectively. This was apparent in 1997-98 in the growing number of strikes in which thousands of demonstrators demanded employment and lower housing costs, as well as back wages and pensions that had not been paid for years. In (former) Kokchetau Oblast, for example, every fourth person is without employment, every third person cannot pay for housing and utilities, and pensioners are only now receiving their March and April payments. The situation can be attributed in part to the fact that Kokchetau Oblast was merged with Northern Kazakhstan Oblast in early 1997. As a result, Kokchetau city was subsequently deprived of the funding it had previously received as a regional center. One major source of the deficit in municipal funds is a severe cutback in funds allocated by the central government.

Municipal governments have little control of their own local budgets because most of their revenue is not raised autonomously. With the approval of the executive branch, a central state budget is established every year by the national legislature from taxes, customs, and sales of state property. Funds are then distributed to each oblast according to the central government's determination of need. In this way, funds are redistributed from wealthier to poorer regions. Targets for the allocation of funds are identified in the central budget, but the local akim can use his authority to redirect these funds. A small part of municipal budgets is based on local tax revenue. In the country's western oblasts, foreign oil companies also serve as a source of local taxation.

6. Do the elected local leaders and local civil servants know how to manage municipal governments effectively? Municipal governments are still managed largely as they were in the Soviet era. Local leaders follow directions from the central authorities in Almaty and, in general, implement centrally-decreed reform programs. Failures to execute such tasks in a timely fashion have led Nazarbayev to dismiss several local leaders.

7. When did the constitutional/legislative changes on local power come into effect? Has there been a reform of the civil service code/system? Are local civil servants employees of the local or central government? To date, the most significant constitutional and legislative reform of Kazakhstan's local power structure has been the new provision to have the akims nominated by the prime minister rather than the president, who then has sole responsibility for actually appointing them. The most substantive change regarding sub-national government occurred in 1997, when

Nazarbayev consolidated several oblasts, thereby reducing the total number of entities from 19 to 14. Each of these is headed by a regional akim.

In January 1996, Nazarbayev issued a decree to begin to reform the civil service code and system. The new law provides civil servants with free housing, pensions, and other entitlements. It also forbids them to engage in partisan activities. In July 1997, Nazarbayev claimed that his reforms of the civil service have saved the country approximately 3 billion *tenge* ($40 million) to date. Local civil servants remain employees of local government.

Rule of Law 5.25/7

1. Is there a post-Communist constitution? How does the judicial system interpret and enforce the constitution? Are there specific examples of judicial enforcement of the constitution in the last year? Kazakhstan's constitution was amended in August 1995 by referendum. In a turnout of approximately 90 percent of registered voters, 89 percent voted to adopt the new constitution. The new document concentrates political power in the executive branch, establishes the Russian language on an equal level with Kazakh in local government, and recognizes the inviolability of private property — particularly regarding land ownership — and the right of individuals to engage in entrepreneurial activity.

Many opposition groups, including the Russian Community, the Independent Trade Union, the Communist Party, and the Social Democrats, opposed the draft constitution as the "undemocratic" creation of authorities who did not consider the views of citizens' groups or public associations. They also objected to the document's vast empowerment of the president at the expense of citizens' rights. Those who supported the draft, including SNEK, the People's Congress Party, and the Democratic Party of Kazakhstan, argued that the centralization of power was necessary in order to continue Kazakhstan's reforms and to solidify its sovereignty.

The Constitutional Court, which had been charged with interpreting the constitution, was replaced by presidential decree on January 9, 1996, when Nazarbayev established a Constitutional Council. The purpose of the council is ostensibly to continue the court's function of ensuring that the country's laws conform to the constitution. Nevertheless, the council is independent in name only. The head of the state has the right to appoint or dismiss its president and up to three of its seven members. In the future, the council will even include former heads of state. In addition to interpreting the constitution, the council also rules on challenges to elections and referenda.

2. Does the constitutional framework provide for human rights? Do the human rights include business and property rights? The legal structure of Kazakhstan, including the new constitution, guarantees human rights but does not fully safeguard them. The law continues to sanction pretrial detention. Police may hold a detainee for 72 hours before bringing charges. With the approval of a prosecutor, they may continue to hold the detainee for up to 10 additional days. In practice, the police routinely hold detainees, with the sanction of a prosecutor, for weeks or months without bringing charges. Defendants enjoy a presumption of innocence, are protected form self-incrimination, and have the right to appeal a decision to a higher court. Nevertheless, judicial corruption — particularly in the form of bribery and political bias — is widespread. The constitution provides for peaceful assembly and association. Under a law issued by Nazarbayev in March 1995 however, organizations must apply to the local authorities for a permit to hold a demonstration or public meeting at least ten days in advance. Political activists have also complained that local authorities have insisted on approving the slogans on banners before allowing demonstrations to take place. The constitution guarantees equal rights of citizens regardless of race, ethnicity, or religion, but in practice, the government discriminates in favor of ethnic Kazakhs in government employment, education, housing, and other areas.

The new constitution provides for the right of emigration and repatriation, both of which are respected in practice. Kazakhs have the right to change their citizenship but are not permitted to hold dual citizenship.

The new constitution also recognizes the inviolability of private property, including land ownership, and the right of individuals to engage in entrepreneurial activity. The Civil Code that took effect in March 1995, established the basic freedom of entrepreneurial activity and defined various forms of business enterprises, including partnerships, limited companies, and joint stock companies. Current law is based upon the equitable distribution of land and asset shares but with the added benefit that the various forms of business enterprise that may be adopted now have a basis in civil law.

3. Has there been basic reform of the criminal code/criminal law? Who authorizes searches and issues warrants? Are suspects and prisoners beaten or abused? Are there excessive delays in the criminal justice system? The Kazakh Criminal Code, which dates from 1986, was amended in 1994. Further revisions to the code were drafted in June 1997. It appears, however, that many of these revisions have not been implemented by local authorities. For example, although the revised code forbids taking individuals into custody without charging them, this is a common practice, especially when the individual in question is a member of the opposition or was engaged in some form of protest against the current government. During the trial of an Almaty's Workers Movement leader, who had been held for several days without being charged, the judge asked the police chief if he was aware that, under the criminal code, a person who is not considered dangerous cannot be imprisoned during a criminal investigation. The investigator replied that he had received his orders "from above" and had never read the relevant chapter of the criminal code.

4. Do most judges rule fairly and impartially? Do many remain from the Communist era? According to Amnesty International, corruption exists at every stage and level of the judicial process. Judges, who are poorly paid, often solicit bribes from participants in trials and then rule in their favor. The government has not made a serious effort to eliminate corruption in the judiciary, although in recent years, several Supreme Court judges have been dismissed or forced to resign due to official allegations of corruption.

The vast majority of judges are holdovers from the Communist era.

5. Are the Courts free of political control and influence? Are the courts linked directly to the Ministry of Justice or any other executive body? Kazakhstan's courts are not free of political control and influence. With the adoption of the new constitution in August 1995, the judiciary was effectively placed under the control of the president and the executive branch. The president nominates judges for appointment to the Supreme Court, and the Senate is obliged to approve them. The president also appoints oblast judges, who are nominated by the Highest Judicial Council, and local judges from a list compiled by the Ministry of Justice. Oblast courts hear cases of serious crimes, such as murder, grand theft, and organized criminal activity. Local courts address less serious crimes, such as petty theft and vandalism. The judgments of local courts may be appealed to the oblast-level courts, while decisions of oblast courts may be appealed to the Supreme Court.

Since June 3, 1996, judges of the Supreme Court and lower courts in Kazakhstan have been required to take examinations that assess their professional qualifications. The tests will be reviewed by a special committee of well-known scholars, lawyers, and parliamentary deputies. Justice minister Konstantin Kolpakov has stated that the certification of judges is part of the country's ongoing judicial reform process. Kazakhstan has already abolished the Soviet-era people's courts, in which the judges were appointed by higher authorities.

6. What proportion of lawyers is in private practice? How does this compare with the previous year? A fairly small, but growing, number of lawyers is engaged in private practice. The American Bar Association has estimated that approximately 20 percent of the lawyers in Almaty are independently employed. The remaining 80 percent are employed by the state. The majority of lawyers engaged in private practice represent new businesses rather than defendants in a public trial.

There are two main organizations of independent lawyers — the Association of Lawyers of Kazakhstan and the social movement known as "Legal Development of Kazakhstan." Both are based in Almaty.

7. Does the state provide public defenders? The state is required by law to provide public defenders in cases involving serious crimes. In practice, however, many defendants are either unaware of their right to a lawyer or are denied this right when detained by police.

8. Are there any effective anti-bias/discrimination laws, including protection of ethnic minority rights? The constitution guarantees equal treatment of Kazakhs regardless of their race, ethnicity, or religion. In practice, however, discrimination exists. In the view of the country's Russian minority, the recognition of the Russian language as equal to Kazakh at the local level of government has not redressed the excessively preferential status of Kazakh as the official state language. This status has expanded under the country's new language policy, which requires that 50 percent of all broadcasting be in Kazakh and that all ethnic Russian state officials be proficient in Kazakh by 2006. At an August 1997 press conference, leaders of the Society of Ethnic Russians in Kazakhstan harshly criticized the country's drive to decrease the importance of the Russian language. They urged the Russian parliament to take firm measures to protect the rights of Kazakhstan's Russian-speakers, who, they claim, constitute more than half of the population.

Since 1996, ethnic tensions in northern Kazakhstan have increased due to alleged government harassment of non-Kazaks. Local residents claim that Russians wearing Cossack uniforms and Chechens are frequently harassed by the Kazakh interior ministry. The head of the Chechen community in North Kazakhstan has stated that the Kazakh militia views all Chechens as "bandits." In

Moscow, members of the Congress of Russian Communities and the Russian-Serb Brotherhood Society have burnt effigies of Nazarbayev on Smolensk Square. Viktor Antoshko, the leader of the Siberian Cossack Army, has stated that the Kazakh government does not defend the rights of the country's non-Kazakh citizens and that crimes committed against non-Kazakhs often go unpunished. He has also claimed that Kazakhs hold every position of authority in the country's banking system, law enforcement agencies, government, and courts.

In 1996, the government initiated a crackdown on Uighur separatist groups after a meeting with representatives from China and neighboring CIS states in Shanghai to discuss border issues. Unlike Kyrgyzstan, Kazakhstan has not banned its local Uighur society, but it has repeatedly endorsed China's efforts to curb Uighurs' support for separatist activities in Xinjiang. This treatment of Uighur organizations in Kazakhstan has continued in 1997-98 with the development of closer political and economic relations between the Kazakh and Chinese governments.

At the end of 1996, the Kazakh government began to reconsider its policy of "special treatment" of Kazakh immigrants in the form of state financial aid and housing. A presidential decree established a ceiling on the number of ethnic Kazakh immigrants who will be eligible to receive financial support. Approximately 4,000 families arriving from neighboring states will receive state aid and housing in 1998. In the first four months of the year, more than 3,400 families moved to Kazakhstan. The government now appears to be questioning its ability to cope with the influx of migrants.

The constitution provides for freedom of religion, and adherents of various faiths worship without government interference. At the same time, however, the constitution requires that the leaders of religious groups be appointed by foreign entities "in coordination with the government." In practice, the government does not interfere in the appointment of religious leaders, although foreign missionaries have complained of harassment by low-level government officials.

Corruption D

1. What is the magnitude of official corruption in the civil service? Must an average person pay a bribe to a bureaucrat in order to receive a service? What services are subject to bribe requests — for example, university entrance, hospital admission, telephone installation, obtaining a license to operate a business, applying for a passport or other official documents? What is the average salary of civil servants at various levels? An increasing majority of Kazakh citizens believe that corruption is widespread and serious throughout the government. According to IFES, 87 percent of Kazakhs believe that corruption is "common." Fifty-three percent believe that it is "very common," while only five percent believe that it is "rare." In a similar poll in 1995, 77 percent of respondents stated that corruption was "common," while 39 percent said that is was "very common."

The problem of corruption is especially acute in business transactions. In a recent survey conducted by the European Bank for Reconstruction and Development (EBRD), more than 3,600 entrepreneurs in 69 countries were asked to respond to the following statement: "It is common for firms in my line of business to have to pay some irregular 'additional payments' to get things done." In Kazakhstan and the other CIS countries, 65 percent of respondents stated that this was frequently, usually, or always true. The regional average for the CIS was 15 percentage points higher than that of the next highest region — sub-Saharan Africa — and 24 points higher than that of Latin America. Respondents were also asked if they could predict in advance how much they would have to pay in bribes if they wanted to "get things done." In the CIS countries, respondents reported a "level of predictability of corruption nearly twice as high as any other region with the exception of Eastern Europe." Participants were also asked to respond to a second statement: "If a firm pays the required additional payment, the service is usually delivered as agreed." More than 80 percent of the respondents agreed.

Until March 1997, the wages of state employees remained at the average level in Kazakhstan: An employee of a state ministry received $80 to $100 per month, and a state minister received approximately $200. Following the governmental reorganization, which decreased the number of ministries and state employees, the wages of state employees were more than doubled in an attempt to combat the practice of taking bribes. Fewer believed that the move would be effective including the president himself, who later launched a broader anti-corruption plan.

2. Do top policy-makers (the President, ministers, vice-ministers, top court justices, and heads of agencies and commissions) have direct ties to businesses? How strong are such connections, and what kinds of businesses are these? Top policy-makers often act as consultants and lobbyists — for example, on licensing procedures and the level of taxation — for privately-owned large enterprises in exchange for payment or gifts. This practice is particularly widespread in the energy sector.

3. Do laws requiring financial disclosure and disallowing conflict of interest exist? Have publicized anti-corruption cases been pursued? To what conclusion? The State Committee for Investigations — the Kazakh equivalent of the U.S. Federal Bureau of Investigation — is responsible for combating corruption. The Kazakh Criminal Code includes special penalties for giving and receiving bribes. In recent years, a small number of low-level government officials have been removed from office for corruption. However, prosecution of officials is extremely rare.

In December 1997, however, Igor Rokov, the presidential legal adviser, introduced an anti-corruption law that required government officials to submit a declaration disclosing their personal and joint spousal property and income, including any gifts and services received.

In 1997, Deputy Prime Minister Asyghat Jabaghin was dismissed for alleged corruption linked to the privatization process. He was then returned to the cabinet in a different post. Education Minister Talgha Mamashev was fired after a scandal in which he and several other officials used their positions to enroll their children in a student exchange program.

4. What major anti-corruption initiatives have been implemented? How often are anti-corruption laws and decrees adopted? In a January 1998 speech on his "Kazakhstan 2030" program, Nazarbayev launched his strongest public attack yet against corruption. He vowed to end the abuse of public office for private gain and warned that the state would soon have two new weapons in its arsenal: Rogov's anti-corruption law, which is expected to be adopted by parliament in the next session, and the formation of a new anti-corruption agency that, based on a presidential list of suspects, will investigate state officials who have profited illegally from privatization. The new agency, which will investigate all cases of abuse of power and financial malfeasance, will be led by former presidential Chief of Staff Oralbay Abdikarimov.

5. How do major corruption-ranking organizations like Transparency International rate this country? According to a new EBRD report, corruption in the CIS is higher than in any other region in the world. The report is based on estimates by the London-based Economist Intelligence Unit and the DRI/McGraw Hill Global Risk Service. The Economist Intelligence Unit asked country experts to assess the "degree to which public officials are involved in corrupt practices" on a scale of zero to four, with four indicating the highest level of corruption. Among the 97 countries surveyed, 18 were former Communist states and received an average rating of 3.35. The report states, "All five CIS countries included in the survey (Azerbajian, Kazakhstan, Russia, Ukraine, and Uzbekistan) received the highest rating — a score of four — for corruption among public officials." DRI/McGraw Hill studied 21 transition economies in its analysis of 33 risk factors in a total of 106 countries. For the 12 CIS countries included in that survey, the average level of corruption was 64 percent, a "level only slightly exceeded by the countries of sub-Saharan Africa."

Privatization 4.25/7

1. What percentage of GDP comes from private ownership? What percentage of the labor force is employed in the private sector? How large is the informal sector in the economy? According to the National Statistics Agency of Kazakhstan, the share of the private sector in Kazakhstan's GDP was 54.9 percent in 1996 and 72 percent in 1997. EBRD estimates for 1996-97 are reportedly consistent with these findings. The 1998 share is expected to increase to 76 percent. There are no available statistics on the percentage of the labor force that is employed in the private sector or on the size of the informal economy.

The informal sector of the economy remains very large. The Chairman of the Customs Committee has reported that 80 percent of imported goods are smuggled.

2. What major privatization legislation has been passed? What were its substantive features? Many important pieces of legislation were developed in the last few months of 1995 and early 1996. On December 26, 1995, President Nazarbayev issued a decree that legalizes private land ownership and allows foreign investors to purchase property. Previously, foreign firms could only lease land for ten years or less. In February 1996, parliament passed a law that provides that ownership of land is open to any person or legal entity, protected by law, irrevocable except through legal proceedings. This protection is also extended to those who have the right to use state-owned land.

In 1997 and 1998, the Kazakh government made concerted efforts to escalate the privatization process primarily in order to encourage greater foreign investment in strategic mineral assets such as gas, oil, and precious metals. Most significantly, it created a State Agency on Investment to streamline the process for the acquisition of state enterprises. As a result, the third phase of the privatization program has been much more successful than the previous two. The first round had included state assets in the small-scale service and retail sectors. The second round included a coupon privatization program. By August 1997, the small-scale privatization program had been completed. A total of 17,000 enterprises were sued. Several important large-scale enterprises, including three major gas companies, were also privatized in 1997.

In a December 1997 move to regulate the privatization process more closely and effectively, the government merged the State Property Committee and the Privatization Committee to form a Privatization Department within the Ministry of Finance. The new department will monitor privatization contracts and the fulfillment of the terms of tenders.

3. What proportion of agriculture, housing and land, industry, and business and services is in private hands? *Agriculture*: A total of 1,671 of 2,500 large agricultural enterprises have been privatized. Unofficially, this number has increased to 1,860. There are also more than 4.4 million privately owned plots of land. As of January 1996, 31,000 family farms occupied 13 million hectares — approximately 5 percent of the country's agricultural land.

Housing and Land: The government estimated that 90 percent of housing has been privatized. While there has been a great deal of resistance to the privatization of land, recent legislation suggests that this is no longer the case. The right to land ownership is now legally enshrined in the constitution as well as a February 1996 law.

Industry: By the end of 1995, the majority share holdings of approximately 800 holding company subsidies had been offered in mass privatizations, and many smaller subsidies had been sold on the local level. After these sales, 8,000 small enterprises were auctioned, most state farms were privatized, and many oil, gas, and mineral reserves were awarded to foreign investors. By the end of 1997, the country had almost completed its process of finding buyers for industry through tenders and deals with companies that were already managing enterprises under trust or leasing agreements. A January 1997 bankruptcy law aided the process.

4. What has been the extent of insider (management, labor, and nomenklatura) participation in the privatization process? What explicit and implicit preferences have been awarded to insiders? Government insiders have benefited from privatization by receiving bonuses from the sale of state assets and industries to foreign companies. In some cases, workers have received shares of the stock in these privatized enterprises, but the Kazakh government can sell them at will.

5. How much public awareness of and support for privatization has there been? What is the nature of support and opposition to privatization by major interests groups? Approximately half of the population would prefer to return to full state control over the economy. According to the Giller Institute poll, 33 percent of Kazakhs stated that they support the current course of economic reforms (including privatization), while 48.6 percent said they did not support it. Only 1.9 percent believe that the economic situation in the country had improved. Nevertheless, 84 percent of Kazakhs believe that citizens should have the right to own land as private property, and 74 percent believe that they should also have the right to buy and sell land.

Macroeconomics 4.50/7

1. Has the taxation system been reformed? (What areas have and have not been overhauled? To what degree are taxpayers complying? Has the level of revenues increased? Is the revenue-collection body overburdened? What is the overall tax burden?) The key changes in the taxation system can be found in a presidential edict issued by Nazarbayev in mid-1995 — "On Taxes and Other Obligatory Payments into the Budget" — which has been in effect since July 1995. Kazakhstan's new tax code, which took effect in July 1995, is considered by many Western legal experts to be the most comprehensive in the former Soviet Union. Its "supremacy provision" supercedes any legislation in conflict with its provisions and prohibits legislation not concerned with taxation from containing provisions that impose taxes. The code also reduces the number of local and national taxes from approximately 45 to 19. Many of the earlier "special taxes" that applied to foreign businesses were eliminated. Foreign investors, however, are still affected by the 20 percent VAT, which, under the 1995 code, is imposed on all transactions within Kazakhstan and on almost all imports. The 1995 code imposed the VAT on all imported capital equipment used for production — a provision that substantially increases the cost of doing business in Kazakhstan. It also established a corporate income tax rate of 30 percent, a graduated personal income tax rate with a maximum rate of 40 percent, a social tax of 30 percent, and an unemployment tax of two percent.

Amendments at the end of 1997 abolished taxes on securities transactions and capital gains. New issues of corporate securities are subject to a five percent tax. Recent amendments also reduced taxes on interest paid to securities holders (dividends, bond interest) by up to 15 percent. Other compulsory payments include social security payments, pension payments, and medical insurance, which constitute approximately 30 percent of the salary fund.

The code has been plagued by problems with tax collection since its inception less than three years ago. In the first nine months of 1996, tax revenues fell by 3.5 billion tenge; the government collected 10 percent less than it had expected and tax revenues have continued to decline in 1997-98. One reason for the decline is that the government has attempted to apply the law retroactively by collecting back payments from businesses and citizens. Tax evasion is endemic. Citizens are not accustomed to paying taxes, entrepreneurs misreport their income to maintain a substantial profit, and tax inspectors have little training or resources for detecting fraud. Evasion occurs even at the highest levels. In November 1996, Nazarbayev ordered all Kazakh state officials to supply personal income declarations to the tax authorities within 10 days.

In order to improve tax collection, a new tax code is being discussed in the Mazhlis. Mazhlis chairman Marat Ospanov has proposed that the tax commission be made independent of finance ministry control. Nazarbayev has also claimed that the collection of taxes from the 20 major enterprises under foreign management was "inadequate." Many foreign companies have been attracted to investing in Kazakhstan largely due to tax exemptions and reduced tax rates. Nazarbayev claimed that the government was partly at fault for not "properly regulating" those businesses.

2. Does fiscal policy encourage private savings, investment, and earnings? (Has there been any reform/alteration of revenue and budget policies? How large are budget deficits and overall debt? Is the financing of the social insurance/pension system sustainable? What proportion of the budget is taken up by subsidies to firms and individuals?) The Kazakh government began to reform its budgetary process at the beginning of 1997. The government is now responsible for determining budgetary priorities, integrating the annual investment program in the country's medium-term fiscal framework, and giving the finance ministry the leading role in budget policy. The budget deficit rose from 2.4 percent of the GDP in 1996 to 3.7 percent in 1997 due to reduced collection rates and the government's payment of outstanding pension arrears. It is expected to increase to 5.5 percent in 1998. The government plans to cover the deficit through the sale of state securities and loans from international financial institutions, including the World Bank and the Asian Development Bank. Currently, more than 70 percent of the budget deficit is financed by external sources. The remainder is covered with long-term bonds, short-term bills, and credits from the National bank of Kazakhstan (NBK). At the end of 1997, the domestic debt stood at $2.5 billion, or 11 percent of GDP.

After a series of demonstrations and strikes, Nazarbayev pledged that all pension arrears would be paid by the end of 1997. By September, more than $250 million had already been paid to pensioners.

The Kazakh government and the World Bank are currently developing a comprehensive pension reform proposal with the assistance of the World Bank. The new system will gradually eliminate the current pay-as-you-go system. Private pensions will replace state pension funds, and a minimum 10 percent employee contribution will be mandatory. The minimum retirement age will be increased to 63 years for men and 58 years for women by the year 2001. According to Russian media, Kazakhstan will receive a $100 million loan from the Asian Development Bank to assist in implementing this reform.

3. Has there been banking reform? (Is the central bank independent? What are its responsibilities? Is it effective in setting and/or implementing monetary policy? What is the actual state of the private banking sector? Does it conform to international standards? Are depositors protected? Since mid-1995, the NBK has been attempting to implement a strict fiscal and monetary policy and promote bank consolidation. At end of 1994, there were 184 banks. By the end of January 1995, there were only 130. In 1995, the scale of 40 state-owned banks yielded $394.61 million in privatization revenue. In 1995, Kazakhstan adopted a restrictive banking code that made it difficult for foreign banks to enter the country, but it is being revised in order to allow five Russian banks to enter the market.

In 1996, 15 banks were closed as the NBK continued its consolidations. In addition, its plan to privatize 13 state-owned banks was largely successful. By mid-January 1998, the number of banks had fallen to 77, including five state banks, one international bank, and 20 joint ventures with foreign firms. The central bank, however, still receives directives from the president.

In large part due to these reforms, Kazakhstan's banking system appears to be improving. The chairman of the NBK reported in January 1998 that the total capital of the banking system was $430 million — an increase of $190 million from the previous year. He also stated that, as of December 1997, bank deposits by Kazakh citizens had increased by 39 percent from the level at the beginning of the year. In order to encourage more foreign interest in the banking sector, the government plans to amend to the existing banking law to allow foreign banks to participate fully in providing the charter capital of local commercial banks. Currently, the law limits their participation to 25 percent.

4. How sound is the national currency? (Is the value of the currency fixed, or does it float? How convertible is the currency? How large are the hard currency reserves? Has exchange

rate policy been stable or predictable?) Since 1994, the NBK has pledged to keep the growth of monetary aggregates under strict control. Its monetary policy is to keep the exchange rate stable with high interest rates and to sterilize the expansionary effects of large capital flows by issuing NBK notes. Nevertheless, inflation remains a serious problem, although it fell from 41.6 percent in 1996 to 19.6 percent in 1997. As a result, the government allowed the exchange rate of the tenge to drop from 73 to 77.4 to the dollar. In October 1997, the NBK reported that it held $1.6 billion in hard currency reserves.

The NBK allows the tenge to float. It is fully convertible with the U.S. dollar. In July 1996, Kazakhstan accepted Article 8 of the International Monetary Fund Charter, which envisages full convertibility of the currency. Nevertheless, Kazakh banks require that legal entities that seek to withdraw funds from hard currency accounts in local banks present an invoice for goods or services to be purchased to prove that the currency is needed. Foreign companies have complained that this requirement is burdensome, since businesses often cannot predict future expenses in any given month.

5. Is there a functioning capital market infrastructure? (Are there existing or planned commodities, bond, and stock markets? What are the mechanisms for investment and lending? What government bodies have authority to regulate capital markets?) In December 1996, Kazakh officials issued the country's first Eurobond. The embattled tenge was strengthened as a result of a doubling of the planned US$100 million issue. The price of the $200 million three-year bond, which was organized by the Dutch bank ABN AMRO Hoare Govett, was set to yield 9.3 percent or 350 basis points above comparable U.S. Treasury notes. Officials admitted that the bond was issued not so much to raise cash as to draw favorable financial attention to the remote former Soviet republic. Dealers at Kazakh banks stated that the issue would temporarily strengthen the tenge, which had fallen sharply against the dollar. Nevertheless, Western economists remain concerned that the issue will adversely affect the republic's commitment to stringent IMF- and World Bank-backed market economic reforms. On September 23, 1997, the Kazakh government issued its second five-year Eurobond for $350 million.

In early 1996, the finance ministry began to issue treasury bills, for which demand remains strong. Some blame the success of these government bills for the lack of activity on Almaty's Central Asian Stock Exchange (CASE), which has operated since mid-1995. Others, such as the chief of the National Commission for Securities in Kazakhstan, an independent organization that supervises private securities exchange, contend that the lack of activity on CASE was not caused by the diversion of capital to government bills, but by investors waiting for the depository system to be instituted and for the opportunity to reap greater profits from share dealing. On March 31, 1998, the National Securities Commission revoked the operating license of CASE, although activity had practically ceased after the establishment of the Kazakhstan Stock Exchange in September 1997. The Kazakhstan Stock Exchange is now the only stock market in the country.

In 1997, demand for government bonds from foreign investors reportedly increased as a result of increasing confidence in the monetary and exchange rate policies of the NBK. Currently, ex-ante yields on three- and six-month bills are 12 and 22 percent, respectively.

In April 1998, the Kazakh government signed an agreement with six investment firms that had been chosen to manage the stock exchange sale of a portion of the state's minority holdings in two major metals companies and two major oil firms.

Microeconomics 4.75/7

1. Are property rights guaranteed? (Are there both formal and de facto protections of private real estate and intellectual property? Is there a land registry with the authority and capability to ensure accurate recording of who owns what? What are the procedures for expropriation, including measures for compensation and challenge? Have any seizures taken place?) The concept of private ownership was introduced in the civil code of March 1995. According to the 1995 constitution, private property is an inviolable right. The concept of private ownership of land was also recognized in December 1995 legislation. In early 1996, the government approved a Land Registry Form for the ownership of land and permanent land use, but its provisions have still not taken effect. In addition, there are still no clear procedures for expropriation.

Despite a number of laws that guarantee the protection of intellectual property — including the Patent Law, the Law on Trademarks, and a special section of the Civil Code — widespread violations continue. These infringements are of special concern to the government because the exercise of intellectual property rights is one of the key prerequisites for admission to the World Trade Organization (WTO).

2. To what extent have prices been liberalized? What subsidies remain? Prices have been liberalized in every economic sector except basic foodstuffs. Enterprises that are still state-owned and all of the agricultural sector continue to receive subsidies.

3. Is it possible to own and operate a business? (Has there been legislation regarding the formation, dissolution, and transfer of businesses, and is the law respected? Do there exist overly cumbersome bureaucratic hurdles that effectively hinder the ability to own and dispose of a business? Are citizens given access to information on commercial law? Is the law applied fairly?) The Civil Code of March 1995 also encoded basic freedoms of entrepreneurial activity including the right to own and operate a private business without governmental interference. Nevertheless, some bureaucratic hurdles effectively limit this right. There is no comprehensive legislation on the formation, dissolution, and transfer of businesses. In addition, business registration procedures change frequently and arbitrarily, and registration can be denied without explanation. In general, citizens outside Almaty also lack information regarding basic commercial law and bankruptcy procedures.

4. Are courts effective, transparent, efficient, and quick in reaching decisions on property and contract disputes? What alternative mechanisms for adjudicating disputes exist? Kazakh courts are not effective, transparent, efficient, or quick in reaching decisions on property and contract disputes. Most foreign investors rely instead on private arbitration and international courts.

5. Is business competition encouraged? (Are monopolistic practices limited in law and in

practice? If so, how? To what degree is "insider" dealing a hindrance to open competition? Are government procurement policies open and unbiased?) Since late 1997, the law has subjected natural monopolies in Kazakhstan to the special regulatory regimes that are imposed on these industries in developed market economies. According to the Department of Anti-monopoly Policy in Kazakhstan's Ministry of Economy and Trade, 39 firms in the energy and basic infrastructure sectors have already been designated as natural monopolies.

6. To what extent has international trade been liberalized? To what degree has there been simplification/overhaul of customs and tariff procedures, and are these applied fairly? What informal trade barriers exist? Kazakhstan is currently a member of several international trade organizations and expects to be admitted to the WTO in the near future. The country's trade turnover with countries of the Economic Cooperation Organization (ECO) amounted to $538 million in the first six months of 1996 — an increase of more than 12 percent from 1995, according to Kazakh Deputy Foreign Minister Vladimir Alesin. The country has launched 184 joint ventures with ECO-members Iran, Pakistan, Turkey, Azerbaijan, Afghanistan, Kazakhstan, Kyrgyzstan, Tajikistan, Turkmenistan, and Uzbekistan.

Kazakhstan's primary trading partners are other former Soviet republics. The country's imports from the CIS increased from 61.2 percent in 1994 to 71.4 percent in 1995. From Russia alone, imports increased to 46.2 percent in 1995 from 31.5 percent in 1994. A January 1995 customs union between Belarus, Russia, and Kazakhstan effectively lowered barriers to trade and investment between the three nations by greatly reducing tariffs and import-export requirements. A March 1996 agreement added Kyrgyzstan to the customs union.

The average tariff rate for Kazakhstan is approximately 12 percent, but tariffs are applied unevenly. Companies that directly negotiate separate agreements with the government can establish different rates. Among the country's other formal and informal trade barriers are the expensive licensing system, including highly paid, mandatory consultancies in many industries; lack of access to government officials with the authority and will to assist investors in resolving commercial and trade problems; disorderly and inconsistent imposition of customs duties; problems associated with quality and safety certifications; vague, weak, and arbitrary implementation of commercial laws; and corruption among customs officials who arbitrarily confiscate imports and exports.

7. To what extent has foreign investment and capital flow been encouraged or constrained? Kazakhstan is open to investment. There are no major sectors of the economy that are closed to foreign investors. By law, foreign investors can participate in all privatization processes. Enterprises can be leased as a first step in the process. In 1994, the government began to allow foreign companies to assume control of major industrial enterprises through long-term management contracts. In 1995, it began to privatize entire large-scale enterprises. Foreign investors do not appear to encounter discrimination after making thin initial investments, but many foreign companies have complained that they must insulate their investments from barrages of decrees, bureaucratic interference, and legislative changes.

As a result of its proactive policies, Kazakhstan enjoys one of the highest rates of foreign direct investment in the CIS. Recent improvements in the country's investment climate include the March

1997 reorganization that created a "one-stop shopping center" for foreign investors; the May 1997 amendments to the 1994 Foreign Investment Law, which simplifies the registration process for foreign investors; and the January 1997 adoption of a Law on Bankruptcy that establishes bankruptcy and liquidation procedures for insolvent debtors.

According to the Director of the States Investments Committee, Kazakhstan attracted $756 million in foreign direct investment during the first half of 1997. In 1996, it attracted $1.638 billion, or 7.9 percent of GDP for 1996. South Korean companies, which are by far the largest foreign investors in the country, invested nearly $400 million of the $756 million for the first half of 1997 and have cumulative investments worth more than $1 billion. In Seoul in October 1997, Kazakhstan and the Daewoo corporation concluded three new investment protocols. These agreements provided for the investment of approximately $370 million in Kazakhstan's telecommunications sector and the construction of a $250 million press center in Almaty.

According to the State Investments Committee, Kazakhstan's foreign direct investment is the fifth largest among post-Communist countries. *Per-capita* Kazakhstan ranks second only to Hungary. These investments have eased Kazakhstan's strained balance-of-payments position. At the same time, because most of these investments are narrowly concentrated in the energy sector, they have yet to generate large returns in other parts of the economy or significantly affect living standards. This rate of foreign direct investment is likely to continue in 1998.

8. Has there been reform of the energy sector? (To what degree has the energy sector been restructured? Is the energy sector more varied, and is it open to private competition? Is the country overly dependent on one or two other countries for energy — including whether exported fuels must pass through one or more countries to reach the markets?) In the former Soviet Union, some republics supplied energy in certain forms to other republics while other energy sources remained untapped. In Central Asia, Kazakhstan has an enormous supply of unexploited oil reserves, but it depends upon Uzbekistan for natural gas. Kyrgyzstan has the potential to develop hydroelectric power, but it is dependent upon Kazakhstan and Uzbekistan for oil and gas respectively; and Uzbekistan has consistently been a large supplier of natural gas to its neighbors, but lacks the resources either to produce gas more efficiently or to develop other sources of energy. Moreover, the Soviet infrastructure, which was designed for the domestic exploitation and transportation of energy resources, is not at all suited to the political reality of independent republics. Oil refineries were built in eastern Kazakhstan, whereas the oil reserves are found in the West, and pipelines were constructed to pass through Russian territory.

Reform in the energy sector has largely taken the form of increased foreign investment, in large part because a great deal of capital is necessary to exploit energy sources. In Moscow on December 6, 1996, participants in the Caspian Pipeline Consortium signed an agreement that determined their respective stakes in the Tengiz pipeline. Fifty percent of the project will be divided between the governments of Russia (24 percent), Kazakhstan (19 percent), and Oman (7 percent). The remaining 50 percent will be divided between Lukoil (12.5 percent), Rosneft (7.5 percent), Chevron (15 percent), Mobil (7.5 percent), Agip (2 percent), British Gas (2 percent), Munaigas (1.75 percent), and Oryx (1.75 percent).

In August 1996, Almaty's state-owned energy utility was sold to Tractebel, a Belgian firm.

Tractebel agreed to invest $358 million in renovating the system and to contribute a further $340 million to the state treasury. The large Yuzhneftegaz oil enterprise, which holds 581 million barrels of oil in central Kazakhstan, was sold to Hurricane Hydrocarbons, a Canadian firm, for $120 million. Hurricane agreed to invest a further $280 million in the enterprise within six years. The Kazakh government anticipated that it will receive more than $2 billion in taxes and royalties from the deal during the next 20 years.

In May 1997, Medco Energy Corporation acquired an 85 percent share of the Mangistaumunaygaz joint stock company, which was then re-sold to Central Asia Petroleum. In June 1997, Chinese National Petroleum bought 60 percent of the Aktyubinskneft joint-stock shares. In July, it acquired 60 percent of the Uzen Oil Fields. These two sales virtually completed the privatization of Kazakhstan's major state oil and gas holdings.

These companies continue to face difficulties in exporting their products due to the lack of pipelines connecting this land-locked country to European and Asian markets. Construction of Kazakhstan's first pipeline — a $2 billion, 1,500 kilometer project — is scheduled to begin in 1999.

KYRGYZ REPUBLIC

Freedom in the World Ratings, 1989-1998

	1989-90	1990-91	1991-92	1992-93	1993-94	1994-95	1995-96	1996-97	1997-98
Political Rights	-	-	3	4	5	4	4	4	4
Civil Liberties	-	-	4	2	3	3	4	4	4
Status	-	-	PF	PF	PF	PF	PF	PF	PF

Polity: Transitional
Economy: Transitional
Population: 4,405,000
PPP: $1,927
Ethnic Groups: Kyrghiz (54 percent), Russian (28 percent), Uzbek (15 percent), German, others
Capital: Bishkek

Political Process 5.00/7

1. When did national legislative elections occur? Were they free and fair? How were they judged by the domestic and international election monitoring organizations? Who composes the government? Prior to independence, elections to the Supreme Soviet took place on February 25 and March 4, 1990. Virtually all of the 350 seats were won by the Communists, who were nevertheless divided between liberal and conservative deputies. The Supreme Court was effectively abolished in a referendum on October 22, 1994. It was replaced by the *Jogorku Kenesh*, a new bicameral legislature that includes a full-time 35-member Legislative Assembly that is elected nationally, and a 70-member Assembly of People's Representatives that meets sporadically and is elected by region. Approximately 1,050 candidates and 12 parties vied for seats in the parliamentary elections of February 5, 1995. Single candidates received majorities in only two electoral districts for the Legislative Assembly and 11 for the Assembly of People's Representatives. Most of the remaining seats were filled in a second electoral round on February 19, 1995. Due to the strong showing of independent candidates, no party won a clear victory. Governing officials, intellectuals, and clan leaders won 82 seats. Both the first and second round of elections, which were monitored by international electoral observers from the U.N., the Organization for Security and Cooperation in Europe (OSCE), and the EU, were marred by irregularities. Violations included ballot-box stuffing, inflation of voter turnout, and interference by local administrations. Nevertheless, the results were validated, in large part due to the estimated high cost of holding another full round of national elections. The next elections are scheduled for 2000. Electoral reforms are under consideration. Political parties favor party lists, while the government prefers a quota system that allocates only one in five seats to candidates on a party list. The Central Electoral Commission also favors the 50 percent threshold of voter turnout for validation of an election. On March 25, 1998, parliament approved a new government, which is led by Prime Minister Kubanchybek Jumaliev.

President Askar Akayev nominated Jumaliev after then-Prime Minister Apas Jumagolov resigned unexpectedly on March 24, 1998. While the prime minister must report to parliament on the activities of the government, the president appoints most government officials in accordance with changes introduced to the constitution in a controversial 1996 referendum. The largely ceremonial post of prime minister is subordinate to the president. On April 3, 1998 the president issued a decree that restructured and, for the second time, reduced the powers of the executive.

2. When did presidential elections occur? Were they free and fair? Askar Akayev was elected president by the Supreme Soviet on October 27, 1990. He was re-elected to a five-year presidential term by popular vote on October 12, 1991. In a January 31, 1994 referendum, his economic reform program received an approval rating of 96.2 percent. In early presidential elections on December 24, 1995, Akayev won 71.6 percent of the vote. The decision to hold the vote ten months early was part of a compromise between the president and the newly-elected parliament. Nevertheless, this attempt to prevent Akayev from extending his term of office by referendum, as other Central Asian leaders had done, raised constitutional problems. By overlooking the 1991 presidential elections and tracing his mandate to the 1990 Soviet-era elections, Akayev contradicted arguments that he had made when he disbanded the Supreme Soviet in September 1994 — namely, that the May 1993 constitution rendered that body null and void. In addition, the Central Electoral Commission obliged candidates to violate the constitution by collecting signatures in every region of the country. The open, multicandidate presidential election of 1995 was marred by the de-registration of three candidates immediately prior to the vote. Of the 11 original opposition candidates, only former Communist Party Secretary Absamat Masaliev and former parliamentary speaker Medtkhan Sherimkulov ran against Akayev. Masaliev received 24.4 percent of the vote, most of which was based in his home province of Osh, while Sherimkulov won 1.7 percent. Masaliev declared that he had won more than 50 percent of the vote in Osh and that the government forged the results in that district. Early elections left the opposition with insufficient time to collect the necessary signatures required to secure places on the ballot and organize political campaigns for their candidates. Two days before the elections, Sherimkulov's campaign chairman and a campaign worker were detained without bail. In April 1996, they were convicted of libel and sentenced to one-year suspended prison sentences for allegedly distributing leaflets stating that President Akayev was an ethnic Kazak. They denied the charges. Nevertheless, the OSCE and the U.N. declared that the elections were "generally free and open."

3. Is the electoral system multiparty-based? Are there at least two viable political parties functioning at all levels of the government? The right to form parties is enshrined in the constitution, and the government encourages the formation of social and political organizations, which are protected under the 1991 Law on Public Organizations. Party leaders have drafted new laws governing political parties, but these proposals have been rejected by the government. There are less than two political parties that function at all levels of government. In general, government and presidential officials resign from their parties before taking office. For example, the former chairwoman of the opposition Ata-Meken Party resigned from her party when she was appointed as a presidential department head in 1994. Although political parties play an insignificant role in elections, elections are strongly contested. Regional and clan ties (fealty to individual leaders within those contexts) play a more important role. Despite legitimate complaints about the 1995 elections, 12 political parties participated and were not restricted in their ability to nominate candidates or in their choice of campaign issues. In the 1991 presidential election, the incumbent faced no opposition. In the 1995 early presidential election, only Masaliyev had the backing of an established party, the Party of Communists of Kyrgyzstan. None of the winners of the 1997 by-elections had any party affiliation, and parties nominated few candidates. In parliament, less than half the deputies claim party affiliation. Ten parties are represented in parliament, where voting seldom follows strict party lines.

4. How many parties have been legalized? Are any particular parties illegal? Eighteen parties are registered in Kyrgyzstan. The Democratic Movement of Kyrgyzstan, which was founded in 1990, was the first significant political organization to emerge. It is an umbrella organization of approximately 30 smaller groups and was registered as a political party in 1993. The Party of Communists of Kyrgyzstan, the successor to the former ruling Kyrgyz Communist Party, was reconstituted in 1992. It is the largest party and claims to have approximately 25,000 members. Although it has staged demonstrations and has a small representation in parliament, it is not considered to be active, adversarial, or influential. In an environment in which parties are not a significant part of the political landscape, the Social Democratic Party of Kyrgyzstan represents the country's ruling elite. It was founded in 1993 to create a base of support for President Akayev and to buttress his reformist pro-market agenda. It claims 22,500 members. The Democratic Party of Free Kyrgyzstan, which was established in 1991, has served as a moderate nationalist, pro-market opposition to the government. Topchubek Turgunaliev, its chairman, was convicted of embezzlement in January 1997 in a trial that may have been politically motivated. Other moderate nationalist parties include Ata-Meken and the Ashar Movement. There are also several ethnic-oriented groupings, including the Accord Slavic Association (*Soglasiye*) and issue-oriented movements, such as the Agrarian Party and Ecological Movement, the Women's Democratic Party, the Party of City-Dwellers, and the Human Rights Movement and Patriotic Party. The Ministry of Justice refused to register the Movement For Deliverance From Poverty in early 1997. Religious-based political parties are forbidden.

5. What proportion of the population belongs to political parties? The percentage of the overall population that belongs to political parties is negligible. Most registered parties have very few members, lack a platform or program, or are inactive. Fewer than one-fifth of the candidates in the 1995 parliamentary elections were affiliated with registered parties, and only a small number were actually elected.

6. What has been the trend of voter turnout at the municipal, provincial, and national levels in recent years? Approximately 90 percent of eligible voters participated in the October 1991 presidential elections. In the January 1994 referendum on President Akayev's performance, 96.9 percent participated. Eighty-seven percent took part in the October 1994 local elections and the constitutional referendum on a new legislative structure. In the 1995 elections, 62 percent participated in the first round and 61 percent participated in the second round. In the December 1995 presidential election, 86 percent voted. In the February 1996 constitutional referendum on enhanced presidential powers, 96.4 participated.

Civil Society 4.50/7

1. How many nongovernmental organizations (NGOs) have come into existence since 1988? What is the number of charitable/nonprofit organizations? Are there locally led efforts to increase philanthropy and volunteerism? What proportion of the population is active in private voluntary activity (from polling data)? Kyrgyzstan's vigorous NGO sector continues to grow. Of the several thousand NGOs that are reportedly registered, an estimated 500 are active. Of these, a core of 70 to 80 are considered dynamic by organizations, such as the National Democratic Institute, that work with them. Among the more active NGOs are the Bureau on Human Rights and the Rule of Law, the Independent Journalists Association, and the Women's Congress. Difficult economic conditions in the country mitigate against a growth in volunteerism and philanthropy.

2. What is the legal and regulatory environment for NGOs (i.e., ease of registration, legal rights, government regulation, taxation, procurement, and access-to-information issues)? To what extent is NGO activism focused on improving the legal and regulatory environment? In general, the government does not interfere with the establishment and development of NGOs, which must register with the Ministry of Justice. At both the national and international levels, exchanges of information and communication are unimpeded. NGOs participate in the drafting of legislation, including a pending land code and a law governing NGO activity. Some groups are involved in lobbying the executive branch and are represented, for example, on the president's Coordinating Council on Sustainable Development.

3. What is the organizational capacity of NGOs? Do management structures clearly delineate authority and responsibility? Is information available on NGO management issues in the native language? Is there a core of experienced practitioners/trainers to serve as consultants or mentors to less developed organizations? The organizational capacity of NGOs has grown due to local determination, external support, and a political climate more favorable than elsewhere in Central Asia. A host of American, European, and international aid organizations have established programs to assist, or work in partnership with, NGOs in Kyrgyzstan. In many cases, active NGOs receive monetary and non-monetary assistance from several external partners simultaneously. Despite the growth of the NGO sector and the enhanced organizational capacity of some organizations, many NGOs are nascent and overly dominated by personalities. Management structures may be absent, with a tiny group of individuals sharing authority and responsibility or one individual dominating a small organization. Most materials germane to organizing and managing an NGO are in Russian rather than Kyrgyz. A core of foreign and local mentors is available to assist less developed organizations. The establishment last year of the 148-strong Forum of NGOs signals further coordination and mutual self-help.

4. Are NGOs financially viable? What is their tax status? Are they obliged to and do they typically disclose revenue sources? Do government procurement opportunities exist for pri-

vate not-for-profit providers of services? A core of viable NGOs exist. In general, their financial resources are not indigenously raised, but rather from international donor agencies, the EU, and U.S.-supported public or private programs. Kyrgyzstan has developed a complex tax system with high rates but does not collect taxes from NGOs. A prospective law on NGOs permits some groups, such as sports clubs, to avoid registration. Most organizations would be tax-exempt, although not all donations to these organizations would necessarily be tax-exempt.

5. Are there free trade unions? How many workers belong to these unions? Is the number of workers belonging to trade unions growing or decreasing? What is the numerical/proportional membership of farmers' groups, small business associations, etc. The 1992 labor law provides for the right of all workers to form and belong to trade unions. It also permits them to join confederations and to affiliate with international trade union bodies. The only trade union umbrella organization is the Federation of Trade Unions of the Kyrgyz Republic, the successor to the former official Soviet-era trade union. It has 20 branches and more than one million members. While it actively cooperates with the government, it has been critical of some policies, especially privatization, and their effect on living standards. A growing number of smaller unions unaffiliated with the umbrella organization have emerged, but their memberships are small. Labor unions are unlikely to grow in size and number in the near future because much of the Kyrgyz Republic's limited industrial base is idle. After 1994, private farmers associations began to grow due to the encouragement of the government and international donor agencies, which funneled inputs and loans through them. According to the Citizens Network on Foreign Affairs, there are 26 general farmers' associations and 15 to 20 other commodity-specific associations. In general, farmers' associations at the district level have from 30 to 50 members, and their regional counterparts have up to 300 members. These organizations typically disseminate information to members through a bulletin or newspaper, hold educational seminars, and attempt to influence elected representatives. Commodity associations, such as the Cotton-Growers' Association of Kara-Su, serve a commercial purpose, such as collective marketing of crops and purchase of agricultural inputs. The larger associations, such as *Diykan Ordo* (Peasants Union) and *Cholpon-Ata* (Sheepbreeders Association) have memberships of approximately 500. Entrepreneurial associations include the Union of Managers and Entrepreneurs and the Union of Entrepreneurs and Small Business Workers, which has tens of thousands of members.

6. What forms of interest group participation in politics are legal? What types of interest groups are active in the political and policy process? The 1993 constitution limits participation in politics to parties. Citizens have the right to associate, and the government generally respects this right in practice. Interest groups, including labor unions, political parties, and public associations, are required to register with the Ministry of Justice in accordance with the 1991 Law on Public Organizations. Religious associations must register with the State Commission on Religious Affairs, which was established in 1996. If they engage in contractual activities, they must also register with the Ministry of Justice. The 1991 law prohibits public associations that adversely affect the public health, morals, or territorial integrity of the country. It also prohibits the formation of groups that provoke religious or ethnic enmity. An Uighur organization was charged with political activity

— promoting the secession of northwest China — and suspended. After a change of leadership, it was re-registered. In general, the participation in politics is limited. Nevertheless, indigenous NGOs working in conjunction with foreign counterpart organizations are active in several areas, including legal and agricultural reform, the media, and human rights.

7. How is the not-for-profit/NGO sector perceived by the public and government officials? What is the nature of media coverage of NGOs? To what extent do government officials engage with NGOs? The NGO sector is viewed positively by the public and government officials, especially those who seek to attract foreign investment and integrate the Kyrgyz Republic into Western political institutions. In general, media coverage is positive, especially in the growing independent electronic media. Officials associated with the presidency and some parliamentary deputies are particularly receptive to engaging with NGOs.

Independent Media 4.25/7

1. Are there legal protections for press freedoms? The constitution provides for a free press. The print and broadcast media operate under the 1992 Law on Mass Media, which prohibits material that promotes violence, ethnic and religious intolerance; the desecration of national norms, ethics, and symbols, and pornography. A new mass media law, which was considered to be more restrictive than the 1972 law, was passed in parliament in 1997 and vetoed by President Akayev. A draft criminal code was to take effect on January 1, 1998, but it remains under consideration in parliament. Its provisions, which appear to be similar to those in the Soviet-era code, could be used to prosecute journalists for criticizing government officials. There is no law on television and radio broadcasting. Media organizations must register with the Ministry of Justice. To produce television and radio programs, an organization must also register with the National Communications Agency, which was established in 1997 and reports to the Office of the President; receive a license; submit its programming schedule; and receive permission to use a frequency. According to *Internews*, of 14 private television and 11 radio stations, only two radio stations are broadcasting legally.

2. Are there legal penalties for libeling officials? Are there legal penalties for "irresponsible" journalism? Have these laws been enforced to harass journalists? According to constitutional amendments, the honor and dignity of the president are inviolable. Libel remains a criminal offense. In November 1997, President Akayev declared his intention to remove libel as an offense under the criminal code and transfer it to the civil code. He later argued that egregious cases of libel would still be subject to prison sentences. Debate on this issue continued in early 1998. In 1995 and 1996, successful criminal libel suits were filed against the newspaper *Res Publica*. In May 1997, two journalists from the newspaper were sentenced to 18 months in prison for criminal libel against a prominent industrialist who held substantial media interests. In June, one of the journalists received a suspended sentence. In August, the other was released by the Supreme Court in what was widely regarded as a politically motivated decision. Earlier in the year, the newspaper *Kriminal* was closed after the appearance of its first issue, which was highly critical of the president, his wife, the prime minister, and other government officials. In September 1997, the president's press secretary announced eight new cases of criminal libel against *Asaba*, an opposition newspaper. Also in

September, an Osh newspaper was threatened with court action for "insulting the honor and dignity" of the police in alleged cases of drug corruption. The number of criminal libel cases increased in 1997. Harassment of print, television, and radio operations continue largely by means of unofficial contacts. Government officials call editors to discourage unflattering coverage. Evidence of economic and legal harassment, including use of the tax inspectorate, continues.

3. What proportion of media is privatized? What are the major private newspapers, television stations, and radio stations? Kyrgyzstan's state-controlled media have not been privatized. Instead, independent media, which are often dependent upon the state for transmission or publishing, have emerged to compete with state-controlled organs. There are four national official newspapers, and every region, district, and town has its own official serial publication. Many regional publications, however, are closing due to insufficient resources. There are two state-owned radio channels and one state television station in Bishkek. Independent media, especially in the electronic sphere, are proliferating. The print media, which are based primarily in Bishkek and Osh, are in decline. Between 20 and 30 official and independent newspapers appear regularly. Major private newspapers include *Vecherniy Bishkek*, which has a daily circulation of 40,000 to 70,000; *Delo Nomer*, a weekly with a circulation of 60,000 to 90,000; *Res Publica*, a weekly with a circulation of 7,000 to 10,000; and *Asaba*. All of these are based in Bishkek. There are several private television and radio stations of widely differing size, staff, and capability. These include Pyramida television and radio in Bishkek and Osh; Independent Bishkek Television; Asman television in Bishkek; Vosst television and radio in Bishkek; and Almaz radio in Bishkek, Karakol, Osh, and Balykchy.

4. Are the private media financially viable? The mass media have made significant strides in development since independence, but still face tremendous hurdles in reaching financial viability. These obstacles include distribution problems and a lack of sufficient advertising revenue, according to a 1998 U.S. AID-funded study. Frequently, newspapers are published for only a few months and then close due to a lack of revenue or a withdrawal of support from sponsors.

5. Are the media editorially independent? Are the media's news gathering functions affected by interference from government or private owners? Self-censorship is widespread. Most news is merely official reporting on government-sponsored events and the activities of the president. Journalists continue to find it difficult to obtain interviews with government officials and to gather information, although in 1997, two vaguely worded laws ("On Access to Information" and "On the Rights and Responsibilities of Journalists") addressed these issues. Private owners, some of whom have significant other business interests and political connections, are also reluctant to publish critical reports on the government.

6. Is the distribution system for newspapers privately or governmentally controlled? All newspaper printing facilities, with the exception of one small commercial plant in Bishkek, were owned and managed by the government until late 1997. The majority of enterprises operating under the umbrella of the state publishing company then became independent. In March 1998, the government declared its readiness to privatize the rump state publishing company.

7. What proportion of the population is connected to the Internet? Are there any restrictions on Internet access to private citizens? The proportion of the population that is connected to the Internet is growing, but remains negligible. E-mail access is now available in Bishkek, Osh, Kara-Balta, and Karakol, but the costs remain prohibitively high for most citizens.

8. What has been the trend in press freedom as measured by Freedom House's *Survey of Press Freedom*? Freedom House's annual *Survey of Press Freedom* rated the Kyrgyz Republic "Not Free" from 1996 and 1998.

Governance and Public Administration 4.25/7

1. Is the legislature the effective rule-making institution? The legislature is empowered to create and enact legislation. Amendments to the constitution in 1996 weakened the legislature and strengthened the executive, which can issue presidential edicts. Nevertheless, parliament has become increasingly active. In 1997, it passed 158 laws; in 1996, 66 laws; and in 1995, 25 laws. Parliament has also over-ridden presidential vetoes. Nevertheless, it is subordinate to the executive and held in low esteem by the public, in large part due to charges of corruption and self-enrichment.

2. Is substantial power decentralized to sub-national levels of government? What specific authority do the sub-national levels have? In Kyrgyzstan, the six *oblasts* (regions) and 44 *raions* (districts) are administered by *akims* (governors), local Councils of Peoples Deputies, and City Councils. The government is considering a merger of four of the regions into two. The president appoints regional, raion-level and town leaders. Regional, district, and town councils are elected. In practice, sub-national levels of government are weak and are dominated by the central authorities and their local representatives. Although the Mayor of Bishkek is an elected position by law, President Akayev appointed the current office-holder.

3. Are subnational officials chosen in free and fair elections? Elections to local legislatures were held concurrently with parliamentary elections in February 1995. Vote-tampering did occur, but at lesser levels than in the national elections. The mayors of Bishkek and Osh were also elected at this time. The authority of governors has been strengthened since 1996. Governors can now cancel any decision reached by locally-elected bodies if they run counter to national directives.

4. Do the executive and legislative bodies operate openly and with transparency? Is draft legislation easily accessible to the media and the public? Government is rarely transparent in Kyrgyzstan. Decisions are often announced publicly just as they are due to take effect. Nevertheless, there has been some progress in increasing public debate and discussion, largely at the instigation of NGOs, independent media, and special interest groups, such as farmers' associations.

5. Do municipal governments have sufficient revenues to carry out their duties? Do municipal governments have control of their own local budgets? Do they raise revenues autonomously or from the central state budget? Municipal governments are responsible for local budget implementation, tax collection, and payment of benefits. In practice, they seldom have sufficient revenues to meet their obligations. In general, they remain dependent upon the central government for a substantial amount of their funding.

6. Do the elected local leaders and local civil servants know how to manage municipal governments effectively? With few exceptions, local and regional governments are ineffective. Dilatory work habits, excessive centralization, and extreme financial constraints make this unlikely to change.

7. When did the constitutional/legislative changes on local power come into effect? Has there been a reform of the civil service code/system? Are local civil servants employees of the local or central government? In 1992 and 1994, amendments to the Law on Self-Governance gave more authority to the local governors at the expense of the regional assemblies. They can call elections, draft the program for socio-economic development, and manage the budget allocation process. Civil servants such as tax inspectors and police officers are employees of the central government. The staffs of local administrations are local government employees.

Rule of Law 4.50/7

1. Is there a post-Communist constitution? How does the judicial system interpret and enforce the constitution? Are there specific examples of judicial enforcement of the constitution in the last year? A post-Communist constitution was approved by the Supreme Soviet on May 5, 1993. It provided for a presidential-parliamentary system with a strong executive. A referendum in 1994 effectively abolished this legislative body and replaced it with a bicameral one. More than half the constitution was amended in a controversial 1996 referendum that concentrated power in the executive branch and expanded the president's authority. The revisions give the president the power to appoint the prime minister and the chairman of the central bank and nominate the chairman of the Central Electoral Commission. Approval for these appointments requires the consent of the Assembly of People's Representatives. Most deputies in this body represent the local and regional administrative leaders who are themselves appointed by the president. According to the constitution, deputies may not serve as governor or officials, though in practice, several do. The president has the power to dissolve parliament if his choice of prime minister is rejected by parliament three times. In general, the executive dominates the judiciary. In November 1996, the Constitutional Court ruled that the speaker of the lower house of parliament had been elected unconstitutionally. The legislature accepted the court's ruling and elected a new speaker. Judicial independence from the executive branch, such as ruling on constitutional amendments adopted in the controversial 1996 referendum, is uncommon.

2. Does the constitutional framework provide for human rights? Do the human rights include business and property rights? The constitution recognizes basic human rights and various forms of property and business rights. Land, minerals, water, and forests remain the property of the state. The new Civil Code of June 1996 guarantees fundamental socio-economic rights and liberties and provides for Kyrgyzstan's adherence to a free-market economic system. It also provides for equality of parties in civil law relationships, the inviolability of the person, equal protection of private and all other forms of property, the right to dispose of private property freely, and freedom of contract. Parliament has explored, without conclusion, the codification of human rights in the International Convention on Civil and Political Rights. According to American Bar Association-sponsored analysis, Kyrgyzstan incorporates a statist theory of rights with an approach that recognizes the people as the ultimate sovereign.

3. Has there been basic reform of the criminal code/criminal law? Who authorizes searches and issues warrants? Are suspects and prisoners beaten or abused? Are there excessive delays in the criminal justice system? A new criminal code remains under discussion in parliament. Many of its provisions reflect those in the Soviet-era code. Searches and warrants are issued by prosecutors at the city, regional, district, or town level. Major cases may only be initiated by the Office of the Prosecutor General. Suspects and prisoners are sometimes beaten.

4. Do most judges rule fairly and impartially? Do many remain from the communist era? Prosecutors have greater power than judges in criminal cases. Judges, who do not hold positions for life and receive low wages, are ill-prepared to rule either fairly or impartially. Nevertheless, the government is continuing its efforts to reform the judicial system. Generally accepted international practices, including the presumption of the innocence of the accused, have been introduced. A new system of court administration is being instituted, and sitting judges must pass examinations that test their knowledge of the law and new civil codes. This requirement has resulted in many dismissals and the appointment by the president of many new, younger judges.

5. Are the courts free of political control and influence? How does this compare with the previous year? The constitution provides for an independent judiciary, but the courts remain subordinate to the Ministry of Justice. A number of constitutional amendments provide for greater oversight of the judicial branch by the executive by enhancing the latter's role in appointing the Procurator General and the chairmen of the Constitutional Court, Supreme Court and Supreme (economic) Arbitration Court. In practice, the court system primarily serves the interests of the prosecution, high-ranking officials, and wealthier litigants.

6. What proportion of lawyers is in private practice? How does this compare with the previous year? Very few lawyers are in private practice, but the number is growing.

7. Does the state provide public defenders? Since 1990, the state has provided legal counsel for anyone arrested or charged with a crime. Defense counsels are appointed by the procurator's office. In practice, defense counsels often see defendants only at trial rather than in the first three days of detention, as required by law.

8. Are there effective anti-bias/discrimination laws, including protection of ethnic minority rights? A December 1993 law conferred citizenship on anyone who was a resident of Kyrgyzstan on December 15, 1991, when independence was declared. The May 1993 constitution provides for the rights and freedom of individuals and prohibits discrimination, including on the basis of language. Even after intense and extensive debate, the Russian language has no formal official or protected status in Kyrgyzstan. In 1997, parliament rejected legislation that would have given it official status. Since 1989, Kyrgyz has been the state language. Unlike in some former Soviet republics, Russian is not an "official" language or a language of inter-ethnic communication in Kyrgyzstan.

Corruption **D**

1. What is the magnitude of official corruption in the civil service? Must an average citizen pay a bribe to a bureaucrat in order to receive a service? What services are subject to bribe requests - for example, university entrance, hospital admission, telephone installation, obtaining a license to operate a business, applying for a passport or other official documents? What is the average salary of civil servants at various levels? Bribe-taking is ubiquitous. Civil servants are poorly paid and compensate by accepting bribes. Bribes are needed to accomplish even mundane tasks, such as purchasing a seat on an "overbooked" airplane, obtaining admission to university, or arranging any kind of official business. Salaries range from the equivalent of $40 per month for lower level bureaucrats to $400 per month for parliamentary deputies. The minimum wage is set at the equivalent of $6 per month.

2. Do top policy-makers (the President, ministers, vice-ministers, top court justices, and heads of agencies and commissions) have direct ties to businesses? How strong are such connections and what kinds of businesses are these? The nexus between politics and business appears to be growing in Kyrgyzstan. Topchubek Turgunaliev, the first prime minister, resigned from his post in December 1993 amid accusations of corruption involving the contract to exploit the Kumtor gold mine. His successor resigned in March 1998, after it was reported that he helped to establish an Austrian firm charged with selling Kyrgyz gold abroad and controlled the country's oil and alcohol industries. Allegations of corruption at the highest levels of the executive branch continue. The privatization process is widely considered to have been manipulated by officials in order to benefit their friends and associates. The legislature, particularly the lower house, is widely regarded as a magnet for individuals involved in illegal or corrupt practices. Many deputies are themselves businessmen, and some have reportedly been linked to dubious business schemes. These deputies reportedly rely on their immunity from prosecution to remain in Kyrgyzstan and continue to operate their businesses. In October 1997, the procurator general published a lengthy list of deputies who were accused of corruption. In December, he claimed that more than 10,000 economic crimes had been registered by his office in three and a half years. He also stated that corruption had cost the country approximately $70 million. Politicians and business are linked in such fields as banking, mineral extraction, and sugar production.

3. Do laws requiring financial disclosure and disallowing conflict of interest exist? Have publicized anti-corruption cases been pursued. To what conclusion? In 1996, parliament debated, but did not pass draft legislation to combat corruption and racketeering. It is now drafting ethics laws that will apply not only to parliamentarians, but also to civil servants involved in policy-making. Economic crimes such as tax evasion, embezzlement, and theft of government property are common. Prosecution for these crimes is relatively rare and appears to be directed at opponents of the government. Topchubek Turgunaliev, the leader of the Erk Kyrgyzstan Party, was convicted of embezzlement, fraud, and abuse of his position as a university rector. In April 1996, he was convicted of defaming President Akayev. In December, after leading a demonstration to protest high unemployment and non-payment of pensions, he was tried and convicted of economic crimes, on charges that had earlier been dismissed. He was sentenced to ten years in prison, a term that was later reduced to four, before being released on parole in November 1997.

4. What major anti-corruption initiatives have been implemented? How often are anti-corruption laws and decrees adopted? President Akayev declared a war against corruption in 1996. At a pre-announced and repeatedly delayed meeting of the Security Council in September, ten high officials were accused of corruption. The security minister who directed the anti-corruption campaign was severely injured in an automobile accident a month after the campaign began. He remained in a coma for 14 months before dying in January 1998. Several of those originally accused have left Kyrgyzstan or had the cases against them closed. One was appointed to an ambassadorship and sent abroad. The procurator general began a campaign against corrupt parliamentary deputies in October 1997. In 1997, 144 government officials, including ten parliamentary deputies, were found guilty of corruption-related offenses.

5. How does major corruption-ranking organizations like Transparency International rate this country? Transparency International has not rated the Kyrgyz Republic.

Privatization 4.00/7

1. What percentage of the GDP comes from private ownership? What percentage of the labor force is employed in the private sector? How large is the informal sector of the economy? According to the U.S. Department of Commerce, there are 66,000 non-state businesses, including 1,300 joint stock companies, registered in the Kyrgyz Republic. EBRD estimates that the private sector share in official GDP is approximately 55 percent. Approximately half of medium-sized to large enterprises have been privatized. Through the country's remaining 14 natural and "permitted" monopolies, however, the state still controls a large percentage of industrial assets, employment and production. Approximately 40 percent of the labor force is engaged in agriculture, which remains largely state-controlled. The size of the informal sector is believed to range from 10 to 30 percent of GDP.

2. What major privatization legislation has been passed? What were its substantive features? After the collapse of the Soviet Union, the Kyrgyz Republic quickly adopted a strategy to transform the economy to a market system. It has remained one of the most active CIS reformers and has received approximately $400 million in support from international lending institutions to assist in the transformation process. A number of market-friendly laws have been passed, including the 1991 Law on General Rudiments of Denationalization, Privatization and Entrepreneurship; the 1992 Regulation of Special Means of Payment; the 1993 Regulation of Terms and Conditions of Denationalization and Privatization of State Property; the 1991 Law on Foreign Investment; and the Plan for Denationalization and Privatization of State Property for 1994-95. According to the International Monetary Fund (IMF), during the first stage of reforms, the government ended controls on most prices, created a national currency, introduced a liberal trade regime, and eliminated most capital controls. Structural reforms included the privatization of small-scale enterprises and housing, the establishment of a two-tiered banking system, and the introduction of the VAT. Between 1991 and 1994, approximately 4,700 enterprises – including small trade outlets and retail and service establishments, were privatized. In the second 1994-95 phase, approximately 1,300 medium- and large-scale enterprises, particularly in industry, transport, and construction, were privatized. In 1996-97, the government completed its divestiture of the state shares of 600 enterprises. In addition, it declared its intent to privatize large strategic entities, including 11 monopolies in fields such as energy and fuel, mining, air transport, and telecommunications. Political opposition has delayed the privatization of public utilities. Concerns over price-rigging led to a temporary halt to privatizations in May 1997. In December 1997, Prime Minister Jumagulov signed a decree to resume the process. The government has not yet determined how it will dispose of the more than 3,000 state enterprises that have not yet been privatized. Kyrgyzstan has established the legislative basis for denationalization and privatization and has effected a marked shift toward a market economy. According to the EBRD, the most successful privatization has been in small businesses in the retail and services sector. According to the IMF, as of June 1997, of 9,989 state concerns in industry, consumer services, trade and catering, agriculture, construction, transport, and other sectors, 3,684 remain to be privatized. Kyrgyzstan has not yet privatized several key sectors of the economy, including agriculture, mining, oil and gas, and telecommunications.

3. What proportion of agriculture, housing and land, industry, and small business and services is in private hands? *Agriculture*: Under the Kyrgyz constitution, all natural resources, including land, are owned by the state and cannot be privatized. As a result of reforms in 1991 and 1992, approximately 480 state and collective farms were reorganized. Of these, 165 were reorganized by August 1993 into 191 agricultural cooperatives, nine shareholder's societies, and approximately 18,000 private farms. By the end of 1993, reforms had stalled, and agricultural production was declining. To revitalize the process, a presidential decree was issued on February 22, 1994, to enable farmers to lease land for 49-year periods. In 1996, another presidential decree provided for 99-year land-use rights.

Housing and Land: According to the IMF, land-use rights were accorded for approximately half of all land. Of the remaining land, approximately half is owned by the National Land Fund, which, in spite of a November 1996 presidential decree that directed it to distribute half of its land through auctions, has yet to formulate a program to sell or distribute the property. The other half is largely located in the Chui region, which, for political reasons, has resisted the distribution of land-use rights. In general, land that has not been allocated to individual farmers is under the control of collective farms. These farms also indirectly control approximately one-third of the land that has been distributed, in part because farmers find it difficult to obtain access to credits and marketing channels. Individual farmers cultivate only one-third of all arable land. According to the IMF, two-thirds of these farmers still work on collective farms. Prior to privatization, between 50 and 60 percent of housing was already privately owned. Most state-owned dwellings are city high-rises.

Industry: According to the State Property Fund, 88.2 percent of industry had been privatized by early 1998.

Small business and services: Small business and services were auctioned by the state between 1991 and 1993 and are now entirely privately-owned.

4. What has been the extent of insider (management, labor, and nomenklatura) participation in the privatization process? What explicit and implicit preferences have been awarded to insiders? In mid-1997, the mass privatization program was halted in order to facilitate an investigation to determine whether enterprises had been sold too cheaply to insiders. In November 1997, the head of the privatization agency was fired amid allegations of financial irregularities and collusive bidding. Another scandal followed the sale of Tsum, the Kyrgyz Republic's largest department store. Former Deputy Prime Minister Atashev purchased the store in 1997 for approximately $20,000 even though the enterprise was valued at more than ten times that amount. According to the EBRD, many enterprises have been privatized by insider management buyouts. These firms are characterized by low-quality products, idle capacity, and a lack of capital. A lack of financial discipline and insider ownership have limited managerial turnover and thereby obstructed the restructuring of newly privatized companies. In many cases, officials do not privatize state-owned enterprises directly and instead manipulate the process to benefit their relatives. Government officials are widely believed to be the real owners of a majority of privatized enterprises in the Kyrgyz Republic.

5. How much public awareness of and support for privatization has there been? What is the nature of support and opposition to privatization by major interest groups? The Kyrgyz public has been adequately informed about privatization since the process was initiated immediately after the collapse of the Soviet Union. The country is united in its support of reform, but disputes arise over the timing, methods, and specific results of the process. In general, individuals with official positions, good connections, and business interests embrace privatization, as they appear to be its major beneficiaries, while the general public views it far more negatively. Critics contend that the process has been manipulated to benefit the nomenklatura and individuals serving in the presidency. They also claim that the process is benefiting the ethnic Kyrgyz, to the detriment of ethnic Russians and Uzbeks, and, more generally, the north over the south. They also claim that land reforms have been delayed or weakened not only due to traditional Kyrgyz opposition to private land ownership, but also due to fears that such reforms would cede the best farmland in the north to its European occupants.

Macroeconomics 3.50/7

1. Has the taxation system been reformed? (What areas have and have not been overhauled? To what degree are taxpayers complying? Is tax compliance difficult to achieve? Has the level of revenues increased? Is the revenue-collection body overburdened? What is the overall tax burden?) Parliament has the authority to introduce and revoke taxes. The Ministry of Finance and the Tax Inspectorate, its enforcement organ, are responsible for implementation. Some specific tax prerogatives are delegated to regional assemblies. For example, the regional assemblies receive a portion of the land tax. In July 1996, Kyrgyzstan introduced a new Tax Code, which includes 181 sections. These sections are divided into sub-sections that address income, profit, excise, customs, land, vehicular traffic, and other taxes.

The Ministry of Finance has prepared and issued a series of "instructions" to interpret and supplement the complex tax code. President Akayev has stated that the tax inspectorate is corrupt "from top to bottom." In addition, officials have claimed that the shadow mafia-run economy is nearly as large as the official state economy. In general, taxes remain high. Although there are some exceptions, profit and income taxes on enterprises range from 30 to 70 percent. The country also imposes a 37-percent and a 20-percent VAT. The legislature is expected to consider 75 amendments to the tax code drafted by the president's legal staff. Tax evasion is widespread, but revenues in 1997 were six percent higher than in 1996.

2. Does fiscal policy encourage private savings, investment and earnings? (Has there been any reform/alteration of revenue and budget policies? How large are budget deficits and overall debt? Is there financing of the social insurance/pension system sustainable? What proportion of the budget is taken up by subsidies to firms and individuals?) According to the IMF, the Kyrgyz Republic's fiscal health improved substantially between 1995 and 1997. The fiscal deficit fell sharply, and the structure and yield of direct taxes and the VAT was improved. Overall expenditures, especially in wages and net lending, were stabilized. Payment arrears were lowered, and budgetary procedures and intergovernmental relations were reformed. According to the IMF, problems remain in the administration and collection of direct taxes, the structure and prioritization of expenditures, pension fund finances, and government guarantees on foreign borrowing. On a cash basis, the fiscal deficit declined from 13.5 percent in 1995 to 6.3 percent in 1996. The 1997 target was 5.7 percent. Fiscal performance in the first half of 1997 was broadly in keeping with the target of the 1997 target of 5.7 percent because expenditures were kept under control and total revenues exceeded targets for the period. In November 1997, parliament approved a draft budget with a projected income of 5,547,973,000 *som* (approximately $326 million) and expenditures of 7,023,691,200 som (approximately $415 million). According to the IMF, total external debt at the end of 1996 was $753 million. Approximately 60 percent is owed to multilateral creditors and 40 percent to bilateral creditors. In December 1997, total external debt was $1.2 billion. Kyrgyzstan's Social Fund was established in 1994 by consolidating the previously independent extra-budgetary Pension Fund, Employment Fund, and Social Insurance Fund, which had provided social protection benefits. In 1997, a Medical Insurance Fund was added. According to the EBRD, the primary source of revenue is a 39 percent payroll tax. The agricultural sector makes virtually no contributions to the Social Fund, and some other sectors enjoy preferential rates.

The Social Fund has been in deficit since 1994, and pension arrears amounted to 0.3 percent of GDP at the end of 1996. In an effort to prevent arrears, budget transfers rose from 1.2 percent to 1.8 percent in 1996. In the same period, revenue collection fell from 6.9 percent of GDP to 6.5 percent due to decreases in formal sector employment, real wages, and levels of compliance.

3. Has there been banking reform? (Is the central bank independent? What are its responsibilities? Is it effective in setting and/or implementing monetary policy? What is the actual state of the private banking sector? Does it conform to international standards? Are depositors protected?) According to the IMF, the Kyrgyz Republic's banking system has become more sound and stable. Banking reform was initiated in 1991 with the Law on the State Bank, the Law on Banks and Banking, and the Law on Pledges. The government launched a restricting program after several banks, including Kyrgyzelbank, Orient, Hang-Fang and Agroprombank, collapsed in 1996. Four banks were put under direct supervision. Two others had their licenses suspended and were subjected to temporary National Bank of the Kyrgyz Republic (NBKR) administration. The systematic reform of the banking system has been termed "successful" by the EBRD. The independent NBKR, the country's central bank, is responsible for monetary and exchange policy, government banking facilities, and the management of relations with foreign banks. In accordance with the 1996 referendum on amendments to the constitution, the chairman of the bank is appointed by the president. The NBKR's general strategy is strongly influenced by the requirements and advice of international lending institutions, including the IMF, the EBRD, and the Asian Development Bank. In April 1997, the bank introduced a new chart of accounts for itself and five commercial banks. It is also modernizing the payments system and strengthening its supervision of banks by issuing new regulations on insider lending, foreign exchange exposure, and loan provisions. According to the IMF, 17 of 18 operating banks are in compliance with prudential regulations. Three new bank licenses were granted in the first half of 1997. Legislation is being prepared for depositors' insurance.

4. How sound is the national currency? (Is the value of the currency fixed or does it float? How convertible is the currency? How large are the hard currency reserves? Has the exchange rate policy been stable and predictable?) In May 1993, the Kyrgyz Republic became the first Central Asian country to introduce its own currency. The som, which has been fully convertible since March 1995, remains the most stable currency in the region. The exchange rate under the NBKR's managed float policy is determined in weekly foreign exchange auctions with commercial banks. There are no surrender or repatriation requirements. In early 1998, the bank's chairman stated that the country had $195 million in hard currency reserves. According to the EBRD, the exchange rate was stable throughout most of 1997.

5. Is there a functioning capital market infrastructure? (Are there existing or planned commodities, bond, and stock markets? What are the mechanisms for investment and lending? What government bodies have authority to regulate capital markets?) Although capital markets are underdeveloped, there are a number of non-banking financial institutions, including 17 investment funds, 47 insurance companies, a stock exchange, a coupon privatization trading center, a state social fund, and two pension funds. The government is amending the prudential regulations that govern investment funds and introducing new legislation on insurance companies and pension funds. The Law on Securities and Stock Exchanges was passed in 1991. In 1994, the Coupon Trading Center began trade in privatization vouchers. The Stock Exchange launched its operations in May 1995. According to the EBRD, an independent share registry and strong listing requirements ensure transparency and the security of property rights. The government plans to attract savings and small private investors by issuing a state investment bond backed by shares of privatized companies. The proceeds will be used to modernize these companies. It also plans to abolish taxes on the revenues of local investment funds from operations on the securities market. The NBKR, the

State Property Fund and two ministries currently control the securities market, however, the government plans to establish a single national securities commission that is accountable only to the president.

Microeconomics 3.50/7

1. Are property rights guaranteed? (Are there both formal and de facto protections of private real estate and intellectual property? Is there a land registry with the authority and capability to ensure accurate recording of who owns what? What are the procedures for expropriation, including measures for compensations and challenge? Have any seizures taken place?) The 1990 property law allows foreign and Kyrgyz citizens to own houses, vehicles, means of production, enterprises, and buildings. These rights are also enshrined in the Law on Foreign Investments and its amendments, which outline procedures for dispute resolution. The civil code, which provides a framework for the legal principles of the new free market system, guarantees the rights of persons to transfer property and the freedom of contract for citizens and foreigners. According to the constitution, the government can only expropriate property by a specific act of parliament and must then pay fair compensation. The Law on Foreign Investment prohibits expropriation of foreign investments unless there is a threat to life or health that the foreign investor refuses to address. Nevertheless, in an attempt to include government revenues, the government has passed a law to nationalize alcohol production. The legal status of land and land rights has not been fully determined. The maximum period for the lease of agricultural land was increased from 49 to 99 years. The system of land registration remains fragmented. Cities have one system for registering residences and another for registering industrial enterprises. Rural areas have different systems for registering farm land, pastures, and forests.

The courts lack the experience, independence, and resources to uphold property rights adequately and to enforce decisions.

2. To what extent have prices been liberalized? What subsidies remain? According to the EBRD, most prices for goods and services have been liberalized, but the prices of some utilities are still directly controlled and subsidized. Tariffs for electricity, hot water, and heating were increased in 1996, but remain relatively low. The government intends to allow an increase of the overall domestic tariff to cover operational costs and depreciation by the end of 1998. At the same time, however, it will provide financial support for low income groups.

3. Is it possible to own and operate a business? (Has there been legislation regarding the formation, dissolution, and transfer of businesses, and is the law respected? Do there exist overly cumbersome bureaucratic hurdles that effectively hinder the ability to own and dispose of a business? Are citizens given access to information on commercial law? Is the law applied fairly? Does regulation (or do licensing requirements) impose significant costs on business and consumers? Do they create significant barriers to entry and seriously hamper competition?) Both domestic and foreign persons may own and operate a business. The legal and regulatory environment for business operations is widely regarded as superior to those in neighboring countries. Nevertheless, personal connections remain the most important asset in the operation of businesses. In December 1993, the country enacted an insolvency law, but, according to the IMF and the EBRD, it has been applied only sporadically. It is sometimes difficult to convince the courts that an enterprise should be declared bankrupt. A new bankruptcy law and insolvency regulations and procedures are being drafted. Much business activity is unregistered. Information on commercial law appears in the Bishkek press, but seldom reaches other parts of the country.

4. Are courts effective, transparent, efficient and quick in reaching decisions on property and contract disputes? What alternative mechanisms for adjudicating disputes exist? The courts have little experience with commercial contracts. Commercial disputes are rarely settled in the courts, which are not considered to be effective, transparent, or efficient. According to the EBRD, a party must wait on average between seven months and one year for a commercial case to be heard. It must wait for a similar period for the execution of a final judgement for monetary payment. Out-of-court settlement procedures for creditors of insolvent enterprises have been introduced to avoid the implementation delays that are endemic in the legal system. Deficiencies in the application of laws are being addressed through a host of programs supported by NGOs and donors, including the American Bar Association, U.S. AID, the Asian Development Bank, and the World Bank.

5. Is business competition encouraged? (Are monopolistic practices limited to law and in practice? If so, how? To what degree is "insider" dealing a hindrance to open competition? Are government procurement policies open and unbiased?) The Kyrgyz Republic has adopted anti-monopoly laws and has established an anti-monopoly department within the Ministry of Finance. Anti-monopoly laws include the 1994 Anti-Monopoly Law and the 1991 Decree on Restriction on Monopolistic Activity, which was supplemented by the Decrees of the State Economic Council. The law defines "monopoly producers" as those with a domestic market share of at least 35 percent. There are seven "natural" monopolies (railways, communications, energy, gas, water, sewerage, and tobacco sectors), seven "permitted" monopolies (including civil aviation, oil, publishing, and the coal and gold mining sectors) and 31 "temporary" monopolies (primarily in the machine-building, textile, and food industries). The Anti-Monopoly Department monitors all monopolies but only regulates the natural monopolies and four of the permitted monopolies. Social, regional, political, and business relationships are intertwined. This represents an obstacle to competition, if not foreign investment. In general, the work of the government is not transparent. Procurement policies are rarely unbiased.

6. To what extent has international trade been liberalized? To what degree has there been simplification/overhaul of customs and tariff procedures, and are these applied fairly? What informal trade barriers exist? The Kyrgyz Republic encourages international trade. In early 1994, the trade regime was substantially liberalized. Remaining import and export licensing agreements were lifted, and export taxes were reduced. In general, customs duties on imports from non-CIS countries are fixed at a rate of 10 percent. After parliament abolished the excise tax on gasoline, electronic goods, furniture, carpets and crystal, the government replaced it with equivalent customs fees. The fees on carpet and crystal were reconverted to excise duties in January 1997. The average tariff rate for agricultural products remains at approximately 10 percent. No duty rate is levied on imports from CIS countries. The average unweighted tariff rate is four percent.

There are no quantitative import restrictions or absolute prohibitions on imports. Import licenses are only required for five categories of goods that must be regulated to protect public health. The Kyrgyz Republic has no export bans or registration requirements for exports. No export duties exist. Export licenses are required only for items such as military arms, explosives, nuclear materials, and narcotics.

7. To what extent has foreign investment and capital flow been encouraged or constrained? The Kyrgyz Republic encourages foreign investment and capital flow. In order to promote foreign investment, it passed the 1991 Law on Foreign Investment, which was amended in 1993. It also issued a 1994 presidential edict on "Supplementary Guarantees for Foreign Investors in Kyrgyzstan." In October 1996, the Kyrgyz Investment and Financial Corporation was established to manage foreign investment and, reportedly, to weaken the power of Goskominvest (the State Commission on Foreign Investments and External Economic Assistance), which had been established in 1992 to manage foreign investment and foreign assistance. In November 1997, President Akayev established the State Agency on Foreign Investments, which is responsible for improving the country's investment climate and which serves as the executive body of the State Commission on Foreign Investments and External Economic Assistance. In order to invest in industries such as natural resource exploitation, foreign investors must have a Kyrgyz partner. Legislation provides for an initial tax exemption for foreign investment entities in which 50 percent or more of the capital is contributed by a foreign source or in which 30 percent or more of the imported cash and equipment are imported. According to the tax code, the principal taxes for foreign investors are the profit tax for legal persons, the tax on non-resident dividends and interest, and the tax on repatriation of earned income. The tax code also provides for a reasonable depreciation of equipment and other assets. The largest foreign direct investment in the Kyrgyz Republic is in the Kumtor gold field, which is considered to be the eighth largest in the world. Two-thirds of the field is owned by the Kyrgyz government. One-third is owned by the Cameco Corporation of Canada. The field's construction and investment phase was completed in December 1996, at a cost of $452 million — approximately 26 percent more than the estimated cost. Production began in 1997. The government expects to receive approximately $172 million in revenue from the project between 1997 and 2002. Opposition politicians and the media claim that the original tendering process was biased and that government officials stand to benefit personally from the exploitation of the field.

8. Has there been reform of the energy sector? (To what degree has the energy sector been restructured? Is the energy sector more varied, and is it open to private competition? Is the country overly dependent on one or two other countries for energy [including whether exported fuels must pass through one or more countries to reach markets]?) The Kyrgyz Republic has insignificant reserves of natural gas and petroleum. It has substantial coal reserves and major potential to generate additional hydroelectric power. Industrial activity was heavily dependent upon fuel subsidies, which disappeared with the collapse of the Soviet Union. Currently, the country can only meet its hydrocarbon needs through imports. While more of its total energy requirements could be met by hydroelectricity, additional investment would be required to develop this domestic energy sector. The coal industry is plagued by increasing extraction costs and a lack of equipment.

Plans for reform and privatization of the energy sector were halted in mid-1997. The government has declared its intention to sell the components of the state energy company Kyrgyzenergo, but has not announced a schedule for the sale. The Kyrgyz Republic is dependent upon natural gas and oil supplies from Uzbekistan. Uzbekistan's decision to charge world-market prices for its natural gas has compounded the Kyrgyz Republic's difficulties in paying for the imports. Payment arrears have repeatedly resulted in gas supply cut-offs. The government is attempting to secure its energy needs in part by selling electricity and water to Uzbekistan and Kahzahkstan.

LATVIA

Freedom in the World Ratings, 1989-1998

	1989-90	1990-91	1991-92	1992-93	1993-94	1994-95	1995-96	1996-97	1997-98
Political Rights	-	-	2	3	3	3	2	2	1
Civil Liberties	-	-	2	3	3	2	2	2	2
Status	-	-	F	PF	PF	F	F	F	F

Polity: Consolidated Democracy
Economy: Consolidated Market
Population: 2,403,000
PPP: $3,273
Ethnic Groups: Latvian (52 percent), Russian (34 percent), Ukrainian, Polish, Belarusian, Lithuanian
Capital: Riga

Political Process 2.00/7

1. When did national legislative elections occur? Were they free and fair? How were they judged by domestic and international election monitoring organizations? Who composes the government? On June 5-6, 1996, Latvia held its first parliamentary election since the restoration of the country's independence in 1991. Latvia's Way won 36 seats and the National Independence Movement won 15. Six other parties and blocs also received votes. The most recent national legislative elections were held on September 30 and October 1, 1995. Members of parliament are elected for three-year terms by proportional representation. In order to win representation, a party must receive at least 5 percent of the total votes cast in the election. Nine of the 19 parties and factions competing for seats in the 100-member parliament (*Saeima*) won seats. The center-left Democratic Party Saimnieks won 15.2 percent of the vote; Joachim Siegeriest's nationalist Popular Movement for Latvia received 14.9 percent; and Latvia's Way, the ruling liberal party, finished third with 14.6 percent of the vote. International organizations declared that the elections had been conducted freely and fairly, but they also noted violations concerning canvassing on election day and flaws in the country's electoral laws. The lack of a clear parliamentary majority necessitated the formation of a six-party coalition that covers a wide ideological spectrum. Andris Skele, a young businessman with no party affiliation, was chosen as prime minister. The years 1996 and 1997 were marked by continuing political instability, including scandals resulting from charges that several high-level ministers had violated the country's anti-corruption laws. In summer 1997, Skele's government fell. Skele resigned as prime minister and was replaced by Guntars Krasts of the Fatherland and Freedom/LNNK bloc. In early 1998, the Democratic Party Saimnieks withdrew from the coalition. Krasts then enlisted two centrist parties, the National Reform Party and the Green

Party, to replace Saimnieks and won a parliamentary vote of confidence for the new broadly centrist, six-party minority coalition. Parliamentary elections are scheduled for October 3-4, 1998.

2. When did presidential elections occur? Were they free and fair? On July 7, 1993, parliament elected Guntis Ulmanis as president of Latvia. According to the constitution, the president is elected for a three-year term by secret ballot by a majority vote in parliament. On June 18, 1996, in the most recent presidential elections, the political parties in parliament nominated four candidates to run for president: incumbent President Guntis Ulmanis; Saeima chairwoman Ilga Kreituse, who was proposed by the ruling Democratic Party Saimnieks; Imants Liepa, a nonparty member who had become a Popular Movement for Latvia (TKL) deputy only after another deputy resigned; and former First Secretary of the Latvian Communist Party Alfred Rubiks, who was nominated by the Socialist Party even though he was serving an eight-year prison sentence for plotting to overthrow the Latvian government in 1991. Under the constitution, any Latvian citizen may be nominated for president, provided that he is at least 40 years old. Although Rubiks had no chance of being elected, the publicity that resulted from his nomination increased the pressure for his release from prison. Of the 99 ballots that were distributed in parliament, 97 were returned. Ulmanis received 53 votes and Kreituse won 25. Liepa received 14 while Rubiks won five. According to the U.S. State Department, parliament elected the president freely and fairly. In his campaign, Ulmanis generally supported moderate policies in Latvia's relations with Russia and opposed efforts to make the citizenship law more restrictive. His election has resulted in continuity in Latvia's internal and foreign policies and curbed internal debate between the coalition partners.

3. Is the electoral system multiparty-based? Are there at least two viable political parties functioning at all levels of government? The electoral system in Latvia is multiparty-based at all levels. In 1993, 23 political parties participated in the national legislative elections. In 1996, 19 parties and factions representing a wide range of political viewpoints competed in the national elections. In the March 1997 local elections, a total of 17 parties won seats on the Riga City Council. The diversity of parties at different levels of government has often made it difficult to reach consensus on many issues. Part of the coalition government, for example, objects to OSCE and Council of Europe recommendations on the alignment of Latvian laws with those of Western Europe. Disagreements such as these have prevented or delayed the adoption of legislation, most notably in the areas of citizenship and knowledge of languages.

4. How many parties have been legalized? Are any particular parties illegal? As of May 1998, 41 political parties were registered in Latvia. The Law on Registering Public Organizations was amended in late 1993 to bar registration of Communist, Nazi, or other organizations that would act in contravention of the constitution.

5. What proportion of the population belongs to political parties? According to the Latvian Prognoze Association of Independent Sociologists, approximately five percent of respondents to a survey indicated membership in a political party or movement. The majority of parties are active only for brief periods during electoral campaigns. Non-citizens are prohibited from forming political organizations.

6. What has been the trend of voter turnout at the municipal, provincial, and national levels in recent years? At the national level, voter turnout increased from the late 1980s through the early 1990s, but then decreased in the mid-1990s. Electoral participation reached its highest level with elections to the Fifth Saeima in 1993, when 90 percent of eligible voters cast their ballots. It decreased to 72 percent in the Sixth Saeima elections. Participation in local government elections has declined from 78 percent in 1989 to 63 percent in 1994 and 57 percent in 1997. This trend reportedly results from the public's decreasing confidence in political leaders and its increasing political alienation in the face of difficulties associated with economic reforms. In addition, noncitizens, who constitute approximately 30 percent of the registered residents of Latvia, were unable to participate in either national or local elections.

Civil Society 2.25/7

1. How many nongovernmental organizations (NGOs) have come into existence since 1988? What is the number of charitable/nonprofit organizations? Are there locally led efforts to increase philanthropy and volunteerism? What proportion of the population is active in private voluntary activity (from polling data)? Although small groups of dissidents were active in Latvia throughout the 1970s and early 1980s, mass political activity outside of the Communist party began in 1986 with a petition and letter-writing campaign against the environmentally dangerous Daugava hydroelectric station. During the next two years, political participation increased dramatically. By autumn 1988, the newly founded nongovernmental Latvian Popular Front, which also worked to promote a variety of minority and religious rights, claimed a membership of between 200,000 and 300,000 people. An increasing number of various types of nongovernmental organizations has been registered in Latvia in recent years. The total number of NGOs registered at the Ministry of Justice rose from 1,676 in 1995 to 2,394 in 1996 and 2,753 in 1997. These include cultural, professional, business, social, charitable, and women's organizations.

The role of NGOs has increased steadily since the late 1980s. In Valmiera in August 1997, a wide-ranging event entitled "Women and Men in Dialogue" increased public awareness of gender equality issues and mobilized state institutions and NGOs. In September 1997, the first NGO Forum attracted hundreds of LatviaNGO representatives. The NGO Center, which provides support for approximately 500 registered NGOs, has also become more active.

Research conducted in order to create a national NGO directory suggests that more than 70 percent of NGOs are based in Riga. Twenty percent are based in the other large towns of Daugavpils, Ventspils, Jurmala, Liepaja, Rezekne, and Jelgava. In regional centers, smaller towns and rural districts, local governments remain the primary force behind social activity.

While the total number of NGOs has increased, only a small segment of the population is involved in NGO activities. According to the Baltic Barometer survey of November 1996, nine percent of Latvians and two percent of non-Latvians were members of NGOs. According to an estimate provided by the NGO Center, only 0.5 to 3.0 percent of the population is active in private voluntary efforts.

2. What is the legal and regulatory environment for NGOs (i.e., ease of registration, legal rights, government regulation, taxation, procurement, and access to information issues)? To

what extent is NGO activism focused on improving the legal and regulatory environment? The primary laws that regulate the work of NGOs in Latvia are the Law on Nonprofit Organizations, which was passed in December 1991 and amended in May 1993; the December 1992 Law on Social Organizations and their Associations; and the Law on the Income of Enterprises. The Law on Social Organizations and their Associations addresses general conditions for the establishment and operation of all social organizations. It also contains specific and supplementary regulations for political organizations, public foundations, professional societies, and sports organizations. The activity of trade unions, religious associations, and some other categories of NGOs are governed by separate laws. Under the law, a social organization may be established by ten or more people who have united to pursue nonprofit-related goals. Social organizations can conduct entrepreneurial and other activities, establish entrepreneurial companies and enterprises, and obtain stocks or shares in those companies in pursuit of their goals. Profit gained from the organization's business activities must be used for the organization's statutory goals and cannot be distributed among its members. To register with the Register of Companies, an NGO must present a charter of statutes, protocol of foundation, verification of legal address, application of registration, and state fee. The state registration fee is 25 *lats* for social organizations and 100 lats for nonprofit organizations. Religious organizations, which are not recognized as NGOs, are registered by the Ministry of Justice.

The Law on Nonprofit Organizations defines a nonprofit organization (NPO) as an entity established for nonprofit service or charity work. Founders of an NPO can be natural or legal persons. State institutions can establish NPOs with approval from the respective ministry. Local governments can form NPOs in accordance with the decisions of local councils. NPOs are registered in the Registry of Enterprises, a governmental agency not connected to the Ministry of Justice. The name of the organization must contain the words "nonprofit organization." Before registering, the founders of an NPO must declare in writing that they will not obtain profit from the activities of the organization and that all profit will be set aside in a special reserve fund and used for the fulfillment of the tasks for which the NPO was established. If the NPO violates this regulation, it will be reregistered within a month as an enterprise, and its activities will be regulated by the laws applying to business establishments. The reserve funds of the NPO will then be transferred to the ownership of the state.

To date, Latvian NGOs have exercised influence in the content or passage of three NGO-related laws: the Law on Social Organizations and their Associations, the Law on State Guardianship, and the Law on Charity, which is still being developed.

3. What is the organizational capacity of NGOs? Do management structures clearly delineate authority and responsibility? Is information available on NGO management issues in the native language? Is there a core of experienced practitioners/trainers to serve as consultants or mentors to less developed organizations? According to a report by the Soros Foundation, one of the leading obstacles confronting NGOs in the Baltic states is a lack of management and organizational skills. According to a report by the NGO Center in Riga, six to ten percent of existing NGOs have a developed management capacity. Information on NGO management issues is available at the NGO Center and is published largely in English. Trainers for NGOs are available, but according to the NGO Center, they meet only 10 to 15 percent of current needs.

4. Are NGOs financially viable? What is their tax status? Are they obliged to and do they typically disclose revenue sources? Do government procurement opportunities exist for private, not-for-profit providers of services? According to a report by the NGO Center, the main sources of income, in decreasing order of prominence, for NGOs in Latvia are membership fees, donations from enterprises and firms, private donations, foreign donations, local government funds, fees for services, income from the organizations' activities, and state budget funds. Businesses may deduct up to 85 percent of the value of their donations to certain foundations and associations, provided the deduction does not exceed 20 percent of their total taxable income. Those foundations and associations to which businesses may contribute and receive a tax deduction are those that have complied each year with a complicated government filing and newspaper publication regimen. There is generally no difference in the tax policy applied to social organizations and for-profit enterprises. Social organizations pay income and social tax, although there are some exceptions for charities. By the end of March of each year, social organizations must submit a report on their income and expenses during the previous year to the State Revenue Service. Journalists are granted access to the reports, have the right to participate in meetings of the governing bodies of social organizations, and can obtain access to the resolutions and decisions adopted by the organizations and their officials.

5. Are there free trade unions? How many workers belong to these unions? Is the number of workers belonging to trade unions growing or decreasing? What is the numerical/proportional membership of farmers' groups, small business associations, etc.? The Constitutional Law of Latvia guarantees the right to strike and the Law on Trade Unions mandates that workers, other than uniformed military, have the right to form and join labor unions of their own choosing. Unions are free to affiliate internationally and are developing contacts with European labor unions and international labor union organizations. Although many state-owned factories are on the verge of bankruptcy and are seriously behind in wage payments, workers fear dismissal if they strike. While the law bans such dismissals, the government has not effectively enforced the law. During 1997, workers in some bankrupt state enterprises sought to defend their economic interests more actively through strikes, picketing, and other forms of protest. Teachers endeavored to start a dialogue with the government through a telephone campaign, while farmers tried to obtain greater support and protection from foreign competition. Labor unions have the right to bargain collectively and are largely free of government interference in their negotiations with employers. Although the law prohibits discrimination against union members and organizers, some emerging private sector businesses have threatened to fire union members. These businesses, however, usually provide better salaries and benefits than are available elsewhere. In general, the trade union movement is undeveloped and still in transition from a socialist to a free-market model. Since independence, the trade union movement has been divided into entities that continue to operate as individual unions, and those that have united to form the Free Trade Union Federation. The latter, which is based primarily in industry, included approximately 40 percent of all trade unions in 1996. Union membership, which constituted approximately 50 percent of the work force in 1993, fell as workers left the Soviet-era unions that had included management or were fired as Soviet-style factories failed. Private farmers have created a number of organizations, but membership in them and in small business associations remains small.

6. What forms of interest group participation in politics are legal? What type of interest groups are active in the political and policy process? The Constitutional Law guarantees the right of citizens to establish political parties. Under Article 31, all people have the right to form public organizations and participate in their activities, provided that they are not contrary to law. Non-citizens are prohibited from forming political organizations. Politically active interest groups included organizations representing businessmen, students, teachers, doctors, non-ethnic Latvians, and pensioners. In late 1993, the Law on Registering Public Organizations was amended to prohibit Communist, Nazi or other organizations that would contravene the constitution.

The government may not legally prohibit public gatherings. Organizers of demonstrations must provide advance notice to local authorities, who may change the time and place of public gatherings for reasons such as fear of public disorder. Numerous public meetings and political demonstrations have taken place without government interference. In January 1998, parliament passed legislation on public demonstrations to require that protesters remain at specified distances from foreign missions, the parliament, and certain other public institutions. While the law comports with Western European statutes, independent human rights organizations in Latvia have found its provisions to be contradictory and confusing. In March 1998, a demonstration of mostly elderly Russian-speakers at Riga City Hall ended when police used force to clear the crowd from the street and onto the sidewalk. This event led some members of the Russian government to accuse Latvia of human rights violations against its Russian speakers and resulted in a marked increase in tensions between the two countries. According to the Latvian government, the rally was unlawful because its organizers had not asked the Riga City Council for advance permission to stage the demonstration. The head of the OSCE mission in Latvia reported to his organization's permanent council that the police actions were directed at restoring public order, not punishing ethnic Russians. His findings were supported by several EU-member and -associated countries as well as the United States. Also in March 1998, a demonstration in Riga to commemorate establishment of the Latvian Nazi SS Legion drew international attention and further condemnation from members of the Russian government. President Ulmanis criticized the participation of top state officials and military personnel in the march, but also asked for understanding by foreigners because most of the Legion's members had been forced to join the unit.

7. How is the not-for-profit/NGO sector perceived by the public and government officials? What is the nature of media coverage of NGOs? To what extent do government officials engage with NGOs? A growing number of NGOs that are engaged in research and advocacy on human rights issues, including prison conditions and children's and women's rights, operate without government interference. Indeed, the government has demonstrated a willingness to engage in dialogue with such organizations. The cabinet has worked with NGOs to adopt the National Program on the Protection and Promotion of Human Rights in Latvia. The establishment of the Latvian National Human Rights Office, which receives its basic financial support from the state and is run by a state-appointed director, was widely supported by human rights NGOs in Latvia. According to a 1997 report by the NGO Center in Riga, 82 percent of NGOs cooperate with national and local governments and 31 percent include representatives of national and local governments in management structures.

Independent Media 1.75/7

1. Are there legal protections for press freedom? The Constitutional Law provides each person with the right to acquire and disseminate information freely; to express his or her views in verbal, written, or any other form; and to freedom from censorship. The 1991 Press Law prohibits censorship of the press or other mass media. Nevertheless, the Law on Radio and Television contains a number of restrictive provisions regulating the content and language of broadcasts. No more than 30 percent of private broadcasts may be in languages other than Latvian. A minimum of 40 percent of prime-time television broadcasts must be of Latvian origin. At least 80 percent must be of European production. These provisions, though, are not always observed in practice. In addition, foreign investment may not exceed 20 percent of the capital in electronic media organizations.

2. Are there legal penalties for libeling officials? Are there legal penalties for "irresponsible" journalism? Have these laws been enforced to harass journalists? Penalties for libel are the same for private and public officials. There are no legal penalties for "irresponsible" journalism. A senior prosecutor in the Latvian Prosecutor-General's office, however, filed criminal charges on March 10, 1998 against Latvian publicist Juris Rudevskis for a series of articles that strongly criticized Russia and the Russians. Rudevskis, who could face up to three years imprisonment if convicted, allegedly violated Article 69 of the Latvian Criminal Code, which forbids incitement of racial or ethnic hatred. In articles in the political weekly *Nacionala Neatkariba* (National Independence), which is published by the center-right Fatherland and Freedom Party, Rudevskis refers to Russia as a "savage" society and cites numerous examples of massacres, court treachery, and murder throughout Russian history. He also analyzes the current rise of chauvinist movements in Russia and asserts that while Russia could be considered an anti-democratic society, it will eventually "come to its senses." According to Index on Censorship, Rudevskis did not use racist terminology in his articles. The investigation represents another in a series of government moves that, while probably intended to reduce ethnic tensions, has had a "chilling effect" on the press. The editor-in-chief of *Dienas Binzness*, a popular business newspaper, has stated that, in his view, Rudevskis was prosecuted due to political pressure in the wake of recently increased Russian-Latvian tensions.

3. What proportion of media is privatized? What are the major private newspapers, television stations, and radio stations? Latvia has two state-owned television networks, LTV-1 and LTV-2, and nine major privately-owned stations. The private Latvian Independent Television has almost twice as many viewers as LTV-1, its nearest competitor. Satellite television enjoys approximately 10 percent of the total Latvian viewership each week and there are numerous independently-owned cable channels. There is also a large number of independent radio outlets that broadcast in both Russian and Latvian. Approximately ten privately-owned stations operate in Riga. The major public radio stations are Latvijas Radio 1, which has the greatest number of listeners each week;

Latvijas Radio 2; and Latvijas Radio 3. Most newspapers and magazines are privately owned. The three most popular daily papers are *Diena* and *Vakara Zinas*, both of which are published in Latvian, and *SM Segodna*, which is published in Russian. The state publishes the weeklies *Fakts* and *Likuma Varda*, as well as *Latvijas Vestnesis*, which appears four times a week. None of these three papers is among the country's top ten most popular non-dailies. All major cities publish their own newspapers.

4. Are the private media financially viable? Since 1992, advertising has accounted for a significant portion of media income. The 1995 banking crisis, in which a number of the country's banks went bankrupt, directly affected the financial viability of many media outlets and sharply diminished the advertising market. In 1996, 43 percent of media advertising was in television, followed by newspapers at 35 percent, radio at 6 percent, magazines at 4 percent, and outdoor venues and other categories comprising the remaining 10 percent. Although new publications continue to appear, economic difficulties have forced others to close.

5. Are the media editorially independent? Are the media's news gathering functions affected by interference from government or private owners? In general, the government respects freedom of speech and the press. Newspapers published in both Latvian and Russian feature a wide range of criticism and political viewpoints. A 1994 city ordinance prohibits the sale of ultra-nationalist Russian-language newspapers in Riga.

The press remains somewhat suspicious of political parties and continues to uncover cases of party stalwarts' conflicts of interest. When the ruling coalition was considering a controversial candidate for finance minister in early 1997, journalists reported on the candidate's dubious business dealings and alleged violations of the country's anti-corruption law. Shortly before the law took effect in late 1996, newspapers reported on the mounting pressure on leading politicians to leave their seats on various enterprise councils. Politicians who continued to hold their posts in violation of the law were subject to attacks by the press. Newspapers have also actively supported state-created "watchdog" institutions such as the Ethics Council. Many journalists criticized the government in early 1997, when the council ceased its operations.

6. Is the distribution system for newspapers privately or governmentally controlled? The distribution system for newspapers is privately controlled.

7. What proportion of the population is connected to the Internet? Are there any restrictions on Internet access to private citizens? According to the RIPE Network Coordination Center, which serves as a regional Internet registry for Europe, there are 34 Internet-connected computers for every 10,000 people in Latvia, or approximately 8,500 Internet-connected computers for a total population of about 2.5 million. According to the most recent edition of *Baltic Media Facts*, there are 15 Internet service providers in Latvia. Major television and radio stations and newspapers have their own web sites.

8. What has been the trend in press freedom as measured by Freedom House's annual *Survey of Press Freedom*? According to Freedom House's annual *Survey of Press Freedom*, Latvia was rated "Free" in 1991, "Partly Free" in 1992 and 1993, and "Free" in 1994-1998.

Governance and Public Administration 2.50/7

1. Is the legislature the effective rule-making institution? The Saeima (parliament) is the country's effective rule-making institution. Although parliament has adopted many news laws, political infighting has limited its ability to function efficiently. The Latvian State Chancellery provides legal and substantive guidance on draft legislation before it is discussed and adopted by the cabinet.

2. Is substantial power decentralized to sub-national levels of government? What specific authority do sub-national levels have? Power was quickly decentralized after the restoration of independence in 1990. Local authorities assumed responsibility not only for functions normally associated with local governments, but also for many of those usually undertaken by central governments. As Latvia has moved toward integration with Europe, however, this trend has been reversed. The current functions of local government are essentially those that cater to local needs and conditions and for which local authorities can determine procedures and funding. Local authorities are responsible for territorial planning, regional and local roads, public transport, housing and community subsidies, primary and secondary education, social services, and primary and secondary health care. Latvia has enacted laws to give local governments, particularly municipalities, substantial authority and allow them to function independently within the limits of the law. Local governments can pass legislation, provided that it does not contradict the laws passed by parliament. In general, councils in smaller municipalities and townships seek guidance from the state before making major decisions. The system of local government in Latvia includes 595 local government units, which are divided into two levels. At the highest level are the 26 *rajoni* (districts) and the 7 largest cities (Riga, Daugavpils, Jelgava, Jurmala, Liepaja, Rezekne, and Ventspils). At the second level are 70 smaller towns and 492 *pagasts* (small rural districts).

3. Are sub-national officials chosen in free and fair elections? Sub-national officials are chosen in free and fair elections. Latvian citizens residing outside the country have the right to vote in local elections. Non-citizen residents of Latvia, however, are barred from voting in local elections. The country's 700,000 primarily Russian-speaking residents are therefore effectively prevented from having direct representation in local politics. Local assemblies elect mayors. On March 9, 1997, in Latvia's most recent local elections, 12,000 candidates competed for 4,445 council seats in 77 city and 489 district councils. The elections proved to be an upset for the national governing coalition. The far-left Social Democratic Party (LSDP), which is not even represented in parliament, won an upset victory over the country's ruling coalition. It won overwhelming control over Daugavpils with 85 percent of the vote. In Riga, it secured 11 of 60 city council seats. The Fatherland and Freedom Party finished second with ten seats. Most of the national coalition parties formed a coalition to control the city council. Rightist parties won majorities in Liepaja and Ventspils. In the local elections of 1994 and 1997, voter turnout was low, 58.5 percent in 1994 and 57 percent in 1997, and many ballots were marked incorrectly due to widespread confusion among voters and the media. Although the share of localities in which two or three electoral lists competed increased from 60.6 percent in 1994 to 64.1 percent in 1997, the number of localities in which there was only one electoral list also increased. In general, these "single list" localities were located in less developed regions where voters were indifferent or where the previous administration or council leader enjoyed considerable authority.

4. Do the executive and legislative bodies operate openly and with transparency? Is draft legislation easily accessible to the media and the public? The executive and legislative bodies generally operate openly and with transparency. Under the constitution, parliamentary sittings are open to the public. Nevertheless, at the request of ten members of parliament, the president, the prime minister, or any one minister, parliament may decide by a majority of not less than two-thirds of the members present, to sit *in camera*. Parliament recently adopted a classified information law that is consistent with international standards and practices. All laws are published in a government newspaper that is available to the general public.

5. Do municipal governments have sufficient revenues to carry out their duties? Do municipal governments have control of their own local budgets? Do they raise revenues autonomously or from the central state budget? In general, local governments do not have sufficient financial resources to undertake their duties at an adequate level. In recent years, various administrative reforms have sharply reduced the finances of the local authorities, while at the same time allotting more functions to local government. Between 1992 and 1995, the work of local authorities constituted more than 24 percent of the state budget. By 1996-97, this figure had fallen to 18 percent and is expected to decrease further to approximately 16 percent in 1998. The reforms have been characterized by a one-third reduction in funding, primarily for education, health, and social assistance, and the transfer of the "savings" to the central government without any accompanying increase in investment in infrastructure. Since local governments receive financing from the central state budget and also raise revenues autonomously, the total revenues available for each region are based largely on the level of economic development of that particular region. On June 10, 1997, in an attempt to promote greater regional-level development and reduce the economic disparities among regions, parliament passed the Law on Regions Requiring Special Assistance. After these regions have been identified according to their income tax revenue, unemployment rate, and population density, the state and local government can actively promote their development. A Regional Fund, which receives money from the state and credits and donations from foreign and international aid institutions, was created to implement support projects. Resources from the fund may be used by the region's businesses and local authorities. During the first six months of 1997, the basic budget of local governments was slightly in surplus. Local government services were not necessarily adequate however, because the aggregate size of local government budgets is and will remain small. In March 1998, parliament adopted a law on municipal finances. The law provides for the equalization of municipal budgets so that, regardless of economic disparities, municipalities will have equal opportunities to perform their functions. Financing will be provided through a special fund as established by the law. Municipal governments have control of their own local budgets.

6. Do the elected local leaders and local civil servants know how to manage municipal governments effectively? Despite the lack of sufficient funds available at the local level, many local leaders in cities and larger towns are competent and manage municipal governments effectively. Training and practical experience are still in short supply in many smaller towns.

7. When did the constitutional/legislative changes on local power come into effect? Has there been a reform of the civil service code/system? Are local civil servants employees of the local or central government? The first post-independence territorial reforms coincided with the 1994 local government elections, when local district authorities in Riga were reorganized as internal departments of the main Riga city authority without elected representatives. The Law on Local Government was adopted in mid-1994. In June 1996, the cabinet adopted a territorial reform "concept" to preserve local authority functions at the regional and local levels and to strengthen local financial independence. Before the March 1997 local elections, a new regulation abolished elections in the *rajoni* and extended the terms of their elected councils to the end of 1997. At the end of its 1997 spring session, parliament passed amendments to the Law on Local Government. These abolished local authorities at the *rajon* level and replaced them with a Cooperation Council that includes representatives from the towns and *pagasts*. After the 1993 parliamentary elections, the government launched a new civil service system by creating a Ministry of State Reform, which will restructure state institutions. A key feature of the Civil Service Law, which was adopted on April 21, 1994, was the creation of a personnel system that provides for entrance by examination, competitive recruitment, adherence to ethical principles, loyalty to constitutional government, and the promotion of competence through education and training. The budget law, which was also passed in 1994, provides for higher salaries for civil servants. An independent non-governmental ethics council was created to implement codes of ethics and standards for government workers. The Ministry of State Reform determined that approximately 14,000 would be subject to the Civil Service Law. The Civil Service Agency (CSA), an implementing agency mandated by the Civil Service Law, was charged with organizing the civil service, implementing civil service laws and regulations, and reviewing the backgrounds and professional qualifications of applicants. Under a separate law passed in late 1994, the CSA became responsible for managing disciplinary procedures for civil servants. Reform began with the highest-level prospective civil servants in order to create a core of people committed, or at least not opposed, to the success of the new system. A requirement that civil servants continue their education and increase their professional competence was incorporated into the Civil Service Law, thereby creating support for the reforms among government workers. The Latvian School of Public Administration and the University of Latvia in Riga are charged with preparing and coordinating training for civil service employment.

Although many elements of civil service reform have already been implemented, limited resources and political opposition have obstructed the implementation of others. A 1996 European Union (EU) study found that bribery of officials at all levels was still not uncommon and that the civil service system had not yet been extended to the local government level. Local civil servants are employees of the local government and must adhere to the same code as all other civil servants.

Rule of Law **2.25/7**

1. Is there a post-Communist constitution? How does the judicial system interpret and enforce the constitution? Are there specific examples of judicial enforcement of the constitution in the last year? The constitution includes the Constitutional Law of Latvia, which was adopted in December 1991, and the 1922 constitution, which dates from Latvia's brief interwar period of independence. The 1922 constitution establishes and defines the separate responsibilities of the executive, legislative, and judicial branches of government. The Constitutional Law, which outlines the basic rights and obligations of citizen and persons, is essentially a declaration with no inherent or practical enforcement mechanism. Unlike amendments to the constitution, the Constitutional Law can be overturned by the judiciary. In December 1997, parliament decided to establish a working group to elaborate a second section of the constitution to strengthen the constitutional protection of basic human rights and freedoms. Consideration of the draft, however, has been delayed due to disagreements among parliamentary factions. In early June 1996, parliament adopted the Law on the Constitutional Court. The court, however, has had difficulties operating because of a failure to allocate sufficient funds from the state budget. In the absence of such a court, parliament has adopted laws that run counter to both the constitution and the country's international obligations. For example, parliament violated the constitution by terminating the mandates of several deputies who allegedly collaborated with the KGB.

2. Does the constitutional framework provide for human rights? Do the human rights include business and property rights? Under Article 12 of the Constitutional Law, all persons in Latvia are equal regardless of race, nationality, sex, language, party affiliation, religion, social status, political preference, or occupation. Article 15 prohibits the use of torture or other cruel, inhuman, or degrading treatment. Each person has the right to engage in entrepreneurial activity that is not contrary to the law, and the state recognizes and protects property and inheritance rights. Under Article 32, freedom of assembly for previously announced peaceful gatherings, meetings, and demonstrations is guaranteed. Under the Constitutional Law, only citizens of Latvia can occupy state positions, establish political parties, and own land. A series of legislative amendments, however, has enlarged the right of non-citizens to own land, both directly and through the use of company shares. Parliament has not yet approved the second section of the constitution, which would include guarantees of human rights.

3. Has there been basic reform of the criminal code/criminal law? Who authorizes searches and issues warrants? Are suspects and prisoners beaten or abused? Are there excessive delays in the criminal justice system? In May 1998, Latvia's parliament adopted a new Criminal Law, which replaced the Latvian Soviet Socialist Republic's Criminal Code in effect since 1961 and which had undergone some basic reforms in 1993. The new law includes provisions for longer jail terms for those sentenced for serious crimes and for broader use of police surveillance for less serious crimes. Against the recommendations of the Organization for Security and Cooperation in Europe (OSCE) and other international organizations, the death penalty can still be imposed in cases of murders that are committed in an especially severe manner. President Krasts, who objected to the clause retaining capital punishment, refused to sign the law and returned it to parliament for revision. In 1994, the responsibility for issuing arrest warrants was transferred from prosecutors to the courts. There have been no reports of imprisonment on political grounds, politically motivated disappearances, or forced exile. There have been credible reports, however, that police and prison personnel have beaten prison inmates, asylum-seekers, and other detainees. Detainees complain that they are subject to physical and psychological intimidation by prison guards. Some law enforcement personnel have been prosecuted for using excessive force against prisoners. Despite new construction and foreign assistance, prison conditions remain poor. The government has stated that it intends to continue to renovate prisons, including the Riga Central Prison, as quickly as its limited finances will allow. By law, the prosecutor's office must make a formal decision whether to charge or release a detainee within 72 hours after an arrest. Charges must be filed within ten days of an arrest. No detainee may be held for more than 18 months without the prosecutor presenting the case to the court and the defendant, who has the right to have an attorney present at any time. There are credible reports that these rights are not always respected in practice, especially outside Riga.

4. Do most judges rule fairly and impartially? Do many remain from the Communist era? Most judges have inadequate judicial training, and the inefficiency of the judiciary sometimes limits the fair administration of justice. Corruption in the judicial system is reportedly widespread. The judiciary suffers from a low level of prestige throughout the country. According to a March 1997 survey, most Latvians do not trust the courts. In August 1996, there were 50 vacant judges' posts — 13 in district courts and 37 in regional courts. Many current judges in Latvia remain from Communist era.

5. Are the courts free of political control and influence? Are the courts linked directly to the Ministry of Justice or any other executive body? The constitution provides for an independent judiciary, and the government generally respects this provision in practice. In November 1997, however, the judges appointed to preside over the trial of the president of the collapsed Bank Baltija resigned from the case after claiming that they were under political pressure from the government. The government continues to reform the judicial system. In 1995, it completed the establishment of regional courts to hear appeals of lower court decisions. In serious criminal cases, two lay assessors join the professional judge on the bench. The courts rely on the Ministry of Justice for administrative support.

6. What proportion of lawyers is in private practice? How does this compare with the previous year? The Latvian College of Sworn Advocates has a membership of more than 1,000 advocates, legal assistants, and consultants. There is a shortage of qualified lawyers. In the mid-1990s, U.N., OSCE, and Council of Europe experts concluded that "there is a chronic lack of lawyers adequately trained in the law of human rights or with adequate competence in international law."

7. Does the state provide public defenders? All defendants have the right to an attorney, and the state will lend funds to destitute defendants for this purpose.

8. Are there effective anti-bias/discrimination laws, including protection of ethnic minority rights? After independence in 1991, citizenship was accorded only to those persons who were citizens of the independent Latvian Republic in 1940 and their descendants. As a result, approximately 700,000 people who had been citizens of the Soviet Union became "non-citizen residents" of Latvia. Under the provisions of a 1994 citizenship law, various categories of non-citizens become eligible to apply for naturalization. The law includes Latvian language and residency requirements, as well as restrictions on the naturalization of several groups, including former Soviet intelligence and military officers. It also requires that applicants possess knowledge of the Latvian constitution and history and take an oath of loyalty to the Latvian state. International observers, including those in the resident OSCE mission, credit the government with establishing a competent and professional naturalization board with offices throughout the country to implement the 1994 law. Nevertheless, the pace of naturalization remains slow. In 1997 alone, only 2,686 of the 31,000 people eligible for naturalization applied. Would-be citizens are reportedly deterred by the language requirements and the naturalization fee. In 1996, the government began to work with the United Nations Development Program (UNDP) to implement a long-term nationwide Latvian language teaching program for adults and children in non-Latvian schools. In December 1997, the government passed regulations to lower the naturalization fee for poor applicants.

Since its passage, there have been many attempts to amend the citizenship law. Max van der Stoel, the OSCE High Commissioner for National Minorities, recommended that the law be amended to grant citizenship to children born in Latvia after August 21, 1991, to non-citizen parents and to close the "naturalization windows," which impose age and birthplace restrictions on candidates. Latvia has found it difficult to follow these recommendations because the citizenship law can be amended only with the support of all the government's ruling factions, one of which opposes the changes. Other parties in parliament support the proposed amendments as a vehicle to facilitate admission into the EU and to improve relations with Russia, which has criticized the law for discriminating against the rights of non-ethnic Latvians. Approximately 65 percent of the non-citizens in Latvia are Russian. On April 22, 1998, the cabinet submitted to parliament a draft amendment to abolish the system of "naturalization windows." In early May, the cabinet accepted amendments to grant citizenship to children born in Latvia after August 21, 1991, to parents who have lived in Latvia for at least five years and who request citizenship. If the parents do not request it, the child may apply for citizenship upon reaching the age of 16, provided that he has completed a school with Latvian as the language of study or has passed a language test. As of late May 1998, both of these amendments were being examined by parliamentary standing committees before presentation to the full parliament. The U.S. Department of State, the EU, the OSCE, and the Council of Baltic Sea States have urged parliament to pass the amendments.

The 1995 Law on the Status of Former Soviet Citizens also provides guarantees of basic human rights and provides non-citizens who have been permanent residents continuously since July 1, 1992, with the rights to establish and change residences, travel abroad, and return to the country. It also requires that non-citizens register regardless of their housing status, thereby facilitating the resolution of cases of persons previously unregistered because they lived in former Soviet military or dormitory housing. The law further provides for the issuance of new travel documents that reflect these rights. Nevertheless, Latvia has continued the Soviet-era practice of requiring the holder's ethnicity to be printed in his passport. Various ethnic groups, including Belarussians and Roma, have complained that since the passport is a basic form of identification in Latvia, the requirement has exposed them to various forms of discrimination based on ethnicity.

Since the majority of people who belong to national and ethnic minorities are not citizens, they find it difficult to participate fully in the country's civic life. In December 1996, the Latvian National Human Rights Office released a study that identified ten differences between the rights of citizens and non-citizens. These differences, which, in its view, violate the International Covenant on Civil and Political Rights, include restrictions on non-citizen employment as firefighters, armed guards, private detectives, members of airline crews, certified attorneys, and licensed pharmacists. Although the restrictions on non-citizens working as firefighters and airline personnel were removed in 1997, the others remain in effect. Some ethnic Russians have complained of discrimination resulting from property laws, which do not allow individual non-citizens to own land. In addition, non-citizens have been given fewer privatization certificates, which can be used to purchase apartments, land, and shares of stock.

The 1995 Law on Religious Organizations specifies that religious organizations can enjoy certain rights and privileges only if they register. Under this law, the justice ministry has registered more than 800 religious congregations, that, without official registration, had found it difficult to obtain visas and residence status for its members. In July 1996, parliament adopted an amendment to reduce the number of persons necessary to seek registration from a minimum of 25 citizens to ten persons residing permanently in Latvia. In June 1997, it further amended the law to allow any citizen or permanent resident to register a religion.

The language law requires employees of the state and of all "institutions, enterprises, and institutes" to possess sufficient knowledge of the Latvian language to perform the duties of their professions. Although Russian is the prevailing language in state-owned industrial enterprises, there have been no reports of widespread dismissals because of a lack of Latvian language skills. Nevertheless, many non-ethnic Latvians claim that the law discriminates against them. In October 1997, the cabinet issued regulations to require Latvian language competence for a person to be registered and to receive unemployment compensation and social security benefits, even if such a person pays social security taxes. There is evidence to suggest that this problem is particularly acute in local government administrations outside of Riga. In May 1998, parliament considered amendments to the language law. The amendments would allow meetings in privately owned companies to be conducted in languages other than Latvian, provided that translation services are available if required by at least one of the participants in the meeting. Meetings and other events must be conducted in Latvian only at fully or partially state-run businesses. These amendments have been opposed by organizations representing Latvia's Russian speakers.

The president's Council on Minorities and Nationalities continues to struggle to define a role for itself. In mid-1997, one of its members resigned to protest what he considered to be the council's passivity. Independent observers have stated that, while individual council members are well-intentioned, as a whole, the council has not played a sufficiently active and public role in addressing minority issues. The council has made no recommendations. By contrast, the Latvian Center for Human Rights and Ethnic Studies received an international democracy and civic society award from the United States and the EU in May 1998. The award is presented to individuals or groups that have contributed to the strengthening of the rule of law, civil society, and democracy. The center was nominated for the award for serving as a leading advocate of human rights education and the peaceful settlement of social conflicts in Latvia. In 1998, the center has focused on the issue of citizenship for children born to non-citizens in Latvia after 1991.

Corruption B

1. What is the magnitude of official corruption in the civil service? Must an average citizen pay a bribe to a bureaucrat in order to receive a service? What services are subject to bribe requests - for example, university entrance, hospital admission, telephone installation, obtaining a license to operate a business, or applying for a passport or other official documents? What is the average salary of civil servants at various levels? Corruption, ranging from small bribe-taking by low-level civil servants for completion of bureaucratic tasks, to the wrongful award of government contracts by high level officials, is widespread in Latvia. Conflicts of interest among government officials are common. A 1996 public opinion survey revealed that 12.7 percent of respondents in Latvia had encountered some form of corruption. Respondents indicated that 36.3 percent of the occasions when bribes were demanded or "suggested" involved civil servants, while 27.9 percent involved customs officials. The police were involved in 10.1 percent of cases, inspectors in 15.6 percent, and other officials in 8.9 percent. The survey results also suggested that citizens complain to the relevant authorities in only 6 percent of cases in which bribes have been extracted. The main reasons provided for not reporting offenses were that the police and other law enforcement agencies could not or had no desire to respond.

2. Do top policy makers (the president, ministers, vice-ministers, top court justices, and heads of agencies and commissions) have direct ties to businesses? How strong are such connections and what kinds of businesses are these? Latvia's anti-corruption law prohibits the President, ministers, parliamentarians, and parliamentary secretaries from employment other than the job to which they have been appointed or elected. They are, however, permitted to work in educational institutions or as artists. In early 1997, the State Revenue Service, which employs 38 people to combat corruption, examined the income declarations of 80 deputies and government representatives and established that 15 had not declared their financial interests in private businesses. Other violations were found in an additional 12 cases. In April and May 1997, further checks on the observance of anti-corruption regulations revealed that half the cabinet and nearly one-third of all deputies had violated the law by holding positions in private businesses. Although there was no evidence that any of the deputies or ministers had used their influence for personal gain, the investigation called into question why the officials were not observing a law that they themselves had passed, and it served to undermine further the public's trust in the political elite.

3. Do laws requiring financial disclosure and disallowing conflict of interest exist? Have publicized anti-corruption cases been pursued? To what conclusion? According to the anti-corruption law, the president, ministers, parliamentarians, and parliamentary secretaries must declare their income to the government. In the corruption scandal of 1997, Prime Minister Andris Skele resigned following allegations the previous year that the Minister of Finance had violated the country's anti-corruption law by holding positions in the private sector. Skele, however, immediately formed a new government with himself once again in charge. In May, new allegations surfaced that several members of parliament, ministers, as well as President Ulmanis also held positions in private companies. In mid-May, Skele learned that economics minister Guntars Krasts held positions in several private companies. Krasts denied the allegations by stating that while these businesses remained on the Enterprise Registry, they had long ago ceased to operate. Skele then asked the Prosecutor General to investigate whether members of parliament and ministers were abiding by the anti-corruption law. The investigation revealed that several other ministers and one-third of parliamentarians held positions in private businesses. The scandal intensified when the press also revealed that, according to the Enterprise Registry, President Ulmanis held still other private positions. Ulmanis was accused of violating not only the anti-corruption law, but also Article 38 of the constitution, which explicitly forbids the president from holding other positions. After reviewing the case, the prosecutor general concluded that the law had not been violated and that the problem stemmed from a failure to update the registry. He also concluded that Krasts had not violated the law. Deputy Prime Minister Juris Kaksitis and the ministers of Agriculture and Education, however, were found to be violating the law. After further revelations, Skele fired the minister of Health, and the Minister of Culture resigned. The prosecutor general continued to review the cases of 40 parliamentarians.

4. What major anti-corruption initiatives have been implemented? How often are anti-corruption laws and decrees adopted? Latvia's anti-corruption law, which was passed in September 1995, prohibits state officials from holding positions in which they are subject to illegal influences and from exercising authority in a situation in which there is a conflict of interest. The law defines 14 categories of state officials beginning with the president, prime minister, parliament, and local government deputies, and ending with officials employed in state and local government institutions and enterprises, policemen, and members of the armed forces. Approximately 34,000 state officials are subject to the law. In 1997, the State Revenue Service, which employs 38 personnel to fight against corruption, introduced an anti-corruption program that led to investigations of the private business activities of a large number of government deputies and ministers. A Coordinating Office for the Prevention of Corruption was established to work with the Crime Prevention Council. It operates under the prime minister together with the Prosecutor General, ministers of justice, interior, and finance, and the Office for the Protection of the Constitution, and the director of the State Chancellery. Additional anti-corruption strategies have or will include various amendments to legislation, including the criminal, criminal procedure, and administrative violation codes. In May 1998, a parliamentary committee rejected proposals to weaken the law. It also determined that state officials would have to declare all forms of income on an annual basis. Also in May, Riga hosted an international conference on the prevention of money laundering and corruption. More than 40 Latvian officials representing various government ministries attended.

5. How do major anti-corruption-ranking organizations like Transparency International rate this country? Transparency International has not yet provided a ranking for the degree of corruption in Latvia. An unofficially published EU report, however, has stated that corruption is widespread in the Latvian government.

Privatization **2.50/7**

1. What percentage of the GDP comes from private ownership? What percentage of the labor force is employed in the private sector? How large is the informal sector of the economy? According to the European Bank for Reconstruction and Development (EBRD), the private sector constituted more than 60 percent of GDP in mid-1997. The private sector accounted for 66 percent of total employment in 1997 — an increase from 64 percent in 1996 and 51 percent in 1993. The size of the informal economy is a matter of some dispute. According to a recent Central Statistics Bureau study, Latvia's shadow economy accounts for approximately 14 percent of GDP. According to another survey, the unofficial economy constituted 35.3 percent of GDP, up slightly from 34.2 percent in 1994.

2. What major privatization legislation has been passed? What were its substantive features? Legislation regarding the privatization of agricultural land includes the 1990 Law on Agricultural Reform, the 1990 Law on Land Reform in Agricultural Regions, and the 1992 Law on the Privatization of Land in Rural Areas. Reprivatization of land in urban areas is covered by the 1991 Law on Land Reforms in Towns and Cities. Reprivatization of housing is covered by the 1991 Laws on Reprivatization of Buildings and the Return of Buildings to Their Legal Owners. The privatization of large enterprises is covered under the 1992 Law on the Order for Privatization of Objects of State and Municipal Property. The 1991 Law on Privatization of Municipally-Owned Small Objects of Trade and Commerce, Restaurants, Cafes, and the Service Sector originally pertained to units below certain size limits, but the size restriction was removed in an amendment passed in February 1992. The Latvian Privatization Agency (LPA), which was established in 1994 to oversee the entire privatization process, began the public phase of the privatization of state property in 1995. It has adopted a case-by-case approach in determining the method to be used for each entity earmarked for privatization. The methods include international tenders of stakes in medium- and large-scale enterprises, restricted tenders and direct sales, domestic auctions or direct sales of smaller enterprises, and public offerings of minority stakes. By early 1996, the Latvian government had passed several decrees to simplify the privatization process. The most widely publicized reform permitted the LPA to sell the land associated with the enterprise that was being privatized. Earlier, only buildings could be sold, while the land itself could only be rented. To encourage the participation of foreign investors, restrictions on the foreign ownership of land were removed in January 1997. Foreign investors had frequently cited these restrictions as a major obstacle to their investment in Latvian enterprises.

3. What proportion of agriculture, housing and land, industry, and small business and services is in private hands? *Agriculture*: Privatization has been particularly successful in the agricultural sector. More than 58,000 private farms have been established, and most remaining collective farms have been converted into private joint-stock companies. Many of Latvia's new farmers are operating at subsistence levels due to a lack of financial resources, credit, and sustainable acreage.

Housing and land: The pace of housing privatization has been slow, with only 15 percent of apartments having been privatized by the beginning of 1998. To accelerate the process, the government has amended the law governing the privatization of housing by establishing timetables for the privatization of housing by local governments, cutting rental subsidies, and eliminating the requirement that the land under the buildings be registered prior to privatization. As of January 1997, 40 percent of land restitution claims had been resolved. In addition, new owners are issued a governmental guarantee against claims by pre-war owners. A real land market is beginning to develop as land is now available for purchase in cash and vouchers.

Industry: The overall pace of privatization of large industrial enterprises has been slow, in part because these industries are often outdated, over sized, and inefficient. The government has now begun to privatize utilities and large energy and transport enterprises, including Latvian Gas, the Latvian Electricity Company Latvenergo, and the Latvian Shipping Company.

Small business and services: The privatization of small enterprises in service and trade, most of which were previously owned by municipalities, is virtually complete.

4. What has been the extent of insider (management, labor, and nomenklatura) participation in the privatization process? What explicit and implicit preferences have been awarded to insiders? In the early stages of privatization, company managers and employees received preferential treatment in the purchase of enterprises from the state. In the privatization of milk processing enterprises, for example, blocks of shares were reserved for enterprise employees and dairy farmers. Currently, foreign investors who have relatively large amounts of funding at their disposal appear to be preferred over domestic investors. In five public offerings of 36 enterprises in 1995-96, strategic investors obtained 46 percent of the shares, while current and retired employees received 16 percent. Management was left with less than one percent of shares.

5. How much public awareness of and support for privatization has there been? What is the nature of support and opposition to privatization by major interest groups? In 1996, in order to increase ordinary citizen's participation in the privatization process, the government launched certificate and voucher programs. The certificate program has been largely unsuccessful for two reasons. First, with no opportunity to invest their certificates in the early stages of the program, many citizens sold their certificates at a fraction of their nominal value. Certificates are transferable and can be bought and sold like securities. Second, certificates are usually used only in the privatization of a minority share of assets. By April 1, 1997, under the public offer program, the shares of 37 enterprises were offered, and approximately 10,000 people became shareholders. The estimated number of potential shareholders in the population is four percent — a negligible amount in light of the fact that certificates were allocated to every citizen. Since privatization certificates may be used to privatize not only state enterprises, but also land and housing, the low level of public participation in the privatization process may also be due to individuals' preference for using these certificates to obtain land and housing.

Macroeconomics 2.50/7

1. Has the taxation system been reformed? (What areas have and have not been overhauled? To what degree are taxpayers complying? Is tax compliance difficult to achieve? Has the

level of revenues increased? Is the revenue-collection body overburdened? What is the overall tax burden?) In 1995, revenue collection fell by one percent of GDP, in part due to fiscal problems that were exacerbated by the year's banking crisis. Poor administration during the period of fiscal reforms led to increases in tax evasion and non-payment of tax debts. During this time, personal income tax returns depended more on the honesty of the individual concerned than on any enforcement measures. In recent years, the tax system has been changed in order to meet EU requirements. In addition, a comprehensive program to improve tax administration is being implemented. Since tax rates are already sufficiently high, the main task of the revenue service is to ensure proper and adequate tax collection. In 1996, tax revenues were 21 percent higher than in 1995. The increased growth resulted from changes to the excise tax rate and improvements in administration. In September 1996, the government introduced the compulsory use of fiscal cash registers, which record the value-added tax (VAT) leveled on each transaction. By May 1998, revenues to the state budget exceeded expenditures by 31.4 million *lats*. The introduction of tax identification numbers for legal and physical persons had been completed and the coverage of the finance ministry's large taxpayers' unit has been increased to include taxpayers that account for nearly half of all tax revenue. The arrears collection department of the treasury had also tightened its procedures for granting tax deferrals. The standard rate is now 18 percent for VAT and 25 percent for corporate and personal income tax. The social tax rate is 37 percent, but this is scheduled to be reduced to 33 percent by the year 2001.

2. Does fiscal policy encourage private savings, investment and earnings? (Has there been any reform/alteration of revenue and budget policies? How large are budget deficits and overall debt? Is the financing of the social insurance/pension system sustainable? What proportion of the budget is taken up by subsidies to firms and individuals?) The banking crisis of 1995 led to widespread distrust of Latvia's commercial banking system. Deposits of private individuals at the failed Banka Baltija, then the country's largest commercial bank, accounted for 40 percent of all individual deposits in Latvia's commercial banks. Fear of future bank failures led clients to withdraw deposits even from banks that were basically stable. Subsequent government reforms in the banking sector helped to stabilize the economy as a whole, creating confidence in the consumer and business sectors, and leading to increased savings. Between April and October 1996, bank deposits by domestic enterprises and private individuals increased from 303.3 million lats to 352.6 million lats. Although the consolidated assets of Latvian commercial banks were 1.68 percent higher in 1997 than in 1996, deposits fell by 4.5 percent during the first quarter of 1998. In 1996, the budget deficit was less than the target figure of 40 million lats — or 2 percent of GDP. By 1997, the basic state budget had collected revenues of 537 million lats against expenditures of 496 million lats. The 1998 central government budget, which was adopted in December 1997, will be balanced. The consumer price index (CPI) as a measure of inflation has decreased consistently throughout the 1990s. In 1993, annual CPI was 109.1 percent. It fell to 36.6 percent in 1994, 26.0 percent in 1995, and 17.6 percent in 1996. By 1997, it had fallen to 8.5 percent. Although Latvia's inflation rate is low by regional standards, price increases still exceed wage increases. In the first nine months of 1997, household incomes rose by 7.1 percent, while consumer prices increased by more than 8 percent. Although the official unemployment rate is approximately 7 percent, the actual rate may be as high as 18 percent. Unemployment is significantly higher in rural areas, especially in the southeastern Latgale region. After a 14.9 percent decline in real GDP in 1993, GDP grew by 0.6 percent in 1994, fell again by 1.6 percent in 1995, and then increased by 2.8 percent in 1996 and 4.0 percent in 1997. An increase of 5 percent is predicted for 1998.

The government has initiated a major overhaul of the social welfare system. Social payroll taxes will be reduced from 38 percent in 1996 to 33 percent by 2001. This will be accompanied by a more equitable division of contributions between employers and employees — 18 percent and 15 percent, respectively. Under the Law on Private Pensions, which was adopted in June 1997, a three-tiered pension system will be established: a modified pay-as-you-go (PAYG) system with stronger links between contributions and benefits, a mandatory funded system of privately managed savings accounts, and voluntary privately managed pensions. The first stage of the reform, the modification of the public PAYG system, took effect in January 1996. The second tier, under which contributors will have an option to assign a portion of their contributions to privately managed savings accounts, was introduced in 1998. On May 1, 1998, retirement pensions that were set before 1996 were increased 15.87 percent. Those that were set thereafter were increased by 5.7 percent. According to Latvia's welfare minister, based on the social insurance budget's revenues in 1998, the state will be able to pay pensions for at least the next two years. For the first time in Latvia's history, the social security fund recorded a surplus, which was aided by a January 1997 legislative change that made it legal to withhold benefits from employees who failed to pay their regular contributions to the social security fund.

3. Has there been banking reform? (Is the central bank independent? What are its responsibilities? Is it effective in setting and/or implementing monetary policy? What is the actual state of the private banking sector? Does it conform to international standards? Are depositors protected?) According to the 1992 Law on the Bank of Latvia, the country's central bank is independent. Under the law, the bank controls the amount of money in circulation, holds exclusive rights to issue the national currency, sets the official exchange rate, and supervises and audits commercial banks and other credit institutions. The bank has designed and implemented an independent and disciplined monetary policy and has successfully reduced inflation and maintained the strength and stability of the national currency. During the late 1980s and early 1990s, banks in Latvia opened under very loose regulations and developed with little supervision from the Bank of Latvia. By 1993, more than 60 banks had been licensed. The underlying weakness of the banking system became apparent in mid-1995, when the largest bank, Banka Baltija, as well as a number of smaller banks, collapsed. The crisis was caused by risky lending practices, unsustainable deposit interest payments, fraud, insider-trading, and inadequate banking laws and regulations. The banks lost approximately 40 percent of their assets and liabilities, and depositors lost an estimated $800 million in savings. The crisis also had a significant impact on the country's overall economy: GDP fell by 1.6 percent, foreign reserves fell by 20 percent, and a budget crisis arose as the government could no longer finance the deficit on the capital markets. The government responded by enacting a strict legal regulatory and supervisory framework, which is among the most stringent in Eastern Europe. The October 1995 Law on Credit Institutions gives the Bank of Latvia a broad range of enforcement powers, including cease-and-desist authority and the power to remove bank managers and fine banks. The law also requires banks to comply with and conduct external audits according to international accounting standards. There are also strict requirements for monthly and quarterly reporting to the Bank of Latvia. The minimum capitalization for existing banks was doubled in March 1998 from one million to two million lats. In 1996, the central bank performed more than 100 on-site inspections and revoked the licenses of eight smaller banks. By 1997, Latvia's commercial banks — led by Parekss Banka, Rietumu Banka, and Latvijas Unibanka — earned 36 percent more net profit than in 1996. As of early 1998, there were 31 commercial banks in Latvia, although only 22 are entitled to take deposits from private citizens, and only two or three banks dominate the relatively small market. With the exception of the Mortgage and Land Bank, Latvia's banking system is completely private. Under a law that will take effect in October 1998, individual bank deposits will be guaranteed through a special reserve fund of contributions from banks and one-time payments from the state budget and the Bank of Latvia. The maximum indemnity to individual depositors will gradually increase from 500 lats per depositor by 2000 to 1,000 lats by 2002 to 3,000 lats by 2004, and is expected to increase to 13,000 lats by 2008. The deposit law will also enable Latvia to meet EU requirements for banking legislation and practices.

4. How sound is the national currency? (Is the value of the currency fixed or does it float? How convertible is the currency? How large are the hard currency reserves? Has exchange rate policy been stable and predictable?) The exchange rate of the lat is determined by market forces with limited intervention by the Bank of Latvia. Although no formal policy has been announced, the lat has been effectively pegged to the Special Drawing Rights (SDR) currencies of the IMF since February 1994. The value of the lat is set at 79.97 *santims* — one santim equals 1/100 of a lat — to one SDR. While the banking crisis of 1995 increased pressure on the lat, the currency recovered strength by late August and remains stable. Some investors have expressed concern that Latvia may be more vulnerable to speculative pressure because it lacks the stabilizing influence of a currency board. Nevertheless, Latvia has maintained sufficient foreign reserves to back each lat in circulation by 113 percent. Based on these reserves, the success of its foreign exchange policies, and the complete and effective convertibility of capital accounts, it is highly unlikely that the government will limit the convertibility of the lat. In 1996, gross reserves, excluding gold, were approximately $654 million. In a recent survey, 80 percent of respondents expressed confidence in Latvia's national currency.

5. Is there a functioning capital market infrastructure? (Are there existing or planned commodities, bond and stock markets? What are the mechanisms for investment and lending? What government bodies have authority to regulate capital markets?) Latvian securities markets are regulated by the Law on Securities and Law on Securities Market Commission. They are supervised by the Securities Market Committee of the Ministry of Finance. The Riga Stock Exchange (RSE) and the Latvian Central Depository began to operate in 1995. Only four stocks were quoted on the RSE during the first day of trading. Both treasury bills and stocks, with the latter subdivided into the primary, secondary, and free lists, are traded. Securities markets are dominated by trade in treasury bills with increasingly lengthening maturities. Foreign banks are allowed to participate in the primary market for treasury bills, and the Bank of Latvia provides repurchase and reverse-repurchase facilities. Stock market capitalization rose to approximately 7 percent of GDP in mid-1997. The Dow Jones RSE Index, which is based on ten stocks that represent approximately 80 percent of the stock market's capitalization, more than tripled between April 1996 and August 1997. Average daily turnover at the stock exchange had increased to approximately $400,000 by mid-1997. Nevertheless, the stock market suffered a correction in October and November 1997, mainly as a secondary effect of the fall in value of Estonian equity at the end of October. As Estonian stocks felt the effect of an international loss of confidence in emerging markets, liquidity on the Estonian stock market ended. Estonian brokers, who held significant stock inventories in Latvia, were forced to liquidate positions in Riga in order to meet commitments in Tallinn. This, in turn, caused a fall in the Dow Jones Riga Stock Exchange (DJRSE) index. On Estonia's "Black Thursday" of October 23, the Latvian index fell by 11.5 percent, and bank stocks were particularly affected. The DJRSE dropped from a high of 488 on October 9 to 324 on November 11, and then rose to 346 on December 30. As of early 1998, approximately 33 legal entities, including 21 banks and 12 brokerages, were licensed to operate on the securities market in Latvia.

Microeconomics 2.50/7

1. **Are property rights guaranteed? (Are there both formal and de facto protections of private real estate and intellectual property? Is there a land registry with the authority and capability to ensure accurate recording of who owns what? What are the procedures for expropriation, including measures for compensation and challenge? Have any seizures taken place?)** Under Article 21 of the Latvian Constitutional Law, the state recognizes and protects the right of a person to own property and the right of inheritance. The Constitutional Law also guarantees freedom for creative work and protects patent rights and copyrights. In 1993, parliament passed additional legislation to protect copyrights, trademarks and patents. Latvia has been a member of the World Intellectual Property Organization since January 1993, a member of the Paris Convention since September 1993, and a member of the Bern Convention since August 1995. While the legal basis for intellectual property rights has been established and some of its enforcement mechanisms are in place, Latvian law has not defined penalties for violations of these rights. Courts may invalidate any patent or trademark that does not meet the legal requirements for the award of a patent or the substantive provisions for registering a trademark. Intellectual property rights may be enforced through Latvian court action. Unauthorized Russian reproductions of copyrighted video recordings are widely distributed in Latvia. In an October 1992 move to halt the use of pirated films imported from Russia by private Latvian television stations, the Latvian Radio and Television Board adopted a ruling under which the license of any domestic television company can be revoked if it is unable to prove that it has legally acquired the rights to the films which it broadcasts.

Since independence, the Latvian government has been de-nationalizing private property seized by Soviet authorities. Although control over urban and rural property is being returned to former owners, legal mechanisms for title registration, sale, and mortgaging of real property are not yet fully developed. Legally transferable rights to private real property are slowly being reestablished as properties are registered in reconstituted land registers. Amendments to the Law on Land Reform in the Cities of the Republic of Latvia, which has been in effect since June 1997, provide that land transactions are allowed only if the land is registered in the land book. According to the Constitutional Law, the forced expropriation of property can occur only through a court decision in accordance with procedures prescribed by law. If property is expropriated for the realization of a public project, the owner is entitled to appropriate compensation. There have been no cases of arbitrary expropriation of private property by the Latvian government.

2. To what extent have prices been liberalized? What subsidies remain? The private sector sets most prices and wages, although the government continues to establish prices for some goods and services, including electricity, rents for government-controlled housing, transportation, and telecommunications. Domestic agricultural prices have been liberalized, and rent subsidies are being cut. Electricity tariffs charged by the state-owned power utility are approaching cost-recovery levels, and authorities predict an increase to full economic cost by 2005. Enterprises must maintain wages at or above a legally specified minimum level. The average gross monthly wage was approximately $191 in the first quarter of 1997. The minimum wage represented about 35 percent of the average gross wage.

3. Is it possible to own and operate a business? (Has there been legislation regarding the formation, dissolution and transfer of businesses, and is the law respected? Do there exist overly cumbersome bureaucratic hurdles that effectively hinder the ability to own and dispose of a business? Are citizens given access to information on commercial law? Is the law applied fairly? Does regulation (or licensing requirements) impose significant costs on business and consumers? Do they create significant barriers to entry and seriously hamper competition?) Business activities in Latvia are regulated by the Law on Entrepreneurial Activities and Business Operations, which serves as the legal framework for establishing, registering, operating, and closing a business. A new Law on Credit Institutions was passed in October 1995 and a modern bankruptcy law was adopted in 1996. A law on commercial activity, which would replace existing laws on entrepreneurship, is likely to be adopted later in 1998. The Latvian Law on Insolvency of Enterprises and Companies, which was enacted in September 1996 and amended in May 1997 provides for reorganization proceedings in which a majority of creditors can reach a binding settlement with the debtor. Establishing a business in Latvia is relatively simple, and many private businesses are opening. Nevertheless, corruption exists and some regulations are applied unevenly. The Register of Enterprises, which registers companies and enterprises, must consider the documents for the formation of an enterprise within 15 days of the date of submission. If the business application is not refused within 30 days, the business is regarded as registered. A Law on Joint Stock Companies was enacted in May 1993. The cost of formation and registration of a joint stock company, including legal, notary, and court fees, but excluding minimum share capital, is estimated at $2,500. The process normally takes less than two months. Latvia has a sound legislative and institutional base for the operation of small- and medium-sized businesses of up to 250 employees. A Central Statistical Bureau survey, however, revealed that the main barriers to business development were lack of finance, limited credit, insufficient knowledge of the market, unfair competition, a low level of technology, and a lack of qualified personnel. Other surveys confirm these findings and also cite frequent changes in legislation and inconsistent implementation as major barriers. In order to stimulate growth and competitiveness in the business sector, the government launched a national program in 1997-1998 for the development of small- and medium-sized businesses. Its provisions include improved business regulation through tax changes and simplification of licensing procedures, a credit guarantee system, coordination of foreign technical and financial assistance, promotion of technological development, encouragement of cooperation among small businesses, and the development of business training.

4. Are courts effective, transparent, efficient, and quick in reaching decisions on property and contract disputes? What alternative mechanisms for adjudicating disputes exist? In general, investment laws are drafted by legally trained personnel and published within one month of their passage. First-instance court decisions can be appealed, and there is an independent right of judicial review of administrative action. On average, a party must wait between seven months and one year for a commercial case to be heard on its merits by a court in the most important commercial center. The average wait is the same for a final judgment for payment of a sum of money to be executed.

5. Is business competition encouraged? (Are monopolistic practices limited in law and in practice? If so, how? To what degree is "insider" dealing a hindrance to open competition? Are government procurement policies open and unbiased?) Under Latvia's 1991 and 1993 laws on competition and restriction of monopolies, businesses are precluded from manipulating prices or quantities of goods offered for sale and may not create artificial shortages in order to increase prices. The Latvian Anti-Monopoly Control Committee, which oversees implementation of the laws, investigates cases of anti-competitive behavior and has the power to issue orders for the termination of unlawful activity. Companies proposing a merger that would result in the concentration of more than 25 percent of the market for a particular good or service must obtain the committee's approval. In 1995-96, the committee's orders and recommendations to the government, municipal authorities, and utilities led to changes in licensing and tendering procedures and price-setting in various markets.

In June 1997, parliament adopted a new Competition Act that is modeled on EU directives. The law defines the concepts of state aid, mergers, unfair competition, and the role of the state in promoting and protecting the competitive environment in the economy. An independent Competition Board was created to oversee the implementation of the new act, which supercedes the 1991 anti-monopoly law. Lattlekom, the Latvian telecommunications company, has been guaranteed a monopoly until 2013. Pressure by the World Trade Organization to advance the opening of the telecom market to 2003 has already generated interest among potential competitors, including Telia Latvija, which has stated its intention to enter the market as soon as the monopoly is lifted. "Insider-dealing" continues to restrict open competition, especially in larger privatization and other transactions. Political connections are important, and corruption and favoritism are not uncommon. In one case of conflict of interest, an employee of the Ministry of Finance opened one of the largest auditing companies in Latvia.

Latvia's Law on Government and Municipal Procurement, which took effect in January 1997, laid the legislative foundation for a modern public procurement system. The law describes public procurement procedures, specifies the general form of procurement contracts and account settlements, provides procedures for resolving disputes, and fixes the responsibilities of each institution and person involved in procurement procedures. The remedies system established by the law is inadequate. It is difficult for tenderers to seek administrative review of mistaken or illegal decisions taken by a public institution. Losing competitors who claim to have suffered loss or damage due to an infringement of the law by the procuring entity in procurement proceedings can apply to the court system. As of early 1998, no competitor had done so. In general, however, the procurement system operates effectively. The EU has provided assistance in the form of training programs for Latvian public procurement agents and legal counsel to analyze current legislation and propose further reforms. Planned future initiatives include harmonizing the law with EU directives and amending the law to clarify the remedies system.

6. To what extent has international trade been liberalized? To what degree has there been simplification/overhaul of customs and tariff procedures, and are these applied fairly? What informal trade barriers exist? Latvia's trade regime is liberal for industrial goods. Its customs tariff system is still evolving. Under a tariff law adopted in December 1994, Latvian customs tariffs on raw materials, spare parts, and capital goods are at rates of 0.5 to 1 percent. Most-favored-nation import tariffs on consumer goods are generally modest and range from 15 to 20 percent. The tariff structure favors investment goods. To protect the ailing farm sector, the government applies its highest rates to agricultural products. A new customs law that was adopted in June 1997 brings anti-dumping and counter-value measures and customs valuation into accord with the requirements of the World Trade Organization, which Latvia may join by the end of 1998. Subsequent amendments to the Law on Custom Tax (Tariffs) simplified customs procedures under the new customs law. The principal non-tariff barrier to trade is the requirement of a license for the import of sugar, grain, alcohol, fuel, and arms. In addition to tariffs, imports are subject to excise taxes and an 18 percent VAT. Excise taxes are applied to alcohol, tobacco, jewelry, automobiles, and gasoline at rates varying from 10 percent for cars to 100 percent for tobacco products. The excise tax on gasoline and diesel fuel is being increased gradually to European levels.

Latvia continues to pursue trade policies consistent with market reforms and the need to extend its primary trade beyond the former Soviet Union. Trade with the EU has increased from nearly 45 percent of total trade in 1996 to 50 percent in 1997. The EU's shares of imports also rose during the same period from approximately 50 percent to 53.5 percent. During the same period, Latvian exports to CIS countries declined from 36.5 percent to 28.8 percent, while imports from the CIS dropped from 24.7 percent to 19.5 percent. Latvia has concluded a free trade agreement with the EU and bilateral free trade agreements with countries of the European Free Trade Area and several countries of the Central European Free Trade Agreement. It is also a signatory to the Baltic Free Trade Agreement. Latvia's trade deficit in the first nine months of 1997 was 400 million lats ($690 million), an increase of 22 percent over the corresponding period in 1996. Exports increased by 22 percent, while imports increased by 24 percent. The fundamental cause of the slower export growth is delays in privatization, which have hampered the badly needed modernization of many enterprises and improvements in the quality and competitiveness of locally manufactured goods. Recently, the government has become more active in export promotion by expanding technical and information assistance for exporters, supporting the creation of overseas chambers of commerce, and developing a mechanism for export credit guarantees.

7. To what extent has foreign investment and capital flow been encouraged or constrained? The Latvian government is actively attempting to encourage foreign direct investment. Under the 1991 Investment Law, Latvian laws apply equally to domestic and foreign investors. In 1996, amendments to the Investment Law removed virtually all restrictions on foreign investment, except in the timber industry. A foreign investor is allowed to lease land for up to 99 years. Companies that are owned by foreigners can purchase land if the foreign investors represent countries with which Latvia has entered into international agreements on the mutual protection of foreign investments. Land can also be purchased by companies in which the controlling share is owned by citizens of Latvia. Although the land law has been liberalized, some restrictions on the purchase of land by individual foreigners still remain. To promote foreign investments, Latvia has concluded bilateral investment agreements with the United States, Canada, France, Germany, the United Kingdom, Vietnam, Israel, and the Scandinavian countries. In addition, the government created the Latvian Development Agency, which provides foreign investors with easy access to advisory services on regulations, local business conditions, and investment opportunities. Special economic zones (SEZs) have been established in the municipalities of Riga, Ventspils, Liepaja, and Rezekne to provide tax and, in some cases, tariff relief to companies established there. Under current plans, SEZs will be established for 20 years and will provide such incentives as an 80 percent reduction in corporate income tax or a suspension of property tax payments. The Liepaja and Rezekne SEZs were formed in order to encourage investment and economic activity in economically distressed areas. No more SEZs are planned because the EU and international financial organizations claim that they distort competition.

According to the Central Statistical Bureau, the total amount of foreign investment from the beginning of the 1990s to the end of 1996 was 369.2 million lats (more than $700 million), an average *per capita* rate of foreign investment for the region. In 1997, foreigners invested 2.15 billion lats in Latvia, representing an increase of 42 percent from 1996. Investors from Denmark provided approximately 19 percent of total foreign investments followed by Russia and the United States with 10 percent each, Germany with nine percent, and Singapore with eight percent The largest investments were in the areas of transportation and warehousing, industrial production, and finance. Foreign investment has reached Latvia mainly through the process of privatization. Obstacles to even greater foreign investment include the troubled financial situation of many local companies, poor management, the low capitalization of the securities market, and the slow pace of land reform. As privatization continues and the economic environment improves further, the volume of direct foreign investment is expected to increase even more.

8. Has there been reform of the energy sector? (To what degree has the energy sector been restructured? Is the energy sector more varied, and is it open to private competition? Is the

country overly dependent on one or two other countries for energy, including whether exported fuels must pass through one or more countries to reach markets?) Latvia's energy sector is being restructured. The first public offering of the state-owned oil company, Ventspils Nafta, through the voucher privatization program took place in October 1997. The sale of nearly five million shares, or five percent of the company's equity, represented the country's largest voucher privatization to date. Russian and German strategic investors bought minority stakes in the state-owned gas company Latvijas Gaze in 1997. There was also a public offering of shares in the company. In March 1998, parliament voted to suspend the privatization of the state power company Latvenergo until a parliamentary committee had completed its investigation of the earlier disappearance of $1.8 million from the company. For more than two decades, Russian gas supplies for consumers in the Baltics and northwestern Russia have been stored seasonally at the Inculkans underground gas storage facility in Latvia. Through this arrangement, Latvia secures a stable supply of gas and collects storage fees. Latvian energy officials have expressed interest in developing other natural gas storage facilities as Russia positions itself to supply greater amounts of gas to the European market. One of the main reasons for the expected rise in consumption of gas is the EU's focus on environmental protection, including the gradual switch from environmentally dangerous fuels to natural gas. In February 1998, parliament adopted a draft power law to regulate the production, purchase, and distribution of various types of energy, the licensing and functioning of power companies, and the supply of energy to consumers. It also provides for Latvia's integration into the international energy market, the attraction of investment, and increased energy efficiency.

LITHUANIA

Freedom in the World Ratings, 1989-1998									
	1989-90	1990-91	1991-92	1992-93	1993-94	1994-95	1995-96	1996-97	1997-98
Political Rights	-	-	2	2	1	1	1	1	1
Civil Liberties	-	-	3	3	3	3	2	2	2
Status	-	-	F	F	F	F	F	F	F

Polity: Consolidated Democracy
Economy: Consolidated Market
Population: 3,705,000
PPP: $3,843
Ethnic Groups: Lithuanian (80 percent), Russian (9 percent), Polish (8 percent), Ukrainian, Belarusian, others
Capital: Vilnius

Political Process 1.75/7

1. When did national legislative elections occur? Were they free and fair? How were they judged by domestic and international election monitoring organizations? Who composes the government? International observers deemed Lithuania's October 20, 1996 election to be "free and fair." The Homeland Union-Conservative Party now holds 70 seats in the country's 138-seat parliament. Three seats remain unoccupied. The Christian Democratic Party holds 16 seats. The Center Union holds 13 seats, while the Democratic Labor Party and the Social Democratic Party each hold 12. Fourteen seats are held by individuals who won in single-mandate districts. Parties must win at least five percent of the total votes that are cast in order to win proportional representation in the parliament. The government is a center-right coalition of the Homeland Union-Conservative Party, the Christian Democratic Party, and the Center Union. Gediminas Vagnorius of the Homeland Union serves as prime minister. The two main opposition parties are the leftist Social Democratic Party and Labor Democratic Party.

2. When did presidential elections occur? Were they free and fair? The most recent presidential elections, which were determined by international observers to be "free and fair," took place on December 21, 1997. U.S. émigré environmentalist Valdas Adamkus was elected by majority vote in the second round of balloting on January 4, 1998. Adamkus defeated Arturas Paulauskas by a margin of less than one percentage point. Voter turnout reached 73.78 percent. Adamkus was supported by the Center Union and other parties, but declared himself an independent when he took office.

3. Is the electoral system multiparty-based? Are there at least two viable political parties func-

tioning at all levels of government? The electoral system is multiparty-based. Half of the seats in the parliament are filled through multiple-mandate proportional balloting, while the other half is identified through polling in single-mandate districts. Parties must receive a minimum of five percent of the votes in order to share in the parliament's proportional representation. Currently, the largest and most influential party is the Homeland Union-Conservative Party. Other major parties that hold parliamentary seats and mayoral posts include the Christian Democratic Party, which is the traditional partner of the Homeland Union; the leftist Social Democratic Party; the Labor Democratic Party, which succeeded the former Communist Party; the Center Union; and the Liberal Union.

4. How many parties have been legalized? Are any particular parties illegal? As of May 1998, 33 political parties were legally registered. No party has been denied registration on political grounds. To be registered, a party must have a minimum of 400 members.

5. What proportion of population belongs to political parties? One to two percent of Lithuania's 3.7 million citizens are registered members of political parties.

6. What has been the trend of voter turnout at the municipal, provincial and national levels in recent years? Voter turnout in Lithuania's national legislative elections fell from more than 70 percent in 1992 to approximately 53 percent in October 1996. In general, turnout is higher in presidential elections. In the 1993 and 1997 presidential elections, more than 70 percent of eligible voters cast their ballots. In municipal elections, the turnout was 45 percent in 1995 and 40 percent in 1997.

Civil Society 2.00/7

1. How many non-governmental organizations (NGOs) have come into existence since 1988? What is the number of charitable/non-profit organizations? Are there locally led efforts to increase philanthropy and volunteerism? What proportion of the population is active in private voluntary activity (from polling data)? The NGO sector has grown steadily in recent years. At the national level, NGOs are registered with the justice and economy ministries, while regional NGOs are registered with municipalities. No governmental or private institution maintains a uniform registry of NGOs. According to the NGO Information and Support Center, there are more than 3,000 non-governmental organizations in Lithuania. Approximately 200 new NGOs are formed each year. In general, individual contributions to NGOs are minimal. NGOs instead focus their fundraising efforts on international foundations and Lithuanian businesses. According to the Department of Statistics, private firms and individuals contribute approximately one-fifth of NGO revenues. NGOs also receive public funding. Volunteerism remains a rare form of support for NGOs. There is no data on the proportion of the population that engages in voluntary activities. The Center for Volunteerism lobbies the legislature and seeks public support for volunteerism.

2. What is the legal and regulatory environment for NGOs (i.e., ease of registration, legal rights, government regulation, taxation, procurement, and access-to-information issues)? To what extent is NGO activism focused on improving the legal and regulatory environment? NGOs are subject to many of the laws that regulate business entities. Certain types of NGOs, for example, are prohibited from selling their products or services. The tax regime for NGOs is similar to that of for-profit companies, but NGOs pay a five percent income tax rather than the regular 29-percent rate. Donations from companies are tax-exempt. Charitable contributions from abroad are not subject to value-added tax (VAT), but, in some cases, are taxed with customs duties. NGOs do not pay stamp duty for registration services. NGOs encounter difficulties in handling complex and inappropriate accounting regulations. They must hire professional accountants to help them tackle accounting. The most active groups urging revision of the legal and regulatory framework for NGOs are international foundations, Lithuanian NGOs and NGO support organizations. In 1996, as a result of heightened policy advocacy from one of Lithuania's NGOs, the Lithuanian Free Market Institute (LFMI), parliament suspended in the third reading the adoption of a draft law on public organizations, returning it to the government for revision. The LFMI consolidated efforts with other institutions and significantly improved the bill. Parliament approved the amended version, which provided for improved operational and financial principles for NGO activities. NGO forums in 1997 and 1998 established coordinating groups to identify and eliminate weaknesses in the NGO regulatory environment.

3. What is the organizational capacity of NGOs? Do management structures clearly delineate authority and responsibility? Is information available on NGO management issues in the native language? Is there a core of experienced practitioners/trainers to serve as consultants or mentors to less developed organizations? According to the NGO Information and Support Center, the U.S.-Baltic Foundation, and the Open Society Fund-Lithuania, the operational and managerial capabilities of NGOs have increased considerably in recent years. The quality of operations and management of approximately 200 major NGOs is comparable to that of leading businesses. The NGO Information and Support Center, other NGO support organizations, and foundations have improved the visibility and effectiveness of Lithuanian NGOs through seminars, publications, and other activities. With support from the Netherlands and Poland, the NGO Information and Support Center has trained 20 professional NGO consultants to assist NGOs in improving their operations.

4. Are NGOs financially viable? What is their tax status? Are they obliged to and do they typically disclose revenue sources? Do government procurement opportunities exist for private, not-for-profit providers of services? Most Lithuanian NGOs are not financially viable because they do not have permanent sources of income. Currently, contributions from international foundations for specific projects constitute the largest portion of NGO income. Funds solicited from local donors account for approximately one-fifth of NGO income. NGOs encounter difficulties in raising unrestricted funds to meet their organizational expenses and development objectives. According to NGO regulations, tax exemptions are valid only for funds that support projects that are approved according to established procedures. Certain types of NGOs, such as associations and foundations, are not allowed to engage in commercial activities. State institutions and municipalities are considering the use of NGOs to provide certain services. To date, government procurements have been limited to social services. Recently, the government prepared a price directory for social services. The directory is expected to improve the prospects of NGOs as providers of services.

5. Are there free trade unions? How many workers belong to these unions? Is the number of workers belonging to trade unions growing or decreasing? What is the numerical/proportional membership of farmers' groups, small business associations, etc.? The Lithuanian Alliance of Trade Unions, the Center of Trade Unions, the Lithuanian Labor Federation, and the Employees' Union link trade union and labor groups. The trade union movement has been adversely affected by industrial restructuring, privatization, and the bankruptcy of large state-owned enterprises. Nevertheless, the number of workers who belong to trade unions has steadily increased. In Lithuania, there are approximately 80 professional organizations with a total of nearly 200,000 members. The largest trade union memberships are in construction, chemical industries, and the energy and food sectors. Trade unions in the educational sector are particularly effective. Newly established professional organizations receive advice and technical support from the Trade Union Fund.

6. What forms of interest group participation in politics are legal? What types of interest groups are active in the political and policy process? Business associations, trade unions, and NGOs are the most active and influential participants in the political process. Trade unions are playing an increasingly significant role due to their large memberships and organizational structures. In general, government officials are attentive, but not always responsive to the views of interest groups. Interest and political advocacy groups are increasingly involved in the policy-making process through their participation in ministerial task forces and other policy initiatives. In recent months, they have played an active role in the development of legislation on private pension funds, taxes, and the budget. Some groups have proposed that lobbying be legalized, while others warn that this would lead to an expansion of governmental authority.

7. How is the not-for-profit/NGO sector perceived by the public and government officials? What is the nature of media coverage of NGOs? To what extent do government officials engage with NGOs? A 1997 survey by the Social Information Center revealed that, in general, Lithuanians are unaware of the existence and activities of Lithuanian NGOs. Thirty-six percent of respondents could not name even one NGO. Many respondents confuse NGOs with private companies and governmental agencies. Local governments often cooperate with NGOs and, in some cases, provide limited financial assistance. Central government officials are also favorably disposed in their dealings with NGOs, but to date, no formal structures for cooperation have been developed. Media coverage of NGO activities is usually in the context of general developments in the country.

Independent Media 1.50/7

1. Are there legal protections for press freedom? The Lithuanian constitution guarantees the freedom to "pursue, receive, and disseminate information and ideas," but this freedom may be limited in order "to protect a man's health, honor, dignity, private life, and morals" or the "constitutional order." The constitutional provision that a "man's personal life is inviolable" has created much political controversy in the country. This provision is also enshrined in the civil code, which provides for compensation of up to 10,000 *litas* if a person sustains moral harm through the publication of information about his personal life without his prior consent. The Journalists Union seeks to limit the involvement of the state in conflicts between press freedom and the right to private life.

Most influential media representatives act professionally in accordance with the Ethical Code of Journalists and Publishers.

2. Are there legal penalties for libeling officials? Are there legal penalties for "irresponsible" journalism? Have these laws been enforced to harass journalists? The law, which holds that all citizens are equal, provides no specific penalties for libeling officials. Article 131 of the Criminal Code provides for two years of imprisonment, two years of penitentiary labor, or a fine for libeling or disseminating false information that defames a person. To date, courts have imposed penalties for libel in only two cases. In April 1998, an editor and the editor-in-chief of the newspaper *Europe* were sentenced to one year in prison for libel. In July 1997, Valery Ivanov, a Russian citizen who led the pro-Soviet organization *Yedinstvo* in Lithuania, was sentenced to one year of penitentiary labor for defamation of the victims of the 1991 failed Soviet coup.

3. What proportion of media is privatized? What are the major newspapers, television stations, and radio stations? The state owns the ELTA news agency and Lithuanian Radio and Television, which holds 30 percent of the radio market and 25 percent of the television market. The remaining media are privately owned. Major daily newspapers includee *Lietuvos Rytas*, which has a circulation of 76,000 on weekdays and 120,000 on weekends; *Kauno Diena*, which has a circulation of 56,000; and *Respublika*, which has a circulation of 40,000 on weekdays and 60,000 on weekends. Popular television stations in addition to Lithuanian Television include LNK, which holds 35 percent of the market the market, and TV-3, which holds a 22-percent market share. Major radio stations include Lithuanian Radio-1, which holds 29 percent of the market; M-1, which holds 19 percent; and Radiocentras, which holds 13 percent.

4. Are the private media financially viable? Some privately-owned media are financially viable. *Lietuvos Rytas*, which has grown steadily in recent years, has expanded its editorial offices and built a modern publishing house. In addition to serving its own printing needs, the newspaper also provides high-quality printing services for other publications, including opposition newspapers that had been subjected to a government crackdown in Belarus. In late 1996, M-1 radio, which is popular with young listeners, established M-1 Plius, a daughter company that is targeting older audiences. In early 1998, the owner of the two stations acquired a controlling, 56-percent share of LNK Television. In recent years, several periodicals have gone out of business. The editor-in-chief of *Pirmadienis* attributed his publication to increased competition from weekend supplements that are now published by the most popular dailies.

5. Are the media editorially independent? Are the media's news gathering functions affected by interference from government or private owners? The media in Lithuania are editorially independent. Publications may be closed and journalists may be penalized only by the courts. Nevertheless, state institutions have on occasion attempted to limit the rights of journalists. In early 1998, the Justice ministry asked parliament to pass an amendment that would have limited the ability of the media to obtain information on legal proceedings. In response to pressure and criticism from the media and the public, the proposal was rejected. The Ministry of Defense refuses to allow its officials to communicate with journalists or to publicize information. State-owned radio and television remains under considerable influence by the government.

6. Is the distribution system for newspapers privately or governmentally controlled? With the exception of the *Lithuanian Post*, which holds a negligible share of the market, Lithuania's newspaper distribution system is privately-owned. The largest periodicals have their own subscription services. The *Lietuvos Rytas* subscription service gives priority to publications that are printed by its publishing house. *Lietuvos Spauda*, which operates 600 kiosks, is the largest press company and was formed from a former Soviet monopolostic enterprise. Today, it is a predominantly employee-owned joint stock company.

7. What proportion of the population is connected to the Internet? Are there any restrictions on Internet access to private citizens? As of 1997, Internet services were being provided by 16 companies, most of which do not release data on the number of clients that they serve. The companies that do release information have from 50 to 6,000 customers. The provision of Internet services is a rapidly developing market. There are no restrictions or regulations on the use of the Internet.

8. What has been the trend in press freedom as measured by Freedom House's Survey of Press Freedom? In Freedom House's annual Survey of Press Freedom, Lithuania was rated "Free" from 1993 to 1998.

Governance and Public Administration 2.50/7

1. Is the legislature the effective rule-making institution? The legislature is the effective rule-making institution. It is frequently criticized for over-regulation and interventionism and for passing laws that express sentiments rather than impose rules. Laws are frequently ambiguous or vague and often duplicate or conflict with other legal provisions. Evidence suggests that laws may be influenced by interest groups.

2. Is substantial power decentralized to sub-national levels of government? What specific authority do sub-national authorities have? Lithuania has one level of local government, which includes 56 municipalities. Most of the municipalities have 30,000 to 50,000 inhabitants. Ten regional administrations, which are territorial units of the central government, are headed by appointed governors. Local government units are largely dependent upon the national government. The responsibilities of local governments are divided into independent functions and functions delegated by the central government. The main independent responsibilities include municipal development, the management of municipal enterprises, the establishment and supervision of protected areas and objects, and sanitation. The main responsibilities that are delegated by the central government include primary and secondary education, primary health care and disease prevention, culture and sports, the development of the leisure and tourism industries, environment protection, social assistance, garbage collection, fire protection, heating, water supply, and sewage. Some responsibilities, including elements of health care and education, have not been clearly assigned to either the central or the local government and are therefore subject to the subjective interpretation of specific laws. Controversy arising from these ambiguities has led to intergovernmental tensions, inefficiencies in the provision of services, and problems in accountability. It may also impede further progress in decentralization and the development of stable municipal fiscal structures.

3. Are sub-national officials chosen in free and fair elections? At the municipal level, sub-national officials are chosen in free and fair elections for three-year terms. Mayors and heads of territorial local government administrations are appointed. The Agrarian Party has called for the direct election of these officials.

4. Do executive and legislative bodies operate openly and with transparency? Is draft legislation easily accessible to the media and public? In recent years, parliament and the government have provided the public with information on their policies. Independent media and NGOs have also monitored and reported on the policy-making process. Executive-level policy-making is not entirely transparent. Policy proposals and bills submitted for governmental consideration are not easily accessible to the public. Cabinet sessions are held in private. Ministries and other executive authorities often adopt new policies and regulations without prior notice or public scrutiny. Parliamentary operations are more transparent, but the parliament has no legal obligations to inform the public and media of its proposals and decisions. Important policy decisions and even laws are sometimes adopted hastily with no time for public comment. There are no procedures for public hearings. The deliberations of local authorities are usually less transparent than those of the parliament.

5. Do municipal governments have sufficient revenues to carry out their duties? Do municipal governments have control over their own budgets? Do they raise revenues autonomously or from the central state budget? In general, municipal governments do not possess sufficient funds to meet their expenditures. Shortfalls may be attributed to mismanagement and the expansion of local government authority. With the exception of functions delegated by the central government, municipalities can re-allocate funds between expenditure categories. Municipal revenues are calculated and transferred by the central government. The formula for local revenues is set by law. Changes are negotiated by municipalities and the central government and approved by parliament every three years. Local authorities are not authorized to introduce or collect taxes. These functions are managed by the Tax Inspectorate and the Finance Ministry. Local governments may, however, introduce local charges and user fees. They can also lower tax rates at the expense of their own revenues. More than 70 percent of municipal revenues derive from personal income tax and subsidies from the central budget. The fiscal capacities of local governments are equalized through revenue-sharing based on an expenditure-need calculus. For example, only 51 percent of personal income tax collected in the city of Vilnius is added to the municipality's budget, while most rural municipalities retain 100 percent of receipts from the tax.

6. Do the elected local leaders and local civil servants know how to manage municipal governments effectively? The managerial ability of local officials varies significantly among municipalities. In most municipalities, local leaders and civil servants lack skills and experience and are inclined toward excessive interventionism.

7. When did the constitutional/legislative changes on local power come into effect? Has there been a reform of the civil service code/system? Are local civil servants employees of the local or central government? Lithuania's system of municipal government was established by the 1992 constitution and the Law on Local Government. In 1997, a new law on local budget revenues brought stability and transparency to the budget process, but did not alter the principles of revenue creation. The government is expected to authorize a gradual increase in the number of municipalities in the near future. In 1995, civil service employees were divided into political appointees and non-appointees. Political appointees must resign when the government changes. Non-appointees are protected from dismissal except for reasons related to competence and performance. Local civil servants are employed by the local governments.

Rule of Law 2.00/7

1. Is there a post-Communist constitution? How does the judicial system interpret and enforce the constitution? Are there specific examples of judicial enforcement of the constitution in the last year? A post-Communist, democratic constitution was adopted by referendum in October 1992. It divides the powers of government on the French model. The constitution may be applied directly as law, but this rarely occurs in practice. The Constitutional Court resolves conflicts between legal provisions and the constitution. In its six years of operations, it has proved to be an independent, powerful, and reliable guardian of constitutional rights and has found many laws to be in conflict with the constitution. In one recent case, it found that a legal prohibition against the public criticism of the government by civil servants was in conflict with the constitution.

2. Does the constitutional framework provide for human rights? Do the human rights include business and property rights? The constitution provides for and protects human rights, including the rights to own property and work in business, in accordance with European and international standards. The constitution allows the state to intervene in economic affairs and promote business. Foreigners have limited opportunities to own land. Only citizens and legal entities of member-states of the European Union (EU), Organization for Economic Cooperation and Development (OECD) and NATO have the right to own non-agricultural land.

3. Has there been basic reform of criminal law/criminal code? Who authorizes searches and issues warrants? Are suspects and prisoners beaten or abused? Are there excessive delays in the criminal justice system? A new draft Criminal Code is under consideration and is scheduled to be enacted in 1999. The country's criminal law and criminal procedural law have been reformed through more than 300 amendments to the Criminal Code. Homosexuality has been decriminalized. Capital punishment, except for murder in aggravated circumstances, has been abolished. Nevertheless, criminal penalties in Lithuania are among the strictest and the country's prison population is among the largest in Europe. The judiciary has been reformed to introduce stricter procedures for criminal prosecutions. Searches are authorized by public prosecutors. Warrants are issued by judges. Prisoners and other detainees are sometimes beaten while imprisoned or under interrogation. Abuse and violence among prisoners and living conditions for prisoners and other detainees are growing causes for concern. Excessive delays in the criminal justice system are another cause for concern. Investigations in criminal cases are often slow. Some suspects spend more than three years in custody before receiving a final court verdict.

4. Do most judges rule fairly and impartially? Do many remain from Communist era? Most judges rule fairly and impartially, but some have accepted bribes. According to opinion polls, the public has little confidence in the judiciary. Most judges are new appointees.

5. Are the courts free of political control and influence? Are the courts linked directly to the Ministry of Justice or any other executive body? The Ministry of Justice has no formal control over court decisions, except in matters of technical support. In practice, however, its influence is significant. Most lawyers and businessmen claim that the state exerts pressure on judges, particularly in cases against state institutions. This influence is more evident in economic than political matters. Judges on the Court of Appeals and the Supreme Court, which hears appeals from appellate courts, are nominated by the president and approved by the legislature. District court judges are appointed by the president. The Constitutional Court, which adjudicates issues of legal constitutionality, has proved to be immune to political pressure. The chairman of the legislature, the chairman of the Supreme Court, and the president each nominate one judge to the Constitutional Court.

6. What proportion of lawyers is in private practice? How does this compare with previous years? There are no official data on the proportion of lawyers who are engaged in private practice.

7. Does the state provide public defenders? By law, the state must provide public defenders. In the face of a dramatic decline in the number of available lawyers, who were poorly compensated for their work, the government now requires that private lawyers provide a certain amount of service to the state.

8. Are there effective anti-bias/discrimination laws, including protection of ethnic minority rights? In general, all citizens are treated equally by law and in practice. There is, however, some evidence of discrimination against women and sexual minorities. Minorities are free to establish their own educational, cultural, and religious institutions. Representatives of national minorities can easily obtain citizenship. As of 1997, more than 90 percent of the country's ethnic minority population were citizens. A requirement that Lithuanian, the official language, be used in the documentation of public and private institutions, has led to controversy. Lithuania has ratified the European Convention on Human Rights and other major international conventions on human rights. The Framework Convention on Protection of National Minorities has been signed, but not ratified.

Corruption B

1. What is the magnitude of official corruption in the civil service? Must average citizen pay a bribe to a bureaucrat in order to receive a service? What services are subject to bribe requests? What is the average salary of civil servants at various levels? Corruption and bribery, two major legacies of the Soviet era, are still widespread in many areas. Most adult citizens are believed to have resorted to bribery for some purposes. Bribes are usually paid to obtain a benefit, obtain more favorable treatment, or hasten the provision of services. The customs department is a well-known center for corruption. Bribes are widely used to lower the costs of customs duties. Bribery is also widespread in tax inspections and hospitals. In hospitals, it is used as an incentive to improve the quality of service. Businesses often have recourse to bribery while obtaining registrations and licenses and seeking compliance with state regulations and controls. Corruption is also pervasive in the police force. Salaries of civil servants, both at the national and sub-national levels, are higher than those paid to individuals with comparable qualifications and responsibility in the private sector. The average salary of a civil servant is 1,200 to 1,300 litas. The salaries of teachers, physicians, and social workers are well below the national average.

2. Do top policy-makers (the President, ministers, vice-ministers, top court justices, and heads of agencies and commissions) have direct ties to businesses? How strong are such connections and what kinds of businesses are these? Links between politicians and businesses are the subject of frequent press reports. In general, businesses have a greater influence on policy-makers than policy-makers have on business. One of the most influential business lobbies is the Lithuanian Industrialists Confederation, which signed a memorandum with the Conservative party before the 1996 parliamentary elections. One of the leaders of the confederation was appointed as economic minister after the Conservatives took power. In a celebrated 1997 bribery case, former Defense Minister Audrius Butkevicius was jailed briefly after being found guilty of accepting a $15,000 payment to mediate with the prosecutor general in a court case. Butkevicius denied the charge. The case demonstrated that corruption has reached the top levels of government and that parliamentarians appear willing to pursue corruption charges on political or other grounds.

3. Do laws requiring financial disclosure and disallowing conflict of interest exist? Have publicized anti-corruption cases been pursued? To what conclusion? The law prohibits conflicts of interest and mandates financial disclosures by politicians, managers of companies, and their spouses. Presidential, parliamentary, and local council candidates must publicly declare their property and income before elections. Elected politicians, political appointees in the civil service, and directors of companies must make annual declarations of their income and property. Most anti-corruption cases that have been publicized are pursued by prosecutors. Many of these cases involve the police or customs or tax inspectors. In 1997, several judges, lawyers, and investigators were sentenced to prison for accepting bribes.

4. What major anti-corruption initiatives have been implemented? How often are anti-corruption laws and decrees adopted? The Conservative Party has honored its pledge to replace "corrupted laws" and enact stricter sanctions for corruption-related crimes. Under the government's "clean hands" policy, an insider commission investigates cases of corruption and abuses of official power. Incentives to curb regulations and bureaucratic authority are beginning to yield results. Some municipalities have adopted measures to curb bureaucracy and corruption, but it is still too early to judge how effective these initiatives will be.

5. How do major corruption-ranking organizations like Transparency International rate this country? Transparency International (TI) has not ranked Lithuania, but maintains that there is insufficient public control over government decisions. The laws provide for control, but it is rarely exercised in practice. In July 1997, TI representatives visited Vilnius at the invitation of the Conservative-controlled Lithuanian parliament, which promised to enact a "clean hands" policy and exercise tight control over government operations. TI concluded that Lithuania's attempts to curb corruption are appropriate, but not yet sufficient. It also concluded that the passage and implementation of clear tax laws would be the best way to curb corruption in the tax inspectorate. It identified customs abuses as a major source of concern. According to TI, civil society is weak, and civic groups do not play a sufficiently strong role in the policy-making process. A Lithuanian branch of the TI may be established to monitor the implementation of anti-corruption legislation.

Privatization 2.25/7

1. What percentage of GDP comes from private ownership? What percentage of the labor force is employed in the private sector? How large is informal sector of the economy? In 1997, the private sector constituted 70 percent of GDP. According to the Department of Statistics, 67.9 percent of the working population was employed in the private sector in the third quarter of 1997. The International Monetary Fund has estimated that the informal or "shadow" economy constituted 25 percent of the country's GDP in 1997.

2. What major privatization legislation has been passed? What where its substantive features? In 1991, parliament passed the Law on Initial Privatization of State Property, the Law on Privatization of the Property of Agricultural Enterprises, and the Law on Privatization of Housing. These laws provided the legal framework for initial privatization through a voucher program, which was used in the sale of approximately 45 percent of state assets, and cash and foreign currency sales, which were used in the divestment of 30 percent of assets. The 1995 privatization law provided a legal basis for cash privatization, which will be used for the sale of most remaining state assets. Legal disputes delayed the launch of the second-stage privatization program, and a lack of transparency led to conflicts of interest and significant public dissent. In 1997, a new law replaced the 1995 law and made changes to procedural rules and privatization authorities.

3. What proportion of agriculture, housing and land, industry, and small business and services is in private hands? Agriculture is privately owned. A process for restitution is still being developed. No precise data on the ownership of agricultural land are available. Ninety-five percent of housing is privately-owned. The state still retains control over approximately 70 percent of industry. Virtually all small businesses and services are in the private sector.

4. What has been the extent of insider (management, labor, and nomenklatura) participation in the privatization process? What explicit and implicit preferences have been awarded to insiders? When free vouchers were distributed in the early stages of privatization, insider participation was extensive. Most citizens bought their own apartments. Many acquired shares of companies that employed them or of investment companies, which later participated in the privatization of bigger enterprises. Since corporate profits were used to increase the share of private capital, a number of companies were privatized under preferential conditions that were not provided by law.

Due to the mismanagement of state enterprises and the absence of a market infrastructures, the nomenklatura obtained a large portion of shares. In the first stage, enterprise workers received preferential treatment. The second phase of privatization was launched in 1996. The sale of items through the stock exchange has been transparent, with no preferences given to specific buyers. Nevertheless, assets may be privatized through tenders and direct negotiations, which invite favoritism and abuse of power. Foreign investors enjoy preferences in the privatization of strategic enterprises.

5. How much public awareness of and support for privatization has there been? What is the nature of support and opposition to privatization by major interest groups? The public generally supports privatization. In a reflection of public confidence in the private sector, the Social Democratic Party failed in its mid-1997 attempt to hold a referendum on the privatization of "strategic" enterprises. Debates over the privatization of Lithuanian Telecom and some other enterprises have been intense, but they have focused on the prevention of monopolies rather than privatization *per se*. Workers at state-owned enterprises often resist privatization for fear of employee retrenchment. Some groups are apprehensive about the possible expansion of the influence of foreign countries in Lithuania. In general, however, the public has been supportive of the privatization process. Elderly citizens are watching closely to ensure that the government honors its commitment to use the proceeds from privatization to compensate for savings lost to currency depreciations and devalued deposits. Businesses, socially active segments of society, and the public at large view privatization as a means of promoting free competition and the effective use of resources.

Macroeconomics 2.25/7

1. Has the taxation system been reformed? The Lithuanian tax system includes income taxes, the VAT, property taxes, customs duties, and other taxes. The general tax burden has increased in recent years. According to the Ministry of Finance, total tax revenues accounted for 30.4 percent of GDP in 1997. In 1998, tax revenues are expected to consitute 32.3 percent of GDP. Personal income tax is charged at a regular rate of 33 percent. Corporate income is subject to a 29-percent tax. The country's income tax laws, which were adopted in 1991, have been repeatedly revised and amended. The main goal of new draft legislation is to broaden the tax base. The 18-percent VAT is the most effective of all Lithuanian taxes. Its revenues account for the largest portion of the state budget. Social insurance contributions, which are financed by a 31-percent payroll tax — with 30 percent paid by the employer and one percent by the employee — augment labor costs and add to the expansion of informal labor relationships. In general, taxpayers have found it difficult to understand the country's convoluted tax regulations, and their inquiries have added substantially to the workload of tax inspectors. The computerization of the tax administration has reduced the amount of manual work for tax inspectors. At the same time, however, new responsibilities – including on-site inspections and a new tax police force – have been added. As of 1997, income and property declaration was mandatory for certain segments of society. A requirement that general income be declared is scheduled to take effect in 1999. Together with a lack of security, Lithuania's complicated, ambiguous rules of income declaration will increase the burden of tax administration imposed on firms and individuals. Firms are responsible for calculating and paying taxes. Only a negligible portion of the tax base is provided by individuals. Severe penalties are imposed for tax evasion. In

April 1998, Lithuania adopted an indirect method for the calculation of incomes by tax inspectors. Taxpayers have the right to question inspectors' calculations.

2. Does fiscal policy encourage private savings, investment and earnings? Lithuania's fiscal policy has been severely criticized for its opaque principles of budget formation, inefficient allocation of resources, and unclear public spending objectives. The criticism has prompted a fundamental budget reform that is intended to secure a shift to program budgeting, with funds being allocated to programs rather than administrators. Lithuania has faced a national budget deficit for five years. According to the Ministry of Finance, federal expenditures exceeded revenues by 8.8 percent in 1997. The estimated budget deficit for 1998 is 7.6 percent. In 1997, the budget deficit constituted 1.9 percent of GDP, while the forecast deficit for 1998 is 1.6 percent. Independent experts claim that the deficit is actually several times larger because the state is still assuming new obligations, such as compensation to individuals for savings lost to currency depreciation and deposits lost in bankrupt banks. By law, the social insurance fund must balance its budget. Deficits are covered with loans taken from banks and guaranteed by the state. Lithuania is facing increasing difficulties in maintaining its pay-as-you-go system. Revenues for the social security budget have fallen dramatically, as have the number of contributors. Adverse demographic trends have further aggravated the under-funded and outmoded system, which represents a drag on the country's economic transition. According to the Ministry of Finance, total state debt in January 1998 constituted 20.16 percent of the projected annual GDP. Foreign debt constituted 14 percent of the anticipated GDP and 24.4 percent of the country's annual volume of exports. Although direct corporate subsidies have been removed, they are reaching companies through corporate welfare programs, including business promotion programs, export insurance, and others. Government expenditures not assigned to major expenditure categories account for more than 20 percent of central government outlays. In the first half of 1998, the central bank instituted interventions to regulate interest rates. Since April 1997, businesses have been allowed to deduct investments from taxable income. Contributions to private pension funds are also expected to be tax-exempt.

3. Has there been banking reform? Lithuania has a two-tiered banking system of commercial banks and a central bank. In April 1994, the country established a currency board that linked litas to the U.S. dollar at a permanently fixed exchange rate of four litas to one dollar. Adopted in early 1997, the Bank of Lithuania's new monetary policy program provoked serious concerns about the plans to restore an independent central bank and raised doubts as to the bank's readiness to pursue discretionary monetary policy. From the traditional point of view, the central bank is independent of the government. In measuring freedom, however, the independence of the central bank can be viewed from a broader perspective, i.e., to what extent legal rules prohibit the central bank from enacting decisions dictated by economic, political, or other interest groups. The creation of the currency board was a safeguard that shielded monetary policy from political pressure. When the Bank of Lithuania announced its monetary policy, it came under pressure from lobbyist groups that demanded a devaluation of the national currency. In late 1995, the suspension of the activities of two large banks, Joint Stock Innovative and Litimpeks Banks, which were facing severe liquidity problems, created a national banking crisis. Joint Stock Innovative Bank ceased operations altogether, while

Litimpeks Bank reopened in June 1996 after a government bailout. Currently, the banking system is being enlarged through merger and acquisition and through a mandatory requirement that authorized capital be increased. The troubled State Commercial Bank merged with the state-run Savings Bank. The second largest state-owned agricultural bank is scheduled for privatization. In October 1997, the Polish Kredyt Bank PBI was the first foreign bank to open a branch office in Lithuania. In June 1998, a second foreign bank, French Societe Generale, was opened. The banking sector relies heavily on traditional governmental safety mechanisms. It adheres to international accounting and risk-management standards. By law, deposits are insured.

4. How sound is the national currency? From 1994 to 1998, Lithuania's currency board supported cash in circulation fully with hard currency and gold reserves and maintained a fixed exchange rate. It also make the national currency fully convertible and shielded the monetary system from political pressure. In addition, it reduced interest rates and curbed inflation, which fell from 35.7 percent in 1995 to 13.1 percent in 1996 and 8.4 percent in 1997. According to the Bank of Lithuania, in late February 1998 foreign reserves totaled $1,074,400,000. The bank's discontent with rule-bound monetary policy provoked some turmoil on the money market. Official statements prompted runs on currency exchange offices. In early 1997, the bank adopted a 1997-99 monetary policy program under which the currency board will be gradually eliminated and "classical" central bank functions restored. The program is to be implemented in three phases. In the first phase, the bank introduced open market operations and began the gradual elimination of the currency board. In the second phase, the bank will amend the Litas Credibility Law by lifting reserve requirements and linking the litas to the *Euro*, the new EU currency, or a basket that includes the Euro and the U.S. dollar. In the third phase, the litas will be linked more closely with European currencies, and exchange rates will be adjusted.

5. Is there a functioning capital market infrastructure? Lithuania has a legal and institutional framework for its capital market. The Securities Commission, which was established in 1992 and which is accountable to parliament, supervises the market. It is responsible for registering all issuances of securities and for licensing financial mediators. The National Stock Exchange was founded in 1993. The stock exchange's Official Trading List includes seven blue-chip issues that meet strict market capitalization, shareholding, and profitability requirements. Official List issues account for approximately 35 percent of the total turnover. In June 1998, the two divisions of the Current List were eliminated, and the number of issues on the list was reduced to 58. The first quarter of 1998 was marked by intense development of the trading system, including a change from single-price auctions to continuous trading at variable prices. Only licensed brokerage firms are allowed to trade in the securities market. The authorized capital requirement will be increased until it reaches EU standards in 2000. The National Brokers Association unites 20 financial brokerage firms and the brokerage departments of four banks. The capital market has faced liquidity problems. In general, institutional investors accumulate large resources from small local investors, thereby enhancing the liquidity and stimulating the growth of the capital market. The stock exchange was highly active in 1997. Enterprises became increasingly involved in the stock market by attracting investments through new stock issues. According to the National Stock Exchange, total trading volume in 1997 was $365.75 million. Total trading volume for the first quarter of 1998 was $90.675 million. In 1997, treasury bill market capitalization rose by nearly 70 percent, while share capitalization rose by 12 percent. In March 1998, treasury bill turnover reached $3.7 million, and the capitalization of the treasury bill market totaled $390.25 million.

Microeconomics 2.75/7

1. Are property rights guaranteed? Property rights and protection mechanisms are guaranteed by the constitution and laws. Court delays, however, are frequent. In general, real estate registers are reliable, but not entirely operational. A mortgage register system is being implemented. Under the constitution, the state reserves the right to appropriate land, but it must provide compensation to owners. The mechanism for compensation, however, is not defined by law. In 1996, the state appropriated the troubled private Joint Stock Innovative Bank and assumed all of the bank's liabilities. Earlier, the Bank of Lithuania had suspended the activities of the bank due to its liquidity problems. Lithuania has made significant progress in securing rights of authorship and industrial ownership. In recent years, violations of authorship rights and the volume of pirate production have declined. The protection of video and audio productions and books has increased markedly. Video tape rentals and computer software, however, remain vulnerable to abuse. Problems are mainly attributable to a lack of experience and technical capacities, inadequate sanctions for offenses, and insufficient authority of supervisory institutions. In addition, there is no tradition of respect for intellectual and industrial property.

2. To what extent have prices been liberalized? What subsidies remain? Price liberalization began in 1991. Currently, a variety of commodities and services – including energy, agricultural commodities, pharmaceuticals, herbs and medicines, medical services, and transport – are subject to price regulations. In the first half of 1998, the government imposed controls on prices charged by state-owned wholesale and retail oil companies. Heating, transport, and local telephone costs are subsidized for pensioners, agricultural workers, the disabled, and individuals whose incomes fall short of the established minimum level. Despite extensive liberalization, prices are affected by other governmental interventions, such as the establishment of set customs values for goods.

3. Is it possible to own and operate a business? The establishment and registration of private firms are regulated by the Law on the Register of Enterprises, laws governing individual types of businesses, and government regulations. A company may be dissolved by the owners or upon a declaration of bankruptcy. Bankruptcy proceedings are regulated by bankruptcy legislation. The government's desire to control the establishment of new businesses resulted in complex, costly, and excessive procedures for their registration. Twenty-five types of economic activities require licensing. The issuance of licenses is regulated by decrees of individual ministries, departments, and other governmental agencies. Licensing procedures are complex and demanding and often necessitate the submission of numerous reports and approvals from various institutions. Entrepreneurs must renew their licenses every year. Laws and regulations frequently conflict or overlap. In addition, they are frequently revised and are inadequately enforced. In some cases, laws and regulations have been applied retroactively. In general, the state's active involvement in economic affairs

— including protection of state-owned companies and corporate welfare programs — undermines competition.

4. Are courts effective, transparent, efficient, and quick in reaching decisions on property and contractual disputes? What alternative mechanisms for adjudicating disputes exist? Courts follow democratic rules, but are frequently ineffective, particularly in addressing economic and business issues. Critics charge that court decisions are often unjust and influenced by state institutions and other parties. This is particularly true in property cases in which the state is involved. Disputes are frequently settled by mutual consent or with recourse to organized crime. In cases with an international dimension, international arbitrage is frequently employed.

5. Is business competition encouraged? (Are monopolistic practices limited in law and in practice? If so, how? To what degree is "insider" dealing a hindrance to open competition? Are government procurement policies open and unbiased? Laws regulate competition. An independent competition commission was established to supervise compliance, although critics charge that the commission is not sufficiently active in protecting competition. Others claim that it is too interventionist in imposing sanctions even for normal business practices. In several cases, enterprises have been punished for imposing uniform prices for their products. Some of the commission's investigations have been initiated by companies that seek to use the commission to constrain their competitors. To date, the commission has not initiated any proceedings against the government for restricting competition. Government procurements that exceed 30,000 litas ($7,500) must be concluded through public tender. There are a variety of exceptions, however, and this provision is frequently ignored in practice. The terms of tenders may be adjusted to favor the desired winner. A newly drafted competition bill that is modeled on the EU competition law is expected to tighten regulations on competition.

6. To what extent has international trade been liberalized? Lithuania's foreign trade is constrained by both tax and non-tax barriers. Differentiated tariffs are applied according to whether similar commodities are manufactured in Lithuania. The weighted average tariff rate is 2 to 3 percent for industrials goods and 12 percent for agricultural commodities. These tariffs are lower than in most other countries in the region. The highest tariff is an 80-percent import duty on sugar. Export duties are imposed on certain wood products and leather. *Ad valorem* taxes are imposed not on the actual value of goods, but on the customs value, which is fixed according to government tabulations. This results in unduly high customs duties. The government is authorized to approve tax-exempt quotas for individual companies. The country's opaque and complex customs procedures have led to numerous scandals and extensive delays in the operations of the customs agencies. Customs activities at warehouses and terminals have been so restricted that many shippers of transit goods now choose to bypass Lithuania. The trade balance is negative. The authorities are trying to handle the deficit by supporting exports, tightening import requirements, and applying other protective measures. In early 1998, an export insurance fund was established.

7. To what extent has foreign investment and capital flow been encouraged or constrained? In the first half of 1997, Lithuania ended its corporate income tax relief for foreign companies that begin operations in the country. The tax breaks remain in effect for companies that enjoyed them prior to the new regulations, which have helped to level the playing field for domestic and foreign investors. Foreigners are prohibited from engaging in business related to state security and defense, the production and sale of narcotics, and the organization of lotteries. The government has adopted an investment promotion program to facilitate "significant" investments not by reducing taxes, but rather by covering labor training expenses, compensating for communications expenses, and providing favorable conditions for the supply of electricity. Business leaders view this program with deep skepticism because, in their view, it discriminates against other investors and invites corruption and government interference in economic affairs.

8. Has there been reform of the energy sector? The price of electricity is regulated by the state. Restructuring of the energy sector began in mid-1995, when electrical plants — with the exception of the Ignalina nuclear power plant — were reorganized into joint-stock companies. Additional restructuring of the energy sector remains in the planning stage.

MACEDONIA

Freedom in the World Ratings, 1989-1998	1989-90	1990-91	1991-92	1992-93	1993-94	1994-95	1995-96	1996-97	1997-98
Political Rights	-	-	-	3	3	4	4	4	4
Civil Liberties	-	-	-	4	3	3	3	3	3
Status	-	-	-	PF	PF	PF	PF	PF	PF

Polity: Transitional
Economy: Transitional
Population: 2,127,000
PPP: $4,058
Ethnic Groups: Macedonian (65 percent), Albanian (22 percent), Turk (5 percent), Macedonian Muslim (3 percent), Roma (2 percent), Serb (2 percent)
Capital: Skopje

Political Process 3.50/7

1. When did national elections occur? Were they free and fair? How were they judged by domestic and international election monitoring organizations? Who composes the government? Parliamentary elections to the unicameral, 120-member Macedonian Assembly (*Sobranje*) took place in October 1994. International observers from the Organization for Security and Cooperation in Europe (OSCE) concluded that they were "marred by irregularities," and the run-off was boycotted by the nationalist opposition Internal Macedonian Revolutionary Organization-Democratic Party for Macedonian Unity (VMRO-DPMNE), the Democratic Party, and others. The ruling Social Democratic Alliance (SDSM), which includes the Social Democratic Union, the Liberal Party, the Socialist Party, and the ethnic Albanian Party for Democratic Prosperity (PDP) won 105 of 120 seats. The People's Democratic Party won four; the Democratic Party of Macedonia, one; the Democratic Party of Turks in Macedonia and Party for Democratic Action-Islamic Way, one; the Party for Total Emancipation of Romanies in Macedonia, one; the Social Democratic Party of Macedonia, one; and independents, seven. Incumbent Branko Crvenkovski of the SDSM was named prime minister. In February 1996, the Liberals, with 29 seats, left the ruling coalition and went into opposition. In March 1997, the prime minister survived a no-confidence vote over the government's handling of organized crime and financial dealings. The collapse of a savings institution led to a cabinet reshuffle in which pro-Western foreign minister Ljoubomir Frckovski and deputy prime minister Jane Miljovski were removed. The current government is dominated by the SDSM and its allies. Parliamentary elections have been scheduled for the latter half of 1998. In March 1998, parliament presented a draft version of a new election law under which 85 deputies would be elected by majority vote and 35 according to a proportional model (The 1994 elections were held under a majoritarian system). Under the proposed law, the majority election will occur in two rounds, with candidates winning more than 7 percent of the vote eligible for participation in the second round. In the proportional part, a party would have to win at least 5 percent of the vote to participate in the second round.

2. When did presidential elections occur? Were they free and fair? President Kiro Gligorov — a former Communist leader, a member of the Yugoslav Collective State Presidency, and the leader of the SDSM — was directly elected on October 16, 1994 to a five-year term. According to OSCE monitors the voting included irregularities. Gligorov received 52 percent of the vote and defeated Ljubisha Georgeievski, who received 14 percent. Gligorov, who was appointed interim president in 1990, survived an assassination attempt in October 1995. The 80-year-old leader is not expected to seek re-election.

3. Is the electoral system multiparty-based? Are there at least two viable political parties functioning at all levels of government? Article 20 of the 1991 constitution gives citizens the right to form parties. Political parties function at every level of government. In the 1996 local elections, VMRO-DPMNE, which is not represented in the national parliament, won more than 300 municipal council seats and several mayoralties.

4. How many parties have been legalized? Are any particular parties illegal? Approximately 50 parties are registered in Macedonia. In 1998, a new party known as the Democratic Alternative (DA) was launched by well-known Yugoslav-era political figure Vasil Tupurkovski and prominent intellectuals and political figures, including representatives from the Liberal Party and SDSM. In early 1998, the PDP formed an alliance with the People's Democratic Party (NDP), a second ethnic Albanian party that held 4 parliamentary seats. The new entity was called the Democratic Party of Albanians. The Liberal and Democratic parties also merged. Other prominent parties include VMRO-DPMNE, the Socialist Party of Macedonia, the Movement for Pan-Macedonian Action, and the Democratic Party of Yugoslavs. No parties are explicitly illegal or outlawed.

5. What proportion of the population belongs to political parties? Reliable party membership figures are impossible to obtain, as most major parties tend to exaggerate their membership rolls. Most Macedonians tell pollsters that they do not identify and are not affiliated with any party. The nationalist VMRO-DPMNE, which was established in 1990, was named after a historic group that was founded in 1893 and had fought for independence from the Turks, and the former-Communist SDSM claim tens of thousands of members, while the embryonic DA claims 25,000 members. In an August 1997 poll, 28 percent of respondents stated that they identified most closely with VMRO-DPMNE. Twenty-two percent identified most closely with the Liberal-Democratic Party, while 18 percent identified most closely with the SDSM.

6. What has been the trend of voter turnout at the municipal, provincial, and national levels in recent years? In the presidential and parliamentary elections of October 1994, 78 percent of eligible voters participated. In the local elections of November 1996, voter turnout was 70 percent.

Civil Society **3.75/7**

1. How many nongovernmental organizations (NGOs) have come into existence since 1988? What is the number of charitable/non-profit organizations? Are there locally led efforts to increase philanthropy and volunteerism? What proportion of the population is active in private voluntary activity (from polling data)? Approximately 300 international associations and indigenous NGOs are registered in Macedonia. According to the Macedonian Center for International Cooperation, most are based in Skopje. The government National Payment Institution reports that there are 3,300 organizations registered, including the autonomous units of national organizations and professional groups. Much of the country's charitable and humanitarian work, including medical assistance and aid to refugees, is overseen by international groups that work with indigenous groups or volunteers. These international groups include the European Community Humanitarian Office (ECHO), Catholic Relief Services, the Civil Volunteer Group, and the International Federation of the Red Cross. ECHO has established several social shelters for orphans, pensioners, and the handicapped. Indigenous organizations include approximately 50 environmental groups, as well as student associations, public policy institutes, women's organizations, and professional associations. Western aid and technical assistance is directed at improving the functioning of local NGOs. Macedonia is a poor country without philanthropic traditions and institutions. According to U.S. AID, by the year 2000, 25 percent of Macedonians will have actively participated in citizen-based organizations and groups – an increase from five percent in 1995.

2. What is the legal and regulatory environment for NGOs (i.e., ease of registration, legal rights, government regulations, taxation, procurement, and access-to-information issues)? To what extent is NGO activism focused on improving the legal and regulatory environment? NGOs must register with the government. In 1996, the government passed several laws on the operations of NGOs and the financing of public organizations, societies, citizens associations, and unions. Under one law, the government has provided assistance to the Macedonian Youth Council, the Movement of Ecologists, the Unions of Women's Organizations, the Helsinki Human Rights Committee, and the Association for the Protection of Children. The Red Cross and other NGOs engaged in humanitarian and charitable work receive tax concessions, but NGOs in general are not tax-exempt. (A new draft Law for Citizen's Associations and Foundations would, however, grant tax-exempt status to NGOs.) Environmental groups have complained of inadequate access to government information. Few NGOs enjoy government procurement opportunities. The Institute for Sociological, Political, and Juridical Research receives less than 5 percent of its revenues from government services. The Center for Environmental Law and Public Participation receives approximately 10 percent of its revenues from government services. Local NGOs work with the International Center for Not-for-Profit Law to improve legislation on the registration and regulation of foreign and domestic NGOs.

3. What is the organizational capacity of NGOs? Do management structures clearly delineate authority and responsibility? Is information available on NGO management issues in the native language? Is there a core of experienced practitioners/trainers to serve as consultants or mentors to less-developed organizations? Most indigenous NGOs are small. Approximately 25 percent of these organizations have annual budgets between $5,000 and $25,000. Larger groups have management structures that delineate authority. The Skopje-based Institute for Sociological, Political, and Juridical Research has a board of directors, 24 professional staff members, and 20 part-time employees. The Center for Environmental Law has five professional staff members and 13 part-time volunteers. Information on NGO management is available in the Macedonian language, but most small NGOs outside of Skopje do not have translating and mass-printing capabilities. Western and international organizations funded by U.S. AID, the European Union (EU), and the U.N. have extensive programs to develop indigenous trainers and practitioners with a focus on building cooperative networks with other NGOs.

4. Are NGOs financially viable? What is their tax status? Are they obliged and do they typically disclose revenue sources? Do government procurement opportunities exist for private, not-for-profit providers of services? Most active NGOs depend on foreign funding and donations from international associations, governments, and private foundations. By law, Macedonian NGOs receive tax concessions. NGOs funded by foreign organizations disclose funding sources and keep accounting records as a condition of grant agreements. Government procurement opportunities are limited, although the government does provide annual allotments for approximately 20 NGOs, most of which are non-political.

5. Are there free trade unions? How many workers belong to these unions? Is the number of workers belonging to trade unions growing or decreasing? What is the numerical/proportional membership of farmers' groups, small business associations, etc.? The 1992 Law on Labor Regulations gives workers the right to form trade unions. The Union of Independent and Autonomous Trade Unions was established in 1992. The Council of Trade Unions of Macedonia, which succeeded and maintains the assets of the country's Communist-era labor federation, is the government's main negotiating partner on labor issues. Unions are registered with the Ministry of Labor and Social Policy. The constitution guarantees the right to strike. The Council of Trade Unions claims approximately 500,000 members, but the actual number is almost certainly much smaller. Newly privatized companies have cut bloated work rolls, and the expanding private service sector is overwhelmingly non-union. Railway workers launched a strike in late 1997. There are over 175,000 private farmers. While cooperatives have been organized throughout the country, precise membership and proportional figures are not available. Formal and informal business and professional associations exist in Skopje and other large cities, but reliable membership figures are not available.

6. What forms of interest group participation in politics is legal? What types of interest groups are active in the political and policy process? The constitution guarantees the right to association and party participation. Article 24 states that "every citizen has a right to petition state and other public bodies." Public demonstrations must be authorized locally, but, as in the largely Albanian cities of Gostivar and Tetovo in July 1997, the police have intervened violently to break up protests. NGOs are beginning to lobby, particularly on environmental issues. Social research and policy groups have disseminated reports and recommendations to government agencies and parliament. Business interests, particularly foreign investors and enterprises, generally have access to high-level government officials.

7. How is the not-for-profit/NGO sector perceived by the public and government officials? What is the nature of media coverage of NGOs? To what extent do government officials engage NGOs? According to a 1997-98 survey of the print media in Macedonia, NGOs and their activities received virtually no media coverage. Legislation affecting NGOs has been published. With the exception of major international humanitarian organizations, most Macedonians are only vaguely aware of NGOs and their work. A number of NGOs have received small government research grants and allotments, but there is little engagement with government officials.

Independent Media 4.00/7

1. Are there legal protections for press freedom? Chapter II, Article 16 of the constitution guarantees free speech and access to information and prohibits censorship of the press.

2. Are there legal penalties for libeling officials? Are there legal penalties for "irresponsible" journalism? Have these laws been enforced to harass journalists? Articles in the criminal code prohibit the spread of false information and slander. Libel laws have led to a measure of self-censorship. Violators are subject to court warnings, fines, or imprisonment. In 1997 and early 1998, there were no prosecutions of journalists under these statutes.

3. What proportion of the media are privatized? What are the major private newspapers, television stations, and radio stations? Most of the major newspapers and electronic media are government-controlled or subsidized. The pro-government NIP Nova Makedonija, which is employee-owned and subsidized by the state, publishes four major dailies: *Vecher*, *Nova Makedonija*, *Flaka* (in Albanian), and *Birlik* (in Turkish). Private, independent newspapers include *Dnevnik,* which reduced its price several times in 1997 to boost circulation; *Denes*, a weekly that was launched in 1997; and *Fokus*, which publishes sensational stories about corruption, scandals, and crime. Private magazines include *Delo*, which is influenced by the nationalist opposition. *Makedonska Sonce*, a weekly, is also nationalist. Party newspapers include the SDSM's *Demokratija,* the Liberal Party's *Liberal* , VMRO-DPMNE's *Glas*; and the Democratic Party's *Demokratski forum*. Daily circulation of all dailies increased from 30,000 in 1996 to 100,000 in 1997, in part because most papers decreased their prices.

Approximately 30 state-owned radio stations and five state television stations operate in the country. A total of 24 private television stations and 91 combined radio and television stations share the airwaves. Most of these stations provide music and entertainment programming. Private television stations include A-1 and Sitel in Skopje and TV-Terra in Bitola. Popular radio stations include Antenna-5; Noma Skopje, Radio Uno, and Pro FM in Skopje; Chanal-77 in Stip; 106 in Bitola, Kiss in Tetovo; and Uno Forte in Ohrid. Controversy arose in February 1998, when the VMRO-DPMNE authorities in Stip moved to take control of Radio Stip and change its name to Radio Glas.

4. Are the media financially viable? Most major publications receive some form of government support. Independent and opposition papers have criticized the government for arbitrary distribution of the modest funds that aid the print media. Control of printing facilities and distribution by the government or the pro-government NIP Nova Makedonija has burdened publications financially. The major private commercial television and radio stations are backed by media companies and do not depend on advertisements. Smaller local broadcasters operate on modest budgets. In November 1997, the official Macedonian Association of Journalists threatened a strike over low wages. Political parties fund party newspapers. A new Law of Radio Diffusion called for higher rates for frequencies, thereby leading independent broadcasters to claim that the law was aimed at bolstering government-owned media. By early 1998, the law had not yet been implemented.

5. Are the media editorially independent? Are the media's news gathering functions affected by interference from government or private owners? Party newspapers reflect the views of their sponsors. The papers published by NIT Nova Makedonija such as *Vecer*, *Nova Makedonija*, *Flaka*, and *Birlik* tend to be pro-government in their coverage, although their editorial boards have declared that they are non-partisan. MRTV, the country's state-owned public-interest broadcasting company, is overseen by parliament, which appoints its general manager, and is financed and controlled by the state. The electronic media are not free from government interference. In 1996, the Liberal Party left the governing coalition over the dismissal of the MRTV director, who was a member of the Liberal Party. In early 1998, local VMRO-DMPNE authorities in Stip took control of Radio Stip, dismissed journalists, and changed the name of the station to Radio "Glas," the name of the party newspaper. The takeover was reportedly orchestrated because Radio Stip was competing favorably with Chanal 77, a private station owned by the son of an VMRO-DPMNE mayor in the region. The dependency of most newspapers on government-controlled printing and distribution facilities has led to "self-censorship."

6. Is the distribution system for newspapers privately or governmentally controlled? The government has a large stake in the distribution system. The pro-government NIP Nova Makedonija has a virtual monopoly on distribution. Attempts by independent papers to create alternative systems through street sales have been met with police pressure. NIP Nova Makedonija owns a distribution network of more than 500 kiosks throughout Macedonia.

7. What proportion of the population is connected to the Internet? Are there restrictions on Internet access to private citizens? Information on the proportion of the population that enjoys access to the Internet is not available. There are two ways of gaining access to the Internet in Macedonia. Universities allow access to students, staff, and faculty. Commercial providers include ITL Communications, Informa, Ultra Communication; and Macedonian Post and Telecommunications.

8. What has been the trend in press freedom as measured by Freedom House's *Survey of Press Freedom*? In its annual *Survey of Press Freedom*, Freedom House rated Macedonia "Partly Free" from 1992 to 1998.

Governance and Public Administration 4.00/7

1. Is The legislature the effective rule-making institution? The unicameral, 120-seat National

Assembly is the effective rule-making body. According to the constitution, the parliament "adopts and changes the constitution," "adopts laws and gives authentic interpretation of laws," and "elects the government of the Republic of Macedonia." Rules of procedure are adopted by a two-thirds vote. The constitutional duties of the president do not provide for the power to issue or rule by decree, although he can appoint and dismiss diplomatic representatives without consulting parliament.

2. Is substantial power decentralized to sub-national levels of government? What specific authorities do sub-national levels have? A 1996 law divided the country into 123 municipalities and communities. Article 114 of the constitution establishes municipalities as units of local self-government. Skopje is a "particular" unit of self-government. Article 115 delineates local areas of authority over "issues of local relevance, particularly in the fields of urban planning, communal activities, culture, sport, social security and child care, pre-school education, primary education, basic health care, and other fields determined by law." A Law on Self-Government was introduced in 1991 and finally passed in 1995. A law on territorial divisions was passed in 1996. Local elections for city councilors and mayors were held in November 1996, but political infighting in Skopje, Bitola, and other cities paralyzed the work of the councils

3. Are sub-national officials chosen in free and fair elections? The country's first local elections since the dissolution of Yugoslavia were held in November 1996, with runoffs through December. Earlier, parliament had passed a local election law under which municipal councils were to be elected by a proportional system. Mayors were to be elected by a majority vote. The OSCE reported no evidence of practices that would have effected the outcome of the elections, and the Council of Europe reported that the vote was "essentially fair and orderly." The ruling SDSM won 503 municipal council seats and a least 13 mayoralties. VMRO-DPMNE and other opposition parties, however, finished strongly and won more than 340 municipal council seats and 11 mayoralties.

4. Do the executive and legislative bodies operate openly and with transparency? Is draft legislation easily accessible to the media and the public? National executive and legislative bodies operate with limited transparency. National Assembly meetings were not opened to the public until 1997, and the non-parliamentary opposition had been barred from proceedings. Journalists can attend parliamentary sessions. Laws are disseminated by the media and the public through the press.

5. Do municipal governments have sufficient revenues to carry out their duties? Do municipal governments have control of their own local budgets? Do they raise revenues autonomously or from the central state budget? Municipal governments can levy taxes. They also receive funding from the central budget. Under Article 114 of the constitution, "municipalities are financed from their own sources of income determined by law, as well as by funds from the Republic." Local governments draft budgets and submit them to the central authorities.

6. Do elected leaders and local civil servants know how to manage municipal governments

effectively? Macedonia's municipal councils are heavily politicized. Many, including those in Skopje and Bitola, are ineffective. Local officials are generally familiar with local and regional issues, and the mayors of Skopje and some other muncipalities have successfully addressed local issues. Nevertheless, many municipal councils have neglected important work. Beginning in November 1997, the three largest municipal councils — in Skopje, Kumanovo, and Bitola — did not function due to political and party infighting. In each area, the councils did not meet for months and deferred decisions on issues such as construction, utility charges, and public lighting. Disputes between the SDSM, VMRO-DPMNE, and other parties were taken to the courts. In Skopje, the merger of the Liberal and Democratic parties led to disputes regarding political legitimacy when some councilors elected from the individual parties did not approve of the merger. In Bitola, several officials were involved in the TAT savings institution scandal. The council's failure to meet throughout most of 1997 led to new elections, as mandated by law. In the March 1998, voting for 24 council seats, the Liberal Democratic Party won eight seats, VMRO-DPMNE won ten, and the SDSM won six. The EU and the U.S. Institute for Public Administration have launched programs to promote reform. Swiss and Danish institutions have established several schools for public administration.

7. When did the constitutional/legislative changes on local power come into effect? Has there been reform of the civil service code/system? Are local civil servants employees of the local or central government? Section V of the constitution, which was adopted in November 1991, addresses local self-government. The Law on Self-Government was passed in 1995. The 1996 Law on Territorial Division created 123 municipalities. Earlier, the country had been divided into 34 administrative units. There have been no major reforms of the civil service system. Local civil servants are employees of local government.

Rule of Law 4.50/7

1. Is there a post-Communist constitution? How does the judicial system interpret and enforce the constitution? Are there specific examples of judicial enforcement in the last year? The constitution was approved by referendum in September 1991 and adopted by parliament one month later. Section IV of the constitution creates a nine-member Constitutional Court that is elected by parliament to a nine-year term without the right to re-election. Under Article 108, the "Constitutional Court of Macedonia is a body of the Republic protecting constitutionality and legality." Article 110 states that the court "decides on the conformity of laws with the constitution." The court heard many cases in 1997. In July, it annulled two articles from the state's collective agreement with workers by ruling that the provisions on temporary leave restricted the workers' legal rights to use legal funds as prescribed in Article 135 of the Law on Labor Relations. In March 1998, the court broadened defendants' rights by ruling that police could not keep defendants in custody for more than 24 hours without taking them before an executive judge. The court ruled that Article 29 of the Law on Internal Affairs violated the constitution, which states that "persons detained shall be brought before a court as soon as possible, within a maximum period of 24 hours from the moment of detention."

2. Does the constitutional framework provide for human rights? Do human rights include business and property rights? The constitution enumerates "civil and political rights," including the presumption of innocence; the proscription of lengthy pre-trial detention; the inviolability of the home; and freedoms of conscience, speech, religion, association, peaceful assembly, and privacy. It also delineates economic, social, and cultural rights, including the "right to ownership of property and the right of inheritance" and the right of "foreign subjects" to "acquire the right of ownership of property under conditions determined by law." It also guarantees "freedom of the market and entrepreneurship."

3. Has there been basic reform of the criminal/code criminal law? Who authorizes searches and issues warrants? Are suspects and prisoners beaten and abused? Are there excessive delays in the criminal justice system? In July 1996, a new criminal code replaced the Yugoslav code from the 1970s. The new code eliminated some of the more political provisions such as anti-state activities and anti-state propaganda and expanded the rights of defendants and other detainees. Under the code, evidence obtained in violation of constitutionally protected rights is inadmissible. Lawyers, doctors, social workers, and psychologists cannot be forced to testify about information supplied by their clients, and correspondence between an attorney and the accused cannot be censored. The law also eliminated the death penalty. In May 1997, a new Code of Criminal Procedure barred police from coercing citizens into so-called "informative talks" without a court order. All detainees must be informed immediately of the reason for their detention and must be given access to a lawyer. A 1995 Law Governing the Ministry of Internal Affairs barred entry without a search warrant and provided that an individual cannot be detained for longer than 24 hours without being charged. Courts issue search warrants. This provision, however, is sometimes ignored by police, and warrants are frequently issued after an arrest. In addition, police have held defendants for more than 24 hours without charging them. Police frequently resort to violence and the excessive use of force. In 1997, there were reports that ethnic Albanians detained during disturbances in Gostivar were beaten by police and deprived of food, water, and sleep. Police violence in those disturbances led to three deaths and the injuries of 200 others. In Bitola in May, there were reports of police beatings during a demonstration by citizens who were demanding compensation for money lost in the failed TAT financial scheme. In general, the judiciary is slow and inefficient. In 1997, the Supreme Court found that 18 of 30 courts were not prompt in performing their duties.

4. Do judges rule fairly and impartially? Do many remain from the Communist era? In 1996 and 1997, opinion polls revealed a broad-based perception that the judiciary is corrupt. More than 50 percent of respondents stated that they had no "trust" in the judicial system. Since 1996, several judges have been removed for bribery. A Republican Judicial Council, which is elected by parliament and is subject to political and party influence, proposes the election and discharge of judges. Most judges, whose judicial education is, in most cases, limited to brief seminars, lack expertise and professionalism. Many judges remain from the Yugoslav era. According to the 1997 report of the Helsinki Committee for Human Rights in the Republic of Macedonia, the "quality of the trials and verdicts is also very low, a fact being confirmed by the great number of annulments." The report also stated that "judges, instead of seeing their role in the protection of civil rights and freedoms and of legality and fairness of the proceeding, see themselves as active partners of the prosecution." The trials of ethnic Albanians after the 1997 disturbances in Gostivar and Tetovo were widely seen as political, with violations of defendants' rights and severe sentences. Rufi Osmani, the Mayor of Gostivar, was sentenced in September 1997 to nearly 14 years in prison for his part in the unrest. Even the nationalist leader of VMRO-DPMNE said that the trial presented further "proof that neither a legal state nor the law function in Macedonian, but rather politics."

5. Are the courts free of political control and influence? Are the courts linked directly to the Ministry of Justice or any other executive body? Macedonia has a three-tiered system of regular municipal and district appellate courts and a Supreme Court. The constitution provides for the creation of a seven-member Republican Judicial Council, which is elected by parliament and which proposes the names of judges in consultation with the justice ministry and other bodies. In a September 1997 *Nova Makedonija* interview, Council President Bugbil Bejzat stated, "The political parties, through their representatives, are present in the parliament, especially the majority party with its coalition partners. They play a crucial role in the election of judges. I consider that efforts should be made to eliminate the political influence in the election of judges and at the same time respect the constitutional position of the Republican Judicial Council and its competence when proposing and dismissing judges." The judiciary does not have its own budget and is therefore financially dependent upon the central government.

6. What proportion of lawyers is in private practice? How does this compare with the previous year? With the advent of privatization, an increasing number of lawyers and law firms work in the commercial sector. Exact figures, however, are not available.

7. Does the state provide public defenders? While the constitution guarantees the right to counsel, the Helsinki Committee for Human Rights in Macedonia reported at the end of 1997 that this provision is often neglected: "The system of free legal aid to the poor is restrictive in laws and inefficient in practice."

8. Are there effective anti-bias/discrimination laws, including protection of ethnic minority rights? The constitution provides that "members of nationalities have a right to freely express, foster, and develop their identity and national attributes" and that the republic "guarantees the protection of the ethnic, cultural, linguistic, and religious identity of the nationalities." Macedonia is a signatory to the Council of Europe's convention on the protection of national minorities. Ethnic Albanians have charged that they are the victims of discrimination in citizenship, government employment, and education and that they are under-represented in the military, police, and judiciary. In July 1997, police attacked ethnic Albanian demonstrators in Gostivar and Tetovo after the mayors of three largely Albanian cities flew the Albanian flag in opposition to a Constitutional Court ruling to express their discontent over discriminatory employment, housing, and education policies. The constitution and laws guarantee equal rights for men and women, but women, particularly in rural areas, face discrimination in employment and education.

Corruption C

1. What is the magnitude of official corruption in the civil service? Must an average citizen pay a bribe to a bureaucrat in order to receive a service? What services are subject to bribe

requests—for example, university entrance, hospital admission, telephone installation, obtaining a license to operate a business, applying for a passport or other official documents? What is the average salary of civil servants at various levels? Corruption and graft are pervasive at all levels of government and in business. In 1997, Macedonia was plagued by a series of high-profile scandals. The collapse of the Bitola-based TAT savings institution, which had bilked 30,000 savers of approximately $90 million, led to the resignation of several officials and ministers. The media also reported that official funds that had been earmarked for the Skopje assembly were diverted for other purposes. In a well-known case reported in October, widespread corruption was revealed in the Interior Ministry, in which companies owned by relatives or friends of ministry officials were given lucrative contracts, even though the bidding process was supposedly open. Slavco Sazdoz, an assistant minister who decided on all public purchases, was ultimately dismissed for receiving kickbacks in the award of contracts for office equipment, automobiles, and the design of passports and drivers' licenses. In the so-called "Saklev" affair, high-ranking members of the intelligence and defense communities were involved in the smuggling of American arms in violation of the international arms embargo. Smuggling of other goods — including cigarettes, drugs, automobiles, and industrial equipment — is endemic and reflects widespread corruption in the customs sector. The pervasiveness of corruption in the civil service and administrative organs and its effect on citizens were detailed in a *Nova Makedonija* article in the wake of the TAT scandal. The article stated that the "small windows manned by clerks in the municipalities, in administrative bodies, wherever they are, should not be underestimated because these are places where on a daily basis the citizen is exposed to mistreatment and to the necessity to bribe in order to receive his basic rights." Of the customs sector, the article stated, "It is a public secret that officials have to be bribed in order to get clearances, where, starting from the various ministries, every import or export permit has its own price, and [continuing with] the companies that pay briefcases full of cash, companies that are neither registered anywhere [on record] nor taxed because the tax and other inspections are bought over lunch."

2. Do top policy-makers (the president, ministers, vice-ministers, top court justices, and heads of agencies and commissions) have direct ties to businesses? How strong are such connections and what kind of businesses are these? There is a close relationship between the country's leading managers of large privatized businesses, government officials, and political parties. The TAT financial scandal implicated local council officials, SDSM leaders, and former ministers. In addition, the TAT savings institution received substantial proceeds from the privatization of a number of Bitola companies, relief money intended for earthquake victims, and money from the Electric Power Enterprise of Macedonia. In general, according to *Nova Makedonija*, the "gray" economy, smuggling, the black market, drug trafficking, crime, and the connection between organized crime and political, judicial, police, and economic power-holders are becoming a dangerous way of life.

3. Do laws requiring financial disclosure and disallowing conflict of interest exist? Have publicized anti-corruption cases been pursued? To what conclusion? Statutes necessitate financial disclosures and prohibit conflicts of interest. Actual conflicts are common, however, because the law is not adequately enforced and because investigations are rare. A businessman and owner of a privatized lottery used his friendship with senior Liberal Party government officials to secure his wife's appointment to the Constitutional Court, which ruled favorably in the privatization of the lottery. Several local officials from Bitola have been indicted in the TAT scandal. Their trials are ongoing.

4. What major anti-corruption initiatives have been implemented? How often are anti-corruption laws and decrees adopted? In the wake of the "Saklev" affair, pervasive corruption in public administration and scandals involving TAT, Karik Bank, Alfa-S, and other companies, the government declared a war on the "octopus of corruption." To date, however, no specific major initiatives have been undertaken. Article 357 of the 1996 Criminal Code prohibits bribery and graft by public officials. Article 358 prohibits offers of bribes to officials. Article 359 prohibits "kick-backs."

5. How do major corruption-ranking organizations like Transparency International rate this country? Information on the ranking of corruption in Macedonia is not available.

Privatization 4.00/7

1. What percentage of the GDP comes from private ownership? What percentage of the labor force is employed in the private sector? How large is the informal sector of the economy? The private sector accounts for approximately 70 percent of Macedonia's GDP. Approximately 62.4 percent of employees work in the private sector and generate 76 percent of all the profit in the economy. The informal sector is substantial. According to unofficial sources, it accounts for $300 million and $500 million in income annually. Western financial officials estimate that the "gray" economy constitutes 20 to 30 percent of GDP.

2. What major privatization legislation has been passed? What were its substantive features? The central legal document governing the privatization of socially-owned enterprises is the 1993 Law on Transformation of Enterprises with Social Capital. Under this law, small enterprises may be privatized through employee buyouts (EBOs), with employees purchasing at least 51 percent of the appraised value of the enterprise; the sale of part of an enterprise in the form of shares or stakes through a public auction, or direct agreements with prospective buyers. Medium-sized companies may be purchased through leveraged management buy-outs or management buy-ins. These agreements can be made with a group of people — employees or outsiders — who offer a business plan for the enterprise. The management group that offers the most attractive program through public tender can obtain the right to control the enterprise through a down payment of only 20 percent of the appraised value. It must then purchase at least 51 percent of shares in no more than five installments with no interest charge. For large enterprises, the leveraged buy-out or buy-in is only 10 percent. Other privatization legislation includes the Foreign Investment Law, the Concessions Law, and the Securities Law, all of which were adopted in 1993; the 1996 Law on Trading Companies; and the 1997 the Law on Issuing and Trading Securities. Under the Law on Transformation of Enterprises, 1,278 enterprises were scheduled for privatization. These included 113 large enterprises, 274 medium-sized enterprises, and 890 small companies. By the end of 1997, 1,041 companies had been privatized. The privatization of an additional 237 additional enterprises was expected to complete the process by mid-1998. In 1996, parliament passed the Law on the Transformation of the Enterprises and Cooperatives with Social Capital That Use Agricultural Land, which targeted 150 enterprises and 210 cooperatives. The most important of these are the so-called *agrokombinats*, which include agricultural and processing industries and which control less than 20 percent of the country's agricultural land. The government expects to complete this phase of privatization in 1998.

3. What proportion of agriculture, housing and land, industry, as small business and service sector is in private hands? *Agriculture:* More than 85 percent of agricultural land is in private hands, and 90 percent of agricultural production is private. Agriculture accounts for 20 to 25 percent of social production.
Housing and land: Most housing has been privatized (Private ownership was permitted in Yugoslavia.) More than 85 percent of land is in private hands. In 1997, the government passed a controversial denationalization law to return property and land or provide compensation to owners whose assets were seized by the Communists.
Industry: Large, state-owned companies, many of which are outmoded, have not been sold or privatized. Twenty-five money-losing enterprises were restructured; companies were divided into smaller entities, and redundant workers were dismissed. Ten enterprises were liquidated. By the end of 1997, more than 1,000 large-, medium-, and small-sized enterprises had been privatized.
Small business and services: Small businesses and the service sector represent the fastest-growing private sector of the economy. Under the 1993 privatization act, more than 800 small businesses, most of which were in the service sector, were privatized. Under the Yugoslav regime, small private businesses were permitted. The government estimates that there are more than 100,000 such entities.

4. What has been the extent of insider (management, labor, and nomenklatura) participation in the privatization process? What explicit and implicit preferences have been awarded to insiders? Insider participation was commonplace in the privatization in Macedonia. Yugoslav-era managers with close connections to politicians and political parties bought many of the country's more successful companies. The enactment of the 1993 Law on Transformation of Enterprises with Socal Capital also seemed initially to favor EBOs. Without ascribing any explicit wrongdoing, a November 1997 Skopje newspaper article on Macedonia's financial oligarchs suggested that prominent manager-owners many of whom had served previously as government officials of banks, tobacco companies, oil and mineral companies, breweries, and other businesses have used inside connections to limit foreign and domestic competition, win lucrative contracts, and obtain other special considerations. In December 1997, the director of the Macedonian Privatization Agency stated that, in 90 percent of privatization cases, only one bid was received, and most of these were from insiders.

5. How much public awareness of and support of privatization has there been? What is the

nature of support and opposition to privatization by major interest groups? The privatization process was widely publicized by the government, media, and the Macedonian Privatization Agency. Completely privatized companies employ more than 175,000 workers, while companies in the process of privatization employ another 90,000 workers. While there are no recent polling data on the seven-year-old privatization process, private enterprise was common in Macedonia during and before the Communist era. Public knowledge of the privatization process, the country's history, and the proliferation of small businesses in the service sector suggest that Macedonians — and particularly younger citizens — have accepted privatization. Labor unions have protested employee lay-offs in inefficient state-owned enterprises, and the collapse of the TAT and other financial schemes have angered thousands of investors. Manager-owners and private businessmen, many of whom enjoy close ties to government officials, have benefited from privatization and make financial contributions to leading political parties.

Macroeconomics 5.00/7

1. Has the taxation system been reformed? (What areas have been overhauled? To what degree are taxpayers complying? Is tax compliance difficult to achieve? Has the level of revenues increased? Is the revenue-collection body overburdened? What is the overall tax burden?) In 1994, Macedonia's post-Yugoslav tax system reduced the number of taxes from 16 to eight. Current taxes include the personal income tax, corporate profit tax, trade tax for goods and services, excise tax, customs tax, property tax, inheritance and gift tax, and estates and rights trade tax. The bases for calculating specific income taxes are determined by special decrees. By the tenth of every month, the average net Macedonian wage (ANMW) for the prior month is published. In general, wages and salaries are stated on a net rather than gross basis. In determining taxable income, a standard deduction of 25 percent of ANMW is granted. Income up to twice the amount of the ANMW is taxed at 23 percent. Income from two to five times the ANMW is taxed at 27 percent. Income more than five times the ANMW is taxed at 35 percent. The basic annual profit tax rate is 30 percent. The Public Revenue Office administers the personal income tax. Tax evasion is common, and collection efforts are inadequate. In October 1997, the Ministry of Finance reported that it found irregularities in more than half of its 9,000 audits. It also reported that tax evasion was a major reason why fewer funds were available for the budget. In addition, it estimated that between 30 and 35 percent of tax liabilities were evaded. More than half of all enterprises did not pay taxes. A November 1997 *Vecer* article contended that the state has been incapable of collecting taxes for several years and must consider the imposition of a value-added tax (VAT) in 1999 in order to increase revenues.

2. Does fiscal policy encourage private savings, investment, and earnings? (Has there been any reform/alteration of revenue and budget policies? How large are budget deficits and overall debt? Is the financing of the social insurance/pension system sustainable? What proportion of the budget is taken up by subsidies to firms and individuals? Tight fiscal and monetary policies reduced inflation from more than 250 percent in 1993 to less than three percent in 1997. The country's small budget deficit – 4.5 million *denars* or 0.3 percent of GDP – produced a measure of macro-economic stability, but unemployment of more than 25 percent, high interest rates, and a weak banking system have discouraged investment. In recent years, many Macedonians invested their money in a series of pyramid schemes, several of which collapsed. The 1998 budget was smaller than in 1997. The Social Insurance system, which includes health insurance and pension disability insurance, is financed through the budget, income or profit of enterprises, and wages. As in most countries of Central Europe and the former Soviet Union, the pension system is based largely on the public pay-as-you-go defined-benefit model. In Macedonia, pensions are administered by an extra-budgetary Pension Fund. The lack of clear relation between years of contribution and pension benefits, loose eligibility criteria, the low retirement age, the declining number of contributors, and weakened tax compliance that reduced revenues have led to a crisis in the pension system. In addition, in 1992 and 1993, Macedonia actually raised the average replacement rate, which is defined as the average pension in terms of the average wage. Recent reform measures have reduced minimum pensions for new retirees and brought benefits in line with contributions. In 1997, public social benefits represented 20 percent of GDP. In a February 1997 *Nova Makedonija* interview, Prime Minister Branko Crvenkovski warned of the possibility of "bankruptcy in the Pension Fund" and the "destruction of the pension system in Macedonia" if steps were not taken to reform the system.

3. Has there been banking reform? (Is the central bank independent? What are its responsibilities? Is it effective in setting or implementing monetary policy? What is the actual state of the private banking sector? Does it conform to international standards? Are depositors protected?) The legal framework for the banking and financial sector was enacted by a series of 1992-93 laws and subsequent amendments, including the National Bank Act, the Banks and Savings Houses Act, the Securities Act, and the Law on Financial Transactions. The banking system includes the National Bank of Macedonia (NBM), which is the country's central bank; commercial banks and savings institutions; insurance companies; and a stock exchange. The NBM, which was established in 1992 as an independent central bank, regulates the quantity of money in circulation, maintains the liquidity of banks and savings institutions, maintains the liquidity of foreign payments, and issues bank notes and coins. The NBM establishes and implements monetary policy. The commercial bank sector includes 21 universal majority private banks, one branch of a foreign bank, and 21 savings institutions. Of the 21 private banks, two have licenses for domestic banking activities, while 19 are authorized for foreign exchange and foreign currency operations. Twelve are completely owned by domestic shareholders. Two have foreign capital participation of more than 70 percent, four of more than 50 percent, and three of more than 10 percent. In general, the banking sector is weak, with low loan collection rates and wide interest rate variations. There is no clear set of banking supervision policies and procedures. In 1997, several savings institutions, many of which were "pyramid" schemes, became insolvent. Thirteen banks and savings institutions then established a Deposit Insurance Fund. If a member-bank fails, the fund will provide 75 percent of each household's deposit. The NBM insures up to 60 percent of savings deposits by a single depositor. The TAT scandal badly eroded already diminished public confidence in the banking system and led parliament to dismiss NBM Governor Borko Stanoevski and Vice Governor Tome Nenovski. In October 1997, a Law on the Re-Compensation of Savers was implemented for the 7,600 households that lost money in the TAT scheme, but the compensation constituted only a fraction of the lost savings. In 1997, groups of depositors staged several demonstrations to blame the government for neglect and collusion in the scandal.

4. How sound is the national currency? (Is the value of the currency fixed, or does it float? How convertible is the currency? How large are the hard currency reserves? Has exchange rate policy been stable and predictable?) The Macedonian denar was introduced in 1992 and was subsequently linked to the German *mark*. The value of the currency floats. Rates are adjusted daily and may vary among institutions. "Internal convertibility" of the denar is permitted, and any foreign currency can be traded for denars in Macedonia. "External convertibility," or trading abroad, may be permitted after the country has met the requirement of the International Monetary Fund. Businesses may freely negotiate foreign currencies with licensed commercial banks. High inflation in the early 1990s led to wide fluctuations in the value of the denar. Inflation has declined from 1,791 percent in 1992 to 122 percent in 1995 and 2.6 percent in 1997. In mid-1997, the denar was devalued by 16 percent against the mark in the face of a growing crisis in the current account of the balance of payments.

5. Is there a functioning capital market infrastructure? (Are there existing or planned commodities, bond, and stock markets? What are the mechanisms for investing and lending? What government bodies have authority to regulate capital markets?) The legal structure for the securities industry was prepared in accordance with the EU's Securities Law Directives. The main law that regulates these issues is the February 1997 Law on Securities Issuance and Trading. The Macedonian Stock Exchange (MSE) was established in March 1996 as a joint-stock company. It has 17 members, including 13 banks, two savings houses, and two insurance companies. There are 140 licensed brokers. Securities are defined by law as shares, bonds, treasury bills, commercial bills, treasury notes, and certificates of deposit. Securities are issued after approval by the Security Exchange Commission (SEC), the main regulatory authority. They are sold in public offerings. A public announcement for the issue and sale of securities is made in the print media within 30 days of an SEC decision. The public offering for securities issued by a foreign entity must be made through a broker. Applicants for a listing on the MSE must be incorporated or otherwise established in Macedonia. The level of trading on the MSE is still low. Among the reasons for the market's non-liquidity include insufficient comprehension of securities and the lack of well-established systems, logistics, and procedures for protection of shareholders' minority rights. International accounting standards are scheduled to be adopted in late 1998. The capital gains tax is 23 percent.

Microeconomics 5.00/7

1. Are property rights guaranteed? (Are there both formal and de facto protections of private real estate and intellectual property? Is there a land registry with the authority and capability to ensure accurate recording of who owns what? What are the procedures for expropriation, including measures for compensation and challenge? Have any seizures taken place? The constitution and laws guarantee property rights. In July 1993, Macedonia became a member of the World Intellectual Property Organization. Industrial property rights include patents, model and sample registrations, and design trade marks. These are overseen by the Office for Protection of Industrial Property. An expropriation law was passed in 1995. Under the law, the expropriating organ is obliged to submit an offer that states the type and level of compensation for property that is to be expropriated, proof of ownership of the property that is being offered as a replacement for the expropriated property, and proof of procured funds for compensation of the expropriated property. The expropriating organ must submit the expropriation proposal to the entity in charge of maintaining public records of properties in order to register the expropriation within eight days upon receipt of the expropriation proposal. Under Article 17 of the law, the "expropriating organ shall arrange a discussion related to the expropriation proposal and summon the proprietor, the possessor of other property rights, and the expropriation beneficiary." The discussion is to determine the existence of public interest, ownership and other property rights, the type and level of compensation, and other facts relevant to the expropriation. Compensation is generally made in the form of cash or comparable property. Complaints and challenges may be lodged with the Office of Legal and Property Affairs. The government continues to struggle with implementation of a denationalization law that would return property to or compensate citizens whose property was seized by the Communists between 1944 and 1968. The law covers 37,000 hectares of agricultural land, 16,000 hectare of forest, 21,000 hectares of pasture, 258 apartment buildings, and other items. It excludes the restitution of church property. In February 1998, a group of citizens whose property in Krivolak was expropriated under the denationalization law threatened to seek redress with the World Bank and international courts.

2. To what extent have prices been liberalized? What subsidies remain? Most price controls have been lifted under a liberalization program. At the time of independence, the control of prices of some products and services amounted to 25 percent of the retail price index. It was decreased to 19 percent in 1995. The government plans to decrease price controls further in 1998. Products that are still under controls include flour, bread, some postal and telephone services, and some community services. In agriculture, protective prices have been set only for corn and tobacco.

3. Is it possible to own and operate a business? (Has there been legislation regarding the formation, dissolution, and transfer of businesses, and is this law respected? Do there exist overly cumbersome bureaucratic hurdles that effectively hinder the ability to own and dispose of a business? Are citizens given access to information on commercial law? Is the law applied fairly? Does regulation (or do licensing requirements) impose significant costs on business and consumers? Do they create significant barriers to entry and seriously hamper competition?) The formation of businesses is controlled by the Law of Commercial Enterprises; the Law on Accounting, Bankruptcy, and Liquidation; the Law on Commercial Registration; and the Law on Commercial Companies. Businesses can be organized by an individual or as a partnership, limited partnership, limited liability company, joint stock company or a limited stock company. Businesses must register with the Trade Register, the Statistics Office, and the Payment Operations Service of the Republic of Macedonia. An unreliable legal framework and bureaucratic delays complicate the registration of businesses. Commercial and all other laws must be published and publicized by the government. While commercial laws are meant to enshrine fair competition, enterprise managers with connections to the government and political parties have received preferential treatment in the development of the private sector and the privatization process.

4. Are courts effective, transparent, efficient, and quick in reaching decisions on property and contract disputes? What alternative mechanism for adjudicating disputes exist? Macedonia's judicial system is plagued by inefficiency and delays. Under the commercial code, business and contract disputes fall within the purview of the Court at the Economic Chamber. In international disputes, contracting parties who cannot reach a mutual agreement within six months can request arbitration by a tribunal that includes an arbitrator from each side. The arbitrators nominate a chairman from a third state that maintains diplomatic relations with the states of both contracting parties. If the parties cannot agree on a chairman within two months, one will be appointed by the International Court of Justice.

5. Is business competition encouraged? (Are monopolistic practices limited in law and practice? If so, how? To what degree is "insider" dealing a hindrance to open competition? Are government procurement policies open and unbiased?) Competition policy in Macedonia is defined by the 1995 Law on Trade. The law includes measures against monopolies and monopolistic behavior. It also defines activities directed toward restriction of free trade and the free enterprise system. Cartels are prohibited. The law provides for the creation of a commission to protect against monopolistic behavior and restrictions of trade. Despite these laws, competition has been hindered by "insider" dealing by managers. For example, the owner of a tobacco company used "insider" influence to bar the entrance of foreign tobacco capital into the country in 1995. He also reportedly instigated the closure of duty free shops, the reduction of tobacco excise taxes, and the removal of the managerial team of a rival company. Government procurement has been marred by corruption, with contracts awarded on the basis of connections and bribes.

6. To what extent has international trade been liberalized? To what degree has there been simplification/overhaul of customs and tariff procedures, and are these applied fairly? What informal trade barriers exist? In 1993, the government passed a foreign trade law. In 1996, it adopted a new customs tariffs law that abolished all protectionist tariff rates that sought to harmonize rates with those of the EU. Customs duties are levied on imported goods. In most cases, the rates vary from zero to 25 percent. Imports of crude oil and essential items are subject to rates of less than five percent. The rate for raw materials and equipment is approximately five percent. Oil derivatives are taxed at approximately 10 percent. Consumer products are taxed at rates between 12 and 15 percent. Rates on luxury goods are higher. The average rate of duty is approximately 12 percent. Services are not subject to duties, levies, or fees. The law provides certain benefits — including duty exemptions on imports of equipment or other assets to be used for capital contributions — for foreign investors, provided that the investor commits to a period of at least five years and holds 20 percent or more of the equity. A number of products, with the exception of those that are free from customs duties, are subject to special import levies in addition to any applicable tariff duties. A special levy of five percent is applied to the import of live animals, meat other than lamb, meat products, fish and fish products, and butter and other fats from milk and cheese. There are no customs duties on exports. The government periodically imposes quotas on some imports and exports to defend the national economy and to prevent the mass export of natural resources. Quotas apply to less than 2 percent of import categories. There are subsidies to promote certain agricultural exports. There is no formal registration requirement for exports or imports. Licenses are required for the export and import of certain goods such as weapons, drugs, and waste materials. In 1997, $1.1 billion of goods were exported, and $1.7 billion of goods were imported. Corruption in the customs sector represents the greatest informal barrier to normal trade.

7. To what extent has foreign investment and capital flow been encouraged or constrained? The government has made a concerted effort to attract foreign direct investment by improving the legal environment. Nevertheless, an abrupt loss of markets, a weak banking sector, political instability in the region, low visibility, and an underdeveloped legal sector have given Macedonia a very small inflow of foreign capital relative to that of other Central and Eastern European countries. The total inflow of direct foreign capital between 1990 and 1996 as $36 million. (In the Czech Republic, it was $4.5 billion). Other factors that deter foreign investment include the low purchasing power of Macedonians and an underdeveloped capital market. According to a September 1997 *Nova Makedonija* article, the World Bank ranked Macedonia 107th — behind Pakistan and Romania — in the world in investment risk. A minister of development has identified other obstacles to foreign investment as the "complicated procedures for obtaining permits," "non-professional procedures" in the banking sector, and the opposition of some bank directors to the entry of foreign capital.

8. Has there been reform in the energy sector? (To what degree has the energy sector been restructured? Is the energy sector more varied, and is it open to private competition? Is the country overly dependent on one or few other countries for energy [including whether exported fuels must pass through one or more countries to reach markets]?) Reform in the energy sector has progressed slowly. Most energy prices have been liberalized. The World Bank has reported that privatization and investment in the energy sector have been inadequate. Four-fifths of the country's energy needs are met through the domestic production of therm-electric and hydro-electric power. The remaining one-fifth is imported from rump Yugoslavia and Bulgaria. As a landlocked nation, Macedonia depends exclusively upon overland shipments and pipelines for its gas and oil needs. Greece imposed an embargo until 1995, when it allowed oil to be shipped by rail from its port in Thessaloniki. Russia remains a key supplier of oil, which is refined in Bulgaria. A natural gas pipeline has been built to carry Russian gas from the Bulgarian border. An independent public utility produces, transmits, and distributes electricity. Macedonia forms part of the European electrical energy system with links to Yugoslavia, Greece, and Bulgaria. The government has announced plans to maintain and upgrade systems with financing from international institutions.

MOLDOVA

Freedom in the World Ratings, 1989-1998

	1989-90	1990-91	1991-92	1992-93	1993-94	1994-95	1995-96	1996-97	1997-98
Political Rights	-	-	5	5	5	4	4	3	3
Civil Liberties	-	-	4	5	5	4	4	4	4
Status	-	-	PF	PF	PF	PF	PF	PF	PF

Polity: Transitional
Economy: Transitional
Population: 4,347,000
PPP: $1,547
Ethnic Groups: Moldovan (64 percent), Ukrainian (14 percent), Russian (13 percent), Gagauz (3.5 percent), Bulgarian (2 percent)
Capital: Chisinau

Political Process 3.50/7

1. When did national legislative elections occur? Were they free and fair? How were they judged by domestic and international election monitoring organizations? Who composes the government? Moldova's first post-Communist parliament was elected on February 27, 1994. International organizations such as the OSCE judged the election to be fair. The centrist Agrarian Democratic Party won an absolute majority in this first election, and ruled cooperatively with the Socialist/Unity Party for the first 18 months of the session. Parties on the right, the Christian Democratic Popular Front and the Peasants and Intellectuals bloc, formed the opposition. On June 26, 1995, President Mircea Snegur resigned from the Agrarian Democratic Party, causing a split in the party and forcing the Agrarians to rely on the Socialists for a majority.

The second parliamentary elections were held on March 22, 1998. As in the first elections, they were held on the basis of proportional representation with party lists. Four parties passed the Five percent threshold for representation. The Party of Moldovan Communists won 30 percent of the popular vote, which translated into 40 seats in the 101-member chamber. The center-right Democratic Convention of Moldova (CDM) won 26 seats. The For a Democratic and Prosperous Moldova Bloc (PMDP), the centrist party most closely associated with President Lucinschi, won 24. The center-right Party of Democratic Forces won 11. The Transdneister authorities prevented some people from voting in the elections and the Helsinki Committee - Moldova noted electoral irregularities.

Despite the Communist victory, the three non-Communist parties formed a coalition called the Alliance for Democracy and Reform in April 1998. Ion Ciubuc was renominated as prime minister. It was agreed that the remaining 13 ministerial positions in the government would be split between the three parties on a 2-2-1 basis with the CDM and PMDP each having two ministers for each one of the Party of Democratic Forces'.

2. When did presidential elections occur? Were they free and fair? Moldova's first presidential election took place in December 1991, when President Snegur was elected without opposition.

The second post-independence presidential election took place in November and December 1996. In the first round, held on November 17, 1996, Snegur, running as the candidate of the new Party of Rebirth and Reconciliation, received 39 percent of the vote; Speaker of the Parliament Petru Lucinschi, running as an independent with the support of the left, received 28 percent; Prime Minister Sangheli, nine percent; Communist Party leader Vladimir Voronin, 10 percent; and leader of the Party on Democratic Forces Valeriu Matei, nine percent. There were also four independents in the race. On December 1, 1996, Lucinschi was elected president by a 54-46 percent margin. He took office on January 15, 1997 and will serve a four-year term. International observers judged the presidential election to be free and fair. After the election Lucinschi nominated Ciubuc as the new prime minister but retained most of Snegur's cabinet.

3. Is the electoral system multiparty-based? Are there at least two viable political parties functioning at all levels of government? Moldova's proportional representation electoral system is multiparty-based. There is open competition between the various parties and blocs at all levels of government.

4. How many parties have been legalized? Are any political parties illegal? Early on, the Communist Party was banned was relegalized following the February 1994 parliamentary elections. In recent years, the creation of parties and voting blocs has been relatively unrestricted and parties have formed and re-formed.

5. What proportion of the population belongs to political parties? Moldovan political organizations are associational. Party identification is fluid and membership is weak. Voters identify more with the personalities and positions of leading political figures than with parties. There is no data available on party membership.

6. What has been the trend of voter turnout at the municipal, provincial, and national levels in recent years? The first post-Communist presidential election in 1991 had an 83-percent voter turnout. The 1994 parliamentary election drew 79 percent. Local and municipal elections in 1995 drew lower rates and some local runoffs failed to attract the requisite 50 percent, especially in the cities where voters seemed to tire of repeated elections. Turnout in Gagauzia for the election to determine regional boundaries in March 1995 was 73 percent. The elections for the Bashkan and Popular Assembly in May and June of 1995 drew approximately 70 percent. The first round of the 1996 election drew 68 percent, and the runoff drew 72 percent of eligible voters.

Civil Society 3.75/7

1. How many nongovernmental organizations have come into existence since 1986? How many charitable/nonprofit organizations? Are there locally led efforts to increase philanthropy and volunteerism? What proportion of the population is active in private voluntary activity (from polling data)? There are several hundred registered NGOs in Moldova, most of which are located in the capital of Chisinau. "Registered" and "active," however, are not synonymous. Less than 100 of these NGOs could be considered active. Charities, as known in the West, are not well understood in Moldova, however, some do exist, mostly with the support of international sponsors.

2. What is the legal and regulatory environment for NGOs (i.e. ease of registration, legal rights, government regulation, taxation, procurement and access-to-information issues)? To what extent is NGO activism focused on improving the legal and regulatory environment? Information not available.

3. What is the organizational capacity of NGOs? Do management structures clearly delineate authority and responsibility? Is information available on NGO management issues in the native language? Is there a core of experienced practitioners/trainers to serve as consultants or mentors to less developed organizations? Information not available.

4. Are NGOs financially viable? What is their tax status? Are they obliged to and do they typically disclose revenue sources? Do government procurement opportunities exist for private, not-for-profit providers of services? Information not available.

5. Are there free trade unions? How many workers belong to these unions? Is the number of workers belonging to trade unions growing or decreasing? What is the numerical/proportional membership of farmers' groups, small business associations, etc.? Legislation provides for the legal formation of trade unions. Over 90 percent of the workforce belongs to the General Federation of Trade Unions (GFTU), which is the successor to the former Communist unions. The GFTU administers the state social insurance system, which makes it difficult to form alternatives to it. Nevertheless, its constituent unions are assuming more independent powers.

Most farmers are members of the former collective farms, now organized as joint-stock companies. For most of those living on the former collective farms, little has changed but the name of the organization. A large U.S. AID supported project to make agricultural privatization a reality has begun, but it is too early to measure any impact. Private farmers constitute a very small proportion of those on the land. Nevertheless, they are increasingly active and have a voice, though little political clout, through the small National Taranist Party.

Businesses, particularly in Chisinau, are becoming increasingly active. This increased activity may result in the organization of business associations and lobbying groups. However, the development of commercial activity is just beginning.

6. What forms of interest group participation in politics are legal? The distinction between interest groups, associations, and political parties is hard to delineate in Moldova. The political process is free and open, so individuals and organizations participate in the political process as they wish.

7. How is the not-for-profit/NGO sector perceived by the public and government officials? What is the nature of media coverage of NGOs? To what extent do government officials en-

gage with NGOs? Information not available.

Independent Media 3.75/7

1. Are there legal protections for press freedom? Press freedom is guaranteed in the constitution and made operational through the Press Law of 1994.

2. Are there legal penalties for libeling officials? Are there legal penalties for "irresponsible" journalism? Have these laws been enforced to harass journalists? The constitution disallows "disputing or defaming the State and the people." These restrictions, however, have not been implemented in law or otherwise enforced. The press law does allow politicians to sue for defamation without distinguishing between their public and private affairs. The suits that have been brought to trial have generally failed.

3. What proportion of the media is privatized? What are the major private newspapers, television stations, and radio stations? Three independent news agencies, Infotag, Basapress, and Flux, plus the government-controlled Moldpress, provide material for the traditional media outlets as well as domestic and international e-mail customers. Most political parties publish their own newspapers. Television and radio are largely controlled by the state owned Teleradio-Moldova. Private Catalan TV debuted in 1995, but its transmissions are limited to Chisinau and 40 kilometers around it. Locally owned radio is also growing slowly. There is only one private radio station, which broadcasts religious material out of Chisinau. Nongovernmental sources are providing an increasing share of the information and are limited more by economic factors than by governmental attempts to restrict information. The most popular weekly newspaper is the independent *Saptamina*.

4. Are the private media financially viable? As in all the post-Communist states, the media have little experience with business operations and thus, are experiencing start-up difficulties. Political party newspapers are similarly short of both cash and management experience. Advertising support is limited, and papers often lose money by increasing circulation.

A new media group, the Association of Independent Press, was launched in October 1997. Its goal is to help finance private media in Moldova.

5. Are the media editorially independent? Are the media's news gathering functions affected by interference from government or private owners? The news services are independent and provide relatively objective coverage. Many of the papers are published by the political parties and thus express a particular point-of-view. They are, however, free from governmental control. The state-owned papers, *Moldova Suverana* and *Nezavisimaya Moldova*, often acted as participants rather than objective sources in the 1996 presidential election. Both serious challengers, parliamentary speaker Lucinschi and Prime Minister Sangheli, received more favorable coverage from the government-controlled print and broadcast outlets than did the incumbent, President Snegur. For example, in a major scandal, national television broadcast an illegally recorded conversation between two of Snegur's top aides in an attempt to embarrass the ex-president. Media not controlled by political parties or the state are growing in number but are still relatively few.

In November 1997, two top directors of Teleradio, Adrian Usatii and Dumitru Turcanu, were replaced after months of fighting in parliament. The Moldovan parliament amended the Law on the Electronic Media in December 1997, and Article 7 was changed to regularize parliamentary power of dismissal over the heads of the state television and radio agencies. President Lucinschi, arguing that this violated the constitution, vetoed the amendment. The veto was overturned later that month.

In 1996, Ion Frunza, the deputy head of Catalan TV, was kidnapped by five men in police uniforms. Three journalists for *Mesagerul*, the party newspaper of the Alliance of Democratic Forces, were beaten in January. Two of them were threatened with death if they continued to write about police involvement in a racketeering ring.

6. Is the distribution system for newspapers privately or governmentally controlled? Most newspapers are printed by the state printing organization. This system has not inhibited opposition media. The kiosk-based distribution system that is used does not appear to serve any particular political interest.

7. What proportion of the population is connected to the Internet? Are there any restrictions on Internet access to private citizens? Information not available.

8. What has been the trend in press freedom as measured by Freedom House's *Survey of Press Freedom*? The media have become increasingly open and competitive. State interference with opposition media is not a problem, though the state-owned outlets were hardly neutral in the election campaign. Some self-censorship is no doubt present as a result of a 1995 press law which forbids "contesting or defaming the Moldovan people." Freedom House's *Survey of Press Freedom* rated Moldova "Partly Free" from 1992-1998.

Governance and Public Administration 4.50/7

1. Is the legislature the effective rule-making institution? Yes. The constitutional structure provides for divided power, or checks-and-balances system. During Snegur's term, both the government and the parliament were able to thwart various presidential initiatives. The Constitutional Court has limited some presidential attempts to bypass parliamentary and governmental prerogatives. Prior to the 1996 presidential election, the president was often at odds with both the government and the parliament. The Lucinschi presidential victory, together with Prime Minister Sangheli's resignation, will likely result in increased cooperation among the institutions.

2. Is substantial power decentralized to subnational levels of government? What specific authority do subnational levels have? Moldova is organized as a unitary state with power concentrated in the central institutions. The constitution, however, allows "special status" for ethnic minority areas. An agreement for special autonomous status for the Gagauz Yeri region was adopted in January 1995.

The Transdniestrian region declared its independence in December 1995, but is not recognized as an independent state by other countries. So far, it has run its own affairs.

3. Are subnational officials chosen in free and fair elections? Local councils are freely elected, with the chairperson selected locally but appointed by the president. Participation in local elections in 1995 was open and fair. Over 27,000 candidates from eight different political parties and 900 independents competed for 2,195 available seats. One mayor, elected in the Gagauz region, was not allowed to take power and the matter is currently under adjudication.

4. Do legislative bodies actually function? Legislative bodies do function. The parliament is effectively organized and passes laws. The Gagauz Popular Assembly has also begun to operate as an effective regional legislature. City and local councils are also elected and operate at the grassroots level, but with limited authority because of the strictures of a unitary state.

5. Do the executive and legislative bodies operate openly and with transparency? The parliament and the Gagauz Popular Assembly operate openly and publish their materials. The executive functions seem to be relatively accessible to the media. Snegur attempted (unsuccessfully) to remove the minister of defense in 1996 because of alleged corruption, but was blocked by the prime minister and the Constitutional Court.

6. Do municipal governments have sufficient revenues to carry out their duties? Do municipal governments have control of their own local budgets? Do they raise revenues autonomously or from the central state budget? The unitary state structure implies that revenues will be provided from the center to the localities. Exceptions are found in Gagauzia and in the proposed Transdniestrian agreement, where local control of many aspects of administration and a local fiscal formula are provided. Central revenues, and thus contributions to the local authorities, have been limited because of Moldova's reduced economic productivity. Thus local authorities still rely heavily on local enterprises for contributions of services.

7. Do the elected local leaders and local civil servants know how to manage municipal governments effectively? Most local leaders had much of their experience working under the Soviet system, and do not know how to manage municipal governments effectively. The Academy of Public Administration is training an increasing number of local officials, but major changes will require additional training and a more productive economy.

8. Has there been constitutional/legislative reform regarding local power? Has there been a reform of the civil service code/ system? Are local civil servants employees of the local or central government? In November 1997, the parliament rejected the government's draft laws on the reorganization of local governments. Local officials are local government employees, however, most of the money still comes from the center.

Rule of Law 4.50/7

1. Is there a post-Communist constitution? How does the judicial system interpret and enforce the constitution? Are there specific examples of judicial enforcement of the constitution in the last year? The post-Communist constitution was adopted on July 28, 1994. It took effect on

August 27, 1994, the anniversary of Moldova's declaration of independence. A powerful and independent Constitutional Court has sole jurisdiction over constitutional disputes and has overturned actions of both the parliament and the president.

In July 1997, the court declared several decrees issued by President Lucinschi, (related to the establishment of an anti-corruption agency) unconstitutional on the grounds that this sort of power is the prerogative of the legislative and not the executive branch.

In March 1996, the bitter feud between then-President Snegur and the Agrarian Democratic Party (PDAM) dominated government headed by Prime Minister Sangheli took an ugly turn. Snegur accused Defense Minister Pavel Creanga of corruption and demanded his resignation. This was despite the fact that, under Moldovan law, only the prime minister has the authority to dismiss ministers. After Creanga refused to resign, Snegur dispatched troops which surrounded the building for several hours before an emergency parliamentary session ended the impasse. In April of that year, the Constitutional Court ruled the dismissal was illegal. Nevertheless, Snegur apparently was intent on defying the court, saying the ruling only aggravated the situation. In June, Snegur warned that if Creanga was not dismissed, he would assume direct control over the army, elements of which showed loyalty to him and not Creanga. Creanga responded by saying he would call troops to arms if attempts were made to forcibly dismiss him. Following this exchange, events stabilized as the November presidential election loomed and Snegur was defeated.

2. Does the constitution provide for human rights? Do the humans rights include business and property rights? The constitution formally protects generally recognized human rights, including property rights.

3. Has there been basic reform of the criminal code/criminal law? Who authorizes searches and issues warrants? Are suspects and prisoners beaten or abused? Are there excessive delays in the criminal justice system? The old Soviet Code on Penal Procedure, with some amendments, is still law. Prosecutors and judges issue warrants. Nevertheless, illegal searches have occurred. There is also no judicial review of search warrants. Prosecutors have an inadequate capability to oversee wiretapping by the police and other security agencies.

There have been some reliable reports that police have beaten prisoners or suspects. Prison conditions are best characterized as grim, especially in cells for those awaiting trial and sentencing. Along with severe overcrowding, disease is epidemic and abuse of prisoners not uncommon. The court system and the criminal code were reformed in 1996. The new structure provided a separation between police functions and the courts. The Ministry of Justice replaced the Ministry of the Interior as the administrator for the prison system.

Another major problem is that the intelligence service and police have been known to monitor Moldovans electronically, especially government opponents. The prosecutor's office, which is supposed to authorize wiretaps, is unable to exert any real check on the activities of these agencies.

4. Do most judges rule fairly and impartially? How many remain from the Communist era? On the whole, judges seem to operate impartially. Nevertheless, there have been some reliable reports that some judges have extorted bribes in exchange for favorable rulings. In October 1997, such charges were brought against a judge and a prosecutor in Cainari.

There has been a serious, ongoing effort to replace personnel from the Communist era with newly-trained judges.

5. Are the courts free of political control and influence? Are the courts linked directly to the Ministry of Justice or any other executive body? The courts operate under the Ministry of Justice but are separate from the Ministry of Internal Affairs. Thirteen district courts, five regional appeals courts, and two higher courts have been established. The president appoints the district judges and the parliament appoints the Supreme Court. Appointments to the new judicial structure were being made during 1995 and 1996. With the help of the Council of Europe, the structures and procedures now in place resemble European models more than the previous Soviet ones.

The independence of the judiciary has increased markedly since the end of the Soviet Union. For example, judges now have tenure. They serve for an initial period of five years and may be reappointed for a ten-year term. Following that, they can serve until retirement. Still, the prosecutor's office has a very strong influence on proceedings. While defendants are considered innocent until proven guilty, prosecutors' recommendations are exceedingly influential. In July 1997, prosecutors obtained the power to open and close investigations without bringing them to a court's attention.

6. What proportion of lawyers is in private practice? A small but growing proportion of lawyers is in private practice.

7. Does the state provide public defenders? Suspects have the right to a public defender under the constitution, but this right is frequently undermined in practice. Access to a lawyer is frequently granted only after a suspect has been detained for a full day. The government requires, but does not pay, the local bar association to provide lawyers for indigent defendants.

8. Has there been a comprehensive reform of anti-bias/discrimination laws, including protection of ethnic minority rights? The constitution formally enshrines the principle of equality before the law. It also assigns special status for regions where ethnic minorities are concentrated. This provision has been utilized in Gagauzia and is central to the negotiations over the Transdniestrian area. Moldova was the first member of the CIS to be accepted into the Council of Europe after close scrutiny of its minority rights practices. Laws on citizenship, voting, language, and education accommodate minorities. Practice, though occasionally uneven, has largely followed the law. The Russian-speaking minority has been uncomfortable with its changed status after Moldovan independence, but actual discrimination has been quite limited. Minorities have claimed discrimination because the state language law requires people in public positions to be able to deal with the public in either the state language, Moldovan, or in Russian. The law itself, however, is quite accommodating to minorities in education, employment, designation of place names, and public services. Those in governmental or public employment were required by the Language Law of 1989 to learn the state language by 1994. The testing, however, required by the law has been delayed indefinitely.

Moldova ratified the Council of Europe's Convention on the Protection of Ethnic Minorities in October 1996.

Corruption C

1. What is the magnitude of official corruption in the civil service? Must an average citizen pay a bribe to a bureaucrat in order to receive a service? What services are subject to bribe requests — for example, university entrance, hospital admission, telephone installation, obtaining a license to operate a business, applying for a passport or other official documents? What is the average salary of civil servants at various levels? Corruption is quite widespread. As of mid-1997, for example, 76 police officers and 32 senior officials at the ministry had been fired, and 50 criminal cases had been filed against police with seven sentenced thus far. In July 1997, for example, all four chief officers of the traffic police were fired after an Interior Ministry investigation revealed they were taking bribes.

The extent of corruption was highlighted in 1996 when the Justice minister was stopped in Austria driving a stolen car.

2. Do top policy makers (the president, ministers, vice-ministers, top court justices, and heads of agencies and commissions) have direct ties to businesses? How strong are such connections and what kinds of businesses are these? In a major case in May 1997, authorities charged Minister of Privatization Ceslav Ciobanu with selling off a state sanitarium to a university founded by his wife.

3. Do laws requiring financial disclosure and disallowing conflict of interest exist? Have publicized anti corruption cases been pursued? To what conclusion? In 1996, the government ordered the interior ministry to form a department to fight crime and corruption. By mid-year, all civil servants were required to declare revenues, bank accounts, and other assets.

4. What major anticorruption initiatives have been implemented? How often are anticorruption laws and decrees adopted? The Minister of the interior under Mihail Plamadeala launched an anti-corruption campaign in February 1997.

In April 1997, President Lucinschi issued decrees which established the Department for Organized Crime and Corruption Prevention within the Ministry of the Interior. In July 1997, the Moldovan Constitutional Court declared these decrees to be unconstitutional. The court ruled that the creation of such new departments was the prerogative of the legislative branch.

5. How do major corruption-ranking organizations like Transparency International rate this country? Transparency International did not rank Moldova in its most recent (1997) survey.

Privatization 4.00/7

1. What percentage of the GDP comes from private ownership? What percentage of the labor force is employed in the private sector? How large is the informal sector of the economy? The private sector accounts for about 45 percent of GDP and employs between 50 and 80 percent of the labor force. The informal sector of the economy was estimated at 15-16 percent of GDP in 1996.

2. What major privatization legislation has been passed? What were its substantive features? Moldova's privatization program was focused on a process similar to the Czech Republic's voucher privatization. So-called national patrimonial bonds were issued to each citizen in proportion to the number of years he worked in the economy. Some 90 percent of Moldovans ultimately participated in the program and about half of state assets were sold.

Privatization bonds could be sold to licensed voucher funds, which emerged as the largest investors in privatized firms. Voucher privatization ended in October 1996. In all, 1,400 small firms and 1,150 medium and large-scale enterprises were privatized through this method.

In June 1996, the government established "Regulation 562" which simplified procedures for privatizing the land on which state assets were located.

Other methods of privatization included cash sales of small enterprises and tenders for large enterprises. While the former has moved quickly, large tender privatization has yet to begin in earnest. Of the 41 large companies selected to be sold in 1995-6, none had been privatized by mid-1997. A major blow to the tender process occured in December 1996, when the state canceled a tobacco company tender. The government had earlier announced that Reemtsma, a German company, had won the tender despite submitting a lower bid than the UK firm BAT. Another problem has been the continual delays in the privatization of Moldtelecom, the telecommunications monopoly. The 1997-8 program, passed in June 1997, lists 580 enterprises targetted for cash privatization.

Ceslav Ciobanu, the privatization minister, was forced to resign in June 1997 over a privatization scandal. Ciobanu was alleged to have sold a sanatorium to a private university in which his wife has a 16-percent share.

3. What proportion of agriculture, housing and land, industry, and small business and services is in private hands? By the end of 1996, there were 61,600 private farms. Agricultural privatization was slow early on. At first, most agriculture was done on collective farms. Later, these were transformed into joint-stock agricultural associations. The government, aided by U.S. AID, launched a program to break up 73 such associations and give land titles to individual farmers. The latest phase of the project was launched in March 1998 with the goal of breaking up 550 more farms over a 15-month period. If this works, then a majority of farmland in Moldova will have been privatized with farmers holding transferable titles to individually-owned pieces of land.

By the end of 1996, about 200,000 homes had been privatized; representing more than 80 percent of the dwellings available for privatization. Of these, 70 percent were privatized free of charge, 28 percent with National Patrimonial Bonds, and 2 percent with cash. An active market for housing has developed in Chisinau and Balti, and the beginning of a private housing boom can be seen around the larger towns and cities. Only 10 percent of land had been privatized by the end of 1995. About 70 percent of trade and services is private.

4. What has been the extent of insider (management, labor, and nomenklatura) participation in the privatization process? What explicit and implicit preferences have been awarded to insiders? Information not available.

5. How much public awareness of and support for privatization has there been? What major interest groups oppose and advocate privatization? Communists and other hard-left political groups virulently oppose privatization. They attempted to launch a popular referendum to nullify the land privatization law passed by the parliament in July 1997. There has not been much pressure by agrarian political forces and farmers themselves against the breakup of collective farms.

Macroeconomics 4.25/7

1. Has the taxation system been reformed? (What areas have and have not been overhauled? To what degree are taxpayers complying? Is tax compliance difficult to achieve? Has the level of revenues increased? Is the revenue-collection body overburdened? What is the overall tax burden?) Moldova relies on five main taxes: a value-added tax (VAT), a company profit tax, a personal income tax, a land tax, and excise taxes. The VAT is the biggest source of income. Its rate is generally a uniform 20 percent, but it discriminates between countries. The profit tax is an even 32 percent. Income taxes range from 10 percent for incomes up to 4,320 *lei* ($940) to 40 percent on incomes above 21,600 lei ($4,695). Average incomes fall in the 10 percent bracket.

Tax arrears were $145 million or 7.5 percent of GDP by the end of 1996. Most of the arrears came from the agricultural sector, with overdue land and excise taxes. In May 1996, the finance ministry launched a new initiative that called for seizing property of tax delinquents.

A simplified tax code came up for parliamentary approval in 1996. It aimed to abolish many exemptions, improve collection and compliance, and rationalize the various components of Moldovan taxes. The parliament adopted the provisions on the profit and income taxes in April 1997. In June 1997, the legislature passed a law exempting firms from penalties for late tax payments. The president vetoed this bill but his veto was overridden in October.

2. Does fiscal policy encourage private savings, investment and earnings? (Has there been any reform/alteration of revenue and budget policies? How large are budget deficits and overall debt? Is the financing of the social insurance/pension system sustainable? What proportion of the budget is taken up by subsidies to firms and individuals)

Government consumption has remained relatively steady at 20 percent of GDP. Debt as a proportion of GDP is 60 percent. Moldova's budget deficit was 7.7 percent of GDP by the end of 1997, an increase from the initial target of 4.5 percent. One major reason for this has been the reluctance of parliament — prior to the March 1998 elections — to penalize politically powerful firms who are delinquent on their tax payments. The economy grew at the rate of 1.3 percent in 1997.

This policy, as well as the decision to suspend energy price liberalization, led the IMF to delay the disbursement of the fourth tranche ($15.5 million) of its extended fund facility loan, the last being made in July 1997. The World Bank signed a new structural adjustment loan agreement in September 1997 for $100 million, but suspended the second installment in November to protest reform backsliding.

The Moody's credit rating agency rates Moldova is sovereign debt at the Ba2 level.

3. Has there been banking reform? (Is the central bank independent? What are its responsi-

bilities? Is it effective in setting and/or implementing monetary policy? What is the actual state of the private banking sector? Does it conform to international standards? Are depositors protected?) Yes, the National Bank of Moldova (NBM) is independent, and has been successful in curbing monetary expansion. A new central bank law adopted in January 1996 further strengthened the NBM. It can now put severely troubled banks into receivership.

There are four state banks and 21 commercial banks. The banking sector is considered generally sound but it is undercapitalized. Average interest rates on loans as of mid -1997 were about 37 percent.

There are numerous Western-style banking regulations, including capital adequacy, ratio of deposits to capital, maximum exposure to single borrowers, risk capital reserves, and a weighted capital asset ratio. Minimal capital requirements were raised to eight million lei ($1.75 million) in 1997. The minimum reserve requirement was eight percent by the end of 1996. International accounting standards were expected to be introduced in all banks by the end of 1997.

4. How sound is the national currency? (To what extent has inflation eroded its value? Is the value of the currency fixed or does it float? Is the currency convertible? How large are the hard currency reserves? Has exchange rate policy been stable and predictable?) The floating Moldovan currency has been relatively stable since 1994. In nominal terms, it has fallen only slightly since 1995. In real terms, it has actually appreciated in value. Depreciation became noticeable, however, in October 1997, dropping to a record low of 4.68 lei to the dollar in January 1998. The leu is convertible on the current account, while capital account conversion requires a license from the central bank. Currency reserves are relatively high; $373 million as of mid-1997. Some $250 million of this is IMF funds. As a result, currency policy is extremely dependent on that institution.

Hyperinflation rocked the economy in 1992 at 1.277 percent and in 1993 at 1.751 percent. Since then, inflation has fallen steadily, dropping to 11.2 percent in 1997.

5. Is there a functioning capital market infrastructure? (Are there existing or planned commodities, bond and stock markets? What are the mechanisms for investment and lending? What government bodies have authority to regulate capital markets?) The Moldovan capital market is underdeveloped but is improving. The electronic Moldovan stock exchange was established in June 1995 with the help of U.S. advisers. Total trade volume has risen rapidly, from $2.5 million in 1996 to $28.4 million in the first ten months of 1997. The number of listed companies, however, is small — less than 20 — and is dominated by the voucher funds created during mass privatization. The capitalization of the market was $670 million as of August 1997.

Moldova lacks a functioning shareholders' register. Minority shareholders do not enjoy many protections.

The State Commission on Securities Markets regulates the capital markets and its participants.

Microeconomics 4.25/7

1. Are property rights guaranteed? (Are there both formal and de facto protections of private real estate and intellectual property? Is there a land registry with the authority and capability to ensure accurate recording of who owns what? What are the procedures for expro-

priation, including measures for compensation and challenge? Have any seizures taken place?) Property rights are explicitly protected in the Moldovan constitution. Law guarantees fair market-price compensation for government "takings" of private land.

A law guaranteeing the sale of land was adopted in July 1997. Nevertheless, the Gagauz Yeri region stated that the law would not be operative in that area of Moldova. The new law overturned a restrictive land code passed in 1995 and set off a campaign by the Communists to hold a plebiscite on the issue. A majority vote of the parliament ended this attempt. Previously, the land code had been amended in February 1995 to restrict the sale of most private land until 2001. This moratorium, however, was declared unconstitutional in October 1996.

Foreigners are not allowed to purchase farmland, and farmland can not be resold within a five-year period.

Moldova adopted a law protecting intellectual property rights in 1995 but has yet to successfully attack massive piracy in software and entertainment products.

Establishing clear land title has been problematic. In November 1997, the parliament rejected a government-proposed law to set up a land registry. This has been a condition of the IMF and World Bank for resuming transfers to Moldova.

2. To what extent have prices been liberalized? What subsidies remain? Most prices, with the exception of energy, were liberalized by 1993. Energy prices were partially liberalized in 1997, but the parliament suspended the incomplete policy in October. Nevertheless, gas and electricity prices are now at cost-recovery levels.

3. Is it possible to own and operate a business? (Has there been legislation regarding the formation, dissolution and transfer of businesses, and is the law respected? Do there exist overly cumbersome bureaucratic hurdles that effectively hinder the ability to own and dispose of a business? Are citizens given access to information on commercial law? Is the law applied fairly? Does regulation (or licensing requirements) impose significant costs on business and consumers? Do they create significant barriers to entry and seriously hamper competition?) Legislation permits ownership and operation of businesses. Regulations, however, are strict and often arbitrarily enforced by an inefficient and often corrupt bureaucracy.

The official cost for registering a new company is between $100 and $1,000, and the process takes one to three months. New private enterprise registrations grew by 150 percent in 1996, although 90 percent of that figure represented sole proprietorships.

A new bankruptcy code was adopted in 1996, and gives new powers to liquidators. The prioritization of wage arrears, tax arrears, credit arrears, and other unpaid claims, however, is uncertain.

4. Are courts effective, transparent, efficient, and quick in reaching decisions on property and contract disputes? What alternative mechanisms for adjudicating disputes exist? Cases are generally heard in a large city court within six months. Decisions are made within approximately six months. Disputants have the right to appeal judgements. Important judgements are not generally published. Judicial review of administrative actions is not yet established. There are no specialized bankruptcy courts.

5. Is business competition encouraged? (Are monopolistic practices limited in law and in practice? If so, how? To what degree is "insider" dealing a hindrance to open competition? Are government procurement policies open and unbiased?) Anti-monopoly legislation was adopted in 1992 but has been largely ineffective. Most of the state-owned monopolies are scheduled for break-up and privatization, but this has yet to occur. Moldova has laws prohibiting insider dealing in shares of public joint-stock companies.

6. To what extent has international trade been liberalized? To what degree has there been simplification/overhaul of customs and tariff procedures, and are these applied fairly? What informal trade barriers exist? Moldova's economy is quite open to foreign trade. It was further liberalized in June and September 1997. Average tariffs are 5 percent. A free trade zone was established in Chisinau in July 1996, and has become a success.

Quotas are present on the imports of unprocessed leather, energy, and cereals.

Russia is Moldova's main trade partner, followed by Romania and Ukraine. Trade with the West has been limited. Moldova launched its application for membership in the World Trade Organization in June 1997.

7. To what extent has foreign investment and capital flow been encouraged or constrained? Current legislation places few formal barriers on foreign investment. Those that exist prohibit full foreign ownership in the financial sector and in natural resource extraction. Barriers are higher, but not total, in the privatization of state enterprises.

Foreign direct investment remains low, with a cumulative total of $161 million by the end of 1996, a mere $37 per capita. Moreover, the majority of this investment is dominated not by private firms, but by the European Bank for Reconstruction and Development. Meanwhile, foreign portfolio investment has increased steadily, to a total of $234 million by mid-1997 ($54 million in 1996).

In May 1998, economics minister Ion Guta announced plans to create ten free economic zones, which would mean 5-10 year tax exemptions for foreign investors.

8. Has there been reform of the energy sector? (To what degree has the energy sector been restructured? Is the energy sector more varied, and is it open to private competition? Is the country overly dependent on one or two other countries for energy [including whether exported fuels must pass through one or more countries to reach markets]?) The energy sector is only partially reformed. External and internal payments arrears are high and unsustainable. Much remains to be privatized and de-monopolized.

Delinquency in payments has resulted in numerous reductions and suspensions in gas supply, most recently during the 1996-7 winter. In September 1997 Moldova owed Gazprom (Russia) $239 million, when a repayment agreement was finally signed with the company. The problem is fueled by nonpayment of gas consumers to the state gas monopoly, Moldovgas. Parliament approved the privatization and merger of Moldovgas and Gazsnabtranzit in February 1998. In partial repayment of its gas liabilities, Gazprom was given a 50 percent share in the company. The state will retain a

35 percent share.

Moldova relies almost exclusively on imports for its energy sources — only 2.3 percent of its supply originated domestically. Moldoveneasca is the country's main electricity generation station, but it is located in Transdnicstr. While oil imports are relatively diversified, the Russian firm Gazprom still dominates gas imports. There has been some recent effort to develop indigenous supplies of gas and oil. The U.S. firm Redeco, for example, has a 20 year concession to explore for oil deposits in the southwest region. The World Bank is financing the installation of energy meters in the housing sector in an effort to reduce consumption and end payment delinquency.

Private fuel importers now account for 80 percent of diesel and gasoline imports.

In May 1998, privatization minister Iurie Badir announced plans to privatize three power plants and five energy distributors in September 1998.

MONGOLIA

Freedom in the World Ratings, 1989-1998

	1989-90	1990-91	1991-92	1992-93	1993-94	1994-95	1995-96	1996-97	1997-98
Political Rights	7	4	2	3	2	2	2	2	2
Civil Liberties	7	4	3	2	3	3	3	3	3
Status	NF	PF	F	F	F	F	F	F	F

Polity: Transitional
Economy: Transitional
Population: 2,323,000
PPP: $3,766
Ethnic Groups: Khalkha Mongol (75 percent), other Mongol (8 percent), Kazakh (5 percent), others
Capital: Ulaanbaatar

Political Process 2.75/7

1. When did national legislative elections occur? Were they free and fair? How were they judged by domestic and international election monitoring organizations? Who composes the government? In May 1990, student-led, pro-democracy demonstrations forced the government to amend the constitution and scrap the ruling Mongolian People's Revolutionary Party's (MPRP) constitutional monopoly, allowing the formation of opposition parties for the first time since 1924. At the country's first multiparty legislative elections in July 1990, the MPRP took 357 of 430 seats in the Great Hural (parliament) against an unprepared opposition. The MPRP also captured 33 of 53 seats in a newly-created Little Hural elected by party preference balloting.

The 1992 post-Communist constitution scrapped the Little Hural in favor of a new, unicameral, 76-member Great Hural. In the June 1992 Great Hural elections, the MPRP — split into factions ranging from orthodox Communists to free market reformers — took a commanding 70 of 76 seats against a confusing array of 12 opposition parties, many of which lacked clear ideological distinctions and the means to campaign effectively. The reform-oriented Democratic Coalition took four seats, the European-influenced Social Democratic Party took one, and an-MPRP affiliated independent took one. The opposition managed to win a credible 43 percent of the popular vote, but was disadvantaged under the first-past-the-post electoral system. Voter turnout was 91 percent. International observers rated the vote as free although not entirely fair, noting that the electoral districts favored the rural areas, where the MPRP draws its bedrock support, and that the MPRP enjoyed ample funding, control over printing equipment and newsprint, and sufficient stocks of gasoline to campaign in the vast countryside. Nevertheless, observers said the victory generally reflected the will of the voters, who blamed the country's severe economic hardship on the free market reforms instituted since 1990 which they associated with the reform-oriented opposition.

In March 1996, the two leading parties in the opposition Democratic Coalition, the Mongolian National Democratic Party, and the Mongolian Social Democratic Party, became the leading members of a new, four-party opposition Democratic Union Coalition (DUC). The DUC ran a well-organized, issues-oriented campaign for Mongolia's second multiparty legislative elections on June 30, 1996. With a 91 percent turnout, the DUC captured 50 seats to sweep the MPRP from parliamentary power after 72 years, as voters sought relief from a severe energy crisis, rising prices, and unemployment. The MPRP won 25 seats. Domestic and international observers rated the vote as free and fair, noting that the main opposition parties had made considerable progress in closing the gap on the MPRP in terms of access to the media and resources. This was true even though changes to the electoral law in February 1996 provided public funds to the election campaigns of existing parliamentary parties in proportion to the number of seats each held, which meant that the ruling MPRP received nearly 92 percent of such funds. In July, the DUC formed a government under Prime Minister Mendsaihan Enksaikhan, a 41 year old economist.

2. When did presidential elections occur? Were they free and fair? In September 1990, an MPRP-dominated parliament appointed Punsalmaagiyn Orchirbat to the newly created post of State President for what was expected to be a five year term. But the 1992 post-Communist constitution established a president who is directly elected for a four year term, thus necessitating the country's first direct, multiparty presidential election. The president can veto Hural decisions (subject to override by a two-thirds majority), and nominate the prime minister in consultation with the largest party or coalition in parliament. He also serves as commander-in-chief of the armed forces.

In April 1993, the MPRP dumped Orchirbat as its candidate for the upcoming direct presidential elections in favor of Lodongiyn Tudev, the hardline Communist editor of the party paper *Unen* (Truth). Later that month, the opposition Democratic Coalition named Orchirbat as its candidate. In the June 7, 1993, elections, held with a 90 percent turnout, Ochirbat won 57.8 percent of the vote to defeat Tudev, with 38.7 percent.

Some 85 percent of registered voters turned out for the country's second multiparty presidential elections on May 18, 1997. The MPRP's Nachagyn Bagabandy, a former parliamentary chairman who capitalized on voters' concerns over the hardships caused by the DUC government's free-market reforms, won with 60.8 percent of the vote against Orchirbat's 29.8 percent. Zhambyn Gombozhab, the candidate of the small Mongolian Traditional Unification Party, rounded out the field. Both the 1993 and 1997 presidential elections were considered free and fair, and each resulted in a decisive opposition victory.

3. Is the electoral system multiparty-based? Are there at least two viable political parties functioning at all levels of government? China controlled this vast Central Asian steppe and mountain region for more than two centuries until the overthrow of the Qing dynasty in 1911, and again in 1919 until Soviet-backed Marxists revolted in 1921. The MPRP formed a Communist state in 1924, following three years of nominal rule by Buddhist lamas. For the next 65 years, the country existed as a virtual republic of the Soviet Union. The country's one-party system began to crack in December 1989 with the formation of an opposition association, the Mongolian Democratic Union (MDU). MDU-organized street protests and hunger strikes forced the resignation of much of the MPRP leadership in March 1990, and in May the government amended the constitution to scrap the party's legal monopoly, making Mongolia both the first Asian country to turn to communism and the first to reject it. Earlier, in February 1990, MDU activists had formed the country's first opposition party, the Mongolian Democratic Party. Since 1990, elections at the national and provincial levels have been multiparty-based.

In January 1996, the MPRP-dominated parliament defeated an electoral reform bill that would have introduced proportional representation. In February 1996, parliament passed a raft of amendments to the 1992 election law, transforming the 26 multi-member constituencies into 76 single-seat districts. The first-past-the-post system, and, more recently, the single-seat districts, have made it difficult for small parties to win seats. Only four parties won seats in the June 1996 parliamentary elections.

4. How many parties have been legalized? Are any particular parties illegal? Mongolia boasts dozens of political parties, although only 11 contested the June 1996 parliamentary elections. The government has not declared any parties illegal.

5. What proportion of the population belongs to political parties? Although voter turnout has been high in post-Communist elections, few Mongolians belong to political parties. In a country with 1.15 million eligible voters, even the largest parties have only several thousand members.

6. What has been the trend of voter turnout at the municipal, provincial and national levels in recent years? The 1992 and 1996 parliamentary elections each had a 91 percent turnout, while the 1993 and 1997 presidential elections had turnouts of 90 percent and 85 percent, respectively. These high figures come even though most rural voters have to travel for miles to reach a polling station. Local election turnouts are considerably lower, with a high of 64.2 percent.

Civil Society 3.25/7

1. How many nongovernmental organizations (NGOs) have come into existence since 1988? What is the number of charitable/nonprofit organizations? Are there locally led efforts to increase philanthropy and volunteerism? What proportion of the population is active in private voluntary activity (from polling data)? There are dozens of NGOs in Mongolia, including smaller numbers of charitable organizations. There are at least 30 NGOs working to improve legal awareness, increase the role of women in administrative and policy making positions, influence public policy on women's issues, and increase public awareness about the work of NGOs. For example, the Women's Federation, an NGO with branches in all of the *aimag* (provincial) centers, played a key role in placing micro-credit schemes and other women's development programs on the government's poverty alleviation agenda, and currently coordinates the disbursal of interest-free loans to female entrepreneurs. A smaller number of NGOs are active in government reform, such as the Ulaanbaatar-based Local Governance Development Foundation. Overall, most NGOs are focused on social welfare and human rights issues rather than on efforts to increase philanthropy or volunteerism. No figures exist on the proportion of the population that is active in private voluntary activity, although given Mongolia's predominantly rural population and the extreme hardship associated with the country's poverty, only a relatively small number of people are likely involved in such activities.

2. What is the legal and regulatory environment for NGOs (i.e. ease of registration, legal rights, government regulation, taxation, procurement and access-to-information issues)? To what extent is NGO activism focused on improving the legal and regulatory environment? There is a relatively straightforward registration process for NGOs. Most NGOs that work on legal issues are generally focused on making citizens aware of their rights, as opposed to improving the legal and regulatory environment.

3. What is the organizational capacity of NGOs? Do management structures clearly delineate authority and responsibility? Is information available on NGO management issues in the native language? Is there a core of experienced practitioners/trainers to serve as consultants or mentors to less developed organizations? Nongovernmental organizations are a new phenomenon in Mongolia, and as such their organizational capacity is limited. Most operate with relatively small staffs, and only a few, such as the Women's Federation, have more than a local presence. Most NGOs do have a board of directors, and the staff often include an executive director, a program coordinator, an accountant, and a public relations officer. There is a small but growing body of literature on NGO management issues in the Mongolian language. Foreign NGOs have provided considerable expertise and training to Mongolian NGOs. Most of the skills training provided by domestic NGOs has involved teaching basic business skills to female entrepreneurs, rather than serving as consultants or mentors to less developed organizations. The nationally-based Liberal Women's Brain Pool (LEOS), however, is running an NGO Capacity Building and Institution Project supported by the United States-based National Endowment for Democracy. LEOS and some other NGOs also conduct training for trainers' seminars on women in development and other issues.

4. Are NGOs financially viable? What is their tax status? Are they obliged to and do they typically disclose revenue sources? Do government procurement opportunities exist for private, not-for-profit providers of services? Most NGOs are not financially viable, and depend at least in part on foreign contributions. Some NGOs have turned to income generating activities, such as teaching, sewing, typing, or other skills at below-market rates to fund their activities. There are no specific barriers to government procurement opportunities for NGOs, although overall procurement procedures in Mongolia are often complex and opaque. An International Monetary Fund-sponsored project aims to promote transparency and accountability in this area by assisting the government in drafting improved regulations and procedures for procurement of goods, civil works and related services, and infrastructure projects.

5. Are there free trade unions? How many workers belong to these unions? Is the number of workers belonging to trade unions growing or decreasing? What is the numerical/proportional membership of farmer's groups, small business associations, etc.? The constitution guarantees workers the right to join independent trade unions, and, in practice, unions are free of government control. Workers have the right to strike, except for those in industries that the government defines as essential, such as law enforcement and transportation. Collective bargaining is also legal, but, in practice, employers generally set wages. The largest federation is the Mongolian Trade Unions Confederation with some workers also belonging to the newer Association of Free Trade Unions. Union officials estimate that more than 400,000 workers belong to trade unions, or somewhat less than half the workforce. This figure is decreasing as large state enterprises are phased out and more workers become self-employed or work at small, non-unionized firms. There are some small business associations such as the Mongolian Trade and Industry Promotion Agency.

6. What forms of interest group participation in politics are legal? What types of interest groups are active in the political and policy process? The Mongolian Democratic Union, a student group, spearheaded the mass demonstrations beginning in 1989 that toppled the MPRP's one-party rule in 1990. There are no legal restrictions on interest group participation in the political and policy process. Student groups continue to participate in the political process through public demonstrations, hunger strikes, petitions, and the media. NGOs played an important role in educating voters, distributing party manifestos, and conducting public opinion polling prior to the June 1996 parliamentary elections. The Women's Federation and other NGOs have also carried out policy advocacy for women's rights in parliament. Nevertheless, after seven decades of Soviet-style governance, preceded by centuries of feudalism, the idea that people can participate in politics is novel and is only beginning to catch on. Moreover, because of the country's huge size, limited communications systems, and scattered population, grassroots activism is difficult and expensive.

7. How is the non-for-profit/NGO sector perceived by the public and government officials? What is the nature of media coverage of NGOs? To what extent do government officials engage with NGOs? The public has generally reacted positively to the work of NGOs. For example, polls showed that 20 percent of the electorate reported being directly influenced by the 1996 pre-election civic education programs of the Ulaanbaatar-based Women for Social Progress. Some old-style politicians are suspicious of the growing political influence of NGOs, but, in general, politicians and government officials tolerate NGO activity. Moreover, more than 36 percent of the MPs elected in the July 1996 elections were beneficiaries of grants from the U.S.-based Asia Foundation, with eight MPs coming directly from NGOs aided by the Asia Foundation. NGOs actively use radio to deliver their messages; newspapers often carry materials prepared by NGOs. The 1993 Law on the Government of Mongolia directs the government to cooperate with NGOs on the protection of human rights, although in practice there is little formal cooperation.

Independent Media 3.25/7

1. Are there legal protections for press freedom? The constitution guarantees freedom of the press; this is respected in practice.

2. Are there legal penalties for libeling officials? Are there legal penalties for "irresponsible" journalism? Have these laws been enforced to harass journalists? Mongolia's libel laws provide a fairly low standard for public officials and other plaintiffs to prove harm. There are no legal penalties for "irresponsible" journalism. The private media occasionally report being threatened by government officials with charges of violating state secrets, but since 1990 the courts have not been used to harass journalists.

3. What proportion of media is privatized? What are the major private newspapers, television stations, and radio stations? There are more than 100 private newspapers and magazines, although due to funding constraints, most are published irregularly and infrequently. Each of the political parties has at least one newspaper, although few parties have the resources to distribute their papers widely. The largest newspaper, *Unen* (Truth), is an MPRP organ with a daily circulation of 150,000. The largest independent newspaper, *Aydyn Erkh* (People's Power), is a former government organ that was privatized in 1996 and has a circulation of 78,000. The Mongolian Trade Union Federation publishes one of the largest private dailies, *Hodolmor* (Labor), with a circulation of 64,900.

There are more than 300 television ground stations with low-powered transmitters. At least three private companies offer cable television in Ulaanbaatar. Nevertheless, the state broadcast media enjoy the best funding and thus maintain a strong market position. The state-run Mongolian Radio is the most important source of information in rural areas. State-run Mongolian Television runs the largest television station.

4. Are the private media financially viable? Hundreds of private newspapers emerged following the 1990 democratic revolution, although most lacked proper funding and folded. Until the mid-1990s, most newspapers generally bartered goods for newsprint; nearly all had to rent printing capacity, when available, from a sole, aging, government-owned press housed in the building of the then-ruling MPRP's daily newspaper in Ulaanbaatar. All newspapers now buy newsprint directly from private suppliers, and supply is no longer a problem. The lack of a sufficient advertising base, however, prevents most newspapers from publishing daily editions.

5. Are the media editorially independent? Are the media's news gathering functions affected by interference from government or private owners? Mongolian newspapers and magazines are editorially independent of the government, although many are owned by political parties, both in the ruling coalition and in opposition, and reflect their respective political views. The privately-owned FM stations are primarily geared towards entertainment and provide little news. The state-run broadcast media offer pluralistic views, but coverage occasionally favors the ruling party. There are few constraints on the media's news gathering function, although independent media sometimes complain of unequal access to government information and officials.

6. Is the distribution system for newspapers privately or governmentally controlled? The distribution system for independent newspapers is privately controlled, although in some areas newspaper delivery is dependent on the postal service.

7. What proportion of the population is connected to the Internet? Are there any restrictions

on Internet access to private citizens? Mongolia has several thousand Internet users, mainly in Ulaanbaatar. There are no restrictions on Internet access for private citizens.

8. What has been the trend in press freedom as measured by Freedom House's *Survey of Press Freedom*? Freedom House's Survey of Press Freedom has rated the Mongolian press as Partly Free since 1990.

Governance and Public Administration 3.50/7

1. Is the legislature the effective rule-making institution? The legislature is the effective rule-making institution. The president nominates the prime minister, who comes from the party or coalition holding the largest number of seats in parliament and who must be approved by parliament. Under the constitution, a presidential veto of any legislation can only be overridden by a two-thirds majority of parliament. Under the DUC government, parliament has become a forum for vigorous debate. Of concern is a frequent lack of implementing regulations in laws. As such, government officials often have disproportionate latitude in interpreting and implementing laws.

2. Is substantial power decentralized to subnational levels of government? What specific authority to subnational levels have? The constitution reserves to the provinces powers not specifically granted to the central government. Local hurals, or legislatures, have legislative responsibilities at the provincial and local levels, and local governments have been given increasing authority and autonomy. Power in Mongolia, however, remains centralized and most decision making is still in the hands of the central government. The 1993 Law on the Government of Mongolia establishes the independence of local governing bodies, but also instructs the central government to "provide centralized management" of the activities of the provincial and capital city governors. The government recognizes the need for greater decentralization and is undertaking public administration reforms aimed at improving expenditure control and accountability to prepare for decentralized decision making.

3. Are subnational officials chosen in free and fair elections? Mongolia is divided into 18 *aimags* (provinces) plus the capital city of Ulaanbaatar, and two other municipalities, Darhan and Erdenet. The aimags are sub-divided into 357 *soums*, or counties, which are subdivided into districts. There have been free and fair elections for legislative bodies at the aimag, municipal (Ulaanbaatar, Darhan and Erdenet), soum and district levels. At present, smaller municipalities within districts have indirect elections. The government has drafted a Local Election Law which, if passed, will establish direct legislative elections in these entities. The prime minister appoints governors of the aimags and the municipalities from among candidates nominated by the legislative bodies of the respective aimags and municipalities. Mongolia's most recent aimag and municipal elections, in October 1996, saw the Mongolian People's Revolutionary Party win 14 out of 21 legislatures.

4. Do the executive and legislative bodies operate openly and with transparency? Is draft legislation easily accessible to the media and the public? The post-Communist MPRP parliament often operated with limited transparency. For example, when parliament amended the electoral law in February 1996, the ruling party did not give the opposition advance notice of the vote; prior to the vote, the public was cleared from the visitors' gallery; and by some accounts there was not a quorum of members present, which would make the vote itself illegal. Parliament also drew up the new electoral districts in relative secrecy. The post-Communist MPRP government did not make voting records and floor statements of parliamentarians available to the public, ostensibly for national security reasons. The DUC government has operated with considerably more transparency.

5. Do municipal governments have sufficient revenues to carry out their duties? Do municipal governments have control of their own local budgets? Do they raise revenue autonomously or from the central state budget? Municipal governments have limited fiscal resources and depend on subsidies from the central government. The government is in the process of implementing public administration reforms that are giving municipal governments control of their own local budgets. According to the Asian Development Bank, the government is also committed to increasing self-financing capabilities for provincial-level infrastructure development by establishing cost-recovery mechanisms for infrastructure projects.

6. Do the elected local leaders and local civil servants know how to manage municipal governments effectively? Local officials lack sufficient human resources and expertise to manage municipal governments and deliver services effectively. In particular, accounting and auditing systems need to be strengthened. The government is currently in the process of adopting resource and performance-based accounting systems and implementing public administration reforms.

7. When did the constitutional/legislative changes on local power come into effect? Has there been a reform of the civil service code/system? Are local civil servants employees of the local or central government? The 1992 constitution delineated the current division of power between the federal and local government. There has not been a sweeping overhaul of the civil service system, although the government is committed to reforming the large and inefficient public sector. The DUC government has initiated civil service reforms that have reduced the number of government ministries from 13 to 9 and reorganized the remaining ministries and agencies and reduced staff. Local civil servants are nominally employees of local governments, although in practice their salaries are often paid for with central government funds.

Rule of Law 3.50/7

1. Is there a post-Communist constitution? How does the judicial system interpret and enforce the constitution? Are there specific examples of judicial enforcement of the constitution in the last year? Mongolia adopted its post-Communist constitution in January 1992, and it took effect in February 1992. The constitution and the Law on the Constitutional Court established an independent nine-member Constitutional Court with the power to interpret the constitution and rule on the constitutionality of laws, decrees, international treaties, national referenda, decisions by the central electoral authority, and other decisions by parliament, the president, and government. While the court has not had the opportunity to issue decisions on crucial constitutional issues, it is respected as an independent arbiter.

2. Does the constitutional framework provide for human rights? Do the human rights include business and property rights? The constitution provides human rights guarantees, including protections against torture and other abuse; discrimination on the basis of ethnicity, language, race, age, gender, social status, property, occupation, religion, creed, or education; and arbitrary searches, arrests, and detentions. The constitution also guarantees the right to a fair trial with due process guarantees; freedom of speech and press; freedom of assembly and association; freedom of religion; freedom of internal travel and emigration; and the right to privacy. The constitution recognizes and protects the "right to fair acquisition, possession, and inheritance of moveable and immovable property," and prohibits "illegal confiscation and requisitioning of the private property of citizens." In addition, the 1994 Civil Code explicitly recognizes the right to hold and transfer private property.

Although Mongolia has a generally positive human rights record, police abuse of prisoners and detainees and unofficial discrimination against women continue to be problems. In November 1996, the MPRP accused the Mongolian Central Intelligence Agency (MCIA) of spying on several party members. The charges were substantiated, and the government reorganized and renamed the MCIA.

3. Has there been basic reform of the criminal code/criminal law? Who authorizes searches and issues warrants? Are suspects and prisoners beaten and abused? Are there excessive delays in the criminal justice system? Basic post-Communist reforms of the criminal code have instituted greater protections for suspects. Prosecutors must issue warrants for searches and for detention of suspects if charges are not brought within 72 hours, or for shorter periods of detention if the police did not actually witness the crime. Police and prison officials reportedly sometimes beat or abuse detainees and prisoners. Prison conditions are poor and rising crime rates have caused severe overcrowding in detention facilities and prisons. In 1997, several dozen prisoners died, in some cases apparently due to negligence and grim prison conditions. There is, however, no evidence that systemic abuse caused these deaths.

4. Do most judges rule fairly and impartially? Do many remain from the Communist era? Judges rule fairly and impartially, with no evidence of discrimination against any group. The constitution guarantees due process rights, including presumption of innocence, the right to a public trial, and protections against self-incrimination. In practice, due process rights are respected. Judges are nominated by the General Council of Courts, an independent administrative body, and are approved by the president. Most judges either served during the Communist era or received their legal education before 1989.

5. Are the courts free of political control and influence? Are the courts linked directly to the Ministry of Justice or any other executive body? The constitution provides for an independent judiciary and this is respected in practice. The judiciary receives its budgetary allowance directly from parliament and is not linked directly to the Ministry of Justice or any other executive body.

The post-Communist State Law of Courts establishes the judicial structure and mechanisms to ensure judicial independence. The court system consists of a Supreme Court, provincial courts, the capital district court, county courts, inter-county courts, and district courts. A 12-member General

Council, which includes the chief justice of the Supreme Court, the state general prosecutor, the justice minister, and several sitting judges, serves as a judicial independence watchdog. The General Council nominates judicial candidates for presidential approval; submits proposals on the required number of court personnel and on remuneration for judges; submits a draft budget for the judiciary to parliament; and operates a judicial discipline committee. Supreme Court and lower court judges are appointed by the president for six-year terms and can be dismissed on the recommendation of the General Council under the terms specified in the State Law of Courts. The Constitutional Court has three members nominated by parliament, three by the president, and three by the Supreme Court, all of whom serve six-year terms.

6. What proportion of lawyers is in private practice? How does this compare with the previous year? Although there are no accurate figures, evidence suggests that most lawyers are now in private practice.

7. Does the state provide public defenders? The constitution guarantees citizens the right of legal assistance. In practice, suspects and defendants have access to an attorney at all stages of the legal process, and the state provides an attorney if the defendant cannot afford one.

8. Are there effective anti-bias/discrimination laws, including protection of ethnic minority rights? Some 76 percent of the population are Khalkha Mongols, with smaller Mongol groups comprising another 13 percent. Turkic-speakers make up seven percent of the population, with Chinese, Russian, and other minorities forming the remainder. There are few reports of discrimination against minorities.

The literacy rate of adult women is around 96 percent, close to that of men. In general, women have equal access to education and are prominent in the professions. Wages for women, however, are generally lower than those for men, and since 1989 the rate of women's employment has fallen. Women also hold just seven of the 76 parliamentary seats. Analysts attribute the general paucity of women in high positions in government, the judiciary and the private sector to both unofficial discrimination, and to traditional norms. Domestic violence is also a problem.

Corruption C

1. What is the magnitude of official corruption in the civil service? Must an average citizen pay a bribe to a bureaucrat in order to receive a service? What services are subject to bribe requests-for example, university entrance, hospital admission, telephone installation, obtaining a license to operate a business, applying for a passport or other official documents? What is the average salary of civil servants at various levels? Petty corruption does exist, but overall, corruption has not been reported as a major problem in post-Communist Mongolia. While no definitive information exists, it is likely that bureaucrats demand bribes for many routine services. In May 1997 the government increased the pay of the 142,000 government employees by 20 percent. Previously, the monthly pay for a typical civil servant was about $25 dollars per month, while a minister made about $50 dollars.

2. Do top policy makers (the president, ministers, vice-ministers, top court justices, and heads of agencies and commissions) have direct ties to businesses? How strong are such connections and what kinds of businesses are these? Top policy makers generally do not have direct ties to business except in cases where they developed private business interests prior to taking office.

3. Do laws requiring financial disclosure and disallowing conflict of interest exist? Have publicized anticorruption cases been pursued? To what conclusion? Laws requiring financial disclosure and disallowing conflict of interest need to be strengthened. There have been some publicized anti-corruption cases. In January 1997, the government announced that investigations by the State Procuratorial and Supervisory Commission and provincial departments into more than 2,200 government offices and state-run businesses found that more than $23 million of public funds had been misused. Authorities said they punished more than 400 people, although the nature of these punishments is unclear.

4. What major anti-corruption initiatives have been implemented? How often are anticorruption laws and decrees adopted? In general, there have been few major anti-corruption initiatives.

5. How do major corruption-ranking organizations like Transparency International rate this country? Transparency International and other major corruption-ranking organizations have not rated Mongolia.

Privatization 4.25/7

1. What percentage of the GDP comes from private ownership? What percentage of the labor force is employed in the private sector? How large is the informal sector of the economy? In 1990, the year that mass protests forced the MPRP to submit to multiparty elections, the public sector accounted for about 90 percent of GDP. Moreover, during the Communist era, Soviet aid made up 30 percent of GDP. In 1997, the state-owned sector still provided nearly 50 percent of GDP.

There is a considerable informal sector, in large part because Mongolia's herdsmen have continued to conduct centuries-old barter trade. Because the governing DUC's free market reforms have caused real incomes to fall dramatically and unemployment to rise, most herdsmen have little incentive to embrace the cash economy, particularly in a nomadic culture which traditionally has placed little emphasis on accumulating luxury goods or commodities. Mongolia lacks a national banking system with local branches which would be needed to draw herdsmen into the cash economy. The informal sector also includes commerce carried out by traders who travel to Russia and China for goods. Moreover, the government's practice of informally intervening in the market to affect supply and demand has created a black market in agricultural goods and other items.

2. What major privatization legislation has been passed? What were its substantive features? Parliament passed the Privatization and Companies Law in June 1991. The law linked the country's privatization program to the development of a capital market under a scheme in which individual citizens would get vouchers that could be exchanged for shares of privatized companies on the stock exchange. In the first phase of privatization, the government distributed vouchers to all citizens free of charge. Citizens could then use the vouchers to buy shares of companies through brokerage firms and the Mongolian Stock Exchange (MSE). By the first half of 1995, the MSE sold shares of 470 companies, with about 1.1 million citizens, or roughly half the population, participating. The 1996 Law on State and Local Property established the manner of valuation of property to be privatized; permissible methods of privatization; and the modalities for carrying out privatization by auction, trade, tender, sale of public shares and stocks, and joint venture.

3. What proportion of agriculture, housing and land, industry, and small business and services is in private hands? Privatization proceeded slowly under the post-1990 MPRP government and was postponed in the run-up to the June 1996 elections. The DUC government accelerated privatization and collected more total revenues from the privatization of state owned assets and enterprises between January and September 1997 than the MPRP government collected in all of 1995 and 1996 combined.

Agriculture: Following the collapse of Communism, the MPRP government ended forced collectivization. In a country in which one-third to two-fifths of the population are nomadic herders, more than 97 percent of the livestock sector has been placed in private hands. Livestock numbers have since soared, from 25 million in 1993 to 29.3 million as of January 1997, the highest level in 50 years. *Housing and Land:* The DUC government has also initiated a housing privatization program. *Industry:* Most large enterprises are still state-owned. The DUC government has pledged to privatize 60 percent of these entities, or more than 800 companies, by the year 2000. The government, however, still owns a majority stake in many factories that are classified as privatized, and it is unclear to what extent the latest round of privatization will actually result in fully privatized companies. *Small Business and Services:* By 1996, 100 percent of small- and medium- sized enterprises and other services had been privatized.

4. What has been the extent of insider (management, labor, and nomenklatura) participation in the privatization process? What explicit and implicit preferences have been awarded to insiders? The 1996 Law on State and Local Property provides mechanisms for adjudicating claims of unfair practices in the privatization process, including appealing to the State Property Commission and to the courts. There have been some allegations of insider preferences in Mongolia's privatization program. For example, in February 1996, the government sold off the profit-making State Department Store to the Tushig Company, headed by a former store director. The media soon published claims that Tushig had received favorable treatment. A special parliamentary committee of inquiry, headed by an opposition Member of Parliament, looked into the allegations and recommended that the government revise the terms of the privatization of the store. The State Privatization Committee ultimately set a higher price, which Tushig was unable to pay, and the store reverted to state control.

5. How much public awareness of and support for privatization has there been? What is the

nature of support and opposition to privatization by major interest groups? The 1996 Law on State and Local Property requires the government to use the media to publicize information on the shares and dividends of a company at least 30 days before it is to be privatized. The government does so and the public appears to have adequate information about the privatization process. Many Mongolians, however, remain wary of privatization which they equate with economic decline and rising unemployment. Most state workers oppose privatization, as do conservative elements of the opposition MPRP.

Macroeconomics 4.00/7

1. Has the taxation system been reformed? (What areas have and have not been overhauled? To what degree are taxpayers complying? Is tax compliance difficult to achieve? Has the level of revenues increased? Is the revenue collection body overburdened? What is the overall tax burden?) In November 1992, parliament passed a General Law of Taxation, which took effect in January 1993. The Law defined the post-Communist tax system, the role of the State Tax Administration and tax inspectors, and the rights, obligations, and responsibilities of taxpayers. Also in November 1992, parliament passed the Personal Income Tax Law, which delineated the country's income tax system. The DUC government has taken tax reform further by nominally lowering tax rates while increasing enforcement, although the revenue collection system continues to suffer from a lack of capacity. The government also plans to shift the tax base to indirect taxes, particularly through the introduction of a Value Added Tax, and to reduce exemptions. Mongolia has a top income tax rate of 40 percent, and a top corporate tax rate of 40 percent. There is also a 10 percent sales tax.

2. Does fiscal policy encourage private savings, investment and earnings? (Has there been any reform/alteration of revenue and budget policies? How large are budget deficits and overall debt? Is the financing of the social insurance/pension system sustainable? What proportion of the budget is taken up by subsidies to firms and individuals?) Following four straight years of contraction (including a 9.5 percent contraction in 1992), GDP grew by 2.3 percent in 1994, the first increase since the end of communism. In 1997, real GDP growth increased 3.3 percent.

Mongolia's tight fiscal policy generally encourages private savings, investment and earnings. The budget deficit, however, continues to be a problem. The previous MPRP government cut capital expenditures from 10 percent of GDP to 8 percent of GDP in 1996, but the fiscal deficit still widened to nine percent that year. The DUC government came to office promising to balance the state budget, but in 1996, world copper prices plunged 33 percent, wiping out nearly a quarter of state revenues. The government has reduced the number of ministries and government departments from 16 to nine, instituted civil service cutbacks and public administration reforms, frozen many areas of government spending, and slashed more than 100,000 women from the pension rolls. The 1997 budget also eliminated most subsidies for state-owned enterprises. The fiscal situation, however, continues to be under pressure due to inadequate tax administration; large interest payments on bank restructuring bonds; the loss of revenue from the government's decision to abolish nearly all import duties; and lower than expected proceeds from asset privatization. In 1997, the fiscal deficit remained at nine percent of GDP. Therefore, concessional assistance from the donor community will continue to be needed to build up adequate foreign exchange reserves and finance public investment. The government's program of reducing the size of the public sector and reforming the tax system is designed to reduce the fiscal deficit to six percent of GDP by the year 2000.

The new government's commitment to reform convinced the International Monetary Fund (IMF) to grant a new three-year, $45 million Enhanced Structural Adjustment Facility (ESAF) in July 1997. In March 1996, the IMF had suspended an ESAF arranged with the previous government.

The social insurance and pension system is not yet sustainable, and the country's fiscal difficulties have adversely affected the quality and delivery of basic health, education and other social services. Besides radically slashing the pension rolls, efforts are underway to shift the pension system to a self-sustaining basis through greater revenue collection. In 1997, the government allowed farmers, herdsmen, and private businessmen to enter the social insurance system, which formerly only covered people listed on government payrolls.

3. Has there been banking reform? (Is the central bank independent? What are its responsibilities? Is it effective in setting and/or implementing monetary policy? What is the actual state of the private banking sector? Does it conform to international standards? Are depositors protected?) The 1991 Banking Law established the legal basis of banking activities in post-Communist Mongolia. The law stops short of creating a truly independent central bank, instead charging the Bank of Mongolia with "implementing the government's monetary policy." The bank's activities include controlling the money supply; ensuring the stability of the currency; determining the capital adequacy ratios banks are required to maintain; setting interest rates; acting as a lender of last resort to commercial banks; making interbank settlements; and supervising commercial banks.

The Bank of Mongolia has adopted tighter credit and monetary policies, but inflation is still a problem. The post-Communist MPRP government had some initial success with macroeconomic stabilization, including bringing inflation down from 325 percent in 1992 to a still high 53 percent in 1995. But in 1996, energy prices rose significantly, the monetary supply expanded by 26 percent, and inflation hit 59 percent. In 1997, the Bank of Mongolia raised the interest rate on its bills to mop up excess liquidity and lower inflation.

The MPRP government postponed banking sector reform in the run-up to the June 1996 parliamentary elections. The new DUC government, facing a severe liquidity crisis in the banking sector, shut down two large, bankrupt state-owned banks in December 1996, and established two new successor banks and an asset recovery agency. In addition, the Bank of Mongolia formalized understandings with individual banks regarding the observance of monthly credit ceilings and minimum reserve requirements, although the banking sector does not yet conform to international capital adequacy and other standards.

The Asian Development Bank's Financial Sector Program loan is working to address what the Bank termed "severe disarray" in the Mongolian banking sector. Key features include upgrading skills in commercial banks; strengthening the legal and regulatory framework for banks; and assisting the Bank of Mongolia in training banking supervisors, developing bank examination procedures, preparing regulations for bank supervision, bringing bank accounting standards in line with international standards, restructuring the operational and financial activities of some banks and liquidating others, and establishing market-determined interest rates.

There is no national banking system with local branches, in part because in the sparsely-populated rural areas, it is difficult to cater to a culture where nomads frequently travel over vast expanses and where there is traditionally little emphasis on savings for material accumulation. Despite these problems, the volume of banks' local currency savings deposits is growing in real terms.

4. How sound is the national currency? (Is the value of the currency fixed or does it float? How convertible is the currency? How large are the hard currency reserves? Has the exchange rate policy been stable and predictable?) The government pegged the currency, the *tugrik*, at 150 to the dollar until May 1993, when it permitted the tugrik to float. The tugrik is fully convertible. An inflow of concessional external finance helped boost net foreign exchange reserves to $89.9 million by the end of 1997, despite a slump in world prices for copper and cashmere, Mongolia's two biggest foreign exchange earners.

Although the exchange rate policy has been stable and predictable, other factors have caused volatility in the value of the thinly-traded tugrik. After the DUC government took power in July 1996, it decontrolled most prices and adopted other radical free market measures that had a short-term inflationary effect. Inflation rose from an annual rate of 16 per cent before the change of government to 66 percent between August and November 1996, pushing the tugrik from 550 to the U.S. dollar in June to 690 by the end of 1996. The tugrik bottomed out at 830 to the U.S. dollar in March 1997, but by September it had stabilized, closing in 1997 at 814.

5. Is there a functioning capital market infrastructure? (Are there existing or planned commodities, bond and stock markets? What are the mechanisms for investing and lending? What government bodies have authority to regulate capital markets?) The Mongolian Stock Exchange (MSE) was created in 1991. In its first operational phase, from February 1992 to August 1995, the MSE allowed individual citizens to buy shares in newly privatized companies. In August 1995, the MSE began trading shares like a regular bourse. Currently there are 400 listed firms. Commodities markets are small and rudimentary. In 1994, parliament passed the Securities Law, which established the legal framework for regulating securities exchanges and set up the Securities Committee to carry out this function.

Microeconomics 3.75/7

1. Are property rights guaranteed? (Are there both formal and de facto protections of private real estate and intellectual property? Is there a land registry with the authority and capability to ensure accurate recording of who owns what? What are the procedures for expropriation, including measures for compensation and challenge? Have any seizures taken place? The constitution guarantees private property rights, including intellectual property. The 1994 Civil Code also explicitly recognizes private property and intellectual property, and guarantees the right to possess, use, and dispose of property. In 1997, the government allowed housing privatization for the first time. As part of the Asian Development Bank's Agriculture Sector Program Loan, the government is establishing a land registry as required under the Civil Code and the 1996 Law on State and Local Property. The latter instructs provincial governors to keep a general registry of local property and make an inventory of local properties.

The Civil Code permits the government to expropriate land on the grounds of "special public need," with the requirement that one year notice be given and compensation be paid to the owner. Unless otherwise provided by law or contract, compensation is to include the price of land and immovable property on it and other expenses incurred by the owner. The owner has the right to challenge an expropriation or compensation package in court. There are no reports of illegal seizures or expropriation of land or other property.

2. To what extent have prices been liberalized? What subsidies remain? The MPRP government began liberalizing prices in 1992. In 1996, the DUC government abolished the Price Consensus Commission which informally set prices for some basic commodities, and fully liberalized most prices. Nevertheless, the government still uses commodity purchasing decisions and other informal means to influence market prices. The government also still sets power and heating tariff, but has raised them significantly and established an automatic increase mechanism to offset the effects of inflation and currency fluctuations. Coal and petroleum prices are decontrolled.

3. Is it possible to own and operate a business? (Has there been legislation regarding the formation, dissolution and transfer of businesses, and is the law respected? Do there exist overly cumbersome bureaucratic hurdles that effectively hinder the ability to own and dispose of a business? Are citizens given access to information on commercial law? Is the law applied fairly? Does the regulation (or licensing requirements) impose significant costs on business and consumers? Do they create significant barriers to entry and seriously hamper competition?) The 1991 Bankruptcy Law established legal procedures for declaring companies bankrupt, dissolving them, and protecting their creditors. While the Bankruptcy Law and commercial laws are respected, the bureaucracy still retains many Communist-era officials who do not yet understand their role in a free-market system. As such, entrepreneurs are sometimes dogged by informal bureaucratic interference in commercial operations. Despite some obstacles, in the capital, Ulaanbaatar, and other cities entrepreneurs have set up numerous hotels, small shops, restaurants, and bars. Urban citizens have access to commercial law, although such access is more difficult across the vast rural expanses. Commercial law appears to be applied fairly. Regulation and licensing requirements appear to be reasonably straightforward and neither impose significant costs nor create significant barriers to entry and hamper competition.

4. Are courts effective, transparent, efficient, and quick in reaching decisions on property and contract disputes? What alternative mechanisms for adjudicating disputes exist? Although Mongolian courts generally adjudicate property and contract disputes in a fair and transparent manner, the court system is still rudimentary and often inefficient. As such, there are often delays in resolving commercial cases.

5. Is business competition encouraged? (Are monopolistic practices limited in law and practice? If so, how? To what degree is "insider" dealing a hindrance to open competition? Are government procurement policies open and unbiased?) The post-Communist Law on Prohibiting Unfair Competition prohibits the government from restricting economic competition, prohibits monopolies and other restraints on fair competition, establishes guidelines for government intervention to ensure fair competition and to regulate natural monopolies, and establishes the role of the courts in determining an entity to be a monopoly and handing down legal remedies. There is no evidence that insider dealing is a significant hindrance to open competition. Government procurement policies are complex and often opaque. An International Monetary Fund-sponsored program is promoting transparency and accountability in procurement by assisting in the drafting and upgrading of regulations and procedures for procurement of goods, civil works and related services, and infrastructure projects.

6. To what extent has international trade been liberalized? To what degree has there been simplification/overhaul of customs and tariff procedures, and are these applied fairly? What informal trade barriers exist? In 1991, the Soviet Union and its former satellites accounted for 99 percent of Mongolia's imports and 94 percent of its exports. By 1997, trade with Russia and the former East Bloc countries accounted for only about half of Mongolia's total trade volume, with China, South Korea, and Japan accounting for much of the rest. In 1997, total export earnings reached $461 million, an increase of about nine percent, owing to increased copper and gold exports.

The government began liberalizing tariffs in 1992, and in April 1997, the reformist government took the radical measure of eliminating tariffs and taxes on all imports. The post-Communist Customs Law established a unified system of customs duties and fees, as well as mechanisms for supervision of trade and enforcement of customs regulations. The government has also streamlined its customs bureau. There are no significant non-tariff barriers.

7. To what extent has foreign investment and capital flow been encouraged or constrained? The 1993 Foreign Investment Law has a stated aim of encouraging foreign investment and establishes guidelines for protecting the rights and property of foreign investors in Mongolia. The Law permits foreign investors to establish wholly-owned companies, dispose of property, and repatriate investment and profits, and explicitly bars nationalization or illegal expropriation of foreign-owned assets. The law also guarantees equal treatment for Mongolian and foreign-owned companies. In practice, the government has encouraged foreign investment, particularly to exploit the country's vast reserves of oil, copper, gold, fluorspar, and other minerals. By December 1997, the country hosted 708 joint or fully foreign-owned ventures in oil, mining, livestock products, food and light industries, and trade and services. Foreigners can lease, but not own, land.

8. Has there been reform of the energy sector? (To what degree has the energy sector been restructured? Is the energy sector more varied, and is it open to private competition? Is the country overly dependent on one or two other country for energy [including whether exported fuels must pass through one or more countries to reach markets]?) Energy sector reform has been limited. The state-owned Energy Authority (EA) controls power supply and distribution, although the government is interested in eventually allowing private sector participation. In line with the Energy Law of 1996, the EA increased tariffs in January 1997 and removed subsidies for small consumers in May 1997. The government has also agreed to implement an automatic quarterly tariff adjustment mechanism to cover cost increases due to higher fuel prices, inflation, and exchange rate depreciation. In Ulaanbaatar, reportedly the world's coldest capital, the Asian Development Bank's Heat Efficiency Project will introduce a pricing and billing system based on metered heat consumption. The Asian Development Bank is also planning an Energy Rehabilitation Project, to commence in the year 2000, that will improve the heat supply to the cities of Ulaanbaatar and Erdenet and boost electricity supply to the 55 percent of the population served by the EA's grid. Monmar, a Mongol-United Kingdom joint venture, is producing portable generators that rely on wind power for use in rural areas where electricity is unavailable.

As recently as 1996, Mongolia imported 99 percent of its oil from Russia. In recent years, there have been electricity service cuts in some areas of Mongolia due to shortages in Russia of mazut, a low-boiling fuel oil imported for use by some coal-fired power stations. Foreign companies have begun developing domestic oilfields, which hold an estimated six billion barrels of oil reserves and should eventually reduce, if not eliminate, this dependence on Russia. Energy exports must go either through Russia or China. Mongolia exports to Russia some of the five million tons of coal it produces each year. In February 1998, Mongolia exported its first crude oil to China, via trucks. An American company, Soco, plans a 100 kilometer pipeline from its operation in eastern Mongolia to the Chinese border, where it could hook up with railway access to refining plants. A planned natural gas pipeline to China from the Kovyktya gas deposit in Russia may be routed through Mongolia, which has no natural gas.

POLAND

Freedom in the World Ratings, 1989-1998

	1989-90	1990-91	1991-92	1992-93	1993-94	1994-95	1995-96	1996-97	1997-98
Political Rights	4	2	2	2	2	2	1	1	1
Civil Liberties	3	2	2	2	2	2	2	2	2
Status	PF	F	F	F	F	F	F	F	F

Polity: Consolidated Democracy
Economy: Consolidated Market
Population: 38,613,000
PPP: $5,442
Ethnic Groups: Polish (98 percent), German, Ukrainian, Belarusian
Capital: Warsaw

Political Process 1.25/7

1. When did national legislative elections take place? Were they free and fair? How were they judged by domestic and international election monitoring organizations? Who composes the government? Elections for the 100-seat Senate and the 460-member *Sejm* were held in September 1997. Under the 1993 electoral law, 391 members of the Sejm are elected by proportional representation in multi-seat constituencies and 69 seats by proportional representation among parties obtaining more than seven percent of the popular vote. The Senate is elected in 47 two-seat constituencies and two three-seat constituencies. The Solidarity Electoral Action (AWS), a coalition of moderate and center-right forces, captured 201 seats in the Sejm and 51 in the Senate. The ruling ex-Communist Democratic Left Alliance (SLD), won 164 and 28; the pro-market Freedom Union (UW), 60 and 8; the Peasant Party (PSL), 27 and 3; the Movement for the Reconstruction of Poland (ROP), 6 and 5; and the German Social and Cultural Society Opole Silesia (MN), won two seats. Five independents were elected to the Senate. The elections were determined to be free and fair by foreign and domestic observers. Jerzy Buzek (AWS), a 57-year-old chemical engineer who played an important role in the Solidarity underground in the 1980s, was named prime minister. Key cabinet posts are held by members of AWS and the UW.

2. When did presidential elections occur? Were they free and fair? In November 1995, SLD leader Alexander Kwasniewski defeated incumbent President Lech Walesa, who had led Poland's independence movement as the head of the Solidarity trade union in the 1980s. Kwasniewski won the runoff election with 51.7 percent of the vote.

3. Is the electoral system multiparty-based? Are there at least two viable political parties func-

tioning at all levels of government? Poland is a multiparty democracy. The Communist Party monopoly ended following roundtable negotiations between the non-Communist opposition and the military regime in 1989, which led to the legalization of Solidarity and other political reforms. A new constitution, ratified by referendum in May 1997, enshrines political pluralism (Article 11) as did the earlier 1992 "Little Constitution." Most major parties function at all levels of government.

4. How many political parties have been legalized? Are any parties illegal? Since 1990, an estimated 300 political parties and associations have registered in Poland, although less than a third actually function. Under a 1993 electoral law aimed at reducing the number of parties in parliament (29 political groupings were represented in parliament after the 1991 vote, and none had more than 13 percent of the vote), parties that failed to receive 5 percent (8 percent for parties campaigning in coalition) of the national vote would not be represented in parliament. In the 1997 elections, only five parties and coalitions cleared the thresholds: the AWS, the SLD, the UW, PSL, and ROP. In November 1997, AWS leader Marian Krzaklewski announced the formation of the AWS Social Movement (RS AWS) as a Christian-Democratic Party, and formally registered in December. Former President Walesa announced the formation of Christian Democracy of the Third Republic (ChD III RP) in February 1998. Article 13 of the constitution bans parties that are "sympathetic to the totalitarian methods of nazism, fascism, and communism."

5. What proportion of the population belongs to political parties? There is low party identification and membership in Poland. Polls in 1997 showed that most voters could identify only eight to 12 parties or groupings, while other studies cited in the press showed that 60 percent of Poles do not feel represented by any existing political party. In terms of membership figures, the largest party is the Peasant Party (PSL), which claims 190,000 members, followed by the Social Democracy Party of Poland (SdRP) — which joined the previously Communist-dominated official union, All-Poland Trade Union Alliance (OPZZ), in 1991 to form the SLD — which claims 60,000 members. The Confederation for an Independent Poland claims 25,000 members, the ROP 12,000, UW, 10,500, and the Christian National Union (ZChN), 5,000. The RS AWS announced it had 15,000 members, and Walesa said in February 1998, that the ChD III RP had 500 members but was hoping to enroll between 10,000 and 15,000 people by the end of the year.

6. What has been the trend of voter turnout at the municipal, provincial, and national levels in recent years? Since 1989, overall voter turnout has decreased slightly in local elections. The turnout for elections since 1989 is as follows: June 1989 (parliamentary), 62 percent; May 1990 (local and regional), 42 percent; November 1990 (presidential), 60 percent; December 1990 (presidential runoff), 53.4 percent; October 1991 (parliamentary), 43.2 percent; September 1993 (parliamentary), 52 percent; June 1994 (local and regional), 34 percent; 1995 (presidential, second round), 68.23 percent; May 1997 constitutional referendum, 43 percent; September 1997 (parliamentary), 48 percent.

Civil Society 1.25/7

1. How many nongovernmental organizations have come into existence since 1988? How many

charitable/nonprofit organizations? Are there locally led efforts to increase philanthropy and volunteerism? What proportion of the population is active in private voluntary activity (from polling data)? The growth of Polish civil society has included the development of NGOs. There are approximately 25,000 non-governmental organizations in Poland, though many are small, underfunded, or inactive. NGOs include professional, cultural, youth, sports, political, ecological, religious, women's, and democracy-building groups, as well as public policy think tanks, educational and academic associations, and charitable organizations. While corporate philanthropy is in its infancy, there are NGOs working with the newly emerging private sector to address pressing social and environmental issues. Voluntary charities, many associated with the Catholic Church, are active in helping the poor and the elderly, and international groups such as the Red Cross, the United Nations Development Program, and others have programs. There is no polling data on private voluntary activity.

2. What is the legal and regulatory environment for NGOs (i.e., ease of registration, legal rights, government regulation, taxation, procurement and access-to-information issues)? To what extent is NGO activism focused on improving the legal and regulatory environment? Although NGOs and public associations must register with the government, there are no serious bureaucratic impediments to the process. Charitable and humanitarian organizations receive tax concessions, but most NGOs are not tax-exempt. The relative openness of Polish society includes access to information, and several NGOs, particularly those dealing with economic transition issues, such as the Adam Smith Research Center and the CASE Foundation/Center for Social and Economic Research, have received fees for doing work with the government. Groups such as the NGO Documentation Center have been working to clarify issues related to taxation and regulation.

3. What is the organizational capacity of NGOs? Do management structures clearly delineate authority and responsibility? Is information available on NGO management issues in the native language? Is there a core of experienced practitioners/trainers to serve as consultants and mentors to less developed organizations? NGOs which have received funding or technical assistance from Western foundations, governments, or international organizations, such as the U.S. Agency for International Development's DemNet project, which has awarded grants and worked with some 67 NGOs, have strong organizational capacity. Small, local NGOs have weak organizational structures, lack fund-raising and media outreach capabilities, and face shortages of funds and equipment. More established NGOs clearly delineate authority and responsibility. The Foundation in Support of Local Democracy, which promotes civic self-governance and works to improve the work of local governments and administrations, has a board of directors, a professional staff of 23, and five part-time volunteers. The Gdansk Institute for Market Economics has a board of directors, a professional staff of 40 full and 80 part-timers, and maintained a budget of $1.5 million in 1996. While NGOs in Poland tend to be isolated and seldom pool resources, efforts to develop national and regional linkages have been spearheaded by the Forum of NGO Initiatives. Part of the program involves the establishment of permanent mechanisms of NGO cooperation that would allow experienced practitioners from more developed organizations to provide assistance to smaller, less-developed groups.

4. Are NGOs financially viable? What is their tax status? Are they obliged and do they typically disclose revenue sources? Do government procurement opportunities exist for private, not-for-profit providers of services? As elsewhere in Central and Eastern Europe and the former Soviet Union, a majority of NGOs in Poland depend on Western organizations and institutions for a substantial part of operating budgets. A growing number of NGOs, however, have found other sources of revenue and are becoming more self-sustainable. The Krakow-based International Center for the Development of Democracy, while relying mainly on foundation grants and international governmental organizations for an overwhelming portion of its revenues, has received fees from non-governmental sources and banks and local businesses. The Institute for Private Enterprise and Democracy in Warsaw gets over a third of its revenues from chambers of commerce. NGOs supported in whole or in part by international organizations do disclose revenue sources and keep accurate accounting as a condition of their grants. Humanitarian and charitable organizations receive tax concessions, but most NGOs are not tax exempt. Government procurement opportunities are limited, although, a number of economic and social policy NGOs have received fees for doing work for the government.

5. Are there free trade unions? How many workers belong to these unions? Is the number of workers belonging to trade unions growing or decreasing? What is the numerical/proportional membership of farmer's groups, small business associations, etc.? The 1997 constitution (Articles 12 and 57) and other legislation allow for the formation of independent trade unions. Under the law, ten persons may form a local union and 30 people may establish a national union. Unions must be registered with the courts. In 1997, the number of unions rose from 318 to 350. The principal union federations are the National Alliance of Trade Unions (OPZZ), the successor of its Communist-era namesake, and the Independent Self-Governing Trade Union Solidarity (NSZZ). Offshoots of mainstream Solidarity include the Christian Trade Union Solidarity and Solidarity '80. In March 1998, the OPZZ claimed it had 2.5 million members, more than 14,000 workplace organizations, and more than 100 industrial federations. The OPZZ reports that membership has dropped in recent years by 50 percent from a high of 4.5 million members. Membership figures could not be verified. The NSZZ has a verified, dues-paying membership of about 1.4 million. The 1994 collective bargaining law does not require union membership figures to be verified or based on dues-paying members in order for unions to be considered "representative" negotiating partners for management and government. Estimates of union participation range from 30 to 40 percent of Poland's roughly 20 million workers, and the rate of unionization is low within the growing private sector (five percent). Union membership has been steadily declining in recent years due to privatization, the growth of the private service sector, and cut-backs at unprofitable, large-scale enterprises. The country's two million private farmers and agricultural workers are organized in local and regional associations, unions, cooperatives, and marketing groups according to crops or species of livestock. Exact membership figures, however, are unavailable. Agrarian interests are represented by the Polish Peasant Party, Rural Solidarity, the Christian Peasant Alliance, and other smaller parties. In 1997, Rural Solidarity staged several demonstrations to protest a planned ten-year transition period for Poland's agriculture following Warsaw's entry into the European Union (EU). Business, trade, and professional associations and groups representing virtually every sector of industry and commerce have mushroomed in Poland with the rise of the private sector. However, no national registry or membership records are kept.

6. What forms of interest group participation in politics are legal? What types of interest groups are active in the political and policy process? The constitution gives citizens the right to petition administrative agencies and public institutions (Article 61), and citizens have the right to lodge complaints with the Constitutional Court (Article 75.1). Lobbying activities are permitted and political endorsements are legal. Freedoms of association and assembly permit public demonstrations. State sector managers, business groups, trade unions, farmers' association, and some NGOs are active in the political and policy process through direct meetings with government officials, providing government agencies with informational materials and media access.

Independent Media 1.50/7

1. Are there legal protections for press freedom? Article 14 of the 1997 constitution safeguards "freedom of the press and other mass media." The 1990 Bill of Annulation of the Law on Control of Publications and Performances, the Abolition of its Control Organs, and the Change of the Press Law abolished censorship and loosened government control of the media. A media law adopted in December 1992 transformed state radio and television into joint-stock companies and led to the growth of private commercial television and radio stations. It prescribed that foreign ownership in broadcasting should not exceed 33 percent. Broadcasting is overseen by a nine-member National Radio and Television Broadcasting Council (KRRiTV).

2. Are there legal penalties for libeling officials? Are there legal penalties for "irresponsible" journalism? Have these laws been used to harass journalists? There are several provisions in the Penal Code dealing with libel and defamation. Article 270 of the Penal Code states that anyone who "publicly insults, ridicules, and derides the Polish Nation, Polish People's Republic, its political system, or its principal organs is punishable by between six months and eight years imprisonment." Article 273 imposes a prison term of up to ten years for anyone who violates Article 270 in print or through the mass media. The Penal Code also prohibits the use of media to "advocate discord" on national, ethnic, racial, or religious grounds, and prohibits offending religious sentiment. The law has been enforced on several occasions, bringing protests from international human rights groups. The 1994 Law on State Secrets was also considered overly broad. In January 1995, the Supreme Court ruled that journalists could be forced to reveal sources whenever it was requested by prosecutors or judges. But in April 1995, the Sejm rejected a measure that would have forced journalists to reveal their sources only in the most serious of crimes. In February 1996, the editor-in-chief of the satirical weekly, *Nie*, was convicted of publishing secret documents, given a one-year suspended sentence, and fined $4,000. Amendments to the press and penal codes in December 1996 held journalists responsible not only for deliberate, but also unintentional, infringements on personal property. The regulation provided that no materials concerning a person's private life may be published, unless they are strictly connected with his or her public activities. In September 1997, President Kwasniewski filed a private lawsuit against the newspapers *Zycie* and *Dziennik Baltycki* for accusing him of having contacts with a Russian spy. *Dziennik Baltycki* retracted the charge. In

January 1997, a journalist for *Gazeta Wyborcza* was charged with refusing to reveal a source who had given him secret court information regarding former Prime Minister Jozef Oleksy, who resigned in January 1996 after allegations that he collaborated with Soviet and Russian intelligence. The case was dismissed, and a new criminal code scheduled to take effect in September 1998 grants journalists the right to protect sources except in cases involving national security, murder, or terrorism.

3. What proportion of the media is privatized? What are the major private newspapers, television stations, and radio stations? Over 85 percent of the media has been privatized. There are over 3,000 newspapers, 119 commercial radio stations (six national stations, five of which are state-owned), as well as ten commercial TV stations. Major private dailies include *Gazeta Wyborcza* (formerly linked to Solidarity) with a circulation of 540,000 daily and 770,000 on weekends; *Rzeczpospolita*, with 300,00 daily and 240,000 on weekends; and *Express Wieczorny*, with 140,000 daily and 400,000 on weekends. State-run television stations, TVP-1 and TVP-2, dominate the market. Polsat remains the most popular commercial television network. In February 1997, a license for central Poland was granted to TVN, which is owned by the Polish company ITI and the Central European Media Enterprises Group, and to Naza Telewizja. Satellite television, including TV Polonia, Atomic TV, and RTL 7, and private cable stations are widely available. The major private national radio stations are Radio ZET in Warsaw, RMF FM from Krakow, and Catholic Radio Maryja from Torun. A new radio station, Radio Trefl, began broadcasting in September 1997.

4. Are the private media financially viable? Private broadcasters face stiff competition from state media but most are partly owned by well-financed foreign media companies. Major newspapers also have foreign investors, though the print media is restricted to no more than 33 percent foreign ownership. A U.S. group, Cox Enterprises, bought a stake in *Gazeta Wyborcza* in 1993. A 30 percent stake in the popular *Super Express* is owned by Bonner A.B., a Swedish group. *Express Wieczorny* belongs to the Swiss Marquard Press. A French group, Socpresse, owns a controlling interest in *Rzeczpospolita*, the former government newspaper. Market saturation, lack of advertising revenues, and printing costs are key factors in the failure of hundreds of newspapers or magazines over the last several years. Small regional and local radio stations have faced financial difficulties.

5. Are the media editorially independent? Are the media's news gathering functions affected by interference from government or private owners? The principle of editorial independence remains a key issue in the Polish media. While newspapers and magazines reflect political diversity and run the gamut from the far-left to the far-right, the independent media are pushing for editorial autonomy from private owners, many of them foreign-based. The International Press Institute reported at the end of 1997 that "struggling newspapers and magazines across the Eastern bloc have welcomed the infusion of foreign capital — and Western media know-how — but there has been a growing backlash against what many journalists perceive as foreign interference in local news." KRRiTV is ostensibly independent of the government but since its nine members are nominated by parliament, the Senate, and the president's office, politics plays a role in the council's makeup. Less then a month before the September 1997 elections won by the AWS-led opposition, the ruling

SLD named new board members to the KRRiTV. Hence, many of the members of the council, which appoints managers and monitors operations of state-owned television and radio stations, were loyal to the former ruling coalition. Reporters, editors, and managers of the state-owned stations were subsequently fired or resigned. Several popular political shows were canceled. Some reporters have jumped to the commercial stations RTL-7 and TVN, which offer news programming.

6. Is the distribution system for newspapers privately or governmentally controlled? According to the U.S. 1997 State Department report on human rights, while RUCH, the national network of newspaper kiosks, remains in state hands, there is no evidence that the government has used its control over distribution to suppress any publications. Plans to privatize the company have been delayed by a civil law suit. Some publications have their own transportation and dissemination structures.

7. What proportion of the population is connected to the Internet? Are there any restrictions on Internet access to private citizens? There are about 500,000 Internet users in Poland. There are currently no laws that restrict Internet use or access.

8. What has been the trend in press freedom? Freedom House's annual *Survey of Press Freedom* rated Poland "Not Free" for 1988, "Partly Free" for 1989, and "Free" from 1990 through 1998.

Governance and Public Administration 1.75/7

1. Is the legislature the effective rule-making institution? Parliament, consisting of a Senate and a lower house, the Sejm, is the effective rule-making institution. The 1997 constitution limited presidential vetoes and clearly delineated separation of powers.

2. Is substantial power decentralized to subnational levels of government? What specific authority do subnational levels have? In 1990, the first Solidarity-led government introduced a local self-government law that laid the foundation for a completely new and decentralized system of local government. The *gmina*, or township, became the basic administrative unit acquiring legal status, ownership of local assets, and responsibility for its own budget. The gmina elected a council which appointed executive officials to run it in accordance with the councilor's resolutions. There are 2465 gmina*s*. Under the 1997 constitution, the gmina remained "the basic unit of local government" (Article 160.1). A key and contentious issue in 1997 and early 1998 was the restructuring of local governments.

3. Are subnational officials chosen in free and fair elections? Local elections were held in Poland in 1990 and 1994 for over 52,000 councilors to 2,383 local councils. The elections were considered free and fair. The SLD and the PSL led all parties in the number of councilors and local council seats. Elections were due in 1998, but the issue of local government restructuring had yet to be finalized as of March 31, 1998. The government said it planned to hold local elections before the end of 1998.

4. Do the executive and legislative bodies operate openly and with transparency? Is draft leg-

islation easily accessible to the media and the public? Executive and legislative bodies at the national level operate openly and with transparency. Article 109 of the 1997 constitution states that "sessions of the Sejm are public," though a majority vote allows for closed session deliberations. Texts of legislation and drafts are published and available to the mass media.

5. Do municipal governments have sufficient revenues to carry out their duties? Do municipal governments have control over their local budgets? Do they raise revenues autonomously or from the central state budget? Municipal governments have control of local budgets and raise revenues autonomously through taxes and fees which are supplemented by state funds. Inefficiency in the distribution of funds due to bureaucratic delays and the need to give local governments greater control over local issues was behind the government's plan to restructure local government. In a March 24, 1998 interview on TV Polonia, Prime Minister Buzek, in outlining the local government reforms, said, "Today, only a few provinces or cities can speak of economic successes attained." He said the new system would expedite development and improve state services.

6. Do elected local leaders and civil servants know how to manage municipal government effectively? While local leaders are familiar with local issues and govern effectively, bureaucratic logjams and confusion over jurisdiction have caused problems. This was evident during the summer of 1997, when Poland was hit by serious flooding. Provisional governors in the effected areas failed to act decisively and there was a lack of coordination between federal, regional, and local officials after the disaster. In the Wroclaw region, for example, responsibility for 95 percent of the levees on the Odra River rests with the province which received funds to repair them. Five percent of the levees are the responsibility of the District Directorate of Water Management which received no funds. While the federal government received foreign aid for flood victims, funds from the central budget and from charitable organizations was spent on emergency aid. The municipality of Wroclaw and poorer localities had to pay for 80 percent of repairs to roads and infrastructure which many areas could not afford.

7. Has there been constitutional/legislative reform regarding local power? Has there been a reform of the civil service code/system? Are local civil servants employees of the local or central government? In March 1998, the government submitted legislation to the Sejm that would reduce the number of provinces (*voivodships)* from 49 to 12, create 300 self-governing districts (*powiats*), and retain the gminas. The three-tiered system is aimed at giving citizens a greater voice in the management of public finances, health care, schools, social welfare assistance, and police. The powiats would take over most of the prerogatives of provinces in determining and managing local issues. The restructuring was opposed by the PSL which objected to the reduction of provinces. The system, if accepted by parliament, would go into effect January 1, 1999. Under the constitution, local governments have the right to determine the amount of taxes and local fees. Reforms of the civil service code and system are ongoing, and a school of public administration trains qualified candidates to serve in government. In October 1996, under a new Civil Service Law, the prime minister appointed 24 politicians, civil servants, and academics to a new Civil Service Council. In March 1998, parliament considered a bill on civil service regulations. Under the measure, which was partly aimed to de-politicize the civil service and make hiring more transparent, the Civil Service Council would oversee the qualification process. All applicants will take tests conducted by independent professional examiners hired by the civil service chief. Only civil service officials will have the right to apply for senior positions such as director general, department director, deputy director, or administration heads, and they will be judged on an open and competitive basis. The law would replace the 1982 and 1996 statutes in force. Recruitment for the civil service was suspended in February pending the new law. Some regional provincial administrative officials are appointed by the federal government, but municipal and local civil servants are employees of local governments.

Rule of Law 1.50/7

1. Is there a post-Communist constitution? How does the judicial system interpret and enforce the constitution? Are there specific examples of judicial enforcement of the constitution in the last year? The Polish parliament adopted a new constitution in April 1997 that was ratified by public referendum in May. Over 53 percent of voters supported the document, with 46 percent against; turnout was 43 percent. The constitution was signed by the president on July 15, and will come into effect in mid-September 1998. The constitution replaced the so-called "Little Constitution" that was signed into law by then-President Lech Walesa in November 1992 mandating a strong presidency. The new constitution diminished presidential powers, widened the prerogatives of the Constitutional Tribunal, and allowed citizens a greater say in legislative matters. It introduced the constructive vote of no-confidence, making it impossible to dismiss a government without appointing a new one at the same time. The new constitution also delineates competencies more precisely and diminishes areas of potential conflict by reducing and more clearly defining the role of the president. The president can still influence legislation through legislative initiatives, but his veto power has been limited. The new constitution enlarged the Constitutional Tribunal from 12 to 15 justices. The new justices were elected in November 1997 by the AWS-dominated parliament. The Little Constitution stipulated that the tribunal could rule only on laws and "other normative acts enacted by main and central state organs," and that tribunal rulings were subject to parliamentary examination. According to Article 188 of the new constitution, the tribunal may rule on conformity to the constitution of statutes, international agreements, legal provisions issued by government bodies, the activities and purposes of political parties, and also settle jurisdictional disputes between state organs. Article 190.1 stipulates that "judgments of the Constitutional Tribunal shall be of universally binding application and shall be final." On May 28, 1997, the Constitutional Tribunal ruled on the amended anti-abortion law. Poland's strict abortion law was amended in October 1996 to allow abortion within the first trimester in cases of difficult financial or personal conditions. In December 1996, a group of 37 UW, Solidarity, and PSL parliamentarians complained to the tribunal that the law violated the constitutional guarantees of the right to life. The tribunal ruled that five articles of the law violated the constitution, including the provisions permitting abortion in certain circumstances, leaving the protection of human life to the decision of parliament and depriving children of the right to sue their mothers for injuries arising before birth.

2. Does the constitutional framework provide for human rights? Do the human rights include

business and property rights? The 1997 constitution enshrines basic human rights and civil liberties, including freedoms of speech, assembly, association, press, and conscience. Chapter II on Rights, Liberties, and Obligations also establishes the principles of equality under the law, the presumption of innocence, and the inviolability of the home. An Ombudsman for Human Rights has the right to investigate alleged violations of human rights and civil liberties. Several articles safeguard the right to property ownership, inheritance, and freedom of economic activity.

3. Has there been reform of the criminal code/criminal law? Who authorizes searches and issues warrants? Are suspects or prisoners beaten or abused? Are there excessive delays in the criminal justice system? In June 1997, the Sejm passed the new Criminal Code and the Code of Criminal Procedure, culminating an eight-year effort to restructure the criminal justice system. The codes, which go into effect September 1, 1998, replace codes from the late 1960s that had been modified piecemeal since 1989. The new law parallels provisions of the new constitution that extend the current 48-hour "initial arrest" phase to 72 hours and provide detainees with a limited right to counsel. Search warrants issued by a court or prosecutors are required in order to enter private residences. In emergency cases, when a prosecutor is not immediately available, police may enter a residence with the approval of the local police commander. There were no reports in 1997 that police abused search warrant procedures. There were sporadic instances of police abuse of detainees. In one 1997 case, three policemen were arrested and charged with raping seven underage detainees. In November, disciplinary proceedings were started against 18 riot police for an attack on soccer fans. Prison conditions are generally poor. In May, the Ombudsman for Human Rights recommended to the prime minister that several detention centers should be closed or renovated and that action be taken to reduce the prison population. The court system suffers from backlogs and inefficiency, often protracting criminal, civil, and commercial cases.

4. Do most judges rule fairly and impartially? How many remain from the Communist era? Judges rule fairly in criminal and civil cases, but the courts are plagued by poor administration, lack of trained personnel, and bureaucratic delays. In December 1997, parliament passed a draft Law on General Courts requiring vetting/lustration of judges. Under the law, judges could be removed for violating judicial independence by having issued unjust verdicts between 1944 and 1989 at the request of Communist authorities. The law was prompted by the acquittal by a Katowice court of police officers accused of murdering nine striking miners in 1981. On February 4, 1998, President Kwasniewski referred the law to the Constitutional Tribunal for review on the grounds that it denies judges the right to a fair trial and due process as well as being retroactive. The case is still pending. Though most judges currently sitting on the courts were appointed prior to 1989, the vetting law would affect no more than 100 of an estimated 7,000 judges.

5. Are courts free of political control and influence? Are the courts linked directly to the Ministry of Justice or any other executive body? Poland's three-tiered court system consists of regional and provincial courts and a Supreme Court. The 1997 constitution expanded the competency of the Constitutional Tribunal. Judges are nominated by the National Judicial Council, created in 1989, and appointed by the president. The National Judicial Council consists of the chief justice of the Supreme Court, the minister of justice, the chief justice of the Superior Administrative Court, a presidential appointee, 15 justices chosen from among the Supreme Court and lower courts, and four members chosen by parliament. Judges are appointed for life and can be reassigned but not dismissed except by a decision of the National Judicial Council. An August 1997 Law Revealing People who were Public Servants in State Security Organs or Cooperated with Them from 1944-1990 (the Vetting Law) called for the creation of a Vetting Court to verify statements made by high-level public officials concerning their involvement with Communist secret services. The court, however, was not constituted when only 20 candidates could be found for the 21 seats on the court. In February 1998, the Senate proposed that vetting should be carried out by the Appeals Court and not by a Vetting Court. The issue was expected to be resolved later in the year. The administration of the judicial system is vested in the hands of the minister of Justice and the courts themselves. Poland's judiciary is independent, but the input of the justice minister, the president, and parliament in the selection of judges does inject politics into the process.

6. What proportion of lawyers is in private practice? Privatization and the proliferation of western companies and law firms in Poland has provided opportunities for thousands of lawyers to work full-or part-time in the private sector. In its 1997 human rights report, the U.S. Department of State said that "many effective judges and prosecutors have left public service for the more lucrative private sector."

7. Does the state provide public defenders? Once formal charges are filed, the defendant is allowed to study the charges and consult with an attorney provided at public expense if necessary. The 1997 constitution (Article 42.2) enshrines the right to counsel at all stages of a criminal proceeding.

8. Has there been comprehensive reform of antibias/discrimination laws, including protection of ethnic minorities? The constitution provides for equal rights regardless of sex (Article 31.2) or ethnic origin (Article 33.1). Poland's population is 98 percent ethnically homogenous with small Ukrainian, Belarusan, Slovak, Lithuanian, and German minorities. The electoral law exempts ethnic minority parties from the requirement to win five percent of the vote nationwide for parliamentary representation. In 1997, a party representing the German minority won a seat in the Sejm. Minority groups enjoy cultural autonomy, and many have established institutions and native-language publications. Lithuanian is taught to pupils of Lithuanian descent in 12 schools in northeastern Poland. In February 1997, parliament passed a law allowing local Jewish groups to submit claims for restitution of communal property owned before World War II. In 1997, anti-Semitic incidents included vandalism of synagogues, cemeteries, and a cultural center. In November, the Gdansk Archbishop suspended Rev. Henryk Jankowski for one year for anti-Semitic remarks. Earlier, charges had been reinstated against the priest for anti-Semitic sermons made in 1995. He was sentenced to two years probation and fined. Roma (Gypsies), who number about 40,000, face discrimination in employment and sporadic violence by skinheads. Though women are equal under the law, the Ministry of Labor found that 57 percent of the unemployed were women and that, despite a generally higher level of education, women earn an average of 25 percent less than men.

Corruption A

1. What is the magnitude of official corruption in the civil service? Must an average citizen pay a bribe to a bureaucrat in order to receive a service? What services are subject to bribe requests — for example, university entrance, hospital admission, telephone installation, obtaining a license to operate a business, applying for a passport or other official documents? What is the average salary of civil servants at various levels? Corruption is less widespread in Poland than in many other post-Communist countries. The source of most corruption is the discretionary power of bureaucrats to issue licenses, conduct inspections, grant waivers, and award contracts. Businesses often find they must pay a "tax" to conduct the desired activity. For example, tax authorities and the Ministry of Finance can arbitrarily decide to cancel tax assessments on a given company. More politically influential firms, such as ailing state-owned enterprises, are far likelier to be the beneficiaries of such action.

2. Do top policy-makers (the president, ministers, vice-ministers, top court justices, and heads of agencies and commissions) have direct ties to businesses? How strong are such connections and what kinds of businesses are these? In 1993, researchers surveyed 1,000 people formerly connected to the Central Committee of the Communist Party in 1988. They compared these to members of the new economic elite and discovered that the overlap in Poland was 28 percent. This compares to 30 percent in Hungary and 19 percent in Russia. The Polish public perceives ties between top party and government officials and financial elites. A February/March 1998 poll revealed that 31.6 percent of the public perceived such ties of the ruling AWS, 25.7 percent of governing partner Freedom Union, and 29.1 percent of the opposition SDL.

3. Do laws requiring financial disclosure and disallowing conflict of interest exist? Have publicized anti-corruption cases been pursued? To what conclusion? The Sejm passed an anti-corruption bill in June 1997 restricting the ability of top state officials to be involved in private business. Such officials include the president, the prime minister, speakers of the Sejm and the Senate, heads of chancelleries of both houses of parliament, the head of the president's Chancellery, the chairman of the Supreme Board of Inspection (NIK), the president of the National Bank of Poland, presidents of the Supreme Court and of the Supreme Administrative Court, judges of the Constitutional Tribunal, the ombudsman, the chairman of the Polish Academy of Sciences (PAN), as well as other central and local government officials. The penalty for violating the law is immediate dismissal. The law also requires top state officials to file asset disclosure statements for themselves as well as for their spouse. A punishment of up to five years in prison is stipulated for those who supply false information. Finally, it requires that the State Electoral Commission maintain a register of substantial gifts and funded trips given to top state officials. In September 1997, the largest corruption trial to date began against the Poz-Sys firm, which is alleged to have bribed high-level officials in the State Fire Department in an attempt to win contracts for that firm's rescue equipment. In late 1996, Minister of Foreign Economic Relations Jacek Buchacz left office after allegations surfaced about the giving of state guarentees to firms that were linked to him. In July 1996, the former mayor of Gdansk was arrested for having accepted a 50,000 *deutsche mark* bribe from a German company for a Gdansk insulation contract.

4. What major anti-corruption initiatives have been implemented? How often are anticorruption laws and decrees adopted? Bribery and other forms of corruption are crimes under Articles 239-245 of the Polish Criminal Code. Article 62 of the Budgetary Law specifies the warnings and penalties (including fines three times the average monthly wage) for such activity. Articles 65-68 of the Law establish commissions to investigate alleged instances of corruption. There are no standing anti-corruption or investigative agencies. One of the most important anti-corruption tools in Poland is the transparent government procurement system with its open bidding at all levels of government. Deputy Prime Minister Leszek Balcerowicz has called for an end to permits and quotas as a way to combat corruption.

5. How do major corruption-ranking organizations like Transparency International rate this country? In July 1997, Transparency International ranked Poland 29th out of the 52 countries it surveyed for its Corruption Perception Index (CPI). Its CPI score was 5.08 in 1997 (on a 1-10 scale, where a lower number equals greater corruption), falling from 5.57 in 1996. Poland's corruption score is similar to the scores of Hungary and the Czech Republic.

Privatization 2.25/7

1. What percentage of the GDP comes from private ownership? What percentage of the labor force is employed in the private sector? How large is the informal sector of the economy? In 1989, the private sector accounted for 18 percent of gross domestic product (GDP). In 1996, an estimated 65 percent of GDP was produced by the private sector, which accounts for 64 percent of total employment. The expansion of the private sector in Poland has been driven more by the spontaneous and vigorous emergence of new enterprises than privatization. According to an Institute for Private Enterprise and Democracy in Poland survey, 15 to 22 percent of the labor force is employed informally and 22 to 25 percent of salaries are paid informally.

2. What major privatization legislation has been passed? What were its substantive features? Privatization in Poland dates to two separate laws passed in August 1990, the Office of the Ministry of Ownership Act, and the Privatization of State-Owned Enterprises (SOEs) Act. Early Polish law defined several principal privatization strategies: sales to foreign investors, initial offerings on the newly organized stock exchange, and the "insider" (management and/or worker) takeover of firms through leasing or outright ownership.

Privatization projects have mostly been handled by regional voivodship (county) offices, not the central privatization ministry, and need to be approved by the firm's managers and employees. This has made the process more spontaneous and decentralized. For these reasons, the pace of privatization of larger firms has been haltingly slow and intensely controversial. Only 1,895 firms, out of a 1989 total of 8,853, were privatized by the end of 1996 through these methods.

On the other hand, "small" privatization — the sale or lease of state-owned stores, shops, and small firms to individuals or groups of private investors — has been relatively successful. In 1990 alone, 35,000 state-owned and cooperative stores were transferred to the private sector.

Poland has still not adopted restitution (reprivatization) legislation returning properties expropriated by Germans during World War II and the Communists afterwards.

In 1990-1991, the government announced a "mass privatization" program that envisaged the commercialization of several hundred of the largest state-owned enterprises. After considerable delay, an amended version of the plan took effect in June 1993. Expected to start in the summer of 1994, mass privatization was stalled again by the SDL-PSL government until June 1995.

Mass privatization in Poland was launched only in 1996 and was based on giving citizens vouchers which represented an ownership stake in all 15 National Investment Funds (NIFs), which are run by state-selected foreign and local management groups. These vouchers went on sale in November 1995 for a nominal amount of 20 *zloty* (approximately $7). By the end of the distribution in November 1996, 90 percent of Poles had participated. These NIFs in turn took a controlling, 33 percent stake in each of 512 large and medium-scale enterprises, while a 27 percent share was distributed to the other 14 NIFs, 10 percent to the firm's workers, and 30 percent went to the state. In early 1997, vouchers in NIFs were transformed into transferable shares. These shares began trading on the Warsaw Stock Exchange in June 1997. With some exceptions, the process has been relatively smooth. There are early signs that individual NIF management teams have sought to become active in restructuring the firms they now control. Apart from the NIFs, the pace of privatization slowed significantly in 1995 and 1996. The privatization of several major SOEs, including the LOT national airline, did not take place as scheduled. The 1998 privatization program is quite ambitious. It envisages the complete and partial privatization of several major large-scale enterprises. The telecommunications monopoly, Telekomunikacja Polska SA, is scheduled to sell 10-25 pecent of its shares both domestically and abroad.

3. What proportion of agriculture, housing and land, industry, and small business and services is in private hands? *Agriculture*: In 1989, one-fifth of the land was state-owned with the rest in private hands. Today, 2.1 million private farmers work on 14.3 million privately-farmed hectares. The Agricultural Ownership Agency was set up four years ago to take over and sell 1495 state farms and 3.1 million hectares of land. By March 1993, new Polish owners were found for a mere 24,000 hectares of former state land and another 204,000 had been leased to individual owners or employee-owned companies. In the first quarter of 1994, the government took over 177 state farms. The large private sector, however, has not necessarily translated into a free market in agriculture. Protection for the agricultural sector in Poland is very significant. According to the National Bank of Poland, this policy fuels price increases that continue to account for a major portion of consumer inflation.

Housing and Land: Poles are allowed to own private housing and land. Real estate may either be owned or leased by way of a perpetual lease. Since June 1996, foreign firms or individuals can own an apartment, 0.4 hectares of urban land, or up to one hectare of agricultural land without a permit. Otherwise, approval from the Ministry of Interior is required.

Industry: The private sector holds a 38 percent share of industry. The privatization of "strategic," i.e. politically significant industries such as the oil, telecommunications, metallurgy, shipbuilding, banking, insurance, mining, airlines, armaments, and portions of the chemical and tobacco industries have been exceedingly slow.

Small Businesses and Services: By 1996, over 90 percent of small business and service sector establishments were in private hands.

4. What has been the extent of insider (management, labor, and nomenklatura) participation in the privatization process? What explicit and implicit preferences have been awarded to insiders? Due to a number of political factors such as the powerful political connections of managerial elites and strong trade union influence, Polish privatization was generally dominated by insiders until the creation of the NIFs. Management and employees at small retail, trade, and consumer services establishments dominated the "small" privatization of their own firms. Where auctions were held, winning bids were approximately the same as the opening price, indicating a very uncompetitive process. This contrasts with the Czech Republic, where winning bids were on average 6.3 times the opening price.

The Law on Commercialization and Privatization of State-Owned Enterprises, in effect from January 1997, reshaped Polish privatization policy. The State Treasury, which assumed control of privatization in August 1996, now had the power to privatize firms without requiring the consent of the firm's insiders as previously practiced. At the same time, employees of a privatized firm were given the right to acquire 15 percent of that firm's shares for free.

5. How much public awareness of and support for privatization has there been? What major interest groups oppose and advocate privatization? The PSL has been the most vocal critic of privatization and bears a large portion of the blame for the slowdown in privatization while in the government. It has stridently opposed liberalization of land sales, in contrast to the ex-Communist SLD party. The new AWS-UW government strongly supports the privatization process. Insiders at enterprises privatized through the NIFs have strongly resisted the exertion of outsider control.

Macroeconomics 1.75/7

1. Has the taxation system been reformed? (What areas have and have not been overhauled? To what degree are taxpayers complying? Is tax compliance difficult to achieve? Has the level of revenues increased? Is the revenue-collection body overburdened? What is the overall tax burden?) The following taxes are levied in Poland: income (three brackets of 20, 32, and 44 percent), social security (aggregate rate of 48.5 percent on income), VAT (22 percent generally and 7 percent on specific goods such as food and medicines), corporate income (38 percent), and capital gains (38 percent). The corporate income tax rate was reduced from 40 to 38 percent in 1997. Further cuts of two percent per year will follow until a 32 percent rate is reached in 2000. These high tax rates encourage private sector activity in the informal economy. High tax rates on wage income also have the unfortunate side effect of making the labor market more rigid. This leads to relatively high unemployment in spite of Poland's impressive growth rate. Many of those unemployed actually work in the informal sector. The introduction of the VAT has considerably improved revenue collection. The biggest laggards in tax payments are large loss-making SOEs in such sectors as mining, steel, and shipbuilding. Tax arrears in the private sector are not a major problem.

2. Does fiscal policy encourage private savings, investment and earnings? (Has there been any reform/alteration of revenue and budget policies? How large are budget deficits and overall debt? Is the financing of the social insurance/pension system sustainable? What proportion of the budget is taken up by subsidies to firms and individuals)? Poland was the first post-Communist nation to embark on macroeconomic reform. The "Balcerowicz Program," began on January 1, 1990 in the face of hyperinflation (600 percent in 1990). Hyperinflationary pressures were extinguished by 1992, and Poland was the first nation to emerge from the post-transition recession with real growth in 1993. Real GDP grew 6.9 percent in 1997, and it has averaged 6.3 percent growth since 1994. The dynamism of the private sector accounts for the majority of this growth in output. Poland has been courageous enough to implement politically painful budget cuts in defense, health care, and education. Subsidies have been cut sharply from 42 percent of state spending in 1988 to 5.6 percent in 1995. In 1997, the deficit was just below 2 percent of GDP and is budgeted to fall to 1.5 percent in 1998 in accordance with the budget enacted by the outgoing SLD government and supported by the new AWS-UW governing coalition. Its macroeconomic progress was recognized by the West when Poland acceded to the OECD in July 1996. Poland's debt rating was raised in April 1996 by Standard & Poor's from BB to BBB. In general, Polish credit ratings are now investment grade, and Poland has also repaid all of its IMF drawings in 1995.

One of the most important issues facing Poland is the solvency and inefficiency of the social insurance system, particularly the national pension. Poland's pay-as-you-go funding system, combined with the youngest retirement age in Europe, led to an unsustainable drain on the state coffers — 39 percent of spending — and extremely high social security taxes levied on wages of current workers. In July 1997, parliament finally reformed the system. The retirement age was raised and sectoral privileges eliminated, and individual pension accounts were introduced. Unlike the current pay-as-you-go scheme, these accounts are fully-funded and will generate a far higher return on contributions. The new multi-tier pension system will take effect in January 1999.

3. Has there been banking reform? (Is the central bank independent? What are its responsibilities? Is it effective in setting and/or implementing monetary policy? What is the actual state of the private banking sector? Does it conform to international standards? Are depositors protected?) Unlike most of its counterparts, the National Bank of Poland (NBP) was strongly independent early in the transition process. Not surprisingly, it has implemented significant monetary restraint, particularly under the stewardship of NBP President Hanna Gronkiewicz-Waltz, who completed her six year term in March 1998. A new nine-member council, which is chaired by the president, was inaugurated in 1998. In addition to the NBP's monetary oversight, it regulates the banking sector through its General Inspectorate of Banking Supervision. Banking regulations are comprehensive. Interest rates were freed in January 1990, but generally follow the interest rate policies of the NBP. By October 1996, there were 88 banks in Poland, 24 of which were state-owned. These state-owned banks, however, only have a 57 percent market share. The financial sector is dominated by nine banking conglomerates spun off from the NBP. A bad debt crisis began plaguing the Polish banking industry in 1990. The problem peaked in 1993, when non-performing loans were 31 percent of total loans. By the end of 1996, this measure had fallen to 12.5 percent. On the whole, bank failures and bail-outs have been minimal in comparison with other post-Communist reformers. Moreover, much of these nonperforming loans were actually held by one troubled bank, BGZ SA. Thirty-two of Poland's leading 50 banks have five percent or less of their portfolios nonperforming. The NBP increased reserve ratio requirements in February and March 1997. A new banking law has been in effect since early 1998, moving Polish banking regulation much closer to European Union norms. Deposit insurance was established by the 1994 Law on the Banking Deposit Guarantee Fund. The bank-funded institution guarentees deposits up to ECU 1,000 fully, and 90 percent of sums up to ECU 3,000.

Polish confidence in the banking system has risen substantially. A September 1997 poll revealed that a record 40 percent of Poles put their savings in banks while only three percent keep them at home.

Bank privatization, however, has been quite slow. While the original target for the completion of bank privatization was the end of 1996, only four of the nine commercial banks spun off from the NBP in 1989 and one specialized bank has been privatized as of mid-1997. This delay was due, in large part, to the SLD government's plan to create two large banking groups centered around Bank Handlowy and Bank Pekao before privatization. The new government will most likely limit this consolidation. Current plans are to privatize the remaining banks by the year 2000.

Foreign investors have taken large positions in Polish banking; 24 banks have majority foreign ownership, and they account for 15.3 percent of total bank loans. The government has committed itself to further liberalizing the bank sector for foreign participation. By the end of 1998, foreign banks will be able to establish their own branches in Poland.

4. How sound is the national currency? (To what extent has inflation eroded its value? Is the value of the currency fixed or does it float? Is the currency convertible? How large are the hard currency reserves? Has exchange rate policy been stable and predictable?) The Balcerowicz reform program made the *zloty* internally convertible on January 1, 1990. The zloty is now fully convertible on the current account and partially convertible on the capital account. The Foreign Exchange Law of October 1995 further liberalized currency exchange rules.

The NBP is responsible for defending the value of the national currency and sets exchange and interest rates. Since 1990, the zloty's value has been pegged (on a downward "crawling" basis) to a basket of Western currencies dominated by the U.S. dollar and the German mark. In May 1995, the exchange rate was allowed to fluctuate in a band of plus or minus seven percent against the basket. Since December 1995, the zloty has been devalued at a constant rate of one percent per month. The new monetary policy, seeking to slow inflationary inertia, council lowered the rate to 0.8 percent in 1998. In real terms, however, the zloty has appreciated because of the difference in inflation rates between Poland and the United States and Germany.

Foreign reserves rose from $6 billion at the end of 1994 to over $21.1 billion in October 1997. Reflecting increasing confidence in the currency, the number of Poles keeping their savings in zloty-denominated accounts rose from 50 percent in 1995 to 56 percent in 1996.

Inflation fell to 15.9 percent in 1997, and has dropped every year since 1990.

5. Is there a functioning capital market infrastructure? (Are there existing or planned commodities, bond and stock markets? What are the mechanisms for investment and lending? What government bodies have authority to regulate capital markets?) Polish capital markets have been maturing slowly but steadily since 1990. The Warsaw Stock Exchange (WSE) was established in April 1991. The Law on Public Trading in Securities and the Act Establishing the Warsaw Stock Exchange provided the basic legal framework. The Securities Commission is considered one of the best in all of East-Central Europe.

Amendments to the Security Law were made in June 1997, allowing for the creation of investment banks, liberalizing and simplifying procedures for initial public offerings, and the trading of warrants and derivatives. A new Investment Fund Act was passed in July 1997. It supplanted the 1991 Law on Trust Funds. The new law expands the types of legal investment funds to include open-ended, closed-ended, mixed, and specialist funds.

In 1991, there were five traded companies, but by mid-1997, 100 firms were regularly traded. There are 51 brokerage houses providing underwriting, auditing, marketing, and consulting services. There are also 843,000 open investment accounts. The WSE is comparable to the Greek and Portuguese stock exchanges in terms of trading volume and quantity of transactions, but lags far behind in capitalization ($9 billion as of November 1996; 7 percent of GDP). The market is one of the most liquid in the region, with an 84.8 percent turnover ratio. The WSE limits daily price movements to about ten percent. A full system of continuous quotations is expected for 1999.

Mass privatization vouchers began trading in July 1996. By September 1996, trading in the vouchers made up about 10-15 percent of the daily trade volume on the WSE. Public trading in individual NIFs began in June 1997, and gave a big boost to investment volume and prices.

The Polish bourse is still underdeveloped in that it lacks large institutional investor-like pension funds and intermediaries like investment banks. This situation should improve with the advent of the new pension system in 1999.

Other exchanges have been late in developing. The Warsaw Grain and Feed Commodity Exchange, Poland's first commodity futures exchange, was created in late 1995. In May 1996, the Council of Ministers Economic Committee decided to establish eight national commodity exchanges and 25 regional exchanges. Poland's over-the-counter securities market, the Central Table of Offers, became operational in December 1996. It was organized by 45 brokerage houses. Few companies, however, trade on it.

Another important development in the evolution of Polish capital markets occurred in November 1996 when 17 Polish financial institutions created Poland's first credit rating agency, the Central European Center for Ratings and Analysis, which rates bond issues of firms, banks, and municipalities.

The private capital markets reflect Poland's evolution. In 1991, bank loans were the only source of capital for expanding companies. Currently, short-term commercial paper, bonds (including convertible bonds), and share issues are now accepted methods of raising short- and medium-term capital. Currency futures and stock market options are also now available. Long-term financing is still difficult to raise because of high inflation and general uncertainty.

Microeconomics 1.75/7

1. Are property rights guaranteed? (Are there both formal and de facto protections of private real estate and intellectual property? Is there a land registry with the authority and capability to ensure accurate recording of who owns what? What are the procedures for expropriation, including measures for compensation and challenge? Have any seizures taken place?) Article 64 of the new constitution states that "every person has the right to ownership, other property rights, and the right of inheritance [which are] subject to legal protection that is equal for all. Ownership may be restricted only by law and only to the extent to which it does not abridge the essence of the right of ownership." A second form of property is the perpetual lease — 40-99 years in duration, and which can be extended for 99 more years. Leases can be sold and inherited.

Article 21 states that "expropriation is admissible only for public purposes and upon equitable compensation." The Law on Land Management and Expropriation of Real Estate limits public "takings" for specified public purposes such as national security. It also provides for full compensation at market value. No cases of expropriations have occurred since reforms began in 1990.

Registries in land, companies, and property liens are not fully developed. For instance, if there is more than one lien on a property, the most recent has priority, the opposite of what happens in the West.

Poland recently liberalized regulations on foreign property holdings which allows foreigners to purchase land without having to apply for a permit from the Ministry of Internal Affairs. Foreign individuals can purchase residential apartments and ownership of land after a five-year residency period. Foreign companies can purchase up to 0.4 hectares of land in cities and up to one hectare of land in the countryside. Regulations and applications remain difficult and confusing. Between 1990 and 1995, only 16.6 percent of permit applications by foreigners were granted.

A Patent Law Act was passed in 1993, followed by a Copyright Law in 1994. Three executive ordinances have been enacted by the Minister of Culture and Arts. A December 1994 ordinance establishes a Copyright Commission. The commission, composed of culture and arts ministry appointees, is charged with two tasks: to approve tables of royalties proposed by "collective administration societies" for the use of works and performances, and to arbitrate disputes concerning royalties. Poland also acceded to the Berne Convention in 1994. These changes in Polish legislation on the protection of intellectual property represent a considerable advance.

Enforcement has also improved. In late 1994, the Polish government closed major television broadcasters that used pirated material. The government has been less effective in curtailing software piracy. The Business Software Alliance, a U.S. anti-piracy trade organization, estimates that 91 percent of software in Poland is pirated. It also estimates that U.S. software vendors lost $201 million as a result of such piracy in 1994. In 1997, Poland was placed on the U.S. government's Special 301 "Watch List" because of U.S. concerns about the high rate of piracy.

One problem created by the lack of legislation on restitution of German- and Communist-expropriated property is that land sales are hampered, and development projects slowed, by confusion over the progress of the legislation. A substantial amount of property, especially in urban areas, has very unclear titles of ownership. When such legislation is enacted, former owners will have first rights of sale or disposal, according to a mid-1996 ruling of the highest administrative court. This will create problems for the current "owners" of restituted property.

2. To what extent have prices been liberalized? What subsidies remain? Prices were liberalized in the 1989 reform program. Controlled prices as a percentage of the goods in the Consumer Price Index fell to 11 percent in 1990, but have remained unchanged since. The major prices that remain controlled are housing rents and energy prices. Changing prices requires permission, the granting of which can take as long as three months.

Overall, energy prices are controlled. In February 1997, however, the government permitted liquid fuel and gasoline price changes without prior approval.

A May 1997 energy law established the Energy Regulation Office, which will award private energy producer licenses, as well as regulate electricity prices. A price increase from the current $0.06 per kWh, to a break-even rate of $0.075 is scheduled to take place in the year 2000. The attainability of this goal, however, is in question because of government-induced delays in scheduled price increases. Electricity prices under the law will be set on a national electricity exchange. At the beginning of May 1996, regional prices were introduced for electricity. These prices will be adjusted based on a number of factors, including reliability and continuity of supply, as well as distance.

3. Is it possible to own and operate a business? (Has there been legislation regarding the formation, dissolution and transfer of businesses, and is the law respected? Do there exist overly cumbersome bureaucratic hurdles that effectively hinder the ability to own and dispose of a business? Are citizens given access to information on commercial law? Is the law applied fairly? Does regulation (or licensing requirements) impose significant costs on business and consumers? Do they create significant barriers to entry and seriously hamper competition?) In general, Polish laws regarding the creation of new businesses are fairly liberal and transparent. There was an explosion of businesses created following the transition, especially of small service firms. Thus, despite the relatively slow speed of Polish privatization, the share of the GDP produced by the private sector is in the top tier among Central European countries.

Nevertheless, there is some degree of complexity and lack of transparency involved in starting and running a business. This is related to the speed with which laws regarding business activity are amended. Over 220 laws, amended over 500 times, regulate business activity. This often means that even small firms must employ professional assistance to comply with the law. Polish regulation remains a barrier to business formation and management. Arbitrary enforcement of labor, health, and safety regulations is one facet of this problem. Another is access to differential levels of protection from imports.

In January 1998, Balcerowicz, who also serves as finance minister, established a commission of businessmen to identify particularly onerous regulations. There is even an anti-bureaucracy "hotline" for people to call with suggestions to simplify regulatory burdens.

Compared with the rest of Central Europe, trade unions are unusually strong in Poland and have, at times, strongly protested the restructuring and management changes in enterprises, especially in those that are newly-privatized. The unions, however, have not seriously disrupted Polish business activity.

The amended 1934 Bankruptcy Act provides procedures for liquidating businesses. After comprehensive post-Communist reforms, bankruptcy filings increased sharply, peaking at 5,249 in 1993 before falling to 2,710 in 1996. There remain some problems in bankruptcy procedures. For example, the law prioritizes government and procedural costs above that of creditors, resulting in the latter having a much diminished incentive to go after debtors.

4. Are courts effective, transparent, efficient, and quick in reaching decisions on property and contract disputes? What alternative mechanisms for adjudicating disputes exist? The Polish legal system is based on French and German models. Important judgements are published with details of the judges' reasoning.

The limited capacity of Polish courts greatly delay adjudication procedures. Commercial cases are generally heard in court between one and two years after filing, and a judgement is rendered in about the same amount of time. Bankruptcy courts are similarly slow. Foreign investors have generally avoided Polish courts to resolve disputes, choosing either international arbitration or informal methods.

Private arbitration tribunals exist in Poland. Under the Code of Civil Procedure, judgements rendered in these tribunals have equal binding force as those done by public courts.

Poland is a signatory of several major international agreements on dispute resolution. Nevertheless, it is very difficult to enforce international arbitration decisions in Polish courts.

5. Is business competition encouraged? (Are monopolistic practices limited in law and in practice? If so, how? To what degree is "insider" dealing a hindrance to open competition? Are government procurement policies open and unbiased?) Poland's 1990 Law on Countering Monopolistic Practices (as amended) prohibits various forms of anti-competitive behavior. The Office of Competition and Consumer Protection executes this law. Monopolies are defined as having a market share exceeding 40 percent. In 1996, the office considered 192 cases; monopolistic practices were found in 80 of them.

Government policy itself often decreases competition. Government sanctioned monopolies exist in many sectors of the economy. In telecommunications, Telekomunikacja Polska has had a sanctioned monopoly. In May 1997, however, the government announced that it would introduce competition in long-distance telephone service by January 1999. The government has increased monopolization by creating industry-wide holding companies (such as Nafta Polska in fuels). The Office of Competition recently ruled that the TPSA could no longer forbid cellular telephone providers from using non-TPSA networks.

Poland's 1994 Government Procurement Law allows for a 20 percent price advantage for domestic firms against their foreign competitors. In addition, there is a 50 percent domestic material and labor content floor for all bids.

6. To what extent has international trade been liberalized? To what degree has there been simplification/overhaul of customs and tariff procedures, and are these applied fairly? What informal trade barriers exist? Poland's average trade-weighted tariff was 15 percent in 1994 and 9.3 percent in January 1995. The January 1996 revision of the customs tariffs established an average 7.7 percent tariff on industrial products and a 19.5 percent tariff on agricultural goods. Further liberalization in January 1997 reduced the average tariff rate to 6.3 percent (5.1 percent on industrial goods and 17.3 percent on agricultural goods).

Poland, however, is still plagued by a proliferating number of barriers to imports affecting approximately 4,000 product groups and 25 percent of imports. Political, not economic, considerations dictate which sector will enjoy protection. Imports from countries outside the EU face much higher protection.

Poland acceded to the Uruguay Round of the General Agreement on Tariffs and Trade (GATT) in July 1995, and as such is a member of the World Trade Organization. Poland is also a member of the European Free Trade Association and the Central European Free Trade Agreement, both of which obligate a substantial reduction in import duties.

Nontariff barriers, such as certification requirements, quotas in agriculture, fuels, alcohol and tobacco products, non-transparent product standards, and fragmented legal regulations, have made up for the ground lost from falling tariff rates. Overworked officials, antiquated methodology, and slow communication between Warsaw and the borders have also hindered trade.

7. To what extent has foreign investment and capital flow been encouraged or constrained? The Foreign Investment Act of 1991 and later amendments to it secured the opening of Poland to foreign investment. With the exception of "strategic" sectors, Poland does not require any local participation, ownership, or management in companies. Foreigners can generally enjoy complete ownership of new or existing Polish firms. Profits and dividends can be fully repatriated with no permit requirement. Final restrictions on foreign investment in joint ventures were removed by the March 1996 Joint Ventures Law. In April 1996, Poland eliminated controls on flows of capital. Polish privatization has, relative to other countries in the region, been quite open to foreign investors. Foreigners can now purchase shares in NIFs (see privatization question #2) that are traded on the stock exchange and which represent ownership of many privatized enterprises. The strategic sectors where there are exceptions to liberal rules on foreign investment include banking, insurance, telecommunications, mining, steel, defense, transportation, energy, and broadcasting. Generally, domestic and foreign firms are treated equally under Polish investment law. One exception is bidding for public procurement contracts. Polish firms enjoy a mandated 20 percent price advantage, and 50 percent of materials and labor in all contracts are required to be Polish. Foreign investors, however, enjoy extensive tax privileges in the so-called "free customs areas," of which eight had been approved as of January 1996. An October 1994 law also established "special economic zones" which extended tax privileges to three areas with high unemployment (and three more to come). Foreign direct investment (FDI) took off in 1995. In 1997, FDI increased to an impressive $6.6 billion. Cumulative investment since 1990 is $20.6 billion, passing Hungary as the largest of all the post-communist countries. The United States is the largest foreign investor in Poland.

8. Has there been reform of the energy sector? (To what degree has the energy sector been restructured? Is the energy sector more varied, and is it open to private competition? Is the country overly dependent on one or two other countries for energy [including whether exported fuels must pass through one or more countries to reach markets]?) Poland's energy sector is among its least reformed sectors. Problems include obsolete technology, poor energy efficiency, excessive waste of raw materials, poor usage of existing capacity, and environmental hazard. The dissolution of state ownership in the energy sector has consisted mostly of "minor privatization" or the contracting out of support services such as repair, transport, storage, and administration to private companies.

The energy market is protected from imports by a number of barriers such as tariffs and quotas.

As a result, imports only account for one-fifth of total supply. The EU agreed in late 1996 to extend protection of the Polish fuel market until the year 2000. Under the agreement, customs duties would be gradually reduced beginning in 1997. In return, Poland is obligated to continue fuel price deregulation, accelerate refinery privatization, remove nontariff barriers such as quotas on fuels, and give equal treatment to all firms dealing with Polish refineries.

The 1990 Law on the Liquidation of the Amalgamated Power Supply and Lignite Authority and the 1993 Law on the Transformation of Strategic Enterprises have shaped the reform of the electricity sector. Polskie Sieci Energetyczne SA, a state-owned firm, has run the Polish electricity grid since 1990. While there are plans to admit private shareholders, the state plans to keep a controlling interest in the company. The new 1996 Energy Law creates an Electricity Regulation Board and is responsible for licensing, supervising and approving rates, levying fines, and arbitrating disputes between users and producers. The law downgrades the powers of the National Electricity Authority which decides the fate of individual power plants. The privatization of a large power plant, Zespol Elektrowni Patnow-Adamow-Konin, set for 1996, has been subject to continual delays.

In May 1996, Poland merged seven state-owned oil refineries and the main gasoline distribution network into Nafta Polska, an industry-wide holding company, in order to increase efficiency. It was hoped that this would attract foreign investment into the industry and the private sector. Individual refineries were to be partially privatized by being able to offer 30 percent of their shares to foreign investors.

The Polish Oil and Gas Company has a monopoly on the importation, transmission, storage, and distribution of natural gas. The Yamal gas pipeline currently being constructed stretches from Siberia to Western Europe across Poland. Construction of the first 107 kilometer stretch was completed in October 1996.

ROMANIA

Freedom in the World Ratings, 1989-1998

	1989-90	1990-91	1991-92	1992-93	1993-94	1994-95	1995-96	1996-97	1997-98
Political Rights	7	6	5	4	4	4	4	2	2
Civil Liberties	7	5	5	4	4	3	3	3	2
Status	NF	NF	PF	PF	PF	PF	PF	F	F

Polity: Transitional
Economy: Transitional
Population: 22,687,000
PPP: $4,431
Ethnic Groups: Romanian (88 percent), Hungarian (9 percent), German, Roma (Gypsy)
Capital: Bucharest

Political Process 3.25/7

1. When did national legislative elections occur? Where they free and fair? How were they judged by domestic and international election monitoring organizations? Who composes the government? Elections for the bicameral legislature took place in two rounds in November 1996. In the vote for the 143-member Senate the results were as follows: the Democratic Convention coalition (CDR), 53 seats; the Social Democracy Party of Romania (PDSR), 41; the Social Democratic Union (USD), 23; the Hungarian Democratic Union (UMDR), 11; the Greater Romania Party (PRM), 8; and the Romanian National Unity Party, (PUNR), 7. In the 328-member lower house, the Chamber of Deputies, the CDR won 122 seats; the PDSR, 91; the USD, 53; the RMDS, 25; the PRM, 19; and the PUNR, 18. In addition, 15 seats were allocated to minority formations that had failed to secure elective membership.

The CDR formed a governing coalition with the USD and the RMDS, giving it control of 300 seats. The opposition is led by the PDSR, headed by former President Ion Iliescu. Victor Ciorbea, a former labor leader and ex-mayor of Bucharest, was named prime minister. On March 30, 1998, he was forced to resign after a three-month-long political crisis sparked when the USD, led by former Prime Minister Petru Roman, walked out of the coalition in January, blaming the prime minister for lagging economic reforms. The Organization for Security and Cooperation in Europe (OSCE) reported the elections were "free and generally fair," citing such problems as incomplete voter registration rolls and irregularities in registering candidates.

2. When did presidential elections occur? Where they free and fair? In November 1996, Emil Constantinescu, head of the Democratic Convention, defeated incumbent Ion Iliescu in a run-off election, 53.8 percent to 46.2 percent. In the first round, Iliescu narrowly defeated Constantinescu,

32.3 percent to 29.2 percent, in a crowded 16-candidate field. The OSCE labeled the vote "free and fair," although there were some discrepancies in signatures supporting several independent candidates. According to the election law, each independent candidate had to have at least 100,000 signatures on a petition.

3. Is the electoral system multi-party based? Are there at least two viable parties functioning at all levels of government? Romania has a pluralistic system. Most of the major parliamentary parties are active at the federal, regional, and local levels. Most major parties get some subsidies from the government.

4. How many parties have been legalized? Are any particular parties illegal? By May 1990, some 200 parties had been legalized under a 1989 law that requires a minimum of 250 people to form a party. In May 1996, Law 27 "On Political Parties" required a political party to have at least 10,000 members before it could be registered, reducing the number of parties to about 50. On May 4, 1994, a Bucharest court authorized a revival of the Romanian Communist Party. A month later, the Romanian Supreme Court revoked the registration under a law barring groups supporting totalitarianism, extremism, fascism, or communism.

5. What proportion of the population belong to political parties? There is no reliable or official data regarding party membership.

6. What was the trend in voter turnout at the municipal, provincial, and national levels in recent years? Legislative elections: 1992, 78 percent; 1996, 76 percent. Presidential elections: 1990, 86 percent; 1992, 76 percent; 1996; 73.2 percent. Local elections: 1992, 72 percent, 1996, 56 percent. The turnout figures have trended downward, particularly in local elections.

Civil Society 3.75/7

1. How many nongovernmental organizations (NGOs) have come into existence since 1988? What is the number of charitable/nonprofit organizations? Are there locally led efforts to increase philanthropy and volunteerism? What proportion of the population is active in private voluntary activity (from polling data)? According to the Foundation for Civil Society Development, approximately 23,000 NGOs have registered since 1990. Of these, only 400 to 500 are functioning. While a number of environmental, human rights, women's organizations, and public policy institutes have obtained foreign support, most Romanian NGOs still lack essential resources and self-sustainability. There are scores of NGOs that deal with health issues and social services. Romania does not have a developed philanthropic tradition or institutions. While most NGOs rely on volunteers, information on public participation is unavailable.

2. What is the legal and regulatory environment for NGOs (i.e., ease of registration, legal rights, government regulation, taxation, procurement and access-to-information issues)? To what extent is NGO activism focused on improving the legal and regulatory environment? NGOs must register with the government but there are no inordinate bureaucratic or legal impediments to registration. Romanian law does require ministry approval prior to registration of a foundation or association. In January 1998, Prime Minister Ciorbea signed a government ordinance which provides the most progressive NGO tax benefits of any country in Central and Eastern Europe. Citizens are able to take tax deductions for contributions to NGOs and corporations are now able to deduct 5-10 percent of donations they make. Television and radio broadcasters will receive favorable tax treatment for airing public service announcements. Several NGOs deal with improving rule-of-law, among them are the Foundation for Democratic Change and Liga Pro Europa.

3. What is the organization capacity of NGOs? Do management structures clearly delineate authority and responsibility? Is information available on NGO management available in the native language? Is there a core of experienced practitioners/trainers to serve as consultants or mentors to less-developed organizations? Most of the better-established NGOs, particularly in the larger cities, have management structures that delineate authority and responsibility. The Foundation for Democratic Change, Liga Pro Europa, the Pro Democracy Association, and the International Center for Entrepreneurial Studies have boards of directors that hold regular meetings. Most, however, continue to be staffed by part-time workers and volunteers. In Romania, NGOs receive training and technical assistance from foreign governments and institutions, among them U.S. AID, through its Democracy Network Program (Freedom House and the International Center for Not-for-Profit Law), the United Nations Development Program (UNDP), the Soros Foundation, the Charles Stewart Mott Foundation, and others. These programs provide training in management, sustainability, government and media outreach, and fund raising. Materials are available in Romanian. Cooperation between NGOs is relatively good. For example, 32 percent of environmental NGOs cooperate closely on joint projects at the local level, and 38 percent collaborate through information exchange at the national level. A core of experienced practitioners is emerging from the older, better-organized organizations.

4. Are NGOs financially viable? What is their tax status? Are they obliged to and do they typically disclose revenue resources? Do government procurement opportunities exist for private, not-for-profit providers of services? Most NGOs are not financially viable without the assistance of Western governments and foreign-based organizations, foundations, and institutions. Half of the environmental groups, for example, have an annual budget of less than $500. The Foundation for Democratic Change receives some 80 percent of its revenue from international sources. The Pro Democracy Association, with a 1996 budget of $265,000, receives over 90 percent of its revenues from foreign foundation grants and international government organizations. Most major NGOs in Bucharest and larger cities typically disclose revenue sources. The Romanian Institute of International Studies operates under the auspices of the Romanian Ministry of Foreign Affairs and the Romanian Academy, but maintains full research autonomy. It does receive service fees for governmental and non-governmental work, but they amount to only about ten percent of revenues. Government procurement opportunities for most private NGOs is limited. The relationship between NGOs and the for-profit sector is sporadic.

5. Are there free trade unions? How many workers belong to these unions? Is the number of

workers belonging to trade unions growing or decreasing? What is the numerical/proportional membership of farmer's groups, small business associations, etc.? The constitution and 1991 legislation stipulate that labor unions should be free from government or political party control. About half of Romania's 11 million workers belong to about 20 labor confederations. The three main unions are the Fratia National Trade Union Confederation (which claims 3.7 million members), the Alfa Worker's Confederation of Labor (which claims 1.2 million members in 29 federations), and the National Union Bloc. In 1995, the three formed a National Inter-Confederate Committee to coordinate activities. Union membership is shrinking as a result of restructuring that has closed money-losing state enterprises. In early 1997, 30,000 workers were laid off. While unions continue to claim some 5-6 million members, the true figure is lower. More than 30 percent of Romania's workforce is employed directly or indirectly in agriculture, and farmers' interests are represented by the Agrarian Democratic Party, the Romanian Peasant Party, the National Association of Private Farmers of Romania, the Agrostar Trade Union, and smaller associations. In March 1997, 7,000 leaders in farmers' trade union in the state and private sector and unionists of farming equipment makers staged a strike to protest planned decreases in subsidies. Farmers also belong to cooperative associations throughout the country. Virtually every major city — Bucharest, Cluj, Brasov, Abad — has active chambers of commerce which include business associations, trade groups, and private enterprises. Precise national figures are unavailable. Several NGOs assist small businesses, including the International Center for Entrepreneurial Studies.

6. What forms of interest participation in politics are legal? What types of interest groups are active in the political and policy process? The constitution protects the rights of assembly and association and the right to petition. Political parties, trade unions, local chambers of commerce, business groups, and a growing number of NGOs are active in the political process. Public demonstrations are still the main mechanism of public pressure on the government. Think tanks and public policy institutes disseminate their findings and recommendations to parliament and the government, and a few receive government research contracts.

7. How is the not-for-profit/NGO sector perceived by the public and government officials? What is the nature of media coverage of NGOs? To what extent do government officials engage with NGOs? The government has made attempts to work with NGOs. For example, President Constantinescu created a position of NGO liaison within his circle of advisors. However, NGOs still do not have adequate outreach programs to government and the media. Senators and parliamentary deputies reported to an advisor for the World Learning Democracy Network Program in 1997 that, although they knew NGOs in their own districts, they had not heard from any of these organizations since the November 1996 elections. Other parliamentarians complained that NGO missions are often vaguely defined. The NGO sector in Romania has yet to form a public image, though the media occasionally cover major conferences in Bucharest involving international institutions.

Independent Media 4.00/7

1. Are there legal protections for press freedom? Romania's 1991 constitution enshrines freedom of expression (Article 30), access to information (Article 31), and autonomy for state-owned broadcast media. The Audiovisual Act No. 48 (1992) introduced a dual system of public and private broadcasters. A significant barrier to press freedom are laws in the 1996 Penal Code dealing with libel and slander.

2. Are there legal penalties for libeling officials? Are there legal penalties for "irresponsible" journalism? Have the laws been enforced to harass journalists? Under Law No. 40 of the 1996 Penal Code, journalists face penalties of up to two years' imprisonment for libel and up to five years for disseminating false information that effects Romania's international relations or national security. On March 24, 1997, a Bucharest court overturned a lower court ruling whereby two journalists were found guilty of "offense to authority" for reporting that former President Iliescu was recruited by the KGB in the 1950s. The two had been sentenced to one year and 14 months, respectively. With the election of Constantinescu in November 1996, no major libel cases affecting journalists have been brought.

3. What proportion of the media is privatized? What are the major newspapers, television stations and radio stations? Most of the print media is private, while electronic media is dominated by state television and radio. The 1992 Audiovisual Act introduced a dual system of public and private broadcasters. The former state broadcasting system was transformed into public corporations in 1994: the Romanian Radio Broadcasting Corporation and the Romanian Television Corporation, described as "editorially independent autonomous public services (acting in the) national interest." Both public and private broadcasters are regulated by the National Audiovisual Council (NAC). The national broadcaster, Television Romania, remains the topmost news provider and has the largest audience share in Romania, particularly in the countryside. Radio Romania Actualitatu, the public radio station, covers the whole country. Private television and radio have proliferated in recent years.

Romania has 15 national dailies, 3 national sports dailies and many local dailies, most of which are privately owned. The main papers include, *Evenimentul Zilei*, the most widely read daily with a distribution of 160,000; *Romania Libera* (120,000); *Adevarul* (120,000); *Libertatea* (50,000); and *Ziua* (30,000). Papers supported by government subsidies include *Vocea Romaniei*, the government paper, and *Dimineata*, the paper of the presidency. The minority press includes *Romaniay Magyar Szo* (Hungarian) and *Deutsche Algemeine Zeitung* (German). Some minority papers receive government subsidies.

There are more than 50 private television stations and over 100 private radio stations. Major private TV broadcasters include Pro-TV, Antena-1, Tele 7 abc, Dacia Europa Nova, Amerom, and TV Sigma. Main private radio broadcasters include Radio Contact, which covers the major part of the country and has a 30 percent audience share; Radio Pro-FM; Radio Total; Radio Delta; Radio 2M+, and several religious stations. Article 19, the London-based anti-censorship group, has noted that state broadcasters reach the largest rural audience, while the reach of private broadcasters is limited to major urban areas.

4. Are the media financially viable? After the 1989 revolution that overthrew the Communist regime, hundreds of new newspapers, magazines and journals flourished. Since then, the print media has shrunk due to economic conditions, high production costs, expensive distribution through state-owned systems, and low demand. Retail prices for newspapers are prohibitively high compared to the average monthly income. *Evenimentul Zilei*, the most popular daily, is part of the Expres media group that includes a magazine, TV station, and radio station. Several papers have websites. The overall majority of private TV stations in the country have a limited range of transmission covering only local audiences. Due to limited funds and very few editorial staff, technical quality and content are poor. The major private TV stations, such as Pro-TV, Antena 1, Tele 7abc, Dacia Europa Nova, and Amerom are well financed by private corporate investors. The major radio stations are also funded by large media companies such as the Media Pro Group, the Hachette-Matra group, and Contact Belgium.

5. Are the media editorially independent? Are the media's news gathering functions affected by interference from government or private owners? Private media reflect the views of the owners. In the 1996 presidential campaign, some newspapers backed the government, while others openly supported the opposition. Sometimes that support led to slanted, non-objective coverage or the tendency to mix news and commentary. The government-owned or public media tend to support official policies. The regulatory agency, the NAC, is subject to political influence, with its top officials appointed by parliament. The chairman of the Board of Management of both state TV and radio, as well its 12 members, are not appointed by the NAC but by parliament. Public media is susceptible to political influence because regulatory bodies are controlled by the parliament where the governing party or coalition has the majority. In both broadcast and print media, political figures appeared as senior managers, shareholders, or owners of the outlets.

6. Is the distribution system for newspapers privately or governmentally controlled? An obstacle to the development of a dynamic print media is the ineffective and monopolistic system of distribution and printing controlled by the government. The state-owned distribution company, Rodipet, has been accused of discriminating against the independent press.

7. What proportion of the population is connected to the Internet? Are there any restrictions on Internet access to private citizens? Information on this subject is not available at this time.

8. What has been the trend in press freedom as measured by Freedom House's *Survey of Press Freedom*? Freedom House's annual press survey rated Romania Not Free from 1988 through 1990, Partly Free for 1991, Free for 1992, and Partly Free from 1993 through 1998.

Governance and Public Administration 4.00/7

1. Is The legislature the effective rule-making institution? Under the 1991 constitution, the bicameral legislature is the effective law-making institution. The government, however, has the power to amend laws and regulations by executive ordinances as "emergency rulings" which are subsequently presented to parliament for approval. In 1997, this procedure was used on several occasions to amend laws related to economic reform, including laws on privatization, transportation, the oil industry, bankruptcy, and the financial system. One such ordinance was used to close 17 money-losing state-run enterprises.

2. Is substantial power decentralized to subnational levels of government? What specific authority do subnational levels have? Romania is essentially a unitary state with little experience with decentralized national authority. While Chapter V, Section 1, Article 119 of the constitution states that public administration is "based on the principle of local autonomy," local authorities have restricted legal authority and even that authority is limited by central government control over financial resources. The new government has promised to amend the law to make local administration more effective. The country's 40 counties are administered by mayors and local councils, county councils, and prefects, who represent the government at the local level. The number of members of each local council is determined by the population of the commune or town and may vary from 11 to 33 members. The municipality of Bucharest has 75 councilors. The county council has from 37 to 45 councilors depending on population. Among anticipated reforms are a clear separation of municipal and state property to increase local governments' financial independence, and transferring health, education, and social policy to local self-governing authorities. The government has signed the European Charter of Local Self-Government.

3. Are subnational officials chosen in free and fair elections? Local elections in 2,954 constituencies (2,686 communes, 182 towns, six districts, and 80 municipalities) were held on June 2, 1996, (with subsequent run-offs) under a system of uninominal elections for mayor and a list-based system for local and country councilors. The PDSR received 24.49 percent of the vote, winning 2,742 mayoralties. The CDR, won 26.25 percent, followed by the Social Democratic Union with 13.5 percent. The PDSR won 23.8 percent of the local councilor posts, the USD 15 percent, and the CDR 13.4 percent. The CDR won the most county councilor posts, followed by the PDSR and USD. Voter turnout was 56.5 percent. There were irregularities and the elections were poorly organized. In Bucharest, 20 percent of the ballots were invalidated.

4. Do executive and legislative bodies operate openly and with transparency? Is draft legislation easily accessible to the media and the public? The constitution does not contain any provisions for publicity and transparency regarding the presidency, but the president holds press conferences and his office releases information. The government press office's role, by law, is to coordinate and support "effective actions of a nature to ensure that the activity of the Government of Romania is known." This includes weekly press conferences, as well as daily briefings, and communiqués. There is no other regulation describing to the citizen the possibility of exercising the constitutional right of requesting and receiving information of public interest from the government. All non-classified debates in the Senate and Chamber of Deputies are transcribed and published in the *Official Gazette of Romania*. Parliamentary sessions are open to the public, but meetings of parliamentary commissions and committees are not. In terms of local administration, Law 69/1991 contains provisions related to transparency and the right to information. The functioning of local councils and county councils are governed by some common rules. Under Article 24, "the agenda is made known to the inhabitants of the commune or the town through the local press or other means of publicity;" "the sessions of the local council are public, except when the councilors decide, with a majority vote, that the session should proceed behind closed doors;" and "budget-related issues will always be discussed in a public session." Under Article 36, "the works of the council may be attended, without voting rights, by the prefect, the chairman of the county council, their representatives, parliamentarians, as well as other invited guests whose presence is deemed necessary."

5. Do municipal governments have sufficient revenues to carry out their duties? Do municipal governments have control over their own local budgets? Do they raise revenues autonomously or from the central state budget? Grant transfers from the Central Budget account for over 80 percent of local revenue. The new government elected in 1996 has promised to increase the level of financial independence for local self-governing authorities. Local authorities can collect local taxes, which account for a small part of the overall budget. Local delivery of social welfare services, health, and education have been hampered by centralized financing. The United Nations Development Program (UNDP), U.S. AID, the European Union (PHARE programs), and the European Bank for Reconstruction and Development are among international institutions assisting local government with public administration and infrastructure development and helping utilities and public institutions raise revenues through tariffs and taxes, making them less reliant on central government grant transfers.

6. Do the elected local leaders and local civil servants know how to manage municipal governments effectively? Competent management remains a problem. The government has pledged that civil servants will be given incentives to improve their performance and reiterated support for a civil service law. As of March 31, 1998, however, no new law had been adopted. Key problems tend to be a lack of coordination, coherence, continuity, policy-making and management capacities, and weak accountability system. The UNDP reported in 1998 that "the institutional capacities of self-government authorities are weak. Professionalism of local self-government staff will be a requirement for self-governing authorities to be able to handle their new responsibilities. Furthermore, the development of a new training system for permanent local officials will have to be developed."

7. When did the constitutional/legislative changes on local power come into effect? Has there been reform of the civil service code/system? Are local civil servants employees of the local or central government? Law No. 69/91 on Public Administration has not been significantly amended. A Civil Service Code has not been adopted. Local councils and mayors are autonomous from the central government. A government-appointed prefect supervises the public services of local units of central government institutions. Technically, civil servants are employed by the central government.

Rule of Law 4.25/7

1. Is there a post-Communist constitution? How does the judicial system interpret and enforce the constitution? Are there specific examples of judicial enforcement of the constitution in the last year? Romania adopted a post-Communist constitution endorsed by referendum in December 1991. The constitution establishes the country as a multiparty state with a bicameral parliamentary system, a directly elected president, and a separate judiciary. The Constitutional Court interprets and enforces the constitution. The court consists of nine justices appointed for nine years: three by the Senate; three by the Chamber of Deputies; and three by the president. Judges may not serve in any other public or private office, except that of professor in higher education. In July 1992, the first nine judges of the Constitutional Court were elected for terms of office of three, six, and nine years. In April 1997, a group of 59 opposition deputies challenged the constitutionality of Article 3 of a new Privatization Law on the distribution of stakes in banking companies. The court ruled the law was constitutional.

2. Does the constitutional framework provide for human rights? Do human rights include business and property rights? The constitution delineates a broad array of human rights, including freedoms of the press, expression, movement, conscience, and equality under law. The right to own private property is guaranteed. Subsequent laws have allowed foreigners to own property and establish businesses.

3. Has there been basic reform of the criminal code/criminal law? Who authorizes searches and issues warrants? Are suspects and prisoners beaten or abused? Are there excessive delays in the criminal justice system? The Communist-era criminal code was replaced by the 1996 Penal Code, which widened the scope of the penal law by adding statutes dealing with felonies such as money-laundering. Controversial components included Article 200, which punished public homosexual relations (the article was upheld by the Constitutional Court); Articles 205 and 206 on libel which opponents said would restrict press freedom and freedom of expression; and Article 238 of offense to public authorities. The constitution provides protection against the search of a residence without a warrant, but this protection is subordinate to "national security or public order." Prosecutors and courts can issue warrants. Security officials may enter a residence without proper authorization from a prosecutor if they deem a threat to national security to be "imminent." One problem with the judiciary is that the Prosecutor's Office still has vast powers and is still a virtually unaccountable institution. A new law curtailed certain powers of the prosecutor general, including the right to overturn court decisions. The law forbids detention for anyone for more than 24 hours without an arrest order from a prosecutor, who may order detention for up to 30 days. Police, who fall under the responsibility of the Ministry of the Interior, often fail to inform citizens of their rights. Police are allowed to hold and question minors for 30 days without restriction. There have been only sporadic reports of prisoner abuses and beatings in police stations and prisons, where conditions are poor. A shortage of trained judges and court personnel has caused delays in court proceedings.

4. Do most judges rule fairly and impartially? Do many remain from the Communist era? Judges are underpaid and generally underqualified, and many are holdovers from the Communist era. Although judges, who are appointed by the president on the proposal of the 15-member Higher Council of the Judiciary, generally rule impartially on civic and petty criminal cases, they are subject to political pressures as well as bribery. Several projects initiated by major international organizations, foundations, and Western governments focus on improving law education and training reform.

5. Are the courts free of political control and influence? Are the courts linked directly to the Ministry of Justice or any other executive body? Under a 1992 law, Romania has a four-tier legal system: the Supreme Court of Justice; courts of appeal; county courts and the Court of the Municipality of Bucharest; and courts of first instance. Under the 1992 law, judges were appointed, promoted, and transferred by the 15-member Higher Council of the Judiciary which is elected for four-year terms by the two chambers of parliament. The members of the council are selected from among the judges of the Supreme Court, public prosecutors, and judges and prosecutors from the Court of Appeals of Bucharest. To diminish the politicization of the process, a 1997 revision of the law called for the Minister of Justice — not parliament — to appoint the members of the Higher Council. Decisions by the Constitutional Court can be overturned by a two-thirds vote in parliament, which undermines the court's effectiveness and independence.

6. What proportion of lawyers are in private practice? How does this compare with the previous year? Most lawyers are employed by the state, but many are in private practice in corporate and commercial law. While precise comparative figures are unavailable, most major cities have bar associations and several areas have regional judges associations.

7. Does the state provide public defenders? The constitution provides that every person has the right to an attorney. The Penal Code requires that an attorney be appointed for a defendant who cannot afford legal representation. In practice, the local bar association provides attorneys to indigents and is compensated the by Ministry of Justice.

8. Are there effective anti-bias/discrimination laws, including protection of ethnic minority rights? The constitution and laws nominally guarantee minority rights. Ethnic Hungarians are estimated to number 1.6 million, and the Roma (Gypsy) population may be as high as 2 million. The UMDR, a Hungarian-based party, has 36 seats in parliament. The Consultative Council for National Minorities, established in 1993, was renamed the Department for the Protection of National Minorities. In 1997, controversial amendments to the education law which struck down provisions that would have allowed the teaching of Romanian geography and history in the native tongue of minorities raised concerns. In December 1997, the Senate, at the urging of Senator George Pruteanu, chairman of the Romanian Senate Education Committee, voted that Romania's history and geography should be taught in Romanian. The UMDR called for Pruteanu's ouster, while Romanian nationalist parties came to his defense. In March 1998, Pruteanu and the press were banned from attending a session of the Chamber of Deputies Education Commission discussing the law, the fate of which remained undecided as of March 31, 1998. The Roma continue to be subjected to societal discrimination, harassment, and violence.

Corruption C

1. What is the magnitude of official corruption in the civil service? Must an average citizen pay a bribe to a bureaucrat in order to receive a service? What services are subject to bribe requests — for example, university entrance, hospital admission, telephone installation, obtaining a license to operate a business, applying for a passport or other official documents? What is the average salary of civil servants at various levels? Corruption is quite extensive in the civil service, particularly in the customs service, municipal zoning offices, local commercial offices, and government procurement. Sectors particularly prone to corruption are health, communication, heavy industry, construction, transportation, banking, and retailing. Demands for bribes have been known to rise to the level of harassment. Small and medium-sized businesses with little political clout are especially vulnerable. Foreign investors cite corruption as one of the two major hurdles to doing business in Romania.

Recorded cases of corruption increased 150 percent in the first nine months of 1997 compared to the same period in 1996. This may be due to increased reporting of incidents rather than an actual increase in corruption.

2. Do top policy-makers (the president, ministers, vice-ministers, top court justices, and heads of agencies and commissions) have direct ties to businesses? How strong are such connections and what kinds of businesses are these? President Constantinescu and former Prime Minister Ciorbea do not have direct ties to business, and are widely lauded for their personal honesty and "clean hands." In fact, Constantinescu and the CDR swept to victory on their promises of launching an anti-corruption campaign. State Police Chief Pavel Abraham was alleged, however, to have received preferential loans from Romania's Foreign Trade Bank, which has been linked to a separate corruption investigation. Abraham was fired in September 1997, ostensibly for "lack of interest" in his job.

Iliescu's ex-Communist PDSR was considered extremely corrupt by both domestic and international observers.

3. Do laws requiring financial disclosure and disallowing conflict of interest exist? Have publicized anticorruption cases been pursued? To what conclusion? Enforcement of anti-corruption laws has been spotty in the past. While low and mid-level bureaucrats have been prosecuted for corruption, no senior officials have been convicted.

The turnover in government has resulted in some apparent changes. For the first time, a judge is being investigated on charges of bribery. In November 1997, a former defense minister and general, Victor Athanasiae Stanculescu, was put on trial with seven other defendants. They were accused of embezzling $8 million in connection with the import of high-tech telephones in 1990. Nevertheless, in September, President Constantinescu complained that economic power was still in the hands of corrupt bureaucrats linked with the former government. Constantinescu said these bureaucrats were still making money through illicit dealings in merchant marine trade, fertilizer exports, and smuggled fuel shipments to Yugoslavia.

In an earlier development in July 1997, the government's Control (Audit) Department charged Foreign Minister Adrian Severin and Transportation Minister Traian Basescu with involvement in illegal dealings involving state-owned apartments. The department also accused Petre Roman, chairman of the Democratic Party, and the junior member of the ruling coalition. The accused denied the charges, which they called politically motivated.

4. What major anticorruption initiatives have been implemented? How often are anticorruption laws and decrees adopted? A high-profile national anti-corruption campaign was initiated by President Constantinescu in January 1997. He became chairman of a newly-established National Council against Corruption and Organized Crime. The council has powers of investigation and arrest, both of which have been employed. It has local representatives in each of Romania's 42 regions.

The national police force has fired a quarter of its county chiefs since Constantinescu came to power. In August 1997, Constantinescu appointed Sorin Moisescu as the new Prosecutor General, succeeding Nicolae Cochinescu who was fired on the recommendation of the justice minister Valeriu Stoica. Cochinescu, an Iliescu appointee, was accused of blocking the new anti-corruption initiative. Victor Ciorbea launched an anti-corruption campaign in 1996 as mayor of Bucharest.

5. How do major corruption-ranking organizations like Transparency International rate this country? In July 1997, Transparency International ranked Romania 37th out of 52 countries it surveyed for its Corruption Perception Index. Its CPI score was 3.44 on a 1-10 scale, where a lower score is worse corruption. Romania was not rated in 1996.

Privatization 4.50/7

1. What percentage of the GDP comes from private ownership? What percentage of the labor force is employed in the private sector? How large is the informal sector of the economy? The percentage of the GDP that comprises the private sector has changed significantly in recent years. In 1997, it was 55 percent of GDP compared to 35 percent in 1994 (according to the EBRD). In 1996, 47 percent of the workforce was in the private sector.

The informal economy is enormous. Virgil Magureanu, the director of the Romanian Information Service, the domestic intelligence agency, has estimated the informal economy at 35-38 percent of GDP. Outside observers contend it is as much as 40-50 percent of GDP.

2. What major privatization legislation has been passed? What were its substantive features? The prerequisites for privatization were established through the corporatization of state-owned companies in 1990 (Law 15/1990). The National Agency for Privatization was set up in December 1991.

The 1991 Privatization Law established the State Ownership Fund (SOF) and five Private Ownership Funds (POF). The SOF was granted 70 percent ownership in 6,400 commercialized enterprises, while the POFs were given the remaining 30 percent. The law specified that shares in the POFs would be freely distributed to all adult Romanian citizens residing in the country.

In 1995, mass privatization received a boost when the government issued vouchers to citizens to be used for direct subscription and transfer of shares in a wide list of commercial companies as well as the POFs. Furthermore, the amount of share capital to be freely distributed was raised to 60 percent. The distribution of vouchers ended in October 1996. The POFs were reorganized in November 1996 into Private Investment Funds (open-ended mutual funds).

A lack of political will and delay by the SOF slowed the privatization process immensely. By the end of 1996 (coinciding with the turnover in political power), the State Ownership Fund had privatized only 45 percent of the enterprises scheduled for privatization, most of them small enterprises. Only 24 percent of medium-sized and 13 percent of large enterprises had been privatized.

To accelerate the process, the new government placed the SOF under the authority of the Ministry of Reform in April 1997 and created a Privatization Ministry in December. This move began to pay off in 1997, when 1,304 companies were privatized. Eighty-three percent of these were small, 13 percent medium, and 4 percent (50 firms) were large. In 1997, the SOF began to sell its minority stakes through the stock exchange.

In June 1997, all the *regimes autonomes* (large industrial monopolies) were commercialized and ordered to be privatized.

Delays in the privatization of large-scale enterprises, especially state-owned monopolies, were due in part to overly bureaucratic procedures of the SOF and also in part to political infighting in the Ciorbea cabinet. Following the resignation of that cabinet in April 1998, it is expected that the privatization of large scale enterprises will accelerate. The 1998 privatization program, approved in March, is ambitious; 1,600 companies are scheduled to be sold off, raising $1 billion in revenue. $180 million had been raised as of April 1998.

As of June 1998, the SOF had total or partial ownership of 5,500 enterprises. Of these, only the 700 largest will be privatized by the central SOF office, while the rest will be sold by its local affiliates in Romania's 42 counties.

The privatization of Romtelecom, the state telecommunications provider, has been among the most eagerly awaited in Romania since reforms began. The privatization of a 35 percent portion to a strategic investor was announced in March 1998, and an initial public offering for 60 percent will be made in September-October. The privatization of the Romanian Postal Service began in April 1998.

3. What proportion of agriculture, housing and land, industry, and business and services is in private hands? Agricultural privatization has been fairly extensive, with 83 percent of farmland reverting to private ownership. The private sector accounts for 87 percent of agricultural production. The state owns the large agricultural intermediaries, as well as the national distribution and storage companies. Livestock farming is still state-dominated.

Tenants in state-owned housing had the option of buying the apartments they resided in for very favorable terms (low real estate prices due to depreciation and long-term credit carrying low interest), and most have taken advantage of this opportunity.

Approximately 98 percent of small trade and service activities are now in the private sector. In the industrial sector, however, only 24 percent of the output is produced by the private sector. Only 2,000 of the 6,300 state firms existing in 1990 had been privatized by the end of 1996.

4. What has been the extent of insider (management, labor, and nomenklatura) participation in the privatization process? What explicit and implicit preferences have been awarded to insiders? Insiders have been the dominant participants in the privatization process, especially in "small privatization." About 80 percent of the firms privatized in Romania were done through management and employee buy-outs.

5. How much public awareness of and support for privatization has there been? What major interest groups oppose and advocate privatization? The Democratic Convention parties as well as the Democratic Union of Magyars in Romania are strongly pro-privatization. The Union of Social Democracy parties are moderately in favor of it. The formerly ruling Party of Social Democracy of Romania is not strongly for or against privatization.

Macroeconomics 4.50/7

1. Has the taxation system been reformed? (What areas have and have not been overhauled? To what degree are taxpayers complying? Is tax compliance difficult to achieve? Has the level of revenues increased? Is the revenue-collection body overburdened? What is the overall tax burden?) The transition to a market economy has made reform of the taxation system both necessary and possible. A value-added tax (VAT) was introduced in July 1993. Its basic rate is 22 percent, increased from 18 percent in February 1998. There is a reduced rate of nine percent for foodstuffs, agricultural raw materials, and services. A small number of products and services such as bread, fuel, and electricity for domestic use are exempt from VAT at the retail level. Excise taxes exist on numerous types of goods, such as liquor, tobacco, luxury items, and electronic equipment.

A new corporate tax structure was introduced in January 1995. The corporate profit tax is 38 percent. Firms with more than 299 employees and 10 billion *Lei* in annual turnover are entitled to index profit and payments to inflation and carry forward losses for a period of five years after the end of the financial year in which they were incurred. Smaller firms can only carry losses forward for 18 months from the day they were incurred. Some companies are taxed at a higher or lower rate. These include entertainment and gambling firms (60 percent), and companies which derive at least 80 percent of their income from agriculture (25 percent). Taxable profits of foreign entities are taxed at an additional rate of 6.2 percent (to a total of 44.2 percent).

Social security contributions paid by employers range from 23 to 33 percent of the employee's salary, depending on the job category. Other payroll taxes include a five percent unemployment fund contribution and a two percent health fund contribution. Employees pay a three percent pension fund tax and a one percent unemployment fund tax. Income taxes range from five percent to 60 percent in several brackets, and the average income is taxed at 28 percent. These high income tax rates have given impetus to the development of the shadow economy.

Local taxes are generally composed of an annual tax (1-1.5 percent) on the book value of buildings and various user fees for such things as the issuance of government documents.

While actual tax rates are clearly set by the government, payment procedures are very complex and cumbersome. For companies, the tax system is much too complicated, requiring monthly reports and very complicated submitting procedures. If a firm fails to submit its reports on time, it can be liable to large, although not always specified, fines at the discretion of the Tax Department of the Ministry of Finances.

The total tax burden is just below 30 percent of GDP. The VAT provides 30.8 percent of the government's revenue, income taxes 21.6 percent, profit taxes 18.3 percent, and excise taxes 12.6 percent.

Tax evasion rose 150 percent in the first nine months of 1997, compared with the same period in 1996.

2. Does fiscal policy encourage private savings, investment and earnings? (Has there been any reform/alteration of revenue and budget policies? How large are budget deficits and overall debt? Is the financing of the social insurance/pension system sustainable? What proportion of the budget is taken up by subsidies to firms and individuals?) The Iliescu government was noted for its profligate spending. Spending was used to raise the government's popularity to the detriment of the state's finances. Unprofitable state enterprises were propped up with subsidies and not allowed to fail. Deficits were financed by printing money, fueling inflation.

The advent of the new Constantinescu/Ciorbea government and its radical reform policy brought a much greater degree of fiscal discipline. The budget deficit in 1997 was 3.7 percent of GDP, a significant improvement from 5.8 percent (actually nearly 10 percent when off-budget subsidies are included) in 1996. The new government's reformist agenda led to the April 1997 IMF approval of a new $430 million loan agreement for Romania. This amount is to be disbursed in four tranches, subject to fulfillment of conditionality agreements by the Romanian government. Failure to conform to the structural reform component of the agreement led the IMF to suspend the loan in October.

By the end of 1996, Romania's external debt was approximately $6.9 billion. Servicing domestic debt cost 3.6 percent in 1997, rising to an estimated 4.5 percent in 1998.

Subsidies have been large — 2.1 percent of GDP in 1996 — and were done in a non-transparent fashion through the central bank. Beginning in 1997, all government subsidies, such as those for agriculture, began to be financed transparently from the state budget. Almost 500 public corporations receive subsides, although the government's goal is to reduce this number to 44. Subsidy levels were substantially reduced in 1997.

The pension system is funded on a pay-as-you-go basis out of payroll taxes and budgetary transfers. In December 1997, Labor Minister Alexandru Athanasiu announced a set of pension reforms which would introduce private pension accounts.

3. Has there been banking reform? (Is the central bank independent? What are its responsibilities? Is it effective in setting and/or implementing monetary policy? What is the actual state of the private banking sector? Does it conform to international standards? Are depositors protected?) Romania initiated reform in its banking system by moving to a two-tier structure and by divesting the National Bank (NBR) of all commercial banking activities. Its main functions are monetary and foreign exchange policymaking, banking system supervision, international reserves (gold, foreign currency, special drawing rights), and the issue of currency.

The NBR has only become relatively independent in the past year. The NBR was forced to provide subsidized credit in the amount of 2.6 percent of GDP in 1996. This practice was abolished in 1997. In May 1997, the government approved three draft laws intended to further enhance its independence.

Interest rates were deregulated in 1991. The number of commercial banks increased from five in 1990 to 33 in 1996, eight of which are branches of foreign banks. Of the 25 Romanian banks, five are entirely state-owned, ten are of mixed-ownership, and ten are private. Despite the increasing role of the private sector in banking, the wholly and party state owned banks dominate the banking sector, accounting for over 70 percent of financial activity. The total assets of commercial banks reached $12.67 billion in June 1995.

All commercial banks are members of the NBR's domestic interbank payment system, which has improved the efficiency of interbank transactions. Most transactions are in cash or through the payment system, as checking is almost unknown. It can take over two weeks to transfer money from a Romanian bank account to a West European or North American account.

The Romanian banking sector is among the weakest in the region. Bank lending as a share of GDP is less than 15 percent, compared with 66 percent in the Czech Republic. Overdue credits as a share of total nongovernment credits were 26.3 percent in September 1997, an increase from 4.3 percent from the beginning of 1993. Low liquidity ratios plague banks.

Two major private banks — Dacia Felix Bank and Credit Bank — failed in 1996. The NBR attempted to bail them out with enormous subsidies while waiting for foreign investors to ultimately salvage them. A year later, no such investors appeared and the NBR initiated liquidation procedures against the two banks. Both banks have appealed this decision in court.

A Bank Privatization Law was adopted in May 1997. It transfers ownership shares from the POFs to the SOF for the purpose of selling them. Nevertheless, actual privatization has lagged. The government intends to privatize three state banks — the Romanian Development Bank, Banc Post, and Banca Agricola. The privatization of these banks has lagged, however, due to their bad debt positions.

In 1996, the National Bank set up a compulsory deposit insurance system in order to protect the population's deposits at commercial banks. Parliament passed a bill that would protect private deposits up to 10 million lei per person per bank (approximately $1,300), an amount to be indexed to inflation.

NBR has also taken steps to identify risky firms and individuals. Romania has very little in the way of credit analysis and risk assessment. In November 1996, a new surveillance arm within NBR became operational. The Department of Banking Risks Pursuit is to develop "blacklists" of banks with financial problems or which are assuming unnecessary risks, e.g. lending without collateral, as well as of clients who have a poor borrowing record.

4. How sound is the national currency? (To what extent has inflation eroded its value? Is the value of the currency fixed or does it float? Is the currency convertible? How large are the hard currency reserves? Has exchange rate policy been stable and predictable?) The lei was freed from heavy regulation in early 1997. Under IMF pressure, it was unified and made convertible in July 1997. It is still not fully convertible on the current account for individuals or for capital exports.

Tight monetary policy led to a decline in inflation from 292 percent in 1993 to 27.8 percent in 1995, although it rose to 56.9 percent in 1996 and 150 percent in 1997 (much of this was due to the end of price controls). Inflation is expected to be almost as bad in 1998.

The lei's value has been continually depreciating since 1990. The average 1996 exchange rate dropped 51.5 percent from 1995 levels. In 1997, the lei fell from 4,000 in the beginning of the year to 8,000 at the end. The high inflation rate, however, has meant that the lei actually appreciated in real terms over the year against the dollar. Foreign exchange reserves were $1.1 billion as of April 1997.

5. Is there a functioning capital market infrastructure? (Are there existing or planned commodities, bond and stock markets? What are the mechanisms for investment and lending? What government bodies have authority to regulate capital markets?) The Bucharest Stock Exchange (BSE) began functioning in June 1995. Trading volume reached $1.1 million per session in May 1997, but only 76 companies are traded as a result of fairly strict listing criteria. In August 1997, total market capitalization was $745 million, or a very low 2.5 percent of GDP.

The RASDAQ over-the-counter market (modeled on the U.S. NASDAQ) was established in September 1996, partly to handle the outcome of the mass privatization effort. Over 5,400 companies are listed on the RASDAQ, and daily trading volume was $1.2 million in May 1997. Total market capitalization was about $2 billion in mid-1997, or seven percent of GDP.

The volume of trading has remained low for several reasons. First, there has been a general lack of confidence by both foreign and domestic investors in these markets. Legislation is lacking which governs foreign portfolio investment, although the government submitted a draft law to address this deficiency in April 1997. Foreign investors have to pay a 1.5 percent tax every time they buy transferable securities.

A securities law was adopted in 1994. It established the National Securities Commission which is responsible for regulating primary and secondary securities markets and their participants.

The Commission established the BSE as a public entity, however, the BSE is effectively governed by its participant private sector members which form the Stock Exchange Association. It has share registry as well as settlement and clearing departments. An Exchange Arbitration Court exists to settle disputes.

In February 1997, the Romanian Commercial Bank launched Romania's first corporate bond, valued at $75 million. A secondary market for government securities is not well developed, though in April 1997 regulations regarding this area were overhauled. The Romanian Commodities Exchange was established in December 1992. Five regional exchanges were established a year later. Trading volume has been thin. There are no capital gains taxes in Romania.

Microeconomics 4.50/7

1. Are property rights guaranteed? (Are there both formal and de facto protections of private real estate and intellectual property? Is there a land registry with the authority and capability to ensure accurate recording of who owns what? What are the procedures for expro-

priation, including measures for compensation and challenge? Have any seizures taken place?) Article 41 of the constitution guarantees the protection of private property. Mineral and air rights are excluded. As a result of Law 18/1995, a land registry was established, although it scarcely functions.

A law protecting intellectual property was passed in early 1996. A new Romanian Office for Copyright Protection also has been established. Romania is a party to numerous international conventions protecting intellectual property rights. Unfortunately, these laws are not respected. After initial enforcement, piracy of software, music, and movies has resumed.

2. To what extent have prices been liberalized? What subsidies remain? The government removed price controls slowly, fearing social unrest and political instability. By mid-1995, however, only three percent of prices on goods and services were controlled. These included prices on energy, foodstuffs, and agricultural products. In early 1997, these controls were lifted.

3. Is it possible to own and operate a business? (Has there been legislation regarding the formation, dissolution and transfer of businesses, and is the law respected? Do there exist overly cumbersome bureaucratic hurdles that effectively hinder the ability to own and dispose of a business? Are citizens given access to information on commercial law? Is the law applied fairly? Does regulation (or licensing requirements) impose significant costs on business and consumers? Do they create significant barriers to entry and seriously hamper competition?) Law 31/1990 regarding the formation, dissolution, and transfer of businesses is generally respected. Its provisions, as well as those of its more recent amendments, not to mention the tax and customs laws, do not particularly help businesses to operate. All laws and regulations are published in the *Official Gazette of Romania* up to six months after adoption.

Forming a joint-stock company costs between $500 and $1,000 and takes between one and three months. Routine business activities, like obtaining zoning permits, property titles, licenses, and utility hook-ups, are burdensome and time-consuming. The lack of sophisticated equipment to process records (especially fiscal records) makes it very difficult to create and run a business, even if the government is not doing anything deliberately to hamper its activities.

A new bankruptcy code was adopted in late 1995 which meets minimum Western standards. It has not, however, been applied against the large loss-making state enterprises.

4. Are courts effective, transparent, efficient, and quick in reaching decisions on property and contract disputes? What alternative mechanisms for adjudicating disputes exist? Legal reform began in 1992. The first level of jurisdiction is the Ordinary Court, which can hear cases limited to no more than 10 million lei. The second level of jurisdiction are the County Courts and the Bucharest City Court, which hear cases above the 10 million lei level. Above these is the Court of Appeal. The highest level is the Supreme Court. Appeals may be made to higher levels of the courts. The wait for a trial averages between seven months and two years in commercial centers. Judgements are executed within seven months to one year afterwards.

Romanian judges, on the whole, have little experience with legal matters in a modern market economy, nor an understanding of international business issues. In the past, courts have been known to make biased decisions and to have been influenced by the executive branch.

As a result, third-party arbitration is an important procedure in adjudicating business disputes. Two important non-government arbitration courts exist. These are the Commercial Arbitration Court administered by the Chamber of Commerce and Industry, and the International Commercial Arbitration Court (which is a non-governmental entity). Romania is a member of the 1958 New York Convention which regularizes recognition and enforcement of foreign arbitration awards. Romania is also a signatory of the European Convention on International Commercial Arbitration of 1961 and the ICSID Convention of 1965. Arbitration decisions are enforceable in Romanian courts.

5. Is business competition encouraged? (Are monopolistic practices limited in law and in practice? If so, how? To what degree is "insider" dealing a hindrance to open competition? Are government procurement policies open and unbiased?) In April 1996, Law 31/1996 on competition was promulgated. This adds to Law 11/1991 on unfair competition, its purpose being to protect and stimulate competition for the benefit of consumers. This is the first time that the concept of "competition" has been defined by law. In January 1997, a new competition law came into force. A Council of Competition has been empowered to investigate anti-competitive practices.

Insider dealing is prohibited by law. Government Decision 156/1992 mandates a generally nondiscriminatory procurement policy. However, it does allow a ten percent price advantage for domestic suppliers.

6. To what extent has international trade been liberalized? To what degree has there been simplification/overhaul of customs and tariff procedures, and are these applied fairly? What informal trade barriers exist? The state monopoly on foreign trade was abolished in 1990, and tariffs with low average rates have become the main instrument of trade policy. The authorities have avoided the use of quantitative restrictions on imports despite difficulties in the balance of payments. A number of export quotas and bans on exports do exist (applicable especially to subsidized goods or those that were subject to price controls), but have steadily been dropping in number. Custom duties range from zero to 60 percent. In July 1995, custom duties were raised on basic raw and processed foods, including meat, butter, sunflower oil, and confectionery. Excise duties range from 15 to 300 percent and are levied on alcoholic drinks, tobacco goods, certain oil and gas products, and "luxuries."

The weighted average of customs duties is 11.7 percent. EU and EFTA members are granted preferential tariff treatment relative to non-members like the United States. In 1997, agricultural tariffs were strongly reduced from an average 67 percent to 22 percent.

Unfortunately, a common feature of Romanian trade policy is the pervasive "temporary" departures from statutory tariff levels. The frequency with which tariffs change presents difficulties for traders who cannot make long-term plans based on the published tariff levels. In 1995, half of Romanian imports were subject to such "special arrangements," making the published tariff schedule partly irrelevant. There are four free trade zones in Romania: Sulina, Constanta-Sud, Galati, and Braila. Romania is a member of the World Trade Organization, and has signed agreements with the EU and the EFTA. It joined the Central European Free Trade Agreement in July 1997. Customs procedures are burdensome and many officials are corrupt. The government has frequently issued very short term customs exemptions for certain goods. The reasons for granting such exemptions are sometimes obviously based on a hidden agenda, and as a result, officials are often accused of corruption.

Import licenses and quotas have been eliminated. Sanitary and safety standards are in place. While these are generally in line with ISO and Western European standards, they are not always applied in a transparent fashion.

Instead of encouraging exports, the government has chosen to try to limit imports, mainly through customs taxes. This policy failed for several reasons, among them the control of the exchange rate, which caused a blockage on the Romanian currency market. On the other hand, the same control of the exchange rate through an overvaluation of the national currency discouraged the exporters. Exporting is also particularly difficult because most markets require a level of quality that Romanian industry finds difficult to meet.

Export restrictions are extensive. In 1996, 52 tariff lines were subject to complete prohibition, and 178 to export quotas. Officially, these are deemed "temporary" but have been renewed annually. Customs duties are not, however, assessed on exports. There is no evidence that Romania is trade-dependent on one or two other countries.

7. To what extent has foreign investment and capital flow been encouraged or constrained? Legislation generally ensures that foreign investors are treated the same as domestic investors, including in the area of access to privatization. Foreign investors are allowed to wholly own firms, as well as to repatriate 100 percent of their profits. They are also allowed to own land. Visa, residence, and work-permit requirements are not discriminatory or overly burdensome.

Capital flow for investment is not restricted, though foreign investors have to pay a 1.5 percent tax every time they buy transferable securities.

Foreigner investors are granted incentives on the basis of a few conditions. For example, investments over $50 million are granted customs exemptions and tax holidays. Further incentives for foreign investors that put them at a distinct advantage vis-a-vis their domestic counterparts were enacted in the form of a government decree in June 1997. After a high-profile battle with parliament, these extra incentives were removed in December.

Since the transition, foreign investment has amounted to a meager $3.5 billion compared to the $17 billion in the much smaller Hungary. Despite the attractions of the Romanian market, foreign investors were turned off by major problems engendered by the previous government, notably an intrusive bureaucracy, much corruption, and the lack of enthusiasm for foreign investment. The new government's reform program has already changed attitudes: in the first quarter of 1997, foreign capital increased 35 percent over the first quarter of 1996.

Article 5 of the Foreign Investment Law stipulates that foreign investments are not subject to expropriation. An exception is made for the "public interest," but only under due process of law and with "prompt, adequate, and effective" compensation.

Regulations such as a prohibition on foreign companies owning land make investors wary. Although the government pursues foreign investment and trade, it has done little to simplify procedures.

8. Has there been reform of the energy sector? (To what degree has the energy sector been restructured? Is the energy sector more varied, and is it open to private competition? Is the country overly dependent on one or two other countries for energy [including whether exported fuels must pass through one or more countries to reach markets]?) There has been only moderate reform of the energy sector and most of that has occurred only recently.

Until recently, energy prices were controlled by the government and were heavily subsidized for both industry and consumers. As a result, energy consumption per capita was among the highest in the region. Previous attempts to raise energy prices resulted in payments arrears to producers. In 1997, however, energy prices were doubled and reached world levels by the end of the year.

The privatization of the state-owned energy monopolies, known as the *regies autonomes*, has been eagerly anticipated by investors. These include Romgaz, the gas provider, and Renel, the electricity provider. These are already being restructured in preparation for a final sale. Romoil, the national oil producer, is also being reading for privatization.

Romania relies on imports of crude oil and natural gas from Russia and the Middle East. These raw materials are then processed in huge refineries at high cost due to old technology. Recently, Romania signed an agreement with Russia regarding imports of gas and oil. In 1996, Romania rejected an offer from the Norwegian Government to connect it to Hungary, Germany, and Norway through a gas distribution pipe system. A parallel network of private gas pumps has appeared and is developing.

Romania has large deposits of oil and gas. In 1996, it produced 6.5 million tons of crude oil and 18.1 billion cubic meters of natural gas. Nevertheless, 7.1 million tons of crude oil and 7 billion cubic meters of gas had to be imported to meet demand. Its proven oil reserves measure 30 years.

In 1992, the refining industry was restructured, and excess capacity of 9 million tons was closed. Petrom, a new national operator, will be established to integrate the production and processing of oil, and further reduce excess refining capacity.

A World Bank/EBRD project to increase oil and gas production through new technology has already begun. Investment by Western Atlas and M.I. Drilling have already raised Romanian production. Other major foreign companies expressing interest in investing are Shell, Amoco, and British Petroleum. Foreign investment in the oil sector amounts to over $130 million.

The nuclear power plant at Cernavoda began operating in 1996, but soon had to be shut down for restructuring. It resumed production in December and its output is expected to account for eight percent of Romania's total energy.

RUSSIA

Freedom in the World Ratings, 1989-1998

	1989-90	1990-91	1991-92	1992-93	1993-94	1994-95	1995-96	1996-97	1997-98
Political Rights	-	-	3	3	3	3	3	3	3
Civil Liberties	-	-	3	4	4	4	4	4	4
Status	-	-	PF	PF	PF	PF	PF	PF	PF

Polity: Transitional
Economy: Transitional
Population: 147,700,000
PPP: $6,140
Ethnic Groups: Russian (82 percent), over 100 ethnic groups
Capital: Moscow

Political Process 3.50/7

1. When did national legislative elections occur? Were they free and fair? How were they judged by domestic and international election monitoring organizations? Who composes the government? Elections to the lower house (State Duma) were held on December 17, 1995. Under the electoral law, each voter cast two votes: one for a single candidate and one for a party. Half of the 450 members were elected in single-seat constituencies; the other 225 were elected according to party lists. 43 parties gained access to the ballot but only four surpassed the five-percent barrier to gain representation on the party list ballot. Final results according to the Central Electoral Committee were as follows: Communist Party of the Russian Federation (KPRF) 22.3 percent of the vote, 99 party-list seats, 58 single-candidate seats for a total of 157; Liberal Democratic Party of Russia (LDPR), 11.18 percent, 50, and 1 for a total of 51; Our Home is Russia, 10.13 percent, 45, and 10 for a total of 55; and Yabloko, 6.89 percent, 31, and 14 for a total of 45. Single-constituent seats went to the following parties: Agrarian Party, 20 seats; Power to the People, 9; Democratic Choice of Russia, 9; Congress of Russian Communities, 5; Women of Russia, 3; Working Russia, 1; Party of Sviatoslav Fyodorov, 1; other parties, 17; Independents, 77. Monitors from the Organization for Security and Cooperation in Europe (OSCE) and other international organizations found the elections were free and fair. Viktor Chernomyrdin was confirmed as Prime Minister after the vote, and was reappointed by President Boris Yeltsin on August 10, 1996, following the presidential election of June 16 and July 3. On March 23, 1998, President Yeltsin dismissed Chernomyrdin and the cabinet, then subsequently announced that 35-year-old Sergei Kiriyenko, a former Energy Minister, would become prime minister.

The first six months of 1997 were marked by a government reshuffle and the ascension of key reformers. Chief of Staff Anatoly Chubais, mastermind of the mass privatization drive and manager of President Yeltsin's re-election, was named deputy prime minister and finance minister responsible for day-to-day economic management, and Boris Nemtsov, a reformer as governor of Nizhny Novgorod, was made deputy prime minister for social affairs, housing, and reform of monopolies. Under an ambitious reform program, the deputy prime ministers forced out corrupt or conservative officials and chipped away at the power of Russia's natural monopolies and the powerful financial institutions, further exacerbating relations with a truculent parliament. After Chubais was weakened by accusations of accepting an exorbitant book fee, parliament threatened a non-confidence motion. In November 1997, Yeltsin fired Chubais's two top aides, and later in the month Chubais was stripped of his job as finance minister. Nemtsov was dismissed as energy minister. The shake-up was partly an effort by Yeltsin to mollify parliament and financial-industrial groups hostile to reform. In dismissing Prime Minister Chernomyrdin, President Yeltsin said he needed a new team that would concentrate more on economics than political infighting. Chernomyrdin is a leading contender in the presidential election scheduled in 2000.

2. When did presidential elections occur? Were they free and fair? Yeltsin was re-elected president in a July 1996 run-off, defeating Communist Party leader Gennady Zyuganov, 53.82 percent to 40.31 percent. In the first round, held June 16, Yeltsin got 35 percent to Zyuganov's 32 percent, with Alexander Lebed getting about 14 percent, Grigory Yavlinsky (Yabloko), nearly 8 percent, and Vladimir Zhirinovsky (LDPR) about 6 percent. Although international monitors for the Organization for Security and Cooperation in Europe deemed the election free and fair, Yeltsin — whose popularity ratings were in the single digits less than a year before the vote — was aided by powerful industrial-financial interests with extensive media holdings and influence. Yeltsin was first elected president of the Russian republic in June 1991, some six months before the Soviet Union collapsed.

3. Is the electoral system multiparty-based? Are there at least two viable political parties functioning at all levels of government? Article 13 of the 1993 constitution provides for a multiparty system and free elections. In parliament, parties have formed coalitions and blocs that often shift through the realignments of factions. After the 1995 parliamentary vote, the liberal-reform bloc, which includes Yabloko, Democratic Choice, Forward Russia and others, controlled 60 seats; the centrists, including Our Home is Russia and Women of Russia, among others, held 64 seats; the Communists-Nationalists, including the Communist party, the Liberal Democrats, the Agrarians, and others, accounted for 245 seats; other smaller parties, 4 seats; and independents, 77 seats. The larger parties, such as the Communists and the Agrarians, function at subnational levels.

4. How many parties have been legalized? Are any particular parties illegal? 43 parties contested the 1996 parliamentary elections, and more than 50 parties and groups are registered. There are several "unregistered" groups, mainly extremists on the left and right. In 1996, the State Duma passed a law stipulating that parties had to have at least 100 members to be recognized. Parties that seek violently to change the constitutional order and violate the territorial integrity of the Russian Federation are prohibited. Armed groups or parties that promote racial, ethnic, and religious hatred are also outlawed.

5. What proportion of the population belongs to political parties? Over the last few years, polls by the U.S. Information Society and Russian polling groups have consistently shown that Russians are disinclined to join political parties. A poll concerning parliamentary elections found that only 10 percent of respondents would pick a candidate on the basis of party affiliation. Voters do identify with certain parties or politicians based on voting patterns: in the 1996 parliamentary vote, the Communists polled 22 percent of the vote, Zhirinovsky's ultra-nationalist LDPR 11 percent, and Prime Minister Viktor Chernomyrdin's centrist Our Home is Russia just over 10 percent. The KPRF claims over 550,000 members; other parties range from the thousands to several hundred.

6. What has been the trend of voter turnout at the municipal, provincial and national levels in recent years? March 17, 1991, referendum on USSR: 75 percent; June 15, 1991 presidential election: 70 percent; April 25, 1993 referendum on Yeltsin's policies: 64.5 percent; December 12, 1993 parliamentary/constitutional election: 54 .8 percent. In March and April, 1994 elections were held for new, streamlined local legislatures in Russia's six *krais* and 49 oblasts, one autonomous oblast's ten autonomous *okrugs*, and two cities of federal importance, Moscow and St. Petersburg. (The 21 republics were left free to decide how to reform their legislatures). Turnouts varied widely (50 percent of eligible voters needed for valid elections) from over 50 percent to as low as 24 percent in some areas. In the June 16, 1996 presidential election, (first round), 72 percent; July (runoff), 68.89 percent. 1996 local elections: turnouts ranged from under 50 percent to 65 percent.

Civil Society 4.00/7

1. How many nongovernmental organizations (NGOs) have come into existence since 1988? What is the number of charitable/nonprofit organizations? Are there locally led efforts to increase philanthropy and volunteerism? What proportion of the population is active in private voluntary activity (from polling data)? According to a report at a May 1997 conference on NGO taxation sponsored by the U.S. based Center for Democracy, there are almost 100,000 NGOs registered in Russia, with 15,000 in Moscow and 4,000 in St. Petersburg. But, according to the report, only about 25-30 percent of them are active. NGOs include language, ecological, cultural, trade union and political movements, charitable organizations, business associations, independent bar associations, polling organizations, veteran's organizations, think tanks, women's and students' organizations, neighborhood associations, cooperatives, and advocacy groups. While all must register with the Ministry of Justice, they can do so in their regions. According to *The Chronicle of Philanthropy,* 17,000 to 35,000 charities have been created in Russia in the past decade; most are struggling due to lack of funds. The *Chronicle* cites a Russian poll that shows 74 percent of Russians could not name a single charity. There are locally led efforts to increase philanthropy and volunteerism. In March 1997, the Russian Volunteers Association called for a national effort to support charitable work. The association, created in 1996, consists of representatives from Irkutsk, Chita, and over a dozen other cities. Numerous humanitarian organizations have proliferated, often started and supported by Western and international institutions. While some of the larger financial-business concerns have funded youth clubs, charitable organizations, and non-political associations, businesses in Russia are struggling under high taxes and heavy regulation which stifle philanthropy, as does a lack of established philanthropic traditions and institutions.

2. What is the legal and regulatory environment for NGOs (i.e., ease of registration, legal rights, government regulation, taxation, procurement, access-to-information issues)? To what extent is NGO activism focused on improving the legal and regulatory environment? The 1993 constitution allows for the creation of nongovernmental organizations, which must be registered with the Ministry of Justice, according to the law. Other legislation governing NGOs include the Civil Code (1994) and a series of 1995 statutes: the Law on Non-Profit Organizations, the Law on Social Organizations, and the Law on Charitable Activities and Charitable Organizations. NGOs were active in planning these drafts. Local laws on concessional taxation for charitable organizations have been passed in St. Petersburg, Moscow, and other cities. Most NGOs, however, are not tax-exempt. NGOs do not generally face unreasonable bureaucratic obstacles in the larger cities. There are several NGOs dealing with improving the legal and regulatory environment for NGO development, among them the Agency for Social Information, the Center for International Cooperation, the Civic Initiatives Program, the Tomsk State University Center Supporting Non-Commercial Organizations, and many others.

3. What is the organizing capacity of NGOs? Do management structures clearly delineate authority and responsibility? Is information available on NGO management issues in the native language? Is there a core of experienced practitioners/trainers to serve as consultants and mentors to less developed organizations? Most larger NGOs, many of which are funded directly by or work closely with Western and international institutions, are well organized with clear management structures. They provide information on NGO development issues in Russian through the use of bulletins, reports, and media outreach. The Agency for Social Information (ASI), which has been supported by the Eurasia Foundation (U.S.), the European Foundation for Freedom of Expression (France) and other groups, prepares 80 weekly bulletins about NGO activities, conferences, and programs, as well as updates concerning legislation concerning NGOs. These reports appear in newspapers 10-12 times per week, on television programs, and periodicals with which the ASI has a contract. The U.S. based Center for Civil Society's *The Post-Soviet Handbook: A Guide to Grassroots Organizations and Internet Resources in the Newly Independent States* lists hundreds of well-established NGOs and humanitarian groups. Thanks largely to technical assistance, seminars, exchanges, and other programs offered by the European Union (PHARE, TACIS), the U.S. Agency for International Development, and Western NGOs, the NGO and voluntary sector is developing an ever-expanding network of NGO practitioners and trainers who can be utilized by less-developed groups.

4. Are NGOs financially viable? What is there tax status? Are they obliged to and do they typically disclose revenue sources? Do government procurement opportunities exist for private, not-for-profit providers of services? As in all of the Newly Independent States and East-Central Europe, most NGOs in Russia face the serious problem of finances and sustainability. According to Olga Starovojtova, a participant from St. Petersburg at a Center for Democracy May 1997 conference on NGOs: "the first problem of NGOs is money; the second — money; the third — money."

Most successful NGOs rely heavily if not exclusively on foreign foundation and government grants and programs. While some charitable organizations are tax-exempt, most NGOs are not, and the fact that Russia has yet to implement a comprehensive tax code further muddles the legal environment. NGOs are subject to government audits, and those supported by Western organizations are required by contract to keep accurate accounts. Government procurements are limited, though some NGOs provide services to the government. The Agency for Social Information, the Institute for the Study of the Russian Economy, the International Center for Research in Economic Reform, and the Institute for the Economy in Transition have done work for the government.

5. Are there free trade unions? How many workers belong to these unions? Is the number of workers belonging to trade unions growing or decreasing? What is the numerical/proportional membership of farmers' groups, small business associations, etc.? Section I, Chapter 2 Article 30 of the constitution states: "everyone shall have the right to association, including the right to create trade unions to protect one's interests." The Federation of Independent Trade Unions of Russia, the successor organization to Communist-era unions, is still the largest labor confederation. The union claims about 65 million of Russia's 72 million workers, but the 1997 U.S. State Department report of staff on human rights estimated that roughly 55 percent of the work force is "nominally unionized," down from 65 percent the year before. When the Soviet Union broke up in 1991, over 80 percent of Russian workers belonged to unions. The closing of money-losing enterprises, lay-offs of hundreds of thousands in the industrial, mining, and public sectors, and the proliferation of non-union jobs in the private service sector have contributed to the decline in membership. A new draft labor code proposed in January 1998 moves away from the concept of permanent employment to fixed-term contracts, which union officials have complained would further undermine workers' rights. There are a number of smaller, independent unions with perhaps two million members. There were several strikes in 1997 and early 1998 by workers protesting wage arrears. The largest farmers' organization is the Association of Peasant Farms and Agricultural Cooperatives. The Agrarian Party of Russia represents collective and state farmers, as well as agro-industrial workers and managers, and opposes privatization of land. The party won 20 constituency seats in 1996 elections. The Peasant Party of Russia favors private land ownership. There are countless hundreds of business associations, trade councils, and economic interest groups throughout Russia, but an exact membership figure is unavailable. Millions of Russians, perhaps as many as 35 percent, belong to consumer cooperatives, which number over 4,000.

6. What forms of interest group participation in politics are legal? What types of interest groups are active in the political and policy process? Section I, Chapter 2, Article 33 of the constitution states, "citizens of the Russian Federation shall have the right to turn personally to, and send individual and collective petitions to state bodies and bodies of local self-government." NGOs and other groups use petitions and public demonstrations to make their views known. The major interest groups involved in the national political and policy process are managers of state farms, state enterprises, and agro-industrial concerns. The seven dominant financial-industrial groups — which control large banks, media, and natural resources — have close contacts with the president, the prime minister, and other government officials, suggesting that they have an inordinate influence on major economic policies.

7. How is the not-for-profit/NGO sector perceived by the public and government officials? What is the nature of media coverage of NGOs? To what extent do government officials engage with NGOs? The issue of public perception and the media are connected as most citizens get their information from television or newspapers. An Agency of Social Information report states that "the general public knows very little about them (NGOs). Information concerning the third sector appears on the pages of the press only episodically." In terms of relations with government officials, NGOs have had successes working with local authorities on specific issues such as housing and public health throughout Russia, but engagement between indigenous NGOs and national officials is limited.

Independent Media 4.25/7

1. Are there legal protections for press freedom? The 1993 constitution guarantees the freedom of mass media (Article 29) and prohibits censorship. Protections were also included in the 1992 Law on Mass Media. The law forbids the use of mass media to commit criminal offenses or to inflame social intolerance or strife. A 1994 government order on "Licensing Television Broadcasting, Radio Broadcasting, and Operating on the Television and Radio Communications System No. 1359" established the Russian Television and Radio Service as the licensing agency and required a second license to operate on a television or radio frequency issued by the Ministry of Communications. The 1995 Federal Law on Communications (Systems) strengthened the Ministry of Communications' right to issue, change the terms, or extend the duration of frequency licenses, as well as to suspend them. While censorship is proscribed by the constitution and the Law on Mass Media, court decisions on libel and defamation have substantially limited journalists' freedom to criticize public figures. Accreditation rules often violate the constitutional right of journalists to access to information (Article 29, Item 4). The U.S. State Department reported that at the beginning of 1997, the public relations department of the Ministry of Internal Affairs revised its accreditation procedure and required journalists to submit their articles for the previous six months in order to be considered for accreditation. In February 1998, the government revoked the accreditation of *Komsomolskaya Pravda* journalist Alexander Gamov for reporting that President Yeltsin's wife had asked him to step down for health reasons. In March, parliament withdrew accreditation from ORT television station journalists on the grounds that their coverage of a Duma debate was not objective. The Supreme Court subsequently ruled the action illegal. Many republican and local governments ignore federal law in contravention of the constitution. For example, in the Bashkortostan Republic, Article 1 of the republican media law states that relations between republican authorities and mass media, including Moscow-based publications, are regulated exclusively by local legislation, while the constitution gives priority to federal law. Another threat to press freedom has been the erosion of media autonomy with the takeover of major electronic and print media by large financial-industrial groups with ties to the government. This has led to slanted coverage and self-censorship.

2. Are there legal penalties for libeling officials? Are there legal penalties for "irresponsible"

journalism? Have these laws been enforced to harass journalists? Libel cases have become a common form of intimidation by public officials and are tried in court on the basis of the Law on the Mass Media and the Law on the Protection of the Honor, Dignity, and Business Reputation of Citizens (1991). A mid-1997 report by the Glasnost Defense Fund noted that libel and defamation actions against journalists increased from 126 cases in the first half of 1996 to 202 in the first half of 1997. In November 1997, First Deputy Prime Minister Anatoly Chubais filed two libel suits against radio station Ekho Moskvy and its journalist Aleksander Minkin, along with the ORT television station and the host of its Vremya news analytical program for defaming his personal honor and reputation by reporting on a lucrative book contract. In December, former Deputy Prime Minister and State Property Minister Maxim Boyko filed a defamation suit for reports linking him to the book scandal. There were 353 incidents in which journalists and media sources were accused by authorities of "abuse of their journalistic privileges." Penalties are normally financial in nature. The president's Judicial Chamber on Information Disputes has ruled that journalists and editors are responsible for disseminating false information, even if an article contains disclaimers such as "it is rumored," "it is said," or "according to unverified information."

3. What proportion of the media is privatized? What are the major newspapers, television stations, and radio stations? While about 80 percent of Russia's 6,000 newspapers and 4,000 magazines have been technically privatized, all but a few receive some form of government subsidies. While about 1,600 television broadcast licenses have been issued, there are an estimated 525 private and state-owned and operated television stations. Russian Television (RTR) and Russian Public Television (ORT) of which the government owns 51 percent of shares, transmit nationwide and to most of the former Soviet Union. Other nationwide TV stations are NTV and TV-6. Increasingly, Russia's powerful financial groups have acquired control or fund most major media assets. In September 1997 a former director of Moscow's powerful Menatep bank was named deputy chief of the government news agency ITAR-TASS. Presidential confidant and former deputy head of the Security Council Boris Berezovsky's LogoVAZ owns shares in ORT and TV 6, and has a controlling stake in *Nezavisimaya Gazeta* through Obedinionny Bank. Vladimir Gusinsky's Media Most controls 70 percent of NTV, an influential station that broadcasts nationwide, and owns *Segodnya* and other leading newspapers. Oneximbank, along with Lukoil, has stakes in several papers, including *Izvestia*. SBS-AGRO is part of a consortium that owns 38 percent of ORT and several newspapers and periodicals. Gazprom, with close ties to Prime Minister Chernomyrdin, owns shares in NTV and ORT, as well as stakes or controlling interests in newspapers. In April 1997, Lukoil moved to gain control of *Izvestia* after it reprinted a controversial article which alleged that the prime minister had accumulated a personal fortune of US $5 billion through his close links with Gazprom. In 1997, Moscow's powerful mayor, Yuri Luzhkov, launched a new television network, Center TV, with financial backing of Moscow city authorities. He is also a major backer of *Moskovsky Komsomolets*. The two most popular newspapers in terms of circulation are *Center Plus* (5 million), a shopper's publication, and *Speed Info* (3.8 million), a racy tabloid. Other major publications include: *Argumenty i Fakty* (3.4 million, weekly); *Komsomolskaya Pravda* (1.5 million, daily); *Trud* (1.4 million, daily); *Ekonomika i Zhizn* (1.2 million, business weekly); *Moskovsky Komsomolets* (1 million, daily); *Izvestiya* (630,000, daily); *Seven Days* (450,000, daily); *Segodnya* (100,000, daily); and *Nezavisimaya Gazeta* (50,000, daily). The major TV stations are ORT, RTR, NTV, and TV-6. Major radio stations are Ekho Moskvy, Mayak, and Radio Rossiya.

4. Are the private media financially viable? Many media organizations face financial problems due to lack of advertising revenue, large decreases or elimination of state subsidies, and increases in material and printing costs. Coincidentally, the public's ability to afford newspapers has declined because of prolonged economic hardship. Only a few newspapers, such as *Argumenty i Fakty*, have sufficient circulation and advertising revenue to be financially independent. Most newspapers rely on subsidies from the government or on business interests close to President Yeltsin. *Nezavisimaya Gazeta*, for example, was forced to suspend publication in 1995 after the editor refused to take state subsidies to protect the paper's independence; it was ultimately reissued after four months following a substantial investment by LogoVAZ. *Obshchaya Gazeta*, which gained a reputation for relative independence during the 1996 presidential campaign, eventually succumbed to financial constraints. In the summer of 1997, the paper revamped its format after investments from Media Most. Classified ad newspapers, business publications, and sex/crime tabloids are doing well. Regional and local newspapers are facing difficult times because few people have the money to subscribe to them. City newspapers have been hardest hit. In February 1996, a law on financial support for the media aimed to help more than 10,000 publications, hundreds of television and radio companies, and several thousand printing presses by making them eligible for new tax breaks and financial privileges as opposed to direct subsidies. In the electronic media, financial-industrial groups with tremendous resources have invested in NTV, ORT, and TV-6. NTV's satellite television project, launched in 1996, required capital investment from the gas giant Gazprom. The radio station Ekho Moskvy was managed by its journalists from 1990 to 1994, but was eventually forced to seek a partnership with Media Most.

5. Are the media editorially independent? Are the media's news gathering functions affected by interference from government or private owners? Because many major media outlets receive some measure of government subsidy and/or have outside sponsors or private owners with connections to the government, editorial independence has been compromised, particularly over the last two or three years. Oblast or local-level officials exert political pressure, particularly in regions and krais where there is competition between local elites. Local authorities and criminal groups routinely threaten and harass journalists. With major media outlets controlled by financial-industrial groups and politicians such as Moscow's Mayor Luzhkov, Russian media now reflects their political biases and the battles of the business concerns controlling them. In a September 1997 interview with Radio Free Europe/Radio Liberty, Iosif Dzialoshinsky, a professor at Moscow University's Faculty of Journalism, said control of powerful media outlets is needed in order to gain political influence. He said this was true for Moscow-based media outlets, as well as for regional media throughout the country. "1997 was the year when Russian journalists had to understand that they were not 'missionaries.' They are no more than company employees." Opinion polls have suggested that televised news and analytical programs, and so-called "respectable" publications have a very limited audience throughout Russia, partly because of the politicization of the media and the internecine squabbling between media elites reflected in the press.

6. Is the distribution system for newspapers privately or governmentally controlled? Private distributors work throughout Russia and compete with the former state-owned monopoly. Subscriptions must still be expedited through the state postal system, but local delivery and distribution through kiosks is now largely in the hands of smaller, private distributors. In broadcasting, however, only a small number of companies own their own transmitters, with the remainder having to lease time on those owned by the state.

7. What proportion of the population is connected to the Internet? Are there any restrictions on Internet access to private citizens? According to the Russian State Committee for Communications and Information (Goskomsvyaz) there were 600,000 Internet users in 1997. The number of Russian-language websites on Russian information servers reached 10,000.

8. What has been the trend in press freedom as measured by Freedom House's *Survey of Press Freedom*? The Freedom House annual *Survey of Press Freedom* has rated Russia "Partly Free" from 1992-98 mainly because of libel laws, harassment and violence against journalists, the politicization of the press, and the influence over media of a small group of financial-industrial moguls with ties to the government.

Governance and Public Administration 4.50/7

1. Is the legislature the effective rule-making institution? According to the constitution, parliament "is the only representative and legislative organ of the Russian Federation." The executive branch, however, has considerable power to "issue edicts and directives that are by nature executive acts and are mandatory for compliance on the entire territory of the Russian Federation." The Constitutional Court provides legal recourse to challenge presidential decrees. Since his election in 1991, President Yeltsin, confronting a recalcitrant parliament, has often issued decrees and executive orders, a right codified in the 1993 constitution. The 1996 gubernatorial elections (executives of regional administrations become members of the Federation Council) saw the emergence of regional directly elected leaders seeking greater autonomy from the center in economic matters and control of natural resources.

2. Is substantial power decentralized to local, regional and other subnational levels of government? What specific authority do subnational levels have? Section I, Chapter 8, Articles 130-133 of the 1993 constitution provide the fundamental underpinnings of local self-government. Under Article 132, "the bodies of local self-government shall independently manage municipal property, form, approve, and execute the local budget, establish local taxes and levies, ensure law and order and solve any other local issues." The constitution also includes considerable provisions on the delineation of authority between federal organs of state power and the authorities of krais, oblasts, Moscow and St. Petersburg, autonomous oblasts, and autonomous okrugs. In the 21 ethnic-based republics, elected executive and legislative officials do have effective power. At the end of October 1997, President Yeltsin signed bilateral treaties with leaders of Astrakhan, Kirov, Murmansk, Ulyanovsk, and Yaroslav oblasts, Krasnoyarsk Krai, and the Taimyr and Evenk autonomous okrugs. This brought the total number of federation "subjects" that have signed such agreements since 1994 to 39. Yeltsin described his treaties with the regions as necessary to prevent "a weak, rag state in which everyone is out for himself." In January 1998, Speaker of the Federation Council Yegor Stroyev criticized the practice of bilateral agreements. Addressing a conference on Russian federalism, he said such power-sharing agreements contribute to the arbitrary nature of relations between Moscow and regional governments and leave relatively weak regions almost entirely dependent of the central government. Under the constitution, krais, oblasts, Moscow and St. Petersburg "effect their own legal regulation...within the framework of their jurisdiction, by way of adopting legal acts." Many key areas fall "within the scope of joint jurisdiction" with the federal government. Autonomous okrugs and autonomous oblasts are bound by the Federation Treaty. Regional and local bodies can pass laws that do not supersede Russian or constitutional laws, but in 1997-98 there was growing concern in Moscow that these bodies were exceeding their constitutional powers. Russia's justice minister reported that roughly one-third of the 16,000 regional laws examined by his ministry since the summer of 1995 were found to violate federal legislation. The state prosecutor complained that nearly 2,000 regional laws have been revoked for contradicting the constitution.

3. Are subnational officials chosen in free and fair elections? Local and regional elections in 1993 and in February-April 1994, saw irregularities, violations, and low voter turnout that nullified the results. In 1996, 48 governors appointed by the President faced elections for the first time; 20 incumbents held on to their jobs and 24 were defeated. Electoral laws varied widely from region to region. Incumbents tended to do better in regions where the law required only that the winner gain a plurality of votes, rather than 50 percent plus one. Turnout figures ranged from well under 50 percent to over 65 percent. Local government control of media outlets in many regions denied opposition candidates access to television, radio, and newspapers; and there were numerous cases of harassment or intimidation of journalists. Nonetheless, the elections were generally "free and fair," with results accepted in almost all cases. In 1997, elections to regional legislative bodies were held in Moscow, St. Petersburg, Chelyabinsk, Tyumen, Tambov, Smolensk, Novosibirsk, Krasnoyarsk, and Tomsk oblasts, while local chief executives were elected in Chuvashia, Komi, Mordoviya, North Ossetia, Ingushetia, and Altai republics. There were no international monitors at these elections, but several of the elections were marked by serious irregularities and disputes over electoral law and jurisdiction. Problems have arisen between regional leaders and mayors and, according to an article in the January 1997, issue of *Obshchaya Gazeta* on the removal of the mayor of Ulan-Ude by the president of Buryatia, "power struggles between the heads of oblasts and the leaders of administrative centers (mayors) are becoming a typical phenomenon of Russian life."

4. Do the executive and legislative bodies operate openly and with transparency? Is draft legislation easily accessible to the media and the public? The government publishes all laws passed by the Duma, and the president's office has published all decrees. The media generally have access to political leaders and government information, although there were several cases in 1997 in which journalists lost their accreditation. Under Section I, Chapter 5, Article 100 of the constitution, "the sessions of the Federation Council and the State Duma shall be open." Each chamber, however, "has the right to hold closed sessions as envisaged by its rules."

5. Do municipal governments have sufficient revenues to carry out their duties? Do municipal governments have control over their own local budgets? Do they raise revenues autonomously or from the central state budget? Municipal governments in the larger cities make their own budgets and do raise some revenue from municipally-owned businesses taxes, but the bulk of municipal revenues still comes from the central state budget. In January 1997, Anatoly Chubais, speaking before the Union of Russian Towns, acknowledged that local administration had to face non-payments from the central government. In a May 1997 article on a meeting on "Rebirth and Reconstruction of Russia's Cities," *Rossiyskaya Gazeta* reported that in the best case, "only half of the 73 percent of state grant money for housing and municipal service payments, which should be allocated from the budget, arrives." In August 1992, the government signed "Measures to Implement the Russian Federation President's Edict 568 of June 11, 1997 on the "Main Avenues of Local Self-Government Reform in the Russian Federation.'" The edict made codifying local self-government reform a top priority. It said that government ministries, in collaboration with unions and associations of municipal formations, "are to ensure that representatives of local self-government organs participate in the implementation of budgetary, housing and utilities, and social reforms and, by agreement with (federal organs), they are to create a system of key areas in which to test said reforms." In November 1997, the Council on Local Self-Government in the Russian Federation noted that while the federal Law on Financial Foundations for Local-Self Government reflected conceptual approaches to the drafts of tax and budget codes, and created a framework for the realization of the constitutional right of local self-government bodies to independent formation, approval, and execution of the local budget, the law was vague on specifics. The council concluded that "without the most rapid examination and adoption by the parliament of draft laws determining the procedure for the delimitation and consolidation of the right of ownership of municipal formations, including land, it is impossible to realize the appropriate provisions of the draft law of the tax code and the Law on Self-Government Financial Foundations." Several mayors recommended that local self-government be left in control of all income tax and land tax revenue. On March 10, 1998, President Yeltsin criticized those local government officials who used federal moneys earmarked for social assistance to pensioners and the handicapped for other purposes.

6. Do the elected local leaders and local civil servants know how to manage municipal governments effectively? Political patronage and a dearth of competent full-time civil servants undermines the effectiveness of local and municipal government. In 1997, many mayors were involved in corruption scandals involving the misuse of funds. In 1996, President Yeltsin approved an edict calling for periodic evaluation of federal civil servants, but no such initiative has been implemented on the regional and local levels.

7. When did the constitutional/legislative changes on local power come into effect? Has there been a reform of the civil service code/system? Are local civil servants employees of the local or central government? The December 1993 constitution delineates regional and local powers, but many have not been codifed into law. In 1997, several decrees and edicts sought to clarify the status and responsibilities of local self-government. Since 1991, there have been several draft laws on reform of the civil service and bureaucracy. In March 1992, Yeltsin's government founded a special organization for the selection and grooming of "fast-track" civil servants, the Main Administration for Training Civil Service Cadres (Roskadry). While only 10 percent of the old-style nomenklatura are still in state or government posts, the system suffers from corruption and an acute shortage of modern managers and civil servants. In July 1996, the State Duma passed the presidential version of the Law on the Basics of the Civil Service, which divides public offices into three categories and bans civil servants from simultaneously holding any other employment, except teaching, research, or other "creative" jobs. Civil servants cannot be members of either federal or regional legislative bodies or serve in local government. Prospective civil servants must report income and property. The same year, President Yeltsin approved a system of evaluating and rating federal civil servants by a special commission. In December 1997, during deliberations on the 1998 budget draft, deputies voted to reduce federal civil service staff by 30 percent. Local civil servants are employees of local governments.

Rule of Law 4.25/7

1. Is there a post-Communist constitution? How does the judicial system interpret and enforce the constitution? Are there specific examples of judicial enforcement of the constitution in the last year? Russians approved a new constitution by referendum on December 12, 1993. It defines Russia as a democratic, federal state with a republican form of government. It provides for a strong executive branch of government and a bicameral legislature, the 178-member Federation Council (upper house) and the 450-member State Duma (lower house). The constitution followed a bitter political struggle between President Yeltsin and a hard-line parliament that culminated in the October 1993 crisis during which the president ordered the use of force to remove obstructionist representatives from parliament. The constitution gives the president strong powers to issue decrees and executive orders, appoint senior members of the judicial and executive branches, and dissolve the State Duma if it repeatedly either declines his choice of prime minister or votes a lack of confidence in him. In December 1997, Yeltsin declared that as long as he was president, he would not allow any changes in the constitution. Grigory Yavlinsky, leader of the reformist opposition Yabloko faction, said that the constitution places too much power in the hands of the president. In an interview with Ekho Moskvy radio, he called for constitutional amendments to increase parliamentary and judicial powers. Section I, Chapter 7, Article 125, calls for the creation of a 19-member Constitutional Court charged with "resolving cases about compliance with the Constitution of the Russian Federation." The court has dominion over federal laws and normative acts, republican constitutions and laws, agreements between Russia and its subnational "subjects," and international agreements that have not gone into force. In July 1997, the Constitutional Court ruled that regional governments cannot charge for the right to live in their territories for this violated Article 27.1 of the constitution. On January 15, 1998, the Court ruled that authorities may not require citizens to produce residency permits *(propiska)* in order to be issued passports for foreign travel.

2. Does the constitutional framework provide for human rights? Do the human rights include business and property rights? Section I, Chapter 2 of the constitution delineates "Rights and Liberties of Man and Citizens." Article 17 guarantees "basic rights and liberties," among them the right to personal inviolability, freedoms of conscience, expression, association, assembly, and movement. Article 35 states that "the right of private property shall be protected by law," and Article 36 states that "citizens and their associations shall have the right to have land in their private ownership." Article 46 declares that "everyone shall have the right to turn to interstate organs concerned with the protection of human rights and liberties when all the means of legal protection available within the state have been exhausted." In February 1998, the State Duma voted overwhelmingly to ratify the European Convention on Human Rights which Russia signed two years earlier. Ratifying the accord allows Russian citizens to file appeals with the European Court, the ruling of which would be binding in Russia. There are scores of human rights NGOs throughout Russia. In 1997, human rights groups called attention to human rights abuses of military recruits and the federal Human Rights Commission reported on the deplorable situation in Russian prisons and detention centers. The commission has also discussed the issue of violation of pensioners' rights due to non-payment by the government. A Land Code prepared by the Agrarian Party and adopted by the Duma provided for extremely severe restrictions on private land ownership, but measures dealing with implementation and other issues have not been passed. As of 1997, the issues of land ownership had not been fully resolved. In January 1998, a final decision on questions concerning land was postponed for three months. In December 1997, when the regional government of Saratov brought in local laws to let farmland be freely bought and sold, 12 more regions promptly followed suit — a show of regional impatience that prompted President Yeltsin and parliamentary leaders to promise a federal law privatizing land.

3. Has there been basic reform of the criminal codes/criminal law? Who authorizes searches and issues warrants? Are suspects and prisoners beaten or abused? Are there excessive delays in the criminal justice system? A new Criminal Code, adopted in May 1996, went into force on January 1, 1997, replacing the RSFSR's Criminal Code of 1960. More reforms of the code are planned for 1998. It retains the death penalty, albeit for five rather than 18 crimes, and increases the maximum sentences for banditry and murder, however, it significantly reduces sentences for non-violent crimes. The code includes about 100 new articles. For the first time, the code includes chapters on liability for crimes against the constitutional rights and freedoms of citizens. There is an article on "piracy" and on liability for environmental crimes. The constitution provides for the presumption of innocence, but prosecutors enjoy numerous built-in procedural advantages. A 1992 draft criminal code gave priority to the defense of the individual, and the interests of property owners and private enterprise. In the same year, parliament approved several amendments to the Criminal Procedure Code, in force since 1960, that granted the judiciary some checks on the Prosecutors Office. There were additional amendments in 1995-96. The Constitutional Court ruled that Article 220 of the Criminal Code, which restricted the legal right to contest arrests, was unconstitutional. In February 1995, the Duma passed an amendment reducing the amount of time suspects can be held in custody without indictment from 30 days to ten. President Yeltsin signed into law reforms to the criminal procedure and penal system that gave certain privileges to prisoners held in isolation, provided for prisoners to serve their sentences in their own regions, and separated first-time offenders from recidivists. At the end of 1997, a draft of a comprehensive Criminal Procedure Code was prepared to replace the 1960 code still in effect. Among safeguards for defendants' rights was a provision giving the accused and their defense attorneys access to prosecutorial evidence before it is sent to the court. The new code will be implemented some time in 1998. The existing code gives procurators authority to issue an order of detention without a judge's authorization and, if police believe that the suspect has committed a crime or is a danger to others, he can be detained up to 48 hours without a warrant. A 1994 presidential decree on combating organized crime allowed law enforcement authorities to detain persons suspected of ties to organized crime for up to 30 days (later changed to ten days) without explanation and without access to a lawyer. The constitution states that officials can enter a private residence only in cases prescribed by federal law or on the basis of a judicial decision. Although search warrants are required, police often enter residences without warrants. There are credible reports that law enforcement personnel use torture to coerce confessions. Prisoner's rights groups have documented numerous cases in which law enforcement and correctional officials beat detainees and suspects. Prisons are extremely overcrowded and health and sanitation standards remain low. Trial delays are common. Although the Criminal Procedure Code requires court consideration to begin no more than 14 days after the judge issues the order designating the location of the trial, congestion in the court system frequently leads to prolonged postponements.

4. Do judges rule fairly and impartially? Do many remain from the Communist era? Under a 1995 law, judges are required to have at least five years of experience in the legal profession. In addition, to attract the best jurists to the profession, the law raised judges' salaries and changed retirement rules. Some regions and republics had demanded the right to appoint their own judges to higher courts. Lower court officials are appointed and paid by regional and local governments. Impartiality is difficult to determine, but most trials are open. A precise number for Communist-era judges is unavailable.

5. Are the courts free of political control and influence? Are the courts linked directly to the Ministry of Justice or any other executive body? A 1996 law separated the courts from the Ministry of Justice and placed them within a separate part of the judicial department. In the 1998 budget, this department is funded independent of the ministry. According to the U.S. State Department report on human rights, judges remain subject to some influence from the executive, military, and security forces, especially in high-profile or political cases. The independence of the judiciary is also threatened by chronic underfunding and by its subordinate position in relation to the executive and the legislature. Despite the 1995 Law on Judges, local courts have serious problems meeting their wage bills, buying equipment, paying phone bills and undertaking building repairs, making them subject to corruption. On July 29, 1997, President Yeltsin ordered a 65-percent pay rise in an attempt to attract new judges to fill approximately 1,500 vacancies in the judiciary.

6. What proportion of lawyers is in private practice? What proportion of lawyers are employed by the state? In 1991, there were only 27,000 practicing advocates. Recent estimates of the number of trained lawyers in Russia range from 22,000 to 50,000 (the latter figure includes judges and prosecutors, as well as defense and business lawyers). Though exact statistics are unavailable, most lawyers continue to be employed by the state, but many moonlight in private practice, working for individuals or private commercial interests. Qualified judges and state procurators have quit and moved into the private sector, undermining the efficiency of the judiciary.

7. Does the state provide public defenders? The Criminal Code provides for the court to appoint a lawyer if the suspect cannot afford one. In many cases, however, the indigent receive little legal assistance because funds are lacking to pay for trial attorneys and public defenders are poorly trained. The Constitutional Court has also ruled that defendants charged under the Law on State Secrets are entitled to choose their own lawyers. The ruling followed complaints that the stipulation in the law that defense lawyers must first obtain security clearance was unconstitutional and gave the prosecution unfair advantage.

8. Are there effective antibias/discrimination laws, including protection of ethnic minorities? Section I, Chapter 2, Article 19.2 guarantees equality of rights and liberties "regardless of race, skin color, nationality, sex, language, social origin, social, property and official position, beliefs, attitude toward religion, involvement in public associations, place of residence, and other circumstances." It also guarantees the "rights and liberties of persons belonging to ethnic minorities." Since 1993, there has been a increase in discrimination and acts against minorities from the Caucasus, Central Asia, and Chechnya under the pretext of anticrime measures. Jews continue to face societal discrimination, and there were numerous reports in 1997 of desecration of Jewish cemeteries and bombings of synagogues. A controversial religious law discriminates against many non-Orthodox religions, particularly Protestant denominations. A Lutheran church was the first one closed under the new religion law. Far-right groups have targeted Central Asians, Roma, and other non-Russians. Women face domestic violence and discrimination in employment, but there are scores of groups and NGOs dealing with women's issues. In March 1998, the Union of Russia's Women launched an initiative to set up a network of commissions for women's rights throughout the country. By the end of 1998, which has been declared the Year of Human Rights in Russia, the Union plans to make public a report on violations of women's rights in Russia. The head of the Union reported that she expected the largest category in the report to be in the sphere of labor relations.

Corruption D

1. What is the magnitude of official corruption in the civil service? Must an average citizen pay a bribe to a bureaucrat in order to receive a service? What services are subject to bribe requests — for example, university entrance, hospital admission, telephone installation, obtaining a license to operate a business, applying for a passport or other official documents? What is the average salary of civil servants at various levels? Corruption and extortion pervade everyday life in Russia. Businessmen routinely pay bribes in order to conduct business, and government officials routinely accept and even demand them.

Press reports name the State Customs Committee; the Tax Police; the State Property Committee; the Central Bank; the Ministries of Defense, Interior, and Agriculture as the most corrupt

From 1994 to 1996, more than 14,000 corruption cases were filed by the Procurator's office. In 1996, 101 tax officials were convicted of corruption, up from 54 in 1995. President Yeltsin stated that 2,500 officials were under investigation for bribery in 1997.

2. Do top policy makers (the president, ministers, vice-ministers, top court justices, and heads of agencies and commissions) have direct ties to businesses? How strong are such connections and what kinds of businesses are these? In 1993, researchers surveyed 1,000 people who were connected to the Central Committee of the Communist Party in 1988. They compared these to members of the new economic elite and discovered that the overlap in Russia was 19 percent. This compares to 30 percent in Hungary and 28 percent in Poland. On the other hand, the former members of the *nomenklatura* in Russia were much more likely to be in the new political, cultural, and state-sector economic elite than their counterparts in Hungary and Poland. A series of scandals which came to light in 1997 in the heat over the disputed privatization process highlighted the way elites move easily between government and business, and use their connections and positions to extract bribes.

The old Soviet underworld has been largely replaced by more sophisticated politico-criminal organizations, staffed by police and former security professionals. Mafia organizations often have close relations with bureaucrats at all levels of Russian government, which in 1997 was amply evident in a string of scandals and mob assassinations. Observers linked the 1997 murder of St. Petersburg deputy mayor Alexander Manevich to an attempt by Moscow businessmen to move into St. Petersburg operations. One common Mafia technique is to obtain inside information from corrupt officials on property about to be privatized. Potential competitors and protesting workers are then pushed aside.

3. Do laws requiring financial disclosure and disallowing conflict of interest exist? Have publicized anti corruption cases been pursued? To what conclusion? President Yeltsin has imposed financial disclosure requirements by decree on several occasions. For example, in May 1997, Yeltsin ordered all top officials to disclose their income. Most officials reported modest, and thus highly dubious, incomes relative to their lifestyles. Little has been done with the information that has been disclosed.

Few publicized anti-corruption cases have been pursued. The Duma audit board reported that some $72 billion in corruption scandals were exposed in 1997, but never investigated. About 219,000 "economic crimes" (largely bribery) were exposed, twice as many as in 1996.

4. What major anticorruption initiatives have been implemented? How often are anticorruption laws and decrees adopted? In November 1997, the Duma passed an anticorruption law, which was ratified by the Federation Council in December. However, it was vetoed by Yeltsin on the grounds that it was unconstitutional. Three previous Duma laws have been also vetoed by Yeltsin.

In May 1997, Yeltsin issued a decree mandating competitive bidding for government contracts.

5. How do major corruption-ranking organizations like Transparency International rate this country? In July 1997, Transparency International ranked Russia 49th out of the 52 countries it surveyed for its Corruption Perception Index. Its CPI score was 2.27 in 1997 (on a 1-10 scale, where lower is worse), worsening from 2.58 in 1996. This means Russia's corruption is worse than Pakistan and Mexico's. Of the rated countries, only Colombia, Bolivia, and Nigeria were worse than Russia.

The Economist Intelligence Unit ranked Russia 4 (on a scale of zero to four) in its corruption survey.

Privatization **3.25/7**

1. What percentage of the GDP comes from private ownership? What percentage of the labor force is employed in the private sector? How large is the informal sector of the economy? As of the beginning of 1997, the private sector accounted for approximately 70 percent of GDP, according to the European Bank for Reconstruction and Finance. Some 60-65 percent of the workforce is employed privately. Nevertheless, the government sector has grown as well. As a percentage of GDP, it has risen from 16 percent in 1992 to 24 percent in 1995. The size of the "invisible" portion of the government budget remains large as well.

The State Statistics Committee (Goskomstat) estimates that the informal economy represents about 25 percent of GDP (as compared with a average of 10 percent in developed nations). Russia's Federal Security Service, on the other hand, estimates this economy at 40 percent of GDP.

2. What major privatization legislation has been passed? What were its substantive features? The first phase of Russia's privatization process began in 1992 on three separate tracks. First, local regions privatized "small" assets like service, retail, and trade firms. Second, workers and management at the large enterprises which dominated the Russian economy were offered preferential access to their company's shares through three separate options, the most popular of which gave workers a 51-percent share of their enterprise for nominal cost. Third, a voucher privatization plan was adopted, similar to the Czechoslovak scheme. A privatization voucher with a face value of 10,000 old *rubles* (about six weeks' average pay) was distributed to each citizen for the nominal price of 25 old rubles. Distribution ended in January 1993, and the vouchers were valid through the end of 1993. The vouchers could be used to buy shares in the person's workplace or in enterprises on the auction block, deposited with voucher investment funds, or sold for cash. More than 15,000 medium and large-sized enterprises, employing over 80 percent of the industrial workforce, were privatized in this phase of privatization. On average, 20 percent of these firms' shares were sold for vouchers.

The first phase of privatization was complete by mid 1994. The second phase, which emphasized cash sales of the remaining state-owned shares in enterprises, began shortly afterward. Although the primary goal was to privatize the "crown jewels" of Russian industry, sell-offs of these large firms languished in 1996 as a result of political pressure from the 1995 loans-for-shares debacle and the 1996 presidential campaign.

The loans-for-shares episode put a major black eye in the public image of privatization, one from which it has yet to recover. In late 1995, the government auctioned off shares in state companies in exchange for long-term loans from Russian banks. Since the government has chosen not to repay the loans, these banks began organizing the sales of the shares they seized as forfeited collateral. Major sales under these rules occurred in mid-1997, including that of oil behemoths Tyumen Oil Co., Yukos, Sidanko, Surgutneftegaz, and metals giant Norilsk Nickel. The banks organizing the share sales biased the auction procedures to heavily favor themselves. Not surprisingly, the organizers won in each case, and most commonly with only a bare minimum increase over the minimum price.

Since the original law on privatization passed by the Duma in June 1992, privatization has been conducted in Russia through a series of executive orders issued by President Yeltsin. A privatization law in July 1997 reintroduced the Duma into privatization policy making. This is important because, in theory, the constitution mandates that adopted laws supersede executive decrees. A lack of controversial portions in the bill and its support for the status quo allowed it to pass with lopsided majorities in parliament and gain presidential approval. The major feature of the law requires the government to agree to an annual privatization program with the Duma at the same time the budget is considered. This may mean a better bargaining position for the legislature given the explicit issue linkage with the budget. The law bans loans-for-shares auctions and investment tenders. It also makes it easier for the government to reverse privatizations where laws were deemed to have been violated. Finally, it establishes more realistic methods of establishing market valuation of asset sales. However, it is vague in several important respects, including what technical grounds are sufficient for renationalization. For example, no statute of limitations is specified, nor is the procedure for reversal of privatization of shares already sold to third parties. This vagueness can be exploited to make overturning a privatization decision relatively easy. This will make property rights even less secure, both for newly privatized firms as well as those privatized earlier.

There were other procedural changes in privatization policy. A government decree adopted in April 1997 mandated that the organizers of future auctions would no longer be the Russian Federal Property Fund by default, but rather the winners of a competition among financial consultants competing on the basis of their privatization plans.

It was only in 1997 that the pace of privatization picked up substantially. Approximately 3,350 enterprises were privatized in 1997, bringing the cumulative total to nearly 127,000 firms, or 58.9 percent of the state-owned firms existing when the process began. There was an unprecedented increase in revenue. In 1997, privatization brought in 18.7 trillion old rubles ($3.1 billion), far in excess of the budgeted R6.5 trillion.

The July 1997 auction of giant telecommunications holding company Svyazinvest marked a turning point in the cash phase of Russian privatization, and can be said to have augured in a third phase of Russian privatization. A 25-percent share in the company was sold to a consortium led by Vladimir Potanin's Oneximbank for $1.9 billion, (significantly above the starting price of $1.2 billion). It was the first time a huge enterprise fetched a fair market price in a government auction. It was also the first time that there was bitter competition between the large banks dominating the cash phase of privatization. Previous cash privatizations were rigged by collusion among major "competitors" who agreed on the winner and phony competitor required by law beforehand. After a failed attempt to lobby then-First Deputy Prime Minister Anatoly Chubais, the cartel broke down and the two consortia unexpectedly became competitors. A second tranche (slightly less than 25 percent) of the state share in Svyazinvestment was to be sold in September 1998.

Alfred Kokh, who was appointed head of privatization in September 1996 was forced to step down in August 1997. It was revealed later that Kokh, his successor Maxim Boyko, Chubais, and two other privatization officials received $90,000 each for an unwritten book on privatization from a firm connected with Oneximbank, the winner of several recent auctions. All were fired except for Chubais. In October 1997, Moscow prosecutors announced criminal proceedings against Kokh based on the payment he received, which they allege was a bribe given by Oneximbank to influence privatization policy.

In March 1998, the government drew up a list of companies in which some of its stake is to be privatized in 1998. These include oil and gas companies (Rosneft, Lukoil, NorsiOil, Tyumen Oil, Slavneft, Transneft, and VNK), Aeroflot and Sheremetyevo Airport, Elektrosvyaz communications, Sibir chemical plant, the Novosibirsk Elektrode Co., and a second share of telecommunications holding company Svyazinvest. All are to be sold through commercial tenders or auctions. If all goes as planned, the government should again raise more than the R9.4 billion budgeted. This program, however, has yet to be approved by the Duma as required by the new privatization law. This is problematic because these privatizations could later be challenged in court.

3. What proportion of agriculture, housing and land, industry, and small business and services is in private hands? *Agriculture*: Some 95 percent of the 24,000 state and collective farms have been reorganized, but are largely unreformed. The overwhelming majority retained some elements of collective labor organizations. 34 percent retained their previous status as state and collective farms, another 47 percent became joint-stock farms of the closed type (in which shares could not be obtained by people outside the farm), and 11 percent formed cooperative agricultural enterprises. The government announced in 1996 that since 1991, the amount of land held by state farms had shrunk from 124 million hectares to 34 million, while the cooperative sector's holdings had increased from 85 million hectares to 137 million and the private sector's from 4 million hectares to 23 million. Only 4 percent of Russian farmers run their own individual farms.
Housing and Land: Millions of Russians, including the new class of business people, have built or bought homes and apartments. A lively independent market in apartment leases has sprung up in Moscow and St. Petersburg. On the other hand, land privatization, especially in urban areas, has moved fairly slowly. Most land in Russian cities has not been privatized. The legislative basis for owning the land on which buildings stand is still unclear, despite constitutional guarantees of an inviolable right to property. There are approximately 55 million individual and 400,000 enterprise landholders.
Industry: Over 70 percent of state-controlled industry has been turned over to private ownership since market reforms began in 1992. Nevertheless, the "crown jewels" of industry remain state monopolies, and they still dominate almost every major industrial sector.
Business and Services: There are about one million small businesses in Russia today, and they employ nine million people, many in the service sector. By mid-1995, over 95 percent of Russia's shops were privately owned. Most medium-and small-sized privately-owned enterprises deal with retail, trade, and hospitality. It appears that this privatization is leading to a fairly significant amount of restructuring. One survey showed that a quarter of managing directors have been replaced since 1992 and one quarter are new.

4. What has been the extent of insider (management, labor, and nomenklatura) participation in the privatization process? What explicit and implicit preferences have been awarded to insiders? The first phase of privatization was explicitly dominated by insiders. Preferential access by firm insiders fell in significance after the end of the first phase in 1994. By 1996, only 31 percent of the shares of newly privatized companies were distributed to insiders, down from 47 percent in 1993.

The new 1997 privatization law officially eliminates most insider preferences. Whether this will hold de facto remains to be seen.

5. How much public awareness of and support for privatization has there been? What major interest groups oppose and advocate privatization? The voucher privatization process was very well publicized. By the deadline of January 1993, 144 million Russians, or 97 percent of those eligible, collected their vouchers from every branch of Sberbank, the state-run savings bank.

The Communists and Agrarians are the most virulent opponents of privatization. These and other populists have labeled privatization a criminal process of giving away the national patrimony. General citizen opinion of privatization has fallen as the process has continued, largely because of a perceived association with the general economic decline.

Macroeconomics 4.25/7

1. Has the taxation system been reformed? (What areas have and have not been overhauled? To what degree are taxpayers complying? Is tax compliance difficult to achieve? Has the level of revenues increased? Is the revenue-collection body overburdened? What is the overall tax burden?) The Russian taxation system remains only partially reformed. It is fragmented, contradictory, excessive, non-transparent, and rife with delinquency.

The following taxes are the major ones levied in Russia: corporate income tax (35 -38 percent); income tax, 12-35 percent; property tax, up to 2 percent; VAT, 20 percent, 10 percent on certain food products, which was reduced by 3 percent in January 1996; social security contributions tax, 28 percent from employers, 1 percent from employees; general social insurance contribution tax, 11 percent of total remuneration by employer; education tax, 1 percent of payroll. The top income tax bracket was increased to from 30 percent to 35 percent in 1997. The average income falls into the 12-percent tax bracket.

The number and the amount of taxes are often a crushing burden to business. It is entirely possible that a company's tax bill can exceed its profits. This invites tax evasion, most commonly by not registering businesses. Tax arrears to the government were some 32 trillion old rubles in August 1996, ($6 billion), and were only 60 percent of budget projections. Despite this, Russia's total tax burden is a relatively heavy 25 percent of GDP. Many firms that owe huge amounts in taxes have political connections. This allows them to avoid unpleasant consequences like bankruptcy. Tax arrears are constantly negotiated and renegotiated. This hidden subsidy, of course, invites more tax evasion.

Tax arrears rose tremendously in 1996 in the laxity engendered by the run-up to the presidential election. An Emergency Tax Commission was formed in late 1996 to go after the biggest tax debtors. The government's efforts paid off in 1997, when large debtors like Gazprom, Sidanko, Sibneft, Rosneft, and UES Rossii settled large portions of their arrears. These one-off payments pumped up tax revenues in 1997 to about 70 percent of the level budgeted (a rather high amount for Russia). They do not, however, signal a systematic solution to Russia's taxation problem.

The federal government has done its part to worsen the arrears problem. By tolerating the growth of monetary surrogates like finance ministry loan guarantees, tax exemption, and bills of exchange, it has allowed tax payments to be made in non-cash form. It has also allowed firms to pay tax arrears through physical goods deliveries. Such non-ruble payments were forbidden in January 1998. Indeed, money payments as a percentage of total receipts rose from 58 percent in September 1996-March 1997 to 91.4 percent in April-November 1997.

A new simplified tax code has been delayed for several years. A tax reform bill passed on its first reading in the Duma in June 1997, under considerable governmental pressure. In October, the Duma rejected the draft code. A revised government bill, reducing the overall tax burden on the economy by 2 percent of GDP, was submitted in February 1998. The chances of the tax code finally being adopted are falling because of the approaching 1999 parliamentary and 2000 presidential elections.

A Constitutional Court decision issued in April 1997 overruled a government decree raising taxes. It said that only the legislature has such power.

2. Does fiscal policy encourage private savings, investment and earnings? (Has there been any reform/alteration of revenue and budget policies? How large are budget deficits and overall debt? Is the financing of the social insurance/pension system sustainable? What proportion of the budget is taken up by subsidies to firms and individuals)? Russian fiscal policy, while much improved, is still unstable and deficit-plagued. In the run-up to the June 1996, presidential election, Yeltsin launched many new spending initiatives to bolster political support. By mid-1996, the budget deficit had risen to 6 percent of GDP. It fell to 4.3 percent by the end of that year when Chubais convinced Yeltsin to cancel some of his campaign promises. In 1998, one-third of the budget was used to pay for interest on previous debt.

For the past several years, budget agreements, while generating much rancorous debate in the opposition-dominated Duma, have been adopted roughly as proposed by the government. The 1998 budget was passed on its fourth reading in the Duma in March 1998.

There were several recent notable milestones of Russian macroeconomic progress. The International Monetary Fund agreed to a multi-year $10.1 billion loan package in March 1996. The Paris Club agreed to reschedule $40 billion of Russian sovereign debt over 25 years in April 1996. Russia also negotiated an agreement with the London Club to reschedule $32.5 million in commercial debt over 25 years in November 1995. This progress has enabled Russia to reenter international capital markets. In October 1996, several international credit rating agencies improved the ranking on Russia's state bonds. The IMF was sufficiently pleased with Russian fiscal discipline to approve in January 1998 the next $700 million tranche of the $10.2 billion extended fund facility loan. It had been delayed in October 1997 over concerns about inadequate tax collection.

Unlike the Central European states, Russia has only barely emerged from the post-transition recession. Russian GDP rose for the first time in 1997, by 0.4 percent.

Russia has a number of extra-budgetary funds which finance social insurance policy. These are funded by payroll taxes and transfers from the main budget. Since they are constructed on a pay-as-you-go basis, their financing is unsustainable and inefficient. Compounding the problems are severe payments arrears by both private and state enterprises to these funds. In mid-1997, arrears to the Pension Fund alone were $12 billion. This situation has led to chronic payment problems to pensioners. Only 29 of Russia's 89 regions are paying out pensions on time.

3. Has there been banking reform? (Is the central bank independent? What are its responsibilities? Is it effective in setting and/or implementing monetary policy? What is the actual state of the private banking sector? Does it conform to international standards? Are depositors protected?) In the early days of transition, the Russian Central Bank (RCB) was neither independent nor competently managed. It often printed money to cover enormous Russian deficits. The new constitution safeguards the independence of the central bank. In 1995, an impressive turnaround at the RCB took place, beginning with the appointment of Sergei Dubinin as its head.

The government, however, decided in June 1996, to transfer $1 billion of the RCB's 1994 profits to the federal budget in order to pay for social spending in the bankrupt Far North. This decision was made under pressure from Yeltsin making extravagant promises during the presidential election campaign. In February 1997, the Duma overrode a Federation Council veto on the law obligating the RCB to transfer 50 percent of its annual profits. The vote was 364-1.

In the first years of transition, RCB regulation of commercial banks was very lax. By the end of 1991, 1,500 banks came into existence and this figure rose to 2,600 by 1994. The RCB, under Dubinin, has made major headway in advancing bank regulation. He has thereby earned much enmity, as was demonstrated in March 1996 when his apartment was shot at. As marketplace and regulatory pressures tightened, the number of banks had fallen to 1,847 by July 1997. The RCB only considers 35 percent of these banks sound; 30 percent are regarded as severly troubled, and are likely to be closed or merged. 265 licenses were revoked in 1996, and 715 more were revoked by mid-1997.

Recent regulations include the increase in minimum capital requirements and minimum risk-weighted capital adequacy ratios, and the tightening of liquidity ratios and exposure limits. International accounting standards were due to be introduced system-wide in early 1998. There are no legal controls on setting interest rates by private banks.

Banking is very immature in Russia. Mortgages are almost unknown, and loans to enterprises for investment are very marginal. In October 1997, loans to non-financial enterprises of a duration greater than six months represented only 3.5 percent of total bank assets. The banking sector is still quite small, with assets less than 30 percent of GDP. Only the two largest banks, Sberbank and Vneshtorgbank, remain majority state-owned. Sberbank, however, controls 30 percent of the entire sector's assets.

Bank services have been improving. Cash settlements, which once took up to two months to complete, can be done in less than two weeks and often overnight. Due to infrastructural and regulatory problems, a reliable inter-bank clearing system does not currently exist. Interest rates are persistently high in real terms. Lending terms are, not surprisingly, long term (over 30 days).

The major Russian banks form the core of what are called financial-industrial groups or FIGs. These banks hold strong equity interests in a variety of industrial enterprises.

Large foreign banks have made substantial inroads in establishing operations, despite two presidential decrees in 1993 and 1994 which restricted the entry of foreign banks. A new commercial banking bill, passed in January 1996, directly authorizes foreign banks to establish full-service banks in Russia. The RCB, however, is given authority to limit foreign banking operations if they grow above a specified level, currently 12 percent of the sector.

The RCB has an "Early Warning System" to monitor bank health. It reviews the statistics of large banks on a daily basis and other banks on a monthly basis. Russia does not currently have a deposit insurance program.

4. How sound is the national currency? (To what extent has inflation eroded its value? Is the value of the currency fixed or does it float? Is the currency convertible? How large are the hard currency reserves? Has exchange rate policy been stable and predictable?) The ruble has been relatively steady in real terms against the dollar since the establishment of a monetary discipline by the RCB and the establishment of a ruble exchange rate corridor in July 1995. The RCB converted the corridor into a "crawling band" with a set rate and a permissible fluctuation of 1.5 percent up or down in July 1996.

The ruble has come under considerable pressure in the wake of the Asian currency crises in 1997. The RCB has strongly resisted devaluing the ruble. Instead, it has pumped up interest rates to shore up its value. It has also spent some of its substantial reserves. These have fallen from $24.5 billion in July 1997 to $16 billion in February 1998.

The ruble is fully convertible on the current account, and somewhat convertible on the capital account. Hard currency accounts with licensed banks are permitted, and currency exchange can take place under the supervision of the Central Bank. In January 1997, the RCB liberalized rules for carrying less than $2,000 of foreign currency outside and into the country.

Russia experienced some of the worst post-transitional inflation in East-Central Europe: 2,600 percent in 1992 and 940 percent in 1993. 70 million investors lost 700 trillion rubles' ($140 billion) worth of savings they had in Sberbank, the national savings bank, because of this hyperinflation. Most of the blame for this massive surge in prices is to be laid at the door of the government and the RCB; the former inducing the latter to inject tremendous amounts of money into the economy, mostly in the form of subsidies. Inflation began to spiral downward once a tighter monetary policy took hold in 1993. Progress has been fairly steady, with price increases falling to 198 percent in 1995 and 48 percent in 1996. Inflation fell further during 1997 to 14.6 percent.

By mid-1996, the Russian people themselves had accumulated $15-20 billion in ruble-denominated domestic savings, symbolizing the new confidence individual Russians place on the relative stability of the ruble.

The ruble was redenominated in January 1998 with 1,000 old rubles equaling one new ruble. This redenomination was a success, and was the first time in decades that the ruble was reformed in a non-confiscatory manner. This has expected to increase confidence in the ruble.

5. Is there a functioning capital market infrastructure? (Are there existing or planned commodities, bond and stock markets? What are the mechanisms for investment and lending? What government bodies have authority to regulate capital markets?) With the adoption of new regulatory requirements, the number of exchanges in Russia fell rapidly from 120 in 1993 to 11 in 1997. Despite recent improvements, Russian stock markets remain non-transparent and illiquid. Trading is active only in a handful of blue chips. Transactions are usually settled offshore.

By the end of 1997, market capitalization on the electronic Russian Trading System (RTS) was $67 billion, up from $20 billion in 1995). Liquidity is still low at $15.7 billion total during 1997, but that is a massive improvement from 1996's $3.5 billion. The market is known for its extreme volatility. By the end of 1997, there were 107 listings on RTS. Nevertheless, 60 percent of RTS's turnover is concentrated in the top 15 companies. RTS-2, the second-tier OTC market for less liquid shares was established in December 1996. 72 companies now trade in it.

The Moscow Interbank Currency Exchange or MICEX, which is owned by 32 commercial banks and other institutions, dominates the trade of currency, derivatives, and government debt. It began trading of equities in March 1997. By December 1992, turnover was $22 million daily.

Large Russian companies have tapped successfully into international equity markets. By the end of 1997, 20 Russian companies had issued American Depositary Receipts. Domestic bond issues by Russian companies , however, have not generally been successful.

There are only about 1,000 private pension funds, with $630 million in assets in early 1997. Only about 40 percent of these are officially licensed, and even those frequently skirt regulations. In July 1995, a presidential decree established the legal framework for mutual funds. By mid-1997, nine mutual funds were licensed. Many existing voucher funds are expected to be converted to mutual funds.

Protection of shareholders' rights is weak in Russia. Firms frequently maintain (and manipulate) their own share registrars, undermine voting procedures, issue new shares to dilute existing shareholder's property, and establish barriers to board representation of outside shareholders. Profits are often siphoned out of companies by management to avoid paying dividends. Employee shareholders are manipulated by enterprise management in various ways. Management finds ways to obtain voting rights to employees' shares. Workers are also often told that they must sell their shares to the management if they leave the company. There have been recent high-profile court cases where shareholders' rights have been upheld, as well as denied.

The ministry-level Russian Federation Commission for Securities Markets (FCSM) was established in November 1994 and began the process of a more Western-style securities market regulation. It is governed by a six-member board, one of whom is chairman. In 1997, the FCSM became truly active for the first time. It and its newly established 15 regional offices relicensed all professional participants in the stock markets. It also instituted new examinations for qualifications. The Commission assumed responsibility for registering new stock issues in July 1997. The FSCM began to regulate share registrars in 1996. This has led the number of share registrars to fall from 500 in 1996 to 201 by the end of 1997. This change should lower transaction costs and improve reliability in securities transactions. In 1997, the FCSM began monitoring of companies operating in the securities markets (RTS, MICEX, etc.) It also issued regulations to improve information disclosure by public companies. The FSCM still does not, however, have broad powers to investigate and punish shareholder rights violations.

The comprehensive Russian Law on Joint-Stock Companies was put into operation in January 1996. It expanded numerous shareholder protections, including the maintenance of independent share registries for companies with over 500 shareholders. Another important regulatory institution is the Professional Association of Securities Market Participants, the industry association which actually organized the RTS market in April 1995. It dictates clear rules to its more than 150 members, among them capital requirements, ethical conduct, and general trading behavior. Enforcement of these regulations has occurred, but remains spotty.

Microeconomics 4.25/7

1. Are property rights guaranteed? Are there both formal and de facto protections of private real estate and intellectual property? Is there a land registry with the authority and capability to ensure accurate recording of who owns what? What are the procedures for expropriation, including measures for compensation and challenge? Have any seizures taken place? Russia's constitution explicitly protects private property. Article 35 establishes the general right to property and the subsidiary right to due process and just compensation when property is nationalized. Article 36 specifically guarantees property rights in land. The checkered protection of such rights by the Duma and the judicial system limits the legal protections afforded by the constitution.

The legal basis for land ownership is only operationalized through presidential decrees, dating from October 1993. The Duma has expressely refused to allow land to be traded freely despite the constitution. This is due to the strong opposition of Communist and agrarian political forces to a liberal land market. The current land code from 1996 permits Russians to inherit and lease farmland, but buying, selling, and mortgaging are prohibited. Russians wishing to buy farmland have to have agricultural training or experience, and "owners" of such land are not allowed to sell it to others. A new land code has been delayed for some time. Federal paralysis on land ownership may be becoming less relevant. The Saratov oblast adopted a liberal land code in November 1997 and other regions are following suit.

Russia lacks a central land registry which would guarantee title to land. Land is registered in many regions with agencies that do not also handle buildings registration. Even where registries exist, the de facto legal protections afforded to such entries remain confused.

There were some worrying developments in 1997 that called into question the security of recently privatized property. In the first high-profile privatization to be reversed, the Moscow Arbitration Court ruled in September 1997 that 41 percent of the chemicals plant Cherepovets Azot be returned to the government. Oneximbank was found to have failed to meet the investment conditions required under the tender that was awarded to it. In November 1997, the Russian Environmental Ministry canceled a 1996 sale (to Exxon) of a 50-percent stake in the Russian Arctic oilfield of Tsentralnaya Khoreiverskaya. Observers attribute this decision to the desire of state-owned Rosneft for a bigger share of the field. The sale of 50 percent of insurance giant Rosgosstrakh was canceled in mid-1997 after Duma criticism of its low price. Most appeals against privatization have, however, been rejected by Russian courts.

Russia is a signatory of all the major international intellectual property treaties such as the Paris Convention, the Trademark Registration Treaty, and the Patent Cooperation Treaty. Russian domestic legal protection for intellectual property was created through four laws passed in October 1992 which covered patents and trademarks. The Copyright Laws of July 1993 and July 1995 followed. In March 1995, Chernomyrdin created an interministry commission to enforce intellectual property laws, composed of representatives from the Russian Anti-Monopoly Committee and the Russian Federation Committee on Patents and Trademarks. In addition, the Russian Criminal and Civil Codes, including sections pertaining to IPR, are in the process of being revised. New features which relate to IPR include increased penalties, the establishment of new specialized courts to resolve disputes, and the training of additional legal personnel such as attorneys and judges.

Despite the existence of institutions protecting intellectual property rights, enforcement and implementation of these protections are notably lagging. Software, motion picture, video, music, and trademark piracy are rampant. An estimated 95 percent of software is pirated, while pirated films (85 percent of the total) are openly broadcast on Russian television. The United States alone is estimated to have lost nearly $1 billion in 1997 because of copyright violations. Patent protection is also deficient. U.S. attorneys in Russia have reported that inexperience in IPR issues in Russian courts is a major problem. Finally, the new IPR interministry commission receives little funding and is only active part-time, limiting its effectiveness.

2. To what extent have prices been liberalized? What subsidies remain? Nearly all prices were liberalized in 1992, when reforms began. Some prices remain controlled. These include the prices of government-controlled monopolies, including gas, electricity, transportation, and telecommunications. Consumer prices for these goods are set much lower than those for producers, although a March 1997 announcement promises to change the situation.

Housing costs are severely controlled. Rents cover only 27 percent of provision costs. These rent subsidies constitute over 40 percent of local government budgets. A recent reform plan envisages the gradual increase of housing prices to cost-recovery levels by 2003.

In July 1996, the Ulyanovsk region abandoned the subsidization of food prices — the last region to do so in Russia.

An excess wage tax is levied on businesses paying more than six times the Russian minimum wage.

3. Is it possible to own and operate a business? (Has there been legislation regarding the formation, dissolution and transfer of businesses, and is the law respected? Do there exist overly cumbersome bureaucratic hurdles that effectively hinder the ability to own and dispose of a business? Are citizens given access to information on commercial law? Is the law applied fairly? Does regulation (or licensing requirements) impose significant costs on business and consumers? Do they create significant barriers to entry and seriously hamper competition?) The Russian business environment is now substantially liberalized. More than 90 percent of wholesale and retail price controls have been removed. They still remain on housing, telephone service, and energy. Regulations are sometimes a hindrance to business operations. In general, enterprises with more than 100 million old rubles in capitalization (currently about $18,000) must register with the government. This can entail lengthy delays.

One major problem for the development of a normal market economy in Russia is the multitude of decrees and regulations issued by the presidential administration, the government, and the various bureaucracies. They are very often vague, overlapping and contradictory. By the end of 1996, Russia had implemented only two-thirds of the Civil Code. In addition, the policymaking process is not very transparent. What is worse, different bureaucracies and jurisdictions apply laws inconsistently. Lines of authority are also unclear, decisions of one institution can be overruled by another. Rapidly changing rules of the game inconsistently applied, make the business environment unpredictable and, as such, not conducive to long-term investment.

Vagueness has been a hallmark of Russian legislation and decrees. This is problematic because vagueness increases business uncertainty and reduces the profitability of forward-looking investment.

Criminal organizations extort "protection money" from both foreign and domestic firms. Figures are obviously hard to come by. One estimate is that 30 percent of Western firms in Moscow pay to the tune of about 10 percent of profits. Even more prevalent is the "sweetener" amount on closing a contract — up to 10 percent of the contract amount. The Ministry of the Interior estimated that organized crime earned 280 trillion old rubles ($128 billion) in 1994.

Bankruptcy is still far from a credible threat. Bankruptcy courts and the Federal Bankruptcy Service's low capacity makes it unable to implement bankruptcies. In fact, only about 1000 bankruptcies have been completed as of mid-1997. Political opposition, especially at the local levels, also slows bankruptcies. Under the new Civil Code, creditors have a relatively low priority.

A new bankruptcy law was enacted in January 1998 and clears up the ambiguities in the bankruptcy legislation previously in force. Decisions regarding firms in bankruptcy proceedings are now to be fully regulated by arbitration courts.

4. Are courts effective, transparent, efficient, and quick in reaching decisions on property and contract disputes? What alternative mechanisms for adjudicating disputes exist? It takes less than six months for cases to be heard, and nearly a year on average for judgement to be made. There are rights of appeal. Important judgements are published.

Independent dispute resolution is difficult to obtain in Russia. In addition to the problems of rapidly changing commercial rules, the judicial system is not equipped to provide prompt and experienced services. The All-Russian Council of Judges has argued that courts have received one-fifth of the money necessary to pay for administrative expenses, while justice minister Valentin says that the $345 million allocated to the system is enough for only one-third of its needs. Judges are often the targets of criminal attacks. In August 1996, Moscow judge Olga Lavrenteva was killed by a street vendor whom she had fined $7 the day before.

Numerous local courts have experienced difficulties in making wage, equipment, and security service payments. In July 1997 *Izvestiya* reported the case of one regional court that was able to function only because a local law firm paid its utility bills and allowed the judge to use its telephone. These conditions not only make the system more vulnerable to the temptations of corruption but, more generally, deter businessmen from using courts to resolve disputes. The lack of resources available for the judiciary means that the most able personnel leave for more lucrative positions, in the private sector.

Even beyond these resource difficulties, the presence of Soviet and inexperienced post-Soviet judges makes the consistent and correct adjudication of complex commercial disputes almost impossible. What is worse, pressure is often applied to obtain a politically desirable outcome. Even judicial decisions are not always binding. The situation is so bad that Western investors seek arbitration outside of Russia to resolve disputes. Within Russia, businesses can turn to the Arbitration Court of the Russian Federation (part of the court system) or the International Commercial Arbitration Court at the Russian Chamber of Commerce and Industry (if both parties agree). Still, arbitration decisions and awards are not always legally binding in courts of law.

Using organized crime as a "dispute resolution" device is popular because it is so hard to settle business problems in Russia legally. A notorious example is sobering. An American businessman, Paul Tatum, was killed by assassins in November 1996. Americom, Tatum's company, had been fighting Moscow city authorities in the courts over the ownership of the Radisson-Slavyanskaya hotel.

5. Is business competition encouraged? (Are monopolistic practices limited in law and in practice? If so, how? To what degree is "insider" dealing a hindrance to open competition? Are government procurement policies open and unbiased?) The legal framework of Russian competition policy was enacted in the Law on Competition and Restriction of Monopolistic Practices in March 1991. It established the State Committee for Anti-Monopoly Policy which became a ministry in March 1995. The committee has a broad mandate to fight anti-competitive behavior by both firms and government bodies. The Anti-Monopoly Committee initiated 1,240 investigations in 1996. In May 1997, a commission composed of the committee and other federal agencies was created to enhance the prosecution of competition policy.

The presence of law does not guarantee enforcement. Laws prohibiting insider dealing of public companies exist but are widely flouted. Although a Law on Financial and Industrial Groups was passed in November 1995, the committee has yet to address anti-competitive aspects of FIG behavior.

Worst of all, cumbersome state and semi-private industrial monopolies (like Gazprom) still dominate large sections of the economy, with the explicit and tacit support of the government. The trade ministry, for example, has in the past encouraged the formation of industry-wide cartels to establish a floor on export prices of "strategically important" commodities.

A recent presidential decree mandates open tendering of all government procurements. The government procurement code, however gives clear preferences to domestic firms. The government has even revoked tenders awarded to foreign businesses and given them to Russian firms.

6. To what extent has international trade been liberalized? To what degree has there been simplification/overhaul of customs and tariff procedures, and are these applied fairly? What informal trade barriers exist? Generally, Russia employs relatively light trade barriers. This has caused Russian trade to boom and the trade sector is one bright spot in the reforming Russian economy. The trend, however, has often not gone in the right direction. In July 1994, for example, the average tariff was increased from 7-8 percent to 11 percent. Another major tariff regime change in July 1995 accentuated this trend, increasing the average tariff from to 12.5 percent, with the minimum duty raised to 5 percent. In April 1996, a presidential decree raised tariffs even further on a broad range of goods, with average tariffs increased to some 13-14 percent. Maximum duties, however, were reduced to 30 percent in late 1996. They have since fallen to an average 10.6 percent tariff in 1997.

Russia is not currently a member of any free-trade organization, although it is in the process of negotiating two (one with Europe, and the other between the Commomwealth of Independent States countries). To Russia's chagrin, it is not yet a member of the World Trade Organization. It has an association agreement with the EU, and MFN trade status with the United States.

Populist and agrarian political forces have been responsible for increasing nontariff barriers on food, through such means as phytosanitary norms and quality standards. The majority of imports face various types of certification, labeling, documentation, and customs requirements. These are constantly revised, and customs officials often impose arbitrary interpretations of such requirements.

In January 1993, a newly-harmonized system for export licensing and quotas on "strategic raw materials" was adopted. A May 1994 presidential decree removed all export quotas as of July 1994. Exporters are required to pay a tax of about 20 percent on cash transactions (30 percent on barter) on most goods. Additional export tariffs exist on most goods, but these have been gradually reduced. Export controls remain on "strategic raw materials" like wheat, soybeans, ethanol, natural gas, electricity, fertilizers, timber, cellulose, uncut diamonds, copper, nickel, and aluminum, as well as on "strategic goods" like weapons. However, the registration procedure necessary to export these goods is not generally difficult. The March 1995 decree further liberalized the export sector.

7. To what extent has foreign investment and capital flow been encouraged or constrained? Legally, the 1991 Investment Code guarantees equal treatment of foreign and native investors. There, however, are many exceptions. In enterprises deemed "strategic" (mostly in the energy and finance sectors), foreigners are forbidden to own more than 15 percent of shares.

That said, foreign investors do enjoy some important privileges. The only controls on profit repatriation are those on short-term government securities. Foreigners may have complete ownership of enterprises. There are no legal requirements on the personnel make-up of the firm. Russia also gives tax amnesties to large foreign investors engaged in manufacturing. Goods imported by firms with foreign investment that are directly necessary for manufacturing machinery can be imported duty-free. Finally, the 1991 Investment Code forbids nationalization of foreign investment except in cases when it serves the "national interest." However, any such nationalization can be appealed and prompt compensation is legally required.

Some $6 billion in FDI came into Russia in 1996 ($12 billion cumulative), a big increase from 1995's $1.9 billion. The United States is by far the largest investor. Still, on a per capita basis, FDI in Russia is very low: approximately $80 per person (compared with $300 for Poland). This is because foreign investors feel that the political and economic risks outweigh the benefits of investment. Foreign portfolio investment is becoming increasingly popular.

Russia has not yet adopted international accounting standards, forcing foreign companies to maintain two sets of books to conform to Russian and their home country's regulations.

8. Has there been reform of the energy sector? (To what degree has the energy sector been restructured? Is the energy sector more varied, and is it open to private competition? Is the country overly dependent on one or two other countries for energy [including whether exported fuels must pass through one or more countries to reach markets]?) Russia's energy sector is one of the biggest in the world. It is first worldwide in natural gas production, third in oil, and fourth in coal. Gazprom, the huge natural gas monopoly, owns a huge network built over twenty years; over 140,000 km of main pipelines. The energy industry is significant also in its intricate ties with political elites. Energy monopolies are thus able to enjoy special privileges like subsidies of various kinds.

The energy sector, however, is plagued numerous problems. The first is payments, wage, and tax arrears. Strikes are prevalent. There exists a vicious cycle of companies not being paid by their customers and not having the cash flow either to pay their workers or their taxes. The debts of power and heating consumers were 71 trillion old rubles ($13 billion) in August 1996. These arrears are partly the legacy of an irrational system of centralized state planning, but they mainly reflect the government's enforcement of an order prohibiting utilities from ending supplies to delinquent customers.

Another major problem is a crumbling and obsolete infrastructure. Gazprom, for example, needs billions of dollars to upgrade its systems, many of which are literally crumbling. Such investment is not likely to happen as long as governments restrict energy prices as well as the entry of foreign investors.

Instead of liberalization, the government has pursued short-term, mutually incompatible solutions to the problems of the energy industry. In September 1996, for example, the government authorized the finance ministry to provide $94 million in loan guarantees for power plants. In August, these guarantees had been restricted to exclude just this sort of subsidy. In February 1996, Yeltsin decreed the conversion of Rosugol, the state coal enterprise, into a joint-stock corporation. Under the pressure of management and unions, however, the state was simultaneously guaranteed complete ownership for three years.

Compared to earlier times, the oil sector substantially liberalized. This industry, unlike gas and electricity, was broken up into a dozen companies as it was privatized. In addition, oil prices as of October 1996, were some 75 percent of world prices, much more realistic than they were at 7-10 percent. Oil export tariffs were phased out entirely in July 1996. Simultaneously, however, oil production excise taxes have been increased.

In January 1998, the oil firms Yukos and Sibneft announced a merger. The enormous new firm, Yuksi, will have a workforce of 200,000. Its combined production 65 million tons of oil in 1997 (22 percent of Russia's output) make it the world's third largest producer after Shell and Exxon.

SLOVAKIA

Freedom in the World Ratings, 1989-1998

	1989-90	1990-91	1991-92	1992-93	1993-94	1994-95	1995-96	1996-97	1997-98
Political Rights	6	2	2	2	3	2	2	2	2
Civil Liberties	6	2	2	2	4	3	3	4	4
Status	NF	F	F	F	PF	F	F	PF	PF

Polity: Transitional
Economy: Transitional
Population: 5,370,000
PPP: $7,320
Ethnic Groups: Slovak (82 percent), Hungarian (11 percent), Roma (5 percent), Czech (1 percent)
Capital: Bratislava

Freedom House ratings through 1992-93 are for the Czechoslovak federal state.

Political Process 3.50/7

1. When did national legislative elections occur? Were they free and fair? How were they judged by domestic and international election monitoring organizations? Who composes the government? Since the collapse of communism in 1989, Slovakia has held three parliamentary elections — in 1990, 1992, and 1994 — all of which were confirmed by international observers to be free and democratic. The first free election to the Slovak National Council, the regional Slovak parliament in the former Czechoslovak federation, in 1990 was a plebiscite against communism. The parties that were critical of the Communist past, e.g., the Public Against Violence and the Hungarian Independent Initiative (VPN/MNI), the Christian Democratic Movement (KDH), the Hungarian Christian Democratic Movement and the Coexistence, the Slovak National Party (SNS), the Democratic Party (DS), and the Green Party, won jointly an overwhelming majority of the vote. The Communist Party of Slovakia (KSS) gained a mere 13.3 percent. Slovakia's first pro-reform government (1990-1992) also comprised representatives of the Hungarian ethnic minority. The 1992 elections were won by the Movement for a Democratic Slovakia (HZDS) which had split off from VPN in 1991. HZDS gained 37.2 percent of the vote and 74 seats in a 150-member strong parliament, the new official name of the parliament after the emergence of an independent Slovakia on January 1, 1993.

In the 1994 elections, the HZDS retained its dominant position after receiving, together with its junior coalition partner, the Agrarian Party, 35 percent of the vote or 61 seats in parliament. HZDS Chairman Vladimir Meciar, who in March 1994 had been ousted as prime minister by a parliamentary no-confidence vote for a second time, became prime minister for the third time. The left-wing parties of the Common Choice coalition, which comprised the Party of the Democratic Left (SDL), Social Democratic Party of Slovakia (SDSS), Green Party (SZS), and the Peasants' Movement, won a mere 10.4 percent of the vote and 18 seats in parliament. Two new political parties entered the parliament: the radical left-wing and populist Association of Slovakia's Workers (ZRS), which received 7.3 percent of the vote and 13 seats, and the liberal Democratic Union (DU), which won 8.6 percent of the vote and 15 seats. The conservative KDH received 10.1 percent and 17 seats, the nationalistic SNS, 5.4 percent and 9 seats. The voting by ethnic Hungarians went along ethnic lines and gave 10.2 percent and 17 seats in parliament to the parties comprising the Hungarian Coalition which included the Hungarian Christian Democratic Movement, Coexistence, and the Hungarian Civic Party. In December 1994, HZDS, ZRS, and the SNS formed a governing coalition that has remained intact.

In the spring of 1998, the coalition government prepared a draft bill to amend Slovakia's election law. According to coalition representatives, the new amendment was necessary to improve Slovakia's election procedures and was fully consistent with electoral norms elsewhere in Europe. Members of the opposition and numerous non-governmental organizations strongly criticized the amendment, not only for introducing major changes to the country's election law just months before the September parliamentary elections, but for what they considered serious substantive flaws. For example, the amendment required that each member of a multiparty coalition reach a 5 percent threshold to gain seats in parliament. This provision was seen as a deliberate attempt to handicap the five-party Slovak Democratic Coalition (SDK), which has led the ruling HZDS in most opinion polls since its origin in July 1997. Another provision strengthened the position of the state administration (which opposition figures do not regard as fully neutral) in the election process at the expense of former electoral commissions composed of political party representatives. In addition, lists of registered voters would no longer be posted in public; voters would still be able to verify their own personal data, but would not be able to check the accuracy of other information on voter lists. The amendment also included other provisions regulating the conduct of the electoral campaign in broadcast media, which critics feared could interfere with the activities of private media covering the campaign. According to the Slovak constitution, amending the electoral law requires only a simple majority which the government coalition currently holds in parliament. Unlike in 1992 and 1994, when it won the elections as an opposition party, HZDS entered the 1998 elections as the strongest party in the ruling parliamentary coalition. The government's powers were, in fact, increased recently by the transfer of certain presidential powers following the expiration of President Michal Kovac's term of office in March 1998. Opposition parties and civic groups have launched a civic campaign for "free and fair elections" while calling for domestic and international election observers and parallel counting of ballots.

2. When did presidential elections occur? Were they free and fair? Under the current constitution, the president is elected by a three-fifths majority in parliament. From March 1993 to March 1998 Michal Kovac served as president. Despite the fact that Kovac had been nominated for the presidency by the HZDS, relations between himself and the HZDS gradually deteriorated. The governing coalition that came to power after the 1994 elections accused the president of having played a role in Meciar's March 1994 removal and of favoring the opposition. The president regarded his office as being above party politics and sought to offset the attempts by the Prime Minister Meciar to increase the powers. In 1994-1998, the confrontation between the president and the prime minister became a hallmark of Slovakia's domestic politics. The ruling coalition unsuccessfully attempted to remove the president from office, adopted legislation that substantially reduced funds allocated to the presidential office, and transferred some presidential powers, including that of appointing the head of the Slovak Information Service (secret service) to the government. The presidency has remained vacant since Kovac left office in March 1998. In the three rounds of presidential elections held by parliament in January, March, and April 1998, none of the nominees for the presidency were able to gain the required three-fifths majority. The political parties were unable to reach consensus on an acceptable head of state, increasing the the risk of a constitutional crisis. In early 1997, opposition parties initiated a public campaign petitioning for a referendum on direct elections for the presidency. President Kovac subsequently announced that a referendum would be held on May 23-24, 1997, combining the question of direct elections for the presidency with three other questions from a parliamentary-approved referendum designed to probe public opinion on Slovakia's prospective NATO membership. The representatives of the ruling coalition repeatedly expressed doubts and questioned the president's right to combine two referendums into one. Several days before the ballots were to be cast, the question about direct presidential elections was removed. While polls by several agencies had indicated that a regular referendum was likely to have attracted more than 50 percent of eligible voters, with most indicating support for direct elections and for Slovakia's membership in NATO, only 9.5 of voters actually participated in a referendum. After President Kovac left office, some presidential powers were transferred to Prime Minister Meciar.

3. Is the electoral system multiparty-based? Are there at least two viable political parties functioning at all levels of government? Slovakia is a multiparty state with as many as 12 organized political parties represented at the national, regional, and local levels. In some cities, local governments have a composition different from that of the national parliament, with opposition parties prevailing, *e.g.* Bratislava, Banska Bystrica, Kosice, Presov, Trnava, Komarno etc.).

4. How many parties have been legalized? Is any particular party illegal? In Slovakia there are about 90 legal political parties and movements. Under current law, political parties can be banned if they violate the constitution and laws, seek to dismantle the democratic foundation of the state, strive to seize and preserve power, prevent other political entities from seeking power by constitutional means, and attempt to suppress the equality of citizens. The same legislation bans parties whose manifesto or actions jeopardize morality, public order, civil rights and freedoms, and undermine the sovereignty and territorial integrity of the Slovak Republic. Since 1990, no political party has been banned in Slovakia, nor has any party been forced underground. In 1997, political developments in Slovakia prompted opposition parties to cooperate more closely. In July 1997, the SDK was established and, as suggested by opinion polls, became a major competitor with the HZDS. The SDK, led by Mikulas Dzurinda, comprises KDH, DU, DS, SDSS, and SZS. In the run-up to the 1998 elections, several new parties emerged. The Civic Understanding Party, led by the mayor of Kosice, Rudolf Schuster, has appeared to be the most successful one, aligning itself with the opposition and committed itself to pro-European integration for Slovakia.

5. What proportion of the population belongs to political parties? The precise membership of political parties operating in Slovakia is unknown. It is estimated that the members of all parties account for about 5 percent of the adult population. This relatively low percentage is due to traditional public mistrust of political parties. In recent years, the HZDS has begun a drive to increase its membership, targeting to recruit 100,000 members.

6. What has been the trend in voter turnout at the municipal, provincial and national level in recent years? Although the voter turnout remains fairly high, it has been declining consistently since the first free elections in 1990. In the 1990 elections in the then-Czechoslovakia, voter turnout was 95.4 percent. In subsequent national legislative elections, the turnout decreased to 84.2 percent in 1992 and 75.7 percent in 1994. Municipal elections, where turnout is traditionally lower than in parliamentary elections, have also recorded diminished voting activity. In the 1990 municipal elections, turnout was 63.8 percent, while in 1994, it was only 52.4 percent. The generally lower municipal elections turnout is due to a lesser intensity of election campaigns, weaker involvement of party structures, and the mass media.

Civil Society 3.00/7

1. How many nongovernmental organizations have come into existence since 1988? What is the number of charitable/nonprofit organizations? Are there locally led efforts to increase philanthropy and volunteerism? What proportion of the population is active in private voluntary activity (from polling data)? Despite decades of political regimentation, the nongovernmental (NGO) or "third" sector has recorded remarkable development. In 1993, there were approximately 6,000 NGOs; in 1994, the number increased to 9,800. As of March 1998, the Ministry of Interior registered the following: 12,000 civil associations such as societies, clubs, associations, movements, trade unions, international non-governmental organizations, various sports clubs or their organizational units; 422 foundations; and 121 non-investment funds. In addition, in April 1998, there were 2,831 registered churches and religious societies or ecclesiastical organizations, 1496 land companies, 329 interest associations of legal entities, 140 professional chambers and bars, and 100 non-profit public benefit organizations. Prior to the adoption of the 1996 Law on Foundations, the number of foundations was higher, but it has declined substantially as a result of a re-registration process required under the new law. From foreign policy, domestic politics, and social policy to health care, economics, education, the environment, culture, media, the judiciary, and public administration, NGOs are attempting to exert a positive influence on public policy by supporting or criticizing governmental proposals, informing citizens, and enhancing diversity and pluralism. They have also been organizing activities related to democracy such as campaigning, educating, and protesting; monitoring the transition process; and attempting to hold elected and government officials accountable to their fellow citizens.

The culture of philanthropy and volunteerism is on the rise with several efforts underway to increase its scope. In 1995, 13 percent of the population was involved in volunteering; in 1996 and in 1997 it was 19 percent. More frequent than volunteering was charitable giving or donating. In 1996, 42 percent of adults donated some material or money to NGOs. In addition, in 1996, almost half of all adult citizens contributed to a church collection and 25 percent to schools and kindergartens. Twelve percent of respondents attended a charity ball or concert in 1996. Volunteering and charitable giving, however, are not evenly distributed among the population. The most likely contributors are persons who are highly educated, middle aged, female, and ethnic Hungarian.

2. What is the legal and regulatory environment for NGOs (i.e. ease of registration, legal rights, government regulations, taxation, procurement and access-to-information issues)? To what extent is NGO activism focused on improvement of the legal and regulatory environment? The majority of NGOs operate under legal norms adopted in the first years after November 1989. Civil associations, the most common legal assemblages, are regulated by the Law on the Associating of Citizens; religious societies are subject to the Law on Freedom of Religious Belief and Status of Churches and Religious Societies and the Law on the Registration of Churches and Religious Societies. The status of interest associations of legal persons is regulated by the Civic Code, Section 20f-20j. There are special laws regulating the functioning of other associations, e.g. professional bars with a compulsory and voluntary membership, non-professional chambers, Slovak Red Cross, hunting associations, a fishermen's union. There are also non-profit legal entities founded under the Commercial Code such as cooperative associations and business companies.

In 1996-1997, extensive public debate transpired over three additional laws. A Law on Foundations imposed new regulations on foundations' activities, composition, and functional life span and clarified the legal status of foundation income, expenditures, and administrative expenses. The Law on Non-Investment Funds established the legal framework for those foundations that do not have their own funds but collect finances on an ad hoc basis or in a permanent way and spend them for a specific purpose or a public utility purpose. A Law on Public Benefit Nonprofit Organizations established guidelines for the creation, termination, and administrative and financial management of nonprofit organizations for both legal entities and private persons. All three laws were challenged by the Gremium of the Third Sector, an umbrella leadership organization of Slovakia's nonprofits, which, in 1996, launched a major "Third Sector SOS" campaign to generate grass-roots opposition to the bill. The participants of the Fifth Conference of Non-Governmental Organizations held in October 1997 declared that legal regulations pertaining to the operations of non-governmental organizations inadequately support, or even in some cases actually hinder, their activities and development. They agreed on the need to prepare the basis for amending pertinent laws and the whole legal context for the existence of the third sector.

3. What is the organizational capacity of NGOs? Do management structures clearly delineate authority and responsibility? Is information available on NGO management issues in native language? Is there a core of experienced practitioners/trainers to serve as consultants or mentors to less developed organizations? Slovakia's NGOs traditionally meet at the so-called Stupava conferences of the nonprofit sector, where they discuss problems and forms of cooperation within the sector, as well as with the government, entrepreneurs, and visitors from foreign countries. The Gremium of the Third Sector, a voluntary, unincorporated, advocacy group, serves as coordinating central body which represents the third sector in relations with the government, parliament, the business sector, and the public. The Service Center for the Third Sector at the Slovak Academic Information Agency and several other institutions gather information about Slovakia's NGOs and offer training to NGO managers. The magazine *NonProfit* serves as a platform for the exchange of information. The number of specialized literature in Slovak is increasing. At the Fifth Stupava Conference in 1997, the participants criticized the unfavorable legislative environment that had been established by the three new laws and called for a law on tax and customs relief suitable for nonprofit entities performing public benefit work. An important step in the institutional building of the NGO sector was the creation of the network of regional *gremia* that have already established contacts with representatives of local state administration, local governments, and businessmen. The Donor's Forum, a new free association, has begun to be active and is made up of leading personalities of grant-making foundations working in Slovakia. A number of community initiatives, both in the villages or towns, are strengthening the vitality in their respective community, attracting and mobilizing new sources, and creating partnerships between citizens, local governments, the business sector, NGOs, state entities, and the media. In the final declaration, the participants of the conference called for improved transparency in the activities of NGOs, especially in the utilization of financial and other sources. At the same time, they demanded the same openness and transparency on the part of the government and the administrators of public resources. They invited representatives of the business sector to cooperate more closely with NGOs and emphasized the need for a closer cooperation with local governments even in the form of the direct participation of representatives of NGOs in community politics.

Despite Slovakia's well developed NGO sector, in comparison with other post-Communist countries, there is much needed improvement. Only a minority of existing NGOs have an appropriately developed organizational structure, and the majority do not have long-term organization, financial, and human resources strategy. There are few organizations with exactly formulated missions and notions how to carry out these missions. Most volunteers do not have skills for building a stable organization although many groups have managed to survive for a remarkably long time.

4. Are NGOs financially viable? What is their tax status? Are they obliged to and do they typically disclose revenue sources? Do government procurement opportunities exist for private, not-for-profit providers of services? The financial situation of the third sector is not favorable. There is growing discussion about the sustainability, diversification of sources, financial management, and strategic planning in the sector. Foundations are obliged to disclose their revenue sources. Some NGOs are subsidized from public budgets. Subsidies are given, in particular, to organizations that provide basic services for the physically or mentally handicapped people and to the state order, i.e. Slovak Red Cross. Financial assistance is also provided by the ministries of labor, social affairs, and family, education, culture, health, interior, and environment as well as from individual state funds administered by the appropriate ministry. Special subsidies are also given for certain activities of non-governmental non-profit organizations, e.g., for publishing children's magazines and literature. Other subsidies may be paid by the state administration to providers of social services. State subsidies are also paid to private and church schools.

Cooperation with local self-governments seems to be promising. The considerable interest in the issue of "community initiatives" at the local level is progressing. A pioneer role in this domain was played by the Healthy City Foundation of Banska Bystrica, which raised funds not only from the city budget but also from entrepreneurs and others in the community. As one of the first domestic foundations, it started to build an endowment in cooperation with a foreign sponsor. While the private sector provides considerable funds, in 1996-1997 there was no reliable data on its real extent. Foreign funds (European, American, or Japanese) represent an invaluable and necessary financial mechanism. Although finances raised by their own activities and membership fees are currently a rather small part of incomes, the larger organizations try to increase incomes from their own activities, such as fees for courses, counseling publications, welfare activities, and the sale of products by the physically or mentally handicapped. Various charity fund-raisers, such as concerts and art auctions, enjoy a growing popularity and have became a regular part of the social life.

According to the Law on Income Taxes, nonprofit organizations are subjected to taxes only in the case of income from activities executed for profit. Incomes acquired by inheritance or donation are not subject to taxation. Membership fees of civic associations, incomes from the main activity of nonprofit organizations, yields from parish collections, and lotteries for public utility purposes are exempt from tax. The same applies to contributions and scholarships that are awarded to individuals by foundations. Donations for the funding of science and education, culture, the education system, protection against fire, promotion and protection of youth, purposes of a social, health, ecological, humanitarian, charitable, religious, sport and physical education can be deducted from the tax base. The value of donations must at a minimum amount to 2,000 Slovak Korunas (SK) in the case of legal entities and 2 percent of the total can be deducted from the tax base. In the case of individuals, it is 1,000 Sk, or 2 percent of the tax base. Donations for public utility purposes are deducted regardless of whether they are given to state, church, or private nonprofit organizations. Contrary to civil associations, foundations are not allowed to engage in enterprise with the exception of the leasing of the property of a foundation, organizing of public collections, operating of lotteries, or organizing of cultural, educational, social, and sports events.

5. Are there free trade unions? How many workers belong to these unions? Is the number of workers belonging to trade unions growing or decreasing? What is the numerical/proportional membership of farmers' groups, small business associations etc.? According to Article 37 of the constitution, trade unions are independent from the state. Data on membership varies, ranging from 50 percent to 65-70 percent of the labor force, however, the general trend indicates a decline in membership. Almost all trade unions are represented in the Confederation of Trade Unions with 1.1 million members uniting 42 branches. Although social peace prevailed generally in 1996-1997, relations between the government and the trade unions have cooled significantly. Following the passage of the law regulating wages in 1997, the trade unionists interrupted their dialogue with the government and refused to continue in further bargaining over a general agreement for the year 1997. As of spring 1998, the negotiations had not been renewed. Small business has attempted to defend its interest also through autonomous political parties.

6. What forms of interest group participation in politics are legal? What types of interest groups are active in the political and policy process? Special interest organizations play an important role both in the political as well as the policy process. The interest representation has different forms, from the pluralist to corporatist ones. Corporatist arrangements, however have gradually become a typical way of interest representation. The old branch structure of industrial production encouraged the promotion of corporatist procedures and led to the development of the tripartite arrangement with the trade unions, associations of employers, and the state as the main actors. A visible trend towards societal corporatism and the creation of umbrella-coordinating organizations in Slovakia has been a natural response to the fact that unassociated and fragmented interests have been ignored by the government. For example, in 1997, the Association of Slovak Periodical Publishers and the Slovak Syndicate of Journalists, supported by private radio and TV broadcasters, organized coordinated action against a proposal to increase the value-added tax (VAT) on periodicals from 6 percent to 23 percent, thus prompting a compromise solution in parliament. A new phenomenon is what some experts call "party-state corporatism" in which the party in power uses its almost exclusive access to public finances and other public resources to establish new party-affiliated organizations or to "colonize" already existing groups.

7. How is the not-for-profit/NGO sector perceived by the public and governmental officials? What is the nature of media coverage of NGOs? To what extent do government officials engage with NGOs? The relations between the NGOs represented by the Gremium of the Third Sector and the government remained tense after the adoption of controversial laws regulating nonprofit field. In February 1997 a new pro-governmental umbrella institution, the Union of Civic Associations and Foundations, was created. In spheres where the present government does not succeed in establishing its domination – due to the still existing democratic conditions, to the strong resistance by a concerned public, or to other circumstances – it implements a strategy of founding alternative, loyal structures, which are usually dependent on governmental resources. Analysts characterize this paradoxical phenomenon as an attempt to disrupt civil society from within, by founding a "parallel polis," that is guaranteed, legitimized, and funded by the state. From June 1995 to November 1997, the third sector received comprehensive media coverage, including more than 22,220 articles. A sociological analysis based on this monitoring confirmed that the majority of Slovak newspapers have reported on NGO efforts favorably. The most visible NGOs were those oriented toward charity, youth, and education. In the majority of newspapers, the nonprofit sector has been frequently placed within the context of civil society.

Independent Media 4.00/7

1. Are there legal protections for press freedom? Yes. Although no new media law has been passed, Article 26 of the Slovak constitution guarantees the "freedom of expression and the right to information." Following the downfall of the Communist regime in 1989, important changes took place in the field of mass media: censorship was officially prohibited, the leading role of the Communist party was abolished, private ownership of mass media was legalized, and a dual system in the field of electronic mass media was introduced. All media operating in Slovakia are subject to the 1966 Law on Mass Media Communications. Since 1990, 16 drafts of a new media law have been prepared but not one has been debated in parliament. Negotiations between professional journalist organizations and governmental officials have been protracted and inconclusive. When by the fall of 1997, the Ministry of Culture still had not prepared a revised bill, the Slovak Syndicate of Journalists, the largest professional organization with approximately 2,300 members, presented its own draft of a media law based on the principles observed in other democratic countries, and in accordance with international treaties signed by the Slovak Republic. As of spring 1998, neither this draft nor the ministry version discussed above had been debated in parliament. Slovak Television and Slovak Radio are defined as public-law institutions; their supervisory boards are appointed by parliament. The opposition, however, considers the composition of these boards unbalanced and having a high degree of pro-government bias.

2. Are there legal protections for libeling officials? Are there legal penalties for irresponsible journalism? Have these laws been enforced to harass journalists? In 1996-1997, the ruling coalition failed to amend the Penal Code. Widely known as "law on the protection of the republic," the proposed amendment included problematic passages outlawing "subversion of the republic" and "damaging the interests of the republic abroad" which would enable prosecution of journalists for "impairing the country" abroad by the dissemination of "false information" about Slovakia. The government's proposal triggered waves of protests from opposition politicians, civic and religious organizations, independent media, trade unions, and many others who feared that its provisions would endanger constitutional freedoms of speech, information, and assembly as well as equality before the law. The bill was vetoed twice by the president. Governmental representatives continue to maintain that independent mass media favor the opposition and are biased against the government. Representatives of the ruling parties frequently blame the independent journalists for working against the national interests of the Slovak Republic. From 1996 to 1998, the government sued the *Sme* daily for "heavy psychological harm" resulting from an article about the murdered Robert Remias. The District Court in Banska Bystrica imposed a fine of Sk 7.5 million ($ 220,000.) upon the daily. The Court of Appeal in Kosice set aside this verdict for procedural reasons, however, the *Slovak Government vs. Sme* court action continues in Bratislava. In April 1998, another court action was started against the editor-in-chief of *Sme* who was taken to court for publishing a record of a discussion between the foreign affairs minister Juraj Schenk and British ambassador Peter Harborne, in which the latter criticized some aspects of the political development in the Slovak Republic. The editor is charged with disclosing a "state secret." In fact, however, the record of the above-mentioned discussion was officially labeled as "secret" by the Ministry of Foreign Affairs as late as after the daily had issued notice of its publication.

Article 103 of the Penal Code penalizes defamation of the president. This paragraph, however, was not applied against the pro-governmental daily, *Slovenska Republika*, which published a fake statement of an alleged bank account held by President Kovac in an Austrian bank. The court fined the publisher of *Slovenska Republika* based on Kovac's court action according to the Civic Code, not the Penal Code. No legal steps were taken against attacks on President Kovac in the pro-governmental media in the period between 1995 and 1997.

3. What proportion of media is privatized? What are the major private newspapers, television stations and radio stations? The media system includes public institutions, i.e. Slovak Television, Slovak Radio, and the TASR - Press Agency of the Slovak Republic, and private media such as television and radio stations, printed periodicals, and an information agency. Public media are financed from the national budget. All major dailies are privatized; *Praca* is published by a company owned by the trade unions associated in the Confederation of Trade Unions. A 1997 poll conducted by AISA agency confirmed the readership of the dailies: *Novy Eas* ranked first with 27 percent market share; *Pravda*, 11 percent; *Sport*, 9 percent; *Sme*, 7 percent; *Praca,* 6 percent; *Slovenska Republika*, 5 percent; and *Uj Szo* (Hungarian daily), 4 percent. *Slovenska Republika* is a pro-governmental daily close to the ruling HZDS.

In 1997, a new private information agency, SITA, was established. In addition, two foreign agencies, the Czech news agency ETK and Reuters, cover Slovakia. These three agencies compete with the public (state-owned) TASR agency. In addition to the state-owned Slovak Radio, there are 20 private radio stations, the most popular being the Fun and the Twist radio stations. While most of them are regional, Fun and Twist have almost national coverage. At the beginning of 1998, Twist Radio was awarded license to operate in eastern Slovakia, expanding its coverage to Slovakia's second largest city, Ko√ice. An important role in informing the citizens is played by the Radio Free Europe station whose license to broadcast in the medium-wave band will expire in July 1998. State-owned Slovak Television, whose signal covers the entire country, broadcasts on two channels (STV1 and STV2). The most popular television station is the private Markiza, which has been broadcasting since August 1996. In the spring of 1997, Markiza was watched by 62 percent of viewers, compared to 40 percent for STV1 and 14 percent for STV2. The VTV, another private television station, broadcasts through satellite and cable networks. In addition, licenses have been issued for six regional television stations, and several dozen licenses have been given to cable television. Parts of Slovakia receive television from the Czech Republic, Hungary, Poland, and Austria. The Czech private station NOVA is the most popular in Western Slovakia, and the Hungarian TV station in southern Slovakia. The cable television system enables urban viewers to watch broadcasts of about 40 national and international television stations, such as CNN, BBC, Euronews, ZDF, ARD, RTL, TV5, ORT.

4. Are the private media financially viable? In 1989, there were 20 publishing houses and five publishers in Slovakia. In 1996, there were 417 publishers and publishing houses of centrally-registered periodicals, plus 343 publishers of regionally-registered periodicals. Most of these publish only one title. The original publishing houses have been transformed into joint-stock or limited-liability companies. Due to international as well as domestic investment, the financial situation of most of the private media was stable in 1997. The majority share of the most popular daily, *Novy Eas,* is held by an Austrian owner. TV Markiza is highly profitable. In 1997, the government proposed to increase the VAT for printed media from 6 percent to 23 percent, which would considerably impair the economic situation of publishers, increase the prices of newspapers and journals, and, consequently, reduce the total circulation as well as the number of readers. Thanks to the resistance of associations of journalists and publishers, the VAT bill was passed in a more acceptable form. Since incomes of newspapers chiefly depend on advertisements, the actual monopolization of the advertisement market by two advertising companies, Artmedia and DONAR, which are close to the HZDS, have raised concerns of possible political influence on the advertisement policy.

5. Are the media editorially independent? Are the media's news gathering functions affected by interference from government or private sector? The state-owned electronic media are closely aligned to the ruling coalition, particularly Slovak Television. In 1996-1997, Slovak Television broadcast attacks on opposition without providing the opposition airtime to respond. Slovak Radio news programs are less biased; in polls by the state-owned Public Opinion Research Institute at the Statistical Office of the Slovak Republic, Slovak Radio ranks as an institution with higher public trust than STV. News and political programs on TV Markiza are more objective and balanced, providing airtime for government and opposition views. In 1997, a balanced coverage was provided by VTV television, however, it is allegedly owned by individuals close to the HZDS. Most of the 20 private radio stations do not focus on politics. Moreover, about 90 percent of Slovak Television's uncollected revenues are owed by two large customers: Slovak Television and Slovak Radio. Among the dailies, *Slovenska Republika* is loyal to the HZDS and the government. In September 1997, the publisher of *Slovenska Republika* became part of a large publishing project called R-Press and H-Press. H-Press began to create a national network of daily newspapers, each named *Hlas* (Voice) of a particular region. The publications combined main news sections prepared in Bratislava with locally-prepared regional supplements with the intent of covering all of Slovakia with pro-government daily newspapers in the crucial pre-election period. In some places, the regional *Hlas* was created by either transforming existing papers or by launching entirely new publications. The new ventures faced stiff competition from existing newspapers and regional weeklies and had problems attracting high-quality journalists to their staffs. Because Slovak law does not require disclosure of ownership in the media, it is difficult to evaluate to what extent owners influence the content of the newspapers. Certain editors have occasionally found themselves restricted by their corporate boards – some of whom are affiliated with the ruling party. In recent years, the editors-in-chief of some dailies were replaced, and the respective editorial staffs underwent considerable changes. These personnel changes took place, as explained by the respective publishers, due to shortcomings in the content of the respective dailies, or due to economic reasons. In the period from 1996 to 1998, the editors-in-chief of *Pravda*, *Uj Szo,* and *Narodna obroda* were replaced. While in 1997 no open pressure of publishers or owners on editorial boards of independent periodicals in connection with the materials published could be observed, the worries regarding the position of the Eastern Slovak Ironworks which published *Narodna obroda,* on Slovakia's media market increased after Julius Rezes, a former minister in Meciar's government and a key figure in the Eastern Slovak Ironworks, became the head of the HZDS electoral staff for the upcoming elections. Repeated cases of cancellation of press conferences by the government, favoritism in selecting journalists for press conferences of the individual ministries, and public authorities' refusal to provide information to private television and radio stations including, for instance, the National Property Fund which does not hold press conferences, may be considered as government interference with the media's news gathering functions.

6. Is the distribution system for newspapers privately or governmentally controlled? With the exception of *Sme*, no daily has its own printing company. The largest printing and publishing company, Danubiaprint, is a private company with alleged links to the HZDS. In February 1998, Danubiaprint acquired First News Service, Slovakia's largest periodical distributor, raising fears among independent publishers that their access to distribution channels may now be in the hands of the ruling coalition. Another private and politically independent distribution network, the Mediaprint Kapa, is able to distribute about one-third of the total number of copies of the dailies.

7. What proportion of the population is connected to the Internet? Are there any restrictions on Internet access to private citizens? The Internet is used by 190,000 people in Slovakia, which amounts to about five percent of adult population; an additional three percent have access but do not use it as yet. There are several private companies providing Internet services. There are no legal or administrative obstacles to Internet use. Connection charges are not high; on the other hand, telecommunication fees may be a limiting factor. The price of the connection to the Internet is also affected by outdated telephone lines and their high failure rate.

8. What has been the trends in press freedom as measured by Freedom Houses *Survey of Press Freedom*? Freedom House's annual *Survey of Press Freedom* rated Czechoslovakia "Not Free" for 1988, "Partly Free" for 1989, and "Free" from 1990 through 1992. The survey rated Slovakia "Partly Free" from 1993 through 1998. The trend for media has gone in two directions. On the positive side, more diverse media environment with a wide range of political, economic, and social perspectives has been developed in the last years through the addition of private television and radio stations and the free commenting of governmental policies in the independent press. On the more problematic side, the ruling coalition's control over publicly-owned media, in particular Slovak television, was strenghtened. The government and other official bodies frequently refuse to provide journalists and citizens with timely, accurate, and complete information about important government activities.

Governance and Public Administration 3.75/7

1. Is the legislature the effective rule-making institution? The parliament is the supreme legislative body and the key rule-making institution. Parliament meets in continuous session unless an adjournment is called by its members. Its 150 deputies serve four-year terms and are elected by "universal, equal, and direct suffrage by secret ballot" on party lists within each administrative region. Seats are awarded to political parties in proportion to votes received. As Meciar's coalition holds a plurality of seats in parliament, he maintains a large degree of influence over the body. Compared with previous years, one can state that the intensity of legislative activity has been declining moderately: every year, the number of bills passed by parliament has decreased by roughly five percent. As one might expect, the most active periods of lawmaking were just after the collapse of the Communist regime in November 1989, and again after the establishment of an independent Slovak Republic in 1993. Over the past three years, the percentage of approved bills introduced by deputies in parliament has declined as the legislature increasingly defers to executive initiative.

2. Is substantial power decentralized to sub-national levels of government? What specific authority does sub-national level have? The original concept of the relationship between national and sub-national levels of government anticipated a dual public administration system in which parallel state- and municipal-level governments would adhere to the European principle of "subsidiarity," where government functions are carried out at levels closest to the people. After laws establishing local branches of the state administration were passed in 1996, however, the position of the central state government was strengthened at the expense of local governments. In July

1996, parliament approved a law establishing a new territorial-administrative division of the Slovak Republic. President Kovac at first criticized the law which divided the country into eight regions and 79 districts and for facilitating an increased centralization of power. The president, however, signed the bill. The new division established a two-tier system for the central government with primary officials in the regions and districts appointed by the central state. Self-governing regional offices have not yet been established. Municipalities remain the basic unit of local administration as outlined in Article 64 of the constitution, and their officials are elected at the local level. Educational administration has become increasingly centralized since April 1995, when the Ministry of Education was given the power to appoint and to dismiss school principals and directors. The replacement of several school officials by the Minister of Education in the summer of 1995 led to protests, particularly in regions containing substantial Hungarian minorities. Legislative assemblies at the municipal level have the power to pass ordinances, to approve budgets, and to call local referenda. Bratislava, which constitutes its own region with eight districts under the new system, contains 17 city municipalities, each with its own local government, executive mayor, and legislative assembly. Municipalities often consult with district officials concerning budgetary matters. In general, the state as the legislative body has sought to curtail the independence of self-governing institutions through legal norms. It interferes with their responsibilities especially by enacting several voluntary duties of towns and settlements and by trying to increase the supervisory rights of the state administration over the self-governments.

3. Are sub-national officials chosen in free and fair elections? Mayors and representatives of municipal assemblies are chosen in local elections based upon "universal, equal and direct suffrage by secret ballot." The mayor serves as the local executive. Independent, i.e., non-partisan candidates, were the most successful in the November 1994 mayoral elections, followed by candidates from SDL and HZDS. The elections were deemed to be free and fair. In the spring of 1998, representatives of the ruling coalition prepared an amendment to the Law on Communal Elections that would introduce a combined system in which candidates would be listed on ballots both as individuals and under political party lists. Critics warned that this change could confuse voters and increase the share of invalid ballots in the November 1998 communal elections. The amendment also requires that the ethnic composition of municipal offices match exactly the ethnic make-up of the locality. This provision, which would favor certain candidates because of their ethnicity, breaches the principle of equality embedded in the constitution. The Association of Slovak Cities and Municipalities and the Union of Towns has opposed the amendment.

4. Do the executive and legislative bodies operate openly and with transparency? Is draft legislation easily accessible to the media and the public? Most sessions of the parliament are open to the public; closed sessions must be defined by law or approved by a three-fifths majority of parliament. The privatization process, directed by the National Property Fund, has exhibited a minimal degree of transparency, however, certain transparency problems exist in the parliament as well. When committees were established in 1994, according to parliament's new rules of procedure, the ruling parties ignored the requests of opposition parties to appoint specific opposition deputies to certain sensitive committees. Opposition parties are not adequately represented in the parliamentary committee overseeing the Slovak Information Service (SIS) (the domestic intelligence service). And although the director of the Slovak Information Service is required by law to submit an annual report on SIS activities to parliament, the current director has not done so for two consecutive years. Drafts of some important bills such as amendments to the election law and the Law on Municipalities, were prepared almost in secrecy by the government. Some ministries and other state administrative bodies have also refused to provide information on their activities to opposition deputies conducting parliamentary oversight. In the spring of 1997, the government canceled regular press conferences at the Office of the Government which reduced the level of information provided to the public. The transparency of municipal and other local government activities, as well as local and regional media coverage of them, varies across the country.

5. Do municipal governments have sufficient revenues to carry out their duties? Do municipal governments have control of their own local budgets? Do they raise revenues autonomously or from the central state budget? According to the constitution, taxes are collected at the national and local levels. Although municipalities receive some subsides from the central government, they often do not have adequate funding to carry out the duties required of them by law. At present, the central state controls 95 percent of tax revenues. Since 1996, the government has reduced the volume of general-purpose subsidies to support self-government functions and has increased the use of subsidies for specified purposes. Critics argue that this gives the central state additional control over local spending. Local governments complain that they do not receive sufficient funding from the central state for schools, health care, public transportation, culture, gas and electricity networks, and other local services. The current relationship between the central state and local government governments has led to unstable local government budgets for the past several years. To cover their deficits, municipalities first decided to sell assets, then to take loans and issue municipal bonds. A growing share of borrowed funds such as loans and bonds in municipal budgets is significantly lowering the share of tax revenues available to fulfill municipal duties and reducing the financial independence of self-governments. Decision-making by municipal officials has become dependent on creditors, i.e., banking institutions and other private institutions, or the state administration, as seen in the 1997 and 1998 state budgets. The expected consequences of these policies include hasty sales of remaining local assets, the decline of investment activities, and the imposition on citizens of additional local taxes and fees.

6. Do the elected local leaders and local civil servants know how to manage municipal governments effectively? The professional education and experience of mayors and other local officials is generally adequate. Many have long-term experience; others have had various sorts of professional training. Representatives of local governments regularly exchange information through a variety of means. The efficiency of local government operations is often undermined by limited financial resources, and by poor, even tense relations between some local governments and the central state administration. The professional skills of local civil servants vary: some work efficiently, others are criticized for not being forthcoming with citizens. According to some members of the opposition, certain higher-level local officials received their positions on the basis of political loyalty to the ruling parties rather than professional skills.

7. When did the constitutional/legislative changes in local power come into effect? Has there been a reform of the civil service code/system? Are local civil servants employees of the local or central government? Legislation in 1996 established eight new regional and 79 new district offices of the central state administration. Officials at the regional and district levels are employees of the central state. Municipal officials such as mayors and assembly members are employees of the local government and are paid with the fees collected by the municipality. According to Article 54 of the constitution, civil servants may be denied the right to strike. Representatives of the opposition have complained about the use of political criteria in selecting these officials. All urban managers of regional and district offices were nominated only after taking their political orientations into account, and a majority of urban managers are members of the ruling HZDS.

Rule of Law 4.00/7

1. Is there a post-Communist constitution ? How does the judicial system interpret and enforce the constitution? Are there specific examples of judicial enforcement of the constitution in the last year? The constitution was adopted on September 1, 1992 and went into effect on October 1, 1992. The constitution guarantees fundamental rights and freedoms: rights to privacy and personal liberty, freedoms of expression, petition, peaceful assembly and association, as well as rights to ownership of property. It is based on the democratic and republican principle, on the principles of pluralism, rule of law, power sharing, checks and balances, and on the principle of judicial review. While it mentions a socially and environmentally-oriented market economy as a desired principle, it also emphasizes that the state shall not subscribe to any particular religion or ideology. Article 124 established a Constitutional Court as an independent organ with jurisdiction over a broad range of constitutional issues and the compatibility of laws with the Constitution of the Slovak Republic. These include conflicts between constitutional provisions and laws passed by parliament, regulations passed by the government, or rules passed by local self-governments, conflicts between different governmental authorities, contested elections to parliament and challenges to the results of a referendum. The court consists of ten judges nominated by the president from a list of 20 nominees approved by the parliament. Judges serve for seven years. Cases may be brought to the Constitutional Court upon request of the president, the government, lower courts, or at least thirty deputies in parliament. Individual citizens who believe their fundamental rights or freedoms have been violated may also bring cases. Despite the controversial nature of many of the cases it is required to adjudicate, the Constitutional Court enjoys wide public support: in 1996-1997, it was regarded as the most credible political institution in the Slovak Republic. In recent years the Constitutional Court has been asked to arbitrate some of the most intractable disputes in the brief history of the Slovak Republic.

While most of the 1997 Constitutional Court's rulings were respected, there were cases which have raised concerns about the efficiency of the judicial enforcement of the constitution. Contrary to decision of the Constitutional Court, parliament refused to reinstate the parliamentary mandate to Deputy Frantisek Gaulieder, who resigned from the HZDS caucus. He was stripped of his mandate on the basis of a resignation letter that he claimed was a fraud. Gaulieder brought suit before the court, which, in July 1997 ruled that the expulsion violated his legal rights. The court, however, added that it could not correct the injustice and that such an action could only be done by the parliament, which has not reversed its decision. The second case was connected with a referendum on direct election of the president initiated on a petition drive that has collected almost 500,000 signatures. President Kovac decided to combine this referendum on direct election with another one on Slovakia's membership in NATO and scheduled both for the weekend of May 23-24, 1997. On May 21, 1997 – two days before the start of the referendum – the Constitutional Court ruled that the constitution does not contain a provision prohibiting its amendment by referendum. The court also ruled that the appendix to the fourth referendum question was inconsistent with the Law on the Referendum, and that an affirmative vote on this question would not be legally binding. The court said, however, that the question was valid and the referendum should be held. Over the vehement objections of the Central Referendum Commission, Minister Krajei removed the question on direct election from the ballot and ordered the reprinting and distribution of more than 4 million copies of a new ballot only with three questions on NATO. While the Central Referendum Commission, which has the legal authority to announce the results, declared the referendum obstructed, the government approved Krajei's measure. In February 1998, the Constitutional Court affirmed that President Kovac had not violated the constitution when he combined the referendum on NATO entry with a referendum on direct presidential elections. In its decision, the court said that the government could not act beyond its competence even in cases when the government believes that the president's action contravened the constitution.

2. Does the constitutional framework provide for human rights? Do the human rights include business and property rights? Article 12 guarantees fundamental rights to individuals "regardless of sex, race, color, language, faith, religion, political affiliation or conviction, national or social origin, nationality or ethnic origin, property, birth or any other status." Rights to privacy and personal liberty, including protection against unjust search and guarantees of freedom of movement and thought, are outlined by Articles 16 through 24. The death penalty is "inadmissible" according to Article 15, and property rights are protected by Article 20.

3. Has there been any substantial reform of the penal code? Who authorizes, searches, and issues warrants? Are suspects and prisoners beaten or abused? Are there excessive delays in the criminal justice system? The Slovak Republic, with minor changes, adopted the Czechoslovak Penal Code in 1994, and few amendments have been made since. Amendments 247/94, 248/94, and 249/94, enacted in 1994, dealt with due process of law and rules for police actions regarding search warrants and other procedural matters. In 1996-1997, the ruling coalition failed to amend the Penal Code. The bill was vetoed twice by President Kovac. The government prepared a complete recodification of criminal law and the Penal Code but it has not been set before the parliament. In 1997, human rights organizations did not record any cases of beating or humiliation of detainees, persons taken into custody, or persons sentenced to imprisonment. Under the constitution, a detainee must be delivered to a court within 24 hours or dismissed, and a judge must see the detainee within 24 hours to decide on his/her taking into custody or dismissing. The maximum admissible length of detention for persons who were taken into custody within a criminal suit and who have not been sentenced is six months; a judge may extend the custody to one year, the Senate may add another year, and the Supreme Court one more year. This means that the maximum possible length of custody before sentencing is three years.

4. Do most judges rule fairly and impartially? Do many remain from the Communist era? At the end of 1997, Slovakia had 1,284 judges reportedly ruling fairly and impartially. The courts, however, are overloaded. Constitutional Court judges are required to withdraw from membership in political organizations and parties including other public offices, and may be required to withdraw from business activities. They must hold a law degree and have 15 years of law experience. According to Article 154, "judges elected under the previous statutory enactments shall be deemed to have been elected to office for indefinite term under this constitution," thereby enabling judges who served under communism to retain their offices. Less than three-fifths of judges active in 1997 had served under communism.

5. Are the courts free of political control and influence? Are the courts linked directly to the Ministry of Justice or any other executive body? The Constitutional Court, seated in Kosice, decides on the matters related to the observance of the constitution and remains independent from the rest of the judiciary. The court has regularly demonstrated its independence of the government. In the period from 1993 to 1998, the Constitutional Court disqualified 13 acts adopted by parliament, two governmental regulations, and one minister's decree as unconstitutional. The Constitutional Court consists of ten judges who are appointed for seven years by the president and are selected from 20 candidates proposed by parliament. The Supreme Court in Bratislava is the highest court of general judiciary and its competence is nation-wide. In the past, some Supreme Court judges, who are also elected by parliament, favored governmental policy and criticized the opposition. The Slovak legal system is based on the principle of the separation of the judiciary from the legislative and executive. The precise jurisdiction of courts is defined by law and not by the constitution, according to Articles 48 and 143. The judiciary is constitutionally "independent of other branches of government at all levels." Judges are selected for a period of four years by the parliament on the advice from the Ministry of Justice and, upon the completion of their first term, the government nominates them to parliament for a reelection for an unlimited tenure.

6. What proportion of lawyers is in private practice? How does this compare with the previous years? Although the proportion of lawyers working for the state was higher in 1997 than the proportion of lawyers in private practice, the number of lawyers choosing private practice has increased significantly. Currently, there are more than 1,100 lawyers registered in the Chamber of Defenders and more than 1,000 in the Chamber of Commercial Lawyers.

7. Does the state provide public defenders? Article 50 of the constitution guarantees the right to public defenders. Public defenders, paid by the state, are provided in courts at all levels for criminal cases. There is reportedly an increasing shortage of public defenders and state judges because the work in the private sector is far more lucrative than in the public sector.

8. Are there effective anti-bias/discrimination laws, including protection of ethnic minorities

rights? The constitution and the laws prohibit discrimination and provide for the equality of all citizens, irrespective of sex, race, color, language, religion, nationality, or ethnic group. Basic rights of the minorities and ethnic groups are enshrined in Articles 33 and 34, which guarantee minorities the right to develop their own culture, to use their mother language, and to establish their own minority associations and cultural and educational institutions. The constitution guarantees minorities the right to education in their native language and the right to employ their language for administration purposes. National or racial intolerance, as well as the support of movements pursuing the suppression of civil rights and liberties, are considered criminal acts under the Penal Code. There are laws, decrees, and programs to protect the rights of children, women, and people with disabilities. There is also a government decree on provision of accessibility with regard to new building construction. Legal norms, however, are not sufficiently implemented in practice, and different minority groups complain about factual discrimination at work or in education. For ethnic Hungarians, who represent the largest minority with a population registered at 567,000, or 10.8 percent of Slovakia's population, the issue of minority rights is tied to political and cultural issues. The Roma (Gypsies), however, whose population is estimated between 76,000 and 300,000, is the focus is social and economic discrimination. The Hungarian minority is characterized by high-level political mobilization, and its interests are represented in the parliament by the Hungarian coalition of three political parties. None of the Roma political groupings has a parliamentary representation. In 1995-1997, there were several attacks against the Roma led by skinheads, and while some of the perpetrators have been prosecuted and sentenced, the Slovak Helsinki Committee Report issued in December 1997 quotes Roma as complaining about slow or insufficient responses by police. Relations between the government and the Hungarian minority were impaired after 1994, when the coalition of the HZDS-ZRS-SNS came to power. Government policy toward the Hungarian minority has been openly confrontational since 1995. The government passed and began enforcing a controversial law on the state language, significantly decreased financial assistance for minority cultural activities, and unsuccessfully attempted to introduce so-called alternative education. On January 1, 1996, a controversial new Law on the State Language took effect. While the Constitutional Court rejected most of the criticism regarding the constitutionality of this law, it upheld an important assertion: that Hungarians do have the right to use their own language in official state contacts. In January 1997, the government accepted an analysis prepared by the Ministry of Culture that minority language rights are already sufficiently protected and additional legislation in this area is unnecessary. In spite of promises given to the representatives of European institutions, in its November 1997 Memorandum on Usage of Minority Languages, the government finally came to conclusion that no legal vacuum exists. According to the memorandum, minority rights are regulated by 26 legal norms, 12 of which deal directly with minority languages usage. The issue, however, has remained on the agenda in negotiations with the European Union (EU) on Slovakia's integration into the Union. In January 1997, the Ministry of Education decided to end a practice dating to 1921 of issuing bilingual student certificates, i.e., grade report cards, in schools with instruction in national minority languages, replacing them with Slovak-only documents. The ministry's decision, based on its reading of the Law on the State Language, generated considerable confusion and ill will among the Hungarian community. Some school directors and teachers defied the order and issued dual-language certificates for which they were warned and even sanctioned. Some pupils and parents initially refused to accept single-language certificates, which created additional problems at the start of the 1997-1998 school year when students were required to present their certificates from the preceding year. In the end, however, teachers, students, and parents were forced to comply with the new policy. In August 1997, Meciar promised to Hungarian Prime Minister Horn to solve this issue. The adopted solution enables to issue the report cards also in Hungarian, but they are issued only on parents' request and do not have validity as legal documents. Hungarian parents and teachers do not consider this measure sufficient.

Corruption	C

1. What is the magnitude of official corruption in the civil service? Must an average citizen pay a bribe to a bureaucrat in order to receive a service? What services are subject to bribe requests – for example, university entrance, hospital admission, telephone installation, obtaining a license to operate a business, applying for a passport or other official documents, what is the average salary of civil servants at various levels? Although the extent of corruption in Slovakia is less than in some former East bloc countries, it is substantially more serious than in the neighboring states of the Visegrad Four — Hungary, the Czech Republic, and Poland. The primary contributing factor is the Slovak privatization practices have become the focus and hotbed of corruption. The Supreme Audit Office (NKU) annually reports to parliament instances of suspected corruption and misuse of office by civil servants, but criminal proceedings have not been launched in a single case. Bribes are customary when dealing with public administration, public health services, or obtaining a licence. Contracts favoring private firms at the expense of state-owned enterprises and institutions are a common occurrence. In 1997, the average salary of civil servants was 11,225Sk compared to nation-wide average wage of 9226Sk .

2. Do top policy makers (the president, ministers, vice-ministers, top court justices and heads of agencies and commissions) have direct ties to businesses? How strong are those connections and what kinds of businesses are these? Independent media have exposed the alleged involvement in privatization projects of high-ranking politicians, including members of parliament of governing parties, as well as the participation of politicians' and top civil servants' relatives in the privatization of enterprises sold at nominal prices. At the end of 1996, the government coalition amended securities legislation by introducing the institute of bearer shares that evades any form of control and supervision. Most businesses privatized since then have been sold to joint-stock companies that issued bearer shares, making it impossible to identify actual owners.

3. Do laws requiring financial disclosure and disallowing conflict of interest exist? Have publicised anticorruption cases been pursued? To what conclusion? Conflict of interest legislation is in place but is being obviated on a mass scale by means of bearer shares as well as business and privatization transactions carried out through relatives or other close persons. Independent (private) media have pursued anti corruption cases. State-controlled media, and in particular, state television, ignore the issue. Although opinion polls suggest growing public discontent because of rampant corruption, the public is yet to exert pressure to bear on political quarters to bring about a real improvement.

4. What major anticorruption initiatives have been implemented? How often are anticorruption laws and decrees adopted? A program called "Clean Hands" was launched in March 1995. Its objective was to counter corruption and protectionism in the civil service. All government agencies were required to formulate principles to counter corruption and generally enhance their anti corruption record. During the first half of the same year, all these agencies submitted progress reports. The main deficiency of the scheme was that it did not apply to the National Property Fund, the main privatizing agency, that is not deemed a part of the civil service. In a March 1996 opinion poll, 56 percent of respondents with a varying degree of conviction did not believe that the "Clean Hands" was relevant, while 20 percent had an opposite view. The tendency of respondents to believe in the effectiveness of the "Clean Hands" program was primarily associated with rural and less-educated segments of the population. Opposition parties believe that the program was a ruse to disguise corruption because government action has been a source of direct or indirect corruption associated with non-transparent privatization and the information blackout imposed on the opposition and independent media.

5. How do major corruption-ranking organizations like Transparency International rate this country? Slovakia has yet to be ranked by Transparency International. The opinion of other organizations has been rather critical in this respect, especially with regards to a lack of transparency in privatisation.

Privatization 3.25/7

1. What percentage of the GDP comes from private ownership? What percentage of the labor force is employed in the private sector? How large is the informal sector of the economy? According to preliminary data from the Statistical Office of the Slovak Republic, in 1997, the private sector accounted for 82.6 percent of gross domestic product (GDP), up 5.8 percent from 1996. The private sector accounted for 73.2 percent of total industrial output, up 5 percent in annual terms, 82.2 percent of the construction industry, down 1.2 percent, and 92.5 percent of trade services. The private sector employed 76.5 percent of employees in industry, 87.8 percent in the construction industry, and 96.7 percent in trade and services. The Transition Report 1997, published by the European Bank for Reconstruction and Development, estimated Slovakia's informal economy at 13 percent of GDP.

2. What major privatization legislation has been passed? What were its substantive features? After the fall of communism, the notion of a radical economic transformation prevailed in the Czech and Slovak Federal Republic (CSFR). Rapid and comprehensive privatization served as one of the four pillars of reform and was perceived not only as an economic phenomenon but also an important part of political changes and a guarantor of their irreversible nature. The process of restitution became a part of privatization and the date of the Communist coup, February 25, 1948, was chosen as the starting point for restitution claims. To be entitled to make a claim, a claimant, i.e., an individual rather than a legal entity, was required to be a Czechoslovak national with permanent residence in Czechoslovakia. The process of privatization was divided into small-scale and large-scale privatization. The exclusive privatization method used in the small-scale scheme was public auction. Property offered was cleared of claims and liabilities; it consisted mostly of retail stores, restaurants, smaller operations and production plants, and small hotels. Bidding in the first round of the small-scale privatization scheme was confined to domestic individuals and enterprises. A second round, involving previously unsold property, was open to foreign buyers as well. Since speed and scope were considered critical, and as there was a lack of available capital funds, voucher privatization was employed along with standard methods. The process of large-scale privatization was divided into two waves during which most of the property earmarked for privatization was to be sold. The division of large-scale privatization into two waves was intended to speed up the process. It was also decided that each wave of large-scale privatization would be accompanied by a wave of voucher privatization.

Three specialized institutions — so-called National Property Funds — were created; one federal, and one for each of the Czech and Slovak Republics. These were independent legal entities charged with the implementation of approved privatization projects, concluding buyer-seller contracts, organizing public tenders and public auctions, and temporarily administrating government holdings in transformed or partially privatized enterprises. Their main bodies included a presidium and a supervisory board whose members were elected by a secret ballot of the respective parliaments. It was decided that the federal Ministry of Finance would be responsible for the demand side of the voucher scheme, while the ministries of privatization in the constituent republics would be in charge of the supply side. During 1990-1991, the Federal Assembly of the CSFR, the Slovak National Council, and the Czech National Council, as well as the respective governments and ministries passed decisive privatization and restitution laws and issued government decrees and ministerial directives. These laws and regulations defined the rules of the game governing the large-scale privatization process. Each state-owned enterprise was assigned to one of the two waves of large-scale privatization. The respective governments, federal and republic, carried out the division into two waves of those enterprises for which it was responsible. Selection was carried out based on proposals submitted by sector ministries after consulting with the enterprises. Deadlines were set by which all enterprises were to prepare so-called basic privatization projects.

An important provision of the law stated that direct sales had to be approved by the government, while other forms of transformation and sale such as public tender, public auctions, and share allocation for voucher privatization were under the authority of the ministries of privatization. The principle was adopted that standard methods would be preferred in basic privatization projects if the management of these enterprises were able to identify a feasible foreign or domestic buyer. In cases where there was no concrete concept of privatization by standard methods before the deadline for submitting basic privatization projects, the transformation of enterprises into joint-stock enterprises and the sale of shares in the voucher scheme was recommended.

Along with basic privatization projects, competitive privatization projects were envisaged which could be proposed by any domestic or foreign individual or enterprise. State enterprises were obligated to provide the information required for the preparation of competitive privatization projects to all interested parties.

Approximately 700 state enterprises worth about 175 billion Czechoslovak crowns *(Kès)* were earmarked for the first wave of privatization in Slovakia. Enterprises participating in the first wave had to prepare and to present their basic privatization projects before the end of October 1991. The deadline for presenting competitive privatization projects was the end of November 1991.

The first wave of the voucher scheme was part of the first privatization wave. The Czech National Property Fund allocated property worth 206 billion Kès for voucher privatization, while the Slovak National Property Fund designated property worth 90 billion Kès for such privatization. In the Czech Republic, this represented 943 joint-stock companies; in the Slovak Republic, 484 joint-stock companies. 5,942,851 citizens in the Czech Republic and 2.6 million citizens in the Slovak Republic registered for the voucher scheme. Thus, the book value of property per holder of investment vouchers was 34,796 Kès.

Small-scale privatization in the Slovak Republic began on February 14, 1991, and was practically concluded by the end of 1992. During this period, 9,676 operational units with a total accounting value of 13.2 billion Kès were auctioned off, generating 14.5 billion Kès in proceeds. The government and the ministry of privatization began approving large-scale privatization projects during the first quarter of 1992. Registration of citizens for the first wave of the voucher scheme began on November 1, 1991. Voucher privatization itself started on May 14, 1992, and was concluded by the end of 1992.

After the June 1992 elections, the Slovak government approved a new concept of privatization that, to a large extent, rejected existing procedures. Greater emphasis was placed on using standard methods, whereas voucher privatization was viewed as only marginal. In addition, the powers of sector ministries in the privatization process increased. There were not, however, sufficient domestic and foreign sources for a rapid and comprehensive privatization: time and capacity constraints of the massive use of standard methods, greater powers vested with sector ministries, and lack of interest on their part in rapid privatization as well as the absence of political will to pursue fast, comprehensive, and transparent privatization caused a significant slowdown of the privatization process. During the autumn of 1992 and throughout 1993, the Law on Large-Scale Privatization was also amended several times. Amendments were aimed at strengthening the authority of the ministry of privatization but also that of the government over the National Property Fund. Privatization only partially accelerated in February-March 1994, when, fearing impending removal from power, the Meciar government went on a direct sales spree.

After the fall of the Meciar government in March 1994, the government led by Jozef Moravceik proceeded with the privatization process using a mechanism similar to that employed before June 1992. The process of approving direct sales was speeded up, and preparations were made for a second wave of the voucher privatization. The registration of citizens for the second wave of the voucher privatization began on September 1, 1994. 3.4 million citizens ultimately registered for the second wave which represented 1.33 times the number who registered in the first wave. On December 15, 1994, the outgoing Moravceik government announced the beginning of the second wave of privatization, but this was canceled by the incoming Meciar government.

An important systemic change took place on the night of November 3-4, 1994, when, at the first session of the newly elected parliament, a parliamentary majority consisting of HZDS, and the ZRS, adopted several modifications. The members of the presidium and the supervisory board of the National Property Fund were recalled; new members, loyal to the parties of the parliamentary majority, were elected. The Law on Large-Scale Privatization was amended so that all decisive authority of the Ministry of Privatization was transferred to the National Property Fund. Several decisions on direct sales approved by the Moraveik government were revoked.

While privatization has proceeded in the Slovak Republic and private enterprises are steadily increasing in their share of GDP, there have been some irregularities in the privatization process and accusations of mismanagement of the process for personal gain.

The second wave of voucher privatization was postponed by the new parliament in November 1994, soon after HZDS regained power. In addition, parliament invalidated projects that the previous government had privatized by direct sales two months earlier. The amendment to the Law on Privatization passed in November 1994, made the National Property Fund the primary actor in the privatization process, removing oversight powers from the government, the Supreme Audit Office, and the Office of the Prosecutor General, thus limiting the transparency of the process. In addition, the September 1995 Law on Strategic Enterprises withdrew several enterprises from the privatization process.

Under the HZDS, privatization has proceeded erratically, and direct sales in the form of employee/management buyouts have become the primary form of privatization with the stated goal of turning enterprises over to direct and experienced management. Irregularities in privatization, such as insider sales, allegations that certain firms were sold at prices well below market value, the lack of transparency, and the fact that six of the nine board members of the National Property Fund were HZDS members, led to a June 1996 challenge by the opposition. By its ruling that the privatization process should be returned to government and parliamentary oversight, the Constitutional Court, in effect, condemned the dominance that the National Property Fund has held over privatization under HZDS rule. Although the Constitutional Court deemed the 1994 legislation unconstitutional, it appears that the decisions made by the National Property Fund will stand due to the practical difficulty of bringing each case up for review.

In 1997, the opposition made several attempts in parliament to amend the Law on Large-scale Privatization. The ruling coalition majority has invariably rejected these motions.

3. What proportion of agriculture, housing and land, industry, and small business services is in private hands? Three types of business enterprises are now typical for the agricultural sector. The first consists of transformed cooperatives, approximately 1,000 of which work 69 percent of arable land. On average, each cooperative works 1,600 hectares of land. The second type is private, mostly family farms typically established by people who left cooperatives. By the end of 1994, there were about 7,600 private farms with an average size of 15 hectares. Many small farmers, however, tend their allotments on a part-time basis, and more than 60 percent of such farms have less than 5 hectares. Moreover, such small farms are typically subdivided into even smaller allotments averaging 0.34 hectares. Finally, there are about sixty businesses, i.e., joint-stock or limited liability companies that farm allotments averaging 290 hectares. In 1994, these, plus private farms accounted for about 9 percent of arable land. Another 22 percent of arable land remains in the care of state-owned farms, whose average size is 2,950 hectares. The privatization of state-owned farms has slowed down due to legislative changes and privatization methods. All state-owned housing has been transferred to the ownership of municipalities and is gradually being privatized. In 1997, 97.3 percent of all economically active profit-making businesses were privately owned. In the small and medium business sector, this ratio was 97.5 percent.

4. What has been the extent of insider (management, labor, and nomenklatura) participation in the privatization process? What explicit and implicit preferences have been awarded to insiders? Since October 1994, the preferred method of privatization has been direct sales to predetermined buyers, frequently at nominal prices. New owners were typically companies incorporated by the management of enterprises being privatized. The Slovak privatization process in 1995-1996 gave birth to a type of cronyism that grew not because of inadequate supervision or legal loopholes, but as a result of legislative amendments (frequently declared unconstitutional after judicial review) that served the interests of narrow groups close to the governing coalition at the expense of other entrepreneurs and taxpayers. Economic favors were most often granted to people who acquired privatized property or who owned the biggest enterprises — Slovakia's so-called industrial lobby. Numerous new laws, amendments, and regulations were passed or implemented during 1995 to 1997 which have impacted the privatization process.

Although the Constitutional Court subsequently ruled most of this legislation was unconstitutional, it was not uncommon for governing executives to ignore these verdicts. This expansion of cronyism resulted in a massive concentration of economic and political power in the hands of a narrow group of people and negatively affects the competitiveness and efficiency of the economy as a whole. In 1996-1997, full-scale and unrestricted privatization at nominal prices was continued. In some companies that had been privatized earlier at higher prices, the initial transaction was canceled and the business was resold again at a far lower price to the same investor acting through an intermediary. New, more profitable, transactions typically benefited individuals close to top executives of National Property Fund or officials of the governing coalition.

5. How much public awareness of and support for privatization has there been? What is the nature of support and opposition to privatization by major interest groups? In early 1997, the public opinion research agency FOCUS conducted a survey in which only 1 percent of respondents agreed that the government's privatization policy was "correct." Nine percent of respondents believed that it was "probably correct rather than incorrect," 27 percent thought it was "incorrect rather than correct," and 45 percent were convinced that it was "incorrect." Eighteen percent of respondents were undecided. At the end of October 1997, the Institute for Public Opinion Research of the Statistical Office of the Slovak Republic released the findings of another survey: 2 percent of respondents "approved" of privatization, 6 percent "approved rather than disapproved," 27 percent "disapproved rather than approved," and as much as 58 percent "totally disapproved." Compared with the FOCUS findings from earlier in the year, broad disapproval had gone up 13 percentage points, to 85 percent. In response to a question about whose living standards would be improved by privatization, 2 percent of respondents replied that it would improve for everyone, 13 percent said it would improve for those who work in industries with good prospects, 40 percent said it would improve for those who have privatized, and 40 percent said it would improve only for a few speculators.

Macroeconomics 3.75/7

1. Has the taxation system been reformed? (What areas have and have not been overhauled? To what degree are taxpayers complying? Is tax compliance difficult to achieve? Has the

level of revenues increased? Is the revenue-collection body overburdened? What is the overall tax burden?) From 1989 to 1992, only partial changes in the Slovak tax system were introduced, e.g., a single tier replaced multiple tiers of turnover tax. On January 1, 1993, however, a comprehensive reform of the Slovak tax system came into force. The new tax system is consistent with a market economy. Standard income tax, both personal and corporate, was introduced along with a value-added tax. The total tax burden was reduced and the taxation system became more transparent. At present the following rates apply: corporate income or profit tax, 40 percent; personal income tax with progressive tax rates of 15, 20, 25, 32, 40, and 42 percent; value-added tax, 23 percent base rate, with a reduced rate of 6 percent for foodstuffs, medicines, periodicals, and books; social insurance (i.e., pension) contributions, 50 percent, of which 38 percent paid by employers and 12 percent by employees; royalties and fees, 10 percent for amounts of up to 3,000 Slovak crowns (Sk) monthly, otherwise regular taxation; dividends, 15 percent; and interest on deposits, 15 percent. Taxation legislation has been amended on several occasions. In February 1998, parliament amended the Law on Income Tax, introducing what is popularly known as "millionaires' tax" which increased the rate of taxation on levied on individuals with net annual earnings in excess of 1.08 million Sk. Under previous regulations, all income in excess of 1.08 million Sk was taxed at 42 percent. The new highest rate rose to 72 percent. Legal entities continue to be taxed at a single rate of 40 percent. The tax burden imposed on businesses and expressed in the composite tax quota increased from 36.8 percent in 1993 to more than 45 percent in 1996. In addition to taxes, businesses are required to make compulsory contributions to social insurance funds (38 percent of the payroll). In 1997, the average tax burden on individuals was 13.5 percent, up 0.9 percent from 1996. This increase in the tax burden was primarily due to growing wages while tax brackets and non-taxable allowances remaining intact. The increase in the tax burden was also affected by the reclassification of telecommunication services in January 1998, from the 6 percent VAT rate to the base rate of 23 percent. In 1997, taxpayer discipline deteriorated dramatically, especially among legal entities. This resulted from increasing tensions on financial markets, i.e. more expensive money, rampant insolvency, from expectations of taxpayers that their liabilities would be waived under the enterprise revitalization law, and a lack of transparency.

In 1997, the state budget collected a mere 59.5 percent of the corporate income tax target.

Personal income tax revenues have been growing largely as a result of rising nominal incomes, while the revenues generated by corporate income tax have been declining.

The tax burden on individuals is also increasing due to tax rate brackets that have not been adjusted to reflect real and nominal (inflation-related) increases to wages and incomes.

2. Does fiscal policy encourage private savings, investment, and earnings? (Has there been any reform/alteration of revenue and budget policies? How large are budget deficits and overall debt? Is the financing of the social insurance/pension system sustainable? What proportion of the budget is taken up by subsidies to firms and individuals?) In 1997, Slovakia's real GDP increased by 6.5 percent. On the demand side, this growth was positively affected by domestic demand and by gross fixed investments going up 14.5 percent. Investments were not accompanied by adequate domestic savings, however, resulting in foreign debt rising by almost $3 billion.

At the end of November 1997, foreign debt was $10.7 billion, of which $5.1 was the debt of enterprises. In 1997, large enterprises increasingly borrowed from abroad, as they found money on the domestic market prohibitively expensive. On a *per capita* basis, the debt increased from $1,473 in 1996 to $2,023 in 1997. Average inflation in 1997 was 6.1 percent, rising to 7 percent in the first quarter of 1998. Interest on deposits and loans has been above 20 percent for quite some time — more than three times the inflation rate. Short-term deposits of up to six months earn the highest rate of interest. In Slovakia, there are virtually no incentives to generate long-term capital; pension funds are not operating yet; and venture capital is non-existent. In 1997, the state budget posted a deficit of 36.7 billion Sk on a cash basis, which was corresponded to 5.75 percent of GDP. Under the 1998 budget legislation, only fiscal deficit will be reported (net of debt principal payments), which is projected to be 5 billion Sk. The central bank has projected that the fiscal deficit of public finances would exceed 20 billion Sk. On a cash basis, the deficit is forecast at 51.3 billion Sk. A serious problem of the 1997 state budget was a 30 percent reduction of corporate income tax revenues from the previous year. Actual collections were only 58 percent of the target. Thus, in 1997, personal income tax for the first time generated more revenue, at 25.64 billion Sk, than legal entities, at 23.4 billion Sk. The government finds it increasingly difficult to finance the growing deficit, as reflected by the high rates of interest offered on treasury securities. The government's expansive fiscal policy is also at odds with the restrictive monetary policy pursued by the National Bank of Slovakia (NBS), and it crowds out private investment. While in 1997 borrowings by enterprises and the population increased by 1.2 percent, net lending to the government went rose by 9.7 percent. In an attempt to cut budgetary expenditures, the government has gradually reduced the base for assessing contributions to insurance funds, i.e. health insurance, pension insurance that it pays on behalf of certain population categories. Along with failure by some enterprises to pay their contributions, this causes problems in financing public health care. Social insurance officials warn that the reduction in reserve funds may jeopardize the payment of pension benefits in January 1999.

3. Has there been banking reform? (Is the central bank independent? What are its responsibilities? Is it effective in setting and/or implementing monetary policy? What is the actual state of the private banking sector? Does it conform to international standards? Are depositors protected?) According to law, the NBS is an independent institution responsible for monetary policy, stability of the national currency, and bank supervision. A bill currently before parliament, however, seeks to reduce central bank independence. In exercising its banking supervision role, the NBS applies prudential regulations that are consistent with international standards. Since 1993, the NBS has pursued a competent monetary policy that was successful in bringing the inflation rate down from 23 percent in 1993 to 6.1 percent in 1997 as well as stabilizing the exchange rate. At present, there are 30 banks operating in Slovakia, including four branches of foreign banks and two state-owned financial institutions, Konsolidaena banka and Slovenska zaruena banka. Ten foreign banks have representative offices in Slovakia. In terms of profit per employee, the best performing financial institutions in 1996 were banks with foreign holdings. The government retains a substantial stake in three banks: Vseobecna uverova banka, Investiena a rozvojova banka (IRB), and Slovenska sporiteoa (SLSP). Significantly, these banks hold most domestic savings — 69 percent as of mid-1997 — and loans — 60 percent. Private banks are eroding this share.

In mid-1997, financial institutions where the government retains a stake had serious problems meeting capital adequacy requirements. Their capital adequacy ratios declined below the generally accepted minimum of 8 percent.

The most serious single problem in the banking sector is the stock of classified loans which the central bank estimated in 1996 at 21 percent of outstanding loans. Significantly, banks with government stakes held most of those classified loans. The crisis in the banking sector came to a head when the third largest bank, IRB, became illiquid in December 1997, and the NBS was forced to appoint a temporary administrator. After the crisis broke out, the NBS was forced to bail out the bank by making available 11 billion Sk, which increased NBS exposure in the IRB to 24 billion Sk. The administrator disclosed that, cleared of 1997 losses, the book value of the bank's share capital was minus 1.2 billion Sk. In April 1998, a general meeting of IRB shareholders decided to increase the bank's own capital by 2 billion Sk. According to the Law on the Protection of Deposits, all non-anonymous deposits by private individuals since July 1, 1996, are insured by a Deposits Protection Fund. Maximum protection is equal to 30 times the average wage of the previous year (8,150 Sk in 1996).

4. How sound is the national currency? (Is the value of the currency fixed or does it float?) How convertible is the currency? How large are the hard currency reserves? Has exchange rate policy been stable and predictable?) The exchange rate of the national currency, the Slovak koruna, is pegged to a currency basket consisting of the German mark (60 percent) and the U.S. dollar (40 percent). The actual rate fluctuates within a ±7 percent central parity band. Throughout most of 1997, the Sk exchange rate was in the devaluation portion of the band. NBS interventions and a relatively low level of speculative foreign capital made possible the preservation of exchange rates during a run on the Slovak currency in May 1997. The most pronounced deviation in the devaluation portion of the fluctuation band (4.25 percent) was observed at the end of January 1998, after the Moody's Investors Service announced that it was considering downgrading Slovakia's sovereign rating to a non-investment grade. Despite pressures on the exchange rate because of the current account deficit, no major adjustments in the exchange rate are expected in the foreseeable future. Under an amendment to legislation on foreign exchange, Slovakia's national currency is fully convertible for all current account operations. Another amendment that came into force in April 1998 revoked the requirement for legal entities to surrender their foreign exchange receipts and lifted limits on purchases of foreign currency by private individuals. The same amendment enabled legal entities to set up foreign currency accounts. The foreign reserves of the central bank have been steady for quite some time at $3.0 billion - $3.4 billion, equivalent to three months' imports in 1997. They dipped significantly ($380 million) in May 1997.

5. Is there a functioning capital market infrastructure? (Are there existing or planned commodities, bond, and stock markets? What are the mechanisms for investment and lending? What government bodies have authority to regulate capital markets?) There are two official securities markets — the Bratislava Stock Exchange (BCPB) and the OTC market RM-system. Capital markets hardly function at all, however, as evidenced by low transaction volumes, diminishing prices of most securities, and declining share indices. Because long-term financial products are unavailable, the enterprise sector is not relying on the capital market to raise capital. The principle reasons for the current situation include the drive by the Ministry of Finance against capital market operators, especially investment companies and investment funds that have been reduced to portfolio investment status, as well as inadequate protection of minority shareholder rights, insufficient foreign investment inflows, non-compliance with securities legislation, price manipulations, and excessively large public issues on the market. After the Bratislava Options Exchange was closed in 1995, there has been no derivatives trading in Slovakia. In May 1998, BCPB filed an application for a derivatives trading license. The main problems of the Slovak capital market are a lack of transparency, inadequate protection of minority shareholders, and destructive conditions for investment funds and investment companies. Public trust in the capital market has been eliminated particularly by the cancellation of the second wave of privatization and by the unlawful state liquidation of Sporofond, the largest open market fund. Oversupply, inadequate demand, and fairly low prices confuse the market. With regard to restructuring needs, a capital market like this cannot adequately promote the inflow of foreign investment and its efficient allocation to various sectors, regions, and enterprises. An excess of demand over supply, particularly with regard to medium and long-term funds, characterizes the lending market. Large banks are burdened with many classified old loans and are forced to create large reserves to cover losses from them. The lack of funds was further aggravated in 1997 by the growing expansion of the fiscal sector. Besides monetary expansion, the NBS has had to cope with the consequences of the 1996 monetary expansion, which means that almost 70 percent of the money supply growth (restricted to 10.7 percent in 1997) will be consumed by government investment. This has resulted in a higher price of money on credit markets, and has made the environment less conducive to restructuring the economy. The government reacted by criticizing the NBS for allegedly excessive restriction and there are indications that the government is trying to limit NBS autonomy.

Microeconomics 3.75/7

1. Are property rights guaranteed? (Are there both formal and de facto protections of private real estate and intellectual property? Is there a land registry with the authority and capability to ensure accurate recording of who owns what? What are the procedures for expropriation, including measures for compensation and challenge? Have any seizures taken place?) Article 20 of the constitution guarantees the protection of property rights, including the right to inheritance. Restrictions on property rights may be imposed to protect the public interest, but resulting losses must be compensated fully. There have been no instances of expropriation. In the business sector, only Slovak legal persons may own real estate; non-residents may hold real estate only through a locally registered company. Provisions relating to real estate are included in the Civil Code and *cadastres* (real estate registries) operate at the district and national levels. The Industrial Property Office is responsible for most intellectual property rights, while the Ministry of Culture deals with copyrights. Slovakia adheres to several intellectual property rights agreements and generally follows European standards in this area. Although property rights are being enforced, the backlog within the court system may result in delays resolving disputes; there are no alternative legal means of property rights enforcement. The constitution guarantees equal treatment of different forms of ownership and the protection of ownership rights. Ownership became less transparent recently, however, as a number of enterprises were privatized by front companies. In 1995, an amendment was enacted to the Law on Securities introducing bearer shares. Another major problem is widespread arrears, totaling approximately 220 billion Sk or one-third of GDP in mid-1997. About 120 billion Sk of this total was accounted for by classified loans and 100 billion Sk represented inter-enterprise debt. The payments discipline of enterprises deteriorated after the enactment of legislation on enterprise revitalization. Under the new law, a revitalization commission consisting of ministry, commercial bank, and central bank officials may waive the liabilities of selected enterprises, including their loan, tax, and insurance fund liabilities. Although more than 700 revitalization proposals have been submitted so far, none of them has been approved yet. In addition, the Law on Bankruptcy is not being enforced. Since the law was enacted in 1993, only two of 4,000 bankruptcy procedures have been successfully completed. A weakness of the current legislation is that it accords the debtor a status superior to that of the creditor.

2. To what extent have prices been liberalized? What subsidies remain? As much as 98 percent of prices have been liberalized. On the other hand, the few prices that continue to be regulated constitute a substantial portion of the consumer basket. These include prices paid for electricity, gas, passenger transport, and housing rent. The prices of basic agricultural commodities are also regulated.

Under the Law on Pricing which took effect in the spring of 1996, the Ministry of Finance has the right to intervene in pricing mechanisms to secure such notions such as "reasonable profits" and "reasonable prices." In practice, however, the ministry has not exercised this right.

3. Is it possible to own and operate a business? (Has there been legislation regarding the formation, dissolution, and transfer of businesses, and is the law respected? Do there exist overly cumbersome bureaucratic hurdles that effectively hinder the ability to own and dispose of a business? Are citizens given access to information on commercial law? Is the law applied fairly? Do regulation or licensing requirements impose significant costs on business and consumers? Do they create significant barriers to entry and seriously hamper competition?) It is possible to own and operate a business; the legal structure for business activity is outlined in the Commercial Code. According to this code, businesses must be listed in the Commercial Register. As noted in the Country Commercial Guide for Slovakia, businesses must hold a lease contract for premises and have local approval for trade and location, a Slovak bank account, and certain minimum capital requirements prior to registration. Individual foreign business owners must hold a long-term residence permit. Enterprises may take four forms: 1) public commercial company with unlimited liability; 2) limited partnership company with at least one partner holding unlimited liability; 3) limited liability company; and 4) joint-stock company. Limited liability companies are the most common, while joint-stock companies tend to emerge primarily in the process of privatization. Professional businesses, such as accounting firms, must be licensed. Foreigners are not restricted from business activities, although they may face some obstacles in the acquisition of property. Commercial laws do not become effective until they appear in the Collection of Laws of the Slovak Republic, which is available to the public. The Commercial Code, which closely adheres to German and European Union legislation, is reportedly applied consistently and fairly. In the first post-Communist years, it was relatively easy to set up a business enterprise in Slovakia. Conditions became more complicated after 1993, due primarily to growing tax and insurance burdens, increased administrative difficulties, and a shortage of loans and capital. These problems primarily confront proprietors and small and medium-sized enterprises since the state favors large enterprises and their owners through direct and indirect transfers and other means. This further aggravates the deficit in state funds and increases the burden on small and medium-size enterprises through various payments. Interest groups that do not sufficiently protect the interests of proprietors of small and medium-size enterprises, and whose leaders are often under the influence of the big business lobby, also share responsibility for this situation. The reason for the inadequate assertion of their demands on the part of the representatives is based on the weak pressure applied by the rank and file members themselves, i.e., by the small and medium-size enterprises, both toward the government and political parties and toward their representatives. The main problem of dissolving an enterprise is the non-existence of a functioning bankruptcy system, which results in high insolvency, the tying up of human, material, and financial resources in loss-making and unpromising enterprises, and limited possibilities for market entry and exit. According to a January 1996 survey of market indicators by the Statistical Office of the Slovak Republic, 69 percent of enterprises were afflicted by insolvency. The courts had received approximately 2,000 bankruptcy petitions by the end of 1995 but fewer than 60 bankruptcies have actually been declared. At the beginning of 1997, the number of such petitions already exceeded 4,000, while only two bankruptcies had actually been carried out. The primary causes of the de facto non-existence of bankruptcies are inadequate bankruptcy law and overburdened commercial courts.

4. Are courts effective, transparent, efficient, and quick in reaching decisions on property and contract disputes? What alternative mechanisms for adjudicating disputes exist? Courts are often overwhelmed and sometimes exposed to subjective pressures; proceedings are relatively long. As insolvency spreads and legal collection enforcement procedures prove ineffective, illegal collection enforcement has become more common recently.

5. Is business competition encouraged? (Are monopolistic practices limited in law and in practice? If so, how? To what degree is "insider" dealing a hindrance to open competition? Are government procurement policies open and unbiased?) Article 55 of the constitution and the Commercial Code provide for the protection and promotion of competition. The Anti-Monopoly Office is responsible for ensuring compliance with competition regulations. The Law on the Protection of Competition, passed in 1994, is the principal regulation in this area. The Anti-Monopoly Office looks into complaints against businesses that abuse their dominant or monopolistic position on the market, anti-competitive agreements, and ownership concentration. It may rule that a deficiency be redressed or apply a financial fine. The independence of the Anti-Monopoly Office was weakened in 1995 when the authority to appoint and to remove its members was transferred from the president to the government. The government also has the power to recall its chairman without giving any reason. In 1995, the Anti-Monopoly Office stopped disclosing the details of its decisions to the public.

6. To what extent has international trade been liberalized? To what degree has there been simplification/overhaul of customs and tariff procedures, and are these applied fairly? What informal trade barriers exist? Slovakia is a member of the World Trade Organization (WTO) and the Central European Free Trade Area (CEFTA). It is also bound by agreements under the General Agreement on Tariffs and Trade, its customs union agreement with the Czech Republic, and its association treaty with the European Union. Slovakia also has bilateral trade agreements with Romania, Slovenia, Bulgaria, and Israel. In 1997, 25 percent of Slovakia's trade was with the Czech Republic, while trade with EU countries accounted for 42 percent of all foreign trade. Trade with CEFTA countries other than the Czech Republic was 8.7 percent, while trade with Russia was 10.1 percent. Customs duties are generally low. In 1996, the average duty was 5.5 percent. Import duties accounted for 1.5 percent of 1997 imports. In May 1997, in an attempt to counter a deteriorating balance of trade, the government introduced compulsory import deposits. In July 1997, a 7 percent import surcharge supplanted these deposits. Following a decision by the WTO Balance of Payments Committee, this surcharge was reduced to 5 percent in January 1998, and to 3 percent in April 1998; it is expected to be eliminated by October 1998. The government's other anti-imports measure in September 1997 was a tightening of import certification requirements, which led to the liquidation of many (particularly smaller) importers. Largely as a result of these measures, the balance of trade deficit was reduced from 64.5 billion Sk (11.1 percent of GDP) in 1996 to 49.5 billion Sk (7.7 percent of GDP) by the end of 1997. Imported goods are subject to VAT of 23 percent or 6 percent. On July 1, 1997, a law on anti-dumping and other legislation to counter excessive imports came into effect. At the end of 1996, a Foreign Trade Promotion Fund was established. Importers and exporters are required to make compulsory contributions, i.e., .1 percent of the value of their imports or exports to the Fund, whose role is to promote Slovak exports through advertising campaigns and participating in trade fairs and exhibitions. A law establishing an Export-Import (EXIM) Bank to fund and to insure export and import loans was approved by parliament in February 1997. The government may also authorize the EXIM Bank to represent Slovakia in international institutions whose business is relevant to its operations. The EXIM Bank was exempted from NBS supervision, a feature criticized by the opposition, the central bank, and representatives of the International Monetary Fund.

7. To what extent has foreign investment and capital flow been encouraged or constrained? Foreign investment and trade are encouraged, and tax holidays may be available to foreign companies. Foreign direct investment may take three forms: joint ventures, green field investment, and participation in privatization by direct sale. There are no restrictions on the repatriation of profits by foreign companies, and the Slovak crown became fully convertible for current account purposes on October 1, 1995. The Statistical Office of the Slovak Republic reported that in 1997, foreign direct investment in Slovak enterprises (excluding the banking sector) increased by 5.4 billion Sk, totaling 41.2 billion Sk. Compared with neighboring countries, foreign investments are low both in absolute and per capita terms. The political situation and privatization methods favoring domestic investors are generally regarded as the main barriers to foreign capital inflows.

8. Has there been reform of the energy sector? (To what degree has the energy sector been

restructured? Is the energy sector more varied, and is it open to private competition? Is the country overly dependent on one or two other countries for energy (including whether exported fuels must pass through one or more countries to reach market)? Slovakia depends on Russia for importing primary raw materials, especially natural gas and oil. The signing of a joint venture contract for natural gas transport and storage by the Slovak Gas Industry and Russia's gas giant *Gazprom* has aggravated fears that Slovakia will become even more dependent on Russia. Although the domestic energy sector is viewed as a "strategic industry," in which the state maintains an interest, some shares in energy sector companies have been sold to domestic firms. In 1996, the National Property Fund sold 45.9 percent of shares in the oil and gas company, NAFTA Gbely, to a virtually unknown business, Druha Obchodna. This sale reportedly involved prices far below those for which NAFTA Gbely shares were then trading, much to the consternation of foreign companies who had previously bought shares at the higher market prices.

There has been virtually no reform in the energy sector. Natural monopolies that are still state-owned dominate natural gas import and distribution as well as electricity generation. Slovnaft, currently a privately-owned refinery, processes oil. Nonetheless, these natural monopolies are facing higher costs that, in a regulated environment, erode their profits.

SLOVENIA

Freedom in the World Ratings, 1989-1998

	1989-90	1990-91	1991-92	1992-93	1993-94	1994-95	1995-96	1996-97	1997-98
Political Rights	-	-	2	2	1	1	1	1	1
Civil Liberties	-	-	3	2	2	2	1	2	2
Status	-	-	F	F	F	F	F	F	F

Polity: Consolidated Democracy
Economy: Consolidated Market
Population: 2,051,522
PPP: $10,594
Ethnic Groups: Slovene (91 percent), Croat (3 percent), Serb (2 percent), Muslim (1 percent), other
Capital: Ljubljana

Political Process 2.00/7

1. When did national legislative elections occur? Were they free and fair? How were they judged by domestic and international election monitoring organizations? Who composes the government? Slovenia held its first multiparty elections in December 1992. Prime Minister Janez Drnovsek's Liberal Democratic Party (LDS), the linchpin of the center-left governing coalition, emerged as a growing force in this contest, which was considered to be generally free of irregularities.

The most recent general elections were held in November 1996. The LDS gave a strong showing, although several once marginal, right-wing parties gained popularity over such issues as European Union (EU) integration, the influx of foreigners and Bosnian refugees, and agricultural protection. The elections were inconclusive: the LDS won 27.1 percent of the vote and 25 of the legislature's 90 seats. Despite a three percent increase in the popular vote, the LDS lost five legislative seats, while its coalition partner, the Christian Democratic Party (SKD), won only nine seats — six fewer than in 1992. These seats were picked up by the Slovenian People's Party (SLS, 19 seats) and the Social Democrats (16 seats). Both of these parties are right-wing and conservative, making it difficult for Drnovsek to assemble a coalition government.

After three months of political deadlock, party leaders put together a left-right coalition of Drnovsek's LDS, Marjan Podobnik's SLS, and the small DeSUS pensioners' party in February 1997. Drnovsek remained prime minister.

Parallel to the November presidential elections, Slovenians also voted for the 40-member National Council, the upper chamber of parliament which has substantially limited powers. Under Article 97 of the constitution, the National Council may propose the enactment of statutes by parliament, give its opinion to parliament, require that parliament reconsider a statute, call a referendum, and call for a parliamentary inquiry. Councilors are elected to five-year terms.

2. When did presidential elections occur? Were they free and fair? Free and fair presidential elections were first held in December 1992, with Milan Kucan winning 63.5 percent of the vote. Kucan, the former local leader and head of the Slovenian League of Communists, won popular support in 1990 when he legalized several alternative political parties and youth movements, thereby advancing political pluralism in the face of Serbian leader Slobodan Milosevic's growing power.

Kucan was re-elected on November 23, 1997 with 65 percent of the vote. Seven other candidates ran as well, including SLS candidate Janez Podobnik, the speaker of parliament. Podobnik came in second with 18.4 percent of the vote. The election was considered to be free and fair.

3. Is the electoral system multiparty based? Are there at least two viable political parties functioning at all levels of government? Of the electoral systems in the former Yugoslavia, Slovenia's most closely resembles those in the West. Differences among the parties result primarily from varying attitudes towards international integration. These parties function at all levels of government, though municipal elections also reflect a larger number of independent candidates. For example, in the December 1994 elections, independent candidates won 29 of the 147 mayoral posts, while an additional 16 had multiparty affiliations.

4. How many parties have been legalized? Are any particular parties illegal? For a country with only 1.5 million eligible voters, Slovenia boasts a considerable number of parties. Thirty political parties are registered, all of which contested the last general elections in 1996. However, the political scene revolves primarily around four: the LDS, SKD, SLS, and the Social Democratic Party of Slovenia (SDSS). Eight national parties are represented in the legislature, including the LDS, the SKD, the United List of Social Democrats (a coalition of four parties composed of the former Communists and their allies), the People's Party (agrarian populists), the Democratic Party, the Green Party, and the SDSS. In addition, the constitution mandates that a single parliamentary seat be given to both the Italian and Hungarian minorities. Though some of the smaller parties have changed in name and constituency, the largest parties remain stable.

5. What proportion of the population belongs to political parties? Exact figures on total party membership are not readily available. According to the European Forum for Democracy and Solidarity, official party figures of the United List of Social Democrats show that the party has some 26,000 members. The youth organization of the right-wing SDSS, the Social Democratic Youth, claims to have 4,000 members.

6. What has been the trend in voter turnout at the municipal, provincial, and national levels in recent years? Voter turnout has been declining since 1992. General elections in 1992 had a turnout of 80 percent. In December 1994, turnout in municipal elections was only 60 percent in the first round and 50 percent in the second round. General elections in 1996 saw a 50 percent turnout.

Civil Society 2.00/7

1. How many nongovernmental organizations (NGOs) have come into existence since 1988? What is the number of charitable/nonprofit organizations? Are there locally led efforts to increase

philanthropy and volunteerism? What proportion of the population is active in private voluntary activity (from polling data)? In 1989, over 100 grassroots organizations were estimated to exist, along with ten alternative parties. Slovenia's relatively liberal political climate made it an exception among Eastern European countries. Since independence, Slovenia's non-governmental sector has declined, reflecting the country's small population and reasonable, though not extraordinary, government safety net. Most NGOs aim to increase levels of technical competence in business and public policy administration or to provide university faculty or media training. Many are involved in environmental issues, and there are also a number of gay and lesbian political and support organizations, marketing associations, religious organizations, and organizations to promote awareness about social issues such as sexual harassment in the workplace. Amnesty International and the Helsinki Monitor have offices in Slovenia as well.

Slovenian NGOs rely mostly on foreign financing which is often distributed to indigenous organizations through regranting organizations.

The debate on the difference between non-governmental organizations and non-profit organizations or non-political organizations in Eastern Eruope has particular relevance in Slovenia. The government has begun to devolve some of its responsibilities to "institutes" or "foundations" that grew out of the Communist system, yet are classified as non-profit. Some of these are financed privately and some publicly, although they are generally independent of direct state administration. The government, however, retains indirect influence through representatives who serve on the institutes' administrative bodies. Since these institutes address broad welfare issues, the government does not fully recognize the contribution of western-style, independent NGOs, and instead perceives them as something of a threat.

2. What is the legal and regulatory environment for NGOs (i.e., ease of registration, legal rights, government regulation, taxation, procurement, and access-to-information issues)? To what extent is NGO activism focused on improving the legal and regulatory environment? This information is not available.

3. What is the organizational capacity of NGOs? Do management structures clearly delineate authority and responsibility? Is information available on NGO management issues in the native language? Is there a core of experienced practitioners/trainers to serve as consultants or mentors to less developed organizations? According to the Regional Environmental Center, which reports on the status of some 120 environmental NGOs in Slovenia, most NGOs have weak organizational structures, small memberships, and very few, if any, paid staff members. Environmental NGOs, however, have been successful at cooperation on common issues despite differences in organizational patterns, working goals, and methods. They recognize the importance of cooperation for effective participation in policy development. More experienced groups guide and provide assistance to others. Information on non-environmental NGOs is not readily available.

4. Are NGOs financially viable? What is their tax status? Are they obliged to and do they typically disclose revenue sources? Do government procurement opportunities exist for private, not-for-profit providers of services? Slovenian NGOs lack financial resources, and tend to generate little income. Thus, they depend on external sources of funding to conduct programs. Few foundations or organizations support NGOs financially; most of the international organizations that support NGOs in other countries do not currently have active granting programs in Slovenia. The U.S. AID closed its office in Slovenia in September 1997.

5. Are there free trade unions? How many workers belong to these unions? Is the number of workers belonging to trade unions growing or decreasing? What is the numerical/proportional membership of farmers' groups, small business associations, etc.? Trade unions are protected by Article 76 of the constitution. Article 77 guarantees the right to strike. In 1993, the National Assembly passed legislation restricting strikes by some public sector employees. After government budget-cutting, however, some public sector professionals, judges, doctors, and educators have become increasingly active on the labor front. According to the European Commission, approximately 50 percent of Slovenians belong to trade unions.

Labor has two main groupings with constituent branches throughout the country. The Association of Free Trade Unions is an independent trade union federation. The Association of Trade Unions is the de facto successor of the communist trade union federation. A third, much smaller, regional labor union operates on the Adriatic coast. Unions are formally and actually independent of the government and political parties, but individual union members hold positions in the legislature.

Radio and television journalists, health-care professionals, railway workers, and university professors all went on strike in 1996, as did some 300,000 factory workers. All of these strikes sought wage increases and improved working conditions; most were resolved with wage increases. In 1997, air traffic controllers and the Aeronautical, Information, and Technical union went on strike for improved working conditions.

Labor concerns continue to dominate the Slovenian political and economic scene. They represent the most developed form of interaction between government and non-government groups. Trade unions play an important part in the 1994 Economic and Social Agreement that sets wage and social policy in conjunction with business and the government. It represents a consensus among all three partners on policies to achieve economic growth, increased employment, lower inflation, and an improvement in social and legal security. Through the Council, consultation and opinions are presented on legislation pending in parliament, and binding decisions are handed down regarding rules of operation for the three Council branches.

Most farmers are represented politically by their political parties. The three major small business associations — the Association of Employers of Slovenia, the Chamber of Small Businesses of Slovenia, and the Association of Employers in Small Businesses, Catering, Intellectual Services, Tourism, Trade, and Freight Transport — signed the economic and social agreement that set up a council to determine wage and social policies. Small business associations are particularly concerned with reorientation towards exports and increasing competitiveness with EU enterprises.

6. What forms of interest group participation in politics is legal? What types of interest groups are active in the political and policy processes? Citizens are free to lobby the government. The constitution explicitly provides for two fundamental forms of direct democracy: referenda and popular initiatives. Though American-style pressure groups such as lobbyists do not exist, other groups are active. Trade unions strike, small business associations conduct policy negotiations with the government, and citizens petition, demonstrate, and engage in media debates. In addition, citizens wishing to unite communities into larger municipalities, and thus gain greater legislative autonomy, can do so by referenda. Certain ethnic Hungarian communities have exercised this right.

According to the 1992 Law on the National Council, 22 of the Council's 40 members are elected by the municipalities to represent their local interests, and the other 18 members are elected by individual interest organizations. According to Article 96 of the constitution, four of these must represent employers, four must represent farmers, small business persons, and independent professionals, and six must represent non-profit organizations.

In July 1997, the government asked employers and labor unions to comment on a draft law on labor relations prior to its submission in parliament. The draft covers a wide number of topics including recruitment and termination, employer and employee obligations, and the treatment of special categories such as the elderly, pregnant women, and disabled workers. This measure is part of a major government effort to bring Slovenia in line with EU standards.

Independent Media 1.75/7

1. Are there legal protections for press freedom? Article 39 of the constitution guarantees the right to "freely collect, receive, and circulate information and opinions." Historically, Slovenia's media were relatively free for a socialist country; unlike its neighbors, Slovenia had fairly free access to Western media. Currently, the greatest threats to freedom of the press stem not from government control, but from self-censorship, indirect political pressure, and journalistic inexperience resulting from over 40 years of authoritarian Communist rule.

2. Are there legal penalties for libeling officials? Are there legal penalties for "irresponsible" journalism? Have these laws been enforced to harass journalists? Article 169 of the Slovenian Civil Code prohibits "insulting" officials. The law was last used in 1996 to prosecute a journalist. Bernard Nezmah of the weekly *Mladina* was given a one-month suspended prison sentence and fined for criticizing a former foreign affairs minister. In November 1997, Justice Minister Tomas Marusic announced that Slovenia would liberalize criminal legislation which allows for the prosecution of journalists who reveal certain state and army secrets. Under the proposed changes, a journalist would not be prosecuted for disclosing a state or army secret if he or she were doing so in order to reveal irregularities in government or army bodies, provided that the disclosure does not harm the state. Slovenia's criminal law, introduced in 1994, is based on legislation prior to its breakaway from Yugoslavia in 1991. The European Commission has said that Slovenia must make its legislation conform to EU laws before formally joining the European Union.

3. What proportion of media is privatized? What are the major private newspapers, television stations, and radio stations? Most Slovenian media have been privatized. Broadcast media are more susceptible to government influence than print media. The major daily newspapers *Delo* (circulation 93,000), *Vecer* (62,000), and *Dnevik* (66,000) are supported with private investment and advertising. Other popular dailies include *Slovenske Novice* (76,000) and *Republika* (25,000). The principal news agency is the Slovenian Press Agency (STA). Radiotelevizija Slovenija (Slovenia Radio-Television) broadcasts in Slovenian over three radio stations and two television channels. It is reportedly moving toward privatization but is still government-subsidized. There are seven other television channels, four of which are independent private stations, and nine major commercial radio stations. Pop TV, founded in 1995, and Kanal A, founded in 1991, are fully private. An early plan to privatize Radio Koper and Radio Maribor came to a halt when journalists argued that a comprehensive legal framework governing the media should be in place prior to the arrival of new investors. Journalists fear that privatization may be insufficient and that the government will continue to dominate the media through legal control. Foreign broadcasts are available via satellite and cable. All major towns in Slovenia have radio stations and cable television. Numerous business and academic publications, as well as foreign newspapers, magazines, and journals, are widely available. Hungarian radio programming is common in the northeast where there are about 8,500 ethnic Hungarians. Bosnian refugees and the Albanian community have newsletters in their own languages.

4. Are the private media financially viable? A small domestic market and lack of a diversified funding base contribute to intense competition among Slovenian media. Private, independent media are more susceptible to financial difficulties, as previously state-owned media tend to have greater capital assets. Immediately after independence, the Slovenian government set up a Fund for Pluralization of the Media which sought to support smaller papers. It was abolished in 1992 for no clear reason. Even well-funded papers, such as *Republika*, cannot count on a diversified funding base to insulate them from sudden financial difficulties.

5. Are the media editorially independent? Are the media's news gathering functions affected by interference from government or private owners? Slovenian media are generally editorially independent, though print media enjoy greater freedom than the broadcast media, which rely to some degree on government funding. Libel legislation and other legal restrictions, as well as journalistic inexperience and the legacy of over 40 years of authoritarian rule, continue to affect the media through political pressure and self-censorship. Slovenian journalists have complained about editorial dependence on economic or political interests, about inexperienced journalists who report crudely or ignorantly, and about economic competition, which gives rise to sensationalism. The media, however, offer a wide variety of opinions and ideas. The election law requires the media to offer free space and time to political parties at election time. Television networks routinely give public figures and opinion makers from across the political spectrum access via a broad range of public interest programming.

6. Is the distribution system for newspapers privately or governmentally controlled? The distribution system for newspapers in Slovenia is privately controlled by independent vendors.

7. What proportion of the population is connected to the Internet? Are there any restrictions on Internet access to private citizens? Internet access in Slovenia is largely unrestricted. As a relatively new phenomenon, the Internet has not been the subject of any specific legislation, though copyright and intellectual property law has been applied to the assignment of domain names and logos. Legal restrictions on violent content and pornography in media have not been used to hinder the flow of information, though one student in Kranj was prosecuted in 1997 for allowing children under 14 years of age to access pornographic material. Dozens of Internet service providers exist to service households, academic institutions, and businesses.

According to a 1997 study by Research on Internet in Slovenia (RIS), some 142,000 Slovenians over age 12 use the Internet with some regularity. RIS conducted a survey in October 1997, which suggested that the number of households with access to the Internet grew by seven percent in the first half of 1997. An additional six percent were planning to obtain access to the Internet in the coming six months, and an additional 12 percent were considering it.

8. What has been the trend in press freedom as measured by Freedom House's *Survey of Press Freedom*? Freedom House's *Survey of Press Freedom* rated Slovenia Partly Free in 1994 and 1995, and Free in 1996, 1997, and 1998.

Governance and Public Administration 2.50/7

1. Is the legislature the effective rule-making institution? The constitution provides for a clear distinction between branches of government, with the legislature clearly in control of rule-making. The legal distinction is fully observed in practice.

2. Is substantial power decentralized to subnational levels of government? What specific authority do subnational levels have? As Slovenia has only two million inhabitants, regional government does not exist. Instead, Slovenia is divided into 58 administrative units whose leaders are appointed by the government upon a proposal by the Minister of the Interior. These leaders carry out decisions made by the central government and oversee the activity of the local authorities.

Local authority in Slovenia is divided into municipalities. The division of Slovenia into municipalities in the Communist period was such that they were very large, with only 62 municipal authorities in the whole area. In 1994, this number was increased to 147, with effective implementation on January 1, 1995, after municipal elections. On March 1, 1997, the European Charter on Local Self-Government came into effect. The number of municipalities is constantly increasing because the small villages forming part of these municipalities have the right, under certain conditions, to become autonomous municipalities.

Municipalities are founded through referenda of the inhabitants of a particular region and they may unite to form broader self-governing communities. One such community is the Hungarian Self-Ruled National Community of Pomursko, which represents 9,000 Prekmurje Hungarians. Article 140 of the constitution defines the duties and functions of self-governing local bodies as "such local matters affecting only the people of that municipality, as the municipality may independently determine." Municipalities administer most local public services and are run by directly elected mayors.

In 1997, a new regionalization process began with the proposal of a Draft Law on Regions by the Ministry of the Interior. This process is part of Slovenia's larger effort to bring its laws and institutions into line with EU standards. The Working Group on Regionalization in Europe held a conference in October 1997 with government representatives and associations of local and regional authorities to examine the bill and discuss its compatibility with the draft European Charter on Local Self-Government. The establishment of regional government is perceived by European experts to be necessary for Slovenia's integration into Europe.

3. Are subnational officials chosen in free and fair elections? The December 1994 elections, the first local elections after independence, occurred without irregularities. The bodies of the municipality include the municipal council, the mayor, and, when necessary, one or more municipal committees and a supervisory committee.

The municipal council makes the basic decisions falling under the jurisdiction of the municipality. The number of council members is set by the municipality itself but legally must be between seven and 45 members. In regions inhabited by Italian and Hungarian communities, these ethnic communities must have at least one representative serving on the municipal council. Members of municipal councils are elected directly for four-year terms, on the basis of universal suffrage, in free and secret ballots. The voter must be a permanent resident of the municipality. In smaller municipalities, the majority system for dividing mandates is used. In medium and larger municipalities, a proportional system is used whereby the electors vote for lists of candidates and preferential voting is possible. The municipal committees are the executive bodies of the municipal councils and are elected by the municipal councils from among their own members and the municipality's citizens.

The mayor, who represents the municipality and heads the municipal administration, is elected for four years by absolute majority in direct elections.

4. Do the executive and legislative bodies operate openly and with transparency? Is draft legislation easily accessible to the media and the public? Executive and legislative bodies operate openly. Most legislation and information about ministries and contacts can be obtained easily through the Internet, by written request, on CD-ROM, or on diskette. Although the constitution provides for it, there is no law at present guaranteeing openness in measures undertaken by the administration. As part of its push for EU membership and in compliance with OECD regulations, the government has attempted to bring its legislation in line with that of the EU and has regularly published economic statistics. Regarding unresolved or ambiguous legislative matters, or certain sensitive economic issues such as privatization, the government is more reticent about disclosing its intentions, if not the relevant statistics.

5. Do municipal governments have sufficient revenues to carry out their duties? Do municipal governments have control of their own local budgets? Do they raise revenues autonomously or from the central state budget? Municipalities generally have sufficient revenues to carry out their duties. Article 142 of the constitution calls upon each municipality to raise its own revenue. Municipalities are normally financed from their own sources, from taxes and other duties, and from revenues received from municipal property. Economically underdeveloped municipalities may receive additional financing from the state. Greater ethnic diversity in a few of these underdeveloped municipalities has caused some tension over the division of revenues.

6. Do the elected local leaders and local civil servants know how to manage municipal govern-

ments effectively? As Slovenia became independent only recently, the development of local government is still underway. To increase the effectiveness of local administration, the government is planning a comprehensive program to modernize the legal, administrative, financial, and organizational aspects of public administration and to boost the training of officials.

In a February 1997, report, the European Commission noted that in public administration, "Professional levels are often good, but in order to provide a sound basis for continued European integration further development of administrative skills will be an important objective." Plans are being developed for a civil service college.

7. When did the constitutional/legislative changes on local power come into effect? Has there been a reform of the civil service code/system? Are local civil servants employees of the local or central government? The division of tasks between the state and local governments was outlined in the 1994 Law on Local Government. The number of municipal authorities was increased from 62 to 147, and responsibility for both state and local tasks was taken out of the hands of local governments. State tasks are now administered locally through administrative units linked to the national ministries; the officials in charge of these units are nominated by the central government. Local tasks are carried out through the municipalities, whose leaders are employees of the local government. Disputes as to jurisdiction between the state and the municipality are decided by the Constitutional Court.

There is currently no full statutory basis for a civil service, nor any clearly stated set of principles governing the role of the civil service. A Civil Service Act is in preparation.

Rule of Law 1.50/7

1. Is there a post-Communist constitution? How does the judicial system interpret and enforce the constitution? Are there specific examples of judicial enforcement of the constitution in the last year? The constitution was adopted in December 1991 after the declaration of independence from the former Yugoslavia. The Constitutional Court is composed of nine judges appointed by parliament for a non-renewable nine-year term of office upon a proposal from the president. By the end of 1998, the mandates of six of the nine current justices will expire, thus forcing a significant change in the court's membership. The court ensures that laws, decrees, and regulatory acts issued by local authorities are consistent with the constitution, international treaties, and the general principles of international law. It also rules on requests from appellants who feel that their constitutional rights have been violated. Under Article 162 of the constitution, any person who can demonstrate that he or she has a case may bring it before the court. The president, the government, or one-third of the members of the national assembly may ask the court to rule on whether an international treaty to be ratified is consistent with the constitution. Article 160 of the constitution empowers the Constitutional Court to rule on jurisdictional disputes between courts and other state bodies.

In November 1997, the Constitutional Court annulled Articles 150-156 of Chapter XV of the Criminal Procedure Code. These articles were part of the preliminary criminal procedure that regulates the powers of the police, state prosecutor, and investigating magistrates in criminal cases. They are also intended to outline special operating methods by police in cases of organized crime. Petitioners challenging the Criminal Procedure Code argued that it violated several articles of the constitution which provide for rule of law and due process. While the Constitutional Court did not find the Criminal Procedure Code provisions unconstitutional, it did annul them pending their adjustment by the National Assembly to conform to constitutional standards for the protection of human rights.

In July 1997, the Constitutional Court decided that Article 68 of the constitution, which restricts the property rights of foreigners, would have to be amended prior to ratification of Slovenia's Association Agreement with the European Union (see next question).

2. Does the constitutional framework provide for human rights? Do the human rights include business and property rights? Section II of the constitution addresses human rights issues explicitly. Although there is a provision for the suspension of these rights in a state of emergency, certain rights, such as the inviolability of human life, may not be suspended at any time. The constitution covers most rights generally found in western constitutions, such as due process, freedom of movement, freedom of expression, and freedom of conscience. Intellectual property rights are also covered in Section II. The rights of ethnic Italians and Hungarians are explicitly detailed, and the constitution grants them the right to use national symbols freely and to bilingual education.

Business and property rights are guaranteed under Articles 66-79, though the property rights of foreigners are limited. Under the Association Agreement with the European Union, signed in 1996, Slovenia promised a gradual deregulation of land ownership. The ratification of the agreement by parliament, however, was clearly in contravention of Article 68, which states that foreigners are permitted to own land in Slovenia only through inheritance and only where there is reciprocity for Slovenian citizens in the country of origin of the foreign national in question. The government asked the Constitutional Court to decide whether the constitution would have to be amended prior to ratification of the agreement. In June 1997 the court ruled that an amendment was necessary. After some political wrangling, the Constitutional Law on Amending Article 68 passed. It allows foreigners to own property in accordance with the law or international agreement ratified by parliament. In either case, the principle of reciprocity must be respected.

3. Has there been basic reform of the criminal code/criminal law? Who authorizes searches and issues warrants? Are suspects and prisoners beaten or abused? Are there excessive delays in the criminal justice system? The Criminal Code was adopted in September 1994 and came into force on January 1, 1995. The constitution prohibits abuse and "humiliating punishment or treatment" of prisoners, and such treatment has not been reported. No human rights organizations have complained about prison conditions or abuse. Changes to the Penal Code and the Law on Criminal Procedure were introduced in November 1997 in order to bring Slovenian legislation into line with European standards and to address "new forms" of crime, such as money laundering, corruption, and computer hacking offenses. New provisions include new measures on the interrogation of underaged persons and witnesses in serious criminal cases and the removal of penalties for journalists who reveal state or military secrets when reporting on cases of official corruption.

Detainees must be advised in writing within 24 hours, and in their own language, of the reasons for arrest. Until charges are brought, detention may last up to six months. Once charges have been brought, detention may be prolonged for a maximum of two years. Because of an overburdened judicial system, justice is frequently a protracted process. In some instances, criminal cases have been reported to take two to five years to come to trial. According to the U.S. State Department, the problem is not widespread, and defendants are released on bail except in the most serious criminal cases.

Searches are authorized by investigating magistrates, and warrants are issued by court order. Articles 150-156 of the Criminal Procedures Code, which provide for special powers of police, the state prosecutor, and investigating magistrates in criminal cases, were annulled in November 1997, pending the adjustments of these measures to constitutional standards for the protection of human rights and freedoms. Two petitioners challenging the measures claimed that their provisions for secret observation, tracking and film recording, and wiretapping violate constitutional provisions for privacy, the inviolability of dwellings, and the protection of personal data.

4. Do most judges rule fairly and impartially? Do many remain from the Communist era? Slovenian judges rule fairly and impartially. The judicial system comprises district courts, regional courts, a court of appeals, and the Supreme Court as the highest court. Judges, elected by parliament on the nomination of the Judicial Council, are constitutionally independent and serve indefinitely, subject to an age limit. The Judicial Council is composed of six sitting judges elected by their peers and five presidential nominees elected by the State Assembly. The nine-member Constitutional Court rules on the constitutionality of legislation.

Judges are appointed for life by the State Assembly upon proposal by the Judicial Council, an 11-member body which administers the judiciary. Five Judicial Council members are elected by parliament upon proposal from the president, while the six others are selected from among sitting judges. To balance the number of Communist-era judges, the government chose judges who had either spent substantial time studying law outside the socialist bloc or who had served on international commissions. Lengthy exposure to international standards of rule of law has created an independent court system.

5. Are the courts free of political control and influence? Are the courts linked directly to the Ministry of Justice or any other executive body? The courts operate as an independent branch of government and are not linked to any executive body. The Judicial Council, which administers the judiciary, is partially elected by parliament upon presidential nomination and partially selected from among sitting judges. According to the European Commission, the main problem facing the Slovenian judiciary is inefficiency. Slovenia lacks judges due to a relatively low level of pay and the statutory requirement that they be at least 30 years of age. A backlog of cases contributes to delays in the judicial system. A plan to equip courts with computers and planned procedural reforms are expected to improve the situation.

6. What proportion of lawyers is in private practice? How does this compare with the previous year? According to the IUS-INFO legal and business information system, Slovenia has about 900 lawyers with special (state approved) status as solicitors, who mostly deal with litigation. All of them are in private practice. There are several thousand other lawyers, working in various companies, administration, institutions, etc. Almost all of these are also private practitioners.

7. Does the state provide public defenders? Article 29 of the constitution provides for public defenders. Other due process protections, such as protection from self-incrimination, public trial, and sufficient defense preparation time, are also guaranteed. These guarantees are respected in practice.

8. Are there effective anti-bias/discrimination laws, including protection of ethnic minority rights? Article 64 of the constitution grants Slovenia's Italian and Hungarian communities the right to education, media, and legal defense in their own languages. These two communities are also granted cultural autonomy in those areas in which they are dominant. Further elaboration of these communities' exclusive rights in statutes must be approved by the communities. Each group is represented by a deputy in the National Assembly who has the power to block the adoption of laws which concern the exercise of the specific rights of these communities or their status. The Italian and Hungarian communities also have the right to promote their ties with Italy and Hungary. Article 62 of the constitution recognizes the right of individuals to use their own languages in dealings with the administration. Article 65 recognizes the special nature of the Roma (gypsy) community, which consists of some 7,000-10,000 people in the country. A law on the protection of gypsies is currently before the National Assembly. They are represented in the municipal councils of the towns in which they live. Though there have been tensions with regard to foreigners living in Slovenia, prompted by an influx of refugees, these rights are respected in practice.

Corruption	A

1. What is the magnitude of official corruption in the civil service? Must an average citizen pay a bribe to a bureaucrat in order to receive a service? What services are subject to bribe requests for example, university entrance, hospital admission, telephone installation, obtaining a license to operate a business, applying for a passport or other official documents? What is the average salary of civil servants at various levels? According to a February 1998 report by the European Commission, public confidence in the civil service is variable, and there is no significant evidence of corruption. Anecdotal evidence suggests that bribe requests are not standard practice in the attainment of services. However, in his December 1997 inaugural speech, President Kucan made the following assertion: "The opinion that corruption reigns in the country is widespread, that there is increasing crime and lawlessness, and that many politicians and officials can be bribed." Accusations of insider deals and a lack of transparency have surrounded the privatization process, which has progressed slowly. It is difficult to ascertain the exact magnitude of official corruption, as until recently, journalists could be penalized for reporting about it.

The European Commission reported that apart from specialized professions, pay levels in the public sector, while lower, are reasonably competitive with the private sector. According to the Slovenian Economic Mirror, public administration employees earn more on average than those in education, real estate, health services, or retail, and less than employees in finance and other personalized services.

2. Do top policy makers (the president, ministers, vice-ministers, top court justices, and heads of agencies and commissions) have direct ties to businesses? How strong are such connections and what kinds of businesses are these? This information is unavailable.

3. Do laws requiring financial disclosure and disallowing conflict of interest exist? Have publicized anticorruption cases been pursued? To what conclusion? Like many other European countries, Slovenia does not have a bribery statute equal in stature to the U.S. Foreign Corrupt Practices Act. The Slovenian Criminal Code (SCC), however, penalizes criminal offenses against the economy. Corruption against the economy can be split into two forms: corruption among private firms and corruption among public officials.

Public officials are held accountable under Article 267 of the SCC which makes it illegal for a public official to request or accept a gift in order to perform or omit an official act within the scope of his official duties. The acceptance of a bribe by a public official may result in a fine or imprisonment of no less than one year up to a maximum sentence of five years. The accepted gift/bribe is also seized.

While Article 267 holds public officials accountable, Article 268 holds the individual offering the gift accountable. Article 267 makes it illegal for persons or legal entities to bribe public officials with gifts. Violation of this article carries a sentence of up to three years. If the individual offering the gift discloses such bribery before it is detected or discovered, punishment may be remitted. Generally, the gift is seized.

The state prosecutor's office is responsible for the enforcement of anti-bribery provisions. The number of cases of actual bribery are few and are generally limited to instances involving inspection and tax collection. Although the prosecutor's office suspects bribery and related corruption practices in the government procurement offices, the ability to ascertain evidence is difficult, thereby making it equally difficult to prosecute. It is the view of the U.S. Embassy in Ljubljana that corruption in Slovenia is not terribly pervasive.

4. What major anticorruption initiatives have been implemented? How often are anticorruption laws and decrees adopted? Initiatives to combat corruption have been included as part of the government's efforts to ensure compliance with EU requirements. One such initiative in 1997 involved amending the Penal Code to ensure that journalists will not be punished for revealing state or military secrets if they do so with the intent to reveal corrupt behavior by public officials. The law, however, contains the condition that the journalist's revelation must not endanger state security. It remains to be seen whether cases of corruption will be reported freely.

5. How do major corruption-ranking organizations like Transparency International rate this country? Transparency International does not rate Slovenia.

Privatization 2.50/7

1. What percentage of the GDP comes from private ownership? What percentage of the labor force is employed in the private sector? How large is the informal sector of the economy? According to a report by the European Commission, the private sector in Slovenia currently accounts for only 50-55 percent of output and employment. The European Commision also reported on the existence of a significant shadow economy, illustrated by the extent of undeclared employment: while recorded unemployment is over 14 percent, an ILO labor market survey put actual unemployment at only 7 percent. Undeclared employment in temporary or contract work accounts for the difference.

2. What major privatization legislation has been passed? What were its substantive features? Slovenia's privatization programs have focused on the transformation of socially-owned enterprises into businesses with "known owners",' i.e., the mass privatization program has not been very open to potential foreign owners. The legal framework for ownership transformation is not yet complete.

Slovenian companies which have now been privatized were not state-owned. Instead, they were "socially owned," with no specific owners, such as the state, individuals, workers, or management. Under this system the responsibility of the state was voluntarily reduced to trade (central planning) and product range definition and investment, or subsidies. As a consequence, foreign investors cannot simply address a ministry or agency in order to buy a company. Another consequence is that after decades of social ownership, individual companies developed a high degree of autonomy. Their managers were not appointed by owners or nominated by the state. They were nominated by staff worker councils, though often with a direct or indirect suggestion by the state. Because of the autonomy of these companies, privatization could not be carried out by the state or by official bodies. After independence, the Slovenian authorities set up a legal framework allowing for a range of privatization routes, and compelled companies to plan and implement their own privatization within this legal framework within set deadlines. The authorities also created the autonomous Agency for Privatization in order to control and monitor the privatization process.

The government-owned Development Fund of Slovenia (SKLAD) has focused its efforts on industrial restructuring, privatizing, and liquidating problem entities. It has rehabilitated and sold a number of the 98 companies under its authority. Only 24 enterprises remained under its control by 1997.

Forty percent of the capital (cash) from selling shares in privatization efforts must be allocated with 20 percent to the Development Fund for needed restructuring, 10 percent to the Pension Funds, and 10 percent to the Compensation Fund for restitution of nationalized property.

In July 1997, parliament passed a Law on Takeovers which gives the government a powerful role in protecting large enterprises from hostile foreign bidders. Under the law, a full bid must be made when an investor seeks to acquire a voting stake of over 25 percent in any company whose shares are publicly traded, and in any company with more than 500 shareholders which was valued at more than one billion *tolars* for privatization. The government will have full discretion to block or approve all takeovers of privatized companies valued at more than 800 million tolars. According to the *Financial Times*, the law will affect between 100 and 150 companies and is valid for five years after the law is enacted.

3. What proportion of agriculture, housing and land, industry, and small business and services is in private hands? According to the World Bank, 93.4 percent of private sector enterprises in 1996 were small, primarily trade and service entities. Over 90 percent of agriculture is in private hands, along with 60 percent of services and 30 percent of industry. Privatization of state-owned industry has not yet begun; it is scheduled to begin in 1998.

4. What has been the extent of insider (management, labor, and nomenklatura) participation in the privatization process? What explicit and implicit preferences have been awarded to insiders? Employees and retirees get up to 20 percent of shares. Ownership certificates were distributed to residents to exchange for shares. The final 40 percent of shares can be purchased through public tender, auction, or offering; transfer of shares to the SKLAD; internal buyouts; and raising additional private equity. Approximately 1,000 of 1,594 eligible companies had been privatized by June 1997. Only 120 of the companies were privatized through public offerings. Management buyouts were behind most privatization efforts.

5. How much public awareness of and support for privatization has there been? What is the nature of support and opposition to privatization by major interest groups? Public awareness of privatization has been high; all citizens of Slovenia were given free, non-transferable certificates in 1994 (equivalent to 40 percent of the total social capital of all the enterprises), which they can use to buy shares in companies or in investment trusts. Management and staff of formerly socially-owned autonomous companies were allowed and encouraged to acquire and buy shares in their own enterprises. Most employees opted to buy shares in their own companies, as they believed that this would help them keep their jobs.

As would be expected, workers tend to be more hesitant about privatization because the necessary restructuring which follows invariably leads to reductions in staff. Preexisting management teams have remained in control at most companies.

Macroeconomics 2.00/7

1. Has the taxation system been reformed? (What areas have and have not been overhauled? To what degree are taxpayers complying? Is tax compliance difficult to achieve? Has the level of revenues increased? Is the revenue-collection body overburdened? What is the overall tax burden?) The Law on Income Tax is expected to undergo a comprehensive renovation to bring it into line with European standards. The new law is introducing taxation based on source of income and is expanding the income tax of residents from abroad and on all sources of income. The new law will also specify the rules that will prevent tax evasion. The Ministry of Finance is expected to send the law to the National Assembly in 1998, with a view to having it implemented in 1999. The new legislation will eliminate ambiguities, loopholes, and general confusion that have occurred in implementing the previous law.

Following a comprehensive tax reform during 1990-1993, corporate profits are taxed at a flat rate of 25 percent. One-fifth of profits may be placed in a tax-free reserve, conditional on reinvestment within four years. Personal income tax is progressive, with a minimum rate of 17 percent and a maximum rate of 50 percent. There is a sales tax of 20 percent for goods and 5 percent for services and equipment. Dividends are taxed at 25 percent for residents and 15 percent for non-residents. In January 1997, a 30 percent capital gains tax on securities held by individuals for less than three years was introduced, though gains made on first sale of shares bought during mass privatization will be exempt.

Slovenia will also coordinate with European legislation in the area of indirect taxes. New laws on excise taxes and on value-added tax will replace the laws on sales tax and special sales taxes on alcoholic beverages and cigarettes. The finance ministry in March 1998 proposed a general value added tax (VAT) rate of 22 percent. The new tax legislation is expected to ensure greater consistency in tax payment.

According to the Slovenian Economic Mirror, social security contributions fell from an average 40.2 percent of gross wages in 1996 to 38 percent in 1997. In the middle of the year, the progressive scale of the payroll tax was changed to ease the burden on lower wages. Furthermore, customs rates were reduced at the beginning of the year, following the adoption of the Europe Agreement, which substantially cut the receipts from this source. On the other hand, sales tax imposed on oil products was raised slightly and a new tax on carbon dioxide was introduced in January 1997 to provide a new tax source as well as an environmental protection fiscal instrument.

The current tax administration is insufficient to ensure a regular collection of taxes, though according to labor market surveys, the gray economy has not increased in recent years. Legislation giving more authority to tax inspectors came into effect in July 1997. Indirect taxes have been increased, while direct taxes, as well as social security contributions, have remained constant.

2. Does fiscal policy encourage private savings, investment, and earnings? (Has there been any reform/alteration of revenue and budget policies? How large are budget deficits and overall debt? Is the financing of the social insurance/pension system sustainable? What proportion of the budget is taken up by subsidies to firms and individuals?) Fiscal policy reflects an overriding concern for entrance into the European Monetary Union. Slovenia already meets three of the five requirements on public debt (less than 60 percent of GDP), budget balance (deficit below 3 percent of GDP), and currency convertibility and stability. Slovenia still falls short on inflation and interest rates, which are both too high. The government's 1998 Budget Memorandum indicates that the general government deficit in 1998 should not exceed one percent of GDP.

According to the European Bank for Reconstruction and Development (EBRD), the payroll tax and its 13.6 percent ratio of pensions to gross domestic product (GDP) are high by European standards. There has been a sharp decrease in the ratio of contributors to pensioners. The elderly dependency ratio is projected to rise from the current 48 percent to 90 percent in 2040. Possible models for reform of the pension system are being evaluated. A White Paper on changes to the state pensions system was published in December 1997. It calls for the introduction of a pension age of 65 for all (currently 58 for men and 54 for women) and for the introduction of a three-tier system consisting of a reduced basic state element supplemented by compulsory personal savings and voluntary additional contributions. Labor groups, however, oppose the proposal's provisions for funding.

3. Has there been banking reform? (Is the central bank independent? What are its responsibilities? Is it effective in setting and/or implementing monetary policy? What is the actual state of the private banking sector? Does it conform to international standards? Are depositors protected? Slovenia has 29 banks, 14 of which are fully licensed. Twelve banks have some foreign participation although only four are majority foreign-owned. The government holds about

40 percent of banking sector assets. Most banks are well capitalized. Only two banks were unprofitable in 1996.

Bank liquidity has varied and one bank was forced into liquidation in 1996. The banking sector has been overregulated, which has restricted competition and limited domestic company access to credit. Although there has been progress in the banking sector, it is still relatively shallow. Banking assets are low at 70 percent of GDP. Use of foreign currencies for deposits, loans, and units of account is widespread. The central bank has been forced to increase restrictions on banks' operations in foreign currencies since 1995. There was a decline in the share of non-performing assets from 1993 (7.6 percent) to 1995 (3.9 percent). Particularly in small banks, productivity and efficiency are low.

A number of regulations adversely affect competition. For example, there are punitive restrictions on companies wishing to finance activities in Slovenia by taking out loans abroad. When these loans are converted into domestic currency, 40 percent must be placed in non-interest bearing accounts at the central bank. This applies for loans up to seven years; for longer credits, a ten percent deposit is required. Foreign banks may not establish branches, and setting up a fully capitalized local bank is an expensive and bureaucratic process. In addition, a cartel agreement among the banks sets a ceiling on interest rates paid to depositors.

The Bank of Slovenia is the bank of issue and the central bank of Slovenia. It was established in 1991 with the passage of the central bank act, the Law on the Bank of Slovenia. The bank's primary task is to ensure currency stability and liquidity of payments within the country and with foreign countries. The Bank is a non-governmental independent institution; it is obliged to present a report on its operation to the parliament once every six months. The bank supervises the banking system but not other financial intermediaries or non-banks. It conducts no corporate business and none with natural persons. The bank is not allowed to take up loans abroad for its own account nor for the account of third persons.

4. How sound is the national currency? (Is the value of the currency fixed or does it float? How convertible is the currency? How large are the hard currency reserves? Has exchange rate policy been stable and predictable?) The Slovenian tolar was introduced in 1991. The government accepted the obligations of the IMF Article VIII to establish full current account convertibility in 1995, though the currency had been de facto convertible for current account purposes since early 1992. At first, the tolar was allowed to float freely, but it depreciated heavily. As it stabilized and inflation dropped, the Bank of Slovenia adopted a managed float against the German *mark*. The aim was to keep the real exchange rate stable and bring down inflation in order to protect competitiveness and boost output. The system was also chosen because Slovenia has a small monetary base and so is susceptible to swings in capital inflows. From mid-1992, these increased as a result of current account surpluses. These inflows were sterilized, at considerable cost, to contain money supply growth and hence inflationary pressure. The policy appears to have been successful. Due to the costs of sterilization, however, the Bank of Slovenia gradually had to restrict capital inflows to be able to maintain the chosen policy objectives. Foreign investors are permitted to repatriate profits and capital.

Inflation in Croatia has been steadily declining: 9.1 percent in 1997, compared to 9.7 percent in 1996 and 12.6 percent in 1995.

5. Is there a functioning capital market infrastructure? (Are there existing or planned commodities, bond, and stock markets? What are the mechanisms for investment and lending? What government bodies have authority to regulate capital markets?) Slovenia's capital market is still very small. According to the EBRD, the Ljubljana Stock Exchange (LSE), founded in 1989, had a total market capitalization of $1.9 billion, or ten percent of GDP, as of April 30, 1997 (75 percent shares and 25 percent bonds). About 60 companies are quoted, including almost 40 which are not fully listed, and 40 bonds are traded on the LSE. In April 1997, average daily turnover was $1.3 million. In January 1995, an over-the-counter market was opened on the LSE with eight companies acting as brokers. Futures trading began in March 1996.

Growth in the equities market has advanced slowly, in line with the progress made with privatization. With few exceptions, Slovenian companies have not yet used the LSE as a means of raising new capital. Constraints such as the recently introduced custody accounts requirements for foreign portfolio investors hinder market development. Banks are not allowed to convert into tolars the foreign currency received for payment of portfolio investments. Fees currently charged by banks for custody accounts reflect the opportunity cost of keeping foreign exchange reserves rather than lending the money domestically. The impact of this measure was a 20 percent fall in share prices within days of the introduction of the decree, while average daily turnover dropped by 70 percent.

The bond market is currently dominated by issues of government bonds. A functioning secondary market for short-term government securities and a more long-term corporate bond market are still to be established. Slovenia is preparing to issue a *Eurobond* in 1998 aimed at investors in the new euro currency. The bond will be launched in ECUs for a minimum of ECU 400 million, but will be transformed into euros with the first interest payments being made in the new European currency due to be launched in January 1999.

Slovenia's capital markets are regulated by the Slovenian Securities and Exchange Commission, which is under the authority of the Ministry of Finance.

Microeconomics 2.00/7

1. Are property rights guaranteed? (Are there both formal and de facto protections of private real estate and intellectual property? Is there a land registry with the authority and capability to ensure accurate recording of who owns what? What are the procedures for expropriation, including measures for compensation and challenge? Have any seizures taken place?) Property rights are guaranteed under Articles 66-79 of the consitution, though the property rights of foreigners are limited. Under the Association Agreement with the EU, signed in 1996, Slovenia promised a gradual deregulation of land ownership. To that end, Article 68, which states that foreigners are permitted to own land in Slovenia only through inheritance and only when there is reciprocity for Slovenian citizens in the country of origin of the foreign national in question, was amended in July 1997. The Constitutional Law on Amending Article 68 allows foreigners to own property in accordance with the law or international agreement ratified by parliament. In either case the principle of reciprocity must be respected.

The 1992 Law on Industrial Property grants and protects patents, model and design rights, trademark and service marks, and appellations of origin. The holder of a patent, model, or design right is entitled to: exclusively work the protected invention, shape, picture, or drawing; exclusively market any products manufactured in accordance with the protected invention, shape, picture, or drawing; dispose of the patent, model, or design right; and prohibit working of the protected invention, model, or design and legal transactions in respect of them, by any person not having his consent.

The holder of a mark has the exclusive right to use the mark in the course of trade to designate his products or services. The authorized user of a protected appellation of origin has the right to use the appellation in the course of trade for marking products to which the appellation refers.

The patent and trademark rights granted by the Law on Industrial Property take effect from the date of filing the appropriate applications. Patents are granted for twenty years from the date of filing, and model and design rights are granted for ten years. Trademarks are granted for ten years but may be renewed an unlimited number of times. The term of an appellation of origin is unlimited. All patents and trademarks are registered through the Slovenian intellectual property office with all registers open to the public. Patent and trademark applications filed in member countries of the International Union for the Protection of Industrial Property are afforded priority rights in Slovenia. The priority period is twelve months for patents and six months for model and design rights. Any person who infringes upon a patent or trademark right may be held liable for damages and prohibited from carrying on the infringing acts.

The Law on Industrial Property also provides for the contractual licensing of patents, model and design rights, and marks. All license agreements must be in writing and specify the duration of the license, the scope of the license, whether the license is exclusive or non-exclusive, and the amount of remuneration for the use if compensation is agreed upon. Compulsory licenses may be granted to another person when the invention is in the public interest or the patentee misuses the rights granted under the patent. A misuse of a patent will occur when the patentee does not work or insufficiently works a patented invention and refuses to license other persons to work the protected invention or imposes unjustified conditions on the licensee. If a compulsory license is granted, the patentee is entitled to compensation.

Slovenia's intellectual property legislation is well-developed and compatible with EU standards. Slovenia negotiated its Trade Related Aspects of Intellectual Property (TRIPs) commitments as a developing country and has implemented those commitments as of 1996. Slovenia is a full member of the TRIPs council of the World Trade Organization and the World Intellectual Property Organization.

The Copyright and Related Rights Act deals with all fields of modern copyright and related rights law, including traditional works and their authors, computer programs and audiovisual works, as well as rental and lending rights. The new act also takes into account new technologies such as storage and electronic memory, original databases, satellite broadcasting, and cable re-transmission.

The 1994 Law on Courts gives the district court of Ljubljana exclusive subject matter jurisdiction over intellectual property disputes. The aim of the law is to assure specialization of the judges and the speed of relevant proceedings. There have been minor complaints, though, by foreign investors regarding the speed of the court system. Slovenian law provides for a number of civil legal sanctions on violations, including injunctive relief and the removal of the infringement, the seizure and destruction of illegal copies and devices, compensatory and punitive damages, and border (customs) measures. Furthermore, these infringements also constitute a misdemeanor with a minimum fine of 400,000 SIT (approximately $2,600) for legal persons and a minimum fine of 80,000 SIT (approximately $520) for natural persons, provided that the reported offenses are not criminal in nature. In such a case, the Slovenian criminal code would apply, which may result in fines or imprisonment in extreme cases.

Since the enactment of the Law on Copyright and Related Rights Act, there have been relatively few reported prosecutions for infringement violations. Most notable are cases of computer software piracy. In 1995, 20 cases were prosecuted for audio, video, and software piracy. Since piracy prosecution is still in the early stages of implementation, Slovenia has dedicated resources to the training of prosecutors and public authorities. Moreover, the Ministry of Culture recently established the Intellectual Property Fund, the Slovenian Copyright Agency, and the Anti-Piracy Association of Software Dealers (BSA) to combat piracy.

According to the U.S. Department of Commerce, there are no outstanding investment expropriation disputes in Slovenia. National law gives adequate protection to all investment. There is an ongoing dispute with those whose property was expropriated by the Communist Yugoslav government after World War II. These claims are being addressed by specific national legislation, though the process is notoriously slow.

2. To what extent have prices been liberalized? What subsidies remain? According to an EC report, the vast majority of prices have been liberalized, most of them by mid-1994. Prices of key commodities, such as energy, telecommunications, and transport, are still administered. Direct budget subsidies are quite limited, and apply only to certain foodstuffs and public services. In total, they add up to about three percent of the budget. Some of the larger enterprises receive support from the Development Fund, which was originally set up to provide emergency funding to stabilize enterprises that were salvageable or initiate procedures to do away with those with no realistic prospects of survival.

According to the European Bank for Reconstruction and Development, electricity prices are steadily being raised and in mid-1996 amounted to just over 70 percent of EU equivalent levels. In the first half of 1997, the energy price was raised by 15 percent and telephone charges by 5 percent. Natural gas prices are close to EU levels. In mid-1997, the government raised the prices of postal services, petrol, and domestic telephone charges.

3. Is it possible to own and operate a business? (Has there been legislation regarding the formation, dissolution, and transfer of businesses, and is the law respected? Do there exist overly cumbersome bureaucratic hurdles that effectively hinder the ability to own and dispose of a business? Are citizens given access to information on commercial law? Is the law applied fairly? Does regulation [or licensing requirements] impose significant costs on business and consumers? Do they create significant barriers to entry and seriously hamper competition?) Private enterprise and ownership are promoted and protected in Slovenia, both by statute and the constitution. As provided for in the law on commercial companies, all business activities within Slovenia are open to domestic and foreign natural and legal persons. The Foreign Investment Act permits foreign investors to establish wholly or partially owned companies in any legal form provided by the Commercial Companies Act (limited, general, and silent partnerships; joint stock companies, limited liability companies, and partnerships limited by shares; and economic interest groups). The Foreign Investment Act gives foreign investors the right to enter contractual joint ventures, which allow the investor to participate in the management of the company and to share in profits. Foreign investors may freely invest Slovenian companies, but to complete a 100 percent takeover of a Slovenian company, the foreign company must first register with the Slovenian courts. Foreign investors are permitted to obtain concessions for the exploitation of renewable and non-renewable natural and public goods.

There are some limitations on the business operations of foreign investors. Wholly foreign-owned companies are not permitted to operate businesses in the fields of military supply, rail and air transport, communications and telecommunications, and insurance. Majority foreign-owned insurance companies may not engage in re-insurance. Some business endeavors are restricted by maximum foreign investment limits (49 percent in auditing companies, 33 percent in publishing and broadcasting, 24 percent in stockbroking companies, and 20 percent in investment companies that deal with the management of investment funds). In all other fields, however, foreign investors enjoy the same opportunities as domestic investors.

Any company registered in Slovenia is granted the status of a Slovenian legal entity, and foreign investors are treated legally the same as domestic companies, with the same rights and obligations as domestic Slovenian companies. The registration process is rather simple and usually takes between three weeks and one month to complete. Foreign investors are legally entitled to own property in Slovenia as long as they are properly registered in Slovenia. Foreign companies, however, have experienced unexplained delays in obtaining land, even though all necessary paper work was complete. Registered foreign companies may be members of the Ljubljana Stock Exchange.

Bureaucratic procedures for starting a business are generally transparent, though current legislation is incomplete and may be rather complex. Commercial laws are generally drafted by legally trained personnel and published within a month of being passed. Regulation and licensing requirements do not impose prohibitively high costs on businesses and consumers, though the cost of formation and registration of a joint-stock company including legal, notary, and court fees, but not minimum share capital, may exceed $1,000. The process takes one to three months.

4. Are courts effective, transparent, efficient, and quick in reaching decisions on property and contract disputes? What alternative mechanisms for adjudicating disputes exist? Important judgments are generally published and accessible to practitioners and provide written reasons for courts' decisions. According to the European Bank for Reconstruction and Development, there is generally a meaningful right of appeal from first-instance court decisions. It appears that there is an independent right of judicial review of administrative action. On average, a party may be expected to wait between seven months and one year for a commercial case to be heard on the merits by a court in the most important commercial center and between seven months and two years for a final judgment for payment of a sum of money to be executed.

Unless the parties to a dispute have agreed to binding arbitration for disputes, the regional court specializing in economic issues has jurisdiction over business disputes. The parties, however, may agree in writing to settle disputes in another court of jurisdiction. The parties may also exclude the court.

5. Is business competition encouraged? (Are monopolistic practices limited in law and in practice? If so, how? To what degree is "insider" dealing a hindrance to open competition? Are government procurement policies open and unbiased?) The 1993 Law on Protection of Competition provided for two new institutions to implement the law: the Competition Protection Bureau (CPB), which handles restrictions on competition, dumping, and subsidized imports, and the Trade Inspectorate, which deals with unfair competition, illicit speculations, and restrictions on free market access by state or local authorities. The CPB is an autonomous body under the auspices of the Ministry for Economic Relations and Development. Of 12 cartel investigations since 1994, the CPB detected and prohibited three. Of nine investigations of vertical agreements, the CPB detected two and prohibited both. Of 12 investigations of abuse of a dominant position, three abuses were prohibited. In July 1997, the Constitutional Court found the mobile telephone monopoly of the state-owned company Mobitel illegal.

Public procurement is regulated by a 1997 framework law, which is intended to implement part of the EU requirements as a first step. Implementing decrees are in the process of being adopted by the government. A Public Procurement Unit under the Ministry of Finance is in charge of monitoring the public procurement system, preparing new legislation, and issuing instructions. According to the law, an independent Audit Committee will be appointed by parliament to rule on all requests for audit of decisions.

6. To what extent has international trade been liberalized? To what degree has there been simplification/overhaul of customs and tariff procedures, and are these applied fairly? What informal trade barriers exist? According to the European Bank for Reconstruction and Development, 98 percent of imports were free from quantitative restrictions by the end of 1994. In 1996, customs rates varied from zero percent to 27 percent and the weighted average MFN tariff rate was about nine percent. The government has committed to further liberalization and to the elimination of all non-tariff barriers, which are still substantial in sectors such as telecommunications and electrical equipment.

Slovenia became a full member of the GATT in 1994 and the World Trade Organization in July 1995, and joined the Central European Free Trade Agreement in January 1996. Its Association Agreement with the EU was signed in June 1996 and came into force in July 1997. Slovenia is among the five Eastern European countries that the European Commission has recommended to be included in negotiations in the next wave of EU enlargement. It has other free trade agreements with the Baltic states, Bulgaria, Macedonia, Israel, and Romania.

7. To what extent has foreign investment and capital flow been encouraged or constrained? Foreign investment in Slovenia has been heavily restricted because of fear that foreigners would buy up the country's most valuable assets. In addition to delays and restrictions in obtaining property (see question #1), foreign investors are restricted in the composition of their management boards.

The Commercial Companies Act requires that the manager or proxy of a company registered in Slovenia be a Slovenian citizen. If there are several managers, the majority of them must be Slovenian. A company's director, however, may be foreign if the manager or proxy is Slovenian, or when the majority of the managers are Slovenian. If the management board is made up of only one person, that person must be Slovenian.

Foreign investors are also restricted in obtaining credit. In order to obtain credit from abroad, a foreign company must deposit 40 percent of the loan amount with a Slovenian bank. This deposit is returned when the foreign debt is paid off.

Foreign companies, while permitted to establish branch offices and legal entities in Slovenia, are also restricted from establishing representative offices in Slovenia.

A further impediment to foreign business practice is difficulty in obtaining business and working visas. Business visas are required for management positions and working visas are required for general staff positions. Typically, visa applications are processed in three weeks, but in some instances may take up to six months.

Despite its ambivalence about foreign investment, Slovenia's actual comparative performance in foreign direct investment (FDI) has been positive. According to the U.S. Department of Commerce, FDI to Slovenia amounted to $2 billion by the end of 1996. Although the share of foreign investment is low in terms of fixed capital formation, it is approximately $1,000 and 11 percent, in terms of total FDI *per capita* and the FDI-to-GDP ratio, respectively. Slovenia, along with Hungary and Estonia, is among the leaders of Central European transitional economies. The small size of the domestic market, however, explains part of the FDI-to-GDP ratio, and growth in FDI has slowed in recent years, suggesting that Slovenia's attractiveness as a destination for foreign capital may have declined.

8. Has there been reform of the energy sector? (To what degree has the energy sector been restructured? Is the energy sector more varied, and is it open to private competition? Is the country overly dependent on one or two other countries for energy[including whether exported fuels must pass through one or more countries to reach markets]?) Slovenia's energy and electricity structure, specifically distribution and production infrastructure, is state-owned. Privatization of this industry is currently being examined. The Law on Privatization of State Assets was submitted to the government in 1996. The draft law states that 51 percent of the energy production companies would remain property of the state. This law has yet to be approved or implemented.

Slovenia's energy production breaks down into nuclear power (37 percent), thermal energy (39 percent), and hydroelectricity (24 percent). Slovenia has minor oil reserves and relies heavily on oil imports. Oil production is less than 500 barrels per day (BBL/D), while proven oil reserves are less than 50 million barrels. Petrol Trgovina, Nafta Lendava, and Istrabenz are three small oil production and refining companies in Slovenia. The Lendava refinery is the sole refinery. Slovenia distills 12,000 BBL/D of crude oil. Oil consumption was 45,000 BBL/D in 1995.

The Adria oil pipeline, with a capacity of approximately 15 million barrels per year, links Slovenia with Croatia and Yugoslavia. Increases in oil consumption have led to an increasingly heavy reliance on imports. Exemplifying this trend, oil imports increased 20 percent in 1994. A lack of sufficient storage capacity for oil is a problem in Slovenia, and without a remedy, Slovenia could face an oil supply shortage.

Slovenia also has minor natural gas resources and is dependent on gas imports. The sole suppliers of gas imports to Slovenia are Algeria and Russia, with a 40 percent and a 60 percent share, respectively. Russia supplied approximately 20.4 billion cubic feet (bcf) in 1995. Domestic gas production is approximately 459 million cubic feet (mcf) annually. Proven reserves of gas in Slovenia are limited. These reserves are only equivalent to half the gas that was imported in 1994. Slovenia has 552 miles of gas pipeline that supplies up to 45 bcf per year of gas. Geoplin, the state-owned gas company, is involved in trade and transit of natural gas and is supported by 12 distribution companies. Gas consumption was 34 bcf in 1995. As in the case of oil, limited storage capacity of natural gas could pose future problems.

TAJIKISTAN

Freedom in the World Ratings, 1989-1998

	1989-90	1990-91	1991-92	1992-93	1993-94	1994-95	1995-96	1996-97	1997-98
Political Rights	-	-	5	6	7	7	7	7	6
Civil Liberties	-	-	5	7	7	7	7	7	6
Status	-	-	PF	NF	NF	NF	NF	NF	NF

Polity: Consolidated Autocracy
Economy: Consolidated Statist
Population: 5,700,000
PPP: $943
Ethnic Groups: Tajik (62 percent), Uzbek (23 percent), Russian, Tatar, and Kyrgyz, others
Capital: Dushanbe

Political Process 5.75/7

1. When did national legislative elections occur? Were they free and fair? How were they judged by domestic and international election monitoring organizations? Who composes the government? This strife-torn Central Asian nation has not held free and fair elections at any level since achieving independence in 1991. The 1994 constitution created a 181-member parliament that is directly elected for a five-year term. As civil conflict continued between the government, composed of former Communist hardliners backed by Russia, and the opposition United Tajik Opposition (UTO), a coalition of Islamic, nationalist, and democratic groups, the UTO boycotted parliamentary elections on February 26 and March 12, 1995. The elections resulted in a parliament dominated by supporters of President Emomali Rakhmonov, with the Communist Party of Tajikistan (CPT) winning about 60 seats; the People's Party, five; the Party of Popular Unity and Accord, two; and the Tajik Party of Economic and Political Renewal, one, with the majority of parliamentarians holding no formal party affiliations. Forty percent of the parliament had held seats in the old Supreme Soviet, which had been elected under Soviet rule in 1990 and had contained 227 Communist members out of 230 deputies. Many were also heads of local and regional governments who had remained in their posts after independence. The Organization for Security and Cooperation in Europe, the United Nations, and the European Union declined to monitor the elections due to the continued fighting and the opposition boycott.

A June 1997 peace accord between the government and the UTO established a National Reconciliation Commission to integrate the opposition into the government and prepare for multiparty elections in 1998. In March 1998, Khodzhi Akbar Turadzhonzoda, a key opposition leader who had spent five years in exile, took office as first deputy premier in the government. Several other opposition figures were also named to the cabinet and other posts. As of March 31, 1998, however, no elections had been scheduled.

2. When did presidential elections occur? Were they free and fair? As the Soviet Union crumbled and Tajikistan declared independence in September 1991, former Communist Party First Secretary Rakhman Nabiyev emerged as president following the resignations of two predecessors. In the November 1991 presidential elections, Nabiyev, backed by the Communist elite from the Leninabad region in the north and by the Kulyab people in the south, defeated six challengers representing democratic, nationalist, and Islamist parties and groups in a vote marred by vote-rigging and other irregularities. Notably, the candidate of the secular, pro-Western, opposition Tajik Democratic Party (TDP), Davlat Koudonazarov, received second-round support from the Islamic Renaissance Party (IRP), thus solidifying a TDP-Islamic opposition alliance that would form a key element in the ensuing civil war.

An April 1992 power-sharing agreement that would have given cabinet posts to the opposition TDP and IRP unraveled and the country plunged into civil war between the Communist old guard and the opposition. As fighting intensified, parliament forced Nabiyev to resign in September 1992 with the government coming into the hands of an IRP-led coalition that included the TDP and other secular and nationalist groups. In the fall, the governing coalition lost effective control of the Kulyab and Kurgan-Tyube regions to Nabiyev supporters, and, in November, an acting president handed power to Rakhmonov, leader of the pro-Nabiyev forces in Kulyab. In December, after a two-month blockade, troops loyal to Rakhmonov and Nabiyev regained control of Dushanbe and pushed the Islamic-TDP forces to the Afghan border. Rakhmonov formed an administration dominated by fellow Kulyabis and the former Leninabadi Communist nomenklatura.

In the November 6, 1994, presidential elections, official results gave Rakhmonov 58 percent of the vote against Abdumalik Abdullajanov, a former premier from the northern Khojent region. The election law effectively prevented opposition candidates from standing, and the IRP and the TDP boycotted the vote, although some secular parties backed Abdullajanov. The voting was marred by massive fraud, including ballot stuffing and intimidation. The state-run media barely covered Abdullajanov's campaign. The United Nations and the Conference on Security and Cooperation in Europe refused invitations to monitor the vote due to the election law. A concurrent constitutional referendum approved a document that established a president who is directly elected for a maximum of two consecutive five-year terms, and can appoint and dismiss the prime minister, judges, and other senior officials subject to parliamentary approval. The president is the head of the executive branch and commander in chief of the armed forces. An April 30, 1997 assassination attempt slightly wounded president Rakhmonov and killed two people.

3. Is the electoral system multiparty-based? Are there at least two viable political parties functioning at all levels of government? Regional rivalries form much of the basis for politics in Tajikistan. The four leading regionally-based tribes are the Leninabad-based clan, the Kulyab, the Gharm, and the Badakhshan. At independence in 1991, a Leninabadi Communist nomenklatura controlled national politics. A power struggle between these northern Leninabadi rulers, who were backed by southern Kulyabis, and an opposition consisting of pro-democratic, nationalist, and Islamic parties and movements, who drew support mainly from the Gharm and the Gorno Badakhshan districts, erupted into civil war in May 1992 after a power-sharing accord collapsed. By the time its most intense phase ended, in December 1992, the war had killed more than 50,000 people and displaced 800,000 others. A coalition consisting of Kulyabi and Leninabadi Communist hardliners emerged victorious, although low-scale fighting continued. The government cracked down on the domestic opposition, forcing many of its leaders and activists to flee the country. In June 1993, parliament banned the four leading opposition groups.

In December 1993, the rural-based Islamic Renaissance Party and the Gorno-Badakhshan-based Tajik Democratic Party formed the UTO, which battled government troops and elements of a Russian-dominated Commonwealth of Independent States border force from its bases in northern Afghanistan. Meanwhile, the Kulyabi leadership gradually marginalized the Leninabadis. After Abdumalik Abdullajanov, a Leninabadi politician, unsuccessfully ran for president in November 1994, Kulyabi politicians asserted control through harassment of activists, arrests, and press controls, and the governing coalition formally collapsed. Many Abdullajanov supporters who had held government posts were demoted or fired.

The November 1994 presidential and February-March 1995 legislative elections, held in the midst of civil conflict, were nominally multiparty-based. The government, however, had outlawed the four key opposition groups in 1993, and, despite a cease-fire agreement in September 1994, they boycotted both votes, claiming violations of the electoral law and official pressure on their candidates. In the legislative elections the government allowed several nominally pro-government parties to participate, but the government-controlled Central Electoral Commission prohibited some candidates from these parties from standing on the grounds of procedural irregularities. Former presidential candidate Abdullajanov was initially refused registration as a candidate; he subsequently stood as a candidate, but not on his party's slate. Some 40 percent of the parliamentary deputies who won seats in the 1995 legislative elections were unaffiliated with any formal party, although they were firmly pro-Rakhmonov.

In December 1996, President Rakhmonov and UTO leader Said Abdullo Nuri signed a cease-fire agreement in Moscow. The deal met the opposition's longstanding demand to create a National Reconciliation Commission (NRC), to be headed by an opposition representative and composed of all political factions, which would implement peace agreements, repatriate and assist refugees, and introduce legislation for fair parliamentary elections. The agreement also included a general amnesty for all participants in the conflict and a full exchange of prisoners under the auspices of the United Nations Observer Mission in Tajikistan and the International Red Cross.

On June 27 1997, the two sides signed the Tajik National Peace Accord in Moscow, which formally ended five years of civil war. The agreement called for opposition soldiers to be merged into the regular army, provided an amnesty to UTO members, and formally established a 26-member NRC, with seats split evenly between the government and the UTO. The NRC, chaired by opposition leader Nuri, held initial working sessions in Moscow before establishing itself in Dushanbe on September 15, 1997. By early 1998, the government had made little movement towards integrating UTO members into 30 percent of posts in ministries and departments, as called for in the Accord.

The government used an April 1997 assassination attempt on President Rakhmonov as a pretext for arresting dozens of political opponents linked to the Leninabadi-based National Resistance Movement (NRM), which was established in early 1996 by three former Leninabadi premiers, including Abdumalik Abdullajanov. In late March 1998, fresh fighting between the government and armed groups ostensibly loyal to the UTO broke out near Dushanbe, while political violence and hostage-taking continue.

Elections for regional and local legislatures have been held irregularly since 1991, and, like the national legislative elections, have been boycotted by the opposition.

4. How many parties have been legalized? Are any particular parties illegal? The CPT had been the sole legal party in the Soviet era. It currently draws its support from the northern industrial region of Khojent (Leninabad) and other areas with ethnic Russian or Uzbek concentrations. After being briefly banned after independence, the CPT regained its dominant status when the government outlawed four main opposition parties in June 1993: the anti-Communist Tajik Democratic Party, which draws its support from the Gorno-Badakhshan region; the rural-based Islamic Renaissance Party, which calls for an Islamic republic; the Badakhshan Ruby Movement, a party of the Pamiri people from Gorno Badakhshan Autonomous Region, who are Ismaeli Muslims, regard themselves as ethnically distinct from Tajiks, and seek true autonomy or outright independence for their homeland; and the Rebirth Movement, an anti-Communist nationalist-religious party.

In 1993 and 1994, several pro-government parties formed the leftist People's Party (PP), former premier Abdumalik Abdullajanov's northern-based Party of Popular Unity and Accord (PPUA), the northern-based People's Democratic Party; the business-oriented Party of Economic and Political Renewal (PEPR), and the Union of Progressive Forces. The PP, PPUA and PEPR won a total of eight seats in the 1995 legislative elections. In July 1995, the government recognized a faction of the TDP.

In July 1996, Abdullajanov, who had lost a November 1994 presidential election marred by fraud and irregularities, founded the Leninabadi-based NRM, with the primary goal of ensuring that all regions in Tajikistan be represented in talks between the government and the UTO then being held under United Nations auspices. The Tajik government tried to crush the NRM through a campaign of arrests and harassment of activists or suspected activists, and by censoring most media coverage of the Leninabad political movement. In May 1996, mass demonstrations in Leninabad called for the removal of officials of southern origin from local police and government posts. In the ensuing year, authorities arrested protest organizers, particularly after an April 1997 assassination attempt on President Rakhmonov. In February 1997, authorities arrested Akhmajon Saidov, a pro-NRM former deputy chairman of the Supreme Soviet of Tajikistan, on charges of abuse of authority and embezzlement. The UTO has called for the NRM to be given seats and ministerial portfolios in the NRC.

Despite the country's ongoing peace process, the opposition parties are still formally banned.

5. What proportion of the population belongs to political parties? It is not clear what proportion of the population belongs to political parties. Most political parties draw their strength from regional strongholds. Only the Communist party has branches in all of the republic's regions, and therefore remains the dominant political force. In addition, the IRP is generally rural-based as opposed to representing a specific region.

6. What has been the trend of voter turnout at the municipal, provincial and national levels in

recent years? Due to the disruption caused by the civil war, municipal and provincial elections have not been held on a regular basis since the dissolution of the Soviet Union. In the national presidential elections and constitutional referendum held on November 6, 1994, turnout was reportedly 90 percent; however, the opposition claims that votes were cast for many citizens who had fled as refugees to Afghanistan and other neighboring states. Similarly, in the February-March 1995 legislative elections, the government maintained that turnout reached 85 percent. Since international organizations declined to send observers due to their concerns over the fairness of the polls, these figures cannot be corroborated.

Civil Society 5.25/7

1. How many nongovernmental organizations (NGOs) have come into existence since 1988? What is the number of charitable/nonprofit organizations? Are there locally led efforts to increase philanthropy and volunteerism? What proportion of the population is active in private voluntary activity (from polling data)? No reliable data exists for the number of NGOs and charitable organizations that have come into existence. The peace agreement between the government and the UTO has improved the political climate for NGOs. Some NGOs are active in cultural affairs and women's and children's welfare, while others represent businesswomen, teachers, and other professionals. Most operate with limited funding, and since there are few locally led efforts to increase philanthropy and volunteerism, many Tajik NGOs are dependent on foreign contributions. There is no accurate data on the proportion of the population that is active in private voluntary activity.

2. What is the legal and regulatory environment for NGOs (i.e. ease of registration, legal rights, government regulation, taxation, procurement and access-to-information issues)? To what extent is NGO activism focused on improving the legal and regulatory environment? The Law on Nongovernmental Organizations requires all NGOs to register with the Ministry of Justice. Documents must be submitted in Russian and Tajik, which often puts a burden on NGOs and delays registration. The government's intolerance of dissent, as well as a security situation in which local warlords hold sway over parts of the country, has been the biggest obstacle to the formation of NGOs.

There is little apparent activism focused on improving the legal and regulatory environment, as most NGOs are focused on providing social services and generally avoid political issues.

3. What is the organizational capacity of NGOs? Do management structures clearly delineate authority and responsibility? Is information available on NGO management issues in the native language? Is there a core of experienced practitioners/trainers to serve as consultants or mentors to less developed organizations? Most NGOs in Tajikistan function at a fairly rudimentary level. Given the small size of the NGO sector and the limited institutional capacity of those that exist, there is little opportunity for the relatively more established NGOs to take on mentor roles to their less developed counterparts.

4. Are NGOs financially viable? What is their tax status? Are they obliged to and do they

typically disclose revenue sources? Do government procurement opportunities exist for private, not-for-profit providers of services? Most NGOs are not financially viable, and often depend on foreign funds to operate. Few government procurement opportunities exist for NGO's in Tajikistan's statist economy.

5. Are there free trade unions? How many workers belong to these unions? Is the number of workers belonging to trade unions growing or decreasing? What is the numerical/proportional membership of farmers' groups, small business associations, etc? Trade unions in Tajikistan are state-controlled. All state enterprise workers belong to the official Confederation of Trade Unions, a Soviet-era umbrella organization of 20 separate labor unions, which controls access to pension funds, health care benefits, housing, day care, and other social services. The confederation claims a membership of 1.5 million workers. The separate, but also state-controlled, Trade Unions of Private Enterprise Workers, includes registered unions in more than 3,000 small and medium-size enterprises, covering some 50,000 employees. Nearly every nonagricultural worker in the formal sector is a member of a trade union. Strikes are legal if arbitration, which is mandatory, fails. Nevertheless, both unions have pledged not to hold strikes given the country's dire financial situation. Workers can also bargain collectively, although the prevailing economic conditions give workers little leverage in such bargaining. Union membership is expected to slowly decrease as Tajikistan continues it ponderous progress toward state enterprise reform.

All farmers belong to the state-controlled Union of Agricultural Workers. Several small business associations exist, including the Dushanbe-based Dilafruz association of businesswomen and the Tajik Center for Entrepreneurship and Management in the northern Leninabad province.

6. What forms of interest group participation in politics are legal? What types of interest groups are active in the political and policy process? Despite constitutional guarantees of freedom of association, the government maintains tight control over NGOs that it believes have any type of political agenda. NGOs must obtain a permit to hold public demonstrations or rallies, and while this right is sometimes granted, authorities have in some cases carried out reprisals against organizers.

The government has also allowed some politically-oriented demonstrations, but reprisals against organizers often follow. In mid-May 1996, several thousand people demonstrated in Khujand, Ura-Teppe, Kanibadam, and other cities in Leninabad region following the murder of a prominent Khujandi businessman, Akhmajon Ashurov. On May 14, as demonstrations in Ura-Teppe turned violent, with protesters vandalizing several government buildings, soldiers reportedly fired into a crowd, killing at least one person. In the months following the demonstrations, authorities searched the houses of many of the organizers.

In 1997, security forces permitted several demonstrations in Khujand, Ura-Teppe, and Kanibadam calling for former premier Abdullajanov's NRM to be included in the ongoing peace and reconciliation process, for a criminal case against Abdullajanov to be closed, and for objective media coverage of the media events in Leninabad. The organizers were later harassed.

7. How is the non-for-profit/NGO sector perceived by the public and government officials?

What is the nature of media coverage of NGOs? To what extent do government officials engage with NGOs? The Tajik government has done little to support the growth of the NGO sector, and its general intolerance of dissent mitigates against the formation of human rights NGOs. Media coverage of NGOs is limited. There is little government engagement or cooperation with NGOs.

Independent Media 6.00/7

1. Are there legal protections for press freedom? Both the 1991 Law on the Press and the 1994 constitution guarantee freedom of the press. The constitution also outlaws all forms of state censorship, and guarantees all citizens the right of access to the media. A December 1996 media law permits independent television stations.

2. Are there legal penalties for libeling officials? Are there legal penalties for "irresponsible" journalism? Have these laws been enforced to harass journalists? The 1991 press law introduced penalties for libeling officials as well as penalties for "irresponsible" journalism, which include jail terms and fines. The government has relied on heavy-handed methods and self-censorship by journalists, rather than legal action, to subjugate the press.

3. What proportion of media is privatized? What are the major private newspapers, television stations, and radio stations? There are some 200 newspapers and magazines published in Tajikistan, including some 50 newspapers that are either independent or affiliated with political parties. During the civil war, several ostensibly-banned opposition newspapers were published abroad and made available within the country.

The broadcast media is dominated by government services. State-run Tajik Radio is the major radio service, although the UTO-controlled Voice of Free Tajikistan broadcasts from northern Afghanistan.

The only national television service is the state-run Tajik Television. There are some ten private television stations, although none have their own facilities meaning that they must use official broadcasting studios for most of their work. An independent television station in the northern city of Khujand, which was closed by the regional government in 1996, remained closed as of early 1998. In 1997, the government closed several other independent television stations. New regulations for the registration of independent television stations allowed several new stations to become operational by the end of the year.

Most major Russian dailies are openly available, and the two leading Russian television channels are available.

4. Are the private media financially viable? Most private media are not financially viable. Due to low advertising revenues and circulation bases, few papers publish daily. Most publications are subsidized by the government, while others are owned or otherwise supported by political parties. One paper with a relatively high circulation, *Biznis I Politika,* is subsidized by a private commodities exchange firm, Sham. The private broadcast media also face serious shortages in funding and technical equipment.

5. Are the media editorially independent? Are the media's news gathering functions affected by interference from government or private owners? Despite legal guarantees of press freedom, in practice the Tajik government substantially controls the content of print and broadcast media. The government's control of the printing presses and the supply of newsprint, as well as subsidies it provides to most publications and television broadcasts, gives it considerable leverage over press content. Government officials also make it clear to journalists what news should not be covered, and journalists practice considerable self-censorship. Independent television stations broadcast little news. The state broadcast media, which Rakhmonov took direct control of in February 1994 under the guise of ensuring its objectivity, do not offer pluralistic views. Many Tajiks say they do not trust the domestic media and rely on foreign radio services for news.

In November 1997, the Moscow-based Glasnost Foundation released a letter by an employee of the Sharki Ozod publishing house questioning a decision not to publish the weekly editions of two newspapers, *Vecherniye Vesti* and *Biznes I Politika*. The letter said the order came from Rakhmonov's office, which denied the charge. According to the Foundation, the papers had recently published an article by Abdullajanov, whom the government has kept out of the peace process, and another that responded to an earlier article by the second secretary of the Russian Embassy in Dushanbe criticizing Russian journalists' coverage of Russian-Tajik relations. According to the U.S. Department of State, in 1997, the government on occasion prevented two newspapers, *Ittihod* (the Socialist party organ), and *Samar*, from publishing articles critical of the government.

In 1997, the U.S.-based Committee to Protect Journalists named Tajikistan one of the most deadly places on earth to be a journalist. According to the Moscow-based Glasnost Foundation, more than 40 journalists were murdered from 1992 until the December 1996 cease-fire between the government and the main opposition. Many of the killings are believed to have been carried out by armed groups not directly linked to either the government or the opposition UTO. The government's criminal investigations into the murders of journalists have failed to bring any substantive results.

According to Human Rights Watch, since 1996, the government has attempted to limit media coverage of the Leninabadi political movement, an April 1997 prison uprising in Khujand in Leninabad that was brutally suppressed by authorities, and other events in the region by arresting and harassing journalists, refusing Leninabadi newspapers permission to print at government-run printing houses, and closing at least one newspaper. As a result, local media have largely failed to report on the Leninabad-based NRM's efforts to be included in the political process. The government also harassed and detained Russian journalists for attempting to cover the 1997 prison massacre in Khujand, an assassination attempt against Rakhmonov the same month, and other local issues and events.

In February, four journalists working for Russian media were among several hostages held for two weeks by an independent opposition commander.

6. Is the distribution system for newspapers privately or governmentally controlled? The government owns and operates printing houses and the major distribution network for newspapers.

7. What proportion of the population is connected to the Internet? Are there any restrictions on Internet access to private citizens? The U.S.-based Central Asia Development Agency first provided Internet access to Tajikistan in 1995. Many people who access the Internet do so through public communications centers. While the number of people who use the Internet is not known, only some 1,500 people in Tajikistan have e-mail addresses.

8. What has been the trend in press freedom as measured by Freedom House's *Survey of Press Freedom*? Freedom House's *Survey of Press Freedom* has rated the Tajikistan press Not Free since the country's independence in 1991.

Governance and Public Administration 6.75/7

1. Is the legislature the effective rule-making institution? The 1994 constitution established a 181-member Supreme Assembly (parliament) that is the highest legislative body and can override a presidential veto by a two-thirds majority. In practice, the legislature is dominated by the executive, and in a broader sense, Rakhmonov's southern Kulyab clan has a virtual monopoly on wealth and power. Policy is often set by presidential decree, bypassing the legislature entirely.

Nevertheless, in 1996 and 1997, parliament did develop and pass several important pieces of legislation, including structural economic reforms conforming to IMF guidelines. The June 1997 peace accord between the government and the United Tajik Opposition established the NRC which is expected to prepare for elections in 1998, raising questions about whether constitutional amendments proposed by the NRC have the same status as those proposed by parliament.

Tajikistan's neighbors exert influence in its politics: Moscow through the presence of the 20,000-member predominantly Russian Commonwealth of Independent States peacekeeping force that has been in the country since 1993, and the provision of economic credits; and Tashkent, because overland and rail transport must pass through Uzbekistan.

2. Is substantial power decentralized to subnational levels of government? What specific authority do subnational levels have? Political power in Tajikistan remains highly centralized. The national parliament can disband local legislatures and call new elections on the grounds that the local bodies are in violation of national law.

Yet even as the central government controls formal political power, large parts of the country are run by local strongmen who vie for control of the country's cotton, metals, and narcotics trade. Tursunzade, for example, has seen various armed groups fight for control of the city and its aluminum plant, one of the largest in the world. Even in some nominally government-controlled areas, Dushanbe's writ extends only in the daytime. In practice, many cities have few institutions of organized government. In some cases, strongmen have prevented Dushanbe-appointed heads of local government from sitting. In the mountainous and isolated eastern region of Gorno-Badakhshan, the central government's influence is most limited and international aid groups carry out many of the functions of government.

3. Are subnational officials chosen in free and fair elections? Tajikistan is divided into 19 regions, plus the capital of Dushanbe. Under the 1994 constitution, the president appoints heads of regional governments, subject to confirmation by local legislatures. The president can also remove local officials, and President Rakhmonov has exercised this power. For example, in 1997, following the April assassination attempt against him, Rakhmonov removed Kodir Bobojanov, the mayor of Khojent and an ally of NRM leader Abdullajanov, from his post. Elections to regional and municipal legislatures have been held irregularly since 1991. The December 1996 ceasefire agreement calls for new regional elections to be held with the full participation of all opposition groups, but this has not been done.

4. Do the executive and legislative bodies operate openly and with transparency? Is draft legislation easily accessible to the media and the public? Under the constitution, citizens are entitled to receive information on the functioning of all branches of government. In practice, government at all levels operates with a minimum amount of transparency. No mechanisms currently exist for transparency in the executive branch. Parliamentary sessions are partially broadcast on national television, and both the legislature and government newspapers publish transcripts of parliamentary deliberations. Substantive debate, however, is carried out in closed-door sessions.

5. Do municipal governments have sufficient revenues to carry out their duties? Do municipal governments have control of their own local budgets? Do they raise revenues autonomously or from the central state budget? Due to the country's anemic economic output, considerable informal sector, and weak tax administration, municipal governments do not have sufficient revenues to carry out their functions. Municipal budgets must be approved by central authorities. In the past, all locally collected revenues were turned over to the national government, which then allocated funds to the regions. Today, under the 1996 Tax Code, regional governments are able to retain a set portion of local revenues as they are collected.

6. Do the elected local leaders and local civil servants know how to manage municipal governments effectively? Entry into and progress within the civil service continues to be dominated by local family and patronage networks, and the majority of civil servants have no specialized training in public administration. Politicians frequently shuffle civil servants, which complicates the situation. As such, local government is generally inefficient and provides few services.

7. When did the constitutional/legislative changes on local power come into effect? Has there been a reform of the civil service code/system? Are local civil servants employees of the local or central government? There have been no substantive constitutional or legislative changes on local power. The 1994 constitution confirms the president's power to appoint the heads of local governments. There have been no local or national reforms of civil service codes. Local civil servants are nominally employees of local governments; in practice, they are controlled by central authorities or by local strongmen.

Rule of Law 6.00/7

1. Is there a post-Communist constitution? How does the judicial system interpret and enforce the constitution? Are there specific examples of judicial enforcement of the constitution in the last year? Tajikistan's post-Communist constitution was approved in a November 6, 1994, referendum that was held concurrently with presidential balloting during a time of civil conflict and boycotted by the Islamic opposition and the TDP. Official results showed more than 90 percent of voters supporting the constitution. The UTO maintains that this referendum was neither free nor fair. The constitution provides for a tripartite division of power with a strong president, who is empowered to appoint the government, the chairman of the National Bank, the head of the Constitutional Court, the state prosecutor, and the heads of regional administrations. Although the constitution provides for an independent judiciary, Tajik judges lack judicial independence and in practice have little power to enforce the constitution.

2. Does the constitutional framework provide for human rights? Do the human rights include business and property rights? The constitution provides for an independent judiciary, the right to privacy in the home, freedoms of speech and press, freedom of assembly and association, freedom of religion, and the right to travel internally and abroad. The constitution also bans discrimination on the basis of nationality, race, gender, and religion. According to the World Bank, existing legislation provides only weak protection for property rights and continues to allow great latitude for state intervention in private commercial activity. The bank has recommended that the 1991 Law on Property Rights be revised to expand protection for private property holders.

Both the government and armed factions violate human rights with impunity. The government controls perhaps only 20 percent of the country, and in some areas, only during the day. A Russian-dominated Commonwealth of Independent States peacekeeping force has been in the country since 1993, and a Tajik-based Russian Border Guard Force, which is responsible to Moscow, defends the Tajik-Afghan border. Government army units often operate outside of government control and have committed numerous abuses.

In 1997, there were scores of extra-judicial killings and disappearances, which were variously attributed to government forces, the opposition, and local strongmen, either on political or ethnic grounds, or simply for settling old scores. Many killings were attributed to disputes between competing military units. In October 1997, gunmen attacked the headquarters of the presidential guards, killing 14. Along the border, a sharp rise in drug trafficking has led to an increase in clashes between border guards and traffickers. During the year, there were several battles over territory and resources involving local warlords, including clashes in January between groups seeking to control the western town of Tursunzade. After renegade Colonel Mahmud Khudoberdiev attempted a mutiny in August in southern Tajikistan, pro-government forces reportedly carried out killings of pro-Khudoberdiev troops and ethnic Uzbeks. The government has carried out few serious investigations into politically-motivated killings.

Armed factions resorted to hostage taking on numerous occasions, including the two-week seizure in February 1997 of 16 people, including the Minister of Security and four United Nations representatives. The situation ended peacefully. On other occasions the kidnappers killed hostages, including members of various armed factions and a French citizen.

On April 30, 1997, after Rakhmonov was wounded slightly by a hand grenade thrown into his entourage, security forces fired directly into the surrounding crowd, killing two people. In the aftermath, authorities arrested dozens of people linked to the Leninabadi-based political opposition, and in some cases reportedly beat family members and relatives. Most are still in jail, and only a few have been tried and sentenced.

Although the December 1996 ceasefire and the June 1997 peace agreement between the government and the UTO has led to a decrease in political violence, the security situation in Dushanbe and other areas remains tense. A series of small explosions ripped through the capital in September just prior to the arrival of exiled opposition leader Nuri who was there to participate in the new NRC. Unexplained night shootings have killed several Russian soldiers and some civilians, and keep most civilians off the streets after dark.

Some opposition figures living abroad have had trouble returning to the country. Domestic violence is reportedly common. According to the U.S. Department of State, abductions of brides are widely reported.

3. Has there been basic reform of the criminal code/criminal law? Who authorizes searches and issues warrants? Are suspects and prisoners beaten or abused? Are there excessive delays in the criminal justice system? The criminal code is a holdover from the Soviet era and has not been reformed since independence. By law, police need the approval of a procurator to search homes, except in exceptional circumstances. In practice, police and soldiers carry out arbitrary searches and seizures. In 1997, authorities carried out scores of politically motivated arrests in the northern Leninabad region following an April 1997 assassination attempt against Rakhmonov, and in the south following an August mutiny attempt by a renegade military commander. Authorities also frequently harass or arrest opposition figures on trumped-up charges of narcotics smuggling. By some estimates there are several hundred political detainees, although by law persons cannot be visited in pre-trial detention, making accurate estimates difficult.

Prison conditions in Tajikistan are life threatening due to overcrowding and unsanitary conditions. In June 1996, the International Committee of the Red Cross (ICRC) instituted an emergency food program in response to reports that many prisoners had died due to starvation and lack of adequate medical care. Nevertheless, the ICRC lacks independent access to prisoners.

Detainees are routinely beaten and are tortured to extract confessions. In mid-April 1997, Tajik security forces massacred scores of prisoners while crushing a prison riot in Khujand in the Leninabad province. According to the U.S.-based Human Rights Watch, the government has obstructed an investigation into the massacre and has covered up the true number of inmate deaths, which was officially reported at 24 but is believed to number between 100 and 150. The prison protests grew out of demands for trials for detainees, hospitalization for those seriously ill, an improvement in prison conditions, and complaints about disproportionate sentences for many of those imprisoned. The immediate catalyst came when inmates learned that some would be transferred to southern Tajikistan, where prison conditions are known to be worse. The Khujand prison itself was built to hold 300 inmates, but at the time of the riots held 800.

In the months following the July 1997 peace agreement between the government and the opposition, both sides exchanged dozens of POWs, although each side is believed to be holding scores of POWs.

The criminal code permits pretrial detention for up to 15 months without judicial approval, subject only to the approval of the local procurator, regional procurator, and the procurator general, depending on the length of time involved. By law, a case that has been entered for trial must be brought before a judge within 28 days. In practice, suspects often wait for months for a trial, even after the case has been entered. As in the Soviet system, defendants are presumed guilty.

4. Do most judges rule fairly and impartially? Do many remain from the Communist era? Many judges are poorly trained and lack sufficient legal competence and experience. Courts in Leninabad, in particular, are accused of handing down disproportionate sentences. For example, according to Human Rights Watch, a court sentenced a person to eight years in prison for stealing two bags of flour, and a 17-year-old received a seven-year sentence for stealing a book from a library. By contrast, a drug trafficking suspect drew just two years in jail, which may also suggest corruption in the system. No available figures document the number of judges who entered the bench since Tajikistan's independence in September 1991.

5. Are the courts free of political control and influence? Are the courts linked directly to the Ministry of Justice or any other executive body? According to the constitution, the judiciary is an independent and autonomous branch of government. The constitution grants judges immunity from arrest and prosecution. Judges of the Supreme Court and the Higher Economic Court are elected, whereas the Ministry of Justice nominates, and the president appoints and can dismiss, judges of military courts, of the Gorno-Badakhshan autonomous region, and of the municipal, regional and provincial governments. Thus, although their independence is nominally guaranteed, most judges depend on the executive branch for their positions.

Judicial officials are pressured by the government, local warlords, armed military groups, and vigilante groups. Prosecutors reportedly have had to abandon some criminal trials due to coercion and pressure from armed groups, while in other cases judges reportedly face pressures to hand down more severe sentences to enemies of armed groups. Bribery of judges is reportedly widespread.

In a case widely viewed as an example of the difficulty defendants face in getting a fair trial in politically-charged cases, on March 12, 1998, the Supreme Court sentenced five men, including Abdullaiev, the brother of NRM leader Abdullajanov, to death on charges of participating in the April 1997 assassination attempt on Rakhmonov, following a closed trial. Human Rights Watch reported that co-defendants were beaten until they incriminated Abdullaiev, who had initially been arrested on apparently fabricated narcotics charges. A judge was removed after ruling in favor of the defendants; the government later claimed the judge was removed for taking a bribe.

6. What proportion of lawyers is in private practice? How does this compare with the previous year? Only a small proportion of lawyers in Tajikistan have entered private practice, although, according to the Independent Lawyers Association, the number is growing. Most legal employment, however, remains with the state.

7. Does the state provide public defenders? The 1994 constitution obligates the state to provide public defenders for the accused at all stages of a criminal investigation and trial. This constitutes a change from Soviet criminal procedure, in which public defenders were often only provided immediately before trial, and therefore were hindered from effectively defending their clients. In practice, however, many of those arrested lack prompt access to an attorney, and some do not receive any legal counsel.

8. Are there effective anti-bias/discrimination laws, including protection of ethnic minority

rights? Tajikistan's population is 65 percent Tajik; 25 percent Uzbek; three percent Russian; with other, smaller minorities. Both the 1994 constitution and the 1990 Law on Language make discrimination on the basis of ethnicity or language illegal. While maintaining that Tajik, a Persian-based language, is the state language, both documents establish Russian as the language of inter-ethnic communication. The Law on Language also mandates that official government documents be made available in three languages: Tajik, Uzbek, and Russian, while the constitution stipulates that a citizen of any of the republic's ethnic groups has the right to demand and receive government information in his or her language. The constitution also forbids discrimination on the basis of religion or gender.

According to human rights monitors, minority groups remain the targets of pervasive discrimination and occasional violence. In Khatlon province, which was formed after the civil war to include the Kulyab and Kurgan Tyube regions, most members of the local population with roots in Gharm (an area east of the capital) supported the opposition during the civil war, and became refugees when the Kulyabi-dominated government factions won. These Gharmis have now mostly returned to Khatlon, but are routinely harassed and beaten, have their property confiscated, and are denied employment. Ethnic Russians, Kazakhs, Kyrgyz, and Uzbeks face discrimination and many are leaving Tajikistan. Tajik minorities in the Uzbek-dominated areas around Tursunzade also reportedly suffer discrimination.

In the wake of a failed August 1997 mutiny attempt by Mahmud Khudoberdiev, an ethnic Uzbek military commander, pro-government forces carried out reprisal killings against ethnic Uzbeks. Many fled Dushanbe and Khatlon oblast for Leninabad or for Uzbekistan, where Khudoberdiev himself fled with many of his supporters.

Under the Law on Freedom of Faith, the Committee on Religious Affairs, which is subordinate to the Council of Ministers, must register religious communities and monitor their formal activities. Several minor, unregistered groups, however, operate with few restrictions, which lends credence to the view that the intent of the registration process is simply to give the government the opportunity to monitor and control Islamic religious affairs so as to prevent organized religion from becoming politicized in this predominantly Muslim country. The government has replaced the independent Muftiyat with a government-controlled Council of the Islamic Center. In rural areas, non-Muslim women are reportedly physically harassed by Muslims for not conforming to a conservative dress code.

Corruption D

1. What is the magnitude of official corruption in the civil service? Must an average citizen must pay a bribe to a bureaucrat in order to receive a service? What services are subject to bribe requests-for example, university entrance, hospital admission, telephone installation, obtaining a license to operate a business, applying for a passport or other official documents? What is the average salary of civil servants at various levels? Bribery is reportedly necessary for many, if not most, public transactions with the government. The average salary in the public sector is about $8 per month, $5 for those working in education and healthcare, with many of these wages in arrears. These low salaries force most civil servants to find other work to supplement their incomes.

2. Do top policy makers (the president, ministers, vice-ministers, top court justices, and heads of agencies and commissions) have direct ties to businesses? How strong are such connections and what kinds of businesses are these? Many top policy makers have direct ties to business through state enterprises. The flawed privatization process has resulted in many companies being sold off to government officials, their relatives, and to leaders of armed factions.

3. Do laws requiring financial disclosure and disallowing conflict of interest exist? Have publicized anti-corruption cases been pursued? To what conclusion? The legal framework regarding financial disclosure and disallowing conflict of interest is inadequate. Observers have viewed the few publicized anti-corruption cases as being politically motivated.

4. What major anti-corruption initiatives have been implemented? How often are anticorruption laws and decrees adopted? Despite rampant smuggling and other forms of corruption, there have been few anti-corruption initiatives. Anti-corruption laws and decrees are inadequate and enforcement is weak.

5. How do major corruption-ranking organizations like Transparency International rate this country? Transparency International and other major corruption-ranking organizations have not rated Tajikistan.

Privatization 6.25/7

1. What percentage of the GDP comes from private ownership? What percentage of the labor force is employed in the private sector? How large is the informal sector of the economy? Tajikistan's economy remains heavily statist, with the private sector contributing only 20-30 percent of GDP. Production from recently privatized joint-stock companies appears to be minimal, reflecting the overall dire state of the economy. During the civil war, the government largely neglected the economy and did not pay civil servants and pensioners for extended periods. As a result, a considerable black market economy developed, along with rampant smuggling. According to the Government Statistics Agency, 95 percent of retail activity during the first half of 1997 was done on the black market.

2. What major privatization legislation has been passed? What were its substantive features? Parliament adopted a privatization law in 1991, but the process of implementing it was largely halted by the civil war. Since 1994, laws on property rights, entrepreneurship, enterprise regulation, and joint-stock companies have also been passed.

Until 1995, the government planned to have the collectives and managers of state enterprises initiate privatization, which would then be approved by the sectoral ministries and local governments. The World Bank pointed out that these interests had the most to lose by ceding control of state assets. At the same time, the collectives were afraid of rising unemployment. In November 1995, the state instead adopted a top-down approach to privatization, identifying enterprises to be sold.

The first stage of privatization began in 1991 and it is continuing to sell off many of the country's shops, restaurants, and other small enterprises. The second phase of the privatization program, in which medium-sized enterprises are being sold, began in 1997. The third and final phase, for large enterprises, is to take place in 1998.

3. What proportion of agriculture, housing and land, industry, and small business and services is in private hands? *Agriculture:* The agriculture sector, which has about 9.6 million hectares of land under cultivation, is still dominated by *kolkhozes* (large collective farms) and *sovkhozes* (state farms). In 1997, 46 percent of agricultural output was in the non-state sector, which includes the kolkhozes. The kolkhozes are to be transformed into individually-run farms, or into farms run by a group of private farmers having the right of inheritance leasing, which allows the lessor to pass control of the property being leased to an heir.

During the Soviet era, farmers were forced into a one-crop cotton culture. Cotton is still the major cash crop and accounts for about two-thirds of the gross production value of the agricultural sector. Although several cotton ginning factories have been sold off, others are still owned by the state cotton procurement agency, Glavkhlopkoprom, which also plays a role in the selling of cotton. Wheat acreage and the total harvest has continued to rise as privatized farmers increase production. In June 1997, the United States granted Tajikistan 35,000 tons of grain under an agreement in which the Tajik government pledged to support the privatization of wholesale trading of agricultural products and promote privatization of agribusiness. The government has begun liberalizing the agricultural market system to reduce the share of production being purchased by the state and give producers the right to sell the remainder of their products not sold to the state.
Small Business and Services: Since 1991, only 3,053 companies, or 16.4 percent of state property subject to privatization, have been sold off. These included most of the small retail enterprises, but few medium and large enterprises. In 1997, 742 companies were privatized; 685 were privatized in 1996. In most cases, the government has maintained a share of more than 40 percent of the privatized enterprises. The slow pace of privatization is widely cited as a key reason for the continued weakness of the economy.

During the civil war, small traders created improvised markets to sell local and foreign products. As a result, many small business and services are now in private hands.

4. What has been the extent of insider (management, labor, and nomenklatura) participation in the privatization process? What explicit and implicit preferences have been awarded to insiders? Privatization in Tajikistan has largely become an insider's game. According to one poll, 74 percent of citizens cannot take part in the privatization process, mostly for financial reasons. Analysts say the average Tajik's savings are equal to about 1,000 Tajik rubles, which corresponds to the price of about two kilograms of meat. Others lost the right to participate because they were refugees at the time the government distributed privatization vouchers. This has resulted in state enterprises largely being sold off to government officials, their relatives, other elements of a newly emerging elite, and to leaders of armed factions, who have gained wealth through drug trafficking, operating road checkpoints, and other illicit activities. Many privatization auctions were reportedly rigged, and insider groups have intimidated potential buyers of shares. The World Bank notes that the process of valuation of state enterprises is inefficient and lacks transparency.

5. How much public awareness of and support for privatization has there been? What is the nature of support and opposition to privatization by major interest groups? Many profitable properties were sold quietly, without advertising or open auctioning. In 1996, the government announced a plan to offer privatization vouchers in exchange for people's savings that had been frozen in state bank accounts. Only 60 percent of the vouchers were distributed by the time of the September 1997 deadline, which analysts interpreted as widespread indifference to privatization.

Macroeconomics 6.25/7

1. Has the taxation system been reformed? (What areas have and have not been overhauled? To what degree are taxpayers complying? Is tax compliance difficult to achieve? Has the level of revenues increased? Is the revenue collection body overburdened? What is the overall tax burden?) The Tajik government has begun reforming the taxation system by applying excises to a larger number of goods and has made an effort to address the growing problem of tax arrears and non-compliance. In practice, however, the tax system is chaotic, rates vary widely, administration is poor, and collection is often arbitrary. The government gets most of its tax revenue from medium and large state enterprises, including the state-owned aluminum operations and the government-dominated cotton industry, and from shares in privatized businesses. There is also a 20 percent value-added tax and a sales tax.

2. Does fiscal policy encourage private savings, investment and earnings? (Has there been any reform/alteration of revenue and budget policies? How large are budget deficits and overall debt? Is the financing of the social insurance/pension system sustainable? What proportion of the budget is taken up by subsidies to firms and individuals?) The government has managed to keep the budget deficit manageable. Nevertheless, inflation is still high and ultimately this discourages private savings, investment, and earnings. The budget deficit as a percentage of GDP has fallen from 31.2 percent in 1992 to 3.4 percent in 1997. By following International Monetary Fund conditions agreed to in 1996, including restraining the budget deficit and adhering to a somewhat tighter monetary policy, the government lowered the inflation rate from over 2,000 percent in 1995 to 60 percent in 1996. In 1997, GDP grew at 1.7 percent, largely due to an increase in agricultural output and higher state spending. Inflation, however, soared to 159.8 percent, in part because of the sharp decline in the currency.

The government has difficulty in meeting its budget obligations and the financing of social welfare provisions is unsustainable. In December 1997, the International Monetary Fund granted Tajikistan $10 million as the first tranche of a credit to help finance the government's 1997-98 budget. In the 1997 budget, 27.7 percent of expenditures went to the "social sphere," consisting of education, culture, health and social welfare, although it is not clear what percentage of these monies went to individuals. Actual social expenditures were only 75 percent of planned expenditures, including 72 percent of planned expenditures actually spent on education and 74 percent of planned expenditures actually spent on health. In practice, the government appears to provide few social services, with most existing services provided by international organizations. As of 1996, the ratio of pensioners to those employed was 27.0 percent versus an average of 39.2 percent (1993) in major advanced economies. The average pension was 23.7 percent of the average wage versus 37.5 percent in major advanced economies. Public pension expenditure was 3 percent of GDP.

3. Has there been banking reform? (Is the central bank independent? What are its responsibilities? Is it effective in setting and/or implementing monetary policy? What is the actual state of the private banking sector? Does it conform to international standards? Are depositors protected?) Several laws regulate the banking sector: The Law on Banks and Banking Activities in the Republic of Tajikistan; The Law of the Republic of Tajikistan on the National Bank of the Republic of Tajikistan; and Gosbank Rules Governing the Regulation of the Activities of Commercial and Cooperative Banks.

The central National Bank of Tajikistan (NBT), whose chairperson is appointed by the president and confirmed by parliament, is a nominally independent entity which has implemented a generally loose, expansionary monetary policy.

Although credit allocation is less centralized than in the past, the government still intervenes through credit directives and NBT intermediation. As a result, credit is not efficiently allocated and existing industries are often propped up regardless of creditworthiness. The central bank also establishes an interest rate for bank refinancing, which is often negative in real terms and tends to discourage savings. Commercial banks can and do set their own rates, which are higher than that set by the NBT. Many of the Russian professional staff of the NBT have left the country, which has eroded its regulatory capacity.

The weak institutional capacity of the NBT and the government's practice of directing credit to favored companies has meant that private banks are poorly supervised, do not adhere to international standards, and continue to lend money to traditional clients regardless of creditworthiness. Long-term overdrafts persist in NBT settlement accounts. The banking system is dominated by three state-owned banks — Agroprombank, Orienbank, and Tajikbankbusiness — which account for more than 96 percent of bank lending, although some 14 other banks exist. Most are partially owned by state-owned enterprises, which are often recipients of loans. The regulatory framework and the accounting system used by banks are largely a holdover from the Soviet era. Cash is often used for commercial transactions; checks are not widely used. As with the NBT, the departure of Russian professional staff from the country has hindered the banks' ability to manage their accounts and upgrade the payments system.

The two state banks are Sberbank, which has a government guarantee on its deposits from households and, with 1.5 million clients, dominates the market for individual savings; and Khatlon Reconstruction and Development Bank, which assists in the development of the Khatlon Region.

4. How sound is the national currency? (Is the value of the currency fixed or does it float? How convertible is the currency? How large are the hard currency reserves? Has the exchange rate policy been stable and predictable?) The Tajik ruble is weak and has little credibility. Much trade in markets takes place in U.S. dollars, Russian rubles, or, in certain areas, Uzbek *sum*, rather than in Tajik rubles. Since May 1995, when the Tajik ruble was introduced as the national currency to replace the Russian ruble, the NBT has set the rate of the ruble through hard currency auctions at the Tajik Interbank Currency Exchange, a closed-stock company established by eight commercial banks. By government decree, these currency auctions are supposed to be held regularly in order to establish the market exchange rate for the ruble. The government, however, controls the auctions, meaning that the rate is effectively fixed. There is often a considerable spread between the NBT's rate for the ruble and the black market rate. For example, in July 1997, the NBT fixed the ruble at 560 to one U.S. dollar, while on the black market one dollar bought 610-620 rubles. On average, the ruble changed hands on the black market at 8-10 percent higher than the official rate.

Although in theory the currency is convertible, in practice foreign exchange offices and banks often refuse to sell U.S. dollars. The exchange rate policy has neither been stable nor predictable. Although the NBT is supposed to hold foreign exchange auctions regularly, the auctions were suspended from May to October 1997 due to foreign exchange shortages. During the year the government devalued the ruble from 320 to the dollar to 820 to the dollar, which contributed to a 159.8 percent inflation rate for the year.

5. Is there a functioning capital market infrastructure? (Are there existing or planned commodities, bond and stock markets? What are the mechanisms for investing and lending? What government bodies have authority to regulate capital markets?) A post-Communist Stock Exchange Law regulates securities trading. Access to credit remains limited, complicated by low bank credit ceilings mandated by the International Monetary Fund. Private commodities markets do exist. Nevertheless, there is still no cotton exchange, even though cotton is the major agricultural commodity. The state cotton procurement agency, Glakhlopkoprom, effectively sets prices and has a monopoly on marketing cotton abroad. Cotton futures contracts are available.

Microeconomics 6.00/7

1. Are property rights guaranteed? (Are there both formal and de facto protections of private real estate and intellectual property? Is there a land registry with the authority and capability to ensure accurate recording of who owns what? What are the procedures for expropriation, including measures for compensation and challenge? Have any seizures taken place? In March 1992, parliament approved land reform legislation that gave Tajik citizens the right to own, lease, and inherit land. Both the constitution and the laws on privatization guarantee property rights, including intellectual property, real estate, and business property. Agricultural land remains under state ownership but can be leased. Lease rights are inheritable and, under a new land code, can also be sold. Land registries are inadequate.

Since privatization of land and property has only recently begun in earnest in Tajikistan, procedures for expropriation, compensation, and challenge of property rights have yet to be worked out in law and in practice. The post-Soviet government initially declared 50,000 hectares of farmland available for private farmers in return for a small levy to the government, but by then farmers had already occupied 30,000 hectares. In 1994, the government legalized this situation by recognizing squatter-occupied farmland and making an additional 20,000 hectares available to private farmers. With the country being 93 percent mountainous, there is considerable potential for conflict over farmland. During the civil war, individual farmers sowed crops on the sides of roads and on mountainsides.

Despite laws protecting intellectual property rights, piracy in computer software continues to be a problem.

2. To what extent have prices been liberalized? What subsidies remain? There are price controls on farm produce, utilities, and transportation. In addition, many prices in the formal sector are effectively set by state-owned enterprises. For example, the state cotton procurement agency, Glavkhlopkoprom, which is involved in both the ginning and selling of cotton fiber, uses its dominant position to set the price for cotton purchases, even though presidential decrees have freed cotton from the state order system. Further, the government continues to distort prices in many sectors through subsidies to industries.

3. Is it possible to own and operate a business? (Has there been legislation regarding the formation, dissolution and transfer of businesses, and is the law respected? Do there exist overly cumbersome bureaucratic hurdles that effectively hinder the ability to own and dispose of a business? Are citizens given access to information on commercial law? Is the law applied fairly? Does the regulation (or licensing requirements) impose significant costs on business and consumers? Do they create significant barriers to entry and seriously hamper competition?) Although legislation governing the ownership and operation of a business exists, according to the World Bank, the barriers to private enterprise remain high. The actual mechanisms provided for in these laws have, in many cases, yet to be implemented.

Entrepreneurs generally must pay bribes to the authorities and criminal syndicates, while bureaucratic inefficiency and delays add to the time and cost involved in setting up a business. The need to bribe local warlords who run road checkpoints can result in transportation costs which can triple the price of many goods.

Limited access to commercial real estate and other physical assets, the vast majority of which are controlled by state enterprises, also remains an obstacle to private enterprise. Other obstacles include difficult entry and exit rules, difficulty in raising working capital, a general lack of access to business information, and an inadequate business law framework. Nevertheless, many traders have banded together into small groups and companies that produce goods and provide construction, transportation, banking, and investment services.

In certain areas, the economy has been effectively outside of central control for extended periods. For example, Colonel Khudoberdiev, commander of the first brigade of the Tajik army stationed in the southern city of Kugonteppa, took control of the southern province's entire economy until other army units re-established central control over the region.

4. Are courts effective, transparent efficient, and quick in reaching decisions on property and contract disputes? What alternative mechanisms for adjudicating disputes exist? In April 1997, the government created a Higher Economic Court, which is governed by the 1995 Legal Code and the 1994 Constitutional Law on Economic Courts. The court consists of legal, appeal, and cassation boards. Previously, decisions were made by one-judge arbitrage courts, whereas now, a verdict is delivered by a group of 15 judges. The economic courts' mandate includes any economic disputes arising from civil, administrative, business, and other economic relationships.

Before a case reaches trial, plaintiffs are required to pay legal expenses of ten percent of the suit sum, which is believed to limit the number of cases brought to the Higher Economic Court. Only legal entities, as opposed to individuals, may bring cases.

Observers generally view the Higher Economic Court as relatively competent, professional, and a positive development in legal reform. In 1997, the Higher Economic Court registered 271 suits and considered 172 of them. In 1998, regional economic courts were established in Gorno Badakhshan, Leninabad, and Khatlon provinces, and in Dushanbe, the capital.

Individuals must bring economic disputes to common courts. The Tajik court system is corrupt and inefficient. Judges are subject to pressure by the executive branch and by local warlords and criminal syndicates. As such, the courts are not an effective, transparent, efficient means of resolving property and contract disputes, and private property is not adequately protected. There are no formal alternative mechanisms for adjudicating disputes.

5. Is business competition encouraged? (Are monopolistic practices limited in law and in practice? If so, how? To what degree is "insider" dealing a hindrance to open competition? Are government procurement policies open and unbiased?) Tajikistan's business culture is based more on personal connections than on competitive processes. Large state enterprises still dominate almost every sector of the economy, including supply networks and transport. Although there has been an anti-monopoly law on the books since 1993, and an anti-monopoly department in the Ministry of the Economy is in charge of enforcing it, little progress has been made. The opposition, along with other groups, have charged that local governments are rife with nepotism and corruption in the control of local economic assets, the operation of private business, and the distribution of land rights.

In October 1997, the government passed a decree allowing for the establishment of "financial-industrial groups" that would pool material and financial resources. Although the ostensible aim is to boost exports, the move could further concentrate industrial production and inhibit domestic competition.

Local warlords, some of which are nominally supporters of President Rakhmonov, have built up shady business concerns. Mafiosi and drug traffickers control a considerable share of economic activity.

As with other areas of the economy, the procurement process is neither open nor unbiased.

6. To what extent has international trade been liberalized? To what degree has there been simplification/overhaul of customs and tariff procedures, and are these applied fairly? What informal trade barriers exist? International trade has been hampered by the country's war-wracked economy, limited foreign currency holdings, and geographical isolation. Most trade is in government hands through state-owned enterprises or stakes in private enterprises. Increasingly, Tajikistan has become a transit point for drugs flowing into Russia and Western Europe from Afghanistan.

In 1996, the Tajik government removed export tariffs on cotton and aluminum — two of the country's main commodities — and also canceled the obligation to turn over foreign currency earnings to the government, with the aim of encouraging foreign trade. In January 1998, the government introduced a uniform five percent duty on all imported goods, although an often predatory customs service reportedly applies tariffs in an arbitrary manner.

Certain informal trade barriers exist. For example, a July 1997 presidential decree made it necessary for exporters to secure advance payments from buyers and obtain government permission before exporting cotton, aluminum, wool, and other goods. At times, the civil war and other fighting sharply curbed imports. Most of Tajikistan's freight and passenger transportation must be run through Uzbek territory. Uzebkistan has intermittently closed critical roads and railways, blocked the entrance and exit of freight, and tightened customs rules, in order to pressure Tajikistan into paying debts for fuel supplies. According to Human Rights Watch, citizens on both sides of the Tajik-Uzbek border are subject to severe and lengthy customs checks. The government has held discussions with China about giving Tajikistan road access to the Karakoram Highway which runs between China and Pakistan.

7. To what extent has foreign investment and capital flow been encouraged or constrained? The government has generally encouraged foreign investment, particularly in the mining and hydroelectric sectors. The 1993 Law on Foreign Investment is favorable to foreign investment. Nevertheless, registration procedures remain cumbersome; decrees are often unclear and contradictory; implementation is frequently stalled by the bureaucracy; and companies face difficulties in repatriating profits and capital due to a lack of a specific legal protection for doing so, and because hard currency shortages frequently lead to difficulties in converting currency. A February 1996 decree liberalized currency operations. Hard currency profits of Tajik exporters are free of any taxes except for profits on cotton and aluminum exports, which are taxed at 5 and 25 percent, respectively. Payments on export-import operations of joint ventures cannot be held in offshore banks. Foreign investors also chafe at a prohibition on land ownership, which makes leasing the only option.

Foreign investors can establish wholly-owned subsidiaries and there are no restrictions on the percentage of foreign ownership in a joint venture. By one estimate, registration of a joint venture takes three weeks of intense work by a Tajik local representative who is familiar with processing the necessary paperwork with the Ministry of Finance, the State Statistical Committee, local administrative and tax officials, and the Ministry of Foreign Economic Relations. There are some 200 registered joint ventures in Tajikistan, although only a minority are currently operational. Seventy percent are involved in production, and the remainder are mostly in trading and services. The main foreign investors are mining companies, which operate mostly in the relatively peaceful north. These companies have cited difficulties due to the lack of formal procedures for operations such as exporting minerals, and an arbitrary and non-transparent bureaucracy. Perhaps not surprisingly, in 1997, Foreign Direct Investment totaled a paltry $20 million. An October 1997 decree allowing the establishment of financial-industrial groups permits foreign participation in providing finance and credit to these companies.

8. Has there been reform of the energy sector? (To what degree has the energy sector been restructured? Is the energy sector more varied, and is it open to private competition? Is the country overly dependent on one or two other country for energy [including whether exported fuels must pass through one or more countries to reach markets]?) There has been little reform of the energy sector, and the country remains highly dependent on outside suppliers. The government does not provide subsidies for energy, and in recent years, fighting has disrupted imports and caused price increases.

In 1996, 35 percent of Tajikistan's oil product imports came from Turkmenistan, 22 percent from Uzbekistan, and 21 percent from Kazakhstan. Tajikistan also remains highly dependent on Uzbekistan for supplies of natural gas, particularly in the fall and winter. In recent years, Uzbekistan has cut off gas and electricity supplies when Tajikistan has fallen behind in its payments, often because Tajik industrial enterprises and even ordinary citizens have tried to avoid paying for gas. The Rakhmonov government has taken steps to reduce the country's energy dependence on Uzbekistan by signing a tripartite agreement covering economic and cultural relations with Turkmenistan and Iran. As part of the deal, Turkmenistan provides Tajikistan with reduced cost fuel and natural gas. The government is also seeking foreign investors for the development of several domestic gas fields.

Tajikistan is the third largest producer of hydroelectric power in the world, after the United States and Russia, but while hydroelectric production represents 76 percent of the country's electricity output, it supplies less than half of its total energy needs. Tajikistan does export electricity, mainly to Uzbekistan, but also imports electricity, mainly from Uzbekistan. The government is attempting to increase hydroelectric power production, which is centered around stations on the Vakhsh River, and claims that the Sangtuda Hydroelectric Plant, which is in the early construction phase, will eventually provide Tajikistan with all of its electricity needs.

TURKMENISTAN

Freedom in the World Ratings, 1989-1998

	1989-90	1990-91	1991-92	1992-93	1993-94	1994-95	1995-96	1996-97	1997-98
Political Rights	-	-	6	7	7	7	7	7	7
Civil Liberties	-	-	5	6	7	7	7	7	7
Status	-	-	PF	NF	NF	NF	NF	NF	NF

Polity: Consolidated Autocracy
Economy: Consolidated Statist
Population: 4,471,000
PPP: $2,345
Ethnic Groups: Turkmen (73 percent), Russian (10 percent), Uzbek (9 percent), Kazakh (3 percent), others
Capital: Ashgabat

Political Process 7.00/7

1. When did national legislative elections occur? Were they free and fair? How were they judged by the domestic and international election monitoring organizations? Who composes the government? Elections to the 175-member Turkmen Supreme Soviet took place on January 7, 1990. This body, however, was supplanted by both the 50-member *Mejlis* (parliament or assembly) in elections which took place on December 11, 1994, and the 150-member *Khalq Maslakhati* (People's Council), which includes Mejlis deputies and appointed officials, and is chaired by the president.

Whereas elections to the Supreme Soviet were contested by two or three candidates in each district, only one seat was contested in elections to the new Mejlis. Deputies were overwhelmingly nominated by the Democratic Party of Turkmenistan, which was the direct successor to the Turkmen Communist Party. The Mejlis was elected in a holiday atmosphere without party registration or campaigning and in the absence of international observers; as such, it can be considered neither free nor fair. The Khalq Maslakhati is effectively an appointed body. Both bodies lack any semblance of independence and are entirely supportive of the president's policies. In 1997, the Mejlis took steps to become a more professional body and undertook to debate and amend some legislation. The next parliamentary elections are scheduled to occur in 1999. New election regulations, providing for candidates to be nominated by uncertain "public organizations" were passed by parliament in November 1997. President Niyazov declared his intent to see the constitution altered to strengthen the role of parliament in February 1998, just prior to visiting the United States.

2. When did presidential elections occur? Were they free and fair? In direct but unopposed elections, former First Secretary of the Turkmen Communist Party and Chairman of the Supreme Soviet Saparmurad Niyazov was elected President on January 27, 1990. Following elections in which he ran unopposed, Niyazov was reinvested as President on June 26, 1992. A referendum on January 15, 1994 extended his term until 2002. The uncontested elections were reminiscent of Soviet-era practices. As such, they can be considered neither free nor fair.

3. Is the electoral system multi-party based? Are there at least two viable political parties functioning at all levels of the government? Turkmenistan is a single party state led by an authoritarian president and his advisors. The ruling National Democratic Party of Turkmenistan is the only registered political party and is headed by President Niyazov. The party is the direct successor to the Turkmen Communist Party. The party's name was changed and adherence to Marxism-Leninism were eschewed at the XXV Party Congress of December 16, 1991.

4. How many parties have been legalized? Are any particular parties illegal? The National Democratic Party of Turkmenistan is the country's only political party. Two small democratic-reform oriented parties, Agzybirlik and the Democratic Party of Turkmenistan (not to be confused with the ruling party), surfaced respectively in 1989 and 1990. Neither party was registered nor permitted to operate. Most of those involved in opposition activity have left Turkmenistan and reside in Russia, Turkey, Sweden, or the Czech Republic.

5. What proportion of the population belongs to political parties? The National Democratic Party claimed a membership of 60,000 in early 1995. Party membership is likely to be of importance mainly to government officials and those seeking government office.

6. What has been the trend of voter turnout at the municipal, provincial and national levels in recent years? October 1990 presidential election: 99.95 percent; June 1992 presidential election: 99.9 percent; 1994 referendum on extending the president's tenure: 99.9 percent (with 99.9 percent voting in favor); December 1994 Mejlis elections: 99.8 percent. Voter turnout, as officially declared, contrasted with reports of low voter turnout at polling stations.

Civil Society **7.00/7**

1. How many nongovernmental organizations (NGOs) have come into existence since 1988? What is the number of charitable/nonprofit organizations? Are there locally led efforts to increase philanthropy and volunteerism? What proportion of the population is active in private voluntary activity (from polling data)? The constitution permits peaceful assembly and association, but severely restricts it in practice. Only a handful of unregistered organizations without a political agenda are permitted to function in Turkmenistan. Among them are the Ashgabat Ecology Club, Dialogue Youth Leadership Center, Information Consultative Center of Turkmenistan, Society for Preservation of Nature, and the Dashkavouz Ecological Club. Other even less formalized organizations exist including those that undertake social work such as assisting battered women. Information on these groups is sketchy; they fear exposure and contact with foreigners as it may result in their work being suspended.

There are several government controlled entities which attempt to occupy a niche filled by NGOs in democratic societies. One of them, the Institute for Democracy and Human Rights, was established in October 1996 and is attached to the Office of the President, helped bring some limited penal reform in 1997.

2. What is the legal and regulatory environment for NGOs (i.e. ease of registration, legal rights, government regulation, taxation, procurement and access-to-information issues)? To what extent is NGO activism focused on improving the legal and regulatory environment? The government of Turkmenistan does not encourage the emergence of NGOs. It uses registration requirements to prevent the emergence of potential opposition groups. The political environment in Turkmenistan is hostile to organized independent activity of almost any variety.

3. What is the organizational capacity of NGOs? Do management structures clearly delineate authority and responsibility? Is information available on NGO management issues in the native language? Is there a core of experienced practitioners/trainers to serve as consultants or mentors to less developed organizations? The handful of NGOs which exist in Turkmenistan do so by remaining uncontroversial and limiting their activities. Given Turkmenistan's totalitarian character, conditions for expanding the NGO sector are poor; little information on the functioning of Turkmen NGOs is available. Presumably, information on NGO management issues trickle in from other Central Asian republics. While some experienced practitioners exist, it is unclear to what extent they are willing to risk confrontation with the authorities by serving as mentors.

4. Are NGOs financially viable? What is their tax status? Are they obliged to and do they typically disclose revenue sources? Do government procurement opportunities exist for private not-for-profit providers of services? Little information concerning the financial status of NGOs is available. Some, however, have received external support and work in conjunction with other organizations based in Central Asia. Some citizens with links to foreigners have been subject to intimidation.

5. Are there free trade unions? How many workers belong to these unions? Is the number of workers belonging to trade unions growing or decreasing? What is the numerical/proportional membership of farmers' groups, small business associations, etc. There are no legal guarantees entitling workers to form or join unions. The central trade union, the Trade Union Federation of Turkmenistan, is the successor to the Soviet-era system of government-controlled trade unions. Its unions are divided along both sectoral and regional lines. Unions may not form or join other federations. The federation claims a membership of 1.6 million. State and collective farms were transformed into Peasant Unions (*Daikhan*) in 1995. Statistics concerning their membership are unavailable. In March 1998, President Niyazov said the Peasant Unions 'did not justify expectations.'

6. What forms of interest group participation in politics are legal? What types of interest groups are active in the political and policy process? Interest group participation is limited to government-controlled organizations which take their cue from the president and his most senior advisors. The only very limited intervention in the policy process which has been accepted, particularly since 1996, has been advice from some international lending institutions.

7. How is the not-for-profit/NGO sector perceived by the public and government officials?

What is the nature of media coverage of NGO's? To what extent do government officials engage with NGO's? The handful of NGOs in Turkmenistan are known only to a limited segment of the intelligentsia. Coverage in the state-controlled media is negligible. NGOs avoid interacting with government officials out of prudence.

Independent Media 7.00/7

1. Are there legal protections for press freedoms? The constitution provides for the right to hold personal convictions and express them freely. The relatively liberal 1991 Law on the Media, identical to the all-Union legislation passed the same year, also supports these notions. In practice, the government completely controls both print and broadcast media. The government prohibits the media from reporting the views of opposition political leaders and critics and rarely allows the mildest form of criticism of the government and its policies.

According to *Internews*, independent media briefly emerged in Turkmenistan in the early 1990s but was throttled in 1994-1995. The print media, which is funded from the state budget, are carefully censored by the Committee for the Protection of State Secrets (a Soviet-era institution). Foreign print media are not widely available and may be confiscated at the border.

Whereas cable television existed in the late 1980s in all of Turkmenistan's cities and three commercial television stations existed in the early 1990s, none currently exist. In the transformation of State TV to National TV and Radio, it appears the new body took effective control over all broadcasting in the republic.

2. Are there legal penalties for libeling officials? Are there legal penalties for "irresponsible" journalism? Have these laws been enforced to harass journalists? Libel is a criminal offense (Articles 132 and 192 of the Criminal Code). Libel in the mass media is punishable by either a fine or up to two years of forced labor. Libel of a state official is punishable by a prison term of up to five years. In practice, libel is not at issue because the media is more strictly controlled than in the Soviet era. Journalists, both foreign and domestic, have experienced harassment and intimidation. The *Izvestiya* office in Ashgabat was closed in 1995. Journalists working for Radio Liberty have experienced problems with the authorities repeatedly. Foreign journalists attempting to cover events in Turkmenistan have been denied visas to enter the country.

3. What proportion of media is privatized? What are the major private newspapers, television stations, and radio stations? None. At present only two papers, *Adalat* (Justice) and G*alkynysh* (Revival), are even notionally independent. However, both were created by presidential decree. In September 1996, President Niyazov was declared the "founder" of all newspapers in Turkmenistan. With the contribution of political exiles, clandestine publications are smuggled into Turkmenistan sporadically from Russia.

4. Are the private media financially viable? The financial viability of the private media is not at issue because the media is state-controlled.

5. Are the media editorially independent? Are the media's news gathering functions affected by interference from government or private owners? Journalists are state employees. News coverage focuses on the activities of the president.

6. Is the distribution system for newspapers privately or governmentally controlled? The distribution system for newspapers is government controlled. For a time, the state-run publishing house existed under a Government Press Committee before that body was abolished, and the publishing house was subordinated directly to the cabinet of ministers.

7. What proportion of the population is connected to the Internet? Are there any restrictions on Internet access to private citizens? E-mail service routed through Russia was available only through the Ashgabat Ecology Club until late 1997. In November of that year, the government announced it had established an Internet center in Ashgabat. The Scientific Information Bureau, in cooperation with the Ministry of Communication and State Telecom and MCI, is expected to increase connectivity to provincial cities in the future.

8. What has been the trend in press freedom as measured by Freedom House's Survey of Press Freedom? Turkmenistan has been consistently rated not free.

Governance and Public Administration 6.75/7

1. Is the legislature the effective rule-making institution? Both the Mejlis and Khalq Maslakhati are subordinate to the executive branch, which itself is dominated by the president. Nominees to both bodies are vetted, if not hand-picked, by the president. The Mejlis is the supreme legislative body in Turkmenistan. While it meets regularly to pass legislation, the Khalq Maslakhati is termed the supreme representative body and meets infrequently, i.e., a minimum of once per year. It is responsible for adopting constitutional amendments, treaties and referenda. The 150-member body, chaired by the president, is composed of 50 Mejlis deputies, the cabinet of ministers, regional, district and city *hakims,* i.e., governors and mayors, and peoples' representatives elected in each of 50 *etrap.*

2. Is substantial power decentralized to subnational levels of government? What specific authority do subnational levels have? Turkmenistan is a unitary, centralized state in which the greatest authority is vested in the president, a self-described "presidential republic." Subnational governments, first and foremost the regional and city hakim — governor and mayor, respectively — are appointed and beholden to the president. A regular feature of Niyazov's exercise of authority has been the bewildering pace at which hakims, like other government officials, have been shuffled, dismissed, and often reappointed.

3. Are subnational officials chosen in free and fair elections? Subnational officials are appointed by the president.

4. Do the executive and legislative bodies operate openly and with transparency? Is draft legislation easily accessible to the media and the public? Neither the executive nor legislative bodies operates openly. Decisions are made at the highest level by the president; the legislature passes all laws put before it; and the media duly publishes them.

5. Do municipal governments have sufficient revenues to carry out their duties? Do municipal governments have control of their own local budgets? Do they raise revenues autonomously or from the central state budget? Turkmenistan's municipal governments are dependent upon the central state budget, which is strained to the breaking point due to a shortfall in revenue from gas, oil, and cotton exports. Economic conditions are poor.

6. Do the elected local leaders and local civil servants know how to manage municipal governments effectively? Local civil servants are notoriously corrupt. Their official status is often exploited for personal benefit and that of their cronies, who are usually connected by clan or regional affiliation.

7. When did the constitutional/legislative changes on local power come into effect? Has there been a reform of the civil service code/system? Are local civil servants employees of the local or central government? No reform of the civil service in Turkmenistan has occurred. Local civil servants are appointed effectively by the central government and are responsible to it.

Rule of Law 6.75/7

1. Is there a post-Communist constitution? How does the judicial system interpret and enforce the constitution? Are there specific examples of judicial enforcement of the constitution in the last year? On May 18, 1992, Turkmenistan's legislature unanimously approved a new constitution. It stresses the country's "neutrality" and identifies the country as a "democratic" state. It clearly outlines the extensive powers of the president, including the right to appoint all executive, judicial, and regional offices, to initiate legislation and budget proposals, and to veto parliamentary proposals. There are no checks on the authority of the president. The judiciary is controlled by the executive and has played no role in interpreting or enforcing the constitution.

President Niyazov has consistently declared that economic reform and national revival requires political stability, which his rule is designed to provide. He claims that his leadership is building a rule of law-based, democratic, and secular country on a gradual basis so as to prevent a decline is the standard of living of the population and to prevent "social confrontations." Most international observers view these claims with great skepticism.

2. Does the constitutional framework provide for human rights? Do the human rights include business and property rights? A wide range of human rights, including the rights to assembly, free speech, free association, and religion, are enshrined in the constitution — along with a caveat restricting them in the event that they threaten the social order. In conjunction with its bid to be recognized as a neutral country by the United Nations, Turkmenistan declared its adherence to the principles of the United Nations Charter and the Universal Declaration on Human Rights. In practice, the government continues to commit human rights abuses, and the authorities severely restrict both political and civil liberties. In 1996, as part of an effort to improve the country's image in the area of human rights and as an ostensible public resource, the National Institute for Democracy and

Human Rights was established in the office of the president. Institute personnel led an investigative tour of prisons and the offices of regional and local authorities. This appears to have played a role in a subsequent declaration of a general amnesty and changes to the criminal code. Before making an official visit to the United States, President Niyazov issued a decree calling on citizens to send letters to the government citing violations of their rights by members of law enforcement bodies.

3. Has there been basic reform of the criminal code/criminal law? Who authorizes searches and issues warrants? Are suspects and prisoners beaten or abused? Are there excessive delays in the criminal justice system? A new criminal code was approved on June 12, 1997. It is not considered a particularly liberal document: it details 17 crimes considered capital offenses, including the possession of narcotics. Although Turkmenistan's laws provide for due process for defendants, including a public trial, the right to a defense attorney, access to accusatory material, and the right to call witnesses to testify on behalf of the accused, these rights are seldom recognized. As in the Soviet era, the authority of the state prosecutor overshadows that of judges or defense attorneys. According to Radio Liberty, suspects and prisoners have been routinely beaten. The criminal justice system is widely feared and considered corrupt.

4. Do most judges rule fairly and impartially? Do many remain from the Communist era? As political appointees in an authoritarian system, judges cannot be considered to rule fairly or impartially. There has been no evidence of reform of the judiciary or court system; it may be presumed many judges remain from the Communist era. Of the 1,400 complaints received by the National Institute of Democracy and Human Rights, over 50 percent concerned the judicial process.

5. Are the courts free of political control and influence? Are the courts linked directly to the Ministry of Justice or any other executive body? All judges are appointed by the president to five-year terms and without legislative review, except the Chairman of the Supreme Court. The president has the authority to remove them from the bench before their terms expire.

6. What proportion of lawyers is in private practice? How does this compare with the previous year? A handful of retired legal officials reportedly practice on an *ad hoc* basis. Otherwise, there are no independent lawyers in Turkmenistan.

7. Does the state provide public defenders? Yes, although their ability to challenge the state's charges is extremely limited. Often, they see their clients only at trial.

8. Are there effective anti-bias/discrimination laws, including protection of ethnic minority rights? The constitution provides for equal rights and freedoms for all citizens. While there is no legal basis for discrimination against women or religious or ethnic minorities, cultural traditions and government policy of promoting ethnic Turkmen limit the employment and educational opportunities of women and non-ethnic Turkmen. The constitution provides for the rights of speakers of languages other than Turkmen to use them. As part of its efforts to promote Turkmen national pride,

Turkmen has been declared the official language; by July 1999, all official documents and declarations are to be in Turkmen. Despite the seemingly privileged status Turkmen enjoys, Russian-language instruction and usage are widespread. Ethnic Russians also have the right to hold dual citizenship, in keeping with a 1995 bilateral treaty between Turkmenistan and Russia. Between 1991 and 1995, some 40,000 ethnic Russians emigrated from Turkmenistan.

Corruption D

1. What is the magnitude of official corruption in the civil service? Must an average citizen pay a bribe to a bureaucrat in order to receive a service? What services are subject to bribe requests for example, university entrance, hospital admission, telephone installation, obtaining a license to operate a business, applying for a passport or other official documents? What is the average salary of civil servants at various levels? Corruption is endemic in Turkmenistan. Government officials at all levels expect payments in order to allow enterprises to operate, to have access to raw materials and equipment, and to sell products. Law enforcement and the justice system are notoriously corrupt, as are regional and local administrations. The threat of imprisonment has been used to collect pay-offs; those in prison must pay bribes to satisfy elementary needs or the hope of release. All services involving interaction with officials require payment. Officials' salaries are on average about $30 per month.

2. Do top policy makers (the president, ministers, vice-ministers, top court justices, and heads of agencies and commissions) have direct ties to businesses? How strong are such connections and what kinds of businesses are these? Contracts have frequently been awarded for political rather than economic reasons with little regard for feasibility, economic viability, or the best company to do the job. Significant commercial contracts require approval at the highest level of government, specifically, the president and his closest advisors. They are widely believed to have direct ties and interests in the agricultural, extractive, i.e., oil and gas, and industrial sectors of the country. Smaller deals must pass muster with ministerial level officials who are frequently shifted, requiring re-negotiation of the contract, as well as additional bribes.

There has been an increase in corruption allegations surrounding the oil and gas sectors. The risk of further government insider deals has risen with the intense foreign interest in exploiting these reserves.

3. Do laws requiring financial disclosure and disallowing conflict of interest exist? Have publicized anti corruption cases been pursued. To what conclusion? Turkmenistan does not have laws, regulations, or penalties to combat corruption effectively. Government officials at all levels have been sacked for corruption. The Minister of Agriculture, Tagandurdy Nuriyev, was sacked, tried, and convicted of corruption. Though sentenced to 13 years imprisonment, he was released after being 'forgiven,' according to Radio Liberty. In 1997, the governor the Balkan province, Rejep Pukhanov, was sacked for corruption, as was Dashauz governor Yagmyr Oevezov.

4. What major anti-corruption initiatives have been implemented? How often are anti-corruption laws and decrees adopted? Most high officials charged with corruption are never formally charged with a crime. In some cases, they are simply re-appointed later to new high level positions. Dismissal on corruption charges is often interpreted as a mere pretext for removal because the practice is so widespread.

5. How do major corruption-ranking organizations like Transparency International rate this country? Transparency International has not rated Turkmenistan.

Privatization 6.75/7

1. What percentage of the GDP comes from private ownership? What percentage of the labor force is employed in the private sector? How large is the informal sector of the economy? Current data on private ownership as a percent of gross domestic product (GDP) is unavailable. According to Turkmen government estimates, the officially recognized private production or service units employed about 22 percent of the labor force and accounted for 10.1 percent of the GDP in 1995 (4.4 excluding private agriculture). Government estimates indicate a total private sector share of GDP of about 18 percent in 1995, including the "home industry" and Sunday market trading. In 1997, the European Bank for Reconstruction and Development (EBRD) estimated the total private sector as unlikely to exceed 25 percent of GDP . The government does not utilize international accounting methods and generally withholds information on the economy. There is no data concerning Turkmenistan's informal economy. Overall, it appears Turkmenistan has experienced six years of deepening economic crisis characterized by output collapse and falling revenues from exports.

2. What major privatization legislation has been passed? What were its substantive features? Turkmenistan's economy remains dependent upon central planning mechanisms and state control, The government, however, has taken a number of steps that appear designed to give the impression that it is being won over to the cause of economic liberalization. Since independence, Niyazov has repeatedly emphasized his desire to undertake a gradual approach to economic transition. In 1993, the State Property and Privatization Agency was established. At the close of the year, the government enacted a law on privatization which resulted in the privatization of about half of the minuscule trade and service sector (catering shops, barbershops, etc.) in 1995 and 1996. In January 1994, a program of economic reform, "Ten Years of Prosperity," was enacted with the approval of the Khalq Maslakhati. Key elements of the plan include the privatization of state enterprises, the reform of land ownership, including the privatization of collective and state farms, and investment in new pipelines for the export of gas and oil outside the Newly Independent States (NIS). According to the EBRD, one of the greatest reform achievements in the area of establishing private ownership rights has been made in agriculture. In December 1996, a land reform initiative was announced allowing for private land ownership. During the first half of 1997, almost all land had been allocated to individual farmers and transfer of land titles into private ownership are envisaged after a two-year lease.

In the spring and summer of 1997, the government issued a presidential order and three presidential decrees privatizing industrial enterprises and allowing the auctioning of small- and medium-size enterprises. Up to 330 firms were concerned. Only 45 firms primarily involved in public utilities were exempted from privatization according to these decrees.

Foreign and Turkmen individuals and legal entities are allowed to participate on an equal footing in privatization. The government intends to auction enterprises that have fewer than 100 workers and do not need significant investment. The transformation of larger state enterprises into private joint stock companies will be more gradual and require the creation of investment funds, a stock exchange (perhaps), and other organizations to handle a securities market. Whether and how fast any such plans materialize are unclear despite declarations the government is preparing a mass privatization program.

In November 1997, President Niyazov declared that the privatization of 50 state-owned enterprises, half of which are in the textile sector, would go forward. According to the EBRD, in the first seven months of 1997, 108 large and small-scale enterprises were privatized raising 63 billion *manats* ($16 million). Of these, 93 were auctioned off, 14 taken over by worker collectives, and one was privatized through an investment tender.

3. What proportion of agriculture, housing and land, industry, and small business and services is in private hands? In 1995, state and collective farms were converted into Peasant Unions. While land has been leased to farmers, they are permitted to hold only an estimated three hectares which cannot be traded. The government retains control over all inputs, access to irrigation and equipment, pricing, transportation and international markets. Land remains controlled by the state. A 1996 law makes Turkmen eligible to own land, but does not grant them the right to sell, exchange, or transfer it. Housing has been privatized to a modest extent and remains heavily subsidized by the government. Industry remains overwhelmingly state-controlled. Most of the tiny service sector was privatized after 1993. According to the U.S. Department of Commerce, there are 23,500 private enterprises operating in Turkmenistan. In the first nine months of 1997, entrepreneurs produced goods and services valued at $49.1 million.

4. What has been the extent of insider (management, labor and nomenklatura) participation in the privatization process? What explicit and implicit preferences have been awarded to insiders? Privatization has not been a priority for the Turkmen authorities. There is no data available on insider participation in the privatization process. Of the 1,856 small enterprises privatized by the end of 1996, one-third went to individuals while the remainder became cooperatives. According to the EBRD, large-scale privatization is usually initiated by line ministries, which formally hold the ownership rights in public enterprises. In 1996, six departments of the Ministry of Agriculture, which is responsible for the bulk of industrial enterprises outside the energy sector; mainly textiles and food processing, were turned into so-called associations that are to act as holding companies in its care. Proposals are submitted to the privatization agency and decided upon by an inter-governmental committee. The incentives for the associations to initiate privatization are contradictory: while attracting a foreign investor can significantly ease access to foreign exchange and government concessions, all sales revenues accrue to the Ministry of Finance and the Council of Ministers, which must approve majority private ownership and can cancel contracts within three months of agreement.

5. How much public awareness of and support for privatization has there been? What is the

nature of support and opposition to privatization by major interest groups? Information on privatization and the functioning of a market economy is not widely available due to the government's information policy and its fundamental hostility to the process. As Turkmenistan is an effectively closed society, it is impossible to determine which groups support or oppose privatization. The steady economic decline the country has experienced, particularly since 1996, may, however, induce a change in policy. It appears possible that Turkmenistan may be forced to follow International Monetary Fund recommendations in order to receive a stand-by loan to stabilize the economy.

Macroeconomics 6.25/7

1. Has the taxation system been reformed? (What areas have and have not been overhauled? To what degree are taxpayers complying? Is tax compliance difficult to achieve? Has the level of revenues increased? Is the revenue-collection body overburdened? What is the overall tax burden?) The government is trying to broaden the tax base in the face of a massive shortfall in gas revenue, particularly in 1997. Although international lending institutions and individual donor countries have undertaken to support the government's avowed desire to do so, it is unclear if a reformed tax system is a government priority. The existing tax system has been built on an *ad hoc* basis without concern for the practical possibility of implementation. Changes to the contradictory and often incoherent tax system were made in 1997, but details are unavailable. Although income and corporate taxes range from 25 percent to 35 percent, there are no tax laws detailing specific rates, liability, and collection procedures. As a result, rates often are applied arbitrarily. The government also imposes a 20 percent value added tax and various taxes on foreign exchange earnings and capital gains. No data on tax compliance is available.

2. Does fiscal policy encourage private savings, investment and earnings? (Has there been any reform/alteration of revenue and budget policies? How large are budget deficits and overall debt? Is there financing of the social insurance/pension system sustainable? What proportion of the budget is taken up by subsidies to firms and individuals)? Private savings, investment and earnings are negligible for most Turkmen citizens who are struggling to meet basic necessities. The government routinely presents ambitious targets which it fails to meet. Major expenditure items are also off-budget, thereby distorting the real versus reported deficit. Delayed payment of wages and pensions, a regular feature of post-Communist Turkmenistan, also serves to artificially improve appearances on the expenditure side. There is no data on the size of the budget deficit. The authorities aim for a 1.4 percent overall fiscal deficit in 1998; in 1997, the target was 0.9 percent. The outcome remains unreported for 1997.

According to the EBRD, the social security system is partly financed by payroll taxes set at 30 percent of wages in the enterprise sector and 20 percent in agricultural associations. The largest components of the social security system are subsidized basic goods, public pensions provided to approximately 425,000 people in 1995, family allowances, and an employment guarantee. In 1996, price subsidies amounted to 4.2 percent of budgetary expenditures and 15 percent to pensions. Another 12 percent was spent on health and education, but because of generally low revenues, social expenditures as a share of GDP did not exceed 3-4 percent. EBRD notes thatconsiderable pressure on the social security system may be anticipated as a result of demographic developments.

The employment guarantee is particularly problematic considering the country's high population growth and significant excess employment in the state sector.

3. Has there been banking reform? (Is the central bank independent? What are its responsibilities? Is it effective in setting and/or implementing monetary policy? What is the actual state of the private banking sector? Does it conform to international standards? Are depositors protected?) Banking by Western standards is still in its infancy in Turkmenistan. The central bank is not independent, but acts as the government's main lending institution. It attempts to implement monetary policy, but lacks the necessary mechanisms and authority to do so. A total of 67 banks, including state and commercial, local and foreign, have registered with the Central Bank of Turkmenistan. This includes two state banks, 52 state agricultural banks, and 13 commercial banks. According to the EBRD, three major state banks established in the 1980s dominate the financial sector with control of over 83 percent of bank credits. As of December 1996, 90 percent of bank credit was extended to state enterprises, which also hold most bank deposits. Bank supervision was strengthened in 1996. The minimum reserve requirements were increased to manat 500 million from 100 million in July 1997. There is no depositor insurance in Turkmenistan.

An Interbank training center was established in 1995 to train staff for commercial banks. An estimated 300 students have gone through its program. In June 1997, the government established the Interbank Council to oversee the reorganization of the banking system. The status of this endeavor and the government's commitment to such a reorganization are uncertain.

4. How sound is the national currency? (Is the value of the currency fixed or does it float? How convertible is the currency? How large are the hard currency reserves? Has the exchange rate policy been stable and predictable?) Turkmenistan introduced it currency, the manat, in November 1993. The Central Bank has declared its desire to unify Turkmenistan's two exchange rates and attempted to do so unsuccessfully in January and April 1996. The main foreign exchange market is controlled by the Central Bank and government. Access to foreign exchange auctions is limited, allowing the Central Bank to set the official rate. There is also a smaller foreign-exchange market operated by commercial banks. The commercial bank of the generally values the manat at 30 percent below the official rate. The black market rate runs slightly below the commercial bank rate. According to the EBRD, since January 1997 the central bank has aimed at stabilizing both the exchange rate and the domestic price level by injecting additional foreign exchange (approximately $15 million per week) into the banking sector. The size of Turkmenistan's hard currency reserves are not known but were estimated to be $1 billion by the U.S. Department of Commerce in August 1997.

5. Is there a functioning capital market infrastructure? (Are there existing or planned commodities, bond and stock markets? What are the mechanisms for investment and lending? What government bodies have authority to regulate capital markets?) Capital markets are undeveloped in Turkmenistan. There is a State Commodity Exchange in Ashgabat. There is no stock market in Turkmenistan. The government has been selling small amounts of Treasury bonds to local commercial banks since August 1996.

Microeconomics 6.25/7

1. Are property rights guaranteed? (Are there both formal and de facto protections of private real estate and intellectual property? Is there a land registry with the authority and capability to ensure accurate recording of who owns what? What are the procedures for expropriation, including measures for compensations and challenge? Have any seizures taken place?) The concept of private property and its protection is not well known or widely accepted in Turkmenistan. The government has been working on developing a civil code, dubbed the "economic constitution" by the authorities, which will guarantee property rights. It is expected to be adopted in 1998, though details are unavailable. A genuine real estate market does not exist; citizens may own property but cannot sell, trade, or transfer it. Commercial businesses exist and are protected under a contradictory mix of laws and regulations.

2. To what extent have prices been liberalized? What subsidies remain? According to the EBRD, during the course of 1995 and 1996, Turkmenistan's formerly comprehensive system of price controls was loosened significantly. A wide range of basic goods, including meat, sugar, vegetable oil, tea, bread, salt, and flour, were subsidized until spring 1998. In March 1998, although accompanied by wage increases, subsidies were removed from the prices of all items sold in state shops, except for flour and meat. Price controls still apply to energy, public services (rent, heating and water), telecommunications, transport, and selected construction materials.

3. Is it possible to own and operate a business? (Has there been legislation regarding the formation, dissolution and transfer of businesses, and is the law respected? Do there exist overly cumbersome bureaucratic hurdles that effectively hinder the ability to own and dispose of a business? Are citizens given access to information on commercial law? Is the law applied fairly? Does regulation (or licensing requirements) impose significant costs on business and consumers? Do they create significant barriers to entry and seriously hamper competition?) Small businesses in the trade and service sector are permitted. The laws which regulate them, including numerous presidential decrees, legislative acts, and administrative rules are not only contradictory, but changes are often applied retroactively. Private citizens are poorly informed concerning commercial law and there are few private lawyers available to provide them with professional advice. Although a bankruptcy law was passed in June 1992, few companies have been forced into bankruptcy to date. The state retains extensive influence and coercive power over the private sector. For example, it has reserved the right to control employment in privatized enterprises. Licensing procedures involve navigating a corrupt bureaucracy. Turkmenistan's economy remains overwhelmingly state-owned and domestic competition is weak.

4. Are courts effective, transparent, efficient and quick in reaching decisions on property and contract disputes? What alternative mechanisms for adjudicating disputes exist? The court system is unreformed. It lacks the resources, independence, and experience necessary to handle commercial disputes. While private parties generally believe that courts may recognize their legal rights against other private parties, they do not believe that courts would enforce such rights against the state. Disputes tend to be resolved through informal channels, not institutionalized ones.

5. Is business competition encouraged? (Are monopolistic practices limited in law and in practice? If so, how? To what degree is "insider" dealing a hindrance to opencompetition? Are government procurement policies open and unbiased?) The state dominates the most profitable, and potentially profitable, sectors of the economy such as energy, agriculture, and industry. Competition is an alien concept and can be seen only to a very modest extent among small businesses which have cropped up. Competition has been introduced to government contracts through international tenders. Previously, they were awarded for purely political reasons, and some still are.

6. To what extent has international trade been liberalized? To what degree has there been simplification/overhaul of customs and tariff procedures, and are these applied fairly? What informal trade barriers exist? Turkmenistan is not a member of any free trade arrangements. There are formally few quota restrictions on imports and exports, but most foreign trade is subject to licensing. Centralized state trading remains a prevalent influence on both foreign trade and production. Outside this system, licenses can be obtained for most imports and exports. Import duties, however, can be very high — (up to 100 percent in selected categories of consumer goods). Since 1994, all domestic and foreign export transactions with the exception of natural gas, and all imports by public enterprises, by law, have to be processed or registered and endorsed at the official State Commodity Exchange.

According to the U.S. Department of Commerce, excise taxes constitute the most significant trade barriers; in 1997, the number of items subject to excise taxes rose from 11 to 104. Delays, paperwork, and corruption constitute informal trade barriers. Although Turkmenistan has established several free economic zones, they are not well utilized due to infrastructure problems

7. To what extent has foreign investment and capital flow been encouraged or constrained? Turkmenistan officially welcomes foreign investment in all areas. Since the passage of a new law on hydrocarbon resources in March 1997, the government has been actively courting energy mul tinationals to participate in the development of Turkmenistan's large oil and gas reserves in particular, through production sharing agreements and as minority joint venture partners. Corruption, forced contract renegotiation, poor infrastructure, and geopolitical realities, notably U.S. policy toward Iran, have dampened investors' ardor to enter the market in Turkmenistan. The tax and legal environment are less than fully satisfactory. According to the profit tax law, foreign investors must pay: a 25 percent profit tax; a 15 percent tax on income and dividends, interest, copyrights, licenses, leases, royalties, and other income earned in any sector of the economy; and a 6 percent tax on income from international cargo transport. These burdens are mutable under varying circumstances.

8. Has there been reform of the energy sector? (To what degree has the energy sector been restructured? Is the energy sector more varied, and is it open to private competition? Is the country overly dependant on one or two other countries for energy [including whether exported fuels must pass through one or more countries to reach markets]?) The energy sector like the agricultural sector is of prime economic importance to Turkmenistan and has not been restructured. The country has huge natural gas reserves, the fourth largest in the world, as well as its substantial on and off-shore oil deposits. It is controlled by the Office of the President. Traditionally, some two-thirds of Turkmenistan's budget comes directly from gas export revenues.

Turkmenistan seeks significant investment and Western participation in the exploration, exploitation, and transport of Turkmenistan's hydrocarbons. Legislation passed to encourage this was passed in 1997, after it became apparent Turkmenistan could not become a new Kuwait, as it declared its intention to do, without attracting foreign investment. The need for doing so was underscored in 1997 when gas production and exports fell to an all-time low due to a pricing and transport disagreement with Russia's Gazprom.

Aside from a small pipeline to Iran which became operational in 1997, Turkmenistan remains dependent upon exporting its gas via the Russian pipeline system. Russia has thwarted Turkmenistan's ambitions to sell its gas to hard-currency paying Western countries and instead directed the flow to insolvent Commonwealth of Independent States countries in the South Caucasus and Ukraine. In the face of this, Turkmenistan has declared its desire to export gas via Iran to Turkey, via Iran or Afghanistan to Pakistan and India, and potentially under the Caspian Sea to Azerbaijan from whence it would cross Georgia into Turkey. All of these potential export routes remain problematic for political and commercial reasons.

UKRAINE

Freedom in the World Ratings, 1989-1998

	1989-90	1990-91	1991-92	1992-93	1993-94	1994-95	1995-96	1996-97	1997-98
Political Rights	-	-	3	3	4	3	3	3	3
Civil Liberties	-	-	3	3	4	4	4	4	4
Status	-	-	PF	PF	PF	PF	PF	PF	PF

Polity: Transitional
Economy: Transitional
Population: 51,148,000
PPP: $2,361
Ethnic Groups: Ukrainian (73 percent), Russian (22 percent), others
Capital: Kyiv

Political Process 3.50/7

1. When did national legislative elections occur? Were they free and fair? How were they judged by domestic and international election monitoring organizations? Who composes the government? The most recent elections for the 450-seat unicameral parliament, the *Verkhovna Rada*, were held on March 29, 1998 in accordance with a new election law, adopted in December 1997. The law changed the previous majoritarian system into proportionate-majoritarian model, with 225 seats to be filled by winners in majoritarian constituencies and the other 225 seats filled by candidates on election lists of political parties and blocs who manage to clear 4 percent threshold for representation. The new election law abolished the 50 percent turnout provision that resulted in numerous runs-off in the 1994 elections, and political parties were given a significant role in the election process for the first time. In all, 21 parties and nine blocs competed in the elections, but only eight received the necessary 4 percent of the votes. The new parliament has eight factions: the Communist faction (121 seats), the bloc of the Socialist and Peasant parties (35 seats), the Rukh faction (47 seats), the Hromada faction (40 seats), the Green Party faction (24 seats), the People's Democratic Party faction (92 seats), the Progressive Socialist faction (16 seats), the faction of the Socialist Democratic Party (United) (25 seats), as well as 39 independent MPs. Re-elections were ordered in several constituencies where the elections were judged invalid by courts due to a number of violations. Although national and international observers (like the nongovernmental Committee of Ukrainian Electors and the OSCE mission) reported violations of the election law (for instance, the lack of space where voters could mark their choices in privacy), the elections were considered free and fair. A major problem was the ineligibility of some 80,000 to 140,000 Crimean Tatars. After the Law "On Election of People's Deputies to the Supreme Council of the Autonomous Republic of the

Crimea" was adopted, actions of civic disobedience, organized by the Crimean Tatar Medjlis, took place in a number of Crimean cities and towns in February-March 1998. Crimean Tatar leaders demanded to maintain the 1994 law "On Election of People's Deputies of the Supreme Council of the Crimea" which granted proportional representation of all former forcibly displaced ethnic groups. In 1994, the Ukrainian legislature made an exception for non-citizens, allowing them to vote at their places of permanent residence, and Crimean Tatars had 14 representatives in the previous Crimean parliament. At its final session on March 24, 1998, the Ukrainian parliament voted down an amendment to the Law "On Election of People's Deputies to the Supreme Council of the Autonomous Republic of the Crimea" designed to permit over 80,000 non-citizen Crimean Tatars to take part in the general and local elections. The rejection of the amendment, mainly due to the vote of Communists and other left-wingers, caused clashes with law-enforcement forces. The Ukrainian government is not formed by a victorious political party or by a coalition. Instead, a prime minister, nominated by the president and approved by the parliament, selects candidates for ministerial positions and submit the nominations to the president for appointment. Therefore, the parliament has practically no control over the government, and its only lever of influence is to reject a nominated candidate for the position of the prime minister or to reject the government's program. Ukrainian Prime Minister Valery Pustovoitenko, who succeeded the ousted Pavlo Lazarenko in July 1997, belongs to the pro-presidential People's Democratic Party (PDP) and, though not formally the party leader, was the lead candidate in the party's election list for the March 1998 parliamentary elections.

2. When did presidential elections occur? Were they free and fair? The first presidential election was held on December 1, 1991. Of 95 candidates allowed to collect petition signatures, seven managed to collect the needed minimum of 100,000 signatures to register as candidates. Then-chairman of the Verkhovna Rada, Leonid Kravchuk, won 61.6 percent of the votes, Rukh leader Vyacheslav Chornovil obtained 23.2 percent, national democrat Levko Lukianenko got 4.5 percent, pro-market economist Volodymyr Hryniov received 4.2 percent, academician Igor Yukhnovsky, MP, obtained 1.7 percent, and chairman of the People's Party of Ukraine Leonid Taburiansky, MP, won 0.6 percent of the votes cast. Seven candidates competed in the second presidential elections held on June 26, 1994. In the July 10 run-off, former Prime Minister Leonid Kuchma defeated incumbent President Leonid Kravchuk, winning 52 percent of the vote. The elections were judged free and fair by international observers and the IFES. The next presidential election will be held in October 1999. In September 1996, President Kuchma virtually announced the start of a new presidential campaign by telling the press that he intended to run for a second term.

3. Is the election system multiparty-based? Are there at least two viable political parties functioning at all levels of government? There are several major political parties that function at all levels of government; eight parties managed to mobilize enough voter support to be represented in parliament. Most political parties share similar agendas with hard-to-enforce socio-economic pledges, which makes it difficult for voters to choose. Subnational and local elected bodies (councils of people's deputies), also comprise representatives of different political parties and non-partisan deputies, though their election is not directly linked to party affiliation.

4. How many parties have been legalized? Are any particular parties illegal? By January 1998, 54 national political parties were formally registered with the Ministry of Justice, though many have similar agendas and many are largely based on the personalities of their leaders. In 1995, the Ministry of Justice annulled registration of the extreme right Ukrainian National Assembly-Ukrainian National Self-Defense (UNA-UNSO), but the registration was renewed after the UNA split from its paramilitary wing, the UNSO. Major political parties include: the Communist party, (led by Petro Symonenko); the Socialist party, (led by Speaker Oleksandr Moroz); the national democratic Ukrainian People's Movement Rukh, (led by Vyacheslav Chornovil); and the Hromada, (overtly oppositional to the president and government, now chaired by Pavlo Lazarenko).

5. What proportion of the population belongs to political parties? Polls conducted by the IFES in 1994 showed that the total membership of Ukraine's political parties amounted to one million people, i.e., about five percent of eligible voters. By January 1998, over two million Ukrainians were members of political parties; (by the parties' own estimates the number of active dues-paying members is much smaller).

6. What has been the trend of voter turnout at the municipal, provincial and national levels in recent years? Voter turnout has dropped gradually from over 84 percent in the 1991 presidential election to 76 percent in the first round of the 1994 parliamentary election, 61 percent in the second round. In subsequent rounds, the turnout usually was slightly over 50 percent. In many areas, especially Kyiv, Kharkiv, Luhansk and southern part of Ukraine, turnouts at the run-offs were significantly lower — 42-44 percent— as voters seemed apathetic about taking part in repeated run-offs. There were two rounds of the 1994 presidential elections with voter turnout of 68 percent and 71 percent, respectively. The pattern remained in the March 1998 parliamentary and local elections. The voter turnout differed from over 70 percent in Western Ukraine (Ternopil, Lviv, Ivano-Frankivsk) to slightly over 40 percent in Kyiv and the Crimea.

Civil Society 4.25/7

1. How many non-governmental organizations have come into existence since 1988? How many charitable/non-profit organizations? Are there locally led efforts to increase philanthropy and volunteerism? What proportion of the population is active in private voluntary activity (from polling data?) Under the law, NGOs (officially referred to in Ukraine as "public associations of citizens") may be registered by the Ministry of Justice and state authorities on regional and local levels. While statistics of national and international NGOs are maintained by the Ministry of Justice, it is rather complicated to obtain accurate data about subnational NGOs. About 3 percent of NGOs are registered as national organizations, about 40 percent are regional, and 30 percent are local organizations. The rest are registered as international NGOs, and many are not registered at all. By the end of 1997, there were over 4,000 registered NGOs. These include over 800 national and international associations, about 300 charities, 36 national youth organizations, 20 national and 92 subnational environmental groups, 61 national minority organizations, 76 art and culture groups and fund, 215 women's groups, 17 human rights organizations, 24 religious organizations, and 22 national charity foundation (most of them with foreign support), as well as 29 public organizations to help victims of Chernobyl. There are also 23 national organizations aiming at helping the disabled and the elderly. Currently, there are 125 non-governmental colleges. Most NGOs operate in major cities including Kyiv (20 percent), Kharkiv (17 percent), Lviv (8.5 percent), Odesa (8.3 percent), and Donetsk (5.5 percent). Philanthropy and volunteerism are not developed in terms of traditions and institutions and are usually connected to election or other publicity campaigns.

2. What is the legal and regulatory environment for NGOs (i.e., ease of registration, legal rights, government regulation, taxation, procurement and access-to-information issues)? To what extent is NGO activism focused on improving the legal and regulatory environment? The draft Law on Non-governmental Organizations is still under discussion in the Verkhovna Rada, and current legislation that regulates the NGO environment does not distinguish between NGOs, political parties, and public associations. Registration of an NGO is onerous and complicated by a large number of documents to be submitted to the local state administration, the local executive committee, or the Ministry of Justice (for national and international NGOs). Registration takes at least two months after all documents i.e., application, four copies of statute documents, minutes of the foundation meeting, information about founders and administration, receipt of payment of registration fee are submitted to the registration body. Then, within a month, the NGO must be registered with the Department of Statistics, the State Taxation Administration, the bank where the NGO's account is opened, the Ministry of the Interior (the department that authorizes making the organization's seal), the Social Insurance Fund, and the Pension Fund. All these authorities also require submission of a number of documents and fees. If the procedure is not completed within a month, the new NGO may be fined by any of the above-mentioned bodies. Due to the lack of clearly identified status, NGOs are effectively excluded from government procurement operations. Formally, tax exemption exists for charities, in accordance with the Law on Charity and Charity Organizations adopted in September 1997, but the provision is not used in practice due to the juridical deficiencies in the law. The draft Civil Code, currently debated by the parliament, does not contain any reference to non-governmental organizations. Currently a number of public policy NGOs, namely the Institute of Civil Society and the Pylyp Orlyk Institute for Democracy, focus on improving the legal and regulatory environment by means of offering expert analysis and alternative draft legislation on NGO issues. Their efforts are undermined by the lack of understanding and support on the part of the government and parliament. Many NGOs that could effectively lobby improvements of NGO status — primarily, veterans organizations and women's groups — rely heavily on state support, while most of educational, children's and sports groups are profit-making organizations.

3. What is the organizational capacity of NGOs? Do management structures clearly delineate authority and responsibility? Is information available on NGO management issues in the native language? Is there a core of experienced practitioners/trainers to serve as consultants or mentors to less developed organizations? Ukrainian NGOs constitute a small and underdeveloped sector; they do not always stick to a strict formal management pattern with clearly specified authority and responsibilities of every member and/or employee. Ukrainian-language information on NGO management issues is available free of charge in major cities and regional centers but is practically absent in smaller towns and rural areas. A dozen foreign assistance programs and joint Ukrainian-

Western projects provide experienced trainers that may serve as consultants to new and developing NGOs.

4. Are NGOs financially viable? What is their tax status? Are they obliged to and do they typically disclose revenue sources? Do government procurement opportunities exist for private, not-for-profit providers of services? Most NGOs rely on state support or grants from foreign sources. Tax benefits exist only for a limited number of veterans', Chernobyl victims', and children's organizations. NGOs are obliged to disclose revenue sources, and most of them do so when acknowledging support for particular activities and in their reports. Government procurement opportunities for private, not-for-profit providers of services are virtually non-existent.

5. Are there free trade unions? How many workers belong to these unions? Is the number of workers belonging to trade unions growing or decreasing? What is numerical/proportional membership of farmers groups, small business associations, etc.? The trade union movement comprises a number of organizations that differ in their relations with employers and the state. These include the official Federation of Trade Unions (a successor to former Soviet state-sponsored trade unions, 20.8 million members), and the National Confederation of Trade Unions (three million). Most trade unions remain mandatory formations at every enterprise and institution, where employers, managers, and workers are members of the same unions. The National Confederation also includes some independent trade unions: the Free Trade Unions of Miners of Donbas, the aviators' PALS, and the Solidarnist federation of regional trade unions that unite workers of co-operatives, as well as small and medium joint-stock entities. Though the Association of Free Trade Unions of Ukraine dissolved due to internal conflicts in April 1996, its constituent unions, including miners, sailors, civil air dispatchers, aviation ground crews, scientists, and locomotive engineers have a total membership of about 150,000. Over 70 percent (up to 97 percent in the state-owned sector) of the labor force is unionized, though membership is mostly formal. Trade unions are practically non-existent in private small and medium businesses. The number of trade union members has been decreasing due to trade unions' inability to protect interests of their members. Farmers' groups exist on local levels but they are not numerous and unite about five percent of farmers. There are only three significant private farmers' groups. The left-wing Peasants' Party and the centrist Agrarian Party claim to represent interests of collective and independent farmers, respectively. Groups representing small and medium business interests have sprouted to lobby through 19 national and some 150 subnational associations of entrepreneurs. An accurate figure for overall membership in these groups does not exist.

6. What forms of interest group participation in politics are legal? What types of interest groups are active in the political and policy process? Legal forms of interest group participation in politics include political parties, business, other public associations, and trade unions. Veterans, Chernobyl groups, minority organizations, and the pensioners seek to influence policy-making mostly by public protests. Businesses and managers of the state-owned agrarian sector lobby their interests through their MPs and political parties. In particular, the "directors' lobby" of large state-owned enterprises and major collective and state farm seeks to influence policy process by means of running for seats in the parliament.

7. How is the not-for-profit/NGO sector perceived by the public and government officials? What is the nature of media coverage of NGOs? To what extent do government officials engage with NGOs? Both the public and governmental officials tend to underestimate the importance of the not-for-profit/NGO sector in handling tasks that the government cannot do or is unwilling to do. NGOs that control distribution of humanitarian assistance and funds are regarded by national and local governments as a welcome ally. Some new NGOs have been established and are run by political leaders. Some governmental institutions, particularly the Ministry of Social Security and the Ministry of Justice, try to engage (or control) NGOs, while other ministries and departments tend to ignore NGOs. Government officials seek the advice of NGO experts (often informally), participate in events organized by NGOs, and receive NGO publications and research materials. Media coverage is usually positive or neutral, depending on affiliation of the NGO.

Independent Media 4.75/7

1. Are there legal protections for press freedom? A 1991 press law declares protection of freedom of speech, but refers only to print media. The constitution (June 28, 1996), the Law on Information (October 1992), and the Television and Radio Broadcasting Law (February 1994) have provisions for freedom of speech, and though overt censorship is illegal, most official and formally independent media are reluctant to publish materials critical of the government. Since most of the print media use state-owned publishing houses and the distribution system, and broadcasters utilize state-owned frequencies and air time, overt censorship is substituted by economic levers of influence. Freedom of the press is limited by the Criminal Code (persecution for "degrading a person's honor and dignity," or "deliberate humiliation"), the Law on Operative-Investigation Work and the Regulation on the General Department for Protection of State Secrets in the Mass Media. The 1994 Television and Radio Broadcasting Law also prohibits dissemination of "state secrets" and envisages liability for "ungrounded refusal to provide relevant information" to law- enforcement agencies and "intentional concealment of information." After his election, President Kuchma disbanded the Council on Broadcast Media on the grounds that this regulatory agency had been biased toward his predecessor.

2. Are there penalties in the law for libeling officials? Are there legal penalties for "irresponsible" journalism? Have these laws been enforced to harass journalists? The law does not explicitly forbid libeling the state's leadership and officials (except for the president) but imposes disciplinary, administrative and criminal liability for "damaging the honor and dignity of a person." Article 125 of the Criminal Code prescribes imprisonment of up to five years for libel. An editor of the *Opositsiya* newspaper, Ivan Makar, was given a two year suspended sentence in 1996 for libeling the president and his staff. His appeal was rejected, and in 1997, a higher court confirmed the sentence. In May 1993, the parliament amended the legislation with a ban on false information "damaging the business reputation of citizens and organizations." A criminal case was opened against Crimean journalist Tatyana Korobova on charges of libeling Crimean MP Lev Mirimskiy who protested against her writing about his criminal connections. The Law on State Secrets specifies an extensive list of topics that may not be addressed by the media. In May 1997, the cabinet adopted a regulation that further defined state secrets to include information on executions, the state of prisons, pretrial detention blocks, and centers for the forcible treatment of alcoholics. Some journalists say they have experienced intimidation, including the threat of arrest, and violent assaults for reporting on crime and official corruption. According to journalists, the deaths of two prominent colleagues — *Kievskiye Vedomosti* correspondent from Luhansk, Petro Shevchenko, and editor of the newspaper *Vechernaya Odesa* Borys Derevyanko — were linked to their journalistic investigations. Journalists believe that a large percentage of the 42 crimes committed against the press community in 1996 and the first half of 1997 was linked to their professional activities.

3. What proportion of the media is privatized? What are the major private newspapers, television stations, and radio stations? There are about 5,500 registered printed media in Ukraine, 70 percent of them are established and co-owned by state entities. Some 25 percent are owned by "working collectives," which in practice means they use funds from sources that choose to remain unnamed. About five percent of print and electronic media are private investments. Some 1,700 newspapers and magazines are disseminated to two and more regions of the country — 451 of them are nation-wide publications — while the rest are local. Only 700 publications have a circulation of 10,000 copies or more. Due to rising subscription rates, overall circulation has dropped dramatically from 63.7 million in 1992 to slightly over 15 million in 1996, with a continued decrease in 1997. There are 25 regional and two national state-owned television and radio stations, and over 70 commercial stations. Many of regional mass media are biased and controlled by regional officials. Of the 451 nation-wide newspapers disseminated through subscription, 208 are published in Ukrainian. There are also a few state-sponsored national minority publications and broadcasts. The official Ukrainian National Information Agency has to compete with independent Interfax-Ukraina, UNIAR, UNIAN, the Ukrainian Press Agency, Nova Mova, and the International Media Center. The major privately-owned media include the newspapers *Zerkalo Nedeli* and *Den*, TV channels Studio 1+1, Inter, and STB, and radio stations Radio Kievskiye Vedomosti, Nashe Radio, Music Radio, and Radio Lux.

4. Are the private media financially viable? Most private media are financially viable, although they have to compete with state-owned media, which are exempt from high taxes and provided with a number of other benefits under the 1994 Law on State Support for the Press. Though private media pay higher taxes and remain substantially dependent on state-owned printing facilities and distribution system, the emergent trend has been the improvement of their financial viability due to attraction of business funds, advertising, and increasing numbers of subscribers and readers. Advertising rates are high, and many newspapers have successfully increased the volume of their advertising, but the revenues raised from advertising are a closely guarded secret.

5. Are the media editorially independent? Are the media's news gathering functions affected by interference from the government or private owners? State-owned media generally reflect government views. Major private media tend to be less biased than state-owned media, though their contents are often controlled by owners and sponsors. Independent, party and business publications often express views at odds with the official line. The news gathering functions of the media are affected by interference from the government. The Law on State Secrets delineates a number of issues off limits to journalists. Private owners often discourage journalists from gathering information that may affect their financial or political supporters.

6. Is the distribution system for newspapers privately or governmentally controlled? Most newspapers and magazines are disseminated through state-owned press kiosks, though there are privately owned newsstands at train stations and other public locations. About 50 percent of the total circulation of newspapers is disseminated by subscription through the state postal service, Ukrposhta.

7. What proportion of the population is connected to the Internet? Are there any restrictions on Internet access to private citizens? Accurate figures are unavailable. The estimated proportion of Internet users among the population is about 0.5 percent, mainly due to a small number of private computers, relatively expensive service (about $4 per hour on-line), and poor quality of telecommunications links. There are no formal restrictions on Internet access to private citizens.

8. What has been the trend in the press freedom as measured by Freedom House's *Survey of Press Freedom*? Freedom House's annual *Survey of Press Freedom* rated Ukraine "Partly Free" from 1992 through 1997. In 1998, the media in Ukraine remain "Partly Free."

Governance and Public Administration 4.75/7

1. Is the legislature the effective rule-making institution? Although the new constitution set the framework for distribution of powers between the president and the parliament, it did not limit the president's control over key appointments, his direct supervision of regional authorities, and the power to issue decrees and competencies which the president had wrested from parliament under the constitutional agreement on June 7, 1995. The presence of 11 parliamentary factions, several dozen MPs who combine work in the parliament with other duties, and internal conflicts between the left and right wings hinder parliament's lawmaking ability. While the parliament passes laws, the president also has lawmaking initiative and power of decree, and the Cabinet of Ministers may adopt decisions that sometimes change the meaning of laws. The previous parliament voted down a package of taxation changes and a radical pro-market budget introduced by the government, and explicitly blamed the executive for the economic crisis and the deterioration of living standards. A strong anti-presidential coalition is likely to function in the new parliament, but it will not have a majority and is being challenged by a strong pro-presidential wing. In practice it means that the new parliament may be even less able to engage in effective lawmaking than its predecessor.

2. Is substantial power decentralized to subnational levels of government? What specific authority do subnational levels have? In August 1994 a presidential decree made local councils and their executive committees ultimately subservient to the president. Heads of regional state administrations — local representatives of the President — hold real power in the regions. According to Article 143 of the constitution and the 1992 Law on Local Councils and Local Self-Governance (amended in 1994 and 1995), territorial communities of village, towns and city — Councils of People's

Deputies — deal with purely local issues such as the establishment of communal enterprises and organizations and control over their activities; development and implementation of local social and cultural projects; and management of communal property. They adopt and control budgets or their territorial unit and establish local taxes. District and regional councils adopt programs of social, economic, and cultural development, and set and control district's and region's budgets. Powers of a local councils may be terminated by parliament if it decides that the council's actions contradict Ukrainian law. The Crimean authorities are granted greater powers than those of any of Ukraine's other regions. The Crimean Council of Ministers operates a budget approved by the Crimean parliament with a substantial degree of independence from central authorities. The Crimean parliament often adopts bills at odds with the national legislation.

3. Are subnational officials chosen in free and fair elections? The structure of local administration is rather complex: it consists of 24 regions (oblasts), divided into "cities-of-oblast-importance" that may consist of several boroughs, and districts (rayons), divided into villages and towns. Members of local councils are elected directly, and the 1998 elections were held at the same time and the same polling stations as the parliamentary elections. Oblast and rayon councils are elected through majoritarian multi-member constituencies while other councils are elected through majoritarian single-member constituencies. Chairmen of city, town, village and borough councils are elected directly through majoritarian constituencies. Local elections, judged by international observers of the OSCE and the IFES as free and fair, were held simultaneously with parliamentary elections on March 29, 1998.

4. Do the executive and legislative bodies operate openly and with transparency? Is draft legislation easily accessible to the media and the public? Independent auditing agencies do not exist, the media are often not allowed to cover committee sessions, and parliamentary voting statistics are recorded irregularly, with some votes taken in closed session. Most documents and draft legislation are not available to the public. The media have assess to government officials and lawmakers, and parliamentary sessions are broadcast regularly on national TV and radio. Draft legislation is relatively easily accessible to the media but practically inaccessible to the public.

5. Do municipal governments have sufficient revenues to carry out their duties? Do municipal governments have control of their own local budgets? Do they raise revenues autonomously or from the central state budget? The national government collects 19 categories of taxes, including VAT, income tax, land and property taxes, and payments to social security funds. Local authorities collect 15 categories of local taxes, including communal, hotel, transport, and market taxes, that go to local budgets. In 1997, local budgets received 14.5 billion *hryvnyas* (121.5 percent of annual budget allocations) and spent 14.4 billion hryvnyas. Only three regions — Donetsk, Dnipropetrovsk, and Kharkiv — and the city of Kyiv donate to the state budget, while other regions live on subsidies from the central government. Municipal governments are traditionally short of funding. Their scarce local budgets make them heavily dependent on the state and largely limit their self-governance abilities. Only the local authorities in Kyiv and Sevastopol, as cities of state subordination, are entitled to gather their own revenues in full. The new package of taxation legislation proposed by the government and currently discussed by the parliament aims at major restructuring of the taxation system and giving local governments more power to raise their own revenues.

6. Do the elected local leaders and local civil servants know how to manage municipal governments effectively? Many of the elected local leaders and appointed local civil servants are former Communist-era apparatchiks. Most local councils lack qualified personnel, and many lack elementary management skills applicable to the changing socio-economic and political conditions. The Institute of Civil Service was established in 1993. Previously, civil servants did not receive special professional training.

7. When did the constitutional/legislative changes on local power come into effect? Has there been a reform of the civil service code/system? Are local civil servants employees of the local or central government? The Law on Local Councils of People's Deputies was adopted in March 1993 and amended in June 1994. It provides for election of heads of local councils directly by citizens and makes local councils accountable to the Cabinet of Ministers and subordinated to higher-ranking councils. Local councils' executive committees are accountable to local state administrations. A new Law on Local Self-Governance, adopted by the parliament in April 1997, stipulated that local councils' powers include management of communal property and operation of local budgets. The bill was vetoed by the president because a number of its provisions contradicted the constitution and created conditions for conflicts between local executive authorities and elected representatives. The Law on State Service, adopted in December 1993 and amended in 1995 and 1996, acts as a civil service statute and defines rights and responsibilities of civil servants. It prohibits civil servants from misusing their authority, but provides for no mechanism to enforce these prohibitions. Civil servants are subordinated to the General Department of Civil Service of the Cabinet of Ministers, though local civil servants are nominally employees of local governments. The law gives civil servants the right to acquire information within their competence from a variety of sources and grants a number of socio-economic benefits. There are seven categories and 15 ranks of civil servants; admission to the civil service and career promotion occurs through the system of a cadre reserve.

Rule of Law 4.00/7

1. Is there a post-Communist constitution? How does the judicial system interpret and enforce the constitution? Are there specific examples of judicial enforcement of the constitution in the last year? Up to mid-1996, Ukraine was governed by the 1978 Constitution of the Ukrainian Soviet Socialist Republic, modified since independence by introduction of a presidency and a multiparty system. A new constitution, based on the draft introduced by the Joint Constitutional Commission, was adopted on June 28, 1996 after a series of debates and a presidential decree to hold a referendum on the constitution on September 25, 1996. The constitution, especially provisions for the presidency and private property, was obstructed by the left, which claimed it violated rights of the "working people." The law adopting and enacting the constitution received 338 votes "for" with 18 votes "against," and five abstentions. Twenty-six MPs did not vote and 37 other members of parliament did not attend the session. However, according to Speaker Oleksandr Moroz, parliament has to adopt some 50 bills to make the new constitution function. The constitution is interpreted by the Constitutional Court. Examples of enforcement of the constitution by the Constitutional Court include introduction of a new party-based election law. Currently, the Constitutional Court is reviewing a protest by a number of MPs against the establishment of the National Bureau of Investigation (NBI) which they see as an illicit military formation. They argue that the presidential decree creating the NBI contradicted the constitution, and question the NBI's non- involvement in politics.

2. Does the constitutional framework provide for human rights? Do the human rights business and property rights? Chapter II of the constitution guarantees broad human rights and civil liberties, including political liberties, religious rights and minority rights. Article 41 stipulates private property rights, and Article 42 guarantees the right to engage in free enterprise and provides for protection of fair competition in business. Before the new constitution was adopted, several statutes and laws dealt with religious, minority, and human rights. A special parliamentary committee for human rights was established, but its powers and enforcement mechanisms remain murky. De facto private property exists but has little respect in the society, and mechanisms intended to protect it are ill-defined. In June 1995, President Kuchma decreed that an enterprise's land and buildings be included in any sale, except in the often-invoked case of historic sites. A draft condominium law proposed in mid-1995 to regulate the rights of co-owners in a building has not been adopted yet.

3. Has there been reform of the criminal code/criminal law? Who authorizes searches and issues warrants? Are suspects and prisoners beaten or abused? Are there excessive delays in the criminal justice system? Reform of the court system and civil codes continues at a slow pace. In November 1991, a new law on the prosecution redefined its powers, stripping it of many of its court oversight functions. In June 1995, Kuchma established a presidential committee on legislative initiatives and a committee to draft new versions of Ukraine's legal and criminal codes. Currently, there are two versions of the draft Criminal Code of Ukraine, one developed by experts of the Cabinet of Ministers, another prepared by the Parliamentary Committee for Law and Law Enforcement. Although both drafts have drawbacks, they are an improvement over the current Criminal Code adopted in 1960 and amended in February 1993. A March 1992 law abolished exile and deportation of Ukrainian citizens as methods of punishment. By law, citizens are allowed to appeal their arrest either to the court or to the prosecutor, and must be released if not charged within 48 hours. A prosecutor must issue an arrest warrant if detention exceeds three days. By law, searches are authorized and warrants are issued by the prosecutor, but, in July 1994 this law was amended by Kuchma's decree on organized crime that permitted police to hold suspected criminals for up to 30 days and to raid suspected criminal locations without search warrants. Although judges must initiate trials within three weeks after the charges are filed, the shortage of judges and delays in the court system have repeatedly led to violations, with suspects detained for months. Torture and abuse of prisoners is prohibited by law, but conditions in overpopulated and underfunded prisons are extreme and at odds with internationally recognized norms. According to independent reports, inmates are sometimes beaten and abused by other inmates or by prison personnel.

4. Do most judges rule fairly and impartially? How many remain from the Communist era? Though impartiality of judges is stipulated and guaranteed by law, many judges on subnational levels remain sensitive to local administrations' pressure (usually exerted in a form of a personal request or order from a high-ranking official). Local authorities provide judges with free housing. Currently there are about 5,600 judges; 35 percent of them specialize in civil law, and 65 percent in criminal law. Though an accurate number of judges who have kept their positions from the Soviet era is unavailable, it is estimated that up to 70 percent remain.

5. Are the courts free of political control and influence? Are the courts linked directly to the Ministry of Justice or any other executive body? According to the 1996 constitution, and the Law on Status of Judges, which was last amended in February 1994, the courts are totally independent and free from political control, and the judiciary is funded independently, not through the Ministry of Justice. However, since the legislature, the executive, and the judiciary have not been completely separated in Ukraine, investigation, interrogation, and prosecution remain within the scope of the executive. The attorney general and deputy attorney general are nominated by the president and confirmed by parliament. Judges are selected by parliament on the basis of recommendations of the Ministry of Justice. State and local prosecutors are appointed by the attorney general. Though the law stipulates liabilities for attempts to influence or limit independence of the judiciary, courts and prosecutors' offices, especially at oblast and local levels, seem to be closely attuned to local administrations' interests. The current system of verification and control over decisions and sentences also requires substantial changes. Although an independent bar exists, the legal profession still faces challenges in defining its role and relationship to other legal structures, as well as finding trained personnel. The judiciary is overburdened and lacks sufficient funding and staff. The Constitutional Court was established in October 1996. It consists of 18 judges who must be citizens of Ukraine, at least 40 years old, graduates in law with at least ten years of relevant professional experience, residents of Ukraine over the last 20 years, and fluent in Ukrainian. The requirement of ten years' professional experience means that all members of the Constitutional Court worked under the Soviet system. The president, parliament, and the Congress of Ukrainian Judges appoint six judges each to the Constitutional Court for a single term of nine years. The Supreme Council of Justice, established in January 1998, is an independent body designed to ensure fairness and professionalism of the judiciary. It consists of two sections: one dealing with nominations and resignations of judges, and a disciplinary section, dealing with complaints and investigation of offenses committed by judges and attorneys. The parliament, president, the Congress of Ukrainian judges, the Congress of Ukrainian Lawyers, Congress of Representatives of Ukrainian Law Schools, and Law Academics appoint three members each to the Supreme Council of Justice, and the national conference of the prosecutions officers appoints two members. Chairman of the Supreme Court, Minister of Justice and Attorney General are members of the Supreme Council of Justice by profession. Activities of this entity are funded from the national budget. A member of the Supreme Council of Justice has to be at least 35 and have at least 10 years of working experience in the judiciary, which in practice means that all members served under the Soviet regime.

6. What proportion of lawyers is in private practice? How does this compare with the previ-

ous year? Of about 50,000 legal professionals in Ukraine, about 17 percent are in private practice. The number of lawyers in private practice is increasing and many combine working for the state and individual private activity. There are 20 national and subnational associations of legal professionals. The major national lawyers' associations are the 1,500-strong Union of Ukrainian Lawyers and the Union of Ukrainian Attorneys that unites 1,250 members.

7. Does the state provide public defenders? The law grants public attorneys from the moment of detention, though private attorneys are usually hired by defendants with the means to afford them. By law, defendants are entitled to have free public attorneys only in criminal cases.

8. Has there been a comprehensive reform of anti- bias/discrimination laws, including protection of ethnic minority rights? In the fall of 1991, Article 66 of the Criminal Code of the Ukrainian SSR was amended with provisions for penalties for acts of discrimination against citizens based on their race, national origin, or religious beliefs. On November 1, 1991, parliament issued a declaration guaranteeing equal political, economic, social, and cultural rights to all individuals and nationalities in Ukraine. Article 24 of the 1996 constitution prohibits any discrimination or privileges based on race, political, religious or other views, gender, ethnic and social origin, language, or other features. Ethnic minority rights are granted by Articles 10 and 11 of the constitution and the Law on National Minorities (June 1992). The law stipulates respect for ethnic minorities' traditions, religions, and languages, and guarantees support of development of national identity and self-expression. The policy is pursued through the national and subnational committees for interethnic relations, operating within legislative bodies, through establishment of national minority advisory committees and departments within local councils and executive authorities. Ukraine's ethnic minority policy is implemented by the State Department of Nationalities; the Council of Representatives of National Minority Associations at the Department monitors the observance of ethnic minority rights. The law guarantees the right of national-cultural autonomy, education in national languages, development of national culture, the use of national symbols, celebration of national holidays and practicing national religions, and the development of literary, cultural, mass media, and education associations. In places where an ethnic minority constitutes the majority of population, the national language may be used alongside Ukrainian in state and public offices and institutions. Representatives of ethnic minorities can be elected or appointed to all levels of government. Citizens of Ukraine are free to choose their nationality and maintain relations with, and receive assistance from, representatives of their ethnic group abroad. Ukraine's national budget allocates funds for ethnic minorities' needs, including the return and re-settlement of some 300,000 representatives of ethnic minorities deported by Stalin from Ukraine.

Corruption | D

1. What is the magnitude of official corruption in the civil service? Must an average citizen pay a bribe to a bureaucrat in order to receive a service? What services are subject to bribe requests - for example, university entrance, hospital admission, telephone installation, obtaining a license to operate a business, applying for a passport or other official documents? What is the average salary of civil servants at various levels? Corruption is widespread at all levels. Many services are subject to bribery, including university entrance, hospital admission, telephone installation, licenses for operating businesses, and processing of official documents. Bribes are taken by the traffic police, by passport and visa registration offices for speeding up the procedure, and by law-enforcement officers for evading or easing punishment. Low salaries (from about 150 to 400 hryvnyas) for civil servants aggravate corruption. Omnipresent corruption in the government has damaged Ukraine's international image and put foreign assistance to Ukraine at risk. In April-September 1997, a number of large foreign investors, among them Coca-Cola, Cargill, Motorola, and Proctor&Gamble complained about corruption in the government and considered canceling investment projects. The U.S. Congress held hearings on mistreatment of American businessmen, which nearly resulted in the suspension of U.S. assistance to Ukraine.

2. Do top policy-makers (the president, ministers, vice- ministers, top court justices, and heads of agencies and commissions) have direct ties to businesses? How strong are such connections and what kind of businesses are these? According to the Law on Combatting Corruption, civil servants at all ranks may not engage in any profit-generating activities. The provision is not enforced effectively. While top officials formally resign from their positions as heads of companies or banks after their appointment, they continue to promote their interests. Numerous articles in the press disclosing corruption and business ties of top-ranking policy- makers were neither refuted nor confirmed. In July 1997, President Kuchma fired his former Dnipropetrovsk ally, Prime Minister Pavlo Lazarenko, after a series articles in Western and Ukrainian press blaming Lazarenko for rampant corruption in the government. Lazarenko was believed to have major personal stake in Ukraine's largest gas trader, the United Energy Systems, a private company, run by a friend, who benefited from government guarantees and patronage.

3. Do laws requiring financial disclosure and disallowing conflict of interests exist? Have publicized anticorruption cases been pursued? To what conclusion? There is no specific law requiring civil servants to disclose their financial affairs, but a number of high-ranking officials have done so. Such declarations tend to understate earnings and property by reporting their "official" salaries, which are relatively low. Article 12 of the Law on Civil Service (Limitations Related to Appointment to the Civil Service) bans election or appointment to a position in a state body and its apparatus of a person who, if appointed, will be directly subordinated to persons who are his or her close relatives by blood or by marriage. The Law on Combatting Corruption specifies limitations with regard to civil servants and other persons authorized to perform state functions: "a civil servant or other person authorized to perform state functions has no right to: (a) assist, using his position, an individual or legal entity in entrepreneurial activities or in receiving subsidies, subventions, loans or benefits, for the purpose of receiving illicit reward in the form of material benefits, services, privileges or other advantages; (b) engage in enterprise directly or through intermediaries, or act as a solicitor for third persons in affairs of state bodies, or do any part-time work (except research, teaching, creative activity, or medical practice); (c) be a member, personally or through a representative, of a board of governors or other executive body of enterprises, loan and finance entities, businesses, organizations, associations, societies, cooperatives engaged in enterprise. The Law on Status of a People's Deputy of Ukraine provides that an MP may not occupy any other business or service position, except teaching, research and "other creative work"; he or she may not receive gifts or awards from foreign governments or foreign and Ukrainian institutions, organizations, and enterprises irrespective of their form of ownership, "except for teaching, research, and other creative work". According to the law, the holding occupation of a paid position is incompatible with the MP's mandate and leads to annulment of his or her membership in parliament. However, the obscurity of the formulation of "other creative work" leaves the provision unenforced.

Notwithstanding numerous statements of top-ranking state officials about corruption in governmental structures and among civil servants, no major public trial of a relatively high-ranking official accused of corruption has occurred so far. Reports of regional representatives of anti-corruption divisions indicate that minor local bureaucrats and commercial structures have been brought to trial. In 1993-1997, the Ukrainian press published over 600 articles that raised the issue of corruption in the top power echelons of the state. The lack of tangible results of fighting corruption, investigative journalism notwithstanding, has led to the public perception of corruption as a phenomenon that nobody wants to tackle and which has become an inevitable part of state power.

4. What major anticorruption initiatives have been implemented? How often are anticorruption laws and decrees adopted? The first measure signed by Kuchma on July 21, 1994 was the Decree on Urgent Measures of Enhancing the Struggle Against Corruption, through which the president ordered the Ministry of the Interior, the Security Service of Ukraine, the State Customs Committee of Ukraine, the State Committee for Protection of the State Border of Ukraine, the Ukrainian National Guards, the government of the Republic of Crimea, local executive bodies, and the Prosecutor General to enhance fighting corruption. The Law on Combatting Corruption (October 1995) defines corruption as an "activity of persons authorized to perform state functions, aiming at illicit usage of their authority for receiving material benefits, services, privileges, and other advantages." The "persons authorized to perform state functions" include state officials and civil servants of all 14 levels. In April 1997, the list was amended to include members of the Ukrainian parliament, members of the Crimean parliament, elected representatives of village, town, city, district, regional councils and chairmen of district and regional councils. In April 1997, Kuchma decreed the establishment of the NBI as part of an effort to show the international community the determination to fight corruption. The NBI is in charge of "information-analytical activities aiming at finding and removing causes and conditions contributing to corruption" and broadening international cooperative efforts to confront proliferation of corruption and organized crime. NBI's key tasks include prevention of corrupt links between civil servants and officials and criminals. In accordance with the National Program for Combatting Corruption, enacted by presidential decree in April 1997, a working group of representatives of ministries, departments, and experts of the Ukrainian Academy of Legal Sciences, led by Minister of Justice of Ukraine Suzanna Stanik, developed a draft Concept of Combatting Corruption in Ukraine in 1998-2005. The draft paper was approved by the Cabinet of Ministers in February 1998, and submitted for confirmation to the president. The Law on Combatting Corruption has been amended several times, and together with other anti-corruption legislation it creates the necessary legal framework for fighting corruption. However, thus far the adoption of anti-corruption laws and decrees has produced few results.

5. How do major corruption-ranking organizations like Transparency International rate this country? Transparency International does not have a chapter in Ukraine, and has not ranked Ukraine.

Privatization 4.50/7

1. What percentage of the GDP comes from private ownership? What percentage of the labor force is employed in the private sector? How large is the informal sector of the economy? About 74.1 percent of Ukrainian enterprises belong to the nongovernmental sector, and their share in the total output is 63.3 percent. Privately-owned entities produce from 45 percent to 50 percent of the GDP (35 percent to 40 percent, according to official estimates). In 1997, the private sector produced 55 percent of the total volume of agricultural products. About 54 percent of the GDP is produced in service sector, 30 percent in processing industries, and 4.3 percent in agriculture. Officially, only 1.1 percent of the workforce is employed in the small business and service sector. The real figure is several times higher. Small businesses' contribution to the economy is 9.3 percent of the GDP. It is estimated that from 50 percent to 60 percent of the GDP is linked to the "shadow economy."

2. What major privatization legislation has been passed? What were its substantive features? The Law on Entrepreneurship (December 1991) opened the way to private enterprise by allowing individuals to own businesses. The Ukrainian Privatization Program (July 1992) set the guidelines for privatization, based on entitling every citizen of Ukraine to receive his or her share of the national wealth, represented by "privatization certificates" or vouchers. According to the privatization program, individuals were supposed to exchange their vouchers, directly or through intermediaries, for shares of enterprises being privatized. Objects of privatization included small enterprises, unfinished construction sites, wholesale and retail trade, catering, services, hotels and tourism facilities, as well as shares in medium and large state-owned enterprises reorganized into open joint-stock companies. According to the Law on Privatization of State Property (1992), objects exempt from privatization include property complexes of enterprises that produce goods and services of national importance (including the military-industrial complex), property of local authorities, land and resources, monetary and securities emission facilities, TV and radio transmitting facilities, objects of the National Space Agency, archives, memorials, national parks, railways, energy transmitting systems, and pipelines. A presidential decree On the Single System of Privatization Organs in Ukraine (February 1994) defined the hierarchy of national and subnational privatization authorities and their responsibilities; a decree On Introduction of Privatization Certificates (April 1994) determined the order of mass voucher privatization; a decree On Measures to Ensure Privatization in 1995 (June 1995) defined the program and scope of privatization for 1995 and allowed foreigners to participate in the privatization of enterprises on equal terms with Ukrainians. Changes and amendments to the Law on Limiting Monopolism and Preventing Unfair Competition in Entrepreneurial Activity (July 1995) prohibited actions that might limit competition. Changes and amendments to the 1992 Law on Privatization of Small State-Owned Enterprises (Small Privatization) (approved in May 1996) defined branches to be privatized in the first turn: processing and local industries, production of construction materials, light and food industries, building industry, some types of transportation, retail trade, public catering, and services. The Law On Specific Features of Privatization of Property in the Agro-Industrial Complex (July 1996) stipulated the order of privatization of the most attractive agro- industrial property. The new privatization program, ratified in February 1998, stated for the first time that the share price is to be based on supply and demand, i.e., above and below par value. Privatization certificates or vouchers, introduced in April 1994, represented individual portions of the aggregated national wealth and were the main method of privatization. They were to be given to all citizens through their local branches of the State Savings Bank and could be exchanged for shares in enterprises being privatized. To date, 45 million people, over 90 percent of the population, have collected their vouchers, and 37 million have invested them directly or through intermediaries in certificate auctions. Some 46 percent of shares in about 7,000 privatized medium and large enterprises were sold to employees and other individuals for vouchers. Privatization of small-scale properties through sale at auction for cash instead of vouchers may be hampered by a 1997 taxation authority decree that stipulated such sales would be subject to 20 percent VAT. In late-1997 to early-1998, the whole privatization process was virtually halted when lawmakers opposed to the previous presidential nominee for the position of chairman of the State Property Fund passed a resolution freezing privatization contracts.

3. What proportion of agriculture, housing and land, industry, and business and services is in private hands? *Agriculture:* By January 1, 1998, the number of private farms was 35,900, an increase of 600 from the previous year. Privatization in agriculture has been slowed by the lack of legislation on mass privatization of land. Currently, there are about 8,000 major collective farms, of which 50 percent are closed stock companies. According to the deputy prime minister for the agrarian sector, nearly half of the Ukraine's agrarian enterprises are bankrupt.

Housing and Land: As of mid-1997, about 60 percent of apartments belonging to the state housing stock were privatized. Rural population (32 percent of the whole) owns 340 million square meters of housing. Though peasants are allowed to privatize small parcels of land adjacent to their houses, mass privatization of land has not started yet.

Industry: Since the beginning of mass privatization in January 1995, some 6,000 medium and large enterprises have been transformed into open joint-stock companies; of them 3,506 medium and large scale enterprises were fully privatized as of October 1996. In 1997, 5,300 enterprises were privatized.

Business and Service: To date, 45,000 small businesses have been privatized, and thousands of retail, trade and service enterprises leased to their "working collectives" who have the right to purchase the entities. About 99 percent of small retail, trade, and service firms have been privatized throughout Ukraine. Many of businesses operate illegally or semi-legally, trying to survive high taxes and tight regulations.

4. What has been the extent of insider (management, labor, and nomenklatura) participation in the privatization process? What explicit and implicit preferences have been awarded to insiders? The privatization legislation gave priority to so-called "working collectives" (formally, all individuals employed at a particular enterprise or institution; de facto, administration and leaders of official trade unions who control the "working collective"), thus enabling them to benefit from privatizing state property at book value and for vouchers. The Law on Specifics of Privatization of Property in the Agro-Industrial Complex (1996) allowed privatization of the most attractive state-owned property of the agriculture and food processing industry only by permission of the Cabinet of Ministers and gave substantial privatization privileges to workers of the enterprises to be privatized. The law stipulated that the property of collective and state farms would be privatized through transforming them into "collective agrarian enterprises" or open joint-stock societies. According to estimates, about 20 percent of privatized small companies remain owned by their work collectives. "Insider privatization" has been widespread, with administrations of enterprises privatized them without competition and at very low cost which comprised only a fraction of the real market value.

5. How much public awareness of and support for privatization has there been? What is the nature of support and opposition to privatization by major interest groups? Notwithstanding broadly publicized voucher privatization, the deadlines for receiving privatization certificates and investing them by the population have been moved several times due to low activity by the population. Although the process began in 1994, by January 1998 about 10 percent of Ukrainians did not receive their privatization certificates. Amidst general disillusionment at privatization as a sound investment and reports about scarcity of dividends, many people have sold their privatization certificates for cash (at a price of about $20). Opposition to privatization comes from Communist and other leftist parties in the parliament, who have repeatedly blocked the appointment of a presidential nominee as chairman of the State Property Fund, and suspended the fund's authority in December 1997. Privatization of large enterprises has been complicated by the competition of a number of financial-political groups whose interests are represented by government officials. Generally, privatization is supported by entrepreneurs and the executive branch.

Macroeconomics 4.50/7

1. Has the taxation system been reformed? (What areas have and have not been overhauled? To what degree are taxpayers complying? Is tax compliance difficult to achieve? Has the level of revenues increased? Is the revenue- collection body overburdened? What is the overall tax burden?) In 1992-1993, taxation system reforms resulted in a heavy tax burden, primarily on non-state owned entities. Taxes of up to 90 percent discouraged production, caused massive tax-evasion, and pushed many new businesses into the "shadow" economy. Kuchma announced a broad taxation reform policy in mid-1994, but the first real attempt was the taxation bills package presented by the government to parliament on November 22, 1996. The proposed changes included reduction of personal income tax from 40 percent to 30 percent; the Chornobyl tax from 12 percent to 6 percent; payments to the unemployment fund from 2 percent to 1 percent; and to the state pension fund from 32 percent to 25 percent. Payments to the salary fund, now a huge burden to businesses and a factor that encourages companies to hide real income amounts would be reduced from 52 percent to 32 percent. The value added tax, now 20 percent, would be reduced. The parliament voted down the reform package, as the reduction of taxes was supposed to be compensated for by the abolition of payments to the Social Security Fund, the Pension Fund, and other non-budget funds, a massive reduction of benefits (currently, there are some 72 kinds of benefits), as well as the increase of retirement age from 55 years (women) and 60 years (men) to 60 and 65 years, respectively. Though the law envisages criminal liability for tax evasion, neither individual nor corporate taxpayers comply. Tax compliance is made difficult by the large number of taxes to be paid and constant changes in amounts and calculations, as well as by the heavy tax burden, with some businesses having to surrender up to 90 percent of earnings. The top income tax rate is 40 percent. The tax rate for an average income (equivalent to about $90 per month) is 20 percent, a reduction from 30 percent rate in 1996. The top corporate tax is 30 percent, plus a 30 percent capital gains tax and 20 percent VAT. Payroll tax remains at a high 51 percent. According to official reports, in 1997 the State Taxation Administration found tax evasion at 217,000 enterprises (58.6 percent of verified entities). To improve collection of taxes, the government increased the number of staff of taxation administrations. Due to the efforts aiming at preventing tax evasion, the level of revenues increased from 15.4 percent of the GDP in 1996 to 17.1 percent of the GDP in 1997. In 1997, the total revenue to the state budget was 15.7 billion hryvnyas, or 72.4 percent of the amount expected in accordance with the approved budget.

2. Does fiscal policy encourage private savings, investment and earnings? (Has there been any reform/alteration of revenue and budget policies? How large are budget deficits and overall debt? Is the financing of the social insurance/pension system sustainable? What proportion of the budget is taken up by subsidies to firms and individuals?) In the first years of independence, the Ukrainian government focused its policies at a sound national financial-economic system. In 1991-1993, the government opted for a inflationary increase of the monetary supply, which caused hyperinflation up to 10,000 percent a month in 1993. In order to cope with hyperinflation, monetary-fiscal restraint was introduced in 1993-1994, and inflation was gradually reduced to 1 or 2 percent a month. Instead of printing money like in 1991-1993, from 1994 onwards the government began the practice of non- payment of salaries and wages to state-employed workers and employees. Financial stabilization began in 1995, a year before the new national currency, the hryvnya, was introduced. Despite the declared course towards financial stabilization, reduction of budget deficit and payment of arrears through improved tax collection, and introduction of strict budget discipline and savings, no significant reform of revenue and budget policies has occurred in the recent years. In 1997, the total state debt increased by 43 percent and by January 1, 1998, it had reached 31.1 billion UAH, which is 10 billion over the revenue share of the 1998 budget. The budget deficit amounted to 6.3 billion hryvnyas (6.8 percent of the GDP) instead of the limit of 5.7 percent set in the 1997 state budget. The state encourages private savings and investment, though provides no insurance or guarantees. Interest rates are not regulated, and there are no state controls regarding the rates of return on investment. There are few restrictions on domestic investment, except in sensitive "strategic" branches like nuclear energy and the military-industrial complex. Individuals can hold and exchange foreign currency and securities. The financing of the social insurance/pension system — which is based on the money that is deducted monthly of everyone's pay and transferred to the state-owned Pension Fund to be re-distributed to all pensioners — is not sustainable due to the constant decrease in funds available for paying benefits as a result of the overwhelming payment crisis and growing budget deficit. Payments of public sector workers and employees amount to 47.6 percent of the GDP, and the government consumes 18.3 percent of the GDP. Subsidies to firms and individuals amount to 13 percent of the budget.

3. Has there been banking reform? (Is the central bank independent? What are its responsibilities? Is it effective in setting and/or implementing monetary policy? What is the actual state of the private banking sector? Does it conform to international standards? Are depositors protected?) According to the Law on Banks and Banking, adopted in March 1991 and amended in 1992, 1993, 1994, 1995, and 1996, banks are (formally) independent institutions, registered by the National Bank. Under the 1991 law, commercial banks are banned from participation in material production, trade and insurance. The state is not responsible for the banks' obligations, unless special agreements stipulate otherwise. The central bank, the National Bank of Ukraine (NBU), is not independent, as it is accountable to the parliament. The NBU governor is nominated by the speaker of parliament and approved by parliament. Thus, the NBU finds it difficult to refuse credit demands from industrial and agrarian interests whose representatives dominate the legislature. The NBU's responsibilities include cash emission, implementation of the state's monetary and credit policies, issuing licenses to banks and coordination of the banking system, maintaining the state treasury, representing Ukraine in relations with central banks of other states and international financial bodies, and regulation of hard currency operations. Within recent years, it has been effective in setting and/or implementing monetary policy. Within five years, about 250 commercial joint stock and private banks have sprouted. By the end of 1995, non-state banks had numbered 231, but only 195 were in operation. Twenty-two banks were undergoing liquidation or merger, nine were bankrupt, and the activities of six were suspended. Only about 25 of major new banks conform to international standards, provide most of usual services and issue major credit cards. The Ukrainian Banking Association counted 113 banks with total assets of 11.8 billion UAH ($5.9 billion) in March 1998. Since 1995, about one-third of the total number of commercial banks have failed to comply with the NBU's requirement about increasing their statute funds and had their licenses revoked. About 40 small and medium banks went bankrupt. Almost every other bank among those registered in 1995 either collapsed or changed owners. Government influence remains pervasive. Starting in 1998, banks have been required to adopt international accounting standards. The NBU raised reserve requirements from 11percent to 15 percent of assets in late 1997. The barriers to market entry for foreign banks are low. Foreign-owned banks are required to open a resident office one year before applying for a banking license. The minimum authorized statutory fund is ECU 10 million. Deposits are confidential, but savings are not safe and are not returned if a bank collapses. In 1997, deposits to personal savings accounts grew 50 percent to the total of 1.6 billion UAH. According to NBU estimates, that accounts to only about 10 percent of the savings accumulated by the population. Credit cards are accepted in about 1,000 restaurants and shops in Kyiv and major cities, but the number of credit card users barely exceeds 10,000.

4. How sound is the national currency? (Is the value of the currency fixed or does it float? How convertible is the currency? How large are the hard currency reserves? Has exchange rate policy been stable and predictable?) In September 1996, the NBU successfully launched a monetary reform and introduced the long-expected Ukrainian national currency, hryvnya, announced in 1992. The currency is "internally convertible", i.e., it can be converted easily into major currencies within Ukraine, but hardly anywhere else. In 1997, the hryvnya exchange rate stayed at under two to the dollar. While the hryvnya has been rather stable, the NBU has to struggle to keep its promised trading band of no more than 2.25 to the dollar for the remainder of the year. Currently the NBU reserves amount to $2.4 billion. In recent years, the exchange rate policy has remained rather stable and predictable, compared to 377 percent inflation rate in 1995 and 80 percent in 1997, although inflation rate remains very high by international standards. Nominally, hryvnya devalued by less than 2 percent in 1997, while real devaluation in proportion to U.S. dollar was 12 percent per year.

5. Is there a functioning capital market infrastructure? (Are there existing or planned commodities, bond and stock markets? What are the mechanisms for investment and lending? What government bodies have authority to regulate capital markets?) The capital market is developing rapidly as the stocks of privatized enterprises and corporations are sold for cash. Currently there are about 100 major companies that are successfully traded. These include 17 most attractive companies such as the oil excavation and distribution monopoly Ukrnafta, the river shipment corporation Ukrrichflot, energy distributing corporations like Dniproenergo, Kyivenergo, Zakhidenergo, metallurgy plants (e.g., Mariupol Metallurgy, Azovstal, Nikopol Ferroalloys, Khartsyzsk Piping) and chemical companies (e.g., Stirol. The government has almost stopped the sale of attractive shares at compensation and privatization certificate auctions for certificates. Non-liquid stocks are sold in cash auctions at the Ukrainian Center for Certificate Auctions. In the bond market, short-term bonds (4- or 5-week bonds) are traded successfully, although in general demand for bonds remains low regardless of high interest rates. Seeking to reduce the budget deficit, the government ordered the issue of long-term (2-3 years) domestic state bonds and Eurobonds with very high interest rates well above inflation: 16.2 percent for 3-year bonds, 50.1 percent for 3-month bonds, and 49.0 percent for 12-month bonds. Although borrowing has helped to maintain the stability of the national currency, the forecasts are that it may cause a major financial crisis when the time comes to pay the interest. Operation of the emergent commodities, bond and stock markets is often hindered by the lack of clearly defined property rights and the complexity of regulations. Major violations of securities legislation involve non-publication of company information in the media, introducing changes to statutory documents without appropriate decisions by a shareholder meeting and violations in provision of notice about meetings. Investment is regulated by "The Law on Investment Activity" (September 1991, amended in 1992) that stipulated equal investment rights to Ukrainian and foreign entities of all forms of ownership and individuals. The law provides for state insurance of Ukrainian state enterprises' investments abroad. Investments are subject to environmental and hygienic expertise. Investments, both domestic and foreign, are protected by state guarantees and cannot be nationalized or expropriated without due compensation. Expropriation is possible only in accordance with the legislation, with full compensation of damages incurred with termination of the investment activity. Investment mechanisms include sale of shares in joint stock and private enterprises through auctions, tender competitions, state investment through banks. Lending is done by all major banks in the standard procedures; interest rates and the kind and size of the collateral vary. Most long-term loans usually do not exceed one year, and borrowers are forced to put up collateral worth 20 percent more than the loan. To help banks properly evaluate collateral, a centralized Property Pledge Registry will open in the second half of 1998. The capital market is controlled by the Securities and Stock Market Commission of Ukraine.

Microeconomics **4.50/7**

1. Are property rights guaranteed? (Are there both formal and de facto protections of private real estate and intellectual property? Is there a land registry with the authority and capability to ensure accurate recording of who owns what? What are the procedures for expropriation, including measures for compensation and challenge? Have any seizures taken place?) Formally, property rights are guaranteed by the constitution and the property law. De facto, the right to own private property remains ill-defined by law. Legislation granting the right to own land has been expected since 1992, but is unlikely to be adopted in the near future. Collective farmers are theoretically eligible to claim their share of land and leave the collective farm, and peasants can privatize small pieces of land adjacent to their houses. Private property must be registered with land registry departments of the local executive authorities. Disputes over private property — usually between a divorced couple or relatives — are settled by the court in a time-consuming, cumbersome, and murky process. Intellectual property rights are formally guaranteed, but the enforcement mechanism is lacking, and unauthorized copying and duplication is widespread. No compensation for property seized and nationalized during the Communist rule has been awarded. According to the new constitution, expropriation is possible only in case of social necessity, on the basis of law, and only after full compensation is given; expropriation without prior compensation is possible only under martial law or emergency. Confiscation of private property can be sanctioned only by the court. No seizures of property have been reported thus far. Investment mechanisms include sale of shares in joint stock and private enterprises through auctions, tender competitions, and state investment through banks.

2. To what extent have prices been liberalized? What subsidies remain? Price liberalization started on a mass scale in 1992, although the government maintains almost 100 percent control over prices for municipal housing, transportation services (local, bus and railway transport), and public utilities. In 1994, the liberalization of prices was limited by introduction of a regulation that prohibited non-state traders to price their goods higher than 25 percent of their initial wholesale value, though the regulation remained inactive. In 1997, prices of natural monopolies (e.g., energy and water prices) increased by 20 to 25 percent and are likely to grow further. Accordingly, market prices for consumer goods and services increased by 10.1 percent, compared to the increase by 39.7 percent in 1996. The state controls prices of basic foodstuffs and offers a number of subsidies for low-income part of the population. In 1997, subsidies for housing and public utilities were provided to 7.2 million families.

3. Is it possible to own and operate a business? (Has there been legislation regarding the formation, dissolution and transfer of businesses, and is the law respected? Do there exist overly cumbersome bureaucratic hurdles that effectively hinder the ability to own and dispose of a business? Are citizens given access to information on commercial law? Is the law applied fairly? Does regulation (or licensing requirements) impose significant costs on business and consumers? Do they create significant barriers to entry and seriously hamper competition?) Since 1992, the introduction of measures that simplified the process of registering and disposing of businesses has contributed to a growing private sector. Currently it takes up to five days and submission of an application and statutory documents to register a business with local authorities. The procedure of disposing of a business has been made more complicated recently in order to discourage creation of one-day "phantom" firms used for converting funds on corporate accounts into cash and for money-laundering. To dispose of a business, a company must undergo an audit, a verification by the taxation authorities and satisfy all creditors' claims. A Bankruptcy Law has been adopted but the bankruptcy procedure practically does not function due to the liquidatory attitude adopted by the state and low liquidity of enterprises' assets. Citizens are given access to information on commercial law. Regulatory barriers include registration, licensing, product certification and export quota systems, as well as strict oversight of business operation by the state through some 26 agencies, from the taxation police and the Ministry of Labor to sanitary control and fire inspection. Though, theoretically, anyone can register and run a business, operating a business is hindered by the heavy taxation burden and growing crime and corruption, as well as by inability of law enforcement bodies to protect businesses and businessmen, many of whom have become victims of racket and contract killings.

4. Are courts effective, transparent, efficient, and quick in reaching decisions on property and contract disputes? What alternative mechanisms for adjudicating disputes exist? According to Ukrainian law, property and contract disputes can be adjudicated in arbitration courts in Ukraine or abroad, or in general courts. State arbitration courts operate reasonably fairly to settle commercial disputes, though the process is neither transparent nor quick. Notwithstanding a number of inadequacies in the Ukrainian legislation and often delays in reaching decisions on property and contract disputes due to the shortage of qualified personnel, many foreign lawyers believe that courts are rather just, unbiased, effective, and transparent, and that the Ukrainian judiciary provides necessary possibilities for protection of rights and interests in such disputes. However, due to reports of widespread corruption, Ukrainians as well as foreigners lack confidence in fairness of the courts. The Arbitration Court consists of 450 judges divided between the Supreme Arbitration Court and 28 regional arbitration courts. Their rules of procedure remain largely unreformed. According to the new constitution, arbitration courts are to be merged into the general court system by 2001. Currently Ukrainian law-makers are considering signing the 1965 Washington Convention on adjudication of investment disputes between states and foreign investors.

5. Is business competition encouraged? (Are monopolistic practices limited in law and in practice? If so, how? To what degree is "insider" dealing a hindrance to open competition? Are government procurement policies open and unbiased?) Formally, business competition is encouraged and monopolies are prohibited by law. Changes and amendments to the Law on Limiting Monopolism and Preventing Unfair Competition in Entrepreneurial Activity (July 1995) and the Law on Protection Against Unfair Competition prohibit actions that might limit competition, i.e., high or low monopolist prices, or control through shares or other interests over more than a quarter of local authorities and agencies, or violations of copyright, or abuse of advertising. The law stipulates liability for forcing entrepreneurs to join associations or to give priority to specific institutions or customers. The Anti-Monopoly Committee, subordinated to the Cabinet and accountable to the parliament, was established in 1992 to protect business rights from monopolies and unfair competition. To date, it has been successful in limiting the sphere of influence on pricing by natural monopolies and companies that deal with natural monopolists' products. In practice, the state remains the major monopolist, and the most attractive branches of energy, oil and gas, metals, and petrochemicals production and trading are controlled by formally non-governmental companies governed by individuals related personally or professionally to key state officials. Corruption is widespread and organized crime has been an impediment on legitimate business interests. Government procurement policies are not open, biased, and often dependent on personal interests and links, or political considerations. Due to widespread "insider" dealing, fair competition remains an underdeveloped concept and a hindrance to privatization and other reforms.

6. To what extent has international trade been liberalized? (To what degree has there been simplification/overhaul of customs and tariff procedures, and are these applied fairly? What informal trade barriers exist? There are no non-tariff barriers on imports except standard rules for safety and the environment, as well as efficacy standards with regard to pharmaceutical and veterinary products. Due to the pressure of international lending institutions, most export controls — introduced in 1993 and often abused by corrupt officials — have been reduced. According to the U.S. Department of State, there are no longer any significant non-tariff barriers, and import licensing requirements have been eased. According to the U.S. Department of Commerce, import duties generally are 16 percent. In 1997, the liberalization of international trade was hindered by the new policy of state protectionism of "national manufacturers" and the adoption of new standardization, certification, and licensing rules. According to the American Chamber of Commerce in Ukraine, main impediments to international trade include the lack of clear rules in the market, general complexity and high price of certification, inconvenient registration process and unjustifiably high commission, divergence from international standards, and instability of requirements. that imposed restrictions on import of some goods and complicated the procedure of import of other goods. Informal trade barriers include high taxes. In January-November 1997, the amount of international trade totaled $28 billion. Ukraine's exports increased by 1.9 percent to $12.8 billion, while imports decreased by 1.5 percent to $15.2 billion. The volumes of foreign trade with the CIS and the Baltic states also decreased (exports by 22.8 percent, imports by 9.7 percent), while operations with countries of the "far abroad" increased by 30.5 percent and 14.2 percent, respectively. The major part of exports were made to Russia (26.2 percent), China (8 percent), Belarus (5.8 percent, Turkey (4.5 percent), Germany (3.9 percent), the major part of imports came from Russia (46.7 percent), Germany (7.4 percent), Turkmenistan (5.1 percent), the US (4 percent), and Poland (3.2 percent). 45.9 percent of the imports are mineral fuel, gas, oil and petroleum products, 15.2 percent are machines and equipment, and 7.1 percent are chemical products. The volume of barter operations decreased to 10.5 percent from 22.6 percent in 1996 and from 33.1 percent in 1995.

7. To what degree has foreign investment and capital flow been encouraged or constrained? Moderate barriers to capital flows and foreign investment exist, although attracting investment, particularly direct foreign investment, has been declared a strategic goal by the government. There are no regulatory restrictions on repatriation of capital or profits. The March 1992 Law on Foreign

Investments, which granted substantial privileges and taxation benefits to enterprises with foreign investments was abolished in March 1996. Instead, after domestic and foreign investors were given equal status in 1995, a number of resolutions were adopted by the government to encourage foreign investment in privatization of lagging industrial enterprises. Foreign investments are protected in accordance with the Ukrainian law and bilateral agreements with foreign states. Ukraine has signed agreements on investment protection with 45 countries. A presidential decree "On Measures to Ensure Privatization in 1995" (June 1995) allowed foreigners to participate in the privatization of enterprises on equal terms with Ukrainians. However, since 1995, the Ukrainian government has been pursuing a policy of protecting national manufacturers, which has meant limiting imports and extending domestic production. There are few restrictions on foreign ownership of businesses. Since April 1996, transformation of strategically important industrial enterprises into open joint-stock companies with foreign capital has been supervised by a governmental commission established by presidential decree. Foreign investments are protected by the "Law on Foreign Investment" (March 1996), which stipulates that foreign investments are immune to nationalization and can be expropriated, with adequate compensation, only in cases of natural disasters and emergencies and when sanctioned by the Cabinet of Ministers. In 1997, direct foreign investment decreased to $759.2 million, compared to $1.2 billion in 1996. By January 1, 1998, the total amount of foreign investments in the Ukrainian economy since 1992 reached $2 million. According to the Ministry of Statistics, main foreign investors in Ukraine are the U.S. (18.6 percent), the Netherlands (10.4 percent), Germany (9 percent), Russia (7.3 percent), Great Britain (7.3 percent), and Cyprus (6.1 percent). A major part of these investments went to foreign and domestic trade (17.8 percent), the food industry (20.6 percent), machine-building and metal-processing (8.2 percent), the chemical industry (6.9 percent), and construction (4.4 percent). Investment abroad by Ukrainian entities and individuals is discouraged by significant restrictions on capital transfers, though the mechanisms of tracking transactions do not work effectively. Travelers abroad are allowed to take out only up to $1,000, either in cash or in traveler's checks, without official permission.

8. Has there been reform of the energy sector? (To what degree has the energy sector been restructured? Is the energy sector more varied, and is it open to private competition? Is the country overly dependent on one or two other countries for energy [including whether exported fuels must pass through one or more countries to reach markets]?) The electric energy market is regulated by a special National Commission established in March 1995. In April 1995, the president issued a decree "On Structural Transformation of the Ukrainian Electric Energy Complex" that envisaged a thorough reform, which, in practice, has only begun. The centralized Energy Exchange System was established in April 1996 in order to introduce market mechanisms of price formation. The energy sector is varied; trading in energy supplies is open for private (domestic and foreign) competition, but production and transportation is controlled by the governmental agencies. Major independent traders on the national oil and gas market include United Energy Systems of Ukraine, Itera, Intergas, Motor-Sich, and state-owned companies, like Ukrgasprom, Ukrnafta, Ukrgas. The emergence of multiple oil and gas traders allowed to reduce the deficit of petrochemicals and gas but did not have a strong impact on energy prices which remain heavily controlled by the state. About 80 percent of oil and gas consumed in Ukraine is supplied from Russia. Ukraine's heavy dependence on Russian oil and gas has made the country vulnerable to political pressure. Natural gas and oil imports accounted for 34 percent of Ukraine's total imports in 1996 and 45.9 percent in 1997. As of May 1, 1998, Ukraine's debt to the Russian Gazprom totaled $1.3 million. To cope with the mounting debt, in mid-1997 the government prohibited the issue of guarantees to independent gas traders and made the state-owned Ukrgaz corporation the only centralized purchaser of gas abroad with the government's guarantees of payment. In February 1998, the president issued a decree On Reforming the Oil and Gas Complex that envisaged creation of the national joint-stock company, Naftogaz Ukrainy, and putting excavation, sale, and transportation of oil and gas under stricter governmental control. Although there have been a number of negotiations of alternative energy no major importers of energy sources other than Russia and, recently, Turkmenistan, have been found.

UZBEKISTAN

Freedom in the World Ratings, 1989-1998	1989-90	1990-91	1991-92	1992-93	1993-94	1994-95	1995-96	1996-97	1997-98
Political Rights	-	-	6	6	7	7	7	7	7
Civil Liberties	-	-	5	6	7	7	7	6	6
Status	-	-	PF	NF	NF	NF	NF	NF	NF

Polity: Consolidated Autocracy
Economy: Consolidated Statist
Population: 23,188,000
PPP: $2,376
Ethnic Groups: Uzbek (71 percent), Russian (8 percent), Tajik, Ukrainian, Turk, others
Capital: Tashkent

Political Process 6.50/7

1. When did national legislative elections occur? Were they free and fair? How were they judged by domestic and international election monitoring organizations? Who composes the government? The most recent national legislative elections took place on December 25, 1994. Runoff elections were held on January 8, 1995 (for 39 seats) and January 22, 1995 (for 6 seats). At that time, 634 candidates vied for the 250 seats in the *Oliy Majlis* (Supreme Council or Soviet). Of these, 243 were from the governing *Halq Tarakiati Partiiasi* (People's Democratic Party, or HDP), 141 were from the *Watan Tarakiati Partiiasi* (Progress of the Fatherland Party, or WTP), and 250 were candidates chosen by local and regional councils and were technically "non-affiliated." The HDP won 69 seats, the WTP captured 14 seats, and the independent candidates won the remaining 167 seats, suggesting that party politics is not important. However, 124 of the independent candidates were actually registered members of the HDP, giving that party control of 193 of the 250 seats in the Oliy Majlis. The elections were not considered free and fair by international observers and organizations. Instances of "family voting" and over inflation of voting results were reported. That said, in recent years, President Islam Karimov has repeatedly stated that the December 1999 elections and the January 2000 presidential elections will be the most open elections to date in Uzbekistan, and has encouraged international observers to scrutinize them. Uzbekistan's political system is a presidential one, thus the legislature has nominal authority to form a government. The government is comprised of presidential appointees, although the chairman of the Oliy Majlis, Erkin Khalilov, was elected by parliamentarians.

2. When did presidential elections occur? Were they free and fair? The only post-independence presidential election took place on December 29, 1991. At that time, the last Soviet-era first secretary of the Uzbek Soviet Socialist Republic (and only president of the Uzbek SSR), Islam Karimov, defeated Muhammed Solih of the opposition party Erk ("Will") by a margin of 86 percent to 14 percent. The election was not considered free by international observers, although domestic analysts note that it was a contested race and therefore "free and fair." Limitations, however, on Solih's campaign, including restrictions on rallies, dissemination of information, and media attention, as well as the prohibition of candidates from other parties, most notably Birlik's Abdurahim Pulatov, supports the international observers' conclusion. On March 26, 1995, a referendum was held to extend President Karimov's term in office until the year 2000. It easily passed with 99.6 percent voter turnout and a 99.3 percent "yes" vote. The Oliy Majlis rejected Karimov's suggestion that this extension be considered his "second term," allowing him to compete in the January 2000 election, if he chooses to run again. An interesting legal situation could arise in that technically, a victory in the January 2000 election could be considered Karimov's "first" using the argument that his 1991 election was under a previous constitution (prior to the passage of the December 1992 constitution), therefore allowing him to run for two full terms, noting that the 1995 referendum was a continuation of the pre-constitutional presidency.

3. Is the electoral system multiparty-based? Are there at least two viable political parties functioning at all levels of government? Technically, Uzbekistan is a multiparty system, with both the 1991 presidential and 1994 legislative elections officially listed as multiparty/multi-candidate races. The reality is that, at all levels, the HDP is the only significant political party in Uzbekistan. As the pro-government party in the country, the HDP is the successor to the Communist Party of Uzbekistan (CPUz), renamed as such in August 1991. Following the failed anti-Gorbachev putsch of that month, Karimov then president of the Uzbek SSR, resigned from the Communist Party and had the CPUz reformed into the HDP. Conveniently, it was able to occupy the office space, publications, and organizational and financial network of the CPUz, making it easy to maintain a prominent position in the country. Because of limitations on other parties, it is difficult to consider Uzbekistan a true multiparty state. The only real challenge to the HDP was the Erk party which was banned in 1993. While there are other political parties in Uzbekistan, none possess the same influence as the HDP. It is also important to note that, at the local level, political party affiliation appears to be unimportant. Local councils (*majlislar*) and executives (*hokimlar*) are often "independent" when it comes to party membership. At the *mahalla* (neighborhood) level, family loyalty, if anything, is more important.

4. How many parties have been legalized? Are any particular parties illegal? At present, there are four political parties that are considered legal in Uzbekistan. In addition to the HDP, there is the WTP, the National Revival Democratic Party (*Milli Tiklanish Demokratik Partiiasi* or MTDP), and the *Adolat* (Justice) Social Democratic Party of Uzbekistan. The WTP was founded in 1993 and, under the chairmanship of Anvar Yuldashev, considers itself to be a loyal opposition to the HDP. The MTDP and Adolat were founded in 1995 and likewise consider themselves to be constructive, or loyal, opposition parties. Adolat, for instance, was founded by 47 previously-declared independent members of the Oliy Majlis. There is also a fledgling People's Unity Movement (*Halq* Birligi, or HB) that will offer candidates in the next legislative election. This movement, to be registered as Uzbekistan's fifth political party, tends to draw support from the ethnic minorities in the country. The most noteworthy illegal parties remain Birlik, Erk, and the Islamic Renaissance Party (IRP). Birlik (Unity) was founded in 1988 as a social movement advocating greater Uzbek cultural and linguistic rights. With independence in 1991, it attempted to become a political force against Karimov's HDP; however, its leader, Abdurahim Polat, was unable to participate in the 1991 presidential election. After a series of crackdowns, the organization was not allowed to re-register in 1993. Its leaders remain in exile, though in 1998, Abdurahim Polat declared his intent to return to Uzbekistan and re-activate Birlik. Erk was formed in April 1990 by members of Birlik who split over ideological and tactical differences with Polat. Its leader, Mohammed Solih, was allowed to participate in the 1991 presidential election, and received 14 percent of the vote. Conflicts over its right to hold rallies and issue its news publication led the government to deny the party's re-registration effort in 1993 and, like Birlik, its leaders went into exile. Former Vice President Shukhrullo Mirsaidov, once an insider in the political system, formed the Forum for Democratic Forces later that year in an attempt to unite the opposition groups, but with no success. Unlike the other figures, Mirsaidov remains in Uzbekistan. Two religious groups — the Islamic Renaissance Party (IRP) and Adolat (Justice, not to be confused with the Adolat Social Democratic Party) — have never been allowed to register. The former was headed by Abdulla Utaev, until his disappearance in December 1992. Since that time, its officials have remained in hiding or in exile. Adolat was founded in 1991, and advocated a return to an Islamic-based political system (predating the Soviet period). Twelve members of its leadership were imprisoned in 1993 for various crimes. And while the current status of these two groups is unclear, in 1997 and 1998 President Karimov has repeatedly warned of an "Islamic threat" in Uzbekistan and the government continues to arrest and try individuals suspected of having links with these organizations. The September 19, 1996 law on political parties explicitly prohibits the formation of political parties based on religious grounds, thus sealing the legal fate of these groups. In that legislation, it is also illegal for all parties to accept financial support from state, foreign, religious, or anonymous sources. In addition, foreigners, military personnel, and "stateless people" may not join political parties.

5. What proportion of the population belongs to political parties? Party membership in Uzbekistan is difficult to gauge, especially if one is trying to include membership in unregistered parties. The HDP claims membership between 300,000-400,000, and the WTP declares that it has at least 35,000 members. These numbers are most likely inflated, with most political organizations membership numbers in the low thousands. In 1996, President Karimov officially left the leadership of the HDP, suggesting that party politics is not strong in Uzbekistan. This was further underscored in an International Foundation for Electrical Systems public opinion survey which discovered that only three percent of those questioned stated that they would be interested in joined a political party at all.

6. What has been the trend in voter turnout at the municipal, provincial and national levels in recent years? Officially, voter turnout is extremely high. These Soviet era-like numbers are mostly for international consumption and to help legitimize the president's image in the country. Anecdotal stories of voter coercion, multiple voting, and fabrication of results from polling places exist, further suggesting that tallies of 93-99 percent voter turnout are not true. Lower figures were found in more recent studies: 81 percent of those surveyed in the IFES poll said they voted in the 1994 legislative election, and 78 percent said that they participated in the 1995 referendum to extend Karimov's mandate. That said, only 39 percent could name their district's deputy to the Oliy Majlis.

Civil Society 6.50/7

1. How many nongovernmental organizations (NGOs) have come into existence since 1988? What is the number of charitable/nonprofit organizations? Are there locally led efforts to increase philanthropy and volunteerism? What proportion of the population is active in private voluntary activity (from polling data)? NGO activity in Uzbekistan has been either prompted by external assistance programs or somehow controlled by the government. Prior to independence, and in the first two years after 1991, there were several truly grass-roots organizations in Uzbekistan: specifically, the political organizations Birlik and Erk, the environmental organization Committee to Save the Aral Sea, and the ethnic-based group Samarkand. Each of these, however, faced problems in registration (or re-registration, if they had been recognized by the government) and all were declared illegal by early 1994. Since that time, the Human Rights Society of Uzbekistan (HRSU) has also tried to register, and in spite of public government claims that it will allow the HRSU to officially exist in Uzbekistan, the organization has yet to receive its official registration documents as of May 1998. In the meantime, the government itself has set up a number of social organizations that fulfill the role of NGOs. Indeed, one Uzbek critic calls these GONGOs (Government-Organized Non-Governmental Organizations). Actually a truism, this typology includes *Kamolot*, a youth organization founded in 1996 that resembles the *Komsomol*, *Watanparvar* or Patriot, which is like volunteer military groups of the Soviet period, and the *Oltin Meros* (Golden Heritage) charity group. The Uzbek government also supports the Uzbek Muslim Board's efforts in building mosques and financing religious education at approved sites. Polling data is not available to give an accurate account of how many people are involved in NGOs.

2. What is the legal and regulatory environment for NGOs (i.e. ease of registration, legal rights, government regulation, taxation, procurement and access-to-information issues)? To what extent is NGO activism focused on improving the legal and regulatory environment? The Law on Associations states that all groups must register with the state, or with the local wilayat government, if they are locally-formed. While the technical aspects of registration are laid out clearly, the governing body's right to reject an application is open to interpretation. Early on, social groups associated with Birlik were deemed "anti-democratic," and thus prevented from registering. In the past two years, religious-based organizations have been subjected to extensive scrutiny as President Karimov feels they could foster "wahabbist" sentiments in the country, a reference to a Sunni Muslim sect.

3. What is the organizational capacity of NGOs? Do management structures clearly delineate authority and responsibility? Is information available on NGO management issues in the native language? Is there a core of experienced practitioners/trainers to serve as consultants or mentors to less developed organizations? As the NGO community is still largely funded through the government or international aid agencies, it is too early to tell the organizational capacity of NGOs in Uzbekistan. On the positive side, there is a high percentage of local staff involved in internationally-funded NGOs, thus a cadre of managers and trainers for future NGOs is developing. Information is becoming more readily available in local languages (especially Russian), although this is mostly concentrated in the larger cities like Tashkent and Samarkand.

4. Are NGOs financially viable? What is their tax status? Are they obliged to and do they typically disclose revenue sources? Do government procurement opportunities exist for private, not-for-profit providers of services? NGOs that are funded by the government or foreign programs are financially viable — at least in the short run. Groups like Kamolot are trying to obtain corporate sponsorship to provide long-term support, but most have not ventured into this arena. The tax status of NGOs is still murky, given that the Uzbek tax law is currently under review. They do pay taxes, although the rates, collection percentages, and record-keeping statistics are all unavailable.

5. Are there free trade unions? How many workers belong to these unions? Is the number of workers belonging to trade unions growing or decreasing? What is the numerical/proportional membership of farmers' groups, small business associations, etc.? While there is no free trade union in Uzbekistan, there are government-sponsored trade unions and shop floor associations. At present, independent union activities are still illegal. About 25 percent of Uzbekistan's labor force is in the main Trade Union that is under the aegis of the Ministry of Labor. In addition, the Employment Service and Employment Fund was set up in 1992 to address issues of social welfare, employment insurance, and health benefits for workers.

6.What form of interest group participation in politics are legal? What types of interest groups are active in the political and policy process? In general, interest groups in Uzbekistan stay clear of political issues. While they may advocate particular issues of importance, for example the rights of farmers and women's health, the role is strictly that of providing information in public forums. Lobbying and advocacy are not, to date, present in the Uzbek political scene. Indeed, "influence-buying" activities are illegal. Interest group activities are made even more difficult by the fact that the government strictly controls public meetings, the dissemination of information via leaflets, radio, newspapers, and television.

7. How is the not-for-profit/NGO sector perceived by the public and government officials? What is the nature of media coverage of NGOs? To what extent to government officials engage with NGOs? Foreign assistance-backed NGOs are still viewed fairly positively in Uzbekistan, as are the developing indigenous ones. Public opinion survey results suggest that individuals would consider joining organizations that help others more than other groups such as political parties or religious organizations. Thus, at least in the abstract, support is present. Government support is still more difficult to obtain, as registration problems and surveillance problems persist. Indeed, autonomous NGOs are sometimes viewed with suspicion — ironically, this is more case with U.S.-backed groups. Media coverage is available for NGOs and, for the most part, it is positive. Usually, this comes in the form of stories about a group — youth, environmental, womens' rights — that has carried out positive duties. NGOs that are critical of the regime or that highlight issues that might embarrass the government are not given the same treatment. It is important to note, though, that such evidence is strictly anecdotal as no comprehensive survey has been published on this aspect of NGO activity in Uzbekistan. Finally, government officials, by their very nature of regulating and monitoring NGO activity, engage with these groups. This is especially true for those NGOs that are government-sponsored.

Independent Media 6.50/7

1. Are there legal protections for press freedom? According to the constitution, the government does provide legal protection for press freedom. In May 1996, a law was passed that outlined the registration process for radio and television media. In 1997, three pieces of legislation were passed that further defined the media's place in Uzbek society. In April, the Oliy Majlis passed two laws: the first provides journalists (and citizens in general) with "freedom of access to information," and the second provides protection for journalists' sources. A Mass Media Law was passed in December 1997 which offers protection of journalists from government prosecution, but at the same time sets restrictions on what types of sources a journalist can use. Specifically, open corroboration of statements must be made, and statements made in a given article, even if quoted from another source, are the responsibility of the writer. In all of these, particularly the Law on the Media, extensive attention is given to the rights of journalists and the role that the press should play in Uzbek society. This latter point is key as it is seen as the justification for limiting press freedoms.

2. Are there legal penalties for libeling officials? Are there legal penalties for irresponsible journalism? Have these laws been enforced to harass journalists? Libel, public defamation of the president, and irresponsible journalism, i.e., spreading falsehoods, are all subject to financial penalty and possible imprisonment. This was underscored in the December 1997 Law on Media, which details the responsibilities and moral obligations of journalists. On occasion, the Uzbek government has criticized foreign journalists, mainly Russians, for reporting libelous stories and have either pressured them to leave the country or prohibited the distribution of their papers. This has been the case for journalists working for *Nezavisimaya gazeta*, *Izvestiia*, and Interfax.

3. What proportion of the media is privatized? What are the major private newspapers, television stations, and radio stations? In all areas, the majority of the media is government-run. In the past several years, however, there has been some growth in the number of privatized media organizations. In a report released in April 1998, it was stated that Uzbekistan has 471 newspapers and magazines currently being published and circulated, which includes dailies, weeklies, and monthlies. Three hundred twenty-eight of these are government papers with 66 national, 68 regional, and the rest either local or municipal; 109 are considered public or organizational representing trade unions, the military, or other associations; and the remaining 34 are commercial, religious-based, or other. This last group is financially independent from the state, making it the genesis of the private media in Uzbekistan. It is important to note that, while these are financially independent of the government, they still are subject to editorial constraints. True opposition papers — those that publicly challenge the state's policies or question Karimov's actions — ceased to exist in 1993. Any opposition paper that appears in Uzbekistan is technically illegal.

Independent radio and television stations are not as developed in Uzbekistan, largely because of the high operating costs. Outside of foreign stations such as Ostankino from Russia, there are independent television stations in Urgench, Samarkand, and Tashkent. Samarkand Independent Television prides itself on receiving no government support, existing exclusively on advertising revenues.

4. Are the private media financially viable? Underground papers such as *Erk*, are financed from abroad. *Mustaqil haftalik*, was also privately financed during its run in 1991-1993, and in its current status being published abroad. The private media based within the country receive some support from the government, international agencies, and advertising revenues. It is too early to tell how viable they will be, as most began operations in the last two years.

5. Are the media editorially independent? Are the media's news gathering functions affected by interference from government or private owners? Censorship of all media continues. More importantly, over the past several years, journalists working for Uzbek publications — even privately financed ones — exercise self-censorship and simply do not publish controversial articles or commentaries. The same holds true for photojournalists who are strongly discouraged from publishing pictures of poverty or crime scenes — unless it is outside of Uzbekistan. Much like their activities during the Soviet period, Uzbek journalists focus on positive issues at home such as presidential visits, developments in the marketplace, and full accounts of decrees or laws passed. International news can, and often does, accentuate problems abroad.

6. Is the distribution system for newspapers privately or governmentally controlled? The newspaper distribution system remains under government control. There are several minor independent papers, particularly in Tashkent, which have a limited circulation and are available at some kiosks. These tend to be business-oriented papers. There are also occasional appearances of illegal papers published by opposition groups in exile, usually in Moscow or Istanbul, that find their way into Uzbekistan.

7. What proportion of the population is connected to the Internet? Are there any restrictions on Internet access to private citizens? Given the low level of computer usage in Uzbekistan, as well as the practical issue of poor communication lines, the majority of Uzbek citizens at present do not have access to the Internet. Those with access almost always live in Tashkent. It is important to note that this is largely due to physical and technical problems as the government has not placed specific restrictions on Internet usage. This has been confirmed by Western computer and software companies which have assessed the market potential of Uzbekistan for their products.

8. What has been the trend in press freedom as measured by Freedom House's Survey of Press Freedom? The media in Uzbekistan are consistently listed as "Not free." And while there have been laws which allow for a free press, in practice pressures and limitations prevent this from actually happening.

Governance and Public Administration 6.00/7

1. Is the legislature the effective rule-making institution? The Uzbek constitution outlines the powers of the Oliy Majlis, calling it the political authority of the country (Chapter 17). It is charged with initiating and passing legislation, as well as executing policies through committee work. It meets on a regular basis — two times a year plus any special sessions — and has both public and close sessions. At the same time, similar authority is given to the president, putting into question the actual powers of the legislature. In addition, the legislature spends most of its two sessions per year discussing and passing presidential proposals and decrees, suggesting that it is not the rule-making body of Uzbekistan. In 1996, President Karimov himself exhorted legislators to act more assertively and to not be a rubber-stamp body, lacking all political initiative.

2. Is substantial power decentralized to subnational levels of government? What specific authority do subnational levels have? Uzbekistan has a centralized political system of government, with ultimate authority resting at the national level. Within this system, there are twelve wilayats (regions), one autonomous region, and one city government (Tashkent). The president has the power to appoint and dismiss regional *hokims* (executive officials). All policies made at the local level must comply with national laws. This holds true for the Autonomous Republic of Karakalpakstan. Local budgetary payments must also be submitted for approval to the national level. In 1997 alone, over half of the regional hokims were dismissed for a variety of reasons, usually due to poor harvests figures from their respective wilayats.

There is also a local level of government called the mahalla, roughly translated as neighborhood. These regional organizations are often selected from among the more senior, traditional leaders (village elders, or *aqsaqals* [white beards]). In the past several years, President Karimov has put greater emphasis on this level of government to address the issues of immediate social need. Public opinion polls also suggest that the mahalla is fast becoming an important organ of government, ranking it second behind the presidency as the most influential and respected level of government for the citizens of Uzbekistan.

3. Are subnational officials chosen in free and fair elections? Regional hokims are appointed and dismissed by the president. Regional councils are selected through local elections with nominal opposition. As with the national level elections, these are not considered to be free and fair. It is interesting to note that party affiliation is not seen as a factor at this level.

4. Do the executive and legislative bodies operate openly and with transparency? Is draft legislation easily accessible to the media and the public? While resolutions, draft laws, and presidential decrees are readily published and announced in the media, the actual political process by which they are developed is very much a closed one. Equally important is the fact that when government decisions are made, explanations are usually not forthcoming.

5. Do municipal governments have sufficient revenues to carry out their duties? Do municipal governments have control of their own local budgets? Do they raise revenues autonomously or from the central state budget? Local governments receive most of their support from the central budget, although certain cities and regions such as Tashkent and Samarkand do have local taxes on businesses that support local government activities. Data on such revenues, however, is unavailable. In general, municipal governments must comply with the national budget plans and, it seems, do not always receive sufficient amounts from the center. This is largely based on the fact that wilayat, raion, and city officials are often criticized — and sometimes removed from office — by the president or one of his subordinates for not keeping up with basic services such as salary payments or equipment and road upkeep.

6. Do the elected local leaders and local civil servants know how to manage municipal government effectively? Even after seven years of independence, the Soviet experience is alive and well among local officials. The practice of simply following orders and not acting until decrees from above are announced seems to hold true for a number of local leaders and civil servants. Anecdotal evidence of innovative hokims or municipal leaders suggests that this is changing, and that there are individuals willing to initiate reform. In addition, since 1995, President Karimov has spoken on the issue of local-level reform and the need for new personnel. To this end, he has replaced a majority of the wilayat and raion hokims, often filling the posts with individuals who have backgrounds in finance or public administration. That said, continued complaints about local leaders operating in a corrupt or inefficient manner, especially during harvest season, for the rural regions, only underscores the belief that problems remain.

7. When did the constitutional/legislative changes on local power come into effect? Has there been a reform of the civil service code/system? Are local civil servants employees of the local or central government? The December 1992 constitution outlines the role of local government, as does the 1994 Law on Elections to Wilayat, Regional, and City Councils of Peoples Deputies. As the system is a unitary one, ultimately all such employees work for the central government. More importantly, as noted above, the practice remains of local officials waiting for presidential decrees or actions to take place before they decide how to act.

Rule of Law 6.50/7

1. Is there a post-Communist constitution? How does the judicial system interpret and enforce the constitution? Are there specific examples of judicial enforcement of the constitution in the last year? The Oliy Majlis approved President Karimov's constitution on December 8, 1992. The document is lengthy and lists a variety of citizens rights and responsibilities, as well as government obligations. Like its Soviet-era predecessor, however, the Uzbek constitution is vague in delineating political power. For example, while the Oliy Majlis is considered the highest body of government, the president is allowed to veto legislation, propose referenda, and dissolve the legislature. Foreign consultants, most notably the American Bar Association's Central and East European Law Initiative project, have raised questions regarding the ambiguous nature of the constitution that have yet to be fully addressed by the government.

At present, it is too early to track how the judicial system would interpret the constitution, as no landmark cases relating to political powers or constitutional oversight have emerged. In the next year, though, there could be several instances where the constitution may need clarification. First,

President Karimov has publicly stated the need to enforce the strict separation of church and state in Uzbekistan, directing his concern at wahabbi groups in the Ferghana Valley. In an effort to become legal participants in the next round of elections, such groups may challenge the presidential decrees on the basis of freedom of religion and freedom of association. The second potential challenge could come from opposition groups who will challenge Karimov's possible election bids in 2000 and 2005, citing that his next term should be his second, and last, as mandated by the constitution. A third challenge, also related to the electoral cycle, related to the law that prohibits individuals with criminal records from running for office. A number of opposition figures, including Shukhrullo Mirsaidov, the former vice-president, have been convicted of various anti-state crimes in the past. Although all were amnestied, their criminal records remain, technically disallowing their possible candidacies. Whether these challenges will take place remain to be seen, however any one of these could begin the process of real constitutional interpretation.

2. Does the constitutional framework provide for human rights? Do the human rights include business and property rights? The constitution lists a wide range of rights (Chapters 7-10), which include the rights to assembly, free speech, due process, ownership of property, and gender and racial equality. While an inalienable quality is suggested, limitations are likewise noted. Specifically, Chapter 11 notes that if these rights infringe upon the rights of society, the state, or other citizens, they can be curtailed. Indeed, enforcement of such limits has already been seen in the government's campaign against opposition parties and religious organizations noted above.

The right to own property is listed in Chapter 9 of the constitution and Chapter 12 provides for freedom to engage in business. Legislation has progressed on these fronts, especially since 1996. In that year, new laws of private property ownership, setting up businesses, and taxation of business were introduced. Economic rights, as outlined in the constitution, have been of particular importance as the government continues to entice foreign investment in Uzbekistan.

3. Has there been basic reform of the criminal code/criminal law? Who authorizes searches and issues warrants? Are suspects and prisoners beaten or abused? Are there excessive delays in the criminal justice system? The current criminal code of Uzbekistan, introduced in 1995, includes capital punishment for the most serious offenses. In an effort to promote law and order, the government has vigorously and publicly enforced these laws. For instance, trials and the carrying out of death sentences for drug traffickers and criminal gang members are regularly noted.

At the same time, President Karimov has tried to present himself as a merciful leader, issuing amnesties to prisoners on a periodic basis. For instance, prior to his June 1996 visit to the United States, he released over 80 prisoners, including two political prisoners.

Search warrants are authorized and issued by local (mahalla and district) militia, and as yet there have been no successful challenges to the legality of such warrants.

Reports continue to appear of prisoners being beaten and abused while in custody. Whether these are anecdotal accounts, or official reports from the U.S. Department of State, Human Rights Watch, or Amnesty International, it is clear that this remains a chronic problem in Uzbekistan. Indeed, a Western official from Human Rights Watch experienced such abuse first-hand in 1996 when he was illegally detained in a local police headquarters. Worse examples can be seen with the treatment of political prisoners, such as the "Namangan 11," who were tried in 1996, and who reported instances of repeated abuse in prison and coerced confessions.

4. Do most judges rule fairly and impartially? Do many remain from the Communist era? To date, fairness and impartiality remain difficult to gauge in Uzbekistan. The judiciary is a passive structure, taking its cue from the president. In light of the numerous cases against dissidents and religious leaders, at least in public cases, fairness and impartiality are most likely compromised. Anecdotal evidence of bribe demands on defendants, especially during sentencing, furthers this claim. While there is no official data, it is likely that most judges in Uzbekistan today were active during the Soviet era. The policy of dismissing Communist-era judges, as seen, for example in states like the Czech Republic, was not carried out in Uzbekistan.

5. Are the courts free of political control and influence? Are the courts linked directly to the Ministry of Justice or any other executive body? While its independence is outlined in the constitution, the judicial system is subservient to the other branches of government, particularly the executive branch. The president has the power to appoint and dismiss judges, dictate the composition of the Supreme Court, the Constitutional Court, and the Higher Arbitration Court, and control the legislation that these courts are to uphold. To date, the courts have not challenged the president's authority, and have never ruled in favor of defendants charged with anti-state crimes. Technically, the courts are not linked to the ministry of Justice; however, as the ministry is part of the presidential apparatus, such a connection is likely.

6. What proportion of lawyers is in private practice? How does this compare with the previous year? While it is permissible to have a private practice, the overwhelming majority of lawyers work for the state. Unfortunately, such data is not available to accurately assess the level of private practice in Uzbekistan.

7. Does the state provide public defenders? Yes. According to Article 117 of the constitution, all defendants are entitled to legal assistance.

8. Are there effective anti-bias/discrimination laws, including protection of ethnic minority rights? In the constitution, the Uzbek legal code, and presidential decrees, the issue of discrimination is addressed. In each instance, government stresses the need to protect minority groups and to create a system of recourse for their complaints. For example, in February 1995, President Karimov appointed a Human Rights Commissioner who is charged with enforcing such legislation. Over the past several years, there have also been efforts to actively support non-Uzbek language media and educational programs. Such efforts are important, given that nearly 25 percent of Uzbekistan's population is non-Uzbek, with the majority of these being Russian and Tajik. The Russian population is of particular concern, as their treatment directly affects Uzbek-Russian relations. To this end, the Uzbek government has permitted the establishment of Russian cultural centers in Tashkent, Ferghana, and Samarkand (cities with large Russian communities). In addition, the language law which was to have Uzbek as the sole language of official communication by 1998 has been modified. No date has been set for this policy to be enacted. At the same time, it must be noted that there have been instances of discrimination and forms of intimidation directed against ethnic minorities. Russians complain of Uzbeks unfairly treating them in social, business, and market settings, while Tajiks claim that their needs are not being met by the Uzbek state. In neither case, have public organizations that promote minority rights been allowed to register and legally participate in the political process.

Corruption C/D

1. What is the magnitude of official corruption in the civil service? Must an average citizen pay a bribe to a bureaucrat in order to receive a service? What services are subject to bribe requests for example, university entrance, hospital admission, telephone installation, obtaining a license to operate a business, applying for a passport or other official documents? What is the average salary of civil servants at various levels? Very little research has been done on the topic of corruption in Uzbekistan, thus, most of the discussion on this topic unfortunately must remain anecdotal and impressionistic. While only two percent of respondents in a public opinion poll conducted in 1996 stated that official corruption was a source of concern, the level of corruption a citizen encounters at the local level is high. Views toward civil servants are not positive and one generally expects to pay some sort of bribe to expedite service. This is particularly true for licenses and permits ranging from kiosk owners to restaurateurs. Not only are university admissions effected by bribe demands, but also final grades and evaluations (at all levels). Unique to Uzbekistan is the need to bribe university officials in order to have a student exempt from the fall cotton harvest, a tradition that goes back to the Soviet era.

2. Do top policy-makers (the president, ministers, vice-ministers, top court justices, and heads of agencies and commissions) have direct ties to businesses? How strong are such connections and what kind of businesses are these? This appears to be less of a problem in Uzbekistan than in other countries, although links are definitely present. For example, President Karimov himself has ties to the largest cotton trading company in Uzbekistan. Of course, given strict government control over the key industries in the country, there is no need to hide such connections.

3. Do laws requiring financial disclosure and disallowing conflict of interest exist? Have publicized anticorruption cases been pursued? To what conclusion? The most interesting anticorruption case to date was the 1994 prosecution of former Vice President Shukhrullo Mirsaidov. In an effort to further reduce his political influence, Mirsaidov was charged with embezzlement and misuse of state funds. After a short trial, he was found guilty and required to pay a fine in excess of $1 million. Although he is challenging the verdict, Mirsaidov remains the highest ranking official to be convicted of this crime. Local hokims and officials have also been periodic targets of anti-corruption campaigns, but most are simply dismissed for mismanagement and poor leadership. There may still exist a residual reluctance to initiate a mass anti-corruption campaign in light of the country's experience with the Soviet-era Cotton Scandal, in which hundreds of Uzbek officials were charged with fraud and embezzlement.

4. What major anticorruption initiatives have been implemented? How often are anticorruption laws and decrees adopted? The constitution and legislation originating from the Oliy Majlis outline penalties for corrupt practices; however, the enforcement of such policies is seen as weak to non-existent.

5. How do major corruption-ranking organizations like Transparency International rate this country? Uzbekistan has not been rated by major corruption-ranking organizations.

Privatization 6.25/7

1. What percentage of the GDP comes from private ownership? What percentage of the labor force is employed in the private sector? How large is the informal sector of the economy? The European Bank for Reconstruction and Development estimated that 45 percent of the economy was in private hands by mid-1997, although some estimates dispute that figure, claiming it is no more than 20-25 percent of GDP. These disputes arise from the nonstandard accounting and statistical practices by the government. Labor force statistics are likewise difficult to ascertain, but estimates range from 25-30 percent of the labor force is employed in the private sector. The higher numbers are attributed to the fact that the labor-intensive agricultural sector is considered largely privatized. There are no valid estimates of the informal sector of the economy, although the government repeatedly complains about a lack of tax collection and true accounting of the economy. In addition, given the discrepancy between the official and unofficial currency exchange rates, one can assume that a reasonable volume of informal trade is taking place. For instance, one survey noted that Uzbekistan has a very high level of activity in the black market, particularly in portable products like cigarettes and computer software.

2. What major privatization legislation has been past? What were its substantive features? The Uzbek government addressed privatization in 1991 Law on Denationalization and Privatization, although no serious effort to implement it took place for several years. In early 1993, 35,000 small-sale enterprises were privatized, followed by the privatization of 15,000 medium-scale enterprises in 1994-1995. In the latter group, the state retained up to a 26 percent stake in each venture, with the collective keeping 25 percent, and the remaining 49 percent being sold off to individuals for cash or as part of the Privatization Investment Funds (PIF). The government issued a more comprehensive set of decrees in 1995 and 1996 to work out discrepancies in the privatization program. Specifically, these decrees addressed land ownership and transfers, taxation of private property, and foreign ownership of private property. Compared to other newly independent states, the government has been deliberately slow in proceeding with privatization legislation, arguing that such step-by-step measures will ensure an orderly development of the economy. Citing the problems of rapid privatization in other CIS states, in particular, Russia , President Karimov was stated that he does not want to go through the same issues of hyperinflation, increased role of criminal associations in the private sector, and the uncertainty of not being able to maintain control of the process. In addition, the government has not changed its position that heavy industry, energy, and major export commodities (especially cotton) remain under state control.

In October 1997, the cabinet established a Republican Commission, chaired by Prime Minister Utkir Sultanov, to study economic reform measures. The commission outlined a proposal that, if implemented, will transfer agricultural production to the private sector. This policy will not apply to cotton and grain export crops, which will remain state-controlled. Nevertheless, this could mean the end of the standard policy of leasing land to farmers. The immediate goal will be to establish a mechanism for examining the legal, economic, and social ramifications of this policy. Specific ministries will be in charge of these issues and will present their findings at a later date.

3. What proportion of agriculture, housing and land, industry, and small business and services is in private hands? *Agriculture*: Given that nearly half of all the country's population lives in rural areas, agricultural privatization has been a delicate undertaking. At present, the agricultural sector has been "officially privatized," although the actual situation has changed less than expected. In essence, the collective farm system of the Soviet era is largely intact, with families, or groups of families, taking over the farms after "privatizing" them. Indeed, one option has been to have families jointly own large tracts of land (paralleling the collective farms), thus avoiding the difficult problem of dividing the land into private farms. The fact that agriculture is the largest sector – 28.5 percent of GNP and 41 percent of the labor force – is one of the reasons given for a slower policy of privatization. Not much has changed in the past year with respect to the privatization of agriculture. Because most agricultural enterprises are collective farms, these were technically privatized when they were turned over to the families that ran them. Payments to the state and guidelines for products remain, though, suggesting that the farms are not completely private. That said, the privatization of the agricultural sector is a politically sensitive issue, given the fact that over half of Uzbekistan's population, and over 40 percent of the labor force, are in this sector.

Housing and Land: As early as September 1992, individuals were given the option of purchasing their apartments for an average cost of three months salary. Homeowners went through a similar process in March 1994. In addition, the government made it possible for individuals to build private residences. By all accounts, this procedure went along fairly well and, at present, a system is in place for citizens to own their own dwelling. In addition, a 1996 decree permitted foreigners to purchase property. In all, this should stimulate the construction sector as new homes, particularly in the suburbs of Tashkent, are being built. To date, the problem of property transfer has not been addressed. Technically, one does not have the right to bequeath property, although anecdotal evidence suggests that it is already being done.

Industry: Privatization has been less successful in the industrial sector, mainly because (as noted above) this sector contains much of what is considered strategic, including heavy industry, energy, and the export production sector. These businesses still rely on quotas from the government and bonuses for plan performance, much like the pre-1991 period.

Business and service: This has been the area with the greatest privatization over the last two years. Beginning in January 1994, and continuing through the present, business and service sector firms have been up for purchase at public auctions. While many of these have been purchased by the former Communist elite, there are instances of entrepreneurs acquiring small-scale businesses. It is estimated that two-thirds of this sector is privatized – an estimated 47,000 of the 68,000 enterprises listed in the country.

4. What has been the extent of insider (management, labor, nomenklatura) participation in the privatization process? What explicit and implicit preferences have been awarded to insiders? As with other states of the former Soviet Union, Uzbekistan has had instances of former managers of businesses and firms buying out companies outright, or at least gaining a majority share. The nomenklatura, in general, has had an unfair advantage since they controlled the privatization auctions and had knowledge of what was to be auctioned. Complete statistics on such activity are unavailable, and most of what is known is anecdotal.

5. How much public awareness of and support for privatization has there been? What is the nature of support and opposition to privatization by major interest groups? In general, public knowledge of the government's privatization program is sketchy. While decrees are published in the daily newspapers, in particular, in *Halq sozi*, the official paper, opinion polls suggest that there is only a passing awareness of the program among the general public. Support, however, seems to be high, as it is unlikely that the general population would question any of Karimov's policies. On November 1, 1997, two agricultural specialists called the recent discussion to privatize more of the agricultural sector unwise, stressing that Uzbekistan is not only unprepared for private ownership of land, but that the whole concept is anathema to the country and is simply bad economics. Professor R. Karimov, who is a member of the Commission for Deepening Economic Reforms in Agriculture, and E. Trushin of the statistics Ministry argued that privatization will only hinder rational land-use, avoid questions of ecology, and does not, in the end, guarantee optimal use of the land. They suggested that, instead, land should be leased on a long-term, even hereditary, basis and include protective measures for the farmers. In this manner, the state would be assured of certain returns from the land and farmers would be given a stable environment within which to work. This is the first time that a serious discussion of government policy is taking place in a public forum. The fact that opposing views are being expressed in the national press is an indication of how serious this next step in economic reform is for the government.

Macroeconomics 6.25/7

1. Has the taxation system been reformed? (What areas have and have not been overhauled? To what degree are taxpayers complying? Is tax compliance difficult to achieve? Has the level of revenues increased? Is the revenue-collection body overburdened? What is the overall tax burden?) The tax system in Uzbekistan is still unreformed and revenue collection is reported to be woefully behind. Tax rates in Uzbekistan include a 20 percent capital gains tax, a 17 percent value-added tax (VAT), and a 40 percent payroll tax. Income and corporate taxes are both on sliding scales, with the highest being 45 percent and 37 percent, respectively. The highest individual rate applies to those whose incomes exceed the minimum wage (750 *soms*, or $9.40) by a factor of 15. These new rates were established in the tax code adopted by the Oliy Majlis in April 1997 and implemented on January 1, 1998. The government hopes that this new code will rectify the current problems in tax compliance.

2. Does fiscal policy encourage private savings, investment and earnings? (Has there been any reform/alteration of revenue and budget policies? How large are budget deficits and overall debt? Is the financing of the social insurance/pension system sustainable? What proportion of the budget is taken up by subsidies to firms and individuals? At present, the Uzbek government is trying to maintain a fiscal deficit at, or under, 3.5 percent as required by international financial institutions. The 1998 predicted deficit is 3.1 percent, or 38.2 billion som, with revenues projected at 399.5 billion som and expenditures at 437.7 billion som. Finally, Uzbekistan still maintains a system of subsidizing consumer goods and welfare measures, particularly for the poor. It is estimated that nearly 50 percent of budget expenditures go to support these measures, although some experts note that this percentage is declining as government investment measures are increasing.

3. Has there been banking reform? (Is the central bank independent? What are its responsibilities? Is it effective in setting and/or implementing monetary policy? What is the actual state of the private banking sector? Does it conform to international standards? Are depositors protected?) Uzbekistan's banking system suffered a severe shock following the collapse of the Soviet Union. It drafted a banking law and established its central bank in 1992. At present, Uzbekistan's banking sector is still in the process of establishing itself as a credible and active entity in the country. Perhaps because of government concerns that the system is too fragile, heavy restrictions are currently in place for just about every aspect of bank activity. This was particularly evident following the dramatic devaluation of the Uzbek som in the fall of 1996 when the government decreed that only two banks could work with hard currencies and additional restrictions were put in place for citizen access to bank accounts. Not surprisingly, this had an adverse effect on international banking in Uzbekistan. One particularly onerous restriction has been the insistence by the central bank that virtually all inter-enterprise transactions be conducted through interbank transfers rather than by cash. Since interbank transfers take up to several months to clear, this has caused severe difficulties for businesses. As a means of coping with these political restrictions, a parallel pricing system has emerged, where cash prices are as little as one-third that of interbank transfer prices. Because the banks are state-run, any reforms or loosening up of regulations will have to come directly from the government. At present, there is a two-tiered banking system, with the Central Bank of Uzbekistan (CBU) and the National Bank for Foreign Economic Activity on one level, and about 30 commercial banks on the second. The first two banks are permitted to purchase and sell hard currencies, while the others are restricted to som activity only. In addition, the CBU is responsible for issuing currency, setting interest rates, and regulating the use of foreign currency in Uzbekistan. These central banks are responsible to the Cabinet of Ministers and ultimately, the presidential apparatus. If banking regulations are loosened, one can expect to see an increase in the number of banks: this is largely due to the fact that the Law on Banks and Banking allows for a bank to be established with as little as six million som in reserve. A decree issued in April 1997 on private banks should allow this to happen. In principle, depositors are protected in Uzbek banks, although it is too early to tell how effective such protection really is.

4. How sound is the national currency? (Is the value of the currency fixed or does it float?

How convertible is the currency? How large are the hard currency reserves? Has exchange rate policy been stable and predictable?) As noted above, a major problem in the Uzbek economy remains the currency, the som. Officially introduced in June 1994 (with a coupon version introduced in November 1993), the Uzbek som remained somewhat stable until the fall of 1996. At that time, the Uzbek government initiated a program to make the som a convertible currency, but within months, found the value of the som dropping precipitously. The value, which stood at 38som/ $1 in the summer of 1996 fell to 55som/$1 at years' end. By the end of 1997, the rate had further dropped to 80som/$1. Making this more problematic was the fact that the unofficial (black market) rate dropped even further. For a short while in 1996, the official and unofficial rates were so close that the black market in som trading was tailing off. However, by the end of 1996, the black market rate was 120som/$1 and by the end of 1997, it stood at almost 200som/$1. In October 1996, the government re-established strict controls on access to hard currency. This decision led the International Monotary Fund to suspend its Stand-By Arrangement financing for Uzbekistan. To obtain hard currency, one needs to apply for a license, and even then a conversion can take a month or more. Moreover, companies earning hard currency are required to exchange 30 percent of their revenues in hard currency for som (at the official rate). The devaluation of the Uzbek som, as well as strict regulations on hard currency access has adversely effected private savings, investment, and earnings. In addition, the high inflation rates of the past (1,100 percent in 1994, 425 percent in 1995, and 105 percent in 1996) have not helped. That said, the 1997 inflation rate dropped to 27 percent and the 1998 goal is 22 percent. If these lower figures can be maintained, one can expect to see increased confidence in the economic system. The total amount of individual savings was also adversely effected by the November 1993 conversion from the ruble to the som-coupon, and the subsequent June 1994 conversion to the official som. In both instances, the government set limits on how much money one could transfer. Reports of people losing 80 to 90 percent of their savings were common.

5. Is there a functioning capital market infrastructure? (Are there existing or planned commodities, bond and stock markets? What are the mechanisms for investing and lending? What government bodies have authority to regulate capital markets?) The capital market in Uzbekistan remains weak, although the government does see this as an area of reform, so the possibility exists of future action. The Central Asian Stock Exchange was established on March 15, 1994, with Karimov's decree on economic communities. This decree allows for the circulation of corporate, employee, and joint-stock company shares, government bonds (both national and local), corporate bonds, and promissory notes (state, commercial, common, and transferable). Securities have to register with the Ministry of Finance before they can be part of the stock exchange. The daily volume of trade remains under $1 billion, thus it is still small enough to not be considered influential at this time. With the inflow of foreign capital, the government hopes to see the volume increase steadily in 1998.

Microeconomics 6.25/7

1. Are property rights guaranteed? (Are there both formal and de facto protections of private real estate and intellectual property? Is there a land registry with the authority and capability to ensure accurate recording of who owns what? What are the procedures for expropriation, including measures for compensation and challenge? Have any seizures taken place?) According to the constitution and the decree on private property, such rights are guaranteed. Housing and land ownership is registered at the ration-level and taxed accordingly. There are also Laws on Expropriation and Compensation, which have been tested in the old city section of Tashkent, where thousands of traditional Uzbek homes were destroyed and replaced with apartment blocks, for sanitary reasons. The issue of property rights has been absent from the legal system, although a citizens' group challenging the urban renewal program will also be a test for the court.

2. To what extent have prices been liberalized? What subsidies remain? Uzbekistan has been slow to liberalize prices, as compared to the other former Soviet states. President Karimov argues that a step-by-step approach is preferable, especially in light of the disastrous price liberalization of January 1992. At that time, Uzbekistan was still in the ruble zone and thus was forced to follow the Russian price liberalization. Since that time, prices on most products have been liberalized with government subsidies existing for basic commodities (bread, flour, tea, cotton seed oil, etc.).

3. Is it possible to own and operate a business? (Has there been legislation regarding the formation, dissolution and transfer of businesses, and is the law respected? Do there exist overly cumbersome bureaucratic hurdles that effectively hinder the ability to own and dispose of a business? Are citizens given access to information on commercial law? Is that law applied fairly? Does regulation (or licensing requirements) impose significant costs on business and consumers? Do they create significant barriers to entry and seriously hamper competition?) It is possible to own and operate a business in Uzbekistan, and laws exist that outline procedures for setting up such enterprises, e.g. the Laws on Entrepreneurship, on Enterprises, and on Foreign Economic Activity. Financial and bureaucratic obstacles exist and are often too difficult to individual entrepreneurs to legally overcome. Rumors of mafia protection rings also plague the business world, especially in the service sector. Citizens do have access to laws and rules on setting up businesses, with the major laws published in the news dailies. Obtaining information at the regional or city offices can be a problem, but again, such documents do exist.

4. Are courts effective, transparent, efficient, and quick in reaching decisions on property and contract disputes? What alternative mechanisms for adjudicating disputes exist? As noted earlier regarding the criminal and civil courts, it can be said that while the institutions exist, their ability to get things done is limited. Uzbek law is often clear on issues of property rights and contract obligations; however, the enforcement of such laws is suspect. Anecdotal evidence suggests that, at the local level, individuals are turning to the mahalla councils and leaders for advice and arbitration. In many ways, this follows upon a legal custom that predates the Soviet period.

There is no data on how many cases have been publicly brought up concerning these issues, nor of their resolution.

5. Is business competition encouraged? (Are monopolistic practices limited in law and in practice? If so, how? Do what degree is insider dealing a hindrance to open competition? Are government procurement policies open and unbiased?) As the state still directly controls the major industries, joint venture partnerships, and export firms such as that for cotton, Uzbekistan's most important crop, competition is not really a factor. Inside dealing is rumored to be very important, especially in landing lucrative joint venture capital. There is some competition, although prices tend to remain constant, among direct competitors. There is no information on government procurements policies and on the bidding process.

6. To what extent has international trade been liberalized? To what degree has there been simplification/overhaul of customs and tariff procedures, and are these applied fairly? What informal trade barriers exist? Foreign trade is encouraged, but obstacles exist that some companies claim are too difficult to address. Tariff barriers at 10-20 percent on average are moderate comparatively. The main barrier to trade is the restrictive rules on currency convertibility and controls on banking transactions. Export tariffs are significant, with duties ranging from 5 to 50 percent. The state retains monopoly status with respect to purchasing key goods for export abroad, such as cotton. In 1997, exports amounted to $4.6085 billion and imports stood at $4.5418, leaving a trade surplus of $66.7 million. Trade with CIS countries was $1.2094 and $1.2751 respectively (about 30 percent of the total trade), signifying that activity with the non-CIS states now takes up a sizeable part of Uzbekistan's trade. Since 1994, trade with these states has increased by more than three-fold. The primary trade product remains cotton, at 30 percent of total exports. Energy makes up a modest 12 percent. Imports are largely machinery and equipment (43 percent). To enhance foreign trade, President Karimov supported the new Customs Code, which was enacted on March 1, 1998. Although it is too early to tell how effective this code will be, on paper it is significant: it lists VAT, duties, licensing fees, costs for storage and transport, and regulations on what companies can export to other CIS states. In short, the government has every intention of spurring the current growth in trade to even higher numbers. How these new regulations will be applied remains to be seen and companies still complain of bribe requirements, especially in working with subcontractors.

7. To what extent has foreign investment and capital flow been encouraged or constrained? Since 1995, this has been a major political issue for President Karimov. Largely in the form of joint-venture (JV) enterprises, foreign investment has been fairly active in Uzbekistan. Significant reform measures were enacted in 1996 that included allowing foreign companies or individuals to own property, take advantage of tax holidays including a seven-year grace period for companies investing in the manufacturing industries, and have monopoly rights in certain sectors. A July 1996 decree on JV investment also eased the requirements on forming such ventures. Logistical and cost barriers still exist, including high tax rates on JV profits, thus dampening enthusiasm on the part of medium foreign companies to get involved. Poor transportation routes and an uncertain regional market are also factors that can dissuade foreign investors. Large corporations such as Newmont Mining (US), Coca-Cola (US), Daewoo (South Korea), British-American Tobacco (UK), and Samsung (South Korea) have had fewer problems in setting up their ventures. Overall, the major investor countries include the United States, Germany, South Korea, the United Kingdom, Turkey, and China. Annual foreign investment reached $150 million in 1996.

8. Has there been reform of the energy sector? (To what degree has the energy sector been restructured? Is the energy sector more varied, and is it open to private competition? Is the country overly dependent on one or two other countries for energy [including whether exported fuels must pass through one or more countries to reach markets]?) The energy sector remains under the control of the state. Uzbekistan has reserves of oil and gas and can become a regional exporter of the latter, once the transport infrastructure is developed more fully. Oil and gas production are managed by the state-owned Uzbekneftegas, which consists of 14 large and 250 smaller enterprises throughout the country. Natural gas production increased from 49 bcm to 51.2 bcm during the period 1996 to 1997, and experts note that this trend should continue. It is already among the world's top ten producers of natural gas. Oil production stands at 8.2 million metric tons (1997). The government considers energy to be a strategic resource and it is unlikely that the sector will be privatized or reformed anytime soon. As the sole proprietor of energy in the country, the government also continues to subsidize energy use, stating that it will do so at least until the year 2000. That the energy sector is state-run does not preclude the involvement of foreign companies. Indeed, Enron Gas has been instrumental in developing the various gas production facilities in the country, and Unocal and Delta have likewise assisted in expanding oil production. In addition, international companies from France, Germany, and Japan are also involved in developing refineries in Bukhara and Nawoi. It is the Uzbek government's position that such assistance is needed to ensure the proper exploitation of these resources.

The biggest single problem facing the energy sector is transportation. Although domestic use will continue to increase with population growth and industrial expansion, the need to export exists. As Uzbekistan is a doubly-landlocked country, pipelines must travel through at least two countries to get to reasonable markets. Recent discussions on whether Uzbek energy will pass through a Trans-Caspian pipeline that the United States supports, or through the energy grid of Russia that currently exists, is a topic of intense debate. The bottom line, though, is that Uzbekistan can at least maintain enough energy to satisfy domestic needs, which is a positive sign for the economy. Only 230 of the country's 800 gasoline refueling stations have been privatized. The inadequacy of the gas distribution system is evident in the fact that it is not uncommon for tanker trucks themselves to stop and serve as mobile refueling stations. Electricity is generated primarily from natural gas-powered thermal plants, though some is produced in coal and hydro-electric plants.

YUGOSLAVIA

Freedom in the World Ratings, 1989-1998

	1989-90	1990-91	1991-92	1992-93	1993-94	1994-95	1995-96	1996-97	1997-98
Political Rights	5	5	6	6	6	6	6	6	6
Civil Liberties	4	4	5	5	6	6	6	6	6
Status	PF	PF	NF	PF	NF	NF	NF	NF	NF

Polity: Transitional
Economy: Transitional
Population: 10,655,000
PPP: na
Ethnic Groups: Serb (67 percent), Kosovar (18 percent), Montenegrin (6 percent), Sanjak Muslim (3.2 percent), Roma, Albanian, others
Capital: Belgrade

Political Process 5.00/7

1. When did national legislative elections occur? Were they free and fair? How were they judged by domestic and international monitoring organizations? Who composed the government? In April 1992, Serbian and Montenegrin delegates in what remainded of the Federal Assembly of the Socialist Federal Republic of Yugoslavia (SFRY) adopted a constitution for a new Federal Republic of Yugoslavia (FRY), composed of Montenegro and Serbia with its two autonomous provinces, Kosovo and Vojvodina. The FRY was proclaimed on April 27, 1992, and in May 1992 elections were held for a body to succeed the SFRY's Federal Assembly. The new FRY constitution created a bicameral Federal Assembly. The upper house comprises a 40-member Chamber of Republics in which Montenegro and Serbia have equal representation. Members of the Chamber of Republics are elected by their respective republican assemblies. Delegates to the 138-member Chamber of Citizens are elected according to a complex formula in which 108 delegates are assigned to Serbia and 30 to Montenegro. In each case, some delegates are popularly elected — 54 in Serbia, and 24 in Montenegro — while the remainder are elected according to constituency majorities. Delegates in both chambers serve four-year terms.

Elections for the Federal Assembly were held in November 1996. An alliance composed of the ruling *Socijalisticka Partija Srbije* (the Socialist Party of Serbia, or SPS), the *Jugoslovenska Udruzena Levica* (the Yugoslav United Left, or YUL), and *Nova Demokratija* (New Democracy, or ND) won a plurality of 64 seats in the 138-member Chamber of Citizens. The SPS's sister party in Montenegro, the Democratic Party of Socialists of Montenegro (*Demokratska Partija Socijalista Crne Gore*, DPSCG) won an additional 20 seats. The three main opposition parties in the *Zajedno* (Together) coalition (the Democratic Party, the Serbian Renewal Movement, or SPO, and the Civic Alliance) won 22 seats, while the main right-wing nationalist opposition party, the *Srpska Radikalna Stranka* (the Serbian Radical Party, or SRS) won 16 seats.

The two republics each have popularly-elected, unicameral assemblies, with delegates serving four-year terms. The Serbian Assembly (*Skupstina Srbije*) has 250 seats. In the December 1993 elections for the Serbian Skupstina, the SPS won 123 seats; a multiparty opposition movement, the *Demokratski Pokret Srbije* (the Democratic Movement of Serbia, or DEPOS) won 45; the SRS won 39; the Democratic Party, 29; the Democratic Party of Serbia, 7; the Democratic Community of Vojvodina Hungarians, 5; and a Sandzak-Moslem Kosovo Albanian coalition, the Party of Democratic Action/Democratic Party of Albanians won 2.

The latest elections for the Serbian Skupstina in September 1997 were boycotted by two leading opposition parties: Zoran Djindjic's Democratic Party and Vesna Pesic's Civic Alliance of Serbia. Milosevic's ruling left-wing coalition lost its governing majority, gaining only 110 seats. The SRS, on the other hand, significantly increased its share of power, gaining 82 seats. Vuk Draskovic's SPO also improved its standing, winning 45 seats in the Skupstina. Other smaller parties, including one representing Vojvodina Hungarians and another representing Sandzak Muslims, shared the remaining 13 seats. Serbian politics took a turn to the nationalist right in March 1998, when SRS president Vojislav Seselj was named Deputy Prime Minister in the new Serbian government.

In the November 1996 elections for the 71-seat Montenegrin Assembly (*Skupstina Crne Gore*), the ruling DPSCG won 45 seats; the Liberal Alliance, 19; the Party of Democratic Action, 3; the Democratic Alliance of Montenegro, 2; and the Democratic Union of Albanians, 2. In 1997, the DPSCG broke into pro-Milosevic and pro-reform factions, and it is widely believed that new elections for the Montenegrin Skupstina would have to be held sometime in 1998.

The Kosovo Albanian population has consistently boycotted Serbian and Yugoslav elections. In 1990, Serbian authorities had promulgated a new republican constitution that rescinded the broad autonomy Serbia's two provinces, Kosovo and Vojvodina, had enjoyed since 1974. Albanian delegates in the Kosovo Assembly responded by declaring Kosovo a constituent republic in Yugoslavia (but independent of Serbia), to which Serbian authorities responded by dissolving the Kosovo Assembly. In May 1992, Kosovo Albanians held elections for a new assembly, and elected Ibrahim Rugova "president" of the self-declared "Republic of Kosovo." Serbian authorities immediately declared the elections illegal. As of March 1998, no one in the international community had recognized the Kosovo Albanians' self-declared state.

Since 1990, the Kosovo Albanians have proceeded to create their own parallel educational, health, and governmental institutions. Serbian authorities generally have not interfered with these efforts. Rugova, for instance, has been allowed to travel freely. In December 1996, however, Serbian security troops did crack down on unauthorized Albanian police forces. A few months earlier, in September 1996, Milosevic and Rugova had reached an agreement providing for an end to the six-year Albanian boycott of state schools. The agreement, however, was never implemented, and the U.S. Department of State blamed both sides for intransigence. Conditions deteriorated in Kosovo during 1997 as the Kosovo Albanian leadership continued to push for independence and the Milosevic regime continued with its repressive policies. At the same time, moderate Albanian leaders urging a policy of non-violence lost influence to more militant factions. During the concurrent anarchy in neighboring Albania in 1997, large stores of weaponry made their way from Albania to Kosovo. By late 1997, an organization called the "Kosovo Liberation Army" (KLA) began attacks on Serbian security forces in Kosovo in which several Serbian policemen were killed. By February 1998, the KLA had claimed responsibility for the assassination of 50 people in the past year, including 20

Albanians accused of being loyal to the Serbian government. The KLA was supported in part by Islamic terrorist organizations with ties to Iran and experience in Bosnia. In March 1998, Serbian security forces responded to KLA attacks with a large-scale campaign to wipe out the KLA, and in fact succeeded in killing one of its leaders. Scores of civilians were killed in the fighting, and the international community condemned the Milosevic government for responding to the KLA's attacks with disproportionate force. The International Criminal Tribunal for the Former Yugoslavia announced that it would begin investigations into the actions of Serbian security forces in Kosovo. On March 9, 1998, the Contact Group imposed new punitive sanctions on Yugoslavia, including denying visas to senior Yugoslav officials believed to be responsible for the crackdown, and an arms embargo. On March 18, 1998, Serbian President Milan Milutinovic called for immediate and unconditional talks on Kosovo based on Serbia's territorial integrity but allowing for "self-rule" for Kosovo. On March 22, 1998, Serbian officials allowed Kosovo Albanians to hold elections for their self-declared parliament and presidency. Despite a boycott of the elections by several smaller Albanian parties, Rugova was again elected "president."

2. When did presidential elections occur? Were they free and fair? The Yugoslav presidency is a largely ceremonial post. The Federal Assembly elects the Yugoslav president, who must obtain the approval of both Montenegrin and Serbian delegates. The Yugoslav president, in turn, nominates the federal prime minister. According to the FRY constitution, the federal president and the federal prime minister cannot be from the same republic, and the federal president is limited to only one four-year term. The first FRY president was Dobrica Cosic, a well-known Serbian writer and dissident during the Titoist period. In June 1993, Cosic was ousted by Milosevic and replaced by Zoran Lilic, a Milosevic protégé with no independent authority. Since Milosevic himself was constitutionally prohibited from serving a third consecutive term as Serbian president, he took over Lilic's position as Yugoslav president in July 1997. At the same time, Milosevic's party also proposed constitutional changes so that the Yugoslav president would henceforth be popularly elected. This was widely seen as a precautionary move, given Milosevic's increasing unpopularity in Montenegro.

The president of Serbia is popularly elected. In the first multi-party elections in December 1990, Milosevic won the position handily, and was re-elected in December 1992. In 1997, Milosevic's SPS nominated Zoran Lilic (see above) as its candidate for the Serbian presidency. After failing to win in the first two rounds in September and October, Lilic was replaced by Milan Milutinovic as the SPS candidate. The primary opponent to both Lilic and Milutinovic was the SRS leader, Vojislav Seselj. In a fourth round of elections in December 1997, Milutinovic beat Seselj amidst widespread rumors of ballot stuffing to assure a 50 percent turnout. Little complaint was heard from the international community, however, because Milutinovic was felt to be an infinitely more acceptable figure than the more nationalist Seselj.

The president of Montenegro is also popularly elected. Milo Djukanovic, the former Montenegrin prime minister who broke with Milosevic and his Montenegrin loyalists during the Serbian opposition protests in the winter of 1996-1997, was elected president of Montenegro in multi-party elections in October 1997. Djukanovic's victory was disputed by his opponent and predecessor as president of Montenegro, Momir Bulatovic, who accused the Djukanovic camp of widespread vote fraud.

Despite rumors that Bulatovic was planning a coup and that Milosevic wanted to impose a state of emergency in Montenegro, strong international support for Djukanovic helped keep him in office through March 1998.

None of the elections held in Yugoslavia over the past several years, whether at the national, republican, or municipal levels, can be considered to have been "free and fair." Regarding the several rounds of presidential and parliamentary elections in Serbia in the latter half of 1997, for instance, an OSCE report noted that the "overall election process in the Republic of Serbia is fundamentally flawed." Opposition parties are routinely denied access to state-owned media (see below), and the Milosevic regime manipulates the electoral process itself in numerous ways.

3. Is the electoral system multi party-based? Are there at least two viable political parties functioning at all levels of government? The FRY Constitution guarantees citizens freedom of political association (Article 41). At the federal Yugoslav, republican, and municipal levels, several parties compete in elections and participate in government. The actual power and influence of the various parties varies significantly. The SPS, for instance, by virtue of its control over the state security forces, the most important mass media, and the most important segments of the economy, has a disproportionate share of power at all levels of government. Nevertheless, over the past few years, the SPS has lost its exclusive control of government institutions, and has been increasingly forced to form coalitions with opposition parties.

4. How many parties have been legalized? Are any particular parties illegal? As of 1995, there were approximately 200 parties functioning at the federal and republican levels. Many of these, however, were small parties with little or no infrastructure or coherent political platform. Article 42 of the FRY constitution forbids any political parties/organizations that advocate the violent overthrow of the constitutional order.

5. What proportion of the population belongs to political parties? Exact figures on political party membership are difficult to come by because many parties are reluctant to release such data. A good rule of thumb for understanding the Serbian electorate, however, is the rule of fourths provided by Prof. Svetozar Stojanovic. Within Serbia itself, if one excludes the Kosovo Albanian population which has been boycotting elections since 1990, and Hungarians in Vojvodina who vote for their own ethnically-based parties, the Serbian electorate can be divided into four segments. The first consists of those who abstain from voting altogether. The second consists of SPS/YUL voters. The third consists of SRS supporters. The fourth segment votes for the rest of the opposition parties, such as the SPO, the DS, the GSS, etc.

The SPS claims a membership of approximately 600,000, making it by far the largest political party in Yugoslavia. *Nova Demokratija* claims to have 40,000 members. In general terms, however, support for a political party can be determined by analyzing voting results since 1990. Public support for Milosevic's SPS, for instance, has declined considerably over the past eight years; in the 1990 elections, the SPS gained over 2.3 million votes, while in the 1997 elections, this number fell to 1,200,000. Vuk Draskovic's SPO has consistently won between 700,000 and one million votes over the past eight years. Support for Vojislav Seselj's SRS also fluctuates considerably; in the elections between 1990 and 1997, the SRS has gained anywhere between 600,000 and 1,038,000.

Reliable figures for Montenegrin political parties are also difficult to obtain. Of Montenegro's approximately 450,000 registered voters, however, it is generally assumed that most Montenegrins who identify themselves more as Serbs, or favor close ties with Serbia, vote for Momir Bulatovic's wing of the DPS-CG. Milo Djukanovic's recent electoral successes, on the other hand, are due to the votes his faction of the DPS-CG has received from Albanians, Croats, and Muslims in Montenegro.

6. What has been the trend of voter turnout at the municipal, provincial, and national levels in recent years? Voter turnout throughout the former Yugoslavia was traditionally high. In the 1990 elections, well over 70 percent of the eligible electorate turned out. In more recent elections there have been signs of "voter fatigue." Due to the boycott of the September 1997 Serbian elections, for instance, many observers questioned the Republican Electoral Commission's claim that 62 percent of the electorate had turned out. In subsequent runoff elections for the Serbian presidency voter turnout hovered at or below the 50 percent level. In the October 1997 presidential elections in Montenegro, voter turnout was approximately 73 percent.

Civil Society 5.00/7

1. How many nongovernmental organizations (NGOs) have come into existence since 1988? What is the number of charitable/nonprofit organizations? Are there locally led efforts to increase philanthropy and volunteerism? What proportion of the population is active in private voluntary activity (from polling data)? Hundreds of organizations have been formed since 1988, although the exact number and the size of their memberships are difficult to determine. NGOs in the FRY are still officially registered as "social organizations" or "associations of citizens" in accord with the terms used during the socialist period. According to the Federal Statistics Office, in 1994 there were 18,937 registered "social organizations" and 1,349 registered "associations of citizens." All of these, however, had originated during the socialist period. Since 1991, observers believe another 500 have been formed, the most numerous being ecological and humanitarian organizations, followed by human rights-oriented NGOs.

In 1991, a Belgrade-based "Center for Anti-War Action" emerged, and a "Humanitarian Law Center" was also founded. There are also Helsinki Committees active in Belgrade, Pristina, and the Sandzak. The Helsinki Committees in Belgrade and Pristina often collaborate in monitoring the human rights situation in Kosovo. The Serbian Orthodox Church is active in providing charitable assistance to refugees and the poor. In Kosovo, a predominantly-Serbian organization of citizens known as the "Serb Resistance Movement" has organized to protest the Milosevic regime's policies in that province. The Students' Club in Belgrade and the Independent Union of Students in Kosovo have also played prominent roles over the past several years. Several environmental and women's rights groups are also active, most notably, the Belgrade-based "Women in Black," and the Pristina-based "League of Albanian Women."

2. What is the legal and regulatory environment for NGOs (i.e., ease of registration, legal rights, government regulation, taxation, procurement and access-to-information issues)? To what extent is NGO activism focused on improving the legal and regulatory environment? In 1997, there was a mild improvement in the position of NGOs in Serbia proper, as some observers noted that the Milosevic regime allowed more foreigners affiliated with international NGOs to enter the country. International monitoring groups claimed that in general they were free to conduct their activities. On the other hand, domestic NGOs have charged that the government was illegally obstructing their activities. For instance, the Center for Free Elections and Democracy (CeSID), a Belgrade-based NGO which monitors elections claimed in November 1997 that the government had denied them the right to monitor the presidential and parliamentary elections in Serbia in September. In subsequent legal proceedings initiated by CeSID, the Serbian Supreme Court upheld the government's refusal to allow CeSID a role in election monitoring. The situation in Montenegro is markedly different, as the government there has for some time promoted more open and liberal policies.

3. What is the organizational capacity of NGOs? Do management structures clearly delineate authority and responsibility? Is information available on NGO management issues in the native language? Is there a core of experienced practitioners/trainers to serve as consultants or mentor to less developed organizations? Information on this subject is not available.

4. Are NGOs financially viable? What is their tax status? Are they obliged to and do they typically disclose revenue sources? Do government procurement opportunities exist for private, not-for-profit providers of services? Information on this subject is not available.

5. Are there free trade unions? How many workers belong to these unions? Is the number of workers belonging to trade unions growing or decreasing? What is the numerical/proportional membership of farmers' groups, small business associations, etc.? Article 41 of the FRY constitution guarantees workers the right to form free trade unions. In addition to the government controlled "Alliance of Independent Labor Unions" with an estimated membership of one million, an independent "United Branch of Independent Labor Unions" with some 157,000 members exists. Numerous smaller unions representing transportation workers, educational employees, journalists, retirees, and others are very active, at least judging by their proclivity to strike. Independent unions suffer from regime attempts to suppress their activities; for instance, unions are often prohibited from busing their members to strikes or demonstrations held in different parts of the country.

6. What forms of interest group participation in politics are legal? What types of interest groups are active in the political and policy process? Articles 39 and 41 of the FRY constitution grant citizens the freedom to form political parties and organizations, and freedom of assembly. There are numerous organized interest groups in the country, representing ethnic constituencies. Especially prominent groups are those representing Albanians, Hungarians, Muslims, and Roma (gypsies), business interests, such as the Yugoslav Chamber of Commerce and Industry, and women's rights groups.

7. How is the not-for-profit/NGO sector perceived by the public and government officials? What is the nature of media coverage of NGOs? To what extent do government officials en-

gage with NGOs? Government officials associated with the ruling regime generally view NGOs, especially those with international connections, as suspect. Often they are accused of being "traitors" or "foreign mercenaries." NGOs also suffer from the fact that they are not a traditional form of social activism in these regions; consequently, the local population often views them as "mercenaries" working for foreign interests. Independent/alternative media treat NGOs more favorably.

Independent Media 4.50/7

1. Are there legal protections for press freedom? Articles 36 and 38 of the FRY constitution guarantee freedom of the press and prohibit censorship, with one stipulation: press/media outlets enjoy these freedoms only if they are registered with the government. In practice, independent and alternative media are frequently subjected to numerous forms of legalistic and bureaucratic harassment. A new media law proposed in February 1998, on the allocation of frequencies for TV and radio stations, for example, drew considerable criticism from the independent media because of its ambiguity. The new regulation imposed undisclosed fees for the allocation of frequencies, leaving officials free to price independent media houses out of business. Another feature of the new regulation warned that applications for a frequency would not be processed if technical details i.e., how far the signal of a certain transmitter will carry, in the application were incorrect. Since the methodologies for testing such things vary, this left considerable scope for arbitrary determinations that an application was "technically incorrect."

2. Are there legal penalties for libeling officials? Are there legal penalties for "irresponsible" journalism? Have these laws been enforced to harass journalists? There are laws on the books against slandering private individuals and government officials, but the Milosevic regime has rarely used such forms of harassment. In 1997, there were no publicized cases of journalists being prosecuted for libel; however, the regime seemed intent on reining in the media with new draft legislation circulated in late 1997 called the "Law on Public Information." According to the draft legislation, the new law included a vaguely-worded prohibition against journalists insulting the honor or reputation of individuals (Article 20); another prohibition against slander and quasi-slander (Article 5) ostensibly intended to force journalists to be more "truthful" in their reporting. Other contentious provisions of the new law called for all print media to provide the republican public prosecutor with a copy of their publications which was interpreted by critics as an attempt to encourage journalistic self-censorship, as well as a call to force all media to make public foreign sources of financing (Articles 14, 16, and 17).

3. What proportion of media is privatized? What are the major private newspapers, television stations, and radio stations? Yugoslavia has a plethora of both electronic and print media outlets. According to one estimate, in 1997 there were 300 privately owned radio stations and 100 privately-owned TV stations in Yugoslavia. Belgrade now has 12 daily newspapers. The largest and most influential media in Yugoslavia, however, both electronic and print, are state-owned. The most important TV station is the only government-owned station, *Radio-Televizija Srbije* (RTS), with a signal covering most of the country. RTS's editorial policy is strictly pro-government. During the 1997 electoral campaign, for instance, the Humanitarian Law Center in Belgrade claimed that all of the opposition parties combined received only one-fourth of the airtime RTS devoted to the ruling SPS coalition. A primary demand by the opposition since 1990 has been greater access to state-owned media. The most memorable feature of the winter 1996-1997 opposition protests was the sight of tens of thousands of demonstrators rattling pots and pans and blowing their car horns during the broadcast of RTS's main evening news program.

Montenegro and each of the provinces have their own state television services as well. In 1997, the relationship between Montenegro's state-run television network, *TV Crna Gora*, and the Milosevic-controlled RTS soured, and *TV Crna Gora* is now broadcasting a much more objective and open news information program. Under *TV Crna Gora's* new editorial leadership, more coverage is devoted to opposition political parties, and collaboration with independent news media in Belgrade, such as Radio B-92 or Belgrade's Studio B television station, is being expanded. By way of contrast, *TV Crna Gora* in 1997 stopped rebroadcasting RTS's main nightly news program.

In both Kosovo and Vojvodina, there are RTS broadcasts in Albanian or Magyar, respectively, although the editorial slant is pro-Milosevic. Yugoslavia also has numerous print media for ethnic minorities published in their native languages, e.g., Novi Sad's *Magyar Szo,* a Hungarian language daily with an estimated circulation of 26,000, or Pristina's *Koha Ditore*, an Albanian language newsmagazine edited by a well-known Albanian activist, Veton Surroi.

The largest print daily in Yugoslavia is the Belgrade-based *Politika* with an estimated circulation of 200-300,000, again with a pro-Milosevic editorial line. There are a variety of opposition publications, and their popularity has increased in recent years. According to one report, the overall circulation of the independent press surpassed that of the state media in 1997. Most important in this category are *Nasa Borba*, a daily formed by the journalists and staff of *Borba* when the Milosevic regime took that paper over. The Belgrade-based newsweeklies *Vreme* and *NIN* are also strongly anti-regime. In recent years, tabloids such as Belgrade's *Blic* have also gained in popularity.

Among the most important privately-owned electronic media are Belgrade's B-92 radio station and Studio B independent television station. B-92 has long been noted for its strong anti-war stance, and during the winter of 1996-1997 Belgrade demonstrations actually gained many new listeners as people tuned in to get more objective reporting as to what was going on around the country. B-92 has also organized a network of 24 opposition radio stations throughout Serbia, Vojvodina, and Montenegro. All told, the network's program reaches 70 percent of Serbia's population.

Over the past several years, Studio B has provided opposition parties with much more coverage than they could receive on RTS. Studio B's signal, however, only reaches limited parts of Belgrade, and over the past several years the government has repeatedly refused to allow Studio B to obtain a stronger transmitter. Opposition cadres from the Zajedno coalition took charge of Studio B after the results of the 1996 municipal elections were recognized, but in September 1996, squabbling among opposition parties led Vuk Draskovic's SPO to purge the station of Zoran Djindjic's supporters.

The most important privately-owned television station is BK Television, owned by three brothers who made their fortune in banking. Although originally close to Milosevic, their television station increasingly began to criticize regime policies, and in March 1997, the state temporarily suspended BK television's broadcasts outside of Belgrade to prevent Serbia's wider population from learning about the extent of the opposition movement.

One interesting development in 1997 was the growing popularity of entertainment-oriented TV and radio stations, and the corresponding decrease in the popularity of news and information-oriented media. For instance, according to some public opinion polls, Radio B-92, which in the immediate aftermath of the Belgrade demonstrations had been the most listened-to radio station in Belgrade, fell to fourth place by September 1997. Similarly, whereas news programs drew the most TV viewers at the beginning of the year, by September 1997, foreign soap operas had become much more popular. Most analysts attributed this turnaround to the electorates' growing disenchantment with politics.

4. Are the private media financially viable? Only a very few, such as BK Television are financially viable. Many, such as *Vreme* and Radio B-92, depend on foreign donations to survive. In March 1997, the Serbian government proposed new draft legislation requiring the various media to disclose any funding they receive from abroad. Another feature of the proposed legislation, prohibiting any radio or television station from broadcasting to more than 25 percent of the population, had to be dropped after the Zajedno coalition threatened to boycott the upcoming elections.

5. Are the media editorially independent? Are the media's news gathering functions affected by interference from government or private owners? State-owned media tow the government/party line. Private and independent media, on the other hand, have completely independent editorial policies. Many newspapers, magazines, and radio stations are vehemently anti-regime. The Milosevic government tolerates this state of affairs because these same media have relatively little impact on public opinion. The limited impact of independent media is mainly the result of two factors. First, given the economic situation, most people simply cannot afford to buy alternative/independent publications. Second, Yugoslavia's rural population relies mainly on state-owned media for information. Nevertheless, on some occasions the regime decides not to take any chances; thus, in the run-up to the Serbian elections in the summer of 1997, the Milosevic government temporarily shut down 77 private radio and television stations around the country.

6. Is the distribution system for newspapers privately or governmentally controlled? Newspapers and other print media are disseminated through several well-established distribution chains, most of which are government affiliated, e.g., the *Politika* publishing house's kiosk chain. In larger cities, independent publications are easily obtained, even at state-owned kiosks. A more common form of government harassment has been to deny independent publications newsprint, or to make the cost of newsprint prohibitively expensive.

7. What proportion of the population is connected to the Internet? Are there any restrictions on Internet access to private citizens? Limited access to the Internet is more the result of a lack of computers than of government restrictions. Although Yugoslav citizens had been in the first wave of Internet users in the early 1990s, a permanent satellite link to the Internet was only established in February 1996, courtesy of a Norwegian provider. According to one estimate, one Yugoslav citizen in one thousand is a regular Internet user. Early in 1998, Yugoslavia's largest Internet services provider, EUNET, signed up its 20,000th subscriber. Many individuals have access to the Internet through academic and governmental institutions, or through various business enterprises; according to some informal estimates, the total figure stands at approximately 300,000 people. Belgrade also has a cyber café where people can stop by and log on. When Radio B-92 was temporarily closed down by the regime in February 1997, its employees resorted to the Internet to publicize what was going on. Rumors, which were impossible to confirm, circulated at the time that the regime had pressured Internet service providers into disconnecting Serbia from the world wide web.

8. What has been the trend in press freedom as measured by Freedom House's *Survey of Press Freedom?* Yugoslavia has been rated as "Not Free" from 1991-1998.

Governance and Public Administration 5.00/7

1. Is the legislature the effective rule-making institution? The trend in recent years, and especially in 1997, has been for the SPS party leadership, and especially Milosevic himself, to determine the outlines of policy, which the SPS-dominated Federal Assembly then rubberstamps. In 1997, the Federal Assembly convened only one time, and one report charged that "decisions are taken at one power center and then take the shape of decrees, written or oral instructions, many of which are not even published." This state of affairs has become more pronounced as the Milosevic regime has slowly lost its exclusive monopoly on state institutions and has had to allow opposition forces into government institutions. In Montenegro, for instance, the reformist victory in October 1997 forced Milosevic loyalists out of office. In Serbia, the opposition parties' victory in the November 1996 municipal elections gave them a toe-hold on power at local levels, and the September 1997 Serbian parliamentary elections gave non-SPS parties a majority in the Serbian Skupstina.

2. Is substantial power decentralized to subnational levels of government? What specific authority do subnational levels have? According to the FRY constitution, the republics enjoy considerable autonomy, and the right to local self-government is guaranteed (Article 6). In practice, however, while Milosevic's Montenegrin protégé, Momir Bulatovic, was president in Serbia's federal partner, most decision-making was centralized. After October 1997, the Djukanovic leadership began to reassert its authority and standing as an equal partner in the federation. Within the republics, there is a high degree of centralization. For instance, the republican education ministries play the determining role in developing school curricula, textbooks, etc., which then have to be implemented throughout the republic. Similarly, prices for various utilities are determined at the republic level, not at the municipality level. Most importantly, the police forces in both republics are highly centralized. Most political parties are highly centralized because of the fact that the support they garner is more a function of their leader's charisma than the party's political program per se.

3. Are subnational officials chosen in free and fair elections? As noted above, the ruling party has numerous ways to influence the outcome of elections. For instance, the OSCE's special representative for Yugoslavia, Felipe Gonzalez, noted in his December 1996 report after a fact-finding trip to Yugoslavia the existence of "deficiencies (of a structural nature) in the electoral system that make it possible to falsify or circumvent the sovereign will of the citizens." Similarly, a recent analysis of the human rights situation in Yugoslavia noted that "in practice, citizens cannot exercise their right to change their government."

Since the first multi-party elections in 1990 at the beginning of the post-Communist era, opposition parties have consistently charged the regime with committing outright vote fraud. The most notorious case of vote fraud came after the November 1996 municipal elections in Serbia. Opposition parties won power in most of Serbia's largest urban areas, including Belgrade, Nis, and Kragujevac. The Milosevic regime, however, refused to acknowledge defeat and declared the elections invalid. Wide-scale, massive protests then erupted throughout Serbia, developing into a three-month long protest movement, with nightly marches and demonstrations by opposition parties. In February 1997, under severe international pressure, Milosevic was forced to back down, and a "*lex specialis*" i.e., a "special law" was passed in the Serbian Skupstina accepting the opposition parties victory — the constitutionality of the law itself, however, was questioned by most observers.

4. Do the executive and legislative bodies operate openly and with transparency? Is draft legislation easily accessible to the media and the public? Sessions of the Federal Yugoslav Assembly, or the Serbian or Montenegrin Skupstina's, are frequently televised or otherwise covered by the press; however, much of the actual decision making takes place behind closed doors. Milosevic's SPS often tries to act unilaterally. For a recent appearance of Yugoslav delegates before the European Parliament, for instance, the SPS tried to send its own cadres, with their own platform, without including opposition members or Montenegrin officials. Nevertheless, as the opposition has increased its representation in state institutions, the Milosevic regime has had less and less opportunity to write and implement legislation unilaterally.

5. Do municipal governments have sufficient revenues to carry out their duties? Do municipal governments have control of their own local budgets? Do they raise revenues autonomously or from the central state budget? Although municipal governments do raise some revenues autonomously (e.g., turnover taxes from the sale of property, issuing various types of personal identification, the sale of vehicle license plates, setting prices of public transportation, etc.), most rely on supplemental funding from the central government. After losing the 1996 municipal elections in several Serbian cities, Milosevic's SPS cadres essentially emptied municipal coffers before the opposition could take power. The Milosevic regime then resorted to punishing municipalities that had voted for the opposition by denying them funds from the republican budget. Central authorities have also begun a campaign to reduce local competencies. For example, municipal governments recently lost the right to grant foreign companies concessions for communal utility services.

6. Do the elected local leaders and local civil servants know how to manage municipal governments effectively? Generally speaking, yes. After the opposition victory in the 1996 municipal elections, however, there were numerous reports of local municipal councils being deadlocked. It also became apparent that, given the fact that many opposition members had never served in government, they had not developed the necessary political or bureaucratic expertise needed to run local governments effectively. Their situation was made even more difficult by the SPS's concerted efforts to portray opposition leaders as incompetent bunglers. In early 1997, the SPS-led Serbian government created a new Ministry for Local Self-Government, which critics charged was intended to maintain the regime's control over municipalities in which the opposition had won.

7. When did the constitutional/legislative changes on local power come into effect? Has there been a reform of the civil service code/system? Are local civil servants employees of the local or central government? Local civil servants are the employees of local municipal governments. This allowed the opposition parties in the 1996 municipal elections to engage in a significant purge of SPS officials at the local level in many of Yugoslavia's biggest cities. For instance, soon after the opposition victory in Belgrade was recognized, the opposition quickly installed its own cadres in Belgrade's Studio B television station, which is officially owned by Belgrade's City Assembly.

Rule of Law 5.00/7

1. Is there a post-Communist constitution? How does the judicial system interpret and enforce the constitution? Are there specific examples of judicial enforcement of the constitution in the last year? A new constitution was promulgated in April 1992. As of March 1998, however, the Serbian republican constitution still had not been brought into agreement with the federal constitution.

The recent election of Milo Djukanovic as Montenegrin president has significantly complicated the FRY's constitutional system; for instance, Montenegro has recently adopted a law by which it no longer recognizes decisions by federal judicial organs.

2. Does the constitutional framework provide for human rights? Do the human rights include business and property rights? The 1992 FRY constitution guarantees Yugoslav citizens all human rights and civil liberties, regardless of ethnicity, race, gender, religion, or political creed, in accordance with international practice. Citizens are guaranteed freedom of assembly, a free press, the right to own property, and national minorities are guaranteed the right to use their own language in educational institutions and in legal proceedings.

In practice, however, these rights have been difficult to uphold, most notably in the case of the Kosovo Albanians. The U.S. State Department report on the human rights situation in Yugoslavia for 1997 noted Yugoslavia had a "poor" record on this note. There were, however, significant differences between the human rights records in Serbia and Montenegro, as the latter's security apparatus was found to have "a relatively clean human rights record since 1995."

3. Has there been basic reform of the criminal code/criminal law? Who authorizes searches and issues warrants? Are suspects and prisoners beaten or abused? Are there excessive delays in the criminal justice system? The former SFRY's Federal Criminal Code remains in force, although work on a new criminal code has been ongoing for the past several years. The FRY constitution prohibits the use of torture against detainees or criminal suspects, but human rights organizations have documented numerous cases of abuse and beatings by security forces, especially in Kosovo and in Belgrade during the winter 1996-1997 demonstrations. In theory, searches are authorized and warrants are issued by judicial authorities; in practice, the police often do these on their own. The criminal justice system is also hampered by the fact that it often takes months, or even years, for cases to reach the courts, and executive institutions generally show little interest in enforcing judicial decisions.

4. Do most judges rule fairly and impartially? Do many remain from the Communist era? The majority of judges are holdovers from the Communist era. Most observers believe that judges do rule fairly and impartially on cases that do not concern politics. Court proceedings are conducted in public, unless there is a perceived need to protect government secrets, public order, or public morality. There have been charges that in the early 1990s many non-Serb judges were dismissed from their positions, particularly in Vojvodina.

Throughout 1997, defense attorneys frequently complained that they were denied access to detainees or had difficulties acquiring copies of official indictments. Some judges were also found to be preventing defense attorneys from reading court files. The judicial system also seems more willing to support human and civil rights in Serbia proper, whereas in Kosovo and the Sandzak, judges frequently are seen to be supporting the actions of the state security apparatus.

On several occasions, judges have proven to be fairly independent of the ruling party. For instance, in a 1998 case in Sremska Mitrovica, the Federal Ministry for Telecommunications confiscated the transmitter and other equipment of a local independent radio station. The local judge, however, ruled in the radio station's favor and ordered the ministry to return the equipment. In February 1998, judges in Novi Sad and Vrsac refused to enforce the controversial "Decree on Measures of Financial Discipline" (see below).

5. Are the courts free of political control and influence? Are the courts linked directly to the Ministry of Justice or any other executive body? According to the FRY constitution, there is a strict separation of powers between the executive, legislative, and judicial branches of government (Article 12), and justices in the Federal Constitutional Court, the Federal Court, and the Federal Public Prosecutor are not allowed to belong to political parties (Article 42). In practice, however, on matters of political importance to the regime, the judicial system often acts as an adjunct of the SPS. Since the tenure of judges and their salaries are not fixed, they are susceptible to regime pressure when deciding on cases with political implications. The prime example of this came in the wake of the 1996 municipal elections when the court system overturned the opposition's victories in several cities throughout Serbia. Similarly, despite the fact that over 60 criminal charges were filed in 1997 in the Serbian court system against Belgrade policemen for using excessive force against demonstrators during the winter 1996-1997 demonstrations, as of November 1997, no one had yet been held accountable for these abuses as of November 1997.

In another example of a judicial ruling having political undertones, in December 1997, the federal state prosecutor overturned a decision by the Montenegrin Supreme Court which declared the anti-Milosevic wing of the DPSCG to be the legitimate successor to the formerly united party. The OSCE's Gonzalez Report noted that reform of the judicial system with regard to the election process was one of the most urgently needed reforms for Yugoslavia.

Over the past several years, criminal investigations have been used to intimidate and harass political opponents of the Milosevic regime. All of the major opposition leaders, including Vuk Draskovic, Zoran Djindjic, and Vojislav Seselj in Serbia, Novak Kilibarda in Montenegro, and

Azem Vlasi in Kosovo, have been charged with criminal wrongdoing for their activities. More recently, in February 1998, the former Montenegrin president, Momir Bulatovic, was also charged with actions destabilizing the "constitutional order" (Article 114 of the Yugoslav Criminal Code) for allegedly organizing a protest demonstration in Podgorica in which several people were hurt.

6. What proportion of lawyers is in private practice? How does this compare with the previous year? Most lawyers are in private practice. In Belgrade alone, there are some 2,900 practicing lawyers.

7. Does the state provide public defenders? Yes. The state is obligated to provide the accused with a public defender if he/she cannot provide his/her own. The accused also has the right to have court proceedings translated into his/her native language.

8. Are there effective anti-bias/discrimination laws, including protection of ethnic minority rights? Numerous anti-bias/discrimination laws exist; for instance, Articles 44-48 guarantee national minorities the right to education and information media in their native language, the right to form educational and cultural institutions, and the right to foster relations with co-nationals outside the borders of the FRY. Article 50 also makes incitement or encouragement of national, racial, or religious hatred or intolerance unconstitutional. It has often proven difficult, however, to enforce these rights in practice.

Corruption D

1. What is the magnitude of official corruption in the civil service? Must an average citizen pay a bribe to a bureaucrat in order to receive a service? What services are subject to bribe requests—for example, university entrance, hospital admission, telephone installation, obtaining a license to operate a business, applying for a passport or other official documents? What is the average salary of civil servants at various levels?) Corruption in Yugoslavia has grown over the past several years, partly as a result of the sanctions, and partly as a result of internal corruption within the regime itself. The extent to which corruption in official circles has proliferated is indicated by the fact that in 1997, several close associates of the Milosevic family were gunned down, gangland style, on the streets of Belgrade. No one has been held responsible for these killings.

Corruption takes numerous forms in Yugoslavia. A longtime Milosevic loyalist, for instance, is in charge of the federal customs agency, which allows Milosevic and the SPS to control the flow of goods into and out of the country and to impose arbitrary financial penalties and fees on individuals crossing the border. Although not officially bribes, a common practice throughout the former Yugoslavia was to provide doctors and nurses with "gifts" as an inducement to provide patients with better care. This practice has become even more widespread since sanctions were imposed in 1992 and the health system has broken down. There have also been charges that some professors at Belgrade University are charging students bribes for passing grades. Protection rackets have become common in larger cities, and municipal authorities often charge kiosk operators considerable sums for the privilege of operating on city property. Because of the overall economic depression, salaries for civil servants have declined considerably. Instructors at Belgrade University, for instance, were reported to have refused to collect their salaries because they were insultingly low. The average monthly salary of a government employee in 1996 was 901 *dinars,* or (approximately $163 according to December 1996 exchange rates).

2. Do top policy makers (the president, ministers, vice-ministers, top court justices, and heads of agencies and commissions) have direct ties to businesses? How strong are such connections and what kinds of businesses are these? Many leading members of the Milosevic regime are the directors of large state-owned enterprises. Directors and top management of other leading economic enterprises also owe their positions to their support for the regime. These ties are especially important in several strategic sectors of the economy, notably those that involve the import of products such as fuel or pharmaceuticals. Enterprises in these sectors have the right to draw hard currency from the National Bank of Yugoslavia (NBY) to pay for their imports at the official exchange rate. They can then quickly sell the hard currency on the black market for a hefty profit. Similar monopolies exist for basic staples such as sugar, or for highly taxed items such as coffee and cigarettes. In 1997, the Yugoslav government decided that henceforth enterprises would only be able to draw hard currency from the NBY for the import of pharmaceutical products and fuel, indicating that they might be trying to clamp down on widespread abuse of the system.

A typical example of the close ties between the Milosevic family, large businesses, and organized crime was Zoran Todorovic, the director of a Belgrade oil company, who was also the secretary-general of YUL, the left-wing political movement founded by Milosevic's wife, Mira Markovic. Todorovic was assassinated in Belgrade in October 1997. Mirko Marjanovic, the premier of the Serbian republican government, is also the director of the "Progres" enterprise, which has exclusive control of the Yugoslav fuel trade market with Russia. The vice-president of the Serbian government, Slobodan Radulovic, is also the director of "S Markets," a chain of small grocery stores. Milorad Vucelic, the vice-president of the SPS, is the owner and director of the "Komuna" publishing conglomerate. Dragan Tomic, the speaker of the Serbian Skupstina, is also the director of Jugopetrol, one of Yugoslavia's largest oil companies.

3. Do laws requiring financial disclosure and disallowing conflict of interest exist? Have publicized anticorruption cases been pursued? To what conclusion? Many prominent officials have been arrested and tried for corruption recently, although some critics charge they were arrested because they had fallen afoul of the regime politically rather than for their criminal activities. In February 1998, for instance, Nenad Djordjevic, the vice-president of YUL and a close political associate of Mira Markovic, Slobodan Milosevic's wife, was arrested for embezzling millions from the republic health insurance fund. Rumors circulating in Belgrade, which were impossible to confirm, however, suggested that Djordjevic's demise was the result of his close ties to the new, anti-Milosevic Montenegrin leadership. Numerous similar such cases have been publicized as well.

4. What major anticorruption initiatives have been implemented? How often are anticorruption laws and decrees adopted? Both government and opposition figures frequently call for crackdowns on corruption. Milan Milutinovic, the SPS candidate for the Serbian presidency in

1997 made a drive against corruption one of the pillars of his electoral campaign. In October 1997, the federal government called on judicial authorities to make corruption trials a priority. However, given the fact that the Milosevic regime is founded on widespread corruption, little may ever come of such calls. The government has not implemented any serious anti-corruption initiatives as of yet. In September 1997, a group of 35 prominent Yugoslav economists published a plan for radical economic reforms in the FRY. Among their proposals was to confiscate all property that was illegally obtained by party, state, and regime functionaries between 1991-1997.

5. How do major corruption-ranking organizations like Transparency International rate this country? In a recent survey of corruption in Central and Eastern Europe by the *Economist,* corruption in Yugoslavia was deemed to be the most severe of any of the former Yugoslav republics.

Privatization 4.50/7

1. What percentage of GDP comes from private ownership? What percentage of the labor force is employed in the private sector? How large is the informal sector of the economy? The private sector accounts for approximately 40 percent of GDP. The vast majority of officially registered businesses are in fact privately owned; according to one estimate, in 1995 this figure stood at 91 percent. Most of these are so-called micro-companies employing less than ten people. All told, some 27 percent of Yugoslavia's workforce is officially registered in the private sector, although, the actual figure is believed to be much higher because many individuals are working in the black or gray markets. In 1994, the private sector accounted for 55.2 percent of all profits in the Yugoslav economy and 29.4 percent of total income, despite the fact that the private sector accounted for less than 3 percent of the total fixed capital in the Yugoslav economy. The "shadow economy" is estimated to have accounted for almost 41 percent of GDP in 1995.

2. What major privatization legislation has been passed? What were its substantive features? The FRY constitution explicitly states that the FRY will have a market economy (Article 13). An initial privatization campaign in 1991-1993 offered managers and workers the right to buy shares in their enterprises on privileged terms, but the campaign went awry when hyperinflation set in and it became difficult to establish the true value of firms and assets. In 1994, the Property Transformation Revaluation Act annulled the privatization of 87 percent of the enterprises that had previously been privatized, effectively, returning the bulk of the economy back to state control.

A new privatization law in Serbia, the Law on Ownership Transformation, was passed by the Serbian Skupstina on July 21, 1997, and came into effect on November 1, 1997. Between 4.5 and 5 million citizens were eligible to take part in this privatization program. According to the new law, 60 percent of the shares in state-controlled and socially-owned enterprises would be distributed free to workers and managers, as well as to public-sector employees, pensioners, and farmers, in the form of coupons. The state pension fund was to be allocated 10 percent of the shares. The remaining shares were to be offered at a discount to employees before being made available to foreign investors. Critics pointed out, however, that the proposed legislation did not make privatization of state-owned and socially-owned enterprises mandatory, nor did it set deadlines according to when privatization had to occur. Moreover, since many of the enterprises up for privatization are unprofitable and perpetually in the red, the actual value of the shares that individuals will receive will be negligible. By March 1998, no enterprises had been privatized according to the new legislation.

Privatization has progressed much further in Montenegro. In 1992, the republican Skupstina had passed the Law on Ownership and Control Transformation, which allowed enterprises to be privatized in various ways including by the issuance and sales of shares under privileged conditions for employees of enterprises to be privatized, debt-equity swapping, investment in an enterprise i.e., raising additional capital, and the sale of enterprises to their respective managements, etc.

According to one estimate, 95 percent of the enterprises in Montenegro had undergone ownership transformation by September 1997. Fifty-six enterprises, with a net worth of 128 million DEM, had been completely privatized, and the private sector was estimated to account for 30-35 percent of Montenegro's GDP. One major enterprise, the Niksic brewery, was bought by a Belgian firm. After Djukanovic was sworn in as president on January 15 1998, the government promised more radical moves towards privatization. Western firms such as Merrill Lynch and Coopers and Lybrand are already involved in deals to privatize a variety of enterprises, including an aluminum combine, a health spa, and a tobacco factory, and to bid for concessions in building a hydro-electric plant.

3. What proportion of agriculture, housing and land, industry, and small business and services is in private hands? *Agriculture*: Over 75 percent of the arable land in Yugoslavia is privately owned.

Industry, Small Business and Services: According to one estimate, of the 219,763 enterprises registered in the industrial sector of the economy in 1996, 143,774 or 65.4 percent, were privately owned. Larger industrial enterprises, such as the steelworks in Smederevo or the Zastava automobile plant in Kragujevac, remain state-owned, although foreign investors are showing some interest in acquiring these enterprises. Of the remaining enterprises that are state-owned, privatization of small enterprises e.g., food processing plants is expected to go the quickest.

Housing: Yugoslavia's housing stock at the end of 1995 was estimated to comprise 3,123,000 units, of which 687,000 were state/socially owned.

4. What has been the extent of insider (management, labor, and nomenklatura) participation in the privatization process? What explicit and implicit preferences have been awarded to insiders? Insiders have taken considerable advantage of the economic "reforms" enacted to date. Under the terms of the Property Transformation Revaluation Act, ownership of many enterprises was turned over to their largest debt-holders, which generally tended to be state-owned banks, thus, bank directors and managers were installed on the managerial boards of most of the largest enterprises in the country. Since the bank managers themselves, however, were generally SPS loyalists, the Milosevic regime succeeded in actually increasing its control over the economy after 1994. Individuals close to the regime are given a wide variety of privileges, such as easier access to credit and hard currency, tax waivers, or special permission to import scarce goods into the country.

5. How much public awareness of and support for privatization has there been? What is the

nature of support and opposition to privatization by major interest groups? Although most government officials claim to support economic reform and restructuring, concrete action has been slow in coming, partly due to the difficulties imposed by the international sanctions, and partly because control of large state-owned enterprises is one of the main instruments the Milosevic regime uses to stay in power. Many leading figures in Milosevic's SPS are the directors of these state-owned enterprises, through which they are able to obtain large loans from the NBY at low interest rates and then sell the funds on the black market. Public support for privatization is also lower among employees of large, unprofitable state owned enterprises who stand to lose their jobs if those enterprises were forced to operate according to market criteria. On the other hand, support for privatization has been strongest among people who own small businesses and firms, primarily found among the younger, better-educated, urban population. A leading reformer in the FRY government, Danko Djunic, has also claimed that there is a critical mass of people in the government itself who are pressing for reform. In Montenegro there has been much more widespread government and popular support for privatization.

Macroeconomics 4.50/7

1. Has the taxation system been reformed? (What areas have and have not been overhauled? To what degree are taxpayers complying? Is tax compliance difficult to achieve? Has the level of revenues increased? Is the revenue-collection body overburdened? What is the overall tax burden?) In July 1996, a new federal tax law significantly modified the previous tax system. The legislation provided for a variety of new taxes including: a surtax on trade and the import of various goods with rates ranging from 5-70 percent, depending on the type of good; a commodity sales tax on all items sold to the end buyer with proportional rates ranging from 10-20 percent; a services sales tax of 10 percent; a profit tax on enterprises ranging from 20-30 percent, with the rate set by the republics; a progressive income tax with rates from 20-40 percent; and a property tax also with rates set by the republics. For the 1998 fiscal year, the FRY government expected to raise 40 percent of its revenue from sales taxes, and 31 percent from customs duties.

Tax compliance has been very difficult to enforce given the fact that most people now prefer to make their transactions in cash using hard currencies. Use of checks and credit cards over the past few years has been minimal, thus, individuals leave no paper trail of their financial activities. Widespread tax avoidance has, to some extent, been accepted by the regime for the past several years for the sake of social peace; moreover, strictly imposing tax regulations would only worsen the Yugoslav economy's liquidity problems. Adding to the overall problem of tax compliance is the fact that regime supporters have frequently been granted tax waivers for various imported goods. For instance, it is estimated that only half of the revenue that should be raised from the sale of cigarettes is actually collected, because many individuals close to the Milosevic regime control the cigarette trade in Yugoslavia.

Recent moves indicate that the government is determined to begin enforcing tax collection more seriously. In February 1998 the Serbian government proposed the very controversial Decree on Measures of Financial Discipline. According to the new law, individuals wishing to sell their private property such as apartments, houses, or automobiles had to go through local municipal officials, who would determine the property's value, and payment had to be made through domestic banks in dinars. Although ostensibly intended to improve the state's ability to collect turnover taxes on the sale of property, the decree immediately met with almost universal condemnation. As of this writing, the decree's ultimate future remains unknown.

The private sector is bearing the brunt of propping up the regime. Since state and socially owned enterprises have been unprofitable for several years, the private sector has had to make up for the public sector's weaknesses. This has resulted in a relatively high tax burden being placed on both individuals and enterprises in the private sector. In February 1998, the federal government began discussing measures to squeeze more money out of the gray economy, including the introduction of a VAT and of non-cash payment mechanisms to reduce the amount of cash in circulation.

2. Does fiscal policy encourage private savings, investment and earnings? (Has there been any reform/alteration of revenue and budget policies? How large are budget deficits and overall debt? Is the financing of the social insurance/pension system sustainable? What proportion of the budget is taken up by subsidies to firms and individuals?) As a result of the regime's decision to confiscate citizens' hard currency accounts in the early 1990s, the collapse of pyramid lending schemes in 1993, and the hyperinflation of 1992-93, individuals have had little incentive to invest or save. In 1997, for instance, it was estimated that FRY citizens, on average, have less than 20 dinars, i.e., less than $3, on deposit in Yugoslav banks. The government is estimated to owe citizens between $3.5-4 billion in hard currency confiscated from private bank accounts. Internal debts to banks and between companies were estimated to be approximately $4 billion in 1996. The budget deficit for 1996 was estimated to be $1 billion, or six percent of GDP. Added to these internal debts are Yugoslavia's external debts, estimated to be $11.2 billion in 1995. Altogether, the FRY's debt as a percentage of GDP was estimated at some 75 percent in 1997.

In 1997, the situation worsened as the FRY pension fund alone ran a deficit of some $1.26 billion, and the payments that were made were only possible due to the sale of a large stake of the Serbian telecommunications system to Italian and Greek investors. Financing of the social insurance system is not sustainable, as is evident by the fact that pensions have been paid out on a very irregular basis over the past several years. According to one estimate, the government owes 1.2 million pensioners some 5,000 dinars or approximately $830 each in pension arrears.

To make up for chronic budget deficits and help fund the government, over the past several years the Milosevic regime has devised several schemes to squeeze money out of the population and/or the shadow economy. One such scheme in the early 1990s involved a well publicized campaign issuing government bonds for the reconstruction of Serbia. Once hyper-inflation set in, however, individuals who had purchased these bonds suffered net losses. Another scheme involved the pyramid lending scandals of 1993, in which millions of citizens invested their hard currency savings in private banks which offered monthly interest rates equivalent to yearly interest rates in western countries. The owners of these banks had close ties to the Milosevic regime. The entire system collapsed within months as soon as the first withdrawals from these banks started a rush on the entire system. Many of the street dealers who buy and sell hard currencies are also believed to be controlled by Milosevic's secret police.

3. Has there been banking reform? (Is the central bank independent? What are its responsi-

bilities? Is it effective in setting and/or implementing monetary policy? What is the actual state of the private banking sector? Does it conform to international standards? Are depositors protected?) Banking reform, as is true of economic reform in general, has been held up by a combination of domestic political obstruction and the constraints imposed by Yugoslavia's diplomatic and economic isolation. In January 1998, Djunic claimed that bank restructuring was impossible without assistance from the IMF or the World Bank.

The individual credited with developing the successful anti-inflation program of 1994, former NBY governor Dragoslav Avramovic, began openly criticizing the Milosevic regime in April 1996, and by May 1996, Avramovic had already been dismissed from his position. Since then, the NBY has lost much of its independence.

The private commercial banking sector is in a desperate situation. Most banks suffer from severe liquidity problems. Many Yugoslav citizens lost faith in the banking system with the collapse of several pyramid lending schemes in 1993. Total current holdings of the 100-odd private commercial banks were estimated to be about $15 billion at the end of 1996. Talks with the London Club of international banks to restructure Yugoslavia's estimated $1.94 billion commercial debt broke off in October 1997 without a settlement. The Yugoslav delegation had requested that 80 percent of their debts' value be written off, and the remainder restructured as a 25-year loan with a nine-year grace period. Yugoslavia's total external debt is believed to be between $10-12 billion.

The Montenegrin government, for its part, has been somewhat more successful in its forays into world financial markets. Over the past few years, the Montenegrin government has assumed responsibility for $170 million in debts to international banks that Montenegrin enterprises had run up; by so doing, however, it reduced Montenegro's external debts by one third, bringing it down to an estimated $340 million.

Individual depositors in Yugoslavia have also suffered from the Milosevic government's policies. In 1992, the regime froze $6.5 billion worth of private hard currency accounts held by Yugoslav depositors to help fund the war effort. In late 1997, the federal government was working on ways to return those monies to restore some confidence in the banking system.

Current plans for bank reform envision a consolidation of the private banking system through a series of mergers among smaller banks. Balance sheets would then be "cleaned up," and non-performing loans transferred into an envisioned "bad loan bank." One aspect of this effort was a decree by the NBY that, as of January 1, 1998, illiquid banks could only allow depositors to withdraw 300,000 dinars or approximately $50,000 unless the bank's reserves could cover the transaction. The move was apparently designed to encourage depositors to begin withdrawing their monies from illiquid banks and depositing them in more liquid banks. In early 1998, the FRY government was reviewing draft legislation that would convert many short-term outstanding loans in agriculture, tourism, and the electrical energy and railway systems into long-term (15 year) credits, or transform current credits into public debt to be repaid in ten years.

4. How sound is the national currency? (Is the value of the currency fixed or does it float? How convertible is the currency? How large are the hard currency reserves? Has exchange rate policy been stable and predictable?) In the late 1980s and early 1990s, the Yugoslav dinar lost much of its value. Inflation began spiraling upward in 1991, averaging 120 percent in that year, but by 1993 it had reached an unprecedented 116,540,000 percent. In January 1994, the NBY, led by Avramovic, initiated an austerity and stabilization program by introducing a new "super dinar" pegged at a fixed rate to the German *mark*. This succeeded in bringing inflation down to 3.3 percent in 1994, but by 1995 it had again risen to an average annual rate of 120 percent. On November 25, 1995, the federal government passed a Foreign Currency Transactions Law pegging the dinar to the mark at a rate of 3.3:1. To control the growth in the money supply, the NBY in August 1996 increased the mandatory reserve requirement for banks to 10 percent, and in November 1996 the mandatory reserve requirement was again increased to 15 percent.

In 1997, inflation was less than 10 percent according to official statistics, although some economists have challenged these estimates. For most of 1997, the dinar was fixed at a rate of 3.5:1 against the mark but fluctuated on the black market anywhere between 3.5 and 5. At the end of 1997, the federal government announced that it planned to maintain a restrictive monetary policy and pledged that it would keep growth in the money supply below GDP growth for 1998. Nevertheless, inflationary pressures continued to mount, and in March 1998, the government was forced to devalue the dinar by bringing the official exchange rate down to 6:1.

Central bank reserves are estimated to be below $200 million — less than one month's worth of imports. In addition to hard currency reserves, the FRY also has 1.3 million troy ounces in its gold reserves. The Milosevic regime has also hidden significant sums of money in secret bank accounts in Cyprus.

5. Is there a functioning capital market infrastructure? (Are there existing or planned commodities, bond and stock markets? What are the mechanisms for investment and lending? What government bodies have authority to regulate capital markets?) The Belgrade Stock Exchange reopened in 1990 after being closed for almost 50 years. Foreign countries, particularly Britain and Italy, are financing its activities. The Podgorica, formerly Titograd Stock Exchange, opened in 1996. Securities trading in both exchanges is limited due to the fact that privatization has just begun, and the regulatory infrastructure for widespread stock and bond trading barely exists. Most activity involves trading short-term (30 day or less) commercial paper and government bonds, while the sale of stocks is practically non-existent. In 1997, both the number of transactions on the Belgrade Stock Exchange and the value of those transactions fell. In the first three months of 1998, 1,808 transactions worth 1.6 billion dinars or approximately $267 million, were made on the Belgrade Stock Exchange, which currently lists 39 different stocks. No stocks are being traded on the Podgorica Stock Exchange as of yet but that is expected to change with the planned distribution of privatization vouchers to 450,000 Montenegrin citizens.

Investors are reluctant to participate in financial markets, as is evident from the fact that less than one percent of financial transactions and deals go through established brokerage houses. Most deals take place directly between buyers and sellers of bonds. Potential investors are at a significant disadvantage because brokerage houses and the stock markets themselves cannot provide them with a good sense of the various risks and costs associated with particular investments. The documentation various firms provide is not reliable, and accounting procedures are also poor.

Given their relative weakness, commercial banks do not play a large role in the capital markets. Consequently, the NBY performs many of the functions commercial banks would typically perform in the West. Foreign observers and domestic critics charge that investment funds and bank credits are often allocated on the basis of political rather than market criteria.

One sign that reform of the capital market infrastructure is underway is the fact that in February 1998 the Yugoslav government signed a deal with a London-based investment bank for long-term cooperation on privatization and foreign investment. As the new privatization law passed in November 1997 takes effect, there will be a greater need to establish exchanges for stocks and investment funds.

Microeconomics 5.00/7

1. Are property rights guaranteed? (Are there both formal and de facto protections of private real estate and intellectual property? Is there a land registry with the authority and capability to ensure accurate recording of who owns what? What are the procedures for expropriation, including measures for compensation and challenge? Have any seizures taken place?) Article 51 of the FRY constitution explicitly recognizes the right to own property, and Article 53 guarantees intellectual property rights. Yugoslavia is also a signatory to numerous international agreements and conventions protecting copyrights and patents. In February 1997, Yugoslavia became a member of the Patent Cooperation Treaty, allowing foreigners to apply for patents in Yugoslavia. Yugoslavia's international isolation, however, has meant that there is often little incentive to prosecute violations of international intellectual property rights.

2. To what extent have prices been liberalized? What subsidies remain? The last SFRY government, led by Ante Markovic, had liberalized prices on the vast majority of goods as early as 1990. During the war, the Milosevic government tried to control the price of basic staples, but the hyperinflation of 1992-1993 made such efforts pointless. The government continues to control prices on approximately 500 goods, ranging from machinery to paper products to food, and producers of these goods must ask the Federal Ministry of Trade for permission to raise prices. The government's ability to control the importation of various goods means that it can also informally set prices for imports by withholding supply whenever prices drop for particular items. Other goods and services for which prices are still set by the government include things such as inland railway traffic, the main postal and telephone services, medicines, and electricity prices. The government also subsidizes various agricultural products such as livestock, edible oil, and other foodstuffs.

3. Is it possible to own and operate a business? (Has there been legislation regarding the formation, dissolution, and transfer of businesses, and is the law respected? Do there exist overly cumbersome bureaucratic hurdles that effectively hinder the ability to own and dispose of a business? Are citizens given access to information on commercial law? Is the law applied fairly? Does regulation (or licensing requirements) impose significant costs on business and consumers? Do they create significant barriers to entry and seriously hamper competition?) All Yugoslav citizens are constitutionally guaranteed the right to own their own businesses. Even during the Communist era, Yugoslav citizens had the right to own and operate small businesses that employed up to five people, or, in the case of agriculture, to own up to ten hectares of land. The formation of businesses is a straightforward procedure, and tens of thousands of Yugoslav citizens have registered their own businesses over the past several years. There is a free flow of information on the various aspects of commercial law, and changes are regularly published in the FRY's Official Gazette (*Sluzbeni Glasnik*). Regulations or licensing requirements, in most cases, are only problematical where business activities can damage the regimes's interests e.g., licensing a media enterprise, or where regime members and supporters have significant personal business interests, in which case the bureaucracy can significantly hamper competition.

4. Are courts effective, transparent, efficient, and quick in reaching decisions on property and contract disputes? What alternative mechanisms for adjudicating disputes exist? The FRY's legislation regarding investment disputes is generally considered to be in accord with international standards. The FRY accepts binding international arbitration for investment disputes between foreign investors and the state. The main problems are inconsistent implementation and lack of enforcement of judicial rulings both for foreign and domestic investors. Foreign observers have also complained that government and judicial decisions often seem to be influenced by the ruling party. Although bureaucratic and regulatory procedures are neither transparent nor efficient, the FRY government is believed to be making legal, regulatory, and accounting systems more transparent in accordance with international standards.

5. Is business competition encouraged? (Are monopolistic practices limited in law and in practice? If so, how? To what degree is "insider" dealing a hindrance to open competition? Are government procurement policies open and unbiased?) The FRY constitution prohibits the creation of monopolies and explicitly states that "terms of business shall be the same for all" (Article 74). In practice, however, individuals and enterprises associated with the Milosevic regime have been granted import monopolies for a wide range of goods, including fuel, pharmaceuticals, and cigarettes. There have also been numerous charges that government employees are frequently instructed to buy goods from individuals and firms with close ties to the regime.

6. To what extent has international trade been liberalized? To what degree has there been simplification/overhaul of customs and tariffs procedures, and are these applied fairly? What informal trade barriers exist? Yugoslavia currently adheres to the "Customs Valuation Agreement" negotiated under GATT but now assumed by the World Trade Organization (WTO), which provides for fair, uniform, and neutral valuations of imports and exports. Yugoslavia is also an adherent to the Convention Covering Anti-Dumping Duties administered by the WTO, and has signed the Convention on Subsidies and Countervailing Duties, although acceptance is pending. Duty rates in 1997, most of which are ad valorem, were in the 0-40 percent range, although most were in the 5-20 percent range. The exception to this is in food products, where, to protect domestic fruit and vegetable producers, duties were raised to as much as 200 percent on April 1, 1997. In addition to customs duties, imports to Yugoslavia are subject to a cumulative 16 percent import tax ad valorem.

In late 1997, the federal government announced a Foreign Trade Regime Liberalization Program that was supposed to become effective in 1998. According to new proposals, 96% of the total monetary value of exports and 90 percent of the total monetary value of imports would be regime-free. In early 1998, amendments to the customs tariff law were being discussed to bring tariffs and duties in line with WTO regulations by 2002. According to the proposed amendments, the average duty rate for imports is to fall from 16 percent to 13.45 percent. The duty rate for consumer goods was scheduled to be between 30-40 percent and for raw material and semi-finished goods, 1-3 percent.

The easing of the sanctions regime in 1995 resulted in a small decline in Yugoslavia's trade deficit. In 1996, exports were only 44.9 percent of imports, while in 1997, exports were 49.3 percent of imports. The trade deficit for 1996 was $2.26 billion or approximately 15 percent of GDP. Two thirds of FRY imports in 1996 consisted of raw materials and semi-finished goods, mainly industrial inputs. Capital goods accounted for 14 percent of imports, and consumer goods the remaining 19 percent. Most FRY exports consist of raw materials, semi-finished goods, and food and chemical products. The FRY's main trading partners are Germany, Italy, Russia, FYR Macedonia, and the Republika Srpska. In 1997, the trade deficit was again estimated to be around $2.2 billion.

7. To what extent has foreign investment and capital flow been encouraged or constrained? Yugoslavia's international trade and ability to attract foreign investment has been extremely limited because of the sanctions regime imposed on Yugoslavia by the UN Security Council in May 1992. After the signing of the Dayton Peace Agreement in December 1995, the UN Security Council suspended the original sanctions regime and allowed Yugoslavia to resume trade with the outside world. In October 1996, the UN Security Council lifted the original sanctions regime completely (Security Council Resolution 1022/1996). In April 1997, the EU granted the FRY preferential trade status, but then revoked it in December after the Milosevic regime failed to make any progress towards democratization as outlined in the Gonzales Report. In contrast to the Europeans, the United States has consistently favored keeping the FRY economically isolated.

Officially, foreigners enjoy the right to own property and businesses on the basis of reciprocity, i.e., to the same extent that Yugoslav citizens enjoy those rights in the foreigner's country. Foreigners also have the right to seek arbitration in foreign courts in disputes. The government does reserve the right to expropriate property "in the public interest." There were no reported cases of such actions in 1997, although in earlier cases compensation for expropriated property fell below market value. Expropriation and nationalization are prohibited in free zones. Repatriation of capital for foreigners is free of restrictions. There have been complaints, however, that high tariffs and surcharges have made it too expensive for foreign firms to import the quantity of goods needed to launch operations on a larger scale. Foreign investment in Yugoslavia is not screened by any particular criteria, and no discriminatory or preferential export or import laws affect foreign investors. Although there is no formal discrimination against foreign investors, there have been charges that FRY law and institutions have been manipulated by domestic firms to give them an advantage over foreign firms.

An important first step in opening Yugoslavia's economy to foreign investment was made in 1989 with the adoption of the Foreign Investment Law, which allowed foreigners to invest in various sectors such as tourism, insurance, and financial services. In 1994, the FRY government passed a foreign investment law. A primary feature of the 1994 legislation set up free economic zones in key import-export zones, such as airports, river and sea ports, and along major international highways. Both domestic and foreign investors in these zones were given a wide variety of customs and tax incentives to stimulate their operations, including extended tax breaks of up to six years in Serbia and ten years in Montenegro. Similar incentives exist for firms operating outside of the free zones. In mid-1996, privatization legislation was further liberalized by the Law on Changes and Supplements to the Law on Foreign Investment. The 1996 legislation allowed foreigners to obtain concessions in the fields of energy production, transportation, telecommunications, and the forest and lumber industries. For example, foreign firms have obtained concessions to build a highway between Nis and Dimitrovgrad, a bridge over the Drina river, and parking lots in Belgrade. A French firm, Saur Internationale, is in negotiations to operate Belgrade's public waterworks system.

In the past two years, the government has made further efforts to encourage foreign investment, but critics charge the government's efforts reflect a need to obtain cash to keep the economy afloat rather than a real desire to restructure the economy. In June 1997, the Serbian government signed a major deal to privatize the Serbian telecommunications system by selling a 49-percent share worth 1.6 billion DEM to two foreign investors: Italy's Stet and Greece's OTE. The money, however, was used to cover back payments to workers and pensioners before the September 1997 elections. Montenegro, for its part, has been promoting itself as a center for offshore business activities. In July 1996, the Montenegrin Skupstina passed the Offshore Companies Act granting substantial tax benefits to foreign entities operating in Montenegro. Montenegro is also trying to attract foreign investors for its plan to privatize its tourist attractions.

Yugoslavia has considerable potential to attract foreign investors: the *Financial Times* called Yugoslavia "Europe's last big untapped market." Part of the attraction is due to the fact that salable assets are significantly undervalued. Moreover, despite the "brain drain" of the 1990s, Yugoslavia still has a well-trained and competitively priced workforce. Potential foreign investors, however, have been put off by the uncertain political climate, most notably, ethnic unrest in Kosovo, political unrest in Montenegro, the continuing problems in Bosnia-Herzegovina, the constant threat of a re-imposition of sanctions against the FRY, and the lack of transparency in the government's privatization program.

Foreign investment and capital flow have also been constrained by an "outer wall" of sanctions the U.S. imposed on Yugoslavia in 1996. After the UN Security Council lifted the original sanctions regime, Yugoslav critics charge that the U.S. "moved the goalposts" by announcing a new set of conditions that Yugoslavia had to fulfill to gain membership in the IMF and the World Bank. Yugoslav economists claim that the FRY has fulfilled all of the economic criteria for re-joining the IMF, but little progress has been made regarding the U.S.'s political conditions, which include handing over war crimes suspects, real progress towards democratization, progress in resolving the Kosovo issue, and agreement with the other former Yugoslav republics on sharing the SFRY's assets. In late 1997, the federal government was working on further legislation to liberalize foreign trade.

8. Has there been reform of the energy sector? (To what degree has the energy sector been restructured? Is the energy sector more varied, and is it open to private competition? Is the country overly dependent on one or two other countries for energy [including whether exported fuels must pass through one or more countries to reach markets?]) Production from the FRY's thermal power stations and hydroelectric power stations fulfill Yugoslavia's electricity needs — the two sectors provide 68 percent of total electricity generated and 32 percent, respectively. Both sectors are still state-owned. Reform of the rest of the energy industry has also been negligible. The government controls who has the right to obtain import licenses for mineral fuels, and these licenses invariably go to individuals with close ties to the regime. During the sanctions, organized smuggling rings earned vast sums of money circumventing the blockade and importing fuel. Currently, Yugoslavia owes some $500 million to Russia for gas, and China for oil, but it continues to import fuel through barter arrangements with these countries. There are rumors that Yugoslavia may have to settle its energy debts to Russia and China by giving them shares of state-owned enterprises scheduled for privatization.

Overall, the energy sector is in desperate shape. Both the state oil company (NIS) and the state electrical company (EPS) in Serbia are running large deficits. In 1996, NIS had debts of approximately 617 million dinars according to the exchange rate then in effect, over $127 million, including some 228 million dinars it owed the federal government in excise taxes. EPS had debts totaling 582 million dinars ($120 million), while at the same time its customers owed EPS 766 million dinars (approximately $158 million). Part of the reason for the deficits is the fact that, despite recent price increases, Serbia still has the lowest electricity prices in Europe, and gasoline prices in Yugoslavia are lower than in western Europe. Many experts believe that overall industrial growth and development will be impossible without significant reform and reconstruction of the energy sector. According to recent estimates, the Yugoslav energy sector needs some $700 million in investments for infrastructure modernization and improvement.

Plans are being made to privatize state energy conglomerates and sell shares to foreign investors, which should significantly restructure the energy sector. Plans are already underway to sell minority stakes in EPS and NIS, which also owns a large network of gas stations.